For Mr. and Mrs. Robert Warden

It has been so nice meeting you both. I look forward to another meeting sometime in Great Falls.

Sincerely,

Alvin M. Josephy Jr.

Helena, Montana
Oct. 15, 1985

Yale Western Americana Series, 10

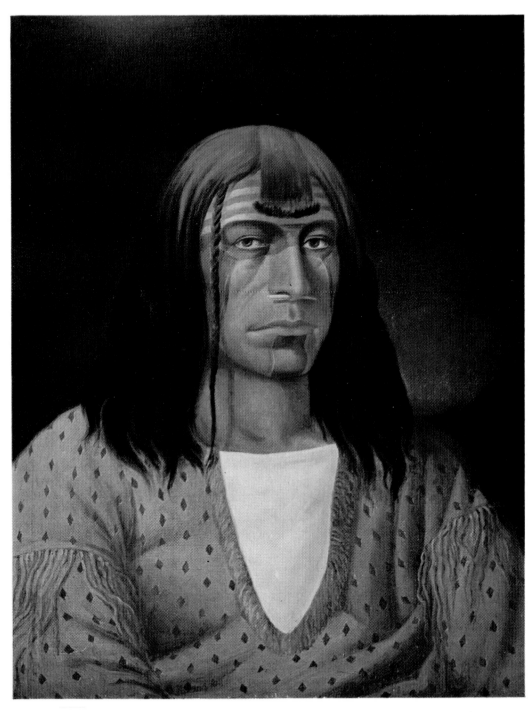

Nez Perce Indian, painting by Paul Kane, after a sketch from life by the artist on the Columbia River near the mouth of the Snake, July 29, 1847. Courtesy Royal Ontario Museum, University of Toronto, and *American Heritage*.

The Nez Perce Indians and
the Opening of the Northwest

by Alvin M. Josephy, Jr.

New Haven and London, Yale University Press, 1965

To the Indian and non-Indian Americans; to the Nez Perce people in Idaho and Washington; to the people of Wallowa County; to my children, Alvin, Allison, Diane, and Katherine; and to my wife, Betty, whose love and understanding sustained the writing of this book.

ACKNOWLEDGMENTS

THIS BOOK was written primarily for the general reader, unacquainted with the Nez Perce story. But it contains considerable detail, including new historical material, that may be of interest to the student and specialist. Some of it, pertaining especially to the early periods of exploration, the fur trade, and the missionaries, has been placed under extended "Discussion Notes" at the end of the volume, where it does not divert the flow of the narrative.

It should also be noted that this work was conceived and written with certain limited objectives. As a history, it does not presume to be an anthropological study. Moreover, it is essentially the story of the conquest and dispossession of the Nez Perces by invaders of their country; and, save for concluding material in the Epilogue, it ends when the last of the people ceased to be free.

Particular mention should be made of the use of the names "Blackfoot" and "Blackfeet" and of the plural spellings for various of the tribes in the text. Anthropologists and ethnologists, for whom I have sincere respect, will forgive me, I trust, if I deviate occasionally from scholarly form in order to use what sounds logical to the English-trained ear. Thus the singular in this work will be "Blackfoot" and the plural will be "Blackfeet," while the plural of tribes like the Nez Perce and Crow will be "Nez Perces" and "Crows."

My bibliography, pruned to a reasonable length, contains the principal sources of manuscript and printed materials on which the book rests. During my many years of research and writing I was provided also with counsel and favors by numerous persons. I have acknowledged the assistance of many of them in footnotes throughout the book, but it is appropriate to mention some of them here and express more formally my appreciation.

I would be remiss if I did not acknowledge at the start my particular debt to Lucullus V. McWhorter, Dale L. Morgan, and Clifford M. Drury. Their research and writings provided valuable source materials without which large portions of this book would have suffered greatly.

I am deeply indebted also to friends who first introduced me to the Nez Perces at Lapwai: Harry Hughes, Earl Bullock, and William Johnston, all of Lewiston, Idaho, and the late Paul Nash of Boise. Among the Nez Perces, many members of the tribe helped on numerous occasions. I wish to thank the Nez Perce Tribal Executive Committee and to acknowledge particular assistance from Richard A. Halfmoon, Angus Wilson, Josiah Redwolf, Allen Slickpoo, James J. Miles, Samuel Watters, Joseph Blackeagle, Otis Halfmoon, Albert Moore, and Sam Tilden, thanking, in addition, Harrison Lott, Mose Thomas, Frank W. Penney, Phil Types, and Earl Gould.

I appreciate the courtesy and aid of the following persons, some of whom have since passed on: Mrs. Rowena L. Alcorn, Tacoma; Haruo Aoki, Tokyo; Nelson A. Ault, Pullman, Washington; Mrs. Emmett Avery, Archivist, Washington State University Library, Pullman, where I was privileged to examine the McWhorter Papers; George B. Hammond, Robert H. Becker, and John Barr Tompkins, always hospitable at the Bancroft Library, University of California, Berkeley; Marius Barbeau, wise and generous friend in Ottawa; J. Neilson Barry, Portland, Oregon; and Mrs. H. E. Bartlett, Joseph, Oregon.

Also: R. A. Skelton and Helen Wallis at the British Museum, London; the late Judge William C. Brown, Okanogan, Washington; Harvey Chalmers II, Amsterdam, N.Y.; Glenn Chaffin, Corvallis, Montana; Sophie J. Cluff, Hawaiian Mission Children's Society, Honolulu; Gwen Coffin, Enterprise, Oregon, my first host in the Wallowa Valley; Gilbert Edward Connor, descendant of Ollokot, Pendleton, Oregon; John Cragun and Donald C. Gormley of Wilkinson, Cragun & Barker, Washington, D.C.; Professor L. S. Cressman, University of Oregon, Eugene; Peter Decker, New York; Ella DeLoria, Vermillion, South Dakota; and Hugh Dempsey of the Glenbow Foundation, Calgary, Alberta, with whom I pursued misty links between the Nez Perces and the earliest fur men in the Oregon country.

In addition: the late Bernard DeVoto; my friend Frederick J. Dockstader, Director of the Museum of the American Indian, Heye Foundation, New York; David C. Duniway, State Archivist, Oregon State Library, Salem; Daphne Gowen, Lewis-Clark Normal School, Lewiston, Idaho; Francis Haines, Sr., Monmouth, Oregon; Archibald Hanna and the staff of the Western Americana Collection, Yale University Library, New Haven; and T. R. Hay, Locust Valley, N.Y.

My gratitude, also, to Robert Hitchman, Seattle; J. S. Holliday, San Francisco; V. G. Hopwood, Vancouver; the late J. H. Horner, Wallowa County, Oregon; R. A. Reynolds and the Governor and Committee, Hudson's Bay Company, London; Robert O. Dougan, Haidee Noya, Lyle H. Wright, and their colleagues at the Henry E. Huntington Library and Art Gallery, San Marino, California; H. J. Swinney and Merle Wells, Idaho Historical Society, Boise; Willard E. Ireland, Provincial Archives of British Columbia, Victoria; Donald Jackson, University of Illinois Press, Urbana; and Thomas E. Jessett, Seattle.

Also: Nard Jones, Seattle; Nyle H. Miller and Robert W. Richmond, Kansas State Historical Society, Topeka; William Kelly, Helena; the late Oliver LaFarge; W. Kaye Lamb, Public Archives of Canada, Ottawa; Bruce LeRoy, Washington State Historical Society, Tacoma; Sol Lewis, New York; Sven S. Liljeblad, Idaho State University, Pocatello; my good friends Theodore Little and the artist, Eve Rockwell Little, Clarkston, Washington; John L. Loos, Louisiana State University, Baton Rouge; Mr. and Mrs. Jack McClaran, Enterprise, Oregon; D'Arcy McNickle, Boulder, Colorado; Marjorie Martin, Enterprise, Oregon; Don Miller, Joseph, Oregon; and George R. Brooks, Mrs. Frances H. Stadler, and their associates at the Missouri Historical Society, St. Louis.

My thanks, also, to Michael Kennedy, Mary K. Dempsey, and Vivian A. Paladin of the Montana Historical Society, Helena; Oliver Wendell Holmes, Herman R. Friis, Jane Smith, Elizabeth Drewery, Carmelita Ryan, and Victor Gondos, Jr., at the National Archives, Washington; Herbert Kahler and Jack R. Williams of the National Park Service; Allan Nevins, who encouraged the completion of this book as a logical successor to my earlier *The Patriot Chiefs;* Thomas Vaughan, Barbara Elkins, and Priscilla Knuth of the Oregon Historical Society, Portland; Helen Peterson, Denver; Mae Reed Porter, Santa Fe; and Eugene S. Rogers, Royal Ontario Museum, University of Toronto.

Also: Mari Sandoz, New York; Harry Shave, Winnipeg; John C. Ewers, Margaret G. Blaker, and Edgar M. Howell of the Smithsonian Institution, Washington; G. W. Spragge, Archives of Ontario, Toronto; Carl S. Dentzel, Southwest Museum, Los Angeles; Ralph S. Space, Orofino, Idaho; John Stands in Timber, Lame Deer, Montana; Earl H. Swanson, Jr., Idaho State University, Pocatello; Gerald Tucker, Joseph, Oregon; Sylvester Vigilante, Croton, New York; Marcus Ware, Lewiston, Idaho; Mr. and Mrs. Ralph Watson, Joseph, Oregon; Carl I. Wheat, Menlo Park, California; Mr. and Mrs. Chester Wiggin, Lewiston, Idaho; the late Cull White, Coulee Dam, Washington; Max Wilson, Joseph, Oregon; and Erskine Wood, Portland, Oregon.

In addition to the institutions mentioned, I appreciate staff help given me while I was doing research at the American Philosophical Society, Philadelphia; the Chicago Historical Society; the Library of Congress; the New York Public Library; and the Spokane, Washington, Public Library.

Finally, I wish to thank the able and dedicated cartographer Charles Staurovsky for the maps that help to illuminate the text of this book; the different institutions that kindly provided the illustrations; Angus Cameron and David Horne, friends as well as editors; the Idaho Historical Society and *American Heritage*, both of which published earlier versions of certain portions of the material in this volume; and my wife, Betty, for long years of aid, comfort, and patience.

A. M. J., Jr.

Greenwich, Connecticut

July 1965

CONTENTS

LIST OF ILLUSTRATIONS

Frontispiece: Nez Perce Indian; painting by Paul Kane of a Nez Perce met near the mouth of the Snake River, July 29, 1847. Courtesy Royal Ontario Museum, University of Toronto, and *American Heritage*.

Following page 705

MAPS

INTRODUCTION

ONE OF THE MOST spectacular and least traveled parts of the United States is the so-called Inland Empire of the Northwest, a ruggedly majestic 150,000 square miles of interior land lying between the Cascades and Rocky Mountains and extending southward from the Canadian border for about 300 miles. From the time of the first white settlers, the area, which encompasses present eastern Washington, northeastern Oregon, the northern panhandle of Idaho, and Montana west of the Continental Divide, has been an economic unit, separated by the Cascades from the populous Pacific Coast, by the formidable Salmon River ranges of central Idaho from Boise and the southern cities of that state, and by the Rockies from the broad plains of eastern Montana.

Local sentiment has occasionally urged combining the region into a separate state. The proposal once came close to succeeding, but although it failed by a pocket veto, by President Cleveland, the logic of terrain still prevails. Today the people of northern Idaho, still without direct rail link to their capital city and connected with it only by a grueling, canyon-and-mountain road, consider themselves somewhat neglected relations of the South and frequently feel closer akin to eastern Washington and western Montana. From the Rockies to the Cascades, the area in a sense revolves about Spokane, a transmountain stranger to the bustling cities of coastal Washington and Oregon, the farmers of southern Idaho, and the ranchers of Montana's eastern plains.

Topographically it is a stupendous country of wide open spaces and unspoiled scenery. Much of it is a high plateau, cut into precipitous up-and-down terrain in which climate and temperature vary abruptly according to altitude. Some canyons and valleys are mild and warm even in winter, but to reach a neighboring valley a traveler must often brave a blizzard on the higher levels or twenty-foot snow drifts in the mountain passes. On the floor of a valley one can experience heat, while cool breezes blow along the hillsides rising above him and snow falls on the higher ridgetops.

West of Spokane the land is almost entirely volcanic lava and dry, sagebrush plains, marked in places by the channels and slices of black-walled coulees. This is the country of the Big Bend of the Columbia River. On the extreme west, irrigation works long ago diverted river water to nourish orchards at Wenatchee and Yakima; elsewhere, Big Bend dryland wheat farmers worked themselves almost to their graves during the early years of the twentieth century, trying to whip the drought-ridden soil. They gave up and moved away, but today water flows through turnpike-wide canals from Grand Coulee Dam, bringing success where the pioneers failed. More than a million green acres of the Columbia Basin Project, one of the largest and most dramatic irrigation developments in the world, have given life since World War II to prosperous towns and to thousands of new Washington farmsteads. The country here is high and windy, cool in winter and hot in summer.

South of Spokane and east of the booming Hanford atomic energy center that owes its existence to Grand Coulee's power, stockmen and wheat farmers have found some of the best dryland in the United States in the Umatilla and Walla Walla valleys and across the rolling, picturesque Palouse. The latter, an unusually rich prairie of high, billowing hills in eastern Washington and part of Idaho's panhandle, is one of the nation's most beautiful and bountiful grain and pea districts (it has rarely known a crop failure), while equally lovely, productive basins like Oregon's Grande Ronde and Wallowa are unsurpassed grazing and grass-raising centers.

North and east of Spokane are numerous populated valleys, including the Okanogan, Colville, Missoula, Bitterroot, Flathead, Mission, Deer Lodge, and Big Hole, lying like friendly corridors among flanking ranges of mountains. Man has settled along the riverbanks and benchlands in those valleys, raising cattle, sheep, grass, grains, dairy herds, beets, and truck crops. From the valley centers miners, timber men and recreation-bent sportsmen have sent groping fingers into the surrounding mountains and high meadows. But they have only probed; the untouched wilderness is still immense. In huge, primitive areas barred to roadbuilders are still some of the greatest hunting and fishing grounds in the nation. Elk, deer, bear, mountain goat and sheep, moose, and cougar roam the forests and cliffs as they always have, and the fast, clear streams and alpine lakes are filled with fighting fish. Most of this virgin land of crags, peaks, silent lakes and meadows, thick stands of evergreens, and rushing, whitewater rivers is government owned (more than half of northern Idaho and western Montana is public land), and access is gained only by packstring or in small planes and helicopters that land on river bars or in meadow clearings. Some of the most rugged area is beyond the reach of all but the boldest adventurers, and the deep, tortuous canyon country of the Salmon and Snake rivers, the latter guarded along the Idaho-Oregon border by a range of rocky peaks called the Seven Devils, includes stretches of the most awesome and inaccessible mountain wilderness in the United

States. In this formidable region, in which even packhorses often fail to find footing, are the steep chasms of the Imnaha, the Grande Ronde, Joseph Creek, and Hell's Canyon, the latter the deepest gorge on the North American continent, 7,900 feet down at its dizziest point, or more than 2,000 feet deeper than the Grand Canyon of Arizona.

After the explorers, Lewis and Clark, the first white men to push into this wilderness were fur traders and trappers, but miners were the first to leave permanent marks. Today mining is concentrated in three principal areas, the rock-bound Metalines in northeastern Washington, the Coeur d'Alenes in northern Idaho, and the barren hills farther east around Butte, Montana. They, and smaller diggings dotting the region elsewhere, have been among the most productive silver, copper, lead, and zinc sources in the country, and have also provided the nation with gold, cobalt, antimony, and mercury. Lumbering is carried on in all the many forests of the area, but the biggest operations are centered in the great pine woods of northern Idaho and northwestern Montana. The Clearwater Forest, carpeting the western slopes of the Bitterroot Mountains east of Lewiston, Idaho, contains the last great stand of white pine in the United States, and the annual colorful, whitewater log drive down the tumbling Clearwater River is among the last of its kind in the nation.

The powerful rivers of the interior, with names that roll like echoes of the past—the Flathead, Kootenai, Yakima, Pend Oreille, Clearwater, Bitterroot, Snake, Salmon, and Clark Fork—are all part of the Columbia Basin and have been partially harnessed to control the region's water resources. Many of the largest multipurpose dams in the world, including Grand Coulee, McNary, Hungry Horse, the Dalles, Chief Joseph, and Ice Harbor, as well as a multitude of smaller dams (though big anywhere else in the country), lie within the area. They are linked by a maze of cross-country transmission lines that feed their power into common pools for the entire Far West. The increase of hydroelectric power during the last twenty-five years has been enormous, and the growth of industry, already accelerated, will in time make inroads into today's wilderness and turn many of the present unused parts of the Inland Empire into new centers of activity. New dams on the Snake River above Hell's Canyon, for instance, have already opened to touring sightseers that once-remote part of the gorge. Hungry Horse electric power is feeding new industries in western Montana and has made possible the building of a sprawling new aluminum installation in a former semi-wilderness area near Glacier Park. And power from Grand Coulee for the Hanford atomic energy center in southeast Washington has built a booming population center around the tri-cities of Richland, Kennewick, and Pasco on the Columbia River.

Stern terrain and inadequate power and irrigation for full-scale growth have combined for generations to keep much of this robust area a last frontier. Matching the spaciousness of their land, the people generally are still proud, self-assured, and individualistic, possibly closer in their raw and rugged surroundings to their pioneer heritage than Americans anywhere else. There are old-timers still alive who remember traveling by covered wagon and stage, erecting cabins and breaking virgin soil, fearing Indians, riding horses over new trails, and being treed near their houses by bears. Persons in their seventies and eighties, the Inland Empire's second generation, are still aware of their parents' early trials, and some are the offspring of pioneers who pulled handcarts from the States to Salt Lake City and then to Idaho, who went placer mining in Montana's gulches during the days of the Vigilantes, who entrenched themselves in sod forts during the Nez Perce and Bannock Indian wars. The environment of big country, abundant space, and small population has helped to maintain the pioneer feeling. There is still much restlessness and moving about, and ample evidence of man still pushing out for himself to get away from populated centers. Upper benches, hillside trails, and mountain meadows are dotted with cabins and small, tilled fields belonging to families that have moved off for privacy, felling timber and breaking soil, raising in the mid-twentieth century squared log buildings with dobe caulking and sod-covered roofs that sprout grass and weeds. Away from the main highways, deep in the Washington woods and the Idaho mountains, the traveler comes on lone dwellings and small log hut settlements, inhabited by families that still hunt bears and cougars and board their children in distant school towns during the winter. In Montana, "rugged individualist" miners and lumberjacks speak up loudly, and the roads are still walked by cocky, free-wheeling itinerant ranch hands, gandy dancers, and bindlestiffs.

On the big, formative developments of the Inland Empire the spirit of independence and self-reliance is also present, among the thousands of hopeful young families working the new land of the Columbia Basin Project, among the many Easterners and midwestern city people who have moved out to build new boom towns on the sage desert, and war veterans and industrial workers who are finding promising lives in dozens of growing Idaho and Montana valley centers like Lewiston, Clarkston, Missoula, and Kalispell. Chambers of Commerce advertise for newcomers. Capital is welcomed, but so are people with ideas, energy, and ambition. "We welcome the sincere young man of vision looking for opportunities." "Come join us and grow with us." "The land of your future." There are land and jobs and opportunity and adventure, and this is the Inland Empire of today, a part of the nation that is building, growing, and filling in empty spaces.

Tucked away from the populated centers of this huge country, all but overlooked and forgotten, there is also a handful of Indian tribes. Generally they are a shy, quiet people, but once their fathers rode across the breadth of the Inland Empire and looked upon it as their own. Today the Indians— Umatillas, Yakimas, Flatheads, Colvilles, Nez Perces, and remnants of smaller tribes—dress and live much like their white neighbors. Their young have received some education; they have fought overseas with non-Indian boys against enemies common to all Americans; their husky youths drive logging trucks and modern road-building equipment, work in sawmills, and spend Saturday nights in the towns. Their families live in frame houses, cook on gas and electric stoves, watch television, join Parent-Teacher Associations and the American Legion, read the daily newspapers, and attend church on Sundays. Though most of them reside on reservations, they feel pressure— principally from white men, but also from some of their own people— to end their special relationship with the federal government and abandon the reservation system. If and when that occurs, tribal unity and commonly held resources will evaporate, and the Indians of the Inland Empire, sharing and maintaining a unique cultural heritage, will be no more. Until that day comes, the reservations, land bases for their development and progress, pro- vide a significant and compelling link with the past, with men and events of yesterday.

No part of the United States had a more colorful and adventurous history in its beginnings. Much of what happened has been obscured or even lost for decades. Much of it has been forgotten in the preoccupation of the latter- day civilizers and builders. But against the panorama of the soaring mountains and wild highlands of the Inland Empire great and exciting dramas were once enacted. Above them all looms one, and it, the epic of the Nez Perce Indians— for no word but epic will do—is the subject of this book.

For seventy-five years the Nez Perces * were intimately associated with most of the historic events of the opening and early development of the Northwest by whites. Their horsemen and villagers ranged far and wide in freedom across the hills and river valleys of the region from the Cascades to the Rockies; and until they were defeated in war and penned on their reservations, they were familiar with almost every land feature of the Inland Empire. American schoolboys of the nineteenth century read of the Nez Perces in vividly written accounts of the Lewis and Clark Expedition and in

---

* French-speaking trappers who came across the Canadian Rockies and entered the Oregon country early in the nineteenth century were among the first white men to meet the Nez Perces. They saw some of them wearing bits of decorative shell in their noses and gave them the name by which they are known today. The French, of course, pronounced it *nay pear- say,* but in the tribe's Idaho homeland people now commonly write it without the French accent mark and pronounce it *nezz purse.*

the Washington Irving histories of Astoria and Captain Bonneville. Mountain men spun the Nez Perces into their narratives of the fabled Rocky Mountain fur trade, and in the 1830s eastern pulpits resounded with the inspiring account of a Nez Perce delegation that journeyed from the little-known Oregon country to St. Louis to seek a teacher of Christianity for their people. The tribe's later welcome to Marcus Whitman and his colleagues who, in turn, helped to induce the covered wagon emigration to Oregon, its roles during the periods of the Whitman massacre, the Indian wars of the 1850s, and the Idaho and Montana gold rushes are at the heart of Northwest history and provide some of the West's most colorful chapters. But all pale before the thundering climax of the Nez Perce story, the valiant attempt by Chief Joseph and a part of the tribe in 1877 to escape their white tormentors in a great 1,700-mile retreat, fighting and defeating American armies all the way until a last tragic battle.

Today the Nez Perces live on their reservation almost in the very center of the Inland Empire, a little to the east of Lewiston, Idaho. Their homes are strung along the valleys of the Clearwater River and its tributaries, across the high prairies, and against the western foothills of the Bitterroot Mountains. A few other Nez Perces live on the Colville reservation near Grand Coulee Dam in northeastern Washington, where their fathers were banished after the 1877 war and where Chief Joseph died and is buried. Few white men pay them attention or know their history, but the Nez Perces have not forgotten the conflicts and the heroes of their past. Each year, during the summer, some fifty or sixty adults of the tribe move off with their children and with Indian friends and descendants of former allies from neighboring reservations to an isolated camping spot at Mud Springs in the forested Idaho mountains south of the town of Winchester. Here for ten days they pitch tipis and live somewhat as their ancestors did a century ago, eating Indian foods, playing the age-old stick game, drumming and singing through the night, and dancing to the warriors' songs in fast, spirited steps around the drums. Even though most of them attend Christian churches, these are the "heathens" of the tribe, so called in impatient manner by some whites and Indians because of the historic past this element represents and from which it stems. They are a part of the Inland Empire today, a very proud and noble fragment of the American Northwest. The book that follows is an attempt to tell their story so that the builders of the new civilization emerging in the Inland Empire and changing it into a great new sector of the nation will have it to treasure if they happen also to obliterate the Indian reservations and the links they provide to this part of their own heritage.

"The earth is part of my body . . . I belong to the land out of which I came. The Earth is my mother."

TOOHOOLHOOLZOTE, THE NEZ PERCE

"You ask me to plow the ground! Shall I take a knife and tear my mother's bosom? Then when I die she will not take me to her bosom to rest.

"You ask me to dig for stone! Shall I dig under her skin for her bones? Then when I die I cannot enter her body to be born again.

"You ask me to cut grass and make hay and sell it, and be rich like white men! But how dare I cut off my mother's hair?"

SMOHALLA, NORTHWEST INDIAN RELIGIOUS TEACHER

"Toohoolhoolzote, the cross-grained growler . . . had the usual long preliminary discussion about the earth being his mother, that she should not be disturbed by hoe or plough, that men should subsist on what grows of itself, etc., etc. He railed against the violence that would separate Indians from lands that were theirs by inheritance . . .

"He was answered: 'We do not wish to interfere with your religion, but you must talk about practicable things. Twenty times over you repeat that the earth is your mother . . . Let us hear it no more, but come to business at once.'"

GENERAL O. O. HOWARD, UNITED STATES ARMY, 1877

Part I. The Tribe

I

"Their Hearts Were Good"

ON SEPTEMBER 11, 1805, the Lewis and Clark Expedition began its westward climb across the maze of the Bitterroot Mountain wilderness from present Montana to Idaho. The "Corps of Discovery," having come up the Missouri River to its head, was trying to find navigable waters of the Columbia. The rugged Salmon River of central Idaho had rebuffed the explorers and turned them north. Now they had heard of a gentler tributary of the Columbia—just across the Bitterroots. On that stream they could build canoes that would carry them the rest of the way to the Pacific.

Guided by a Shoshoni Indian and his son, the expedition members followed an old Indian trail that led them along the highest ridges. In the stupendous, forested mountains—"the most terrible mountains I ever beheld," wrote Sergeant Patrick Gass—there was practically nothing to eat. It was fall, the first storms had occurred in the heights, and most of the game had already moved to lower ground. The men had been on short rations ever since leaving the buffalo country of the plains. Now they began to starve. The route made steep ascents and descents, through thick woods choked with underbrush and waist-high piles of windfall, over boulders and slides of shale, and along slippery cliffs where wind, rain, and sleet beat at the travelers. Chilling fog hung low among the trees, and horses lost their footing and rolled down the steep hills. The explorers built big fires, drank soup made from concentrated stock (emergency rations hoarded until now), and by the side of a stream they called Colt Killed Creek, near its junction with the rocky Lochsa River, slaughtered one of their horses for meat. Then came hail and snow, eight inches of it on one day, ten inches during a night, obscuring the path and numbing the men. Day followed day in the cold and snow, and the going became worse.

On September 18, a week after they had entered the mountains, William Clark and six hunters set out in advance of the main party, determined to find something to kill and send back to revive the spirits of the others. After going twenty miles without luck, still heading west through the seemingly endless chain of ranges, they reached the summit of what is called today Sherman Peak and at a great distance across the wilderness sighted the end of their troubles, "an emence Plain and *leavel* Countrey to the S W. & West." They hurried on another twelve miles, part of the way along a narrow, rocky path on the side of a steep, dangerous precipice, and that night camped by a stream which they called "*Hungery* Creek as at that place we had nothing to eate." [1]

The next day, with the promise of an end to the mountains driving them on, Clark and the hunters made their way six miles up Hungry Creek and suddenly, in the woods, saw a horse, a sign that Indians must be near. They killed the animal, skinned and butchered it, and cooked some of the meat for breakfast, hanging the rest on a tree for Lewis' party. Refreshed by the food, they hurried two miles more up the creek and continued over more mountainous country, where they had to keep climbing over and around criss-crossed piles of fallen timber. They made a total of twenty-two miles that day, edging along the sides of more cliffs, killing two grouse in the woods, and noticing thankfully that the air seemed to be getting milder. Tired, stiff, and hungry again, they lay down in their blankets that night, confident that the end of the mountains was near at hand.

Early in the morning they were off again. ". . . proceeded on through a Countrey as ruged as usial," Clark wrote, and finally, after crossing the headwaters of several streams that flowed into Idaho's Lolo Creek, "at 12 miles decended the mountain to a leavel pine Countrey." Clark continued: "Proceeded on through a butifull Countrey for three miles to a Small Plain in which I found maney Indian lodges, at the distance of 1 mile from the lodges,

1. *Original Journals of the Lewis and Clark Expedition 1804–1806*, ed. Reuben Gold Thwaites (rep. New York, 1959), 3, 72. The earlier Gass quotation is from Patrick Gass, *Journals of the Lewis and Clark Expedition* (rep. Minneapolis, 1958), p. 164. Other Expedition quotations in this chapter are from Thwaites, the one by Whitehouse being in 7, 168. Geographic information is based on the Expedition's maps, mostly in Thwaites, Vol. 8; on Clark's manuscript map of the West, undated, but finished possibly in 1812, and published in facsimile by its owner, the Yale University Library, in 1950; on Olin D. Wheeler, *The Trail of Lewis and Clark* (New York, 1904); on studies of the explorers' route across the Lolo Trail by Ralph S. Space, former supervisor of the Clearwater National Forest, including *The Clearwater Story*, published by the U. S. Forest Service (Missoula, Montana, 1964), and *Lewis and Clark through Idaho* (Lewiston, Idaho, n.d.); and on my own field research in the Bitterroot Mountains and the Northwest.

I met 3 Indian boys, when they saw me [they] ran and hid themselves, in the grass I desmounted gave my gun and horse to one of the men, searched in the grass and found 2 of the boys gave them Small pieces of ribin & Sent them forward to the village Soon after a man Came out to meet me with great caution & Conducted me to a large Spacious Lodge which he told me (by Signs) was the Lodge of his great Chief who had Set out 3 days previous with all the Warriers of the nation to war on a South West derection & would return in 15 or 18 days. the fiew men that were left in the Village and great numbers of women geathered around me with much apparent signs of fear, and apr. pleased they those people gave us a Small piece of Buffalow meat, Some dried Salmon beries & roots in different States . . . I gave them a fiew Small articles as preasants . . ."

Thus, on September 20, 1805, about three miles south of the present town of Weippe, Idaho, William Clark recorded the entrance of the first known white men, weary, bedraggled, and starving, into the Nez Perce homeland.

After a brief halt with the Indians, who were gathering an "emence" quantity of camas roots from the prairie, Clark and his companions continued on, looking for the river, which they understood was called the Kooskooske.[2] A throng of curious natives moved along with them, and that night, September 20, the explorers stayed at one of the Indians' villages, still short of the river.

"I find myself verry unwell . . . from eateing the fish & roots too freely," Clark wrote. The next morning he was still sick, but his hunters failed to find game in the nearby woods, and he had to trade for more dried salmon, roots, and berries, some of which he sent back with one of his men to Lewis' party, which was still struggling through the mountains. That afternoon the travelers went on through a "butifull Pine Country badly watered, thinly timbered & covered with grass." At sundown they at last reached the heights above the Kooskooske, the present-day Clearwater River. The men made a long, difficult climb down the bluffs to the river valley and two miles down the stream came on the fishing village of a headman whom they understood was named The Twisted Hair.[3] "I found him a Chearfull man of about 65 with apparent siencerity," Clark noted.

The explorers camped with him that night, giving him an Indian trade medal bearing President Jefferson's likeness, and smoking with him until 1:00

2. Actually a misunderstanding of the Nez Perce term *koos keich keich*, meaning clear water. White men who read the explorers' narrative and went to the Nez Perce country kept calling it the Kooskooske, and when many of the Indians themselves picked it up from the whites, the Clearwater and the Kooskooske became synomomous.

3. According to Lucullus McWhorter, friend and historian of the Nez Perces, this man's name was Walammottinin, signifying "hair or forelock bunched and tied." McWhorter, *Hear Me, My Chiefs!* (Caldwell, Idaho, 1952), p. 18.

NEZ PERCE COUNTRY

+ + + + LEWIS AND CLARK ROUTE
WESTWARD, 1805

→ → → DEVIATIONS ON THE
RETURN TRIP, 1806

1. The Northwest at the Time of Lewis and Clark 1805–06

A.M. In the village they also saw an Indian woman who, they made out by sign language, had once been captured by an enemy tribe on the plains and taken to a place where she had seen white men.

In the morning Clark and his men, accompanied by The Twisted Hair, climbed the bluff and started back to find Lewis' party. They discovered its weak and starving members already arrived on the Weippe Prairie, which was "covered with Spectators viewing the white men and the articles which we had." The Indians gave food to the newcomers, after which The Twisted Hair and several knowledgable natives obliged the two captains by drawing maps on whitened elk skins that showed the river route ahead. The explorers had already noticed white and blue beads and bits of brass and copper among some of the Indians. They were manufactured items that must have been left on the Pacific Coast by sea traders and been bartered inland. Now, the Indians pointed out on their maps where they believed white people lived, near some falls on a big river. It was obviously the Columbia, close to its mouth, and Lewis and Clark saw they could get there all the way from the Kooskooske by canoe.

After distributing more medals, two American flags (one for the important war leader who was away), some tobacco, and various trinkets, the combined party made its way during the next two days to The Twisted Hair's village on the river. The journey suddenly became a nightmare, for most of the men, including Lewis, were stricken with dysentery caused by the fish and roots they had eaten. "8 or 9 men So unwell that they were Compelled to lie on the Side of the road . . . Capt. Lewis verry sick . . . I gave Some Salts & Tarter *emetic*," wrote Clark.

The disabled group eventually hobbled down the Clearwater to a stand of large pine trees opposite the mouth of the river's North Fork. There, as hunters began to bring in deer meat and the men's health improved, the expedition members fashioned canoes, cached their saddles and boxes of spare powder and balls, and turned their branded horses over to The Twisted Hair and members of his family, who promised to take care of the animals until the explorers returned from the Pacific. On October 7 the men loaded their canoes and set off down the Clearwater.

In some places the river was deep and gentle, but in others the canoes shot through dangerous rapids or grounded on shallow bars. The men made good progress, passing many small Nez Perce fishing settlements of grass mat lodges. A serious accident held them up for a day; Gass's canoe split open against some rocks and sank, and the water-soaked supplies had to be opened and dried. In the rescuing of the men and the retrieving of the equipment, the Indians, Clark wrote, "appeared disposed to give us every assistance in their power during our distress." While the expedition dried the baggage and repaired the damaged canoe, the men fraternized with the Indians. It was "verry mery," Clark wrote, and Private Joseph Whitehouse recorded that "we played the fiddle and danced a little."

The accident frightened the two Shoshonis who had guided the expedition across the mountains, and they left the travelers abruptly to return to their own people. On October 10 the expedition set off downstream again, passing more villages and small, mound-shaped sweat houses, and arriving at the juncture of the Snake River, whose deep, bluish-green waters flowed past them between the high bluffs of the almost treeless plateau country. As groups of mounted Indians, clad in leather shirts and leggings, watched from the benches and hillsides, the explorers swept around the bend into the current of the Snake and headed down it against a stiff wind. After a mile, they pulled ashore and made camp on the north bank. Indians gathered around them, gazing at them with interest, and some of them rode boldly into the camp and made friendly signs.

East of the mountains, the Shoshonis had referred to this country west of the Bitterroots as the land of pierced-nosed Indians. Ever since the explorers had arrived at the Weippe Prairie, they had heard the natives calling themselves something that sounded like Chopunnish. But they had also seen a few of the people wearing decorative bits of shell in their nostrils, and they had grown used to calling them the Pierced Noses.[4]

In the first camp on the Snake River, Clark wrote more fully than previously about this numerous people, whose settlements had lined the Clearwater and were still around them. "The *Cho-pun-nish* or Pierced nose Indians," he noted, "are Stout likely men, handsom women, and verry dressey in their way, the dress of the men are a White Buffalow robe or Elk Skin dressed with Beeds which are generally white, Sea Shells & the Mother of Pirl hung to their hair & on a piece of otter skin about their necks hair Ceewed in two parsels hanging forward over their Sholders, feathers, and different Coloured Paints which they find in their Countrey Generally white, Green & light Blue. Some fiew were a Shirt of Dressed Skins and long legins & Mockersons Painted, which appears to be their winters dress, with a plat of twisted grass about their Necks. The women dress in a Shirt of Ibex or Goat Skins which reach quite down to their anckles with a girdle, their heads are not ornemented, their Shirts are ornemented with quilled Brass, Small peces of Brass Cut into different forms, Beeds, Shells & curious bones &c. The men expose those parts which are generally kept from view by other nations but the women are more perticular than any other nation which I have passed in *secreting the parts*."

4. See below, p. 645.

The following morning, after the Indians had told them more about the geography of the area, the expedition members began their descent of the Snake, which they called Lewis' River, for Meriwether Lewis. Several Indians, including The Twisted Hair, who had hastened down the Clearwater after them, went along to assist them, and groups of natives, mounted and on foot, chased along the banks, keeping them company part of the way and enjoying the excitement. The explorers stopped several times at villages to purchase provisions, and at one place bought seven dogs to eat.[5] They inspected an underground sweat house in which the Indians dashed water on heated rocks to send up clouds of steam, and observed the fishing villages and paraphernalia of the natives' fish economy: weirs extending into the river where there were rapids; spears and nets; drying scaffolds; and caches where dried salmon were stored. Most of the villages were empty. It was not the best time for fishing, and the explorers learned that the inhabitants were on the prairie above the bluffs, "hunting the antelope."

Gradually the expedition left the country of the Chopunnish behind, and on October 16 reached the long-sought Columbia. As far down that river as the present city of The Dalles, they met bands with Sahaptin dialects similar to that of the Chopunnish, and The Twisted Hair and another Indian from the Clearwater helped the explorers negotiate with each group. At the site of The Dalles, which was a great, intertribal fishing and trading center, the two Chopunnish said good-by, and the expedition members continued on past Chinookan-speaking fishing settlements to the Pacific Coast. On March 23, 1806, after having wintered near the ocean and not seeing any other white men, the explorers started up the Columbia again. By early May they were back on the Clearwater River and had recovered most of their horses from The Twisted Hair.

During their absence, the travelers' fame had spread among the Chopunnish villages. The Captains had had success in the fall administering soothing lotion to Indians with eye afflictions, and native patients now besieged them. At the same time, headmen more influential than The Twisted Hair had returned from war and wanted to meet them. Guided by The Twisted Hair and a headman named Neesh-ne-park-ke-ook, whom the explorers called The

5. Unable to secure meat, the explorers were occasionally forced to eat dogs. It disgusted the Nez Perces, who, unlike some of the plains tribes, did not eat dog meat. Clark reported that at one time a Nez Perce "very impertinently threw a half starved puppy into the plate of Capt. Lewis by way of derision for our eating dogs and laughed very hartily at his own impertinence; Capt. L.—— was so provoked at the insolence that he caught the puppy and threw it with great violence at him and struck him in the breast and face, seazed his tomahawk, and shewed him by sign that if he repeeted his insolence that he would tomahawk him,   the fellow withdrew apparently much mortified and we continued our Dinner without further molestation."

Cutnose for a wound he had suffered from the lance of an enemy, the expedition members climbed to the plateau south of the Clearwater and made their way to the village of a great war chief named Tunnachemootoolt, or The Broken Arm.

The settlement, lying in the broad Kamiah Valley of the Clearwater, actually consisted of a single long building, like that seen by the explorers in several other villages. It was about 150 feet in length and contained twenty-four fires down its center and about twice that many families. Clark guessed that the village numbered 100 fighting men. Women nearby were pounding and grinding root meal in their mortars, the noise reminding Clark of a nail factory. More impressive to the explorers was the sight of the American flag they had left for The Broken Arm in the fall, flying from a pole near his lodge.

The war chief greeted the explorers at the flagpole, gave them horses to kill for food, and ordered a leather tipi erected for their use. After a meal of horse beef and root bread, Clark wrote with good will: "Those people has shown much greater acts of hospitality than we have witnessed from any nation or tribe since we have passed the rocky Mountains. in short be it spoken to their immortal honor it is the only act which diserves the appelation of hospitality which we have witnessed in this quarter."

That day and the next, two more powerful war leaders and their retinues arrived and were introduced to the explorers. One of them, accompanied by a mounted group of fifty warriors, was named Hohots Ilppilp, which meant Red Grizzly Bear. He wore a tippet of human scalps ornamented with the thumbs and forefingers of enemies he had slain in battle, and he carried the scars of many wounds. The other leader, a stout, good-looking man of about forty named Yoom-park-kar-tim, who lived farther south, had lost his left eye.[6]

6. Lewis and Clark spelled Hohots Ilppilp "Ho-hast-ill-pilp." White men of later days who got to know this headman called him The Bloody Chief, but whether it referred to his bleeding grizzly bear Wyakin or to his numerous battle scars is not clear. Wheeler, *The Trail of Lewis and Clark*, 2, 267, was wide of the mark in saying that his name meant red flute. Hohots Ilppilp's principal home was in the Salmon River country near the mouth of Whitebird Creek. Wheeler, 2, 267, says that Yoom-park-kar-tim meant Five Big Hearts. (The Nez Perce word for five is Pahkatos). The explorers mentioned the assistance of another strong Nez Perce headman who joined the tribe's councils with the Americans. They called him We-ark-koomt and indicated that he lived in the vicinity of present-day Asotin, Wash., on the Snake River slightly above its confluence with the Clearwater. He was actually Apash Wyakaikt (Flint Necklace), and men with the same name, who might have been his son and grandson, became famous Nez Perce leaders. The former was known as Looking Glass Sr., and the latter, also known as Looking Glass, was for a time the principal war leader of the Nez Perces during the war of 1877.

After the Americans distributed medals to the newcomers, the leaders and elders of the different bands crowded into the captains' tipi, and while some of the important fighting men filled the entrance of the lodge to watch, the headmen held a council with Lewis and Clark. The expedition leaders drew a map of the continent and with the help of Sacajawea, the Shoshoni woman interpreter of their group, and a Shoshoni prisoner in The Broken Arm's village, described the powerful American nation that had sent them across the mountains. One of their hopes, they told the Indians, was to establish peace among all the warring western tribes so that they could establish trading houses where the natives could acquire white men's goods. The headmen watched gravely as the visitors pointed out on a map where they might set up trading posts at the mouth of the Marias River and other places across the Bitterroots on the upper Missouri (within the United States–owned territory of the Louisiana Purchase).

At the conclusion of the captains' talk, the Indians said that they would consider the visitors' words and meet with the white leaders again. Outside, the explorers demonstrated the use of some of the objects they had with them, "the power of magnetism, the spye glass, compass, watch, *air gun* and sundery other articles equally novel and incomprehensible to them." The Indians "appeared highly pleased" and told the captains that the previous fall three of their people, who had crossed the plains to visit the Hidatsa Indians on the middle Missouri, had heard about the white men's expedition—which by then had already left the Hidatsa—and had come back with news of "such things in our possession, but that they could not place confidence in the information untill they had now witnessed it themselves."

The next morning the chiefs held a council of their own and agreed to recommend to their bands "confidence in the information they had received." Leaving the meeting, Broken Arm addressed all the people, "making known the deliberations of their council and impressing the necessity of unanimity among them . . . he concluded by inviting all such men as had resolved to abide by the decrees of the council to come and eat and requested such as would not be so bound to shew themselves by not partaking of the feast." There was not a dissenting vote, although many of the women, fearing the placing of too much trust in the strangers' intentions, cried and showed their distress by wringing their hands and tearing their hair.

After the Indians had finished eating, the leading men and elders returned to the captains' tipi and had another meeting, this time with Lewis alone, for they had asked Clark to attend to some of their sick people. An old man, whom Lewis understood was the father of Hohots Ilppilp, announced that the people had agreed to accept the white men's words and that they were "convinced of the advantages of peace and ardently wished to cultivate peace with their neighbors." Early the previous summer, he related, his people had sent three of their brave young men with a pipe of peace to the Snake bands up Snake River. The pipe had been disregarded, and the three emissaries had been slain, and it had resulted in the war expedition against the Snakes which The Broken Arm had led the previous fall. The warriors had found the Snakes and had killed forty-two of them, losing three of their own number. This had satisfied "the blood of the deceased," and they would now hope that the visitors' words of peace would spread to all the Snakes, and they would never have to make war on them again.

As for a people whom they called the "Pahkees," the treacherous Blackfeet and Gros Ventres who frequented the upper Missouri River across the mountains, the white visitors had not yet seen them, and until they managed to do so and convince them to make peace, that part of the country would not be safe. If the white men brought about such a peace and established trading forts on the Missouri, the people of the Clearwater would go over and trade for arms, ammunition, and other things, and would be glad to live around the white men's houses. The old man, Lewis wrote, concluded with the promise "that the whitemen might be assured of their warmest attatchment and that they would alwas give them every assistance in their power; that they were poor but their hearts were good." [7]

Because of the snow in the mountains, which was deeper that year than usual, the expedition was forced to remain for several weeks in the warm valleys of the Nez Perce homeland. Game was scarce, and the Captains sent men off in small parties, looking for villages that had food to trade. One group of three men journeyed up present Lawyer's Creek and across the high Camas Prairie to the confluence of the Snake and Salmon rivers, eyeing the mighty gorges of those rivers, and returning with two Spanish silver dollars that a Nez Perce had taken from around the neck of a dead Snake Indian.

The longer the explorers were with the Nez Perces, the higher grew their regard for them. They found the people industrious and able, cheerful "but not gay," somewhat reticent and reserved, with a dignified, proud bearing

7. Within the context of Nez Perce history this promise had enduring significance. It was a sign from the Nez Perces of an understanding of friendship and alliance, based primarily on the hope that the Nez Perces would profit from it. Word of the agreement was spread among the villages, and knowledge was passed from generation to generation that the Nez Perce leaders had given their word to Lewis and Clark, the first white men in their country. The Indians who could later say that they had met or seen the Captains boasted about it with increasing pride and saw to it that the young men understood the promise given in the Kamiah Valley, and that they honored it. Despite persecution and pressure, the tribe's friendship for Americans persisted with few interruptions until 1877, and white men in their country lived in debt to the respect, honesty, and fairness with which the two Captains had first treated the Nez Perces.

and high ethical standards. Gass called them "the most friendly, honest, and ingenuous" of all tribes. Clark, who Nez Perce tradition says left behind him a Nez Perce woman with child, called them "much more clenly in their persons and habitations than any nation we have seen sence we left the Illinois," and the Captains, who twice (on May 7 and May 13) described them as wearing "a single shell of Wampom" in their pierced noses, said they were fond of gambling, shooting arrows at targets, and horseback riding, and called them "expirt marksmen & good riders." [8]

Early in June, word arrived in the Indians' village that the Snake Indians in the south had heard of the white men's appeal for peace among the tribes and wanted to have a council with the Nez Perces. With much ceremony, The Broken Arm, Hohots Ilppilp, The Cutnose, and most of the Indians responded happily and, saying good-by to the expedition's members, left for the meeting.[9] Soon afterward, the Americans made a start for the mountains. The men were turned back once by snow, but on a second attempt succeeded in crossing the range. On July 1, at the eastern base of the Bitterroots, they set their course for home.

8. Clark, May 7, 1806: "The orniments worn by the Chopunnish are, in their nose a single shell of Wampom . . ." Lewis, May 13, 1806: "the ornament of the nose is a single shell of the wampum." It was usually a small, tusk-shaped dentalium shell that came originally from Vancouver Island and—employed by many coastal peoples as decorations, standards of wealth, and articles of barter—were traded inland. Concerning Clark's Nez Perce offspring: Prior to the 1877 war, William H. Jackson, the western photographer, met a Nez Perce hunting band and took a picture of one of its members whom he said the Indians had told him was the son of William Clark. He was a halfblood with blue eyes and light hair, said Jackson. A copy of Jackson's photograph, with this information, is in the Iconographic Collections of the Wisconsin Historical Society, Madison. In addition, Nelson Miles and his men learned that among the Nez Perce prisoners who had surrendered with Chief Joseph at the Bear Paws was an aged son of William Clark. He was presumably the same person Jackson had photographed.

9. The Indians first went up present-day Lawyer's Creek and across the Camas Prairie to an ancient Nez Perce rendezvous site called Tepahlewam (Split Rocks), meadows at the head of a rocky canyon near present Cottonwood, Idaho. (At this same rendezvous site in 1877 the Nez Perce War with the Americans began.) A few weeks after the Indians had left, The Cut Nose's brother and two other Nez Perces returned to the Clearwater and told the Americans that the Nez Perces and their allies had concluded a peace with the Shoshonis "agreeable to our late advice to them." On the basis of a report by members of the U. S. Naval Exploring Expedition under Charles Wilkes, who made a rapid tour through part of the Nez Perce country in 1841 and learned some of the tribe's history, Thwaites understood that the peace council had occurred in the Grande Ronde Valley of eastern Oregon. (Thwaites, 5, 117 n.). The Cutnose had merely told Clark that he would meet with the Shoshonis at "Lewis's River" (the Snake), but he may have been referring to a general southerly direction, rather than a specific location. The peace, however, turned out to be temporary; soon the bands were fighting again.

The people whom the Lewis and Clark Expedition called the Chopunnish or Pierced Nosed Indians had become a part of the white man's history.

At the time of the explorers' visit, the tribe was one of the more numerous and powerful in the Northwest, estimated to number between 4,000 and 6,000 persons. Their small, independent wintering communities and fishing settlements which the Americans had seen were established mostly near the mouths of lateral streams along the Salmon, Clearwater, and other tributaries of the Snake River in present-day northern Idaho, southeastern Washington, and northeastern Oregon. But the tribal hunting and food-gathering lands that surrounded those riverine settlements extended over hundreds of square miles from the Bitterroots to the Blue Mountains of Oregon, and centered approximately at the site of today's Lewiston, Idaho.

Much is known of the tribe's prehistory, but almost nothing of its origins.

About 10,000 or more years ago, according to one theory, a group of people speaking a parent "Macro-Penutian" tongue came south from Alaska on the western side of the Rockies and somewhere in the mountainous region north of the Great Basin ran into a group of earlier arrivals. The newcomers, it is believed, may thereupon have separated gradually into several elements, some of them turning east toward the present Nez Perce country and eventually becoming the ancestors of many people, including the Nez Perces. [10] Another theory, giving the name Old Cordilleran Culture to a people also presumed to have come south on the western side of the Rockies perhaps 12,000–13,000 years ago, suggests that that culture first became based west of the modern Nez Perce country and gradually spread eastward across the plateau from the axis of the Cascades about 9,000 years ago. Those people may have reached the present Nez Perce area shortly thereafter, possibly even finding other men—so far unknown—already inhabiting the region.[11]

There is no doubt that the Nez Perces and other speakers of Penutian tongues stem from one of the oldest known language superstocks in the present United States, and that humans occupied the Nez Perce country for millennia in prehistoric times. A recent discovery has revealed man's presence in the lower Snake River Valley 6,000–8,000 years ago; and caves and rock shelters elsewhere in the Nez Perce region have yielded combs, woven grasses, wedges, and spear points at least three or four thousand years old, if not older.

Although archaeological findings indicate considerable cultural stability during most of that time, wandering people in search of food occasionally moved through the middle Columbia Basin, entering districts in which others

10. See below, p. 646.
11. Butler, *The Old Cordilleran Culture.*

had previously settled. None of the people seems to have been warlike, and undoubtedly some peaceful combinations and absorptions occurred. Eventually large families and related groups became dominant in various areas, and the Nez Perces may have been one such people. Small, food-foraging bands among the nameless ones who had come south on the western side of the Rockies and who had made their way from Canada's Fraser River or Washington's Cascades to the Columbia and the Snake-Clearwater region, may have been the earliest of their ancestors. Later, other arrivals may have appeared and combined with the descendants of these first groups, and by historic times, after ages of unions, divisions, and intermixings, may have developed into the modern Nez Perces. By that time, the people would have had no knowledge of migrations into the area, and the legends of the villages would only have been able to tell them—as they did—that many, many winters before, when the world was newly made and populated only by animals, their first fathers had sprung to life, fully formed, from the heart of a monster that lived in the Kamiah Valley along the Clearwater, where many then dwelled.

By that time, too, the different languages and dialects of the region would have developed from the parent stocks. Divergencies from the original Penutian would have given rise, among other tongues, to the Sahaptin dialects of the Nez Perces, Wallawallas, Yakimas, and various groups along the middle Columbia. None of those people became well-defined tribes until comparatively recent times. Mutual defense, continuing associations in trade and the gathering of food supplies, unions between persons of different bands, and the shifting of individuals and groups from their own villages to those of friends all played a role in giving somewhat common traditions and identity to related bands. But villages remained autonomous, and the unification of the peoples into tribes in the political sense occurred only after the arrival of white men.

Whoever they originally were and wherever they came from, the Nez Perces occupied a good land but not an easy one, and the struggle for survival in the rugged, hilly plateau country helped during the prehistoric days to mold them into a virile people. In the earliest times they probably wore little clothing—perhaps breechclouts, capes of shredded bark, and fur robes and leg wrappings when it was cold. Later, untailored skin garments came into use, and women took to wearing hats made of twined basketry. By the end of the eighteenth century, dress was carefully tailored and decorated with beads, shells, elk's teeth, and other ornaments, and reflected the influences of Indians of both the Pacific Coast (which had possibly begun reaching them some 800 years ago) and the Great Plains (arriving among them only in the late prehistoric period).

In the narrow valleys along the rivers, where the fishing was good and there was winter warmth beneath towering hills, the people who became the Nez Perces built their permanent settlements, clusters of circular pit-houses with flat, earthern roofs, as well as lodges covered with mats of reeds and grasses. As families moved together and sought increased comfort and social contact, the buildings grew in size and sophistication. Floors were still dug below the level of the earth, and the spare dirt banked for cold-weather protection around the bases of the lodges; but to accommodate many families under a single roof, some of the shelters were extended into long houses up to one hundred feet or more in length. The people slept along the inner walls of the buildings, placing their family fires in rows down the centers, and letting the smoke escape through openings in the roofs along the ridgepoles.

The Nez Perces, like all the Northwest peoples, practiced no agriculture and suffered for it. The gathering of food supplies was an almost constant preoccupation, and although the villagers stored some of their surplus food, they knew lean periods. They were shrewd hunters and artful fishermen, but the wild game came and went, and fish were plentiful only during the seasonal runs. Each spring after the floods of melting snow, the rivers filled with salmon from the Pacific, fighting their way to upper waters to spawn. The Indians waited expectantly for the first sign of their arrival, calling the exciting June period when they usually appeared *hillal,* "the time of the first run of the salmon." Men and boys built rock and driftwood platforms out from the shorelines and splashed into the rapids, gathering large harvests of struggling fish with spears, nets, and weirs of willow brush and poles, which were lashed together and anchored with stones in the streambeds. What fish were not eaten at once were split open, cleaned, and dried on wooden racks in the sun, or smoked and stored away for use in trade or at hungry times in later months.

A second food staple came from the ground. During the winter the higher country that rimmed the valleys was cold and bitter, but when the spring warmed the plateau, the people climbed the tall, grassy slopes and journeyed to favored root-gathering grounds. With sharpened digging sticks, the women poked in the muddy ground and through patches of melting snow, turning up cormlike roots called *kouse,* which they boiled into a mealy mush or cooked and shaped into small cakes to be saved for later use. In the following months there were other roots to be gathered, as well as wild plants, nuts, and berries. In the sparkling meadows of the mountain foothills were wild onions and carrots and pink-blossomed bitterroots. Higher up, in the underbrush of the mountainsides, were hawthorn and service berries, blackberries and strawberries, and gritty huckleberries, all carried down to the camps in large basketfuls to be pressed into cakes and saved for winter, when they would be used to flavor dried fish, meat, and roots.

In late June and July there was another harvest, this time of the favorite camas, a wild lily bulb whose delicate flowers carpeted the prairies with a bluish sheen. The bulbs resembled small onions but, eaten cooked or raw, tasted agreeably sweet. In the summer, when the blossoms had faded, the people of many villages gathered together at the camas grounds, pitched camps of mat-covered lodges, and while the women dug the bulbs with their curved sticks, the men and boys hunted, gambled, and played at games. It was the Nez Perces' happiest communal meeting, an annual combination vacation and time of food-gathering, when the people of the different bands came to know one another. After the camas bulbs had been gathered, steamed, made into dough or pounded into gruel, and some of it packed away for use in later months, the lodge mats were pulled down and rolled into bundles, and the people trooped back to their respective settlements in the valleys.

The most uncertain food, and also the most arduous and difficult to secure, was meat. Without horses, the hunters were limited in the ground they could cover, and often the men who went after game returned unsuccessfully or with scarcely enough meat to feed the waiting villagers. On the chase the men beat through groves of willows and cottonwoods along the canyon riverbanks, looking for the shaded resting places of deer. When they had no luck, they climbed the hot draws of the hillsides, pushing through bunchgrass and underbrush, and avoiding the sudden whirr of rattlesnakes coiled beneath the lava outcroppings. On the plateau they hurried across the open country, searching for deer droppings and signs of trails, sometimes following animals into thick stands of pine that covered the higher shoulders of the hills above the prairies. Often they went for days, ranging into the foothills and forested mountains, making their way across high meadows and along precipitous ridgetops, daring the land of swirling fogs, sudden snows, and many unknown spirits to seek elk, bear, or the prized mountain sheep with the curved horns.

Many times the long chase was in vain. Even if it were sighted, the quarry was frequently hard to reach and kill, though the hunters used stratagems that fathers had taught their sons for generations. Sometimes they cloaked themselves in the skins and antlers of animals they had previously killed and, creeping across the open ground, tried to get close to the game before being detected. Or with great patience they strung out in encircling lines to surround the quarry and, by closing in slowly, attempt to run the animals into a small, confined area where they could easily kill them. In the high grass of the prairies they used nets and nooses to snare rabbits and blue grouse, and when they discovered a coyote or wolf, they tried to lure it into a dead fall. In the dark woods they might suddenly come on a grizzly bear, the most dangerous and fearsome of all the animals, and then it was sometimes a life-and-death struggle between the hunter and hunted. Rearing up to face its attackers, the huge bear could sweep a man from the ground and crush and tear him to death before his companions could save him. Only by the concerted action of several persons or by an individual's exceedingly courageous or lucky attack could a grizzly be brought down. A lone man who accomplished the deed gained the praise of his people and, in later days particularly, would string the bear's claws in a necklace to wear as a badge of bravery.

The Nez Perce hunters in time perfected a variety of weapons, but the best was a distinctive bow which eventually won fame among other Indians who eagerly sought it in intertribal trade. The Nez Perces made the bow, which was about three feet long, from a section of the curled horn of a mountain sheep. After straightening it by a patient process of steaming and stretching, they backed it with deer sinew attached by a glue made from the scraped skin of a salmon or the boiled and dried blood of a sturgeon caught in the Snake River. The finished bow was handsome and powerful, and with it the Nez Perces could whip arrows, as long as the bow itself, clear through the bodies of running animals. Sometimes, when they used the bow against human enemies, the Nez Perces provoked captured rattlesnakes into striking at pieces of liver and then smeared their arrowheads with the venom—though the venom was not as poisonous when it dried.

The roots, berries, and dried fish and meat that the Nez Perces could save from spring through fall were hoarded against the winter starving times, which were sometimes serious. If the hunts had been successful and the root harvests plentiful, the stores could be stretched to go a long way until the return of spring and its new supply of fish and roots. Winter hunters on snowshoes were sometimes lucky to find deer or elk forced down from higher ground. But people often existed for weeks, and even months, on a meager diet of camas and dried salmon, and occasionally, when the food gave out entirely, villagers had to forage for anything edible, including the inner fibers of the bark of trees, or moss which they gathered from tree trunks and then roasted, ground, and made into mush.

There are traditions, and scientific evidence as well, that in prehistoric days buffalo roamed near the Nez Perce homeland in eastern Washington and possibly southeastern Oregon and southwestern Idaho.[12] The animals were no longer that far west when the first white men arrived, but the earliest explorers and fur traders found them still on the southeastern Idaho plains and in the valleys of western Montana, across the Bitterroot range from the Nez Perces. Tribal traditions, stemming from times at least prior to the middle of

12. "Association of Bison with Artifacts in Eastern Washington" by Earl H. Swanson, Jr., *American Antiquity*, 24 (1959), 429–31; Douglas Osborne, "Archaeological Occurrences of Pronghorn Antelope, Bison, and Horse in the Columbia Plateau," *Scientific Monthly*, 77 (1953), 260–69.

the eighteenth century, say that parties of venturesome Nez Perce hunters, following game on foot farther away from their summer camps each year, eventually pushed across the mountains and came down into Montana's Bitterroot Valley. There they met Salish-speaking Flatheads who taught them to hunt buffalo by surrounds, by creeping up on them, or by stampeding them over cliffs. Groups of Nez Perce hunters and their families undoubtedly did get across the Bitterroots to make contact with buffalo-hunting peoples long before any of the Indians of the region got their first horses, and such visits may have become regular. But the number of Nez Perces who made the long trip to hunt buffalo on foot was so few, and the loads they could carry back home across the mountains were so small, that influences from the plains culture made little impact on the tribe as a whole, which continued to have a culture affected primarily by its own Columbia Basin environment and by the other groups that lived there.

The Nez Perces had had close relationships with many of the other northwestern peoples for countless generations. About the mouth of the Snake River and along the middle Columbia and its tributaries they often visited settlements of Wallawallas, Yakimas, Umatillas, Palouse, and river-dwelling Wanapams, all of whom had a plateau culture similar to that of the Nez Perce and spoke Sahaptin dialects closely related to the Nez Perce language. Slightly south of those people, in the Blue Mountains and Grande Ronde Valley of present Oregon, they knew the Cayuse, whose language, like that of the Sahaptin-speakers, stemmed from the Penutian parent stock. Some groups of Nez Perces had their own settlements along the routes to those bands, both on the lower Snake and in northeastern Oregon's Imnaha and lower Grande Ronde valleys and in the Wallowa Valley.

Other Nez Perces had drifted north from the Clearwater and Snake rivers, across high-rolling Palouse plains to the forested country of the Coeur d'Alenes, Spokans, Colvilles, Kalispels, and other northeastern Washington and northern Idaho tribes, who also had a plateau culture but spoke Salish tongues. Most of the Salish-speaking bands, particularly the Flatheads who appeared at Lakes Pend Oreille and Coeur d'Alene from their homeland in the Bitterroot Valley east of the Bitterroot Mountains, got on peaceably with the Nez Perces, and unions between members of the various bands were frequent. When the Nez Perces had trouble, it was usually with the Coeur d'Alenes or Spokans, their closest neighbors in the area, who carried on sporadic feuds with the Nez Perces and sometimes warred with them over rivalries and insults, real or fancied.

The bitterest enemies of the Nez Perces lived in the south. They were the various bands of Shoshonean-speaking peoples of the desert or Great Basin culture who dwelled among the mountains and on the arid plains of southwestern Idaho and southeastern Oregon, and whom Lewis and Clark and other white men later referred to as Snake Indians.[13] Nez Perce hunting parties, moving up the Salmon and Little Salmon rivers toward the lush meadows near Payette Lake north of present-day Boise, ran into groups of those people and waged almost continuous touch-and-go warfare with them. The Shoshonis, one of the most widespread family groups in the West, occupied territory from Montana to southern Oregon, neighboring in part of the western regions with a related people known today as the Northern Paiutes. In southwestern Idaho, the Nez Perce enemies included Western Shoshonis, Northern Paiutes, and Bannocks, the latter an offshoot of the Northern Paiutes who had come to live with the Shoshonis.[14]

Usually, each year in early summer there was a period of truce in order to trade, and groups of Nez Perces, Cayuses, and various Sahaptin-speaking peoples traveled to the region of the mouths of the Weiser, Payette, and Boise rivers in southwestern Idaho to meet peaceably with the Shoshonis and Paiutes. After the trade was concluded and the bands had filed home, the sporadic warfare was resumed. Raids and counter-raids frequently resulted in fierce skirmishes and massacres, and along the Columbia there was so much fear of the southern enemies that most of the Indian fishing villages were located on the river's north bank beyond the reach of the marauders. The Nez Perces, however, taunted the Shoshonis on the southern border of their homeland and drew them into ambushes in the canyons of the Salmon and Snake rivers, and the Shoshonis in anger retaliated with daring invasions of Nez Perce territory. Sometimes, when blood flowed close to home, the Nez Perce bands organized large parties of revenge, joined by Umatillas, Wallawallas, and Cayuses, all dancing and chanting for the righting of wrongs. The intense hostility between the Nez Perces and the Bannocks and Western Shoshonis, whom the Nez Perces called *Teewalka*, "an enemy to be fought," [15] lasted into historic times—as did the annual periods of truce for the summer trade meetings.

13. William Clark believed that the Snakes got their name "by their being remarkable for taming snakes of which they have many in their country" (*Letters of the Lewis and Clark Expedition with Related Documents, 1783–1854*, ed. Donald Jackson, Urbana, Ill., 1962, p. 544). The derivation of the name cannot be established with certainty, but during the first half of the eighteenth century tribes in central Canada and on the middle Missouri were telling French traders that the Indians in the Shoshonis' country were known to them as People of the Serpent.

14. Once called Plateau Shoshoneans, the Northern Paiutes, Shoshonis, and Bannocks are now sometimes linguistically referred to as Numians. See Sydney M. Lamb, "Linguistic Prehistory in the Great Basin," *International Journal of American Linguistics*, 24 (1958).

15. McWhorter, *Hear Me*, p. 10.

Elsewhere, farther toward the northwest and along the Columbia River, the Nez Perces met regularly in peace with other peoples, Sahaptins, Salish, and Chinookan-speaking groups from the lower Columbia and Pacific coastal regions, joining some of them in intertribal gatherings at camas grounds and meeting others at trading centers that had flourished without interruption since ancient times. Many of the Nez Perces, individually or in family groups, traveled across the Columbia plains on foot, following long-known routes to the meeting places. Others, in shovel-nosed dugouts, hollowed by fire from driftwood logs from fourteen to forty feet long, navigated the fast-flowing rivers to the distant gathering sites, guiding their flimsy craft through dangerous rapids with poles and crude paddles. Two of the favored grounds for counciling, trading, and visiting were at the junction of the Snake and Columbia rivers and across the Columbia on the plains of the Yakima Valley. But the biggest trade center of all was far down the Columbia at the busy fishing grounds near today's city of The Dalles, where the river narrowed and boiled between high basalt ledges before it approached the Cascades. There, where Wishram, Wasco, and Wyampam Indians maintained permanent fishing villages, the Nez Perces and other natives from the plateau country met small, unkempt Chinookan-speaking people from the forests and waters of the lower Columbia, people who were somewhat bandy-legged from squatting in their big, high-prowed, deep-water canoes, and who wore shell decorations in their noses and flattened the heads of their children as a mark of beauty and nobility.

The Nez Perces found it adventurous and profitable to travel to this faraway mart. At the Dalles were Indians from all over the Northwest, their many temporary camps, boisterous with dogs and children and foul with the stench of decaying fishheads, lining the rocky shores above the turbulent river. The area was busy with constant visiting between villages. At night there was dancing, gambling, and the telling of stories, and during the day gossiping and trading. The Chinookan-speaking people haggled for slaves to take back to the coast and also for dried meat, furs, animal hides, elk's teeth, camas roots, bear claws, and other articles of the plateau country that the Nez Perces had brought with them. The latter got, in return, dried clams, fish oil, baskets, carved wooden implements, wappatoo roots, and dentalium shells that had come originally in coastal trade from Vancouver Island.

The long practice of gathering at the Dalles and other intertribal meeting places tended inevitably to intermix some of the cultural traits of the different peoples. In the trading of tales, the lore and traditions of the various bands, much of it already stemming from common roots in antiquity, were sometimes blended anew. The legends of the creation of people, which grandparents told the children, often with moral points, were somewhat similar among many different bands, and the monster whose blood had given birth to the first Nez Perces in the Clearwater Valley had its counterparts in monsters that had lived on the Yakima or the Palouse or in Lake Cle Elum in the northern Cascades. The ancient animal heroes of many tribes were also much alike in their characteristics, and some of the most popular myths of different peoples, including the Nez Perces, concerned the same culture hero, Coyote, a supernatural trickster who could accomplish bold and courageous deeds but frequently outsmarted himself with comical results. It was Coyote who, in most tales, slew the fearsome monster that had been devouring all the other animals; he jumped down the monster's throat and sawed up his heart with a flint. When the monster was dead, Coyote cut its body into small pieces, creating the different tribes from the various parts. In each case, the group telling the story had sprung from the monster's blood and was therefore "the bravest and the smartest" of all people.[16]

The bands also acquired new skills, habits, and methods from each other. As hunters, fishermen, and root-gatherers, the Nez Perces traded knowledge with the other peoples, and over the years the intermingling influenced their own culture. They adopted new tools, learned new weaving techniques and designs for their baskets, and copied styles of personal dress, adornment, and decoration. The Dalles was as far west as most of the Nez Perces dared venture, but even the coastal tribesmen they met at the trading center left imprints on their way of life. Some of the Nez Perce family groups flattened their children's heads, as did the people of the lower Columbia and the coast, by binding them tightly between the cradleboard and a pad of hardened skin so that the pressure would give the child's forehead a slanted shape.[17] Other Nez Perces, as well as many of the people on the middle Columbia, pierced their noses and wore thin dentalium shells in their septums, a practice that would later be responsible for giving the entire tribe its historic name.[18]

16. Ella E. Clark, "The Mythology of the Indians in the Pacific Northwest," *Oregon Historical Quarterly*, 54 (1953), 164. Also, the same author's "George Gibbs' Account of Indian Mythology in Oregon and Washington Territories," *Oregon Historical Quarterly*, 56 (1955), 323.

17. See below, p. 646.

18. On March 24, 1826, the famed botanical collector David Douglas was befriended by a Cayuse chief near the Dalles. In return, he wrote: "I bored a hole in the only shilling I had . . . and, the septum of his nose being perforated, I suspended it to it with a brass wire. This was to him the great seal of friendship." *Journal Kept by David Douglas, 1823–1827*, ed. W. Wilks (rep. New York, 1959), p. 159. Eleven years later the westering artist Alfred Jacob Miller painted the portrait of a Nez Perce near Fort Laramie with a ring suspended from his nose. And as late as July 29, 1847, Paul Kane drew the portrait of a Nez Perce with a decorative dentalium shell in his nose whom he met near the junction of the Snake and the Columbia (see frontispiece). For additional

In their travels through the lonely reaches of their homeland, the Nez Perces identified themselves closely with all the natural features of the earth. The enormous ranges of mountains; the vast, forested highlands, often overhung with fog; the maze of canyons and silver threads of rushing rivers; the towering, barren hills; the hot sage plains, scarred with basalt—all were familiar and intimate to the Indians. The earth, in the Nez Perce's belief, was his mother who nourished him, as any mother provides for a child, with the free bounty of her land and waters. The Nez Perces, without the amenities of civilization but with respect for the earth, lived in a state of balance and harmony with their surroundings, almost a natural part of the country itself. They were brothers to the animals and trees, to the grasses seared by the sun, to the insects on the rocks, the brooks running through snowbanks in winter, and the rain dropping from the leaves of bushes. Everything about them, the inanimate objects as well as the creatures that lived, was bound like themselves to the earth and possessed a spiritual being that was joined through a great unseen world of powers to the spirit within an individual Indian.

All peoples have felt the need for supernatural forms of assistance: for gods, magic, four-leaf clovers, or, as white men taught the Indians to call it, a "medicine" that would help them make their way through the world, achieving personal goals and providing protection against dangers. The earliest Nez Perces undoubtedly placed reliance on effigies, dreams, and symbolic rock carvings and drawings. The power of dreams for good and evil remained strong among them, but eventually, perhaps through their intermingling with others, they refined their methods of identifying themselves more intimately with the forces of the natural world. Though they observed no formal religion or organized religious ceremonies, they possessed both men and women shamans—persons with miraculous powers, who could bring good weather, cure the sick by singing sacred songs and prescribing herb medicines, and inflict the bad with illness and misfortune. But the link to nature was even more personal. In all the phases of their daily lives the Nez Perces regarded the spirits of the forces and objects around them, as well as of small token possessions that symbolized spirits, as supernatural guardian forms which they called in a personal way their *Wyakin*.

The Wyakin belief reflected a Nez Perce universe filled with individual spirits that existed in dreams and in real life, and to which Nez Perces could appeal for assistance: thunder, lightning, a soaring eagle, a grizzly bear, and so

---

citations of contemporary observers and more recent research on the subject of Nez Perce and Sahaptin nose-piercing (e.g. Alexander Ross, *Fur Hunters of the Far West,* London, 1855, *1,* 185; and Teit, *The Salishan Tribes,* pp. 82, 147, 340), see Alvin M. Josephy, Jr., "The Naming of the Nez Perces," *Montana, The Magazine of Western History,* 5 (Autumn, 1955), 1–18.

forth. Each spirit could harm or protect a man according to its powers and inclination.[19] The Wyakin could be a single force or a combination of forces acting in concert. Each man had a personal Wyakin, warning him, protecting him, and assisting him through his life on earth. It was the spirit of something in nature around him, a forest fire, a wounded bear, a one-antlered elk, and its presence was made known to the Indian only through his dreams, feelings, instincts, and emotions. When danger was near, a sleeping Nez Perce might be stirred and wakened by his Wyakin. When a man started across a danger- ous river, he could appeal to his Wyakin for assistance and the guarantee of a safe crossing. Many Wounds, a modern-day Nez Perce, explained it to his Christian friend, the chronicler of Nez Perce history Lucullus McWhorter: "It is this way. You have faith, and ask maybe some saint to help with some- thing where you probably are stalled. It is the same way climbing a mountain. You ask Wyakin to help you." [20]

Women could also have a Wyakin, and sometimes they possessed guardian spirits as powerful as those of the men. The process of acquiring a Wyakin was one of the Nez Perces' most sacred and solemn experiences, and was ob- served by both boys and girls. At a certain age, usually between the ninth and fifteenth birthdays, after several years of instruction from an elderly man or woman who already possessed a strong Wyakin, a Nez Perce youth would depart from his village, alone, unarmed, and without food or water, to seek his personal guardian. Frightened, steeling himself for the most awesome of all ordeals, the youth would make his way to a silent and lonely place, per- haps on a mountainside or by a lava outcropping on the plains, to fast and wait for an appearance by the Wyakin.

He would build up a pile of stones and sit by it—not unlike a devout youth of any other faith, seeking a vision or revelation from his god—patiently waiting, night and day, trying to keep his mind on the object of his sacred

19. McWhorter, *Hear Me*, p. 67, reported (from interviews with modern Indians) that the Nez Perces believed in a spirit above all spirits, an idea expressed in many ways, a "Hunyawat or Ahkinkenekii (Man Above, Above All, Deity) who had but two countries, Earth for this life, and Ahkinkenekia (Place of Happiness or Happy Here- after)." In his recent linguistic studies among the Nez Perces, Haruo Aoki perhaps more precisely translated *hunyawat* as meaning a maker or creator (related to a Nez Perce verb, "huneesa," or "make"); Ahkinkenekii: a high one; and Ahkinkenekia: a high region. Early fur traders among the Nez Perces heard Indians refer to a Master of Life which some whites translated into the Great Spirit or Spirit over all spirits in the Indians' supernatural world. All such references, however, including those of McWhorter, prob- ably reflect a degree of Christian influence.

20. McWhorter, *Yellow Wolf* (Caldwell, Idaho, 1948), p. 296. See also George L. Coale, "Notes on the Guardian Spirit Concept among the Nez Perce," *National Archives of Ethnography, 48* (1958).

quest, hoping for a sign that would seize his imagination and surge through him, binding him emotionally to the spirit of something outside of him. The wilder and more frightening his surroundings the quicker his imagination would be stimulated. Sometimes the candidate would be back home after only one night, having recognized his Wyakin unmistakably in a sudden flash of lightning that illuminated a deer, or in the glimpse of a huge grizzly standing on a precipice and looking red in the sunset, or in a rush of wind that whipped toward him and filled his ears with a roar. If the terrifying surroundings failed to produce a Wyakin, the ordeal of contemplation, fasting, and thirst, day after day, might eventually induce a state of dreaminess and unreality in which the Wyakin would be almost bound to appear. The youth would be startled by the apparition of an elk standing over him, or a yellow bird darting back and forth, or perhaps the long howl of a wolf, or the sudden blackening of the sky and the falling of a bundle of arrows from the darkness. The vision might be of something real, or it might be a dream or an hallucination. But when it had gripped the youth and become part of him, he knew that the new bond then existed, and he was ready to hurry back to his village, possessed with a power he had not had before.

Whatever he had glimpsed and absorbed was his own, and he could interpret its powers for himself alone. The spirit of the wind, under certain conditions, could turn enemy arrows from his body. Thunder and lightning would make him brave in battle. A grizzly bear or a bull buffalo would give him strength, the coyote cunning in stalking enemies; the blue grouse would help him hide from danger, and a deer would make him fleet. The Wyakin was his secret guardian spirit, what he later referred to as his good "medicine." It would counteract and protect him from the bad "medicine" of an enemy, or from a sickness or something in nature, and in war he might carry the symbols of his Wyakin—feathers, a bird's head, bits of fur, or other charmlike representations—wrapped in a small medicine bundle which he carefully guarded. At any time, in danger or stress—before setting out on a trip or on the morning of a hunt or a raid against an enemy—he might appeal to his Wyakin for assistance.

But the rights of help and protection were also circumscribed by complicated restrictions, and if the Indian violated a rule stipulated by the Wyakin, dire results, rather than assistance, was bound to follow. Thus a poor hunt, a wound in battle, an accident during a trip, or some other adversity would inevitably be explained by a broken rule, a situation often known in advance by the doomed Indian, who would set out with the ominous knowledge that because he had placed his Wyakin symbol in a forbidden position the night before, or had allowed his woman to do something which the Wyakin had told him to prevent her from doing, or because he was entering battle in the rain when the Wyakin had warned him not to fight in the rain, he had lost protection.

Not all the young men and women who embarked on a sacred vigil found a guardian spirit. Some became so frightened or homesick that they hurried back to their villages before they had seen a vision. Others were unable to concentrate on their quest and eventually lost patience and gave up. It was forbidden to pretend to have received a Wyakin, and the young candidates were made to understand that a false claim would ensure the enmity rather than the protection of the spirit. Those whose lonely vigils were rewarded came back to the villages proud and happy, but made no public announcement of the results. The first occasion in which their families and friends could guess the nature of their newly acquired Wyakins was the Guardian Spirit Dance, which was usually held during the winter when the young men and women, one after the other, would join a dancing circle and chant hints about their Wyakins.

The songs they sang were cryptic, supposedly communicated to the singers by their Wyakins at the time of the sacred vigil, and often only the chanters knew what the words meant. Each singer would refer to his Wyakin with words like, "The wolf comes, now comes the wolf," stating it differently each time, and accompanying the song with wild and repetitive calls, howls, and contortions that suggested the nature of the Wyakin. In the ceremony the singers tried to become one with their guardian spirits. They painted themselves with symbolic designs suggestive of a wolf, an eagle, or whatever their Wyakin was, and older dancers would help arouse them to hypnotic frenzy by joining in their cries and mimicry. Often the dancing became so fevered that youths would drop in a stupor and seem dead. After the ceremony, the ones who had announced the identities of their Wyakins could adopt the names of their guardian spirits. From then on, an Indian might be known by four or five different names. They included the ancestral name first bestowed upon him when he was a child, his guardian spirit name, and various nicknames given him at different times by other members of his village to point up one of his physical or mental characteristics, or to celebrate a feat he had performed.

Sometime between 1700 and 1730, a significant development affected Nez Perce life. The horse, which the Spaniards had brought with them to Mexico and which was spreading north among the Indians from the Spaniards' Rio Grande colonies in New Mexico, first began appearing on the borders of the Nez Perce homeland. The Shoshonis had the animals by 1700, and from the southern Idaho country of those bands horses spread to the Flatheads and other tribes east of the Bitterroots and to the Nez Perces and their neighbors west of that range.[21]

It is not known exactly when or how the Nez Perces acquired their first stock. Nez Perce lore relates that the people first became aware of horses among the Cayuses and, learning that they had come from the Shoshonis, sent an expedition south to trade for some. They purchased, among other animals, a white mare heavy with foal, and that mare and its colt, according to the legend, became the basis of the Nez Perce herds.

It perhaps took the Nez Perces a generation to become fully acclimated to the use of the horse. The younger men probably learned quickly to ride the animals on hunts and in war, while the older and less venturesome people may have preferred to continue to walk, though they would have been happy to let the horses, like big dogs, carry their baggage and possessions. In time, all the villagers found the horses a boon. They welcomed their assistance in getting themselves and their equipment up the steep slopes of the hills and across the rough plateau country to the camas grounds. Travelers journeying farther—members of long-ranging war and hunting bands, families that trekked to distant trading marts, and adventurers who had been used to walking across the Bitterroots to the buffalo country—all took to riding. By the mid-eighteenth century, the Nez Perces were a mounted people.

At the same time, the natural advantages of the Nez Perces' land helped them build up some of the largest horse herds on the continent. Almost everywhere beneath the forested mountains were rich grasslands, carpeting the hills and canyon floors and stretching across the plateau prairies. In summer the high, green meadows, drained by the Grande Ronde, Wallowa, and other streams, made perfect pasture, and when it grew cold, the people

21. Studies on the northward dispersal of horses and their adoption by the Nez Perces include several by Francis Haines: "Where Did the Plains Indians Get Their Horses?" *American Anthropologist*, 40 (1938); "The Northward Spread of Horses among the Plains Indians," ibid.; and, with George B. Hatley and Robert Peckinpah, *The Appaloosa Horse* (Lewiston, Idaho, 1950). My treatment of the subject is greatly in debt to these fine studies by Dr. Haines, as well as to the following works: Robert M. Denhardt, *The Horse of the Americas* (Norman, Okla., 1947); Frank G. Roe, *The Indian and the Horse* (Norman, Okla., 1955); Teit, *The Salishan Tribes*, pp. 109, 351; John C. Ewers, *The Horse in Blackfoot Indian Culture*, Bureau of American Ethnology, Bulletin 159 (Washington, D.C., 1955); Thwaites, *Lewis and Clark Journals*; and *David Thompson's Narrative of His Explorations in Western America, 1784–1812*, ed. J. B. Tyrrell (Toronto, 1916), p. 334. In addition, I have engaged in field research of my own and have received counsel and assistance on the subject of the Nez Perces and their horses from various members of the Nez Perce tribe and from non-Indian stockmen in Idaho, Oregon, Washington, and Montana. I particularly acknowledge the friendly assistance and research done in my behalf by my friend, the late Cull White, horseman and long-time friend of many Northwest Indians.

could drive the animals into the warm, protected valleys and canyons that were grown with protein-rich bunchgrass and dotted with groves of willows. The natural barriers of mountains and chasms that protected the Nez Perces from serious inroads by invaders also helped keep the horse herds from dispersing and moving elsewhere, and wild animals that normally attacked horses were relatively few in the region.

Through the valley of the lower Snake, across the Palouse prairie, and on the broad Columbia plains, wherever conditions were favorable, the horses multiplied. The Wallawalla, Cayuse, and Yakima countries, like that of the Nez Perce, filled with the animals, and when the different peoples gathered for intertribal meetings, thousands of grazing horses covered the landscape. At the Dalles the horse domain ended; on the forest-hemmed lower Columbia, where natural conditions did not favor the horse or its use, the Chinookan-speaking natives never did adopt the animal, but continued to travel on foot or by canoe.

Almost alone among all the Indian peoples on the continent, the Nez Perces also learned how to practice selective breeding. No one knows how they acquired the skill, or why, in their own region, they were the only Indians who became horse breeders. Their ability was the more remarkable in that they acquired it rapidly. In 1806, during his stay with the Nez Perces, Meriwether Lewis let one of the natives geld some of the expedition's horses and, on the animals' surprisingly quick recovery, noted, "I have no hesitation in declaring my beleif that the indian method of gelding is preferable to that practiced by ourselves." Yet the Nez Perces at that time had possessed horses for probably less than one hundred years.

Lewis also noted that some of the Nez Perces' "lofty eligantly formed active and durable" horses were pied "with large spots of white irregularly scattered and intermixed with the black brown bey or some other dark colour." This was perhaps a reference to a horse known today as the Appaloosa, which is marked with distinctive spots, often on the rump only. The Nez Perces acquired some spotted horses along with others that had come up from Mexico, and by selective breeding maintained a number of them among their herds. Contrary to a popular modern story, however, there is no proof that they specially bred spotted horses or favored them above any others.[22]

With the acquisition of the horse, the Nez Perces' horizons expanded, especially in the direction of the buffalo country to the east. Instead of a few friends banding together for the long trip on foot, an entire village or group of villages would now set off on horseback, following one of several trails that led across the mountains. Three of the routes took them over the high country, the most northerly one being the Lolo Trail, which Lewis and Clark

22. See below, p. 648.

traveled, and which began at the Weippe Prairie and emerged in the Flatheads' lands of the Bitterroot Valley. The middle route followed the rugged
divide between the Lochsa and Selway rivers and descended into the Bitterroot Valley via Lost Horse Pass, and the third, or most southerly, ran from
the South Fork of the Clearwater across the divide between the Clearwater
and Salmon rivers to a crossing of the Selway River. There it forked, one
branch emerging in the southern part of the Bitterroot Valley and the other
leading to the Salmon.[23]

All three of these trails were rugged, and from November to June were
blocked by deep snow. A fourth route, longer but less difficult, followed
water level. By traveling to Lake Pend Oreille in the north, the Nez Perces
could move eastward through the mountains along the banks of the Clark
Fork River, emerging in the Flatheads' country near present-day Missoula,
Montana, just north of the Bitterroot Valley. This route was one of the
busiest Indian trade highways in the Northwest and took the Nez Perces
through country frequented by Coeur d'Alenes, Spokans, Kalispels, southern
Kutenais, and Flatheads.[24]

The Salishan-speaking Flatheads had a plateau culture somewhat similar to
that of the Nez Perces, although it was modified by the possession of many
traits of the buffalo-hunting plains tribes. Small herds of buffalo had long
roamed the valleys between the Bitterroots and Rockies that adjoined Flathead lands. But sometime before the Flatheads had acquired horses, large eastern herds of bison had begun moving westward through passes of the Continental Divide, and the Flathead hunting grounds had become some of the best
on the continent. Like the plains tribes, the Flatheads, especially after they
were mounted, pursued the buffalo herds and used many parts of the animals
for food, robes, leather lodge covers, sinews, and bone and horn utensils.

Through the years, Nez Perces who had crossed the Bitterroots had attached themselves to Flathead camps, living, hunting, and intermarrying with
those people, and, while they remained east of the mountains, adopting the
traits of buffalo hunters. Before the period of the horse, those relatively few
adventurers, as previously noted, had made little impact on the ways of life of
their home villages. But with the arrival of the horse and the increased number of Indians who rode to the buffalo country, Nez Perce culture began to
feel the influence of plains traits. The Nez Perces packed their horses at home
with dried fish, salmon oil in sealed fish skins, berries and roots, cakes of

23. Sister M. Alfreda Elsensohn, *Pioneer Days in Idaho County* (Caldwell, Idaho,
1951), Vol. 2, passim; Robert G. Bailey, *River of No Return* (Lewiston, Idaho, 1947),
passim; and Alvin M. Josephy, Jr., "The Lolo Trail," *The Westerners New York Posse
Brand Book, 4* (1958), 82–85.
24. See Teit, *The Salishan Tribes,* pp. 322, 355–57.

camas and huckleberries, bows and arrows of horn and wood, mountain grass hemp, and shells they had purchased at the Dalles. In the camps on the east side of the Bitterroots they traded these goods with their Flathead friends, peaceful Shoshonis, and small bands of Blackfeet from the northeast for dressed buffalo robes, rawhide skins, lodge covers, and a variety of eastern products such as beads, feathered bonnets, and stone pipes that had come across the plains in intertribal trade. With horses, they could take these articles home, and gradually the growing wealth of cultural material from the plains enriched the Nez Perce way of life. Dried buffalo meat was added to the diet; many tipis were covered with long-lasting leather covers; buffalo bone implements and painted rawhide bags and pouches were employed; and showy plains decoration, ornamentation, and costuming, including feathered headdresses, were adopted.

A generally peaceful period of trade and hunting continued east of the mountains for perhaps two or three decades after the Nez Perces first began to use horses. About 1755, however, the confederated Blackfoot tribes (Blackfeet, Piegans, and Bloods) of the Saskatchewan Valley, together with their allies, the Atsinas, or Canadian Gros Ventres, who lived farther east in the region of the Saskatchewan's forks, began to receive British and French guns through fur trade channels.[25] The new arms emboldened the Canadian bands, and their raiding parties—sometimes accompanied by Sarcis, who lived north of the Blackfeet—began to strike savagely at all the western tribes, none of whom had guns. The Kutenais retreated west across the Canadian Rockies, and the Shoshonis withdrew into mountain hiding places in Wyoming and Idaho. Many Nez Perces, hunting with Flatheads in western Montana, were caught in the raids, and survivors of mauled villages sent messengers across the Bitterroots for help.[26]

25. Since approximately 1740 those tribes had been acquiring horses, first in trade with the Kutenais, Flatheads, and Nez Perces, and then in occasional raids against those same people and the Shoshonis. Interesting evidence of Blackfoot trade with the Kutenais for horses is found in a previously unpublished journal entry of 1801 by Peter Fidler, the Hudson's Bay Company trader on the east side of the Canadian Rockies. Two French-Canadian *engagés* of the North West Company had wintered with the Kutenais west of the mountains in 1800–01, the first white men known to have crossed the Canadian Rockies into the Columbia Basin, and on their return Fidler, who heard of their experiences, wrote that they had reported that the Kutenais possessed hatchets, kettles, knives, etc., "formerly traded from the Muddy river Indians [Piegans] for Horses." (Hudson's Bay Company Archives, London, E.3/2, fol. 20, used with the kind permission of the Governor and Committee of the Hudson's Bay Company). During the period of peaceful trade, many of the Kutenais lived east of the Rockies. By Fidler's time the Blackfeet had turned on them and driven them across the mountains.

26. Teit, *The Salishan Tribes*, pp. 316–19, 359–60. Also John C. Ewers, *The Story of the Blackfeet* (Washington, D.C., 1952), pp. 9–20.

Nez Perce warriors and allied Sahaptin and Salish Indians, perhaps realizing the danger to their own homelands if the aggressor were not halted, trailed into western Montana in sufficient numbers to halt the Blackfeet and eventually to stabilize a dangerous frontier with them. But a pattern of conflict was set for a century. The Blackfeet roamed almost at will on the northern plains, raiding the herds of any bands in their path, and acquiring a reputation for belligerency and terror. Their guns were still too few and inaccurate to allow them to establish unchallenged supremacy over all their enemies; but their hit-and-run attacks kept much of what is now western Montana in a state of constant warfare, and their depredations and thefts of horses sent one enraged band against another in desperate attempts to regain honor and replenish lost stock. From time to time, Shoshonis emerged from their hiding places to hunt and, on occasion, managed to hold their own against, or drub, a Blackfoot raiding party. More serious punishment was sometimes meted out to the Canadian invaders by superior-sized bands of Flatheads and Nez Perces who not only met the Blackfeet head on in the Flathead country but ventured across the principal passes of the Continental Divide to the broad plains of the Missouri Basin, where they knew they risked attack. When parties of Blackfeet showed up to contest the hunting grounds, the Nez Perce–Flathead groups engaged them in sharp skirmishes that frequently ended in victory for the westerners, who rode off triumphantly with enemy scalps and horses.[27]

During long years of such hunting and fighting, the Nez Perces acquired many of the characteristics of the plains tribes. Not all of the bands or villages were yet making the trip to the plains. Many of the older people in the fishing settlements at home frowned on the long journeys that sometimes seemed to be little more than excuses for seeking trouble. But those who did cross the mountains returned regularly with scalps, trophies, handsome plains regalia, and stories of bold and dangerous deeds, and the tribe's fish-and-root plateau culture continued to change coloration with added plains traits.

Tribal organization, however, became no more cohesive than it had been. Each village still retained its autonomy under its own civil headman. Sometimes one leader was accepted by several settlements, but no headman could speak for any but his own followers. Authority, also, had its limitations. Headmen usually gave counsel, advice, and leadership, rather than orders. Agreement was by persuasion, and if an individual villager disagreed, he could follow his own bent. Tribal councils of headmen, shamans, elders, and, occasionally, respected war leaders of the different bands or villages could similarly make decisions, but villages, as well as individuals, might comply or not, as they saw fit.

On hunts and in times of war the leading men of the groups that were in-

27. Teit, p. 320.

volved would name a respected hunting or war chief as the leader of the combined party. But the man selected held that power only by the consent of those he led, and exercised it only for the duration of the hunt or hostilities. Each village or band went to the hunting or war grounds with its own subordinate leaders, and these men, who might also attract followers from other bands, could advise the supreme leader or select another if the original one were slain or failed to provide acceptable leadership.

During the latter part of the eighteenth century the buffalo-hunting Nez Perces, frequently traveling in mixed groups with Flatheads and other Salish-speaking peoples, gradually expanded their roaming across enormous areas of the West, coming to know almost as intimately as they knew their own homeland hundreds of square miles of lonely reaches of plains, deserts, and mountains. A principal avenue to the buffalo grasslands of central Montana led through the dangerous Hellgate defile at the site of present-day Missoula, where painted Blackfoot warriors frequently lay in ambush. Once the western Indians had passed safely through that dark gap, they followed the Blackfoot River to the passes of the Rockies north of present-day Helena, and descended cautiously to the high, billowing plains of the Missouri, across which they could roam to the valleys of the Judith, Musselshell, and Yellowstone. Another route took them up the Bitterroot Valley to the Big Hole and Beaverhead regions of southwestern Montana, and on eastward past the forested mountains of today's Yellowstone Park area to the wide Bighorn Basin and the craggy Big Horns of Wyoming. Other passes from the upper Madison and the Beaverhead area led south into the sage and lava flats of eastern Idaho, to the upper Snake River, the northern deserts of present-day Utah, and across the Tetons to Jackson Hole and the valley of Wyoming's Green River. It was big country, but in their travels the Nez Perces became familiar with landmarks, passes, and animal trails over which they would later play out much of their affairs with white men.

At the same time, they came to know many of the nomadic plains peoples and met for the first time Cheyennes, Arapahoes, Kiowas, Comanches, and Utes. Far in the east, Chippewa pressure on the Sioux was driving that people westward onto the Dakota plains. Other eastern tribes, mounted and armed with fur-trade guns, were also in motion, and near the end of the eighteenth century Plains Crees and Assiniboines appeared on the Montana plains from central Canada. Hidatsa, relatives of Crows who had previously broken with them and moved westward as far as Wyoming's Wind River Valley, roamed on horses from their villages on the middle Missouri in present-day North Dakota to the headwaters of the Missouri in southwestern Montana and, like the Blackfoot tribes and Gros Ventres of Canada (the Hidatsa were also known as Gros Ventres), raided the herds of the western bands. There were periods of truce and trade, but enmities festered and intertribal raids were common.

The Nez Perces on the plains lived the warriors' life of the other nomadic bands. A youth proved his manhood and courage and reaped honors and adulation by brave deeds on the hunt or against an enemy. Horse stealing was part of the way of existence which plains war leaders taught the young. Stealing a horse from under an enemy's nose was a dangerous deed, worthy of acclaim. It took courage to slip into an enemy's camp at night, cut the rawhide hobble of a horse, and get away on the animal without being detected. Driving off a whole herd was an especially notable act that carried a fighting man well along the path to chieftainship, a title of bravery and ability that Nez Perces generally earned after ten successful raids.

White men of later times frequently misconstrued raiding—both of band against band and Indian against white—as war; but what they regarded as war was often only the attempt of a daring individual or small group to accomplish a brave deed and win honors. Sometimes the raids had other objectives: the securing of prisoners or scalps, the opportunity to win an honor by counting coup (touching an enemy with one's hand or with a special coup stick, and getting away unharmed), or—at the harshest extreme—the annihilation of an enemy camp in revenge for an insult or injury suffered by one's own people. Tribal headmen and chiefs might make truces with an enemy and promise to halt such raids, but they could not be responsible for the conduct of any bands save their own, and even then they could not always prevent rash and unauthorized actions by their honor-seeking braves.

The loss of one's own men on a raid was not taken lightly. If a chief or respected warrior were slain or too many casualties were being suffered, the raid might be broken off abruptly, and the attackers would retreat, miserable with failure. Back at camp, the fighting men might receive humiliating reproaches.[28] The men would blacken their faces in mourning; the women would wail and mutilate themselves, tear their hair, and smear their bodies with blood from their wounds. All the village would cry for another raid to avenge the losses. Then the warriors might strike at the same enemy or, in their fury, might turn against another band, raiding its herd and killing innocent people to satisfy their honor. But rarely were there prolonged tribal wars or sustained battles in which large numbers of combatants were killed.

Whatever the roaming Nez Perces had not previously known about these ways of the life of the plains tribes, they learned during the closing decades of the eighteenth century as they continued to travel with the Salish tribes and clash with Blackfeet and Gros Ventres from Canada and with Hidatsa, Crows,

28. Leaders of Blackfoot war parties generally understood that they risked humiliation and disgrace if they lost any of their own men.

Assiniboines, and other peoples from the East. The Nez Perce herds were raided and some of their people killed or taken prisoner. When that happened, the Nez Perces, usually in company with Flatheads, reacted in the furious, dramatic way of the plains. In their camps, excitement ruled, and everyone prepared for a counter-raid. The dogs barked, the children gathered to watch the fighting men get ready, the women rocked back and forth, crying for the dead, and the older men gathered in council to talk and raise the war spirit. As the drums boomed, the young men stripped to breechclout and moccasins and took out their war paint. The powdered tints were mixed with water or grease and applied with all the fastidious care of dandies at their toilet. A red streak went down the part in the center of the hair. The forehead was smeared solidly with red or orange for strength. Dots and lines of yellow, red, green, or black covered the cheeks, eyelids, and body, often in a special individual pattern that represented the man's guardian spirit. After the paint came feathers and symbolic decorations. Some of the warriors donned eagle-feathered warbonnets which they had copied from the eastern tribes. Others put on headdresses made from animals with powers sacred to themselves—the heads of wolves, or of young buffalo with the horns still in place, or sashes, necklaces, armbands, and garters fashioned from animal tails, strips of ermine and otter skins, birds' heads, bones, grizzly bear claws, elks' teeth, and feathers. Each item had a strong and personal meaning to the fighting man, denoting his rank or valorous deeds, or linking him to his guardian for protection and strength on the dangerous mission.

The horses were often painted, too, the white ones best showing the striking war designs. The head and neck were streaked with yellow and red, the mane blackened, the body covered with meaningful stripes, circles, and zigzag lines; and the tail, clubbed in a knot, was tied short, painted red, and hung with colored streamers. From the horse's head festoons of feathers, streamers, and trinkets became animal warbonnets; and when the warrior looped a rawhide bridle to the underjaw of his horse and leaped on its back, man and animal almost blended in a single wild apparition of colors and decorations. The first men, mounted and ready with hide shields, bows, lances, warclubs, and arrows whose tips had sometimes been smeared with rattlesnake venom, raced back and forth through the camp, shouting boasts of what they would do to the enemy, and exhorting the others to hurry and join them. Often there were ceremonies to help ensure good fortune for the party. War dances were held, their movements copied from the war dances of the Crows on whose camps Nez Perce scouts had spied to learn the routines, and the older chiefs and fighting men would dig out the emblems of their ranks and brave deeds of the past and hurry to the affair with medicine rattles, decorated clubs, quirts, pipes, and spears hung with eagle feathers and ceremonial sticks with decorated hoops or crooked ends, each of which had symbolic importance to its possessor or to the village as a whole. Afterward there would be a frenzied display of equestrian feats and a mock attack on horseback by the warriors, which was reviewed by the chiefs and the excited villagers.

On the war trail the party observed strict discipline under the war chief's leadership. Scouts traveled ahead of the main body, moving cautiously toward every rise, searching for horse tracks, footprints, signs of campfires, herds of disturbed animals, and other evidence of the enemy. At first the group moved by day and rested at night. As signs of the enemy increased, the party rode at night. When spies found the enemy's camp, they watched it for a while, studying its size and location, the nature of the surrounding terrain, the guard over the horse herd, and the activities of the people. The main body of Nez Perces and Flatheads would wait in hiding behind a hill or in a wooded area until darkness. Late at night a few men on foot would make their way quietly into the enemy camp, throwing pieces of meat to silence the dogs. After working their way cautiously into the herd, they would cut the rawhide picket lines and slowly and quietly lead the animals out of camp.

If any of the enemy awoke, or if barking dogs revealed the raiders' presence, the main group of Nez Perces and Flatheads would make a sudden, wild charge into the camp, yelling like demons, shooting arrows at the dark tipis, and stampeding all the horses in a panicked flight away from the village. Some of the men would fall behind to divert the awakening enemy and hold off pursurers while the main body hurried the horses homeward as fast as possible along the trail. The enemy was almost sure to come after them, but if the raiders got a long-enough head start, rode night and day with few pauses, and were careful to cover their trail, they were frequently able to evade their pursuers and reach the safety of their camp, where the people would greet them with rejoicing. If any were fortunate enough also to have brought home a prisoner or a scalp, it was an occasion for another dance and celebration, during which the heroes of the raid could recount the coups they had scored and the glorious exploits they had achieved. For a few days, if there were a prisoner, he was made to hold aloft the scalps of his friends on a pole, while the women danced fiendishly around him and tortured him. Afterward he was given the liberty of the camp and, though regarded as a slave, was treated kindly and, quite often, adopted by a Nez Perce family.

By 1800 the white man's presence on the continent, which had already forced the movement of many eastern tribes onto the plains, was beginning to have an indirect impact on intertribal plains warfare. Increasing numbers of guns were appearing in the hands of Canadian and Missouri River Indians from the east, and for the first time an inequality of power was threatening the Nez Perces and other western tribes that had no way of acquiring firearms and powder and shot.[29] Some Nez Perces, taken prisoner on the plains and brought to the Saskatchewan or the Missouri by their captors, apparently saw white men but were in no position to trade with them.[30] Although the rest of the tribe were still to glimpse their first white men, there is no doubt that they had an awareness of a particularly powerful people beyond the borders of any band that they had yet met. A great quantity of beads and pieces of metal, which the Indians used mostly for decoration, had been coming inland from Pacific Coast sea traders, and on the Columbia the Nez Perces had been hearing descriptions of those men and had come to believe that they lived on the lower part of the big river. From the Shoshonis, who were getting Spanish bridles and other articles stolen in New Mexico, they had picked up gossip about powerful, bearded men in that direction. And from the Crows who visited the Hidatsa and Mandans on the middle Missouri, they had heard increasingly of the white traders who came up that river and supplied the Indians with metal knives, hatchets, and guns.

According to the Nez Perces, the first of their own people to see white men and return to tell about them was a woman who, sometime late in the eighteenth century, was captured by Blackfeet or Atsinas during a raid in the Montana buffalo country and taken to Canada. There she was sold to another tribe living farther east, perhaps the Assiniboines or Plains Crees. Eventually she was purchased by a white man, probably a French Canadian or halfblood, and lived for a while among the whites. They treated her with kindness and gave her medicine to help her trachoma, a contagious conjunctivitis that raged among the Nez Perces. The girl gave birth to a child, after which things apparently did not go well for her, for she ran away and after several months of wandering, during which her child died, she reached a band of friendly Salish who restored her to her own people.

The Nez Perces called her Watkuweis which meant "returned from a far

29. The plight of the Kutenais, for example, was reported by Duncan M'Gillivray, the North West Company trader, who noted in his journal at Fort George on the Saskatchewan River east of the Rockies on February 22, 1795: "the Coutonées a tribe from the Southwest are determined to force their way this year to the Fort or perish in the attempt . . . The Coutonées have already made several attempts to visit us, but they have been always obstructed by their enemies [the Blackfeet] and forced to relinquish their design with loss . . ." *The Journal of Duncan M'Gillivray, 1794–95*, ed. Arthur S. Morton (Toronto, 1929), p. 56. Some of the Kutenais got past the Blackfeet soon afterward and secured guns, for Peter Fidler noted that on May 23, 1801, the two Canadians, mentioned above, n. 25, who had wintered with the Kutenais, reported that those Indians already used guns, and that "the Bow" was "much upon the Decline" (Hudson's Bay Company Archives E.3/2, fols. 19d, 20, printed with the permission of the Governor and Committee of the Hudson's Bay Company).

30. See below, p. 649.

away country," and her stories of the white men whom she called Soyappo (a Salish term for long knives, by which eastern tribes designated whites, though usually Americans in particular), or, in another version, Allimah ("big blade"), spread among the different Nez Perce villages. The Nez Perces say that it was Watkuweis, now aged and dying, whom William Clark saw in The Twisted Hair's village on the Clearwater the night after the explorer's arrival in the Nez Perce country. Clark noted in his journal that she "had formerly been taken by the Minitarries of the north [the Atsinas] & seen white men," but the Nez Perces add that, although Clark did not know it, it was on her recommendation that the Indians received the expedition in a friendly manner. "These are the people who helped me," tribal tradition quotes the old woman as telling her people. "Do them no hurt." [31]

Equally compelling as a motive for the Nez Perces' friendship to Lewis and Clark was the Indians' desire for white men's guns and other powerful articles. In the spring of 1805, as the Nez Perces told Lewis and Clark, three Nez Perces had made a bold expedition to the Hidatsa on the middle Missouri. They had probably traveled eastward to present-day North Dakota with a band of Crows who regularly visited the Hidatsa to trade plains articles and horses for corn and guns. Before the Nez Perces left the Hidatsa, they heard about the expedition of white men who had already gone on with their powerful goods toward the region of the western mountains.

Either those three Nez Perces or another group at about the same time secured six guns from the Hidatsa.[32] They were the first guns the Nez Perces ever owned. The travelers got safely back to their homeland with the firearms, and during Lewis and Clark's stay with the Nez Perces, the explorers gave the Indians some ammunition for the weapons.

To the Nez Perces the visit of Lewis and Clark was the promise of more white visitors—traders with all the articles, including guns, that the white man was supplying the Nez Perces' enemies. The greater significance of the

31. McWhorter, *Hear Me*, pp. 17–18. Kate C. McBeth, in *The Nez Perces since Lewis and Clark* (New York, 1908), pp. 24–26, tells the story also, but says that Soyappo meant the crowned ones, referring to the fact that the white men wore hats. At the time Miss McBeth wrote, the word had come to have that significance. But until the middle of the nineteenth century most Indians in the Midwest called Americans the Long Knives, and the term had traveled from tribe to tribe as far as the Rockies. At the fur trappers' rendezvous of 1834 William Marshall Anderson took pains to discover what each of the tribes called the Americans. "So far as I can learn," he wrote, "they are all synonyms of 'long knife,' 'big blade,' or 'sword' . . . the Nez Perces say we are Alaim—big blade; the Flatheads, Sooi-api—sword or long knife . . ." See "Anderson's Narrative of a Ride to the Rocky Mountains in 1834," ed. Albert J. Partoll, in *Frontier Omnibus*, ed. John W. Hakola (Missoula, Montana, 1962), p. 78.
32. They were members of The Broken Arm's band. Thwaites, *Journals*, 5, 23.

explorers' arrival could not be understood. The Nez Perces had had nothing in their experience to tell them that, from then on, their homeland would be a part of the great arena of struggle between white men and Indians for possession of the continent. Of that, Lewis and Clark gave no hint.

2

Fur Trade Embroilments

THE THREE DECADES after the departure of Lewis and Clark from the Northwest were important ones for the Nez Perces. It was the period when the fur
trade of the white men swirled around the tribe, when the Nez Perces became
armed and enriched with manufactured goods, and when they reached a new
position of power and influence, while at the same time becoming enmeshed
in forces that would ultimately crush them.

Five Nez Perces guided Lewis and Clark eastward across the perilous Bitterroots and put one division of the expedition under Lewis on the route to
the Blackfoot country of the upper Missouri, hoping dimly that the Americans could talk those belligerent people into a peace and then establish a trading post near the mouth of the Marias River. Lewis' effort failed, as the Nez
Perces thought it would. South of present-day Cut Bank, Montana, on the
upper waters of the Marias, the American Captain and three of his men ran
into a hunting party of eight Piegans. Lewis' plea—that their tribe make
peace with the western Indians and that all then come to trade for guns and
other goods at a post the Americans would build on the Marias River—fell on
deaf ears. The Piegans attacked; the explorer and his men, after killing two of
the assailants, barely got away with their lives.[1]

If word of the debacle reached the Nez Perces, their disappointment was
short-lived, for the next year, as if making good the promise of Lewis and
Clark, white traders arrived in the Northwest. Early in the summer of 1807,
David Thompson, heading a party of the North West Company of Montreal,
which had long wanted to open trade with the Kutenais and other Indians of
the Columbia Basin, crossed the Canadian Rockies over Howse Pass and es-

1. See below, p. 651.

tablished a trading post, the Kootanae House, on the upper part of the Columbia River north of the present British Columbia-Montana border.[2] News of the white men's arrival reached a group of Flatheads and Nez Perces in northwestern Montana, and they tried to visit the northerly post. A band of Piegans, Bloods, and Blackfeet cut them off, and the Nez Perces and Flatheads sent word to Thompson via two Kutenai Indians that they had gone, instead, "to a military Post" of some Americans, who were also in the Northwest. By way of explanation regarding the presence of that group, the Kutenais, Thompson noted in his journal on August 13, "informed me that about 3 weeks ago the Americans to the number of 42 arrived to settle a military Post, at the confluence of the two most southern & considerable Branches of the Columbia & that they were preparing to make a small advance post lower down on the River. 2 of those who were with Capt. Lewis were also with them of whom the poor Kootenaes related several dreadful stories."[3]

Who these Americans were, who had sent them, where they had located their military post, or what eventually happened to them are all mysteries. But further information about them, provided by Thompson, makes it clear that Nez Perces were with them. On that same August 13, the two Kutenais gave Thompson a letter from the Americans which was dated "Fort Lewis, Yellow River, Columbia, July 10, 1807." It was signed "James Roseman Lieutenant" and "Zachary Perch Captain & Commanding Officer," and, notifying Thompson erroneously that he was in territory "within the jurisdiction of Congress," contained in addition a set of regulations for foreigners trading with Indians within the United States.[4] Thompson ignored the letter, but on December 24 the Kutenais brought him a second and more sternly written communication, this one dated September 29, 1807, at "Poltitopalton Lake" and signed "Jeremy Pinch Lieut."

The new letter informed the British trader that "a chief of the Poltitopalton" Indians had told the Americans that the first message had reached Thompson and that the Americans considered his failure to reply to it as "tacit disrespect." It threatened Thompson with force and blamed him for difficulties the Americans were having with Blackfeet and their allies, who had received arms from the British traders. "The Pichenees [Atsinas]," the letter stated, "with their bloodthirsty allies made an inroad into the Territories of the Poltito palton, our friends and wounded one of our brave soldiers." Thompson replied to this letter, via the Kutenais, saying that he was not authorized to discuss the question of ownership of the area in which he

2. See below, p. 653.
3. See below, p. 655.
4. See below, p. 656.

was trading, and at the same time sent the Americans' note to his colleagues of the North West Company on the eastern side of the Canadian Rockies with an explanation that the Poltito Paltons were the "Green Wood Indians," a name by which the British traders at the time referred to the Nez Perces, whom they had not yet met but knew about from other tribes.[5]

The Nez Perces have no tribal memory of these Americans, the first that any of them presumably had met since Lewis and Clark's departure the year before. Neither U.S. Army nor militia records reveal a trace of a "James Roseman," a "Zachary Perch," or a "Jeremy Pinch" (which may have been a misreading on the second letter of "Zachary Perch"). There is no record of the departure of such an expedition to the Northwest, or of its return to the States. "Fort Lewis, Yellow River, Columbia," could have been one of several places, including the junction of the Clark Fork and Bitterroot rivers near present-day Missoula or the junction of the Snake and Clearwater or Snake and Columbia, and "Paltitopalton Lake" could have been Montana's Flathead Lake or northern Idaho's Lake Pend Oreille.

The name "Paltitopalton" is reminiscent of "Pelloat Pallah," which Lewis and Clark had reported that certain bands of the Chopunnish, or Nez Perce, tribe had called themselves.[6] Conceivably, the American group could have been dispatched from St. Louis in 1806 on a secret exploring and spying mission, its military leader disguising his identity and also doing some private trading along the way. (A skein of evidence, in fact, suggests that just such an expedition, sent up the Missouri River in 1806 by the master intriguer General James Wilkinson, who was then Governor of Louisiana Territory in St. Louis, and led by a Captain John McClallen, an ex-artillery officer who had served Wilkinson in public and private ventures, may have gone to the Northwest and been wiped out by Blackfeet. But no proof of these speculations has yet been found.)[7] Conceivably, too, the group, whose ranks included two veterans of service with Lewis and Clark, made contact with friendly Flatheads and Nez Perces, hovered about the area of present-day Missoula, the Clark Fork Valley and Flathead Lake, and eventually met total disaster at the hands of the Saskatchewan River Indians. Whatever the facts

5. The text of the "Pinch" letter is in Tyrrell, "Letter of Roseman and Perch." Thompson's explanatory comments to his colleagues on the eastern side of the Rockies include the following: "It seems this officer [Pinch] was on a party of Discovery when he wrote the above. His Poltito paltons are the Green Wood Indians—his Pilchenees the Fall Indians [Atsinas], I suppose, as it was they wounded the soldier—not one of these petty officers but what has as much arrogance as Buonaparte at the head of his invincibles." For the identity of Green Wood Indians as Nez Perces see Coues, *New Light*, 2, 712.

6. See below, p. 649.

7. See below, p. 657.

were, Thompson's testimony, coupling the Americans with the Nez Perces, is all that is definitely known of the group.

During the next few years, Thompson and his associates, mostly French-Canadian and halfblood trappers from eastern and central Canada, traveled the streams and trails of the upper Columbia Basin, generally exploring and following the main Indian transportation arteries on the northern and western fringes of the Nez Perce country. In northwestern Montana, northern Idaho, and eastern Washington the trader-explorer and his clerks built a succession of posts, opening trade with all the tribes in the region. In December 1807 two Nez Perces, in company with Flatheads, finally made their first visit to the Kootanae House. Thereafter, Nez Perces, singly and in groups, appeared at the different posts, and Thompson recorded his trade with them, referring to them occasionally as Green Wood Indians, but usually as Shawpatins or other variants of Sahaptin, which the Salish tribes called them. At the Kullyspell House, which the trader built on Lake Pend Oreille in September 1809, for the Kalispels and other Indians in that area, he noted the arrival that same month of Green Wood Indians who, using sign language, presented him with "a Bear skin, 1 Beaver . . . 5 Rats with 2 parcels of dried fish & 2 Mares." Thompson gave them each some tobacco and an awl, showed them how to stretch the skins of the different animals they killed, and sent them away with a promise of more goods when they returned with furs.

Another of his posts, the Saleesh House, erected in November 1809 on the Clark Fork River near Thompson Falls, Montana, catered principally to the Flatheads, although it was also frequented by Nez Perces on their way to or from the buffalo grounds. There, on March 11, 1810, Thompson noted in his journal, "Traded a very trifle of provisions from the Nez Perce . . ." The French Canadians, taking their cue from the sign language for the tribe, or from the shells which some of the Nez Perces wore in their noses, had already been calling them Nez Perces, but Thompson's notation of that date was the first written reference to them by that name. From then on, through continual use by French-speaking trappers and traders, the name clung to the tribe, though its members eventually dropped the practice of nose-piercing.

By the spring of 1810 Thompson had distributed more than 20 guns and 100 iron arrowheads among the western natives, and in the summer of that year a band of 150 Flatheads and Nez Perces, some with guns, met a Piegan war party on the plains and for the first time used the new weapons in battle. The Piegans recoiled in fury, and during the winter, when Thompson had gone east for more supplies, they blocked the pass he normally used, forcing him to return to the Columbia Basin by a more northerly route. In his absence in the East, two of his men, Finan McDonald and Jaco Finlay, had built a new post, the Spokane House, about ten miles northwest of the present

Washington city of that name, and had traded more guns to Spokans, Kalispels, and Nez Perces in the area. Thompson arrived at that post to find a war party of those Indians ready to test their new weapons in a raid against the Okanogans, a Salish-speaking group in northeastern Washington that did not yet have firearms. After a stern lecture from the trader, the Indians called off the raid and rode eastward instead, in search of Blackfeet.

Busy elsewhere, Thompson never entered the Nez Perce homeland, and his trade with members of that tribe was limited to Nez Perce hunting bands and small groups that visited other people's countries. Some guns, iron arrowheads, kettles, awls, cloth, woolen shirts, and other manufactured articles were brought back to the Nez Perce villages, but they were few in number and resulted in little change in the ways of the people as a whole.

With other Nor'Westers from Canada coming into the Columbia Basin to continue the trade he had begun, Thompson left the region in 1812. Before then, Nez Perce buffalo hunters had been meeting and doing a smattering of trade with more Americans who had been pushing westward up the Missouri and across the plains. As early as the winter of 1807–08, Nez Perces and Flatheads may have come on John Colter on the western side of the Teton Mountains.[8] Late of the Lewis and Clark Expedition, Colter was then in the employ of the St. Louis fur entrepreneur Manuel Lisa. The American had few trade goods with him, but he was searching for tribes to induce to go to Manuel's new post at the mouth of the Bighorn River, and he would have urged the Nez Perces and Flatheads to make that trip. The Indians may have guided Colter part way back to Manuel's fort, but, not wishing to undertake so distant a journey, some of it through Blackfoot regions, may have made an appointment to meet the American again in the spring. Certainly in the spring of 1808 Flatheads—and quite likely Nez Perces—traveling with a band of Crows did meet Colter on western Montana's Gallatin River and started for Manuel's post with him. The party ran into Blackfeet, and after a bruising fight in which the wounded Colter enraged the Canadian warriors by helping the western Indians with his gun, the Blackfeet withdrew, and the Flatheads and their allies decided they had had enough trouble and let Colter go on to the American post without them.[9]

8. Colter reported that on this trip he had gone from the Crows "to several other tribes" (Henry M. Brackenridge, *Views of Louisiana*, Pittsburgh, 1814, p. 92). On the western side of the Teton Mountains, beyond the Crow country, these would have been bands of Shoshonis, Bannocks, Flatheads, and Nez Perces. There is reason to believe that all the evidence concerning Colter's 1807–08 trip has not yet been found, and that in time it may be discovered that he did not travel alone, that on his return trip he journeyed northward west of the Tetons, perhaps with Flatheads and Nez Perces, and that he was west of the Continental Divide in Montana.

9. The assumption that Nez Perces may have been with the Flatheads and Crows in this battle is based on descriptive evidence in Thomas James, *Three Years among the*

For several years after that, Lisa's beaver hunters fanned westward across the plains and into Nez Perce–frequented regions in the mountains. Peter Wiser, another Lewis and Clark veteran, found a route from the Three Forks of the Missouri to the Henry Fork of the Snake River in southeastern Idaho near the country Colter had visited in the winter of 1807–08. Nez Perces and Flatheads may also have guided Wiser on that trip, for soon afterward Americans equated the Idaho area with those tribes, as well as with the Shoshonis, all of whom they considered friendly to whites. As other trappers, including Colter, kept returning to the Three Forks, each time being struck and scattered by Blackfeet, the theme became insistent: the Flatheads and their allies were on the side of the Americans. In the fall of 1808, the members of one Lisa group, under a hunter named Casé Fortin, cached their furs at the Three Forks and, leaving the area to the Blackfeet, sent word to other trappers that they were heading across the Continental Divide to the Flatheads' country, which must have seemed a sanctuary to them. They would probably have wintered with Flatheads and Nez Perces on the Clark Fork River or in the area of Missoula. But history knows nothing of what happened to them, nor even whether they got safely over the mountains.[10]

A little more is known of a man named Charles Courtin, a French Canadian who became an American. Courtin went up the Missouri ahead of Manuel Lisa's group in 1807, established a post in the Three Forks area, and sometime later, presumably under Blackfoot pressure, crossed one of the passes of the Rocky Mountains, emerging through the Hellgate defile into the Flathead country of present-day Missoula. He built another post among the Flatheads on the Clark Fork, and Nez Perces in that part of Montana would have known of him. Finally, in February 1810, when David Thompson happened to be close enough to record the event, Blackfoot raiders pounced on Courtin and killed him in the Flathead country near present-day Dixon, Montana.[11]

By 1811 straggling American trappers who had survived Blackfoot attacks were wandering through several parts of the West, and Flatheads and Nez Perces were bringing horrendous reports of their disasters to David Thompson, who was still in northwestern Montana. One teen-aged youth named

---

Indians and Mexicans (St. Louis, 1916), pp. 52–53. The year after the fight, Colter told James about the battle, and after recounting its details James characterized the Flatheads who had been in the scrap as "a noble race of men, brave, generous and hospitable. They might be called the Spartans of Oregon. Lewis and Clark received much kindness from them in their expedition to the Columbia, which waters their country . . ." The description would have fit either tribe, but they regularly traveled together, and the trappers, like Lewis and Clark, used "Flathead" for both of them.

10. See below, p. 660.
11. See below, p. 660.

Archibald Pelton, who had come originally from Northampton, Massachusetts, was even living in a Nez Perce village, his mind crazed by his experiences. With a group of Lisa's men, he had been driven south from the Three Forks to the Henry Fork of the Snake over the route Peter Wiser had found. There in the winter of 1810–11 Pelton had become deranged and, straying from his companions, had traveled westward across Idaho's Snake plains, living among settlements of Shoshoni and Bannock Indians, and spreading wild-eyed stories of Blackfoot massacres of his fellow-trappers. In time he had fallen in with some Nez Perces and had gone with them to their homeland. He stayed with them along the Clearwater until late in 1811, when another group of Americans appeared suddenly in the Nez Perce country from the south.[12]

The newcomers were members of Wilson Price Hunt's Astorians, bound overland from St. Louis to erect a post at the mouth of the Columbia for John Jacob Astor's Pacific Fur Company. After a canoe accident in the canyons of the upper Snake River in southern Idaho, the party had disintegrated into several desperate groups that had tried to force their way northward toward the Columbia through the immense, lava-bound Hell's Canyon of the Snake. Most of them had suffered greatly and, after turning back, had found an alternate route to the Columbia over Oregon's Blue Mountains. But eleven men, thanks principally to the forceful leadership of a herculean, 300-pound trader named Donald McKenzie, had got through part of the canyon, then climbed the rugged mountains to the Little Salmon River. Living on five beaver and two mountain goats that they had shot, they had reached the main Salmon and, ragged and starving, had arrived finally among the southernmost Nez Perce settlements.[13] In a repetition of their services to Lewis and Clark, the Nez Perces gave the men food and guided them to the Clearwater. On

12. See J. Neilson Barry, "Archibald Pelton, the First Follower of Lewis and Clark," *Washington Historical Quarterly, 19* (1928), 199–201; Ross Cox, *The Columbia River*, ed. Edgar I. and Jane R. Stewart (Norman, Okla., 1957), p. 60; and Gabriel Franchère, *Narrative of a Voyage to the Northwest Coast of America in the Years 1811, 1812, 1813, and 1814* (New York, 1854), pp. 149–50. After he was taken to the coast by the Astorians who picked him up in the Nez Perce country, Pelton's last days were equally unfortunate. In "An Account of the Tonquin's Voyage," in *The Discovery of the Oregon Trail*, ed. Philip Ashton Rollins (New York, 1935), p. 279, he is represented as having been held a prisoner by the "Cathlapoutles" in western Oregon for two months. In *The Oregon Country under the Union Jack* (Postscript Edition), comp. B. C. Payette (Montreal, 1962), p. 118, a Joseph Pelton "Idiot" is listed at Fort George in 1814, and on p. 190 a roll of Pacific Fur Company employees "in the Columbia for Winter 1813/14" lists Joseph Pelton "Fool" at Fort George, citing Hudson's Bay Company Archives F. 4/61 fols. 6–7d. Pelton was finally murdered with an axe by a Coast Indian.

13. See below, p. 663.

their way to that river, the group came upon Pelton in one of the Indian villages and added him to their party. They fashioned canoes on the Clearwater and continued their trip by water, reaching safely the lower Columbia, where they found that the previously arrived Astorians had already erected a fort.

One of the Astorians' purposes was to open trade with the tribes in the interior, and in August 1812 McKenzie and a party of Americans reappeared up the Snake River to establish a post for the Nez Perces. There was no reason to doubt the success of the venture. The Astorians had discovered unhappily that the Canadian North West Company was already doing business with many inland tribes, and that in most areas the Americans would have to compete with a well-established opposition. But McKenzie himself had seen that no traders had yet come among the Nez Perces, although the previous March Thompson had informed two of the tribe's hunting chiefs in northwestern Montana that he had meant to get to their country and would definitely send someone to them in the autumn "to trade their Furrs & Provisions." But no Canadian had arrived, and during McKenzie's stay with the Nez Perces on his westward trip the Indians had assured him that they would welcome his return to them with trade goods. Still, his undertaking was a failure.

Hurrying his canoes up the Snake, which the whites now knew by several names—the Shahaptian, for the people who lived along it; the Kimooenim, which some of the Nez Perces called it for a hemp vine that trailed along its banks; and Lewis' River, the name Lewis and Clark had given it—McKenzie turned into the Clearwater and landed on that stream's north bank opposite present-day Lewiston. There he selected a site for his post close to several Nez Perce settlements of mat-covered lodges, and along what he understood was a principal route which the Indians traveled in passing between the Lower Snake and the upper Clearwater Valley.[14]

While he built his post, a small group of men under John Reed, one of the Astorians who had come through the Snake Canyon with him, left for the south, intending to retrace the route to the Snake plains and recover goods that Wilson Price Hunt had cached after the canoe accident on the upper

---

14. The principal sources for the activities of the Astorians are Wilson Price Hunt's "Diary," Robert Stuart's "Narratives," and "An Account of the Tonquin's Voyage"—all in Rollins, *The Discovery of the Oregon Trail;* Washington Irving, *Astoria* (Philadelphia, 1836); Alexander Ross, *Adventures of the First Settlers on the Oregon and Columbia River,* ed. R. G. Thwaites (Cleveland, 1904); Cox, *The Columbia River;* Franchère, *Narrative of a Voyage;* Payette, *The Oregon Country;* J. Neilson Barry, "Madame Dorion of the Astorians," *Oregon Historical Quarterly, 30* (1929); and "The Trail of the Astorians," ibid., *13* (1912); Miles Cannon, "Snake River in History," ibid., *20* (1919); Constance Lindsey Skinner, *Adventurers of Oregon* (New Haven, Conn., 1921); and W. C. Brown, *Early Okanogan History* (Okanogan, Wash., 1911).

Snake River. McKenzie, meanwhile, sought out the Indians he had met the previous winter, and for a time the Nez Perces were undoubtedly pleased by his presence among them. But after the first cordial smokes and exchanges of professions of friendship, the realities of the white men's conditions of trade apparently confused them. They badly wanted McKenzie's goods, which they could see heaped under guard in his camp, but those articles were available only for beaver skins. In the area of their home villages the people had neither the experience nor the inclination to wander about, trapping beaver. The difficult, year-round routine of getting enough to eat required all their time and attention, they said. Going after beaver would be a dangerous diversion of their labor, and would demand knowledge and skills which they did not possess.[15] The leading men must have counciled again and again with the trader, pleading for his goods, evading exhortations to hunt, and promising perhaps to take instruction in how to use traps after the white men first sold them articles for something else. In time, their expectations turned to disillusionment and angry frustration, and McKenzie, in turn, became disgusted too.

Soon the Indians began to ignore the whites, who seemed stingy and demanding, a people unlike Lewis and Clark. McKenzie sent out his own men to trap the nearby streams, but they had little luck. As the summer waned, game too became scarce, and the white men had to ask the Indians to trade for food. Nursing their disappointment and hurt pride, the Nez Perces

15. The Nez Perces were not unique in this reaction. Even though most tribes desired white men's goods, particularly firearms for use in war against their enemies, some of them disappointed—and even irritated—the first traders among them by a reluctance to hunt beaver, which often required a fundamental, and not always desired change in their habits and ways of life. In the middle of the eighteenth century the buffalo-hunting Blackfeet of the Canadian plains rejected the urgings of the Hudson's Bay Company to change their cultural habits, trap beaver, and bring the pelts by canoe to the British at Hudson Bay. Similarly, in the early years of the nineteenth century, Pierre-Antoine Tabeau, a St. Louis trader on the Upper Missouri, saw difficulties in enlisting the nomadic plains tribes in the fur trade, noting among the reasons the following: "They disregard all other hunting [save the buffalo] and are unskilful at it . . . The facility of buffalo-hunting with the arrow, as it requires only going to meet the animals, makes them dislike all fatigue. The beaver can be obtained only by activity and industry as they are nowhere common enough to be hunted with the arrow or the gun . . . They find in the buffalo cow . . . everything necessary to them and much that is superfluous and, for this hunt, they rightly prefer the bow and arrow to our guns and ammunition. If they desire the latter, it is for war alone, as they do not even dare to use them against the black bear . . ." (*Tabeau's Narrative of Loisel's Expedition to the Upper Missouri*, ed. Annie H. Abel, Norman, Okla., 1939, p. 163). Similar thinking motivated the Nez Perces, who were making a satisfactory living from roots, fish, berries, small game, and—when they crossed the mountains—buffalo.

offered horses at what the Astorians considered exorbitant prices. McKenzie, angered, called the Nez Perces a "rascally tribe," but it was either trade with them on their terms or starve, and goods that had been brought in to barter for beaver skins were finally given to the Nez Perces for horse meat.

Late in the fall, after John Reed had returned from the south, McKenzie decided that he had had enough. Leaving Reed in charge of the foundering Nez Perce post, he traveled north across the Idaho and Washington Palouse hills to tell John Clarke, an Astorian who was trading with the Spokan Indians, that he was going to withdraw from the Clearwater. Shortly after McKenzie reached Clarke, Nor'Westers from Canada arrived at the nearby Spokane House with word that the United States and Great Britain were at war and that an armed British vessel was on its way to the mouth of the Columbia. Realizing that he had to warn the partners at Astoria, McKenzie hastened back to the Clearwater, cached his goods, and, pulling out John Reed and all his men, left the Nez Perces abruptly and paddled to the coast.

Isolated in a country already swarming with Nor'Westers, and threatened by attack from the sea, the partners at Astoria decided to abandon the Columbia Basin to the rival Canadians and return eastward across the Rocky Mountains as soon as possible. McKenzie and Reed hurried upriver again, planning to retrieve the goods they had cached at the Nez Perce post, inform Clarke and the other Astorians in the interior of the proposal to withdraw, and buy provisions and horses from the Indians for the overland trip to the East. At the Clearwater, however, McKenzie found to his chagrin that the Nez Perces had plundered his caches during his absence.

Summoning the leading men in the vicinity, he demanded the immediate return of his possessions. The headmen indicated their regret but told the trader that they knew nothing of the thefts. The next morning the angry Astorians marched on the nearest Nez Perce village, and while the white men stood with their guns at the ready, the burly McKenzie entered one of the lodges and searched it. As the Indians of the settlement gathered in silence to watch, the trader repeated the performance at one lodge after the other. Finally, the village headman, stirred by the humiliating spectacle, asked McKenzie to withdraw his men and promised to conduct the search himself. McKenzie refused, and soon afterward some of the Indians began to appear with the missing articles.

When all the goods that could be found were laid before them, the Astorians returned to their own camp. Dispatching Reed to the other Astorians in the interior with a message to meet him at the junction of the Columbia and Walla Walla rivers, McKenzie next turned to purchasing provisions and horses from the Nez Perces. At first he met with a cold reception from the Indians, who refused sullenly to have anything to do with him. But, at length, in a show of determination, he began to shoot their horses, leaving an equal value in trade goods on the ground for the owners. The Nez Perces finally relented enough to sell him a few horses, though not enough for the homeward trip. When he finally gave up and departed from the Clearwater to meet the other Astorians, he had the opinion that the Nez Perces would never welcome traders again.

At the Walla Walla River, where the other Astorians joined him, he learned to his dismay of an even more serious conflict that Clarke had had with Indians at the mouth of the Palouse River. On his way inland the year before to establish his post for the Spokans, Clarke had paddled up the Snake to the Palouse, where he had found a fishing settlement of some forty rush-covered lodges of Palouse and Nez Perce Indians. Intending to leave his canoes there and go overland the rest of the way to the Spokan country, Clarke had tried to trade for horses and, like McKenzie, had been annoyed by the high prices the Indians had asked for their animals. The trading had dragged out for a week, during which time the natives had further irritated the Astorians by pilfering articles from them.

Just a year earlier, David Thompson had visited the same settlement on the western border of the Nez Perce country and had found the villagers friendly and eager for trade. What had caused the change is not known, although it can be surmised that Clarke and the Astorians were neither as diplomatic nor as understanding in dealing with Indians as Thompson had been. Clarke himself was overbearing and quick-tempered, and it is possible that a misunderstanding had occurred that had caused him to offend the villagers. Whatever the reason for the strained relations, the impatient trader had finally given the Indians some presents to take care of his canoes for him and had gone on with packhorses to the Spokans.

Now, hurrying back in response to McKenzie's summons, Clarke had had a much more serious clash at the same village. He had found his boats in good order, but again the Indians had pilfered objects from his camp. Among the missing articles this time had been a silver drinking cup that Clarke had prized. Thoroughly angered, Clarke had demanded that the stolen goods be returned. When the Indians had failed to produce them, he had threatened to hang any native he caught stealing. That night his men had trapped an Indian in the act of robbery, and the next morning Clarke had carried out his threat. Forcing all the villagers to watch, he had erected a gallows, pinioned the arms and legs of the prisoner—apparently a Nez Perce from a village farther up the Snake River—and hanged him.

McKenzie and the other Astorians were concerned by the news. McKenzie had had his own troubles with the Nez Perces, and he had dealt firmly with them. But firmness, in his opinion, meant fairness rather than intimidation, and the hanging at the Palouse settlement seemed unjust and cruel. Furthermore, at the moment it was unwise. A number of company men were still at some of the interior posts, guarding Astorian interests until evacuation was ordered, and Clarke's harsh measure could provoke widespread resentment among the inland tribes that would endanger the isolated men. There was no way to undo the harm, however, and the Astorians left the Walla Walla and hurried down the Columbia.

On October 16, 1813, the Americans sold all their interests in the Columbia country, including the fort at Astoria and the inland posts, to representatives of the North West Company. But without horses and provisions, the men could not return east that year. Some of the Astorians took employment with the Canadian firm, and the Nor'Westers agreed to provide transportation east the following year, via ship or overland passage across Canada, to those who wished it. Meanwhile, during the wait, various groups of Astorians went inland again to continue to trade and trap.

Repercussions of the hanging on the Palouse greeted them. On the middle Columbia, Clarke and other Astorians, bound for the Spokans and Okanogans, found the once-friendly bands in the vicinity of the mouths of the Walla Walla and Snake rivers surly and hostile. At one point, only the presence of a brass four-pounder aboard one of the traders' boats prevented the Indians from attacking them. Even the usually hospitable Wallawalla Indians were angry and accused the Astorians of having returned the Indians' many acts of friendship by spilling "blood on our lands." Clarke found it expedient to make a long detour to the Spokans, avoiding the usual route via the Palouse River. Soon afterward another group of Astorians, riding across country from the Wallawallas to the Spokans, was chased on the Palouse prairie by a band of thirty or forty Nez Perces and Palouses. The whites finally halted and dismounted and, firing at their pursuers, brought down two of the Indians' horses. The rest of the natives wheeled about and rode off, but it was not the last of the whites' troubles with the Nez Perces.

In April 1814 McKenzie and the other Astorians who had not changed their allegiance to the North West Company left the country with a canoe brigade of the Canadian firm. On their way up the Columbia, bound for the Canadian Rockies, they learned of a final Astorian misfortune. Along the Boise River in southern Idaho, Indians had slain John Reed and most of the members of a trapping group he had taken to the lands of the Snakes. McKenzie assumed that the massacre had been the work of revenge-seeking Nez Perces, but some years later he learned that the murderers had actually been Bannocks.[16]

16. Alexander Ross, *The Fur Hunters of the Far West*, ed. Kenneth A. Spaulding (Norman, Okla., 1956), p. 171.

The anger of the Nez Perces and their allies had not died, however. Astoria, renamed Fort George and used as a depot for sea-borne supplies from British vessels, became the Nor'Westers' principal post, and the Canadians, moving up and down the Columbia between the coastal base and the inland posts, inherited the Indians' hostility. The month after the Astorians departed, Alexander Ross, a North West Company clerk, and five companions visited a large spring gathering of Sahaptin-speaking bands in Washington's Yakima Valley to buy horses for the company's interior trade. Ross ignored warnings from friendly Salish to stay away from the Sahaptins—who, they said, would surely kill them—and, putting on a bold front, entered the mammoth camp of 3,000 men and "treble that number of horses . . . a grand and imposing sight . . . covering more than six miles in every direction." [17]

There were Nez Perces, Yakimas, Wallawallas, Cayuses, Palouses, and others present, and as soon as the whites dismounted, the Indians surrounded them angrily, accusing them of being "the men who kill our relations, the people who have caused us to mourn . . ." For three days Ross and his companions were held as virtual prisoners, their horses and guns taken from them. Finally, Ross won the friendship of a headman, and with his help the traders procured twenty-five horses and rode out of the camp, although still harassed and jeered at by most of the Indians.

More serious encounters occurred along the Columbia. Nor'Wester canoes going past the mouth of the Snake River were shot at and, on occasion, forced to land, their occupants bullied by Nez Perce and Cayuse Indians into giving them tobacco. In August 1814 some Wallawallas again cautioned a group of traders to be careful of the Nez Perces, who, they said, were still vowing to kill a white man as satisfaction for their relative whom Clarke had hanged. Sometime later more than sixty Nor'Westers in eight canoes loaded with trade goods for the interior posts tried to hurry past a large group of Indians gathered on shore near the mouth of the Snake. A number of natives pursued the traders in canoes, demanding tobacco and trying to wrestle bales of goods out of the white men's boats.

Blows were traded over the gunwales, and when an Indian raised his bow menacingly, the Nor'Westers opened fire. Two Indians were killed and another wounded. The natives broke off the fight and, lying prostrate out of sight in their craft, drifted off in the current. But the Canadians' difficulties had just begun. It was growing dark, and the whites camped for the night on a sandbar in the middle of the river. A storm arose, churning up the Columbia and pinning the men on the sandbar all the next day and the following night. During the entire time, the Indians laid siege to their position. On both shores of the river, the Nor'Westers, huddled wet and miserable behind sandbanks

17. Ibid., p. 23.

and stones, saw signal fires burning, and in the choppy waters around them made out natives threatening them from canoes. Once, in the rain, Indians tried to land on the island, but retreated when the whites fired at them.

Realizing the seriousness of the situation, the Canadians decided they would have to try to effect a peaceable meeting with the Indians and atone for the deaths of the two men they had killed, lest the entire area—lying athwart the trade route between Fort George and the interior posts—erupt in war. When the storm finally lifted, the Nor'Westers made their way safely to the main shore and with the aid of a white flag managed to convey to a large group of Indians, mostly Nez Perces, Yakimas, and Wallawallas, that they wished to pay the relatives of the dead men for their loss. The natives rebuffed them angrily, and for a time it seemed that the whites would have to fight for their lives. The tension was broken by the sudden arrival of a powerful young chief and twelve mounted warriors who, instead of being hostile, dismounted hurriedly and shook the traders' hands in friendship. The young Indian was a Wallawalla war chief who had often taken groups of Sahaptins into battle against the Shoshonis, and who had arrived on the riverbank in response to a summons to lead the Indians in their fight against the whites. Instead, he turned on the natives, admonishing them for having tried to rob the white men's canoes and reminding them of their reliance on the traders for guns and ammunition, which had made them powerful against their real enemies, the Shoshonis. If the whites left the country, he told them, the Indians would soon use up their ammunition, their guns would be useless, and their enemies would drive them from their homes.

His authority and logic stirred the natives, and after the Nor'Westers distributed goods in payment for the men they had killed, peace and good will suddenly reigned. The Canadians were speeded on their way with assurances that all was forgiven, and the incident was the last one in which arms were used between the Sahaptins on the river and the traders, who were careful in the future to pause for a smoke whenever they passed Indians on that part of the Columbia.[18] The following spring, a North West Company group, descending the river, halted at a Sahaptin camp near the Walla Walla River. "We recognized several of the party who had attacked us the preceding autumn," one of the men reported. "They came however among us unarmed, and all recollections of that unpleasant affair seemed to have vanished from their memories."[19]

In 1816 Donald McKenzie, whom John Jacob Astor had partially blamed for what he had considered an unnecessary and cowardly sell-out of Astorian interests in the Northwest, returned to the Columbia country. Troubled by

18. Cox, *The Columbia River*, pp. 194–205, has details of this episode.
19. Ibid., p. 212.

inefficient management and lack of zeal, the North West Company had been doing poorly in the Columbia district, and the Canadian firm had hired the former Astorian, who combined knowledge of the area and an aggressive, dynamic spirit. McKenzie had a plan for the expansion of the Nor'Westers' trade and profits. Instead of repeating the kind of venture he had tried among the Nez Perces and building new posts among Indians who might have no desire to hunt furs, he intended to lead trapping brigades of his own through the virtually unexploited Snake country of southern Idaho, which he knew from the reports of the few Astorians who had been there was rich in beaver. His brigades, composed of veteran French-Canadian, halfblood, and Iroquois and other eastern Indian trappers, would employ horses instead of canoes and, traveling in large bodies for mutual protection, would move from one beaver stream to another. As a base for his brigades he planned, also, to build a new post on the Columbia River near the mouth of the Snake—a more advantageous location for a source of horses and provisions, for communication with Fort George, and as a jump-off point for his trappers than was the site of the company's Spokane House, which was farther north and away from the Columbia.

His first problem was to overcome and eliminate any lingering resentment toward him among the Nez Perces and their allies, on whose good will he would have to depend for horses and provisions, for the security of his new post, and for safety in passing through their lands and trapping in the country of their southern enemies.[20] Early in 1817, despite some jealous foot-dragging by his Nor'Wester colleagues at Fort George, he took an expedition of 36 men to the Nez Perce country. Some Hawaiians, whom the Canadian firm had been bringing to the Columbia River from the Sandwich Islands, were in his group, and McKenzie later reported that the Nez Perces "did not half relish the swarthy aspect of these invincibles and fancied I intended to

20. Since the departure of the Astorians, no trader had gone east from the Columbia to visit the homeland of the Nez Perces. In their isolation from the trade, the only evidence those Indians had had of the presence of white men had been the stories brought back to them by their people who had traveled to the Columbia or to the Nor'Westers' posts among the Spokans and Flatheads—and the guns, ammunition, and manufactured articles which the travelers had purchased with horses from the Salish. Trade had flourished particularly between the Nez Perces and Spokan Indians, and a steady supply of white men's goods had come into the Nez Perce villages via that source. Nez Perces had also come home with reports of wonders: the white men had brought strange birds and animals—chickens, goats, and hogs—to the Spokane House to raise for food, and had gashed the surface of the earth, the mother of life, with iron tools, placing seeds in the upturned dirt to grow other foods—potatoes, turnips, cabbages, melons, and cucumbers. Like the Nez Perces, the Salish peoples had been horrified by the wounding of the earth, and the traders had made small progress in inducing the Spokans to grow gardens of their own.

resent former grudges." [21] He went out of his way, however, to win the Indians' confidence and, managing to purchase horses from them without trouble, satisfied himself that the Nez Perces would offer no opposition to brigades passing through their lands.

He established no permanent camp among the Nez Perces this time but for more than a month moved through their country, counciling with the headmen of different villages, pleading for good will and friendship, and examining the region and various routes to the south. At the same time, he realized that the hostility between the Sahaptin-speaking peoples and the Snake bands, renewed since the time of Lewis and Clark, would threaten his brigades with disruptions and attacks by both sides in the war areas of the south, and he recognized that before he could launch his expeditions, he would have to try to bring about another peace treaty between the two peoples.

McKenzie's only difficulty during this new stay with the Nez Perces was with unruly Iroquois in his own party. Some of those hunters got into an altercation with McKenzie and concocting a plot to kill him tried to enlist the aid of several Nez Perces on whom they intended to place the blame for the murder. The Nez Perces, instead, warned McKenzie, and the trader, at first not believing the Indians, finally thwarted the plot and sent the Iroquois off to the Okanogan and Spokane posts.

Hobbled by continued opposition and inertia among his fellow-Nor'Westers, McKenzie was unable to set his plans in motion until the middle of 1818.[22] In July of that year, with a group of ninety-five men, including Canadians, Iroquois, and "Owhyhees," he commenced building a log post one hundred feet square on the left, or east, shore of the Columbia about half a mile north of the mouth of the Walla Walla River. Although the site was actually in the homeland of Wallawalla and Cayuse Indians, the whites were still using the term Nez Perces for most of the people along that part of the Columbia, and McKenzie named the post Fort Nez Perces. A large number of Indians gathered to watch the builders, who had to float driftwood and other timber from upriver. The natives were fearful of the traders' intentions, some warning each other that the white men had come to kill them. Others threatened the intruders, demanding payment for the site and the timber. McKenzie was patient and diplomatic, and by the time he had erected a rough enclosure, he had won the Indians over and had begun a friendly trade with them.

Convincing them to agree to a peace with the Snakes was more difficult. The trader held a round of councils with the headmen, telling them of his

21. Cecil W. Mackenzie, *Donald Mackenzie, King of the Northwest* (Los Angeles, 1937), p. 114.
22. In the meantime, he had made a second visit to the Nez Perces, reinforcing the improvement of his relations with them.

PACIFIC OCEAN

CASCADE MOUNTAINS

Okanogan

Fort
Okanogan

OKANOGAN R.

COLUMBIA R.

Fort
Colvile

COLUMBIA R.

Spokane
House

Kalispel

Spokan

Palouse

PALOUSE R.

Hanging,
1813

SNAKE R.

McK
CLEA

Coeu

YAKIMA R.

Astoria

Fort
Vancouver

Yakima

River Fight,
1814

COLUMBIA R.

Wallawalla
Fort Nez Perces
[Walla Walla]

Kar

Cayuse

GRANDE RONDE R.

Wallowa

IMNAHA R.

WILLAMETTE R.

DESCHUTES R.

JOHN DAY R.

Grande
Ronde

BLUE MTS.

POWDER R.

Hells Can

BURNT R.

WEISER

Sn
[Fo

OWYHEE R.

BO

- - - - - Route across Blue Mountains
from Fort Nez Perces
to Snake Country

Kootanae
House

KOOTENAY R.

Blackfeet Tribes

MARIAS R.

Flathead
Lake

Saleesh
House
Flathead
Post

Flathead

CLARK FK.

Continental Divide

MISSOURI R.

Manuel's
Post

Hellgate
[Missoula]

Lolo Trail

LOCHSA R.

SELWAY R.

BITTERROOT R.

BITTERROOT MTS.

Deer Lodge
Valley

Three
Forks

YELLOWSTONE R.

BIG HORN R.

z Perce

ALMON R.

Big Hole
Valley

JEFFERSON R.

MADISON R.

GALLATIN R.

Crow

Wintering
Camps

Lemhi
Pass

LEMHI R.

SALMON R.

Monida
Pass

BIRCH CR.

Yellowstone
Lake

ette
e

HENRY FK.

Pierre's
Hole

TETONS

Jackson
Hole

Crow

Bannock

Fort
Hall

Battle
1832

Teton
Pass

WIND R.

shoni

SNAKE RIVER

PORTNEUF R.

BEAR R.

Bear
Lake

Continental Divide

WIND RIVER MTS.

GREEN R.

Great
Salt
Lake

Cache
Valley

2. The Fur Trade Period, 1806–36

plans to go south to trap, but he finally realized that no one in the area could speak with authority and that he would have to wait for the return of a war party which even then was in the south fighting the Snakes. In time, the war band of almost 500 Sahaptins, including Nez Perces, arrived home with "hideous yells, mangled prisoners, and bloody scalps . . ." After waiting through their victory celebrations, McKenzie counciled with their leaders, notably a Wallawalla named Tamtappam and a Cayuse named Quahat, and at last got them to agree that if he could persuade the Snakes to make peace, they would do so too and would permit the trappers to travel to and from the Snakes' country without molestation.[23]

Leaving Alexander Ross to finish the fort, McKenzie purchased 195 horses from the Indians and at the end of September departed for the south with fifty-four men, intending to trap beaver and talk the Snakes into making peace. Crossing Oregon's Blue Mountains by a route that some of his men, former Astorians, had pioneered during their westward trek with Wilson Price Hunt in 1811, he reached the Snake Basin and moved slowly eastward, exploring and trapping its streams and giving many of the rivers their modern names. Along the way he met numerous groups of Shoshonis and Bannocks, reporting that "to each we communicated the welcome tidings of peace on the part of the Nez Perces . . ." The Snake bands all seemed pleased by the news and assured McKenzie that they, too, wished to live in peace.[24]

The abundance of beaver, which surprised McKenzie and made him regret that he "had been so long deprived of the riches of such a country," also gave him the idea that the Snake River, from its mouth to this area in southern Idaho, might prove a faster and easier route between his new post on the Columbia and the Snake beaver lands. Leaving most of his men to continue their trapping, he hastened back to Fort Nez Perces to test his theory. Ross by

23. The claim that Tamtappam, the Wallawalla, was Yelleppit—who had been friendly to Lewis and Clark and David Thompson, and had acquired a second name, Tom-o-top-po, after Lewis and Clark had treated his rheumatism—is found in Wheeler, *The Trail of Lewis and Clark*, 2, 254–60. "Quahat," the Cayuse leader, was probably Ollokot, whom Lewis and Clark had also met and called Ar-lo-quat, describing him as "of the Chopunnish Nation," though he was actually a Cayuse. (Thwaites, *Original Journals*, 3, 132 n.). Ollokot in Cayuse meant Frog. Chief Joseph's father, born ca. 1785–90, was the son of a Cayuse leader and had a younger Cayuse half-brother named Ollokot who married a Wallawalla and lived in the vicinity of present-day Pendleton, Oregon. This may have been he. At a later time Chief Joseph had a brother, also named Ollokot.

24. The principal sources for McKenzie's Snake country activities, 1818–21, are Ross, *Fur Hunters; Peter Skene Ogden's Snake Country Journals, 1824–25 and 1825–26*, ed. E. E. Rich, Hudson's Bay Record Society (London, 1950); *Ogden's Snake Country Journal, 1826–27*, ed. K. G. Davies, Hudson's Bay Record Society (London, 1961); *Fur Trade and Empire*, ed. Frederick Merk (Cambridge, Mass., 1931); and Alexander Ross's map of the Columbia, 1821–49 (British Museum, Additional MSS 31,358B).

then had completed the post, which he regarded as a veritable "Gibraltar of the Columbia," composed of stone buildings guarded by a rampart, firing gallery, and bastions, with cannons, swivel guns, and a main gate of iron. Resting there for a week, McKenzie took off in canoes with six Canadians, bound for the Snake River. He went through the Nez Perce country and two months later, having pushed, pulled, and portaged his boats upriver through the rapids of the entire Grand Canyon of the Snake, including the dark narrows of Hells Canyon, emerged from the chasm's upper end, shaken by the experience. He never tried it again, and no man ever repeated his feat.

Ross, meanwhile, had dispatched a party with provisions and trade goods across the Blue Mountains to him. Near the Boise that group found McKenzie, who had just gathered the year's Snake country fur catch from his trappers. The new party left the provisions and with the furs started back to Fort Nez Perces, intending to return to McKenzie and accompany him on a new tour of the Snake Basin trapping grounds. While McKenzie waited with three Iroquois on the banks of the Boise, a party of Bannocks appeared and tried to seize his store of goods. The trader held them off dramatically by getting behind a keg of gunpowder and lighting a match, threatening to blow them all up, himself included, if they came closer. The Bannocks hesitated in confusion, then abruptly galloped away as a mounted party of some 200 Nez Perces, painted and feathered for battle, appeared on the opposite shore. McKenzie's prospects had not improved. Cornered, with trade goods that were destined for the Snakes, the trader was legitimate prey for an aroused, prize-seeking raiding band that was searching for those Indians. The Nez Perces shouted angrily at McKenzie to come across the river for a smoke. When he made no response, some of the warriors tried to force their way over to him. The current was too swift, however, and after several unsuccessful attempts to cross, the band turned away from the river and disappeared. Trailing northward, its members overtook the party with McKenzie's furs and in their frustration fell on it, killing a French Canadian and an Iroquois trapper. The rest of the Nor'Wester group, furious at the Nez Perces, got safely back to Ross's fort with the furs, delivered the peltry, and started back to rejoin McKenzie.

Shortly afterward, the marauding Nez Perce band appeared at the post, having in the meantime also fallen on and slaughtered a group of Snakes. Now a war party of infuriated Snakes, pursuing the Nez Perces, also arrived in the neighborhood and struck at a group of Wallawallas three miles from the fort, killing five adults and five children and escaping with three prisoners. Consternation struck the Sahaptin peoples around the post. Carrying the corpses of the Wallawallas to the front gate of the fort, they berated the traders for having given guns and ammunition to their enemies. Ross assured

them that McKenzie had not yet traded guns to the Snakes and satisfied them
that the Snakes had killed the Wallawallas with arrows. Then he reproached
the Nez Perce war party for having started the entire affair by having violated the peace that McKenzie had been trying to arrange. ". . . not content
with having killed their enemies they killed their friends also!" he added.
"They killed two of the whites!" [25]

His lecture was persuasive, and the Sahaptins soon began quarreling among
themselves. Ross at length calmed them down and, inviting the headmen of
the different bands into the fort for a smoke, counseled them sternly on the
benefits of accepting, and abiding by, a peace with the Snakes. The best they
gave him, after a week of meetings, was a promise not to renew hostilities
with their enemies until McKenzie had safely withdrawn his trappers from
the southern country. Their resentments meanwhile simmered against the
whites, who somehow, they felt, should have been more on their side. Ross
complained of the "anxiety and vexation" they caused him, and despaired
that anyone could ever effect a peace between them and their foes.

In the Snake country McKenzie had ample reason to arrive at the same
conclusion. Joined by his reinforcements, he zealously exploited the streams
on the northern fringe of the Snake plains, again running into bands of Bannocks and Shoshonis but this time having his pleas for peace rebuffed. Soon
he learned the reason: no fewer than five Nez Perce war parties were in the
area, scattering small, frightened settlements of Snakes every which way into
the mountains. At length a large war band of Blackfeet showed up, and the
Nez Perces left the country quickly.

In eastern Idaho, McKenzie finally heard that the two most powerful war
chiefs of the eastern Shoshonis were nearby, and that if they agreed to peace
with the Sahaptins, they might be able to effect a truce council with the
northern Indians and end hostilities throughout the Snake country. McKenzie
left his trappers and, guided by an eastern Shoshoni, traveled south across the
Snake River, along a stream where he sighted some Blackfeet (and therefore
named it the Blackfoot River), and through the mountains southeast of
present-day Pocatello to the region of "Black Bears' Lake," probably the
present Bear Lake.

There he came on the main body of eastern Shoshonis, buffalo hunters
who had adopted many of the cultural traits of the plains tribes. They owned
large horse herds, traded and fought on the plains, and were friendlier to the
Nez Perces than were the Shoshonis who lived farther west on the Snake
plains.[26] He induced the eastern Shoshoni leaders to bring their people back

25. Ross, *Fur Hunters*, p. 159.
26. Band organization among the Shoshoni and Bannock peoples of the Great Basin
was very loose. Individuals could come and go as they pleased from one band or settle-

to where he had left his trappers, and on Birch Creek north of the Snake plains sat down with 54 headmen of the eastern and western Shoshonis and the Bannocks, pleading with them to unite in making peace with the Nez Perces. The eastern Shoshoni headmen claimed that they were already at peace with the Nez Perces and that their only enemies were the Blackfeet but, recognizing the authority of their voices, told the weaker western Shoshonis and Bannocks that if they did not listen to the whites and observe the peace, to which McKenzie said the Nez Perces had already agreed, the eastern Shoshonis would punish them with death.

Their threat was hollow. It was not the affair of the easterners, and the western Shoshonis knew it. As soon as the eastern Indians had departed, the western Shoshonis and Bannocks stole traps and horses from McKenzie's men and disappeared. Later, Bannocks killed three of McKenzie's Hawaiian trappers on a river that has ever since been known as the Owhyee, and the trader concluded that it would be a long and difficult task to get the western tribes, the Sahaptins as well as the Snakes, to reform.

Nevertheless, while he remained in the area, he continued his peace-making efforts with both sides, and when he finally left the Snake country for the last time in July 1821 his patience had begun to have results. Around Fort Nez Perces he had made considerable progress in ameliorating the deep-seated resentments of the Nez Perces and other Sahaptins toward the high-handedness and superior attitudes of the white invaders squatting in their midst. Those Indians, gradually corrupted by the flow of trade goods and beginning to accept the conclusion that a friendly policy toward the traders would be of material benefit to themselves, were bringing in beaver pelts in increasing numbers to sell for the goods at the post. War and trade parties of Nez Perces

---

ment to another, and "chiefs," who were usually men of wealth, good judgment—and therefore of influence—exercised little authority, save as voluntarily accepted leaders in times of hunts, wars, or crises. Even then, individuals or groups, if they wished, had perfect freedom to ignore the course of action suggested by the leader. Since the bands, moreover, were composed of fluid elements—families and groups that often wandered from one part of the region to another, leaving one band and attaching themselves temporarily to another—the names by which they called themselves had little permanent meaning for individuals. Most Shoshoni names referred to the principal food which the people ate. At one time, while living in the west, a family might be "fish eaters"; later, the same people might have attached themselves to a buffalo-hunting band in the east and become "buffalo eaters." Generally, wherever the people lived, they designated themselves by the principal food they ate, as it was conditioned by the particular environment. In the west, the food supply, principally fish, was more precarious, and the people were poorer. In the East, people hunted buffalo and enjoyed a higher standard of living in their richer environment. For excellent, brief summaries of the subject, see Sven Liljeblad, *The Indians of Idaho* (Boise, 1960), and "The Bannock of Idaho," a critique by the same writer in *Idaho Yesterdays*, 2 (Spring 1958), 22–25.

were starting to hold truce meetings with bands and villages of Snakes in the
south, trading for furs that the Snakes had trapped along the mountain streams
in their own country, and then as middlemen bringing the furs to Fort Nez
Perces to sell to the whites. Most Nez Perces still had an aversion to trapping
beaver themselves, and those who felt a need for white men's goods could get
what they wanted as middlemen or by trading with Spokans and Flatheads.
But other Indians around Fort Nez Perces, particularly the Cayuses who had
longer journeys to make to the Spokans and Flatheads, were leaving the post
with traps of their own and working some of the waters of northern and central Oregon where they were relatively safe from Snake enemies. Their returns early in 1822 helped to swell the fur receipts at Fort Nez Perces to
1,200 skins, a 50 per cent rise over the previous year.[27]

At the same time, the friendliness of the Nez Perce villages, which were
still isolated from the theaters of trade and most of whose people still behaved
scornfully independent of the men who demanded the killing of so many beavers, continued questionable to the whites. In 1821, after years of rivalry, the
Hudson's Bay and North West Companies merged, keeping the name of the
former firm, and George Simpson, the peppery resident governor of the combined company, brought changes to the Columbia Department. McKenzie returned to the East, where he eventually became Governor of the Hudson's
Bay Company's Red River Colony in central Canada, and other men took
over the leadership of the trapping brigades to the rich beaver waters of the
Snake country. But, commencing in 1822, Simpson ordered the brigades to
leave from the Flathead Post on the Clark Fork River in northwestern Montana and travel south to the Snake plains along the eastern side of the Bitterroots and Salmon River mountains.

There were several motives for this change. One, an economic reason, was
Simpson's belief that the brigades could trap beaver, as well as provision
themselves by hunting buffalo, while passing through the regions between the
Flathead Post and the Snake country, whereas they could do neither in the
long stretch, where there was little beaver or game, between Fort Nez Perces
and the Snake lands. The new, eastern route would thus save the company
food expenses for the brigades, while at the same time providing the men with
added furs from the previously untrapped beaver streams in the Montana valleys. In addition, Simpson was familiar with the history of clashes between
the traders and the Sahaptin peoples on the Columbia and Snake rivers, as
well as with the hostility between the Sahaptins and the Snakes, and he believed that the Nez Perces were still a potentially dangerous people who at
any time might turn on the whites and disrupt the western route and communications to the Snake country.

27. Merk, *Fur Trade and Empire*, p. 177.

He put his fears on paper two years later when he was pressed to allow the Snake expeditions to depart once again from Fort Nez Perces. He refused, and noted in his journal that the Nez Perces might "identify us with their enemies the Snakes on account of our furnishing them with the Sinews of War Arms and Ammunition . . ." Moreover, quarrels between unruly members of the brigades and the Nez Perces might break out with consequences "fatal both to the Establishment and Expedition." [28] McKenzie had faced these possibilities since 1818, but by expert relations in the field with the Sahaptin and Snake peoples, he had gradually improved the security of the trapping brigades. Nevertheless, Simpson regarded the risk too great to take, and brigades in the immediate future departed from the Flathead Post.

Fort Nez Perces remained in operation, continuing to trade with Indians in the vicinity, and eventually Snake country brigades used it again. In the meantime, Flatheads guided the brigades from the Clark Fork River along the old hunting routes through the Deer Lodge, Big Hole, Beaverhead, Lemhi, and other valleys in western Montana and eastern Idaho. Nez Perce visitors had long fraternized and traded with the Iroquois and other trappers around the British posts on the Clark Fork, and now in concert with the Flatheads and other Salish in the area their roaming bands began to associate with the members of the brigades, sometimes joining them in camps and sometimes moving along with them for several days. On the way to the Snake country through the mountain-girt valleys the whites frequently had skirmishes with Blackfoot raiders. In 1823 a Hudson's Bay Company brigade under David Thompson's former clerk, Finan McDonald, almost annihilated a war party of seventy-five Piegans. It was good news to the Nez Perce and Flathead bands in the region and gave them a heightened sense of alliance with the traders against a common foe.

The 1824 brigade, taken south from the Flathead Post by Alexander Ross, met large Nez Perce parties in the Bitterroot Valley, and Ross, whose experiences at Fort Nez Perces had given him a jaundiced opinion of the tribe, was pleased by how friendly the buffalo-hunting Nez Perces were to the whites. Later, on the Boise River north of the Snake plains, he experienced another pleasant surprise: in a hot, crowded lodge he witnessed a band of Cayuses from Fort Nez Perces and some western Shoshonis conclude a peace, solemnly formalized by the smoking of a pipe filled with horse dung. Having watched the efforts toward peace between the Sahaptin peoples and the western Snakes "occasionally progressing for the last seven years," he said, he now "for the first time began to entertain hopes that it might, after all, possibly succeed."

In eastern Idaho, meanwhile, a group of Ross's Iroquois hunters spent some

28. See below, p. 663.

time in 1824 just west of the Teton peaks in a meadowed valley which trappers later called Pierre's Hole, for Pierre Tivanitagon, the Iroquois' leader. Then, after some Snakes robbed them of most of their possessions, they fell in with a group of Americans led by tall, intelligent, 25-year-old American trapper-explorer, Jedediah Smith. Smith and his six companions, the advance element of a new wave of American beaver hunters working their way westward to challenge the British in the Rockies and the Oregon country, accompanied the Iroquois back to Ross's main party. Although shocked to see them in a region the British had been working for so long as their own, Ross believed that the Americans' purpose was to lure his men and their beaver furs away from his brigade and, thinking it best to keep the newcomers under observation, let them travel with him all the way back to the Flathead Post.

The reappearance of the Americans, known as "Bostons" to the Northwest tribes since Astorian days, opened a new era for the Nez Perces. On the Clark Fork River the visitors watched the British conduct trade with more than 1,000 Nez Perces and Flatheads. The Americans hinted future trade of their own with those Indians, whetting their interest with suggestions that they would pay more for beaver than the British did, and William Sublette, one of Smith's men, reported that the natives expressed "a great desire that the Americans would go more among them." [29] Planning a return to the area, the Yankees departed from the Flathead Post late in December 1824, returning to the Snake country with a new British brigade under Peter Skene Ogden, a short, powerfully built former Nor'Wester.

Ogden was relieved when Smith's group left him in southeastern Idaho. But on the streams of northeastern Utah, where the British leader took his brigade, he found more Americans. After numerous difficulties with these rivals, who with offers of higher prices seduced some of the brigade members and their beaver catch away from him, Ogden retreated angrily to the Snake plains. There he met a hunting party of Flatheads and Nez Perces who further irritated him by telling him that they had heard "many wonderful accounts" of the newly arrived Americans.

Circumstances forced Ogden to take his brigade out of the Snake country in 1825 by way of Fort Nez Perces. His fears about the on-coming Americans were already shared by his superiors of the Hudson's Bay Company, and further changes were occurring along the Columbia. Although various problems since the War of 1812 had deterred Americans from returning pre-

29. William H. Ashley, conveying information received from Sublette, to Joseph Charless, St. Louis, June 5, 1827 (Dale L. Morgan, *The West of William H. Ashley*, Denver, 1964). Ashley's letter to Charless was published in the *Missouri Republican* on June 7, according to Donald M. Frost, *Notes on General Ashley* (Barre, Mass., 1960), p. 139.

viously to the Northwest, they possessed equal rights with the British to the region. But the Convention of 1818, which had extended joint occupancy of the Oregon country, would, unless renewed, expire in 1828, and the British were hoping for a permanent boundary settlement along a line that would run westward from where Lewis and Clark had crossed the Rockies to the Clearwater, Snake, and Columbia rivers. Everything south of that line, including Fort George, which the Treaty of Ghent in 1814 had restored to United States ownership—though Americans had never physically repossessed it—would be American.

In 1824–25, Governor Simpson, a waspish man with great energy and a mania for detail, had buzzed through the Columbia Department, reorganizing its administration, effecting economies, and bracing it for the reappearance of the Americans. Over the entire Department he had placed a single chief factor, Dr. John McLoughlin, a huge man of wisdom and administrative ability, and had directed him to abandon Fort George and construct a new post on the north bank of the Columbia, which, it was assumed, would remain British soil. Opposite the mouth of the Willamette River, McLoughlin had erected Fort Vancouver, where in succeeding years he would establish grain fields and vegetable gardens, build up herds of cattle and swine, locate mills and salmon fisheries, and develop a great provisioning center for the region.

In the interior, Simpson had ordered additional changes. He had reduced the complement of Fort Nez Perces to a chief trader and eight men, and had directed them to prepare to build a new post on the north shore of the Columbia if a boundary decision awarded their present location to the United States. He had noted that most of the fort's furs were now supplied to it by Cayuses, but he had taken a dim view of an increase in future returns, since the Indians were still "very independent of us requiring but few of our supplies and it is not until absolutely in need of an essential article or an article of finery such as Guns & Beads that they will take the trouble of hunting." While he was at the fort, he had had to take a hand in halting a threatened attack by some Nez Perces and other Indians who had been angered by the indiscretions of the post's interpreter. He had removed the interpreter from the area and had held a peace council with the displeased headmen, giving them presents, and finally winning their promise "to exert themselves in hunting, to respect the whites, [and] to protect us while on their Lands . . ." But he had judged the natives around the fort as still "capricious and treacherous." [30]

In economy moves farther north, he had ordered the Spokane House and Flathead Post closed as soon as possible, and a new post constructed on the main Columbia trade route near the mouth of the Colville River in northeast-

30. Merk, *Fur Trade and Empire*, pp. 54, 57, 127–28.

ern Washington. He had then left the country, and in 1825—while Ogden was having his difficulties with the Americans in the south—John Work, a dour, heavy-set Hudson's Bay Company trader, had set about closing the northern posts and erecting a new one on the Colville.

Requiring horses for the transfer of supplies, Work journeyed to the Nez Perce villages on the Clearwater. In the years since McKenzie's tours through the area, white men had rarely visited the settlements, going to them only to purchase horses or dried salmon and camas, or—in the cases of a few free trappers—to try their luck on the mountain streams. Work discovered that trading with the horse-wealthy Nez Perces was no easier than it had been in earlier days. Left largely to themselves, the people had lost none of their pride and feeling of independence. Aided by a French-Canadian interpreter named Jean Toupin, who had been attached to Fort Nez Perces since 1821, and by an accommodating Nez Perce the whites called Charlie, who lived at present-day Alpowa Creek on the Snake River below the mouth of the Clearwater, Work finally collected a large gathering of Indians around his camp and, by trading presents with two influential men—one of them old Cut Nose and the other the son of the equally aged Broken Arm—managed to buy 106 horses.[31] When trade was finished, Work traveled to the Spokane House and then to the Colville River, where he supervised the construction of the new post, whose name, Fort Colvile, for a director of the Hudson's Bay Company, eventually endowed the river with the same name, though custom slightly misspelled it.

Ogden, meanwhile, had reached Fort Nez Perces and had written Simpson that he had learned that the Americans were planning to come up to the Marias River, where they would build a post and compete with the British for the trade of the northern Indians.[32] The threat did not materialize,

31. Toupin, whom we will meet on several future occasions, was living with an interesting woman, the stoic Madame Dorion, Iowa Indian widow of a Missouri River interpreter with whom she had trudged across the continent in 1811 as a member of the Wilson Price Hunt party. She had also survived the John Reed massacre on the Boise River in 1814. See Davies, *Ogden's Snake Country Journals*, p. xxxiii n; H. H. Bancroft, *The History of Oregon*, Vol. 1 (San Francisco, 1886), 119; Clifford M. Drury, *Marcus Whitman* (Caldwell, Idaho, 1937), pp. 194–95; McWhorter, *Hear Me*, p. 58; Payette, *The Oregon Country*, p. 630. The Nez Perce, Charlie, more ambitious than most of the rest of his countrymen for the favor of the whites, was well known at Fort Nez Perces, where he had often visited and made himself useful as a guide and middle party between the whites and Indians.

32. Rich, *Ogden's Snake Country Journals*, p. 256. American preoccupation with the Marias River of the Missouri as a site for a post is interesting. Lewis and Clark had first proposed that location for a trade center for the Blackfeet as well as for their enemies. In 1823 Missouri Fur Company men under Michael Immell and Robert Jones had told Piegans that they hoped to erect a post on the Marias, but Bloods had killed

however, and in the winter of 1825–26 Work traveled to the old Flathead Post and conducted the usual trade with the Nez Perces and Flatheads who had been coming there for years.

In 1826 Fort Colvile was finished, and the Spokane House, to the distress of the Indians in the vicinity, was stripped and abandoned. Work returned to Fort Nez Perces, finding new difficulties there. The Indians had learned of the British plan to move to the opposite shore of the Columbia and were offering vigorous objection. Finally, McLoughlin, reasoning that removal of the fort against the will of the natives "would Expose it to Great Danger and also the Communication Up and Down the River and Greatly Injure the Whole of the Columbia Trade of the Interior," ordered the traders to stay where they were and await the results of the boundary negotiations between Great Britain and the United States.[33]

From Fort Nez Perces, Work again in July 1826 visited the Nez Perce villages on the Clearwater to buy horses. Helped once more by the intermediary, Charlie, he managed a trade with some 200 Nez Perces under the leadership of two headmen whom he called "Old Alumie" and "Towishpal," the latter of whom was probably Apash Wyakaikt (Flint Necklace), the leader of the Asotin band. The trade was marred by a quarrel between Charlie and Work's interpreter, Toupin. An aged Nez Perce female shaman had examined the sore hands of one of Work's men, and although the whites thought she had done nothing to aid the man, she demanded payment. Toupin turned her down, and when Charlie interceded, an argument started during which Charlie called Toupin a dog. Toupin returned the epithet, Charlie struck him with his gun, and the two men went at each other. Work finally got them separated and smoothed the affair with gifts. After a peaceful smoke, the traders parted from the Nez Perces, having purchased seventy-nine horses.[34]

Work went on to the new Fort Colvile, and that fall learned to his dismay that Ogden's warning had at last materialized, that Americans were trading farther east in the Flathead country. During the summer of 1826 one of the American trapping parties, accompanied by some of Ogden's deserters, had moved north from the Snake Basin to the vicinity of the Flathead Post on the

---

Immell and Jones before they could carry out their plans. Although Jedediah Smith, who had since visited the Flathead country, would shortly convince his colleagues that the Clark Fork River was the place to compete with the British, other American trappers in the south, who had not yet reached the Flathead country, would probably still have thought of the Marias as the best site for a post. From that location, they could try to pacify the Blackfeet and win them, as well as the Flatheads, Nez Perces, and Kutenais, away from the British.

33. *McLoughlin's Fort Vancouver Letters, 1st Series, 1825–1838*, ed. E. E. Rich (Toronto, 1941), p. 26.
34. See below, p. 664.

Clark Fork River. Nez Perces and Flatheads may have traveled with them; at least, Work received reports that several of their bands had seen the Americans. Grimly, the British trader hurried to the Clark Fork to see what was happening. The Americans had already gone, but Work learned that John Gray, a halfblood Iroquois who had resented the British traders and had led the desertion from Ogden's brigade in Utah the year before, had acted as intermediary between the Americans and the northern Indians. He had given the natives tobacco and scarlet cloth as presents from the Americans and, accompanied by a number of Nez Perces and Flatheads, had departed with a promise that the Americans would return with 150 horse loads of goods, that another American company was coming with a quantity of supplies equally large, and that many American supply ships were on their way to the Columbia.

Work found that the Flatheads and Nez Perces had been won to the newcomers, whose expansive promises had been calculated to delight them. Moreover, he learned that the Americans had made capital of the abandonment of the Spokane and Flathead posts, both of which had now been closed. The Americans, the Indians said they had been told, were to take over the country which the British seemed to be evacuating. Work tried to persuade them that the information was false; but he had a difficult time getting the Indians to trade with him, and he finally returned unhappily to Fort Colvile.

The American threat to push into the heartland of the Columbia Basin had not been hollow. That same spring of 1826 American trappers, led possibly by William Sublette and David Jackson, had moved eastward through the Snake Basin in the direction of Fort Nez Perces. They had not gone that far, but had trapped all the way to Payette Lake at present-day McCall, Idaho, on the southern fringe of the Nez Perces' homeland.[35] Fortunately for them, the truce between the Sahaptins and Snakes that Alexander Ross had witnessed in 1824 had been renewed in 1825, and was being formalized again that season in a big intertribal council at the mouth of the Burnt River on the Snake, and the Americans had been able to hunt in peace.[36] In July they had gone to Bear River in northeastern Utah, arriving soon after the close of a rendezvous in nearby Cache Valley between other American trappers and William H. Ashley's supply train from St. Louis. On Bear River, Ashley had sold out his mountain interests to Jedediah Smith, David Jackson, and William Sublette, and the three partners had made plans that had included a trapping expedition toward the Flathead country. Sublette and Jackson had led a party in that direction, but had apparently fallen short of reaching the Clark Fork

35. Morgan, *The West of William H. Ashley*, p. 147.
36. Merk, *Fur Trade and Empire*, p. 273, and Rich, *Ogden's Snake Country Journals*, p. 174 (June 2, 1826).

—although another group, perhaps mostly of Iroquois who had started north directly after the rendezvous with Ashley, and had included John Gray among its members—had gone the full distance and had told the Flatheads, as Work had learned, that more Americans would soon be arriving.[37]

In the early part of 1827 Sublette returned to St. Louis and took out a license for the Indian trade that pointed to keener competition with the Hudson's Bay Company. It authorized the American partnership to establish three posts, including one at Horse Prairie on the Clark Fork, where Gray had talked to the Flatheads and Nez Perces, and another at the mouth of the Snake River in the vicinity of Fort Nez Perces. Returning west with a supply train, Sublette reached the mountains in time for the 1827 rendezvous, which was held at Bear Lake in the Idaho-Utah border country.

For the first time Indians were present to participate in the boisterous frolic of the American mountain men. Near the camps of the trappers, Snakes and Utes, newly brought together in peace by the Americans, erected villages of tipis. On the Snake plains a group of trappers had also invited a band of Nez Perces to come to the trade meeting, and the Nez Perces came in cautiously, with guns and lances aloft, riding with stiff dignity and prepared to trade or not, depending on the behavior of the "Bostons" and the terms they offered. The democratic welcome and friendly jollity of the Americans surprised them, and they soon abandoned the reserve that had so long characterized their attitude toward the more formal and demanding British traders. In time they were drinking, laughing, racing, and gambling with the trappers, and learning to swear in mountain-man English. Blackfeet also showed up in the neighborhood and, as enemies of everyone at the rendezvous, managed occasionally to pick off one or more of the Indian celebrants. At such times the entire camp, red men and white, whooped off together into the hills on punitive chases.

From then on, Nez Perces and Flatheads traveled from time to time in close relationship with American trapping groups. Ogden, who was back in the Snake country in the fall of 1827 with another British brigade, came on them together almost everywhere. On the Weiser River in southwestern Idaho he found Nez Perces acting as guides for the mountain men. Later, when he wintered near the mouth of the Portneuf River at the site of present-day Pocatello, he learned that Nez Perces were with two different American groups, and that the Indians had discovered another reason to like the "Bos-

---

37. It may be inferred that Gray's party had started north before Ashley had sold out to Smith, Jackson, and Sublette on Bear River, for the Iroquois, according to Work, had given the Flatheads presents from the American chief, "Ashley." I owe a great debt to Dale L. Morgan's *The West of William H. Ashley* for my knowledge of the movements of Ashley, Smith, Jackson, and Sublette.

tons." The U.S. trappers, he commented indignantly, had "traded 49 horses from the Nez Perces at an extravagant rate averaging $50."

During the winter, also, Ogden heard that the previous fall Robert Campbell of the Smith, Jackson, and Sublette partnership had taken a party toward the Flathead country. He did not discover how far it had gotten, but Campbell and his men must have traveled to within rumor's distance of the Clark Fork, for Iroquois trappers with him had learned that, as a result of the Americans' competition, the British in that area had greatly increased the prices they would pay for beaver and were now offering more than the Americans. Fourteen of the Iroquois had promptly quit the American group to return to the British, and Blackfeet had seriously buffeted Campbell and his weakened party before the trappers had got back to winter quarters in the south.

In the spring Ogden reported the departure again of Campbell and a Smith, Jackson, and Sublette group for the Flathead country. The Americans safely reached the Clark Fork area that season, and Campbell, apparently raising his own prices, conducted a highly successful trade with Nez Perces and Flatheads. He did not erect a post, but hastened back to the 1828 rendezvous at Bear Lake. Just short of the lake, he was attacked by Blackfeet. With a companion he got through to the rendezvous area for help, and numerous trappers, as well as Nez Perces, Flatheads, and Snakes, who were already gathered for the trade, galloped back with him to the rescue of his beleaguered men, helping to drive the Blackfeet away.

That same summer, Jedediah Smith, who had meanwhile made two pioneering trips across the Southwest to California, appeared suddenly at Fort Vancouver. Smith had been leading a group of American trappers up the coast from California, intending to reach the mouth of the Columbia at the very nerve center of British interests. On the headwaters of the Umpqua River in southwestern Oregon, Indians had all but wiped out his party, and with difficulty Smith and three other survivors had struggled the rest of the way to Fort Vancouver. Dr. McLoughlin was bewildered by their appearance, but he received them hospitably and dispatched an expedition to the Umpqua to punish the Oregon natives and retrieve Smith's property. Smith stayed at Fort Vancouver during the winter and in March 1829, hearing that Americans were on the Clark Fork River, journeyed with an escort of Hudson's Bay Company men up the Columbia and along the usual British route past the Nez Perces and Colvile posts to the Flathead country.

The northwestern Montana haunts of the Flatheads and buffalo-hunting Nez Perces were filled with Americans that spring. Near Flathead Lake, Smith found his partner, David Jackson, who, accompanied from time to time by Flathead and Nez Perce bands, had brought one of the partnership's trapping groups north after the 1828 rendezvous and had wintered on the shore of the lake. Nearby was another American party, an independent group under Joshua Pilcher, a veteran Missouri River trader who had come to the mountains in 1827. Pilcher and his men had dogged Jackson's tracks from the rendezvous to the Flathead country, trying unsuccessfully to cut themselves in on some of the Flathead and Nez Perce trade. But they had done so poorly —even having one of their men killed by the usually friendly Kutenais in the area—that soon after Jed Smith showed up Pilcher sold out to the Smith, Jackson, and Sublette firm and returned east with a Hudson's Bay Company brigade through Canada.

In 1828, meanwhile, the United States and Great Britain had extended joint occupancy of Oregon for another ten years, subject to termination at any time after a year's notice by either government. The postponement of the boundary settlement left the entire Oregon country open to the fur men of both nations, and during the rest of the 1820s and early 1830s more American trappers and traders arrived in the area, and competition increased. British policy shifted to the goal of trying to discourage and turn back Americans from penetration of the richer fur regions in the north by trapping the Snake Basin to exhaustion, thus creating a buffer wasteland, and by out-trading Americans for the furs that the natives of the region caught themselves. But though beaver became scarcer in the streams of the Snake Basin, American trappers joined the unrestrained exploitation and continued to hunt every likely water.

Jedediah Smith gave up the mountain trade and returned east, being killed on the Santa Fe Trail in 1831. He and his partners had sold their interests in the West to five trappers who, doing business as the Rocky Mountain Fur Company, still fingered units of mountain men every which way through the beaver country, meanwhile traveling and trading on occasion with bands of Nez Perces and Flatheads. The mountains also filled with free trappers and with brigades of a new competitor, the American Fur Company, which in 1831 at last established uneasy trade relations with the Blackfeet and opened a post for those Indians at the mouth of the Marias River, the location first suggested for an American post by Lewis and Clark.

In their homeland the Nez Perce villagers, still with only horses and provisions to trade, continued to attract few of the beaver men. But outside the borders of their country the heady competition increased the wealth of the roaming Nez Perces, providing them with a choice of sources for guns, ammunition, knives, cloth, blankets, tobacco, paint, fishhooks, decorative articles like ribbons, beads, and bells, and other manufactured goods in return for beaver, robes, saddle blankets of buffalo skin called apishamons, dressed skins, buffalo meat, saddles, and articles of clothing made by the Indian women.

The Nez Perces particularly enjoyed traveling and trading with the rough and easy-going Americans, who often paid no attention to fixed prices, as the British did, but offered goods in accordance with their own needs and desires. Nez Perces became regular participants in the annual rendezvous, wintered in sheltered valleys with the Americans, fought side by side with them against the Blackfeet, and frequently gave Nez Perce women to the mountain men as wives.

In turn, to the Americans in the beaver country there soon came to be no Indians quite like the Nez Perces and Flatheads. Both peoples were often praised as an unusual species of red men, unlike any that the past had conditioned Americans to expect to find anywhere on the continent. In the East generations of interracial conflict had established among frontiersmen the axiom that the only good Indian was a dead one. To pioneer hunters and settlers the unconquered or "wild" Indian was a treacherous and deceitful savage, and the conquered Indian was a worthless beggar, thief, and drunk. They had no morals, according to the borderer's view; they would never accept civilized standards; and the white man had a duty or divine right to brush them aside or exterminate them. In the 1830s frontier warfare, which had moved west to the Missouri and the edge of the plains, appeared to confirm this traditional image of the Indian. Sauk, Foxes, Pawnees, Arikaras, Sioux, Kiowas, Comanches, and other tribes immediately in the path of advancing civilization were considered barbarous enemies. Even Americans who came west from the Atlantic seaboard, where the Indian menace had long since disappeared and where public opinion had become more humane and even romantically sentimental about Indians, changed their minds as they started onto the plains, gripping their rifles in readiness for attacks by wild savages.

The trappers who set out for the Rocky Mountains for the first time actually knew little about the Indians who lived west of the plains. What knowledge they had was derived mostly from the narrative of Lewis and Clark and from the tales and newspaper reports of returned mountain men. On starting west they were made generally aware that their business would require that they get on peaceably with the Indians of the Rockies, for certain of the tribes provided the Americans with furs and granted them permission to trap in safety on their lands. But the veterans described the Flatheads and Nez Perces in unprecedented terms. In many ways, they said, they were like white men, honorable, sincere, and trustworthy.

These Indians—often companionable mixings of Nez Perces, Flatheads, Pend d'Oreilles, Kutenais, Coeur d'Alenes, and Spokans, and sometimes even of Palouses, Wallawallas, Cayuses, and Yakimas—favorably impressed the new arrivals. In their letters and journals the Americans commented on their manliness, pride, and dignified bearing, on their cleanliness, handsome garments, and combed and plaited hair, and on their arms and wealth in horses; and, because the Nez Perces and Flatheads were the Americans' reliable allies against the Blackfeet, they spoke with appreciation of their courage and valor in battle. Most frequently, however—and after 1830 with an increasing persistence that is significant—they mentioned qualities of character that they were surprised to find among wild Indians. They are "a sincere people," wrote John B. Wyeth, who arrived in the West in 1832 and met Nez Perces and various Salish peoples at the trappers' rendezvous that year. "We had many instances of their honesty and humanity. They do not lie, steal, nor rob any one, unless when driven too near starvation; and then any man black, white, or red will seize any thing to save himself from an agonizing death . . . There certainly appeared among them an honor, or conscience, and sense of justice . . ." [38]

Similar judgments, found in the writings of many other Americans in the mountains after 1830, were at variance with long-settled British opinions about the Nez Perces. The North West Company and Hudson's Bay Company traders had lived amicably near them, but, like Governor Simpson, they had often grumbled about the frustrations of trading with them and the vexations they caused their brigades. Unlike the American trappers, the British, who treated the Indians formally and as colonial subjects, had had little or nothing to say about their ethics and had confined their comments to churlish observations like that of John Work, who only a short time before, in contrast to the Americans' feelings about the Nez Perces, had written, "the Nez Perces are really an annoyance." [39] (What the Indians thought about the British traders who, in turn, must often have been vexatious and annoying to the natives was, of course, not recorded.)

By coincidence, the beginning of the close association between the Sahaptin-Salish peoples and large numbers of American trappers which became significant about 1830, occurred simultaneously with a dramatic and remarkably influential introduction of Christian ideas among the home villages of those Indians. The Americans in the mountains had nothing to do

38. John B. Wyeth, "Oregon: A Short History of a Long Journey," in *Early Western Travels, 1748–1846*, ed. Reuben Gold Thwaites, Vol. 21 (Cleveland, 1905), 74–75. Other samples: The Flatheads "are noted for humanity, courage, prudence, candour, forebearance, integrity, trustfulness, piety, and honesty" (the trapper Warren Ferris, May 1831, in *Life in the Rocky Mountains, 1830–1835*, ed. J. Cecil Alter, Salt Lake City, 1940, p. 73); "the best Indians and incomparably the best people in the world, the Flatheads and Nez-Perces tribes" (William Marshall Anderson at the trappers' rendezvous, August 3, 1834, courtesy Dale L. Morgan, editor of Anderson's journals, which are owned by the Huntington Library, San Marino, Calif.).

39. See below, p. 664.

with it and were unaware of what was taking place. But, as will be shown in the next chapter, it worked abrupt and profound changes in the behavior of many of the plateau tribes beginning in the winter of 1829–30, and accounted in large measure for some of the Americans' attitudes about them that differed sharply from earlier British estimates of their conduct.

At the same time, some of the characteristics that so pleased the Americans about the Nez Perces and Flatheads had resulted from British influence. The integrity, sense of justice, and standard of morality of both peoples had always been commendable to those white men who, like Lewis and Clark and David Thompson, had been wise enough to be understanding of the differences between white and native cultures—and, in truth, the natives from their point of view had certainly judged the various white men they had met and found many of them wanting. But much credit for such changes for the better, according to European-based standards, as had occurred among the tribes belonged to Dr. McLoughlin's Indian policy. Since 1824 he had encouraged the cultivation of the friendship and support of the various tribal leaders in the Columbia Department and by ordering swift punishments that fit crimes had made it clear to the natives of the region that the traders would no longer tolerate pilfering, threats with arms, or the molestation of white men in their midst. On the other hand, he had left the Indian peoples and their institutions entirely alone, making no attempt to interfere with or endanger their freedom and ways of life, and had visited stern justice on any white man who mistreated a native or gave Indians cause for offense.

Under that colonial policy, benign and fair to its subjects, the roaming Nez Perces had gradually acclimated themselves to conforming to the standards of relations that the British traders demanded. At the heart of the Indians' change were such things as a continued desire for access to the white man and his trade and alliance with him against common enemies, as well as a wish to avoid trouble—all of which were guaranteed only by the stoppage of horse thefts, pilfering, threats with arms, and other acts that angered the traders. As the Indians had abandoned those traits, their relations with the British had grown more harmonious; and by February 1833 an American who was traveling with a Hudson's Bay Company group through Sahaptin country could visit the area at the junction of the Palouse and Snake rivers, where John Clarke had once hanged an Indian, and write, "The people who are most used to this country are so little afraid of the Indians that they either travel without guns or with them unloaded." [40] But the British could never be anything but calculating and officious traders to the Indians; and because the Ameri-

40. "The Correspondence and Journals of Captain Nathaniel J. Wyeth, 1831–1836," ed. F. G. Young, in *Sources of the History of Oregon*, Vol. 1, Parts III–VI (Eugene, Ore., 1899), p. 185.

cans usually offered better prices the Nez Perces and Flatheads responded to them and found, in addition, a delight in the friendship and equality that the more democratic mountain men accorded them.

Under such conditions the Flatheads and Nez Perces by 1830 were shifting their attentions increasingly from the British to the Americans. That year John Work, now leading the Snake country expedition, discovered large new brigades of the American Fur Company in the Snake Basin, buying horses from the Indians for "high prices" and starting north to trap and trade in the Flathead country. Work returned to Fort Nez Perces, deposited his furs, and headed his own men for the Flathead country, this time by way of the Nez Perces' homeland and the direct route of the Lolo Trail across the Bitter-roots.

Although roaming halfbloods, small groups of free hunters and trappers, and emissaries of the fur companies, usually guided by Indians, had occasionally crossed the formidable, ridgetop trail, no known white expedition had dared take it since Lewis and Clark. Work left Fort Nez Perces on September 11, 1831, and traveled over the high, bare Walla Walla prairies to the Nez Perce villages on the Snake River. He moved up the Clearwater, finding the Nez Perces in a friendly mood, and after counciling with two headmen whose names he recorded as Sowities and Sauwashen, he crossed the camas grounds of the Weippe Prairie and ascended the pine-covered mountains to "the great road" of Lewis and Clark.[41] It was still no more than a narrow, beaten trail, obscured in places by deadfall and underbrush, but a Nez Perce Indian guided the long pack train through the woods and across the exposed ridges. Though Work's men experienced rain, snow, and freezing cold, they had no serious difficulty, and after crossing the pass followed "Loloo's river" down to the warm Bitterroot Valley of the Flatheads, arriving on October 18.[42]

The Americans had been there ahead of Work. As he moved his brigade south through the trapping and hunting valleys of western Montana, he not only found evidence almost everywhere of recent trapping by parties of both the American and Rocky Mountain Fur Companies but learned that Nez Perces and Flatheads had traveled with the "Bostons." Deep in the valley where the Lemhi joined the Salmon River, near present-day Salmon City, Idaho, he finally came on the competition—several different American parties camped with Nez Perces, Flatheads, and other Salish in a snug wintering retreat that Indians had first revealed to Thomas McKay, one of Ogden's men, in the winter of 1827–28. The area swarmed with American trappers whom Work found living in skin lodges, trading for robes and dried meat with the

41. "Sowities" must have been Se-wat-is (Cloud).
42. See below, p. 665.

Indians, gambling with the natives in card and stick games, and joining them in boastful story-telling sessions.

It was no place for the British. Work pushed his men on to more trapping, had two desperate clashes with Blackfeet, in one of which he was wounded, and in the spring suffered a final misfortune when he sent four of his men in a small skin canoe down the main Salmon River to hunt. "This part of the river is not known to have ever been hunted by whites," he recorded. There was good reason for it. Coursing through the furious rapids of the "river of no return," the men upset in one of the Salmon's canyons. Two men were drowned in the current, and the other two reached Fort Nez Perces months later "quite naked," after having been cared for, said Work, "with the utmost kindness" by Nez Perces who lived along the Salmon.[43]

Work went on to Fort Vancouver and took his next expedition to northern Nevada and California. The eastern country of the upper Snake River and the Flathead lands along the Continental Divide were now obviously too filled with Americans for the British to hope ever again to outcompete their rivals or force them from the region. The Hudson's Bay Company, Dr. McLoughlin could see, must accept the competition on the frontier of Oregon and learn to live with it. Being a realist, he would have to think of how to turn adversity into a boon and make profits for the company from the new state of affairs.

Meanwhile, for the time being, the American trappers had this border area of the Columbia Basin almost entirely to themselves. In the spring the different groups parted from the Indians at the Lemhi and Salmon and continued trapping, but the Indians joined them again at the summer rendezvous at Pierre's Hole on the west side of the Tetons. Near the head of the Lemhi River a large group of Nez Perces and Flatheads had fought a desperate two-day battle with Blackfeet, armed with guns received from the new American Fur Company post on the Marias, and the western Indians came into the rendezvous dragging their wounded on buffalo robe litters bound to travois poles.

Two new American companies were in the mountains that year. One, led by Captain Benjamin L. E. Bonneville, a West Pointer on leave from the Army, had stopped in Wyoming's Green River Valley to build a post and missed the rendezvous. Romantically inclined, Bonneville may have been taking a fling at fur trading, or he may have been secretly observing the West for the Army and using fur trading as a cover; his motive in the mountains has never been clear. The second group was a party of greenhorns under a 29-year-old Cambridge, Massachusetts, ice dealer named Nathaniel Wyeth. An otherwise practical businessman with an abundance of energy and deter-

43. Lewis and Phillips, *Journal of John Work*, pp. 174–75.

mination, Wyeth was leading his companions to the Columbia River to try to make a fortune from the Oregon country's unexploited resources. By the time they got to the rendezvous, all but eleven members of his party had had enough of the rugged life and had decided to return home.

The rendezvous progressed according to traditional pattern, commencing with a grand and general alcoholic debauch among the trappers. The Nez Perces and Flatheads had a rousing time, too, racing and demonstrating equestrian stunts for pay, selling dried meat, horses, moccasins, and leather clothing, visiting and gambling with the white men, and buying powder and balls, knives and blankets, and decorative cloth, bells, and beads for their women. When it was over and the various parties started on their different ways, there was an explosive climax. Toward the southern end of Pierre's Hole, a combined party of several trapper groups and Wyeth and his loyal companions, all bound for points farther west, ran into a large band of Gros Ventres, on their way home from a visit to the Arapahoes in Colorado.

A fight started, and the ensuing battle, joined by all the whites and friendly Indians still at the rendezvous site, lasted all day. The Nez Perces and Flatheads fought bravely by the side of the trappers, pinning the Gros Ventres in a thick grove of willows and cottonwoods, choked with marshy underbrush. After dark, the Gros Ventres managed to slip away, and at dawn the Nez Perces and Flatheads rushed into the abandoned enemy fortification, finding many dead and wounded. As well as they could reckon it, more than 25 Gros Ventres had been killed. But five trappers and seven Nez Perces and Flatheads had lost their lives, and many more, including William Sublette, had been wounded.[44] Among the injured Indians were two Nez Perce leaders who would become intimate associates of the Americans and in time play significant roles in the whites' conquest of their own tribe. One was a "tall, commanding-looking fellow" named Tackensuatis, whose severe stomach wound resulted in the trappers thereafter calling him Rotten Belly.[45] He was

44. Several participants of this battle of Pierre's Hole of July 18, 1832, left eyewitness accounts, although most of them differ in details. One of the best versions is in a letter penned from the scene of conflict on the following day, July 19, by Robert Campbell to his brother, Hugh, in Philadelphia, and printed in *The Rocky Mountain Letters of Robert Campbell* (New York, 1955), for Frederick W. Beinecke. Other known accounts are those of William Sublette (a letter in the *Missouri Republican*, October 16, 1832); Nathaniel J. Wyeth (*The Correspondence and Journals*, pp. 158–59); George Nidever (*The Life and Adventures of George Nidever, 1802–1883* ed., William H. Ellison, Berkeley, Calif., 1937, pp. 26–30); John B. Wyeth (*Oregon: A Short History of a Long Journey*, pp. 69–72); Warren A. Ferris (*Life in the Rocky Mountains*, p. 124); and Zenas Leonard (*Adventures of Zenas Leonard, Fur Trader*, ed. John C. Ewers, Norman, Okla., 1959, pp. 42–46).

45. Partoll, "Anderson's Narrative of a Ride to the Rocky Mountains in 1834," in *Frontier Omnibus*, p. 77. Partoll's identification of Tackensuatis as a noted Crow chief

from the vicinity of present-day Stites, Idaho, on the South Fork of the Clearwater River. The other Indian was a shrewd and ambitious young man, part Nez Perce and part Flathead, from the Kamiah region of the Clearwater. His name Hallalhotsoot, was Salish, but the Americans called him The Lawyer because of his ability in argument.

Eventually, all the groups started off again. The trappers returned to the mountain streams, Wyeth made it safely all the way to Fort Vancouver, and the Indians, exultant over the battle and the flight of the Gros Ventres, headed toward the Salmon River. From there, some of the Indians went on, the Flatheads to the Clark Fork Valley and the Nez Perces up and over the Bitterroots to their homes.

The latter Indians were at another turning point in their history. Armed adequately with guns and bound in close friendship to the Americans, they had reached the height of their power. Their bands were as free and independent as always. They had as much of the trade as they wanted, and could acquire what they needed from the American trappers without being made to feel subservient. Their strength, and the source of their supplies, gave them greater confidence than ever before that they could hold their own on contested buffalo grounds, even in the countries of their enemies. Their home villages were secure, free at last from the menace of raids from the south. No one threatened the Nez Perces, least of all, it appeared, the white men who had crushed and wiped away so many of the other native peoples on the continent.

But in this heyday of their affairs, the seed of their destruction was being planted. On March 1, 1833, a Methodist publication in New York City carried a dramatic story about four "Flathead" Indians who had journeyed all the way from the Rocky Mountains to St. Louis in 1831, seeking information about the white man's religion. Those Indians were Nez Perces, and the article, which swept through eastern churches and inspired a frenetic missionary movement, changed the course of Northwest history and led to the doom of the Nez Perces.

---

named Arapooish, whom the whites called Rotten Belly, is an error, although it continues to be copied by almost every writer on the battle of Pierre's Hole. There were no Crows present.

Part II. The Aggressor

3

"Creatures So Far Below"

THE SAHAPTIN AND SALISH PEOPLES had been dimly aware of white men's Christian beliefs and practices ever since the days of Lewis and Clark and David Thompson, when Indians around the explorers' camps had first seen some of the white men at prayer and had heard them read from their Bibles and discuss their single Great Spirit. For years, it was a curiosity to the western Indians, worthy of occasional wonder, but with little meaning to their daily lives. Around Fort Nez Perces and among the Salish peoples on the main routes of the fur trade, where French-Canadian voyageurs and eastern Indians were commonly seen, certain ideas and practices of the more devout Iroquois and other easterners who had been reared in the Roman Catholic faith impressed some of the western natives. Iroquois who witnessed Salish and Sahaptin dances and observed the practices of the western shamans probably took occasion to uphold their own religious beliefs, and even to scoff at the ways of the Columbia Basin Indians. Some of them may have informed the western natives that they were wandering in error, and ascribed instances of their misfortune, including illness, death, starvation, a poor hunt, or a defeat in battle, to the anger of the true Great Spirit whom they were ignoring. At other times, they may have aroused envy among their hearers, instilling in some of them the belief that the white man's spiritual strength and material wealth came from the possession of an intimate relationship with the supernatural world, different and more powerful than that enjoyed by the natives' shamans.

What that relationship was, and how it was acquired, would have been difficult for the comprehension of the Salish and Sahaptins, who followed the faiths of their ancestors in the powers of village shamans and personal guard-

ian spirits. Some of the voyageurs and Iroquois are known to have told them
about the priests in the East, whom they called blackrobes and, because they
taught the religion of the French, French chiefs; and they discussed some of
the things the priests had taught them. But their efforts to instruct the western natives could not have been compelling enough to have seriously challenged the power of the Indians' shamans. Although a few of the easterners
were more religious than others, most of the Iroquois, who mixed freely with
the western Indians and would have been best able to convert them, were
characterized by the British traders as dissolute and semicivilized, and they
could not have been effective teachers. In the environment of the Salish and
Sahaptin villages, moreover, cultural influences ran both ways; and in a short
time, contemporary accounts make clear, the eastern Indians usually acquired
more traits from the westerners than they were able to impart themselves.
The spreading of information that the white man had a strong and advantageous relationship with the spirit world, and that there were special men who
could teach its secrets, can undoubtedly be credited to some of the Iroquois
and French-Canadian voyageurs; but there is no reliable evidence that their
Catholicism made either a deep or a widely felt spiritual mark—even remotely
equal to the changes wrought by the economics of the fur trade—on the cultures of any of the Northwest tribes.[1]

On the other hand, a Christian impact that led to a profound change
throughout the area came eventually from Anglicans connected with the
Hudson's Bay Company. The British fur firm had traditionally shown little
interest in the natives' religious beliefs, or in attempting to influence them.
But in 1824 a directive from the London Committee called attention to the
need for consideration of missionary work in the Northwest. By its 1821 license from the British government the company had accepted an obligation
to provide for the religious instruction of natives within the territories it controlled. In the Columbia district it had ignored the obligation up to that time;
but now a religious revival was astir in England, and many influential persons
had taken an interest in the moral and spiritual welfare of native peoples in
overseas countries that were under British sovereignty. Among the leaders of
the revival movement was one of the directors of the Hudson's Bay Company,
a philanthropist named Benjamin Harrison; and largely as a result of his pressure, together with that of the Church of England Missionary Society in
London, the Committee on March 11, 1824, reminded Governor Simpson
that "It is incumbent on the Company . . . at least to allow missions to be
established at proper places for the conversion of the Indians, indeed it wd be
extremely impolitic in the present temper & disposition of the public in this
Country to show any unwillingness to assist in such an object."[2]

1. See below, p. 666.
2. Merk, *Fur Trade and Empire*, p. 205.

It was the year that Simpson was making his tour of inspection and reorganization of the Columbia district, but he seemed willing to accept the directive. In June, before he left the Red River settlement near present-day Winnipeg, Manitoba, he had a conversation with the Reverend David T. Jones, who conducted a Church of England Missionary Society school at that location, regarding the possibility of enrolling Indian boys, including "2 From the Columbia," and in August he addressed a letter to Benjamin Harrison in London, telling him of his thoughts on the subject. "The poverty of the country in large animals," he wrote, "renders it impossible to do any good among the Indians by Missionaries and the only practical mode of instructing and enlightening them appears to be by getting a few children from each Tribe to the Societys School at Red River where they could be educated with a due regard to morality and Religion and afterwards sent back to their relations for the purpose of instructing them . . . While in the Columbia I shall endeavour to procure a few children (from those Tribes on the coast who live in Villages) for the Missionary Society School." [3]

Simpson went on to Fort George, where he discussed the subject with his reached the Spokane House on his way to Fort George, wrote to Alexander Ross, who at the moment was unhappily bringing his Snake country expedition back to the Flathead Post with Jedediah Smith and his Americans in tow. Simpson had apparently already decided to remove Ross as leader of the trapping brigades, and he offered him the post of schoolmaster at the Red River settlement, adding, "I could wish that two Indian boys of about eight years of age of the Spokan and Nez Perce Tribe were got from their relations for the purpose of being educated at the School and taken out with your Family; a present to the value of £2.3 or 4. might be given to the friends of each as an inducement to part with them." [4]

Simpson went on to Fort George, where he discussed the subject with his traders at that post. In November he came to the conclusion that it would be possible to establish missions in the Columbia country, provided that sites were selected where the Indians were settled in villages and did not roam, and

3. J. Orin Oliphant, "George Simpson and Oregon Missions," *Pacific Historical Review, 6* (1937), 234; Clifford M. Drury, "Oregon Indians in the Red River School," *Pacific Historical Review,* 7 (1938), 52. Simpson's letter to Harrison of August 1, 1824, quoted by Drury, is in the Hudson's Bay Company Archives, D. 4/3, pp. 140 ff.

4. Drury, "Oregon Indians in the Red River School," pp. 52–53, quoting Hudson's Bay Company Archives D. 4/5, fol. 2d. Ross eventually went to Red River, and during the winter of 1843–44 a visitor there wrote of him as follows: "Though somewhat stiff and pedantic in his appearance he is a very well-informed man—he is familiarly styled 'the Professor'—from his having, at one period of his life exercised his talents and his toes, as a dancing master . . . he is considerable of a Screw; he holds the office of sheriff." "A Red River Gossip," the letters of Robert Clouston, ed. Elaine Allan Mitchell, *The Beaver* (Spring 1961), p. 8.

where the land was favorable for cultivation and the raising of livestock to supplement a supply of fish. Two locations that he considered suitable were the Spokane House and the neighborhood of the Cascade portage on the Columbia. But missionaries who came to the western country, he thought, would have to be mild, even-tempered men, not too quick to criticize the morals of the Indians. Moreover, they would have to come for a minimum of five years' service, since a succession of new faces would only confuse the Indians, and it would take five years, in his opinion, for a newcomer to master the different native languages in any one area. Finally, as a sound businessman, he reminded his factors and traders that the conversion of the natives might prove profitable to them, for it would place the Indians in greater need of white men's goods and thus increase the company's profits.

Before he left Fort George, Simpson made plans to take two youths with him from the lower Columbia to the Red River school, and on March 10, 1825, he wrote Benjamin Harrison that "Two boys of the Cheenook Tribe accompany me across the Mountain this season for the purpose of being put under the charge of the Revd. Mr. Jones; one of them belongs to a family of the first rank in the River, he is the Grandson of Comcomly or Chief of the Cheenooks . . ." [5] Something went awry with his plan, however, and when he started upriver six days later, the Indian boys were not with him. But on April 7, in the vicinity of the Spokane House, he met Alexander Ross, who had received his letter of October 29 and had arranged for the two youths whom Simpson had requested from that part of the country. Ross reported that when he had first taken up the matter with Salish leaders in the Flathead lands, they had been indignant with him. They had "asked him if they 'were looked upon as dogs—willing to give up their children to go they knew not whither,' but when he told them they were going to a minister of religion to learn how to know and to serve God, they said he might have '*hundreds of children in an hour's time*.' and he selected two, being the sons of the most powerful chiefs in the part of the country." [6]

A more precise account of what Ross had told the Salish headmen would be interesting to read, for it is certain that they could have had no clear idea of the white man's religion, nor a realization that Ross meant to end their sons' attachments to their own spiritual beliefs and shamanistic practices. Learning about the white man's God and how to serve Him could only have been understood at that time as an opportunity to acquire a new supernatural power which they could add to the ones they already possessed, and Ross

5. Drury, "Oregon Indians," p. 53, quoting Hudson's Bay Company Archives D. 4/5, fol. 13.

6. Oliphant, "George Simpson and Oregon Missions," p. 239; Thomas E. Jessett, *Chief Spokan Garry* (Minneapolis, 1960), p. 22.

must have given the headmen the belief that their sons were being accorded the privilege of receiving the secrets of that power for the use of their people. At any rate, on April 8 Ross introduced Simpson to some of the Kutenai and Salish leaders in his camp near the Spokane House, and Simpson recorded that "The Spokan & Flat Head Chiefs put a son each under my care to be Educated at the Missionary School Red River." At the same time, he noted that "all the Chiefs joined in a most earnest request that a Missionary or religious instructor should be placed among them . . ." [7]

The following day two Nez Perce leaders arrived at Simpson's camp, having come "a distance of between 2 & 300 Miles" to see the Governor. They told him that their people had heard of him and that some of them understood that he was one of the "Master of Life's Sons" sent to see if their hearts were good, while others believed that he was the "War Chief" of the Master of Life and had bad medicine to dispense if their hearts were bad.

Simpson lingered in the neighborhood of the Spokane House for several days, but the problems of settling accounts with his traders and reorganizing the trade of the interior prevented him for the time being from establishing a mission at that location. Instead, on April 12 he accepted charge of the two Indian youths, one a Spokan and the other a Kutenai, whom he would take to Red River. "Baptised the Indian boys," he noted in his journal, "they are the Sons of the Principal Spokan and Coutonais War Chiefs, men of great Weight and Consequence in this part of the country. They are named Coutonais Pelly and Spokan Garry." [8]

The boys, both in their early teens, had been honored with the names of J. H. Pelly and Nicholas Garry, officials of the Hudson's Bay Company. The youths accompanied Simpson's party over the Canadian Rockies, and eventually reached the Red River school. Other Indian boys from elsewhere in Canada were already enrolled in the school, and when two of them died there soon afterward, Simpson wrote to Jones, "Let me entreat that the utmost care be taken of the two boys 'Pelly' and 'Garry' brought by me from the Columbia this summer, they are the Sons of Two Chiefs of considerable influence and any accident to them would be likely to involve us in eternal warfare with their Tribes which are very powerful." [9]

At the mission the boys were taught reading, writing, history, and geography, and by 1827, when the Scottish botanist, David Douglas, who stopped at Red River on his way home from the Columbia River, met Garry, he reported that he spoke good English and had almost forgotten his own language. In addition, the youths learned to plant and tend crops, and their reli-

7. Merk, *Fur Trade*, pp. 135–36.
8. Ibid., p. 138.
9. Drury, "Oregon Indians," p. 54.

gious instruction proceeded so well that on June 27, 1827, the Reverend Jones baptized them again, deeming their knowledge of the Scriptures "satisfactory." [10] Significantly, in view of later history, other Indians from various parts of Canada visited Red River from time to time and referred to the Anglican missionaries as the "Black Robes," distinguishing them from the Roman Catholic priests at the French Canadian center across the river, whom they called the "Long Robes." Garry and Pelly, also, probably learned to use those terms and eventually carried them back to their homelands with them. Its importance arose in the future, when their peoples' interest in having "Blackrobes" come to instruct them led to bitterness between Protestants and Catholics over what kind of missionaries the Indians actually meant. [11]

In the summer of 1829, after having attended the school for four years, the two boys, now grown to young manhood, accompanied the Hudson's Bay Company's express back across the Canadian Rockies to their families. Both of them had been given leather-bound copies of the King James Version of the Bible, a New Testament, and the Book of Common Prayer of the Church of England. Dressed in white men's clothes, speaking English, and behaving like youths used to civilized society, they created sensations in their home villages. Little is known of the activities of Kutenai Pelly among his people, but news of the return of Spokan Garry, and of the white man's ways and powers he had acquired, spread excitedly among the different Salish and Sahaptin peoples, including the Nez Perces. Garry's father, Illim-Spokanee, the most influential of the Spokans' headmen, had died during the youths' absence; and Garry, who was now eighteen, was treated with grave respect, not only as a youthful shaman of a sort, who was endowed with special material and supernatural powers, but as a leader's son who was old enough to be heard on matters affecting the welfare of his people.

Throughout the winter of 1829–30, he lectured and preached to groups of Indians of different tribes, telling them about the white man's God and Jesus, his Heaven and Hell, the Ten Commandments, and the need to observe Sundays and to say prayers in the morning and before meals. He sang hymns to his audiences and read to them from his Bible, explaining its lessons and describing it as the guide to the supernatural powers that men must have if they wished to go to heaven. [12] Indians traveled great distances to see the Bible and to listen to Garry read from it, and some of them, including a number of Nez Perce leaders, became envious of the new influence that possession of the book and its powers gave to the Spokans. They were anxious for their own

10. Jessett, *Chief Spokan Garry*, p. 30.

11. John West, *The Substance of a Journal during a Residence at the Red River Colony, British North America* (London, 1824), p. 91.

12. Jessett, pp. 32–34.

copy, and for the knowledge of the supernatural that the book seemed to contain, but acquiring one for themselves presented a problem. In the intervening years, the Hudson's Bay Company had forgotten its earlier missionary intentions. Simpson had ordered that divine services be read at company posts on Sundays, and those weekly rites had played a role in continuing to increase the Indians' awareness of Christianity. But as moral pressures from England had slackened, Simpson had postponed and then abandoned his plan to establish missions west of the mountains and to send missionaries to the tribes in that region, and the Nez Perces and other peoples of the area were without a source to whom to appeal for Bibles of their own.

Kutenai Pelly, also, must have contributed that winter to the interest in Christianity that spread rapidly among tribes of the upper Columbia Basin and resulted in the adoption by many villages of a few basic Christian practices, as well as in the partial acceptance of new ideas, including the concept of the brotherhood of Indians and white men under God and the idea that making war except in defense was wrong. In certain areas something similar in fervor to a white man's religious revival may have occurred, though evidence regarding it is scant. On July 25, 1831, the Reverend Jones, recording his knowledge of what had been happening in the Columbia country, wrote from Red River to the Church Missionary Society in London that "The impression which Pelly and Garry *made*, in their relation of what they had learned, upon them [the Indians], seems to have been very great, according to the account of Company's Officers residing in that quarter . . . the Indians on the Upper part of the Columbia paid utmost attention to the information conveyed to them through the boys, Spokan and . . . Pelly, and readily received whatever instruction or doctrines they thought proper to inculcate . . . and ever since they assemble every Sunday to keep the Sabbath in the ways the boys directed." [13] The youths' influence traveled even farther, for John McLean, a Hudson's Bay Company trader at Stuart Lake in northern British Columbia, reported during the winter of 1835–36 that "Two young men, natives of Oregon, who had received a little education at Red River, had, on their return to their own country, introduced a sort of religion whose groundwork seemed to be Christianity, accompanied with some heathen ceremonies of the natives. This religion spread with amazing rapidity all over the country. It reached Fort Alexandria, the lower post of the district, in the autumn 1834 or 1835 . . ." [14]

13. Ibid., pp. 35, 38.
14. *John McLean's Notes of a Twenty-Five Year's Service in the Hudson's Bay Territory*, ed. W. S. Wallace (Toronto, 1932), pp. 159–60. The manuscript text of Father Nicholas Point's "Recollections of the Rocky Mountains," pp. 77–78, also confirms the curiosity that Garry's return excited among the various tribes. Speaking

An opportunity for other tribes to share the Spokans' new power and influence came suddenly in 1830, when the Hudson's Bay Company announced it would take five more Indian boys from the Columbia country to Red River that spring, in addition to Garry and Pelly, who were returning to the school. Five boys were immediately produced by eager tribal leaders, and were taken to Fort Colvile to join the company's express canoe for the Canadian Rockies. All of them were between twelve and seventeen years of age, and were related to influential headmen. Two of them were Nez Perces. One, a grandson of the powerful old war chief Hohots Ilppilp, who had met Lewis and Clark, was given the name Ellice by the traders. The second Nez Perce was called Pitt. The other new boys were the nephew of a Cayuse leader named Tauitau, sometimes called the Young Chief; the son of a Spokan leader known as Big Head; and a relative of Kutenai headmen.[15] The traders renamed the

---

of the Coeur d'Alenes, whom he met in the early 1840s, Father Point relates that a member of that tribe had heard about Garry and had told his people about the Spokan, after which the report had spread far and wide. Many Coeur d'Alenes, northern neighbors of the Nez Perces, had flocked to hear Garry, curious about what he had learned, said the priest. Finally, as Jessett points out, the anthropologist Leslie Spier, while studying the religious life of Indians in the Northwest, came to the conclusion that a great interest in Christianity had permeated the interior tribes "about 1830 or a little later," and that "the revival must have spread from the Spokan country." See Leslie Spier, *The Prophet Dance in the Northwest and Its Derivatives: The Source of the Ghost Dance*, General Series in Anthropology, (Menasha, Wis., 1935), p. 38. In 1958 the Reverend Don M. Chase, in *He Opened the West*, a study of Jedediah Smith published in Sacramento, advanced the belief that the deeply religious Smith had been responsible for the interest of the Salish and Sahaptins in Christianity. His thesis rests on the fact that when those Indians finally sent messengers to bring missionaries to their homelands, they dispatched them to St. Louis rather than to the Red River. It is an interesting theory, one suggested earlier by Edwin L. Sabin in *Kit Carson Days* (Chicago, 1914), but it ignores the chain of events I describe; and although I cannot prove (though I can assume, as I do later) why the Indians did not go to Red River, I cannot without evidence attribute the sudden interest in Christianity among the tribes in 1830 to Smith, who made no known attempt to influence any of the numerous other Indian tribes he met, and who would have had small influence among the native peoples around the Flathead Post.

15. The identities of these boys might be kept in mind, since they help to illuminate some of the later history of their tribes. For example, Big Head, the father of Spokan Berens, became the friend and protector of the Walkers and Eellses, Protestant missionaries who settled among the Spokans in 1837. Halket's uncle, Tauitau, a proud Cayuse, who often had conflicts with British traders, became a Catholic after Halket died at Red River. But Tauitau's brother, Five Crows, known as Hezekiah (who may have been Halket's father), and his half-brother, Tuekakas, the Nez Perce Wallowa chieftain, later known as Old Joseph, were two of the few Indians baptized by Henry H. Spalding, the Protestant missionary. All of these men, soon to play leading roles in Indian-white relations in Oregon, undoubtedly had a close interest in the boys who went to the Red River school, and thus also an early curiosity about the white man's

youths Cayuse Halket, Spokan Berens, and Kutenai Collins, after Hudson's Bay Company officials, and the seven youths departed from Fort Colvile on April 30, 1830, reaching the school that summer. There the newcomers began an education and training similar to that of Garry and Pelly.

When he had been home, Pelly had fallen from a horse. He had never fully recovered his strength, and in April, 1831, he died at the school. Garry was sent back to the Columbia country that summer to tell the Kutenais what had happened. He did not return to Red River, but settled among his people, opening a school and continuing to teach and preach to Spokans, Coeur d'Alenes, Colvilles, Nez Perces, Pend d'Oreilles, Flatheads, and other Indians who came to hear him. Ellice, Pitt, Cayuse Halket, and Kutenai Collins returned to their homes in the summer of 1833, all of them versed in English and in the rudiments of Christianity. Spokan Berens was ill, and remained at Red River, where he died on July 19, 1834. Kutenai Collins also died, soon after his return to his people. Ellice, Pitt, and Halket took up lives in their own villages again, but none of them created the sensation that Garry and Pelly had first made when they had come back from Red River in 1829. In their own settlements they contributed to the work begun by Garry and enjoyed brief periods of influence. Cayuse Halket eventually returned to Red River, where he had an accident and died in 1837. Pitt gradually sank into obscurity among the people of his village, and he is believed to have died about 1839, unmentioned even by the American missionaries who had settled among the Nez Perces by that time.[16] Ellice's power as a religious force also

---

supernatural world. For Berens' relationship to Big Head see Drury, *First White Women over the Rockies, 2,* 131 n.; for that of Halket to Tauitau see ibid., *1,* 123.

16. Jessett, *Spokan Garry,* pp. 41–46. The Whitmans did hear about Cayuse Halket, for on January 2, 1837, Narcissa Whitman, soon after she and her husband had settled among the Cayuses, wrote about "Young Cayuse Halket now at Red River Mission whom we expect to return this fall & to whom the chieftainship belongs by inheritance" (Drury, *First White Women, 1,* 123). Of interest also is a statement regarding the deaths at Red River of Kutenai Pelly and Spokan Berens by Father Joseph Joset, a Jesuit missionary to the Salish, which Jessett quotes, p. 35, from the Joset Papers, Vol. 23, Jesuit Historical Archives, Mount St. Michaels, Spokane, Wash.: "Hudson's Bay Company had sent some savages to a Protestant school at the Red River. Among them there was a Coeur d'Alene and a Coutenais: they died there: and it is very probably necessary to attribute to this fact that these two tribes are now Catholic. Two of these young men came back, one a Spokane and one a Nez Perce, and were the cause that the sacred teachings were spread among their people." Too little attention, I believe, has been paid to Catholic references to the Red River school, like this one and the quotation cited above from Father Point's "Recollections." Even such a recently published work as Bischoff's "Jesuits in Old Oregon" (1945), which cites the Joset Papers in its bibliography, continues to credit the first Christian influences among the Salish and Sahaptins solely to Iroquois "warriors," and fails to include a single mention of the Red River school.

faded, although as a grandson of Hohots Ilppilp he continued under the name Twvish Sisimnen (Sparkling Horn) as a civil leader among the Indians in his home region of Kamiah on the Clearwater River. In later years, when white missionaries reached the area, they singled him out as a tribal headman, although more because of his English training than for his religious influence.

The impact of Garry and Pelly, in the meantime, had been felt, to a greater or lesser degree, in most of the Nez Perce villages. The bands that crossed the mountains after buffalo carried smatterings of Christian ideas onto the plains with them, and commencing soon after 1830 American trappers who had never expected to find Christian influences among Rocky Mountain Indians were startled by practices among the natives that seemed to indicate a genuine religious piety. In their astonishment and enthusiasm the more devout trappers, like later observers, failing to realize that the Indians regarded the white man's religion as an addition to their own beliefs of the universe—albeit one that might increase their power and improve their welfare—often jumped to the conclusion that the Indians were ripe for conversion.

"The Flatheads," wrote Warren Ferris, the American Fur Company trapper, in May 1831, referring to a band that also included Nez Perces and Pend d'Oreilles, "have received some notions of religion either from pious traders or from transient ministers who have visited the Columbia. Their ancient superstitions have given place to the more enlightened views of the christian faith, and they seem to have become deeply and profitably impressed with the great truth of the gospel. They appear to be very devout and orderly, and never eat, drink, or sleep without giving thanks to God." [17]

Captain Bonneville was even more misled by appearances when a year later, after building his fort on the Green River, he moved north to the upper Salmon near present-day Salmon City, Idaho, and met Nez Perces for the first time. Relating Bonneville's adventures as the Captain had reported them to him, Washington Irving told how Bonneville had suggested to this band of Nez Perces, who had come from the upper Clearwater River, that they join one of his hunting parties:

> To his surprise they promptly declined . . . It was a sacred day with them, and the Great Spirit would be angry should they devote it to hunting. They offered, however, to accompany the party if it would delay its departure until the following day; but this the pinching demands of hunger would not permit, and the detachment proceeded. A few days afterward, four of them signified to Captain Bonneville that they were about to hunt. "What!" exclaimed he, "without guns or ar-

17. Ferris, *Life in the Rocky Mountains*, p. 75. I have used the Salt Lake City edition of 1940.

rows; and with only one old spear? What do you expect to kill?" They smiled among themselves, but made no answer. Preparatory to the chase they performed some religious rites, and offered up to the Great Spirit a few short prayers for safety and success; then, having received the blessings of their wives, they leaped upon their horses and departed, leaving the whole party of Christian spectators amazed and rebuked by this lesson of faith and dependence on a supreme and benevolent Being. "Accustomed," adds Captain Bonneville, "as I had heretofore been, to find the wretched Indian reveling in blood and stained by every vice which can degrade human nature, I could scarcely realize the scene I had witnessed. Wonder at such unaffected tenderness and piety, where it was least to have been sought, contended in all our bosoms with shame and confusion, at receiving such pure and wholesome instructions from creatures so far below us in all the arts and comforts of life.

The "simple prayers," moreover, were answered, according to Bonneville; and a few days later the Indians, who had ridden down and tired some buffalo and dispatched them with their spear, came back laden with meat, which they shared, "charitable as they had been pious," with the whites. "A further and more intimate intercourse with this tribe," Irving added, "gave Captain Bonneville still greater cause to admire their strong devotional feeling. 'Simply to call these people religious,' says he, 'would convey but a faint idea of the deep hue of piety and devotion which pervades their whole conduct. Their honesty is immaculate, and their purity of purpose, and their observance of the rites of their religion, are most uniform and remarkable. They are certainly more like a nation of saints than a horde of savages.' "[18]

Although his interest in the Indians' souls blinded him to an appreciation of the continued strength of their own cultural traits, Bonneville did not overstate the ritualistic atmosphere that pervaded their daily lives. In the case of some of them, he described the outward signs of their grafting of Christian ideas on their own customs and habits but, unaware of their Anglican derivation, ascribed some of their practices, which were obviously not those of American Protestant faiths, to Roman Catholic teachers.

It would appear that they had imbibed some notions of the Christian faith from Catholic missionaries and traders who had been among them. They even had a rude calendar of the fasts and festivals of the Romish Church, and some traces of its ceremonials. These have become blended with their own wild rites, and present a strange medley; civilized and barbarous. On the Sabbath, men, women, and children array them-

18. Irving, *The Adventures of Captain Bonneville*, pp. 87-88. My citations in this chapter are to the New York edition of 1904.

selves in their best style, and assemble round a pole erected at the head of the camp. Here they go through a wild fantastic ceremonial; strongly resembling the religious dance of the Shaking Quakers; but, from its enthusiasm, much more striking and impressive. During the intervals of the ceremony, the principal chiefs, who officiate as priests, instruct them in their duties, and exhort them to virtue and good deeds.[19]

In the spring of 1833 Nathaniel Wyeth, traveling through parts of Idaho and western Montana with bands of Nez Perce, Flathead, and other Salish Indians, was also impressed by the outward manifestations of the Indians' religious enthusiasm. He repeatedly mentioned their "praying, dancing & singing," and on April 30 dwelled at length in his journal on the manner of their practices. "Every morning some important indian addresses either heaven or his countrymen or both I believe exhorting the one to good conduct to each other and to the strangers among them and the other to bestow its blessings he finishes with 'I am done' the whole set up an exclamation in concord during the whole time Sunday there is more parade of prayer as above nothing is done Sunday in the way of trade with these Indians nor in playing games and they seldom fish or kill game or raise camp while prayers are being said on week days everyone ceases whatever vocation he is about if on horseback he dismounts and holds his horse on the spot until all is done . . ."[20]

On the following Sunday, Wyeth provided a suggestion of the superficial nature of Christianity's attraction to the Indians. "There is a new great man now getting up in the Camp and like the rest of the world he covers his designs under the great cloak religion," he wrote. "His followers are now dancing to their own vocal music in the plain perhaps ⅕ of the Camp follow him when he gets enough followers he will branch off and be an independent chief he is getting up some new form of religion among the Indians more simple than himself . . ." And two weeks after that, still with the Flatheads and Nez Perces, he wrote, "The medicine chief had devotional exercises with his followers," indicating again that shamanism was yet the dominant spiritual chord of those tribes, and that, even though the shamans might have added and adapted certain Christian ideas to their own practices, they were still the people's leaders in affairs of the supernatural.[21]

Among the ethical teachings that Garry had apparently communicated to them, the command not to kill had impressed many of the Indians, and some of the Nez Perces and Flatheads, Bonneville noted impatiently, seemed to be

19. Ibid., p. 88.
20. Wyeth, *Correspondence and Journals*, p. 192.
21. Ibid., pp. 193–94, 196.

losing their fighting spirit, allowing the Blackfeet to raid their camps and steal their horses with impunity. To the men of his command, who needed allies against the Blackfeet, this ironic result of Christian influence was irritating; and although Bonneville must have recognized that to the logical Indians it would have been a reasonable law from the white man's Great Spirit, he nevertheless became angry with the Nez Perces, who seemed too mild and unwarlike.

On one occasion, after Blackfeet had twice raided Nez Perce horse herds on the upper Salmon River without retaliation by the Nez Perces, Irving wrote that Bonneville's impatience became exhausted. "Accordingly, convoking their chiefs, he inveighed against their craven policy, and urged the necessity of vigorous and retributive measures that would check the confidence and presumption of their enemies, if not inspire them with awe. For this purpose, he advised that a war party should be immediately sent off on the trail of the marauders, to follow them, if necessary, into the very heart of the Blackfoot country, and not to leave them until they had taken signal vengeance. Besides this, he recommended the organization of minor war parties, to make repraisals to the extent of the losses sustained. 'Unless you rouse yourselves from your apathy,' said he, 'and strike some bold and decisive blow, you will cease to be considered men, or objects of manly warfare. The very squaws and children of the Blackfeet will be sent against you, while their warriors reserve themselves for nobler antagonists.' "

"This harangue," Irving reported, "had evidently a momentary effect upon the pride of the hearers." But then came the blow. After a short pause, one of the Indian orators arose. "It was bad, he said, to go to war for revenge. The Great Spirit had given them a heart for peace, not for war." [22]

Although Bonneville, in this instance, failed in his appeal, the Nez Perces and Flatheads had not become nations of pacifists. Their participation in the Battle of Pierre's Hole had occurred only a few months before, and their bands, later in the same year, would continue to show that they could still fight aggressively and with reckless daring against their enemies. But even as Bonneville was lecturing them, a very real inhibiting influence was beginning to be aimed against them as the result of a dramatic event that had taken place the year before, without the knowledge of the British or that of most of the Americans in the West. Four Nez Perces, as previously stated, had gone to St. Louis from the Rocky Mountains, and several persons in that city had got the idea that the Indians had made the long trip to secure spiritual salvation for their people.

The Nez Perce mission to the East has been romanticized and distorted by so many generations of religious partisans and writers of drama and fiction that

22. Irving, *Bonneville*, p. 109.

some of the truth concerning it can only be pieced together by conjecture. The known events began on June 19, 1831, approximately a year and a half after Garry and Pelly had first returned to their people from Red River. On that day, according to Warren Ferris, who was with an American Fur Company brigade north of Monida Pass on the present Montana-Idaho border, a party of thirty men under Lucien Fontenelle and Andrew Drips, bound ultimately for St. Louis to bring back supplies for their men in the field, departed for Cache Valley, Utah, where they were to rendezvous with a Rocky Mountain Fur Company group with whom they had agreed to make the trip to the States. Some twenty "Flatheads"—that is, Flatheads and Nez Perces—accompanied Fontenelle and Drips from the Monida Pass encampment, Ferris said.[23] From Cache Valley seven of the Indians, whose object—the missionary Marcus Whitman later reported that Fontenelle told him—"was to gain religious knowledge," went on with the American Fur Company leaders to the East.[24] Drips halted at Council Bluffs to make up a supply train for an immediate return to the mountains from that place, and three of the Indians stayed there with him. The other four went on to St. Louis with Fontenelle, who planned to go back to the mountains the following spring. Drips started west again from Council Bluffs on or about October 1, 1831, but winter weather held him up, and he only rejoined his men on Muddy Creek in southwestern Wyoming on April 24, 1832, a few months before the Pierre's Hole rendezvous. His arrival back, according to Ferris, was heralded by the appearance of "a well known Flathead Indian, named Pascal, who accompanied Fontenelle and Drips to St. Louis last summer" but was one of the three who turned around at Council Bluffs with Drips.[25] The other four Indians who had gone all the way to St. Louis were not mentioned by Ferris, and they were the ones who were making history.

The composition and purpose of that quartet have long been the subject of controversy. The Nez Perces who were with the Flatheads and Ferris's American Fur Company group near Monida Pass on June 19, 1831, included Indians from villages in the Kamiah Valley and along the South Fork of the Clearwater River, where the people had been greatly influenced by Garry's teachings, and from where the year before they had sent one of their youths, Ellice, to the Red River school. In 1839, A. B. Smith, a Congregationalist missionary who settled briefly among the Indians in that area, quoted Hallalhotsoot, The Lawyer, who also came from the Kamiah region, as saying that as a result of Spokan Garry's teachings, six Nez Perces had set out from the Kamiah villages for the United States in search of Christian teachers. Two of

23. Ferris, *Life in the Rocky Mountains*, p. 80.
24. Clifford M. Drury, *Henry Harmon Spalding* (Caldwell, Idaho, 1936), pp. 81–82.
25. Ferris, p. 113.

them, he reported, had turned back in the mountains and the other four had gone on to St. Louis.[26] In 1894 a Nez Perce convert named Billy Williams told another missionary, Kate McBeth, somewhat the same story, recalling that when he was about eight or ten years old, he had ridden a few miles along the trail from Kamiah with men who were going in search of the white men's "book." [27]

It is probable that, under the impact of Garry's teaching during the winter of 1829–30, some of the shamans and headmen of the Nez Perces in the Kamiah Valley and elsewhere had held councils to consider how to secure a teacher with a copy of the white men's "book." They must have been filled with envy of the Spokans, as well as with an intense curiosity about this new subject; for their ignorance of it kept them from identifying themselves with it and achieving the importance and influence among their own people that its knowledge would give them. It is difficult to reconstruct the thinking that led them finally to send some of their people to St. Louis. There are no explanations in the writings of British traders or American trappers, and the Nez Perces themselves have no tradition today of exactly what happened. The logical place to have sent emissaries would seem to have been Red River, where Garry and Pelly had got their education and Bibles. But the Nez Perces had just provided two of their own youths, Ellice and Pitt, to go to Red River, and it is possible that the Hudson's Bay Company had told them that the school was only for their sons, and that their canoes could not take grown men to Canada. No British trader in the Columbia country, on his own, would have authorized sending adult Indians to Red River, and even Governor Simpson would not have known what to do with them once they arrived. At the same time, the Nez Perce headmen, having decided to seek for themselves what the Hudson's Bay Company was putting into the hands of their children, would not have asked their emissaries to attempt the journey to Red River by themselves. The Nez Perces not only would have been ignorant of the route but would have had to travel much of the way directly through the homelands of their mortal enemies, the Blackfoot tribes.

On the other hand, it is possible that the Nez Perces' trade relations at the time with the British and the Americans decided them from the beginning to try to send their messengers to the country of the rivals of the British, hoping perhaps for additional favor and gain for themselves. They had no love for the men at Fort Nez Perces or for other British traders like John Work, with whom at the time they were bargaining hard and often quarreling; and their pride may well have dictated against their approaching the British for so personal a favor. In the Kamiah Valley, however, memory of the good-

26. See below, p. 667.
27. McBeth, *The Nez Perces since Lewis and Clark*, p. 30.

hearted Lewis and Clark, who had stayed among their villages in that area for almost two months some twenty-five years before, was still strong. Many people from Kamiah had vivid recollections of the explorers, and those among them who crossed over to the buffalo grounds often reminisced to the American trappers about the expedition's visit to their country. Now, on the eastern side of the mountains, they had established a warm relationship with more Americans. Some of them, they knew, went regularly east to the States to get trade goods. Perhaps, if the British would only take boys to Red River, the Nez Perces would please the Americans by the friendship they would indicate in asking that they take some of their men to their country with their traders. The Americans could not help understanding the point. Far from seeking a favor, the Nez Perces would be showing a preference for the Americans as against the British, and the "Bostons" would respond more liberally than would the cold and tight-fisted men of the Hudson's Bay Company.

However the Nez Perces finally did reach their decision, it seems likely that the men they selected to make the trip traveled across the Bitterroots with a buffalo-hunting band and held council with the Flatheads, who decided to send some of their own people with the mission. The first opportunity for the Indians to accompany American fur men to their distant country came in the late summer of 1831; and so when Drips and Fontenelle headed back to the States from Cache Valley, the group of seven Nez Perces and Flatheads might well have "girded up their loins," in the theatric words of a later romanticist, "and set forth on a pathless Venture, over mountains and plains and down winding rivers, for thousands of miles."

There is no doubt about the identity of the four Indians who traveled all the way with Fontenelle and in the early fall of 1831 reached the busy fur-outfitting city of St. Louis. One of them was a Nez Perce warrior of about 44 years of age from the Kamiah Valley, who was known as both Tipyahlanah (Eagle) and Kipkip Pahlekin, a term whose meaning is not known today. He seems to have come from the village of the powerful Kamiah leader whom Lewis and Clark had met and called Tunnachemootoolt. The others were two young Nez Perces, each about 20 years old, named Hi-yuts-to-henin (Rabbit Skin Leggings) and Tawis Geejumnin (No Horns on His Head, or Horns Worn Down Like Those on an Old Buffalo); and a second older Indian warrior named Ka-ou-pu (Man of the Morning, or of the Dawn Light), the son of a Nez Perce buffalo-hunting leader from the Kooskia-Stites area of the upper Clearwater, and of a Flathead woman. Hi-yuts-to-henin was related to Tipyahlahnah, and it may have been that the entire mission was concocted and carried out in behalf of only a limited number of Nez Perces, possibly the leaders of the villages in the Kamiah-Kooskia-Stites region.

The four Indians stayed close to Fontenelle and his men in the strange city. Eventually they were taken to call on General William Clark, who was Superintendent of Indian Affairs. It was the first time since his expedition with Meriwether Lewis that Clark had seen transmountain Indians from what he still referred to as the Flathead region, and he was interested in conversing with them and learning the purpose of their mission. During the course of the interview he was told of their people's growing interest in the white man's religion, and was led to understand that the Indians would welcome receiving a missionary who could instruct them in the Bible.

Also in the fall, apparently, Fontenelle's men took the Indians to the Catholic church in the city. The Right Reverend Joseph Rosati, Bishop of St. Louis, was out of town; but he was told of their visit, and on December 31, 1831, after his return, he wrote that the Indians had seemed "exceedingly well pleased" with the church, although "unfortunately, there was no one who understood their language." Soon afterward two of the Indians became seriously ill, and two priests went to see them. Bishop Rosati wrote: "The poor Indians seemed delighted with the visit. They made the sign of the Cross and other signs which appeared to have some relation to baptism. The sacrament was administered to them; they gave expressions of satisfaction. A little cross was presented to them. They took it with eagerness, kissed it repeatedly, and it could be taken from them only after death." Significantly, he added in this same account, written on December 31, 1831, "We have since learned from a Canadian, who has crossed the country which they inhabit, that they belong to the nation of Flat Heads who, as also another nation called Blackfeet, had received some notions of the Catholic religion from two Indians who had been to Canada, and who had related what they had seen, giving a striking description of the beautiful ceremonies of the Catholic worship, and telling them that it was also the religion of the whites. They have retained what they could of it and they have learned to make the sign of the Cross and to pray." Despite the garbled elements of some of his information, it appears obvious that Bishop Rosati was referring to Spokan Garry and Kutenai Pelly, although he did not know their names and was unaware that the influence under which they had fallen was Anglican and not Catholic.[28]

When the two Indians died, they were taken to the Catholic church and buried, the Nez Perce chief, The Eagle (whom the church authorities called Keepellele, a corruption of either Tipyahlanah or Kipkip Pahlekin, "of the Nez Perce, of the tribe of Chopoweck Nation called Flat Heads") on October 31, 1831, and Ka-ou-pu (called "Paul, savage of the Nation of the Flat

28. Palladino, *Indian and White in the Northwest*, p. 11. Even in 1922, when Palladino reprinted Bishop Rosati's 1831 letter in a second edition of *Indian and White*, he seemed unaware that the two Indians mentioned had been to the Red River school.

Heads") on December 17.[29] The two young survivors melted into the ranks of other Indian delegations that regularly visited St. Louis, and on March 26, 1832, departed from the city with Fontenelle and his men aboard the American Fur Company's steamboat, the *Yellowstone*, bound up the Missouri for Fort Union at the mouth of the Yellowstone River, from which place Fontenelle was to take his supply outfit overland by packhorses to the 1832 summer rendezvous at Pierre's Hole.

On board the steamer, the two Nez Perces were introduced to the celebrated painter of Indians George Catlin, who was a fellow-passenger; and when the boat reached Fort Pierre, Catlin had the Nez Perces don "Sioux dresses, which had been presented to them in a talk with the Sioux," and painted their portraits. The vessel continued on with them toward Fort Union, and somewhere near the mouth of the Yellowstone, No Horns on His Head also died, according to Catlin, "with disease which he had contracted in the civilized district." [30] The lone survivor, Rabbit Skin Leggings, accompanied Fontenelle's pack train back to the mountains, reaching Green River too late for the Pierre's Hole rendezvous and the big battle that had been fought there with the Gros Ventres. Soon afterward he joined a band of his people and told them all that had befallen the four adventurers who had journeyed on from Council Bluffs to St. Louis the previous fall. Some months later, in the middle of March 1833, the buffalo-hunting band he had joined got into a battle with Blackfeet near the Salmon forks winter grounds, and Rabbit Skin Leggings was killed.[31] None of the members of the mission, therefore, ever returned to the Nez Perce homeland; but Rabbit Skin Leggings' report, traveling among the Nez Perce and Flathead bands and villages, spread the tale of the four men's journey.

In the East, meanwhile, a significant chain of events had begun to be forged. Sometime during the fall of 1831 a visitor to St. Louis named William Walker had learned of the arrival of the four western Indians in that city. Walker, a white man who had married a Wyandot Indian woman, had become one of the influential leaders of the Wyandot tribe, which was composed mostly of the remnants of the Hurons in northern Ohio. Those debauched and poverty-stricken people, hounded by midwestern settlers ever since the end of the War of 1812, had been ordered to move onto a reservation west of the Mississippi River; and while on his way to western Missouri to inspect the lands on which the government proposed to resettle them, Walker had stopped in St. Louis to visit the Superintendent of Indian Affairs. According

29. Chittenden and Richardson, *Life, Letters and Travels of De Smet, 1,* 22.

30. George Catlin, *Letters and Notes on the Manners, Customs, and Condition of the North American Indians* (New York, 1842), *2,* 108–09.

31. McWhorter, *Hear Me,* p. 29. The details are given below, p. 104.

to Walker, General Clark "informed me that three chiefs from the Flathead nation were in his house, and were quite sick, and that one (the fourth) had died a few days ago. They were from the west of the Rocky mountains. Curiosity prompted me to step into the adjoining room to see them, having never seen any, but often heard of them."

What Walker claimed he saw moved him greatly; and when he got back to Ohio, on January 19, 1833, he wrote a letter to a Methodist friend in New York, G. P. Disosway, a prominent layman who was actively interested in the support of Methodist missionary work. Though he was an intelligent man, Walker had a vivid imagination, which he put to work with passion in describing what the "Flatheads" he had seen a year previously had looked like. "I was struck with their appearance," he wrote Disosway. "They differ in appearance from any tribe of Indians I have ever seen: small in size, delicately formed, small limbs, and the most exact symmetry throughout, except the head. I had always supposed from their being called 'Flatheads,' that the head was actually flat on top; but this was not the case. The head is flattened thus." And on the letter paper, he drew a portrait of an Indian whose head tapered to a sharp point on top.

The description of the normally strong and portly Nez Perces as small and delicately formed, and the inclusion of the sketch, both cast doubt on whether Walker actually saw the Indians, none of whom certainly would have had flattened heads. More likely, Clark or somebody had merely told him about the visit of "Flatheads," and Walker had then copied a sketch that Clark had made at the mouth of the Columbia River, during the winter of 1805–06, of Chinookan Clatsop Indians, who did flatten their heads.[32] At any rate, after further describing their appearance, and informing Disosway that the Indians had traveled "on foot . . . nearly three thousand miles," he continued:

> Gen. C related to me the object of their mission, and, my dear friend, it is impossible for me to describe to you my feelings while listening to his narrative. I will here relate it as briefly as I well can. It appeared that some white man had penetrated into their country, and happened to be a spectator at one of their religious ceremonies, which they scrupulously perform at stated periods. He informed them that their mode of worshipping the supreme Being was radically wrong, and instead of being acceptable and pleasing, it was displeasing to him; he also informed them that the white people *away* toward the rising of the sun

32. Compare Walker's sketch reproduced in *Westward on the Oregon Trail*, by the editors of American Heritage (New York, 1962), p. 59, with Clark's 1805–06 sketches in Thwaites, *Original Journals, 4,* 10.

had been put in possession of the true mode of worshipping the great Spirit. They had a book containing directions how to conduct themselves in order to enjoy his favor and hold converse with him; and with his guide, no one need go astray; but every one that would follow the directions laid down there could enjoy, in this life, his favor, and after death would be received into the country where the great Spirit resides, and live for ever with him.

Upon receiving this information, they called a national council to take this subject into consideration. Some said, if this be true, it is certainly high time we were put in possession of this mode, and if *our* mode of worshipping be wrong and displeasing to the great Spirit, it is time we had laid it aside. We must know something about this, it is a matter that cannot be put off, the sooner we know it the better. They accordingly deputed four of the chiefs to proceed to St. Louis to see their great father, Gen. Clark, to inquire of him, having no doubt but he would tell them the whole truth about it.

Walker went on to relate that the Indians had found General Clark, who had confirmed to them that "what they had been told by the white men in their own country was true," and concluded, "Poor fellows, they were not all permitted to return home to their people with the intelligence. Two died in St. Louis, and the remaining two, though somewhat indisposed, set out for their native land. Whether they reached home or not is not known . . . If they died on their way home, peace be to their names! They died inquirers after the truth!" [33]

Disosway was so aroused by Walker's letter that he sent it, with an explanatory message of his own, to the *Christian Advocate and Journal and Zion's Herald* in New York, which published them both on March 1, 1833. Disosway's letter was even more imaginative than Walker's, and lest the editor and his readers miss some of the Wyandot's impressive points, he elaborated freely upon them, dwelling first at great length on the "human face Divine" which the western savages in their innocence and ignorance deformed, and then coming to the main reason for his interest:

> How deeply touching is the circumstance of the four natives traveling on foot 3,000 miles through thick forests and extensive prairies, sincere searchers after truth! The story had scarcely a parallel in history. What a touching theme does it form for the imagination and pen of a

33. The text of this letter of Walker's can be found in Chittenden, *A History of the American Fur Trade of the Far West* (Stanford, Calif., 1954), 2, 915–17. The recipient's name was spelled correctly, as I have made it, although Chittenden published it as Disoway. See Drury, *Henry Harmon Spalding*, pp. 72, 92.

Montgomery, a Mrs. Hemans, or our own fair Sigourney! With what intense concern will men of God whose souls are fired with holy zeal for the salvation of their fellow beings, read their history! There are immense plains, mountains, and forests in those regions whence they came, the abodes of numerous savage tribes. But no apostle of Christ has yet had the courage to penetrate into their moral darkness . . . May we not indulge the hope that the day is not far distant when the missionaries will penetrate into these wilds where the Sabbath bell has never yet tolled since the world began! . . . Let the Church awake from her slumbers and go forth in her strength to the salvation of these wandering sons of our native forests.[34]

The publication of the letters fired the zealous throughout the East. The messages were reprinted in other religous periodicals, read from pulpits, and discussed in church circles. On March 22 the *Advocate* ran a "ringing editorial" that contained a cry for action: "Hear! Hear! Who will respond to the call from beyond the Rocky mountains? The communication of Brother G. P. Disosway, including one from the Wyandot agent, on the subject of the deputation of the Flathead Indians to General Clark, has excited in many in this section intense interest. And to be short about it, we are for having a mission established there at once . . . All we want is men. Who will go? Who?" [35]

The appeal grew rapidly into a spirited race among many different denominations to be the first to send men to the Rockies. Congregations raised money, and volunteer missionaries stepped forward for the glorious task of saving the Flatheads' souls and straightening their heads. A few persons, more cautious than others, wrote to friends in St. Louis for confirmation of Walker's story and, aware that no one in the East knew anything about the Flatheads or the land in which they dwelled, asked for information that might be useful to a missionary before he embarked on the inspired venture. The St. Louis friends called on General Clark and learned enough to become excited themselves.

"Gen. Clark informed me that the publication which had appeared in the *Advocate* was correct," wrote the Reverend E. W. Sehon. "He informed me the cause of their visit was the following: Two of their number had received an education at some Jesuitical school in Montreal, Canada, had returned to the tribe, and endeavored, as far as possible, to instruct their brethren how the whites approached the Great Spirit. The consequence was a spirit of inquiry was aroused, a deputation appointed, and a tedious journey of three

34. Chittenden, *Fur Trade*, 2, 919–20.
35. Ibid., 2, 646.

thousand miles performed, to learn for themselves of Jesus and him crucified. Will not these Indians," he added passionately, "rise up in the day of judgment to the condemnation of hundreds and thousands who live and die unforgiven in Christian lands?" [36]

The Reverend Sehon, who had thus provided additional evidence of the influence of Garry and Pelly and the Red River Anglican school, had also had the good fortune, he informed his friends in the East, to have met the veteran Rocky Mountain fur trader Robert Campbell; and Campbell had replied to some questions he had put to him concerning the proposal to send a mission to the Flatheads. "I cannot pretend to say what prospects there would be in a religious point of view," Campbell had said. "The Flat Head Indians are proverbial for their mild disposition and friendship to the whites, and I have little hesitation in saying a missionary would be treated by them with kindness." But Campbell knew the Indians well, and when asked about the availability of suitable interpreters, he had probably thought more of the problems that a missionary would have with Indian cultures than with their languages. "There would be some difficulty to have religious matters explained," he had commented cautiously, "because the best interpreters are half-Indians, that you could not explain to their minds the matter you would require to have told to the Indians." When asked about the number of Flatheads, he had assumed that the Reverend Sehon had meant that one single tribe, and not the Nez Perces, and he had said, "There are about forty lodges of these Indians, averaging, say seven Indians to a lodge."

The last two replies could have been discouraging, but the first of them was overlooked, and the second was quickly noticed and clarified by another St. Louis correspondent who reassured the church people in the East that, "this statement, though strictly true and fully covering the inquiry proposed, might induce many not otherwise informed to suppose that the Flat Heads constitute a mere handful of people buried in the deep recesses of the stony mountains, near three thousand miles from the abodes of civilized man, and are scarcely worth looking after. This is not the fact: the deputation was from the Cho-pun-ish tribe, residing on Lewis river, above and below the mouth of the Koos-koos-ka river, and a small band of Flat Heads who live with them. The Cho-pun-ish or Pierce Nose Indians are about seven thousand in number, according to Gen. Clark's account." [37]

36. So far, neither I—nor anyone else—have been able to find a reference to this Nez Perce visit to St. Louis in the papers or official reports of William Clark. All likely places have been searched, including the National Archives and the depositories of Clark papers at the Missouri and Kansas Historical Societies. The episode seems not to have been of unusual significance to the busy Indian superintendent.

37. Chittenden, *Fur Trade,* 2, 921–24.

So the information from St. Louis fortified the anxious, and in the East different churches hurried to organize missionary parties to leave for the Rockies as soon as possible.

In the West, meanwhile, the only kind of Americans the Nez Perces yet knew—the rugged beaver hunters—had paid their first visits to Nez Perce home villages. The first known to have done so were members of a party under William Sublette's brother, Milton, who had trapped their way to Payette Lake in western Idaho in the fall of 1832. In the group was a 22-year-old Virginian named Joe Meek, who had come West originally with William Sublette in 1829. From Payette Lake, Meek and three companions continued to hunt farther north through the mountains, crossing the Salmon River and reaching an area just south of present-day Grangeville, Idaho. Meek was alone in camp one day, broiling some deer meat, when he saw "A band of about a hundred Indians approaching." He took flight, but was chagrined, on looking about, to see that the Indians had halted in his camp and were calmly eating his venison. He returned cautiously, and discovered that they were friendly Nez Perces from a nearby settlement. They invited the four trappers to come to their village with them, and when the rest of Sublette's outfit came up, looking for Meek and his companions, they found them enjoying themselves among the Nez Perces.[38]

About a year later a more important visit was paid the Nez Perce country by Captain Bonneville. To follow the episode we must digress to certain events occurring in the fur trade. The former West Pointer–turned–fur trader met Nez Perces for the first time in eastern Idaho in 1832. He had left the fort he had built at Green River and had led his men to Idaho's Lemhi Valley, where late in the fall he had come on a band of Nez Perce and Salish Indians. The natives had conducted him to the sheltered wintering quarters near present-day Salmon City, and a few miles below the junction of the Lemhi and Salmon rivers he had built a new post consisting of several log cabins. Delighted to make the acquaintance of new Americans with an abundant supply of trade goods, the Indians had gone into camp around him, and Bonneville and his men, as already related, had found the Nez Perces and Flatheads surprisingly pious and honest. Rabbit Skin Leggings, who had recently returned from St. Louis, was with the Nez Perces, and his presence may have had something to do with the moral tone of the Indians. But Bonneville was unaware of Rabbit Skin Leggings or of an influence that might have resulted from his trip, and he guessed that the natives' conduct stemmed from the work of Christians who had visited their home villages.

The large assemblage of whites and Indians soon drove the wild game from

38. Frances Fuller Victor, *The River of the West* (Hartford, Conn., 1871), pp. 129–30.

the area, and Bonneville sent out hunting parties accompanied by Nez Perces and Flatheads. On the east side of Lemhi Pass on the present Idaho-Montana border, they ran into Blackfeet, and the Nez Perces proved, despite Bonneville's concern over their pacifism, that they could still fight. On December 9 the scarcity of food finally compelled both Bonneville and his Indian friends to move to the North Fork of the Salmon River, where game was more plentiful. There, on Christmas Day, the whites were guests at a feast of venison, elk meat, and roots given by the principal Nez Perce leader of the hunting band, whom they called Kowsoter, "after which," according to Washington Irving's account, "various games of strength and agility by both white men and Indians closed the Christmas festivities."

The Nez Perces were from villages on the upper Clearwater River, and the trappers spent most of the winter with them in "the most perfect harmony." On March 15 Bonneville finally left them to commence his spring hunt on the Big Wood River, but he assigned a clerk named Hodgkiss with a supply of goods to stay with the Nez Perces and trade for the beaver they trapped. Soon after Bonneville had departed, a band of 300 Blackfeet appeared in the neighborhood. One of the leading Nez Perce warriors, whom the whites had named Blue John, called for volunteers to join him in a raid on the enemy's horse herd. Some thirty Indians, including Rabbit Skin Leggings, responded, and the small group rode off to a canyon through which they hoped to make a secret approach to the Blackfoot camp. Blue John, according to Hodgkiss' later report to Bonneville, consulted his guardian spirit and was advised that the enterprise would meet with success, provided that no rain fell before the Nez Perces and Flatheads got through the canyon. The weather was clear until they reached the defile; but as they entered it the sky darkened, rain began to fall, and their powder got wet. Soon afterward they were sighted by a Blackfoot scouting party. They routed this small group, but the main band of Blackfeet whooped into the canyon and pressed the Nez Perces into a side draw. The fight was short, but furious. All the western Indians except one were slain, and among the dead was Rabbit Skin Leggings. The lone survivor, a Flathead, got away unnoticed and returned to tell the mournful story.[39]

Bonneville trapped the mountain wilderness of central Idaho that spring of 1833, then in June rejoined his clerk Hodgkiss and the Indians on the eastern Snake plains. Something had gone amiss; the natives had trapped beaver, but although they were as warm and friendly to the Americans as always, they had refused to sell their furs to Hodgkiss. The answer became clear with the

39. Bernard De Voto, *Across the Wide Missouri* (Boston, 1947), p. 93; Irving, *Bonneville*, p. 140; Wyeth, *Correspondence and Journals*, pp. 197–98; McWhorter, *Hear Me*, p. 29.

arrival of that year's Hudson's Bay Company Snake expedition led by a jovial but business-like trader named Francis Ermatinger. A large number of Nez Perces, Flatheads, and other western Indians had traveled with the British brigade from the Clark Fork Valley, and native messengers, urging the Indians to wait for higher prices from the British, had maintained constant communication between the Indians with Ermatinger and the smaller group of Nez Perces and Flatheads, numbering some sixteen lodges, who were with Hodgkiss.[40] Ermatinger won the day; while Bonneville looked on helplessly, the Nez Perces cheerfully sold their beaver to the British.

Also with Ermatinger was Nathaniel Wyeth, the Massachusetts ice dealer, who had spent the winter at Fort Vancouver as the guest of the chivalrous Dr. McLoughlin and who was now returning to the States with a set of ambitious, new plans in his head. Wyeth and the companions who had remained loyal to him had had a disappointing time on the Columbia. They had visited Fort Nez Perces, which the British were beginning to call Fort Walla Walla, for the river and the Indian tribe in the immediate vicinity. There the Americans had begun to see the strength of British entrenchment in the Northwest. At Fort Vancouver they had learned that a ship on which they had dispatched their supplies for doing business on the Columbia had been wrecked in the Society Islands. Wyeth had gradually realized that he could not compete with the Hudson's Bay Company in the fur trade; but instead of admitting defeat, he had convinced himself that other opportunities in Oregon, including salmon packing, farming, and supplying trade goods to independent American trappers in the mountains, were still open to him.

With those ends in view, he had planned to return to Boston, send another vessel with trade goods and supplies to the Columbia, and come West again himself the following year. Before he had left Fort Vancouver, he had released his eleven companions from further loyalty to him. One of them, John Ball, had been hired by McLoughlin to teach school to the halfblood children at the fort. Later, Ball and another Wyeth man moved to the Willamette Valley, built a home, and farmed for a while. Eventually they lost enthusiasm for the region and left the country, but two other Wyeth men, Solomon Smith and Calvin Tibbetts, became permanent settlers in the Willamette, teaching the children of retired Hudson's Bay Company employees who were grouped in a little settlement called French Prairie, and helping to raise the curtain on a new day when American homebuilders, arriving via the Oregon Trail, would fill the same valley.

Wyeth, meanwhile, had left for the States with Ermatinger, who was bound for the company's interior posts and the Snake country. They had followed the well-traveled route past Fort Walla Walla and the abandoned Spo-

40. Wyeth, *Correspondence and Journals*, p. 198.

kane House to Fort Colvile, and from there Wyeth, still alert to opportunities, had written Governor Simpson, outlining some of his plans to supply
American trappers the next year, and proposing an arrangement in which
Wyeth would gather furs south and east of the Columbia River and sell them
to McLoughlin.[41] Simpson in time turned Wyeth down; but part of the
scheme had been an echo of one of McLoughlin's own ideas of how to derive
profits from the American trappers, whom the British now knew they could
not turn back. The following year, doing exactly what Wyeth proposed
doing himself, McLoughlin sent Tom McKay with a Hudson's Bay Company supply train to trade with the United States trappers at the American
rendezvous, "so as to Introduce Our Goods Among them." [42]

From Fort Colvile, Wyeth had continued on with Ermatinger's column to
the Flatheads on the Clark Fork River and in the Bitterroot Valley, and then
south to the Snake plains, recording in his journal along the way the deep impression made upon him by the piety, virtue, and honor of the Nez Perce and
Salish peoples, numbering some 120 lodges, who traveled with the British brigade. Accompaning Wyeth were a halfblood Flathead boy named Baptiste,
the son of a Hudson's Bay Company employee, François Payette, and a
twenty-year-old Nez Perce youth, both of whom he had agreed to take to
the States with him and bring back the following year.[43] It was a reflection,
again, of tribal curiosity about the ways of the Americans. The youths would
look, listen, and learn, and come back with knowledge for their people.

On the Snake plains, Wyeth made an unsuccessful attempt to arrange a
partnership undertaking with Bonneville, then went on to the 1833 rendezvous and the East.[44] Bonneville, meanwhile, dispatched Hodgkiss and four or
five of his men to accompany a party of free trappers who planned to ignore
the rendezvous and hunt beaver in the mountains north of the Snake plains.
For their protection, Bonneville prevailed on the Nez Perces and Salish to go
with them, and if there were Nez Perces at the rendezvous that year, they
were so few that white men did not mention them in their accounts.[45]

It was a good year for the trappers. Prices as high as nine dollars a pound
were paid for pelts at the trade gathering, and huge promises were given the
veteran mountain men to sign up with the competing companies, including
Bonneville's, for the next twelve months. But an ominous cloud was on the
horizon. In the East, machinery was beginning to manufacture felt from

41. Ibid., pp. 56–58.
42. Rich, *McLoughlin's Fort Vancouver Letters, 1st Series, 1825–1838*, p. 168.
43. Wyeth, *Correspondence and Journals*, p. 141.
44. Ibid., pp. 58–62.
45. Many writers have stated that Nez Perces and Flatheads came to the rendezvous,
expecting the arrival of missionaries from the East; but I am not aware of a single
contemporary source to support that assumption.

cheaper materials, and silk hats were already coming on the market. By the time the caravans arrived home from the rendezvous, beaver in St. Louis had fallen to $3.50 a pound, heralding the beginning of the end of the Rocky Mountain fur trade. It would not collapse for several more years, but high prices in the field and a failing market in the States would mean an intensification of competition and the elimination of the weaker American fur companies.

After the rendezvous the trappers and traders dispersed. Bonneville sent an expedition of between 40 and 50 men to trap the shores of Great Salt Lake, but his actual orders are a mystery. Under Joseph Reddeford Walker, a 35-year-old veteran mountain man, the group went all the way to California. Bonneville claimed publically that Walker had had no business going there, but some of the party's members, including Joe Meek, had seemed to know from the beginning that they were going to the Mexican province.[46] With another group Bonneville went to the Bighorn River in Wyoming, and by November was back in winter camp on the Portneuf River in southeastern Idaho.

From there, he launched his first visit to the Nez Perces' homeland. On Christmas Day 1833 he and three companions left the winter camp, bound, said Washington Irving, on a "reconnoitering expedition . . . to penetrate to the Hudson's Bay establishments on the banks of the Columbia, and to make himself acquainted with the country and the Indian tribes; it being one part of his scheme to establish a trading-post somewhere on the lower part of the river, so as to participate in the trade lost to the United States by the capture of Astoria."[47] It was a logical summation of Bonneville's motives: reconnaisance, exploration, and competition with the British, whose trader, Francis Ermatinger, had nettled him in eastern Idaho.

Wyeth had made the trip to Fort Walla Walla from approximately the same area in 1832 without unusual difficulty by following the Blue Mountain route that was already well known to the whites. That route, pioneered by Wilson Price Hunt, left the Snake River above its Grand Canyon and cut diagonally northwestward across present-day Oregon to the Columbia. Almost everyone still used it in going between Walla Walla and the Snake country. But Bonneville ignored or missed it. He and his companions followed the Snake River across Idaho, then, instead of veering northwestward near present-day Ontario, Oregon, took the advice of some Shoshoni Indians and kept along the river's banks past the Powder River until, like Donald Mc-

46. See Ewers, *Adventures of Zenas Leonard, Fur Trader*, pp. 63–65; and Ellison, *The Life and Adventures of George Nidever*, pp. 31–32.

47. It is too bad that whatever journals or notes Bonneville supplied Irving are now lost. Here, again, it would be interesting to know more of Bonneville's motives.

Kenzie's Astorians, twenty-two years before them, they were lost and floundering, without a guide, deep within the frightening mountains of Hell's Canyon. By sheer perseverance, they climbed the wall of the chasm, after being turned back once. Then, appalled by the rocky wilderness in which they found themselves, they struggled for days along the icy shoulders and steep slopes of the dividing ridge between the Snake and Imnaha rivers until at last, on the verge of starvation and collapse, they got across the immense divide and descended to the warm, grassy valley of the Imnaha River, whose sight "inspired almost a frenzy of delight." [48]

It was February 16, 1834, and they had entered the home country of the Nez Perces who lived west of the Snake River, in Oregon's high Wallowa Valley during the summer and in the deep canyons on the eastern and northern borders of the valley in the winter. Those Indians, like their Cayuse and Wallawalla neighbors, had been trading regularly with the British at Fort Walla Walla, and few of them had been in the buffalo country in recent years. Although they had not yet seen American trappers, they had heard increasingly about them from other Nez Perces, who called the Americans "the big hearts of the east" and talked of their liberality to the Indians in terms that made the British seem stingy in comparison. Bonneville, in turn, had heard about this branch of the tribe from the Clearwater Nez Perces whom he had met in eastern Idaho. They had called them their "cousins," he said, and had told him that they owned huge horse herds. To get them straight in his thinking, Bonneville termed them Lower Nez Perces, distinguishing them from the bands on the Idaho side of the Snake River, whom he already knew and whom he now called the Upper Nez Perces. Irving's narrative of Bonne-

---

48. Many persons familiar with the area have tried to work out Bonneville's route through this mountainous wilderness. Though no two men have agreed precisely, three former residents of the Wallowa region, John W. Himelwright, J. F. Winneford, and Thomas Lathrop, all local stockmen or Forest Rangers, helped J. H. Horner, the late Wallowa County historian, figure out the route, and they came to somewhat similar conclusions. My own research, though less exact than theirs, tends to support them. Generally, it would appear that Bonneville and his men descended the Snake to approximately Squaw or Buck Creek on the western bank. They were frustrated in attempting to ascend the mountain at that point and, dropping back down the river about four miles, managed to get part way toward the top. They then made their way along the shoulders of the divide and were able to cross the summit somewhere beyond the head of 32 Point Creek, after which they struck the head of Trail Creek. They descended that stream to Summit Creek and went on to the Imnaha. Later, after following down the Imnaha almost all the way to its mouth, they were guided by Indians up Tulley Creek, past Cherry and Cook creeks, and across rough country to Joseph Creek. I am indebted to the late Mr. Horner for his valuable research, and to Mrs. Marjorie Martin, County Clerk, Enterprise, Oregon, for allowing me to see Mr. Horner's notes.

ville's travels popularized those expressions, and although they had no meaning to the Indians, white men used them for many years when referring to the different Nez Perce bands.

Bonneville's arrival among the Wallowa Nez Perces awakened their hopes that they were now to enjoy the trade of the big-hearted Americans, and Bonneville found them as friendly and hospitable as their relatives in the east. The day of his arrival in the Imnaha Valley, "a fine, haughty-looking savage, fancifully decorated, and mounted on a high-mettled steed, with gaudy trappings and equipments," appeared along a trail and, approaching the four weary and starving travelers "with an air of protection, gave them his hand, and, in the Nez Perce language, invited them to his camp, which was only a few miles distant; where he had plenty to eat, and plenty of horses, and would cheerfully share his good things with them."

Bonneville was too exhausted and weak to continue farther that day, but after a night of "heavy sleep," he reached a settlement of twelve Nez Perce families, "living together under the patriarchal sway of an ancient and venerable chief [village headman]." The Nez Perces treated him "with the hospitality of the golden age," took care of his horses, and surprised him with the information that they already knew about him, having heard of him from their cousins in Idaho. They were even familiar with his name, according to Washington Irving, but soon bestowed upon him a new one, by which he was ever afterward remembered among the Wallowa Indians. "As he sat chatting and smoking in the midst of them," said Irving, "he would occasionally take off his cap. Whenever he did so, there was a sensation in the surrounding circle. The Indians would half rise from their recumbent posture, and gaze upon his uncovered head with their usual exclamation of astonishment. The worthy captain was completely bald; a phenomenon very surprising in their eyes. They were at a loss to know whether he had been scalped in battle, or enjoyed a natural immunity from that belligerent infliction. In a little while he became known among them by an Indian name signifying 'the bald chief.'"

He remained in that settlement overnight, cutting his plaid coat into strips and making colorful "turbans *a la Turque*" for the Indian women in exchange for provisions. During the next two days, after leaving that village, he and his companions traveled down the valley of the Imnaha, coming upon another friendly group of Nez Perces, the name of whose headman sounded to them like "Yo-mus-ro-y-e-cut." Again, they were treated with "loving-kindness," and the headman told them that he, too, had often heard from his buffalo-hunting brethren in Idaho about the big-hearted whites of the east who were the very good friends of the Nez Perce people. When it came time to leave that settlement, they were accompanied by the headman and a young

Indian, who guided them up and down steep draws and across high, broken country from the lower valley of the Imnaha to the deep canyon of Joseph Creek. They reached that stream near its junction with the Grande Ronde, which Bonneville called the Way-lee-way, close to where it flowed past high goosenecks of land to empty into the Snake. As the travelers approached the mouth of Joseph Creek, their guide informed them that he had sent word of their arrival ahead to an important village at the junction of the Grande Ronde. Rounding a high, grassy hill, they came on the Indian settlement, the sheltered winter camp of the principal chief of the Wallowa Nez Perces, Tuekakas. The father of the more celebrated Chief Joseph (who would be born in this vicinity six years later, in 1840), Tuekakas—himself to be called Old Joseph—was in his late forties.[49] This was history's first note of him, and around him in the camp that day were many young men who, as aged warriors in later years, would take up arms with his two sons when the Americans drove them from this ancient home.

No white man knew of the Wallowa Valley, much less wanted it at that time, however, and the Indians welcomed Bonneville and his companions as representatives of a friendly and honorable people. The meeting, said Irving, was an impressive one, the first view of the travelers being of the whole population of the village "drawn out in the most imposing style, and arrayed in all their finery." In the front rank, as Bonneville and his men rode up to them, "were the chiefs and principal warriors, glaringly painted and decorated; behind them were arranged the rest of the people, men, women and children." Bonneville and his party moved toward them slowly, exchanging salutes of firearms. "When arrived within a respectful distance they dismounted. The chiefs then came forward successively, according to their respective characters and consequence, to offer the hand of good-fellowship; each filing off when he had shaken hands, to make way for his successor. Those in the next rank followed in the same order, and so on, until all had given the pledge of friendship. During all this time, the chief, according to custom, took his stand beside the guests."

After the reception, a lodge was constructed for the Americans, and they were treated to a sumptuous banquet of deer, elk, and buffalo meat, and fish and roots. Then, said Irving, "a long talk ensued. The chief showed the same curiosity evinced by his tribe generally to obtain information concerning the United States, of which they knew little but what they derived through their cousins, the Upper Nez Perces . . . Captain Bonneville did his best to set forth the merits of his nation, and the importance of their friendship to the red men, in which he was ably seconded by his worthy friend, the old chief with the hard name [Yo-mus-ro-y-e-cut], who did all that he could to glo-

49. See below, p. 668.

rify the Big Hearts of the East. The chief and all present listened with profound attention, and evidently with great interest; nor were the important facts thus set forth confined to the audience in the lodge; for sentence after sentence was loudly repeated by a crier for the benefit of the whole village . . . Captain Bonneville," Irving concluded about these Indians who were later to be persecuted and driven from the area by the Americans, "passed some short time among these good people, more and more impressed with the general excellence of their character."

Leaving them, Bonneville and his men, still accompanied by Yo-mus-ro-y-e-cut and the young Indian guide, traveled down the winding banks of the Grande Ronde River, being greeted by more Nez Perces along the way, and reached the Snake again. They were below Hell's Canyon now, but the mountains hemming the river were still high and formidable. The Indians conducted them down the Snake, and at one place they paused to call across to an upper Nez Perce on the opposite side of the river. He came over to them in a canoe and, mounting a horse behind one of Bonneville's men, joined them as they "jogged on very sociably and cheerily together."

Farther down, they came on more settlements, and at each stop they were greeted with warmth and friendship. At one place the Americans met an Indian whom they had known in the beaver country of eastern Idaho, and he "welcomed them with open arms." They stayed overnight in the lodge of another Indian, where "the evening passed away in perfect harmony and good humor"; and the next day, near present-day Asotin, Washington, in the village of an important buffalo-hunting and war leader whom Bonneville called O-push-y-e-cut, they were given another ceremonial reception and banquet. This headman of the Asotin band of Nez Perces was Apash Wyakaikt (Flint Color, or Flint Necklace). White men who met him at a later time heard him referred to as Meiway (Chief), and gave him still another name, Looking Glass, for a small, round trade mirror that he wore. His son, who would eventually become known by that name also, would be one of the principal Nez Perce military leaders in the war of 1877.[50]

Apash Wyakaikt had had long experience in trading with the British at Fort Walla Walla and with John Work and other Hudson's Bay Company men on the Snake and Clearwater rivers, and in recent years had met American mountain men in the beaver country of the Rockies. Aware that the Americans gave better terms to the Indians than the British, he discussed with his visitors the prospects of their opening trade with the Nez Perces in their

50. McWhorter, *Hear Me*, p. 94 n.; A. J. Splawn, *Ka-mi-akin* (Portland, Oregon, 1944), p. 17; Hazard Stevens, *The Life of Isaac Ingalls Stevens* (Boston, 1900), Vol. 2, drawing by Gustav Sohon, opposite page 54; Drury, *Diaries and Letters of Spalding and Smith*, pp. 197 ff.

own country, an aim that Bonneville already had in mind. Irving gave no hint of what agreement they reached, but later events suggest that Bonneville promised Apash Wyakaikt to bring American trade to his people and to undercut Fort Walla Walla by offering higher prices for beaver than the British paid. At any rate, he endeared himself to the Indian leader by acting the role of physician to his sixteen-year-old daughter, who for three days had been racked with pain from some ailment. The American's prescription of a sweat bath, followed by a dose of gunpowder dissolved in cold water, eased the girl's suffering, and Apash Wyakaikt was so delighted that he gave Bonneville one of his best horses.

At Asotin Creek, slightly south of the junction of the Snake and Clearwater rivers, the travelers finally left the Snake and, turning westward, climbed to the plateau and rode across "a gently undulating country, of such fertility that it excited the rapturous admiration of two of the captain's followers, a Kentuckian and a native of Ohio. They declared that it surpassed any land that they had ever seen, and often exclaimed what a delight it would be just to run a plow through such a rich and teeming soil, and see its bountiful promise before the share." This was the beginning of the high, rolling country of the southeastern part of the present state of Washington, which white men would develop one day into some of the richest wheat-producing land in the world. Bonneville and his men continued across it, stopping overnight on Alpowa Creek with a headman named Hemene Ilppilp (Red Wolf), who would eventually become well known to Americans; seeing huge Indian horse herds; and meeting more Nez Perces "by whom they were invariably treated with the utmost kindness." On March 4, 1834, a week after leaving Red Wolf's village, they reached Fort Walla Walla.

There they were hospitably received by the clerk in charge, Pierre C. Pambrun, a courteous and gentlemanly 42-year-old Canadian who had been with the Hudson's Bay Company since 1815, and who had come into the Columbia district in 1831, assuming his post at Walla Walla the following year. Just before Pambrun's arrival, there had been trouble at the post. In an attempt to meet competition, both in the Snake country and at the mouth of the Columbia, where an American sea trader had disrupted British business by offering the Indians higher prices for their furs, the Hudson's Bay Company had been forced to pay more for pelts in those areas than it was paying at Walla Walla, where there was no competition. Word of those price boosts had reached the Indians who brought their furs to Walla Walla, and they had clamored for equal treatment.

A succession of clerks in charge, during 1830 and 1831, had held them off, though the traders had written anxious letters regarding their plight to Dr. McLoughlin at Fort Vancouver. On June 29, 1830, McLoughlin replied to chief clerk Samuel Black, praising him for keeping up the number of beaver skins he demanded for goods at Walla Walla "in spite of all the means employed by the natives to make you lower them." Five months later, he wrote a similar letter to a new clerk at the post, George Barnston, telling him that he knew how difficult it was for him to continue asking five beaver for one blanket, when at Fort George, which was competing with American coastal traders, they had to accept only one beaver for a blanket. After Pambrun's arrival at the post, the unrest quieted, but eventually it flared up again, this time largely as an aftermath of Bonneville's appearance and the promises the American had made to many Indians similar to the one he must have given Apash Wyakaikt. Soon after Bonneville had left the scene, the Indians asked Pambrun to pay them the same prices the Americans paid. When Pambrun refused, the Indians became angry; and in 1836, a group of Nez Perces and Cayuses, led by Apash Wyakaikt and the 37-year-old Cayuse headman, Tauitau, or the Young Chief, the uncle of Cayuse Halket and the half-brother of Tuekakas, seized Pambrun, tied him up, and refused to release him until he had promised to increase the prices he paid for horses and furs.

Pambrun, a courageous little man, was also a wily strategist who thereafter used a "divide and conquer" policy in handling his clients. Apash Wyakaikt returned to his own people, whom the British trader could not easily influence; but in the country closer to the post Pambrun played upon the jealousies of certain of the young Cayuses who aspired to positions of influence and wealth among their people. By showering favors upon those younger men and winning them to his support, he craftily undermined the authority of the more threatening Cayuses who had made trouble for him. He managed to advance Tauitau's brother, Five Crows, to a position of prestige higher than that of Tauitau, and in the end was able to restore prices to their earlier levels without encountering opposition. His troubles, however, had been a reflection of the Indians' ideas of the Americans versus the British; and the significance of those conceptions, which Bonneville had furthered, was to become even more evident when American missionaries, with no idea or understanding of the trade background and rivalries in the area, innocently took up residence in the region.

Pambrun was also a Roman Catholic, and Bonneville, who had noticed religious influences among the Sahaptin bands on the west side of the Snake River, reported that the British clerk "had been at some pains to introduce the Christian religions, in the Roman Catholic form, among them, where it had evidently taken root; but had become altered and modified to suit their peculiar habits of thought and motives of action; retaining, however, the principal points of faith and its entire precepts of morality. The same gentleman had given them a code of laws, to which they conformed with scrupulous fidelity. Polygamy, which once prevailed among them to a great extent, was now rarely indulged. All the crimes denounced by the Christian faith met with severe punishment among them. Even theft, so venial a crime among the Indians, had recently been punished with hanging, by sentence of a chief." The Lower Nez Perces, particularly, Bonneville thought, had profited by this instruction, being "one of the very, very few that have benefited in morals and manners by an intercourse with white men." The Wallawallas, for instance, once the friendliest of people to Lewis and Clark and the Nor'Westers, he found now to have become "a degenerate, wornout tribe."[51]

Bonneville and his companions stayed at the fort for only two days. They had told their men at the Portneuf River that they would return to them early in March, and that period was already upon them. "He had seen enough," said Irving, "to convince him that an American trade might be carried on with advantage in this quarter; and he determined soon to return with a stronger party more completely fitted for the purpose." When he tried to buy provisions from Pambrun for his journey back to the Portneuf, however, he gained an insight into the kind of competition an American would have to face in this area. Pambrun sold him a roll of tobacco and some dry goods at the usual high prices he charged freemen, and that was all. Even so, Pambrun was later reprimanded by McLoughlin for having provided a rival trader with goods that were supposed to have been sold to Indians at even higher prices.[52]

Bonneville departed on March 6, declining Pambrun's proposal that he avoid trying to return over the difficult and dangerous Snake canyon route by which he had come and travel, instead, with a Hudson's Bay Company

51. Jessett, *Chief Spokan Garry*, pp. 67–68, calls this passage in Irving "fanciful," arguing that "polygamy was common when the Protestant missionaries arrived," and questioning whether Pambrun himself was "sufficiently instructed in the Roman Catholic faith" to teach the Indians, since "he had his son, Pierre Chrysologue, baptized by the Rev. David T. Jones, an Anglican clergyman, at the Red River settlement." In his autobiography, Pambrun's son states that his father taught the Indians the Lord's Prayer and the Apostles' Creed (Erwin Thompson, *Pacific Northwest Quarterly, 52,* 1961, 116), but on January 2, 1837, shortly after Narcissa Whitman and her husband had settled among the Cayuses, she wrote: "The Cayuses as well as the Nez Perces are very strict in attending to their worship which they have regularly every morning at day break & eve at twilight and once on the Sab. They sing & repeat a form of prayers very devoutly after which the Chief gives them a talk. The tunes & prayers were taught them by a Roman Catholic trader" (Drury, *First White Women, 1,* 123). Mrs. Whitman may not have recognized an influence that had actually derived from the Red River school; but it is also possible that the Cayuses had learned the tunes and prayers from Pambrun. Later portions of this book will present sufficient evidence that Pambrun was a devout Catholic.

52. Rich, *McLoughlin Letters, 1st Series,* p. 195.

brigade under François Payette that would take him back to the Snake country on the long, round-about trading circuit via the Clearwater River, Fort Colvile, and the Flatheads. Retracing his path across the Walla Walla hills to the Snake River, he passed the different Nez Perce villages he had previously visited, went up the Snake to the Grande Ronde River and, accompanied by Nez Perces who found it a lark trailing along with him, traveled up Joseph Creek and the Imnaha Valley again. Everywhere, he and his companions were once more "welcomed with cordiality, and everything," said Irving, "was done to cheer them on their journey."

They had difficulties getting across the snow-covered heights of the Wallowa Mountains, from the upper Imnaha to the Snake River; but this time Nez Perce guides aided them, and they completed the passage without the anxiety and strain of hunger and exhaustion that had made a nightmare of the outward-bound trip. With the worst of the mountains behind them, they parted from their Indian guides, "exchanging many farewells and kind wishes," and the rest of the journey back to the Portneuf passed without serious incident. Bonneville rejoined his men on June 1, and about three weeks later on the Bear River met Joe Walker's party, returned from California and waiting for him. The reunion celebration was enjoyed by the men, but not by Bonneville, who, said Irving, registered only "horror and indignation" at Walker's report of his long and unprofitable expedition.

On July 3, after assigning one party to return to St. Louis with his furs and another to trap the Crow country of Wyoming, Bonneville started out again with twenty-three men for the Columbia River to establish trade among the Nez Perces and Cayuses and to examine Fort Vancouver and the Willamette Valley, about which he had heard from Nathaniel Wyeth. This time he left the Snake River before entering its fearful chasm and, arriving safely in Oregon's Grande Ronde Valley, whose borders were almost completely ablaze with prairie and mountain fires, halted amid clouds of smoke in a camp on a headwater of the Grande Ronde River and sent out scouts to find a westward overland route to the Willamette. British Snake country brigades had struggled back and forth through the central Oregon wilderness and knew that there was no easy passage by land. But again Bonneville had no one to tell him that the quickest and surest way to Fort Vancouver and the Willamette was down the Columbia River, and he waited for twenty days until his scouts straggled back to him, hopelessly defeated by the rugged wilderness. During their absence, Bonneville met some Nez Perces, as well as Cayuses, who roamed through the Grande Ronde Valley, and at this time he might have had conversations with Tauitau and other Cayuse headmen about the better terms of trade which he and other Americans would offer them in their home country. He was much struck by the Indians' huge horse herds, pronouncing their ponies "infinitely superior to any in the United States," and he found a strong religious influence among the Cayuses, similar to that among the Nez Perces and Flatheads, "successfully cultivated," he thought, by the Hudson's Bay Company. He was again seeing a grafting of Christian forms onto ancestral beliefs and practices; for while the Cayuses prayed reverently to a Deity, kept Sundays sacred, and observed "the cardinal holidays of the Roman Catholic Church," they continued to possess a "medicine man" and mingle old ceremonials with their new religion.

Bonneville also judged that these natives were ready for "a considerable degree of civilization. A few farmers settled among them," he said, "might lead them . . . to till the earth and cultivate grain," adding, "a Christian missionary or two, and some trifling assistance from government, to protect them from the predatory and warlike tribes, might lay the foundation of a Christian people in the midst of the great western wilderness, who would 'wear the Americans near their hearts.' "

An event that Irving did not mention might have moved Bonneville to express those sentiments. While he lay in camp in the Grande Ronde, with the tipis of friendly Cayuses and Nez Perces near him, two parties of Oregon-bound travelers who had left the States that spring went past him. One of them, which will soon be described, included the first group of missionaries to respond to the Nez Perce appeal. They were on their way to find a suitable mission station, and they probably spoke to Bonneville of their hopes and plans, and received encouragement from him.

Soon afterward, the second westward-bound party reached the Grande Ronde. It included Nathaniel Wyeth, on his return trip to the West, and a number of companions, among them John K. Townsend, a prominent physician and ornithologist of Philadelphia, who had made the journey as a scientific venture. Townsend found every new sight a source of interest and wonder; and when Bonneville came over to his camp, accompanied by "a whole troop" of Cayuses and Nez Perces, the scientist wrote of the Indians, "they were very friendly towards us, each of the chiefs taking us by the hand with great cordiality, appearing pleased to see us, and anxious to point out to us the easiest and most expeditious route to the lower country . . . I observed one young and very pretty looking woman, dressed in a great superabundance of finery, glittering with rings and beads, and flaunting in broad bands of scarlet cloth. She was mounted astride,—Indian fashion,—upon a fine bay horse, whose head and tail were decorated with scarlet and blue ribbons, and the saddle, upon which the fair one sat, was ornamented all over with beads and little hawk's bells. This damsel did not do us the honor to dismount, but seemed to keep warily aloof, as though she feared that some of us might be inordinately fascinated by her fine person and splendid equipments, and her whole deportment proved to us, pretty satisfactorily, that she was no common beauty, but the favored companion of one high in office, who was jealous of her slightest movement." [53]

Again, Irving made no mention of it, but Wyeth and Bonneville apparently had another business discussion at this time. After Wyeth started to move on toward the Columbia River, Bonneville sent him a note, and that day, September 1, 1834, while he was still in the Grande Ronde, Wyeth sent a letter back to him. Bonneville had probably told him of his plans to bring the American trade to the Cayuses and Nez Perces, under the noses of the British, and in his note he seems to have urged Wyeth to do the same. Wyeth responded eagerly, agreeing to return with trade goods in about seven weeks, after he first got to Fort Vancouver where he intended to meet his supply vessel from Boston. He would "trade with them [the Indians] personally at your present camp, if they will be there, or I will send a clerk to them at any place they shall designate," he wrote Bonneville, adding, "it is likely that we might make a joint business of it." [54]

He and Bonneville may have been talking principally of the Nez Perces; for Bonneville appears to have rushed another note to him, and Wyeth replied, still on the same day, September 1: "I got your note of to day late this evening, and am obliged to you for the trouble you have taken. I will meet the Nez Perces at the A-show-to River within 8 weeks. I Hope to meet you before this, and would be pleased to make a joint affair of it much better than to proceed alone." Bonneville must also have told him that he had traded furs from the Cayuses in the Grande Ronde, for Wyeth added, "Your beaver traded from the Skiuses is so much seized from the common enemy in trade, so far so good."

Bonneville's "A-show-to River," where he suggested that Wyeth take his goods to trade, was undoubtedly Asotin Creek, the home of Apash Wyakaikt on the Snake River south of the Clearwater's mouth. It was an indication that the captain had talked to that powerful Nez Perce chief of bringing the American trade to him; but Wyeth had never been there, and without Bonneville or someone knowledgeable to show him the way and introduce him, he might never get there. As it turned out, neither he nor Bonneville ever did show up at Asotin, and the frustrated Apash Wyakaikt, without the lower-priced American goods, eventually turned his anger against Pambrun whom, he correctly surmised, stood between him and the Americans and thus man-

53. "Narrative of a Journey across the Rocky Mountains" by John K. Townsend, reprinted in Thwaites, *Early Western Travels, 21* (Cleveland, 1905), 272–73.
54. Wyeth, *Correspondence and Journals,* pp. 141–42.

aged to keep the prices of British goods higher than what the Americans charged.[55]

Bonneville did not remain in the Grande Ronde, waiting for Wyeth's return. Dejected by his scouts' information, and pressed for food and supplies, he left the valley and, crossing the Blue Mountains to the Umatilla River, sent some men to Fort Walla Walla, the "enemy," to buy provisions. Pambrun, now thoroughly aware of Bonneville's connivings among the Nez Perces and Cayuses, turned the captain's messengers down cold, refusing this time to provide them with the slightest assistance, but trying, instead—though unsuccessfully—to lure them into the employ of the Hudson's Bay Company. Pinched by increasing hunger, Bonneville hurried down the Umatilla to the Columbia but was again rebuffed by the river bands of Sahaptins, who refused to sell him fish or other provisions, being, said Irving, "under the influence of the Hudson's Bay Company, who had forbidden them to trade or hold any communion with him."

In desperation, Bonneville abandoned his plans, believing that even if he reached the Willamette, McLoughlin would deny him food for the winter. Turning up the John Day River, he followed a southeasterly course back to the Snake River and was soon again on the Portneuf, far from the Columbia peoples for whom he had intended building a trading post. He was through. After wintering among Shoshonis and Utes on the upper Bear River, he moved east during the spring of 1835, hunting the Green and Wind River countries, and finally in August returning to the States, where Washington Irving eventually publicized his three years of adventures among the Indians and trappers.[56]

In the meantime, the world of the Nez Perces' mountain men friends had been changing. In 1834, while Bonneville had been starting off on his second trip to the Columbia, the annual rendezvous had been held at Green River. William Sublette, bringing a supply caravan to the trappers, had detached thirteen men en route to build a post at Laramie Fork on the North Platte River.

55. For some time after he reached Fort Vancouver, Wyeth seems to have intended going to the Nez Perces and building a trading post for them. See his *Correspondence and Journals*, pp. 143 ff., for a number of his letters, all dated October 6, 1834, from "Columbia River," notifying persons in the East that he planned to build two new posts, including one "up Lewis River" [the Snake]. His intentions may again have been blasted, however, when twelve Hawaiian employees soon afterward deserted his trading party in the vicinity of Fort Walla Walla. At any rate, he never visited the Nez Perce homeland.

56. It is interesting, too, that in his narrative of Bonneville's adventures, published only one year after his book *Astoria*, Irving presented an entirely different image of the Nez Perces, who in the first work were characterized as rogues and rascals, and in the second as saints.

Designed to lure the Sioux from American Fur Company forts on the Missouri, Sublette's strategically located post, soon to be called Fort Laramie, would become one of the best known in the West.[57] Nathaniel Wyeth, who had sent another vessel with supplies and salmon packing equipment from Boston to the Columbia, was also back, returning with the Nez Perce youth and Payette's halfblood son, both of whom had received a little formal education in Boston during the winter. At the rendezvous Wyeth received another blow. The year before he had made a contract to bring supplies this year to the Rocky Mountain Fur Company. But Tom Fitzpatrick gave the company's business to William Sublette, who had beaten Wyeth to the rendezvous, and refused to honor Wyeth's contract when the latter appeared. Something else went smash too. The Rocky Mountain Fur Company could no longer compete with the American Fur Company, and at the trade gathering the partnership was dissolved. Although another combine was formed, high costs and falling beaver prices soon caused its collapse.

The era of the Rocky Mountain trade was beginning to reach its end. But new types of pioneers in the Far West were already on hand. Trailing along with Wyeth's caravan, new arrivals, some of them already mentioned, had reached the rendezvous and become incongruous objects of wonder to the mountaineers. There were two scientists, Thomas Nuttall, a Harvard botanist, and Townsend, the Philadelphia ornithologist, both of them more interested in the plants and birds of the American West than in its beaver. Also, there was a strange and uneasy party of five men, three of them traveling to save the souls of the Flatheads, and the other two, their hired hands, going along to help the Bible-carrying trio as well as to see for themselves what the Rockies and Oregon looked like. The missionaries, responding to the eastern visit of the Nez Perces, had finally come. But the shadow they would cast on the Indians' West was going to be longer and different than that of the trappers. In the midst of the profane and drunken revelry that marked a rendezvous, the leader of the missionary party, the Reverend Jason Lee, sat in his tent trying to shut out the noise of the mountain men's carousing and cursing, and wrote in his diary, "My God, my God, is there nothing that will have any effect on them?"

57. William Sublette was engaged in a sharp maneuver. In February 1834 he had met in New York City with representatives of the American Fur Company and had agreed with them on a division of the western country. The American Fur Company had taken the upper Missouri River region for trade, and Sublette had agreed to confine his activities to the tribes of the Rocky Mountains and avoid the Missouri.

4

Children of Grace

JASON LEE was a tall, slightly stooped, and slow-moving man. He was powerfully built and had a heavy jaw, and looked more like a gangling frontiersman than a minister. He was convinced, moreover, that Divine Providence
directed him, and it made him unafraid of any mortal, whether an Indian or a
contemptuous trapper. Soon after Lee's arrival at the rendezvous, Nathaniel
Wyeth warned him to be on his guard, as some of William Sublette's men
had threatened to "give them missionaries 'hell.' " Lee responded by making
Wyeth lead him over to Sublette's camp and introduce him to the mountain
men who were lolling about. His straightforward and fearless manner disarmed them, and he soon satisfied himself that their threats were just bold
talk.

Lee was 31 years old. He had been born in Stanstead, Quebec, a border
town which at the time had been considered a part of Vermont. At 23 he had
experienced a religious awakening and soon afterward had become a Methodist minister, preaching to whites and Indians along the border. In 1833 the
New England Conference of the Methodist Episcopal Church had reacted
with excitement to the *Christian Advocate*'s dramatic account of the Nez
Perce visit to St. Louis, and Lee had volunteered at once to head a Methodist
mission to the Northwest Indians. His offer had been accepted, and during
the winter he had prepared for the trip, enlisting his nephew, Daniel Lee,
who was almost as old as he, to make the journey with him. In Boston, he had
met Wyeth, who had returned to prepare for his second expedition to Oregon, and who had with him the Flathead and Nez Perce youths he had
brought back from the Columbia country. Wyeth agreeably made personal
appearances with Lee, helping him raise money for the missionary effort; and

the exhibition of Wyeth's young Indians, one of whom fortunately had been born with a head that looked as if it might have been artificially flattened, had moved audiences to wondrous gasps and opened their pocketbooks for Lee's mission. Lee had also arranged to travel west with Wyeth's caravan and ship his mission supplies and equipment in Wyeth's chartered brig, the *May Dacre*, which was carrying the trader's goods and salmon-packing equipment to the mouth of the Columbia. Finally, on his way to the frontier jump-off point in the spring, Lee had added three more members to his missionary party, Cyrus Shepard, a frail but dedicated layman from the Boston area, and two young lay assistants, Philip M. Edwards and Courtney M. Walker, whom he had hired at Independence, Mo., to drive a small herd of cattle and to help with his outfit.

Lee had left the Missouri frontier "as Paul went to Jerusalem," certain that God would lead him to the Flatheads and show him where and how to establish a mission for those Indians, whom he had never seen and about whom he knew almost nothing. His trip across the plains with Wyeth had passed without serious difficulty, and in his diary he had continually recorded his expectations of being able to bring the light to the innocent charges whom he was traveling west to meet. But at the rendezvous on Ham's Fork of the Green River his interest in the Indians, as evidenced by his journal entries, suddenly seemed to change. In that wild, lawless setting, he saw his first Flatheads and Nez Perces. Some of them were gathered around Sublette's camp, probably gambling with old acquaintances among the trappers. After going over and talking to the mountain men, Lee recounted that "Some of the men told the Pierced Nose and Flat Head Indians our object in coming into the country and they came and shook hands very cordially and seemed to welcome me to their country." [1]

There must have been some wondering looks among the trappers, and a reaction of pleasure and interest among the Indians, who perhaps withdrew to announce to their people the sudden appearance of the long-awaited teacher of the white men's supernatural powers. The next day Lee wrote in his diary, "Have had a visit from some 10 or 12 Pierced Nose and 1 or 2 Flat Heads today and conversed a little with them through an indifferent interpreter. But being busy arranging our things we requested them to come again when we were more at leisure." [2]

One of William Sublette's companions, William Marshall Anderson, kept a diary at the rendezvous that year and named the principal Nez Perce leaders whom he met at the trade gathering. In the end pages of his diary he noted: "As near as I can write them, names of chiefs of the Nez-percé tribe—Cut

1. "Diary of Reverend Jason Lee," *Oregon Historical Quarterly*, 17 (1916), 138.
2. Ibid., p. 139.

nose – nose nicion – Cowso tum – Ot lot cou ts sum do or the Lawyer – red
crow—& then others pusherahikati – Melmelstin tinton & Kokokelpip – Koul
& koultamin or red lead – Tieltickinickiti Takinswhaitish – or rotten belly."
On another end page he wrote again: "Chiefs of the Sapaten or Nez percé
tribe Nouse nacéon – or Cut nose—Cowsotum. Otlotcoutson – or the Lawyer
—Ko ho kelpip the red crow. Pushwahikite—Mel. meltohhintintini—
Koulkoultamin or the red beard – Tiellickinickito – Takinshaitish or rotten
belly." [3]

Some or all of those headmen were undoubtedly among the Nez Perces
who made the first call on Jason Lee at the 1834 rendezvous, and most of
them can be identified as men who had participated in events mentioned earlier in this narrative or who would play important roles in later history.
"Nose nicion" (The Cut Nose)) bore the same name as Neesh ne park kee
ook, The Cut Nose from the vicinity of Colter's Creek on the Clearwater,
who had welcomed Lewis and Clark in 1806. "Cowsotum," whom Bonneville
had met near the forks of the Salmon River in 1832 and had called Kowsoter,
was perhaps a Nez Perce; but because his name was Salish, he may have had a
Flathead father or been called after a Flathead leader. "Otlotcoutson" was
Hallalhotsoot (The Lawyer) from Kamiah, who had been wounded at the
Battle of Pierre's Hole in 1832. He was the man who had heard Spokan
Garry preach during the winter of 1829–30 and who would later tell the missionary A. B. Smith that his people had sent the messengers to St. Louis. "Ko
ho kelpip" was Qoh Qoh Ilppilp (Red Crow, or Red Raven) from the area
of present-day Stites, Idaho, on the Clearwater River above Kamiah. "Pushwahikite" was Bonneville's friend, Apash Wyakaikt (Flint Necklace, later
known as the senior Looking Glass) from Asotin on the Snake River.

3. Soon after he returned home, Anderson reframed his diary into a journal, and
again listed the chiefs "of the Sâapeten or Nez Percé Tribe," this time with slightly
different spellings, as follows: "1st Nose—nési-ow – Cut nose. 2nd Cow-so.tum—3rd—
Ot-lot-coat-sum The talker. The whites know him by the name of the lawyer. 4th
Ko-ko-kel-pip, the red crow, 5th Push-wa-hi-kite, 6th Mel-wel-tshin-tin-tini- 7th Koul-
koul-ta min or the red beard, Tiel-licki-nichiti, 8th Ta kin-shwai tish – Known to the
whites as rotten Belley – Wounded by the Black-feet at the same time that Sublette
was shot.—" About the Nez Perces as a whole, Anderson wrote: "This tribe like the
flatheads is remarkable for their more than Christian practice of honesty, veracity
and very moral virtue which every philosopher and professor so much laud, and practice so little. There are now four missionaries on their route to the nation of flat-heads.
If they can only succeed in making them such as the white-men *are*, not such as they
should be, it would be charity for these messengers of civilization to desist." I am indebted to Dale L. Morgan for his generosity in making available to me these excerpts
from the 1834 diary and journals of William Marshall Anderson, which are owned by
the Henry L. Huntington Library in San Marino, Calif., and which Morgan has edited
and annotated for publication.

"Melmelstin tinton" was a Cayuse. "Koulkoultamin" was Koolkooltami, a noted warrior from the Stites area. "Tieltickinickiti" may have been Tilaukait, a Cayuse leader from the Walla Walla Valley; and "Takinswhaitish" was the Nez Perce whose stomach wound at the Battle of Pierre's Hole had gained him the name Rotten Belly.

Lee's meager notation about his first visit from the Nez Perces and Flatheads whom he had come so far to save seemed strangely casual. He provided no suggestion that he had any curiosity about where or how he would establish a mission for them, nor did he comment on how the Indians looked and behaved, or on his own reactions to their interest in him. After his high expectations and long trip, he may have been disillusioned, and even shocked, by the "wild" Indians they really were, as well as by the arid and lonely country in which he had met them. Farther west, in the more pleasant and friendlier clime of the Columbia River, which Wyeth would have described to him, he might already have been thinking that there were other Flatheads—the ones who, as Wyeth would have told him, really did flatten their heads. They were, perhaps, a more tamed people, already settled in a green, fertile land with trees, grass, and shaded brooks, where a missionary could build a comfortable dwelling, plant gardens, and instruct docile and attentive audiences.

The following day, Sunday, June 22, after he had taken a long nap, the Indians came to see him again.

> Soon after I awoke, as many Indians as could enter our tent came to see us and we told them our object in coming, showed them the Bible, told them some of the commandments and how they were given, to all of which they listened with the utmost attention and then replied that it was all good. They inquired if we could build houses and said that the Indians at Walla Wallah gave horses to a white man to build them a house and when he got the horses he went off and did not build it. We of course expressed our strong disapprobation of his conduct. They said if we could build a house for them they would catch plenty of Beaver for us which we take as a favorable indication showing their desire for improvement. One said he was going to St. Louis next year but he would leave his three children with his friends who was present and he would give them to us that we might teach them to read and write and be good. Some of them shook hands very heartily when they left. One of the men went to purchase meat of the Indians but they would not bring it to him because it was Sunday. Thus while the whites who have been educated in a Christian land pay no regard whatever to the Sabbath these poor savages who have at most only some vague idea of the Christian religion respect the Sabbath of the Lord our God.[4]

4. "Diary of Reverend Jason Lee," p. 139.

Lee's reference to the Indian who was going to St. Louis the following year is interesting. Five years later, on October 20, 1839, Bishop Joseph Rosati of St. Louis appealed to Father John Roothan, General of the Society of Jesus, to assign Jesuit missionaries to the Flatheads. In his letter the Bishop informed Father Roothan that a number of delegations of Flatheads and Iroquois had arrived in St. Louis in various years, beginning in 1831, to plead for religious teachers. The Indians he referred to included the original Nez Perce group of 1831, and also a delegation that came in 1835, the year after Lee's presence at the rendezvous.

This latter party was led by an Iroquois named Old Ignace La Mousse, who had come from Canada and settled among the Salish, probably about 1820.[5] Like the other Iroquois with him, including a man named Pierre Gaucher (Left Hand) and another known as Aeneas or Ignace Chapped Lips, he was a Catholic, and Bishop Rosati credited Old Ignace and his companions with having "sown the first seeds of Catholicity in the midst of the infidel nations among whom they live."[6] Old Ignace had three children by a Pend d'Oreille woman, and in 1835, he took two of them, boys 14 and 12 years old, to St. Louis with him. Other Indians went along also, perhaps, for High Bear, a Nez Perce from the area near the junction of the Snake and Salmon rivers, later embraced Catholicism and told white men, when he was known to them as Salmon River Billy, that he too had gone to see the priests in St. Louis in 1835.[7] There is no doubt that that journey occurred the year after Jason Lee's arrival at the rendezvous, for Ignace's two sons were baptized in St. Louis on December 2, 1835, with the Christian names Francis and Charles. Both were later prominent among traders in western Montana, and Francis was alive at Arlee, Montana, in 1903, where he confirmed the facts of his 1835 trip.[8]

If Old Ignace, the Catholic Iroquois, was therefore with the Flatheads at the 1834 rendezvous, a question is raised concerning the motive for his journey to St. Louis the next year. Bishop Rosati stated that the Iroquois made their trips to the States to seek priests for the Flatheads, thus leaving the impression that

5. He was probably a free trapper, since Hudson's Bay Company rolls fail to list his name. However, he must have been among the Salish by 1820, for he had a son by a Pend d'Oreille woman, and the boy was 14 years old in 1835. See George F. Weisel, *Men and Trade on the Northwest Frontier* (Missoula, Montana, 1955), p. 26.
6. Bischoff, *The Jesuits in Old Oregon*, p. 9. See below, p. 670.
7. Ibid., p. 142; Elsensohn, *Pioneer Days in Idaho County*, 2, 490.
8. Chittenden and Richardson, *De Smet, 1*, 29, 292. In May and June 1854 Gustavus Sohon, a soldier artist with I. I. Stevens' Pacific Railroad Survey party in Montana, drew pencil portraits of Aeneas and Charles La Mousse. He called the latter "½ Iroquois ½ Pend-d-oreile" and said he "speaks English and French and lives with the Flatheads." The drawings are in the ethnology branch of the Smithsonian Institution in Washington, D.C.

each of the journeys was inspired by the desire to secure Catholic rather than Protestant teachers for the Salish. Of Ignace and the other Iroquois, he wrote in 1839 to Father Roothan: "Not only have they planted the faith in those wild countries, but they have besides defended it against the encroachments of the Protestant ministers. When these pretended ministers presented themselves among them, our good Catholics refused to accept them. 'These are not the priests about whom we have spoken to you,' they would say to the Flatheads, 'these are not the long black-robed priests who have no wives, who say mass, who carry the crucifix with them, etc." [9] Father Lawrence B. Palladino, a later priest among the Flatheads, said even more specifically that when the Flatheads discovered that the Protestant missionaries at the rendezvous were not priests, they "would not consent to have them come" among their people.[10]

It is possible that Old Ignace and the Iroquois at the rendezvous cautioned the Flatheads against the Protestants, but the evidence today would not seem to support that conclusion. The diary entries of the various Protestant missionaries at the rendezvous of 1834, 1835, and 1836 not only fail to reflect Flathead skepticism of their brand of Christianity but, on the contrary, record accounts of warm and enthusiastic receptions given them by the Flatheads, as well as evidence of eager attentiveness by both Flatheads and Nez Perces to what they had to say. Unless Lee, for example, grossly distorted in his diary the facts of his June 22 discussion with the Indians, it does not seem plausible that they would have conversed with him as they did had Old Ignace already told them that Lee was not a true "long blackrobe" and that he, Ignace, would bring them real teachers in 1835. Nor, if Lee had been turned down because he was considered a "pretended minister," does it appear logical that Ignace would have proposed leaving his three children with him for instruction while he journeyed to St. Louis for acceptable teachers.[11]

Still, as the 1834 rendezvous progressed, Lee, the Methodist, who had arrived in the mountains before the representatives of any other denomination, showed a puzzling lack of interest in the natives. Despite the later writings of Catholic missionaries who said specifically that Ignace had warned a distinguished and influential Flathead leader named Insula, or The Little Chief (because of his small stature), against the Protestants, that Indian—although he later became a Catholic—did his best to let Lee know that his people would welcome him as a teacher. But Lee was coldly indifferent to him. He saw other Indians, behaving in a manner that dismayed him. One, an impulsive, fun-loving, young Nez Perce named The Bull's Head, whom the trappers

9. Bischoff, *The Jesuits in Old Oregon*, p. 11.
10. Chittenden and Richardson, *De Smet, 1*, 267.
11. See below, p. 669.

nicknamed Kentuck (because he continually tried to sing the popular ballad, "The Hunters of Kentucky," which the Americans had taught him), came charging through the white men's camp one day, chasing a frightened buffalo and yelling, "Hokahey!" as the mountain men cheered and fired their guns in the air. Another Nez Perce, Tackensuatis, offended Lee by sousing himself in drink and swearing in English with the trappers.

Lee watched the undignified proceedings that showed much work to be done and, thinking of his experiences with more civilized eastern Indians on the Canadian border, wrote to his superiors in the States, "It is easier converting a tribe of Indians at a missionary meeting than in the wilderness." One evening, he noted hopefully, "Heard the Indians in one lodge praying and singing. Went to listen to them but they were just closing as we approached. How encouraging to see these red men thus religiously inclined." But later he added gloomily, "Soon after dark a fire was built in the Prairie for the purpose of a war dance." [12]

On July 4, still without having made an effort to reach an understanding with the Indians, he packed up and prepared to continue west with Wyeth, who had decided to build a trading post on the Snake River and try to sell to the Indians and trappers in that area the trade goods that Fitzpatrick and the Rocky Mountain Fur Company had refused to accept from him at the rendezvous. "Just as we were on the point of starting," Lee wrote, "the Indians came and informed us that they were about to leave us and wished to know if we intended to come back and stop with the Flat Head camp. We told them we could not say positively now. We did not know as we would find their Camp. I asked them if they would like to have their children learn to read &c. One said he would give me his. Some said they would like to learn to cultivate land. And they seemed desirous that we should locate among *them*. I told them if they came where Capt. Wyeth proposed to build up a Fort that if it were not too far I would go and see the Chief and talk with him about it and if we did not come this winter, that we would come next or the following. When we arrived at the place of separation they all shook hands with me in the most cordial hearty and friendly manner. I was very much affected with this parting scene . . . O that these sons of nature may soon be the children of grace." [13]

So the Reverend Jason Lee and his colleagues left the Flatheads and Nez Perces. They had shipped their equipment on Wyeth's brig to the Columbia River, and it was logical for them to continue to that point, get their supplies, and then decide where to locate a mission. But from his indifference to the Indians at the rendezvous, it seems apparent that already Lee had little idea of

12. "Diary of Reverend Jason Lee," p. 140.
13. Ibid., Friday, July 4.

ever returning to them. He continued on with Wyeth, giving infrequent thought to the natives he had left, and reached the trappers' old wintering grounds near present-day Pocatello, Idaho, at the junction of the Portneuf and Snake rivers. There, Wyeth halted and in the vicinity built a post which he named Fort Hall, for one of his financial backers.[14] While Wyeth lingered to complete the structure and select men to garrison it, Lee went on with a Hudson's Bay Company brigade under Tom McKay that was headed for Walla Walla. They followed the route across southern Idaho, and six miles above the mouth of the Boise River, McKay, in turn, halted with most of his men and started to build a British post to divert trade from Wyeth's new fort. McKay called his small, rough structure Snake Fort. Lee, with no interest in the competitive activities of the fur men, hurried on with some of McKay's trappers to Walla Walla and eventually to Fort Vancouver, where Dr. McLoughlin, as usual, provided the travelers with a courteous welcome.

On the advice of the Hudson's Bay Company factor, Lee visited the beautiful, well-watered Willamette Valley, which revived his spirits and enthusiasm. He was far from the Flatheads now, but this was the West's New England, one of the loveliest and most promising valleys he had ever seen, and roaming through it, he once again earnestly sought the Lord's guidance. "Oh, My God," he wrote in his diary, "direct us to the right spot where we can best glorify thee and be most useful to these degraded red men." The next day he pleaded again, "My mind is yet much exercised in respect to our location. I know not what to do." But on September 27, 1834, he wrote, "I have nearly concluded to go to the Willamette," and on October 1 he finally found peace: "To the Willamette we have concluded to go." [15]

Some ten miles northwest of present-day Salem, Oregon, in a pleasant setting on the Willamette River, he built a mission for a handful of white settlers in the area, mostly retired employees of the Hudson's Bay Company, and for the remnants of the real flathead Indians of the Northwest, the white-dominated survivors of devastating epidemics that since the late 1820s had all but wiped out the once-numerous Chinookan-speaking peoples of the lower Columbia. But Lee's interest in ministering even to those few disoriented natives soon faltered under the over-shadowing influence of a new goal. Failing to convert Indians, he became interested in real estate. In 1837 two groups of missionaries arrived from the East to reinforce him. Although they came with high ideals, it was obvious to Lee that they constituted a vanguard of settlers who would soon be coming to Oregon to acquire new homes. The Indians, to him, had already become a "lost" race, and about his mission in the Willam-

14. For details see Richard G. Beidleman, "Nathaniel Wyeth's Fort Hall," *Oregon Historical Quarterly*, *58* (1957), 197 ff.
15. "Diary of Reverend Jason Lee," p. 264.

ette Valley he realized that there was one white for every Indian, or one civilizer for every savage. There was no future in that, and he began to turn increasingly to material affairs. He promoted the acquisition of land, sent for farmers, mechanics, and workmen from the East to settle around his mission, and in 1838 went to Washington to petition for the establishment of a territorial government in Oregon. He remained in the East for a year, addressing public meetings, stirring interest in the rich and fertile Oregon country, and urging settlers to follow him back to the Willamette. He presented his petition to Congress and wrote in confidence to Senator Caleb Cushing of Massachusetts that the settlers needed a government guarantee of ownership of the land they claimed. "These settlements," he informed Cushing, "will greatly increase the value of the government domain in that country, should the Indian title ever be extinguished. And we cannot but expect, therefore, that those who have been pioneers in this arduous work will be liberally dealt with in this matter." [16]

In confidence, also, Lee managed to get the Cabinet to appropriate money from its secret service fund to help him charter a ship on which to take people back to Oregon. The government gave him $50 a head for each person carried by the vessel, and in October 1839 he sailed from New York with a "Great Reinforcement" of settlers and a number of additional missionaries. The ship reached the Columbia in May 1840. Although he was still the religious head of the mission, Lee spent most of his time on real estate matters and in consolidating the position of the Americans in the Willamette. In 1841 he presided over a meeting that called for United States acquisition of the area, and two years later he guided the beginnings of a provisional government for Oregon. In 1844, he was suddenly relieved as mission head. He went East again, and during a visit to his home in Quebec caught a cold and died.

Lee had turned out to be an empire builder and an important instrument of American Manifest Destiny rather than a missionary to the Indians. In the face of increasing opposition from the Hudson's Bay Company, he had started the movement that would eventually take the country away not only from the British traders but from the Indians whom he had originally intended to save. His role was clearly assessed by a later chronicler of his paltry missionary achievements, a Reverend A. S. Atwood, who wrote in his book, *The Conquerors:* "One of the most potential factors in the work of the Methodist Mission [Lee's] was its colonization feature. This was the determining element in the establishment of American institutions in Oregon." [17]

The first missionary to reach the Nez Perce homeland went west the year

16. Hubert H. Bancroft, *History of Oregon*, Vol. 1, 1834–1848 (San Francisco, 1886), p. 173.
17. See below, p. 671.

after Jason Lee. He was Samuel Parker, and although he was a rather elderly man, officious and often arrogant, he respected Indians and regarded them as brothers of the white men. Parker was an unusual man to be risking the hardships and perils of a western trip. He was 56 years old, the father of three children, a somewhat cultured instructor who was more at home in the quiet study of a parsonage than in the outdoors. A Congregationalist, he had preached in New York and Massachusetts and had taught at a girl's school in Ithaca, New York. Although he was parsimonious to an extreme (a Hudson's Bay Company employee in Oregon characterized him as "a very good old fanatic with some few peculiarities, such as licking his plate"), and often angered others by his begging attitude and manner of helping himself to whatever he wished, he was inspired to self-sacrifice by the report of the Nez Perce deputation, and promptly offered to go to their country as a missionary.[18] At first, the American Board of Commissioners for Foreign Missions, representing Congregationalists, Presbyterians, and two smaller denominations, rejected him on account of his age; but he would not be turned away, and it was finally agreed that he would undertake an exploring tour to select suitable sites for mission stations among the western tribes. He started eagerly for the West in 1834, the same year as the Lees, but missed a steamboat connection and arrived on the frontier after the fur caravans had already departed for that year's rendezvous.

Forced to postpone his excursion until the following year, he returned to the East and raised additional funds during the winter. In Wheeler, N.Y., he recruited a 33-year-old Presbyterian physician named Marcus Whitman as a companion on the venture. Whitman, a hard-working, dedicated man, described as "rather forbidding at first, but makes a good impression soon and is respected," was strongly built and of medium height. In later years another missionary who knew him in Oregon, in trying to explain why the Indians had not appreciated Whitman, said of him, "I need hardly tell you he cared for no man under heaven—perfectly fearless & independent. Secondly he could never stop to *parley*. It was always *yes* or *no*. In the 3d place he had no sense of etiquette or personal dignity—manners, I mean. 4. And in the fourth place *he was always at work* . . . What would such a man have in common with an Indian? How could they sympathize with each other?" [19]

In early life Whitman had planned to be a minister, but the death of a clergyman who was instructing him caused him to abandon that career, and he became, instead, a doctor, receiving an exceptionally good medical educa-

18. The quotation characterizing Parker can be found in a letter written by George B. Roberts to Mrs. Frances Fuller Victor on November 28, 1878, and published in the *Oregon Historical Quarterly*, *63* (1962), 195.

19. Clifford M. Drury, *Marcus Whitman, M.D.* (Caldwell, Idaho, 1937), p. 458.

tion in upstate New York.[20] He remained close to his church, however, and several times offered to go west as a missionary. Because of a discomforting pain in his side, the American Board was afraid to enlist him; but finally, after Parker interceded for him, he was accepted as an assistant to the older man on the exploring expedition.

In the spring of 1835 the two men journeyed to St. Louis and received permission from the American Fur Company to travel with its supply caravan, led by Lucien Fontenelle, as far as the rendezvous. The group left Liberty, across the river from Independence, Missouri, on May 15 and moved up the Missouri to a fur post at Bellevue near the mouth of the Platte River to organize for the trip across the plains. Whitman, even more than Parker, was headed for enduring fame as a man who would help to change the course of Northwestern history; but on this leg of the journey, the rough and irreverent members of the caravan saw him and his older companion only as two praying persons who were incongruously out of their element. Parker was constantly critical of the fur men's conduct and refused to move with the caravan on Sundays, and Fontenelle's employees answered his disapproving remarks with ridicule of both men. They cut loose a raft which was to carry the missionaries' outfit across a river, pelted Whitman with rotten eggs, and made Parker believe that they were plotting to murder the two of them once they got out on the plains.

At Bellevue things changed. Cholera struck the members of the caravan, and for twelve days Whitman, using knowledge he had gained during an earlier outbreak of cholera in New York State, administered to the sick men, laboring alone and unselfishly, nursing them with calomel, and finally saving the lives of all but three of them by having the outfit move to a higher and more sanitary campsite. Fontenelle himself was stricken; after his recovery he conveyed the thanks of all of the men and assured the missionaries that there would be no further trouble. After that, it was more pleasant for Parker and Whitman. The group moved out along the Platte, almost a month behind schedule, and east of Fort Laramie met Tom Fitzpatrick and a party of mountain men who had ridden east from the rendezvous to see what was delaying their supplies. At Fort Laramie, which William Sublette and Robert Campbell had just sold to the American Fur Company, the caravan found a large village of Oglalla Sioux who had come down from their home country east of the Black Hills in present-day South Dakota. Sublette's men had lured them to the new trading post, and from that time on, bands of Teton Sioux, extending their roamings, would appear increasingly along the Platte and its north fork in Nebraska and Wyoming.

20. Frederick C. Waite, "Medical Education of Dr. Whitman," *Oregon Historical Quarterly, 38* (1936), 192–216.

At the fort Fitzpatrick replaced Fontenelle as leader of the caravan. The travelers struck off again, and on August 12 reached the rendezvous at the mouth of New Fork on the Green River, where trappers and Indians had been waiting impatiently for a month. Parker and Whitman were no more approving of the high-jinks and debauchery of the rendezvous than the Lees had been the year before; but on the trail they had at least shown themselves able to become more tolerant of the ways of the mountaineers, and their attitude at the gathering was less pious and hand-wringing than that of their Methodist predecessors. The hard-working young Whitman, particularly, had become more respected by the trappers; and when the medical services that he had rendered to the caravan during the attack of cholera were related around the campfires, some of the men found reasons to call on him. The first to come over was the grizzled Jim Bridger, who was carrying a Blackfoot arrowhead in his back. While mountain men and Indians watched, Whitman operated on him, removing a three-inch, barbed arrowhead from under his skin. Another trapper had an arrow removed from his shoulder, and "after these operations," Parker reported, "calls for surgical and medical aid were constant every hour in the day."

At the rendezvous, Parker also recorded a thrilling gun duel on horseback between Kit Carson and a liquored-up bully named "Shunar." Parker deplored the duel, but wrote it off as a typical "pastime" of men who were leading a "wild and wandering life" and who "appear to have sought for a place where, as they would say, human nature is not oppressed by the tyranny of religion, and pleasure is not awed by the frown of virtue." More distressing to him was the example the trappers were setting for the Indians. "Their demoralizing influence with the Indians has been lamentable," he wrote, "and they have imposed upon them, in all the ways that sinful propensities dictate. It is said they have sold them packs of cards at high prices, calling them the bible; and have told them, if they should refuse to give white men wives, God would be angry with them and punish them eternally: and on almost any occasion when their wishes have been resisted, they have threatened them with the wrath of God." [21]

This was probably nonsense, and Parker admitted that he did not always believe the stories that were told to him for their effect. But he was filled with the superior attitude of a zealous guardian. He considered the uncivilized Indians as children who required protection until white men could elevate them, and missionaries in his view were God's instruments to provide the natives with both services. Fortunately, at the rendezvous he could make a start at weaning the Indians away from the trappers' influence. There were Utes

21. Samuel Parker, *Journal of an Exploring Tour beyond the Rocky Mountains* (Ithaca, N.Y., 1838), pp. 80–81.

present, a large village of some 2,000 Shoshonis, and forty lodges of Flatheads and Nez Perces. Although he was "disappointed to see nothing peculiar in the shape of the Flathead Indians," he was drawn to them and the Nez Perces because they had been the ones who had sent the mission to St. Louis.

For several days, he and Whitman secured information from participants at the gathering who knew something about the Flathead and Nez Perce country, and Whitman was shocked to learn that the Lees had by-passed those Indians and settled in the Willamette Valley. Then they secured the services of a French-Canadian Catholic trapper named Charles Compo who had taken a Nez Perce woman as his wife and, using him as their interpreter, "had an interesting interview with the chiefs" of the two tribes, inquiring "whether they wished to have teachers come among them and instruct them in the knowledge of God, his worship, and the way to be saved; and what they would do to aid them in their labors." The chiefs had all been present at the rendezvous the year before; but although they had had the same kind of conversation with Jason Lee, and had gone over similar ground with him, Parker got the idea that they had "never heard of the Methodist missionaries." [22]

"The oldest chief of the Flatheads arose," Parker reported, "and said, he was old, and did not expect to know much more; he was deaf and could not hear, but his heart was made glad, very glad, to see what he had never seen before, a man near to God (meaning a minister of the gospel). Next arose Insula, the most influential chief among the Flathead nation, and said, he had heard a man near God was coming to visit them, and he, with some of his people joined with some white men, went out three days' journey to meet him, but missed us. A war party of Crow Indians came upon them, and took away some of their horses, and one from him which he greatly loved, but now he forgets all, his heart is made so glad to see a man near to God." [23]

Insula, of course, had talked to Lee the year before, and was the same chief whom Catholic missionaries later quoted as having said he had opposed the entry of Protestant teachers into the Flatheads' country. If that had been so, Insula must have acquired the point of view after 1835. Tackensuatis, the whites' friend Rotten Belly, was also present. He arose, said Parker, "and said, he had heard from white men a little about God, which had only gone into his ears; he wished to know enough to have it go down into his heart, to influence his life, and to teach his people. Others spoke to the same import, and they all made as many promises as we could desire."

The apparent hunger of the Indians for salvation warmed the missionaries' hearts, and Parker wrote, "We came to the conclusion, that, though many other important stations might be found, this would be one." To hasten the

22. Drury, *Spalding*, p. 93, quoting a letter from Parker, August 17, 1835.
23. Parker, *Journal*, p. 77.

establishment of a mission, the two men decided that Whitman would return to the East with the fur caravan, recruit reinforcements, and come back the next year to set up a station. It would save a whole year, but it would mean that Parker would have to continue the exploring trip by himself. The doughty, old man was unafraid, and reassured Whitman that "we could not go safely together without divine protection, and with it, I could go alone." With "the presence of God" protecting him, he would make his way through the Oregon country to Walla Walla and Fort Vancouver, visiting other tribes in the region and selecting suitable sites for missions, and would come back to meet Whitman at the 1836 rendezvous. It disappointed him that he could do nothing for the Utes and Shoshonis at the rendezvous, but those Indians lived in a different part of the West, and he decided not to approach them at that time, "lest we should excite expectations which would not soon be fulfilled."

The missionaries had another conference with the Nez Perce and Flathead headmen and told them what they had decided. The Nez Perces must have been delighted with the news. At last an American was promising to go with them into their country. "They were much pleased," Parker wrote of their reaction, "and promised to assist me, and to send a convoy with me from their country to Fort Walla Walla on the Columbia river. They selected one of their principal young men for my particular assistant, as long as I should have need of him, who was called Kentuc." This was the irrepressible Bull's Head, who had chased a buffalo through the camp during the 1834 rendezvous, and who liked to sing "The Hunters of Kentucky." Parker also enlisted Compo to accompany him as his interpreter. At the same time, Whitman had become interested in a Nez Perce boy named Tackitonitis who could speak a little English, and he secured permission from the boy's father to take him east with him, so that they could learn each other's languages during the winter.[24] Whitman renamed the youth Richard, and a day later another Nez Perce brought over his son, Ais, and urged the missionary to take him also, and start his education in the white man's ways. Whitman consented, and called the second boy John, promising to bring both of the youths back to their people the following year.

From the rendezvous, Jim Bridger planned to take a brigade north to the Yellowstone country and the headwaters of the Missouri, and he invited Parker to travel with him to the Snake River. The Nez Perces and Flatheads would move along with the trappers, at least to Pierre's Hole, and the com-

---

24. In his various works, Clifford Drury called this boy the son of Rotten Belly, but only, as he wrote me, because Tackitonitis sounded like Tackensuatis. This is far-fetched. At the rendezvous of 1836, Mrs. Whitman wrote that Richard's "father is not here," although Tackensuatis was present. Drury, *First White Women over the Rockies* (Glendale, Calif., 1963), *1*, 58.

bined party would help get the missionary safely started on his bold journey. Parker accepted the proposal gratefully, and on August 22 he said farewell to Whitman and started up the Green River with the trappers and Indians. Whitman waited for almost a week while Fitzpatrick wound up the rendezvous, and then set off for the East on August 27 with the fur caravan and the two Nez Perce youths.

Parker's journey was one of the most unusual in the annals of the West. From the start he rode with the Indians. They clustered around him and, treating him like a precious cargo, convoyed him tenderly and affectionately over the rugged route, vieing "with each other to see which could do the most for my comfort, so that they more than anticipated my wants." Little Indian girls brought him wild strawberries. Others cut green bushes to set up a shade for him when he rested, and once the wife of Tackensuatis and some other women collected the fragrant leaves of a mintlike plant and "strewed them in my tent." He rode at the head of the column in a position of honor "with the first chief," and he was pleased to record that "they consult me upon all their important business, and are very ready to follow my counsels."

With Bridger's brigade, the party crossed the difficult divide from the Green River to the Hoback, pausing on the trail at the head of the dangerous Hoback Canyon for Parker to conduct Sunday services for the trappers, who included Kit Carson and Joe Meek. "I did not feel any disposition to upbraid them for their sins," Parker said. Continuing on to Jackson Hole, they climbed the Teton Pass and descended to Pierre's Hole, where the mountain men showed Parker the scene of the battle of 1832. There, Bridger and his men said goodbye and headed north with Insula and some of the Flatheads, leaving Parker alone with the rest of the Indians, who promised to take him safely through the Nez Perce homeland to Fort Walla Walla. As they started for the Salmon River, the journey took on the quality of an epic, centered around the stoic figure of the elderly divine. It was a fabulous ride through some of the most rugged wilderness in the West. Parker had no idea where he was, or where he was going. The Indians continued to be considerate and gentle, and he trusted them completely, urging his horse on manfully, as his companions helped him along precipices, through dense woods, and across wind-blown ridgetops. At night, he lay down with his portmanteau for a pillow, aware that Blackfeet and grizzly bears lurked nearby, but his faith in God and the Nez Perces eased both discomfort and anxiety.

The route took them first from Pierre's Hole to Medicine Lodge Creek and the Continental Divide. The going was rough, but Parker found the Indians "very kind to each other, and if one meets with any disaster, the others will wait and assist him." When a horse once "turned a saddle under him upon which a child was fastened, and started to run . . . those near hovered at once around with their horses so as to enclose the one to which the child was attached, and it was extricated without hurt."

In the companionship of the trail, Parker felt that he was making progress with his instruction of the Indians. At one point, he wrote that Tackensuatis "came to me and requested me to meet in his lodge a number of their people who had separated, husbands from their wives, and wives from their husbands, and explain to them what God has said upon the subject . . . When they were assembled, I read to them and explained what God has said about the duty of husbands to wives, and of wives to their husbands; and of the duty of parents to their children, and children to their parents. I commented upon the subject, and told them, that when they marry, it must be for life. They all but two agreed to go back to their former husbands and wives. It was interesting," he added, "to see that they are ready to put in practice instructions as soon as received. The chief said they wish me to instruct them in all that God has said; for they wish to do right. After I left them, they stayed a long time in the lodge of the chief, which was near my tent, and I heard them conversing on the subject until I went to sleep . . ." [25]

On September 5 they were joined by another band of Nez Perces, led by a man named Charle, who may have been John Work's friend, Charley, from the lower Snake River. The newcomers arrived on Medicine Lodge Creek, "the principal chief marching in front with his aid, carrying an American flag by his side. They all sung a march, while a few beat a sort of drum. As they drew near, they displayed columns, and made quite an imposing appearance." In the evening Parker met with the new chief and his people and explained the object of his mission. Charle, he reported, "arose and spoke very sensibly for a considerable time—mentioned his ignorance, his desire to know more about God, and his gladness of heart to see one who can teach him." In turn, Parker told them that the next day was Sunday, which they should keep holy. If they agreed not to travel, he would help them worship God.

The result was all that he could have wished for. Early in the morning one of the eldest Indians went through the camp, crying to the people that it was the Sabbath day, "and they must prepare for worship." At eight o'clock the chiefs asked Parker where they should assemble.

> I asked them if they could not be accomodated in the willows which skirted the stream of water on which we were encamped. They thought not. I then enquired if they could not take the poles of some of their lodges and construct a shade. They thought they could; and without any other directions went out and made preparation, and about eleven o'clock

25. Parker, *Journal*, pp. 93–94.

came and said they were ready for worship. I found them all assembled, men, women and children, between four and five hundred, in what I would call a sanctuary of God, constructed with their lodges, nearly one hundred feet long and about twenty feet wide; and all were arranged in rows, through the length of the building, upon their knees . . . The whole area within was carpeted with their dressed skins, and they were all attired in their best . . . The whole sight, taken together, sensibly affected me, and filled me with astonishment; and I felt as though it was the house of God and the gate of heaven.

Parker led them in singing and prayer and then talked to them with the help of his interpreter on the fall of man "and the ruined and sinful condition of all mankind; the law of God, and that all are transgressors of this law, and as such are exposed to the wrath of God, both in this life and the life to come; and then told them of the mercy of God in giving his son to die for us; and of the love of the Savior, and though he desires our salvation, yet he will not save us unless we hate sin and put our trust in him, and love and obey him with all our heart. I also endeavored to show them the necessity of renovation of heart by the power and grace of the Holy Spirit." It was a strange and difficult lesson for the Indians to understand; but perhaps a few of them had heard similar talks from Garry, and it was now an exciting experience for all of them to listen to it from the lips of the American teacher. His talk was perhaps not clear, and where it would lead and what it would accomplish could not yet be told. But Parker's voice must have rung with earnestness and drama, and the Indians listened to the sounds of his words in spellbound silence, except "when some truth arrested their mind forcibly, a little humming sound was made through the whole assembly, occupying two or three seconds."

Later in the day, at the funeral of an Indian boy, Parker spoke again to the awed Indians, this time on the resurrection and the judgment. When the missionary had finished, Tackensuatis came to him "and said, what I had said was 'tois,' (good), it was spiritual, and now he knew more about God." There was "medicine" in what Parker was giving them, new and so mystic that it must be extremely powerful to those who possessed it in their hearts. It was what the Indians had wanted to receive, and it pleased them. They were proud that Parker was traveling with them.[26]

From Medicine Lodge Creek the group, now joined by Charle's band, crossed the Continental Divide into Montana. Parker became sick, first with a cold and then with a soreness in his breast that became "inflammation in my head," with "throbbing, pain, and fever." He rode stubbornly on across wild and precipitous country, suffering each mile, and wondering whether he was

26. Ibid., pp. 97–99.

going to die. The Indians buoyed him along, persevering in their kindness. Once they stopped to hunt buffalo and dry the meat for their ride across the Salmon River mountains that still lay ahead. They gradually made their way northward and westward, recrossing the Divide again, and reaching the Lemhi River part way down its course. Tackensuatis and most of the Nez Perces and Flatheads, content now in the belief that their people at last possessed a white teacher, left the party to remain in the buffalo country; but about 150 Nez Perces, led by Charle, continued on with the ailing Parker.[27] Miserable as he felt, he was interested in all that he saw, and he took copious notes about the mountainous country. The route led down the Lemhi to the wintering grounds near the junction with the Salmon River, and Parker viewed Bonneville's old fort and the vicinity where Blue John and his volunteers, including Rabbit Skin Leggings, one of the four Indians responsible for Parker's being there, had been killed by Blackfeet in 1833.

As they moved along the Salmon to where the river turned west, Parker fretted at their slow progress. They entered the mountains again, staying east of the North Fork, and headed due north. On September 18 Parker's impatience got the better of him, and certain that he could not survive if he had to spend many more days in the mountains, he prevailed upon Charle and nine other Indians to press forward with him at a faster rate of speed. Hurrying toward the start of the southern Nez Perce Trail, they cut across the high, tangled wilderness, stopping to rest only on a Sunday near the site of present-day Alta, Montana.[28] Parker could hardly walk, and he bled himself, which increased his weakness. "I found my heart sinking into despondency, and was ready to say, I shall perish in these wild, cold mountains," he wrote. But he gamely conducted a Sabbath service for his companions, and sang a hymn and prayed.

The next day the route was even more rugged and difficult. As they reentered Idaho and started on the Nez Perce Trail, the southernmost of the Indians' routes across the Bitterroots, he wrote, "Parts of the way the ascent and descent was at an angle of 45° and some places even more steep; and sometimes on the verge of dizzy precipices; sometimes down shelves of rocks where my Indian horse would have to jump from one to another; and in other places where he would brace himself upon all fours and slide down; and

27. Many Nez Perces, possibly including the members of Tackensuatis' band, showed up now and then at Wyeth's newly built Fort Hall during the summer and fall to trade dried meat and buffalo tongues.

28. Stanley Davison, "Worker in God's Wilderness," *Montana, Magazine of Western History*, 7 (January, 1957), pp. 8–17, tried to work out the exact route taken by Parker and the Indians from Pierre's Hole to the southern Nez Perce Trail. However, additional studies, still unpublished, disagree with some of Davison's conclusions.

I had become so weak that I could not walk on foot, but was obliged to keep upon his back."

The torment went on for a week, as they crossed ridge after ridge, pushed along steep hillsides covered with fallen trees, passed the Selway River, and finally reached the upper waters of the Clearwater. On September 27, another Sunday, Parker took a pint of blood from his arm, but somehow still possessed enough strength to conduct religious services both in the morning and afternoon. Charle, too, encouraged him that day. The chief, Parker said, had prayed every morning and evening with his men, and had also asked a blessing whenever they ate. Now, he took Compo, the interpreter, and sitting down by Parker's side, said, "We are now near our country, and when we come into it, I wish you to look over it, and see if it is good for missionaries to live in. I know but little about God—my people know but little—I wish my people to know more about God."

The next day they came to the end of the mountains, and Parker suddenly felt much better. They made a long ride, and in the afternoon reached some Nez Perce lodges on the South Fork of the Clearwater. As the Indians welcomed them with a feast of dried salmon, Parker "rejoiced to find myself wholly through the Salmon river mountains, and convalescent." The poor man was tottering and emaciated, but his strong heart drove him forward, and with his little Indian troupe he continued down the Clearwater and across the high country from Kamiah to the villages near the Snake River. Indians greeted him as he passed their lodges; and wherever they paused, Charle, with a show of self-importance that gave Parker the impression that he was "their first chief," explained the object of the missionary's presence.

"A squalid looking Indian" ferried them across the Snake in a canoe, and they continued down that river past the confluence of the Clearwater. At the point where the two rivers joined, the site of present-day Lewiston, Idaho—which Donald McKenzie some twenty-three years before had selected as the best location for a fur-trading post—Parker studied the broad banks under the tall, bare hills and noted that the area "combines many advantages for a missionary station." He was feeling decidedly stronger now, and at Alpowa, near the home village of Hemene Ilppilp (Red Wolf), whom Bonneville had visited, he started overland for Walla Walla, remarking the next day that "no country can possess a climate more conducive to health." October 4 was again a Sunday, and Nez Perces from three nearby lodges attended his services. The next day he reached the Walla Walla River, and on October 6, forty-five days after Parker had left the rendezvous, Pierre Pambrun greeted him at the gate of Fort Walla Walla. "I never felt more joy," the missionary said. "I felt that I had great cause of thankfulness, that God, in his great mercy, and by his watchful providence, had brought me in safety and with restored health to this place."

He sank down in the comfort of a chair and ate at a table "upon which was placed ducks, bread and butter, sugar and milk." He had arrived at the fort from the Snake country over a mountainous Indian route that the Hudson's Bay Company had never taken, and Pambrun would have been interested to know all about it. But Parker did not tarry long. His goal was Fort Vancouver, and he was anxious to get there. He settled with Compo, gave presents to his Nez Perce friends and, promising to return to them, departed in a canoe with three Wallawalla Indians for Fort Vancouver.[29] On October 16, 1835, he arrived at the Hudson's Bay Company headquarters, where Dr. McLoughlin "received me with many expressions of kindness, and invited me to make his residence my home for the winter, and as long as it would suit my convenience. Never," he added gratefully, "could such an invitation be more thankfully received."

During the winter he did make the fort his home, but managed to do considerable sight-seeing through the country of the lower Columbia. He visited the mouth of the river, toured the Willamette Valley, and paid a call on Jason and Daniel Lee at their mission. The fertile and pleasant Willamette intrigued him. At the falls of the river he wondered, "Can the period be far distant, when there will be here a busy population? . . . I called to remembrance that in the year 1809 I stood by the falls of Genesee river, and all was still except the roar of the cataract. But it is not so now; for Rochester stands where I then stood." He was another advance prospector of American Manifest Destiny; near where he stood and mused by the Willamette falls is present-day Portland, Oregon.

Parker found time also during the winter to gain perspective about the Northwest Indian tribes. The natives of the lower Columbia, he thought, were miserable souls. "Since 1829, probably seven-eighths if not, as Doct. McLoughlin believes, nine-tenths, have been swept away by disease." Let the Lees administer to the pitiful remnants, Parker thought. He was far more attracted to the Nez Perces of the interior, whom he described in nostalgic retrospect as "truly dignified and respectable in their manners and general appearance . . . and have much of the proud independence of freemen." Those upriver Indians were "far more neat than those of the lower coun-

29. Beidleman, "Nathaniel Wyeth's Fort Hall," p. 237, says a trapper named Baptiste Bonaparte "rode express" to Samuel Parker, apparently from Fort Hall to Fort Walla Walla sometime late that summer or early in the fall, but he fails to indicate the nature of his message or mission. Parker gave no hint that he had contact with the Snake country trappers and traders, once he left Bridger at Pierre's Hole.

try . . . They are cheerful and often gay, sociable, kind, and affectionate; and anxious to receive instruction in whatever may conduce to their happiness here or hereafter."

He cast a challenge at racial superiority theorists by declaring that he "saw no special difference between them and other nations. As a part of the human family, they have the same natural propensities and the same social affections . . . It is worse than idle to speak of 'physical insensibility inwrought into the animal nature of the Indians, so that their bodies approximate to the insensibility of horses' hoofs.' The influence of this kind of remarks," he wrote reprovingly, "is to produce, in the bosoms of all who read them, the same insensibility which is charged upon the native character of the Indians." Finally, he seconded the verdict of the trappers: the Nez Perces and Flatheads were "kind to strangers, and remarkably so to each other . . . they are scrupulously honest in all their dealings, and lying is scarcely known. They say they fear to sin against the Great Spirit, and therefore, they have but one heart, and their tongue is straight and not forked." They were fit pupils, in his opinion, for a missionary, and the sooner they received one, the better.[30]

For a fleeting moment that winter, Parker speculated on the future of the region he was visiting. "Whose country is this?" he asked. "The natives claim it as theirs, and say they only permit white men to reside among them. But the governments of Great Britain and of the United States have assumed the right to lay their claims." Parker would soon leave the area, and many of the missionaries who would follow him to Oregon would, like Jason Lee, become empire builders for American settlers. Parker, at that period anyway, was of a different sort. The "deep and intricate questions," concerning ownership of the land, he said, he would "leave for learned diplomats to decide, retaining my private opinion that the Indians have a priority of claim." [31]

On April 14, 1836, he started upriver again, planning to meet Whitman at the rendezvous. He reached Fort Walla Walla on April 25 and found a group of Cayuse Indians and Nez Perce friends waiting for him. Both peoples appealed to him to continue his inspirational meetings, and he remained at the fort for two weeks, preaching to the Indians and delivering sermons on moral and religious themes. "They always gave good attention," he reported, although there was one instance of "opposition . . . A chief of the Cayuses, who several times came to hear, disliked what was said about a plurality of wives. He said he would not part with any of his; for he had always lived in sin, and was going to the place of burning, and it was too late for him, now he was getting old, to repent and be saved; and as he must go to that place, he

30. Parker, *Journal*, pp. 231, 237–38.
31. Ibid., pp. 261–62.

would go in all his sins, and would not alter his life." Parker accepted it philosophically as proof of "the truth of the scriptures, that the Savior is set for the fall and rising of those who hear."

On May 9, accompanied by several Nez Perces who had ridden from their own country to get him, he set out for the Clearwater River. The group reached Alpowa after three days of travel, and stopped at a small settlement of Nez Perces. That night a little Indian girl died, and Parker participated at the burial ceremony the next morning. The Nez Perces, "probably having been told to do so by some Iroquois Indians, a few of whom, not in the capacity of teachers, but as trappers in the employ of the fur companies, I saw west of the mountains," had prepared a cross to erect over the grave. "But," said Parker, "as I viewed a cross of wood made by men's hands of no avail, to benefit either the dead or the living, and far more likely to operate as a salvo to a guilty conscience, or a stepping-stone to idolatry, than to be understood in its spiritual sense to refer to a crucifixion of our sins, I took this, which the Indians had prepared, and broke it to pieces. I then told them we place a stone at the head and foot of the grave, only to mark the place." The Indians "cheerfully acquiesced, and adopted our custom," he reported, although future puzzlement over such differences among the white men regarding their own spiritual beliefs and practices would one day result in serious trouble.[32]

Parker continued on to the confluence of the Clearwater and Snake, where British fur traders had so often found the Nez Perces difficult to deal with. But times had changed, and news of this special kind of white man had spread throughout the nation. Indians were assembling, Parker wrote, "in great numbers from different and distant parts of the country," probably from each of the different centers of population from the upper Salmon and Clearwater rivers to the Wallowa Valley, gathering with curiosity "to enquire about the religion that is to guide them to God and heaven; and which," he added with a hint that he recognized the gap in communication that lay between a missionary and the Indians, "they also think, has power to elevate

32. Ibid., pp. 275–76. In his thesis that Christian customs among the Indians, which the Americans thought had stemmed from Catholic teaching, had actually derived from the Anglican school at Red River, Jessett (*Chief Spokan Garry*, pp. 69–70) says: "All of the Christian observances and practices current among these Indian tribes of the interior region of the Oregon country are consistent with Anglicanism. Not only that, but they are the very practices which an Anglican layman could teach and tell about to others. The observance of Sunday, the calling to worship with a bell, the keeping of holidays such as Christmas, the practice of daily morning and evening prayers, the congregational use of 'amen,' the wearing of the best clothes (insisted upon by one of the rubrics in the Book of Common Prayer), kneeling for prayer, bowing (not genuflecting, which is Roman Catholic), chanting and hymn singing, grace at meals and the placing of a cross over a grave . . .""

them in the scale of society in this world, and place them on a level with intelligent as well as christian white men." Someone, it would appear, had made an impression on Parker that the Indians' motive was not entirely that of spiritual salvation.

While he waited for the arrival of an interpreter from Walla Walla, he treated the "opthalmy with which the people are much afflicted, not only at the present time, but which I should think is a prevalent endemic. Calomel, applied in about the quantity of one grain to each eye, once in twenty-four hours, I found to be an efficacious remedy." At least, he noted, somewhat like Lewis and Clark, who had also tried to help many of the Indians who suffered from trachoma, "no injuries were known to have occurred from its use."

Sunday came, but the interpreter, quarrelsome Jean Toupin of Fort Walla Walla, failed to arrive, and Parker was at a loss what to do. The chiefs told him that the people wanted to celebrate the Sabbath in a Christian manner, and Parker finally instructed them to "collect the people into an assembly and spend the hours of this sacred day in prayer and singing, and in conversation on those things about which I formally instructed them." They did so, he reported, "and it was truly affecting to see their apparent reverence, order, and devotion, while I could not but know that their knowledge was limited indeed."

Later, his former assistant and traveling companion, Kentuck, who had learned to speak some English from the trappers, came to him and told him that he wanted to describe the different manner in which he regarded the sincerity of the worship of two of the chiefs. Charle, the self-important headman who had guided him across the Salmon River Mountains, prayed with his lips, Kentuck said, but a chief named "Tuetacus" prayed with his heart. The latter was Tuekakas, the Wallowa Valley leader whom Bonneville had met on Joseph Creek. After observing this benign Indian, the father of the future Chief Joseph, Parker wrote significantly, "Confession of sin appears to occupy much of his prayers, and if there is one among this multitude, who it may be hoped, has been everlastingly benefited by the gospel, I should believe it is this man." [33]

The next day, the missionary made a change in his plans. In order to avoid the Blackfeet, the Nez Perces, he learned, intended to return to the rendezvous over the same mountain route by which they had brought Parker to the Clearwater the previous fall. The missionary could not face the prospect of another trip through that rugged wilderness in which he had suffered so desperately; and when he failed to persuade the Indians to go south, instead, by way of the Blue Mountains and the Grande Ronde Valley, the Hudson's Bay

33. Parker, *Journal*, p. 279.

Company route in present-day Oregon which McLoughlin and Pambrun had told him about, he decided to return to Fort Walla Walla, procure guides and assistants, and visit tribes farther up the Columbia that he had not yet met. "I informed the Indians of my determination," he said, "who, though they evidently preferred that I should accompany them, yet acquiesced in the decision and showed more kindness than I expected." They appointed a young Nez Perce whom he called Haminilpilt, who was undoubtedly Red Wolf of Alpowa, to escort him back to the fort; and after he wrote some letters to Whitman and friends in the East, which he gave to the Indians to take to the rendezvous for him, he started back to Walla Walla on May 16.

Riding overland again, he reached the upper part of the Walla Walla River, and decided that it would make "a delightful situation for a missionary establishment." It was close to where Marcus Whitman would soon settle and where in later years farmers would harvest bounteous wheat crops. Parker, again the visionary, was enthusiastic: "How easily might the plough go through these vallies, and what rich and abundant harvest might be gathered by the hand of industry." The "hand of industry" that he saw, however, was that not of the white man but of the civilized Indian, for "a mission located on this fertile field," he said, "would draw around an interesting settlement, who would fix down to cultivate the soil, and to be instructed."

At Walla Walla, Parker enlisted the services of two French voyageurs and some Indian guides, and set out to visit the Spokans. He followed the fur traders' route to the crossing of the Snake at the Palouse River, continued up that stream, and struck off across he prairies to the ruins of the Spokane House.[34] Among the Spokans, Parker met Spokan Garry, who assisted him as interpreter at a gathering of the Indians. Some Nez Perces were also present, and a Nez Perce leader who understood the Spokan language "collected his people a little back of the Spokeins, and translated the discourse as it was delivered." Parker also saw a garden of potatoes, peas, beans, and other vegetables, growing at a Spokan village, the result of the Hudson's Bay Company's teaching, and "the first," the missionary noted, that "I had seen springing up under Indian industry west of the mountains." He recorded that the Spokan country would provide an ideal site for another mission station, and went on farther north to visit Fort Colvile, everywhere meeting Indians who showed the results of Garry's religious influence among various Salish peoples. From the Colvile post, he started down the Columbia, exploring part of the Grand Coulee, meeting Okanogan Indians, and returning at last to Fort Walla Walla.

34. Jaco Finley, one of its builders, had remained living in the area for many years. But he was now dead, and Parker found only one bastion of the famous old post still standing.

On June 6, 1836, he left the interior country for the last time, heading down the Columbia River to Fort Vancouver. He reached McLoughlin's headquarters safely, and on June 28 sailed aboard a Hudson's Bay Company vessel for Hawaii. In December he was able to secure passage on a ship from those islands, and the following May he was back in Ithaca, preparing his reports for the American Board and a book for publication. Marcus Whitman was in the West by then, but Parker's comments about the Indians, the country, and the suggested mission sites were to prove valuable to future parties of missionaries. His book, a narrative of his journey, published in 1838, was the first general account of the Northwest country to appear in print since Lewis and Clark's narrative, and it was widely read in the East by people who were beginning to be attracted to the prospect of emigration to Oregon. In retrospect, two passages in it serve as well as any to describe the Nez Perces as Parker, the pioneer missionary, left them.

"The Nez Perces," he said, "have been celebrated for their skill and bravery in war. This they have mentioned to me, but they say they now are afraid to go to war; for they do not now believe that all who fall in battle go to a happy country. They now believe there is no other way to be happy here or hereafter, but by knowing and doing what God requires. They have learned enough to fear the consequences of dying unforgiven, but not sufficient to embrace the hope and consolation of the gospel." [35]

Parker's generalization in that passage applied to only a part of the Nez Perces. There were many who were still unaffected by Christian teaching, and still unafraid to go to war and die in battle. But some, without doubt, had been started toward a partial acceptance, at least, of new ideas that would eventually turn them against their cultural heritage, make them deny their traditions, and prepare them for the white man's conquest.

Elsewhere, in another statement, Parker spoke of all the leaders and people he had met in the region. "Probably," he wrote, "there is no government upon earth where there is so much personal and political freedom, and at the same time so little anarchy; and I can unhesitatingly say, that I have no where witnessed so much subordination, peace, and friendship as among the Indians in the Oregon Territory. The day may be rued," he added with an awareness of what the white man's civilization had done to eastern Indians, "when their order and harmony shall be interrupted by any instrumentality whatever." [36]

Those words had little meaning for the expanding American nation. Parker's explorations were overshadowed by more dramatic activities of some of those who followed him; and when he died in 1866, he was out of history's

35. Parker, *Journal*, pp. 277–78.
36. Ibid., p. 251.

limelight.[37] Meanwhile, the course of events that he had helped to set in motion had continued to unfold in the States and Oregon. In the fall of 1835, Whitman arrived back in the East, after having left Parker in the mountains, and placed his two young Nez Perce charges in school. Richard Tackitonitis stayed with the Whitman family at Rushville, N.Y., and John Ais boarded with Parker's relatives in Ithaca. Whitman had unusual plans for the mission party that he would take west the following year, and he had to work quickly to have all in readiness on the frontier for a spring departure with the fur caravan. He was engaged to an attractive 27-year-old Angelica, N.Y., schoolteacher named Narcissa Prentiss, and he wanted to marry her and take her with him. Narcissa was a strong-willed young woman, with blue eyes, a fine, full figure, and reddish blonde hair. She was well-bred and intelligent, and was liked by almost everyone who knew her. Parker had met her the previous year when he had been looking for a companion for his trip, and it is believed that he had not only introduced her to Whitman at that time but had aroused in her an enthusiasm to become a missionary herself. She had applied to the American Board and had been accepted, with the apparent understanding that she would wait for the return of Parker and Whitman before being assigned, as a married woman, to a western station.

Although no white women had yet tried to cross the plains, Whitman was sure after his inspection of the West that the use of wagons would make the journey possible for them. Wheeled vehicles had already been to Green River, and he saw no reason why he could not take a wagon all the way to Oregon. His mission, however, required the enlisting of a second married couple to accompany Narcissa and himself; and after many disappointments and delays, he prevailed somewhat desperately on another missionary team, the Reverend Henry H. Spalding and his wife, Eliza, to change their destination from the Osage Indians, to whom they had previously been assigned, and go, instead, to the Northwest. Though the choice was unavoidable, it was an unfortunate one. Spalding was a severe and bitter man of 33, with a thin-skinned, jealous nature and a sudden, furious temper. He had been born out of wedlock at Wheeler, N.Y., to an "unfeeling mother," who had turned him over to others for rearing when he was 14 years old. His foster father had treated him harshly and, when Henry was 17, had cast him out with the reminder that he was "a bastard." [38] He had gone to live with other people and had finally studied for the ministry at Hamilton College and Western Reserve, but the scars of his youth had left him with feelings of guilt and shame.

To make matters worse, he had known Narcissa earlier in life, and had

37. A biography of Parker, utilizing his various reports, letters, and other writings—many of them still unpublished—would be a worthwhile undertaking.
38. Drury, *Diaries and Letters of Spalding and Smith*, p. 228.

once proposed marriage to her and been rejected. He was now married to a
tall, thin woman of 27, with whom he had corresponded for a full year before they had met; but he still harbored bitter feelings toward Narcissa. When
Whitman enlisted the Spaldings, he was unaware of that past episode, although he learned about it soon afterward. By then it was too late to do anything about it, and he could only hope naïvely that it would not interfere
with the harmony of his honeymoon trip west or with the establishment of
the mission. Narcissa, however, was more concerned; and at her insistence
Spalding had an interviw with her father regarding the propriety of the
Spaldings accompanying the Whitmans. Apparently, the meeting satisfied
Mr. Prentiss; but later, Narcissa heard that Spalding had said publicly, "I will
not go into the same mission with Narcissa for I question her judgment," and
she wrote to her parents that, "The man who came with us is one who never
ought to have come . . . This pretended settlement with father, before we
started, was only an excuse, and from all we have seen and heard, both during
the journey and since we have been here, the same bitter feeling exists." [39]

At least, the Spaldings did not attend the Whitmans' wedding. They
started ahead to the frontier, while Marcus and Narcissa were married in
Angelica on February 18, 1836. It was an emotional ceremony, during
which Narcissa, with a fine voice, sang to the sobbing guests, including the
two Nez Perce boys, the hymn, "Yes, My Native Land," whose words went:
"In the deserts let me labor, On the mountains let me tell, How he died—the
blessed Savior—To redeem a world from Hell! Let me hasten, Far in heathen
lands to dwell." The next day, amid tearful farewells, the couple started on
their wedding journey to Oregon.

In Cincinnati they overtook the Spaldings, who had shipped a light wagon
to St. Louis. They reached the latter city together on March 29, and went on
to Liberty, where they prepared for the trip across the plains. They made a
conical tent, large enough to accommodate them all, and purchased sidesad-
dles for the women, twelve horses and six mules, a large farm wagon to carry
their supplies, and seventeen head of cattle, including four milch cows and
two calves. Marcus bought one of the mules for Narcissa to ride, in addition
to a horse, and she was amused when the Nez Perce boy, Richard, shook his
head over the mule and said, "Thats very bad mule, can't catch Buffaloe!" [40]

The party's number was increased, also, by the appearance from the East
of an ambitious, self-assured young man of 26 named William H. Gray,
who announced that the American Board had appointed him to join the group
as a mechanic and helper. Gray had been a cabinet-maker and had studied to
be a physician. He had been a poor student, but he was energetic and healthy;

39. Drury, *Spalding*, pp. 115, 117.
40. Drury, *First White Women*, *1*, 48.

and when he had volunteered for missionary work, the Board had remembered Whitman's desperate search for colleagues and, without conducting an adequate investigation of him, had sent Gray hastening to the frontier. Further examination would have shown that he, too, was an unhappy choice to dispatch to the Indians, for in time he proved to be a restless, impatient fault-finder as well as narrow and bigoted.

Before leaving Liberty, also, Whitman and Spalding hired a young man by the name of Dulin to assist them, and somehow picked up another Nez Perce youth who had reached the States—perhaps with Flatheads from the 1835 rendezvous—whom Whitman called Samuel Temoni.[41] Finally, after they started up the Missouri for Bellevue, where they were to meet the fur caravan, they were joined by a ragged, 19-year-old youth named Miles Goodyear, who had come west to seek his fortune. Whitman accepted him as a member of the party in return for his promise to help Dulin with the horses, and the red-headed Goodyear stayed with the missionaries as far as Fort Hall, when he left them to hunt beaver with trappers and Bannock Indians. Later, as a celebrated mountain man, he built a cabin for himself in northern Utah and became the first permanent white settler in that future state.

Moving up the Missouri, the party was beset with accidents and delays. Spalding was kicked in the chest by a mule, toppled from a ferryboat with a cow, and had his tent and blankets blown away during the night by a severe wind and rainstorm. By the time the missionaries reached the Platte River, Tom Fitzpatrick and the fur caravan had already started for the 1836 rendezvous, but with hard driving, the Whitmans and Spaldings finally caught up with them and joined the rear of the procession. The novelty of having white women along, one of whom was attractive as well as congenial, gave an unusual flavor to the caravan, and almost all the fur men went out of their way to be gallant and protective to the female travelers. Narcissa's letters on the journey showed that she enjoyed herself immensely, delighting in the strange sights of the trip, and responding with pleasure to the attentions of the members of the caravan. Wearing heavy boots and swathed in long skirts, she sometimes rode sidesaddle and sometimes traveled in the light wagon with the frail and ailing Eliza Spalding, to whom the trip seemed merely a painful trial of duty.

41. At one time during the trip Mrs. Whitman wrote, "There are five Nez Perces in the company" (ibid., p. 54). Samuel Temoni (the last name meant "heart" in Nez Perce), whom she described as old enough to hunt buffalo, may have been the Nez Perce later known as Salmon River Billy, who claimed that he had gone east with the Flatheads in 1835. Billy lived on Salmon River at a crossing place later known as Craig's Ferry, or the Craig Billy Crossing. Nothing else is known about the other Nez Perces, who might have been Flatheads, also returning from the 1835 trip to the East.

On June 13 the caravan reached Fort Laramie, and Whitman agreed to abandon the cumbersome farm wagon but insisted on keeping the light wagon for the convenience of the ladies. The travelers were off again on June 21, following the regular fur supply route up the North Platte to the Sweetwater River, pausing to mark their names on Independence Rock, and reaching South Pass on July 4. It was an historic day, embellished unnecessarily in later years by romanticists who envisioned an imaginary ceremony taking place, in which the missionaries knelt on the crest of the pass with Bibles and an American flag. Although some of the members of the caravan may have realized the significance, for the future, of this first crossing of the Continental Divide by white women, there was no halt for ceremony. They were close to the rendezvous area, and Fitzpatrick was hurrying the caravan to do business. As they neared the Green River, he dispatched a rider to the gathering to tell them of his approach, and of the white women who were with him.

The news caused a sensation among the mountain men who were waiting at the Horse Creek tributary of the Green. As word spread excitedly among them, a group of about fifteen trappers and Nez Perce and Flathead Indians galloped over the plains to give the caravan a rousing welcome. Led by the fun-loving Joe Meek, they sighted the travelers plodding along, still two days east of the rendezvous, and, charging across the sagebrush flats toward them, frightened the missionaries by firing their guns in the air and yelling like a band of attacking enemies. As they came nearer, they were recognized as friends, and the members of the caravan answered their shots by firing their own guns. The newcomers whooped back and forth along the length of the column, zigzagging at a wild gallop, jumping sagebrush, and putting on a joyous show for the ladies. When the caravan stopped to camp, the Indians and trappers finally flung themselves from their mounts and shook hands exuberantly, showing a special eye for the members of the missionary party. The Nez Perces and Flatheads had never seen white women before, and some of the trappers had not seen one for several years. But from the accounts of the meeting, it appeared that the tall, dark-eyed Joe Meek, above all the rest, was most captivated by Narcissa and for the duration of the rendezvous behaved like a smitten man.

As they set up camp, Spalding and Whitman began to converse with the Indians. According to Spalding, the discussion was conducted from English to Iroquois to Flathead and Nez Perce, which seems strange, because Meek or the Nez Perce boys could have done the translating. The reference to Iroquois suggests that among the members of Fitzpatrick's caravan was Big Ignace or another Iroquois, returning to the mountains from the 1835 visit to St. Louis. If this was true, it would indicate, in addition, that the Iroquois were at least still cooperative to the Presbyterian missionaries. The Nez Perces included Parker's friend Tackensuatis, who had come down to the rendezvous from a year in the buffalo country, and Hallalhotsoot, The Lawyer.

Both the Nez Perces and the Flatheads were delighted with Whitman's return, and were especially pleased that this time the missionaries had plans to locate permanently among them. One of the Nez Perces gave Whitman the letter that Parker had written him on May 14 from Fort Walla Walla. The missionaries were distressed to learn that Parker was going to Fort Vancouver and would not meet them at the rendezvous, and they were particularly concerned because his letter failed to give them information concerning the country west of Green River, or suggestions of where to establish a mission.

The next day, however, the caravan moved on to the Green River and, escorted by Meek's welcoming committee, reached the rendezvous on July 6. The greeting on the plains was only a prelude to the reception at Horse Creek. Indians and trappers crowded around the missionaries, and Narcissa and Eliza were overwhelmed by the friendliness of the Nez Perce women, who examined their clothes and equipment, as well as the wagon, and who, said Eliza, "were not satisfied, short of saluting Mrs. Whitman and myself with a kiss," which was the way the trappers had told them that white women greeted each other. The Indians also found interest in the missionaries' cattle, and studied the animals with admiration and wonder, while the mountain men put on an unusual performance of their own. Many of them amazed Whitman by their restrained conduct and by the willingness with which they took the Bibles offered them by Narcissa and Eliza, and accepted Spalding's invitation to join in the missionaries' daily devotions. Some of the men, including William Craig and Robert Newell, two trappers who had been in the mountains since 1829, suggested that if the missionaries got a station safely established on the Columbia, they might come down and settle near it. Joe Meek who, according to Gray, had a native wife and an infant son just learning to speak, but who could already say, "God damn you," was particularly interested in the possibility of having an edifying environment in which to settle in later years. And to underscore the point, he hovered continually about Narcissa, making himself useful in the missionaries' camp and regaling the ladies with fearful stories of close calls with death from Blackfeet and grizzly bears.

Soon after they arrived, Whitman and Spalding returned the two Nez Perce boys to their people, and Narcissa wrote that "Richard was affected to tears" by the reunion with his friends and family.[42] At the rendezvous were Cayuses, Shoshonis, Bannocks, and Utes, as well as the Nez Perces and Flatheads, and to honor the missionaries the Indians put on a combined parade past the camps of the whites. The natives were "all dressed and

42. Drury, *First White Women*, 1, 58.

painted in their gayest uniforms," said William Gray, "each having a company of warriors in war garb, that is, naked." The long procession, at once
dignified, noisy, and colorful, was composed of both men and women, who
rode by, yelling, shaking rattles, and beating skin drums, and carrying guns
and lances with feathers and medicines fluttering in the wind. The "native
belles," Gray noted, were "covered with beads." The Shoshoni and Nez
Perce girls were among the most beautiful of all Indian women and, sitting
with pride and noble grace on their high-pommeled, wooden saddles, knew
how to show off their handsome riding habits that were colorfully decorated
with shells, feathers, beads, and animals' teeth.

As the rendezvous progressed, Whitman and Spalding found themselves in a
quandary over what to do after the gathering ended. The Indians, fearful of
losing them again, wanted their company to the Clearwater River over the
same mountainous route that they had taken Parker. But the trappers told the
missionaries of the difficulties of that route, and urged them to cross the
Snake plains to Fort Walla Walla where they could get advice about where
to settle, and could also arrange for supplies and assistance in establishing
their mission. Arguments broke out between the Nez Perce and Cayuse
women over which people the missionaries were going to live with, and
Narcissa wrote that "the contradiction was so sharp they nearly came to
blows." The problem was finally solved by John McLeod, who arrived at the
rendezvous with a Hudson's Bay Company brigade, accompanied by Tom
McKay and Nathaniel Wyeth. The British had come boldly into the American
gathering that year, determined to try to sell company trade goods to the
trappers and thus make something out of the competition. On their way from
the Columbia River they had paused at Fort Hall, which Wyeth had about
decided to abandon. After four years of desperate planning and trying, he was
at last giving up in the Northwest. He would take a brief look at the prospects
of the Santa Fe trade and then returned to the ice business in Massachusetts,
letting his agent in charge at Fort Hall finally sell that post to the Hudson's
Bay Company in 1837.

McLeod had another letter from Parker for Whitman, and this one advised
Whitman to travel to the Columbia with the British brigade. The missionaries
were glad to accept McLeod's hospitality, and on July 14, accompanied by a
Negro trapper named John Hinds who wanted to go to the Columbia, they
moved their equipment to the Hudson's Bay Company camp.[43] Spalding still
had his light wagon, and the missionaries were anxious to keep it "for the

43. Hinds, who had worked for Nathaniel Wyeth, helped Marcus Whitman build
and establish the Waiilatpu mission, and died there late in November or early in December 1836. The missionaries rarely referred to him, and although he was a Negro
pioneer in the Northwest, few writers have ever mentioned him.

benefit it will be to us when we get there." Although no wagon had ever gone beyond the Green River, McLeod, who showed extreme gallantry toward the American ladies, agreed to take it along, and on July 18 they started west again. The Indians were disappointed that the white teachers had decided to take the southern route to Walla Walla, but Tackensuatis, Lawyer, and a group of Nez Perces and Flatheads struck their tipis and trailed along with them, letting the missionaries know that they would now not be able to hunt buffalo for their winter supply of meat. Spalding said that he tried to dissuade them from coming along, but Tackensuatis, he understood, replied, "I shall go no more with my people, but with you; where you settle I shall settle."

Though the missionaries were impressed with the Indians' friendship and enthusiasm for them, they fretted over the language barrier that frustrated communication. Narcissa spent much time riding with Indian women during the day and sitting with them in camp at night. "I am making some little progress in their language," she wrote, but added, "Long to be able to converse with them about the Saviour. They all appear anxious to converse with us & to be understood by us." As she observed the Indians, the lot of the native women distressed her. "They do all the work, such as getting the wood, preparing food, picking their lodges, packing & driving their animals, the complete slaves of their husbands," she noted. Spalding was perturbed by this too, and apparently the missionaries were eventually able to do something about it. Tackensuatis prayed daily and kept the Sabbath, Spalding wrote, and soon he also began to help his Flathead wife with the packing and unpacking of the horses. "Long before we closed our journey," Spalding recorded with quiet satisfaction, "the chief did his part of the labor, rode by the side of his wife and was very sociable and attentive, a thing looked upon as degrading among Indians." The missionary did not recognize that he was causing the proud headman to degrade himself in front of the other Indians. Nor did he attach special significance to another item he recorded, the fact that the Nez Perces referred to him as a "black coat."

The route to Fort Hall via the Bear River lay across steep, broken, and hilly country; and although the Indians hunted for smooth roads for the wagon, which they called a "chick-chick-shauile-kai-kash" for the monotonous creaking, grinding, and clicking of the wheels and dried-out axles, Whitman, who was driving it, found it difficult each day to keep up with the pack train. After nursing the vehicle through deep sand, over draws and sharp-edged lava, down precipitous hillsides on which it often upset, and across shallow streams in which it got stuck, he was finally forced to convert it into a two-wheeled cart when its front axletree splintered and broke.

The tiring labor and the vexations of the trail also shortened the missionaries' tempers. Traveling so close to Narcissa during her honeymoon trip with another man had tortured the soul of Henry Spalding. But it had not been easy for Marcus and Narcissa either, and there had been considerable discord between the two families during the trip. Now the heat and oppressiveness of the arid country, the monotony of the diet of unpalatable dried buffalo meat, a series of accidents and frustrations, and days of sickness suffered by one or another member of the group had them all on nerves' ends. William Gray was of no help, either. He continually criticized Spalding and the Whitmans, bickered, complained about everything, and worked up a hostility toward McLeod and the British that reached a feverish climax when he became sick one day in the desert and was unable to convince the Hudson's Bay men to halt their brigade and wait for him to recover. As he lagged behind, he was joined by the Whitmans, who remained with him until he finally lay down in the sand and moaned that he could go no farther. The brigade by then had got far ahead, and Whitman rode anxiously after it, intending to return for the sick man with the cart which Spalding was driving. Before Whitman arrived back, Lawyer appeared, having ridden back to see what had happened, and he hoisted Gray from the ground. "The Indian helped him on his horse," Narcissa wrote, "got on behind him, supported him in his arms & in this manner rode slowly into camp." Gray was saved, but he never forgave McLeod or the British for their unfeelingness toward him.

On August 3 the party reached Fort Hall, where young Miles Goodyear left the missionaries to try his luck with the beaver trappers in the vicinity. Also, the Flatheads and most of the Nez Perces, after making another vain effort to divert the travelers toward the route that Parker had taken, decided, after all, to head for the buffalo country, and veered off toward Henry's Fork. Tackensuatis and a few of the Nez Perces, including Lawyer and Parker's friend Kentuck, remained behind, agreeing to help the missionaries drive their cattle, and on August 4 they all started west again along the Snake River.[44] It was the hottest time of the year, and the shimmering heat waves, rising from the lava and sagebrush plain, caused Narcissa to write, "the Heavens over us were brass & the earth iron under our feet." Still, they struggled on with their cattle and cart and on August 19 reached the little post of Snake Fort that McKay had built on the Boise River. There the weary Whitman was at last persuaded to leave his battered two-wheeled cart.

Crossing the Snake, they started up the west side of the river, where tensions and difficulties finally made them decide to separate. Their footsore stock was traveling too slowly for McLeod, and he pushed ahead with the Whitmans and Gray, who agreed that some of them ought to speed their progress if

44. Kentuck, according to Whitman, "did not do well," and soon left the mission party (Drury, *First White Women*, *1*, 80 n.).

they hoped to catch Parker before he left Fort Vancouver for Hawaii. The Spaldings and the Indians followed with the animals and most of the baggage, and the party crossed the Grande Ronde and the steep, forested slopes of the Blue Mountains in two groups. The Whitmans reached Fort Walla Walla on September 1, but two days later, while they were still resting there, the Spaldings arrived with Tackensuatis, the other Indians, and the livestock.

Pambrun gave them a cordial welcome and, with unconcealed admiration for the first white women to come across the continent, put the post's rough facilities at their disposal. The missionaries also met Parker's interpreter Charles Compo, who added another tale to the ones they had been hearing about the niggardliness of the elderly divine. Compo's complaint was that after he had given up his chance to trap beaver for an entire year in order to assist Parker, he had been paid only $18 in Indian goods by the old man and had then been left stranded at Walla Walla when Parker had decided not to return to the rendezvous. Destitute, he had been forced to accept employment from the Hudson's Bay Company.

There was no message at the post from Parker, and Pambrun advised the Whitmans to accompany him to Fort Vancouver, where the minister might still be waiting for them. The Spaldings decided to go along with them, since nothing could "be done by either of the party about location, untill the Indians return from their Summer hunt"; and on September 6, promising to return to Takensuatis, Lawyer, and the other Nez Perces, including the youths, Richard and John, who waited at Walla Walla, they started by boat, together again, down the Columbia. Six days later they reached the big post, and were welcomed graciously by Dr. McLoughlin, who made them comfortable in his own house and treated them to fresh vegetables, fruits, and other luxuries of civilization that they had done so long without.

To their bitter disappointment they found that Parker had already left the mainland for Hawaii, but McLoughlin told them that Parker had suggested the Walla Walla and Clearwater rivers as suitable locations for a mission. Gray, whom McLoughlin had greeted as a subordinate member of the missionary party and who therefore felt himself slighted by the caste-conscious chief factor, had by that time worked up a hearty dislike for all Hudson's Bay Company people and later said that there was a discussion about establishing a station in the Cowlitz or Puget Sound districts, but that the British had not approved of those sites because they were north of the Columbia. Besides, he recounted, Pambrun argued for the Nez Perces and Cayuses, and "his interests and arguments prevailed." McLoughlin apparently offered no objection to an inland establishment, although it was later said that he had done so to Jason Lee two years before, and, in fact, he assured the missionaries that they could obtain all the supplies and equipment they would need for such a station from the stores at Fort Vancouver. While the men returned upriver to select a site and erect buildings in which to live, it was decided that the women would rest at the fort.

Even before Spalding, Whitman, Gray, and Pambrun started up the Columbia in boats heavily laden with supplies, the missionaries had agreed that there would be two stations. The Spaldings and Whitmans, who had continued their quarreling, had realized that they could not live together. Narcissa, who was now pregnant and who undoubtedly loathed Spalding for his unconcealed envy and ill will, must have been firm on that point with Marcus. When the men reached Fort Walla Walla, they found that the Nez Perces had gone back to their own country but had left word that they would return for the missionaries. Without waiting for them, Spalding, Whitman, and Gray took Pambrun's advice and with two Cayuse Indians and a member of the post as guides explored up the Walla Walla River with a packhorse loaded with camping equipment, looking for a suitable mission location for the Whitmans.

They were in country belonging to one of the bands of Cayuse, some of whose people had told Parker the year before that they wanted a missionary, and at this year's rendezvous had favorably struck the Whitmans and Spaldings with their pleadings that the two families settle on their lands. On October 5 Whitman selected a spot about twenty-two miles upriver, near the mouth of a small creek that flowed into the main stream. A few Indians who showed up around the camp in the evening to stare at them called the region Waiilatpu, "place of the rye grass." Most of the visitors were Cayuses, but with them was an influential leader of the Wallawallas who lived lower down near the mouth of the Walla Walla River. His name was Peopeo Moxmox (Yellow Bird), and he was a strong and intelligent man of dignified bearing. Accompanying him was his 12-year-old son who had been attending Jason Lee's Willamette Valley mission school, where the Methodists had baptized him, given him the name Elijah Hedding, and taught him some English. The newly arrived missionaries at Waiilatpu failed to record their meeting that first night with the Wallawalla father and son, but they would soon come to know both of them well.

The next day the party marked the site with a stake and returned to Fort Walla Walla. Tackensuatis and some twenty or thirty Nez Perces had meanwhile ridden back with extra horses to conduct the missionaries to their own country, and they were distressed to find that some of the American teachers had decided to settle among the Cayuses and let those people share the knowledge of the white men's powers, which the Nez Perces had hoped to acquire alone. The Cayuses, they were quick to inform the missionaries, were bad and untrustworthy people. Marcus wrote to Narcissa, repeating their warnings, and she, in turn, without fully comprehending the Indians' motives, noted in her diary that the Nez Perces "do not like to have us stop with the Cayouses. Say *they* do not have difficulty with the white men as the Cayouses do & that we shall find it so."

Despite the Nez Perces' appeals, Whitman and Spalding directed Gray to start moving supplies out to the Waiilatpu location and begin building a house, while they traveled to the Nez Perces' country to search for a site for the Spaldings. Before they left, however, they apparently agreed to a demand which Gray had been pressing upon them ever since they had come upriver from Fort Vancouver. Not wishing to continue in a subordinate position, Gray had been asking for the right to establish a mission of his own; and at Fort Walla Walla it seems that Whitman and Spalding finally promised to let him open a station in the Flathead country after he helped them get the Cayuse and Nez Perce missions built.[45] On October 8 Gray went happily back to Waiilatpu, and Whitman and Spalding set out for the Clearwater River with Tackensuatis and the Nez Perces. The youths, Richard and John, were probably not with them, for during the journey Spalding attempted to hold services, but found it difficult to communicate with the natives. "Oh that I may soon be settled among them, and master of their language, so as to point them to the Lamb of God that taketh away the sins of the world," he wrote.

At the mouth of the Clearwater they reported witnessing a large group of Nez Perces assembled on their knees in a circle, saying the Lord's Prayer. Spalding understood that they had learned it from Parker. The latter had thought that the juncture of the Clearwater and Snake would make a good location for a mission, but Tackensuatis had another site in mind, and he led Whitman and Spalding up the Clearwater about twelve miles to where a small stream flowed into the river from the south. It was called Lapwai, "place of the butterflies." The bare hills around the junction rose more than a thousand feet close to the riverbanks, leaving little room for cultivation. Spalding was distressed and wrote, "The appearance of the country for the last half day greatly discouraged us. It was very mountainous and broken; the vallies were narrow and without good soil. As we drew near the place we were still more discouraged . . . I was riding far behind, almost disheartened. I thought it was all over with the poor Nez Perces. To take them from their country would prove ruinous to the nation, and to commence an establishment, without soil or timber, would prove equally ruinous to the mission." However, Tackensuatis turned up the valley of the Lapwai, and after about two miles, "with his hand to his face, he turned to Doct. Whitman and said: 'We are now near the place where there is good land, if any where in

45. Ibid., *1*, 197.

the Nez Perce country. Perhaps it will not answer, but if it does I am happy. This is all my country and where he (meaning myself) [Spalding] settles, I shall settle. And he need not think he will work by himself: only let us know what he wants done, and it shall be done.' " [46]

Unless Spalding misunderstood him, Tackensuatis, who was from the region of present-day Stites on the upper Clearwater, was speaking broadly in calling Lapwai his country. The site was actually occupied by a group of people under Hin-mah-tute-ke-kaikt (Thunder Strikes, or Thunder Eyes), a civil leader and *tewats* (shaman), who often went to the buffalo country, where he was popular with the American trappers. Later, Spalding gave him the biblical name James. The valley was about half a mile wide, and there was timber along the creek. At the foot of a hill near the village of Thunder Eyes, Spalding finally decided that the soil was sufficiently good, and he agreed with the Nez Perces that this might be the place. "The Indians could scarcely contain themselves for joy," he said, "when they heard us pronounce the word good. They had watched every motion with trembling anxiety, as though life and death were at stake." After carefully selecting a site for the mission building, he agreed with Whitman that he would go back to Fort Vancouver for the women, and told the Indians to meet him at Walla Walla in five weeks to help him bring his goods to Lapwai.

The two missionaries returned to Pambrun's post, and while Whitman went out to Waiilatpu to help Gray, Spalding went down the Columbia with a Hudson's Bay Company express, which was on its way to Fort Vancouver from Montreal. On November 3 he started up the river again with the two women and all their baggage and supplies. Almost 125 Nez Perces were waiting for them at Walla Walla. On November 22 the Spaldings and Whitmans parted, and the former couple, guided by their Indian escort and accompanied by Gray, started for Lapwai. The Nez Perces showed them their great pleasure. At last they had their teacher. On the trip, "they took the entire direction of everything," Spalding said, "pitched & struck our tent, saddled our horses, and gladly would have put our victuals to our mouths, had we wished it." [47]

The party reached the Lapwai site on November 29, and for three weeks the Spaldings lived in a buffalo hide tipi while Gray and the Indians helped them build a log house 42 by 18 feet. "It is due to those Indians," Gray wrote, "that they labored freely and faithfully, and showed the best of feelings toward Mr. and Mrs. Spalding, paying good attention to instructions given

46. Drury, *Spalding*, p. 159.
47. Spalding to Reverend David Greene, Secretary, American Board of Commissioners for Foreign Missions, Boston, February 16, 1837. "Spalding and Whitman Letters, 1837," *Oregon Historical Quarterly*, 37 (1936), 113.

them, and appeared quite anxious to learn all they could of their teachers. It is also due to truth to state that Mr. Spalding paid them liberally for their services . . . say, for bringing a pine-log ten feet long and one foot in diameter from the Clearwater River to the station, it usually took about twelve Indians; for this service Mr. Spalding paid them about six inches of trail-rope tobacco each." Most of the logs for the house had to be carried up from the Clearwater, more than two miles away, and the manual labor was something the male Indians had never done before. "I put an axe upon the shoulder of my friend, Tack-en-su-a-tis," Spalding said, "and told the other chiefs to follow me with their men. A shout echoed through the camp, & every countenance said yes. We were soon all at the timber hard at work. Being better acquainted with the use of the axe, the wife of Tack-en-su-a-tis soon relieved her husband from his awkwardness, and he, with the other chiefs and people, applied themselves diligently to carrying timber." [48]

Some of the Nez Perces hung back, puzzled, concerned, and full of contempt for their fellow warriors who were doing a woman's job. But Spalding had already decided that he had to teach the Indians the skills of civilized men as a preliminary to getting them settled in one place where he could work at Christianizing them; and the enthusiasm of those who followed his directions dulled him to the uncertainties and fears of the others who were not sure what he was going to do for them.

On December 23, the Spaldings were able to move into their new building. It was a log hut, divided by a partition into two sections—a living quarters for Eliza and himself, and an assembly and classroom for the Indians. The roof was made of grass and clay, and in rainy weather it leaked mud into the rooms. But the Spaldings had a home, and the Nez Perces at last possessed the prestige of having a white teacher and a white man's house in their country.

48. Ibid., p. 114.

5

"The Scene, The Most Awful
and Interesting"

In THE BEGINNING things went well at the mission. Spalding's immediate problem, food for the winter, was met by the Indians who supplied him with fish and game and rode to Fort Colvile for him, returning with pork, peas, corn, and flour which the Hudson's Bay Company sold him on credit. Crowds of Nez Perces gathered regularly around Eliza and himself, delighted with the novelty of their presence in their country, and watching attentively for opportunities to be helpful. "The Indians," Spalding wrote, ". . . are remarkably kind, possess industrious habits, with scarcely the appearance of the savage or heathen about them. We consider them perfectly honest, and do not fear to trust them with any article we possess." [1]

From the start, both of the Spaldings dedicated themselves to the many difficult challenges of their situation. In addition to struggling with the new and laborious tasks of making their own home in an uncivilized country, without a single white neighbor for companionship, they faced a multitude of daily burdens connected with the mission. Spalding conducted morning and evening prayers, and on Sundays spoke to large assemblages of Indians. Young Richard had gone to Waiilatpu to live with the Whitmans as interpreter and assistant, but John Ais remained at Lapwai, and Spalding used him during the services to translate his sermons. Mrs. Spalding also painted pictures of biblical scenes, and Spalding held them up to make the subjects of his

1. Spalding to Reverend David Greene, Secretary of the American Board of Commissioners for Foreign Missions, February 16, 1837, in *Oregon Historical Quarterly*, 37 (1936), 116.

talks more graphic to his audiences. "My manner of preaching," he wrote, "is as follows: We have represented in paintings, several events recorded in the Scriptures, such as the passage through the Red Sea, the crucifixion of Christ, etc. These I explain first to my crier. I then go over with the subject to the people, the crier correcting my language & carrying out the history . . ." [2]

Spalding's Bible stories and the morals he drew from them impressed many of the Indians, and they repeated them from village to village, so that Spalding was sometimes surprised to learn how widely they had circulated. He also taught the members of his assemblages to sing hymns, using the English words at first but eventually trying to translate them into Nez Perce. Even if they did not understand the words, the Indians enjoyed the gospel tunes, and the enthusiasm of their group singing often moved some of the Nez Perces to tears.

There were also secular demands. Although Spalding had studied medicine for only a few weeks, he was visited by Indians with every sort of ailment. "I am no physician," he wrote sometime later, "but have more or less sickness to look after, sometimes eight or ten cases on my hands at once, usually bowel complaints caused by eating bad food or too much of it, or in other words gluttony, requiring, as I suppose, cathartics. These I issue at order sometimes five or six before I am dressed in the morning, not often finding time to go near the patients, especially if they are any distance off; besides by my ignorance I can do as well by ear as by the eye . . . Blood letting is a favorite remedy among them, and I often go by the lot, opening five or six at a time and go about more pressing business, leaving them to stop the blood when they please. If they cannot get me to open their veins for them they do it themselves with an arrow; digging away until they find the blood from the veins or artery, which they usually dig for, occasioning swelled arms, legs, and sometimes, I believe death." [3]

On January 27, 1837, two months after they arrived, Mrs. Spalding opened a school for the Indians. "Here a scene commenced," her husband recorded, "more interesting, if possible, than any we had before witnessed. Nothing but actual observation can give an idea of the indefatigable application of old and young, mothers with babes in their arms, Grand-parents & Grand-children. Having no books, Mrs. S. with her numerous other cares, is obliged to supply the deficiency with her pen, & print her own books, consequently, she can spend but a short time each day in school. But her abscence does not close the school. From morning till night they are assembled in clusters, with one teaching a number of others." [4] About one hundred Indians attended the

2. Ibid., p. 115.
3. Drury, *Spalding*, p. 173.
4. *Oregon Historical Quarterly*, 37 (1936), 115–16.

classes, most of them women, children, and a few of the important older men who hoped that what they learned would increase their prestige and influence among the people. Spalding was delighted with their zeal. "Their progress is astonishing," he wrote. "Today a stranger will enter the room, not knowing a letter. Tomorrow he will be teaching others." Mrs. Spalding also organized a class of Indian girls, teaching them how to sew and assist in the chores of running a white man's house.

With the approach of spring, Spalding also had to give attention to the planting of crops. His aim was eventually to make the Nez Perces a nation of farmers, no longer anxious to leave their homes to chase buffalo on the plains, but settled happily around him and accessible to his religious instruction the full year. Ignorant of the Indians' deeply felt love of travel, adventure, hunting, and daring against enemies, he could only foresee a future when white men would spread across the West and the buffalo would disappear, and he considered it his duty to get the Nez Perces collected and living prosperously on farms before they endured a tragic fate. His immediate problem, therefore, seemed to be to keep them under his wing so that he could teach them as rapidly as possible and without interruption. "How much grain I shall be able to get in the coming season, I do not know," he wrote in February 1837, "but . . . I count upon 100 acres. This will enable me to furnish a good number with seed for the coming year & keep many children at school, who are now obliged to leave frequently to go with their parents in search of food." [5]

During the cold months he labored to have farm implements ready, and by plowing time he was able to distribute about thirty hoes among the Indians. After furnishing them with seed, he showed them how to break the ground and tend their plantings, and directed them to work a week for himself and two weeks on their own plots. It was a strange undertaking for the Nez Perces, and they were not adept at it. Some of them were aghast at the idea of cutting and wounding the breast of their mother, the Earth, and they refused to accept Spalding's instructions. But others who had seen the Spokans' efforts at farming or had heard about the white men's gardens at Fort Vancouver were less reluctant to try it, and by May 1 the Indians had fifteen acres of their own under cultivation and had helped Spalding set out a nursery of apple trees and sow two bushels of peas, seven bushels of potatoes, and a variety of garden vegetables on his own land. In addition, the Nez Perces so trusted Spalding's promise that their efforts would provide them with all the food they would need for that year that for the first time they stayed home during the summer instead of crossing the mountains for buffalo.

To communicate with the Indians the Spaldings also had to work hard

5. Ibid., p. 117.

studying their language. Spalding thought that he would soon be able to teach the Nez Perces English and conduct his instruction in that language; but in the meantime, he wrote, "the constant intercourse with them in every kind of work, compelled me to use every effort to acquire their language. Frequently while putting up our house, a word must be had, or a stick of timber fall at the risk of life; and on the Sabbath while going over some event recorded in the bible, a new word must be learned or the story must stop half told." [6] At first the Nez Perce tongue seemed easy to him, and Spalding was pleased with his progress. But he proved, actually, to be both a poor student of Nez Perce and an unsuccessful teacher of English; and as the Nez Perces seemed unwilling or unable to learn English from him, and he, at the same time, found their tongue more difficult than he had thought it would be, he became discouraged at the realization that the religious knowledge the Indians were acquiring from him was full of misunderstandings and errors.

His inability to communicate as well as he wished was overshadowed by an even more serious deficiency, his lack of understanding of the Indians' cultural background and habits of thinking. He was more aware than the Whitmans were that such a gap existed between the missionary families and the Indians, but he had no interest in trying to bridge the gulf on the Indians' terms, and was intolerant of native beliefs and practices that he did not understand or of which he failed to approve. His well-meant dedication to the uplifting of the Nez Perces was often harmed by his sudden bursts of anger at Indians who seemed to disobey or ignore his directions. He had learned that the Hudson's Bay Company traders had sometimes employed headmen to use the lash on unruly members of their own bands around the British posts, and in his impatience and fits of temper he began to threaten to whip Nez Perces who displeased him. By their silence, some of the leading Indians appeared to offer no objection to his use of a whip, and when, on occasion, some of them seemed to side with him in his quarrels with more independent-minded younger men, his threats became a reality. Such punishment, however, was alien to the Nez Perces, who maintained discipline by voluntary action and showed disapproval of offenders by shaming or ostracizing them; and Spalding's use of the lash dismayed them. Sometimes Spalding did the whipping himself, but often he copied the method of the Hudson's Bay Company and tried to get leading men to administer the punishment. Although a few of them obliged him, they had never before assumed responsibility for the actions of one of their own people, and each time Spalding got out his whip and directed them to execute a sentence of fifty or seventy-five lashes on a young man whom he had judged insolent or guilty of a misdeed, they were torn with distress.

It was a remarkable manner for a man of God to conduct himself with In-

6. Ibid., p. 115.

ST. JO

ST. MARIES' R.

PALOUSE R.

COLUMBIA R.

SNAKE R.

TUCANNON R.

N. FORK

Lewiston

POTLATCH R.

8

CLEARWATER R.

11

ALPOWA CR.

2nd Spalding
Mission, 1838-47

We
Pr

TOUCHET R.

9

10

1st Spalding
Mission, 1836-38

Asotin

LAPWAI CR.

Whitman
Mission
(Waiilatpu),
1836-47

7

12

Smith, 1839-41

13

Ka

Fort
Walla Walla

1

2

Craig,
1840

LAWYERS CR.

WALLA

Camas
Prairie

3

WALLA R.

GRANDE RONDE R.

SALMON R.

UMATILLA R.

4

6

16

JOSEPH CR.

BLUE MTS.

WALLOWA R.

5

IMNAHA R.

SNAKE RIVER

Hells Canyon

Pa
La

Wallowa
Lake

WALLOWA MTS.

LITTLE SALMON R.

POWDER R.

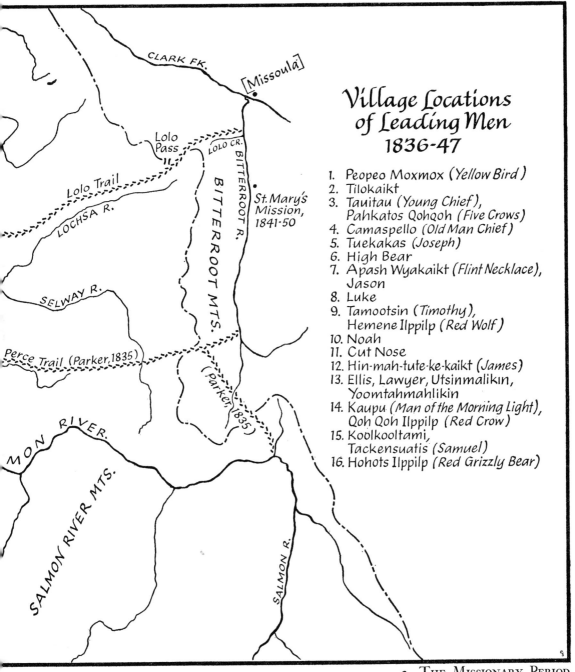

Village Locations of Leading Men 1836-47

1. Peopeo Moxmox (*Yellow Bird*)
2. Tilokaikt
3. Tauitau (*Young Chief*), Pahkatos Qohqoh (*Five Crows*)
4. Camaspello (*Old Man Chief*)
5. Tuekakas (*Joseph*)
6. High Bear
7. Apash Wyakaikt (*Flint Necklace*), Jason
8. Luke
9. Tamootsin (*Timothy*), Hemene Ilppilp (*Red Wolf*)
10. Noah
11. Cut Nose
12. Hin-mah-tute-ke-kaikt (*James*)
13. Ellis, Lawyer, Utsinmalikin, Yoomtahmahlikin
14. Kaupu (*Man of the Morning Light*), Qoh Qoh Ilppilp (*Red Crow*)
15. Koolkooltami, Tackensuatis (*Samuel*)
16. Hohots Ilppilp (*Red Grizzly Bear*)

3. THE MISSIONARY PERIOD

dians who had invited him to their land to instruct them in Christianity. Spalding may have rationalized that he had to enforce discipline in order to impart the religion of the gentle Christ, which is what it came down to, but he proved that he was no less a conqueror than any of the other white men who had trampled on the rights and dignity of Indians. The willingness of the proud Nez Perces to accept punishment of any kind, particularly that of a degrading whip, was a reflection of their fear of the power of Spalding, the teacher who was in touch with the white man's God. Submission to his whip was an attempt to appease his anger, as well as to atone for having followed what he said was a wrong path. Like the Bible, the whip could be regarded as an instrument of God's purpose, especially because it helped men avoid the place called Hell. In the Indians' tradition there had been only two worlds, the earth for this life and a single hereafter of comfort and contentment. But Spalding spoke in tones of doom and terror of a third world, a dark, wide, rimless fire country, the awful destination of those who failed to abide by his instructions. It was a frightening place, and their fear of going to it helped to bend many of the Indians to the missionary's orders. Young warriors may have smoldered with resentment while they endured the lash, but the rest of the people, including the leading men, were usually too afraid to object or to intercede for the victim.

Inevitably, as the Indians became aware of the weaknesses in Spalding's character, their respect for his authority and teachings began to deteriorate, and some of them commenced to turn away from him. The first serious breach between the missionary and the Nez Perces occurred within a year after the Spaldings had settled at Lapwai and resulted from what had started as a sincere attempt by Spalding to improve their material condition. Soon after the two missionary families had founded their stations, the restless William Gray had held Whitman and Spalding to their promise and had departed for the Flathead country with Francis Ermatinger of the Hudson's Bay Company, intending to live among the Salish for a year and learn whether those Indians would welcome a station for themselves. On March 31, 1837, only a short time after Gray had started on his journey, Spalding and five Nez Perces, making a trip to Fort Colvile, arrived in the Spokans' country and met Gray.[7] The latter told Spalding that he now planned to take some Indian horses to the States that summer to exchange for cattle for the Salish, and while in the East would visit the American Board of Commissioners for Foreign Missions in Boston and ask its members to send out a reinforcement of personnel to help him establish a mission for the Salish-speaking peoples. Af-

7. H. H. Spalding to Levi Chamberlain, Hawaii, October 12, 1837, courtesy the Hawaiian Mission Children's Society Archives, Honolulu. I am indebted to Mrs. Sophie J. Cluff for transcribing this letter for me from the original.

ter meeting Spokan Garry, who impressed him with the Spokans' desire for a station of their own, Spalding gave his support to Gray's proposal, but partly because it also coincided with his own thoughts. His Nez Perces had been fascinated with the white man's cattle and wanted stock of their own, and Spalding was anxious to help them get started raising herds so that they would lose their desire to hunt buffalo.

When he went back to Lapwai, Spalding discussed the idea with the leading Nez Perces, and finally prevailed on a number of them to give him some horses which Gray would take to the States to trade for cattle for them. In addition, four Indians agreed to make the trip with Gray to help him bring back the animals. Among them were Ellice (whose name Spalding and other Americans spelled Ellis) and two headmen named Blue Cloak and The Hat, the latter of whom had acquired his name when he had begun wearing a tall silk hat that a fun-loving mountain man had given him.[8] Ellis, who had been back from the Red River school for almost four years, was now 27 years old, and his knowledge of the white men's customs and language, together with the fact that he was the grandson of the respected Hohots Ilppilp, made him an important civil leader. Before the Nez Perces departed, Spalding and Gray also sent messages to Whitman to see if some Cayuses would want to go along.

Whitman had not been having an easy time with his Indians. First, he had discovered that he had built his mission on ground claimed by an elderly headman named Umtippe. The Cayuse was used to the cool formality of the British traders at Fort Walla Walla, who paid for what they received, and he must have expected a liberal reward from the newly arrived Americans, who had a reputation for being more generous than the British. When nothing but words were forthcoming, Umtippe became disillusioned and resentful. Narcissa, with no understanding of the Indians' past relations with British and American traders, reacted to his unfriendliness by writing that he was full of "hypocracy deceit and guile . . . a mortal beggar as all Indians are. If you ask a favour of him, sometimes it is granted or not just as he feels, if granted it must be well paid for." [9]

The Whitmans were allowed to stay put, and Umtippe died shortly afterward. But the Waiilatpu mission had started its activities on the wrong foot. By their treatment of Umtippe, the Whitmans had served notice on all the Cayuses that they were a different type of "Bostons." They were not only not "big hearts," like the trappers in the mountains, but they were stingy and hollow-talking people, who took whatever they wanted without paying for it. As a result, it soon seemed to the Whitmans that the Cayuses were less in-

8. M. Morgan Estergreen, *Kit Carson* (Norman, Okla., 1962), p. 74.
9. Drury, *First White Women*, *1*, 123.

terested in having a missionary among them than they had earlier indicated. A number of boys showed up to stare curiously at the Whitmans' family worship and to enjoy the fun of learning to sing gospel hymns under the direction of the attractive, blonde-haired Narcissa; but few of the older Indians stayed around the station, and those who did refused to do manual labor. The Whitmans were forced to do all of their work themselves and had little time in which to learn the Cayuse language and try to communicate with the Indians. After helping them interpret Bible readings to the Cayuse youths, even Richard offended them by running away one day with some of the Whitmans' property, which, with his clothes and books, he shortly afterward lost in gambling. When Richard later came back to the mission, Whitman expelled him.[10]

In March the principal Cayuse hunting parties returned from the buffalo country, but Whitman and his wife were again disappointed. For a while, some of the chiefs and leading men displayed curiosity and friendship, and Tilokaikt, who succeeded Umtippe as headman of the Cayuses in that area, professed a warm and generous feeling for the Whitmans. But most of the adult Cayuses avoided the mission station and moved about indifferently at their own affairs, as if no white man was among them. Much of the problem stemmed from the behavior and attitude of the Whitmans themselves. Narcissa particularly had little understanding of or sympathy for Indian habits and thinking, and although she tried dutifully to show interest in the welfare of the Cayuses, she was unable to win the confidence of more than a handful of them. Years later, after her death, another missionary who had observed her at Waiilatpu wrote, "Her carriage towards them was always considered *haughty*. It was the common remark among them that Mrs. Whitman was 'very proud' . . . [She] was not adapted to savage but *civilized* life." [11] It was a way of saying that, like her hard-working husband, she meant well, but no matter how long she lived among them, she could not acclimate herself to the people whom she had come to change and whom she would always regard as "mortal beggars," or worse.

Whitman gave his approval to Gray's returning to the States for more mission workers, but he was not as secure among the Cayuses as Spalding was among the Nez Perces, and he did not think it wise to suggest to his Indians that they send some of their horses on the long trading expedition. "For want of sufficient notice & on account of some horse given to an American Trader by the Cayuses for which they received no return as promised & also on account of some horses given the Rev. Messers Lee finding a disaffection I do

10. Whitman to Rev. David Greene, May 5, 1837, in *Oregon Historical Quarterly*, 37 (1936), 124; and Drury, *Marcus Whitman*, p. 172 n.
11. Drury, *Whitman*, pp. 459–60; and *First White Women*, *1*, 155.

not like to take the responsibility of sending their animals & therefore no Cayuses will accompany him," he explained.[12]

Gray left the Spokan country for the States on April 5 with Ermatinger's Hudson's Bay Company brigade, apparently arranging to meet the four Nez Perces at the American trappers' rendezvous on the plains. Crossing the Bitterroots via the Clark Fork River, he paused with the British at the Flathead House where a large part of that tribe and some of the Iroquois members of their villages joined them. The combined party then moved south along the usual fur route through western Montana, reaching the Big Hole Basin on May 31. Gray did some preaching to the Flatheads and aroused their interest in having him establish a mission for them at some future date. As they continued to travel south, they had troubles with bands of Blackfeet. Finally, Gray and some of the Indians hurried ahead of the slower-moving brigade, halted briefly at Fort Hall, and a short time later overtook another Hudson's Bay group under John McLeod. Spalding's four Nez Perces and their horses were with this brigade, and the two parties, soon joined by some American trappers led by Andrew Drips, went on together to the 1837 rendezvous, which was held on the Green River between Horse Creek and New Fork.

There were Snakes and Crows at the gathering, but few Nez Perces. Most of them had stayed at home on the Clearwater River with Spalding. A small number of them showed up with mountain men, however, and six Nez Perces boasted of a beating they had just helped Jim Bridger, Joe Meek, Robert Newell (whom the Americans called "Doc"), and a group of other trappers administer to a band of raiding Bannocks.[13]

At the rendezvous Gray had no interest in the revelry and trade, but was impatient to be off for the States. For some reason, Ellis and two of the Nez Perces decided not to continue with him, and only The Hat agreed to remain in his party. Perhaps Gray had offended the others. His impatience and officiousness had already got him in trouble with the Flatheads; and the trappers, who thought he was about as obnoxious a human as had ever come into the West, sided with the Indians against him whenever an argument arose. Gray pestered Drips, Bridger, and others to hurry the rendezvous so that Tom Fitzpatrick's caravan, with which he intended to travel, could start for the East. When they would have none of his nagging, he threatened to start out alone. The mountain men warned him not to try it, but his impatience finally got the better of him, and on July 25 he set out for the States, leading his own private party of three French Canadians (one of them probably a halfblood youth), The Hat, Big Ignace, the Iroquois, and four Flatheads. Ignace, who had been to St. Louis in 1835 with his sons, was probably taking

12. *Oregon Historical Quarterly*, 37 (1936), 124.
13. Harvie E. Tobie, *No Man Like Joe* (Portland, Ore., 1949), p. 65.

the Flatheads to visit Catholic authorities in that city. But Gray made no mention of the purpose of their trip, and two of the Flatheads, sons of a war chief named The Grand Visage, were solemnly entrusted to the Protestant's care by their father, who told Gray that he wanted them to learn about the white men's religion and did not want him to "make fools of them by making them drunken and bad men when they returned."

The mountain men thought Gray was courting disaster by starting east alone, but there was no stopping him. He was warned again at Fort Laramie, where one of his white companions abandoned him. But he pushed on blithely, down the Platte. On August 7 the catastrophe of which he had been warned finally overtook him. Near Ash Hollow on the North Platte River, the little party was attacked by Sioux and forced to scramble to a defensive position on top of a small bluff. A French trader who was with the Sioux called across to Gray that the Indians with him only wanted to kill the Flatheads, and that Gray and his white companions could save themselves by coming out and surrendering. What happened next brought lasting disgrace to Gray's name among the trappers who later heard about the fight. Prevailing on the two white men and the youth to accompany him, Gray abandoned the Indians and walked out in the open to surrender. The next moment, the Sioux swept past him and fell upon his former companions. Big Ignace, The Hat, and the four Flatheads were butchered, although they managed to kill three of the Sioux before they died.

Gray and the others were made prisoner, but the next day were set free and given a few horses on which to subsist as they made their way to the settlements.[14] Gray had been wounded twice in the head, and thought himself lucky to have survived. But the Sioux and their French friend spread the story across the plains about the white man's cowardice, and in the mountains the Flatheads and their trapper allies waited angrily for Gray's return. There was to be trouble, too, along the Clearwater when the Nez Perces heard of The Hat's death; but before that time, Spalding became involved in a tense situation of his own, occasioned by the return of Ellis and Blue Cloak from the 1837 rendezvous where they had left Gray.

Those two Nez Perces got back to Lapwai in the fall with their herd of horses. Their unexpected reappearance, ahead of time and without cattle, aroused Spalding's ire. He wondered why they had deserted Gray, and possibly also felt a sense of failure with his Indians for which both Gray and Whitman would inevitably criticize him. At any rate, he railed at the two Nez Perces for having disobeyed him, and accused them of having impeded the progress of the entire Nez Perce nation by having returned without cat-

14. Spalding to missionaries in Hawaii, December 17, 1838, courtesy Hawaiian Mission Children's Society Archives, Honolulu.

tle. In later years, during the tensions of a bitter Protestant-Catholic controversy in Oregon over the causes of the Whitman massacre, Father J. B. A. Brouillet, a priest who by then had been among the Cayuses and was familiar with Hudson's Bay Company personnel at Fort Walla Walla, published a lurid version of this early conflict between Spalding and the Nez Perces, using it as an illustration of the Indians' gradual disenchantment with the Spaldings and Whitmans. Father Brouillet's account was based on what he had been told by Jean Toupin, the Catholic interpreter at Fort Walla Walla. Toupin's religious partisanship and record for unreliability must be taken into account, but the fact that that moment in the relationship between Spalding and the Nez Perces could provide an opportunity for the telling of such a story years after its alleged occurrence was an indication, at least, that a conflict of serious dimensions did take place. Moreover, the tale was never convincingly denied.

According to Toupin, Spalding ordered the Indian leaders, Ellis and Blue Cloak, to receive fifty lashes apiece, and to give him two good horses. When Ellis heard what was in store for him, he simply rode off to Kamiah with his people, but the dignified Blue Cloak, thinking that the missionary would not dare to humiliate him, calmly appeared at a prayer meeting, and was astounded when Spalding directed the other Indians to seize him. At first, Toupin recounted, no Indian moved. Then a young Nez Perce took hold of Blue Cloak, and as he made no effort to resist, solemnly tied his arms. While the others watched in breathless fear, the young Indian turned to Spalding and said, "Now, whip him." Spalding shook his head and stated that he would not do the whipping himself. "I stand in the place of God," he announced. "I command. God does not whip. He commands." The young Indian then called Spalding a liar, and pointing to one of Mrs. Spalding's paintings that illustrated a conception of God, the punisher of wrongdoing, said, "Look. You have painted two men in it, and God behind them with a bundle of rods to whip them. Whip him, or if not, we will put you in his place and whip you." Spalding, said Toupin, obeyed, whipping the chief, and later receiving the horse he had demanded.[15]

Whatever the facts actually were, there is no doubt that there was a sharp clash between Spalding and the two chiefs, and although the period of tension eventually passed, Spalding's prestige among the Nez Perces suffered serious damage at that time. Most of the Indians, perhaps from fear or with the hope of gain or because of a genuine desire to prove their goodness and piety, still remained loyal to the missionary couple, continuing to listen faith-

15. J. B. A. Brouillet, S.J., *Protestantism in Oregon* (New York, 1853), reprinted in *House Executive Document No. 38*, 35th Congress, 1st Session (Washington, D.C., 1858), pp. 18–19; also McWhorter, *Hear Me*, p. 57.

fully to them and to do their bidding. But some of the young men and leaders were emboldened by the incident, and they turned away from the Spaldings to join fellow tribesmen who had already been questioning the Indians' wisdom in listening to the white man and woman. This group was still small, and its minority position made its members hesitate to oppose openly the continued presence of the missionaries in the Nez Perce country. A few of them were shamans who resented the competition of the Spaldings and the eclipse of their own influence among the people; but the others, whose numbers gradually increased, were Indians who became disappointed when their friendship to the missionaries and their loyal attention to his sermons failed to improve their fortunes or bring them greater material rewards than they had been getting from the Hudson's Bay Company. Among this group, in time, was the missionaries' warm friend, Tackensuatis, who decided one day that his goodness was never going to be appreciated. After a quarrel with Spalding, he struck the tipi in which he had been living near the mission and rode back to his own country in the Stites area, farther up the Clearwater. His defection was a serious blow to the Spaldings, who had regarded him as their most reliable friend, and potentially their first convert. Spalding harbored angry feelings against him and characterized him so bitterly that in 1840 a missionary colleague, in commenting on Tackensuatis, said that "he . . . proves to be a very wicked man & now spends much of his time in the buffalo country. It is now very evident what his motives were in being so kind & obliging, & when his selfish expectations were not gratified, he showed out his wickedness." [16]

On March 14, 1837, Narcissa Whitman gave birth to a daughter, Alice Clarissa, the first white child born in the Northwest, and eight months later, on November 7, a girl was born to the Spaldings and given the name Eliza. Mrs. Spalding was a gentle, kindly woman with compassionate feelings for the Indians. Two months before the birth of her child she had won the respect of many of the Nez Perces by an incident of firmness and courage. Spalding had left her alone with Indians at the mission while he had started off with twenty Nez Perces and eighty horses, for supplies at Fort Colvile. A few days after he left, he recounted later, a cry was raised at Lapwai that a war party of Snake Indians was approaching. "Mrs. S. by the glass discovered it to be a band of wild horses, & told them to be quiet. A few nights after, a woman came crying into camp late at night, with 2 or 3 children. The Snakes came upon her not far distant, fired upon her, shot horse through. She said the blood poured from each side as he fell, & she barely escaped with her children. Mrs. S. told them to be quiet, the Snakes would not shoot horses but steal them. That the woman's horse had become tired of its load & stopped.

16. A. B. Smith to Greene, February 6, 1840, in Drury, *The Diaries and Letters of Spalding and Smith*, p. 127.

However, many asked the privilege of staying in the house as they saw the white woman had a big heart, others held their horses by the rope two or three nights ready to flee. Mrs. S.," said Spalding, "slept soundly every night without any fear. The woman's horse was found in a few days unhurt." [17] In addition to observing her qualities of courage, the Nez Perces saw her often trying to calm her husband's fierce temper, and many of the Indians came to respect and love her as a human as well as a teacher. The birth of her child aroused an even warmer affection for her, and helped to strengthen the sympathy and friendship of the majority element of the tribe who still remained loyal to herself and her husband—although Spalding must frequently have strained that relationship.

In April 1838 Jason Lee paid a visit to Lapwai on his way to the States with his plea that Congress take possession of Oregon. While he wrote that he found the Spaldings "getting on well with their Indians," he noted that Spalding had "his troubles with them," used "highhanded" measures, "and when they deserve it let them feel the *lash*." Returning to Fort Walla Walla to join the Hudson's Bay Company brigade to the rendezvous, he reported, too, that Spalding "did not tell me, but Mr. Pambrun says that he was obliged to fly to his double barrel gun to protect himself from some rascals who were laying hold on him." [18] No other account of this episode is known, unless it was part of Spalding's clash with Ellis and Blue Cloak. Although such a crisis was probably rare, it reflected the difficulties into which Spalding occasionally got himself. That spring, after Lee's departure, Spalding had further trouble with some of the Indians when he decided to move his mission site to the mouth of Lapwai Creek on the south bank of the Clearwater, to an area that was cooler and less bothered by mosquitoes. Whitman went farther up the Clearwater with him to help him float logs down the river for the new house; but when Spalding tried to press the Nez Perces into service, he found that most of them labored unwillingly, and he had to resort to constant threats and punishment, including the use of the whip, to keep them working for him. His cruelty during that period must have been severe, for it is the principal example of his wrongdoing that the Indians kept alive in their tribal memories.

By winter, Spalding had finished a new two-story home of cedar and pine logs and cedar shingles, divided into "2 large rooms with fire places, 2 bedrooms & a buttery" downstairs, and "3 small rooms & a store room" upstairs. During the summer, three Hawaiians had arrived at Fort Walla Walla with some sheep for the Whitmans and Spaldings from the missions on the Sand-

17. Spalding to Levi Chamberlain, Hawaii, October 12, 1837, Archives of the Hawaiian Mission Children's Society.
18. Drury, *Spalding*, pp. 180–81.

wich Islands, and one of the Hawaiians had gone to Lapwai to live with Spalding. With his help, and with that of others who reached Oregon with William Gray later in the year, Spalding also erected a blacksmith shop, a schoolhouse, a two-room dwelling for Indian children who boarded with the Spaldings while they received instruction, and a small house for the Hawaiian to occupy. It made an impressive little settlement, but the construction of so many buildings was accomplished only at the expense of numerous conflicts with the Nez Perces, who disliked having to do manual labor and who at the end of the year were smoldering with resentments against the missionaries.

In August 1838 Whitman asked Spalding to join him at Waiilatpu for some intensive religious meetings with the Cayuses. Whitman's success in administering to some of the Cayuses' physical ailments, as well as the impression he made on them through the productivity of his farm, were beginning to gain the attention and good will of a large number of them, and they had even begun to show an interest in his religious talks. Spalding left his Hawaiian assistant in charge at Lapwai and took his family on horseback to Waiilatpu, where he conducted services for the Cayuses each day for a week. At the same time, he and Whitman formally organized themselves into the First Presbyterian Church in the Oregon Territory, accepting into membership their wives, the two Hawaiians who were living with the Whitmans and who were named Mr. and Mrs. Joseph Maki, and the Catholic-born French Canadian Charles Compo, who had been Parker's guide and had settled on a small plot of land near the Waiilatpu mission with his Nez Perce wife. From time to time during the previous two years he had helped the Whitmans and had attended their family worship. Although Pierre Pambrun, who was also a Catholic, advised Compo "to consider the matter well before he left his own religion to join another," the French Canadian willingly received Spalding's baptism and entered the new church of his friends.

Just as Spalding was preparing to return to Lapwai, word was received at Waiilatpu that Gray was nearing the mission, on his way back from the States with reinforcements; and the Spaldings decided to wait and join in welcoming the newcomers. The reinforcements arrived on August 29, and proved to be even more unsuited for the tasks ahead of them than the Spaldings and Whitmans had been. The party was composed of Gray and a woman he had married while in the East, three new missionary couples, the Cushing Eellses, the Elkanah Walkers, and the Asa B. Smiths, and a 23-year-old unmarried man named Cornelius Rogers. All of them had quarreled and fought during the crossing of the country, and they were scarcely speaking to each other when they arrived at Waiilatpu.

Spalding was crestfallen to hear from Gray of the death of The Hat and the loss of the Nez Perces' horses, and worried how the Indians at Lapwai would react to the news, especially after his altercation with Ellis and Blue Cloak. But the Nez Perces, for a time, were to be the least of his problems. The new missionaries were full of frustrations and disillusionments that made them envious and complaining. Their arrival was a misfortune for the Indians, with whom they had no possible chance of finding common ground, but it was also an unhappy turn for Spalding, whose quick-tempered, dictatorial nature would soon make him the target of their animosity.

The Reverend Asa B. Smith and his wife, Sarah, were the pettiest of the three new couples. Smith was a well educated, young man, 29 years old, with an arrogant, superior attitude. He had been born in Williamstown, Vermont, and after experiencing a spiritual regeneration in 1832 had attended the Andover Theological Seminary and the Yale Divinity School. In addition to becoming a Congregationalist minister, he was a militant advocate of temperance. Just before coming west, he had married a woman who was eminently suited to him, a small, prudish soul who seemed to be "a little dear," as one of her traveling companions described her after first meeting her, but who during the trip as well as in Oregon proved to be a vicious gossip and troublemaker, constantly bursting into tears and complaining about her miserable lot. The Walkers and Eellses were little better, although they affected a sanctimonious self-righteousness and piety that made them appear to be more reserved and less malicious. Eells was the sterner and more forthright of the two, Walker—six feet, four inches tall—sometimes betraying an awkward timidity and indecisiveness that rendered him incapable of dealing with the people he had come to save. All of them were strict Calvinists, without tolerance, sympathy, or humor but with an enormous dedication to the cause of ending depravity, of which the earth seemed fuller to them than at any time since the Great Flood. Their companion, Rogers, was younger, more accommodating, and less bigoted, but he had already become prissy. Looking them all over in the East before they set out, Gray must have considered that he alone, among the entire group, possessed the adaptability and common sense to bring the party safely through the perils of the overland trip and the soul-shattering experience of the trappers' rendezvous.[19]

Gray, however, had lost none of his own stubbornness in the East. From the beginning, the year had been eventful for him. After his arrival in the States, minus The Hat and the unfortunate Flatheads, he had gone to Boston, where the surprised Board had given him a sharp reprimand for having returned to the East without permission. By some fast talking, aided by enthusi-

---

19. For a detailed insight into these missionaries see their letters and diaries in Drury's two principal collections of their writings, *The Diaries and Letters of Spalding and Smith* and *First White Women over the Rockies*. Unless otherwise noted, the quotations in this chapter are from those collections.

astic letters about the missions which the Board had already received from Whitman and Spalding, he had won approval to study medicine during the winter and guide reinforcements back to Oregon the following year. He spent about three months listening to lectures on the practice of medicine, affixed the title "Dr." to his name (which Whitman eventually found offensive and made him drop), and cast about eagerly for a wife. In Ithaca Samuel Parker introduced him to a young lady named Mary Augusta Dix, 28 years old, and he proposed to her immediately, pressing his suit the next day with a letter that included the plea that she join him in missionary work in Oregon. "Thousands will immediately feel your influence," he wrote her, "and tens of thousands must in time, and unnumbered souls may bless the hour in which you did decide to devote your life to the Salvation of 6,277,000 natives on our own continent . . ." [20] Apparently inspired by the scope of the challenge, Miss Dix married Gray six days later, and in March set off with him for Independence, Missouri, to join the new missionaries whom the Board had promised would meet them on the frontier. The Board's candidates were all newly married couples. The Walkers came from Maine, and the Eellses from Massachusetts. Both had previously been assigned to go to South Africa to work among the Zulus, but there had been delays; and upon being offered positions in Oregon, they had readily accepted. The two couples had been wed on the same day, March 5, 1838, and two weeks later had been joined in New York by the Smiths, who themselves had been married only two days before.

The Smiths were unhappy even before they began the trip. In 1834 Sarah's sister had been sent on mission work to Singapore, where she had married another missionary. The couple had written to Sarah and Asa, urging them to become missionaries also, and to seek the post in Siam. The two sisters would then be relatively near together, and could occasionally visit each other. The idea appealed to Asa. Siam was a virgin field, and he envisioned himself as a pioneer missionary, opening that remote country to Christianity. He offered himself to the American Board, and was tentatively accepted. The betrothed couple were delighted and began to make plans to leave, looking forward to a pleasant sea voyage, a happy reunion with Sarah's sister, and an important future in the "heathen" but civilized centers of Siam.

During the winter of 1837–38, however, the Board abruptly informed Asa that it could not open a new field in Siam, but wished to send him instead to assist the Whitmans and Spaldings in Oregon. It was a shattering blow to the Smiths, who were now expected not only to labor in an uncivilized wilderness among dangerous Indians but to play subsidiary roles to two other missionary families who were already receiving attention for their pioneer work.

20. Drury, *First White Women, 1,* 239.

Confused and unhappy, they hesitated as long as they could, hinting to the Board that the overland trip might not be conducive to Sarah's health, and hoping that there might be a last-minute change. When it failed to materialize, they finally accepted, but they did not like it, and they never would. They quickly married, joined the Walkers and Eellses in New York, and on March 20, 1838, set off dispiritedly to meet Gray in Missouri.[21]

Rogers joined the group in Cincinnati, and together they continued on by steamboat to St. Louis and then to Independence, where they found Mr. and Mrs. Gray.[22] Smith, who would not be outdone in officiousness, immediately had a quarrel with the man who was to guide them west. "Mr. Gray did not like Mr. Smith's movements," Mrs. Walker noted, "and considering it was the first time, we came very near having unpleasant feelings." It was a portent of things to come.

The fur caravan was led that year by Andrew Drips, who got an unfavorable impression of the missionary group and tried without success to persuade Gray and his party to travel by themselves. Such a course was unthink-

21. Their first serious problem arose before they reached Pittsburgh: whether or not to travel on the Sabbath. In Cincinnati the distinguished Reverend Lyman Beecher advised them not to be too particular. "If I were crossing the Atlantic, I certainly would not jump overboard when Saturday night came," he told them. (Myron Eells, *Father Eells*, Boston, 1894, p. 39.) It was not what they wished to hear, and on the plains their diaries overflowed with conscience-stricken entries whenever the fur caravan refused to allow them to halt on Sundays. Dr. Beecher also had a comment to make about their mission. "Go on and save all the souls you can," he said, "for soon there will be no Indians left on the continent" (Drury, *Diaries of Spalding and Smith*, p. 126). The remark made an impression on the Smiths, who to their other misgivings now added a concern that they were wasting time by going to a people who were headed for early extinction.

22. "Not having time to receive an appointment from the Board [Rogers] came on his own responsibility," Spalding informed the missionaries in Hawaii in his letter to them on December 17, 1838. At Louisville, Kentucky, the Swiss adventurer Johann Augustus Sutter, then 35 years old, came aboard the steamboat on which the missionaries were traveling. Bound also for Oregon, he accompanied the missionary party to Independence, joined the fur caravan, and eventually, by way of Oregon, went on to California.

While crossing the Midwest, the New England missionaries were shocked by the sinfulness of their fellow-Americans. "I must confess that the most high handed wickedness I ever witnessed was seen here," commented the Reverend Walker in one town. "It would seem the imagination of the very devil himself, of which he could be ashamed to be known that he was so wicked, were continually being poured forth. I rejoiced when we left this very seat & I might with all propriety call it the very contemplation of the lower regions. I was rejoiced feeling assured that we could not possibly be in a more debased place on the face of the earth." There is no indication that the Reverend Walker wondered at the logic or propriety of missionaries going all the way to Oregon to save Indians when they could not save their own fellow-citizens at home.

able, but Drips quickly antagonized the missionaries by setting out on a Sunday, knowing that they would not move with him on that day. It was not until the following Saturday that the missionaries caught up with the caravan, and when Drips persisted in traveling again the next day, another Sabbath, the missionaries finally decided that they had better tag along.

Smith was a complainer throughout the trip, but the others were a good match for him. In the intimacy of their close quarters they discovered one another's faults and weaknesses, and by the time they reached the Platte River they were all looking down their noses at each other. "Mr. Smith acted hogish," Mrs. Eells noted in her diary one day. Mary Walker made a more serious charge. "Mrs. Smith undertook to help Mr. W. correct me for dictating Mr. Gray," she wrote. "Mrs. S. tries my patience talking abut Gray as she calls him all the time. I wish she could see how much like him only worse she gets." Later she added, "A strange company of missionaries. Scarcely one who is not intolerable on some account."

When the party reached the rendezvous, the Smiths, who could stand nobody else, moved out of the tent they had been sharing with the Walkers and built a brush shelter for themselves. At the same time, the newcomers had had enough of Gray's orders, and Smith took it on himself to send a letter about their leader to the Board in the East. Smith was a master at character assassination, but in the case of Gray, he reported facts. "What I am now to write I whisper in your ear, but would not say it to the world," he wrote the Board members in Boston. "We have not found Mr. Gray such a man as we hoped to find . . . He is not judicious in all his movements. He is rash & inconsiderate & not at all calculated properly to fill the station he now does—He has assumed a great deal of authority over us, & talked to us in a very harsh & unbecoming, & I may say abusive manner, regardless of the feelings of others, even of the ladies . . . These things have been a severe trial to us."

Gray found other difficulties waiting for him at the rendezvous on the Popo Agie River. On July 4 the trappers' carousing reached a patriotic pitch, and that night some of the mountain men, who had been eyeing Gray, decided to avenge the deaths of their Flathead friends. "We were awakened by the barking of dogs," Mrs. Eells wrote, "soon we heard a rush of drunken men coming directly towards our tent. Mr. Eells got up immediately and went to the door of the tent; in a moment, four men came swearing and blaspheming, inquiring for Mr. Gray . . . They said they wished to settle accounts with Mr. Gray, then they should be off." Gray was hiding behind a curtain in the tent, and luck was with him. The men kept yelling and swearing, and then began to sing. Gradually, they became good natured and tried to get Eells to sing along with them. At length they mellowed enough to apologize for waking him up, and staggered away. The trappers made no further trouble for Gray during the rendezvous, but they let the other missionaries know their feelings about him, and Smith made certain to pass them on to Boston. "Mr. G.," he wrote the Board, "is censured very much by the Company on account of the loss of the Indians last fall . . . All the men who were killed, Mr. Bridger told me, had left widows & orphans. If I have done wrong in writing thus, pardon me, for I thought you would wish to know the facts."

Bridger's brigade had arrived at the trade gathering in good spirits. Just a year before, an American Fur Company steamboat had gone up the Missouri carrying several cases of smallpox among its passengers. The white men's scourge had spread across the northern plains, almost wiping out the entire Mandan population and causing frightful and frightening deaths to a thousand or more Blackfeet. When the epidemic had finally passed, much of the ability of the Blackfeet to strike terror among their enemies had disappeared. The mountain men were filled with rejoicing. There was safety now from the Blackfeet, and Bridger's men, arriving at the rendezvous after a season without interference from those Indians, carried a Blackfoot scalp in symbolic triumph. When they saw the missionaries, the trappers came whooping over, banging an Indian hand drum and flaunting the scalp before the white women. Then they danced, Indian-style, around the scalp, roaring and yelling, celebrating the terrible fate of their enemies, and looking, according to the horrified Mrs. Eells, "like the emissaries of the Devil worshiping their own master."

The gaiety of the trappers was short-lived. Prices for beaver were low, and rumors circulated that the American Fur Company would send no more supply caravans to the mountains, and that this might be the last rendezvous. Robert Newell, who was present with his close companions, Joe Meek and William Craig, had already mourned how hard it was getting to be to find beaver. The streams, he had complained, were being trapped out, and "all peltries are on the decline." Joseph Reddeford Walker, for one, had begun to turn away from the beaver trade to enter the horse business, and had arrived at the rendezvous from farther west with a herd of horses to sell to the caravan. Newell looked around and saw ominous signs among some of the other trappers. ". . . men who had been in the company a long time," he wrote, "commenced leaving owing to the Company being So hard   some run off Stole horses traps and other articles of value." [23]

There were Snakes, Crows, Arapahoes, and Flatheads at the rendezvous also, and many of the Nez Perces had come back again. But even the Indians could feel the effect of the dwindling fur trade. Prices of goods ran high, and

23. *Robert Newell's Memoranda*, ed. Dorothy O. Johansen (Portland, Ore., 1959), p. 37.

the Americans were not so free with their property. Some of the Nez Perces might have thought of Spalding's warning to them that times would inevitably change in the buffalo country, and one Nez Perce came over to the missionaries' camp and sought out Gray to ask for his cow. He claimed that the previous year he had sold Spalding a horse, which The Hat was to take east for him and exchange for a cow. When Gray told him that the Sioux had run off with all the Nez Perce horses, he went away unhappily to spread the bad news among his friends.

On July 8 a Hudson's Bay Company brigade under Francis Ermatinger appeared at the rendezvous from Fort Walla Walla. Accompanying it was Jason Lee with cheering letters from Whitman for the missionaries, telling them that fresh provisions would be sent to await them at Fort Hall. Lee left them to continue to the East, and on July 12 the westward-bound party joined Ermatinger, who had managed to do a little trading, and started for Fort Hall. A number of Nez Perces traveled along with the missionaries, and among them was Joe Meek's Indian wife, who had had a quarrel with her husband and had decided to return to her homeland. Meek had been doing considerable drinking, and when he learned that his Nez Perce mate had left him, he saddled up and started boozily after her. His alcoholic haze might have got the better of him, but according to a story he told in later years he trailed the caravan for several days, almost dying of thirst, and finally on the sandy desert west of South Pass came on "a solitary woman's figure, standing in the trail, and two riding horses near her, whose drooping heads expressed their dejection."

On coming up to the woman, he discovered it to be Mrs. Smith, whose husband, Asa, "was lying on the ground, dying, as the poor sufferer believed himself for water." Mrs. Smith made "a weeping appeal" for water, but since Meek had none, he offered her alcohol instead. Realizing that the couple would actually die unless he could goad Asa to his feet and keep him going, Meek began to revile the prostrate missionary for his unmanliness. "You're a —— pretty fellow to be lying on the ground here, lolling your tongue out of your mouth, and trying to die," he claimed he said, although his language was probably a good deal more intemperate. "Die, if you want to, you're of no account and will never be missed. Here's your wife, who you are keeping standing here in the hot sun; why don't *she* die? She's got more pluck than a white-livered chap like you." Then, according to Meek's tale, he hoisted the protesting Mrs. Smith to his saddle and started on again after the caravan, calling back to Smith, "You can follow us if you choose, or you can stay where you are. Mrs. Smith can find plenty of better men than you." Before Meek had ridden out of sight, he looked back and saw Smith sitting up, and that night after Meek had caught up with the brigade, Smith wandered in also, to the relief of Sarah, if not to the pleasure of everyone else, whose conduct in abandoning the Smiths on the desert was never explained.[24]

Another Nez Perce with the brigade happened to be Hin-mah-tute-ke-kaikt (Thunder Eyes), the influential headman and shaman of the village on whose land at Lapwai Spalding had built his mission, and to whom the Spaldings had given the name James. The latter was not certain how he felt about the white teachers. He liked American trappers, and at the rendezvous that had just ended he had let one of his daughters, whom the mountain men called Isabel, become the wife of Bill Craig. But he did not like Spalding, and after a year of attendance at the Lapwai mission, during which he had tried without success to acquire an understanding of the white man's medicine, he had ridden away again to the buffalo lands. Now he was returning home, keeping a close watch on the new religious teachers who were coming to his country and wondering whether they would do better than the Spaldings. Near the Soda Springs on the Bear River the missionaries prevailed on him to sing one of the hymns that Spalding had taught him. Afterward, they gave him a hot biscuit for his performance. Meek had been watching and later, collaring James at the edge of camp, pleaded with him to go back and get him a biscuit too. James returned, sang an encore, and received another biscuit, which he gave to the hungry Meek.[25]

On July 27 the party reached Fort Hall and found six Nez Perces waiting for the newcomers with provisions from Lapwai. The missionaries were delighted with the Indians from Spalding's station and found them well started along the path to salvation. "It was truly interesting to hear them sing the songs of Zion," wrote Smith, who lost no time in giving them some of his own religious instruction. "They appeared very solemn during these exercises," he said, "and it may be that the Spirit of God has already touched their hearts."

At the fort Meek called it quits with his Nez Perce wife and rode off to rejoin his trapper friends. The missionaries rested for four days, still complaining and scrapping with each other, and Mrs. Walker wrote another letter home, reporting that a room she used in the post "resembles a hog sty" and adding for good measure that "unless someone should like Mr. S. better than at present, he will have to settle alone." Before starting off again, they hired a mountain man, James Conner, who had a Nez Perce wife, and on July 31 they were once more on the trail. At the Hudson's Bay Company's Snake Fort, which was beginning to be called Fort Boise, they were courteously received by François Payette, who provided the weary travelers with butter, milk, and fresh vegetables. The missionaries had abandoned their light wagon

24. Mrs. F. F. Victor, *The River of the West* (Hartford, Conn., 1871), pp. 240–41.
25. Ibid., pp. 241–42.

long ago, at Fort Laramie; but even so, their slow pace made Gray impatient; and with an excuse about preparing the Whitmans for their arrival, he and his wife started out from Fort Boise ahead of the others, and reached Waiilatpu on August 21. The rest, glad of the holiday from Gray but still grumbling with one another, arrived nine days later.[26]

Even with the journey ended, there was no cessation of complaints. Mrs. Eells inspected the Whitmans' house and noted that "There are doors and windows, but they are of the roughest kind; the boards being sawed by hand and put together by no carpenter, but by one who knew nothing about such work, as is evident from its appearance." When the missionaries sat down to decide where everyone would live during the winter, it turned out that the new arrivals "decidedly . . . would not be associated with Mr. Gray." No one wanted to live with the Smiths either, so the Spaldings generously offered to take in the Grays, as well as Cornelius Rogers, and the Whitmans made room in their home for the Smiths. The enthusiasm that the Spokans had shown for a mission of their own in 1837 decided the Eells and Walkers to start a new station for those Indians, and on September 8 those two men left to explore the Spokan country for a suitable location. Before they left, all of the group met to pass several resolutions, including one to accept an offer by the Sandwich Islands missionaries to send them a small printing press and equipment to make books for the Indians.

The Spaldings returned to Lapwai on September 4, accompanied by the Grays, Compo, and Conner, whom Spalding hired to assist him in a new building program that included the construction of a flour mill and a mill race. Rogers lingered for a while at Waiilatpu but arrived soon afterward at Lapwai, guided by some Nez Perces. The presence of so many white people in their country seemed to give the Nez Perces a new feeling of prestige; and they were pleased when headmen from the Pend d'Oreilles and Coeur d'Alenes, showing up at Lapwai to see if they could get missionaries for themselves, were told by Spalding that none could be spared. The Coeur d'Alene chief "said his heart broke & he left the next day, greatly disap-

26. Since the time of Wilson Price Hunt's party, many persons had toiled across the plains and mountains to the Columbia, suffering privations and dangers in order to find and make known the route that the missionaries in 1838 followed with comparative security. Few of them, including the pioneer women on the route, Narcissa Whitman and Eliza Spalding, ever complained as much about the difficulties as did Asa Smith. The memory of the journey was a hideous nightmare to him for years. Long after it was over, he continued to dwell on the torments he had endured. "The trials, hardships & perplexities of such a journey no one can realize but those who have undertaken it," he wrote the American Board in Boston. "I never could be induced to undertake this journey again under the same circumstances . . ." (Drury, *Diaries of Spalding and Smith,* p. 144).

pointed," Spalding reported, unaware that, as a consequence, those Indians would soon afterward welcome Jesuits to their country.

Despite their pride in having the white men with them, some of the Nez Perces were ready for trouble. They had heard rumors of The Hat's death, and when Gray confirmed it to them, they gathered in an angry group at the mission. Spalding's friends and loyal followers among the Indians either disappeared or stood fearfully in the background, while the others taunted Spalding and reminded him that Ellis and Blue Cloak would also have been killed if they had gone with Gray. Once again, the only account of what happened is contained in the publication of Father J. B. A. Brouillet, who was quoting the Fort Walla Walla interpreter, Jean Toupin. According to Toupin, Spalding tried to make explanations, but the Indians became more irate, and finally, as the situation grew threatening, all the whites retreated into Spalding's house. News of their plight reached Fort Walla Walla, and Toupin claimed that Pambrun sent him hurrying to Lapwai to intercede for the besieged American missionaries. He found the whites hiding in the mission building, surrounded by Indians. Toupin reported that, altogether, the Nez Perces kept Spalding's group blockaded for more than a month, and he had to make three different trips from the fort to "induce them to accept tobacco, sign of peace, and to retire." [27]

In later years William Gray, who was one of those allegedly besieged, wrote: "We were two years at Mr. Spalding's station, on returning from the States, and saw the whole Nez Perce tribe, and employed them for days and months, and worked with them, and explored their country to select farms for them, and know that the Nez Perces never, on any occasion, made the least disturbance about the station, or in any other place, on account of the death of that Indian; and we know that neither Mr. Spalding nor any of the people at his place were ever confined in their houses for an hour on account of it; and we further know that the statement made by Brouillet, as coming from old Toupin, is false and malicious, and only shows the ignorance and malice of this priest, who has made these false statements . . . to cover his own guilt in the infamous crime charged upon him and his associates [alleged complicity in the massacre of the Whitmans]." [28] Unfortunately, all three principals in the telling of this episode—Gray, Brouillet, and Toupin—were stirred by intense partisan feelings, and the truth of what happened will probably never be known. Regarding the incident, however, Spalding himself furnished strong evidence that Toupin might have come close to accuracy in what he recounted to Brouillet, for Spalding noted at the time that he was

27. House Executive Document No. 38, 35th Congress, 1st Session (Washington, D. C., 1858), p. 19.
28. William H. Gray, *History of Oregon* (Portland, Ore., 1870), p. 511.

living through a tense period with the Indians as a result of The Hat's death. "It is said they will demand my head or all my property," he wrote. In the end, he recorded that he had to furnish cows from his mission herd to some of the Indians in order to restore peace.[29]

Sometime in the fall two mountain men, the advance guard of others who would become discouraged with the beaver trade and head for Oregon, appeared at Lapwai. They were George Ebberts and Richard Williams, and Spalding gave both of them employment for the winter. They helped Gray and the others complete a schoolhouse and dig a mill race half a mile long, but again Spalding had to coerce many of the Nez Perces into assisting him, and once more there was grumbling and resentment over the manual labor. Ebberts, Williams, and Conner, who understood the Indians better than the missionaries did and had little interest in wanting to change their habits so drastically, sympathized with the Nez Perces and offended Spalding by their rough advice and criticism of his conduct. Conner and Ebberts even moved a short distance away from the mission to live by themselves, but they were at Spalding's mercy for food and supplies, and they insisted that they were anxious to learn to be good Christians and get on peaceably with everyone at the mission.

With so many others to help with the labor, Spalding had more time to devote to the religious instruction of the Nez Perces, and in December 1838 there was a sudden revival of interest in his teaching among many of the Indians. Perhaps Spalding exhibited more patience and understanding, but beginning in the early part of the month large crowds of Nez Perces began to show up on Sundays, and Spalding responded with some powerful and emotional sermons that held the Indians' attention and, when translated, moved many of them to tears. Among the most affected was Tuekakas, the chief from the Wallowa Valley, who had met Bonneville and had later impressed Samuel Parker. Teukakas had been attending the mission for many months, living in a tipi near the missionaries and showing a warm loyalty to Spalding, who had given him the name Joseph. On December 2 Joseph helped Spalding conduct a service, speaking to the other Indians "most affectingly, urging all present to give their hearts to Jesus Christ without delay." Spalding was also aided by another leading Indian, Tamootsin, a mild, sensitive man who had found genuine interest and comfort in the ideas of the white men's religion and had given the name Alpowa, meaning the place where the Sabbath is observed, to his village, near that of Red Wolf's, on the Snake River below the confluence of the Clearwater. Spalding called him Timothy, and in time had the satisfaction of seeing Christianity take strong hold of him and make him a loyal, lifelong friend of the whites.

29. Drury, *Spalding*, p. 201.

Throughout December and January, Spalding's preaching had everyone in tears, including the rough mountain men. On December 18 Spalding reported that Conner "has found peace of soul is happy." Two days later Ebberts was "anxious" and an Indian whom Spalding called Luke "slept none." The Sabbath service on December 23 was memorable. "Before the Sermon closed Timothy was before the stand in tears. Connor gives a brief history of his wicked life & concludes by saying he hates now what he once loved & is determined to serve & love no one but Jesus Christ in future . . . After which Timothy commenced but soon was overwhelmed with grief & cried aloud. Before we closed many more were before the stand, men and women & the scene, the most awful and interesting I have ever witnessed . . ." It went on in similar vein for many days, with high moments reached on the following Sunday, when even young Richard showed up again to confess his wickedness to the other Indians, and on January 3, when Spalding managed to get many of the Nez Perces to sign their marks to a temperance pledge.[30]

Things were going so well that Spalding sent for Whitman to come over and assist him, and the two missionaries held a full week of prayer meetings at Lapwai for the Indians. At their conclusion, Spalding wrote, "Probably 2000 have made a public confession of their sins & pledged themselves to live to God, but few of these in all probability have any just sense of sin or holiness, however many give evidence of a change of heart, & among these are three or four of the principal men of the nation."

Whitman, again, had been having a difficult winter at Waiilatpu, but this time it was because of the new missionaries who had moved in with him. Walker and Eells had found a promising site for a station for themselves about 25 miles northwest of present-day Spokane at a place the Salish-speaking Indians called Tshimakain (the place of springs). But it was too late in the year to move there, and they returned to Waiilatpu to winter with the Whitmans and Smiths. Four families were now crowded into a house built to accommodate three people, and within a few weeks the ill will that had already existed among the reinforcements spread to include the Whitmans. Each couple criticized the others; the Walkers and Eellses could scarcely wait to get to their own station; and by spring Narcissa wrote bitterly to her sister, "How do you think I have lived with such folks right in my kitchen for the whole winter?"[31] The Smiths, as usual, were the most offensive. Smith had

30. Drury, *Diaries of Spalding and Smith*, pp. 248–51.
31. No one was happy. "Find it very unpleasant being with the Indians, the smell of them is so offensive," Mrs. Walker wrote from Waiilatpu. "I shall try to associate more with the Indians & learn of them when my senses become less acute." Regarding her companion, Mrs. Eells, she added, "She is rather unreconciled to the idea of spending the winter here. She does not seem to like Mrs. Whitman very well." Drury, *First White Women*, 2, 130 n.

scarcely arrived at Waiilatpu before he began writing criticisms to Boston, including the observation, less than two weeks after he had been in the country, that "it is very evident" that the hearts of the Indians for whom the Whitmans and Spaldings had been laboring for two years were still "opposed to God & we find them extremely selfish . . . with most of them the character of the Pharisee is plain to see." [32] The Smiths and the Whitmans quickly grew to dislike each other, and it became clear that the two couples could not continue at the same station. A solution was eventually provided by the Nez Perce, Lawyer, whom Whitman had hired to live at Waiilatpu during the winter and teach the Salish tongue to the Walkers and Eellses, as well as Nez Perce to the Smiths. Lawyer talked long and glowingly about his own country around Kamiah on the upper Clearwater and suggested to Smith that one of the missionary families ought to settle there.

After a preliminary exploration of the Tucannon River country that convinced him that he would not be happy locating in that area, Smith journeyed to Kamiah in February, being guided by a Nez Perce whom he called the Green Cap. Three days later he came back to Lapwai, not overjoyed with the prospect of dwelling in isolation at Kamiah, but preferring it to staying at Waiilatpu with the Whitmans. Spalding was distressed to hear of the friction between the Whitmans and Smiths, and he tried to soothe Smith's feelings. When Smith proved insistent about moving, saying that "he would leave the Mission rather than be connected with Dr. Whitman," Spalding sent for the other missionaries to meet with them at Lapwai. They gathered on February 22, and after a fruitless attempt to restore good feelings between Whitman and Smith formally voted disapproval of Smith's request to locate at Kamiah. Then, in an attempt to solve the impasse, Spalding, Walker, and Eells suggested the advisability of having a doctor centrally located among all the missions and proposed that Whitman turn over Waiilatpu to the Smiths and found a new medical station in the region of the Tucannon or Palouse rivers. Smith was delighted with the idea; and although Whitman was at first taken aback, he finally agreed, and the next week rode through the Tucannon country with Spalding looking for a site. When they failed to find a suitable one, Whitman changed his mind, largely because of Narcissa's unwillingness to abandon her home to the newcomers. Whitman informed the other missionaries of his decision, and they acquiesced with him; but although Smith pretended that he was willing to try again to get on with the Whitmans, he was bitterly unhappy and wrote to Walker, "I lament the day that connected me with this mission. Why it is that I am here I know not . . . Should this mission be broken up, I should not be disappointed." [33]

32. Drury, *Diaries of Spalding and Smith*, p. 88.
33. Ibid., p. 95.

The Walkers and Eellses, meanwhile, had packed their belongings and with a feeling of relief had ridden north on March 5, 1839, to establish their own mission for the Spokans at Tshimakain. Left alone with the Whitmans, the Smiths continued to nurse their frustrations and unhappiness, and by the end of April had decided to go to Kamiah, whether the others liked it or not. Their excuse was that they would spend only the summer in that area, studying the Nez Perce language, and Whitman proved agreeable to that limited proposal. On April 17 news arrived that a Mr. and Mrs. Edwin O. Hall, who were bringing the printing press from Hawaii, had arrived at Fort Vancouver, and a week later Spalding started for Waiilatpu to help with preparations to welcome them. At the Whitman mission he found the Smiths preparing "to leave soon for the Lawyer's country to spend the summer in the language." Spalding offered no opposition, and a few days later, while he and Whitman were journeying to Fort Walla Walla to greet the Halls, the Smiths set out for Kamiah, probably guided by Lawyer. It had been decided to set up the press at Lapwai, perhaps because Spalding had had previous experience with printing; and by the time that he and the Halls arrived at Lapwai with the new equipment, the Smiths had passed that mission on their way to Kamiah.

The Smiths settled on the Clearwater River, about sixty miles above Lapwai, in the area where Lewis and Clark had spent two months with the hospitable Nez Perces and made their treaty of friendship between the United States and The Cut Nose, The Broken Arm, Hohots Ilppilp, and other headmen thirty-three years before. A few weeks after the couple arrived there, William Gray came up the river to help them build a crude cedar house with a dirt roof and floor, and without windows. After several days Gray returned to Lapwai, and Smith began his Nez Perce language studies, giving Lawyer and the members of his family food and clothing in return for his labor as their instructor. Occupying so important a position, and receiving such gifts, the buffalo-hunting Lawyer, son of a Flathead father, started a climb in prestige that would one day—because of his closeness to the whites and his acculturation to their ways of life and thinking—see him made head chief of all the Nez Perces.

Spalding had been having increasing difficulties with the Nez Perce language, but Smith, an exceedingly able student, mastered the tongue quickly. While he eventually used that knowledge to undermine Spalding and imperil the mission, he did make an important contribution to all the missionaries by reducing the Nez Perce language to writing and compiling the first Nez Perce dictionary and grammar. Although he had little use for most of the Indians, he also acknowledged his debt to Lawyer as his teacher, and wrote east that "he exhibits more mind than I have witnessed in any other Indian" and has "stood by me during the summer & been faithful in giving me instruction." [34]

The loneliness and rough camp life in the wilderness were a far cry from the dreams of civilized comforts in Siam which the Smiths had not abandoned, and their hardships were much on their minds. "To live a whole summer on the bare ground is something which is almost unknown in civilized regions," Smith complained to his diary, "yet such have been the sacrifices we have made by coming to this region." Later, in a letter home, he wrote that "many a time should we have been thankful for such accomodations as we could have found in our father's barn among the cattle." In her isolation among the Nez Perces at Kamiah, the frail Sarah was despondent and sick much of the time, and Smith had to take care of her and do the chores around the house, while he tried to continue with his studies.

Still, he found time to write complaining letters, and in his unhappiness he began to aim his attacks at Spalding. In reports that had been carried east by Hudson's Bay Company expresses, or via Fort Vancouver and the Sandwich Islands, or on other occasions by persons returning overland to the States, Spalding had furnished the Prudential Committee of the American Board with most of the information it had received, up to then, on the Nez Perces. Despite his occasional outbursts of anger and his frequent clashes with various Indians, Spalding was enthusiastic about the tribe. He liked and respected the Nez Perce people, and he was sincerely dedicated to the tasks he had set out to accomplish for their benefit. He had reflected his optimism in his letters to the Board, and much of what he had written in praise of the Indians' interest in Christianity, their high morals and ethics, and the friendship they had shown the missionaries when they had first arrived among them, had been published in eastern religious periodicals. Now Smith began communicating a different assessment of the Nez Perces, and by assuming the role of an unbiased and objective observer, who having learned the Nez Perce language could judge the true situation, he skillfully commenced to destroy the Board's faith in Spalding.

First, concerning Spalding's report of his wife's devoted schoolroom work, teaching English to the Nez Perces so that they could receive religious instruction in that language, Smith wrote that "after witnessing what has been accomplished towards instructing the people in the English language for three years, I must say it appears folly in the extreme . . . Not a child can be found who can read a single sentence of English intelligibly." About the Nez Perces themselves, whose religious interest both Parker and Spalding had praised so highly, Smith commented somberly, "The accounts given of this people's religious character by worldly men, cannot be depended on—& the

34. Ibid., p. 104.

first accounts of missionaries even merely from their first appearances & first impressions wh. ought not to be too much relied on . . . There is no doubt but that much of this desire has been the hope of temporal gain . . . They are like the Pharisees of old . . . They often tell of their own goodness & labor hard to convince us that they are good. They are self righteous in the extreme. They have no fondness for the plain truths of the gospel. As long as they listened to the interesting historical parts of the bible, they were pleased, but the great truth that all are under condemnation & exposed to the penalty of the law while in their present situation, is very offensive to them.

"No longer can we be born along by the current of popular favor among this people," he went on to warn. "The novelty of having missionaries among them is now gone." But even so, he felt that Spalding's hoodwinking had led the Board into the wasteful error of sending too many valuable missionaries to this part of the world. "There are probably from 3000 to 4000 speaking this language," he noted pointedly, with his mind again on Siam. "The thought of spending one's life in translating for such a little handful of people while millions speaking the same language are sitting in darkness, is truly heart-sickening. Had I known what I now do before I left the States, I can not say that I should have been here." Finally, he took issue with Spalding's policy of supplying the Indians with seeds, hoes, and cattle to get them settled so that they could be taught. It was wrong to cater to the Indians' avarice for material goods, he counseled. They would do or say anything to get hoes and cattle, "and the more we do to encourage their selfish desires, the more difficult it will be to bring them under the influence of the gospel. My only hope is in giving them the pure unadulterated word of God & enabling them to understand it. This & this alone I believe will benefit them in this life & in the life to come." [35]

Smith's analyses of the Nez Perces, which became more damaging to Spalding as time went on, were the result of more than the unhappiness of a misdirected missionary. Almost everything that Smith wrote about the Indians' difficulties in comprehending the differences between the white men's religion and their own relationship to the supernatural world was true, and Spalding, even reluctantly, would have had to agree with him if he had known what Smith was writing. But Spalding believed that he had a duty to change the Indians, and that he could do it, and it never occurred to him to be a defeatist, or to write pessimistic reports to the East.

In his way, Spalding was grappling with the impossible, because he could not get on common ground with the Indians, and failed to realize that the Indians would not be changed easily or quickly. But Smith was demanding that

35. Ibid., pp. 106–09.

the task be made even more impossible. He could make the same objective assessments of the Indians as Spalding, pass them on to the East as Spalding did not do, and come to conclusions about what to do that were totally different from Spalding's ideas, and not half as realistic—showing that he understood the Indians even less than Spalding. If Spalding was to have any chance of success, he had to settle the Indians about him and encourage their interest in Christianity by bringing them along slowly, and on their own terms, as he was trying to do. But Smith, the bigoted, puritanical zealot, could not stand for that. His first and only goal was to make the Indians accept the teaching that they were sinners, condemned by Adam's fall, and that they would remain sinners, headed straight for the fire country of Hell, until they showed, not by words or protestations but with proof of action beyond all doubt, that they had received Jesus Christ in their souls.

Smith was expecting from Indians, with thousands of years of traditions and distinct spiritual ideas of their own, exactly what he would have expected from Christian-oriented New Englanders, and the absurdity of it never occurred to him. The Nez Perces, a proud, free people, living by their own codes of conduct which had always seemed fair and just to them and which in practice were more ethical than those of many white men, could not easily understand the charge that they were sinners because of the act of some white man many thousand years before, and they found it difficult to comprehend how to experience a truthful repentence for a wrong that, so far as they could see, none of their people had committed. At least, they understood and took to heart Spalding's Bible stories and his admonishments to believe and live like Christians. But they could not fathom what Smith was talking about. So they became offensive to him, and because he could not bend them to his will, he turned on Spalding with increasing venom, and accused him of having misled the Board about the Indians.[36]

Spalding, on his part, needed no one to tell him that a wide and frustrating gulf still lay between himself and many of the Nez Perces, and during 1839 his troubles with some of them worried him deeply. In March an Indian threatened to whip Gray, and when Spalding interceded and called some of the headmen together, they too turned on Gray and wanted to whip him. Spalding punished them by refusing to worship with them until they lashed

36. On February 17, 1839, Mrs. Walker noted in her diary at Waiilatpu that the Indians there were "very anxious to devise some way to get to heaven without repenting & renouncing their sins." And a week later she wrote that the Indians on that Sunday were "more noisy & mischievous than I ever knew them. They say the Dr. [Whitman] says they will go to hell any way & they are not going to restrain their children to try to be good any more." Drury, *First White Women*, 2, 145–46.

the Indian who had threatened Gray, and soon he too found himself in difficulties. His chief antagonist was Bonneville's old friend, Apash Wyakaikt, whom Spalding called Meiway (chief) and who took pains to tell the missionary how three years before he had tied up Pambrun in a dispute over fur prices and had learned on that occasion how to make white men do what the Indians wanted. But even James, the headman and shaman of the Lapwai district who was a friend of Joe Meek's and had sung for the missionaries' biscuits at Bear River, became hostile. While "multitudes" of Indians stood around, threatening to tie and whip Spalding, James exhorted them happily, urging them to stop all work for the Spaldings.

In the end, as Spalding put it, it was "all wind," and after thirty-six hours of threats the headmen came to him to "say they have done wrong, ask pardon, promise to whip the man, and wish to commence worship with them again." Spalding consented, but as the Nez Perces, including James, went conscientiously back to work, helping Spalding build a fence, he wrote with puzzlement in his diary, "What is the character of Indians?" [37] The next month he had his fight with Tackensuatis, and as that erstwhile loyal friend rode away, the missionary was even more concerned about what he did not understand. "I do not know," he confided to his journal, "that I ever felt discouraged in the least before in relation to this people . . . Surely many of them appear like another race of beings from what they did when we first came among them." [38]

His hopes centered increasingly on the two chiefs Joseph and Timothy, whose acceptance of Christianity and evidence of repentance seemed sincere. In March 1839 Spalding thought that they showed convincing evidence of conversion. The year before, prior to the arrival of the reinforcements, he had baptized two dying Indian girls at the mission, but since their deaths neither he nor Whitman had accepted a single Indian into the church. Now he proposed baptizing Joseph and Timothy and making them church members. Smith, Walker, and Eells, however, protested that the two Indians had still not demonstrated enough evidence that they had been born again, and Spalding agreed to wait. During the year 1839 he continued to work closely with both Nez Perces, and in July he made a visit to Joseph's beautiful Wallowa Valley in northeastern Oregon.

It was the first time that a white man is known to have been in that valley, just west of the deep Imnaha canyon through which Bonneville had traveled, and Spalding was guided along the rugged route from Lapwai by Timothy and a large retinue of Nez Perces. After crossing the Snake River, he and the

37. Drury, *Diaries of Spalding and Smith*, p. 259.
38. Ibid., p. 261.

Indians rode south across a high prairie and through pine woods to the edge of the steep Grande Ronde canyon, in whose depths they eventually met Joseph and his people. After a Sabbath service along the river, Joseph led them up the opposite side of the canyon to high ground, where Spalding soon got a breathtaking view of the chasm of the Snake River and its junction with the Salmon. Three days later, after trailing through meadows and stands of pine filled with bear and other game, they emerged in the luxuriant Wallowa Valley, threaded by the clear, rushing Wallowa River and backed by the majestic, snow-crowned peaks of the Wallowa Mountains. It was the Alpine paradise home of the Wellamotkin band of Joseph, and while many of the Indians at once went fishing in "fifty or more" holes in the river, Joseph on July 26 took Spalding to see the grandest sight of all, a deep blue, four-mile-long lake, tucked between a high glacial moraine and the base of the towering mountain range. This was Wallowa Lake, beloved by Joseph and his people; and Spalding, who referred to it in his diary as "Spalding lake," was so enthusiastic that the sight of it "paid me for my journey." There were many white-headed eagles about, and Joseph caught one for Spalding, after which the missionary and his host went bathing in the lake. In the evening they returned to camp and found that the Indians had taken "about 600 salmon" from the Wallowa River while they had been gone.[39]

During the following days the Nez Perces showed Spalding all over the valley, pointing out the site of a battle they had once fought with Snake Indians who occasionally came marauding into the area from the south. Spalding was enormously impressed with the quality of the soil, finding the ground covered with grass, clover, and rich growths of weeds. Although he thought it might be frosty, he called it "the best land I have seen in this country" and, thinking of the day when Joseph's band would be Christianized and happily settled as farmers in the valley, added, "On the whole I consider this a delightful & desirable country for a Christian settlement & may the time soon come when the Snakes shall be Christianized so that it can be safely occupied." On July 29 he finally left the lovely valley, from which the government of the United States would one day evict Joseph's son by force, and two days later he was back at Lapwai with renewed determination to convert Joseph.

He had to wait until November, but on the 17th of that month, with Whitman's approval, he finally "lawfully" married Joseph and his wife, Khapkhaponimi, to whom he gave the name Asenoth, and Timothy and his wife, "Tamar," and then baptized Joseph and Timothy, as well as James Conner, the mountain man, and welcomed them all into membership in the church. A week later he baptized Timothy's two small children, "Willard

39. Ibid., pp. 269–73.

James & Amos," and "Joseph's 4—Mary Noyes, Abigail, Hannah More & Manassa." [40] Later, Joseph was to have three more children. One, born early in 1840, was baptized Ephraim by Spalding on April 12, 1840. [41] This was probably the future Chief Joseph. Another, born a year or two afterward, was named Ollokot. As Presbyterians, both Spalding and Whitman were within their rights to take action alone in accepting Timothy, Joseph, and Conner for baptism. But in the Congregational Church new members were received by vote of the church members. Smith was a Congregational minister, and when he learned of Spalding's action, he was furious. The deed was done, however, and he could not undo it.

The Smiths, by then, were permanently situated at Kamiah. In September there had been another general meeting of the missionaries at Lapwai. The summer was ended, and the Smiths were faced with returning to Waiilatpu. Rather than have to do that, Smith once more requested permission to open a new station at Kamiah among the Nez Perces whose language he now knew, and despite Spalding's opposition the majority this time gave him approval. On September 24 he and his wife returned to Kamiah to build a more substantial home and to begin a more intensive program of instruction of the Indians. Four days later they were joined by Cornelius Rogers, who had recently come back from the buffalo country, where he had journeyed with some of the Nez Perces. Earlier in the year Spalding had realized that he was not yet in a position to object to the continued trips of the Nez Perces for buffalo meat. His attempt to turn them into farmers was still at a rude beginning, and it would be a long time before he would have enough hoes, seed, and stock to get the whole tribe settled down. In the meantime, they would have to continue to rely on buffalo. When the bands that year began to start toward the mountains, he decided to send Rogers with them so that their religious instruction would not be interrupted. Rogers left with one of the groups on June 25, rode across the Bitterroots, and traveled with the Indians on their hunts. There is no record of his adventures, which must have been many, but he returned on September 4, in time to go to Kamiah and assist the Smiths with his increased knowledge of the Nez Perce people.

Meanwhile, the band with which he had traveled had left the Clearwater country so late that it had missed that year's rendezvous, which began on July 5. The assemblage was at Horse Creek on the Green River, but the condition of the fur trade was no better than it had been the year before. The

40. Ibid., p. 281. Spaldings's record does not coincide with modern Nez Perce knowledge about Old Joseph's children. Members of the tribe today know of only two children, Celia and Elawinonmi, who were older than Young Joseph, who was not born until 1840.

41. Drury, *Diaries of Spalding and Smith*, p. 288.

American Fur Company had been absorbed by the firm of Pierre Chouteau Jr. and Company of St. Louis, and although the new organization had sent out a caravan, its terms to the trappers were worse than ever. Pay for beaver was low, there was little drinking or gambling, and the mountain men were sunk in sullenness and gloom. Joe Meek was there, this time with a new Nez Perce wife. After he had parted from the other one at Fort Hall the previous year, he had joined two trapper friends, Cotton Mansfield and Caleb Wilkins, and had headed for the streams of the Beaverhead Valley in Montana, where he and his companions had joined a village of Flatheads and Nez Perces led by the buffalo-hunting chief, Kowsoter. The area was full of straggling bands of trappers, left on their own by the collapse of organized company brigades, and several of the veterans, including a man named John Larison, soon attached themselves to Meek and his friends. The entire group wintered with Kowsoter and his Indians at the sheltered forks of the Salmon River, and there entered into many religious discussions with Nez Perces who had been attending the Lapwai mission.

Meek's knowledge of the Bible received a workout when he was smitten by one of Kowsoter's daughters and asked the chief for her hand. Kowsoter had already given one of his daughters to Doc Newell and another one to Caleb Wilkins, but he turned Meek down brusquely, claiming that Spalding had preached to the Nez Perces on the sin of polygamy, and that Meek was still united to the Nez Perce woman he had abandoned at Fort Hall. Meek was nettled, but after thinking of the Bible stories he knew, he lectured Kowsoter on the many wives of David and Solomon. His arguments finally won the day, and the chief relented, announcing that there was "no man like Joe"—a good man, a good hunter, and a good human being who would make a worthy son-in-law. Joe called his new wife Virginia, and they stayed with the village until March, when he took her off trapping with him, and eventually to the Horse Creek rendezvous.

From the East that year there also arrived at the trade gathering a new party of greenhorns who had traveled across the plains with the fur caravan. One was a man named William Geiger from Angelica, New York, where the Whitmans had been married. Geiger was probably the first emigrant bound for the Northwest as a result of the interest which the Whitmans' reports were beginning to arouse in the East. He was accompanied by a Mr. Johnson, and was on an "exploring tour with a view of being followed by settlers." In the same party were two missionary couples, the John S. Griffins and the Asahel Mungers. The Reverend Griffin was an old friend of Spalding and was traveling west without the support of any church, perhaps also having been inspired to go to Oregon by the published letters of the two pioneer missionary families. Munger was a trained carpenter and mechanic but was somewhat unstable mentally. He wanted to be a missionary to the Indians and was traveling with the tenuous backing of a Congregational Association in North Litchfield, Connecticut. Munger and Griffin had quarreled crossing the plains, and the trappers at the rendezvous found them no more appealing than the missionary group that had come west the previous year.

Munger, however, showed considerable broadmindedness for a missionary by his compassionate observation of the dismal future faced by the fur men. "The scene we left is really distressing," he wrote when the trade fair broke up. "Those poor mountain men are receiving payment in alcohol at an enormous price. These men now scatter off . . . and seek a home and employment where they can, many of them are so poor that they cannot go down to the States—what to do they know not—." [42]

As it turned out, many of them moved along with the missionaries and emigrants to Fort Hall, and at the post some fifteen of them finally decided to abandon trapping and go to the Columbia River and seek new starts in life. The Mungers and Griffins, meanwhile, continued to bicker on the way to Fort Hall, and lost some of their horses to Shoshonis or Bannocks. At the post the Griffins finally left the Mungers and went ahead. The Hudson's Bay Company's Frank Ermatinger took pity on the stranded Mungers, loaned them horses and provisions, and let them accompany his brigade to Fort Walla Walla. The other travelers, in the meantime, also split up. Geiger and Johnson were the first to arrive at Waiilatpu. They halted briefly while Geiger paid his respects to an old acquaintance, Mr. Hall, who had brought the printing press from Hawaii, and then went on to the Willamette Valley. When the Griffins arrived, they went to Lapwai to see Spalding. The Mungers came wearily into Waiilatpu and sought shelter there.

The Whitmans and Spaldings were heartened by the arrival in Oregon of more white people from the East. It seemed to break the loneliness of their isolation, and made them wonder if more of their countrymen, particularly substantial farmers and settlers, would follow in future years to help found a strong American civilization around their missions. But the Griffins and Mungers were something of a problem. Although they had come as independent, "self-supporting" missionaries, with no connection to the American Board, they were destitute and without plans, and with winter approaching they had little chance of being able to care for themselves. Whitman finally hired Munger to work for him at Waiilatpu for room and board and eight dollars a month, and Spalding took on Griffin to assist him at Lapwai.

In the same season two other outsiders were employed by the missions. The first was a kindly old man known today only as W. Blair. He had started

42. "Diary of Asahel Munger and Wife," *Oregon Historical Quarterly, 8* (1907), 395–96; and Tobie, *No Man Like Joe,* p. 78.

across the country from Peoria, Illinois, in a party of eighteen men who had
called themselves the Oregon Dragoons and had hoped to establish an American colony in Oregon. On the way West the group had quarreled and divided, and only three of its members had reached the Columbia. Two of them
went on to the Willamette, while Blair visited Lapwai and hired himself out
to help Spalding construct the flour mill and a sawmill. The second new employee was Tom McKay, the veteran British fur brigade leader and erstwhile
assistant to Peter Skene Ogden. In the Willamette Valley, McKay had become sympathetic to the Americans, and he had sent three sons to the East
with Jason Lee to receive education in the States. Now, after he had come up
from the Snake country with Ermatinger and the Mungers, McKay accepted
employment from Asa Smith and went to Kamiah to assist him for a few
months with his friends, the Nez Perces.

Throughout the fall of 1839, Smith's contempt for Spalding had been
growing. He thought the Nez Perces were hopeless, and he continued to
brood over the fact that he would not have been in the Northwest, wasting
his time, if it had not been for Spalding's exaggerated descriptions of those
Indians. He resented the baptizing of Joseph and Timothy, believing that it
had been done in secrecy behind his back. From his own experience he convinced himself that all of Spalding's policies with the Indians were wrong,
and that Spalding himself was an inadequate man to be running the Lapwai
mission. During the winter his wife and he were both sick much of the time,
and early in 1840 his cup of bitterness, already full, ran over when his only
milch cow died after eating a poisonous plant. He asked Spalding to send him
another one from the Lapwai mission herd, and when Spalding replied that he
had given the only spare cow he owned to James Conner for some labor,
Smith became furious.

On February 6, 1840, again in the guise of an objective report on mission
affairs, he sent a long letter to the Board, attacking Spalding. "High expectations have been raised respecting this mission among the churches at home—
expectations which can never be realized," he wrote. "It is easy for any one
of an excitable temperament & vivid imagination to write a most flattering
account . . . but I am confident that if Mr. S. had had more experience, a
better knowledge of human nature & less imagination, he would have written
different from what he did." He listed a bill of particulars, first contradicting
once again Spalding's favorable account of the character of the Nez Perces.
"Almost every days experience shows me more of their selfishness & of the
awful depravity of their hearts," he wrote. "With but few exceptions, I believe it to be true that their only desire for missionaries is the temporal benefit
which they hope to derive from them & that they desire instruction only that
they may appear wise & gain influence among their people."

Nez Perce society, without formal organization or law, also annoyed Smith, and although Spalding had never discussed that problem, Smith felt that the Board ought to know how difficult it made the task of Christian instruction. "They know nothing of the restraints of law," he stated, "have no idea of penalty, & apparently no idea of justice . . . Hence it seems impossible to make them understand the nature of divine law, its holiness & justice, the nature of its penalty, &c."

Having straightened out the Board about the Nez Perces, he proceeded to list specific charges against Spalding. He criticized his teaching methods and his use of pictures, as the "natives filled up the pictures from their own imaginations & in this way have acquired a vast amount of error which I find no easy matter to eradicate." He deprecated Spalding's knowledge of the language and his inability to make himself correctly understood by the people. In 1838 Spalding had reported that he had completed an alphabet in the Nez Perce language, and in 1839, after the arrival of the press from Hawaii, he and Hall had printed 400 copies of an eight-page primer, and later in the year 500 copies of a twenty-page Nez Perce alphabet. "That alphabet," Smith now commented, "has been thrown away, it being found . . . not only 'unclasical & outlandish,' but also attended with such difficulties, as to render it entirely impracticable to use it." Respecting the book, "before it went to press, it was sent to me for correction. On examining it, I found scarcely a correct sentence of Nez Perce in the whole of it." He cast doubt on everything Spalding had written concerning his farming efforts, by quoting an earlier statement in which Spalding had told of his hope of being able to cultivate one hundred acres. After reminding the Board that Whitman had supplied Lapwai with "considerable corn & potatoes," he asked why, and answered, "To tell the truth," Spalding's one hundred acres had been "sown only in the air."

Regarding the baptism of Joseph and Timothy, he hinted at a conspiracy to admit the Indians to the church before they were ready, and added testily that while he would not say that "those individuals are not christians . . . certainly they are not intelligent christians . . . I do not believe they know *why* they are in the church, nor that they are able to give a satisfactory reason for 'the hope that is in them.' " Finally, he questioned the wisdom of the mission itself under such leadership, and reminded the Board of the money that had been expended on it. "By the time this reaches you," he pointed out, "the mission will have cost the Board not less than $17,000 . . . not less than $12,000 of which must be considered as belonging to the Nez Perces mission, making an expense of at least *four dollars* to each individual of the whole tribe. And as yet the work can scarcely be said to be begun . . . I must say that in view of the present condition of the church & the world, I am ready to

give up the cause of Indian missions in despair." What would he do, instead?
"The same array of means, the same machinery is necessary here for 3,000, as
needed for the millions of Siam, or of China," he noted meaningfully.[43]

Smith's complaints were to prove serious enough by themselves, but unfortunately at about the same time Spalding had also aroused the enmity of
Gray. The latter had never lost his ambition to have his own station, and in
September 1839 the other missionaries had granted him permission merely to
explore for a site for a new mission. Although Spalding had been opposed
even to that, Gray had taken it to mean that he could found his own mission.
He made a tour of the Sahaptin lands along the middle Columbia, meeting a
strong and distinguished-looking young Yakima headman named Kamiakin,
who invited him to establish a station for his people near the mouth of the
Yakima River. Kamiakin accompanied Gray back to Waiilatpu to plead for
the mission; but when Gray returned to Lapwai to make preparations to
move, Spalding told him bluntly that he had not been authorized to establish
a new station and, besides, there was plenty of work waiting for him to do at
the other missions.[44] The two men had an angry argument, which ended
with Gray packing up again and going to Fort Vancouver, ignoring
Kamiakin, who returned to his people without an American teacher. Gray's
efforts to gain employment from the Hudson's Bay Company as a schoolmaster or in some other capacity came to nothing, and shortly afterward he
was obliged to return in chagrin to Walla Walla. At another meeting of the
missionaries in November, he again raised his request to open a new station,
and this time he was clearly rebuffed and ordered to carry out the original
duties to which he had been assigned. Gray blamed Spalding for his humiliation, and although he returned to Lapwai, he sulked through most of the winter, doing little work, and taking advantage of every opportunity to criticize
and oppose Spalding.[45]

Spalding's conduct, in retaliation, was far from wise. He resented Gray's

43. Drury, *Diaries of Spalding and Smith*, pp. 124–44.
44. Gray, *History of Oregon*, p. 94.
45. The following year Gray was finally given permission to establish his station at
the mouth of the Yakima; but when he and Dr. Whitman went to the site that Gray
had selected, they found that the ground had been flooded. Gray reluctantly postponed
his plans for a year, but in 1841 the other missionaries again reversed themselves and
directed him not to start the new mission. The Protestants' oscillations had an effect—
heretofore overlooked by writers—on Kamiakin and the Yakimas, who had expected to
acquire a white teacher for themselves. When the missionaries raised and then dashed
their hopes on two occasions, the Yakimas began to wonder at the value of the Americans' word. Eventually, when the Catholics offered them a mission, they accepted it;
and as Americans broke other promises to them in ensuing years, the Yakimas' regard
for the "Bostons" turned to contempt and hostility.

opposition, lost his temper, and got into angry fights with Gray in front of the Indians. Sometimes he involved the Nez Perces, directing them not to take orders from Gray; and on one occasion, when he tried unsuccessfully to make James and his people halt some work they were doing for Gray, he accused the little Nez Perce headman of having "gone over" to Gray, adding that he "expected that he would be taking the land & giving it to Mr. Gray next."

This intemperateness played into the hands of his enemies. The neutral members of the mission were appalled by Spalding's violent outbursts and by some of the things he said in moments of heat; and when Whitman visited Lapwai late in January 1840, they told him their fears. Whitman knew Spalding's fierce temper, and he was still carrying resentments of his own. Through all the years, Spalding had continued to be rude to Narcissa, and had many times said things that hurt her. He had let the other members of the mission know that he disliked her, and both Marcus and Narcissa blamed him for the vote the previous year that had ordered them to abandon Waiilatpu to the Asa Smiths. On January 28 Whitman, Gray, Hall, and Rogers had a stormy session with Spalding in which they accused him of harming the mission. Spalding fought back, and as tempers flared, the charges against him were broadened. He was accused of having come under the influence of Mr. Griffin, who was not a member of the mission and who had ideas contrary to their own, of ordering Griffin not to work for Gray, of devoting too much time to secular activities, and even of engaging in some kind of conspiracy against the rest of them by educating the natives to believe that the missionaries were going to give them farms, homes, livestock, and provisions. Spalding insisted that he was only trying to tell the Indians that they must become settled as soon as possible, but the others were already in agreement with Smith that that was a wrong policy, and Whitman now took their side. As a result of Spalding's activities, he charged, the Indians had come to believe that a free distribution of plows, cows, or anything else that they needed to become settled was a part of the duty of a missionary, and when he himself had not been able to give the Cayuses what they wanted, a headman had replied that "God is stingy."

In trying to defend himself, Spalding must have made an ill-advised reference to the personal rift between himself and the Whitmans, and the old sore over Narcissa was again laid open. Whitman left Lapwai, incensed at Spalding, and the scandalous fighting that had occurred at the session was spread as gossip among all the members of the mission. Both Gray and Rogers carried reports of it almost immediately to Kamiah, where they found a sympathetic audience in the Smiths. As a result of their discussions, Gray on March 20 wrote to Boston, suggesting that the American Board send someone to

Oregon to investigate what was going on, or at least recall certain members of the mission. A week later, Whitman also wrote a letter which, while not openly critical of Spalding, plainly indicated that he was not sympathetic to him. At the same time, Mr. Hall sent a letter of his own, informing the Board that "The state of things is truly lamentable, and I have been exceedingly grieved to find such a want of confidence and brotherly-love (in fact common politeness) among those who bear the name of missionaries." [46]

As time went on, the discord and ill will became worse, exacerbated by letters that the missionaries wrote back and forth to each other and by numerous injudicious remarks and petty arguments. Because of his stubbornness and temper, Spalding was considered the key to all the difficulties, but both Smith and Gray managed also to find displeasure with the Walkers and Whitmans, as well as with each other. Much of the fighting was done in front of the Indians, who were either confused or contemptuous, and many of the Nez Perces began to regard the missionaries as ridiculous and childish. On April 2, as Spalding was preparing to do his spring planting, Gray suddenly took possession of Lapwai and announced that Spalding was not to be allowed to do any cultivating. Spalding was bewildered, but was unwilling to put up a fight. Two weeks later he received a letter from the Secretary of the Prudential Committee of the Board, approving his policy of settling the Indians, and Gray abruptly turned the mission back to him, content to fire off another letter to Boston full of innuendoes about "the character of Mr. Sp."

Nothing that Gray wrote, however, could compare with the damage that Smith did to Spalding. During the year Smith sent a volley of complaining letters to the Prudential Committee, repeating all of the gossip, expanding on his old charges and adding new ones, and making the Board feel that Spalding had personally brought the entire Oregon Mission to the edge of destruction. In a letter of February 25 he had told the Board that he and Rogers had made a census of the Nez Perce nation and had found that they numbered fewer than 3,000, fewer even than he had originally imagined. "Their hearts are enmity against God," he wrote, and even Lawyer "gives me reason to doubt the sincerity of his seriousness. His heart is full of pride & he is evidently resting on his own good works. Sometimes I think he makes these pretenses in order to please me, as he is very submissive to me, for he feels himself some what dependent on me, & wishes to obtain favors from me."

Spalding's role in this deterioration was clearly placed in context in a long letter of September 3. There had been another unpleasant meeting of all the missionaries at Lapwai from July 4 to 9, and Smith had been directed to send a report of it to Boston. His letter was fifty-two pages long, and forty of them were a diatribe against Spalding. Earlier, he had noted that Spalding's policies

46. Drury, *Spalding*, p. 245.

and instruction of the natives were all wrong. They had led to errors among the Indians and had promoted attitudes that defeated the aims of the mission. Now he could report that Spalding's actions had been a deliberate conspiracy. He was an enemy of the Board and was only interested in his personal enrichment. "He has been buying a large number of horses from the Indians," he wrote, adding: "Said I, 'What will you do with them & what do you want of them.' Said he, 'I shall have something to depend upon, if the Board should throw me off.' But said I, 'The property is not yours, it belongs to the Board. It will do you no good.' But said he, 'I think they will never come to get the property, & if they order any of the members of the mission to take it, I will not give it up to them.' " Mr. Rogers, Smith went on, also "mentioned to me that during the year he spent in Mr. Spalding's family 'many a time had he defended the policy of the Board when assailed by Mr. Spalding' " and "Mr. Hall also, the first time I saw him which was at this place a few weeks after his arrival, in conversation respecting what he had heard Mr. Spalding say, remarked that 'if the Board knew of Mr. Spalding's remarks & of the feelings he cherishes towards the Board, they would say to him "come home & answer to these things" '." [47]

Everything Spalding did, according to Smith, contributed to the downfall of the mission. He revealed that Spalding whipped the Indians, and reported a number of incidents and trouble occasioned by Spalding's irascible temper and use of the lash. He accused Spalding of having taken Griffin as "his counsellor, to the rejection of his brethren at the mission," of quarreling with Whitman, of endangering the missionaries' relations with Pambrun, their chief means of protection and support at Fort Walla Walla, of making conditions intolerable for Gray, of wasting mission funds and resources, and even of making them all ridiculous by causing to be published in the East a "perfectly visionary" prophecy that a railroad would one day connect Oregon with the States.

He ended that letter with a recommendation that the mission be transferred to the Methodists before it completely broke up, and a month later repeated the suggestion, adding that the only way to salvage the present mission was to conduct an investigation of Spalding, which would result in undesirable publicity. For Spalding, he now charged, was becoming insane. "His conduct has evidently been governed & modified much by the peculiarities of his mind, his peculiar temperment & disposition," he commented. "He is certainly to be pitied. At times, he seems unable to control himself & this makes him a dangerous person in a mission . . . It is my earnest desire & prayer that the Board will treat him as *tenderly* as the case will possibly admit of, & if possible get him back to his native land & dismiss him from the service of the

47. Drury, *Diaries of Spalding and Smith*, pp. 157–80.

Board without bringing him to any trial respecting his conduct here. From what I have seen & know of him, I greatly fear that the man will become deranged should any heavy calamity befall him."

Though Smith's reports were a mass of falsehoods, half truths, fears, and jealousies, the work of a miserably unhappy man who wanted to be elsewhere and was no less neurotic than Spalding himself, they horrified the Board and seemed to be confirmed by the letters of Hall, Gray, and Whitman, the last two of whom had written again. Spalding had no idea of what was being charged behind his back, and had sent no letters of complaint of his own, or defenses of his policies and actions. Far removed from the scene, the Board felt that it had to do something, and in February 1842 the members of its Prudential Committee in Boston resolved to recall to the States the three men who appeared to be in most serious conflict, Spalding, Gray, and Smith. At the same time they voted to direct Whitman and Rogers to close out both Lapwai and Waiilatpu, which according to Smith's letters had made no progress among the Indians, and join Walker and Eells at Tshimakain, against which no complaints had been made. The Nez Perces, who had sent the original mission to St. Louis for religious teachers, were written off by the Board as a failure.

6

Chiefs, Laws, and Massacre

It took considerable time for mail to reach Boston from Oregon. The missionaries' letters of complaint had been written in 1840, and had been received by the Board during the year 1841. The Board had taken its action early in 1842, and it would be months before the orders would arrive in Oregon. During that long period, before those at the missions learned what had happened, additional problems arose to harry them.

On October 12, 1837, Spalding had written his fellow-missionaries in Hawaii that two Catholic priests were expected soon in the Northwest from Montreal. Spalding and most of the other Protestant missionaries, reflecting the intense religious feelings of the times, were bitterly anti-Catholic; and when, a year later, the priests did arrive, and Spalding heard that one of them would settle in the Willamette Valley near Jason Lee's mission while the other would come upriver to the vicinity of Waiilatpu and Lapwai, he wrote in distress, "The Lord in great mercy watch his own cause in the dark regions."

Ever since they had talked to the first Nez Perce delegation in 1831, Catholic officials in St. Louis had felt the need of sending missionaries to the Northwest. But they had lacked the personnel and resources for such an undertaking, and the first priests who reached the area came from a different place, and in response to a different appeal. There were a number of French Canadians, former Hudson's Bay Company servants, settled in the Willamette Valley with their Indian wives and halfblood children; and on July 3, 1834, even before the arrival of Jason Lee in Oregon, those among them who had received Catholic education in their youth had addressed a petition to Joseph N. Provencher, the titular Bishop of Juliopolis, with headquarters at Red

River, asking him to send a priest to the lower Columbia. They wrote a second petition on Febuary 23, 1835, and Dr. McLoughlin forwarded both appeals by company express to Red River.

On June 6, 1835, Provencher addressed a letter to McLoughlin, explaining that he had no priest available at Red River to assign to Oregon, but that he was going to Europe that year and would endeavor to find someone to send to the Columbia. He enclosed a message for the freemen in the Willamette, telling them the same thing and asking them to have patience. On his way east, Provencher discussed the settlers' appeal with Joseph Signay, the Bishop of Quebec, and Signay agreed to provide the priests. He wrote the Hudson's Bay Company, asking permission to send missionaries to the Northwest with the company's express, and the request was forwarded to London. By then Jason Lee had become settled in the Willamette, and at first the London Committee expressed doubt about allowing priests to go there too, thinking that the presence in the same region of both Catholic and Protestant missionaries would lead to Indian troubles. But McLoughlin wrote to London, arguing that Catholic teachers "would prevent the American missionaries acquiring influence over the Canadians" there, and Signay finally received permission to send his priests on condition that they set up no mission south of the Columbia River where the Americans were. The Catholics agreed to that stipulation, but a year later managed to have it withdrawn.

On February 17, 1838, Simpson wrote to Signay, advising him to have his priests ready to accompany the canoes of a westbound brigade, embarking at Lachine for the interior on April 25. At Vancouver, he informed them, a Hudson's Bay Company representative would "facilitate the establishment of the mission, and the carrying into effect the objects thereof generally." Signay chose two Canadian-born priests, Fathers Francis Norbert Blanchet, 43 years old, and Modeste Demers, 29, who had served for a few months at the Catholic mission at Red River. He appointed Blanchet Vicar General of the Oregon country, and instructed both men to preach the gospel in private and public, learn native tongues, baptize those who were sufficiently instructed, remarry those who had taken wives without church blessing, establish schools, and plant crosses in important places "so as to take possession of those various places in the name of the Catholic religion." [1]

The priests crossed the continent safely with the fur men and halted briefly at Fort Colvile, where they preached and baptized nineteen persons, mostly halfbloods. At Fort Walla Walla they met the Cayuse headman, Tauitau, or the Young Chief, Joseph's half-brother, who several years before had helped Apash Wyakaikt attack Pambrun. Since then, Pambrun had undermined Tauitau's power by playing up to his brother, Five Crows, and other

1. Bischoff, *The Jesuits in Old Oregon*, pp. 2–5.

Cayuses; and the chastened Tauitau had eventually changed his attitude and become friendly to Pambrun. During the fall of 1837, in fact, the British trader had built a house for Tauitau on the Umatilla River, where the band headed by Five Crows and Tauitau dwelled; and after that, Pambrun had made considerable progress in converting Tauitau to Catholicism.[2] When the priests arrived at the fort, Pambrun persuaded the Cayuse leader to have one of his children baptized. The event was witnessed by other Indians and caused excitement throughout the region among Cayuses, Wallawallas, Nez Perces, and Yakimas, who exclaimed in wonder at the garments, altar, and ritual of the Catholics, which were so unlike those of the Protestants. Some of the Indians also listened to the two priests talk, and their confusion increased when Toupin, the Catholic interpreter, advised them that the newcomers' spiritual powers were different from those of the Whitmans and Spaldings and were the only effective ones.[3] On this first visit the priests stayed only briefly at the fort, conducting but two other baptisms, and then continued on to Fort Vancouver, which they reached on November 24, 1838.

For a time they confined their activities to the French-Canadian settlement at French Prairie in the Willamette, south of the Columbia, and on April 17, 1839, Spalding reported the receipt of a disquieting letter from one of the Methodist ministers there, and noted that "the Catholic priests disregarding all law and propriety are marrying over those whom Mr. Lee, Mr. Beaver and himself have heretofore married. Also that they baptize again. That they do not recognize him [the Methodist] as a minister of the gospel." [4] But the priests also had an interest in converting Indians, and soon they began to move upriver again, visiting the different tribes and finding that the Protestant influence over the natives was fragile. Wearing long gowns, disclaiming an interest in wives, conducting visually exciting services, and drawing distinctions between their own lessons and those of the other religious teachers,

2. Gray, *History of Oregon*, p. 480. On August 30, 1837, soon after Mary Walker's arrival in the Northwest, she had met Tauitau at Waiilatpu and had noted that he "said he liked what the [Protestant] Missionaries said to them [the Indians] but he was always concerned about trade, and pointed out Pambre [Pambrun] as a bad man" (Drury, *First White Women*, p. 117). It must have been soon after this that Pambrun began to win over the young Cayuse chief.

3. Gray, *History of Oregon*, p. 180. Pambrun, Mrs. Walker noted at this time, invited the Protestant missionaries to come over to Fort Walla Walla and meet the priests. "They hardly knew what to do about accepting it," she wrote, "but finally concluded it was best. So Dr. W. [Whitman] Mr. W [Walker] & Eells have gone. Mr. S. [Spalding] declined saying that it looked too much like countenancing Romanism. Hope our husbands will manage discreetly" (Drury, *First White Women*, p. 132). There was no problem, because the priests were delayed farther up the Columbia, and the Protestants missed seeing them.

4. Drury, *Diaries of Spalding and Smith*, p. 260.

the priests were a novelty to the Indians, many of whom recognized the Catholics' hostility to the Protestants and were quick to take advantage of it by pouring out complaints about the Protestants and appealing to the new-comers for better treatment and promises of more liberal favors.[5]

Spalding and Whitman finally met one of the priests on July 1 at Walla Walla. A week earlier, on June 23, the Whitmans' 27-month-old daughter, Alice Clarissa, had accidentally drowned in the river at Waiilatpu, and the Spaldings had hurried over from Lapwai to be of assistance to the stricken parents. After the funeral, word had arrived that the Hudson's Bay Company express was coming up the Columbia with supplies and mail for the missionaries, and Spalding and Whitman had ridden to Fort Walla Walla to meet the express. Among those who landed were Peter Skene Ogden, who was traveling to company posts in northern British Columbia, and Father Demers, who was on his way to Fort Colvile. Regarding the priest, Spalding said only that he stayed at Walla Walla for two days. On September 13, however, Asa Smith, who had come to Waiilatpu, wrote an unhappy letter to Boston about what was happening at the nearby British fur post, to which Demers had again returned after his visit to Fort Colvile. "Catholicism," Smith warned, "is now making his appearance, & the errors of that church are beginning to be diffused among this people. At this very moment the Catholic priest is at Walla Walla instructing the people & the Indians are gathering together there to listen to the false doctrines which he inculcates. Already has the priest denounced us because we have wives & the people told that they are going to hell because they are unbaptised. How much influence this will have on the people we know not. One thing is certain, the natural heart loves such kind of instruction as the Catholics usually give, & we have reason to fear that our work will soon be done up along this people." [6]

In calling attention to the difference between the Catholics' missionary methods and those of the Protestants, Smith also unwittingly underscored the manner in which he was impeding Spalding's efforts. The Catholics laid emphasis on forms and rites and on the necessity of baptism, and they administered that sacrament to the Indians as soon as possible, giving them fuller

---

5. See below, p. 672.

6. Note that the bigoted Smith could match anything that Fathers Demers or Blanchet might have said about him. During this visit to Fort Colvile, Father Demers wrote: "the nearness of Protestant ministers [Walker and Eells at Tshimakain] . . . injure the development of this growing Christianity . . . the latitude given to morals by the ministers, and the prejudices inspired by them against the *black robes* are the expedients of the spirit of error for dragging into heresy these tribes . . . They distribute Bibles in profusion; but that ridiculous means of conversion for the inhabitants of the forest does not bear fruit to suit the ministers, especially if they are forced to set up a comparison with the Catholic missions" (*Notices & Voyages*, p. 33).

religious instruction after baptism. The Congregationalists and Presbyterians, on the other hand, dwelled on instruction, reserving baptism only for those whom they felt were ready beyond a doubt for membership in the church. Spalding was more lenient than his colleagues in deciding when applicants were ready for baptism, but the opposition that Smith raised against him inhibited him and kept him from bringing more Indians into the church. With the exception of infants, who could be baptized prior to receiving instruction, no Indian other than Joseph and Timothy were counted as converts at any of the missions for a long time, which made the efforts at Waiilatpu, Lapwai, Kamiah, and Tshimakain seem ineffective, especially when compared to the numbers of baptisms administered in a short time by the Catholics.

In September, Whitman wrote to Spalding on the same matter that was troubling Smith. The Catholic priest, Spalding noted in his diary, "is now at Walla Walla calling the Indians & telling the Indians that we are false teachers because we do not feed & clothe the people, that we have wives as other men, & wear pantaloons as common men & not frocks as he does. The people are told not come near the Doct as he is a bad man, & has made no christians as yet but he will fix them all for heaven soon." The concern that this gave Spalding was emphasized a month later, when he received letters from the missionaries in Hawaii and recorded again in his diary, that those islands had been "visited by a French Man of War threatening entire extermination to the inhabitants, especially the Missionaries if the Gov. did not in 48 hours proclaim the Catholic religion free, give a lot of land in Honolulu for a church, pay $20,000 & permit wine, brandy &c to be sold, which was complied with & many precious lives saved." [7]

The Protestant missionaries tried to defend themselves against the new teachings by delivering sermons and lectures that attacked the priests in violent terms, and they warned the Indians against listening to their instruction. Some of the Indians who harbored resentments against Whitman and Spalding paid no attention to the advice but, regarding the priests as "bigger hearts" than the Protestants, welcomed their arrival and showed an interest in what they had to say. Other natives were simply confused, or thought it best to remain loyal to Whitman and Spalding. On October 30, 1839, Spalding noted that one Wallawalla chief at the fort had "refused to have his boy baptised by the Catholic priest on condition that he should never go into the house of the Am Missionary." [8] But William Gray later reported that from this time, some of Spalding's "own pet Indians" began to turn Catholic, and that even James, the headman who claimed the land on which Spalding had built his mission, "had been induced to receive a cross and a string of beads"

7. Drury, *Diaries of Spalding and Smith*, pp. 276, 278.
8. Ibid., p. 279.

through the influence of Pambrun and one of the priests, although James had no serious intention of turning either Protestant or Catholic.[9]

In 1840 the menace to the Protestants seemed to increase, as reports arrived from the buffalo country that a priest had finally come west from St. Louis and was traveling with the Flatheads east of the Bitterroots. This was a Belgian Jesuit, Father Pierre Jean De Smet, who had been engaged in missionary work among the Indians on the eastern fringe of the plains and in the spring of 1840 had crossed to the mountains with the fur caravan. At the rendezvous he had found the Flatheads, who had been eager for so long to have a religious teacher of their own. During the summer the Salish escorted him through their hunting country from Pierre's Hole to the Three Forks of the Missouri, and listened with enthusiasm to his plans to return to the East and come back to them the following year with more priests to establish a permanent mission in their lands. Lawyer and many of the Nez Perces were in the buffalo country with the Flatheads that summer, and in the fall some of them hurried home, bewildered by the new things they had heard and wondering which breed of religious teacher, after all, was the more powerful and influential in the country of the whites. At Kamiah, they informed Smith of De Smet's visit, and from their excited reports he concluded that the danger to the Protestant missions from the Bitterroot Valley was "ten times as much" as from the Canadian priests on the Columbia. "A considerable number," he wrote to Elkanah Walker at Tshimakain on October 12, 1840, "the Indians say, a great many children both Flat Head and Nez Perces have been baptized & have been presented with the image of the cross or other emblems of Popery." [10]

According to Lawyer, some of the Indians had also told Father De Smet many unpleasant things about the Protestant missions, "saddest of all," wrote Smith, "what has been exceptionable in the conduct of Mr. Spalding, & [he] is using it with great effect in prejudicing the minds of the Indians against the mission . . . To hear of such things is indeed painful & we have reason to fear for the consequences." The Lawyer, he went on, saw the priest "two days & he says they tried to get the cross on him. He heard considerable from the priest & says the priest inquired of him about the mission & according to his account, he defended the mission very well, tho' he did not deny the reports about Mr. S." [11]

9. Gray, *History of Oregon*, pp. 211, 563.

10. Drury, *Diaries*, p. 192.

11. Ibid., pp. 192–93 (Smith to Elkanah Walker, October 12, 1840). On August 10, 1840, while he was traveling with the Indians in western Montana, Father De Smet sent a letter by courier to Father Blanchet on the Columbia, informing him that "The Nez Perces appeared to me tired of their self-styled ministers with wives, and show a great

Smith sent the news of what he had heard to Spalding and Whitman; but if he informed Spalding of how the Indians were discussing his conduct in front of the Catholic missionary, Spalding failed to comment on it in his diary, noting only that "great multitudes of Flathead children & also Nez Perces children" had been baptized, and that four priests were to return to the country east of the Bitterroots the following year, one to establish on the Salmon River, and three on the "Flathead," meaning the Bitterroot River.[12]

The arrival of Father De Smet was not the only ominous development for the Protestant missionaries in 1840. The previous winter had marked the final collapse of the big company fur brigades, and the mountains were full of small bands of wandering, destitute mountain men, wondering what to do next. Some of them had begun to steal horses and supplies from the Indians and from each other, and the profitless fighting had decided many of them to return to the States or to try their luck on the Columbia or in California as soon as the weather enabled them to get there. In partnership with Philip M. Thompson and Prouett Sinclair, William Craig had established a rude log post, called Fort Davy Crockett, on the Green River in Brown's Hole, a favorite Indian wintering site in the northwest corner of Colorado; and from time to time Joe Meek and Doc Newell and their Indian families, as well as Kit Carson and other footloose trappers, had put in there. In the spring of 1840 most of the men who had decided to remain in the mountains had gone out to do more trapping, and in July they showed up at the Green River for another rendezvous. It was to be the final gathering. Bridger and a brigade appeared, and also a caravan from St. Louis under Drips, who announced that this would definitely be the last time a supply train would come to the mountains.

In addition to shepherding Father De Smet across the plains that year, Drips' caravan had in tow a new set of independent Protestant missionary couples who were hopeful that they could labor on their own in Oregon. They were the Harvey Clarks, the Philo P. Littlejohns, and the Alvin T. Smiths, and with them across the plains had traveled the first bona fide family of settlers, Joel P. Walker, his wife, and five children, and a companion named Herman Ehrenberg. Walker, a brother of Joseph Walker, the former lieutenant of Bonneville, was the herald of a new era in the Northwest. He was a typical "westering" American, who had successively moved from Vir-

---

preference in favor of Catholic priests" (*Notices & Voyages*, p. 72). The following year, in the Bitterroot Valley, he wrote: "the Nez Perces . . . are disgusted at the conduct of the Protestant ministers that have settled among them." On Christmas Day of that year, 1841, he baptized thirty Nez Perces at St. Mary's Mission, which he had established for the Flatheads in Montana. (Chittenden and Richardson, *Life, Letters and Travels of Father De Smet, 1*, 318, 338.)

12. Spalding, October 8, 1840. Drury, *Diaries*, p. 301.

ginia to Tennessee to Missouri, with time out to fight the Creeks and Semi-
noles in Alabama and Florida. Now, still in search of good free land, he was
following the sun to the newest place he had heard about.

The rendezvous was subdued and sad, and it ended quickly. There was little beaver to trade, prices were the lowest ever, and, for the first time, there
was no carousing to annoy the missionaries. When it was over, the trappers
drifted silently away. Some headed back to the States and a few set their
courses for California, Oregon, or the Mexican settlements of Taos and Santa
Fe. Many stayed in the mountains, because it was the only place they wished
to be. But the great days of the beaver trade were ended.

The three old friends, Bill Craig, Joe Meek, and Doc Newell, fared better
than the majority. After the rendezvous, Newell got himself hired to guide
the new missionary couples to Fort Hall, and Meek went along with him. At
the fort, the missionaries gave Newell their two wagons as pay. Joel Walker
also abandoned a wagon at the post, and Caleb Wilkins, another of the old
trappers, claimed it. Meek left the post to do some trapping, but at the Bear
River he received a message that Newell wanted to see him again at the fort.
He hurried back and found Newell, Craig, Wilkins, John Larison, and a
number of other trappers assembled with their Indian families, all of them
having decided to abandon the mountains and head for a new life in Oregon.
Meek threw in his lot with them, and on September 27 they all left the post
with their Indian wives and children, driving the three wagons, as well as a
small herd of cattle that the missionaries had also left behind.

At Fort Boise the group halted for five days, then pushed on toward the
Blue Mountains. Whitman had taken his two-wheeled cart as far as Fort
Boise in 1836, but no wheeled vehicle had ever gone farther. Now the trappers and their families, forging the last link of the Oregon Trail, guided their
wagons successfully over the rugged mountains, and one day late in October
1840 streamed in to Waiilatpu, to the amazement of the Whitmans and the
Indians. Word of the feat spread to the Willamette, and eventually back to
the States, announcing the exciting information that at last it was possible to
travel in wagons all the way from the Missouri to the Columbia. A route for
family emigration was opened.

With Meek was his daughter by his first Nez Perce wife, a two-year-old
child, more Indian than white, whom Meek had named Helen Mar after a
character in the book *Scottish Chiefs*, which he had read at one of the rendezvous. While the party rested at Waiilatpu, Meek's admiration for Narcissa
revived, and he asked the Whitmans to accept the care and training of Helen
Mar. The Whitmans agreed, and took the child into their household, and in
time she came to fill, to a degree, the place that had been occupied by their
own Alice Clarissa.

After two days the mountain men left Waiilatpu and went on to Fort Walla Walla, where they finally abandoned their wagons. Meek, Newell, and most of the others continued on horseback with their families to the Dalles mission, and later to the Willamette, where they joined the settlers. They had a difficult time at first, trying to adjust to the new life, but eventually they became respected members of the colony. Craig and Larison did not go on with them from Fort Walla Walla. Craig was married to a daughter of James, the Nez Perce leader in the Lapwai area, and at the fort he decided to take his wife to visit her father. Larison went with them, and they arrived at Spalding's mission on November 20. Spalding was not pleased to see them. "I have seen enough of mountain men," he wrote in his diary, thinking of unhappy experiences he had had with Ebberts, Williams, and even Conner, whose religious conversion at times did not seem to have taken satisfactorily.

Conner was still at Lapwai, but that mission and the others had experienced several changes in personnel during the year. Ebberts, Williams, and Mr. Blair had gone to the Willamette, and the Halls had returned to Hawaii. In March the Griffins had departed for the Snake country, intending to establish an independent mission of their own for the Shoshonis and Bannocks. Two of Spalding's Nez Perces had guided them as far as they dared to go, the Salmon River border between their own lands and those of the Snakes, and from there the couple had had a hazardous time, wandering alone through the rugged and perplexing country. By the time they had reached Fort Boise they had had enough, and after returning to Waiilatpu they continued to the Willamette where they finally settled down. At Waiilatpu, Whitman's Hawaiian assistant, Joseph Maki, had died, and his wife had been sent back to the islands. The Mungers remained with the Whitmans, and when the new, independent missionaries, the Clarks, Littlejohns, and A. T. Smiths arrived from the rendezvous in the fall, they too moved in with the Whitmans until they could make plans of their own. Eventually, the Clarks were sent to spend the winter with Asa Smith and his wife at Kamiah, and the A. T. Smiths joined the Spaldings at Lapwai.

Both Spalding and Asa Smith had been having difficulties with the Nez Perces, and the sudden appearance at Lapwai of Bill Craig, the Indians' old friend from the mountains, gave the disgruntled Indians a sympathetic and powerful ally. Exactly what had aroused the Nez Perces just before Craig's arrival is not clear, but since a number of them began suddenly and simultaneously to show their resentment against the whites at both Lapwai and Kamiah, it is possible that they had been conferring among themselves and had decided to show the missionaries that the white teachers were not the Indians' masters, and that the Nez Perce people did not fear them or have to take orders from them.

On October 9 Spalding recorded a serious set-to with the Indians. "A most disgraceful circumstance today," he wrote in his diary. "Two young painted [Indians] rode up to the door of the school house as Mrs. Spalding was about to open the school with pray. She requested them to turn away. They came the nearer & glanced their hellish looks directly at her. She moved to another part of the room, they moved their position so as to look her again in the face. She then put a blanket at the door. They then commenced their savage talk. She sent for me. I requested them to leave, they refused. I sent for Old James, as they belonged to his lodge. He refused to come. I went to him & found to my great surprise & sore grief that he countenanced the evil doers. Mark, George, & the whole camp joined the heathen party. Red Wolf turned away from me & the two or three who discountenanced the deed, & joined the heathen party. Timothy, the Eagle, & Conner's father-in-law were the only three who openly discountenanced the evil doers." [13]

Protestant missionaries of the period regularly used the term heathen for the non-Christian peoples of the world, particularly those whom they intended to convert, but Spalding and his colleagues had gradually begun to use the word to characterize those Indians who most stubbornly resisted their instruction. This was the first time that Spalding had referred to a heathen party among the Nez Perces, and it showed the extent to which he had already created a division within the tribe. It was an ideological split, political and social as well as religious, between those who clung to their Indian beliefs and practices and those whose hearts and minds the Spaldings had won. As time went on, the rupture among the people became sharper until it rent the tribe into Christian and "heathen" factions and, in the end, proved to be a major legacy bequeathed to the Nez Perces by those who tried to force Christianity and civilization on them.

On October 12 Asa Smith at Kamiah heard of Spalding's new difficulties with the Indians, and noted the additional information that James had become tired of being an unwilling host to members of other bands who were squatting about the mission buildings on his land at Lapwai and paying homage to his rival, Spalding. James was trying, said Smith, "to drive away Joseph and

13. Ibid., p. 300. On September 22, 1840, Spalding had written Greene at Boston: "Most of our perplexities with the natives, I believe arise from our trading in Indian goods— Our powder measure is not as large as that at Walla Walla . . . we do not give as much for this thing or that thing as the French etc are frequent speeches." Spalding said he would rather trade provisions from farms than Indian goods, such as ammunition, knives, blankets, and so on, for favors (buying a horse) or errands. He indicated his feeling that most of his problems with the Indians were caused by petty, temporary grudges, such as could happen anywhere, and he added that the Nez Perces, including James, whom he called an "old man," were generally friendly and kind. (Text of letter courtesy of Clifford M. Drury.)

Timothy & all who do not belong there." The news "discouraged" Smith, but the next day he had his own troubles. While he was harrowing his wheat field, two of the principal men in the Kamiah district, brothers named Utsin-malikin and Yoomtahmahlikin, who, he wrote, "pretend to own this soil came & insulted me with the most abusive language—demanding pay for the land &c & then in the most absolute terms ordered me to leave the place on the next day. After hearing their abuse for a time I began to think it was time to begin to think about moving & I told them I would go but must have time to get ready." The following morning, some of the headmen came to talk to him, and soon afterward the two brothers forced their way in "full of rage . . . & such a scene I never witnessed in my life. The talk was principally between the Indians & it was warm, I can assure you. They seemed more like demons from the bottomless pit than human beings . . . I have ascertained that the Meoway as he is called set them on somewhat, & it was an attempt to force me to give them goods. He told them that he tied Mr. Pambrun & made him a slave & since that he had been a little good." [14]

Smith's troubles, stemming from his ignorance of Nez Perce culture and backgrounds, were undoubtedly compounded by his arrogance. Utsin-malikin, who later proved to be a worthy and influential friend of white men, had the feelings of a proud and free Indian and a leader of his people. In time, he would sign treaties for them, and even journey to Washington at the request of American negotiators.[15] The Meoway—which the missionaries sometimes spelled Meiway or Meaway, and was merely an Indian term for a strong chief—was actually the war and buffalo-hunting leader Apash Wyakaikt, otherwise known as Flint Necklace or Looking Glass, from Asotin. He was not a man for the untutored missionaries to trifle with.

Eventually the other Indians calmed the two brothers and led them away, but the Smiths had received a scare, and Asa sent for Spalding to come to his help. Despite his own problems, Spalding hastened immediately to Kamiah with some of his loyal Nez Perces, and found Sarah sick and in tears and her husband alternately furious and frightened. Spalding gradually managed to

14. Drury, *Diaries*, pp. 194–97.

15. In 1855, at the Walla Walla Treaty Council, Governor I. I. Stevens referred to him as Spotted Eagle. Gustavus Sohon, an artist with Stevens, drew Spotted Eagle's portrait, but titled it "Te-pe-lah na- Te-many," which actually meant Eagle Heart, or Heart of an Eagle. Lucullus McWhorter's research also confirmed that the Spotted Eagle of the 1855 treaty came from Kamiah, the home of Utsinmalikin. But the minutes of the 1863 treaty council at Lapwai state that the negotiators met with two different men, "Ute-si-mi-la-kin" and "Tipu-lana-tima-ni, or Spotted Eagle." Proceedings of the Treaty Council at Lapwai, May–June, 1863, p. 32. National Archives, Record Group No. 75. Also, Hazard Stevens, *Life of General Isaac I. Stevens* (Boston, 1900), 2, 40, and McWhorter, *Hear Me*, pp. 608, 610.

mollify the Indians, and both brothers at length showed up to request for-
giveness. But it was plain that most of the Nez Perces around Kamiah disliked
Smith and knew of his feelings toward them. In the various letters he had
written during the year, he had called them evil and sinful and had said they
possessed "stupid degenerated minds," and it was unlikely that he had successfully concealed those opinions from them.[16] After the attack, he was un-
decided what to do. Whitman wanted him to leave Kamiah, but he had no
desire to return to Waiilatpu. As the tension eased, he hung on, and felt more
secure when one of the brothers departed for the fishing center at the Dalles
to spend the winter. But there was no future for him among these Indians,
and he knew it. Amid growing despondency, he wrote to Boston, pleading
with the Board to "send me to some other field," reminding its members again
that "Siam is the field which early attracted my attention & it is the place
where I should still like to labor," and adding almost desperately, "We feel to
leave ourselves in the hands of God & at the disposal of the Board, praying
that they may be guided to make such a disposition of us as shall be most for
the glory of God & advancement of his cause." [17]

At Lapwai, meanwhile, Spalding's troubles with James and others in that
area were multiplied when Craig and Larison decided to settle down on
Lapwai Creek near James' village. The old headman recited to his white son-
in-law all his resentments against Spalding, and the rough-hewn, plain-
speaking mountain man, who had little respect for the Puritanical, narrow-
minded missionaries, agreed with James that the preacher was an interloper
on his lands who had no right to behave the way he did. A few days after
Craig's arrival, Spalding's worst fears regarding him were borne out. "Old
James & others," he wrote in his diary, "say they have been stopped from
going after timber by Cragge who tells them I am making dogs & slaves of
them." [18] Spalding had a talk with the two mountain men, and finally persuaded Larison to do some work for him in return for beef and clothing. But
Craig remained hostile, continuing to sympathize with James' people, and in
February 1841 Spalding rounded up Mr. A. T. Smith, Rogers, Conner, and
Larison for support and visited Craig again "to give him an opportunity to
clear himself before the Indians if he is not guilty of the charges alleged
against him. For some time," he said,

> in very ambiguous language, he denied the charges. But his brother-in-
> law, Thomas [an Indian loyal to Spalding], told him to his face that he
> told them as follows: when he learned we were coming to a miserable

16. Drury, *Diaries*, p. 190.
17. Ibid., p. 202.
18. Ibid., p. 304.

people to benefit them he was rejoiced but on arriving & beholding with his own eyes he is astonished to see us sell property to the people & not clothe & feed them & give cattle & build houses for the people without taking any thing in return. This would be blessing the people, but now while they are obliged to plant their own lands & build their own houses & feed themselves & clothe themselves by the labor of their hands, their missionaries are a great curse to them. We are only treating them as dogs & hogs. Also that the land & water privilege which has been sold should be sold again. After Thomas had exposed him so clearly, he made no further effort to deny but attempted to justify his course by calling up a great many things which had been done here which he considered wrong . . . It also appears from his own statements that he came here greatly prejudiced against me, & from what the Indians say & from what his wife said there in the lodge, that he came telling the Indians he would set things right & giving them to understand that I must be sent away & he take the place, mills, property. My heart sickened at the discovery of such a dark plot . . .[19]

The next day, some of the Indians angrily demolished Spalding's mill dam, and the following evening, wondering how it was possible "for a man born of Christian parents . . . to be guilty of such deeds of darkness," Spalding visited Craig alone, managing to talk to him on religion and, before leaving, praying with him and giving him "a testament, a sermon & tract." When Sunday came around, however, there was more trouble with James. The old shaman showed up at Spalding's service and rose and "said I had made the people miserable & was ruining them, that he learned this from his son-in-law Craig who tells the people that if I was a true teacher I would not even think about or look at the earth much less build houses, look after wood, water, fish, cattle, & cultivate the land. That I would sit still & keep my heart in heaven till the bell called me to my meals . . . Such is the management of a selfish, lawless, self-ruined scape goat from the States who having rejected the offer of mercy hates above all things to any body else in a way to be benefited." [20]

On March 2 Craig and Larison left Lapwai to visit their trapper friends in the Willamette Valley, and Spalding sighed, "I hope to see peaceful times soon." He had rebuilt the mill dam, but Craig's influence lingered among some of the Indians, and in April a group of them again damaged part of the irrigation works. Spalding was disheartened by Conner, who had begun to side with Craig and who finally turned wholeheartedly against the man who

19. Ibid., pp. 307–08.
20. Ibid., pp. 308–09.

had baptized him. Spalding called him a "finished rogue & a liar," and offered no opposition when Conner at last took his Nez Perce wife and left the mission to follow Craig and Larison to the Willamette.

In April, also, the Asa Smiths finally departed. Smith had a dozen reasons for giving up, but he explained to Boston and to everyone in Oregon that the principal one was concern for his wife's health. Sarah had been sick and despondent all winter, and had cried steadily, so that the Nez Perces remembered her ever afterward as "the weeping one." As missionaries and teachers, the couple had accomplished nothing with the Indians since the tension of the previous fall, and Smith's stream of letters of gossip and complaint to the other missionaries had resulted finally in his becoming insulted on learning that his colleagues considered him a trouble-maker who had stirred them up against each other.[21] On April 19, 1841, he and his wife, ignored by most of the Indians who had generally been indifferent to the couple during the winter, left Kamiah by canoe and, after a brief stop at Lapwai, went on to Forts Walla Walla and Vancouver. Early the following January they reached the Hawaiian Islands, where they remained, happier and in better health, for three years, finally sailing around the world (but not seeing Siam), and returning to the United States in 1846. During the rest of his life, Smith preached in Massachusetts, Connecticut, and Tennessee, where he died in 1886.

Smith's departure was a signal also for Cornelius Rogers to withdraw from the mission. He had not got on well with Spalding and, becoming sick, had gone to Waiilatpu to recover. He was already a favorite of Pambrun, and during his convalescence he spent much time with the Hudson's Bay Company trader. While the two men were riding on May 11, 1841, Pambrun was thrown from his horse, and died four days later from internal injuries. Soon afterward, Rogers went down the Columbia, where he eventually was drowned in a canoe accident on the Willamette River.

With the departure of the Asa Smiths, Nez Perce opposition to Spalding quieted again, and during the spring of 1841 the missionary felt more at peace than he had in a long time. His repose came to an abrupt end, however, at the regular meeting of the missionaries, which took place at Waiilatpu June 9–13. There, Spalding had another bitter quarrel with the Whitmans, and in the heat of charges and countercharges he learned for the first time of the many letters of criticism and complaint that Smith, Hall, Gray, Rogers, and even Whitman had sent to Boston behind his back. He was shocked by the knowledge and that night wrote in his diary, "The Lord in great mercy look upon these men and forgive their sins to sustain his unworthy servant to kindness

21. Ibid., p. 188. This letter from Smith to Elkanah Walker is erroneously dated by Drury. It should read February 22, 1841.

under these accumulating trials." Although stunned and humbled for a while, he went back to Lapwai, puzzling about his colleagues and their conduct, and wondering if he, after all, were right and they wrong. A week after his return to the mission, five members of a United States Naval expedition appeared suddenly at Lapwai. The expedition, led by Commander Charles Wilkes, was on a four-year exploration of the Pacific, and the visitors were part of a group that had been sent inland to examine a portion of the Oregon country. Spalding showed them around the mission and asked for their opinion of whether he should feel discouraged. According to Spalding, they told him that he had less cause to feel discouraged than any missionaries they had seen anywhere during their three years' voyage. They were particularly impressed with Joseph, and one of them remarked that he "never expected this of a N. American savage." [22] After they had left, Spalding felt considerably better.

The revelation of the complaints that had been made against him sobered his hasty temper somewhat, and for a while, with the help of his wife who gently restrained him when he began to grow upset, he became less impatient and rash with the Indians. But his nature was too authoritarian for easy control, and he was soon again using the whip to punish offenders. On August 10, after he had lectured two young Nez Perces on the evils of gambling, they tried to set fire to his house. He caught one of them, but before he could use the lash on him, the Indian broke away and, with the aid of some of his friends, escaped by plunging into the Clearwater. A week later the harsh extent of Spalding's attempts at discipline was reflected by a brief note in his diary: "Cause three children to be whiped for stealing corn." [23] Some of the Indians retaliated with petty annoyances that were little more than pitiable gestures to assert their independence, but one day Spalding found two of his best cows dead, evidently poisoned by the Indians.

On October 7 there was a double dose of bad news. Craig and Larison returned from the Willamette, having stopped at Waiilatpu on their way back and picked up the information that Whitman was in serious trouble with the Cayuses. To some extent the problem stemmed from the increasing competition between Whitman and the Catholics for the allegiance of the Indians. Before his death, Pambrun had continued to assist the priests from time to

22. Drury, *Spalding*, p. 267. One of the members of the Wilkes group to visit Lapwai was William D. Brackenridge, "horticulturalist" with the Exploring Expedition. The men were at Lapwai, June 25–26, and Brackenridge wrote with enthusiasm of the Spaldings' many accomplishments. At a large meeting with the Indians at the mission, the visitors, he said, encouraged the Nez Perces to take the advice and follow the example of Spalding "in cultivating the Soil & raising Cattle, to which the[y] all agreed . . ." McKelvey, *Botanical Exploration of the Trans-Mississippi West*, p. 698.

23. Drury, *Diaries*, p. 319.

time by introducing them to Indians with whom the Whitmans had been trying to work. After Pambrun's death Archibald McKinlay, a Scotch Presbyterian who had married the daughter of Peter Skene Ogden, had become
chief trader at the fort; but by that time a number of Cayuses had turned to
the priests, and Whitman considered that great damage had been done to his
position at Waiilatpu. As he tried to make up lost ground by lecturing the
Indians severely on what he considered the evils of Catholicism, the rivalry
between the spokesmen of the two branches of the white men's religion became the uppermost subject of discussion among the confused Indians around
Waiilatpu, and played into the hands of a halfblood Iroquois free trapper
named Joe Gray, who was living with the Cayuses and seemed to be aspiring
to a position of influence and leadership among them.[24]

As Craig had done at Lapwai, Gray took the Indians' side against the missionaries and told the Cayuses that they ought to make the Whitmans pay
for the use of their land. Eventually, Tilokaikt, the leader of the Cayuses
around the mission, whom Whitman claimed had been "practicing the ceremonies of the Papists," struck the Protestant missionary, and shortly afterward got into a fight with William Gray, who was still living with Whitman,
and ordered him to leave the country. When Whitman tried to intercede in
that quarrel, the Indian pulled Whitman's ears and threw his hat in the water.
At the fort, McKinlay heard of what had happened, and told the Indians that
they had behaved like dogs. That got the Indians angrier, and on October 2 a
group of them battered their way into Whitman's house with an axe,
assaulted him, tore his clothes, and threatened him with a gun. When he stood
his ground boldly, showing no sign of fear, they withdrew, but the next day
broke some of his windows and continued making threatening gestures. Craig
and Larison, arriving at Waiilatpu about that time, helped calm them down,
but a number of the Indians left for Fort Walla Walla, intending to teach
McKinlay a lesson also.

When Spalding heard these reports from the two mountain men, he gathered a group of Nez Perces and hurried over to Waiilatpu. Although peace
had returned to the Whitman mission, he learned that a fire had swept
through part of Fort Walla Walla. It had been an accident, but it had helped
to appease the Indians' unrest. After showing that he was ready to fight them,

24. Although Whitman called him Joe Gray, Clifford Drury states that he had once
been in the service of the Hudson's Bay Company, and it is therefore possible that he
was actually John Gray, the Iroquois halfblood who had deserted Ogden's Snake country
brigade in Utah in 1825. During the summer of 1841 John Gray, still a familiar figure
in the West, had accompanied Father De Smet and his missionary party from the States
to the Rockies. He was at Fort Hall on August 15, and could have gone on from there
to Waiilatpu with Cayuse friends. See Drury, *Marcus Whitman*, pp. 259-61, and "Mengarini's Narrative of the Rockies," ed. Albert J. Partoll, in *Frontier Omnibus*, p. 141.

McKinlay made peace with the Cayuses and sent them home in a more tranquil mood. Then he set about rebuilding his post, this time with adobes. Spalding did not visit the fort; but assuring himself that the passion of the Cayuses was spent and that the Whitmans were safe, he returned to Lapwai, where he found great numbers of Nez Perces collected from all parts of their country for religious services.

The missionary had planned to hold another series of protracted meetings, and according to his estimate some 2,000 Indians had responded, including many from Kamiah and elsewhere who were not friendly to himself or his teachings, but who had come as they might have traveled to a fur trappers' rendezvous, for the interest and holiday atmosphere of the gathering. Spalding preached to them for eight days, managing again to irritate James, who "seeing too much light for his sorcery rose in a rage & said he had received the Waiikin [his spiritual power, in his case the thunder] when young & could not throw it away & by this he had power over the winds & clouds." Timothy tried to answer the desperately upset little shaman, but James "soon stoped him by force, & attempting to speak, I told him to sit down." [25] Early the next morning, James came to see Spalding and told him that Craig was once more advising him to demand pay for his land. Spalding felt that there were now too many friendly Indians around him for James to be able to make trouble, and he ignored him. In time, the headman quieted down again; and although Craig never approved of Spalding, he stopped stirring up his father-in-law and eventually went to work for the missionary as a hired hand.

From the fall of 1841 to the spring of 1842, Spalding saw the Indians around the mission make their best progress to date, both with their farms and in the schoolhouse. In letters to the East he wrote of "the satisfaction of seeing the people coming to the mill with their horses loaded with grain, the fruits of their own industry," and said that at the school, attendance averaged "about 85, including a class of ten adults, six of whom are chiefs & principal men." Mrs. Spalding was still in charge of the school, being assisted by four Nez Perce youths who lived in the Spalding home.[26] In a letter to the

25. Drury, *Diaries*, p. 324.
26. Drury, *Spalding*, pp. 272–73. On February 14, 1842, Mrs. Spalding wrote Mrs. A. T. Smith that Ellis had also assisted her at the school for several weeks during the winter. Ellis, she said, had obtained a cow and two "young cattle" from Fort Walla Walla, and was going to settle down as a farmer at Kamiah. "He is also expecting Mr. McKinlay to furnish him with farming utensils and some mechanic tools, tin ware, etc." From this time on, Ellis and an increasing number of Indians would begin to build up herds of cattle, which would assume great importance to them. Later that year, on June 22, Mrs. William Gray, who was at Waiilatpu, noted Indians returning from the Willamette Valley with cattle which they had secured at Fort Vancouver. Drury, *First White Women*, 1, 214, 257.

A. T. Smiths, who had gone to live in the Willamette, she identified the adults who attended her class, most of them by the biblical names that her husband had given them. They were Joseph, Timothy, Luke, Lawyer, Stephen, Jason, Hezekiah, Lot, Mary, and Ellis. Hezekiah was the proud, young Cayuse chief Pahkatos Qohqoh (Five Crows), who shared the leadership of the Umatilla Valley band of Cayuses with his brother Tauitau, the Catholic. Both men were brothers-in-law of the Wallawalla headman, Peopeo Moxmox, as well as half-brothers of Joseph, the Nez Perce.[27] In December 1841 Spalding examined Hezekiah, Luke, and a number of other Indians in Mrs. Spalding's class and thought them ready for membership in the church; but when Whitman came over to Lapwai, he became embroiled in another quarrel with Spalding, revived all his old resentments against Spalding's remarks about Narcissa and, in a display of pique, refused to allow Spalding to baptize the Indians.

In February, all of the missionaries were saddened by news of the suicide of Mr. Munger in the Willamette. Early in 1841, while living at Waiilatpu, he had shown signs of insanity, and Whitman had arranged for the Mungers to return to the East, traveling with a Hudson's Bay Company party to the vicinity of Green River, where, he hoped, they could be given into the care of Americans going back to the States. But there were no more rendezvous, and no more fur caravans, and the only people making their way across the plains that year were a group of travelers that included Father De Smet, who was returning to the Flatheads with some colleagues to establish a mission, a lone Methodist preacher named Joseph Williams, and a group of emigrants known as the Bidwell-Bartleson company—all of them employing Tom Fitzpatrick as their guide for part of the way. The emigrants were farmers and adventurers from the Midwest and constituted the first sizable party of settlers bound for homes in the Far West. When they reached Soda Springs on the Bear River, some of them struck off for California, but twenty-four, on horseback, "two families with small children from Missouri," headed for the fabled Oregon of Hall Kelley, Nathaniel Wyeth, and Jason Lee. They halted briefly at Waiilatpu before starting down the Columbia, and their appearance in Oregon gave the dispirited Whitmans a feeling of renewed hope. After all their years of labor among the Cayuses, the missionary couple had begun to wonder if, like the Asa Smiths, they were doomed to failure. Christianity, it now seemed clear to them, required the disciplining of undisciplined Indians, something that could only be provided by the presence of a strong, civilized community that would force the Indians into a pattern of life which they had so far chosen to ignore or resist. Now, the civilizers were coming at

27. "The Gun Powder Story, Letter of Archibald McKinlay," ed. T. C. Elliott, *Oregon Historical Quarterly, 12* (1911).

last, and in their talk of crops, soil, and rainfall the Whitmans sensed a possible salvation for the mission. The newcomers were only a handful, but their numbers would swell. They would take the Indians' land and confine them into small areas, but they would also make them settle down and become farmers and Christians.[28]

The emigrants left the Whitmans after a few days and continued to the Willamette. About the same time, the Mungers straggled back from the plains, bringing with them Jim Bridger's six-year-old halfblood daughter, Mary Ann, whom the veteran trapper wished the Whitmans to care for and educate as they were doing with Joe Meek's daughter, Helen Mar. The Whitmans placed sheltering arms around the little Bridger girl and sent the Mungers down the Columbia. In the Willamette Valley, Munger found employment with the Methodist mission, but eventually his derangement became worse, and he believed himself able to perform miracles. One day, in an effort to prove his spiritual powers, he nailed himself through the hand to the wall above the fireplace in his shop, and was burned to death.

In May 1842 the missionaries gathered for another of their regular meetings. It was held at Waiilatpu and proved to be climactic, for Whitman was determined to force a showdown with Spalding, whose manner, if not his remarks, was continuing to disturb Narcissa and himself. Apparently, Whitman thought he might force Spalding out of the mission; and if that failed, he was ready to leave himself unless Spalding guaranteed to change his attitude. "We hope soon to be able to say *all* are *united* either in a final separation, or in everlasting *union & cooperation*," he wrote the Board just before the meeting.[29] When the men came together, Whitman invited the women also to listen to what he had to say, and Mrs. Walker noted in her diary that they heard "much to make our ears tingle . . ." There is no record of what Whitman related to the others, but the missionaries from Tshimakain were shocked,

28. The missionaries, of course, made a sharp distinction between solid farm families from the East and mountain men like Craig and Larison, who often seemed more like Indians than white men. From time to time trappers, abandoning their trade in the Rockies, appeared at the missions, but they were not welcomed, save as hired hands willing to do work around the stations. Most of them soon drifted on to the Willamette Valley. Among the best known of the mountain men to call at Waiilatpu was Kit Carson's friend, Philip M. Thompson, who arrived at Whitman's station in July 1842 with his Indian wife and children and with two other trappers, Joseph Matt and a man named Banks, and their Shoshoni wives. In noting their arrival "from New Mexico" on July 30, Mrs. William Gray wrote: "They are very anxious to settle here & the Indians are quite as anxious to have them. Husband & Dr. W. [Whitman] do not feel at liberty to encourage them." Thompson and his companions apparently lingered at Waiilatpu for only a short time, and then went on to the Willamette. Drury, *First White Women,* 1, 258–61.
29. Drury, *Whitman,* p. 266.

and Walker reported that "there was so much bad feeling manifested that I said that I thought it was an abomination for us to meet to pray." Eventually, Walker felt that he had to do something to restore peace if the mission were to be saved, and on June 2 he noted that he "felt much & said considerable." Not all of his blame was directed at Spalding, for the neutral missionaries thought that Whitman was showing unreasonable pettiness and resentment for whatever it was that he was complaining about, and they were irritated by his selfishness and obstinancy in threatening to abandon the mission and leave them all without a doctor "if he is not to have his own way entirely."

The next day, perhaps sobered by the stern lecture, Spalding and Whitman had a long, private talk together and finally managed to effect a peace between themselves that was to prove enduring. When they emerged from their discussion, Spalding made a public "confession" to the whole group, which, Mrs. Walker said, was "as humble as could be wished." It satisfied Whitman and started a new era of good relations among all the missionaries; and before they broke up their meeting, they wrote a letter to the Board, announcing that they had settled all their differences and difficulties and had reason "to hope for permanent peace and harmony." At the same time, fearing that the Board might already have taken some drastic action on the basis of all the complaining letters that had been sent previously about Spalding, they voted to do nothing about any harmful order that might come from the East until they received an answer to the happy information they were now sending.

That decision proved to be an important one, for in early September, Dr. Elijah White, who was leading a large group of emigrants across the country to Oregon, arrived at Waiilatpu, carrying the Board's fateful letter that ordered the dismissal of Spalding, the return of Gray and Asa Smith, and the abandonment of Lapwai and Waiilatpu. Dr. White appeared at the mission ahead of the emigrants and stayed for two days with Whitman. He was a scheming man, swollen with the importance of an appointment as subagent for Indian relations in the Oregon country, the first officer of any kind named by the United States for that region, which was still jointly claimed by Great Britain and the United States.

White had been in Oregon before as an assistant to Jason Lee in the Willamette. But the two men had quarreled, and White had resigned from the Methodist mission, under attack for having spent funds in an unauthorized manner and for having taken liberties with Indian women. In 1840 he had returned to the East by sea and, posing as an authority on Oregon, had lobbied for an appointment as governor or chief magistrate of the distant territory. Because of the joint occupancy of the country, the government could make no such appointment, and White had then focused his appeals on the need, as he saw it, for the naming of someone who could act for the United States in dealings with the Northwest Indians. With the help of influential persons who were interested in seeing Oregon become American, but who knew nothing of White's troubles with Lee, he had finally secured an appointment as subagent to the Oregon Indians. In addition, he had been encouraged to enlist American settlers to return with him to the Willamette Valley, and had been authorized to draw upon the government's Secret Service funds for the payment of expenses incurred by their emigration.

In the spring of 1842 he had left the Atlantic Coast for the frontier, carrying the order for Spalding's recall, which the American Board had entrusted to him. On the way to Missouri he had stopped at several places, enlisting recruits for the overland trek to Oregon, and on May 15 had started across the plains at the head of the first large emigration to the Columbia—more than 100 people, with their horses, cattle, pack mules, and nineteen white-topped Pennsylvania wagons. On the trip he had made himself unpopular and had been deposed as captain. The party had gradually abandoned its wagons, and from Fort Hall had pushed on only with packhorses and mules. In the Grande Ronde of Eastern Oregon the travelers had come on a large group of Nez Perces and Cayuses with their horse herds. Although many of the emigrants had regarded all Indians as treacherous enemies, there had been some who could make a distinction, and one of them, Medorem Crawford, had written in his journal, "I have seen no Indians since I started which appear so happy & well provided for as these. The beneficial influence of the Missionary Society appears to have reached here. They attended morning and evening devotion in our camp." When some of the emigrants' horses had strayed into the Indians' herds and become mixed with their animals, Crawford had reported that those Indians, moreover, had "showed moral honesty by bringing horses to us." [30]

As the party had neared the Columbia, White had ridden ahead with a Cayuse guide. At Waiilatpu he delivered the American Board's letter to Whitman, then hurried on to the Willamette where the American settlers—save those of Lee's mission, who were dismayed by his reappearance and possession of governmental authority—hailed him as the personification of Washington's interest in their protection and welfare.

The severity of the letter he had left at Waiilatpu stunned the missionaries. Aside from the recall of Spalding, which all agreed was now unwarranted and unnecessary, it seemed that the two most important and promising missions were being closed, while Tshimakain, where the timid and ineffective Walkers and Eellses were having only minor success among the Spokans, was to be reinforced. Whitman was particularly upset by the order to abandon

30. "Journal of Medorem Crawford," ed. F. G. Young, *Sources of the History of Oregon*, Vol. 1, No. 1 (Portland, Ore., 1897), p. 19.

Waiilatpu. It had resulted from the many complaints that Asa Smith and William Gray had leveled at Whitman in their letters to Boston, and Whitman must have considered the Board's decision a stern rebuke to himself as well as to Spalding.

The missionaries had voted not to do anything until they received a reply from Boston to the last letter they had sent, announcing their reconciliation; but Whitman believed that action was now necessary. Someone would have to return to Boston at once and inform the Board of the true situation at the missions. Spalding was in favor of the proposal, for his good name as well as the continuation of Lapwai were at stake, but the Walkers and Eellses were not sure. Whitman was insistent, however, undoubtedly being more worried over himself and Waiilatpu than about Spalding; and when he announced that he wanted to make the trip, he won agreement from the others. In the meantime, Gray was indifferent to the Board's order concerning himself. He had been offered a position with the Methodists in the Willamette, and he now formally resigned from the mission in which for so long he had done little but make trouble.

Whitman made immediate plans to leave for the East. It was already the end of September, a late and dangerous time to be considering a ride across the country, but the missionary felt that he had no choice. The big and impressive emigration that White had started west had already arrived at Waiilatpu on its way to the Willamette, and Whitman had heard of a number of persons who had gone back to the States with plans to return the following year with friends and relatives. The emigration the next year would be the biggest yet, and Whitman had a reason for wanting to come back with it. The hard-working missionary families, aware of the great amount of time they had to expend simply on their own affairs, desperately needed farmers, carpenters, and other skilled people to help them with their chores, and Whitman hoped to enlist a few settlers to work at the missions. At the same time he had an additional and larger hope. If Waiilatpu was saved in Boston, as he expected it would be, it was going to be worth while, he believed, to try to surround it in the future with a colony of intelligent and pious laymen who would help him civilize the Indians so that he could make more progress with his efforts to Christianize them. Thus, if he could get across the mountains this year before snow blocked his route, he would make his plea in Boston, and then do something to help get the right kind of settlers to join the 1843 emigration and come out to settle around Waiilatpu.[31]

31. A long, earnest letter by Elkanah Walker to Greene in Boston on October 3, 1842, the same day Whitman left for the East, reveals how greatly the Protestants' point of view about their mission in the Northwest had changed since they had originally enlisted to bring Christianity to the Indians. Pleading with Greene not to close the missions,

Whitman left the mission on October 3, accompanied by Asa Lovejoy, a 34-year-old lawyer who had just arrived with the emigrants but had agreed to go east again so the missionary would not have to ride alone. It was a daring and adventurous trip, but the two men made fast time. Although the danger of meeting hostile Sioux on the Platte forced them to take a long southward detour via the Colorado Rockies and Taos, they reached Bent's Fort on the Arkansas River safely. From there Whitman went on with mountain men to St. Louis, arriving early in March, five months after he had left Waiilatpu.[32] In Boston, after brief stops in Washington and New York, he received a cold reception from the Prudential Committee, whose members were distressed to see him in the East. He made a successful appeal to them, however, telling them of the changed conditions at the missions, and on April 4 the Committee agreed to reverse its position, and authorized Whitman and Spalding "to continue to occupy the stations at Waiilatpu and Clear Water."[33] Permission was also granted Whitman to take back to Oregon with him "a small company of intelligent and pious laymen," if he could do so without expense to the Board.

This aim of his ride was doomed not to be realized. He had little time left to get back to the frontier to join the new emigration, and although, after

---

Walker expounded on the agricultural, commercial, and manufacturing possibilities of the region and argued that "a numerous white population" would inevitably be coming to the area in a short time. Since much of the immigration would consist of Catholics, "and no one need be told that they need the pure influence of the gospel . . . the importance of the Mission could not be doubted." After continuing at length on the reasons why Protestants must stay in the Northwest to combat the Catholics, he mentioned the Indians: "One thing is very certain, that the influence of the gospel will have the tendency to make them more submissive to the rule of the whites and will be the means of preventing them from wars with their new neighbors, and save them from utter extinction. It seems the only [way] they can be saved from being destroyed from the face of the earth is by their yielding to the control of the whites, and nothing will induce them to do this but a cordial reception of the gospel, and how can this be done without the labors of the christian missionary." "The Oregon Missions as Shown in the Walker Letters, 1839–1851," ed. Paul C. Phillips, in *Frontier Omnibus*, pp. 105–11.

32. See below, p. 673.

33. The Committee's action gave Spalding permission to remain at the mission "for the present." When Spalding learned of the qualified support, he accepted it without protest, but it remained on his mind. On October 17, 1845, in a letter to Greene, he explained that he had not written east very often during the preceding two years, as he had felt that he was "on trial," and was being suffered to stay till the Board could man the mission "anew." He added that he still felt that his fate was unsettled, and wondered if he was still on trial. A few months later, on January 24, 1846, he again wrote Greene, saying that he now took it for granted "that confidence is somewhat restored & that statements I may make will not be received altogether as accounts of a 'paper mission.'" The texts of these letters were made available to me by Clifford M. Drury.

leaving Boston, he made stops at his home and at many other places en route to Missouri, he was able to enlist only one young man, his 13-year-old nephew, Perrin Whitman. The propaganda work on behalf of Oregon that Lee, Whitman, and others had already done with their letters to newspapers and personal visits had contributed importantly, however, to an "Oregon fever" that was spreading through many parts of the States; and when Whitman and his nephew arrived at Independence in mid-May, they were overwhelmed to find an assemblage of a thousand emigrants, with 125 heavily loaded covered wagons and between 3,000 and 5,000 head of cattle, horses, and mules. "It is now decided," Whitman wrote enthusiastically to eastern friends, "that Oregon will be occupied by American citizens. Those who go only open the way for more another year." What reaction he thought this would have on the Indians—if he thought about it at all—he did not say.

On the trail, Whitman aided the emigrants with advice and assistance at river crossings and along difficult parts of the route, and administered to their medical needs. At Fort Hall, when the British trader in charge told the settlers that they would never get their wagons the rest of the way, the missionary remembered the three wagons that Joe Meek and his companions had driven to Waiilatpu three years before and insisted that wheeled vehicles could get through. The emigrants took his advice, and Whitman himself guided the train to the Grande Ronde, where a band of Cayuses, under a chief named Stickus who was a friend of the Whitmans, met them. Then, when Whitman hurried on ahead, Stickus took over the duties of a guide and piloted the wagons across the Blue Mountains. By the end of September 1843 the first of them rolled safely down to the Walla Walla River near Whitman's mission.

It was a momentous event for the Northwest. Five years before, on February 7, 1838, J. H. Pelly, Governor of the Hudson's Bay Company, had written a letter to the Lords of the Committee of the Privy Council for Trade in London, informing them that the Hudson's Bay Company had pressed its enterprise so vigorously in the Columbia district that the American fur men had all but disappeared from that territory. The future of the region, he was confident, would henceforth be firmly in the hands of the British.[34] But now the die was being cast differently. American settlers, more dangerous to the British than the trappers had ever been, had found Oregon and the road to it, and the balance of power along the Columbia was about to make its final shift.[35]

34. Merk, *Fur Trade and Empire*, p. 343.

35. Governor George Simpson and other officials of the Hudson's Bay Company were aghast at the sheer numbers of American settlers coming into the country. Even Dr. McLoughlin, who greeted all arrivals with consideration and kindness, became alarmed by the prospect of no longer being able to contain the newcomers south of the Columbia River. See Rich, *Hudson's Bay Company*, 2, 717.

Some of the Indians were as uneasy as the British. The Nez Perces, whose original mission to St. Louis had unwittingly helped to lead to this new invasion, watched the "Bostons" and their women and children stream through the Grande Ronde Valley and over the Blue Mountains to the Walla Walla, and with many of the Cayuses and other Indians of the area did not know what to think of it. A few of them saw new sources of gain for themselves. In the Grande Ronde, those Indians who wanted to own white men's cattle—the possession of which, like that of horses, was becoming a mark of influence and wealth—found that they could trade their sturdy western ponies for some of the settlers' scraggly, trailworn livestock, which they could fatten on their own ranges. Other Indians who had learned to farm and were raising produce and grain could follow the example of the missionaries at Lapwai and Waiilatpu and sell their agricultural products along the trail to the emigrants.

Many of the Indians, however, had longer visions, and some of the shamans and headmen worried their people with ominous talk of the future. Although the whites were headed down the Columbia to the country of the Chinookans, and had no interest in settling in this arid, upriver country east of the Cascades, there would be others coming after them, all hungry for land. The Indians had heard terrible stories of what had been happening to tribes in the East; on the plains and in the mountains, Delaware trappers and others had been telling them of lands stolen and peoples uprooted, of tribes forced on long marches from their homelands east of the Mississippi to new places in hot, disease-ridden country on the southern plains. And closer to home, the Sahaptins knew what was occurring in the Willamette, where the Americans were also taking the Indians' land and the native peoples were becoming beggars and thieves, and dying like insects from the white man's sicknesses. Eventually, the tribal prophets warned, some of the "Bostons" would halt on the Sahaptins' lands, and then there would be trouble in that part of the country too.

Whitman himself had hoped that some of the white families whom he had helped to pilot west would settle around Waiilatpu. But although many of them paused, none remained. They stopped long enough to rest or to purchase supplies, paying a dollar a bushel for the mission's wheat and forty cents a bushel for potatoes, and buying so much of Whitman's beef, pork, corn, and other provisions that he had to call on Spalding to supply him for the winter. Then the emigrants moved on, taking to boats and rafts at the Dalles, and finally straggling in to Fort Vancouver where, with the assistance of Dr. McLoughlin, they were given supplies and launched on their way to creating new homes and settlements in the wilderness country of the lower Columbia.

Although he was unhappy that none of the newcomers had elected to stay with him, Whitman at least had saved Waiilatpu for future years. There would be emigrations each year from then on, he assured the other missionaries when they gathered again, and eventually some of the settlers would build homes in that part of Oregon too. Meanwhile, from his colleagues, he learned what had happened during his absence. Only three days after he had left Waiilatpu the previous fall, an Indian intruder had tried to break into Narcissa's bedroom in the middle of the night. The Grays had already left the station to go to the Willamette, and she had been the only white person at the mission at the time. She had frightened the intruder away with her screams; but at the insistence of McKinlay, who had hurried over to get her, she had moved to the safety of Fort Walla Walla, and eventually to the Methodist mission at the Dalles. Shortly after she had left the fort, disgruntled Cayuses had set fire to the grist mill at Waiilatpu and burned some two hundred bushels of wheat and corn.

News of both occurrences had traveled quickly down the Columbia River and reached the ears of the newly arrived Dr. Elijah White who, as Indian agent, believed he had a duty to protect the American mission. Although he had little money for expenses, he enlisted an escort that included Tom McKay, six armed guards, and Cornelius Rogers and Baptiste Dorion as interpreters, and started upriver on November 15, 1842, to investigate what was happening. Dorion was a link with earlier events in the Northwest. With his mother, the stoic Iowa Indian wife of Pierre Dorion, he had crossed the country with the Wilson Price Hunt expedition of 1811, and had survived the massacre of John Reed's trapping party on the Boise River in 1814. His mother, who in 1824 had become the wife of Jean Toupin, the interpreter at Fort Nez Perces, was still alive; and on July 19, 1841, Father Blanchet had formally solemnized that union with a Catholic ceremony in the Willamette Valley.[36] Now, a year later, White hired Baptiste, who had occasionally served the Hudson's Bay Company as a Sahaptin interpreter. As a devout Catholic, young Dorion's value in helping to straighten out the difficulties at the Protestant missions was questionable; and soon after White's mission had ended, rumors were abroad that Dorion, indeed, had spread tales among the Indians that were harmful to the missionaries' future.

Buffeted by heavy winds, White's party made slow progress up the Columbia, and on November 24 reached the mission at the Dalles, where Narcissa was resting. worn and lonely, "her noble and intellectual mind and spirit . . . much depressed, and her health suffering," [37] William Geiger and the Littlejohns were also there. William Gray had enlisted Geiger to take care of Waiilatpu until Whitman returned, and Littlejohn agreed to keep

36. W. J. Ghent, *The Early Far West* (New York, 1931), p. 326 n.
37. A. J. Allen, *Ten Years in Oregon* (Ithaca, New York, 1850), p. 181.

Geiger company for a while at the mission. So both men went on with White to Fort Walla Walla, which they reached on November 20. There, McKinlay also joined the group, and the next day they all rode out to Waiilatpu. White was "shocked and pained at beholding the sad work of savage destruction" that the Indians had caused during the absence of the whites. He wanted to have a conference with the Cayuses, but only a few frightened Indians lurked about the area. He directed them to tell their chiefs to gather the tribe and be ready to meet him in a few days, then turned his attention to Lapwai. Reports of Nez Perce opposition to their mission had also reached him, and thinking that he ought to support Spalding's position too, he started with his companions for the Clearwater River, sending a messenger ahead to ask that the chiefs be assembled to meet him.

He arrived at Lapwai on December 3 and found the Nez Perces beginning to collect around the mission. The Spaldings, White said, greeted him "with joyful countenances and glad hearts," while "the chiefs met us with civility, gravity and dignified reserve." For two days, while his party waited for all of the principal men to come in, the Indians wondered at his presence. He was neither a trader nor a teacher of the white man's religion, but was more like the Captains Lewis and Clark, whose memory they still respected. Looking up to him as a representative of the Americans' chiefs in the East, they must have thought that he was going to council with them with the same degree of fairness and equality that Lewis and Clark had accorded them; and as he visited their lodges, inspected their farms and watched them at Spalding's classes, they waited with expectant politeness. White, in turn, was "happily surprised and greatly interested at seeing such numbers so far advanced and so eagerly pursuing after knowledge" and found it "most gratifying to witness their fondness and care for their little herds, pigs, poultry, etc." [38]

His council with them began on December 5, when he was "ushered into the presence of the assembled chiefs, to the number of twenty-two, with some lesser dignitaries, and a large number of the common people." The Indians listened to him with grave expressions while he told them first that the American government had sent him with "kind intentions" to assure them that from this time, sad consequences would befall any white man "who should invade their rights, by stealing, murder, selling them damaged for good articles, or alcohol." Having thus ingratiated himself with this irresponsible and false promise, mere words which government agents had used time and again on every frontier with little thought of enforcement, White went on to shore up Spalding's position. "I gave them to understand," he reported, "how highly Mr. and Mrs. Spalding were prized by the numerous whites, and with what pleasure the great chief gave them a passport to encourage them to

38. Ibid., p. 182.

come here to teach them what they were now so diligently employed in obtaining, in order that they and their children might become good, wise and happy." [39] It was only the beginning of what he had to say, for in discussions with Spalding, White had convinced himself that he understood the reasons for the missionaries' troubles, and he now planned to offer his solution. First, however, he called on McKinlay, Rogers, and McKay to prepare the ground for him, and each one, in turn, asked the Nez Perces whether they were of heart to listen to the advice which their new protector, Dr. White, had come to present to them.

A number of the Indians arose to give an affirmative response, including the Cayuse, Five Crows, who, under the name Hezekiah, had been attending Spalding's classes, as well as an old and respected leader, "not less than ninety years," whom White called the Bloody Chief. He was Ellis' grandfather, Hohots Ilppilp, the venerable war chief, Red Grizzly Bear, also known as Many Wounds, who had counciled with Lewis and Clark. "I am the oldest chief of the tribe," he told White in a tremulous voice. "Was the high chief when your great brothers, Lewis and Clark, visited this country; they visited me, and honored me with their friendship and counsel. I showed them my numerous wounds received in bloody battles with the Snakes; they told me it was not good, it was better to be at peace; gave me a flag of truce; I held it up high; we met and talked, but never fought again. Clark pointed to this day, to you, and this occasion; we have long waited in expectation; sent three of our sons to Red river school to prepare for it; two of them sleep with their fathers; the other is here, and can be ears, mouth, and pen for us. I can say no more; I am quickly tired; my voice and limbs tremble. I am glad I live to see you and this day, but I shall soon be still and quiet in death." [40]

The aged Indian's dignified speech was the voice of another age. White was affected, his ego undoubtedly touched by the realization that he was being linked by history with the great Lewis and Clark. But there was a difference between him and the explorers. Lewis and Clark had regarded the Nez Perces as a free people. White did not. This was not yet United States territory. No white nation, in fact, had as yet established sovereignty over the land which the Nez Perces considered their own. But it made no difference to White. He was an agent of the United States government and, indifferent to the fact that the Indians to whom he was talking were still independent peo-

39. An assumption, of course, that the Indians had not been any of these things before the missionaries' arrival.

40. Allen, *Ten Years in Oregon*, p. 185. The three "sons" sent to the Red River school were Ellis, Pitt, and Cayuse Halket. Halket, as noted earlier, died at the school, and Pitt in the Nez Perce country. The reference to Ellis, present at the council, as "ears, mouth, and pen" of the Nez Perces made a strong impression on White.

ple, owing nothing to any white man, he treated them as being under his supervision and therefore bound by his directions. And he was prepared now not to propose a treaty with them, as was done with tribes in United States territory, but arrogantly and arbitrarily to impose upon them a set of "laws" by which they should henceforth live.

While the Indians listened in silence, he read the regulations he wanted them to accept:

"1) Whoever wilfully takes life shall be hung.

"2) Whoever burns a dwelling house shall be hung.

"3) Whoever burns an outbuilding shall be imprisoned six months, receive fifty lashes, and pay all damages.

"4) Whoever carelessly burns a house, or any property, shall pay damages.

"5) If any one enter a dwelling, without permission of the occupant, the chiefs shall punish him as they think proper. Public rooms are excepted.

"6) If any one steal he shall pay back two fold; and if it be the value of a beaver skin or less, he shall receive twenty-five lashes; and if the value is over a beaver skin he shall pay back two fold, and receive fifty lashes.

"7) If any one take a horse, and ride it, without permission, or take any article and use it, without liberty, he shall pay for the use of it, and receive from twenty to fifty lashes, as the chief shall direct.

"8) If any one enter a field, and injure the crops, or throw down the fence, so that cattle or horses go in and do damage, he shall pay all damages, and receive twenty-five lashes for every offence.

"9) Those only may keep dogs who travel or live among the game; if a dog kill a lamb, calf, or any domestic animal, the owner shall pay the damage, and kill the dog.

"10) If an Indian raise a gun or other weapon against a white man, it shall be reported to the chiefs, and they shall punish him. If a white person do the same to an Indian, it shall be reported to Dr. White, and he shall redress it.

"11) If an Indian break these laws, he shall be punished by his chiefs; if a white men break them, he shall be reported to the agent, and be punished at his instance."

White may have meant well, and considered that these provisions would effectively halt all of the principal offenses by the Indians which the Spaldings and Whitmans had experienced. Spalding himself probably had a strong hand in devising and framing them. But in time, the laws would prove damaging to both the Indians and the white men. On the missionaries' part, they signified the abandonment of any further pretense of divine disapproval of the Indians' bad conduct. The Americans, not God, were now admitted to be the directors of the giving of punishment, and the realization of that fact by the Indians soon stripped the missionaries of what had long been one of their most powerful means of control. On the Indians' part, the laws substituted the hangman's noose, the lash, and cruel imprisonment for the humane, ethical forms of social disapproval under which the Indians, without Christianity or civilization, had long maintained village and family discipline. As the old ways came into question, the ground was inevitably prepared for the dissolution of Indian self-discipline and morale.

White reported that he read the laws to the Nez Perces, "clause by clause, leaving them as free to reject as to accept," and that "they were greatly pleased with all proposed." But the significance and consequences, if not the meaning itself, of what they were hearing were beyond them, for few, if any, could foresee how the laws would be used to divide and subjugate them. It would be one thing, for example, for an Indian wrongdoer to be turned over to a headman for punishment while Spalding or other white men watched, and were satisfied. But the Indians would discover that the laws could not be made to apply to white men. Articles ten and eleven, which exempted white offenders from Indian jurisdiction, even in Indian-owned country, would give whites liberty to exploit, rob, persecute, and murder Indians, for no Indian agent would ever have the power or ability to bring a white man to justice in the face of the public opinion and political opposition of the white settlers, who recognized no rights of the Indians and protected each other against the native peoples.

Even after the Indians indicated their acceptance of the laws, White was not finished with them. One of the missionaries' most difficult problems, he understood, resulted from the loose social and political organization within the tribes. Headmen, or chiefs (the latter term usually referring to warriors, who had no authority at all), had jurisdiction only over the people of their own villages. When Indians from many villages clustered around the missions, it was impossible to make a headman responsible for the actions of wrongdoers if they were not members of his band. James had avoided helping Spalding many times by disclaiming responsibility for brash, young men around the mission, and Spalding had often been unable to find anyone to assume leadership over Indians who were making trouble for him. If the new laws were to be carried out, White felt, a new, organized system of responsibility would have to be instituted among the headmen and chiefs. His proposal was to direct that all of the bands of the Nez Perces, for the first time in their history, choose a single "high chief of the tribe, and acknowledge him as such by universal consent." All the other chiefs were to become subordinate, with equal power among themselves, and with five men each "as a body guard, to execute all their lawful commands." Thus, the high chief, giving orders to the subordinate chiefs, would become responsible to the whites for the effective enforcement of the new laws.

White's undemocratic and tyrannical scheme was too great a break with cultural traditions for the leaders of the autonomous Nez Perce bands and villages to understand. No headman had ever given orders to, or spoken for, any people but his own, except when others had elected him to lead war parties or buffalo-hunting groups, and even then he had guided and advised rather than ordered. The proposal, White said, "was a new and delicate task," and the Indians "soon saw and felt it." They withdrew in consternation and tried to select the kind of leader the white man had described; but after two hours, during which the responsible headmen must have shrunk from the immodesty of the proposed new position, they returned and told White he would have to pick such a man himself. He refused to do it, though he reported that the Nez Perces were "somewhat puzzled." Eventually, he gave them permission to counsel with McKay and Rogers. They "worked poor Rogers and McKay severely for many hours," he said, "but altogether at length figured it out, and in great good humor" finally chose Ellis. The selection was made possibly in deference to Ellis' grandfather, old Hohots Ilppilp, who had earlier told White that the young man "can be ears, mouth, and pen for us." But Rogers and McKay, and perhaps White himself, may have had a hand in it too, since Ellis was the only member of the tribe who had received a Christian education at Red River, and could read, write, and speak English satisfactorily.

The choosing of any one as the single, head chief of the whole tribe was unfortunate, for it was bound to lead to misunderstanding and trouble. The Indians could not comprehend the new position, and they had no idea of abandoning the traditional autonomy and independence of their individual villages. But to the white men, the head chief was now responsible for the whole tribe; and although the different bands still did not recognize him as spokesman for any but his own people—and the embarrassed "head chief" himself often protested that he did not speak for everyone—the whites made him act the role, whether he liked it or not. The situation, dangerous from the start, had within it the seeds of turmoil and war. The choice of Ellis, moreover, was of no help. He lived in the Kamiah region, had his own farm and some sheep and cattle, as well as a herd of more than 1,100 horses, and White considered him "a sensible man . . . quite as correct in his conclusions and firm in his decisions as could have been expected." [41] But he was only 32 years old, and although he enjoyed prestige because he had been to Red River, he had never won honors in warfare or on hunts. After his selection as head chief, he became conceited, and grew offensive to his fellow tribesmen. He aroused the jealousy of older and more experienced leaders, including Lawyer and Joseph, and when he tried to exert authority, they and other able and respected headmen and shamans refused to recognize his posi-

41. Ibid., pp. 186–87.

tion, and further undermined the Indians' acceptance of any one person's
right to usurp the role of the tribal council as the voice of all the people.

White's party remained at Lapwai for two weeks after the council, and
Spalding used the opportunity to strengthen his position on another front.
He had already decided to stay with the Nez Perces as an independent missionary if Whitman proved unable to save his job; but it would be better, he
knew, if the Board could be made to see that it had committed an error in its
judgment of him. He showed his guests the work he had done, and the progress that he and Mrs. Spalding had achieved with the Nez Perces, and asked
them for testimonials to the Board in his behalf. White, McKinlay, and Mc-
Kay all seemed thoroughly impressed with his work at Lapwai, and obliged
him with letters. "I . . . was most agreeably surprised at the great progress
of the school," McKinlay wrote. "I had formed no adequate idea of the labors of himself & Mrs. Spalding." McKay was even more enthusiastic. "I am
happy to inform you," he wrote to Boston, "that the Mission under the care
of Revd H. H. Spalding is above all Missions, in this country that is it sur-
passes them all, notwithstanding all what has been said against him he stands
aloof like a pillar; unshaken by his opponents." [42] And White informed the
Board that "I found nearer approaches [at Lapwai] to civilization and more
manifest desire for improvement than I have elsewhere met with in this or
any other Indian country." [43] Later, in his report to the Commissioner of Indian Affairs in Washington, White added another pat on the back for the
Spaldings. Their "zeal and untiring industry for the people of their charge,"
he made a part of his official record, "entitle them to our best considerations." [44]

42. Drury, *Spalding*, p. 293.
43. Ibid., p. 297.
44. Allen, *Ten Years in Oregon*, p. 194. As pointed above, n. 33, Spalding continued
to nurse hurt feelings, and seek visitors' testimony in his behalf, even after he learned
that the Board had rescinded its action in recalling him. In June 1844 a German botanist,
Karl A. Geyer, who was making an extended tour through the Northwest, traveled from
Tshimakain to Lapwai and stayed with the Spaldings for a while. Geyer interested the
missionary couple in collecting varieties of local plants and flowers, and Spalding accompanied the botanist on several trips through the Clearwater Valley, and possibly on one
occasion to the mouth of the Salmon River. He must have poured out his troubles to
Geyer, for in 1845 and 1846, when the scientist published the notes of his tour in the
London Journal of Botany, he apologized to his readers for digressing at one point to do
"justice" to Spalding. That missionary's work, he said, was "propitious beyond my
expectation," and he went on: "Mr. S. is by far the most successful Indian missionary
deputed by the American Board of Foreign Missions . . . He boldly left off the absurd
custom of teaching the Indian to pray, before endeavouring to fill his hungry stomach . . . The American Board of Foreign Missions has committed an error in not aiding
Mr. Spalding, or giving and entrusting to his hands the surveillance of all the Missions

White and his companions left Lapwai about December 20 and returned to Waiilatpu, where they found a few of the Cayuse chiefs waiting for them. Most of them were still in the buffalo country, however, and those who were present were "manifestly uneasy." When White told them of the laws that the Nez Perces had accepted, they showed "great concern and anxiety." Rogers and McKay lectured them about their bad conduct, and although one of the headmen most hostile to the Whitmans, a Cayuse whom Narcissa called Feathercap, burst into tears, another one told the party boldly that "the whites were much more to blame than the Indians; that three-fourths of them, though they taught the purest doctrines, practiced the greatest abominations—alluding," said White, "to the base conduct of many in the Rocky Mountains where they meet them on their buffalo hunts during the summer season, and witness the greatest extravagances." [45] White was unable to make progress with them, and told them that he would return to Waiilatpu at the "new moon of April" to meet with the whole tribe. Then, leaving Geiger at the station, the party returned to the Dalles, where White prevailed upon the Indians at that trading center along the river to adopt the Nez Perce laws. "Succeeded in like happy manner, with them as the Nez Perces," he noted. At the Dalles, also, the Littlejohns, who had originally planned to spend the winter at Waiilatpu with Geiger, now agreed with White's suggestion to help the Spaldings at Lapwai, instead. They parted from White and the others, who continued downriver to Fort Vancouver.

For some time after the adoption of the laws, Spalding had an easier time with the Nez Perces. White's visit had made an impression on them, and if there was opposition either to the laws or to the missionaries, it was kept quietly among the Indians themselves. Spalding printed the laws as quickly as he could and, before the end of the year, distributed them to the villages in an eight-page booklet. White had asked him for a report on the mission to send to Washington, and Spalding's reply, also sent that winter, reflected the peace that reigned at Lapwai. Some 225 Indian students, half of them adults, showed up daily for school, and Mrs. Spalding, who conducted classes, had about one hundred of them "printing their own books with a pen." Concerning agriculture, 140 Indians, Spalding reported, had cultivated from one-quarter of an acre to four or five acres each the previous season. "One chief raised about one hundred and seventy-six bushels of peas . . . one hundred of corn, and four hundred of potatoes." Others had also done well, and eight Indians already had plows. A few, he added, had livestock: "Thirty-two head

---

of that Board in Oregon. They leave him to struggle alone, and consequently the credit and praise belong solely to him . . ." McKelvey, *Botanical Exploration of the Trans-Mississippi West*, pp. 783–84.
45. Allen, *Ten Years in Oregon*, p. 191.

of cattle are possessed by two individuals; ten sheep by four; some forty hogs." The Nez Perces were a "very industrious people . . . Doubtless many more would cultivate, but for the want of means." As to arts and sciences, ten "females" were knitting under Mrs. Spalding's instruction, many were sewing, six carding and spinning, and three weaving.[46]

Much of the progress the Spaldings were making would have a lasting effect on the tribe. Many of those who were now learning the skills and beliefs of a Christian civilization would never abandon them, and slowly a cadre of "civilized" Nez Perces was forming within the nation. It was a significant development, and in the long run would confirm the Spaldings as the most successful of the early Protestant missionaries in the Northwest. Waiilatpu with the Cayuses was an utter failure. The Walkers and Eellses at Tshimakain made practically no progress with the Spokans, and the Methodists at the Dalles and along the lower Columbia were of more importance to the whites than to Indians.[47] But the Spaldings, passionately devoted to the elevation of their Indians, were teaching a strong, vital native people to read and write, to raise livestock and make a living from the soil, to spin, sew, and weave, to grind wheat into flour, to saw logs into boards for buildings, and to make hoes and plows out of iron. Only a part of the tribe welcomed their labors, and only a fraction of that part responded wholeheartedly to their instructions. But the seed was being planted, and in time the secular education begun at Lapwai resulted in what Spalding had hoped for, the settling of a large part of the tribe in farm homes around churches.

The seeds of catastrophe that the Spaldings, with White's help, were also planting were harder to see. For a while the new laws and punishments were enforced around the mission. But by the early spring of 1843 the laws were beginning to prove so unpopular that enforcement gradually broke down. When Spalding urged the chiefs to carry out their duties, some of them refused to do so, unwilling to face the resentment and opposition of their people. The fact that the new order existed, even in theory, further weakened the position of Spalding's loyal Indians. They were looked on as women, and as servants of the whites, and many of them were torn between abiding by their agreement with Elijah White and maintaining their prestige and influence among their people. Even Ellis felt the sting of censure and became a problem. To prove his independence and disdain for Spalding, he rode down to Lapwai and created a commotion, ordering a drumming and dance around the mission, and advising the Indians to paint their faces in the schoolroom. Many of the Nez Perces obeyed him, and when the shocked and scandalized Spalding upbraided him, Ellis replied in a manner that Spalding termed

46. Ibid., pp. 205–06.
47. See below, p. 673.

haughty. The missionary couple thought that his authority had gone to his head, and Mrs. Spalding described the incident as one in which Ellis had come "filled with pride, vanity, and wrath and made an attempt to frighten Mr. S. and all the chiefs here with great swelling words." [48]

The young head chief finally calmed down and became "humble, respectful, and friendly as we could wish," but Spalding thought that the time had come for another sobering talk by Dr. White. He wrote White a letter, telling him of the difficulties he was beginning to have in getting the laws enforced, and complaining of Ellis' behavior, and gave it to Ellis himself to deliver to Dr. White in the Willamette, hoping that the Indian agent would diplomatically straighten out the chief in the impressive environment of the numerous white settlements of the lower Columbia. Ellis went down the river by canoe with several companions, and White apparently successfully impressed him, for after the Indian's return, Spalding did not have occasion to complain about him again.

Spalding's letter to White, however, served as a stimulus for another upriver trip by the Indian agent, who was again receiving alarming advice from Waiilatpu and the Dalles. The Cayuses were once more threatening trouble. Their buffalo hunting bands had returned from the plains, and the whole tribe, Geiger wrote, was upset and full of dangerous rumors. Some of the Indians believed that great numbers of "Boston men" were coming from the East with Dr. Whitman to take their lands. Others thought that Whitman had gone to get American soldiers to fight them. The laws that the Nez Perces had adopted had increased their alarm, and some of the young men were even proposing to form a war party to attack the whites in the Willamette Valley. Their anxieties and resentments had spread to the Indians at the Dalles, and the missionaries there were even more excited than Geiger. Mrs. Whitman, however, was calm. While the others at the Dalles appealed to Dr. White to hurry upriver again, she wrote her husband an understanding account of what was happening: "The principal cause of the excitement," she told Marcus with a perception that was rare for a white interpreter of Indians anywhere in the United States at that time, "is the Kayuses do not wish to be *forced* to adopt the laws. They say the laws in themselves are good, they do not object to them—but do not wish to be compelled to adopt them (enforce them). This arises from what was said at the meeting to this effect; We advise you to adopt these laws, but if you do not *we will put you in a way to do it.* They took exceptions to such language as this. Call it threatening them—and are jealous and complain of Ellis—the High Chief and the Nez Perces for so soon and so readily entering into the new measures of the Americans." [49]

48. Drury, *Spalding*, p. 303.
49. Drury, *Whitman*, p. 287.

In addition to the Cayuses' objection to dictation and threats by White, the commotion, she observed, had also been stirred by members of the agent's party the previous fall. Baptiste Dorion, in particular, was said to have informed the Indians secretly that when White returned to Waiilatpu in April, he would have troops with him to force the Indians to accept the laws.[50]

Mrs. Whitman was strongly opposed to White's meddling any further with the Cayuses. In the absence of Marcus, she thought of them as "sheep without a shepherd," and until her husband's return believed it would be better for the Indian agent to stay away from Waiilatpu. White, she maintained, was "quite ignorant of the Indian character and especially of the character of the Kaiuses," and at Fort Vancouver Dr. McLoughlin agreed with her. The influx of inept and narrow-minded missionaries who through the years had poured into the Northwest "to bewilder our poor Indians," who, McLoughlin said, were "already perplexed beyond measure by the number and variety of their instructors," worried the Hudson's Bay Company leader and made him wonder when the Indians would react.[51] He was particularly concerned about the Cayuses, who had always showed the traders at Fort Walla Walla that they had a fiercely independent spirit, and he advised White not to try to force them to accept the laws.

But White thought he knew better, and he wrote Mrs. Whitman to meet him at Waiilatpu. His first aim was to restore quiet among the Cayuses by proving that he had no intention of bringing troops upon them, and when he arrived at the Whitman station on May 9, 1843, he was accompanied by only a small party that included two Methodist missionaries, the Reverends H. K. W. Perkins and Gustavus Hines. The Cayuses, he found, were more

---

50. To Mary Walker, on April 11, 1843, Narcissa wrote: "Dorion that came up with Doct White last fall has told them many things that has excited them greatly such as— there are troops coming into the mouth of the Columbia this spring. The Agent is coming up this spring with an armed force to take away their lands & compel them to adopt & enforce laws to regulate their own people & redress the wrongs of the whites." Drury, *First White Women*, 2, 249–50 n. See also Johansen, *Robert Newell's Memoranda*, p. 94. At about the same time, March 8, 1843, Father Blanchet wrote to the Bishop of Quebec: "The Cayuse tribe, the wealthiest of all the native tribes in the vicinity, finds itself divided between the minister Whitman and a young native, named Pierre, who was taught at our mission of the Walamette. In the month of April 1842 he went to the falls of the Walamette, and left there only after having acquired new powers and secured new knowledge. He baptizes children and adults in danger of death, and says his prayers every day of the week, as well as the one on Sunday. This young man, who has the zeal of a missionary, has succeeded in deriving some of his [people] from the ministerial prayer . . ." (*Notices & Voyages*, pp. 172–73). Pierre, who seems to have been active among the Cayuses during the absence of the Whitmans, is not further identified.

51. Dorothy O. Johansen and Charles M. Gates, *Empire of the Columbia* (New York, 1957), p. 217.

frightened than warlike, and he was soon able to reassure them that he had no soldiers "concealed somewhere near," ready "to open fire upon, and cut them all off at a blow." [52] Among the Indians in the vicinity he found some sixty working at small farms. They included the Wallawalla chief, Peopeo Moxmox, and his son, Elijah, now 18 years old. Both men were considered loyal friends of the whites, and the Indian agent felt sure that they would support his plea for the adoption of the laws. But the Cayuses were still too fearful to council with him. The stern punishments which the laws provided for actions which the Indians considered normal conduct or, at worst, trivial offenses fed other fears and made them believe that the code was simply a means of subjugating them and making them slaves so that Whitman and the "Bostons" he was bringing back with him could more easily take their lands away from them. Before discussing the laws, some of the Indians wanted to wait for the return of Whitman, and see whether he would try to give their lands to new white people. Others wanted to know more about how the laws actually worked, and wished, first, to discuss them with Ellis and the Nez Perces.

To the impatient White there seemed only one solution. He had formed a good opinion of Ellis during the Nez Perce chief's visit to the Willamette, and he was certain that he could count on his assistance in the impasse. Instead of leaning on white soldiers to force the Cayuses to his will, he would let the Nez Perces do his arguing for him. Informing the Indians at Waiilatpu that he would return in a short time to make a treaty with them, "if we could agree on the terms," he hastened to Lapwai with the two Methodists, arriving on May 13 and finding the Nez Perces in a friendly mood. Spalding had been conducting special religious meetings and, without the presence of Asa Smith, William Gray, Whitman, or the others to inhibit him, was planning the next day to accept nine Indians into the church. White and the Methodists witnessed the ceremony, during which Spalding baptized four men and five women, including Asenoth and Tamar, the wives of Joseph and Timothy respectively. Some 200 Nez Perces participated, and Hines, in a burst of enthusiasm for Spalding's work, wrote in his journal, "This is evidently the most promising Indian mission to Oregon." Spalding's Cayuse student, Hezekiah, was also scheduled to be baptized; but although he was absent that day and

52. There must have been considerable confusion, as well as division, among the Indians at this time. The fears and warlike rumblings among some of the Cayuses had reached the ears of other tribes, and there is an indication that moderates, who wanted no trouble with the white men, had brought their influence to bear on the Cayuses. The whites had little way of knowing what was going on among the Indians, and their councils would not have been recorded. But on April 27 Mrs. Walker at Tshimakain wrote of news from the Flathead post in northwestern Montana that the Indians there (probably Nez Perces) were going to Waiilatpu "to receive their laws and protect Mr. Spalding if necessary" (Drury, *White Women*, 2, 250).

his baptism was therefore delayed until June 16, he was remembered by White as one of the chiefs who had spoken during his earlier visit to Lapwai, and the agent probably discussed with Spalding the advisability of his becoming the Cayuse counterpart of Ellis. After the ceremony, White made a flattering appeal to the Nez Perces and, playing them off against the Cayuses, reported that "they accepted my invitation to visit with me the Keyuses and Wallawallas, and assist by their influence to bring them into the same regulations they had previously adopted."

Somewhat in a carnival mood, the Nez Perces gathered their people and, with more curiosity than crusading zeal, rode over to Waiilatpu with White's party and Spalding. White said that there were "some four or five hundred of the men and their women," including Ellis, old Hohots Ilppilp, and "every other chief and brave of importance." News of their trek preceded them, and the missionaries found the Cayuses and Wallawallas waiting for them "in mass." With the help of Ellis and some of the Nez Perce leaders, White finally got the council started. According to Hines, who later reported some of the details of the proceedings, the laws, which were now referred to as "the Nez Perce laws," were first read aloud in English, and then in Nez Perce. Most of the Cayuses were quiet, one of the few serious questions being voiced by the Wallawalla leader, Peopeo Moxmox, who "rose and said to the white men, 'I have a message to you. Where are these laws from? Are they from God or from the earth? I would that you might say they were from God. But I think that they are from the earth, because, from what I know of white men, they did not honor these laws.' " For decades, Americans in the East had been deceiving Indians with untruths and half truths, and Elijah White was the advance element of generations of negotiators who would bring such dishonesty to the Northwest. In answer to Peopeo Moxmox, Hines said that White blithely assured the Cayuses that "the laws were recognized by God, and imposed on men in all civilized countries." The Wallawalla chief then replied that he "was very glad to learn that it was so, because many of his people had been angry with him when he had whipped them for crime, and had told him that God would send him to hell for it." He was "glad to know that it was pleasing to God," he told the unabashed white men.[53]

After two days of discussion, the Cayuses finally agreed to accept the laws. There was a momentary problem when they elected as their high chief Joseph's half-brother, Tauitau, who was the only Catholic among the leading men of the tribe. But the next day, Tauitau, undoubtedly under pressure from the Protestant missionaries, resigned the position, stating publicly that it was better to do so because the majority of his people did not "follow the Catholic worship," and White was able to install his brother, Hezekiah, in his

53. Gustavus Hines, *History of the Oregon Missions* (Buffalo, N.Y., 1850), p. 179.

place. Satisfied that he had averted the danger of a Cayuse uprising, White and his party left Geiger in charge of the mission and returned to Fort Walla Walla. Mrs. Whitman accompanied the Indian agent, and went all the way down the Columbia for a rest with friends in the Willamette Valley. Her health, as well as her interest in the mission, had deteriorated, and she remained in the lower country during the summer of 1843, going back upriver to join her husband when he returned to Waiilatpu from the East in September.

After Whitman's return there was harmony among the missionaries. The shock of the preceding year's events had sobered Spalding, and the antagonism between himself and Whitman became an unpleasantness of the past. From the emigration of 1843 Spalding managed to entice an accommodating young assistant named Henry A. G. Lee, who helped him with the school. A member of the famous Virginia family, Lee, who was 25 years old, stayed at Lapwai during the winter, studied the Nez Perce language, and in March 1844 finally went on to the Willamette, where he became an aid and interpreter for Dr. White.

At both Lapwai and Waiilatpu, also, there seemed for a time to be better relations with the Indians, although beneath the surface profound fears and confusions still disturbed the natives. The large emigration of 1843 had confirmed the anxieties of many of them who were sure that, as invaders, the white settlers would soon turn out to be robbers of their lands. Some of the Indians, Dr. White wrote to Washington in November 1843, "are becoming considerably enlightened on the subject of the white man's policy, and begin to quake in view of their future doom." [54] In April 1844, after his first winter back at Waiilatpu, Whitman wrote east about a Delaware halfblood named Tom Hill, who was beginning to make new difficulties around the missions. Hill had been on the plains and in the mountains for many years as a hunter and trapper, and had been a companion of Kit Carson, Joe Meek, and others. After the collapse of the fur trade he had joined a band of Nez Perces in the Montana buffalo country, marrying one of the Nez Perce women and rising rapidly to a position of respect and influence among the western Indians. By the time he had trailed into the Sahaptins' homeland with his in-laws, he had become a prominent war leader, enjoying the support of eight or nine Nez Perce chiefs and their warriors. As a Delaware whose people had been treated unjustly and pushed out of the East by white men, he had little use for American settlers or for their Christian religion, which he considered hypocritical, and, like Craig, he soon began to side with the Northwest Indians against the missionaries. He talked against their teachings, told the Indians to return to their old ways of life, including the taking of as many wives as

54. Allen, *Ten Years in Oregon*, p. 219.

they wished, accused Spalding and Whitman of using the Indians' land, water, and air without paying for them, warned the Nez Perces and Cayuses that the religious teachers were bringing the white settlers into the area to steal their country, as they had taken it from the Indian tribes in the East, and even counseled them to oust the whites from the region before it was too late. As a border figure of the times, Hill was not an unusual type. Like many half-bloods nursing resentments against advancing white settlers, he espoused the cause of the offended Indians and was a patriotic voice for Indian freedom and justice. But Spalding called him a "blasphemous and debassed infidel," and he and Whitman smarted under the stirrings of renewed opposition among the Indians which his agitation promoted.

In 1844 an unfortunate event in California quickened the Indians' unrest. During the summer a group of about fifty Wallawallas, Nez Perces, Cayuses, and Spokans had set off on an enterprising trip to the California settlements, hundreds of miles away across the mountains in the south. All of those Indians had become eager to own cattle, but the Hudson's Bay Company had refused to sell them any, and the few head they had obtained from settlers had only increased their desire to possess more. Peopeo Moxmox knew that the California ranchers owned enormous herds, and his son, Elijah Hedding, had told him that the British company and the settlers in the Willamette Valley, where he had attended Jason Lee's school, had sometimes received cattle from California. It was a long and dangerous journey, but the Indians had determined to undertake a trading expedition of their own to the distant country. Traveling like a war party and including in their ranks many leading men of the different tribes—including Peopeo Moxmox, Elijah Hedding, Tauitau, Spokan Garry, and Kipkip Pahlekin, a Nez Perce from the Kamiah area—they started south with a band of horses and a supply of furs to trade for cattle. They drove their horses up the John Day River, across Oregon's mountains, and through the wild and rugged lands of the Klamath and Shasta Indians, who were unfriendly and threatening to them, and after many perils and adventures, reached the valley of California's Sacramento River.[55] There they found a fort and settlement that had been built by John Sutter, whom some of them had met when the Swiss emigrant had been in Oregon, and

55. The Sahaptins were not altogether unfamiliar with the route. Since the early part of the nineteenth century, Cayuses, Wallawallas, and Nez Perces had periodically made their way to California to steal horses from the large Spanish ranches. According to A. J. Splawn, author of *Ka-mi-akin* (Portland, Ore., 1944), p. 367, old Indians had told him that Peopeo Moxmox had begun his California horse raids when he was a small boy, going on a trip with his father and a band of warriors. And in 1826 Peter Skene Ogden discovered that Nez Perce and Cayuse war parties "for many years past" had been traveling through southwestern Oregon, almost on the northern California border, searching for Klamath Indian settlements. Davies, *Peter Skene Ogden's Snake Country Journal, 1826–27*, pp. xxxiii, 33.

they managed to make a good trade for their horses and other wares with ranchers in the vicinity, many of whom were Americans who had come down from the Willamette to live in California.

Before setting out for home, the travelers went off on a hunt in the mountains, got into a fight with a group of California Indians, and captured twenty-two horses and mules from them. When they brought their booty back to Sutter's, some of the settlers claimed that the horses and mules had been stolen originally from herds belonging to themselves, and they demanded that the animals be returned to them. The Oregon Indians refused to give them up, and a conflict ensued in which an American named Grove Cook, already notorious as a man who hated Indians and shot them without provocation, killed Elijah in Sutter's apartment in the fort. The violence aroused other settlers, who spread word that the Northwest visitors were known as bad Indians, and the members of the little band fled from the area without their cattle.[56]

By the time they got back to Fort Walla Walla that fall, they were enraged against all Americans. The headmen who had made the trip sent messengers to villages throughout the area, telling them of the murder of Elijah Hedding and calling on them to unite in a war of revenge. Great excitement spread among the tribes, and a council was held among Wallawallas, Cayuses, Spokans, Nez Perces, Pend d'Oreilles, and various villages of Shoshonis, who for many years had been allies together against the Blackfeet. Some of the chiefs suggested raising a party of 2,000 warriors to exterminate the whites on the Sacramento, while Peopeo Moxmox was also for wiping out the Americans on the Willamette, who, he felt, were responsible for the whites' sentiment against them in California. Nothing could be done, however, until the spring, when the snow melted in the mountain passes; and in the meantime, calmer advice prevailed. By prearrangement, Peopeo Moxmox met with Dr. McLoughlin, who told him that a war against the Americans would be a disastrous undertaking for the Indians, and that the warriors could not count on help from the British fur company. Reminding him that the Nez Perce laws also provided for the punishment of white offenders, Dr. McLoughlin advised the chief to send an emissary to Dr. White, and see what he proposed. The Indians selected Ellis to go to the Willamette to see the Indian agent, and urged him to demand punishment for the slayers of Elijah, as promised by the laws.

Both Spalding and Whitman had heard what was going on, and Whitman

56. *James Clyman, Frontiersman*, ed. Charles L. Camp (Portland, Oregon, 1960), pp. 148–52, 328. Peopeo Moxmox not only was an influential leader among the Wallawallas but was related to important men of several different tribes, including the Cayuses and Nez Perces. The murder of Elijah therefore became a personal as well as an interracial matter to various leaders of the offended tribes.

had already sent a worried letter to the Indian agent, warning him that the Indians might avenge Elijah's death by killing all the whites in the upper country. The letter had just reached Dr. White, when Ellis appeared in the Willamette. White still referred to the Nez Perce chief as "this honest man, this *real* friend, though an Indian," but he was hard put to know how to answer his demand. As the representative of the American government and the author of the Nez Perce laws, White had an obligation to hang the man who had slain Elijah. But that was obviously impossible. For a while, he stalled Ellis. "I feasted him well," he wrote his superiors in Washington, "and took at once unobserved measures to have him invited to every respectable place abroad, where the ladies and gentlemen received him so cordially, and feasted him so richly and delicately, that he almost forgot the object of his embassy." But Ellis managed to remember what he was there for, and finally, "with a view to divert attention," White, who behaved little better than a confidence man, wrote a delaying letter for the Indian to take back to the other chiefs, inviting them to visit him in the Willamette that fall, when he promised he would give them five hundred dollars from his own funds with which to purchase cattle, and also present each one with a cow and a calf "out of my own herds," in exchange for some ten-dollar drafts he had earlier given them. Those drafts had been meant for the Indians to use to buy cattle from the emigrants; but the settlers had refused to honor them, and the Indians had come to look upon them as articles of bad faith. In addition, White wrote them that in the fall he would establish "a good manual labor literary institution" for the Sahaptin-speaking peoples, where their sons and daughters could receive an English education. Meanwhile, concerning the murder in California, he would immediately "write to the governor of California, to captain Suter, and to our great chiefs, respecting this matter . . . I would use every measure to get the unhappy affair adjusted." Ellis, he noted in his report, "more than properly appreciated my motives and profers, and said he was of the full belief that the chiefs would accede to my proposition." [57]

In time, nothing came of the Indians' excitement, or of White's promises to them. The Indians agreed to wait; and in May 1845 White sent some complaining letters to California, using as his courier old Jim Clyman, a former mountain man and companion of Jedediah Smith, who had helped to find South Pass and explore Great Salt Lake in the early 1820s and who had come to Oregon with the emigrants of 1844 after having spent more than a decade following the comparatively tame existence of a farmer in Illinois and Wisconsin. "Could the Murderer be givin up and Safely forward to Me I have No doubt but this would be the surest and Safest Manner to dispose of the affair—but Sir as this May be impracticable I with pleasure and confi-

57. Allen, *Ten Years*, pp. 247–51.

dence, leave the whole Matter in the hands of Yourself and Mr Clyman for adjustment and rectification . . ." White wrote to Thomas Larkin, the American consul at Monterey, California.[58] Although Larkin did not relish the thought of an invasion of California by Oregon Indians, neither he nor Clyman could do anything about apprehending Grove Cook. The consul sent a copy of White's letter to Governor Pio Pico of California, but apparently that Mexican worthy never even bothered to respond to it. In the end there was no satisfaction offered to the Indians from California; but even if there had been, Dr. White would not have been around to accept credit for it.

He had become involved in political quarrels in the Willamette Valley; and on August 15, even before he received a reply from California, he left suddenly with a party of travelers, bound overland for the States, carrying with him a resolution of the American settlers' provisional legislature in Oregon that asked Congress to assume jurisdiction over the area. His departure increased the opposition to him in Oregon, especially since the settlers thought that he meant to use the resolution to get himself named territorial delegate by Congress. When he reached Washington D.C. in the fall, however, he spent most of his time lobbying unsuccessfully for an increase in salary. Finally, word of the settlers' displeasure with him reached the capital, and the newly inaugurated Polk Administration dismissed him from the government's service. He went back to his home in New York State and forgot everything he had promised or planned for the Indians.

Although he had left a threatening situation in the upper Columbia country, no Indian uprising occurred. Some of the tension was eased by Dr. Mc-Loughlin, who summoned the disturbed headmen to a friendly council at Fort Vancouver. A number of Indians who were not mollified by the British trader continued to talk of revenge, however, and in July 1846 a mixed band of some 40 Sahaptins, led by Peopeo Moxmox and Tom Hill, the Delaware, and composed of veteran warriors of the plains, including Samuel Parker's old companion, the jolly Bull's Head known as Kentuck, started back to the Sacramento River.[59] Some of the Californians were alarmed by the reappearance of the Oregon Indians, but the visitors' mission was dramatically diverted and overshadowed by a larger and more important conflict that had the Mexican province in a turmoil and many of its inhabitants organized under arms. The Bear Flag Revolt had occurred in June, and at Sutter's Fort, Tom Hill met some Delaware Indians and many of his old trapper friends, including Kit Carson, who were part of the forces of Frémont. The Sahap-

58. Larkin Documents, III:155, "Larkin Papers," Vol. 3, p. 187, Bancroft Library, Berkeley, Calif.; included in Camp, *James Clyman*, p. 150.

59. Gray, *History of Oregon*, p. 564, and "Diary of Rev. George Gary," *Oregon Historical Quarterly*, 24 (1923), 319.

tins related their grievances to Frémont, who promised them redress, and in
the confusion of the moment Tom Hill and the Indians under Peopeo Moxmox abandoned their purpose in coming, and some of them enlisted under
Frémont's banner in the California Battalion. Hill became a trusted dispatch
bearer and a member of Frémont's bodyguard, and the Indians who stayed
with the troops, including Kentuck and some Nez Perces, had an adventurous
time as scouts and spies through the boisterous events of the Conquest of
California.[60] The other Indians headed home in 1847, and on the way were
struck by measles, which they blamed on the white men. By the time they
straggled back to their homeland that summer the survivors were as an-
guished and bitter as they had been eighteen months before when they had
left the Columbia River. The warriors who had remained in California also
returned later that year, but Tom Hill did not go back to Oregon with them.
Eventually he settled on the Delaware Indian reservation in Kansas, where his
military service earned him a grant of land. He died there about 1860.

At the missions, meanwhile, the position of the Spaldings and Whitmans
had gradually deteriorated. Covered wagon trains had continued to stream
through the country each year, bringing new settlers into the Northwest. In
1844 a former mountain man, Moses Harris, had guided almost 500 newcomers to the Columbia. Some 3,000 emigrants had arrived in 1845, and more
than 1,500 in 1846, including Mrs. Spalding's brother, Horace Hart, who had
come to live at Lapwai. Although many Nez Perces and Cayuses had lined
the route in the Grande Ronde and on the rolling hills north of the Blue
Mountains to barter horses and provisions with the emigrants, they had frequently been offended and badly treated by the whites, who knew nothing
about the Oregon Indians and who were filled with the Easterners' prejudices
and fears of all "Injuns." With the attitude that the lands of the Northwest
were already theirs to claim, no longer the property of either the British or the
Indians, large numbers of the emigrants regarded the Nez Perces and Cayuses
as horse thieves and treacherous scalpers, and rode past them with hostile countenances and itching trigger fingers.

Their arrogance and ominous appearance were not lost on the Indians, and
in September 1845 some of the worried Cayuses planned to halt the emigration in the Grande Ronde Valley. Whitman learned of their scheme from Indians who were friendly to him and, accompanied by a few Nez Perces, made
a hurried ride to the Powder River, where he joined the wagon train. When
the emigrants came into the Grande Ronde and met the waiting Cayuses, the
latter were surprised to find that the settlers had been warned and were on
guard. The Cayuse chiefs argued for a while with Whitman, and finally let
the emigrants move past them; but the episode helped to establish in the Indi-

60. Splawn, *Ka-mi-akin*, pp. 366–67.

ans' minds, more strongly than before, the belief that the missionary was the man who was bringing the whites from the East to take their country from them.

Slowly, the feeling of fear spread among the tribes, and increasing numbers of Indians, inflamed by rumors and gossip that were frequently started by halfbloods and interpreters, saw a future in which they would be enslaved by overwhelming numbers of "Bostons." Those Indians who remained loyal to the Spaldings and Whitmans and counted themselves "Christians" became defensive, and their strength and influence waned. Timothy and others who cultivated land were harassed and threatened, and many of their improvements were destroyed. During the winter of 1845–46 Spalding and Whitman hired several helpers from among the members of the 1845 emigration, and sent one of them up to Kamiah to try taking up where Asa Smith had left off. Only a handful of Indians, including Ellis and two Delaware hunters who were living with the Nez Perces, showed up for instruction, and the missionaries abandoned the effort in the spring. At Lapwai and Waiilatpu, during the same time, there seemed to be no one to enforce Dr. White's laws, and observance of them was almost forgotten. Many of the Indians returned to their shamans and old ways, and openly flaunted the missionaries' teachings. In the fall of 1845 a group of Nez Perces gathered defiantly near Spalding's home one night to gamble, feeding their fire with his cedar fence rails and making "the whole valley [ring] with their gambling songs & hideous yells." When Spalding went out to protest against this revival of their own singing and other cultural traits, the Indians seized them and wrestled him onto the fire. He was saved by the big buffalo coat he was wearing; and when they let him return to his house, he went to his room, he said, and wept. Soon afterward his mill dam was destroyed, his fence rails pulled down, and he was ordered to leave the area. When he ignored the demand, some of the Indians broke his meetinghouse windows, spat into the house, and insulted Mrs. Spalding and their children. Craig turned against him again, also, and tried to file a claim to land that included all of the mission property. The former mountain man failed, but he continued to urge the Indians to drive the missionaries away.

Some of the Indians who remained friendly to the Americans did so not because they were among the "Christian" group, but because of their ambition or desire for material goods. On June 9, 1846, the Methodist Reverend George Gary, who had succeeded Jason Lee, visited the Dalles and met Ellis with fourteen men and 150 horses on their way to the Willamette Valley to sell their horses for cattle.[61] Lawyer was probably with them, for on July 4 he occupied an honored position as a guest at a settlers' celebration of the national holiday in Oregon City. At a banquet he sat at the left hand of George

61. "Diary of Rev. George Gary," *Oregon Historical Quarterly, 24,* 315.

Abernethy, who on June 3, 1845, had been elected governor of the Americans' provisional government in Oregon, and he and many other Indians participated in a pioneers' party and dance that "went on without interruption for three whole days and nights." [62] Later, on July 13, the Reverend Gary noted the return, past the Dalles, of Ellis and the other Nez Perces, on their way home from the Willamette. Such flattery and contacts with the settlers as had taken place at Oregon City kept ambitious leaders like Ellis and Lawyer satisfied with the Americans and hopeful of greater favors and influence in the future, but they also served to widen the breach between those Indians and their fellow tribesmen who regarded them as servants of the "Bostons."

On June 26 Gary also wrote that Spalding appeared at the Dalles. The Lapwai missionary poured out to him his discouragement over the deteriorating situation at the missions, and blamed it on the influence of "Romanism" and "depraved whites" from the mountains. Spalding showed particular concern for what he considered a deliberate and sinister conspiracy to turn the Indians against Whitman and himself.[63] In his opinion, the Hudson's Bay Company was now helping the priests to gain influence over the Indians in order to keep them loyal to the British and to the fur company in case of a rupture over Oregon between the United States and Great Britain—who, unknown to himself and others in the West, had just signed a treaty on June 15 that finally settled the boundary at the 49th Parallel and ended the long-simmering Oregon controversy.

In their efforts to maintain their own position, the British company's factors and traders had often given Spalding and many settlers in the Willamette Valley reason to suspect that such a conspiracy actually existed. During conflicts between the company and American settlers in the Willamette Valley, the priests—who were British subjects and under obligation to the Hudson's Bay Company—had frequently sided against the Americans, influencing many of their French-Canadian parishioners to the same course. At the same time, Hudson's Bay Company traders, interpreters, and employees in the vicinity of Fort Walla Walla had sometimes seemed to aid the priests against the Protestant missionaries, or to say things to the Indians that Whitman and Spalding felt were calculated to turn the Indians against the Protestants.

But historical evidence shows that no conspiracy existed. It was easy, in a time of partisan passion, to discover hidden motives everywhere; and as the settlers' fears of the Indians increased—as a result of the tensions that the American settlers themselves furthered—the newcomers envisioned a repetition of the old frontier pattern of the Midwest, where British agents had

62. Dan E. Clark, "Pioneer Pastimes," *Oregon Historical Quarterly,* 57 (1956), 335–36, taken from the *Morning Oregonian,* Portland, March 25, 1900.
63. "Diary of Rev. Gary," p. 318.

aroused Indians against American settlers before and during the War of 1812. In the Willamette Valley, many settlers, imagining the worst about the up-river Sahaptin and Cayuse tribesmen through whose lands they had passed, lived in dread of the day when the British would inflame them against the settlements. In such a mood the Americans spread tales and rumors, and many people, including William H. Gray, who was not living in the Willamette, even believed that the Hudson's Bay Company had deliberately duped Dr. White into combining the bands of the different tribes under head chiefs to make them more formidable to the Americans. It was one of many misreadings of appearances, but it seemed no more fanciful at the time than Spalding's fears that the British were directing the vigorous activities of the priests.

During the fall of 1846 the tension at Lapwai and Waiilatpu appeared to lessen somewhat, but it was only temporary. Conflicts continued to arise, and by February 1847 the hopes of a decade of hard labor at the two missions had almost collapsed. At Lapwai the so-called "heathen" element of the Nez Perces had become the majority, and the "Christian" Indians were cowed and silent. "Our prospects as missionaries," Spalding wrote his former helper, A. T. Smith, "has become very dark. The large and interesting school at this place . . . has entirely ceased. Not one attends this winter, and there is not the least prospect that there ever will be another school here." [64] In June 1844 Spalding had celebrated his last triumph. He had taken ten more Nez Perces into membership in the church, bringing the total number of his adult converts to twenty-one. Most of them were still quietly loyal to him and to their new religion, but the rest of the tribe was stepping backward. Sundays were being ignored. There were no more mass congregations singing hymns and listening to sermons and prayers.

At Waiilatpu, Whitman was faring even worse with the Cayuses, few of whom felt anything but hatred for him. On April 1, 1847, he wrote east that he would perhaps locate a claim in the lower Columbia country that summer "to be ready in case of retirement." [65] The Indians, according to Geiger, who was still at Waiilatpu with the Whitmans, kept telling the missionaries that the priests at Fort Walla Walla were warning them that they had been following the wrong road, and "would continue to die. If they followed the Catholics, it would be otherwise with them; only now and then would one

64. Drury, *Spalding*, p. 326. On February 3, 1847, Spalding also wrote to Greene, announcing the collapse of the missions and blaming, in order, the "Papists"; Tom Hill, the Delaware; the emigrants and mountain men; the Indians' feeling that the Spaldings had not let them learn English, which they now believed was the only language God understood (i.e. it was the means to get material rewards); the Indians' disillusionment with Christianity which had not brought them wordly gain; and sorcery (James' band was now driving other Indians out of the Lapwai area).
65. Drury, *Spalding*, p. 326.

die of age. That they would get presents—would become rich in every thing." [66] To the wearied and discouraged Whitman the pressure of the priests began to seem too strong. Both Spalding and he had tried to halt their influence, but at Waiilatpu particularly their efforts had only confused and disgusted the Indians, some of whom thought that the unseemly quarrels of the Christian teachers were setting a bad example, while others turned with spite and hopes of gain to listen to the Catholics. As early as 1841 the priests had been using a picture chart of a "tree" or "ladder" to help instruct the Indians. It was basically an anti-Protestant propaganda device, for it showed the Protestants as the withered ends of the "true" Christian faith, falling down into the flames of hell. Its use infuriated the Protestant missionaries, and with the help of his wife Spalding drew another "tree," which was "6 feet long and 2 wide," and showed Martin Luther's path as the only correct one.[67] Spalding used this "Protestant tree" at Lapwai, but it seemed to have little effect on the Indians, for on April 2, 1847, he wrote the Board in Boston that "perhaps one fourth of this tribe have turned Papists, and are very bitter against the Protestant religion. Villages, lodges, and even families have been separated." [68]

Priests had not yet appeared in the Nez Perce villages, and despite Spalding's fears, their influence over those Indians was not widespread, having taken hold principally among small groups of Nez Perces who had met Father De Smet's Jesuits with the Flatheads and Coeur d'Alenes, or who had listened to the priests at Walla Walla. Nevertheless, it had added another division within the tribe, and the restlessness and dissatisfaction it had created among the Cayuses were spreading to the Nez Perces. Whatever happened at Waiilatpu was followed anxiously at Lapwai, and Indian actions against the Whitmans found supporters among the Nez Perces, who were always capable of doing the same thing to the Spaldings.[69]

The dangerous competition among the religious teachers reached its climax in 1847. William McBean, a Catholic, had succeeded the Whitmans' Protestant friend Archibald McKinlay as chief clerk at Fort Walla Walla. On September 5 McBean welcomed a group of Catholics to the post, including the Right Reverend Augustine M. Blanchet, who had been appointed Bishop of Walla Walla, and discussed with them the establishment of Catholic missions for the Indians of the region. At the request of the Yakima headman,

66. Gray, *History of Oregon*, pp. 495–96.

67. A picture of the Catholic Ladder is printed in *Notices & Voyages* opposite p. 44. The Protestant Ladder is pictured in the *Oregon Historical Quarterly*, 37 (1936), opposite p. 237.

68. Drury, *Spalding*, p. 330.

69. See below, p. 674.

Kamiakin (for whom William Gray had once been prevented from establishing a mission), Bishop Blanchet sent two Oblate fathers, Pascal Ricard and Eugene Chirouse, to open a station at a place called Simcoe on an upper tributary of the Yakima River.[70] The Catholics' plans for activities among the Cayuses were also discussed, and came, wrote Bishop Blanchet, as "a thunderbolt" to Whitman, who was "wounded to the heart." [71] The Reverend John Baptiste Brouillet, who was to establish the Cayuse station, added that Whitman "made a furious charge against the Catholics, accusing them of having persecuted Protestants," and said that he would not assist the new missionaries "unless he saw them in starvation." [72] The Bishop and his party waited at the fort until October 26 for Tauitau, the leading Catholic among the Cayuses, who had been on a buffalo hunt. On that day Tauitau arrived at the fort and told the Bishop that the priests could use as their mission station the house that Pambrun had built for him in the Umatilla Valley. There was a discussion concerning the need for "reuniting the Cayuses" and finding a more central location where religious instruction would be more available to all the tribe, and Tauitau was said to have suggested establishing the mission "near Dr. Whitman's, at the camp of Tiloukaikt."

In view of the bitter feelings of the Cayuses against the Whitmans and the American emigrants, the Canadian Catholics were playing with fire; but on October 29 they sent for Tilokaikt, and on November 4 that chief joined the discussions. Tom McKay was also present, and according to his testimony, "one of the chiefs told the bishop that they would send the Doctor [Whitman] off very soon; they would give him [Bishop Blanchet] his house if he wished. The bishop answered that he would not take the Doctor's house, that he did not wish him to send the Doctor away, and that there was room for two missions." Tilokaikt then offered some of his own land, and on November 8, Father Brouillet went to look at it. While the priest was there, he stated, Tilokaikt changed his mind and again suggested that he take Whitman's mission. Brouillet said he refused, and finally, instead, went to Tauitau's house and accepted it for the mission. He returned to the fort on November 10, and the next day men went to Tauitau's camp to repair the house and put it in order. It was on the Umatilla River, only 25 miles from Whitman's station.

At a later date other versions of what had happened also appeared in print, including a deposition by an emigrant who halted at Fort Walla Walla while the Catholics were there and claimed that McBean had said that the priests

70. Splawn, *Ka-mi-akin*, p. 357.

71. Bischoff, *The Jesuits in Old Oregon*, p. 207.

72. Drury, *Whitman*, p. 378; also House Executive Document, No. 38, 35th Congress, 1st Session (Washington, D. C., 1858).

had offered to buy Whitman's station, but that Whitman had refused to sell it to them.[73] Whatever the true story was, the realization that the Catholics were finally to open a mission among the Cayuses shattered Whitman and made it seem even more doubtful to him that he could continue to hold on at Waiilatpu.

In the end, the decision was not his to make. The Catholic competition had increased the danger to him, but other forces were leading inexorably to tragedy. The winter of 1846–47 had been an unusually severe one. Many of the Indians' horses and cattle had perished, the wild game had suffered, and the Indians' vitality and resistance to disease had become lowered. In the late summer the first wagons of the 1847 emigrants began to appear at Waiilatpu. It was a large emigration, numbering between 4,000 and 5,000 people. Again, the Indians were filled with fear, and from the Grande Ronde to the Dalles small bodies of warriors began to strike angrily at the passing invaders, killing stragglers and plundering and burning their wagons. That year, however, the emigrants brought with them a virulent form of measles that spread among the Indians with devastating effect. Almost the entire Cayuse nation, whose raids against the emigrants were blackening the tribe's name in the Willamette, caught the dread illness. It was made worse by dysentery, and perhaps half of the tribe died. In their misery and panic the Indians became desperate. A halfblood from Maine named Joe Lewis, who had arrived at Waiilatpu with the emigrants, settled Whitman's fate. Like Tom Hill, the Delaware, he hated the white settlers, but he was less principled than Hill. Whitman found Lewis destitute and surly, and after fitting him out with new clothes, tried to pack him off to the Willamette. But Lewis returned to the mission, and began to strike up acquaintances among the Cayuses. It was a ready-made situation for him. Soon he was circulating the story that he had overheard Whitman and Spalding plotting to poison the Indians so that they could more quickly take their land.

To the distraught Cayuses, ready to believe anything, the tale was plausible. Whitman's medicine was not saving them. Perhaps it *was* poison. They remembered stories they had heard on the plains about American traders who had brought the smallpox up the Missouri to wipe out the Blackfeet. Two other men, whom the Indians trusted, also whispered to the Cayuses, agreeing with what Lewis had told them. One was a French Canadian named Joseph Stanfield, and the other was Nicholas Finlay, a mixed-blood from the Spokan country, whom the Cayuses had known for many years and who was probably a son of Jacques Raphael Finlay, David Thompson's associate. If that were so, the era of the fur trade was helping to seal the doom of the period of the missionaries.

73. Gray, *History of Oregon,* p. 463.

November 29, 1847, was the last day on earth for Marcus and Narcissa Whitman. They were both tired and defeated. There were many people living with them in the crowded mission buildings, but these were mostly transients and helpers, members of the emigration who had become sick, who needed a rest, or who had paused to winter at Waiilatpu and assist the Whitmans with their secular chores. No settlers had ever stopped to build a new community around the mission, and since 1845 most of the emigrants had been taking short-cuts across northeastern Oregon to the Columbia that bypassed Waiilatpu. On September 7 Whitman had purchased the Dalles mission from the Methodists and had installed his 17-year-old nephew, Perrin, at that station to try to work with the Indians who still came on periodic visits to the old fishing and trading center. But even the Dalles was an isolated and lonely outpost, far from the settlements of the lower Columbia where a new day had already arrived. Everything south of the 49th parallel was now American. Further negotiations would be necessary to liquidate the Hudson's Bay Company's properties in Oregon, and until then the various posts, including Fort Walla Walla, would continue to do business. But Dr. McLoughlin had resigned from the company and, under the new sovereignty of the United States, had settled down as a private citizen in the country over which he had so long ruled supreme. Together with oldtimers and newcomers, he was helping to build a grand, new civilization in the country of the lower Columbia, west of the Cascades. But up the river, at Waiilatpu and Lapwai in the interior, there were still only loneliness, heartbreak, and strife.

On November 27, Spalding, who had brought his daughter, Eliza, now 10 years old, to Waiilatpu to attend the Whitman school, accompanied Marcus on a visit to some Cayuse measles patients in the long, multifamily winter lodge of Hezekiah on the Umatilla River, near the new Catholic mission. As the two men rode away from the Whitman station, it was the last time that Spalding would see Narcissa. On the way to the Umatilla, Spalding's horse fell, and the missionary was badly bruised. When they reached the Cayuse villages, Spalding rested at the lodge of the friendly Stickus, who had guided the emigrants across the Blue Mountains in 1843. Whitman went about his medical duties, and during the afternoon stopped at the Catholic mission. Its repair had just been completed, and Bishop Blanchet, Father Brouillet, and several other priests had arrived only the day before. They invited Whitman to dine with them, but he refused. He apparently discussed with them, however, their purchase of Waiilatpu whenever the majority of Cayuses showed that they no longer wanted the Whitmans, and before he left he asked Brouillet to visit him. He returned to the lodge of Stickus; and finding Spalding still not well enough to ride, started off ahead of him for Waiilatpu. He reached home late in the evening, after picking up rumors that the Cayuses were plotting to kill him. He and Narcissa were filled with a sense of impending doom. Still, they took no measures for the safety of themselves or the other seventy-two persons who were living in the various buildings at the mission.

The following day was a bleak and cold Monday. About two in the afternoon the neighboring Cayuse chief, Tilokaikt, who had offered land to Bishop Blanchet and had then withdrawn the offer, entered the Whitman home and asked the Doctor for some medicine. While Whitman's back was turned, a second Indian named Tomahas struck the missionary on the head from behind with a pipe tomahawk. In the struggle that followed, Whitman was hit several times, and his face was slashed and mutilated. Other Cayuses, by signal, joined the attack, shooting and butchering whites inside and outside the buildings. While the Doctor was still alive, Narcissa was shot in the arm. Later, weak from the loss of blood, she was carried outside the house on a settee, shot again and again by frenzied Indians, dumped in the mud, and beaten with a leather quirt. The enraged bloodletting paused, went on, and paused once more over a period of several days. By the time it ended, the Whitmans and eleven other whites had been slain, three more persons, including Joe Meek's daughter, Helen Mar, had died, unattended, of illness, or while trying to escape, and forty-seven were being held captive. The rest of the people at the station had escaped or, like Joe Lewis, were not considered enemies by the Indians. The Cayuses looted and burned the mission buildings, then started to look for Spalding.

7

Vengeance on the Walla Walla

ON THE AFTERNOON of Tuesday, November 30, the day following the massacre, Father Brouillet, unaware of what had happened at Waiilatpu, set out from the Catholic mission on the Umatilla. He planned to pay a call on Whitman and visit the sick Indians at Tilokaikt's camp near Waiilatpu "for the purpose of baptizing the infants and such dying adults as might desire this favor." [1] Spalding, who also had no inkling of the danger that threatened him, still felt too sore to travel and decided to stay another day at Hezekiah's.

Father Brouillet rode into Tilokaikt's village late in the evening. Feeling certain that the priest would approve of the Cayuses' action, the somber-faced chief announced what the Indians had done, and told him that Spalding would also die. The priest was horrified but, fearful for his own safety, said nothing. He sat with the Indians, worried for Spalding and tense about his own situation, and that night scarcely closed his eyes. The next morning, still pretending that what had happened was an affair between the Indians and the Protestants, he baptized three native children, and finally rode over to the Whitman mission.

"What a sight did I then behold!" he wrote. "Ten bodies lying here and there, covered with blood, and bearing the marks of the most atrocious cruelty—some pierced with balls, others more or less gashed by the hatchet. Dr. Whitman had received three gashes on the face. Three others had their skulls crushed so that their brains were oozing out." [2] The stricken prisoners, mostly women and children who had seen their husbands and fathers slain in front of their eyes, moved him to tears which, he said, "I was obliged to con-

1. Gray, *History of Oregon*, p. 490.
2. Ibid., quoting letter from Brouillet to Colonel Gilliam.

ceal, for I was the greater part of the day in the presence of the murderers, and closely watched by them; and if I had shown too marked an interest in behalf of the sufferers, it would only have endangered their lives and mine." He helped Joseph Stanfield, the French Canadian whom the Indians had spared, bury the hacked and mutilated corpses, but was "far from feeling safe, being obliged to go here and there gathering up the dead bodies in the midst of the assassins, whose hands were still stained with blood, and who, by their manners, their countenances, and the arms which they still carried, sufficiently announced that their thirst for blood was yet unsatiated."

Despite his fears, Brouillet was regarded as a sympathetic ally by the Cayuses, and that afternoon, without interference, he left for his mission, sickened by what he had witnessed. He hoped that in some way he could save Spalding, whom he had left at Hezekiah's; but as he started away with his interpreter, he was joined suddenly by one of Tilokait's sons, whom the missionaries had named Edward. The young Indian had been ordered to carry the news of the killings to the leaders of the two Cayuse bands that made their homes in the Umatilla Valley, and he told Brouillet that he would accompany him to Hezekiah's lodge and ask that chief what to do with the captives. Edward's appearance gave the priest a new fright, and as the three men rode off across the hills, Brouillet worried again for his own safety, wondering what would happen to him when the Cayuses learned that he had not told them where Spalding was.

After several miles of travel, Edward and the interpreter paused on the trail to light their pipes, and Brouillet continued on. A few moments later, by a lucky chance, he spied the lone figure of Spalding, making his way back to Waiilatpu from the Umatilla. Racing forward, he managed to intercept him, telling him breathlessly what had happened. Spalding listened in a daze, not knowing what to do, and the next instant Edward and the interpreter appeared. As Spalding tried to collect his thoughts, Brouillet pleaded with the young Cayuse for the Protestant's life, and after a moment of hesitation the Indian wheeled his horse and galloped back to tell his father that he had found Spalding.[3]

There was no time to lose. With Brouillet urging him to flee, Spalding took some food from the priest, gave his pack horses to the interpreter, and set off as fast as he could away from the direction of Waiilatpu. He might have ridden directly to safety at Fort Walla Walla, but his mind was on Lapwai and his wife, and at the Touchet River he headed up the trail that led to the

3. A slightly different account, written sometime later by Spalding, said that Edward actually fired at him but that his pistol was not loaded. The Indian then went back along the trail to reload secretly and wait for Spalding. When the missionary did not appear, the Indian galloped after the priest.

distant Nez Perce country. Soon after Spalding had left Brouillet, three armed Cayuses came up to where the priest was waiting, and were enraged when they heard that Spalding had escaped. They paused only a moment with Brouillet, then set off in search of their prey, who they were sure could not have got far. Fortunately for Spalding, it was already late in the afternoon, and a heavy fog settled down on the wooded river valleys and helped to conceal his flight. He rode frantically all that night, hid in the brush the next day, and rode again after dark. During the second night he was panicked by the sounds of horses and the cries of pursuers and, taking cover in tall grass, cowered in the blackness with his heart pounding and his body shaking with fear, as a group of warriors rode by without seeing him. Later the same night he paused to rest, but this time his horse strayed away from him, and he had to continue his flight on foot.

It was a painful ordeal. He had little food, his shoes were so tight that he had to take them off and wrap his feet in leggings, and his water-soaked blankets became so heavy that he had to abandon them. But his fear drove him on, and in two nights he traveled sixty miles. "My feet suffered from the frozen ground," he wrote later. "I avoided the places of encampment and forded the streams far from the trail, lest the Cayuse might be way-laying. I secreted myself on the Sabbath—and hunger, pain in my feet, and weakness were very great; I wanted sleep, but could get none, for the cold. From the moment I stopped traveling in the morning till I started at night, I shook to the center of every bone, with cold." [4] After four days of suffering, he finally reached the Snake River near Alpowa, and after hiding until night, crept forward to search for the lodge of his friend, Timothy. A heavy rain was falling, and in one of the lodges he heard Indians singing at their evening worship. His spirits rose but plummeted as fast when he suddenly heard the Indians begin to talk of the murder of the Whitmans. Their conversation made him think that they had turned against him, and when he failed to see Timothy among them, he decided not to trust them but to try to reach Lapwai. Finding a canoe in the darkness, he crossed the Snake River, and the next day used another dugout to ferry himself across a deserted part of the Clearwater. Still unseen by the Indians, he finally reached a high hill overlooking the mission. When he peered down at it, however, the last of his courage fled. The grounds at the confluence of the Clearwater and Lapwai Creek were filled with Indians, many of whom were looting the buildings. Confused and not knowing what to do next, he tried to hide in some bushes; but a Nez Perce woman, passing by on horseback, saw him and stopped. At first, she did not recognize the missionary, but when his cap fell off, revealing his bald head, she saw who it was, and hurried down to the mission buildings to announce

4. Drury, *Spalding*, p. 339.

his presence, explaining to the Indians, Spalding said later, that "the bald head and the Nez Perce language were mine, but that the voice and appearance was not." [5]

A group of friendly Nez Perces, led by Luke, one of his converts who was still loyal to him, hurried up the hill and crowded around him. Helping him to his feet, they led him, disheveled and bleeding, down the slope to the mission, where they tenderly bathed and bandaged his feet, gave him a bowl of corn meal pudding and milk, and made a bed for him. Although his wife was not there, he was told that she was safe. Two days before, the Indians said, an emigrant named William Canfield, who had escaped from Waiilatpu with a bullet wound in his hip, had staggered into Lapwai with the first news of the murders. Besides Mrs. Spalding and her three small children, the only whites at Lapwai at the time were her brother, Horace Hart, a helper named Jackson, and a young emigrant woman named Mary Johnson, who had been assisting Mrs. Spalding with her household chores. Canfield thought that Cayuse pursuers were on his trail, and he pleaded with the other whites to flee with him to the eastern plains without telling the Nez Perces what had happened. But Mrs. Spalding trusted the Indians who were loyal to her, and she told the news secretly to a few of them, including Timothy, Jacob, and The Eagle, sending one of them to inform Craig, who still lived a couple of miles up Lapwai Creek, and dispatching Timothy and The Eagle to Waiilatpu to try to rescue the Spaldings' little girl, Eliza.[6] The next day an Indian messenger arrived at Lapwai with word that Spalding had escaped from the Cayuses. At the same time Craig came down from his home and invited the whites to move from the mission to his own house, where, under the protection of his father-in-law, the old shaman James, they might be safer.

The mountain man's friendly offer came none too soon. As Mrs. Spalding and the others were preparing to leave the mission, a band of Nez Perces rode up, headed by an Indian who had been at Waiilatpu during the killings. The group was composed of Indians who shared the Cayuses' fears and were determined to join them in driving all American missionaries and settlers from their country. They were angry to find the whites being guarded by Craig and by a large number of their own people, many of whom were critical of the Cayuses' violence. Although the Nez Perces differed among themselves in their feelings about the Spaldings, those who were protecting the missionaries were determined not to spill the blood of white men on their own lands, and

5. Ibid., p. 340.

6. The Eagle was Asa Smith's former antagonist, Utsinmalikin from Kamiah, who since Smith's time had prospered as a farmer and stockman and had become warmly sympathetic and loyal to the Spaldings.

they threatened to fight anyone who tried to harm the whites.[7] The new arrivals sat by sullenly on their horses, while Mrs. Spalding and the others were taken off in a wagon to Craig's house. Then, with jeers and shouts of triumph, they began to plunder the mission buildings.

Soon afterward Spalding himself arrived and saw the pillaging from the hill. Most of the Indians were young warriors who had gathered from different villages. Spalding later thought that many of them were Joseph's people, who had close personal ties to the Cayuse bands of the Umatilla. But it is certain that Joseph, a man of deep principles and a high regard for the teachings of the Bible, was not with them, and that he played no part in the looting. By the time that the friendly Indians had brought Spalding down to the mission grounds, the fury of the others was spent and they moved away from the missionary, unwilling to risk bloodshed among their own people by attacking Spalding. The next day Spalding, his nerves shattered by his experiences, was led up to Craig's house, where his wife and children welcomed him with sobs and tears of gratitude.

As the whites settled in for what amounted to a siege in the isolated Nez Perce country, word of what had happened at Waiilatpu was traveling to the outside world. The day after the massacre one of the men who had escaped from Whitman's mission during the turmoil reached Fort Walla Walla, half-naked and covered with blood. He blurted out his story to McBean, the chief clerk, who immediately sent an interpreter to Waiilatpu with a warning to the Cayuses to stop the killings. At the same time he hurried a messenger downriver to Fort Vancouver, and set to work preparing the defenses of Fort Walla Walla in case the aroused Indians turned their anger against the post.

McBean's courier arrived at Vancouver on the evening of December 6, a week after the massacre, and James Douglas, who had succeeded Dr. McLoughlin as chief factor at the fort, rushed word to Governor George Abernethy, the head of the settlers' provisional government in the Willamette Valley. Consternation struck the Americans. The upriver Indians, whose reputation had already been blackened by the angry tales of plundered emigrants, loomed suddenly as bloodthirsty savages who had taken the warpath

7. At this critical moment in the Nez Perces' history, Ellis and Lawyer were both in the buffalo country. Ellis and sixty members of the band caught the measles and died on the plains. Soon afterward, news of the Whitmans' massacre reached the rest of the group. "We were perfectly bewildered, we knew not which way to turn . . ." Lawyer said later. "I was confident then, that there would be fighting amongst the Indians of this country. I sent word to my people here, to have nothing to do with the war, that would arise from this murder . . ." Official Proceedings of the Treaty Council at Lapwai (May–June, 1863), p. 63; National Archives, Record Group 75.

without provocation against all settlers in the Northwest. Many of the pioneers, constitutionally dedicated to the belief that Oregon would one day
have to be swept clean of Indians, demanded the forming of an army to
march at once against the Cayuses and any other tribes that got in the way.
But wiser leaders, who realized the danger of uniting the Indians against the
small and weak settlements, argued against any action that would lead to a
large-scale war, and won approval for the more limited goal of capturing and
punishing only the individual Indians who were responsible for the murders,
while at the same time making every effort to keep the Cayuses' neighbors at
peace.

On December 9 the settlers' legislature voted to raise and equip a company
of fifty riflemen and officers to proceed immediately to the old Indian trading
mart at The Dalles and hold the mission station at that site until reinforcements could join them in an expedition to capture the guilty Cayuses. In succeeding days the emotion-charged legislature also passed bills to enlist up to
500 volunteers, to dispatch a messenger to Washington with an appeal for
help from the federal government, to select a three-man "peace" delegation
to go to Walla Walla and try to council with all the other tribes of the area
"to prevent, if possible, the coalition with the Cayuse tribe, in the present
difficulties," and to appoint commissioners to raise money to pay for the
troops. The commissioners at once tried to borrow funds from the Hudson's
Bay Company, but Douglas was under orders from London to make no more
loans to an American governmental agency because the United States had not
yet repaid money that Dr. White had borrowed while he had been Indian
subagent. The commissioners finally gave their pledges as private citizens to
Douglas and got an advance of $999, to which were added loans of $2,600
from Oregon City merchants and the Methodist mission. In the meantime
Douglas, who had no wish for an Indian war that would ruin the British company's trade in the Columbia country, urged the settlers not to take action
that would further frighten the upriver tribes and make them feel that they
had to combine in a war of defense against the Americans. The proper policy,
he advised them, was to rescue the captives as quickly as possible and then
punish the murderers, so that the Indians would realize that a repetition of the
crime would be followed by swift and certain retaliation.

To accomplish the first aim he had already taken the initiative, and on the
evening of December 7, without waiting for the Americans, had dispatched
the veteran fur trader Peter Skene Ogden and sixteen Hudson's Bay Company men to Fort Walla Walla, directing them to halt the killings and rescue
the prisoners before the outraged settlers could take action that might set off
a general Indian uprising. Ogden's familiarity with the Cayuses and the other
interior tribes made him the best possible man for the assignment. In his mid-

fifties, he now shared the management of Fort Vancouver with Douglas and was respected by Indian leaders throughout the Northwest, wherever Hudson's Bay Company traders still had influence. Hastening up the Columbia, he found that Indian fears and hostility had spread as far west as The Dalles, and he advised the American missionaries to evacuate that place. At Fort Walla Walla, which he reached on December 19, he learned that none of the captives had been killed since the first week of the outbreak. But since that time much else had happened to them.

When Father Brouillet had returned to the Umatilla after warning Spalding to flee, Bishop Blanchet, who was still at the Catholic mission with the Umatilla Cayuses, had summoned Tauitau and Five Crows (Hezekiah), and had pleaded with the two chiefs to protect the lives of the widows and orphans of the massacre. The brothers had said that they had had nothing to do with the murders, which were solely the affair of the Walla Walla band of Cayuses, but they had promised to do what they could for the survivors. It had turned out, however, to be a moment of personal crisis for Five Crows. He was a dignified and kindly man in his middle forties, and he had no wish to harm the captives. But he had been educated and converted by Spalding, who had given him the name Hezekiah, and he had come to desire a white woman as a wife. Now, he saw an opportunity to acquire one. Some of the Cayuses at Waiilatpu, reacting as they would have done after a triumphant war raid on an enemy village, had already taken women for themselves from among the prisoners; and eleven days after the massacre word arrived at Whitman's mission that Five Crows of the Umatilla band wanted one of the female captives for himself. A young woman named Lorinda Bewley, who was still sick, was told that by going to the Umatilla she would receive the protection of the powerful Five Crows. She agreed to the transfer and was delivered first to the Catholic mission house, where she learned the real reason for the move. She cried and begged the priests for help, but Bishop Blanchet was powerless to intercede for her. At first Five Crows was gentlemanly and courteous to her, and allowed her to remain at the mission house to think it over. But finally he dragged her to his lodge. She endured her trial for more than two weeks, staying at the bishop's house during the days and accompanying the Indian to his lodge at night. Her deposition, one of many that rescued survivors gave at a later date concerning events that occurred during and after the massacre, stirred angry emotions among the settlers in the Willamette and aroused them even more bitterly against both the upriver Indians and the Catholics.[8]

8. The priests, Lorinda Bewley charged, not only failed to protect her but for their own safety "ordered me to go" with Five Crows, and even asked "in a good deal of glee, how I liked my companion." Whether true or the product of an emotionally ex-

At Craig's house on the Lapwai, Spalding, too, was experiencing an unpleasant time. Although he and his wife knew that their daughter was alive, the Cayuses refused to send her back to Lapwai, and the missionary couple were fearful for her safety. Moreover, Ellis and Lawyer were in the buffalo country, and in the absence of those two influential friends of the Americans, the Nez Perces themselves were becoming uncertain about the future and, in their doubts, were growing more threatening. What had happened at Waiilatpu had created an unprecedented situation for the tribe. The Nez Perces had never made war against the white men, and although the young men and warriors were not afraid, few of the people wanted to risk trouble for their villages. As the Indians talked about what the whites would do, the older men became more worried that the settlers would soon send an army from the Willamette to attack everyone, and then they would have to fight. To avoid such a conflict the leaders finally agreed on a diplomatic course, and in a council with Spalding urged him to write letters to prevent American soldiers from coming upriver to avenge the murders. They would have to hold the missionary and the other members of his party as "hostages of peace," they told Spalding, and would not be able to protect them from the young men if troops from the Willamette appeared in the Indians' country. The threat frightened Spalding again, and on December 10 he wrote pleading letters to McBean and the bishop at the Umatilla, desperately begging both of them to use their influence to keep American soldiers from coming up the river.

The Nez Perces carried Spalding's letter to Bishop Blanchet on the Umatilla. Supporting it with their own appeals, they urged the Catholic to write to the American governor, Abernethy, and advise him not to send an army but to come himself in the spring and make a peace treaty with the Cayuses, who, they argued, would then release the prisoners. Bishop Blanchet told them that he would first have to talk to the Cayuses themselves to see if they would agree, and on December 20 he met in council at the Umatilla mission house with Tauitau, Five Crows, Tilokaikt, Camaspello, and many of the lesser Cayuse chiefs, and asked for their consent to the Nez Perce proposals.[9] The Cayuses were angrier toward the whites than the Nez Perces were, but after pouring out to the bishop a long record of wrongs they felt they had suffered from the Protestant missionaries and the American settlers who had invaded their country, they agreed to forget the past injustices and "hoped

---

cited girl, the deposition made a powerful piece of propaganda. William Gray, as would be expected, never questioned its veracity but published it in his history of Oregon, pp. 486, 501.

9. Camaspello, known as the Old Man Chief, or Olaman Chief, headed one of the two Cayuse bands in the Umatilla Valley. Tauitau and Five Crows (Hezekiah) headed the other one. Tilokaikt, of course, was the leader of the Cayuses who lived along the Walla Walla, the band that had committed the murders.

that the Americans would also forget what had recently been done." In their name Blanchet, who could see the right that lay on their side, where the inflamed Americans could not, then prepared a lengthy statement to Abernethy, asking that the Americans not make war on the Indians, that they forget the murders at Waiilatpu as the Indians would forget the killing of Peopeo Moxmox's son in California, and that two or three American leaders come upriver to make peace with the Indians. In addition, he wrote, the Cayuses promised to do no further harm to the captives and to release them when peace was concluded, and finally they begged that "Americans may not travel any more through their country, as their young men might do them harm." [10]

The night before this assemblage on the Umatilla, Ogden and his sixteen-member rescue group reached Fort Walla Walla, where they heard that the captives were still alive. Ogden immediately dispatched messengers to the Cayuses for a council at the fort, and on December 23 the Cayuse leaders, accompanied by Peopeo Moxmox and two Nez Perces, showed up, wondering at the role of the British trader in their quarrel with the "Bostons." Ogden made them a short, blunt speech, determined, he explained, to accomplish only the rescue of the prisoners without turning the Indians against the Hudson's Bay Company, or presuming to tell the Indians what the Americans would or would not do. "We have been among you for thirty years," he reminded the Cayuses, "without the shedding of blood. We are traders, and of a different nation from the Americans. But recollect, we supply you with ammunition, not to kill Americans, who are of the same color, speak the same language, and worship the same God as ourselves, and whose cruel fate causes our hearts to bleed . . . I give you only advice, and promise you nothing . . . If you wish it, on my return, I will see what can be done for you; but I do not promise to prevent war. Deliver me the prisoners to return to their friends, and I will pay you a ransom. That is all." [11]

Ogden's words unsettled the Indians. Despite his assurance of neutrality, his demand for the prisoners was the voice of the still-powerful Hudson's Bay Company, the principal supplier of arms to the bands. To oppose his request would be to risk uniting the British traders with the "Bostons" against the Indians. On the other hand, if they listened to Ogden, he would be a strong ally in helping persuade the Willamette settlers not to make war. Gradually, the Indians weakened in their intention to hold the captives until peace was made with the Americans; and at last Tauitau and Tilokaikt agreed that the Cayuses should accept the ransom. Ogden paid them 62 three-point blankets, 63 cotton shirts, 12 guns, 600 loads of ammunition, 37 pounds of tobacco,

10. Gray, *History of Oregon*, p. 515.
11. Hubert H. Bancroft, *The History of Oregon*, *1* (San Francisco, 1886), 693–94.

and 12 flints, and six days later, the Cayuses came back to the post with all of the captives, 51 in number, from Waiilatpu and the Umatilla. The two Nez Perces, meanwhile, agreed to return to Lapwai and provide safe conduct for the Spaldings out of the Nez Perce country if the couple wished to leave. Ogden gave them a letter to take to Spalding, in which he urged the missionary to lose no time in joining him at Fort Walla Walla, advising him, in addition, to make no promises or payments to the Indians.

The two Nez Perces rode off to Lapwai, but before they returned with the Spaldings, rumors began to circulate among the Indians around Fort Walla Walla that American troops from the Willamette were on their way upriver to fight the Indians, and had already arrived at The Dalles. Ogden kept the ransomed captives from Waiilatpu and the Umatilla inside the security of the fort's walls, while he waited anxiously for Spalding; and as the rumors increased and the Indians grew threatening, he worried whether he could get the prisoners safely downriver. Fortunately, on January 1, 1848, Henry and Eliza Spalding and the other whites from Lapwai rode up to the post, escorted by a solemn group of fifty Nez Perces, who were still friendly to the missionaries and were troubled to see them leave. Unhappy farewells, in which Timothy and some of the Christianized Nez Perces promised to remain loyal to their new religion, were mixed with the tears of a joyful reunion between the Spaldings and their daughter, Eliza, whom Spalding later described as "too weak to stand, a mere skeleton, and her mind much impaired as her health" by the experiences she had been through.[12]

Before leaving the fort, Spalding wrote hurriedly to Walker and Eells, who were still at their Tshimakain mission, urging them to flee to safety at Fort Colvile. Those missionaries, however, had received assurances of protection from the Spokans; and despite threats by the Cayuses to come and kill them, they remained at Tshimakain, unharmed, until March 15, when they finally went to Fort Colvile, where American volunteers met them and escorted them to the Willamette.[13]

12. Drury, *Spalding*, p. 345.

13. During the weeks after the Waiilatpu massacre, the Walkers and Eells lived through a period of terror at Tshimakain. The Spokans told them that the Cayuses planned to kill them, or to ask the Spokans to do so, if an American army made war on the Indians. Despite Spokan promises to defend the missionaries, the air was filled with alarms. At one time, the Spokans, many of whose people also were dying from measles and dysentery, began to whisper—like the Cayuses—that the Americans were poisoning them. When the missionaries discussed moving to the safety of Fort Colvile, the Spokan chiefs asked them to stay, explaining that the Spokans would be made laughingstocks for not having been able to defend their teachers but at the same time adding to the anxiety of the missionaries by telling them that it would be better for them to stay and die there than to leave. At another time, Nicholas Finlay, who had been with the Cayuses at Waiilatpu, arrived in the vicinity of Tshimakain to tell the

On January 2, 1848, Ogden started down the Columbia in three boats with the rescued prisoners. They left Fort Walla Walla just in time, for a few hours after the group departed, some fifty young Cayuses arrived at the post, looking for Spalding. They were angered by reports that American soldiers were coming to attack them, and were determined to kill Spalding. When they learned that he had eluded them, they rode bitterly back to their people, whose concern was mounting over the prospect of having to defend themselves against the "Bostons." The leaders and older men, who had hoped that they could make peace with the settlers and had agreed to surrender the captives even before a peace meeting occurred, felt that they had been deceived. After a worried council, they sent messages to the Nez Perces, Yakimas, and other interior tribes, telling them that the Americans were on their way to attack them all and offering bounties of horses and cattle if they would join them in a war of defense. The answers were slow in coming and were generally unfavorable to them. The Nez Perces, the most numerous and powerful of their neighbors, were divided among themselves and could not agree on what course to follow. The Yakimas and Spokans decided to remain neutral, and Kamiakin even sent the Cayuses a sharp reprimand for what they had done at Waiilatpu. The Americans, he said, had not bothered his people, who lived off the routes which the settlers followed, and therefore the Yakimas had no reason to become involved in the difficulties which the Cayuses had brought upon themselves.[14] Only the Palouses of the lower Snake River responded favorably. They were as fearful of the soldiers as the Cayuses were, and they agreed to fight in defense of their country if it were necessary.

When the Spaldings and other ransomed captives reached the Willamette,

---

Spokans that an American army was coming upriver and to urge them to join the Cayuses in a war against the Americans. Finally, the news that American troops had had a success against the Cayuses in a battle on February 24 and that 100 Nez Perces were on their way to join the Americans seemed to stiffen the Spokan determination to avoid trouble. When the Americans moved north into the Palouse country and the war appeared to be approaching the lands of the Spokans, the latter agreed that it was best for the Walkers and Eellses to depart for Fort Colvile. See Drury, *First White Women,* 2, 324–38, for excerpts from the Walkers' diaries during this tense period.

On the Umatilla, meanwhile, Father Brouillet and another priest also remained in the Indian country, although Bishop Blanchet joined Ogden and the ransomed captives and returned to the Willamette. Without Protestant competition Brouillet tried for a while to win the friendship of the Cayuses, but the situation was too turbulent, and when American troops arrived in the area, he finally abandoned the mission. The Oblate fathers with the Yakimas also hung on for a while, but eventually they withdrew, too, although they were able to return to those Indians in 1849.

14. The Yakimas' rebuke to the Cayuses angered the latter people and hurt relations between the two tribes for several years. In 1849 their warriors even engaged in a battle north of the Columbia River.

their accounts of what had occurred at the missions fanned the settlers' anger even higher against the interior Indians. A punitive army, however, was already under way from the settlements, and the Northwest's first Indian war had become inevitable. On December 21 an advance group of some fifty volunteer riflemen led by Major Henry A. G. Lee, the young Virginian who had assisted the Spaldings as a teacher at Lapwai during the winter of 1843-44, had reached The Dalles mission. In the Willamette a larger force was being formed under the command of Colonel Cornelius Gilliam, an impulsive, 49-year-old veteran of the Black Hawk and Seminole Indian wars in the East. An ordained minister of the Freewill Baptist denomination, Gilliam was a belligerent, narrow-minded man, who had participated in the expulsion of the Mormons from Missouri and now believed that the Catholics and the Hudson's Bay Company had combined to incite the Indians against the Protestant missionaries. Although Governor Abernathy and the members of the settlers' legislature had recommended punishing only the Indians who had committed the murders, Gilliam hated all Indians, and believed that the best policy was to exterminate them as quickly as possible.

On the same day that Ogden and the prisoners arrived at the Willamette, Gilliam and a second group of soldiers set out to join Lee at The Dalles. With them went Joe Meek, who had been directed by the legislature to carry a memorial overland to Washington, informing the government of the Whitman massacre and the troubles with the Indians, and soliciting federal aid for the settlers. Meek, accompanied by an old companion of the mountains, George Ebberts, had been told to go by way of California, where he was to request military help from California's governor and from the United States Naval squadron in the Pacific. The easiest route to California ran southward from The Dalles, but at that place Meek decided that it was too dangerous a trip for that time of the year; and after being swept into the military actions against the Cayuses he reached Waiilatpu and finally took the Oregon Trail across the continent. Traveling with Ebberts in midwinter, he hastened across the mountains and plains and arrived in St. Louis in May 1848, two months after he had left Oregon. He went on to Washington, creating a stir with his outlandish trapper's clothes and his dramatic news of what was happening in the Northwest, and personally laid before President James Polk, to whom one of his cousins was married, the information regarding the plight of the settlers in Oregon. Overnight he became a celebrity in the capital, and was lionized and entertained by political and social leaders. While Meek waited, Congress responded to an appeal from Polk, the members of the legislature arguing at first, through long sessions, over the slavery issue in the distant northwestern region, but finally establishing Oregon as a territory on August 14, 1848. Provision was made to furnish the Willamette settlers with men,

Pend
Oreille
Lake

Coeur
d'Alene
Lake

• Tshimakain

■ Fort
Colvile

Spokan

SPOKANE R.

COLUMBIA R.

PALOUSE R.

Palouse

SNAKE R.

CLEARWATER RIVER

Spalding
Mission

LAPWAI CR.

• Craig

Nez Perce

SALMON R.

SNAKE R.

Red Wolf's
Village

ALPOWA CR.

TUCANNON R.

SNAKE R.

TOUCHET R.

Wallawalla
Waiilatpu

RONDE R.

GRANDE

WALLA WALLA R.

Cayuse

UMATILLA R.

Umatilla

WALLOWA
VALLEY

WALLOWA R.

BLUE MTS.

YAKIMA R.

Fort
Walla Walla

Yakima

COLUMBIA R.

AHTANUM CR.

St. Joseph's
Mission

KLICKITAT R.

COLUMBIA R.

The Dalles

Tenino

DESCHUTES R.

JOHN DAY R.

Fort
Gilliam

COLUMBIA R.

Fort
Vancouver

Oregon City

WILLAMETTE R.

CASCADE MTS.

✗ Battle or skirmish
∎▪∎▪ Gilliam

4. THE CAYUSE WAR, 1848

arms, and ammunition from forces in California that had just concluded the war with Mexico, and General Joseph Lane of Indiana, a distinguished veteran of that war, was named new governor of the territory and Joe Meek United States marshal.

In Oregon, meanwhile, Gilliam, Lee, and the army of citizen soldiers were finally beginning the violent phase of the white man's conquest of that newest corner of the Republic. On January 8, before Gilliam and his reinforcements reached The Dalles, Lee and his advance unit of riflemen had a skirmish with some Indians whom they discovered rounding up cattle that immigrants had left at The Dalles mission until they could drive them to the Willamette in the spring. The Indians, who included eight Cayuses from farther up the river, lost three of their own people in a two-hour, running fight, but managed to wound one of the white men and drive off about 300 head of cattle. The next day, as the Cayuses spread the word up the Columbia that American soldiers were starting a war against the Indians, some of Lee's troops came on an Indian horse herd and captured sixty horses in reprisal.

Soon afterward, Gilliam joined Lee with several companies of fresh troops. In the settlements of the lower Columbia more units were forming, including one comprised of French Canadians and halfbloods under Tom Mc-Kay. At the Cascades, Gilliam had erected a depot for supplies which he named Fort Gilliam, and at The Dalles Lee had built a stockade called Fort Lee. When Gilliam reached the latter post and heard of Lee's skirmish, he at once ordered a punitive expedition against the Indians who had stolen the 300 head of cattle. Riding with 130 men to the east side of the Deschutes River, he spied a group of Sahaptin-speaking Indians, members of small family groups that lived along the Columbia west of the Umatilla River. Although they had not been implicated in the Cayuse murders at Waiilatpu, they had carried out angry raids on emigrants who had passed through their lands, and Gilliam regarded them as enemies. Lee and and a small detachment were sent after them, and in a sudden skirmish, one of the Indians was killed and two women and some horses captured. On the way back to the main body of troops, Lee's men were ambushed in a narrow canyon and had to dismount and hide among the boulders until after dark. None of the whites was injured, and the next day Gilliam pursued the fleeing Indians with his entire force, charging in and killing between twenty and thirty of them. The Indians' camp was destroyed and some horses and cattle seized, but many of the Indians escaped, and skirmishing continued in the rugged country for several days, during which three whites were killed and two others wounded.

In Oregon City, in the meantime, Governor Abernethy had appointed a prominent pioneer named Joel Palmer as superintendent of Indian Affairs and had named him, together with Meek's old trapper companion, Robert Newell, and Major Lee, who was already in the field, as members of the "peace commission" that the legislature had authorized. The three men were directed to proceed to Walla Walla, hold a council with the interior tribes, particularly with the powerful Nez Perces, and try to keep them from combining with the Cayuses by assuring them that the American troops would leave the Indians' country as soon as the murderers of the Whitmans were surrendered to them. From the Indians' point of view it was a good group. Palmer, who had been an Indiana farmer, was a tolerant, genial man, who respected the Indians' rights to their lands. Newell, the former mountaineer, was aware of the Indians' problems and sympathized with their difficult position, and even Lee had made many friends among the upriver Indians during his stay with the Spaldings. Moreover, the commission's assignment coincided, to some extent, with the aim of the Indians themselves. They had asked for just such an American group to make a peace treaty with them.

Palmer and Newell, who recognized the delicacy—but also the importance —of interposing themselves between the Indians and the army that would frighten them, left the Willamette early in February with a small party that included Marcus Whitman's youthful nephew, Perrin, and an Indian named Old Elijah, who was probably a Nez Perce and was taken along to be employed as an intermediary if one were needed. They carried several letters to the interior tribes, including one from Spalding to his friends among the Nez Perces. It was written in the style in which Spalding had been accustomed to speaking to large groups of Indians through a crier, and was meant to be read aloud to them.

"Nez Perce chiefs!" it read. "My friends, Ellis, Kancoot [probably Lawyer, or Kentuck], James, Yuainimalkin [Utsinmalikin], Luke, Jacob, Pucatash [Pahkatos], Yamohmohnim, Yumtamilkin:—quick, meet them; with these flags meet them. From us, from the Americans, five go to meet you: Mr. Palmer, Dr. Newell, Mr. McKay, Mr. Lee, and Mr. Gilliam. These meet you, with good hearts they meet you. They bear a message from the great chief, they bear it; therefore they call you to meet them. Keep quiet ye young men; do not go over to the Cayuses. Wait till these speak closely to you. The good are not to be punished; only the bad are to be punished. The Nez Perces, the Americans are one, therefore do you not depart from us. Very many Americans are going to seek the bad Cayuses, and the bad only. There will soon be large ships from California; therefore they offer to you a proposal of peace. They send you tobacco, therefore meet them without delay. My youngest child is sick, therefore I cannot meet you. When he is well, I will see you by the blessing of God. Ever make yourselves good hearts. By the blessing of God, may we see each other. H. H. Spalding." [15]

Traveling upriver, Palmer and Newell reached The Dalles on February 10 and met Gilliam, who had just returned from his punitive sortie against the

15. Bancroft, *Oregon, 1,* 713 n.

Sahaptins at the Deschutes River. A conference was held, and Palmer made known the governor's hope that the commissioners could go on ahead and call an Indian meeting in an atmosphere in which the Indians would not be frightened by the presence of troops. A letter from the governor to Gilliam, however, added a note of confusion by authorizing the colonel to proceed at once to Waiilatpu and erect a fort there if he thought the situation warranted it. Gilliam was in favor of just such a course; and the next day, to the chagrin and disappointment of the commissioners, he informed them that he could not divide his forces by giving them the armed escort they had requested and, overriding their dismay, told them bluntly that the entire army would march with them to the council.

The die was now cast for hostilities, and on February 14 Gilliam and the unhappy commissioners left The Dalles with more than 400 men, bound for the Cayuse country. Before they started, they received messages from the Yakimas and the Sahaptins on the Deschutes that those peoples would not join the Cayuses. But the commissioners were principally concerned about keeping the powerful Nez Perces neutral, and on February 20, at the John Day River, Palmer sent Old Elijah to McBean at Fort Walla Walla with a flag and some tobacco, as well as Spalding's letter, to be forwarded by the Hudson's Bay Company trader to the Nez Perces. In the packet containing Spaldings's letter was also one from Gilliam, to be sent by McBean to Father Brouillet on the Umatilla, asking the priest for facts concerning his role in the massacre and the events that followed it, an accounting which the Americans eagerly desired having as a result of the stories they had heard from Spalding and the ransomed captives. On his way to Fort Walla Walla, Elijah met some Cayuses under Tauitau, who took the flag and tobacco from him but sent the packet of letters to the fort. At the post, McBean gave Spalding's letter to Timothy and Red Wolf, who happened to be there at the time, and the two Nez Perce leaders hurried back to the Clearwater with the message. Brouillet, in the meantime, had realized that hostilities were about to occur between the Cayuses and the approaching Americans, and on February 20 he moved from the Umatilla to the safety of the British fort. He and McBean both wrote letters to Gilliam, but again Tauitau intercepted the messenger, and this time the Cayuse chief destroyed the packet of letters.

The American troops had halted about twenty-five miles west of the Umatilla River to wait for replies to their messages. When none came, the assumption grew that the Nez Perces had joined the Cayuses, and the dispirited commissioners agreed with Gilliam to continue the march to Waiilatpu.[16] The troops started out in the morning, the three commissioners rid-

16. On February 23 thirteen frightened members of the Sahaptin bands whom Gilliam and Lee had fought earlier near the Deschutes River appeared at the Americans' camp

ing in advance and carrying a white flag. They were entering the country of the Umatilla Cayuses of the band of Tauitau and Hezekiah, and just before noon they sighted two Indians, watching them from a distance. When the commissioners advanced toward them, the Indians backed off and disappeared. Soon a large war party appeared on the hills ahead. Newell tried to ride up to them, carrying the white flag, but their leader called to him to keep away. He returned to the troops, followed by the Indians who ranged boldly on both flanks of the army, hooting and shouting at the Americans. There had never before been a battle between these Indians and the "Bostons," who had once been good friends and allies in the Rockies; and the Indians, underestimating the settlers' fierce racial animosity, envisioned a fight not unlike those they had waged many times against the Blackfeet and Snakes—one in which a strong stand made the enemy break off the engagement and go away.

The two forces were almost equal in size. The Indians, mostly Cayuses, numbered more than 400, but one hundred of them were unarmed women and spectators who circled noisily in the background, waiting to help celebrate the victory. As the Indians moved closer, the Americans deployed in a circle around their wagons and cattle, and kept advancing. Suddenly, one of the Indians raised his rifle and, in a derisive gesture, shot a dog belonging to one of the volunteers. Immediately everyone began shooting. The troops continued moving ahead, firing as they went, and the Indians charged back and forth, answering their shots. At one point two Indian leaders rode desperately toward McKay's unit of French Canadians and halfbloods, shouting belief in their strong medicine. One of them, a Cayuse shaman named Grey Eagle, was shot through the head by Tom McKay and killed instantly. The other Indian was Spalding's Christian convert Hezekiah. He was stopped and driven off by Tom's brother, Charles, with a shot that shattered his arm. Other troops soon took to charging the Indians, forcing them to scatter behind nearby hills, where they regrouped and came galloping back at the soldiers. After several hours of inconclusive fighting, the Indians finally withdrew for the night, and the tired soldiers went into camp on the open plains without wood or water. Five of their number had been wounded, while the Cayuses had lost eight dead.

In the evening, Nicholas Finlay and his two brothers, who had been with

---

and announced their desire to join the war against the Cayuses. They explained that they had not meant to be hostile to the Americans, but that Lee's men had fired on their people and had made them afraid. Now they "hoped never to be at war with the Americans." Newell wrote that Gilliam "was in favor of killing those people," but the commissioners prevailed on the Colonel to let them go peaceably to The Dalles and await the army's return, when the Americans would make a peace treaty with them. Johansen, *Robert Newell's Memoranda*, pp. 108–09.

the Cayuses, came into the American camp. Nicholas was already suspected of having played a role in arousing the Cayuses against the Whitmans, and Newell wrote that he "is a friend to the enemy in my Opinion." However, Gilliam gave him a letter, which he promised to deliver to McBean.

The next day the troops started out again, and once more the Cayuses, defending their homeland, surrounded the soldiers and kept up an harassing fire on them. But there was now obvious dissension among the Indians, many of them arguing that it was no good to keep on fighting, and riding close to the Americans to try to make known their desire to end the battle. Finally, the warriors sent messengers to the soldiers' lines, asking for a council of peace. Gilliam replied that the army would not halt until it reached water, and a half-hearted skirmishing continued until sundown, when the troops reached the Umatilla River. The next morning the army crossed the stream, and the Cayuses appeared again, swarming at a safe distance along the Americans' line of march but still making defiant demonstrations. That evening, after Gilliam's men had encamped, several Cayuses rode up, showing peaceful signs. One of them was Whitman's loyal friend Chief Stickus, who had guided the 1843 emigrants across the Blue Mountains. Stickus appealed for a peace council but was told by the commissioners to meet them at Waiilatpu. The next morning no Indians were in sight, and the army marched to the Walla Walla River and camped near the fort, receiving a letter from McBean that gave them the happy news that the Nez Perces were still peaceful. The commissioners "would have been in a position to treat with the Cayuses, a majority of whom would gladly have accepted peace on the governor's terms—the surrender of the murderers," the British trader wrote. "But with the guilty ones striving to prevent a peace on these terms, and the commissioners coming with an army and hesitating to hold a council, the multitude were alarmed, and uncertain to a degree which impelled them to self-defense, if not to aggressive warfare." [17] If Gilliam smarted at this rebuke to his belligerency, from which so much damage in the form of fear and hostility had resulted, the commissioners made no mention of it in their report. Nor would any white man during the constant troubles of the ensuing years in eastern Oregon ever understand the enduring harm to interracial relations that Gilliam had caused by his refusal to give an escort of troops, as police, to the commissioners when they had asked to be allowed to precede the army. The harvest of his stubbornness was to be an increasing suspicion and hate on both sides.

At the fort, Gilliam and the commissioners finally met with McBean and Brouillet and, after listening to their accounts of the massacre and the events that had taken place since then, were apparently satisfied that the Catholics

17. Ibid., p. 122 n.

were not implicated, as Spalding and the ransomed captives had charged. Gilliam moved his men six miles up the Walla Walla the next day and camped near the village of Peopeo Moxmox, who convinced the Americans that he was peaceable and sold them some beef cattle. "He is our friend," Newell wrote of the old Wallawalla chief, whose son had been killed in California.[18]

Two days later Gilliam learned that the Cayuses, frightened by their inability to stop the Americans, had retreated to the east in the direction of the Nez Perce country, and were seeking the protection and aid of that tribe. Previously, the commissioners had been told by McBean that Timothy and Red Wolf had taken Spalding's letter to the Nez Perces, and they were satisfied that those Indians knew of the Americans' wish to hold a council of peace with them at Waiilatpu. But again Palmer and his colleagues were concerned. They still had no idea of the Nez Perces' ultimate intentions. All that seemed clear was that there was a division among them and that some of them wanted to fight the Americans with the Cayuses, while others felt that the Cayuses had bad hearts and wanted nothing to do with them. There was no choice but to wait and hope.

In the absence of hostile Cayuses, Gilliam moved his men closer to Waiilatpu and on March 2 took two companies of men to the site of the ruined mission. The buildings had been burned and everything destroyed or taken away; but littering the ground were the remains of many of the victims, disinterred from their shallow graves by wolves. Joe Meek, bound for Washington, was still with Gilliam's men, and he helped rebury the mutilated corpses, one of which was that of his own daughter, Helen Mar. The scene sickened the troops, and so incensed Gilliam that he returned to camp determined to end attempts to council with the Indians and, instead, continue the war. He moved his entire command to the mission site and from adobes of Whitman's ruined buildings erected a post, which he called Fort Waters in honor of his lieutenant colonel.

On March 4 a French Canadian named Gervais, who had established contact with the Nez Perces, arrived at the fort with Peopeo Moxmox and several Nez Perces.[19] "Good news," Newell finally reported. "Our Mission is

18. The British and Americans called him Yellow Serpent, although Peopeo Moxmox actually meant Yellow Bird.

19. Dale L. Morgan suspects that this was Jean Baptiste Gervais, a one-time partner in the Rocky Mountain Fur Company, who had settled in the Willamette Valley. See Morgan's review of *Robert Newell's Memoranda* in *Oregon Historical Quarterly*, *61* (1960), 73. If so, he had accompanied Gilliam's troops up the Columbia and had been sent to the Clearwater to establish contact with the Nez Perces, whom he would have known from his days in the mountains. There were a number of former trappers and mountain men with Gilliam's troops, among them Philip M. Thompson, who had stayed briefly at Waiilatpu in 1842 while he was on his way to the Willamette Valley.

not altogether *Cultus* [Chinook Jargon for bad medicine, meaning that the mission still had a chance to succeed] but much it appears has been effected." The commissioners had a talk with the Nez Perces, who gave them reason to hope that their leaders would soon be coming to meet with the commissioners. The turn of events failed to satisfy Gilliam. "Col Gilliam left the council in a huff," said Newell, "and declared he has come to fight and fight he will . . . Most of the officers and men of the Army are disposed to adhere to what the Commissioners say with regard to the war but the Col is altogether against them and no unity apparent among them." [20]

That night Meek and Ebberts, wearing Hudson's Bay Company Scotch capotes to help them get past Indians who still respected the British if not the Americans, started for the States. Doc Newell and William Craig, who had joined Gilliam's command to try to help him with the Nez Perces, gave their old companions of the mountains a confident farewell and watched Meek and Ebberts head south, escorted across the Cayuse country as far as the Grande Ronde by one hundred of Gilliam's men. The next day there were rumors that a large party of Nez Perces was on its way from Lapwai to meet the commissioners, and Craig and Gervais left the camp to meet them. "Col Gilliam is much displeased with the Commissioners, and says for the future he will have his own way, and also says on tomorrow he will march to battle," Newell wrote. "If so we are in a desperate State of Civilization. The porobability is the men will not obey."

The commissioners finally managed to convince Gilliam to be patient and give the Nez Perces a chance to be heard, and on March 6, about noon, Craig appeared and announced that the Indians were nearby. A short time later some 250 Nez Perces, richly attired and led by Gervais, rode proudly into the Americans' camp. They were greeted with cheers by the settler-soldiers, who had heard many stories of their bravery and power and now hoped that Craig had brought them in as allies against the Cayuses.

The Nez Perces set up their tipis near the troops' encampment, and the next day the chiefs sat down to council with Gilliam and the commissioners. Their head chief, Ellis, they explained, was in the buffalo country with a hunting party, but among the leaders who had journeyed to Waiilatpu were old friends of Spalding, including Joseph, Timothy, James, Red Wolf, Jacob, Richard, Kentuck, Luke, and Yoomtamalikin. Camaspello, the Old Man Chief of one of the Umatilla bands of Cayuse, was also present. All of them represented bands that had no desire to fight the Americans.

Among the first to speak was Joseph, who Spalding thought had turned against the missionaries. A disinclination to accept Ellis as a single head chief and spokesman for all the bands, including the Wallowa people, to-

20. *Newell's Memoranda*, p. 111.

gether with a mounting concern over the many settlers who were coming into the country, had undoubtedly filled Joseph with misgivings about the Americans prior to the massacre; and after that event he had perhaps shown understanding and sympathy for the Cayuses' difficulties and, later, for his half-brother, Five Crows, who had reacted to the appearance of the American troops by going out to defend his village. But Joseph wished only to have the Indians left alone on their own lands; and as a headman whose wisdom commanded the respect of all elements of the Nez Perces, as well as of the handful of Cayuses who were present, he had been selected by the Indians as their chief spokesman in the absence of Ellis.

After the commissioners read aloud a letter from Governor Abernethy, Joseph arose to speak. "When I left my home," he said, "I took the book [one of the gospels that Spalding had printed in the Nez Perce language] in my hand and brought it with me. It is my light. I heard the Americans were coming to kill me. Still I held my book before me, and came on. I have heard the words of your chief. I speak for all the Cayuses present, and all my people. I do not want my children engaged in this war, although my brother is wounded. You speak of the murderers. I shall not meddle with them. I bow my head. This much I speak."

He was followed by Jacob, James, Red Wolf, and Timothy, all of whom disassociated themselves from the Cayuses who had perpetrated the massacre, and then by Richard and Kentuck, who, stating that their old chiefs, now dead, had told them to be friends of the Americans, reminded the commissioners of their past close associations with the trappers and missionaries. Finally, Camaspello, speaking for the Cayuses, said that his tribe was divided and that many of his people had no wish to protect the murderers.

When the Indians had finished speaking, Palmer stunned them by announcing that the Cayuses had forfeited their right to their lands because of their hostile actions. He softened the blow, however, by adding that the Americans did not want the country, but would return to the Willamette as soon as the Cayuses handed over the murderers. He asked the Nez Perces to go to the Cayuse camp, believed to be about twenty-five miles away, and convince them to surrender the guilty men. Then he advised the Nez Perces to return to their own country and take up peaceful farming, as Spalding had taught them to do. As an earnest of good faith he would assign their friend William Craig to live among them as an Indian agent to help them and to settle their disputes, and would assure them that no other white man would be allowed to live on their lands without their consent. Later, after peace was restored, he would also send them a schoolteacher and a blacksmith, but in the meantime they were not to molest travelers passing through their country, or Americans coming to trade with them. To all of these proposals the Nez

Perces agreed, and after Colonel Gilliam and the other commissioners had spoken to them, Newell gave them some tobacco and an American flag "to hoist . . . on all national occasions." The commissioners were pleased with the Indians' reactions. "I am aware of their cincerity and know much good has ben done by the interview," Newell wrote. That evening the Nez Perces performed "a war dance" for the entertainment of the troops, and the commissioners reported, "We do them but bare justice when we say the performance was well timed, the parts well acted, characters represented to the very life, and the whole *first rate*." [21]

More importantly, the commissioners noted, "We felt gratified with our success in our efforts to prevent a general war with the Indians—in saving the Nez Perces which had been a matter of much anxiety with us—in breaking the ranks of the enemy by calling off their allies—and especially in separating the innocent from the guilty." To aid the accomplishment of the latter aim, the Nez Perces struck their tipis on March 8 and, accompanied by Craig, their new agent, started for the Cayuse camp. Gilliam agreed to wait a day and then follow them, and on March 9 he started the army on the march. After traveling three miles toward the Touchet River, which came into the Walla Walla from the north, the column met a Nez Perce, Stickus, and two other Cayuses with a white flag. They were on their way from the Cayuse camp and had some money, personal property, and several head of cattle that had been stolen at Waiilatpu and from emigrants during the past year. Stickus gave it all to Colonel Gilliam, and asked for a council to discuss the advice given the Cayuses by the Nez Perces. Gilliam again suspected a trick, and wanted to push ahead to the Cayuse camp before the murderers had time to escape, but Palmer and Newell argued successfully for a council, and once more the troops encamped. In the talk that followed, Stickus announced that the Cayuses had decided not to surrender Tauitau and Tamsucky, two of the Indians whom the whites had considered guilty of the murders, and Gilliam, in a sudden bargaining mood, said that he would drop the pursuit of five of the Indians on his list of wanted men if the Cayuses would deliver the man he most wanted to catch, the halfblood Joe Lewis. This angered Palmer and Newell, who considered it a betrayal of the "eye for an eye" form of justice which the Indians would respect. They got into an argument with Gilliam and withdrew from further participation in negotiations. The two commissioners returned to Waiilatpu with an officer and forty-two men whom Gilliam sent back with the cattle; and soon afterward, escorted as far as The Dalles by some of McBean's men, they went down the Columbia to the Willamette, leaving future events completely in Gilliam's hands.

The military leader was glad to be rid of the commissioners. Stickus had

21. Ibid., pp. 112, 135.

already gone back to the Cayuse camp, and on March 11 Gilliam set his troops on the march again, determined to find the Cayuses and have a final settling with them. The Indians had moved, but Gilliam followed their trail; and two days later, near the upper part of the Tucannon River, he received a message from Tauitau, who had moved off by himself to live alone. The Young Chief professed friendship for the Americans and said that Tilokaikt, one of Whitman's murderers, and the rest of the Cayuses were moving down the Tucannon to its mouth, intending to cross Snake River into the country of the Palouse Indians. Ordering a forced march during the night, Gilliam arrived at dawn a few miles above the mouth of the Tucannon, where he sighted an Indian camp. He waited for daylight, then began to move closer, but halted when he met an old Indian who, with one hand pressed to his heart, told him that this was the camp of the friendly Peopeo Moxmox, and that Tilokaikt and the Cayuses had already crossed the Snake. Gilliam may have misunderstood the old man's information, because it was actually a winter camp shared by Palouses and Wallawallas, who had dwelled in long lodges in the low, sheltered area during the cold weather. With the coming of milder days, the Indians had separated and moved to higher grounds, and were now living in single-fire tipis in the surrounding countryside. The Americans entered the camp, finding only a few Indians, all of whom seemed friendly. According to one account, the Indians pointed to cattle grazing on the surrounding hills, and said that Tilokaikt had left them behind. But there is no evidence that Tilokaikt had ever been there, and the cattle actually belonged to the Palouse and Wallawallas in the vicinity. Disappointed at having missed the Cayuse leader, Gilliam ordered his men to round up the cattle.

White and Indian versions differ as to what happened next. The soldiers said they had a difficult time securing the stock. To get to the top of the hills, they had to climb a long draw, and when they reached the plateau, they said they saw that they had been tricked. Most of the cattle had been driven down another draw and under their eyes were being herded across the Snake, apparently by Cayuses. Unhappily, Gilliam had his men round up some horses and a few head of cattle that the Indians had left behind, and ordered a return to the Touchet River. They had scarcely started out when from behind the hills on all sides of them, some 400 mounted warriors, mostly Palouse—who, they believed, were now in alliance with the Cayuses against the Americans —swooped down around them. The Indian version, repeated to this day by descendants of participants in the clash, is probably more accurate. When the soldiers started after the cattle, the Indians say, some of the natives tried to protest, but were driven away. The stock was theirs, however—not Tilokaikt's, as the soldiers' account says—and they sent messengers to the scattered Palouse camps in the vicinity to tell the people what the troops were

doing. The alarmed Indians gathered during the day, and late in the afternoon decided to attack the soldiers and rescue their cattle. After that, the two
accounts are virtually the same. The Palouse came over the hills, and a running fight began. The army halted for the night at a small stream, but the
Indians continued to fire at them, and the troops finally turned loose the captured stock, hoping to satisfy the Indians, who would then go away.

But several Indians had already been killed or wounded, and the others had
no intention of breaking off the engagement before the invaders were out of
their country. The next morning they were again on the hills around the
camp, and Gilliam's troops were forced to engage in an all-day, running
fight. As the soldiers pressed steadily across the hilly country toward the
Touchet, with the Indians whooping and firing at them from their flanks,
their withdrawal became a retreat. Some two hundred and fifty warriors
harried them, but another hundred and fifty Indian women rode noisily with
their men, shrieking invectives at the white trespassers and urging the young
men to kill them. Late in the evening the soldiers finally reached the Touchet,
and the next morning they recrossed it safely with their wounded, leaving a
small rear guard to defend the south bank. Some of the Indians threatened to
ford the stream and continue the pursuit, but the leaders and women pleaded
with them not to risk further casualties, and they finally broke off the engagement and headed back to their camps. Ten white men had been wounded
in the long battle, and it was believed that four Indians had been killed and
fourteen injured. On March 16 the tired and bedraggled army trailed back to
Fort Waters at Waiilatpu, short of horses, provisions, and ammunition and
worried that their punitive expedition against the Cayuses had resulted in
what the Hudson's Bay Company men had warned them to avoid—a full-
scale war by all the tribes.

On March 20 Colonel Gilliam and two companies of troops started back to
The Dalles for more ammunition and supplies. That night, in camp near the
Umatilla River, Gilliam was pulling a rope from a wagon to tether his horse.
The rope caught in the trigger of his gun, accidentally discharging the
weapon and killing him instantly. With the body of their commander, the
men went on to The Dalles and sent an appeal to Oregon City for provisions
and more troops to take the places of the volunteers whose terms of enlist-
ment were expiring. Another 250 men responded in the settlements and
started upriver. Lieutenant Colonel James Waters succeeded Gilliam in command at Waiilatpu, and H. A. G. Lee was named Superintendent of Indian
Affairs to succeed Joel Palmer, who had resigned.

Under their new commander the troops at the old Whitman station took
stock of their situation and tried to decide which tribes were now hostile to
them, and how many enemies they would have to face. In the north they

learned that the Yakimas and Spokans were still peaceful. The Sahaptins at the Deschutes River in their rear were again becoming restless, and Peopeo Moxmox and his Wallawallas, who had been disturbed by the invasion of the Palouse country, were making open threats against the Americans. Despite the advice of the Hudson's Bay Company traders, who had kept the good will of friendly tribes by supplying them with arms and ammunition for hunting, the settlers in the Willamette had passed a law prohibiting the further sale of weapons to the Indians; and Peopeo Moxmox was saying that the law, which denied him firearms that had become a necessity for the livelihood of his people, had automatically classed him with the enemies of the Americans. Among the Cayuses, who now had the help of the Palouses, there was still fear, and divided opinion concerning what to do. An almost unbelievable piece of information had come from the Hudson's Bay Company post at Fort Hall that a new city of 3,000 Mormons, with 600 houses, had "sprung up, as if by enchantment, in the midst of the desert, near the southern extremity of great Salt Lake," and McBean told Colonel Waters that Joe Lewis and some of the guilty Cayuses were on the road to Fort Hall, intending to seek safety in the new Mormon city.[22] Other Cayuses, including Stickus, Camaspello, and Tauitau, had gone to the mountains to wait until the war was over, while the rest of the tribe had had a great feast with the Nez Perces, about whom there was new reason to be concerned. From the buffalo plains the Nez Perces had received word that their head chief, Ellis, and sixty members of his band had died of measles, and the news was stirring the feelings of his followers against the whites. The wounded Five Crows was with Joseph in the Wallowa Valley, and other Nez Perce leaders, McBean heard, were providing shelter for some of the Cayuses whom the Americans wanted.

While the troops were awaiting their reinforcements, however, Nez Perce messengers showed up with a request for another council, and early in May H. A. G. Lee met with several of their leaders at Waiilatpu. Lee learned that in their home villages some of the bands were arguing again over what course to take with the Americans, and that the chiefs who had come to Waiilatpu, and who represented a majority of the tribe, were genuinely angry with the Cayuses for continuing to try to force them into a war. After making clear their determination to remain at peace, they asked Lee to appoint one of them as a new head chief to succeed the unfortunate Ellis. Lee selected Richard, the young man who had gone to the States with Whitman in 1835 and who, he thought, would be the most amenable Nez Perce in future dealings with the whites. William H. Gray later wrote, without further explanation, that Richard was "murdered by a Catholic Indian" after Lee had appointed

22. Gray, *History of Oregon*, p. 565, quoting a letter from James Douglas at Fort Vancouver to Governor Abernethy, March 15, 1848.

him.[23] Whatever his fate actually was, he did not enjoy the respect of the older and more experienced chiefs, and he was soon superseded by the shrewder and more aggressive Lawyer as head chief of the pro-white element of Nez Perces.[24] At the same time Lee also appointed a tribal war chief, a person usually selected by the bands that combined to travel into buffalo or enemy country. Undoubtedly, it was a tactical attempt by the young superintendent to appease a potential troublemaker, for the man he thus tried to flatter was the powerful Apash Wyakaikt, or Looking Glass, of Asotin, who had once cowed Pambrun and had later opposed Asa Smith and Spalding.[25] Looking Glass was also a close friend of Peopeo Moxmox and of Kamiakin, whose grandfather had been a Nez Perce from Asotin, and Lee probably hoped that the Nez Perce chief's influence could be employed to keep those leaders and their tribes at peace.

Soon after the Nez Perces started for home, a group of Wallawallas and Cayuses appeared suddenly at Waiilatpu. Among them were Peopeo Moxmox and the Cayuse leaders, Tauitau, Stickus, and Camaspello, who had returned from hiding. They, too, asked for a council with Lee and again announced their innocence and asked what they could do to bring about a restoration of peace so that they could return to their homes and live again without fear. Lee told them to deliver Tilokaikt and the other murderers to him; but although they rode off, promising to try to return with the wanted men, Lee recognized that he could not count on them. The three Indian leaders were in an unfortunate quandary, anxious to end their exile wanderings but unwilling to turn traitor to their people and risk war with other Indians who regarded the fugitives as men of courage and patriotism. Before they left, however, they satisfied Lee that most of the Cayuses he wanted were now living with the Nez Perces; and in an impatient mood the American leaders decided abruptly to invade the country of the Nez Perces—whether or not they professed friendship—and conduct their own search.

23. Ibid., p. 563.

24. Lawyer only returned home from the buffalo country after the excitement of the Cayuse war was over. Demonstrating his political acumen, he soon afterward went to the Willamette, convinced the territorial officials that the Nez Perces were pro-American, and returned to the Nez Perce country to bind together the tribe's Christian elements into a peace-abiding "Lawyer's party." This activity, together with American support, led to his becoming head chief. Proceedings of the Treaty Council (1863), p. 64; National Archives, Record Group 75.

25. H. H. Bancroft and recent writers who have borrowed from him have been misled in stating that the person Lee appointed to the position of war chief was "Meaway, a man of little note." (Bancroft, *Oregon*, *I*, 731.) On reflection, it seems obvious that Lee would have been a fool to name a man "of little note" to such a position. "Meaway," a Nez Perce–Sahaptin word for a strong chief, was used by the Indians when referring to Apash Wyakaikt, one of their most respected leaders.

On May 17, 1848, Colonel Waters marched out of Waiilatpu with 400 men, headed for the Snake River. The next day, believing that the fugitives were with Nez Perces somewhere along the Snake west of its junction with the Clearwater, he divided his command into two groups, sending Lee and 121 men to Red Wolf's village near the mouth of the Alpowa, and hurrying north with the rest of the army to the junction of the Palouse and Snake rivers. The pincers movement, designed to trap the Cayuses between the two principal crossings of the Snake, failed to accomplish its purpose. At Red Wolf's camp Lee learned that Tilokaikt and his Cayuses had already moved farther east, toward Lapwai. Lee set out in pursuit, passing the future site of Lewiston, and on May 21 reached the area of Spalding's abandoned mission, where he discovered that the Cayuse refugees had fled to the safety of the mountains. Chagrined at losing his quarry, Lee had his men round up some of the Cayuses' horses and cattle and, without opposition from the Nez Perces, who were too stunned and confused to object to this first American invasion of their country, moved back down the Snake River and rejoined Waters. The latter's campaign had also come to nothing. His men had reached the Snake, occupied a day and a half in crossing it, and amid many false rumors of the near-presence of Tilokaikt had scoured the countryside in vain, shooting at least one innocent Indian who looked suspicious. Finally, Waters had marched his column eastward toward Red Wolf's village and on the way had come to the camp of Richard, the newly appointed head chief, who told him the bad news that Tilokaikt had escaped to the mountains. Soon afterward, Lee rejoined him to confirm Richard's information.

The fruitless expedition had discouraged the men, and Waters led them back to Waiilatpu. On the way, they rounded up some more Indian cattle, believing that it belonged to the Cayuses. When a friendly and dignified-looking Indian rode up to insist that the stock was his, one of the soldiers shot him down. The temper of the volunteers was so bad that Colonel Waters had to permit the guilty man to go unpunished, and the army's report of the incident stated that the troops would have been more satisfied to have been allowed "to wipe from the face of existence" all of the professedly friendly Indians.[26] This from white Christians, who ten years before had lived two thousand miles and more from Oregon!

At Waiilatpu, Waters called a council of his officers. The situation, it was clear, had become a stalemate. The Americans could not hope to capture the men they had come to punish, and the continued presence of troops in the Indian country was leading only to conflicts with bands and leaders with whom the settlers had no quarrel, each incident creating new enemies and risking the broadening of the war. Deciding to abandon further efforts at

26. Bancroft, *Oregon*, *1*, 735 n.

pursuit, Waters sent a group of men to evacuate the Walkers and Eellses, who were still at Tshimakain. With the exception of leaving small military units at Waiilatpu and The Dalles to guard the emigrant routes and act as restraining influences on the Indians, he decided to abandon the entire Indian country to the natives, promising them a reward if they changed their minds and surrendered the fugitives. When he tried to form a garrison to remain at Waiilatpu, however, he was unable at first to secure volunteers for the lonely duty. Finally, using his authority as Superintendent of Indian Affairs, Lee announced that the Cayuses had forfeited title to their lands on the Walla Walla, and that any volunteer who stayed there could assert a claim, the legal right to which Lee would support. With that assurance, fifty men agreed to remain, and Waters and Lee with the rest of the troops set off for the lower Columbia, promising to send back more settlers from the Willamette to help colonize the Walla Walla Valley. At Oregon City, Governor Abernethy promptly endorsed Lee's pledge to the men at Waiilatpu, and the Willamette settlers' newspaper, the *Oregon Spectator*, announced the seizure of the Indians' country with a proclamation headed, "Forfeiture of the Cayuse Lands." There followed a glowing account of the valley, with a statement by Lee to prospective settlers, assuring them that there were already in the area (meaning at the two mission sites), in the Nez Perce country as well as at Waiilatpu, grist and saw mills, a blacksmith's anvil and bellows, tools, plows, harrows, hoes, ironware, and a crop of wheat, peas, potatoes, and corn.[27]

Although the Americans justified the confiscation of the Cayuses' country as punishment of the Indians who would not deliver the Whitmans' murderers, Lee's action was a violation of promises to the Indians that the whites did not want their lands and wished only to bring justice to the guilty men. To the Indians it was a shocking act of mass punishment that went far beyond the code of laws which Dr. White had given them. Moreover, because it was arbitrary and unsanctioned by law or treaty, it set no geographic limits to white settlement and, in effect, served notice on all the tribes that they now faced the real danger of sharing the fate of the Indians of the Willamette Valley and the lower Columbia. As the climactic act of the Northwest Indians' first war with the "Bostons," it also established a clear end to previous relationships between the races. Gone for good was the possibility of peaceful development between the Americans and the Indians in the upriver country. Gone were the hopes of a friendly and mutually respectful coexistence, or of the voluntary adoption by the Indians of the white man's way of life that would save them before they were overrun—as Spalding had once hoped would happen.

27. Ibid., p. 740 n.

Because of the perilous situation that existed in the Walla Walla Valley and its remoteness from the protection of the government in the Willamette, and because of the abundance of desirable land that was still available to home-seekers closer to the downriver settlements, few persons responded immediately to Lee's opening of the Walla Walla country. But the invitation was there, and in time settlers began to arrive. When they did, harmonious relationships between the Americans and Indians no longer existed. The volunteer troops of Gilliam, Waters, and Lee had shown the tribes the bitter face of the land-hungry, Indian-hating settler. The era was past when an authoritarian agency like the Hudson's Bay Company, whose profits required Indian tranquillity and good will, could restrain white men from committing outrages on the Indians. There was no police force to protect the Indians, and aggressors more powerful than the Blackfeet were moving into their lands. Although the Indians had no tradition of united action, save that of the buffalo-hunting bands that had fought together on the plains, all of them faced the greatest crisis in their history. There was no agreement on how to meet the threat. Some would fight with a patriotic determination to defend their homelands. Some would try to save their lives by submitting humbly, and some would try to buy their way to favor, and perhaps to new prestige and power for themselves, by taking the white man's side against their own people. It was the legacy of the division wrought by the missionaries and Dr. White.

Outside of the Walla Walla district, which was guarded by the military post at Waiilatpu and by the British traders at Fort Walla Walla, Lee considered the rest of the interior country unsafe and urged the evacuation of all unprotected whites east of the Cascades until United States troops arrived from California or the East to establish authority in the region. Spalding, who had wanted to return to the Nez Perces, was denied permission to do so, and for a number of years he lived with friends in the lower Columbia country, where, in January 1851, his loyal wife, Eliza, died. At the same time, Lee directed all of the Catholic missionaries to leave the Indians' country, but in various ways some of them managed to evade his order and remain. Bishop Blanchet asked to be allowed to return to the Umatilla. When his request was denied, he returned to the Cayuses anyway and wandered with them for a while, administering to them in their temporary camps in exile, where he also met and was able to instruct some of the Nez Perces. At The Dalles, where Catholics had already begun to establish themselves in place of the departed Protestants, one priest contrived to remain as a settler on a land claim among the Indians in that area; and in the Yakima country the Oblate fathers built a mission, called St. Joseph's, on the upper part of Ahtanum Creek, a tributary of the Yakima. Elsewhere, Catholics maintained stations among the Coeur d'Alenes in northern Idaho, the Kalispels and Flatheads in northeastern Washington and the Bitterroot Valley of Montana, and among the Indians at Kettle Falls near Fort Colvile on the upper Columbia. But those missions for Salish-speaking tribes, established during the 1840s by Father De Smet and his Jesuits from a base among the Flatheads east of the Bitterroots, were in a remote territory little known to the newly arrived American settlers, and were beyond the effective reach of government authorities in the Willamette Valley.

The prohibition against Protestant missionaries in the Indians' country angered many persons on the lower Columbia who, like Spalding and William H. Gray, feared Catholic activity. Occasionally, incidents which on the surface made it appear that the priests were arming the upriver Indians against the Americans or were advising and protecting Indians who were hostile inflamed the Protestant population against the continued presence of Catholics in the tribal areas, and in December 1848, a number of citizens went so far as to petition the Oregon legislature to expel Catholics from the territory. Although their appeal was refused, their bigotry and distrust reflected fears whose roots lay partially in the intense competition which the priests had provided the Protestant missionaries who had tried to work with the Indians. Eventually, many of the interior Indians themselves, including some of the Flatheads who had once earnestly sought Christian teachers, lost interest in the priests, whose promises of greater happiness proved to be no more substantial on this earth than those of the Whitmans and Spaldings. The missionaries had started with baptisms, wrote the wise, old mountain man Tom Fitzpatrick, now a United States Indian agent at Bent's Fort on the upper Arkansas River, and the Indians, "thinking the cerimony some great 'Medicine' which will render him invulnerable or produce some good luck will submit to the ceremony with a good grace, until they find that those who have passed through all the ceremonies of religion, have no better luck in hunting, and war, than they had before, come to the conclusion that the white man's 'medicine' is not so strong as his own, and therefore loses all faith in the white man 'Medicine.' " [28] Such disinterest, sometimes marked by defiance and hostility, discouraged some of the Jesuits who were also harassed by raiding Blackfeet; and when the California gold rush of 1848–49 created a demand for spiritual workers in that part of the West, the Catholic missionary movement shifted much of its emphasis from the Northwest to the new mining regions, temporarily abandoning the Flatheads, withdrawing from the lower

28. Fitzpatrick, from Bent's Fort, October 19, 1847, to Thomas H. Harvey, Superintendent of Indian Affairs at St. Louis. Upper Platte Agency File, 1846–51, National Archives.

Columbia, and transferring some of its personnel from the Indians in Oregon to the white men in California.[29]

But wherever missionaries had been, their influence, whether Protestant or Catholic, managed to survive among some of the Indians with whom they had lived. Along the Snake and Clearwater rivers many of Spalding's loyal Nez Perce followers, like Lawyer and Timothy, continued to hold regular religious services and keep alive much of what the Spaldings had taught them. The Cayuses, drawn more closely to Catholicism by Bishop Blanchet, wandered dispiritedly through the mountains and on the plains, wishing to end their exile and return to their homes, but not daring to do so. Finally, in April 1850, the Indians learned that the settlers who had led the provisional government in the Willamette had been replaced by more important territorial officials appointed by the Great Chief in the East. Lawyer, who had been extending his influence over the Christian and pro-white Nez Perces, went downriver almost immediately with a small party of Indians to assure the new governor, Joseph Lane, that the Nez Perces were friends of the Americans. Lane flattered Lawyer, told him to enforce the old Nez Perce laws that Elijah White had given the tribe, and asked him to help secure the surrender of the murderers of the Whitmans. The reference to the laws made a deep impression on the new Nez Perce head chief. White and Spalding had insisted that the laws derived their authority from the Creator of men, and that the American government operated by, and under, such heaven-given commandments. If men obeyed them and lived by them, they received protection and stayed out of trouble. Similarly, a tribe, guiding its conduct by a strict observance of the laws, would retain the friendship and respect of the American government. From that moment until the end of his life, Lawyer spoke to Nez Perces and Americans alike of the importance of living by law, and of the necessity of knowing what the American law was, so that his people could conform to it.

Returning to the Clearwater from his meeting with Lane, Lawyer later reported that "[I] addressed my people, and Timothy and his people, and my brother . . . and his people. I said to them, there is a great work for us to do. The murderers of Dr. Whitman must be delivered up to the Whites, that

29. For a fuller discussion of the reasons for the closing of St. Mary's, the Jesuit mission among the Flatheads in the Bitterroot Valley, in 1850, see Palladino, *Indian and White in the Northwest*, pp. 64–66, and *The Journals and Letters of Major John Owen*, ed. Seymour Dunbar and Paul C. Phillips (New York, 1927), pp. 6–7. Apparently an important contributing factor was a policy of retrenchment in "liberality" to the Indians practiced by De Smet's successor at St. Mary's, Father Gregory Mengarini. While his superior in the East approved of this policy—at the same time charging De Smet with having been too generous and wasteful—the Indians thought differently and showed their disapproval.

they may be put to death. This is the Law. They were taken and delivered up." [30] The actual facts of the surrender of the Cayuses soon afterward are not known. But still feeling that they had sinned less than the white men, and that they could expect understanding and justice from the new officials in the Willamette Valley, Tilokaikt, Tomahas, and three other Cayuse leaders came out of hiding to seek a conference. They were immediately seized and sent to Oregon City, where they were put on trial and convicted. Their resignation to their fate led to the spreading of a story that they had voluntarily surrendered so that the rest of their people might win pardon and permission to end their exile and return to their homes. When Tilokaikt was asked why he had surrendered, it was said that he had replied, "Did not your missionaries teach us that Christ died to save his people? Thus die we, if we must, to save our people." [31]

The condemned Indians refused Spalding's offer of spiritual comfort but accepted the ministrations of a priest. They were hanged on June 3, 1850, among the first of many Northwest Indian patriots who were to forfeit their lives trying to save their people and their land. The halfblood Joe Lewis, who had quickened the Indians' fears of the Whitmans, was never captured; but in 1862 he was reported to have been mortally wounded when he tried to rob an express in southern Idaho. The rest of the Cayuses, smoldering with resentment and hate, came down from their hiding places and separated into several groups. Some returned to the Walla Walla Valley, saw that it had been taken from them, and rode off to the Umatilla, where they reestablished themselves. Others settled among their Nez Perce friends and relatives in the Wallowa Valley and along the Snake and Clearwater rivers, submerging their language and cultural identity among bands of that still proud and powerful people who had so far managed to avoid trouble.

30. Proceedings of the Treaty Council at Lapwai (1863), p. 64; National Archives, Record Group 75.
31. Frances F. Victor, *Early Indian Wars of Oregon* (Salem, Oregon, 1894), p. 249.

8

A Most Satisfactory Council

AT BEST, united Indian action in the Northwest could only have delayed the inevitable. Armed unity among the tribes immediately after the Whitman massacre might have brought calamities to the Willamette settlers, but Indian victories would have been temporary ones, and the vengeance that the whites would have visited ultimately on the Indians would have been more catastrophic than it was.

In the period of uneasy truce between the Indians and the settlers which followed the abandonment of the punitive war against the Cayuses, the scales tipped completely and with finality against the native peoples of the Northwest. Oregon, now joined politically and economically to the United States, changed from a rough frontier wilderness to a civilized corner of the nation. The Overland Trail, with numerous cutoffs, side roads, and parallel routes, became the Emigrant Road, carrying American white culture westward year after year to the goldfields of California and the new villages and towns of Oregon. In 1849 regular army troops came with the settlers, some of them halting in the Indians' country to establish guardian posts for the emigrants at Fort Laramie and Fort Hall, others continuing on to garrison the Northwest at The Dalles and other strategic points. Headquarters were established at the old Hudson's Bay center at Fort Vancouver, and there, in new military buildings called first Columbia Barracks and later Vancouver Barracks, many professional soldiers, including Ulysses S. Grant, George B. McClellan, Philip Sheridan, and George Pickett, who were soon to win fame in the Civil War, saw service as junior officers during the 1850s.

For a brief period the California gold rush slowed Oregon's development by drawing many of the Willamette settlers to the mines in the south. But the nation's westward surge, accelerated by the gold rush itself, soon more than compensated for the exodus. As trains of covered wagons continued to reach the Northwest, the better lands in the older, settled regions became filled and pioneer families began moving north of the Columbia, still staying west of the Cascades in well-watered country more suitable for farming than the arid lands of the interior. The new districts they entered belonged to Indian tribes too, but that was of no consequence to the newcomers. By the end of 1852 several thousand white people were living north of the Columbia River in the valley of the Cowlitz and along the southern and eastern shores of Puget Sound, impinging on the villages and hunting grounds of Indians who were faced suddenly with starvation and extinction. The remoteness of the new settlements from the Willamette, and the feeling that the Oregon government was not attentive to the needs and problems of the people north of the Columbia, aroused a desire among the new pioneers for a territorial organization of their own; and on March 2, 1853, the federal government established Washington Territory, including within its boundaries all land from the Pacific to the summit of the Rockies and from the border on the 49th Parallel to the Columbia River as far east as the Walla Walla, and from there along the 46th Parallel to the Continental Divide. The Indian tribes that still held title to most of the land within both territories played no role in the considerations or decisions that involved their country, and the new line, as an example, cut directly across the homeland of the Nez Perces, dividing jurisdiction over the area between the governments of Washington and Oregon.

Inevitably, as the white population increased in both territories, the legal right to the Indians' lands assumed a growing importance. Under the federal government's Oregon Donation Land Law of 1850 settlers were given a free choice of lands from the Northwest's public domain—every male citizen over 18 years of age was entitled to 320 acres and his wife was able to bring him 320 acres more. But since no public domain yet existed, Congress the same year passed an Indian Treaty Act, authorizing commissions to purchase the lands of the different Northwest tribes and then remove the Indians from the acquired lands, in the style of the removal of the Cherokees and other Southeastern tribes, to areas unwanted by the whites.

The policy in the Northwest was a failure from the beginning. White settlers, assuming the land was theirs to take, moved into the Indians' country, especially north of the Columbia River, without waiting for the government to acquire title to it. The usurpation of the Indians' village sites and hunting areas resulted in conflicts which white commissioners belatedly tried to settle. When they finally met with the Indians, the latter would not agree to the terms proposed to them. Usually, they were willing to sell some of their land, but they insisted on retaining a portion of it for their own use. Suggestions to move them from the west side of the Cascades to the east were also opposed by all of the tribes. The western, canoe-using and forest-dwelling Indians did not want to be exiled among alien peoples in a hot, dry country where the horse was a necessity; and the Sahaptins and Salish, who feared the spread of diseases that were common among the coastal tribes, did not want the strangers in their midst. In the impasse the commissioners disregarded their instructions from Washington and between 1851 and 1853 made treaties with a number of tribes in the Willamette Valley and along the Coast, in which the Indians ceded most of their lands but retained portions on which they could continue to dwell.

Nor did this work. On March 3, 1849, the Indian Bureau of the War Department had been transferred to the newly created Department of Interior. When the new treaties reached Washington, the Commissioner of Indian Affairs noted their deviation from what had been established Indian policy since the removal of the Southeastern tribes. The provision to allow the Northwestern Indians to retain sovereignty over a portion of their country, which would be reserved for their exclusive use, seemed to inaugurate a new policy, "the practical operation of which could not be foreseen," and the Indian Bureau sent the treaties to Congress without either recommendation or opposition. In turn, the Senate failed to ratify them, and the Bureau advised its Superintendent in Oregon to enter into no more treaties, unless forced to do so in order to preserve peace.[1] The unresolved situation resulted in further trouble. As white settlers continued to move onto Indian lands west of the Cascades, the Indians found themselves now without either the protection of a treaty or the guarantee of remuneration. In 1852 gold was discovered in southern Oregon, and prospectors, whose luck had played out in California, hastened north to the new El Dorado in the valleys of the Rogue and Umpqua rivers. There was soon conflict in that area, and in 1853 a brief but bitter war broke out in the forested mountains where Indians had once massacred Jedediah Smith's trappers. An emergency treaty brought the conflict to a temporary halt, but the ruthless violation of the Indians' rights by the miners served to heighten the fears of many other tribes on the western side of the Cascades, whose leaders were already talking of the possibility of having to fight for their own lands.[2]

For a while the Sahaptin and Salish peoples east of the Cascades escaped the whites' pressure. In the interior country white men were still few and widely

1. C. F. Coan, "The First Stage of the Federal Indian Policy in the Pacific Northwest, 1849–1852," *Oregon Historical Quarterly, 22* (1921), 56. Oregon Superintendency, Microfilm Roll 12, 1852, Letter No. 73, L. Lea, Commissioner of Indian Affairs, to Anson Dart, September 3, 1852, National Archives. At almost the same time, the reservation system, which the nation would eventually adopt, was also evolving in California. In 1853–54 Edward F. Beale, Superintendent of Indian Affairs for California and Nevada, established the Tejon Reserve, the first one accepted by the government.

2. War with the Rogue River Indians erupted again in 1855–56.

separated. The centers of non-Indian population, such as they were, were in the Walla Walla and Colville valleys. American volunteer troops no longer garrisoned the site of Whitman's mission. In the fall of 1852, claim to that land had been filed by three partners, S. Lloyd Brooks, George C. Bomford, and John F. Noble, who had come upriver from Fort Vancouver, seeking a location in which to engage in the raising of stock. Brooks had been chief clerk to the army quartermaster at Fort Vancouver and was a friend of Ulysses S. Grant, who was then a lieutenant at the fort. On February 23, 1853, Brooks and Bomford, with Grant as a "silent partner," received a license to operate a "store" for Indians and white travelers on their Walla Walla Valley property.[3]

Under a treaty agreement, pending the settlement of a purchase price by the United States, the Hudson's Bay Company still operated Forts Walla Walla and Colvile, and in their vicinities were small centers of retired French-Canadian employees who lived with their Indian wives and children. Their colony near Fort Walla Walla was known as Frenchtown. William Craig still occupied his claim at Lapwai, and, nearby, another white settler, Henri M. Chase, had established a home for his family in the Nez Perce country, probably close to the site of Spalding's mission. Chase had originally settled on the Umatilla River in 1851, and a year later had discovered some gold traces in a creek that flowed into the Grande Ronde River. It had been a small find, not rewarding enough to work, and late in 1852 he had come up to Lapwai and become a stock raiser among the Indians, who did not object to his presence. Somewhere nearby, also in the Nez Perce country, were two other white men who found occasional employment with Craig, Chase, or Brooks, and engaged in a desultory trade with the Indians. They were W. A. "Al" Tall-man and Peter M. Lafontaine, the latter a 22-year-old adventurer who had come west from Vermont.

On the Tucannon River, along the route between the Clearwater and Walla Walla, an American of Illinois French stock named Louis Raboin lived with a Flathead woman and six children. Raboin was a former American Fur Company trapper and had first settled in the Bitterroot Valley with the Flat-heads. He had left there to get away from the Blackfeet, and had crossed to the Nez Perce country. The French halfbloods called him "Maringouin" (Mosquito), and the site of his home on the Tucannon is the present town of Marengo, Washington. In time, Henri Chase, who became his friend, married one of his daughters and settled for a while nearby.[4]

3. *The Journals and Letters of Major John Owen*, ed. Dunbar and Phillips, *1*, 58, 74. Click Relander, *Strangers on the Land* (Yakima, Washington, 1962), p. 40.

4. Frank T. Gilbert, *Historic Sketches of Walla Walla, Whitman, Columbia and Gar-field Counties, Washington Territory* (Portland, Oregon, 1882), pp. 163–64, 389,

Hundreds of miles to the east, in Montana's Bitterroot Valley, dwelled another trader, John Owen. A 34-year-old Pennsylvanian, he had come west in 1849 as a sutler, accompanying a regiment of United States mounted riflemen bound for military duty in Oregon. The troops, commanded by Lieutenant Colonel William F. Loring, had followed the Oregon Trail and had halted in winter quarters near Fort Hall in southeastern Idaho. Before the troops continued to the Northwest in the spring of 1850, Owen resigned his sutlership to enter trade with the emigrants and Indians in the mountains. He took a Shoshoni Indian woman as his wife and later in the year made his way with a group of employees and followers, probably guided by Flatheads, to the Jesuits' St. Mary's mission, which Father De Smet had founded in 1841 for the Flatheads near the present town of Stevensville in the Bitterroot Valley. Owen arrived to find De Smet's Jesuit successors discouraged by the growing antagonism of their Flathead charges and by repeated Blackfoot raids in the area, and preparing to close the mission. For $250 he bought the buildings from the Catholics and, erecting a palisaded fort, turned the station into a trading post which became the haunt of trappers, hunters, old mountain men, and Indians, and was called by them Fort Owen.

Elsewhere in the interior region Catholic missionaries were still in the Walla Walla, Yakima, Colville, and Coeur d'Alene countries, and Tom McKay's son, William, who had been educated in the East, was living among the Cayuses on the Umatilla River near present-day Pendleton. Except for a few others, mostly wanderers who found occasional employment with Brooks or Owen, they were the only white men in the Sahaptin and Salish countries in the early 1850s, and they constituted no threat to the Indians among whom they dwelled.

Despite their freedom from friction with whites during those years, however, the Nez Perces were already well launched on the road to tribal disunity and decline. Lawyer, Timothy, and many of the Indians who had remained loyal to the missionaries continued on their own initiative to follow the Spaldings' teachings, and in the absence of Spalding and other whites who had given offense to the Indians and caused resentments among them the "Christian" leaders were able to expand their influence among the bands. By example and persuasion they promoted farming and a good and peaceful way of life that seemed attractive and necessary to Indians who feared military defeat by the white men. They repeated the lessons of Spalding, to settle down and "follow the road of the whites"; and with their tilled fields, herds of cattle, and Christian devotions, they promised a hope of safety from the invader.

---

414. Weisel, *Men and Trade on the Northwest Frontier*, pp. 119, 135, 139, 164. Raboin eventually became an interpreter for the treaty Nez Perces, and there is still a family of that name in the tribe.

From time to time white men who visited the tribe saw the marks of the missionary element's influence. Many of the Nez Perces, they reported, were tending plots of land on which they raised grain and vegetables. Some of them had livestock; others, like Red Wolf at Alpowa, had thrifty orchards that Spalding had helped them start. Christianity, or certain borrowings from it, was also widespread, and some white visitors reported that entire bands assembled daily for morning and evening prayers and observed the Sabbath with religious services that were led by one of their own number and were conducted in their own language.[5]

The spread of the civilizing and Christianizing processes, which the Spaldings had initiated, in turn broadened and strengthened the tribe's pro-white groups. As the economic influence of Lawyer and Timothy increased, their political counsel, supported by William Craig, gained stature, and their advice to follow the laws of the white men and not to try to oppose a power that could destroy them all received acceptance, even by leaders like the Kamiah chief Utsinmalikin, who had once clashed bitterly with Asa Smith. Traders in the Nez Perce country observed this attitude also, and Anson Dart, Oregon's new Superintendent of Indian Affairs, who journeyed uneasily to Walla Walla and Lapwai, was cheered by the Nez Perces' warm professions of friendship.

Dart, who employed Elkanah Walker and Perrin Whitman as interpreters, went up the Columbia in June 1851. The Sahaptins had already heard of the first attempts to force coastal tribes to cede their lands, and rumors had preceded the Superintendent to the effect that he would try to make the same sort of treaties with the peoples of the interior. Dart was realistic enough to know that the peace on the upper Columbia was more of a tense truce, and at the Umatilla he was not surprised to find the Cayuses still sullen and suspicious. He met with a small group of them, then went on to Lapwai, where some four hundred Nez Perce leaders and warriors, including Joseph and a group from the Wallowa, came riding in with a proud show of strength, beating drums, whooping, firing their guns, and, finally, putting on a huge war dance. When the Nez Perces learned that Dart had no idea of proposing that they give up any of their lands, their defensiveness vanished, and they convinced him that they intended to remain friendly to the Americans.[6]

But the protestations of friendship by the pro-white Nez Perce spokesmen and their evidence of continued interest in Christianity and the ways of civilization—although important to the agents and other whites because they

5. Gray, *History of Oregon*, p. 599.

6. House Executive Document 1, 33rd Congress, 1st Session, Part I, p. 450, Palmer to Manypenny. *Elkanah and Mary Walker*, Clifford M. Drury (Caldwell, Idaho, 1940), pp. 231–33. Phillips, "The Oregon Missions," in *Frontier Omnibus*, pp. 118–19.

were signs of Indian "progress," and gave hope of future harmony—were only a part of the picture. The Indian villages of the interior country were full of reports of what was happening to Indians elsewhere, and the air was electric with suspicion and distrust of what the white man would do next. Rumors and alarms circulated constantly from band to band, and even Lawyer and the "Christian" Nez Perces viewed with fear the motive of each new group of white visitors that came up the river from the Willamette Valley. The position of the pro-white Indians, at best, was insecure. As in Spalding's time there were many Nez Perces, including powerful war leaders like Apash Wyakaikt, who wanted nothing to do with the ways of the white man and wished no more than to be left alone by them. Even among the chiefs who nodded approval to the counsel of the pro-white leaders, there were many who did so only half-heartedly and who retained doubts about the Americans, whom they had come to believe were all liars and hypocrites. Some of those Indians were willing to be friendly if it would protect their villages and their people, but they were also ready, if necessary, to follow militant leaders and join other tribes in a war of all the Indians against the whites. Those Indians had little or nothing to do with gardens and orchards and Christian services. They appealed to their *wyakins* and to the counsel of the shamans, and continued to leave the settled "Christians" in the villages, while they sought manly adventure and danger beyond their homeland. As their fathers had done, they joined under Apash Wyakaikt and other war leaders and set off in summer and fall on buffalo-hunting excursions, past the Coeur d'Alenes to the old Clark Fork River route, or directly east across the Bitterroots on the Lolo or southern Nez Perce trails, to join the Flatheads.

In the east they found the country changing too. They halted temporarily among the halfbloods and old mountain men at John Owen's trading post in the Bitterroot Valley, where they could purchase guns, ammunition, and supplies, and then moved on to the Big Hole, the Lemhi Valley, and the Snake plains, watching the wagon traffic on the Emigrant Trail and hearing of American soldiers at Fort Laramie and of the Mormon city the whites had built at Salt Lake. Emigrants going west to Utah, California, and Oregon glimpsed the Nez Perces now and then as far east as the Platte River, and made notes about them in their diaries. On July 8, 1851, Robert Robe, a young minister from Ohio taking more religion to Oregon, camped with his party near a band of Nez Perces in the old trapping grounds of the Bear River Valley and recorded that "one of their company says she has a white husband and can talk considerably in English. Another can converse and has learned to swear in English." [7] Two years later William H. Gray, who was returning to Oregon after a trip to the East, met several families of Flatheads

7. *Washington Historical Quarterly, 19* (1928), p. 58.

and Nez Perces on the Portneuf River. As luck would have it, one of them was an Indian who had traveled with him as far as Fort Laramie on his ill-fated trip east in 1837, when The Hat had been killed. There were no recriminations, however, for what had happened sixteen years before, and the Flatheads and Nez Perces rode off peaceably.[8]

There were still large expanses of wilderness, free of Americans, in which to continue hunting buffalo and counting coup on enemies, and the Nez Perces generally stayed away from the white men's roads. They followed the familiar Indian routes to the upper Salmon, and east across the mountains and plains to the Yellowstone, the Musselshell, and the Bighorn. The Sioux were on the western plains now, and the Nez Perces, still allied with bands of Salish and Kutenais, clashed with them, as well as with their older rivals, the Blackfeet, Bannocks, Cheyennes, and Crows. They stole horses, had them stolen from their own camps, and fought battles with daring and courage. Eventually, they turned homeward again, recrossing the passes with horse loads of dried buffalo meat, skins, and trophies, to exult in the villages on the Clearwater and the Snake over victories which their life of freedom still permitted them to celebrate.[9]

Through all their adventures, however, they could never forget the threat that hung over them. In the west their old trading ground at The Dalles was gone, occupied by a white settlement and a garrison of troops that threatened to make war on the Bannocks and Shoshonis in southern Idaho, who were harassing the emigrants passing through the Snake country on the Emigrant Road. In the Grande Ronde and the Umatilla Valley, Cayuses and Nez Perces from the Wallowa still watched unhappily as long trains of wagons continued to roll by. In the north, on the trails between Fort Colvile and the country of the Salish, where the Jesuits operated a mission on the Coeur d'Alene River, Nez Perces saw increasing numbers of traders, and knew that the first settlers would not be long in coming. The question of what to do kept the chiefs and old men talking, but there was no unanimity of feeling. Some were for fighting, and some were for doing anything that was necessary to avoid trouble.

Trouble that they could not avoid came suddenly upon them in 1853 in the person of Isaac I. Stevens, an impatient, politically ambitious military man who arrived in the Northwest wearing three official hats simultaneously. Originally from Massachusetts, Stevens was a West Point graduate who had served with distinction in the Engineer Corps during the Mexican War and

8. "From Ithaca to Clatsop Plains: Miss Ketchum's Journal of Travel," Part II, ed. Leo M. Kaiser and Priscilla Knuth, *Oregon Historical Quarterly, 62* (1961), 372.

9. For Nez Perce accounts of the wars and adventures of some of these buffalo hunting bands in the period 1850–75, see McWhorter, *Hear Me,* pp. 31–49, 561–93.

had later received scientific training with the United States Coast Survey. An efficient organizer, he had helped Franklin Pierce's presidential campaign in 1852 and had then applied successfully for the governorship of the newly created Washington Territory, which carried with it the position of Superintendent of Indian Affairs for the territory. Not content with that, he had conducted a whirlwind campaign of letter writing and lobbying in the capital, and had also won the role of leader of the most northerly of four Pacific Railroad Survey groups being dispatched by the War Department in parallel paths across the trans-Mississippi West to discover the most feasible route for a railroad to the Pacific.

Still a young man of 35, a dynamo of energy who moved with speed and decisiveness, Stevens saw all three of his jobs complementing each other toward a single grand end. As a governor who would build up the population and prosperity of his territory, he was intent on winning Congressional approval for a railroad that would terminate at Puget Sound. That meant not only finding a northern route through the mountains, cheaper and more practicable for a railroad than any route farther south, but also ensuring its safety from Indians. At the same time, he would increase the public domain in Washington and make land available for the settlers who would come to the new territory. He bore no ill will against Indians, and even fancied that he admired and respected them. But as an instrument of advancing American civilization he had a job to carry out, and with a flair for publicity he expected to win notice in the East for what he would achieve. As Superintendent of Indian Affairs he would try to treat the Indians justly and peaceably, but he was determined to bend them to his wishes.

Stevens assembled an outstanding body of civilians and military men for his survey party, equipped them elaborately, and started them west in several groups. His plan was to lead the largest party himself, surveying west from St. Paul, Minnesota, across the northern plains and mountains to Washington Territory. A second group would go up the Missouri River and meet him at Fort Union. A third party under Captain George B. McClellan, who would later lead the Army of the Potomac during the Civil War, would go by way of Panama to Fort Vancouver on the Columbia and come eastward across the Cascades, exploring for feasible railroad passes and joining Stevens somewhere on the eastern side of those mountains. McClellan, in addition, would send supplies with part of his command under Lieutenant Rufus Saxton even farther east to the Bitterroot Valley, where Stevens would meet him. The focal location of the plans, unnoticed by Stevens and unknown to the Indians, was in the lands of the Sahaptins and Salish.

On June 6, 1853, Stevens' large party set out from Minnesota, bound for Fort Benton and the Montana Rockies. Several weeks later McClellan reached Fort Vancouver, and on July 18, after dispatching Saxton's pack train with supplies to the Bitterroot Valley, he started east to explore the Cascades. McClellan's party numbered 66 men and 173 mules and horses. As he headed east across a pass just north of the Columbia River, he was forced to hire a number of Sahaptin-speaking Klickitat Indian guides, who soon had word circulating from one Indian camp to another of the movements of this new body of soldiers. On the eastern side of the mountains the Sahaptin Yakimas, whose plateau culture was very much like that of the Nez Perces, responded with alarm. Kamiakin sent his younger brother, Skloom, who was also known as "Ice," up to the summit of the Cascades to discover the purpose of the troops, and somehow the Yakima picked up the information from McClellan, or from members of his party, that the next year a Great Chief from the East (Stevens) would come to buy the Yakimas' land and open it to white settlers.[10]

The news startled the Yakimas, and as McClellan went on, he was met by delegations of Sahaptins whom he noted were much disturbed by "false reports of the character of his party." [11] At length he reached the eastern side of the Cascades and turned north to the Yakima Valley, intending to explore passes from that side of the mountains. In mid-August he descended Ahtanum Creek, a tributary of the Yakima River near the present city of Yakima, and came on St. Joseph's mission, which was administered by Father Charles M. Pandosy for the Yakimas. A few miles up the creek were the home and gardens of Kamiakin.

That headman, the strongest and best known of the Yakima leaders, was related as already noted, to the Nez Perces through one of his grandfathers, who had been born in the Asotin region, the home also of Apash Wyakaikt's family. During his frequent visits to the Spokan country, Kamiakin's grandfather had met a Spokan girl and had settled down with her people. They had had a son named Ki-yi-yah who had become a headman among the Spokans and who had eventually established homes also in the region of the Palouse and lower Snake rivers. During the latter years of the eighteenth century there had been frequent migrations of Nez Perces, Spokans, and Yakimas into the Palouse country, where the fine grazing hills favored the building of big horse herds, and Ki-yi-yah had gradually become something of an inter-tribal leader of all the villages in that region. In time he had taken as his wife the daughter of a headman of the lower Yakimas, and they had had three sons, Show-away, Kamiakin, and Skloom. Kamiakin, the middle one, had been born about 1800.

10. See Splawn, *Ka-mi-akin*, p. 21.
11. *Explorations and Surveys for a Railroad Route from the Mississippi River to the Pacific Ocean*, Vol. 12, Part I (Washington, D.C., 1859), p. 107.

During his youth Kamiakin had spent most of his time with his father in the Palouse and Spokan countries. But about 1825 he had married a Yakima girl named Sal-kow and had moved to her country on the Yakima River. Sal-kow was a member of the most powerful family among the Yakimas. Her grandfather had been a venerated Yakima leader named Weowikt, and her father, Te-i-as, was the headman of all the Indians on the lower part of the Yakima River. His younger brother, Owhi, held an equally important station among the Yakimas farther up the valley toward the mountains.[12] Kamiakin's connections with the leaders of so many different peoples helped to give him an importance among all of them, but they also made for complications that white men did not grasp and that led to serious misunderstandings between the Indians and Stevens. Kamiakin, over six feet tall, was a forceful and forthright man who quickly won the respect and following of many of the young Yakimas. He also counted such leaders as Apash Wyakaikt and Peopeo Moxmox as close friends, and he already enjoyed the admiration of many Nez Perces, Spokans, Palouses, and Coeur d'Alenes. But the members of the powerful clan of Weowikt of the Yakimas, into which he had married, eyed him jealously and often reminded him that the country in which he resided was that of his wife. Their differences increased after 1843, when he took two more wives, both of them the daughters of a prominent Klickitat chief named Tennaks who lived near The Dalles.

Despite their hereditary positions of leadership, however, both Te-i-as and Owhi, his chief rivals, were relatively weak men, and Kamiakin's star continued to ascend. He traded in the Grande Ronde and the Willamette and at The Dalles for cattle, and about 1845 established irrigated gardens around his home on the Ahtanum. He was influenced by both the British fur traders and the missionaries and, although he had no interest in becoming a Christian, he desired the material benefits of the white man's civilization and tried for a while to get William H. Gray to live with his band. In 1847 he welcomed the Oblate fathers to the Ahtanum, and after the massacre at Waiilatpu he excoriated the Cayuses and gave protection to Jesuit priests who had joined the Oblates. By 1853 he possessed large horse and cattle herds and extensive gardens of potatoes, melons, and squashes, and is believed to have employed other Indians to tend his stock and fields.[13]

12. Most contemporary accounts by white men called Owhi the brother or brother-in-law of Kamiakin. Actually, he was the uncle of Kamiakin's wife.

13. The biographical material on Kamiakin and the interpretation of his position in the tribe are based on the author's interviews with Yakima Indians over a period of several years, and on William C. Brown, *The Indian Side of the Story* (Spokane, Wash., 1961), pp. 66–80, and Splawn, *Ka-mi-akin*, pp. 17–20. Brown, at one time a Superior Court Judge in Washington, knew the Yakimas and other tribes of eastern Washington

Overland Trail

ERRITORY→ ←— NEBRASKA TERRITORY

Marias
Pass

MARIAS R.

Blackfeet

Gros Ventre

MISSOURI R.

Flathead
Lake

TETON R.

Fort
Benton

Pend d'Oreille

MISSOURI R.

JUDITH R.

Flathead

CLARK FK.

Hellgate
[Missoula]

Cadotte's
Pass

[Helena]

Lolo Trail

BLACKFOOT R.

BITTERROOT R.

Fort
Owen

Mullan
Pass

YELLOWSTONE R.

BIG HORN R.

Nez Perce   Trail

Perce

MON R.

Yellowstone
Lake

Bannock

Fort
Hall

ROCKY

Shoshoni

R.

MTS.

Continental Divide

Shoshoni

5. The Coming of I. I. Stevens, 1854–55

Although he was careful not to act as a spokesman for any but his own followers, his wealth, ability, and powerful connections gave him an influence and authority that Te-i-as and Owhi could not match. He was a natural leader and a convincing orator, and in times of difficulty headmen of other bands came to seek his counsel. As a result many of the interior Indians regarded him as the strongest and most important leader among the Yakimas, and they communicated that opinion to white men, who were quick to assume that he was therefore the head chief of the entire tribe. Theodore Winthrop, a young writer and adventurer who traveled through the Yakima country in 1853 and described his journey in a popular book, *Canoe and Saddle,* told of meeting Kamiakin, "a majestic Indian . . . chiefest of Yakimah chiefs." Winthrop went on: "He was a tall, large man, very dark, with a massive square face, and grave, reflective look. Without the senatorial coxcombry of Owhhigh, his manner was strikingly distinguished, quiet and dignified." [14] McClellan, similarly, had come to understand that Kamiakin was the principal chief of all the Yakimas, and when he met him at Father Pandosy's mission and sat down to talk with him, he made a determined effort to assure him that he had no reason to fear the presence of the government survey party. Kamiakin remained skeptical, however, and McClellan later reported that "the favorable influence of the Catholic priests was here of great benefit . . . and probably prevented trouble." [15]

Soon afterward, McClellan established a camp on the nearby Wenas River, while he and his men examined the Naches Pass and the Yakima River. The Indians watched them closely, and one day Kamiakin rode over to the American camp and had another talk with McClellan. Again, the officer's explanation of what the soldiers were doing in the area failed to satisfy him. McClellan may have told him frankly that he was searching for a good route across the Cascades, but if so, it would only have concerned the Indians the more. For although the Indians were unhappy about it, they knew that white men from the settlements at Puget Sound were already familiar with the Naches

---

for more than half a century, becoming their friend, confidant, and historian. His book was the first to publish a clarification of Kamiakin's position among the different tribes. My own research on the history and culture of the Yakimas convinces me that almost everything written on this tribe in the past has been based, too largely, on writings by early settlers, missionaries, and military men. Only in comparatively recent years have knowledgeable researchers, like Lucullus McWhorter, Judge Brown, and Click Relander, begun to cut through the distortions and misrepresentations that have passed for history. These men have understood that the historian of Indian-white relationships must also know something about the Indians and their culture.

14. Theodore Winthrop, *Canoe and Saddle,* Nisqually Edition (Portland, Ore., n.d.), pp. 150–51.

15. *Pacific Railroad Reports,* Vol. 12, Part I, p. 139.

Pass and were even then building a wagon road over it. The highway would come out at the Yakima River and run all the way through the Yakimas' lands to Fort Walla Walla, where it would connect with the Oregon Trail and give emigrants an opportunity to go to Puget Sound rather than to the Willamette. The whites, in fact, had known of the pass since 1840, when Pierre Pambrun and his young friend, Cornelius Rogers, had explored it. In 1850 the Puget Sound settlers had tried to clear a road across it but had abandoned their attempt. With increased funds and more men to work on it, they had commenced again in 1853, and were now making better progress. Kamiakin would probably not have understood McClellan's need to find grades suitable for rails, rather than for packhorses and wagons, and his puzzlement would only have increased his suspicions.

When he left McClellan, he visited the village of Owhi and told that chief of his concern. McClellan had informed Kamiakin that he intended to continue moving north, exploring the various passes, and Owhi, who had a close relationship with the leaders of the Wenatchi and other Salish-speaking bands that lived north of the Yakimas along the Columbia, agreed to remain close to the Americans and try to discover their true motives. On September 3 McClellan moved his camp from the Wenas to the Yakima Valley and reported that "a large band of Indians, under Ouhi, a brother of Kamiakan, encamped near, and were very friendly, their chief being the most good natured Indian yet seen in the country." [16] Owhi, who was actually the uncle of Kamiakin's Yakima wife and not Kamiakin's brother, may have appeared amicable, but he was no less troubled than Kamiakin. Joined by another Indian leader named Quil-ten-e-nock, who was the headman of a Salish band that lived on the eastern side of the Columbia near the Grand Coulee, he accompanied McClellan's party north to the Wenatchis and then returned to Kamiakin to tell him that he had learned that a great chief of the Americans was actually on his way from the East to join McClellan and to force the Indians to make a treaty to sell their lands to the whites. If the Indians refused to sell, he had been told, the soldiers would drive them away and seize their country as they had done to the Cayuses.

Kamiakin had guessed as much. He and the other Yakimas met and agreed not to accede to such a treaty. At the same time, they sent messengers to Salish and Sahaptin bands in every part of the country, informing them what Owhi had learned. They suggested that they wait for the principal American chief and then act together.

In the meantime, Lieutenant Saxton, who had left The Dalles on July 18 with supplies for Stevens, had observed alarm among other tribes. With a party of fifty-one men he moved up the Columbia and at the Umatilla River

16. Ibid., pp. 140–41.

reported that he "was met by a deputation of Cayuse braves, sent by the chief to ascertain his object in passing through their country, they having been told that he was coming to make war upon them and take away their horses." He assured them that they had been misinformed and, after smoking with them, moved on to Fort Walla Walla, where he was advised to go to the Bitterroot Valley by way of the old trade route along the Clark Fork River, rather than try to take the difficult Lolo Trail across the mountains. He struck off north to the junction of the Palouse and Snake rivers, and at the crossing "met a delegation of fifty Peluse and Nez Perces warriors, who came in full costume and with great formality to have a great war talk. After a smoke, the chief made inquiries as to his objects in going through their territory with so many horses and so much merchandise." Lieutenant Saxton's explanation of his mission to meet Stevens seemed to satisfy them, and he related that he further won their good will by a demonstration of shooting with new rapid-firing army rifles, which they had not seen before. They "made a very favorable impression in regard to their means of defence," he reported.[17]

He crossed the Snake and traveled north to the Spokan country, meeting Spokan Garry and again finding the Indians concerned by rumors that he was going to make war on them. Once more he did his best to win their confidence, and after being joined by John Owen, who was going back to his trading post in the Bitterroot Valley, proceeded to Lake Pend Oreille and the Clark Fork River, passing the site of the old, abandoned Flathead Post and reaching Owen's fort on August 28. There he divided his group. In order to conserve as many of the supplies as possible for the Stevens party, he sent Lieutenant Robert MacFeeley and nineteen men back to Fort Vancouver, directing them to return by way of the Nez Perce trail across the mountains, which he had failed to explore in going east. MacFeeley took eight days getting over the mountains, running into some snow and losing a number of his horses, but he finally emerged on the Clearwater River, where Nez Perce Indians gave him assistance and sent him on his way to Fort Walla Walla. At Owen's fort, Saxton also left Lieutenant Richard Arnold with five men to establish a depot for Stevens' supplies, then, with the rest of the men and a guide, started for the Missouri River to look for the governor and his party.

Stevens had reached Fort Benton near the junction of the Teton and Missouri rivers in northern Montana on September 1. By the time he arrived at that American Fur Company post, which traded with the Blackfoot tribes, he was thoroughly convinced that the northern railroad route which he was surveying would be the best one for the nation to adopt. As he had come across the plains of present-day North Dakota and Montana, he had pursued

17. Ibid., p. 108.

his mission with vigor and optimism, and several side parties, generally paralleling his route, had given him encouraging reports that had increased his enthusiasm. There remained the problem of security from Indian war parties on the northern plains, but he had a solution for that too. The Gros Ventres and Blackfoot tribes were friendly to the American Fur Company men with whom they traded, but they still looked with hostility on white men who armed and supplied the western Indians. More than that, they resented the continued intrusions by the western tribes into the buffalo lands of central Montana, and they still tried to drive them away whenever they came on them. The intertribal wars, Stevens realized, would endanger the exploration and settlement of the northern country, as well as the building of a railroad and the passage of emigrants on their way to Washington Territory. In 1851 a council of Indians at Fort Laramie had achieved an intertribal truce among the tribes that hunted on the central plains, and had secured their promise not to molest travelers on the Overland Trail. With that recent treaty as his model, Stevens now proposed to the Blackfeet that they meet with him in council the following spring at Fort Benton and make a lasting peace with Americans and with the Flatheads, Nez Perces, and other tribes that came from west of the mountains to hunt buffalo. His arguments, including a promise to give the Blackfeet white men's goods and presents, were persuasive, and after several meetings the Blackfeet and Gros Ventres agreed to participate in such a council.

Stevens' next problem were the Rocky Mountains. The Blackfeet raised his hopes, however, by telling him there was an easy pass to the Bitterroot Valley. It was the old buffalo road via Hellgate that the Flatheads and Nez Perces often took to the plains. On September 9, hearing that a party of Flatheads was hunting on the Musselshell River somewhere to the southeast, he dispatched Lieutenant John Mullan, a Piegan guide, and several men to find them, tell them of his desire to bring peace between the Blackfeet and the western Indians, and ask them to meet him in the Bitterroot Valley. Lieutenant Saxton had meanwhile arrived at Fort Benton and confirmed the feasibility of movement across the Rockies. After sending Saxton and another group of men on their way down the Missouri with messages for Washington, including a request for permission to hold the Blackfoot treaty council at Fort Benton—which was actually in the Territory of Nebraska, beyond his jurisdiction—Stevens prepared to cross the mountains. He left James Doty, the son of a former governor of Wisconsin, at Fort Benton as a special Indian agent, and directed him to examine the country around the post during the winter and become better acquainted with the Blackfoot bands in the vicinity. Then, on September 22, he set out for the Continental Divide. The comparative ease with which he crossed it at Cadotte's Pass further cheered him, and the rest of the way to Hellgate and the Bitterroot Valley provided no obstacles. On September 28 he reached Owen's fort and found the supplies that Saxton had left for him with Lieutenant Arnold.

In the meantime, Lieutenant Mullan had found a large hunting camp of Flatheads and Nez Perces south of the Musselshell River. The Flathead population, never great, had been dwindling steadily during the years of fighting with the Blackfeet, and Flathead villages were now a conglomerate of Pend d'Oreilles, Kutenais, and Iroquois, as well as Nez Perces, Flatheads, and a few other Salish peoples. Mullan reported that there were twenty-five lodges of Nez Perces, each containing two men and a number of women and children, in the Flathead camp. After being "astonished" by a prayer meeting that the Indians conducted on his arrival, he sat down for a council with them, using a French-speaking Flathead, possibly an Iroquois, as his interpreter. The Flatheads and Nez Perces welcomed hearing that the Americans wished to establish a peace between the Blackfeet and the western tribes, and they agreed to send four of their important men with Mullan to meet with Stevens in the Bitterroot Valley. Three of the men chosen were Flatheads, and the fourth was a Nez Perce, whom Mullan understood was named Cohoxolockny, but was possibly Hohots Moxmox (Yellow Grizzly). They guided the members of Mullan's party to the heads of the Musselshell and Smith rivers, across the Missouri, and over the present-day Mullan Pass near Helena, Montana, to the Blackfoot River and Hellgate, reaching Owen's fort two days after Stevens had arrived there.

Stevens, who was also intrigued by the evidence of Christianity among the Flatheads, was glad to see them and immediately informed them that the Blackfeet had signified their intention of giving up war and stealing horses. The four Indians were skeptical but agreed to participate in any peacemaking council that Stevens held at Fort Benton the next year. The buffalo country woud be much better if there were peace, they admitted, but it remained to be seen whether the Blackfeet would make such a promise and keep it. After telling them that he would leave Lieutenant Mullan and a party of Americans in the Bitterroot Valley during the winter to "see to their wants" and help guarantee their safety against any Blackfeet who persisted in making war, he turned his attention to the next leg of the railroad route.

Directing Mullan to keep records of the snow and climate in the Bitterroot Valley during the winter, and to explore the country between Fort Hall in the south and Flathead Lake in the north, as well as maintain a protective watch over the Flatheads, Stevens departed from the valley on October 4 and moved down the Bitterroot River. Near Hellgate he visited Victor, the head chief of the Flatheads, and repeated his invitation to join the Fort Benton council the next year. He delayed briefly in the area, waiting for one of his men, an old friend and able assistant named Abiel W. Tinkham, who had left the main party near Cadotte's Pass to explore a more northerly route across the Rockies. Tinkham finally arrived, reporting that he had been through country too difficult for a railroad, and Stevens promptly reassigned him to head north again to Marias Pass on the southern boundary of present-day Glacier National Park, explore that route back to Fort Benton, return to the Bitterroot Valley by the Hellgate route, and then take the most southerly Nez Perce trail over the Bitterroots to the Clearwater River and Fort Walla Walla. It was a formidable mission over a great expanse of high mountain territory, to be undertaken at a late period in the year; but Tinkham had already demonstrated that he was one of the most efficient explorers and best wilderness travelers with the expedition, and he set out at once for the Marias Pass, accompanied by a Flathead guide.

On October 7 Stevens started down the Clark Fork River. The next day he met large bands of Nez Perce and Coeur d'Alenes bound for the buffalo country. They told him that they usually traveled to the plains at that time of year and returned in March. Stevens informed them, also, of his talks at Fort Benton and related the promise of the Blackfeet to hold a council the next spring and make peace with all tribes. "This intelligence," he said, "was most gratefully received." Continuing on his way, he separated from his main party, which followed the Clark Fork River over the old trail to Lake Pend Oreille, and took the more southerly route up the St. Regis River to Lookout Pass, which he called Stevens Pass. On the western side of the divide he descended the Coeur d'Alene River and stopped at the Jesuit mission, run by Fathers Anthony Ravalli and Gregory Gazzoli for the Coeur d'Alene Indians near Lake Coeur d'Alene. While Stevens was there, a Nez Perce Indian arrived from Fort Walla Walla with the news that the first group of emigrants from the States had gone successfully from Walla Walla to Puget Sound the month before over the new Naches Pass road. It had been a party of between 100 and 200 men, women, and children, with some fifty wagons, under the leadership of a man named James Longmire. Some of Peopeo Moxmox's people had been paid to ferry them across the Columbia River, and the emigrants had trailed west across the Yakimas' land.[18]

From the mission Stevens circled to the western side of Coeur d'Alene Lake, passing several groups of Nez Perces, Coeur d'Alenes, and Spokans on their way to buffalo, and soon reached the Spokan country, where he observed Indians holding Christian religious services. After meeting Spokan Garry, who, he reported, "is not frank, and I do not understand him," he turned north to Fort Colville (which the Americans were now spelling with

18. Ibid., pp. 134, 136, 153; also Hubert Howe Bancroft, *The History of Washington, Idaho, and Montana, 1845–1889* (San Francisco, 1890), p. 65.

two "ll's"), arriving there almost simultaneously with McClellan, who was concluding his exploration of the eastern slopes of the Cascades.

Stevens was disappointed with McClellan's report. His own explorations, as far west as that point, had convinced him that a northern railroad was feasible, but McClellan had found no satisfactory pass through the Cascades, except possibly the Snoqualmie Pass at the head of the Yakima River. He could not even say that that pass would be suitable, however, since Indians had told him that some twenty to twenty-five feet of snow blocked it in winter, and he himself had made only a cursory examination of it for three miles beyond the summit. McClellan's failure rankled Stevens, but he refused to accept his judgment as final and determined to send him back for another try.

The Americans were entertained liberally at Fort Colville by its Hudson's Bay Company factor, Angus McDonald, a tall, heavily bearded, fun-loving man who had requisitioned a supply of "50 imperial gallons" in expectation of their arrival. Stevens and McClellan were not bashful about accepting the trader's hospitality, but their lack of capacity and endurance failed to win McDonald's approval.[19] Two days later the Americans moved south to the Spokane River, pausing to visit the site of the Tshimakain mission, which the Walkers and Eellses had abandoned five years before. After meeting Spokan Garry again, Stevens established a camp south of the Spokane River, where he soon welcomed the arrival of his main party that had taken the longer route across the Bitterroots by way of the Clark Fork River and Lake Pend Oreille. He had persuaded McClellan to return to the Cascades and try again to run a line across Snoqualmie Pass to Puget Sound; but while they were in the Spokan country it began to snow, and McClellan convinced him that it was now too late in the season to make the attempt. Stevens finally acquiesced and, calling off further exploration for that year, reluctantly directed all of his parties to head for Olympia, the Washington territorial capital, by way of Walla Walla, The Dalles, and Fort Vancouver.

Striking out ahead of the others with Spokan Garry as his guide, he went down the Palouse River to the Snake and reached Fort Walla Walla on November 2. The view of the Blue Mountains, still free of snow, convinced him that the Cascades could not be too formidable, and his irritation with McClellan increased. He examined the Walla Walla Valley, visiting the home of John McBean, the former chief factor at Fort Walla Walla, and a Jesuit mission run by Father Eugene Chirouse, and calling at the ranch of Brooks and Bomford on the site of the Whitman mission. On his return to Fort Walla Walla he met Peopeo Moxmox, noting that he was "of dignified manner, and

19. "Angus McDonald: A Few Items of the West," ed. F. W. Howay, W. S. Lewis, and J. A. Mayers, *Washington Historical Quarterly*, 8 (1917), 188–229; and Terry Pettus, "Frolic at Fort Nisqually," *The Beaver* (Summer, 1961), p. 11.

well qualified to manage men." The old chief, he reported, had "saved up a large amount of money (probably as much as $5000); still he is generous, and frequently gives an ox and other articles of value to the neighbors." The cash, an unusually high amount for an Indian to possess, had probably been accumulated through the sale of horses, cattle, and produce to the fort and to emigrants. Few Indians beside Peopeo Moxmox would even have had a desire to own cash, the value of which to most Indians at that time did not seem comparable to that of material possessions.

A few days later McClellan and the other members of the expedition reached the fort, and Stevens, still chafing over his uncompleted railroad survey, persuaded Frederick W. Lander, one of the civilians in the party, to go up the Yakima River and try to get across the Naches Pass to Puget Sound. After Lander set out, Stevens started down the Columbia, still accompanied by Spokan Garry, who had finally ingratiated himself to the governor by a series of friendly favors, and whom Stevens, as a result, now considered "a man of judgment, forecast, and great reliability." At The Dalles military leaders in command of the post pulled Stevens up short with the one problem that had so far escaped him. The country was on the verge of an Indian explosion, they told him. Commissioners had started to make treaties with some of the tribes, buying their land and guaranteeing them protection on reserves. But the Senate had refused to ratify the pacts. Captain Benjamin Alvord of the 4th Infantry at The Dalles had written repeatedly to the Superintendent of Indian Affairs in Oregon and to the headquarters of the Pacific Department of the Army in San Francisco, asking for "laws, rules and regulations relating to the Indian tribes, especially such as might concern this frontier." The Yakimas and other Sahaptin tribes of the interior were filled with alarm at the increasing number of settlers. Some sort of treaties had to be made "at an early date before the crowding in of the whites . . . produces collision and war." [20] Alvord's fears of the Indian danger east of the Cascades had been discredited, and he had been relieved of his command. But his successor, Major Gabriel J. Rains, poured out the same warning to Stevens.

Although Stevens seems to have heard nothing of this before, he recognized the dangers inherent in the situation, especially when on the next day at the Cascades he met several men who claimed they had examined the Yakimas' country "for new locations" and had found it an excellent agricultural and grazing region.[21] Here was a second insecure area lying athwart the proposed route for the northern railroad, but the problem of its safety was more

20. Oregon Superintendency, Microfilm Roll 12, Letter No. 86, November 28, 1852, National Archives, quoted by Relander, *Strangers on the Land*, p. 38 n.
21. *Pacific Railroad Reports*, Vol. 12, Part I, p. 155. Hazard Stevens, *The Life of Isaac Ingalls Stevens* (Boston and New York, 1900), 2, 25–26.

urgent than that of the Montana plains. This country was within his own jurisdiction, close to the coastal centers of white population. A wagon road already ran through it, and settlers were about to demand the region. An impasse had resulted from the Senate's refusal to ratify the treaties with the coastal tribes. But Stevens was the Superintendent of Indian Affairs. It was his problem, and with characteristic self-assuredness he convinced himself that he could deal with it.

Continuing down the Columbia, he reached Fort Vancouver on November 16 and was welcomed by its commanding officer, the same Colonel B. L. E. Bonneville whom the Hudson's Bay Company had once forced to withdraw from the Oregon country. Three days later, after sending Spokan Garry back to the Bitterroot Valley with messages for Lieutenant Mullan, Stevens left the fort and, ascending the Cowlitz River, reached his capital at Olympia. Soon afterward, the other members of his party began to arrive, including Lander, who bewildered Stevens by reporting that he had abandoned his attempt to cross the Naches Pass because he had suddenly realized that it was not the route that Stevens had had in mind for the railroad. Stevens' feeling of frustration was great, but it only renewed his determination to get someone across the Cascades that year. His reliable friend Tinkham was still in the field, making his way across the southern Nez Perce trail to the Clearwater and Walla Walla. Dispatching a message to Fort Walla Walla, he directed Tinkham to come from that point to Puget Sound by way of the Snoqualmie Pass "to get at some facts," he wrote, "which would decisively settle the question of the depth of the snow, in regard to which Captain McClellan and myself differed, as well as really to connect our work with the Sound itself." A couple of days later McClellan reached Olympia, and Stevens sent him back also, ordering him to go through the Snoqualmie Pass from the western side. Again, McClellan failed. The future commander of the Union armies started up the pass, ran into snow, and turned around when an Indian told him that the higher country was so deep in snow that "it was positively impracticable to use snowshoes." His report further angered Stevens, who from that time on had small regard for McClellan's abilities or courage.

In the end Tinkham succeeded in crossing the Cascades and gave Stevens the information he required to prove his northern route practicable. Tinkham's trip was a remarkable one. After leaving Stevens at Hellgate, he had gone eastward across the Montana Rockies by the Marias Pass, reached Fort Benton, recrossed the Divide to the Bitterroot Valley, and then gone up that valley to the start of the southern Nez Perce trail. That rugged and difficult route across the Bitterroot wilderness was the same one over which the Nez Perces had conveyed Samuel Parker to their homeland in 1835. The difference was that it was now winter, and Tinkham and his small party, striking snow almost as soon as they entered the mountains, had to abandon their horses and take to snowshoes. It was a laborious and perilous trip over high, precipitous ranges; but on December 17, after more than fifteen days of carrying their packs on their backs across the snow-covered ridges, the travelers reached some Nez Perce villages near the South Fork of the Clearwater River. There, they reported, the Indians' "horses and cattle, with some young calves, were grazing in the valley, where the grass was bright and green; and young pea-vines were several inches high, the whole valley being strongly contrasted with the mountains . . ." Tinkham stayed with the Nez Perces for nearly a week and then went on to Fort Walla Walla, where he received Stevens' orders to cross the Snoqualmie Pass. He did so by ascending the Yakima River, and although it was now mid-January he found the snow only six or seven feet deep at the summit. Descending to Puget Sound, he reported to Olympia, giving Stevens a favorable report on the Snoqualmie Pass as a railroad route and allowing the governor the satisfaction of watching McClellan redden with embarrassment.

Stevens had confirmed the practicability of a northern railroad, but the explorations of the members of his party had, in addition, provided the expedition with considerable information about the geography of the Sahaptin and Salish lands and the best and fastest routes of travel through them. Most of this great interior country had already been well known to the British traders; but at Olympia, Stevens and his men prepared detailed and accurate maps and compiled minute traveling memoranda that revealed the secrets of the region for the first time to the American settlers who had bypassed the area on their way to the coast. This information was to be useful during the next few years.

Stevens turned his attention now to the country west of the Cascades, where the Indian threat, being closer to the settlements, was even more urgent than on the other side of the mountains. He visited the tribes of Puget Sound and western Washington, promising them protection, trying wherever possible to calm their fears, but urging them, at the same time, to "follow the white man's road" to civilized ways. He appointed Indian agents for them, simultaneously naming A. J. Bolon as agent for all the Indians on the eastern side of the Cascades. When the first territorial legislature met in Olympia in February 1854, Stevens addressed it, calling attention to the need of a memorial to Congress asking for a law to help extinguish the Indians' land title. He also asked for the creation of a militia to be ready for emergencies, but the legislators saw no need yet for such a force and rejected that request. The same session divided the territory into sixteen counties, creating a huge Walla Walla county for all of the country from a line opposite the mouth of the Deschutes River to the Rocky Mountains, and from the Columbia River to the British border. Embracing approximately all of present-day eastern Washington, northern Idaho, and western Montana, it provided a form for the civil government of most of the lands of the Nez Perces and other Sahaptins north of the Columbia, the countries of the Spokans, Flatheads, and numerous other Salish tribes, and the hunting grounds of many of the western plains Indians. The Waiilatpu home of Lloyd Brooks was designated as the headquarters of the county government, and Brooks was named probate judge, county treasurer, and county auditor. John Owen, far off in the Bitterroot Valley, Brooks' partner, Bomford, and A. Dominique Pambrun, who lived at Fort Walla Walla, were appointed county commissioners. It was a paper government, based on information about the region and its inhabitants that Stevens personally supplied the legislature, and Pambrun did not even learn of his appointment until someone told him about it several years later.

Meanwhile, Stevens had received a blow from the national capital. The selection of a route for a railroad to the Pacific, already enmeshed in the growing sectional quarrel between northern and southern congressmen, was running afoul of Jefferson Davis, the Secretary of War, who meant to see that the route chosen would favor the South and would run through the new, potentially pro-slave territories of the Southwest, reaching the Pacific at San Diego. Whether or not he was motivated, in this case, by his antagonism to a northern route, Davis wrote Stevens a sharp note, pointing out to him that he had exceeded his appropriations without authorization and that the payment of his overdrafts was being protested. He expressed disapproval of any further activity and curtly ordered him to call in his wintering parties and end his survey.

Stevens was stung, but his personal friendship with President Pierce, who had appointed him, gave him a sense of security. He had a number of reasons for wanting to return to Washington, including the securing of permission from the Secretary of Interior to hold the Blackfoot treaty council at Fort Benton, and the pressing of the right to make treaties with Washington Indians which Congress would ratify; and he quickly got the territorial legislature to justify his departure for the national capital by passing a resolution that "no disadvantage would result to the Territory should the governor visit Washington, if, in his judgment, the interests of the Northern Pacific Railroad survey could thereby be promoted." On March 26, after sending messages to Doty at Fort Benton and Mullan in the Bitterroot Valley to quit the interior and come to Olympia with their parties, Stevens left for San Francisco and the East.

His personal appeal on behalf of the northern railroad failed. Davis agreed to cover the financial deficiency, but he persisted in his demand that Stevens end his survey. When he presented the railroad reports to Congress, he deprecated the northern route, emphasizing Stevens' difficulties in finding a suitable pass across the Cascades. By that time, however, it was irrelevant. The southern congressmen would not have supported a northern line, even if there had been no mountains in its way. Agreement on any route was impossible until after the Civil War, when, in the absence of southern opposition, Congress finally chose the central route to San Francisco. The situation at the moment, however, was not that clear-cut as far as Stevens was concerned, and he continued in the belief that Davis would not succeed in blocking the northern line and that the safety of the northwestern country had to be secured. In that matter he had better success. He secured permission and a $10,-000 allotment for a treaty council at Fort Benton, and won what he thought was sufficient acceptance for his views regarding the kind of treaties that had to be made in Washington Territory. Essentially, they were pacts similar to those that Congress had earlier refused to ratify, calling for the purchase of some of the Indians' lands but reserving the remainder as permanently guaranteed homes for the Indians. Stevens was actually courting trouble. It is possible that he won support from the President, the Secretary of Interior, and appropriate committee heads in the Senate. But the votes of many other men were necessary also, and by the time the treaties were made, there might well have been a new administration and many new faces in Washington, in and out of Congress.

At any rate Stevens, joined by his wife and four children, sailed from New York and was back in Olympia on December 1, 1854. Mullan and Doty had already arrived from the interior, and their reports made up the final portions of the northern railroad survey. Both men had spent an active year, exploring large sections of the Rockies. Mullan, particularly, had covered a huge expanse of territory, although most of it was already thoroughly familiar to the trappers and traders. From the Bitterroot Valley, where he had built his own camp, called Cantonment Stevens, about ten miles above Owen's fort, he had ranged between Fort Hall on Idaho's Snake River to the British border above Flathead Lake, following all the Hudson's Bay Company routes through such regions as Alexander Ross's Hole and the Big Hole, Beaverhead, and Deer Lodge valleys. He had spent much of his time with Salish Indians and Nez Perces, whose hunting bands missed the old Hudson's Bay brigades and the American fur trapping parties, and appreciated traveling along with Mullan's men. The presence of the explorers gave them some measure of security from the Blackfeet, but it was the fun of companionship and the opportunity to trade with whites that mattered the most. It was like old times.

When Mullan finally left them for Olympia, he took the Lolo Trail across to the Nez Perces' country, following the high ridge route, but being the first person of record to note that although the region seemed to be a mass of wooded mountains, "yet there is some probability that a large level valley might exist, and be quite hidden" from where he was. There was such a gap —although not a large, level valley—through which the Lochsa River flowed, and in 1962, one hundred and eight years after Mullan made the crossing, engineers completed a highway through it, finally linking the Bitterroot and Clearwater valleys. Mullan went on across the Nez Perces' country to the Snake River and Alpowa Creek, and reached Fort Walla Walla on October 9, where he found James Doty, who had come from Fort Benton via Hellgate and the Coeur d'Alene country.

Both men had done their jobs well, and Stevens welcomed the new geographical information they brought him. But they could also tell the governor much about the Indians. "The report of the council at Fort Benton has spread throughout the whole Indian country as on the wings of lightning, and has been received as a harbinger of glad tidings to all," Mullan had written him earlier in the year.[22] Now, they confirmed the excitement. The Blackfeet were ready for the treaty, and so were the Flatheads and their allies on the plains.

But that was on the plains. Nearer home, the Indians' situation had not improved during the governor's absence. There were rumors in the settlements of secret Indian councils, and of plots and conspiracies. White pressure on the tribes around Puget Sound and in southwestern Washington was greater than ever. And across the mountains the white man's traffic through the Yakimas' country was increasing. Another group of emigrants from the East had taken the road in September from Walla Walla to Naches Pass. Others were going regularly to look over the Yakimas' land or to steal across it to the Colville country, where there were whispers of gold. Stevens had a responsibility to protect the Indians. That, to his mind, did not mean policing their countries to keep the whites away—obviously impossible, he assumed, even if he had wanted to do so—but extinguishing their rights to their lands and getting them out of the paths of the whites. If he were to avoid war, the time to act was now.

In six weeks, during January and February, he swept through the Puget Sound region, gathering the tribes, presenting them with hurriedly prepared treaties, and getting the headmen to sign. His pace was breathless, and although he had the terms read to the Indians, he gave them little time to understand or consider their meanings. When they balked at signing, Stevens cajoled them and made lavish, high-sounding promises to them. When they still objected, he became impatient and threatening. He played on the fears of the most timorous of the headmen, and after frightening them into signing, he dragooned the others by making them feel that the majority of their people

22. *Pacific Railroad Reports,* Vol. 12, Part I, p. 182.

would no longer look to them for leadership. In at least one instance he was accused later of having forged the "X" mark of a chief who had refused to sign.[23]

By four separate treaties, embracing all the individual bands and tribes in the region, he permanently extinguished the Indian title to almost the entire Puget Sound Basin in Washington Territory. The agreements, secured in large measure by coercion and fraud, defined a number of small reservations and imposed various terms on the Indians. In return for annuities and, in some cases, permission to continue to fish, hunt, and gather roots and berries on lands off the reservations which white men had not yet claimed, he wrung from the bands their promise to move to their new homes and stay there, to cease violence against whites, and to submit all their grievances to the government "for settlement." To make it possible to confine the Indians on an even fewer number of reservations in the future, or to remove them entirely from the region, the treaties also gave the government the right to move the Indians to other reservations at any time "when the interests of the Territory require it."

In southwestern Washington the tribes rebuffed Stevens and for the time being refused to sign the treaties. But Stevens humiliated some of their leaders and caused divisions within their bands, and a year later they too agreed to his terms. None of the treaties were supposed to go into effect until the President and the Senate had ratified them; but Stevens' announcement of their signing was a signal to the settlers that the Indians' lands were now opened, and they rushed in. By the treaties' terms the Indians, who had not yet moved, had no right to defend themselves, and their appeals to the government brought them little help. The era of the American politician had arrived in the Northwest, and the politician, just and humane as he might wish to be, was the instrument of the source of his position and power. The Puget Sound tribes, harassed, goaded, and left no choice but to fight back, were the first to learn the hard truths of a treaty with Stevens.

The Governor saw it the other way. For the moment he viewed the treaties as models of justice and sent them to Washington with the self-righteous feeling that he had protected the Indians and saved the peace. Then he turned to the tribes east of the Cascades. The rumors of gold in the Colville country, northeast of the Yakimas, had become insistent. There was little time to lose to protect the Indians of the interior. In March he sent two Indian agents, A. J. Bolon and R. H. Lansdale, accompanied by James Doty, now his secretary, up the Columbia to visit the different tribes and make arrangements with them for a single great treaty-making council. Unknown to

23. See Ezra Meeker, *Pioneer Reminiscences of Puget Sound* (Seattle, 1905), pp. 236, 242, 250–51, 255, 268, 342.

him, those Indians had been expecting just such a visit for more than a year.

The headmen of the interior tribes had been nervous ever since the arrival of McClellan on the Yakimas' land in 1853, when Owhi had learned that the new governor intended to force the Indians from their homes. Neither Stevens nor any of his men who had since traveled through the Sahaptin and Salish countries are known to have discussed the subject during their meetings with the Indians; but their words and conduct had done nothing to allay the Indians' fears. The man most suspicious of the troops' intentions was Kamiakin, who had been following closely the reports of the Indians' travail at Puget Sound and in western Oregon. Messengers from the villages on the Sound had come to him periodically, and he himself had made frequent trips to The Dalles, where he had heard of the white man's pressure on the Indians of Oregon.

A.J. Splawn, a prominent pioneer of Washington who spent some fifty years among the Yakimas collecting their versions of what happened in the 1850s and then publishing them in *Ka-mi-akin*, a history of the tribe and its country, stated that in the summer of 1854 Kamiakin, Peopeo Moxmox of the Wallawallas, and the Nez Perce war leader, Apash Wyakaikt, whom the Americans were now calling Looking Glass, joined forces to call a large intertribal council in the Grande Ronde Valley. According to Splawn, headmen from many tribes and bands of the middle and upper Columbia Basin gathered for five days, listening to Kamiakin's accounts of what was happening to the Indians west of the Cascades and debating how to avoid a similar fate for their own peoples. Kamiakin, Splawn said, urged that the bands unite in a confederacy and fight the whites together. Everyone agreed to this except Spokan Garry, Stickus of the Cayuses, and Lawyer, who felt that the Indians were not strong enough to wage a successful war against the soldiers and argued that the bands ought to meet Stevens in a council and hear what he had to say. In the end the headmen were said to have arranged a compromise, deciding to meet the Governor if he came for a treaty council but resolving to stand together in refusing to give up any of their lands. Each chief would rise at the council, define the boundaries of his country, and ask for all of it as a reservation for his people. In that way no land would be sold.[24] There is no way of knowing for sure today whether that intertribal council actually occurred or, if it did, whether it was in 1854, as Splawn said, or in 1855. Splawn stated that it was motivated by a meeting between Stevens and Owhi early in the summer of 1854, during which Stevens told the Indian point-blank that he intended to meet with the Indians the next year and purchase their lands, and that if the Indians refused to sell, soldiers would be sent to their countries to wipe them off the face of the earth. But Stevens was in Washington during

24. Splawn, *Ka-mi-akin*, pp. 24–26.

the summer of 1854, and his own records give no evidence that he ever had such a meeting with Owhi. Moreover, it seems improbable that Stevens would have talked that way to the Indian leader if he had hoped for a successful council. It is possible, though, that some irresponsible member of one of Stevens' parties had actually made such a threat to Owhi, who had then communicated it to Kamiakin. On the other hand, there is evidence that the tribes did hold a great council in the Grande Ronde Valley in 1855, after Stevens had signed his treaties with them. Kamiakin's brother, Skloom, as well as Lawyer, were reported to have told A. J. Bolon, the Indian agent, about it, and Splawn's Indian informants, long after that period, may have confused him about the date and purpose of the meeting.[25]

Whether or not such a council occurred, it is certain that Kamiakin did work busily throughout 1854 and early in 1855, keeping the headmen of the interior bands informed about what was happening on the western side of the Cascades. He sent emissaries on constant rounds through the interior country, and traveled to many of the bands himself, stirring the Indians with eloquent oratory that aroused their determination to defend the lands of their fathers. Some of the headmen who had been meeting members of Stevens' survey parties did not share the intensity of Kamiakin's alarm; but he won the young warriors and buffalo hunters to his side, and the various leaders were forced to listen to him. At the same time, a strong, organized opposition to his war talk developed among chiefs upon whom Christianity had had its greatest effect. Lawyer, Timothy, Stickus, and even the more reticent Spokan Garry were deadset against risking trouble with the Americans. For the moment their position was a delicate one. They could counsel patience and urge their peoples to listen to what Stevens might say; but they could not suggest what to do if the Americans demanded that they sell their lands. It made them uneasy, for they sensed that at some point they might either have to support Kamiakin in a war or face the scorn and fury of their bands. But until a crisis arose, they managed to hold the loyalty of their followers, winning support with attacks on the hotheads and, in the process, widening gulfs that already existed among the Indians.

In the fall of 1854 there was trouble in the Snake country in the south, and word of it swept along the middle Columbia. Shoshoni Indians, retaliating for ill treatment by emigrants on the Overland Trail, had begun to kill whites. They had almost wiped out one party near Fort Boise, and American soldiers from Fort Dalles under Major Granville O. Haller were ordered to the Snake country to punish them. On his way to the south Haller met Lawyer, who offered to send some Nez Perces with the Americans. Two of Lawyer's followers, Jason, a chief from Asotin, and an Indian called Captain John, who

25. Bancroft, *History of Washington*, p. 109 n.

was headman of a small village on the eastern side of the Snake River south of present-day Lewiston, joined the American troops with some of their people and made the foray into the Shoshonis' country. Lawyer later said that the Nez Perces "killed some of the Snakes, and delivered others up at the Dalles," but most of the Shoshonis disappeared in the mountains, and with the approach of winter, the troops abandoned the pursuit and returned to The Dalles, promising to go back the next year and kill the Indians responsible for the murder of the emigrants.[26]

Even as the Sahaptins contemplated this new conflict on their southern border, word from the west heightened the tension. Early in 1855 Klickitats came down the Yakima River with news of the treaties that Stevens was forcing the Puget Sound Indians to accept. Shortly afterward, the moment that all the interior tribes had been dreading arrived. On Sunday, April 1, 1855, James Doty and A. J. Bolon appeared at Father Pandosy's mission on the Ahtanum, met Kamiakin and Te-i-as, and informed them that he had come to arrange for a treaty council between the American officials of Washington and Oregon and all the tribes east of the Cascades.

Finding that Kamiakin was "either silent or sulky and declined meeting the whites or discussing the subject of a treaty," Doty met the next day with Te-i-as, Skloom, and Show-away, who were "very friendly." Kamiakin "sat down in the willows" a quarter of a mile away and paid no attention to the meeting; but on the day after that, when some 200 Yakimas showed up, Doty called a general council, and Kamiakin agreed to participate. One by one, all the headmen, including Kamiakin, assented to meet with Stevens, and Kamiakin suggested that the meeting place be in the Walla Walla Valley, where it had been the custom for the tribes to gather when they wished to have a council. Doty promised to suggest the site to Governor Stevens and notify the bands when to meet; and after the different leaders emphasized that they wanted to be friends of the Americans, he offered them presents of shirts, calico, and tobacco to divide among their people. Kamiakin at once took offense, stating that he "had never accepted from the Americans the value of a grain of wheat without paying for it" and did not wish to buy the goods now being offered to him, since he had heard that that was a trick by which the Americans later claimed that they had bought the Indians' land. His anger gave pause to the other headmen, and Doty closed the council without distributing the presents.

The next day, however, Te-i-as came to see Doty and told him that he had misunderstood what had been said about the presents, and would now like to accept them for himself and Owhi. Then, in a statement that undoubtedly was aimed at Kamiakin, he said, "Te-i-as and Owhi are not the slaves of any

26. Proceedings of the Treaty Council at Lapwai (1863), p. 64. National Archives, Record Group 75.

man. They are independent and act for themselves." [27] The significance of the division within the tribe seemed to elude Doty, for when he left the Yakimas he took with him the understanding that Kamiakin was not only their principal headman but also the chief spokesman for many bands on the vast Columbia plateau. Father Pandosy, who attended the meetings, may have given him that impression by telling him of Kamiakin's family relationships to other tribes and of his hold on the young warriors of many bands beside his own. But Kamiakin could not have been their spokesman; the bands were still autonomous and had their own headmen.

Doty went on to the Nez Perces, the Wallawallas, and the Cayuses, persuading their leaders to attend the council, and set the meeting place at Mill Creek, some six miles above Waiilatpu in the Walla Walla Valley. The gathering was called for the latter part of May, and in the middle of that month Stevens sent a number of keelboats up the Columbia with presents for the tribes, and followed with a large entourage. At The Dalles he met Joel Palmer, now Superintendent of Indian Affairs in Oregon, who would have jurisdiction at the council over the tribes living in his territory. The two men discussed the possibility of trouble with the Indians, a fear that lay heavily on Palmer's mind, and Stevens induced Major Rains to send a detachment of forty-seven soldiers to the council as a guard. "There were unquestionably a great many malcontents in each tribe," Stevens noted in his diary. "A few determined spirits, if not controlled, might embolden all not well disposed, and defeat the negotiations. Should this spirit be shown, they must be seized; the well affected would then govern in the deliberations, and I anticipated little or no difficulty in negotiating." [28]

Much has been written about the ensuing council, both in defense and in condemnation of Stevens. But there is no doubt of the attitude with which the Governor approached the meeting. Strong and proud peoples, intent on preserving their right to continue to dwell in the lands of their fathers, were coming to talk to him as equals. Yet those who opposed his plans to oust them would be regarded as "malcontents," whatever that meant, and would be seized. The rest, he was sure, would accept his orders meekly.

On May 21 Stevens, Palmer, and their parties reached the council grounds, where an advance group had erected tents, a log storehouse for the Indian presents, and two arbors of poles and boughs, one to serve as a council chamber, the other "as a banqueting-hall for distinguished chiefs, so that, as in civilized lands, gastronomy might aid diplomacy." [29] On May 24 a great part of the Nez Perce nation, some 2,500 Indians of the different bands and

27. Brown, *The Indian Side of the Story*, pp. 86–90.
28. H. Stevens, *Stevens*, 2, 29.
29. Ibid., p. 31.

villages from the Wallowa Valley to the upper waters of the Clearwater, arrived. When about a mile distant from the council grounds, they halted, and the leading men, including Lawyer, Joseph, old James, Utsinmalikin, Metat Waptass, Red Wolf, and several others, rode forward with William Craig to be introduced formally to Stevens and Palmer. Then, as the chiefs dismounted and joined the commissioners' party in a reviewing group at the council's flagpole, the rest of the Nez Perces started toward them and circled about the pole. They made a dramatic sight, "a thousand warriors mounted on fine horses and riding at a gallop, two abreast, naked to the breech-clout, their faces covered with white, red, and yellow paint in fanciful designs, and decked with plumes and feathers and trinkets fluttering in the sunshine." They put on a series of equestrian displays for the commissioners, "charging at full gallop . . . firing their guns, brandishing their shields, beating their drums, and yelling their war-whoops," and then, after a war dance, filed off to a location a half mile away that had been selected for their camp. Stevens was pleased by the grand show, but he missed part of its significance. It was the Indians' way not only of according him a salute but of demonstrating that they were strong and unafraid, and expected to be treated as a powerful people.

Still, some of the most important Nez Perces—because of their prowess and leadership in war—were not there. Looking Glass and many of the tribe's ablest warriors and hunters were in the buffalo country. Stevens must have been delighted to receive that information. In the absence of Looking Glass, there was less chance of his encountering difficulty with the more tractable head chief, Lawyer, who in his opinion was "wise, enlightened, and magnanimous . . . head and shoulders above the other chiefs, whether in intellect, nobility of soul, or influence." [30]

To the members of the council who were meeting the Nez Perces for the first time, Lawyer and his people were remarkable Indians. "There is an odd mixture of this world and the next in some of the Nez Perces,—an equal love for fighting and [religious] devotion, the wildest Indian traits with a strictness in some religious rites which might shame those 'who profess and call themselves Christians,'" wrote Lieutenant Lawrence Kip, a member of Stevens' military escort. "They have prayers in their lodges every morning and evening—service several times on Sunday—and nothing will induce them on that day to engage in any trading." Later, after the council began, Kip was impressed when he learned that "two or three of the half-civilized Nez Perces, who could write, were keeping a minute account of all that transpired at these meetings." Nevertheless, there was still a gap between those friendly Indians and the whites. When Lieutenant Archibald Gracie, who com-

30. Ibid., p. 36.

manded the military escort, strove to "test" Lawyer by asking him if he would welcome having Gracie make a brief visit to the Nez Perces' country, the head chief evaded the question and then answered only, "Perhaps so." It was a measure of the narrow line Lawyer was trying to walk between accommodating the whites and retaining his hold over his people, but Lieutenant Gracie did not recognize it.[31]

When the Cayuses, Wallawallas, and Umatillas arrived, they were less friendly than the Nez Perces and "went into camp without any parade or salutations." With them was Peopeo Moxmox, who reflected the deep distrust of those tribes by sending word to Stevens that they had brought their own provisions with them, and did not want any from the whites. Even the Wallawalla leader's messenger refused to accept any tobacco for his chief, "a very unfriendly sign," and rode off muttering, "You will find out by and by why we won't take provisions." Soon afterward, Tauitau, known to Stevens as the Young Chief, and several of the Cayuse headmen rode into Stevens' camp and, refusing to smoke, "shook hands in a very cold manner." Nevertheless, Stevens wrote in his diary, "The haughty carriage of these chiefs and their manly character have, for the first time in my Indian experience, realized the descriptions of the writers of fiction."

Fathers Chirouse of the Walla Walla Valley and Pandosy of the Yakima mission also appeared, reporting to Stevens that all the Indians they knew, except Kamiakin, were well disposed toward the whites. Some Indians had told them, "Kamiakin will come with his young men with powder and ball." Stevens added Kamiakin to his list of potential "malcontents" that now included Peopeo Moxmox and the Young Chief; but when the Yakima leader arrived with Owhi, Skloom, and a number of warriors, he shook hands in a friendly manner and sat down for a smoke, although he refused tobacco from the commissioners.

The day before the council opened, Peopeo Moxmox, having insisted that he, the Young Chief, Lawyer, and Kamiakin do all the talking for the Indians, asked Stevens for more than one interpreter, "that they might know they translated truly." When Stevens agreed to the request, the old chief looked around the area at young Nez Perces who loitered about and said with scorn, "I do not wish my boys running around the camp of the whites like these young men."

The distinction between distrust and hostility was a thin one, but Stevens, the optimist, was still sure that he could win over men like Peopeo Moxmox without using force. Palmer and some of the others were not so sure. And if it came to force, forty-seven troopers were slim security against several thou-

31. Lawrence Kip, "The Indian Council at Walla Walla," in *Sources of the History of Oregon*, Vol. 1, Part II (Eugene, Ore., 1897), pp. 12, 13, 16.

sand Indians. There was always Lawyer, however, and through him Stevens continued to count on the Nez Perces. He cultivated the Nez Perce chiefs and at a banquet for thirty of them piled their tin plates to the brim "again and again." A mess was maintained for them throughout the council, "and every day was well attended."

Before the council started, a number of other Indians arrived, including members of several bands that lived along the Columbia, a headman of the Palouses who reported that his people "were indifferent to the matter," and Spokan Garry, who came as an observer. Altogether, some 5,000 Indians were in attendance. On the morning the council was to begin, the commissioners visited Lawyer, who was in great pain from the old wound he had received at the Battle of Pierre's Hole more than twenty years before. While they were with Lawyer, Utsinmalikin appeared and told the commissioners that Peopeo Moxmox, Kamiakin, and the Cayuses had asked him and two other Nez Perce chiefs to come to their camp for a council. He claimed he had rebuffed them angrily. "Why do you come here and ask three chiefs to come to a council, while to the head chief [Lawyer] and the rest you say nothing?" he reported he had said. The news confirmed to the commissioners that the "malcontents" were already at work, plotting some conspiracy; but it seemed evident also that the friendly Lawyer was still in firm control of the Nez Perces, and there were as many of them as all the other Indians together.

The council began on the afternoon of May 29. The minutes of the proceedings are astounding to read. The transparency of the speeches of Governor Stevens and Superintendent Palmer is so obvious that it is a wonder the commissioners could not realize the ease with which the Indians saw through what they were saying. One can only assume either that their ignorance of the Indians' mentality was appalling or that they were so intent on having their way with the tribes that they blinded themselves to the flagrancy of their hypocrisy. It was so clear to the Indians, however, that it soon placed Lawyer and the friendly Nez Perce headmen in an awkward position, undermining their ability to cope with the Indians who were opposed to selling their lands, and finally even embarrassed Palmer, who, more attuned to Indian reactions than Stevens, suddenly realized the harm that was being done.

The council met in front of an arbor erected near Stevens' tent. Stevens and Palmer sat on a bench, and the Indians gathered around them on the ground in a large circle. The chiefs sat in the front row, with some 1,000 of their people ranged behind them. As the white men spoke, Craig and the other interpreters translated each sentence to Indian criers, who announced it in loud voices to the assemblage. After the interpreters were sworn in on the first day, it began to rain, and the council was adjourned. The next day Stevens opened the proceedings with a speech, praising the individual tribes for their friendship to whites and for their accomplishments so far in adopting the ways of life of the white man.[32] "I went back to the Great Father last year to say that you had been good, you have been kind, *he must do something for you*," he told the Indians. Getting to what that "something" was took him through a long, circuitous, and tortuous explanation. There were bad white men, he said, who made trouble for Indians. But east of the mountains, the Great Father had taken measures to protect his Indian children from the bad white men. He had guided "the red man across a great river into a fine country," where he could take care of them, away from the trouble-making white men. He even named the Great Father, Andrew Jackson, but he was on thin ground. Although he omitted references to the coercion, misery, starvation, and deaths of the "trail of tears" that marked the enforced removal of Indians from their homelands east of the Mississippi, some of the Northwestern Indians were not as uninformed as he thought they were. Delawares, Iroquois, and plains Indians had been telling them for fifteen years of what had happened to the eastern Indians. As they sat and listened to Stevens, the governor was already beginning to lose ground.

But he went on. The Great Father had done wonderful things for the Indians whom he had moved to new homes. In fact, they were so happy that Stevens wanted to do the same thing for the western tribes. "This brings us now to the question. What shall we do at this council? We want you and ourselves to agree upon tracts of lands where you shall live; in those tracts of land we want each man who will work to have his own land, his own horses, his own cattle, and his home for himself and his children." Among the Indians who were absorbing this, he was now in trouble. He may have recognized that he was moving too fast, for he checked himself, and switched quickly to a long list of things he wanted to give the Indians: schools, blacksmiths, carpenters, farmers, plows, wagons, saw mills, grist mills, and instructors who would teach them to spin, weave, make clothes, and become mechanics, farmers, doctors, and lawyers. Then suddenly it was out: "Now we want you to agree with us to such a state of things: You to have your tract with all these things; the rest to be the Great Father's for his white children." There must have been an awful pause, for he immediately reverted to a repetition of all the things the Great Father would give the Indians. "Besides all these things, these shops, these mills and these schools which I have mentioned, we must pay you for the land which you give to the Great Father," he summed up, finally saying, "I am tired of speaking; you are tired of listening. I will speak tomorrow."

32. Quotations from the council's minutes are from the L. V. McWhorter Manuscript Collection, Washington State University Library, 201, No. 48, and are used with the kind permission of the University Library at Pullman, Washington.

Palmer must already have sensed that the Indians were not reacting well. He took over for a moment with an explanation: "It is not expected that we can come together with one day's talk; nor do we expect you can understand with what has been said all that we want . . . Sometimes when people have a matter to settle, they commence way off; but as they understand each other they come together. With us, if we commenced way off, I hope we are a little nearer now, and by and by I hope we shall come quite together." The minutes show that the Indians made no reply, and the council was adjourned until the next day.

On May 31 Stevens made another speech, repeating several times the many things the Great Father wished to give the Indians. "We want you to have schools and mills and shops and farms . . . there will be blankets and cloth for leggings . . . we want in your houses plates and cups and brass and tin kettles, frying pans to cook your meat and bake ovens to bake your bread . . . you will have your own smiths, your own wheelwrights, your own carpenters, your own physicians and lawyers and other learned men . . ." He went on, appearing as if he had a compulsion to keep talking about gifts but obviously doing everything possible to postpone coming to the main point— acquisition of the Indians' lands. None of what he was saying could have been helpful to him. Save perhaps for Lawyer and a few other headmen, the Indians had not the slightest interest in abandoning their own ways and adopting the white man's culture. Few of them could have understood the desirability of acquiring all that Stevens was offering them, but they could see clearly that he was bargaining with promises of gifts if they sold him what they did not wish to sell.

Eventually, Stevens changed his tack and told them about his plan to end the Blackfoot menace to their buffalo-hunting parties. The Blackfeet would be friends of the western tribes, but Stevens would want the western tribes to be models for the Blackfeet and teach the Blackfeet how to settle down on prosperous farms like white men. This the western tribes could do to help Stevens.

He then called on Palmer, who spoke as if he did not know what to say. Launching into a discussion of "the course pursued by the government towards the Indians on the other side of the mountains," he gave a long, rambling, and distorted version of the history of Indian-white relations in the East, commencing with Columbus. It was a hodge-podge of colonial and mid-western episodes, showing, if anything, Palmer's ignorance of what he was talking about. However, it led abruptly to a relevant point, which Palmer recognized was worth emphasizing for several moments: There had always been bad white men from whom the Indians had needed protection, and there were bad men now scheming "to get your horses," and do other evil things to the Indians. "It is these men I am told who would rob you of your property," he said, suddenly adding a new idea, "who are giving you advice not to treat with us. Whose councils do you prefer to take? These men who would rob you, or ours who come to befriend you?" These men, he concluded, even married Indian women in order to steal the Indians' horses. "All such men need watching . . . who are your friends, such men, or myself and my brother [Stevens] who have come here to act for your good?" On that note, the council adjourned till the next day.

But the council did not meet the next day, "as the Indians," said Lieutenant Kip, "wished time to consider the proposals." It is obvious that in the private meetings among the headmen the purpose of the white commissioners was clear to all, and Kamiakin and Peopeo Moxmox must have found it easy to muster support for their policy of opposition to the sale of the Indians' lands. The talk of history, presents, and other matters that had clothed the commissioners' central point, their hope that the Indians would give up some of their country, must, in fact, have angered men like Kamiakin who would have characterized it as the glibness of crooked tongues. With the Nez Perces at the council was a Delaware Indian, Jim Simonds, who had lived and traveled with the Sahaptins since 1849 or 1850. Well known both to the whites and Indians as Delaware Jim, he would have been able to give the Northwestern Indians a different version of Stevens' account of Andrew Jackson's removal of the eastern Indians, and the council proceedings later indicated that he did just that.[33]

At any rate, when the council convened again on June 2, Palmer knew that the Indians' opposition was hardening, and he made a more forthright appeal to them, stating that "like grasshoppers on the plains," the white settlers were coming to this country, and no one would be able to stop them. It simply could not be done, any more than one could "stop the waters of the Columbia River from flowing." But the land, like the air, the water, the fish, and the game, was "made for the white man and the red man," and that was why the commissioners wished to have the Indians choose the lands they wanted to keep for themselves before the settlers arrived. "We did not come here to scare you or to drive you away, but we came here to talk to you like men . . . if we enter into a treaty now we can select a good country for

33. Weisel, *Men and Trade*, pp. 117–18, says that Simonds probably came west with Frémont, and later spent much time in the Flathead country. John Owen's accounts show that he traded in the Bitterroot Valley but that he was often with the Flatheads and Nez Perces. He came to the council with the latter tribe but later became a guide for Stevens.

you; but if we wait till the country is filled up with whites, where will we find such a place? . . . If we make a treaty with you . . . you can rely on all its provisions being carried out strictly." [34]

When Palmer was done, Stevens announced that the time had come for the Indians to be heard. There was a pause. "We are tired," said Five Crows. Palmer assured him that the whites had nothing more to say, and Five Crows then spoke briefly. He was the Cayuse half-brother of Joseph, who had taken one of the female prisoners to live with him on the Umatilla after the massacre at Waiilatpu, and had been wounded in battle with the volunteers during the Cayuse war. Spalding had converted him and given him the name Hezekiah, but the events of the months after the massacre had destroyed his faith in the white man's religion. The Father in Heaven had made the earth, and had made man of earth, but he had given man no gardens to plow, he pointed out to the commissioners in a reply to Stevens' talk about turning the Indians into farmers.

He was followed by Peopeo Moxmox, who was full of anger. "We have listened to all you have to say, and we desire you to listen when any Indian speaks . . . I know the value of your speech from having experienced the same in California." The memory of his son's death, still unpunished, flooded through his mind, but it would have meant nothing to Stevens or Palmer. "We have not seen in a true light the object of your speeches . . . you have spoken in a round about way. Speak straight. I have ears to hear you, and here is my heart . . . You have spoken in a manner partly tending to evil. Speak plain to us . . ."

The session ended tensely. The old Wallawalla had been blunt. Moreover, he had embarrassed Lawyer by stating that he knew that Craig was putting pressure on the Nez Perces for an immediate answer, without giving them time to think. "The whole has been prearranged," he had said.

What happened among the Indians that evening will probably never be clear. Long after the entire council was over, Stevens claimed that Lawyer had come to his tent alone after midnight that night and had told him that he had just learned that during the day the Cayuses had formed a plot to massacre all the whites at the council, and that the Yakimas and Wallawallas were now about to join them. The conspirators did not trust the Nez Perces, he had said, and he had announced to Stevens, "I will come with my family and pitch my lodge in the midst of your camp, that those Cayuses may see that you and your party are under the protection of the head chief of the Nez

34. Indians have never forgotten this false statement, typical of those which have been responsible for characterizing so many government officials in their eyes—even to this day—as men with "forked tongues." My narrative will show how hollow this particular promise was.

Perces." Lawyer did move into Stevens' camp, but his story, if indeed that is what he told Stevens, is questionable. Stevens made no mention of it in the contemporary records of the council, and the Indians have always laughed at his later report of the plot. They have insisted that there was no such plan, that Lawyer would not have been so stupid as to move his family to the site of an intended attack, and that more likely the truth of what had happened was that after Peopeo Moxmox's speech many of the Nez Perces had turned against Lawyer, and he had left his people for his own safety.

There is no doubt that Lawyer was in a difficult position, and that he was frightened. On Monday, June 4, when the council reconvened, Stevens called on him to talk. The head chief orated in a confused manner, trying not to offend Stevens, but at the same time attempting not to arouse the ire of the Indians who were listening to him. After posing somewhat as an intermediary, and telling Stevens that the Indians were poor and did not want to lose their lands, he pleaded, "There are a good many men here who wish to speak. Let them speak."

But no one had much to say. Kamiakin stated that he was afraid of the white man; Utsinmalikin said he agreed with Lawyer; Stickus the Cayuse asked Stevens to speak plainly; and Peopeo Moxmox demanded that the commissioners mention the specific lands they were talking about. "You have spoken for lands generally. You have not spoken of any particular ones." Then Tipyahlanah Ka-ou-pu, the Eagle of the Morning Light, or of the Dawn (known to whites variously as Eagle of the Light, Eagle From the Light, and Eagle of Delight), rose to review the history of Nez Perce relations with the white men, telling the commissioners of his "brother," whom the Astorians had hanged many years before "for no offense" at the mouth of the Palouse River. "This I say to my brother here that he may think of it," he said bitterly. He also told them of The Hat, "my Father," whom Spalding had sent to the States with William H. Gray. "His body was never returned . . . that is another thing to think of." [35] And during the Cayuse war the Nez Perces had remained friendly to the whites, but his chief, Ellis, had gone to the East to look for counsel, "and there his body lies beyond here. He has never returned." He condemned Spalding, who, he claimed, had come to teach the Indians but had stayed to become a trader. "He made a farm and raised grain and bought our stock . . . and I do not wish another preacher to come."

When Eagle From the Light sat down, no other Indian wished to speak,

35. It is possible that the Eagle From the Light was here referring to Ka-ou-pu, Man of the Morning Light, whose name he bore and who had been one of the members of the delegation that went to St. Louis in 1831. Ka-ou-pu, it will be remembered, died in that city.

and Stevens rose hesitantly to answer Peopeo Moxmox's question and make
clear the specifics of the treaty. Feeling his way carefully, he announced that
he had two reservations in mind, one in the Nez Perce country from the Blue
Mountains to the Bitterroots and from the Palouse River to the Grande
Ronde and Salmon rivers, and the other in the Yakima country between the
Yakima and Columbia rivers. On the first reservation he proposed that the
Spokans, Cayuses, Wallawallas, and Umatillas move in with the Nez Perces,
and on the second reservation he hoped to gather all the tribes and bands
along the Columbia River from The Dalles to the Okanogan and Colville valleys far in the north. Both schemes had been carefully worked out and were
already delineated on maps which he showed the Indians. He did not, however, tell them his purposes, which were to select lands for them that no
white man yet wanted, and to clear all the areas which the settlers were already eyeing or entering, or which he would have to secure for the building
of a railroad and highways. Thus he planned to have the Indians vacate regions like the Umatilla, Walla Walla, and Colville valleys, as well as the
Spokan and Palouse countries and the Yakima River valley through which his
projected northern railroad would run.

He spent the next two days explaining the reservations more fully, tracing
their boundaries on his map, and describing the payments the government
would give the tribes for the lands they sold. But he made little headway.
With the exception of Lawyer and a few of the Nez Perce headmen whose
homelands were untouched by Stevens' proposals, the Indians reacted coldly
and with bitterness. "There is evidently a more hostile feeling toward the
whites getting up among some of the tribes," Lieutenant Kip noted on one of
the evenings, adding that when he and Lieutenant Gracie attempted to visit
the Cayuse camp, a group of young warriors stood in their way and mo-
tioned them to leave.

In addition to having to surrender their lands, none of the tribes liked the
prospect of being forced to live together like a single people. Few of the Columbia River bands that were supposed to move in with the Yakimas were
even present at the council, and no one could speak for them. Some of them
were Salish and some Sahaptins, but the Yakimas wanted none of them on
their lands. Similarly, the Cayuses, Wallawallas, and Umatillas had no intention of moving onto Nez Perce lands, and few of the Nez Perces looked forward happily to welcoming them. Spokan Garry, merely a witness at the
council, sat glumly, worrying how to inform his people that they would have
to join the Nez Perces, and Joseph and Chief Plenty Bears from the Wallowa
and Grande Ronde River districts were concerned that the treaty called for
them to sell their parts of the Nez Perce domain.

Nevertheless, Lawyer conferred privately with the commissioners at night and, after ascertaining that he would receive added benefits and payments befitting his position as head chief, he worked on Spotted Eagle, James, Red Wolf, Timothy, and some of the other headmen and won their approval of the treaty. On June 7 he got up in the council meeting and again played the role of politician and diplomat for Stevens, making a long speech about the history of Indians and white men. In the course of it he amused everyone with a recital of the story of Columbus and the egg, which the Spaldings must have taught him, and then inadvertently revealed that Delaware Jim, who was sitting with the Nez Perces, had related to the Indians how the white men had come steadily pushing against the Indians all across the continent, and now "they are here." In closing, he expressed his approval of the treaty, but reminded Stevens that the Indians were poor people, and begged him to "take care of us well."

The spokesmen for the other tribes were smoldering. All of the Cayuses, including Stickus, made known their opposition to abandoning their own country and moving in with the Nez Perces. Tauitau, the Young Chief of the Umatilla Valley, who had already lived through many crises, was angry. What Lawyer could see well, "us Indians" could not see. "The reason . . . is I do not see the offer you have made us yet. If I had the money in my hand then I would see . . . I wonder if this ground has anything to say? I wonder if the ground is listening to what is said? I wonder if the ground would come to life and what is on it? I hear what this earth says. The earth says, God has placed me here. The earth says that God tells me to take care of the Indians on this earth. The earth says to the Indians that stop on the earth, feed them right. God named the roots that he should feed the Indians on. The water speaks the same way: God says, feed the Indians upon the earth. The grass says the same thing: feed the horses and cattle. The earth and water and grass says, God has given our names and we are told those names. Neither the Indians or the whites have a right to change those names. The earth says, God has placed me here to produce all that grows upon me . . . The same way the earth says it was from her man was made. God on placing them on the earth . . . said, you Indians who take care of the earth and do each other no harm. God said, you Indians who take care of a certain portion of the country should not trade it off unless you get a fair price."

There it was, the Indians' sacred belief in their Earth Mother, a deeply held feeling, already twisted somewhat by some of the leaders who were trying to adjust to white culture. But Stevens could not see it. Five Crows supported the Young Chief; and Peopeo Moxmox, now fighting for the valley of his ancestors, the land where his forebear the great Yellepit had welcomed Lewis and Clark and David Thompson, told the commissioners that they were treating him as if he were a child or a feather. He wanted to go slower, to have time to think. "I request another meeting," he asked. "It is not only by one meeting that we can come to a decision."

Kamiakin, also feeling the pressure that the whites, with Lawyer's help, were beginning to place upon him, had nothing to say. But Owhi reminded the commissioners that God had made the earth and given it to the Indians. Could the Indians now steal it and sell it? "God made our bodies from the earth . . . What shall I do? Shall I give the lands that are a part of my body?" When the Yakima had finished, Stevens again asked Kamiakin to talk. It is possible that Kamiakin was thinking of the many unrepresented Columbia River bands that would be moved onto the Yakima reservation if he agreed to the treaty. He had no right to speak in their names. "What have I to be talking about?" he said to Stevens.

Now Palmer was impatient. He told the Indians he could not understand what more information they needed. He and Governor Stevens had informed them of everything the government would give them. "Can we bring these sawmills and these grist mills here on our backs . . . can we cause farms of wheat and corn to spring up in a day . . . ?" How long would the Indians remain blind? "We don't come to steal your lands; we pay you more than it is worth." Gold had been discovered in the Colville region, he told them. Bad men would soon be coming onto their lands. He and Governor Stevens wanted to protect them. Peopeo Moxmox had asked for another council. But there could not be another council. There was no time. "We want to help you . . . we want to open your eyes and give you light . . . we want to make you a good people. Will you receive our talk or will you throw it behind you?"

The tempo was speeding up, and the Indians could sense the hurry. Howlish Wompoon, a Cayuse, glared at Palmer. "I have listened to your speech without any impression . . . The Nez Perces have given you their land. You want us to go there . . . I cannot think of leaving this land. Your words since you came here have been crooked. That is all I have to say."

For a moment, Palmer tried hurriedly to answer the different objections. Then Five Crows spoke again, looking at the Nez Perces in anger. "Listen to me, you chiefs. We have been as one people with the Nez Perces heretofore. This day we are divided." At that point, Stevens took over, maintaining the pressure on the Indians that Palmer had begun. "I must say a few words. My Brother and I have talked straight. Have all of you talked straight? . . . The treaty will have to be drawn up tonight. You can see it tomorrow. The Nez Perces must not be put off any longer. This business must be dispatched . . ." The council then adjourned.

That night Lieutenant Kip wrote that in all the Indian camps save that of the Nez Perces there was violent confusion. "The Cayuse and other tribes were very much incensed against the Nez Perces." But the next day the com-missioners found that the pressure was working. At the council the Young Chief suddenly began to give in. "The reason why we could not understand you," he said to Stevens and Palmer, "was that you selected this country for us to live in without our having any voice in the matter . . . Wait, we may come to an agreement . . ." He pleaded, however, for more time to consider a division of the country between the whites and the Indians. He did not want to abandon his own homeland—"the land where my forefathers are buried should be mine. That is the place that I am speaking for. We shall talk about it," and his words seemed suddenly almost begging, "we shall then know, my brothers, that is what I have to show you, that is what I love—the place we get our roots to live upon—the salmon comes up the stream—. That is all."

He sat down, but Palmer had good news for him. The night before, as a result of the Cayuse, Wallawalla, and Umatilla opposition to going onto the Nez Perce reservation, the commissioners had changed their plans, and Pal-mer now offered them a single reservation of their own, centering on the Umatilla Valley. In a long speech aimed directly at the recalcitrant headmen, he made many new promises of things the government would do for them personally if they accepted this reservation: "We will build a good house for Peopeo Moxmox, and a good house for the chief of the Cayuses . . . we will plow and fence ten acres of land for Peopeo Moxmox; we will plow and fence the same for the chief of the Cayuses . . . we will give him [Peopeo Moxmox] . . . $500 in money, we will give him three yoke of oxen, wagon and two plows . . . we give him a salary, and also the chief of the Cayuses $500 a year in money, this to continue for twenty years—the same as is to be given to the Lawyer . . ." Moreover, "you will not be required to go onto the reservation till our chief the President and his council sees this paper and says it is good, and we build the houses, the mills and the blacksmith shop . . . How long will it take you to decide?"

The new promises had their effect. The Wallawalla, Cayuse, and Umatilla spokesmen were won over, and Peopeo Moxmox promised to go on the reser-vation as soon as his new house was built. Stevens was delighted, and ordered the treaties prepared for signature. Only Kamiakin and the Yakimas still held out. Suddenly, wrote Lieutenant Kip, "a new explosive element dropped into this little political caldron. Just before the Council adjourned, an Indian run-ner arrived with the news that Looking Glass, the war chief of the Nez Perces, was coming." It is probable that both Lawyer and Stevens were thrown into confusion. Stevens recovered quickly. "I am glad Looking Glass . . . is coming," he announced. "He is a friend of Kamiakin . . . he has come away from the Blackfeet . . . let his first glance be upon you sit-ting here. When he is close by two or three of us will go and take him by the hand and set him down by his chief in the presence of his friend Kamiakin. Let us now have Kamiakin's heart."

The Yakima's reply, at last, was one of submission. But it indicated that he had received a dressing down from the chiefs of his wife's people, Te-i-as and Owhi, who had told him that they intended signing the treaty. The significance of what he had to say was apparently not noticed by Stevens and Palmer. Let the Americans settle down by the Yakima Valley wagon route, Kamiakin said. Let them settle about the road so that the Indians may go and see them. "I do not speak this for myself; it is my people's wish. Owhi and Te-i-as and the chiefs. I, Kamiakin, do not wish for goods for myself. The forest knows me. He knows my heart . . . I am tired. I am anxious to get back to my garden."

So Kamiakin capitulated, and after him Joseph, Red Wolf, and Skloom spoke. Joseph appealed to the commissioners to think of the future generations of Nez Perces, and to be certain to include his Wallowa land in the Nez Perce reservation. Red Wolf asked that Craig be allowed to stay with the Nez Perces "because he understands us . . . when there is any news that comes into the country we can go to him and hear it straight." Skloom, Kamiakin's brother, asked merely that the Americans pay what the Yakimas' land was worth. Stevens agreed, and on a note of complete victory announced that the treaties would be signed the next day. Then he adjourned the council.

A few minutes later the Indians hurried off to meet Looking Glass, who came riding onto the council grounds with three elderly buffalo-hunting chiefs and a retinue of about twenty warriors. Their arrival created a commotion. All were in buffalo robes and were painted for war. They had been in fights with the Blackfeet and had got back to the Bitterroot Valley when they had heard of the council. Looking Glass had left most of his band behind to travel slowly, and with the small group that now appeared with him had hastened across the mountains by the Coeur d'Alene route. As Stevens and Palmer came up to meet them, they noticed that one of the warriors carried a staff from which dangled a Blackfoot scalp. Looking Glass received the commissioners coldly. He looked around at the Indians, and launched suddenly into a tirade: "My people, what have you done? While I was gone, you have sold my country. I have come home, and there is not left me a place on which to pitch my lodge. Go home to your lodges. I will talk to you."

All of Stevens' work fell suddenly apart. The 70-year-old war chief—"old, irascible, and treacherous," Stevens called him—whipped scorn that night on the headmen who had agreed to sign the treaty. The next day, June 9, Lawyer told Stevens that Looking Glass would probably calm down in a day or two, but Stevens' determination had now risen, and he had no intention of letting Looking Glass defeat him at the last moment.[36] Before the council started, the Governor met privately with Peopeo Moxmox and Kamiakin and won promises from them to abide by their word and sign the treaties. Then he asked Kamiakin for a list of the tribes over which he had authority as head chief. The Yakima, according to Stevens' secretary, Doty, named the tribes, but the only one other than the Yakimas which Doty recorded at that time was the Palouse.[37]

When the council reconvened, Stevens presented the Indians with finished versions of the treaties for the three reservations, all ready to be signed. With studied indifference to Looking Glass, he reviewed what the treaties said, reminding the chiefs that they did not have to move their people onto the reservations "for two or three years." Certain points were glossed over: Kamiakin, for instance, was to be considered the head chief of a long list of Columbia River bands that were not present but whose people Stevens wished to move onto the Yakima reservation, out of the way of the whites. Stevens was talking quickly, and probably did not even reveal the role he was assigning Kamiakin, for the Yakima would not willingly have accepted it, and it is not likely that the Indian had included those bands in the list he had given Stevens and Doty earlier that morning. All of them had their own headmen, and Kamiakin had nothing to do with their affairs.[38] But Stevens brushed past the

36. When Stevens had decided to create a third reservation for the Wallawallas, Cayuses, and Umatillas, he had intimated that he would make the Nez Perce reservation smaller, since space on it was no longer required for the other three tribes. He now said that Lawyer told him that although Looking Glass would eventually calm down, the old war Chief's return "would make it impossible to reduce the Nez Perce reservation . . . and it was determined to make it a general reservation for other tribes, not exceeding in numbers those for whom it was at first designed." Some writers have deduced from this the possibility that Looking Glass and Lawyer were in league, and that Looking Glass timed his arrival and stirred up the commotion deliberately so that Lawyer would have a bargaining point to keep the Nez Perce reservation its original size. See Haines, *The Nez Perces*, p. 122. These writers, however, knew little about the history and background of Looking Glass, which this book presents for the first time. Such a performance, in league with Lawyer, of all people, would have been out of character for Looking Glass. But on other counts, too, the idea seems implausible. Nez Perce history, the traits and character of the headmen involved, the forces at work within the tribe, even the surrounding evidence of the treaty council, the testimony of Stevens, and the minutes of the proceedings, make it appear unbelievable. It would be interesting to know, however, what Stevens meant by suggesting that other tribes would move onto the Nez Perce reservation; none ever did.

37. Brown, *The Indian Side of the Story*, p. 122, quoting from James Doty's "Journal of Operations of Governor Isaac I. Stevens" in the Library of the University of Washington, Seattle.

38. The introduction to the text of the Yakima Treaty read, in part, "Articles of agreement . . . between . . . the United States, and the undersigned head chiefs, chiefs

point and kept talking. He offered to read the treaties, article by article, but told the Indians they had already heard everything in them, "not once but two or three times." Then he asked if anyone still wanted to be heard.

That gave Looking Glass his chance. He did not tell white men where to go, he snapped at Stevens angrily, and if anybody was going to tell his people where to go, it would be he, not a white man. "I am going to talk straight," he said. He looked around, pointing to the other headmen. "I am not like those people who hang their heads and say nothing." He paused a moment, and the Young Chief suddenly said, "That is the reason I told the Governor to let it be till another time . . ." Stevens patiently cautioned the Young Chief to let Looking Glass finish. The old war chief suddenly ran his finger along Stevens' map, outlining the borders of the Nez Perce lands. That was the reservation he wanted for the Nez Perces. It was the stratagem that Kamiakin, Peopeo Moxmox, and Looking Glass had originally devised. They would designate all their land as reservations, and there would be no country to sell. Then he asked for a second council, later on. One of the Nez Perces, a follower of Lawyer named Billy, called out that that was just putting it off. He was answered by Metat Waptass, the Three Feathers: "Looking Glass is speaking. We look upon him as a chief."

"I thought we had appointed Lawyer our head chief, and he was to do our talking," Billy replied.

Stevens and Palmer both tried to argue with Looking Glass, but to no avail. The war chief argued for *his* line, not the one defined in the treaty. Stevens turned away from him to ask the tribes if they were ready to sign. "What the

---

head-men, and delegates of the Yakima, Palouse, Pisquouse, Wenatshapam, Klikitat, Klinquit, Kow-was-say-ee, Li-ay-was, Skin-pah, Wash-ham, Shyiks, Ochechotes, Kah-milt-pah, and Se-ap-cat . . . who for the purpose of this treaty are to be considered as one nation, under the name of Yakima, with Kamiakin as its head chief, on behalf of and acting for said tribes and bands, and being duly authorized thereto by them." This was an old trick, almost standard operating procedure since the time of General Anthony Wayne, for American officials who wanted to acquire title to Indian land quickly. Often a venal chief, for a bribe, would claim that he spoke for other tribes and would then sell their lands without telling them anything about it. This had been a common practice in the Ohio Valley and the Southeast. The difference here was that Kamiakin was honest and turned down American offers of payment. It is extremely doubtful that he knew he was being made a tool, because it appears that Stevens did not even read the treaty aloud to him, either before or during the council. It is unlikely, also, that Stevens had misunderstood Kamiakin during the private meeting in the morning, and had actually thought that the Yakima could speak for those Chinookan, Salish, and Sahaptin bands. The assumption ran counter to the strongest Indian traditions: Kamiakin never before or afterward posed as spokesman for those bands that had their own councils of headmen. If he had done so at Walla Walla, he would have known that he had committed a crime against other Indians.

Looking Glass says, I say," said the Young Chief. "I ask you whether you are ready to sign?" Stevens repeated. "The papers are drawn. We ask are you now ready to sign those papers and let them go to the President."

". . . to the line I marked myself. Not to your line," Looking Glass insisted.

Stevens faced the old war chief. "I will say to the Looking Glass, we cannot agree."

"Why do you talk so much about it?" Palmer snapped angrily at the Nez Perce.

"It was my children that spoke yesterday, and now I come . . ." said Looking Glass.

Stevens sat back resignedly, as Palmer argued with the old man. It did him no good. "I am not going to say anymore today," Looking Glass said. Stevens finally adjourned the council, urging Looking Glass to think the matter over and talk to the other Nez Perces.

After the meeting, Peopeo Moxmox signed the treaty for the Wallawallas. Stevens maintained that Kamiakin also signed, having "yielded to the advice of the other [Yakima] chiefs." But Kamiakin later insisted that he only made a pledge of friendship by touching a little stick as it made a mark.[39] Later in the evening Lawyer came to see Stevens, and told him that he should have reminded Looking Glass that he, Lawyer, was the head chief, that the whole Nez Perce tribe had said in council that he was the head chief, and that the tribe had agreed to the treaty and had pledged its word. Stevens, he said, should have insisted that the Nez Perces live up to their pledge.

"In reply," Stevens wrote, "I told the Lawyer . . . your authority will be sustained, and your people will be called upon to keep their word . . . The Looking Glass will not be allowed to speak as head chief. You, and you alone, will be recognized. Should Looking Glass persist, the appeal will be made to your people. They must sign the treaty agreed to by them through you as head chief . . ." Lawyer then went to the Nez Perce camp, and in a stormy council that lasted through most of the next day managed to muster enough support to reaffirm his position as head chief. Looking Glass, the war leader of Asotin, apparently accepted his position as second to Lawyer in the council, and the headmen drew up a paper that pledged the tribe to honor its word to Governor Stevens.

Early on the morning of June 11 Stevens told Lawyer that he was about to call the council. "I shall call upon your people to keep their word, and upon you as head chief to sign first. We want no speeches. This will be the last day of the council." Lawyer assured him that that was the right course, and it was the way it finally happened. The council convened, Stevens reminded the

39. McWhorter, *Hear Me,* p. 91 n.

Nez Perces that they had all originally agreed that Lawyer was their head chief and spokesman, and that Lawyer had given his word to the treaty. "I shall call upon Lawyer the head chief, and then I shall call on the other chiefs to sign. Will Lawyer now come forward."

Lawyer signed. Then Stevens called on Looking Glass and Joseph, and both of them stepped up and made their marks without a word. The other Nez Perce headmen followed in a line, and after them, the Cayuses signed their treaty.

"Thus ended in the most satisfactory manner this great council," Stevens wrote in his journal.

9

The Bloody Shirt

FEW OF THE INDIANS who had been at the council were pleased by what had happened. Many were ashamed that they had sold their lands, and many were angry at the way the white men had dictated to them and hurried them along as if they were children.[1] It is no idle affair to be forced to give up one's home. There are few things that any man, red or white, will fight harder to protect. But to almost every Indian who has been dispossessed, anywhere in the present-day United States, home has been more than a domicile. An Indian's land is his faith, his religion, the repository of the bones of his fathers, part of his own being—everything, save the lives of his people, that he holds most sacred.[2] Even the Nez Perces, who had managed to retain most of their

1. Although white men generally seemed to forget Indian treaties—their stipulations, as well as the conditions under which they were signed—Indians did not. In 1878, the year after the Nez Perce war, Duncan McDonald, the halfblood son of the Hudson's Bay Company trader Angus McDonald and of a Nez Perce woman, interviewed Indian survivors of the war and wrote: "In 1855 the Indians were told on the treaty grounds that 'If they did not sell their lands they would be taken from them.' These words were never forgotten. They were the chief arrows in the quiver of the Kayuse war of that year. It was all compulsion, and the author of them, with his friends, would not have lived to repeat them had the Nez Perces yielded to the proposition of striking him then and there. But the kind, brave and unscrupulous Stevens met a braver death years afterward in the battles of his own people [in the Civil War]." *The New Northwest*, Deer Lodge, Montana, June 14, 1878.

2. This is as true today as it ever was. Most non-Indian Americans who regard with horror and indignation the exile and migrations which totalitarian states have forced on peoples abroad are either unaware of or indifferent to constant removals which they still force on American Indians. In different parts of the United States agencies like the Army Corps of Engineers, the Bureau of Reclamation, and federal and state roadbuilding groups—with the cynical attitude of, "Oh, we can get away with it. They are only

333

country intact, including Joseph's Wallowa Valley, were ill at ease over the arrogance with which Stevens had treated the tribes and forced them to sell part of their lands. It was not only that they had been rushed and brow-beaten. At the council, it was plain, they had lost some of their pride and self-respect. The Governor had told them what to do, and they had obeyed.

Fifty-six band or village headmen signed the Nez Perce treaty, each man, including Joseph, being satisfied merely that he had retained possession of the land that belonged to his own band.[3] By the terms of the treaty—from the point of view of Stevens, who lumped all the bands together as a tribe—the Nez Perces accepted a reservation of approximately five thousand square miles, roughly from the upper Grande Ronde River in northeastern Oregon to the crest of the Bitterroot Range on the present Idaho-Montana border, and from the St. Joe and Palouse rivers in northern Idaho to the Wallowa Mountains and the neighborhood of Payette Lake in the south.[4] The head-

---

Indians"—continue to cause distress and hardship to Indian communities that occupy lands the white man still wants. Newspapers and citizens generally are as unconcerned about what happens to Indians as they ever were, and administration officials, members of Congress, and state officers, reflecting the indifference of public opinion, continue to trample on Indian rights. In 1965, for example, Senecas, Dakotas, Flatheads, and Alaskan Natives, among others, were in turmoil over actual or threatened removals, but relatively few non-Indians had the slightest concern for their distress.

3. All except Lawyer made "X" marks. The head chief printed the word "Aleiya," which some have speculated was a transliteration into Nez Perce of Lawyer, but which was more likely a corruption of *Alaim* (big blade), used originally for Americans but at this date signifying, literally, a big person, or head man. If it was a transliteration of "Lawyer," there was irony to it, for the treaty in time raised a fine legalistic point of great consequence to the Nez Perces. If any one of the Nez Perces was aware that he had signed the document as a spokesman for the entire tribe, rather than for his own individual band, it was Lawyer, and Lawyer alone. Despite the fact that the band leaders, ever since the time of Dr. Elijah White, had acknowledged the existence of a head chief, they still considered that they spoke for their bands alone, which were still autonomous. Lawyer, for example, would never have been allowed to speak for the Wallowa country and the people who lived there. That was Joseph's right, and to an historian it seems clear that Joseph understood that he was speaking for the Wallowa, and only for the Wallowa, when he signed. The government, however—basing its view on Stevens' version of the treaty—maintained that all who signed did so for the entire tribe and for all of the land in question. By that interpretation, it has been maintained ever since that Joseph agreed to cede lands that did not belong to his band, and that another chief could therefore, at a later time, cede Joseph's land if he signed for the tribe as a whole. This legalistic interpretation, however, seems to rest on deception practiced by Stevens, first on the Nez Perces themselves, and then on the United States government—i.e. on Stevens' fraudulent reporting of the treaty council and of the Indians' understanding of the position in which he was placing them.

4. Article I of the treaty defined the full extent of the Nez Perce country as the Indians originally claimed it to be. Article II then defined the reservation as follows: "Com-

— Reservation boundary as understood by Lawyer, 1855

▨ Lands ceded, 1855

--- Eastern and southern reservation boundary line of 1855 as established by Indian Claims Commission, 1957

•••• 1957 Nez Perce tribal understanding of the southern, eastern, and northern boundaries of 1855 reservation

ST. JOE R.

BITTER ROOT MTS.

ST. MARIES R.

LOCHSA R.

N. FORK

SELWAY R.

M. FORK

S. FORK

SALMON RIVER

MIDDLE FORK

[Salmon City]

SALMON R.

LEMHI R.

N. FORK

PAHSIMEROI R.

SOUTH FORK

Payette Lake

LITTLE SALMON R.

Kamiah

CLEARWATER R.

POTLATCH R.

N. FORK

Fort Lapwai

LAPWAI CR.

SALMON R.

[Lewiston]

[Colfax]

PALOUSE RIVER

S. FORK PALOUSE R.

SNAKE R.

TUCANNON R.

ALPOWA CR.

WASHINGTON TERRITORY

OREGON TERRITORY

GRAND RONDE RIVER

JOSEPH CR.

IMNAHA R.

SNAKE RIVER

WALLOWA R.

WALLOWA MTS.

POWDER RIVER

[Elgin]

BLUE MTS.

6. The Nez Perce Reservation, 1855

men relinquished very little land the tribe regarded as its own: an area north and south of the Snake River west and north of Alpowa Creek, much of it actually the home of Palouse Indians, and a narrow strip of hunting grounds in the south, running mostly across Idaho eastwardly from the junction of the Snake and Powder rivers.

For the cession (that is, for the Nez Perces' acquiescence and assistance at the council), the tribe was promised $200,000 in improvements on the reservation or in goods and services, payable at the rate of $60,000 within the first year after the ratification of the treaty, and then in graduated amounts annually for twenty years. The government also promised to establish, furnish, and operate two schools; to provide an agent and two teachers; to build blacksmith, tinsmith, gunsmith, and carpenter shops, and a sawmill, gristmill, and hospital; and to employ ten persons on the reservation to keep the buildings in repair for twenty years. In addition, Lawyer, as head chief, was to receive a personal annuity of $500 for twenty years, and would have a house built for him and ten acres of land plowed and fenced at government expense. At the request of the Indians, William Craig's claim and homestead were confirmed to him as an enclave within the reservation's boundaries, but it was expressly guaranteed that no other white men, except employees of the

---

mencing where the Moh-ha-na-she or southern tributary of the Palouse River [actually the mainstream of the present-day Palouse River] flows from the spurs of the Bitter Root Mountains; thence down said tributary to the mouth of the Ti-nat-pan-up Creek [the South Fork of the Palouse at the site of Colfax, Washington], thence southerly to the crossing of the Snake River ten miles below the mouth of the Al-po-wa-wi River [Alpowa Creek, below Lewiston, Idaho]; thence to the source of the Al-po-wa-wi River in the Blue Mountains; thence along the crest of the Blue Mountains; thence to the crossing of the Grande Ronde River, midway between the Grande Ronde and the mouth of the Woll-low-how River [approximately the present site of Elgin, Oregon, on the Grande Ronde River above the mouth of the Wallowa River]; thence along the divide between the waters of the Woll-low-how and Powder Rivers [the crest of the Wallowa Mountains]; thence to the crossing of the Snake River fifteen miles below the mouth of the Powder River; thence to the Salmon River above the crossing [it is not clear which crossing was meant, but it probably referred to the neighborhood of the junction of the Salmon and the Pahsimeroi rivers in northeastern Idaho, just north of land claimed by the Lemhi Shoshonis]; thence by the spurs of the Bitter Root Mountains to the place of beginning." See Francis Haines, Sr., "The Old Nez Perce Reservation," *Idaho Yesterdays,* 2 (Winter, 1958–59), 16–19; *Indian Affairs, Laws, and Treaties,* ed. Charles J. Kappler (Washington, 1904), 2, 702; "The Nez Perce Tribe of Indians v. The United States of America," Indian Claims Commission, Docket No. 175-A, Petitioner's Proposed Findings of Fact and Brief (1958), p. 9; also map of Nez Perce Tract, "Economic Land Use and Area Distribution," Plate 1, Docket No. 175–180, in possession of Nez Perce Tribal Council, Lapwai, Idaho. I appreciate assistance rendered by the Executive Committee of the Tribal Council and by Donald C. Gormley of Wilkinson, Cragun & Barker, Washington, D.C.

Indian Bureau, would be allowed on the reservation without the tribe's permission.

The other tribes fared less fortunately. The new Umatilla reservation for the Cayuses, Wallawallas, and Umatillas comprised only eight hundred square miles. The Yakima reservation was larger, but the Yakimas were to give up all their lands north of Ahtanum Creek, including the valleys of the Naches and Wenas rivers and the upper part of the Yakima, and several tribes and bands were to be crowded in with them. The Wallawallas were entirely dispossessed of their ancestral homeland. The Palouse bands were to abandon their grazing grounds and fishing villages and move westward across the Columbia to the Yakima reservation. A number of bands that lived along the Columbia and on the plateau east of that river in the general areas of the Grand Coulee and Moses Lake had not even been at the council, but they were to move in with the Yakimas. Nothing had been decided for the Spokans; Stevens would hold another council for them and their Salish neighbors.

Before leaving the council grounds, Stevens appointed William H. Tappan as the new agent for the Nez Perces, with William Craig as his interpreter, and A. J. Bolon as agent for the Yakimas. He also announced to the Indians that he intended to start shortly for the Blackfoot council at Fort Benton, and asked each tribe to send a delegation to the meeting, requesting specifically that the Nez Perces send "a hundred chiefs and braves, the whole under the head chief, or some chief of acknowledged authority, as Looking Glass." After the tribes started for their homes, Stevens lingered at the council grounds for several days, preparing his reports of the treaties, and on June 14 sent them with W. H. Pearson, an express rider, to Olympia. His messages included a serious violation of the promises he had made the Indians. Under the terms of the treaties—and according to his personal assurances to the headmen—nothing in the interior country was to change until Stevens notified the tribes that the Senate had ratified the treaties and the President had signed them. It would take perhaps two or three years, he had told them, and until then, when he would build new homes for the headmen, no one would have to move. Implicit in this was the understanding that during that time the Indians would be secure on their present lands, and no white men would come to bother them.

Nevertheless, Stevens' reports, supported by those of Palmer, caused to be published in Washington and Oregon newspapers an announcement that the treaties at Walla Walla had opened for immediate settlement all Indian lands east of the Cascade Mountains except areas specifically reserved for the Indians. On June 23, 1855, only twelve days after the treaties had been signed, the *Oregon Weekly Times* carried an article signed by Stevens and Palmer, describing the regions ceded by the Indians and announcing that "By an express provision of the treaty the country embraced in these cessions and not included in the reservation is open to settlement, excepting that the Indians are secured in the possession of their buildings and implements till removal to the reservation. This notice is published for the benefit of the public . . . Oregon and Washington papers please copy." [5] They did. The *Puget Sound Courier*, the *Table Rock Sentinel*, and the *Umpqua Gazette* were some of the papers that informed their readers that the interior lands were open to settlers.[6] There was no excuse for the premature announcement, and it had its expected result. Almost immediately, land-hunters and prospectors headed across the Cascades, hoping to beat the rush into the new country. If the Walla Walla treaties would not lead to war, this betrayal of the Indians was guaranteed to do so.

Stevens and his party left the Walla Walla Valley for the Blackfoot council on June 16, while Palmer and the Oregon delegation returned to The Dalles to make treaties with the tribes of the central part of Oregon. The Stevens group traveled across country to the villages of Red Wolf and Timothy at the junction of Alpowa Creek and the Snake River and stopped to admire Red Wolf's orchards and fenced and irrigated corn fields, in which "men as well as women and children were at work" with plows. Lawyer joined them there to discuss arrangements for the delegation the Nez Perces would send to the meeting with the Blackfeet, and the Americans had a supper of salmon with the three friendly chiefs. Then the Indians, exacting "a stiff toll," ferried the whites across the Snake, and Stevens' party continued through the high Palouse country toward Lake Coeur d'Alene. The governor was impressed with the fertility and beauty of the region, and although it had been guaranteed to the Nez Perces as part of their new reservation, his glowing references to it, when published in his final report on the railroad survey, could not have done other than stimulate the appetite of land-hunting whites. "The Nez Perces country is exceedingly well adapted to grazing, and is for the most part a remarkably fine arable country," he wrote. ". . . I was astonished, not simply at the luxuriance of the grass and the richness of the soil. The whole view presents to the eye a vast bed of flowers in all their varied beauty. The country is a rolling table-land, and the soil like that of the prairies of Illinois . . . I say again, the whole country was, apparently, exceedingly rich and luxuriant . . . the whole country is arable, the soil as rich as the best prairies of Minnesota, and every convenience for the house and farm at hand —water, wood for fires, and timber for building." [7] Such repetitive descrip-

5. Chester Anders Fee, *Chief Joseph* (New York, 1936), p. 37.
6. Relander, *Strangers on the Land*, p. 45.
7. *Pacific Railroad Reports*, Vol. 12, Part I, pp. 199, 201.

tions were little short of an open invitation to come and put the region to productive use.

As he crossed the prairies, Stevens passed large groups of Nez Perces gathering camas, and at one place met a band of Palouses under a minor headman named Kahlotus, the only Palouse who had signed the Walla Walla treaty. Soon, those Indians would have to move to the Yakima reservation. Farther on, he met Coeur d'Alene Indians, also digging camas, and another group of Palouses under a chief who had refused to attend the council. That leader, nevertheless, told the governor that his people regarded themselves as part of the Yakima tribe and looked upon Kamiakin as their head chief.

At the Coeur d'Alene mission Stevens found much excitement over the recent gold discoveries on the Pend Oreille River farther north. Prospectors had not yet reached the area, but he learned that a Hudson's Bay Company employee was already on his way to Fort Vancouver with news of the find, and Stevens must have realized that miners would soon be arriving in the region. He met with some thirty Coeur d'Alene leaders, won their agreement to meet him in a treaty council with the Spokans when he returned from Fort Benton, but was unable to persuade them to send a delegation to the Blackfoot council. Only a few of their people went to the buffalo country any more, the Coeur d'Alenes said, and they feared the Blackfeet too much to go to the meeting.

Stevens went on, up the Coeur d'Alene River and over the divide of the Bitterroots to the St. Regis River. He had sent a messenger ahead to the Flatheads, and on July 7 in the valley near present-day Missoula he met a large assemblage of Flatheads, Pend d'Oreilles, and Kutenais, under their head chiefs Victor, Alexander, and Michelle respectively. They agreed to hold a treaty council with Stevens, similar to the one he had conducted at Walla Walla, and two days later they met in a formal gathering. There was no question about the friendship of those Indians toward white men. They had long been under the influence of Christianity, and many of them had been baptized by Father De Smet. Nevertheless, they disliked the proposals Stevens made to them, and stubbornly resisted him for eight days. He told them that he regarded them all as one people, since they were all Salish (the Kutenais were not), and he asked them to combine on a single reservation either at the head of the Bitterroot Valley in Victor's country in the south, or farther north on Pend d'Oreille lands at Horse Plains and along the Flathead and Jocko rivers. At first, they saw no need for a reservation that would confine them to any one part of the country over which they still roamed without conflict with whites. "Talk about treaty," said one of the Pend d'Oreilles. "When did I kill you? When did you kill me? What is the reason we are talking about treaties? We are friends. We never spilt the blood of one of you. I never saw your blood. I want my country. I thought no one would ever want to talk about my country . . ."

As Stevens persisted, the older chiefs finally acquiesced, but they could not agree on which area to accept. The Flatheads did not want to abandon the Bitterroot Valley, and the Pend d'Oreilles did not want to leave the northern area. With growing impatience, Stevens spoke harshly to the headmen, putting more pressure on them than he had exerted on the tribes at Walla Walla. Finally, after the governor had asked the friendly Victor if he was "an old woman . . . dumb as a dog," the Flathead leader walked out of the council, badly hurt. Several days later, when Stevens induced him to return, Victor proposed that the government look over both areas and decide which one was best for the Indians. They would then accept that decision, and whichever group had to move would do so.

To break the impasse and get on to the Blackfoot council, Stevens agreed to the proposal, and the chiefs signed a treaty that established a reservation in the northern area but allowed the Flatheads to remain in the Bitterroot Valley above Lolo Creek until the government surveyed that region and determined whether the Indians could retain it permanently. It was a poor decision that led eventually to friction with settlers and further injustices to the Flatheads; but Stevens was in a hurry and probably thought he could settle the matter when he had more time. Meanwhile, he told the headmen that from then on, the government would regard their people as a single Flathead nation, with Victor as head chief, and that he hoped that he could also place other groups like the Coeur d'Alenes on their reservation with them.

The council seriously disturbed the Salish and Kutenais and, for the first time, filled them with bitterness against white men. Moses, a Flathead leader, spoke for many of the Indians when he said to Stevens, "You have pulled all my wings off." The Indians ceded some 25,000 square miles, including the Hellgate-Missoula region and the Clark Fork Valley trade route, both of which Stevens wanted for the railroad. With utter cynicism Stevens reported that the council had terminated happily, "every man pleased and every man satisfied," and that the principal reason why the Flatheads had not wanted to move to the northern lands was that a Jesuit mission was already established there and the Flatheads did not want to have anything to do with it. It was probable, he explained, that the Jesuit missionaries who had once lived with the Flatheads in the Bitterroot Valley had been too strict and exacting for the Indians' independent nature.[8] Nevertheless, after their long comradeship with whites the tribes were stunned by what Stevens did to them, and to this day their descendants regard the 1855 treaty as a bullying betrayal of their friendship.

8. H. Stevens, *Stevens*, 2, 89–90.

During the council William Tappan and Bill Craig arrived with the Nez Perce delegation for the Blackfoot meeting. The chiefs, comprising the tribe's principal leaders of bands that regularly crossed to the plains and fought the Blackfeet, included Looking Glass, Eagle From the Light, Metat Waptass, Spotted Eagle, White Bird from Salmon River, Plenty Bears from the Grande Ronde River, Stabbing Man, and Jason.[9] With some trepidation the Salish also agreed to come to the council, and Stevens suggested that they and the Nez Perces, accompanied by their agents, hunt on the plains south of the Missouri until the council was ready to begin and he sent for them. With his party he then crossed the Continental Divide via the Hellgate route and arrived at the American Fur Company post near the Marias River. Indian Superintendent Alfred Cumming of Nebraska Territory reached the fort soon afterward, but incurred Stevens' displeasure by informing him that the Indian presents he was sending up the Missouri for the council would be delayed in arriving.

Stevens fretted while the weeks passed. The Blackfeet were hunting north of the Missouri and the western tribes south of it, and by messengers he kept the Indians informed of the postponement of the meeting. Finally, just as the hunting bands began to drift farther away in pursuit of the wandering herds, the supply boats were reported to have reached the mouth of the Judith River, and Stevens impatiently changed the location of the council to that place. He had wanted the Snakes and Crows at the meeting also, but they were hunting elsewhere, and his agents could not bring them in. By October 15 large camps of Gros Ventres, Piegans, Bloods, and Blackfeet, as well as Nez Perces, Pend d'Oreilles, Kutenais, and Flatheads—some 3,500 Indians altogether—had assembled at the council grounds near the mouth of the Judith. The Canadian and western tribes, bitter enemies for more than a century, were friendly but cautious, waiting to hear what Stevens would say.

The Governor opened the proceedings on October 16, calling on all the tribes to live in peace on the plains, and reading the terms of the treaty he had prepared for their approval. At the Fort Laramie Treaty in 1851 a large portion of the northwestern plains had been designated as belonging to the Blackfeet. Now Stevens suggested that that part of the Blackfoot country south of the Missouri River be established as a common hunting ground for all the tribes signing the new treaty, while the part north of the Missouri be reserved for the Blackfeet alone, although the western Indians could enter it to trade and visit. The tribes were asked to allow whites to pass through and

9. Lawyer later said that he had directed the sending of these men and had told them on their departure that "if you go and are killed by unfriendly Indians, it will be in defence of Law." *Proceedings of the Treaty Council at Lapwai* (1863), p. 65; National Archives, Record Group 75.

live in Indian territory without molestation, to permit the building of roads, telegraph lines, and military posts in the country, and to guarantee peace with white men and with each other. In addition, annuities, teachers, farm implements, shops, and schools, similar to those offered the western Indians at Walla Walla and Hellgate, were promised the Blackfeet, who were urged to learn to settle down and become farmers.

The Blackfeet had conditioned themselves for two years to the acceptance of peace with the western Indians, and save for reminding Stevens that they could not speak for bands that still lived in Canada and had not come to the council, they readily assented to the terms. Only one Indian, a Pend d'Oreille headman, objected to the treaty, pointing out that his people, who lived farther north than the other western Indians, usually crossed to the plains by the Marias Pass near present-day Glacier Park, and would have to make a long trip in the future if they had to hunt south of the Missouri River. The Blackfeet gave his band permission to hunt in the northern country, and on the second day of the council all of the tribes were ready to sign. It had been a remarkably happy meeting, and for once none of the Indians had reason to resent what had occurred. Some of them, perhaps, could not believe that a new day had actually arrived on the plains. The Nez Perce chief Metat Waptass, or the Three Feathers, called on the Blackfeet to say again publicly that they meant to live in peace with all their neighbors. The Blackfeet responded to his satisfaction, and Metat Waptass sat down, murmuring, "It is good. The Blackfeet agree." [10]

For a few years the tribes actually lived up to their promises not to steal horses or make war upon each other, and Blackfoot bands even made friendly visits to Salish camps in the Bitterroot Valley. Credit for the truce belonged to Stevens, who on this occasion parleyed on terms of equality with the Indians, since he was not trying to coerce them into an unwilling act. Except when they visited the Blackfeet to trade, the western tribes stayed south of the Missouri, along the Musselshell and the Yellowstone; and although in time young men began to raid and draw their bands into clashes again, the old days of fierce, tribal-wide hostility between the westerners and the Blackfeet were ended.

For the first time in generations, also, the home villages of the Salish and Sahaptin peoples were secure against enemy war bands. The Snakes no longer raided the Sahaptins, and the Blackfoot threat was ended. But the historic moment, which should have been cause for rejoicing by the western tribes, had little actual meaning for them. The white men, invaders more powerful and menacing than any previous enemy, were already accomplishing what

10. For the minutes of the proceedings of the Blackfoot council see "The Blackfoot Indian Peace Council," ed. Albert J. Partoll, in *Frontier Omnibus*, pp. 197–207.

neither the Snakes nor the Blackfeet had been able to do, and many of the chiefs recognized that they were achieving it so far without resistance from the warrior protectors of the villages.

On October 24, after the various tribes had started for home from the Judith River council grounds, Stevens and his party returned to Fort Benton, and on October 28 headed for the Continental Divide. Stevens had reason to feel pleased with himself; everything up to then had gone according to his hopes. Two months before, on August 27, while he had been waiting for the Blackfoot council goods to arrive from the lower Missouri, his express rider, W. H. Pearson, had ridden in from Washington Territory to report to him that "everything was quiet and favorable west of the mountains, and that many miners and settlers were going into the upper country," where the discovery of gold had finally been confirmed.[11] The news had not given Stevens reason for concern; on the way home he would stop to make a treaty with the Spokans, Coeur d'Alenes, and other tribes in the region of the gold strikes, and that would be that.

But suddenly, on October 29, as Stevens and his men were on Montana's Teton River on the eastern side of the Continental Divide, Pearson, who had since made another trip to Olympia and back, rode exhaustedly into camp, "emaciated, wild, and haggard," and announced the horrendous news that war had exploded on both sides of the Cascades. The Indians of Puget Sound had attacked the settlements in that district, and along the Columbia River from the Cascades to the Colville Valley tribes had gone on the warpath. The Cayuses, Wallawallas, Umatillas, Palouses, and Yakimas were fighting under Kamiakin, Peopeo Moxmox, the Young Chief, and Five Crows. Indian agent A. J. Bolon had been murdered and an expedition of federal troops under Major Haller had been defeated and forced to retreat from the Yakima country. Settlers and miner were being killed; all whites were fleeing from the interior. The Spokans and Coeur d'Alenes were about to join the hostiles, and even many of the Nez Perces were threatening to enter the war.

Stevens and his party, said Pearson, were cut off. A large Indian army lay in wait in the Walla Walla Valley to wipe them out. Pearson himself had been chased by warriors from the Umatilla to the Nez Perce country, where Red Wolf and other friendly Indians had taken care of him.[12] Then a Nez Perce had guided him hurriedly across the Lolo Trail to bring the news to

---

11. H. Stevens, *Stevens*, 2, 101.

12. "An Express [Pearson] to give notice to Gov. Stevens came to my camp in the night," Lawyer reported later. "My horses had been in use, were tired, almost worn out, but such was the nature of the case, no time to be lost, that I told the Messenger, take my horse, follow after Gov. Stevens. The prospect was fair for war, all the tribes were in commotion." Proceedings at Treaty Council at Lapwai (1863), pp. 65–66.

Stevens. The express rider also carried letters from Acting Governor Charles H. Mason and others in Olympia, urging Stevens not to try to come back by way of the mountains, but to go to New York and return to the coast by boat.

Stevens was thunderstruck by the news. His immediate reaction was one of fury at the tribes that had signed his treaties and then treacherously gone to war. His plans had been smashed, his authority rebuffed, and his future thrown in jeopardy. He had no intention of running away from the Indians and returning to Olympia by way of New York. It was a measure of his feeling of superiority over the headmen whom he had bossed at Walla Walla; he would outface them again and teach them an enduring lesson. "His decision," said his youthful son, Hazard, who was with him at the time, "was instant and unwavering. It was to force his way back to his Territory by the direct route through all opposition and obstacles . . . his determination was unalterably fixed sternly to confront them all, and by a bold, decided course and rapid movements to force a passage through the hostile country and hostile savages." [13] Leaving the main party to follow more slowly, the Governor, accompanied by the guide Delaware Jim and one other man, hurried as fast as he could toward the Divide and the Bitterroot Valley, not knowing what he was getting into.

Events west of the Bitterroots were as serious as Pearson had reported them. As soon as the Indians had got back to their homelands after the Walla Walla council in June, they had begun to discuss and argue about the treaties they had signed. For the moment, the Nez Perces, Wallawallas, Cayuses, and Umatillas had supported their headmen's agreements to the documents, but elsewhere there had been great unrest. Father J. B. A. Brouillet, who was still in the Indians' country, had come to Father Pandosy's mission on the Ahtanum, and the priests had helped explain to the Indians what the Yakima treaty entailed. The Yakimas had met repeatedly, and leaders of many bands that had not been at Walla Walla but were affected by what had happened there had joined the Yakima chiefs in angry sessions. All along the Columbia River, from The Dalles to the Okanogan country in the north, bands had learned that Kamiakin had signed a paper that had sold their lands and committed them to moving in with the Yakimas. Kamiakin had maintained his innocence, and he had been as bitter as the headmen of the cheated bands. The angriest, apparently, had been Quil-ten-e-nock and his younger brother, Que-tal-a-kin, known later as Chief Moses, who were the leaders of the Sinkiuse, a Salish-speaking group of people living just north and east of the Yakimas along the Columbia River and in the region that stretched from

13. H. Stevens, *Stevens*, 2, 124.

Moses Lake to Grand Coulee. The two headmen, both of them courageous and manly, had condemned Kamiakin for having allowed himself to be tricked into speaking for them, and they had announced their intention to fight any white man who tried to move them from their lands. The Palouses, who had acknowledged Kamiakin's right to represent them, had said that they wished to fight also. But others had been less bellicose. The Wanapums, who lived south of Quil-ten-e-nock's people on the Columbia River, had also blamed Kamiakin and had said they would not move; but they reflected the feelings of most of the unwarlike fishing bands along the Columbia by protesting that they did not want a war. The Yakimas themselves had divided. Timorous, old Te-i-as had been willing to abide by the treaty. His brother, Owhi, had suggested waiting to see what happened. Many of the young warriors had wanted to fight as soon as white men showed up.

Smarting under the blame he had received, Kamiakin had made many warlike statements, some of them in the presence of the priests. But, like Owhi, he had been willing to let events take their course. Meanwhile, white men, responding to the announcement that the interior land had been opened to them, had begun to come across the passes of the Cascades. When news of the gold strike had been confirmed, the intruders' numbers had grown. Rough, impatient prospectors had hurried through the Indians' country to the Colville Valley, often treating the Indians with high-handedness and telling them that they no longer owned the land. News of such episodes had circulated quickly among the bands and had increased their alarm. The younger Indians had begun to chafe at the restraints on them. Kamiakin had sent messengers to most of the powerful interior tribes and to Indian friends at Puget Sound and along the lower Columbia. More meetings had followed, and the Yakimas and Klickitats had placed headmen and warriors atop the passes of the Cascades to warn white invaders to turn back. Some of the whites had done so, but some had ignored the advice and ridden past the Indians. Those who had returned home had begun to spread the alarm that the Indians in the interior seemed about to go on the warpath.

They had not been wrong. Early in September, three months after the Walla Walla council had ended, an impetuous Yakima warrior named Qualchin, the son of Owhi, and five other young men had finally attacked a party of six white men who were traveling down the Yakima River, and had killed them all. Other murders had occurred soon afterward on the lands of the Yakimas and Wenatchis. Returning miners had brought back rumors of the slayings to the settlements, and on September 20 the Indian agent A. J. Bolon, who had been at The Dalles preparing to travel to the Spokan country

to meet Stevens on his way back from Fort Benton, had left for the Yakimas'
lands to investigate the reports.[14] Bolon had been well liked by many of the
Yakimas, but he had recently had a stormy session with some of their leaders,
during which he had threatened to send government troops into their country
to protect white travelers. At length, on the advice of Kamiakin's younger
brother, Show-away, also known as Ice, he had started back to The Dalles
on September 22. Along the way he had been trailed and overtaken by
Me-chiel, the 20-year-old son of Ice, and two other young Yakimas. When
the group had stopped to make a fire and warm themselves, the Indians had
murdered the agent, cutting his throat and burning his body in the fire.

Bolon's failure to reappear at The Dalles had caused Nathan Olney, another Indian agent, concern, and he had sent a Des Chutes Indian to the Yakimas as a spy to find out where Bolon was. The Indian had returned with the
alarming news that Bolon had been slain. This information, coupled with the
reports of other murders of white travelers in the Indian country, had inflamed the population on the lower Columbia and around Puget Sound. In
the absence of Stevens, Acting Governor Mason of Washington Territory
had asked for federal troops at Forts Vancouver and Steilacoom to protect
travelers on the eastern side of the Cascades. Major Gabriel Rains, in command at Fort Vancouver, had earlier received Stevens' report of what the
Governor had termed the Indians' satisfaction with the Walla Walla treaties,
and he was now puzzled by the Indians' hostility. Stevens and Palmer had referred to Kamiakin and Peopeo Moxmox as potential troublemakers, and a
letter from Father Brouillet at Ahtanum, stating that Kamiakin had talked
steadily of war since the meeting at Walla Walla, had seemed to confirm that
the Yakima headman had been responsible for all the killings. To discover the
cause of the outbreaks as well as to make a display of armed strength to the
Indians, Rains had ordered Major Haller, who was at The Dalles, to proceed
to the Yakima country with a force of some 100 men and a howitzer and cooperate with a unit being dispatched across the Naches Pass from Fort
Steilacoom on Puget Sound.

The appearance of the troops, as Bolon had promised the Yakimas, had
been the final betrayal of the Walla Walla treaties that the Indians had fearfully
come to expect. The treaties had not been ratified, no reservations had been

14. H. H. Bancroft, *History of Washington, Idaho, and Montana*, p. 109, says that
it was Spokan Garry who told Bolon about the murders. Bolon was going to take Indian
goods to the Spokan country for the treaty council that Stevens intended to hold with
that tribe and the Coeur d'Alenes, and presumably Garry came to tell Bolon that the
killings had made the time an unfavorable one for the council. Garry, however, knew
where Stevens was; and if he had wanted to postpone the council, it seems more likely
that he would have sent a messenger to Stevens and not made the long trip to The Dalles.

established, and no bands had been moved; but white men had entered the Indians' countries, had refused to leave, and had told the Indians that they had come because Governor Stevens had announced that the lands no longer belonged to the Indians. Among the tribes themselves, no headman, including Kamiakin, had been known to condone the killings of the whites. The Yakima chiefs, in fact, had been stricken by the senseless murder of Bolon. But the young men had had enough of the enemy; their passions had risen, and they had reached the point where the only chiefs they would follow were the ones who led them to war.

On October 5, near the Toppenish River south of the Ahtanum, Haller's troops had sighted some Indians. Shots had been exchanged, and a fierce battle had begun. More than 500 Indians, mostly Yakimas under Kamiakin and Qualchin—but also some Columbia River Salish led by Quil-ten-e-nock—had brought the regulars to a halt, fought them all the next two days, and finally forced them to bury their howitzer, burn their baggage and supplies, and retreat to The Dalles. The soldiers had had five men killed and 17 wounded, and had lost most of their supplies; the Indians had claimed they had had only two men killed and four wounded. When the troops from Fort Steilacoom had learned of Haller's defeat, they too had withdrawn.

The Indian victory had caused great excitement west of the Cascades. At almost the same time, trouble had broken out with the bands around Puget Sound which had signed Stevens' treaties, as well as with the Rogue River Indians in southern Oregon, and little had been required to convince the people of both Washington and Oregon that they were now facing the start of a coordinated, general uprising of Indians throughout the Northwest, probably masterminded by Kamiakin. Deciding on a punitive expedition against the Yakimas, Major Rains had hurriedly assembled a new force at The Dalles consisting of some 335 regulars and three howitzers. He was to be joined also by a unit of regulars from Fort Steilacoom and by a group of 19 dragoons under Lieutenant Philip Sheridan from Fort Vancouver. In addition he had asked Acting Governor Mason for two companies of Washington volunteers and Governor George L. Curry of Oregon for four companies. He had wanted those forces to serve under his command with the regulars, but units of Oregon volunteers had had difficulties earlier with federal officers, particularly with Major General John E. Wool, commander of the Department of the Pacific, with headquarters at San Francisco, who had regarded the volunteers with disdain, and Curry had refused to let his troops serve under Rains. Instead, he had organized a First Regiment of Oregon Mounted Volunteers and had sent them to The Dalles under Colonel J. W. Nesmith, a prominent resident of Portland. Mason, meanwhile, had deployed one of the Washington companies as a defensive unit to guard the western side of the Cascade passes against a sudden foray by the Yakimas toward Puget Sound, and had ordered the other company to prepare to go to the rescue of Stevens, who was still at the Blackfoot council.

All of this had happened while Stevens was on the eastern side of the Rocky Mountains, and had been blurted out to the Governor by Pearson, his express rider. No one quite knew the disposition of the interior tribes, other than the Yakimas, but Pearson had picked up enough information during his long, exciting ride to Stevens to believe that all the tribes and bands had combined in war, or were about to do so, and that Kamiakin and Peopeo Moxmox seemed to be directing the uprising.

Stevens and his two companions, hurrying back to the trouble zone, overtook William Craig, Looking Glass, and the delegation of Nez Perce chiefs, who were returning to their homes from the Blackfoot council and who had already heard of the outbreak of hostilities.[15] The Nez Perces continued to seem friendly to the Governor, however; and even after he received confirmation in the Bitterroot Valley that Peopeo Moxmox and Kamiakin had assembled a great war party to intercept him on the western side of the Bitterroot Mountains, the Nez Perce leaders agreed to accompany him across the mountains and try to help him. Reports indicated that the Coeur d'Alenes and Spokans were still wavering over whether or not to go to war, and Stevens noted in his journal that it seemed important to him to "cross the mountains and throw ourselves into the nearest tribes without their having the slightest notice of our coming . . . if I could bring this about, I could handle enough tribes, and conciliate the friendship of enough Indians, to be sufficiently strong to defy the rest." The Stevens Pass, which led directly to the Coeur d'Alene Indians, was already blocked by snow, and for that reason, he decided, the Indians would not expect him to take it. He therefore selected that route, and, accompanied by fourteen Nez Perces and his main party, which had now caught up with him, he crossed the Bitterroots through snow up to three feet deep and on November 23 reached the neighborhood of the Coeur d'Alene mission. The next day, with Craig, Pearson, and four Nez Perces, including Looking Glass, he galloped into the principal Coeur d'Alene village, rifle in hand and ready to fire, and shouted at the startled Indians, "Are you friends or enemies? Do you want peace or war?" At the sign of a hostile action, Stevens had instructed his companions to open fire, killing as many of the Coeur d'Alenes as possible, and then fall back to a knoll until the main party came up.

15. Letter from I. I. Stevens to Secretary of War Jefferson Davis, February 19, 1856, I. I. Stevens Correspondence, 1848–1857, Western Americana Collection, Yale University Library.

The Coeur d'Alenes insisted they were friendly, and the next day Stevens had a council with them. They admitted that many of them were in sympathy with the Yakimas and were disturbed by the miners in their own country, that some of their young men had already joined the war, and that a delegation of Kamiakin's warriors had been at their village until five days before. Nevertheless, the headmen wished to avoid war, and when Stevens threatened them with stern punishment they agreed to do everything possible to restrain their younger men. At the same time, Stevens learned of the dangers still facing him on the road ahead. The tribes farther south had gathered to block his route, and Peopeo Moxmox was said to have boasted that he would take Stevens' scalp himself. In the Spokan country fifteen miners, as well as four men who had brought up the Indian goods for the Spokan council, were virtually under siege at the home of Antoine Plante, a halfblood. Deciding to go to their rescue, Stevens dispatched William Craig and most of the Nez Perces to Lapwai to discover the disposition of that tribe and let him know if he could count on their assistance, and then set out for the Spokans' country.

With Stevens were Looking Glass, Spotted Eagle, and Three Feathers. The entire party of some thirty men rode into the principal Spokan village near Plante's home on November 27, taking the Indians by surprise and again demanding whether they were for war or peace. The Indians replied that they were friendly, and Stevens found that the white men had built a blockhouse and were unharmed. He sent messengers to the other Spokan villages and to the Colville Valley, summoning all the Indians, as well as Angus McDonald and the Jesuit missionaries at Colville, to a council, and organized the miners into a military unit which he named the Spokane Invincibles. His own men he formed into a fighting group called the Stevens Guards.[16]

Spokan Garry arrived on November 29, obviously ill at ease but still friendly to Stevens. Large numbers of Spokans and Coeur d'Alenes also appeared, and on December 2 McDonald and the Jesuits came in with headmen from the Colville region. The meeting began on December 3 and lasted three days, and Stevens later called it "one of the most stormy councils . . . that ever occurred in my whole Indian experience." The Indians were openly sympathetic to the Yakimas and were filled with grievances of their own. They resented the miners who had come brusquely onto their lands, and ob-

16. Among the Stevens Guards were the Nez Perces, including Captain John, who had been with Haller in the punitive expedition against the Shoshonis. In 1863, this Indian, who had also gone to the Blackfoot council with Stevens, still carried a well-worn and unpaid certificate for a private's pay in the Stevens Guards (Proceedings of the Lapwai Council, 1863, p. 25). Captain John was still on the troops' side during the war against his own people in 1877, as will be seen.

Kutenai

PEND OREILLE R.

Pend
Oreille
Lake

Flathead
Lake

[Spokane]

Four Lakes,
1858

Coeur d'Alene
Mission

COEUR D'ALENE R.

Coeur
d'Alene
Lake

CLARK FK.

Stevens
Pass

ST. REGIS R.

FLATHEAD R.

Coeur d'Alene

✕ Steptoe's
Defeat, 1858

Flathead

CLARK FK.

[Missoula]

Lolo
Pass

LOLO CR.

NORTH FK.

Lolo Trail

BITTERROOT R.

Fort
Owen

SNAKE R.

Red Wolf's Crossing

CLEARWATER RIVER

LOCHSA R.

ALPOWA CR.

LAPWAI CR.

Craig

Chase

Nez Perce

MIDDLE FK.

SELWAY R.

BITTERROOT MOUNTAINS

ANDE RONDE R.

SALMON R.

WASHINGTON TERRITORY

OREGON TERRITORY

SOUTH FK.

SNAKE R.

LLOWA R.

1856

SALMON R.

7. THE WARS IN THE INTERIOR COUNTRY, 1855–58

jected to the former Hudson's Bay Company employees who had filed claims in the Colville Valley under the Donation Act. Kamiakin's emissaries, said Hazard Stevens, who again was present with his father, "had imbued them with all kinds of falsehoods concerning the war and its causes, and the purposes of the whites, particularly of Governor Stevens, and what he did and said at the Walla Walla council." [17] One of the "falsehoods" was that they were to be driven by soldiers from their own country onto the Nez Perce reservation. None of them wanted war, but they were angry and frightened. A rumor was current that the troops had driven the Yakimas across the Columbia into the camas grounds of the Spokans. Unless Stevens made peace with the Yakimas, the fighting, they said, would involve the Spokans, who would have to defend the lands where they gathered their roots.

Isolated in the heart of hostile country, Stevens was in a dangerous, almost desperate situation. He spoke like a man deeply hurt, but for once he recognized the peril of trying to rush the Indians. Still, he could not give up trying to have his way. "I think it best for you to sell a portion of your lands . . ." he told the Indians. "I want every man here to believe that I am and will be his friend, and that his rights will be protected, and that even if I *should* talk to you about lands, and the selling of them, it is not true that soldiers are coming here to take them by force . . . I do not think we could agree now. We want more time to think of it . . . When you want to talk to me about your lands, by and by, I shall be ready to talk." [18]

The Indians wanted no delay; they were ready to talk then. Few of them recognized Spokan Garry as one of their leaders, but his education and acceptance as a friend by Stevens and other white men made the Indians feel that they would achieve more if Garry were their spokesman. He was forty-four years old, a tired, emotionally torn man between two worlds, once the hope of his people and now a lonely, discredited collaborator with the enemy. But at this moment of crisis for the Spokans, Garry suddenly cast aside the fears and doubts of his past and became a patriot. It was his time for greatness, and though he had become a little man, he lived up to the large challenge.

As the Spokans, Coeur d'Alenes, and Colville Indians listened to his angry oratory, he rose again and again to shame and humiliate Stevens. "Since I heard of trouble among the Indians, I have had you on my mind all the time . . ." he told the Governor. "From the time of my first recollection, no blood has ever been upon the hands of my people. Now that I am grown

17. H. Stevens, *Stevens*, 2, 133.

18. Excerpts of the speeches at the Spokan Council are reprinted from Jessett, *Spokan Garry*, pp. 117 ff., quoting from James Doty's "Journal of Operations of Governor Isaac I. Stevens," in the Library of the University of Washington, Seattle.

up, I am afraid that we may have the blood of whites on our hands . . . I would not like it if the troops should come to the junction of the Columbia and Snake rivers—I would not like to have the Yakimas driven this way . . . I am an Indian. I was the first one to spill my blood for the whites in the Spanish country [in California, when he and the Wallawallas had helped Frémont], and afterwards when blood was spilled in the Cayuses Country. The Indians are always thinking of this—of an Indian who was killed in California by an American [another reference to the murder of Elijah Hedding, which the Northwest Indians would never forget] . . . Governor, I will not hide my mind. Those troubles are on my mind and I will not hide them . . . Those who killed Peopeo Moxmox's son in California, they were Americans. Why are those three Americans alive now? Why are they not hung? That is what the Indians think, that it will be Indians only who are hung for murder."

About the reservation he had something else to say. "When you first commenced to speak [at Walla Walla], you said the Wallawallas, Cayuses, and Umatillas were to move onto the Nez Perce Reservation, and that the Spokans were to move there also. Then I thought you spoke bad. Then I thought when you said that, you would strike the Indian to the heart."

Stevens' answer was a defensive quibble. "What Garry said as to what I said, is right," he stammered. "I did say it. I asked Garry would his people like to go to the Nez Perce Reservation? . . . I never said to Garry, though, your people *shall* be moved to the Nez Perce River. If Garry's people were willing to go, I would like it, that was what I said . . ."

On the final day of the council Garry spoke suddenly for all Indians of all time. "Governor," he said. "See the difference there is between these Indians and you. See how everybody is red and you are white. The Indians think they are not poor. When you look at yourself, you see you are white. You see the Indian is red, what do you think? Do you think they are poor when you look at them that way? When you look at those Red men, you think you have more heart, more sense than those poor Indians. I think the difference between us and you Americans is in the Clothing; the blood and body are the same. Do you think because your mother was white, and theirs black that you are higher or better? We are black, yet if we cut ourselves, the blood will be red—and so with the whites it is the same, though their skin is white. I do not think we are poor, because we belong to another nation. I am of another nation. When I speak you do not understand me . . . Since we have been speaking, it is as if we had been talking for nothing . . . If you take those Indians for men, treat them so now. The Indians are proud, they are not poor. If you talk truth to the Indians to make a peace, the Indians will do the same for you. You see now the Indians are proud."

Then he summed up, bluntly exposing to the other whites who were present the real reason for the Indians' hostility. "On account of one of your remarks," he said to Stevens, "some of your people have already fallen on the ground. The Indians are not satisfied with the land you gave them . . . If all those Indians had marked out their own Reservation, this trouble would not have happened . . . If I had the business to do I could fix it by giving them a little more land. Talking about land I am only telling you my mind." But on another matter, he could give a serious warning. "What I said yesterday about not crossing the soldiers to this side of the Columbia, is my business. Those Indians have gone to war, and I don't know how myself to fix it up again. That is your business."

Stevens was nettled. The war was being blamed on him and on the treaties that he had reported to Washington as being entirely satisfactory to the Indians.[19] There were white witnesses here, and he could not let Garry's accusation go unchallenged. Most of what the Indians were saying about him, he replied angrily to the Spokan, were lies. The Nez Perces, Wallawallas, Cayuses, and Umatillas were all satisfied with their reservations. So were the Yakimas. He did not know why Kamiakin had gone on the warpath, but it was not over the reservation. He denied responsibility for the war, and in his heat he ignored Garry's demand that troops be kept south of the Columbia and the Snake rivers. Then, going suddenly on the offensive and overlooking the Indians' complaints about the miners and former Hudson's Bay Company men who were claiming the tribes' lands, he demanded sharply: "Have you anything further that you wish to speak about? Do you want to speak about lands? Do you wish to point out lands you want the whites to have? I call on Garry to answer."

The moment must have been a tense one. Every Indian present had known that Stevens had talked with a crooked tongue. Not one tribe he had mentioned was satisfied with its reservation. Their emissaries had come to the Spokans and told them so. Stevens had had nothing to say about protecting the Spokans and their friends from the miners and settlers. He had ignored Garry's question about keeping troops out of their country. As if he knew that the future was dark and without hope, Garry rose and gave Stevens his answer: "All these things we have been speaking of had better be tied together as they are, like a bundle of sticks, because you are in a hurry. There is

19. Other Indians who spoke at the council also accused Stevens of being responsible for the war. Said Quin-quim-moe-se, a Spokan headman: "one thing was not right. You alone arranged the Indian's land. The Indians did not speak . . . It is all your fault the Indians are at war. It is your fault, because you have said that the Cayuses and Wallawallas will be moved to the Yakima land. They who owned the land did not speak, and yet you divided the land." H. Stevens, *Stevens*, 2, 139.

not time to talk of them. But afterwards you can come back, when you find time and see us."

The council broke up, and Stevens later reported its results to the nation in these words: "having gone there with the most anxious desire to prevent their entering into the war, but with a firm determination to tell them plainly and candidly the truth, I succeeded both in convincing them of the facts and gaining their entire confidence." [20]

After the council the Indians seemed more friendly. They were relieved, at least, that they had not been forced to decide on a treaty, nor been asked to move to the Nez Perce reservation. They traded horses to the Americans, and Stevens said that he even turned down a Spokan offer to provide him with a protective escort to the lower Columbia. He had decided to go now to the Nez Perce country, hoping that Craig had found those people at peace, and that they would give him assistance through the Walla Walla Valley where Peopeo Moxmox was supposed to be waiting for him. Looking Glass was also apparently causing him anxiety. An interpreter had reported that he had overheard the old Nez Perce war chief tell a Spokan of his intention to trap Stevens in the Nez Perce country. Stevens said nothing to Looking Glass, but decided to trust his luck and run for it, if he had to.

On December 6 the Governor and his party left the Spokans for the Clearwater River. The next day they were met by a messenger from Craig with the cheering news that the Nez Perces had not joined the war and would help Stevens. The party reached Lapwai on December 11 and found Lawyer assembled with some 2,000 Indians, who promised to provide the Americans with an escort of 250 warriors through the Wallawalla and Cayuse countries. A council was held, in which all the headmen, including Looking Glass, agreed to protect Stevens with their lives. Such a united show of friendship at that juncture of the tribe's history was deceptive and concealed from the Americans the deep division that actually existed among the Nez Perces. The individual bands had been under great pressure from Yakima, Wallawalla, Palouse, and Cayuse emissaries to join those tribes against the whites, and many of the headmen and warriors saw the justice of Kamiakin's case and were within a hair's breadth of entering the war. But at a tribal council, where the matter had been vigorously debated, Lawyer's arguments had been persuasive: the Nez Perces had done well for themselves at the Walla Walla meeting; the bands had no business looking for trouble; entering the war would only bring misery and death to the people. No one was under greater pressure from the Cayuses and Wallawallas than Joseph, whose Wallowa and Grande Ronde country bordered the troubled area, and whose people were linked by marriage and friendship with families already in the war. But Jo-

20. *Pacific Railroad Reports,* Vol. 12, Part I, p. 224.

seph supported Lawyer; concern for the safety of his own people was upper-most in his mind, and he wanted no troops in the Wallowa Valley. Even the most belligerent of the headmen were pulled up short by the realization that the Nez Perce villagers were afraid of the consequences of joining the war. Although their hearts were with the embattled tribes, they therefore went along with Lawyer and his supporters, and agreed reluctantly to do what was necessary to preserve the tribe's security.

Stevens appreciated the Nez Perces' offer of help, but it proved unneces-sary. During the course of the council an Indian messenger arrived with news that a large army of Oregon volunteers had defeated the hostile Indians in a great, four-day battle in the Walla Walla Valley, and had killed Peopeo Moxmox and scattered the Indians. Stevens felt vastly relieved, and realized that he had been able to travel from the Spokans to the Nez Perces without trouble, because the Palouses of the region through which he had passed had been engaged at the time in the battle at the Walla Walla. Perhaps not quite sure that the danger was entirely past, he invited a group of sixty-nine of the Nez Perces led by Spotted Eagle to accompany him "as a guard of honor" to Walla Walla, and soon afterward left Lapwai.

The column of Indians, miners, and members of Stevens' party rode down the Clearwater, ferried across the Snake, and traveled overland to Walla Walla in good humor. Stevens reported that a gay cameraderie existed be-tween the whites and the Nez Perces, whom his son, Hazard, described as "the most devoted and enthusiastic auxiliaries that ever marched in behalf of the whites." No trouble was encountered, and on December 20 the group reached the vicinity of Waiilatpu and was greeted happily by the army of Oregon volunteers.[21]

From Lieutenant Colonel James K. Kelly, commander of the Oregonians, Stevens now learned all that had happened since Pearson had brought him the first news of the war's outbreak. American forces since then had had impor-

---

21. Lawyer's version of the Nez Perce assistance to Stevens at this tense period is interesting. When Stevens first reached Lapwai from the Spokans, the Governor, according to Lawyer, said, "My friend, Lawyer, what shall I do?" Lawyer said he replied: "My friend, Governor Stevens, we will take you in our arms as a child, and as a child, deliver you safely to your own people. And I have only to ask of you, in return for our care of you, that you will deal as kindly and tenderly with me and my people, as I now deal with you; and as I conduct you through this danger in safety, so do you conduct me and my people when we need your aid." Lawyer went on: "Eighty of my warriors were supplied with arms by Governor Stevens. We carried him safely to Walla Walla. When he arrived there, he was met by forces, and the governor said to them, 'My White Friends, I introduce you to our *true* friends, who have brought and delivered me here in safety. These who are with me are here as representatives.'" Proceedings of the Lapwai Council (1863), pp. 66–67.

tant successes on two fronts. From The Dalles a large army of regulars under Major Rains—joined by Nesmith's regiment of Oregon Mounted Volunteers and two other companies of citizens, one of them led by Robert Newell—had invaded the Yakima country in November to punish those Indians for the defeat of Major Haller. In the face of the overwhelming force of more than 700 men most of the Yakimas had abandoned their villages and fled with as much of their livestock as they could move. Some of the warriors, led by Kamiakin, Skloom, Ice, and Qualchin and joined by Quil-ten-e-nock and Moses, with a number of Spokans and other Salish, had stayed behind and tried to make a stand. After a hot fight, in which many Indians had been killed, shells from a howitzer had dispersed the rest, and the Indians had scattered after their families. Some had gone north, but Kamiakin and most of the others had hurried eastward across the Columbia River toward the Spokan and Palouse countries. They had suffered great hardships in their flight, and many old men and women had perished in the cold. The volunteers had not pursued them, but their pell-mell retreat across the Columbia had occasioned the Spokans' concern that Garry had communicated to Stevens.

After the battle the troops had marched to the Ahtanum mission and had found it deserted. On a table Major Rains had discovered a letter written by Father Pandosy at the request of Kamiakin, offering "terms of peace" to the Americans. Feeling affronted, Rains had written an angry, intemperate message in reply. "Fugitives and vagabonds shall you also be, all that remain of you, upon the face of the earth . . . until you are gone," he had responded to the Indian whose crime had been to oppose the violation of the treaty he had signed. "You say now, '*If we will be quiet and make friendship, you will not war with us; but give a piece of land to all the tribes.*' We will not be quiet, but war forever until not a Yakima breathes in the land he calls his own. The river only will we let retain this name, to show to all people that here the Yakimas once lived . . . We are thirsting for your blood . . . my advice to you, as you will see, is to scatter yourselves among the Indian tribes more peaceable and there forget you ever were Yakimas." [22] The volunteers had then looted and burned the mission; and after scouting around to flush and shoot down several Indian stragglers, the expedition had returned to The Dalles.

On another front, a second group of Oregon volunteers under Colonel Kelly had defeated the Wallawallas, Cayuses, and Palouses, as Stevens had already learned. The justice of that campaign was even more questionable than

22. Victor, *Early Indian Wars of Oregon*, pp. 430–31. In all the lurid literature of Indian-white warfare, no document—as Judge William C. Brown points out—was ever more asinine than this one, nor—in the light of the cause of hostilities—more unjust.

the one against Kamiakin—although Stevens and the volunteers, of course, saw it in a different light. The Indian agent Nathan Olney had borne the major responsibility for it. Immediately after the defeat of Haller, Olney had hurried to Fort Walla Walla to try to persuade the Indians in that region not to join the Yakimas. The tribes there had made no move up to then to indicate that they had intended to join Kamiakin, but they too had been disgruntled about the treaties they had signed with Stevens, and their complaints had soon frightened Olney and convinced him that Peopeo Moxmox was hostile to whites. The old Wallawalla, prosperous and unwarlike, had always spoken his mind frankly and bluntly, but there is no evidence that he had contemplated joining the conflict. Nevertheless, Olney had finally panicked and announced that Peopeo Moxmox was about to lead a general Indian uprising. He had persuaded James Sinclair, who was in charge of the Hudson's Bay Company's Fort Walla Walla at the time, to dump a large supply of powder and ball into the Columbia and abandon the post, and had also warned all whites in the area to be ready to flee to safety. Some had taken him seriously, but many had thought he was exaggerating the danger. Olney, a typical westering American, had come to The Dalles in 1843, where he had erected a store, and he had all the fears and prejudices about Indians that marked most of the settlers.[23] In November, however, Oregon volunteers had appeared in the Umatilla Valley and had built a fort there. Additional companies had kept arriving, and early in December a large force under Colonel Kelly had started for the Walla Walla. When the Americans had reached the abandoned British fort, they had found that Indians had pillaged and burned it, writing an end to the famous old fur post that had seen so much history.[24]

23. At one time in his life, while he was protecting some emigrants against an Indian attack, Olney had been struck in the head by an arrow. The point was imbedded in his skull and could not be removed. In 1866 Olney fell from a horse, and the shock caused the arrowhead to penetrate his brain and kill him.

24. About the same time the Hudson's Bay Company also finally abandoned Forts Boise and Hall because of Indian warfare in the Snake country, and the consequent difficulty of communicating with those posts. The British, whose only remaining active post on American territory at the time was Fort Colvile, were indignant and claimed that Stevens' policy of buying the Indians' lands and putting the Indians on reservations not only had disrupted their trade, thus violating the terms of the Treaty of 1846, but had been responsible for the wars. "I am of opinion," wrote James Douglas, Chief Factor of the Hudson's Bay Company, "that there must have been some great mismanagement on the part of the American authorities or it is hardly credible that the natives of Oregon, whose character has been softened and improved by fifty years of commercial intercourse with the establishment of the Hudson's Bay Company, would otherwise exhibit so determined a Spirit of hostility against any white people." It was an understatement. Rich, *Hudson's Bay Company*, 2, 744–45.

The volunteers had ranged through the valley, seizing Indian horses and cattle and shooting any Indian they had seen. Reports of their violence had reached Peopeo Moxmox, and on December 4 he and a group of five or six companions had left their people and, carrying a white flag of truce, had approached Colonel Kelly's camp and asked for a parley. When the Wallawalla had asked why the troops had come into his country, Kelly had replied that he had come to punish the chief and his people for crimes against the whites. Peopeo Moxmox had denied committing any crimes, but admitted that some of the young men had looted the abandoned British post. He had promised to restore whatever goods he could find, but the council had ended with Kelly violating the flag of truce and holding the chief and his companions as hostages under guard.

The news had soon reached Indian camps in the vicinity, and angry Indians had begun to show up on the hills around the Americans. Kelly had marched his men into Peopeo Moxmox's village on the Touchet, finding it deserted, but the numbers of Indians observing them from a distance had increased. On December 7, with the Indians becoming more menacing, Kelly had started to move his troops to Waiilatpu to build a fort. He still had Peopeo Moxmox and the other hostages with him, and had warned them that he would shoot them if they tried to escape. That morning, some of the Indians on the hills had opened fire, and a general battle had begun. It had raged for four days, in the first three of which the Indians had had the advantage and had inflicted serious casualties on the volunteers. During its course, Peopeo Moxmox and the other hostages had been murdered by their guards. Kelly claimed that they had cheered the attacking Indians and that he had ordered the guards to tie them up and shoot them if they resisted. The precise details of the murders were never revealed, but after the death of the stately old Wallawalla chief, whose intelligence and pride had made him too dangerous to the Americans, the volunteers had had a ghoulish time, mutilating his corpse and cutting off his fingers, ears, and bits of his scalp as souvenirs. One man reported that "They skinned him from head to foot, and made razor-straps of his skin." [25] So died the descendant of Lewis and Clark's host Yellepit, the friend of fur traders and missionaries and the father of the slain Elijah Hedding, an Indian leader with every reason to turn with bitterness against the Americans, but a man who had remained to the end a peace chief, and not a warrior.

On December 10 Kelly had received reinforcements and had finally driven off the Indians, most of whom had retreated north toward the Snake River and the Palouse country. The weary troops had moved two miles above Waiilatpu and had built a fort. There Stevens and his party from Lapwai had met them.

25. Bancroft, *History of Washington*, p. 141 n.

Stevens' troubles were far from over. The Indians, although beaten in battle, were still unsubdued and, under angry war leaders, were gathered in dangerous strength north and east of the Snake and Columbia rivers. Working from interior lines of communication and aided by reinforcements from the Spokans and other tribes that had so far been neutral, they could attack the whites at any time. But there were even more compelling problems elsewhere. The Indian uprising at Puget Sound, close to the towns of Washington, had become serious. The Indians were on the offensive, and the settlers had taken to blockhouses. Moreover, General Wool, who had come up to Fort Vancouver from San Francisco, had implied that the whites and Stevens' treaties were more to blame than the Indians for the uprising, and he had angered the people of the territories by demanding that the volunteers get out of the Indian country and let the regulars restore peace.

General Wool, a veteran of the Mexican War, was not the most tactful man, and his outspokenness and lack of political acumen did much to exacerbate his conflict with the citizens of the two territories. But he saw the situation with better perspective than Stevens or the settlers. As ranking military representative of the federal government in the Far West, he was charged with maintaining peace between the Indians and whites, and from experience in northern California and southern Oregon he had come to recognize that most of the conflicts were caused by the aggressions of whites. He knew the treaties Stevens had signed, and they seemed clear to him: no whites were to settle on the Indians' lands until certain conditions were met by the government, and those conditions, particularly the ratification and presidential signing of the treaties, had not yet been observed. The whites were aggressors in Washington and Oregon, and Stevens not only had failed to protect the Indians but had encouraged the violation of his own treaties. Moreover, Wool saw no prospect of protection for the Indians, or of peace in the region unless he interposed the force and authority of federal troops between the settlers and the Indians. The volunteers were like unrestrained vigilante mobs, lacking responsible command and running off under their individual leaders in indiscriminate raids and shootings that only increased the Indians' bitterness and made the situation more uncontrollable. On top of that, Wool sensed that unless he brought the war to a halt the settlers would encourage it to go on and on, for the demand for military supplies and equipment was bringing prosperity to the commercial and mercantile interests of the two territories.

So far, the governments of the territories, angrily resenting Wool's attacks on them, had refused to allow him to muster their volunteer units into the ranks of the regulars. His point of view about the war, moreover, had not only widened the breach with the volunteer units but had led many of the settlers to charge that Wool and the regulars were on the side of the Indians.

When all of this was communicated to Stevens at Walla Walla, he was quick to agree with the aggrieved volunteers. Stevens had had no personal brush with Wool; but in 1854, during his return from the East, he had stopped in San Francisco and in Wool's presence had questioned the General's right to claim credit for the victory of Buena Vista in the Mexican War. Stevens had thought at the time that he might have offended the General, and now he heard something that made him feel sure that Wool, indeed, had taken personal revenge on him. It angered him enough to know that Wool was blaming his treaties for the uprisings, but when he learned that Acting Governor Mason had raised a company of Washington volunteers to come to Stevens' rescue while he was still in the mountains, and that Wool had halted the unit by refusing to recognize or equip it, he was stung. The more he brooded about it, the more irate he became; and when he got back to Olympia, he fired off a bitter letter to Secretary of War Jefferson Davis:

> When remonstrated with by Capt. Wm. McKay in command of the company raised to push forward to my assistance, [and] when informed of the objects for which this Company was enlisted and that if it was not pushed forward at once, or if some other force were not sent Gov. Stevens and his Party would be in the most imminent danger, the General replied that in his opinion the danger was greatly exaggerated, that probably Gov. Stevens would be able to protect himself, but that if he could not, then Gov. Stevens could obtain an escort from Genl. Harney [in command of troops in Nebraska Territory, far east of Fort Benton]. What a reply was this? . . . Major General Woll [sic] very cooly says Gov. Stevens can take care of himself . . . Mr. Secretary, Major Genl. Woll Commanding the Pacific Division neglected and refused to send a force to the relief of myself and Party when known to be in imminent danger and believed, by those who were best capable of jud[g]ing, to be coming on to certain death . . .[26]

It was the harbinger of more trouble to come with Wool. Meanwhile, Stevens conferred in the Walla Walla Valley with the volunteers about pushing

---

26. Stevens to Jefferson Davis, February 19, 1856, I.I. Stevens Correspondence, 1848–1857, Yale University Library. Stevens also wrote to Wool, telling him that he was complaining to Washington about his action. In reply, Wool wrote Stevens: "In your frankness and determination to represent me to the department, I trust you will be governed by truth, and by truth only. I disbanded no troops raised for your relief; and your communication gave me the first intelligence that any were raised for such a purpose." Stevens responded, in turn, by citing evidence that Wool had been told the purpose of the company, and by urging him to be governed, also, "by the truth, and the truth only." H. Stevens, *Stevens*, 2, 175, 183.

north across the Snake River after the Indians, but abandoned the idea because of the lack of boats with which to cross the Snake, as well as a shortage of rations for the troops. After thanking the Nez Perces, he sent them back to Lapwai with Bill Craig, instructing the old mountain man to muster them out of service, as if they had been a regularly enlisted body in the American forces, and to prepare a muster roll for them so that the government could pay them for their assistance. It was a calculated move, designed to keep them loyal by flattering them with a prospect of future pay, as well as to arouse a desire among other Nez Perces to share similar honor and favor from the Americans. At the same time, Stevens appointed one of his Indian agents, B. F. Shaw, a colonel in the Washington Territorial militia and directed him to organize the Walla Walla Valley whites and some friendly Wallawalla and Cayuse Indians in the vicinity into a military force and cooperate with the Oregon volunteers in guarding the area. Then, on January 1, 1856, he left for Olympia, planning to return in the spring to finish the job against the hostiles of the interior.

For the next few months his hands were full with the quelling of the Puget Sound uprising. But a good part of the time he fought with Wool. The old General was adamant in insisting that the settlers and territorial officials exaggerated the Indian threat and, in fact, kept stirring it up. He was particularly incensed at the volunteer units east of the Cascades, who, in his opinion, had no one to protect, since any American settlers in that part of the territory were there either illegally or with the permission of Indians who were therefore no threat to them. He had heard of the murder of Peopeo Moxmox and the revolting indignities to his corpse, as well as other atrocities committed by the volunteers against Indians in the interior, and he condemned those actions to Stevens and in reports to Washington, stating in addition that their net result was to turn friendly and neutral Indians into hostiles—an observation that should also have been clear to Stevens, but was not. Repeatedly, Wool argued that if the volunteers stopped provoking the Indians and got out of the interior country, the Indians would again become peaceful. He communicated that view to his field officers and directed them not to fight the Indians unless forced to do so, but to try to persuade them to become peaceful again. This so-called "peace policy" incurred the further wrath of Stevens and the settlers, who felt that the Indians had to be rendered powerless; as a result, the regular and volunteer units in the field during the following months often pursued separate and contradictory ends, which only confused them both, as well as the Indians.

At the same time, Wool persisted in trying to force the disbanding of the volunteer groups or their enrollment in the regular army, and Stevens as stubbornly continued to resist him.[27] Neither Wool nor Stevens accepted the strategic and tactical war plans of the other, and as hostilities dragged on, they blamed each other for the continuation of the war. Nevertheless, in western Washington, Stevens had his way, and by determined and vigorous action against the Indians gradually smashed their principal war bands and scattered or killed their leaders. A few companies of federal troops, as well as pro-white Indian auxiliaries, frightened, venal, or convinced that the Indians could not win, cooperated with him in a campaign that was mainly a series of skirmishes and forest ambushes. On at least two occasions Qualchin and war parties of Yakimas and Klickitats who were related to some of the Puget Sound natives crossed the Cascades to help the embattled Indians; but their assistance had little effect, and by the middle of March 1856 Stevens had broken forever the Indian power in western Washington. The next two months were marked by mopping up actions at the Sound and by the executions of Indian leaders. Some of the headmen and their families managed to flee across the mountains and find refuge with the Yakimas, but many others died in the woods and swamps of the Pacific slope, resisting to the end.

On the eastern side of the Cascades, meanwhile, Oregon volunteers, now under the command of Colonel Thomas R. Cornelius, were still based in the Walla Walla Valley, where they had the assistance of a military company composed of ten white men who lived in the vicinity and forty-three Nez Perces under Craig's friend and neighbor at Lapwai, Henri M. Chase. That group's origin had stemmed from Stevens' directive to B. F. Shaw in December 1855 to organize the whites in the valley into a militia unit. Shaw had had little success in doing so; and when he had left for Olympia, he had turned his orders over to Chase, who had enrolled a group of friendly Nez Perces in the unit, which appeared on Stevens' official rolls as Company "M" of mounted men of the Washington Territorial Volunteers.

Through the winter Cornelius' forces waged war on any questionable Indians they could find in the area, and provided Wool with numerous examples

27. Governor Curry of Oregon also opposed Wool. But Stevens, with a national reputation and powerful friends in Washington, was the more prominent of the two governors, and the controversy was waged principally between him and Wool. Joel Palmer, the Oregon Superintendent of Indian Affairs, it is interesting to note, did not always see eye to eye with Stevens. On November 21, 1855, he wrote Wool: "The reported combination of all these tribes with intent to wage a war of extermination against the whites, is, I apprehend, but a phantom conjured up in the brains of alarmists . . . and the plot said to have been nearly consummated of cutting off those engaged in the negotiations last June, I regard as of the same character." Helen Addison Howard and Dan L. McGrath, *War Chief Joseph* (Caldwell, Idaho, 1952), p. 51. The reference to the Indian "plot" at the Walla Walla council is strong evidence that Lawyer, or someone, was responsible for a hoax.

of provocative conduct. On one occasion a loitering Nez Perce was accused of being a spy and was hanged. The news horrified the federal officers, who were sure that the episode would play into the hands of the war faction of the powerful tribe. They were correct; the continued presence of the volunteers in the Walla Walla Valley, and their ruthlessness toward Indians, strained the collective patience of the Nez Perces almost to the breaking point. Yakima, Wallawalla, Palouse, and Cayuse warriors made frequent visits to the Nez Perce villages and whipped up a war fever that tested the oratorical powers of Lawyer, Timothy, Spotted Eagle, Jason, and others to the utmost. But, aided by Craig, those leaders managed to restrain the anger of such men as Looking Glass, Three Feathers, and Eagle From the Light; and Lawyer and Jason even persuaded their followers to demonstrate their continued respect for "the Law" by supporting the continued existence of Chase's troop and selling more than forty horses to Colonel Cornelius' forces. The use of the animals was provided to the Oregon Volunteers on credit, and in 1863 Lawyer and Jason were still complaining that although Cornelius had thus been enabled "to proceed and fight the Indians who were hostile, and many were killed both of men and horses," they had not yet been paid for the mounts.[28] Nor had the tribe been paid by 1877, when Lawyer and Jason were both dead.

In March 1856 the Oregon troops, having built six boats, finally crossed the Snake River and moved north through the Palouse country, seizing Indians' stock and shooting any Indians they came on. Toward the end of March they turned west toward the Columbia. When they reached the river, Cornelius sent part of his command back to the Walla Walla Valley and led the rest of it across the Columbia and up the Yakima River, searching for hostiles. On April 10, in an area of rocky hills and canyons on the lower part of the river, the volunteers ran into several hundred Yakimas and fought an all-day battle, in which few casualties were suffered by either side. The Indians disappeared at nightfall, and the next day Cornelius, whose men were running out of food, abandoned the Yakima country and hurried to The Dalles. The foray of the Oregonians had been fruitless, but it had served again to fire up the Nez Perces. White soldiers had now gone north and east of the Snake and Columbia rivers into country shared by Nez Perces, Palouses, and Spokans, and had frightened many Indians who had fled to Nez Perce villages. Henri M. Chase led his Indian detachment back to the Clearwater and disbanded it, and soon afterward the tribal leaders came together once more. In their debates during the following months Red Wolf and Joseph for the first time swung away from Lawyer and refused to argue against Looking Glass. Still, by a slim margin, no decision was made concerning what to do.

28. Proceedings of the Treaty Council at Lapwai (1863), pp. 24, 67, 101.

On the lower Columbia, in the meantime, eight companies of the 9th U.S. Infantry, under Colonel George H. Wright, had arrived from San Francisco to take over the conduct of the war against the interior tribes. Wright established headquarters at The Dalles; but on March 26 Indians came suddenly out of the wooded mountains at the portage of the Cascades, lower down on the river, and for several, terror-filled days laid siege to whites at several points in the vicinity. Yakimas and Klickitats, angered by the harassing actions of the volunteers, apparently led the retaliatory attack, although they were joined by a large number of the remnants of Chinookan bands that had lived along that part of the Columbia and were then known collectively to the settlers as Cascade Indians. It was the last defiant gesture of those once numerous people who had been debauched and decimated by the white man and his diseases, and they killed fifteen people before soldiers from Fort Vancouver and The Dalles arrived to overwhelm them and drive them away.

The territorial governors were quick to criticize Wright and the regulars for not having left an adequate guard at the vulnerable Cascades portage in their rear, but Wright's next move angered Stevens even more. Late in April the federal officer left The Dalles with an army of regulars on a peace-making excursion into the Yakimas' country. After a brief flurry of skirmishing, Wright reached the Naches River on May 9 and established a camp. The Yakima Indians had been observing his movements, but a controversy that had broken out among the headmen held back the warriors. The family bitterness that had long been brewing between Owhi and Kamiakin had finally steamed over, and Te-i-as and Owhi, supported by Quil-ten-e-nock and Moses, now decided that they had had enough fighting and wanted to try to make peace with the regulars. Kamiakin, still for resistance, could not launch an attack, and with about half of the warriors withdrew from the area and rode away to the Palouse country. The other chiefs, left with some 200 fighting men, took their time about treating with Wright. Messengers went back and forth; the headmen agreed to meetings and then, apparently remembering the fate of Peopeo Moxmox, thought better about it and failed to show up. Wright heard of interminable councils going on among the chiefs and of decisions that were made one day and changed the next. But he was patient. On May 27 his second in command, Lieutenant Colonel Edward J. Steptoe, joined him with more troops, bringing his total to more than 500 men.

Finally, on June 9, Te-i-as and Owhi crossed the Naches River and came into Wright's camp. They had a frank talk, during which the Yakimas told Wright that the Walla Walla treaty, which Stevens had forced them to accept, had caused the war. Wright replied with understanding, but told the Indians that if they continued fighting, he had a force "large enough to wipe them off the earth." He was willing to spare them, however, and directed them to bring in all their people and surrender everything they had captured or stolen from white people, and to comply within five days. "I have never seen Indians more delighted than these were," he wrote of Te-i-as and Owhi.[29] The chiefs left; but they either changed their minds or were still too distrustful of white men's motives, for instead of surrendering, they and most of their people trailed peacefully off to fishing camps on rivers in the mountains farther west and north. After waiting in vain for them, Wright finally left Steptoe and a detachment of troops at the Naches and marched north toward the Wenatchi country. There was no concentration of warriors now to oppose his movements, and from time to time he came on frightened and unprotected camps of Indians. Without having to resort to arms, he rounded up almost 500 men, women, and children, mostly Yakimas and Klickitats, and sent them to The Dalles to be placed on the newly established Warm Springs reservation in central Oregon. Then, returning to the south, he located a site for a permanent fort on Simcoe Creek south of the Ahtanum, left a detail of men to build and garrison it, and, considering that he had successfully ended the difficulties with the Yakimas, withdrew the bulk of his command to The Dalles. "The whole country between the Cascade Mountains and the Columbia River should be given over to the Indians, as it is not necessary to the whites," he reported on his return.

Stevens meanwhile had concluded his campaign in western Washington, and had turned his attention to the eastern side of the Cascades, where Wright at the time was still in contact with the Yakima chiefs. Stevens had little patience with Wright's peacemaking operation, and on June 12, believing that Kamiakin and the Yakimas would eventually have to be crushed in battle, sent a force of 175 mounted Washington territorial volunteers under Colonel B. F. Shaw across the Cascades to offer their services to Wright's infantrymen.[30] Shaw, a tall, angular man with long, red hair and the beard of a biblical prophet, arrived to find Wright treating peaceably not only with the Yakimas but with several of the Indian leaders of the Puget Sound uprising

29. Splawn, *Ka-mi-akin*, p. 78.

30. The wide divergence between the aims of Stevens and Wright at this time is well illustrated by a letter Stevens wrote Jefferson Davis from Olympia on May 23, 1856. He hoped, he said, that the Yakimas would strike Wright, because he knew that the federal troops would drive the Indians back and across the Columbia River. But he thought that the wily Indians, instead, would choose to harass Wright's foot soldiers and make them use up their provisions. In that kind of warfare the mounted volunteers would be needed to pursue the Indians to their hiding places, so he was organizing a force of 200 horsemen to send to Wright. The idea of peace could not enter Stevens' thinking, because he was committed to clearing the Indians from land needed by settlers and the railroad. I. I. Stevens Correspondence, 1848–1857, Yale University Library.

who had fled across the mountains. He was angry, but Wright quickly let him know that the volunteers were not welcome; and Shaw, still looking for a fight somewhere, and following Stevens' directions regarding what to do if Wright did not need him, headed his command toward the Walla Walla Valley, where the Oregon volunteers had not yet felt the restraining hand of the regulars.[31]

Stevens regarded possession of the Walla Walla Valley as the key to a successful campaign against the interior tribes. From there, troops could smash at the Wallawallas, Cayuses, Umatillas, and other hostile tribes in the south, and at the Palouses, Yakimas, and other enemies in the north, whom the volunteers would sweep westward across the Columbia to entrap between themselves and Wright's regulars in the Yakima country. Equally important, volunteers working out of the Walla Walla Valley could establish liaison with Nez Perce auxiliaries and with their help act as a wall between the hostiles and peoples like the Coeur d'Alenes and Spokans who were still neutral. He was particularly concerned about isolating the neutrals from agitators who came to them from hostile bands, and, as if unaware that Indians could see and judge for themselves, spoke constantly of enemy Indians who were "infecting" uncommitted tribes.

The disposition of the Nez Perces, the most powerful of the interior tribes, was constantly on his mind, and with reason. On both May 29 and June 8 Craig wrote him rather desperate letters from Lapwai, telling him of the alarming surge of war fever among the headmen and reminding him that supplies, arms, and ammunition that Stevens had promised the Nez Perces had not yet arrived. The situation was so bad, in fact, said Craig, that he and Henri Chase might soon have to flee for their lives with a small group of Indians under Lawyer, Spotted Eagle, and Timothy, who were still loyal to the Americans.[32] The appeals moved Stevens to action. He wrote Wright that Kamiakin was making "every exertion to induce the tribes thus far friendly

31. On June 6, 1856, Wool had written Assistant Adjutant General Lorenzo Thomas in New York: "Colonel Wright is now in the Yakima country . . . He has had several interviews with a number of chiefs who appear to want peace, and remarks, 'I believe these Indians desire peace and I must find out what outside influence is operating to keep them from coming in.' It is reported to me that Governor Stevens had ordered two hundred volunteers to the Yakima country . . . If this should be true, I should consider it very unfortunate, for they are not wanted in that region . . . Colonel Wright required no volunteers to bring the Indians to terms and he so informed Governor Stevens. The latter, however, as I believe, is determined, if possible, to prevent the regulars from terminating the war . . ." Splawn, *Ka-mi-akin*, p. 76.

32. In 1863 Lawyer claimed that "eighty of our people gathered themselves for the defense of Craig and Chase." Proceedings of the Lapwai Treaty Council (1863), p. 68.

to join in the war," that "he has flattered the Spokanes, where he was on the 25th of May, and has endeavored to browbeat the Nez Perces," and that he hoped the regulars would cooperate in a plan to push the hostiles eastward from the Cascades and westward from the Palouse country and "prevent the extension of the war." [33] At the same time he went to The Dalles himself and on June 22 personally supervised the dispatch of another column of Washington volunteers to the Walla Walla Valley with the promised supplies and ammunition for the Nez Perces. Some of these men left the train at the Umatilla, where they turned south to help the Oregon volunteers who had become enmeshed in hostilities with a number of bands between the John Day River and the Snake; but the rest reached the Walla Walla Valley on July 9 and joined Shaw's men, who had just arrived from the Yakima country. A message had also been sent to Lapwai, where Craig's position was still a risky one; and on the same day, the former mountain man, now carrying the title of lieutenant colonel in the Washington forces, appeared with a troop of seventy-five Nez Perces under Spotted Eagle, the most respected buffalo hunter and war leader of the part of the tribe that Lawyer still controlled.[34] Those Indians gave Shaw assurances that the tribe as a whole was still friendly to the Americans, and, accepting their word, Shaw assigned only one man, A. H. Robie, to take the train of Indian goods to the Nez Perce country, with Craig and Spotted Eagle's troop going along as escort.

Shaw, meanwhile, scouted around for hostiles. According to his acting adjutant, Captain Walter W. DeLacy, who kept the official account of the vol-

33. H. Stevens, *Stevens*, 2, 199.

34. This new unit, composed principally of Indians who had served with Chase under Colonel Cornelius, and who had then provided security for Chase and Craig at Lapwai, became known simply as Shaw's "Indian Auxiliaries." On July 9, 1856, Captain Walter W. DeLacy, Acting Adjutant in Shaw's group, who was keeping an official account of the activities of Shaw's command, described the meeting between the Washington volunteers and Craig's troop under Spotted Eagle at Mill Creek in the upper Walla Walla Valley: "In 4 miles we perceived the Nez Perce Camp and the Nez Perce warriors probably to the number of 100 approaching, singing, dressed in their gayest attire, splendidly mounted and bearing aloft a large American Flag which had been presented to them at the Council last year by Gov. Stevens. They formed in line on the prairie with the regularity of Dragoons, the Flag in the centre, still continuing their chant. The Battalion was then formed by the Adjutant in close column of two, and moved steadily past the line. As it passed they fired a salute. The Volunteers gave three lusty cheers for the stars and stripes—and drawing their revolvers returned the salute, and without halting continued their march." "Itinerary of the March of the Right Wing of the Second Regiment of W. T. Vols. under Command of Lt. Col. Shaw," report to Stevens written by Walter W. DeLacy, MS in Isaac I. Stevens Correspondence, 1848–1857, Western Americana Collection, Yale Library. The volunteers and the Nez Perces were equally fond of the formalities of a military spectacle.

unteers' actions, the impatient, red-haired colonel now believed that the arch enemy, Kamiakin, was well beyond his reach and that he would therefore take a look through the Grande Ronde Valley in the south, because large groups of hostiles often frequented that area. "A trusty guide was found among the Nez Perce indians who engaged to take us thither by a new route," DeLacy wrote.

The Indian guide was Lawyer's friend, Captain John, who had accompanied Stevens to the Blackfoot council and had been a private in the Stevens Guards. He now led the volunteers across the Blue Mountains and into the Grande Ronde. Part of that grassy prairie had been specifically reserved for Joseph's Nez Perce band under the Walla Walla treaty, and the rest was still legally the possession of Cayuses and Umatillas, who had traditionally shared the valley with the Nez Perces. Shaw's invasion, almost forgotten today, was a trouble-making trespass. On July 17, about eight miles southeast of present-day Elgin, the volunteers from Washington—now in Oregon—came on a large camp, composed principally of Cayuse and Wallawalla women, children, and old men. A few warriors were present, but none of the tribal spokesmen or principal war leaders were in the vicinity. The Indians were thrown into a panic by the appearance of the soldiers, and commenced packing. Some of the warriors rode forward in an attempt to screen the people, and Shaw directed Captain John to go up to them and ask for a parley. The Nez Perce started forward but wheeled around suddenly and came back, claiming that the Cayuses had called out to each other to shoot him. Thereupon, Shaw ordered the volunteers to charge the camp. The Indians broke and fled, scattering in all directions, as the whites swooped savagely in among them. Several times, small knots of warriors tried to make a stand among rocks and trees, but the volunteers dispersed them. Men, women, and children ran in terror, and Shaw's men, inflamed with racial hatred, chased them and cut them down. Many of the Indians managed to find cover in the brush along the river bottom, and eventually they got away to high, rocky ground. But Shaw's report summarized the massacre: "The enemy was run on the gallop for 15 miles, and most of those who fell were shot with the revolver. It is impossible to state how many of the enemy were killed. Twenty-seven bodies were counted by one individual, and many others we know to have fallen and been left, but were so scattered about that it was impossible to get count of them." The volunteers also destroyed everything they found in the Indians' camp, including some 150 horse loads of camas roots, dried beef, flour, tents, and other provisions and supplies.[35]

35. Historians have generally relied on Colonel Shaw's official report for their version and interpretation of this so-called Battle of the Grande Ronde. However, that document was presented by Stevens to the Washington Territorial legislature that

After the raid, which cost Shaw five men killed and four wounded, the volunteers returned to the Walla Walla Valley. They exulted in their "victory," and Shaw, with Stevens' help, publicized the episode as a great triumph by the Washington volunteer army over an important body of hostiles, contrasting the action with Wright's peaceful—and seemingly ineffective—policy against the Yakimas. As soon as they reached the Walla Walla, however, the volunteers received a shock. Robie, who had taken the train of supplies to the Nez Perces, was back, having been driven out of the Nez Perce country by angry Indians. The anti-Lawyer element had seemed to be in control, at last, and their leaders had announced that they were going to order every white man, including Craig and Henri Chase, out of their lands. Fearing for his life, Robie had turned his train around at once and had hastened back to the Walla Walla, marching 100 miles without halting.[36]

Robie had not been wrong about the Nez Perces' temper. The reappearance of volunteers in the Walla Walla Valley had confirmed the correctness of Wool's policy. Once again, the anti-Lawyer leaders of the tribe had maintained that the settlers' soldiers had had no business being there, and again the unruly and free-wheeling troopers had committed outrages on the Indians. In their march from the Yakima country, and during their brief stay in the Walla Walla Valley before they had started for the Grande Ronde, some of Shaw's men had shot Indians for the sport of it, and had stolen and killed livestock that had belonged to friendly Indians. Many of the Washington volunteers had refused to accept the discipline of their commanders, and Shaw had not even been able to hold his companies together. The depredations and brigandage had been reported to the Nez Perces, and those among them who were for peace at any price had been forced further on the defensive. When Robie had arrived, the tribe had been close to a decision to fight if the volunteers moved toward their country. They had ordered Stevens' emissary to get out with his goods but for the moment had allowed Craig to stay. The former mountain man still lived on his Lapwai claim with his Nez Perce wife and children. His father-in-law, old James, was still alive, but he could make no promise to protect Craig. From their homes, Craig and Henri Chase sent

convened in December 1856, and shows evidence of having been edited to make it conform to Stevens' point of view. A better source for the volunteers' point of view of what happened is the original report, prepared by DeLacy for Stevens. The manuscript is in the Stevens Correspondence, 1848–57, file in the Western Americana Collection of the Yale Library. The Indians' point of view, communicated by the Cayuse headman, "Howlish Wampum," to Wright, was sent by Wright to Major W. W. Mackall, Assistant Adjutant General, Department of the Pacific, on October 31, 1856, and is found in Brown, *The Indian Side of the Story*, pp. 159–60.

36. Stevens to Jefferson Davis, August 14, 1856, Stevens Correspondence, 1848–1857, Yale University Library.

letters across the Bitterroots to their friend, John Owen, informing him of their dangerous situation. "Col Wm. Craig writes that he May be obliged to leave the Country after being with them some 15 years," Owen noted in his journal on July 31, 1856. "Married & reared a family among them. Their hearts are Sore about something." Another letter about the Nez Perces, written by Pearson, the express rider, who was still traveling regularly between Olympia and the Flatheads, reached Owen at the same time, and the trader noted that "the leaders of this Warlike Party are Old Looking Glass Three Feather Joseph & two or three others." [37]

Robie's report of the Nez Perces' hostility was ominous, but Shaw was flushed with victory, and he reacted as if he were ready to cope with the whole Nez Perce nation. He sent Captain John to Lapwai with a letter, offering peace to the headmen but threatening that "if they beat their drums for war, he would parade his men for battle." Captain John returned soon afterward with a buoyant message from Craig, saying that news of the Grande Ronde fight had just reached the Nez Perces and was having a chastening effect on them. Lawyer once more seemed to be in control, and the Nez Perces had announced that they still wanted to obey the laws and be friends of the Americans. The report pleased Shaw and gave support to his contention—later seconded by Stevens—that the determined actions of the volunteers and the raid in the Grande Ronde had been responsible for maintaining the loyalty of the Nez Perces. The reasons that their loyalty had wavered in the first place, Stevens eventually maintained, were that hostile Cayuses had visited their kindred among the Nez Perces and stirred up disaffection among them, and Yakimas, whom Wright should have kept away from the Nez Perces, had got to the tribe too and had threatened them with punishment unless they joined the war. [38]

Actually, Nez Perce fear of the Yakimas had nothing to do with their war feeling. But Shaw and Stevens were right in their conclusions about the effect of the Battle of the Grande Ronde, as it was called. The raid had stripped the Cayuses and Wallawallas of much of their food and many of their possessions and had hurt their morale. But it had also disheartened many of the Nez Perce villagers who were already riddled with doubts about what would happen to them if they decided to fight the Americans. As Craig noted, the battle resulted in a braking of the Nez Perce trend to war, and provided new sup-

---

37. Dunbar and Phillips, *Journals and Letters of John Owen*, 1, 137. However, H. H. Bancroft, quoting a letter by Pearson that appeared in a newspaper west of the Cascades early in August 1856, says the express rider named the hostile chiefs as Looking Glass, Three Feathers, Red Bear, Eagle From the Light, Red Wolf, and "Man with a Rope in His Mouth." Bancroft, *History of Washington*, p. 168 n.
38. H. Stevens, *Stevens*, 2, 202.

port for the pacifism of men like Lawyer. But at the same time, the anger of Looking Glass, who still wanted to go to war, increased, as did the bitterness and frustrations of men like Red Wolf and Joseph, who by now had adopted an animosity against white men, although they believed that the welfare and safety of their people were more important than the misery that would come with a war. They had no interest any longer in Spalding's Christian teachings, which now seemed unmasked as white men's hypocrisy and deceit, and they turned their backs on Craig and other whites who said they were their friends. On August 1, as an indication of the tense atmosphere that existed among the tribe, Henri Chase finally departed from Lapwai with his family and rode across the Bitterroots to find a safer home for himself near John Owen in the Bitterroot Valley.[39]

At Olympia, meanwhile, Stevens was following the events in the interior and chafing over his remoteness from the scenes of action. In late July, after he had heard of the fight in the Grande Ronde and Robie's trouble with the Nez Perces, he decided to go to Walla Walla and hold another council with the tribes. The purpose of his decision is not clear, but it appears that Wool's charge that Stevens was deliberately prolonging the war and did not want peace was getting under his skin, and that he felt that he had to make some sort of a gesture to convince the regular officers in the field that Wool was wrong. At the same time, he may have hoped that he could bully the tribes, face to face, into submitting to his authority, and by ending the war on his own terms eliminate Wool from the scene. Whatever his reasons were, he sent messages to Shaw and Craig to summon all the neutral tribes in the interior to meet him at the head of the Walla Walla Valley in the middle of September, and to invite all hostile bands to attend also, with the condition that they come unarmed under a guarantee of safe conduct and agree to end the war and submit to the government.

Stevens left Olympia on August 11 and stopped at Fort Vancouver, where he asked Wright to accompany him to the Walla Walla and see for himself whether he was fair to the Indians. He made no impression on the federal officer, who had just received instructions from Wool to send regulars to the Walla Walla country, oust Shaw's volunteers, and establish peace among the tribes in that region. Wright told Stevens that he could not make the trip himself but that he would order Lieutenant Colonel Steptoe and four companies of regulars to go to the council, relieve the volunteers, and build a permanent post there. The two men traveled together to The Dalles to talk to Steptoe; and although Stevens promised to send his volunteers home as soon as Steptoe took over on the Walla Walla, Wright secretly gave his junior officer General Wool's orders, telling him that if the volunteers refused to leave, he

39. Dunbar and Phillips, *Journals of John Owen, 1,* 139.

was to arrest and disarm them, and expel them, forcibly if necessary, from the Indian country. Stevens' council with the tribes, Wright hoped, would result in the end of hostilities; but if it did not, Wright meant to establish peace himself, and that could only be done by removing the volunteers who had been harassing the Indians.

Unaware of those instructions to Steptoe, Stevens left The Dalles on August 19, traveling with a large train of Indian goods in advance of the column of regulars. He reached Shaw's men in the valley on August 23 and a few days later was upset when a band of Indians captured part of the pack train a few miles from his camp. In a stern lecture to the volunteers, he told them that even when they were outnumbered they could defeat the Indians by bold and repeated charges. "In this way only can the superiority of our race be established," he said.

On August 30 the Indians began to arrive, and by September 11 the council was ready to begin. A large number of Nez Perces, some of whom had come with Craig, were on hand, although Looking Glass had stayed away. Cayuses, Umatillas, and Wallawallas, many of them with unconcealed hostility, were there, as well as members of bands from the John Day and Deschutes river regions of Oregon. The Spokans and Coeur d'Alenes had declined to come, and none of the Yakimas or upper Columbia River bands were represented, although there were rumors that Kamiakin and other Yakimas were on their way.

The council was an awkward one. For two days Stevens lectured the Indians on the justice of the treaties he had signed with them, and the treachery of the Indians who had murdered white men and gone to war. Most of the Indians listened in hostile silence. On the second day Stevens asked them to speak their minds, but none of the headmen wished to talk. Finally, two chiefs exclaimed that the Indians were determined to have their lands, and would fight for them. Eagle From the Light reminded the Governor of the Nez Perce whom the Oregon volunteers had hanged in the Walla Walla Valley the previous winter. Stevens replied that he did not know the facts of the case but would find out. Then, when he made no further progress, he adjourned the council for the day.

Steptoe and the regulars had arrived previously and had established a camp eight miles above the council grounds. True to his promise, Stevens had then started Shaw's volunteers on their way home, keeping only one company of 69 men for his protection at the council. But the meeting with the Indians was now going so badly that, on the morning of the third day, he sent a message to Steptoe, asking him for a company of regulars to help safeguard his camp. Before he received an answer, he opened the day's session, which went from bad to worse. He explained that the Nez Perce who had been hanged had been accused of being a spy. But a Nez Perce leader named Speaking Owl abruptly changed the subject. "Will you give us back our lands?" he demanded. "That is what we all want to hear about; that is what troubles us. I ask plainly to have a plain answer." [40] Stevens ignored him, and urged Lawyer to say something. The head chief, called on to repeat his performance of the original Walla Walla council, obliged, reminding the other Nez Perces that they had signed the treaty, and should stand by it. Timothy and James said they agreed, but Joseph, Red Wolf, Eagle From the Light, and Speaking Owl all rose to argue with Lawyer and tell Stevens that they had not understood the treaty, that they had had no intention of giving away any land, and that Lawyer had sold it unfairly.

Stevens could see that he was getting nowhere, and that the friendly headmen among the Nez Perces no longer held the balance of power in the tribe. Although his situation was not dangerous, it could become so at any time, especially because there were reports that Kamiakin and Owhi were somewhere in the neighborhood. In the afternoon, however, the Governor was stunned by a message from Steptoe, who stated that "in execution of certain instructions received from General Wool," he could not detach a portion of his command to send to Stevens' assistance, and suggested, instead, that Stevens move his party to Steptoe's camp. Stevens considered it an insult, but he held his temper, and the next day, as his uneasiness increased, he moved his party to the camp of the regulars. On the way, he came suddenly on Kamiakin, Owhi, and Qualchin, who had encamped the night before on the Touchet River not far from the council grounds. To Stevens they were the most dangerous Indians present; but Judge William Brown's many years of research among the Yakimas, summarized in his study *The Indian Side of the Story*, reveals significant information concerning Kamiakin at that stage of his career that Stevens would not have known about. Since part of it was confirmed independently by A. J. Splawn, another long-time researcher of Yakima history, it is relevant to mention it here.

It will be recalled that during the Yakimas' negotiations with Colonel Wright, Kamiakin's plea to continue the fighting had been outvoted by the other headmen, and Kamiakin had ridden away, leaving the peacemaking to Te-i-as and Owhi. During the following months he had lived with his father's relatives in the Palouse country but had made occasional visits to the Spokans

40. Speaking Owl was probably a young headman from the present-day Stites area of the South Fork of the Clearwater, who was named Koolkool Snehee (Salish for Red Owl), and was just beginning to gain prominence as a leading spokesman of the anti-white faction of the Nez Perces. In 1878 Duncan McDonald described him as "eloquent, sagacious . . . noted as an Apollo among belles of the tribe." The *New Northwest*, Deer Lodge, Montana, June 7, 1878.

and Coeur d'Alenes, recounting his grievances against the white men and urging support for continued resistance. Farther west, meanwhile, Quil-ten-e-nock, the leader of the Sinkiuse (the Salish who lived in the country bordering the Columbia River northeast of the Yakima lands), had had a greater grievance. Kamiakin had signed away the country of the Sinkiuse at the Walla Walla council, and Quil-ten-e-nock, a young patriot in his early 30s, had fought by the side of the Yakimas in some of their engagements with the whites. But he, too, had made peace with Wright, and the federal officer had then given him a letter "acknowledging his valuable services in bringing about the peace of the Yakima." [41] According to Brown, when Quil-ten-e-nock learned of Stevens' second council at Walla Walla, he decided to go there, tell Stevens that Kamiakin had had no authority to sell his country, and get the Governor to promise that his people could continue to occupy their villages. He had persuaded Owhi, Qualchin, and Kamiakin to come with him to confirm to Stevens that a mistake had been made at the first council, and that an injustice had been done to the Sinkiuse.

The evidence supports this story. The Yakimas made no sign of hostility during Stevens' second council, and neither Kamiakin nor Owhi attended the sessions. But Quil-ten-e-nock did show his letter from Wright to the Governor and, apparently, made an unsuccessful attempt to discuss his land problem with him. Stevens, however, must have brushed him aside—perhaps not understanding what he was talking about—and when the council ended, Quil-ten-e-nock was enraged, as will be seen, and attacked the Governor's party. There is no other explanation for the Sinkiuse chief's sudden anger.[42]

Meanwhile, the council met again for two more days near Steptoe's camp, and Stevens' position failed to improve. Lawyer and his followers among the Nez Perces, whom Stevens reckoned as numbering half the tribe, supported the treaties, but everyone else demanded that the agreements be done away with. Reaching an impasse, the Governor finally ended the council on September 17, telling the Indians, "Follow your hearts; those who wish to go into the war go." When it was over, the friendly Nez Perces advised him that the tribe was so wrought up that they could no longer guarantee Craig's safety among them, and Stevens ordered the former mountain man to leave Lapwai and establish his agency near Steptoe's camp in the Walla Walla Valley. On the day after the council, Stevens watched in anger as Steptoe met with the Indians and announced to them, "My mission is pacific. I have not come to fight you, but to live among you . . . I trust we shall live together as friends."

Still, the Governor's troubles were not over. The only Indians who seemed

41. H. Stevens, *Stevens*, 2, 223.
42. For the full account see Brown, *The Indian Side of the Story*, pp. 169–76.

willing to remain friendly to him were a band of fifty Nez Perce warriors loyal to Lawyer and led by Spotted Eagle. On September 19 they set off with Craig and the one company of Washington volunteers to help escort Stevens back to The Dalles. Meanwhile, the angry Sinkiuse chief, Quil-ten-e-nock, aroused a group of young Indians with his complaints, and despite Steptoe's speech of friendship to them they suddenly set fire to the grass needed by Steptoe's horses. Other mounted warriors from different bands joined them, and the party, swollen now to an excited mob, started after Stevens to show him their contempt. Coming upon the Governor about three miles from Steptoe's camp, they opened fire. Stevens made a corral of his wagons, and a crackling firefight raged all afternoon. The only leaders Stevens could make out were Quil-ten-e-nock and Owhi's tempestuous son, Qualchin, but he claimed that the party included Yakimas, Palouses, Wallawallas, Umatillas, and 120 of the hostile Nez Perces, numbering in all about 450 warriors. It is probable that he exaggerated the size of the combatant group, since the Indians later reported that most of their people were merely spectators who had ridden along to watch the excitement from the background. The charges and countercharges were wild, yelling affairs, and at one point the Indians called out to Stevens' escort of friendly Nez Perces, "We came not to fight the Nez Perces, but the whites; go to your camp, or we wipe it out." Stevens was afraid for Spotted Eagle's group, and he directed the chief to withdraw with his warriors, lest the whites shoot some of them by mistake. After the loyal troop had left, Stevens continued the battle, and managed to hold off the enemy through the rest of the day. In the evening he sent to Steptoe for help, and the federal officer dispatched some dragoons with a mountain howitzer to bring Stevens' men back to his camp. The next morning the Indians attacked Steptoe's position, but the regulars soon drove them off and dispersed them with rounds from the howitzer.

Steptoe was disillusioned by the Indians' action, which seemed to vindicate Stevens' views concerning the only way to deal with the tribes. Aided by the Governor's men, he built a blockhouse and stockade during the next three days, left one company to defend it, and on September 23 marched the rest of his force down the Columbia with Stevens' party. On the way he sent Colonel Wright a note, reflecting his altered opinion of the Indians. "In general terms," he wrote, "I may say that in my judgment we are reduced to the necessity of waging a vigorous war, striking the Cayuses at the Grande Ronde, and Kam-i-ah-kan wherever he may be found."

Wright, still taking orders from Wool, overruled him. Steptoe and Stevens reached The Dalles on October 2, and the Governor, who had now withdrawn all his volunteers from the interior, returned to Olympia. On October 5

Wright and Steptoe with an enlarged force of regulars, started upriver again. In the Walla Walla Valley, Wright once more called in the tribal leaders for a meeting. Few of the bands responded, and only five of the important chiefs, three Cayuses and two Nez Perces—Red Wolf and Eagle From the Light— showed up. In a council with them, however, the federal officer won their attention and respect by seeming to show, at last, that a white chief understood the Indians' complaints against Stevens. Wright told them that he was satisfied that the Indians wanted only to be left alone by the whites, and that he accepted their statements that the Walla Walla treaties had been the cause of the war. The treaties, he assured them, had not yet been ratified, and until they were, his troops would keep white men out of their lands. Then, offering them peace and good will, he said, "The bloody shirt shall now be washed and not a spot left on it . . . All past differences must be thrown behind us . . . Let peace and friendship remain forever."

The delighted headmen quickly spread the news through the interior country. By November 1856 peace had settled over the land. At Wright's direction Steptoe constructed a permanent military post, Fort Walla Walla, on Mill Creek, six miles from its juncture with the Walla Walla River, and it became the beginning of the present Washington city of that same name. Then, by order of General Wool, Steptoe issued a proclamation formally barring the country east of the Cascades to all whites except missionaries, Hudson's Bay Company employees, and prospectors going to the northern mining districts.

The glad tidings wrought a change over the Nez Perces. With white settlers excluded, the fears and hostility of the bands subsided. Lawyer and his followers were uneasy because the treaties were not yet signed by the President, and other Indians were beginning to tell them laughingly that they would never get the payments and gifts that Stevens had promised them at the Walla Walla council. But Lawyer was shrewd enough to know that his position as leader continued to rest primarily on the white men's acceptance of him as the tribe's head chief, and he was willing to be patient. He visited Fort Walla Walla regularly, and, as Looking Glass's influence declined and other headmen like Red Wolf swung again to his support, he invited Craig to come back to Lapwai. The old mountain man returned with his family and took up his claim again on the reservation.

Stevens was furious at the abandonment of the country and the barring of settlers. In a scorching letter to Jefferson Davis he attacked Wright for having made peace with Red Wolf and the very Indians who, he claimed, had assaulted him at his last meeting in the Walla Walla Valley, and added, "It seems to me that we have in this Territory fallen upon evil times. I hope and trust some energetic action may be taken to stop this trifling with great public interests, and to make our flag respected by the Indians of the interior." [43] The Governor's active role with the upriver tribes, however, was finished. At Olympia he became embroiled in political quarrels with the settlers, and early in 1857, during a legal controversy, he was censured by the territorial legislature. Nevertheless, the same year he ran successfully for the office of delegate to Congress, and in the fall departed for the national capital with his family. He occupied much of his time in Washington attacking the federal officers who had opposed him in the West, defending his Indian policies, and working for the ratification of the treaties he had negotiated at Walla Walla. They were finally accepted by the Senate and signed by the President in 1859, four years after the council. When the Civil War came, Stevens entered it as a Union officer and at the age of 44 was killed at the Battle of Chantilly on September 1, 1862. History's judgment of him must be that he was a brave, capable, and energetic executive. His work on the Pacific railroad survey was outstanding, and his achievements in connection with that project were breathtaking when compared to the results of the other survey parties. But his Indian policies were unjust and led to wars that need not have occurred, and his ambition and stubbornness resulted in death and misery to many Indians.

Wool also left the West. The territorial governments continued their agitation against him, and in the spring of 1857 General Newman S. Clarke replaced him as commanding officer of the Department of the Pacific. Clarke, however, continued Wool's policies, and the settlers, for the time being, were no better off. In another change, the office of territorial governor in Washington was stripped of its authority over Indian affairs, and Colonel J. W. Nesmith, who had led the Oregon volunteers against the Yakimas in 1855, was appointed Superintendent of Indian Affairs for both Oregon and Washington.

The peace in the interior country, which lasted throughout 1857, turned out to be more of an armed truce. By early 1858—even though the treaties had not yet been ratified—the inexorable pressure of the whites to get into the Indian country was again stirring trouble. Large numbers of miners, in groups of a few up to more than a hundred, crossed the Indians' lands, beating their way back and forth between the coast and the mining centers at Colville and the Fraser River in British Columbia. Many of the prospectors had come from California, where miners' posses had held the lives of Indians to be cheap and had exterminated whole bands of Indians for the sport of killing; and their hostility and arrogance, unchanged in the north, soon led to Indian

---

43. Stevens to Davis, November 21, 1856, Stevens Correspondence, 1848–1857, Yale University Library.

retaliation and fights in which both Indians and miners were killed. Qualchin and Quil-ten-e-nock were among the most active in opposition to the miners, and when Quil-ten-e-nock was slain in one of the skirmishes on his own land, many warriors were roused to avenge his death.

At the same time there were additional causes of unrest. Lieutenant John Mullan had been ordered to survey a route for a wagon road from Fort Benton at the head of navigation on the Missouri to the site of the old Walla Walla fur-trading post on the Columbia; and the Coeur d'Alenes, who had made no treaty with Stevens, were dismayed to learn that the white man's road would go directly through their country. They told their fears to Father Joseph Joset, the Jesuit priest at the Sacred Heart mission on their lands, but he was unable to interfere with the government's plans. Farther south, there was increasing trouble also in the vicinities of Fort Simcoe among the Yakimas and the new Fort Walla Walla, which Steptoe still commanded. Both forts were gathering places for Indians, many of whom were considered friendly and who were employed as interpreters, scouts, and spies among the bands in the surrounding countryside.

The so-called "friendlies" sometimes played the double game of keeping their own people informed of the intentions and movements of the troops; but a few of them were troublemakers who, for reasons of revenge, ambition, or personal gain, created misunderstandings and whipped up conflicts between inoffensive bands and the soldiers. Frequently, difficulties began when a "friendly" known to the other Indians as an agent of the troops would steal horses or cattle from Indian herds. In time the Indians' patience would crack, and warriors would retaliate with raids on the troopers' herds.

The ferment in all parts of the interior increased gradually, but by March 1858 the unrest north of the Snake River and east of the Columbia had become critical. Many miners, as well as Indians, had been killed, and rumors were prevalent that Kamiakin, Qualchin, Owhi, and a number of Spokan, Palouse, Coeur d'Alene, and Columbia River headmen were again plotting an uprising.[44] Steptoe had watched events in the north uneasily. At one point he had received a petition signed by forty white men in the Colville area asking for military protection. Finally, on April 17, after some Palouse Indians had raided horse and cattle herds in the Walla Walla Valley, he decided to lead an

---

44. Jack Dozier, "The Coeur d'Alene Indians in the War of 1858," *Idaho Yesterdays*, 5 (Fall, 1961), 23, states that Kamiakin held a council with the Coeur d'Alenes, Palouses, Cayuses, Spokans, and Nez Perces in the early spring of 1858 and "made an impassioned plea for a general uprising," telling them that "the military would soon invade them to take their tribal holdings and enslave their women." The young men of the Coeur d'Alenes, says Dozier, were for immediate war, but cooler heads prevailed, and it was decided to fight only if invaded.

expedition into the Palouse and Spokan countries from Fort Walla Walla "to stop this thieving." He did not get going until early May, by which time he wrote his superiors that he expected to encounter "considerable disturbance among the neighboring tribes, but I hope to check it."

He left the fort on May 6 with more than 150 mounted men, two howitzers, and a long pack train that included civilian and Indian packers, guides, and interpreters. At the mouth of Alpowa Creek, Timothy's people helped ferry the command across the Snake River, and Timothy, together with his brother Levi, Levi's son, and a few members of Timothy's band, accompanied the troops on their march.[45]

Proceeding north up Skalassams Creek, the expedition reached the Palouse River, where it was visited by a delegation of worried Spokans who asked Steptoe why he was invading their country. He told them that he had not come to fight, that he was on his way to the Colville country, where there was some trouble between the miners and the Indians, and that his only aim was to find out what had happened there and try to restore peace. But Steptoe was far east of the usual route to the Colville country, which trailed north from the mouth of the Palouse River, where he should have crossed the Snake if he was telling the truth, and his answer failed to satisfy the Indians. They guessed that his real interest was in the countries of the Palouses, Spokans, and Coeur d'Alenes.

Steptoe pushed forward, and on the morning of May 16, after he had passed the vicinity of present-day Rosalia, southeast of Spokane, he found himself suddenly in trouble. Scouts reported that Indians were watching the troops from their flanks and that scattered bands of Palouses, Spokans, Coeur d'Alenes, and Yakimas were gathering in the hills ahead. Toward noon the main body of soldiers sighted the Indians, "all armed, painted, and defiant." [46]

The warriors offered no resistance, but rode ominously along with the troops. Twice, delegations of headmen came over to ask Steptoe to go back, but he repeated that he was merely traveling through their country and meant them no harm.

As the Indians' numbers increased, Steptoe realized the gravity of his situation. In camp that night he decided to withdraw, and at daylight on the 17th, with the Indians taunting his men and calling on them to fight, he sent a Nez Perce scout to Fort Walla Walla with a call for reinforcements, and began a retreat to the Snake River. Father Joset, who had hurried to the scene from the Sacred Heart mission to try to keep the Coeur d'Alenes out of trouble,

45. Historians have long argued over whether Timothy actually went with Steptoe. But all of them seem to have overlooked Lawyer's statement at the 1863 treaty council at Lapwai: "Timothy and some of my people accompanied him." Proceedings of the Treaty Council at Lapwai (1863), p. 67.

46. Annual Report of the Secretary of War (1858; Washington, D.C., 1859), p. 346.

brought their head chief, Vincent, to Steptoe, and for a while they rode together, while Joset explained the Coeur d'Alenes' fears to the officer. When Steptoe indicated that the withdrawal of the troops showed that the Americans would not invade the Coeur d'Alenes' lands, Vincent seemed pleased and rode back to his people with Father Joset. A quarrel ensued among the Coeur d'Alene leaders over whether to attack the Americans, and after Joset thought he had settled the matter peaceably and ended the threat of violence, he left to return to his mission. But a short time later one of the aggrieved Coeur d'Alenes "galloped to the troops and began to shoot." [47] Firing immediately became general, and Steptoe's orderly withdrawal suddenly became an anxious retreat. Some of his officers and men began to drop, and when the Indians closed around the head of the column the command veered to the east and took up a defensive position on a hill. There, near the present town of Rosalia, they fought the rest of the day, without water or shade and surrounded by several hundred Indians. That night, after dark, the troops left their equipment on the hill and managed to escape, undetected, through the encircling enemy. [48]

The entire command got away and made a grueling dash for the Snake River, eighty-five miles distant. A handful of men fell by the wayside and were found by pursuing Indians, but the rest reached the Snake after twenty-four hours of hard riding, and Timothy and his Nez Perces ferried them safely across the river. The Nez Perce scout whom Steptoe had sent back for reinforcements had meanwhile carried the message to his own people, and south of the Snake, Lawyer and a large group of Nez Perce warriors joined the tired troopers and offered to accompany them back to punish the Indians in the north. Two of the Nez Perces with Steptoe had been wounded, and Lawyer was eager for revenge. [49] But the soldiers were in no condition to fight again; Steptoe had lost twenty-five men, a little less than a fifth of his command.

47. Dozier, "The Coeur d'Alene Indians in the War of 1858," p. 26, quoting from Joseph Joset, "An Account of 1858 War," p. 6, Joset Papers, File 67, Oregon Provincial Archives, S.J., Crosby Library, Gonzaga University, Spokane, Wash.

48. It is generally believed that Timothy guided the troops through an unguarded avenue of escape in the darkness. But Brown, *The Indian Side of the Story*, pp. 192–93, suggests that Steptoe, in some manner, was able to effect a deal with some of the Coeur d'Alenes to let the whites slip through them. In return, the troops would leave their equipment for the Coeur d'Alenes, and would treat that tribe leniently in the future.

49. Lawyer often repeated the story of how his warriors had "mingled their blood on the ground" with that of Steptoe's soldiers, and had therefore proved that the Nez Perces were "in alliance with the white people." Proceedings of the Treaty Council at Lapwai (1863), p. 67, and Lawyer's speech to Governor Caleb Lyon, Lewiston, 1864, titled "Grievances of the Nez Perce," *Idaho Yesterdays, 4* (Fall, 1960), 7.

The rout of the regulars turned out to be a calamity for the Indians, who, as soon as Steptoe had disappeared, must have realized that a bigger army would come back. General Clarke could not accept the defeat of his forces, whatever its cause had been, and overnight he abandoned the Indian policy of Wool. Becoming harsher than Stevens had ever been, he held a stern council of war with Wright, Steptoe, and Major R. S. Garnett, commander at Fort Simcoe, and directed them to end the Indian problem in the interior, once and for all, by showing no mercy and employing any measure necessary to crush every sign of hostility and punish the offending tribes.

There was neither legality nor logic to what happened next. With greatly enlarged forces, augmented by reinforcements from California, Garnett and Wright swept through the Indians' country from the Cascades to Lake Coeur d'Alene, attacking villages, burning provisions and supplies, taking hostages, and shooting and hanging Indians, without knowing for sure who they were or what they had done. Garnett's men, striking out from Fort Simcoe, broke the last trace of power of the Yakimas and allied peoples of the Columbia River, killing many of their warriors and headmen and scattering the bands. Wright, leading a large army out of Fort Walla Walla, roughly retraced Steptoe's route, determined to whip the Palouses, Spokans, and Coeur d'Alenes. Before he left the fort, he summoned the Nez Perce chiefs to meet with him and, to bind them securely to his side, offered them another treaty of friendship, requiring them to aid the United States in war against the other tribes, and promising to furnish them arms and defend them against any enemy. "I answered, by tomorrow [I would let you know]," Lawyer later reported he replied. "Colonel Wright said, 'This is no boys play. We enter into this truly and solemnly. We will together defend and protect this country that is not yet in a state of war. The Law by which we are governed is unchangeable.' " [50]

Twenty-one Nez Perce leaders, still hopefully waiting for their original treaty to be ratified and too alarmed to risk offending the American officer, signed the new compact on August 6, 1858. They included Lawyer, Timothy, Spotted Eagle, Three Feathers, and the man still known as Richard, who, as a youth, had been in the East with Marcus Whitman. After the paper had been signed, Wright formed a unit of thirty Nez Perce scouts again led by Spotted Eagle, put them in the blue uniforms of the regular army, and placed them under the command of Lieutenant John Mullan, whose road-surveying project had been temporarily postponed after Steptoe's defeat. When the command of 700 men left the post, the Nez Perces rode in the advance, the first members of their tribe to be employed as a formal unit of the regular army.

50. Proceedings at the Lapwai Treaty Council (1863), pp. 67–68.

Wright's troops, armed with mountain howitzers and new long-range rifles using minie balls, shattered a combined force of Spokans, Coeur d'Alenes, Palouses, and a few Yakimas at the Battles of Four Lakes and Spokane Plains on September 1 and 5, respectively. The Nez Perces scouted and skirmished for Wright at both battles, and Mullan cited Utsinmalikin for particular bravery at the Four Lakes.[51] The two fights, waged close to the modern city of Spokane, took the heart out of the resisting tribes and ended forever their belief that they could successfully defend their lands, or even bargain as equals with the white men. After the second battle Spokan Garry, again reduced to the pitiable role of pleader for his people, appeared and told Wright that the Spokans had turned against him because he had refused to join the warriors in the fight, but that they now wished him to tell the Americans that they wanted to make peace. Wright made plans to meet the Spokans but in the meantime heard from Father Joset that the Coeur d'Alenes also wanted to treat for peace. Going to the Coeur d'Alene mission, he signed a treaty with the Coeur d'Alenes on September 17. The tribe, now entirely submissive, returned property taken during the battle with Steptoe, surrendered some of their people as hostages, agreed not to molest any white man going through their country, and promised to treat their neighbors, the Nez Perces—some of whom had fought them, and might therefore have expected acts of revenge—in peace and friendship. Because of Father Joset's intercession on their behalf, the Coeur d'Alenes got off rather lightly; Wright, on his part, promised that if the tribe behaved, he would not injure the hostages but would send them back to their villages after a year.

On September 23 Wright met with the Spokans and a scattering of headmen of other tribes and signed an almost identical treaty with them. As soon as he had the documents, however, he adopted a totally new and savage attitude. The military power of the tribes was broken; there was no combination of war parties left to oppose him. As master of the land, he now began to hang individual Indians, demonstrating to the tribes what would happen to them if they ever broke the treaties they had signed. A few hours after the council with the Spokans had ended, Owhi, also wanting to make peace, rode into Wright's camp. The officer had him seized and put in irons. The next day, Owhi's son, Qualchin, not knowing what had happened to his father, also appeared at the Americans' camp. Fifteen minutes later Wright had him hanged without a trial. He hanged another Indian, a Palouse, and then, taking Owhi with him, started the troops back to Fort Walla Walla. Along the way he met a band of noncombatant Palouses, who had been in none of the battles. "After calling them together in council," he wrote in his

51. Wright to Major W. W. Mackall, September 2, 1858, *Report of the Secretary of War* (1858), p. 389.

official report, "I addressed them in severe language . . . I then demanded the murderers of the two miners in April last. One man was brought out and hung forthwith. Two of the men who stole the cattle from Walla Walla were hung at my camp on the Nedwhauld . . . I then brought out my Indian prisoners, and found three of them were either Walla Wallas or Yakimas. They were hung on the spot. One of the murderers of the miners had been hung on the Spokane." His "severe language" to the frightened Palouses, as reported by Lieutenant Lawrence Kip, an eyewitness who had also been at Stevens' Walla Walla council, included the following: "Tell them they are a set of rascals, and deserve to be hung . . . and if I catch one of them on the other side of Snake River, I will hang him . . . If they behave themselves and do all that I direct them, I will make a written treaty with them next spring . . . If they do not submit to these terms, I will make war on them; and if I come here again to war, I will hang them all, men, women, and children." To underscore his threat, he proceeded to hang several members of this group from nearby trees and, while the victims expired, kicking and squirming desperately, he made the other Indians continue their council with him.

Three days later, on October 3, Owhi was also killed. While crossing a ford at the Tucannon River, the Yakima, whose feet were bound by a rope under his horse, tried suddenly to escape. Troopers wounded him, and he was brought to bay in the dead end of a steep draw. He sat on his horse like a trapped animal, looking piteously at his captors as they rode up to him. One of the men took deliberate aim and shot him in the head at close range, but he clung to life for several hours. On October 5 Wright reached Fort Walla Walla, where he hanged four more Indians. The campaign was closed, but many of the Nez Perces would never forget how the American army had treated the Indians who had surrendered.

And so permanent peace finally came to the land that Stevens had tried to clear of Indians. All the greatest of the resisting patriots were dead, save Kamiakin. He had been injured at the Battle of Spokane Plains by a tree limb that had been shattered by a howitzer shell, and with the principal Palouse war chiefs and warriors had managed to escape from Wright. With his family, he fled to the safety of the Kootenai country in British Columbia. Sometime later he returned to the United States, lived with the Crows on the plains, and in 1861 returned to his homeland. He dwelled in obscurity and poverty in the Palouse country for many years, and finally died about 1878. After his death, white men who knew who he was opened his grave and twisted his head off the decomposing body. Since white men had similarly decapitated the corpses of King Philip of New England, Osceola the Seminole, and Black Hawk the Sauk—and were later to do the same to the remains of old Joseph in the Wallowa Valley—Kamiakin was in good company. Besides, he was dead, and the indignity could no longer offend him.

On September 13, 1858, the Army's Department of the Pacific was divided into the Department of California and the Department of Oregon, the latter also encompassing Washington Territory. General Clarke retained command in California, and on October 29 General W. S. Harney, a stern Indian fighter who had handled the Sioux with extreme brutality on the plains in 1855, arrived at Fort Vancouver to assume command of the northern district. Two days later—although Congress still had not ratified the Stevens treaties of 1855—Harney issued orders that killed Wool's policy for good, and declared the Walla Walla Valley finally open to white settlement. By April of the following year some 2,000 settlers had poured into the valley and begun to spread across the lands of eastern Washington. By then, there was nothing the Nez Perces could do about it. They were an unbeaten people, but their allies were gone. They were alone—and divided among themselves.

IO

Ho for Idaho!

IN 1859 the Nez Perces were clearly divided. The bands of Lawyer and his followers, numbering perhaps two-thirds of the total Nez Perce population of approximately 4,000 people, placed their reliance on "the laws" that the American missionaries, soldiers, and agents had revealed to them. They were God's laws, and Lawyer's portion of the tribe respected Christianity, whose teachings made the laws clear to them. The laws were also the guiding principles of a just American President and Congress in the East, and obedience to the wishes of the representatives of the government would demonstrate to the whites the goodness of heart of the Nez Perces, and would safeguard the people from punishment and unhappiness. The laws, spelled out, were still what Elijah White had given the tribe in 1842; but their essence was that of the Golden Rule. They required conduct that carried charity and meekness to an extreme, and a strict observance of them would have turned the Nez Perces into a nation of saints and angels. No one could be that good, but Lawyer and the headmen who accepted his chieftaincy tried to do their best, especially in their dealings with American officials.

At the same time, the laws taught that there were bad men among both the whites and the Indians. That recognition prepared Lawyer's people for troubles with ill-intentioned white men and increased their dependence on an alliance with the representatives of the American government, the agents and soldiers, who as upholders of the laws would, they thought, give them protection and assistance. They had greater problems with the anti-Lawyer part of the tribe, the people whom they came to regard as "bad Indians." Those were Nez Perces who saw hypocrisy in the laws, who believed that they worked for the benefit of white men and against the Indians, and who consid-

386

ered that what was good for the white man was bad for the Indian. They were people who had lost friends and relatives during the wars of the 1850s, and who lived with resentments and fears that the white man would one day try to visit the same fate on the Nez Perces. Christianity to them was the carrier of the unjust laws, and they would have nothing to do with the white man's religion. Nor were they as willing as Lawyer's followers to settle down in their villages and live like white men. Many of them owned cattle, which like horses meant wealth, and some of them built up large herds. But the earth was still regarded as their mother, and they would not tear its breast and farm. In 1858, after the Nez Perce scouts aided the Americans in their campaign against the Spokans, Coeur d'Alenes, and Palouses, Colonel Wright asked Lawyer what the chiefs wished for their people. "Peace, plows, and schools," Lawyer replied. But he was speaking only for his own followers, who genuinely wished to enjoy the material advantages of the white man's way of life. The other Indians were content to follow their old manner of existence, unmolested by the white man, free to travel to the buffalo country when they wished and to return to their home villages after the hunt.

The divergent attitudes about the white man and his works were enough to arouse bitter feelings between the two factions. But the anti-whites had an additional weapon that sorely tried and hurt Lawyer's people. By the end of 1858 Stevens' treaties of 1855 still had not been ratified. There had been no payments to the Nez Perces, and none of Stevens' many promises to the Indians who had signed the treaty had come true. When the wars had ended, Lawyer had written to Stevens: "At this place about three years since we had our talk, and since that time I have been waiting to hear from our big father. We are very poor . . ." [1] Still, nothing had happened, and the anti-treaty Indians had taken advantage of the silence to mock Lawyer's people, telling them that Stevens had tricked the head chief and that—as had happened to the Wallawallas and Yakimas—the soldiers would find an excuse to take the Nez Perce lands by force before the treaty terms were carried out. Lawyer had continued to defend the treaty, confident that the government would ratify it; but as his defensiveness had increased, so had the gap between the two factions. In Lawyer's estimation the anti-treaty leaders like Eagle From the Light, who had begun to eclipse the aged and failing Looking Glass, had become "bad men" whom he could not force into goodness and with whom he wanted nothing to do. And Eagle From the Light, in turn, had little but contempt for Lawyer and pro-American headmen like him.

In Washington the wars in the Northwest and Wool's opposition to Stevens' Indian policies, casting doubt on the wisdom of the 1855 treaties, had been responsible for the delay in the ratification of the agreements. But even-

1. Report of the Commssioner of Indian Affairs (1858), p. 277.

tually Stevens' intensive lobbying for them began to have results, and on March 8, 1859, the Senate finally approved the documents. President Buchanan signed them on April 29, and on July 22 Indian agent A. J. Cain appeared at the Weippe Prairie, where many of the Nez Perce bands were gathered at their annual camp on the camas grounds, and announced that the treaty was in force. Leaders of both factions were present, and all of them except Eagle From the Light were grateful that the American government seemed at last to be living up to its word—although there was still no sign of annuities or funds to pay for the many promises that Stevens had made. Cain reported that Eagle From the Light continued to claim that the Indians "had not been properly treated by the whites," but that Joseph, who had long since decided to have nothing to do with white men, was pleased by the news because the treaty ensured the Wallowa country as a home for his children. "The line [in the treaty] was made as I wanted it," Joseph said to Cain, "not for me but my children that will follow me. There is where I live and there is where I want to leave my body." [2] The chief's words were overlooked by most whites who read the agent's report, but their significance was to have increasing importance in the years that followed.

Cain assured the Indians that the first annuity money should be arriving soon; and when the bands departed for their home villages, it seemed possible to them that Lawyer's long-held trust in the Americans might be vindicated. But in the moment of new hope all was suddenly lost. The worst disaster that had yet befallen the Nez Perces was about to occur.

In the Walla Walla Valley and along the streams in eastern Washington, the white population had been increasing. The settlers were mostly ranchers who raised stock in the high hills and farmed in the protected valleys. All through 1859 they arrived from Puget Sound and the lower Columbia, spreading across what had recently been the lands of the Wallawallas, Cayuses, Palouses, and Yakimas. Among the new arrivals was Henry Spalding, who had been living west of the Cascades since 1847 but had never abandoned the hope of being able to go back to the Nez Perces. After Eliza had died in 1851, Spalding had remarried and had made several attempts to win support from both the American Board and the Indian Bureau for his return to Lapwai. Since his experiences during the massacre period in 1847, however, his erratic temperament had become worse. He was fanatic and tempestuous, particularly in his attitude toward Catholics, and he was quick to quarrel with and make wild accusations against persons who did not agree with him. Both Eells and Walker thought he was "wholly unfitted in body and mind" to be sent back to the Nez Perces, and Spalding did not receive the permission he sought. In 1859 his daughter, Eliza, and her husband, A. J.

2. Ibid. (1859), p. 420.

Warren, arrived on the Touchet River not far from Waiilatpu and took up a land claim. Spalding soon followed them and in August staked out a claim nearby for himself. For the next three years, he and his wife occupied the claim, farming and raising stock. Spalding occasionally preached, there and at Walla Walla, and several times Timothy and some of his friends among the Nez Perces came to visit him.

Walla Walla, first called Steptoe City, grew up around the military post that Wright had established. In the winter of 1858–59 Craig left his family at Lapwai and moved to the new town to become its postmaster. Indians of all the tribes that had frequented the region were still commonly seen, but the history of every frontier in the East was repeated. The tribes were broken and powerless; the headmen and military leaders were weak, venal, and without authority; and the Indians lacked cultural standards and self respect. As village life and traditional traits disintegrated, many of the Indians turned from hunting, fishing, and root-gathering to hanging about the white men's farms and settlements, begging, trading, and selling their labor. Liquor was plentiful, and a large number of Indians found an escape in alcohol from their unhappy existence. The white attitude toward the Indians, ranging from fear to contempt, made them an unwanted minority, and constant appeals were addressed to the military to get the Indians out of the way by forcing them onto the new reservations. From time to time it was done. Individuals and villages were scooped up and sent packing; and when the distraught Indians had departed, white men moved in and claimed the river bottom sites they had abandoned. The Palouses and Wallawallas almost disappeared as peoples, the former among the Yakimas and other Indians being herded onto the Yakima reservation, and the latter among the Cayuses on the Umatilla reservation.

The great wheat potential of the region had not yet been realized. Few people considered that the dry, barren hills were fit for anything but grazing, and the whites' attention was focused on the rivers. But the principal traffic along the waterways was of miners. The interior country had seen one gold strike after another, none of them matching the bonanza of California but all of them luring increasing numbers of footloose prospectors to the area east of the Cascades. When the wars had ended, fortune hunters had swarmed into the Colville country, fanning out through the mountains of northeastern Washington, and in May 1859 the government had garrisoned Fort Colville for their protection. The prospectors had had luck in a series of widely separated locations, and each one had had its excited rush. The most promising had been in the valley of the Similkameen, just over the border in southern British Columbia. But it, too, had fallen short of expectation. Nevertheless, the miners had played an important role in changing the country. The Columbia River had become a busy highway, breasted by sternwheeled steam-

boats that carried miners, merchants, supplies, and mail back and forth between The Dalles and the Walla Walla Valley. Occasionally a steamer
churned even farther up the Columbia or to the Palouse River on the Snake,
where passengers debarked to take the overland route to the mines. The new
settlements in the interior that were based on the miners' trade were little
more than clusters of canvas shacks, saloons, and merchants' shanties, but
they and a host of new roads, ferries, and farms that supplied the prospectors
with provisions stamped the rough beginnings of a permanent civilization
across much of what until recently had been a forbidden Indian country.

   East of this region, protected by the Stevens treaty against inroads by the
whites, the Nez Perces lived on their large reservation in splendid isolation.
But if an invisible wall guarded their land, it was not strong enough to turn
back the influences of the white man's culture. Most of the anti-treaty bands
were located more distantly than the others from the Walla Walla country,
and their members, following the stern injunctions of their leaders, generally
refrained from traveling to the white centers. But those who followed Lawyer found it adventurous and profitable to go to Walla Walla and hang on
the heels of the whites. The market for produce and livestock promised the
Indians new wealth, and many of them increased the size of their garden
plots, or turned to farming for the first time. Their frequent trips to the
merchants at Walla Walla put American cash in their pockets, and newly
prosperous Nez Perces, able to buy white men's clothes, groceries, hardware,
and guns, also began to have problems with liquor. Lawyer and the headmen
lectured them against the use of alcohol, but their warnings had little effect.
Even in the Wallowa Valley, where Joseph's people did not farm, young
men returned from livestock-selling expeditions reeling from whiskey and
carrying more of the liquor with them to those who had stayed at home. It
led to quarrels and fights in the camps, and Joseph, still trying to keep his
people out of harm's way, saw increased reason for continuing to isolate his
band from American civilizers.

   The barrier of an unseen reservation line could not protect the Nez Perces
forever. Since 1858 prospectors worming their way through the ravines and
gulches of eastern Washington had eyed with interest the great mountain
mass of the Bitterroots farther east. The relatively slim pickings of the areas
they were combing convinced them that they were working so far only on
the western fringe of a rich mineral source that must lie in the Bitterroots.
Moreover, there were constant rumors to support that theory. Father De
Smet and some of the Jesuits were quoted as having seen gold in the Bitterroot country. Halfbloods and mysterious prospectors, some real, some leg-
endary, were reported to have discovered traces of the metal in half a dozen
different localities in the Bitterroots, and on at least one occasion gold had

been traded to a white man by Spokan Indians.[3] The most tantalizing center of a new El Dorado seemed to lie in the Nez Perce country—somewhere in the mountains on the eastern side of that tribe's reservation. But getting there was a problem. Stevens' treaty forbade white entrance on the reservation. And if the dragoons from Fort Walla Walla did not go after a man and eject him, Indian hostility was not to be taken lightly. The Nez Perces were known to be fighters who did not want whites on their land. A miner who got in trouble with them could expect no help from the military.

Still, a few prospectors undoubtedly did get into the mountains on Nez Perce land. As early as 1856 a man named Martin, heading across the Bitter-roots via the southern Nez Perce Trail, is said to have panned some gold on the South Fork of the Clearwater, and the following year a trapper named Jack Lassier is also believed to have found gold on Orofino Creek, a tributary of the Clearwater above its North Fork.[4] News of the discoveries may have reached others, and several men may have tried to pursue the rumors. One of the earliest of the known gold hunters in the area was Elias D. Pierce, who claimed that he first visited the Nez Perce country as a trader in 1852 and was satisfied at that time that it was a gold-bearing region.[5] Pierce, a veteran of the Mexican War and the California gold rush, was diverted back to California, however, and then to the British Columbia mines, and it was 1858 before he returned to the border of the Nez Perce reservation. He began to trade with Indians in the Walla Walla region, and during 1858 he revisited the Clearwater country, stopping at the village of an elderly headman named Wislaneqa, a follower of Lawyer. The village was near the mouth of the North Fork of the Clearwater, on the same site where Lewis and Clark had built their canoes to travel to the lower Columbia in 1805, and there, during his first visit in 1852, Pierce had apparently found gold. Although he confirmed his original belief that he was in a rich mineral area, he decided that the times were too dangerous for him to prospect on the reservation, and he withdrew again, planning to wait until the Indian wars had ended and the Nez Perce treaty had been ratified.

At Pierce's base, Walla Walla, it was taken for granted that somebody would sooner or later challenge the hostility of the Nez Perces and make a strike on the Indians' land. Although many whites opposed the idea of prospecting on the Nez Perce reservation, fearing that it might lead to another

3. Bancroft, *History of Washington, Idaho, and Montana*, p. 234.
4. Merle W. Wells, *Rush to Idaho*, Idaho Bureau of Mines and Geology, Bulletin 19 (Moscow, Idaho, 1963), p. 2. John C. Reed, *Gold-Bearing Gravel of the Nezperce National Forest, Idaho County*, Idaho Bureau of Mines and Geology, Pamphlet 40 (Moscow, June 1934), p. 4.
5. "Orofino Gold," ed. Ralph Burcham, *Idaho Yesterdays*, 4 (Fall, 1960), 5.

Indian war, others earnestly hoped that such a strike would occur, bringing with it a rush of people and business to the Walla Walla area. But until 1860 there was no certain knowledge of anyone having penetrated the Nez Perce reservation and come out with gold. Then, on February 12 of that year, Pierce and a 25-year-old companion named Seth Ferrell quietly left Walla Walla for the Nez Perces. "It was generally supposed that we had gone for the purpose of trading," Pierce wrote at a later date. "I had taken the precaution of putting our prospecting implements up safe and secure so no one could tell what they were." [6] The pair reached the Clearwater safely and camped for several days at Wislaneqa's village. The Indians were curious about Pierce's prospecting tools, and examined them closely. When Pierce told them what they were for, the Indians did not seem to be concerned. "One evening," Pierce reported, "I said to Wishlanuker that tomorrow I intended going up the river, and if he would accompany us, I would show him some gold dust if there was any gold in the country."

The next morning, February 20, the headman accompanied the two whites up the river to a low bar. "I shoveled off the sand and surplus soil," said Pierce, "dug up some of the gravel and dirt that seemed more compact, filled the pan, [and] went to the water to wash it. Mr. Ferrel and the Chief followed me to see what would be the result. In reducing the pan of dirt, I soon discovered I had a floating prospect of gold. Mr. Ferrel and [the] Chief seemed wonderfully elated. I still continued to prospect and got from three to five cents of float gold to the pan. It was evident that there was a fountain head or feeder further up in the mountains. I remarked to Mr. Ferrel [that] this is a key to a rich and extensive gold field."

They returned to their camp, and the headman showed the gold to the Indians. The next day Pierce and Ferrell did some more prospecting and "found gold in every place we tried." When they got back to camp, a large group of Indians were gathered excitedly to see the results. There was no question of their opposing Pierce's activity. The two white men seemed harmless; they were not farmers, and had no intention of settling on the Indians' land. Pierce and Wislaneqa directed the Indians to keep the news secret "even from their own people," and Pierce, who needed provisions for a longer stay, arranged to take the headman and eight members of his village to Walla Walla for prospecting equipment and supplies, and then return and try his luck with them on the headwaters of the North Fork, where he believed he would find the rich "fountain head." They started for Walla Walla on February 28, and Pierce said, "[I] knew I had the shaping or the destiny of that country, and that I could flood the entire region with good reliable men at my own option."

6. Ibid., p. 2.

At Walla Walla, which they reached early in March, Pierce reported his discovery to a few friends and to Indian agent A. J. Cain.[7] "The Indians were perfectly willing I should come in there to explore," he told Cain. They were "agreeable to arrangements I had made with the chief . . . It is not my intention to create any excitement, but to go quietly and not cause any disturbance." He explained falsely to Cain that he had made his discovery east of the reservation, outside the boundary as defined in the Stevens treaty, and only wished to cross the reservation to get to the mining area. "Mr. Cain talked reasonable," he reported, but he asked Pierce to come back the next day and discuss the matter further. When Pierce called on him again, he found that Cain "had changed his mind and views, and said it would never do to go into the Nez Perce Nation prospecting." The intrusion would cause a war between the Nez Perces and the whites, the agent said, and "one hundred well armed men could not go in there with any degree of safety." Cain's injunction fell on deaf ears. "With all due regard to Mr. Cain," said Pierce, "I soon saw where the shoe fit too close, and in my case the 'power behind the throne' was greater than that 'on the throne.' We agreed to disagree in opinion and I withdrew from the council chamber." [8]

Pierce outfitted Wislaneqa and the other Indians and sent them back to their country. Then he and three companions went down to The Dalles for supplies and equipment for a four months' expedition. They returned to Walla Walla and went on to Lapwai, where Cain had sent a man named Charles H. Frush to act as subagent for the Nez Perces. Frush stopped the miners and asked if they had a written permit to pass through the reservation. When they said they did not, Frush told them, "I am not allowed to let anyone pass through without a written permit of permission from the Agent Cain."

"I don't think anything of that kind would be of any service to us on that trip," Pierce said he replied. "I am sorry, Mr. Frush, that you cannot carry out your strict orders, but we will pass quietly along . . ." As they rode ahead, Frush accompanied them, "still insisting that it was absolutely necessary for us to have a pass. 'Well, so far as our having a pass Mr. Frush, giving me the liberty to travel through this country, I would just as soon have that much brown paper,'" Pierce retorted. Frush "then proposed to write out a permit, if I would accept it. 'Most assuredly I will.' He then gave us a permit to pass through the Nation to the Bitterroot country. He handed it to me,

7. Bancroft, *History of Washington*, says that Pierce reached Walla Walla in early April. If so, the dates in Pierce's account—dictated years after the gold rush—are wrong by a month, and the first discovery actually occurred on March 20 rather than February 20. The latter date, however, is believed to be correct.

8. Burcham, "Orofino Gold," p. 4.

and asked me if it was all right. 'It is correct, but if you had said through to the Bitter country, and left the Root out [you] would have had it near right."

The subagent let them go, apparently satisfied that he had done his duty, and Pierce reported that all the Indians they passed knew that they were coming to their country to prospect, but were friendly and made no objection. When they arrived at Wislaneqa's village, they found the chief waiting for them with a problem. Cain had informed him, the Nez Perce told Pierce, that if he let prospectors into the country, and they found gold, the reservation would be flooded with miners who would steal the Indians' livestock and not pay for it. "Now you say to us," the Indian explained, "there is gold in our country . . . and if we are willing for the whites to come in and mine, they soon will build towns all through the mountains; bring all kinds of provisions and goods [so] that we can buy anything we want here at home. That the whites will buy our horses and cattle and pay us money for them. We can learn to mine the same as the whites. We believe what you say and all our people are willing for you to stay in our country and go where you please, but I would rather you would remain here, and I will send my son to Lawyer's Camp and have him come here and we will talk the matter over and get his consent."

Pierce agreed, and the next day Lawyer and a delegation of headmen arrived. "The day following," Pierce said, "all assembled in council, discussing the subject. The Lawyer (Head Peace Chief of the Nation) was in favor of our prospecting." To Pierce's sad surprise, however, the council was interrupted at that favorable moment by the unexpected appearance of two white men. Pierce did not say who they were, but the implication is that they were authorities from Fort Walla Walla. At any rate, their arrival forced the miners to abandon their plans, and Pierce and his companions told the Indians that they would have to return to Walla Walla, but would come back at a later time.

At Walla Walla, Pierce turned the pressure on Cain. He made no attempt to keep his plans a secret, but joined the leaders of the town in holding a mass meeting to arouse support for the prospecting of the Nez Perce country. Cain was even invited to attend and make known his objections. At the rally, held about July 20, Pierce announced his belief that he could find "rich and extensive mines" in the Clearwater region. He described the area in which he was interested as lying east of the reservation. "This country has been bought and paid for by the United States Government and consequently is not on holy ground," he told the gathering. "On this expedition I propose to make, I don't even intend to pass through the reservation, but will travel to the north."

The Walla Walla audience, impatient for the prosperity that a gold discovery would bring them, put Cain in an awkward position. The agent spoke meekly, assuring the audience that if Pierce kept to his promise and avoided trespassing on the reservation, the government could have no objection to his movements. "He did not claim any right for the Indians outside the reservation," Pierce said with satisfaction, "and had nothing more to say on the subject."

A large party of men planned to go with Pierce, but when Craig arrived from Lapwai with news that the Indians were making preparations for resistance and would halt a big group, most of the hopefuls backed out, and on August 12 Pierce departed with only ten men. They traveled to the mouth of the Tucannon, where Pierce said they "procured a guide who was familiar with the country." The following year a story sprang up that the guide was Timothy's daughter, Jane, who in 1858 had married John McBean, the post interpreter at Fort Walla Walla. Young McBean was the halfblood son of William McBean, who had been in charge of the Hudson's Bay Company's Walla Walla fur post at the time of the Whitman murders. Although Jane may have felt closer to the white men than to her own people, none of the members of the party ever said that their guide had been a woman, or even an Indian, and there is no evidence that the story is true.

Crossing the Snake River, the party moved up the Palouse River and, entering the heavily wooded mountains east of present-day Moscow, Idaho, reached the North Fork of the Clearwater. They ascended its banks through rugged country for seven days, then forded the stream and made their way south for more than a month through thick forests and across difficult mountains and canyons, heading generally toward the Weippe Prairie. At the end of September they reached the vicinity of present-day Pierce, Idaho, and began prospecting. On the 30th of that month one of the men, W. F. Bassett, made a rich strike on Canal Gulch, a headwater of Orofino Creek, which is a tributary of the Clearwater River. Immediately afterward, the members of the group found gold in every part of the stream— ". . . in the flats and banks and gold generally diffused from the surface of the bed rock," said Pierce. "I never saw a party of men so much excited; they made the hills and mountains ring with shouts of joy." [9]

The men worked their rockers until October 12, and then returned to Walla Walla for provisions for the winter. They left the country without being detected, though at Walla Walla they learned that eighteen Indians whom Cain had sent to trail them had tried unsuccessfully to find them in the mountains. The announcement of their discovery, supported by the gold dust they displayed, electrified the town. The news traveled down the Columbia

9. Ibid., p. 9.

to The Dalles, Portland, and Puget Sound, and newspapers as far away as Sacramento reported the find, pointing out that the miners had had no trouble with the Nez Perces. The reaction was instantaneous; prospectors everywhere hungered for more news that would reveal the extent of the new strike.

In Walla Walla a party was formed to return to the Clearwater, and word was spread that the Indians wanted the miners and would be pleased by their presence. But the *Weekly Portland Times* of October 27, 1860, questioning Pierce's assurance that the discovery was east of the reservation's boundary, suggested that the government would have to make some arrangement with the Nez Perces before the mines could be worked, though it added darkly, "Some, however, assert that they will go there and mine without any regard to the Indians, whatever . . ." [10] While Pierce went to Olympia to seek a charter to construct a wagon road from Fort Boise to Walla Walla via the Clearwater River, that would divert emigrants from the Overland Trail to the Nez Perce mining country, the new party of some 40 prospectors left Walla Walla on November 14. At Cain's request, a group of 100 dragoons from the fort pursued them for several days, but abandoned the chase and turned back when the weather became cold and snowy. The miners reached Orofino Creek on December 3, established a townsite which they called Pierce, and commenced building cabins for the winter. After a discussion with the military commander at Fort Walla Walla, who contended that the miners were within their rights if, as they asserted, they were operating outside the reservation boundaries, Cain himself made a trip to Canal Gulch late in the year. Deciding perhaps that there was nothing he could do to oust the determined prospectors, he left, and one of the miners wrote to friends in the outside world that the Indian agent had "expressed himself well pleased with their behavior." [11]

Cain, however, was in a quandary. Recognizing that the mining area was actually on the reservation and that no force possible could halt the rush that would come with good weather in the spring, he wrote to Edward R. Geary, the Superintendent of Indian Affairs for Oregon and Washington, describing the ominous situation. Geary consulted with General Wright at Fort Vancouver and came to the conclusion that he would have to meet with the Nez Perces and, in some fashion, amend the 1855 treaty in order to secure the right of access for the prospectors to the mining area. On Wright's part, he was

10. "Gold in 1860," *Idaho Yesterdays*, 3 (Fall, 1959), 15. My thanks go to H. J. Swinney, Merle Wells, and the staff of the Idaho Historical Society and its publication, *Idaho Yesterdays*, for the excellent compilations of gold rush material which they published and on which I have relied so heavily.

11. Olympia, Wash., *Pioneer and Democrat*, January 18, 1861.

violating all the promises he had made to his friends, the Nez Perces, but like Geary he thought that he had little choice, for public opinion was already snapping at both men. Newspapers and politicians would not have supported military protection of the reservation, and Geary himself soon realized that he would have to hustle if he were to hold his job. "I would respectfully urge . . . that the Department of the Interior be memorialized to dispatch a Commissioner to this Territory with authority to define the boundaries of the reservation, and acquire the cession of the lands on which the mines are situated," the Governor of Washington had said to the territory's legislature in his annual message at the beginning of January 1861.[12]

Asking the Nez Perces for another land cession was not a pleasant task to have to face, but early in February 1861 four men reached Walla Walla with more gold from the mines, and Geary watched the excitement increase. Despite the fact that winter snow in the mountains made travel near the mines all but impossible except on snowshoes, several prospectors started immediately for the Clearwater. Farther down the Columbia, hundreds of other men made plans to move upriver at once in order to be ready to leave Walla Walla by April 1. During the next two months, to Geary's discomfiture, more of the miners returned from Pierce, each with a glowing story of the gold region. By March 4 more than 200 impatient men had departed from Walla Walla for the mines. On March 12 a shipment of approximately $1,000 in gold dust reached the town from the Clearwater, and the rush quickened. Returning miners were full of news. Men were prospecting farther up the Clearwater and were finding gold almost everywhere. Some of the parties had run into Indian opposition, but it had not been serious. The head chief, Lawyer, welcomed the prospectors. One "young and intelligent" Nez Perce headman named Reuben was even said to be building a warehouse and ferry to accommodate the miners at the crossing of the Snake River near the mouth of the Clearwater. On March 10, Reuben himself arrived in Walla Walla to post a notice advertising his ferry. Three years before, as a 30-year-old Nez Perce warrior known as Tipyahlanah Oikelazikin, he had been in battle against the Crows on the plains.[13] Now, with hired white men running his ferry for him, he was about to become a wealthy man. Two months later he would be wearing white men's clothes and would be living in a log house three miles up the Clearwater, the owner of 2,500 horses and a farm on several hundred acres of ground.[14]

In mid-March a newspaper correspondent reached Walla Walla from Cali-

12. "Gold in 1860," p. 20 n.
13. McWhorter, *Hear Me*, p. 555.
14. "Henry Miller's Letters from the Upper Columbia," *Idaho Yesterdays*, 4 (Winter, 1960–61), 19.

WASHINGTON TERRITORY

PALOUSE R.

Hahtalekin

Husishusis
Kute

SNAKE RIVER

SNAKE R.

COLUMBIA R.

TUCANNON R.

ALPOWA CR.

Timoth

TOUCHET R.

Wallula

Walla Walla

WALLA WALLA R.

COLUMBIA R.

GRANDE RON

OREGON

JOS

UMATILLA R.

Josep

[Pendleton]

BLUE MTS.

WALLOWA R.

RESERVATION OF 1855
(WESTERN BOUNDARY)

------ RESERVATION OF 1863

WALLOWA MTS.

NORTH FK.

Lolo Trail

POTLATCH R.

CLEARWATER R.

OROFINO CR.
• Pierce

LOCHSA R.

Lewiston

Fort
Lapwai
Lapwai Agency

LAPWAI CR.

LAWYERS CR.

• Oro Fino

Weippe
Prairie

*Big
Thunder*

Kamiah

[Kooskia]

MIDDLE FK.

SELWAY R.

Koolkool Snehee

[Stites]

Looking Glass, Jr.

CLEAR CR.

Toohoolhoolzote

SALMON RIVER

Camas
Prairie

Mt.
Idaho

*Eagle From
the Light*

Elk City

IMNAHA R.

Whitebird

WHITE BIRD CR.

SOUTH FORK

IDAHO TERRITORY

SNAKE R.

SNAKE R.

SLATE CR.

• Dixie

• Florence

LITTLE SALMON

SALMON R.

SALMON RIVER MOUNTAINS

SOUTH FORK

Warrens

8. THE IDAHO GOLD RUSH AND THE NEZ PERCE RESERVATION OF 1863

fornia. His reports would soon set a stream of prospectors on their way from that state. At Pierce, at approximately the same time, the first of the new men began to arrive at the mines. They sent out word at once for others to hurry and join them. Numbers meant security against the Indians, as well as a harder job for the government if it intended to evict them. The newcomers also appealed for merchants to come with supplies and provisions. Stores would preclude the necessity of having to make the long trip back to Walla Walla for food and equipment, and would mean a town, entertainment, and the feeling of civilization in the mountains.

All through the end of March and the month of April the tide of men rolling toward the Clearwater increased. A dozen routes were used, but the principal one, now called the Big Nez Perces Trail, was the old route between Walla Walla and Lapwai. On the way, the miners passed Alpowa and the extensive gardens of Timothy, who was friendly and cordial to everyone. A new Indian subagent named Thomas Hughes had just established himself near Timothy, although he did not interfere with the movement of prospectors. At the mouth of Lapwai Creek, where Henry Spalding had once had his mission, the miners could pause at a new Nez Perce agency under subagent Charles Frush. Early in 1861 Cain received the first treaty payments for the tribe.[15] Only a part of the promised money and annuity goods arrived, and some of what did reach the Northwest was pocketed or squandered by Cain before it got to the Nez Perces. What was left was used to support Hughes and Frush and to dole out in token annuity payments to the headmen. Joseph and some of the anti-treaty leaders refused to accept anything, intending in that way to demonstrate their insistence that they had signed away nothing to the Americans and were therefore owed nothing. Lawyer and his followers accepted what was offered to them but complained because the payments were not as large as promised, because there were no funds for schools and other buildings that should already have been erected, and because the Indian goods were inferior and insultingly shoddy. More than one supplier had obviously profiteered, but neither Cain nor anyone else concerned appeared to be in a position to call the kettle black. An uninhibited era of wholesale stealing of Indian funds had begun.

After the agency was established, Lawyer settled himself nearby, and greeted the miners as they passed by on their way up the Clearwater. Henry Miller, a visiting newspaperman from Portland, described the appearance of the head chief: "This interesting gentleman is apparently fifty years of age," he wrote. (Lawyer was actually about 65). "He is about five feet eight inches in height, and awkwardly framed. His features are rather more oval than common among Indians, with a nose straight but not high. Eyes small and ex-

15. Report of the Commissioner of Indian Affairs (1865), p. 236.

pressive and a smile always about the corner of his mouth, completes his picture. His whole bearing is extremely amiable. He wore elegantly beaded moccasins, blue cloth pants, calico shirt, alpaca sack and a preposterous, white plug-hat . . . he carried a plain hickory cane, the usual three-tailed tobacco pouch, and an Indian pipe." [16] Another correspondent who met the head chief and called him "Sawyer," remarked that "it appears to me that he is not entirely satisfied that the whites should come into his country. After asking him three separate times he refused to answer . . . 'Sawyer' says he tells his people that they are rich now, but if they should go to war with the whites, they will loose [sic] all their horses and cattle as the Cayuses have, and become reduced to poverty; that the whites are too strong for them, but yet most of his sub-chiefs are complaining to him, while many of the people are understood to be satisfied that miners shall come in . . ." [17]

Upriver from Lapwai, a white man had already built a ferry across the North Fork not far from Wislaneqa's village. That headman had apparently not taken to prospecting with the tools that Pierce had given him, and had even been dealt out of a claim when Pierce's party had made its first big strike on Orofino Creek in September. Since then, the chief, who was also rumored to be a medicine man, had had an additional disappointment. In March a miner had plied his 15-year-old daughter with liquor, got her drunk, and seduced her. "The old man heard of it," a correspondent reported, "and was much grieved." [18] A month or two later, the miners had begun to call the old headman "whisky Knocker," but by then he may not have minded it. He had opened a ferry of his own across the Clearwater, and was making money from miners the easy way.

On April 1 the first express was opened between Walla Walla and the mines. A new town of Oro Fino was established two miles from Pierce, and merchants were arriving to set up canvas-walled shops and saloons. The use of liquor by Indians was already worrying some of the responsible miners, and on April 8, in response to their appeals to the agents to take action against men who sold whiskey to the Indians, Dr. Augustus J. Thibodo, who had been hired as agency physician at Lapwai, and Captain C. H. Armstrong, a special agent, journeyed to Pierce to see what they could do. The trip was little more than a formality. The miners welcomed them and promised to cooperate and never to sell whiskey to Indians. At a mass meeting the prospectors passed a resolution calling for the arrest of anyone "who, by proof,

16. "Miller's Letters from the Upper Columbia," p. 20.

17. "News from the Nez Perce Mines," *Idaho Yesterdays, 3* (Winter, 1959–60), 26, quoting dispatch by C. L. Goodrich, Oro Fino, March 30, 1861, to the *Daily Alta California*, April 23, 1861, p. 1.

18. Ibid., p. 26.

has already been guilty" of such a sale. A committee was named to enforce the resolution, which all too soon turned out to be unenforceable. At the same meeting another resolution—easier to enforce—was passed, barring Chinese "and the Asiatic race" from the mines. Armstrong and Thibodo departed and the Captain returned to Portland, where a newspaper interview with him dwelled principally on his report that some 2,000 claims had already been taken up at the mines, "as good as any in California."[19]

On April 10 Superintendent Geary and Agent Cain finally arrived at Lapwai and went into council with Lawyer and a large assemblage of his followers. Geary was prepared for a painful ordeal, trying to convince Lawyer to part with the region around Pierce and Oro Fino. But his fears were unnecessary. The head chief had already decided that the mining grounds in the mountains on the north side of the Clearwater were actually of no use to his people, and that he would gladly sell them for a "big price." [20] Giving the headman no opportunity to change his mind, Geary offered him $50,000, payable as soon as the Senate and the President approved the transaction. When Lawyer reminded him that the Indians were still waiting for the government to live up to its promises of the 1855 treaty, Geary assured him that he would speed the delinquent funds and annuities. The chief then agreed to the deal, and he and Geary settled on an ambiguously worded compromise concerning the ownership of the mining grounds. A treaty, written that day, said that the part of the Nez Perce reservation lying north of the Clearwater River and the Lolo Trail "is hereby opened to the whites, but shall remain for the exclusive use and benefit of the Indians." No whites were to be allowed south of the new line without the permission of the superintendent, agent, or tribe, and a military unit would be settled on the reservation to enforce the agreement and protect the Indians.

Lawyer and forty-nine of his followers signed the document, which was dated April 10. For Geary it was a satisfying end to a nightmarish situation. The treaty was sent to Washington, and in time it was approved. Only forty thousand dollars were appropriated to pay for the land, however, and there is no record that even that sum ever reached the Nez Perces. But in the context of what was occurring, the amount soon proved irrelevant, and the agreement itself became a farce.

Within a month after the signing of the treaty, there were 1,000 whites, including women and children, at the mines, and thousands more were on their way to the Clearwater from all parts of the West. On May 6 a little sternwheeler, the *Colonel Wright*, jammed with miners and supplies, pushed all the way up the Snake, turned into the Clearwater, and proceeded thirty-

19. "Clearwater Gold Rush," *Idaho Yesterdays*, 4 (Spring, 1960), 14.
20. "News from the Nez Perce Mines," p. 26.

seven miles up that stream, almost to the foot of the mountain trail that led to the mines. Where the vessel was finally forced to halt and unload, a town named Slaterville came into being. The settlement lasted only briefly, for the violence of the water in that part of the river, known as Big Eddy, made it unsafe for boats, and on the *Colonel Wright's* next trip the vessel halted at the mouth of the Clearwater. On May 13 passengers and goods were unloaded on the south bank of the river, close to the junction with the Snake, the narrow strip of ground beneath the towering hills on the Clearwater's northern shore proving unsuitable for a boat landing and a warehouse.

The site was ideal for a base depot for the mines. Tents and canvas shacks sprang up, and six days later a man named Vic Trevitt, agent for a firm of Portland merchants, named the location Lewiston in honor of Meriwether Lewis, who had been there fifty-six years before. The settlement was in flagrant violation of the treaty of April 10, and Nez Perces, Indian agents, and military officials tried unsuccessfully to get the interlopers to depart. Finally, Lawyer granted special permission for the building of a wharf and a warehouse, provided that no other permanent structure was erected on the site. What induced Lawyer to agree to the violation, a month after he had signed the new treaty, was never made clear; but it was stated publicly in Lewiston that the whites gave him "some compensation," through the agent (who probably shared it with the chief), and a rumor was soon in circulation that a Nez Perce had spied the head chief and a few of his followers counting gold pieces one night at the agency building, in company with the agent and Louis Raboin, who had been hired as the agency interpreter.[21]

At any rate, the new treaty that was supposed to safeguard the Nez Perces had been breached. Within a month, steamboats were arriving regularly at Lewiston with hundreds of merchants, miners, and other newcomers, and in October the whites laid out a permanent townsite. By that time the April agreement was in shreds. At Pierce and Oro Fino all the promising mining locations had been claimed, and the overflow of prospectors had pushed farther up the Clearwater Valley, finding gold in one tributary after the other. Oro Fino itself had become a flourishing town, with sixty houses and ten business places, including butcher shops, stores, and a saloon. There were 500 people in the settlement in June, and 5,000 a month later. Belatedly, William Craig, the first white settler in the Nez Perce country, had also joined the rush, and was operating a ferry across the Clearwater near the mines.

All activity through the end of April had been confined to the region north of the Clearwater, and the Indians in contact with the miners had been members of friendly bands that followed Lawyer. But in mid-May fifty-two men,

21. McWhorter, *Hear Me*, pp. 100–01.

still believing that the gold that had been discovered so far was merely the edge of a much greater "fountainhead," left Oro Fino and explored far up the Clearwater. After passing the junction of the South and Middle forks of the river at present-day Kooskia, they continued up the South Fork. Near the location of the present town of Stites they came suddenly on the village of the anti-treaty headman, Koolkool Snehee, or Red Owl, the chief who had given Stevens trouble at the second Walla Walla council in 1856. Koolkool Snehee had no love for Lawyer. He had been a noted buffalo hunter and warrior in the band of old Looking Glass, and had risen to become a prominent subchief under the aged war leader. Part of the region near his village belonged to Looking Glass, and the old headman had made it his second home. Just to the east, on Clear Creek that flowed into the Middle Fork of the Clearwater, was the village of Looking Glass's son, also a noted war and buffalo hunting leader, who would soon inherit his father's name and position.

Koolkool Snehee stopped the miners and told them that they were violating the April agreement that Lawyer had signed. After a long discussion, thirty of the prospectors agreed to abandon the quest and return to Oro Fino. The others crossed the river, slipped past the Indians, and striking the Old Nez Perce Trail to the buffalo country, followed it into the mountains. Near the present site of Elk City, deep in the wilderness north of the Salmon River, they made a rich gold strike. About June 6 some of the men returned to Oro Fino for provisions and announced their new discovery—and another rush was on. By July 1 400 men were at Elk City, and a month later there were 2,000 there. The Indians protested the invasion, and there were rumors that they would fight to eject the whites. But the stampede south of the line that had been established on April 10 continued, and neither the Indians nor the agents took any action that might have discouraged or halted it. New strikes were made elsewhere in the southern mountains, and on August 20 the richest discovery in the entire Northwest was made at Florence, southwest of Elk City. It started still another excited scramble of miners all through the Salmon River country, and by early fall, pack trails, wagon roads, ferries, rough, overnight "hotels," and the first log houses of settlers who intended to grow produce to sell to the miners began to appear in many parts of what was still the treaty-guaranteed reservation of the Nez Perces.

The rapid developments brought swift changes, as well as new divisions and crises, to the Indians. In many of the bands and villages, Nez Perce culture degenerated overnight, as the Indians participated eagerly in the dynamic economy of the gold rush. Indians supplied food, livestock, and labor to the miners. They hung around the whites, visited their camps, helped them with their pack trains, and traveled the trails with them as guides and messengers. They ate the miners' food, donned white men's shirts and pants, drank their liquor, and began to swear, talk, and think like the prospectors. Within a few months, as the Nez Perces adopted the white man's traits, the gold rush accomplished what fur traders, missionaries, soldiers, and agents had failed to do in decades.

The temptations of the gold dust prosperity, in which the Indians shared, were more than flesh could stand, and the abundance of material benefits suddenly available to the Indians overcame the resistance even of some of the anti-treaty leaders. Villagers who lived along the routes to the mines could not hold out while Lawyer's followers prospered and lorded it over them. The principal anti-treaty peoples affected were those of the bands of Koolkool Snehee, Eagle From the Light, and White Bird, who lived along the trails to Elk City, Florence, and the Salmon River country and used the Nez Perce Trail past the mines when they went to the Bitterroot Valley. From time to time they stopped pack strings and groups of miners and ordered them to abide by Lawyer's April 10 treaty and go back; but when the whites slipped around them through the wilderness, the Indians did little except murmur threats. In August a large number of Nez Perces passed Elk City on their way to the Bitterroot Valley, and a correspondent wrote to a Sacramento newspaper that the miners in that settlement had heard that after a three days' journey, the Indians had had an important council in which Eagle From the Light and Koolkool Snehee had fallen out over whether to make war against the whites. Eagle From the Light had proposed that, with the Shoshonis, the Nez Perces exterminate the miners. But Koolkool Snehee had revealed a change of heart about white men. "My eyes are now open," the correspondent quoted him as saying. "The white men dig up and take the gold; what then? *We* get some of it. They buy our beef and pay for it with some of this gold. Our buffalo robes they exchange for gold or blankets. I am an Indian, and don't know how to farm; but I am going to learn . . . they will buy my corn and other things that I shall grow on my farm. No! I have so far been for war, but now my eyes are open. I say peace." Other headmen and leaders had apparently supported him, and in a huff Eagle From the Light "gathered together his lodges—abjured his nation forever as slaves to the whites, and took his departure for the Shoshones, with whom in the future he intends to cast his lot." [22]

By October, however, Eagle From the Light was back in his own country, once again trying to halt the miners. On October 20 a correspondent at Elk City wrote to Oregon City that the chief and a band of about 200 Indians

22. Donald N. Wells, "Farmers Forgotten," *Idaho Yesterdays,* 2 (Summer, 1958), p. 30, quoting Elk City correspondence, August 27, 1861, to the Sacramento *Daily Union,* September 16, 1861, p. 3.

had forbidden the whites to go to the Salmon River country, and had detained three pack trains on the Camas Prairie south of Lewiston. "Lawyer discountances the action of Eagle-of-the-Light," he added, "and has sent a messenger to him, to command him and his band to disperse and not molest the whites, or he (Lawyer) with 600 braves would come out and scalp the last man of them." [23] The threat could not have been serious. In the same month, a man who had come from California wrote that Salmon River miners had told him that Indians "had stretched a rope across the trail leading to the mines, and declared they would kill every white man they found over that limit. The miners were collecting forces," he said, "and would go back with about 400 men to open the trail and protect those who had already gone through . . . We would not be surprised to hear that our California Volunteers would soon be in that country, to aid our people in dispersing the hostile Indians." [24] Soon after that, it appears that Eagle From the Light must have recognized the hopelessness of his position, for in December he and White Bird, the headman in the Salmon River country, sent a delegation to the miners to tell them that they did not wish to fight.

Yet all was not peaceful. No funds arrived to make up the deficiencies in annuity payments for the years 1859 through 1861; and although some money did arrive in November 1862, it amounted to only $6,396 and was mostly diverted into white men's pockets.[25] Lawyer knew he was being cheated, and his complaints grew louder and more insistent. At the same time, he and the other friendly headmen recognized the manner in which parts of the reservation were being converted into a white man's domain under their noses. Lewiston, it was clear, was there to stay; it was on Nez Perce reservation land, but white men were in authority and were talking of forming a local government. Elsewhere, settlements were increasing, and in the countryside between the mining camps whites moved freely wherever they pleased. Individual Indians began to sell reservation land, the most notable native realtor being Stevens' friend Captain John, whom other Indians were calling Jokais (Worthless). In 1861 he sold some of his village land at Slate Creek on the route to Florence to a man named Charles Silverman, who immediately built what is believed to be the first white man's dwelling on the Salmon River. The next year Silverman sold the house to another white man for $1,000, and Captain John shared in the proceeds.[26]

23. "The Salmon River Mines," *Idaho Yesterdays*, 6 (Spring, 1962), p. 44, quoting *Oregon Argus*, Oregon City, November 23, 1861.

24. Ibid., quoting *Daily Portland Times*, October 28, 1861.

25. Report of the Commissioner of Indian Affairs (1865), p. 236.

26. Sister M. Alfreda Elsensohn, *Pioneer Days in Idaho County* (Caldwell, Idaho, 1947), *1*, 279.

There were still uncompromising anti-treaty chiefs, like Joseph in the Wallowa Valley and several along the Snake and Salmon rivers, who continued to demonstrate their contempt for Lawyer and headmen like Captain John. In addition, the erratic James, now known to the white men as Big Thunder (although his name actually meant Thunder Strikes), was making as much trouble for the Indian agent at Lapwai Creek as he had once made for Spalding. Again, jealousy was at the root of it, for both the agency and Lawyer had moved in on top of James, and the latter was getting little out of it but Lawyer's high-handedness. Driven by envy and resentment at slights, the old shaman roared and fussed, and gradually got himself the reputation of being one of the ringleaders of the "anti-treaty party." Lawyer, however, had few defenses against the legitimate evidences of white men's aggrandizement, for which the anti-treaty headmen held him responsible; and in his frustration he subscribed to their grievances and passed them on to the agent at Lapwai Creek, who, in turn, forwarded them helplessly to his superiors at Portland and Washington.

Still, the situation grew worse. By December 1861 the white population east of the Cascades was two-thirds greater than that west of the mountains.[27] The Washington territorial legislature at Olympia recognized the approach of the day when it would have to provide government for the distant mining country. As long as it was Indian reservation land, it could not assume authority; but the Indians, it began to be clear, could not be allowed to possess the region much longer, and in 1861–62, the legislators marked the interior region between the Snake and the Rockies into counties with the names Shoshone, Missoula, Nez Perce, and Idaho (the latter being an apparently meaningless word concocted in Washington, D.C., in 1860 to apply to Colorado territory, but transferred to the Northwest after a Columbia River steamboat adopted the name and popularized it among miners bound for the Clearwater region).[28] The unusual mineral wealth of this country, also, was just beginning to be recognized. In January 1862 it was estimated that $3,000,000 in gold had already been shipped from mines on the Nez Perce res-

27. Bancroft, *History of Idaho*, p. 252.

28. *New Notes on the Word "Idaho,"* Idaho Historical Series, 1, Idaho Historical Society (Boise, 1959). The word (originally spelled "Idahoe"), according to this study, "seems to have been thought up" early in the spring of 1860 by S. W. Beall, "a lobbyist promoting the creation of the new territory" (Colorado), who said that it meant "gem of the mountains." Though it is improbable that any Indian tribe had a word with such a meaning, there has long been a popular story that the term was of Arapaho derivation, and Beall may erroneously have attributed it to that Colorado tribe when he first advanced it. At any rate, the word was not used by the territory that became Colorado. Instead, by June 1860 it also reached the Northwest and was so well regarded there that it was given to a boat, then to a county, a territory, and, finally, a state.

ervation, and it seemed to be just the start.[29] Although the winter of 1861–62 was a severe one in the mountains, some 600 prospectors stayed in the isolated Salmon River region, many of them suffering from hunger and cold in the deep snows of the high country. When the snow started to melt, the rush of newcomers began again, and in May one correspondent reported that from 600 to 1,000 men were arriving daily in the Salmon River area. The influx of new miners accelerated the tempo of change. Dozens of families crossed overland from Walla Walla and went up the Snake and Clearwater rivers to find new homes where they could raise food for the mines and share in the boom. The new town of Wallula, established on the site of the old Fort Walla Walla fur post, became a thriving inland port, serving as a transshipment point for the mining country. The invasion of merchants and traders increased, as did the stream of adventurers, men and women of shady morals, and desperadoes, who arrived at the new bonanza from the California and Colorado mining regions.

In the tumultuous environment of the reservation, lacking any order save that of the miners' law, the social bonds in the Nez Perce villages that neighbored the whites all but disintegrated. Liquor became a desperate problem for the Indians. In 1861 Robert Newell, the Nez Perces' friend, returned to the reservation. "The worst sign I see about here," he wrote to friends, "is the presence of sellers of whiskey to Indians . . . many of the Indians are continually drunk, and consequently sooner or later, we must have a flare up . . . The Nez Perces are more dissipated than formerly. Yesterday I was lecturing an Indian on the evils of getting drunk, when he cooly informed me that he knew what was good as well as a white man. I caved, of course." [30] As expected, Captain Armstrong's admonition to the miners had not worked. For a while, whiskey was brought onto the reservation disguised as vinegar. ". . . you would see whole trains passing through freighted with half barrels of 'vinegar' for the relief of the poor suffering, maybe, honest miners," a correspondent wrote to a Salem, Oregon, paper. But a year later, he added, all pretense had vanished. ". . . horses pass out of the Indians' hands daily by the score for merchandise at the average rate of one horse for two bottles of merchandise." The reason that Eagle From the Light had become friendly, he reported, was to secure liquor from the whites. And another miner wrote: "What a miracle rum has wrought. What Christianity

29. "Fabulous Florence," *Idaho Yesterdays*, 6 (Summer, 1962), 22–23, quoting the Portland *Oregonian*, January 18, 1862, p. 2. From 1860 to 1867 it is estimated that $5–7 million in gold was taken from the Nez Perce reservation.

30. "Clearwater Gold Rush," p. 26, quoting *Oregon Argus*, Oregon City, June 22, 1861, p. 2.

and civilization could not accomplish in decades, liquor has accomplished in a few short months." [31]

The "accomplishment" was not a happy one. The acculturation of the Nez Perces, occurring with such speed, was marked principally by the abandonment of Indian standards and the degeneration of large numbers of Indians to the level of the roughest, most unethical class of whites with whom they were in contact. The flareups that Newell had foreseen were quick in coming, though they were limited to clashes between individuals and small groups. Sometimes they were little more than quarrels, in which the Indians usually came off second best and from which they slunk away to nurse their grudges. But frequently they stemmed from injustices on the part of the whites. Drunken Indians were cheated, robbed, and murdered. Fraud and deceit were practiced on any Indian, drunk or sober. Indians were shortchanged and given false measures. Thefts of horses and cattle by white men were blamed on innocent Indians, who were then punished. Springs were claimed by white squatters, and Indians were forced to pay to use them for themselves or their livestock, or they were driven away at gunpoint. Indian women were seduced and abandoned, raped and left injured and uncared for. The Indians complained about the wrongs, but rarely received satisfaction. When they dared to try to seek redress themselves, they got into worse trouble.

Lawyer and the friendly headmen made repeated appeals to the agency authorities, popularizing a statement that possessed neither truth nor—in the existing state of affairs—self-respect: "The Nez Perces have never killed a white man." The idea was that the Nez Perces and whites had always lived in harmony, and that they should continue to do so. It was like braying at a hurricane. Nevertheless, the increasing friction and conflict could not be ignored, and to Lawyer's complaints were added a growing number of appeals to the national and territorial governments by responsible white men, some of whom saw justice in the Nez Perces' travail, but all of whom wanted something done before there was an explosion and an Indian war.

In Portland, Olympia, and Washington, D.C., only one solution seemed possible—although it was not what Lawyer would have proposed. The military could not interpose itself between the Indians and the miners, the white men would not withdraw from the mines, and historic precedent said that in

31. Wells, "Farmers Forgotten," pp. 31–32. The comment about Eagle From the Light may have been unfair. In March 1866, according to Nez Perce Indian Agent James O'Neill, that chief came to the agency at Lapwai to ask for help in ejecting whiskey sellers from his land. Report of the Commissioner of Indian Affairs (1866), p. 193. There is no evidence that Eagle From the Light ever used or encouraged the use of alcohol.

such cases the Indians must get out. As conflict and tension continued on the reservation, public opinion in the centers of white population focused on a single idea, and hardened. The military leaders at Fort Vancouver, the politicians at Olympia and in the Willamette Valley, and the newspapers from Walla Walla to the Pacific Coast talked the same line, and the elected officials in the national capital finally responded. On August 2, 1862, in the very first issue of *The Golden Age,* the first newspaper published at Lewiston, editor A. S. Gould headlined the news that the miners had waited expectantly to hear: On May 14 the United States Senate had appropriated $50,000 "to negotiate a treaty with the Nez Perces Indians of Oregon and Washington Territory, for the relinquishment of a portion of their present reservation, or its exchange for other lands."

The act, an amendment to the Indian Appropriation Bill, was the work of Senator J. W. Nesmith of Oregon, which had won its statehood in 1859. Nesmith had led the Oregon volunteers against the Yakimas in 1856, and had later been Superintendent of Indian Affairs for Oregon and Washington. He knew the Indians, and he pulled the Senate's heartstrings in a speech that painted a deplorable picture of the government's broken promises to the Nez Perces. "White men have . . . overspread and occupied the reservation in violation of the treaty, and to the great detriment of the Indians," he said. ". . . the annuities which were promised to be paid in stock and substantial improvement, were, in a great part, paid in utterly worthless articles; whistles and shoe strings, pod augurs and gimlets, and old worthless, shelf-worn goods, purchased by some swindling agent in New York at three times their value . . ." It was not the Nez Perces' fault what happened; "it is their boast that the blood of the white man never stained their hands." But now "exterminating war" threatens. "For the purpose of preserving peace, to say nothing about our treaty obligations to these Indians," they should be removed from danger. There was something a bit twisted in his thinking that the Nez Perces should be ousted from their homes in order to live up to past treaty obligations to them, but Nesmith had a piece of private information that made everything understandable. It would have startled the Nez Perces to have heard it, but he told the Senate without a twinge of conscience: "The Indians are anxious to dispose of the reservation and remove to some point where they will not be intruded upon . . . They can be taken to some valley which will be more remote than the present position which they occupy, from the line of travel across the continent."

That satisfied the senators, and the treaty was authorized. The order for its execution was sent to W. H. Rector and Calvin H. Hale, the Superintendents of Indian Affairs in Oregon and Washington Territory, respectively. Relations between Indian agents in the Northwest and the Nez Perces had not been entirely successful since the signing of the April 1861 treaty with Geary. Soon after that agreement had been made, Agent A. J. Cain (who maintained his headquarters in the more comfortable and entertaining surroundings at Walla Walla, far removed from his Nez Perce charges) and the first set of agency employees at Lapwai Creek had been replaced by the Lincoln Administration, and B. F. Kendall, the new Superintendent of Indian Affairs in Washington Territory, had visited the reservation. He had been shocked by what he had found, but his annual report to the Commissioner of Indian Affairs had reflected a preoccupation with carrying out the terms of the Nez Perce treaties and satisfying the head chief, Lawyer, rather than with coping with the increasing friction between Indians and miners. "Not far from sixty thousand dollars have been expended by the agent [Cain] heretofore in charge of the tribe," he had written, "and I regret to say that the visible results of this liberal expenditure are meagre indeed. The buildings erected by Mr. Cain for the agency and employes were mere shells, hardly fit for human habitation . . . I sought in vain to find the first foot of land fenced or broken by him or his employes; and the only product of the agricultural department that I could discover consisted of some three tons of oats in the straw, piled up within a rude, uncovered enclosure of rails, to raise which must have cost the government more than seven thousand dollars." [32]

Kendall had placed a new agent, Charles Hutchins, in residence at Lapwai, but treaty obligations had fared little better. Hutchins had arrived soon after the signing of the April 1861 agreement with the Nez Perces, and had lived through some of the wildest days of the violation of that document. As miners had pushed south of the 1861 line to establish Lewiston and open up Elk City and the Salmon River country, Hutchins had decided that no one could protect the Nez Perces, and that the government should remove the Indians entirely from their reservation. He had written the Commissioner of Indian Affairs to that effect on March 20, 1862, and his letter had provided ammunition to Nesmith in the Senate.[33] With that defeatist attitude, Hutchins had been of no value to the Indians. In the summer of 1862 Kendall was succeeded by Calvin Hale, and when the latter visited Hutchins at the Nez Perce reservation in September, he was even more disturbed with conditions than Kendall had been. "I found there was not so much done as you had the right to expect nor as much as the U. S. Government supposed," he confessed to the Nez Perce headmen when he met with them in council the following year. "I was surprised to see so little improvement made, in view of the large appropriations, which I know have been made. Your head chief had no house

32. Report of the Secretary of the Interior (1861–62), p. 447.
33. Office of Indian Affairs, Letters Received, Washington Superintendency, H-473 (1862), National Archives.

built, and no farm fenced or ploughed. The money for this had been appropriated . . . Your head chief, Lawyer, was entitled to pay. The money had been appropriated, but I found none had been paid . . . I found that you had no school house, although a teacher had been sent; that you had no hospital built, and your mills were not finished . . ."[34]

Hale transferred Hutchins to the Flatheads and replaced him at Lapwai with J. W. Anderson. The new team of Hale and Anderson made a better record than their predecessors, and during 1862–63 they took care of many of the omissions that Hale had noted. Lawyer received his salary, his house was built, part of his land was ploughed and fenced, and the mills and schoolhouse were constructed. But Hale had received his instructions for the new treaty meeting, and he knew that it was worth his while to hurry and eliminate some of the sore points that would otherwise hurt his chance of success with the Indians. Despite the government's intention to hold the council as quickly as possible, Hale recommended delaying it until the spring of 1863.

Many others who visited the reservation in 1862 also noted the injustice of the Indians' position. In May and June, Edward Giddings, Chief Clerk of the Surveyor General's Office in Washington Territory, came from Olympia to investigate the country occupied by the miners. He reported that there were approximately 18,690 whites already living on the Nez Perces' land. Lewiston had a population of 2,000, he said, and there were 3,514 in Pierce City and 9,200 in Florence.[35] In November, Superintendent Rector of Oregon and Brigadier General Benjamin Alvord, in command at Fort Vancouver, arrived on the reservation. Rector thought the situation was so bad that the treaty council should have been held that fall, and he wrote the Commissioner of Indian Affairs on November 12, criticizing the delay.[36] Nevertheless, he and Alvord called the friendly headmen together and announced that the government wished to have another treaty gathering with them in the spring. The Indians were apparently too startled to reply, and Rector told them that he would ask Agent Anderson to set a date with them for the meeting. On their return to Fort Vancouver, Alvord sent a dismal letter to Senator Nesmith in Washington, in which he said nothing about the Indians' reaction to the council but commented freely on the state of affairs on the reservation:

34. Proceedings at Lapwai Treaty Council (1863), National Archives, Record Group 75, pp. 54–55.

35. Giddings Report, August 28, 1862, House Executive Document No. 1, 37th Congress, 3rd Session.

36. Hale's recommendation to delay the council can be found in Office of Indian Affairs, Letters Received, Washington Superintendency, H-580, H-581, H-595 (1862), National Archives. Rector's criticism is in the Office of Indian Affairs, Letters Received, Oregon, R-1919 (1862), National Archives.

After their long and unswerving friendship & fidelity to us & to our flag, it is melancholy to see so little care taken to carry out treaty stipulations, and that with a tribe who have adhered to us through thick and thin. It is a miracle considering the mass of people upon that reservation the last year or two, that last month the first alleged murders by Indians occurred—One of the accused is a son of Peu-peu-mox-mox by a Nez Perces wife.—The other is a boy of Big Thunders band of Nez Perces. His guilt is doubtful but if guilty, it is the very first Nez Perces known to kill a white man in the scores of years Craig & Newell have known that tribe. I left here for the reservation before I had heard of the murders. The tribe was much excited & were also alarmed because the military were to have been withdrawn for the winter by the order of Genl Wright the *Department* Commander. I had to assume the responsibility to establish a military fort there & have no doubt when the facts are known, that General Wright will approve of my course. The step is pleasing to all factions of the tribe, as they are habituated to look to the military for protection. It will serve to put the tribe in good heart— seeing some show of earnest protection under the *old* treaty, will put them in better heart for a *new* treaty next spring.[37]

The military post that Alvord established and manned with western volunteers sworn into the federal service was named Fort Lapwai, and was located in Big Thunder's territory in the Lapwai Valley, several miles above the agency buildings. At the same time, noting the rapid turnover of agents that had distressed the friendly headmen, the General informed Nesmith that he and Rector concurred in the belief that the old mountain man, Robert Newell, now making his home among the Nez Perces, should be appointed as their agent. "I urge it mainly," he said, "because my recent visit to that Reservation has shown me how desirable it is that some one should be appointed, who would take a permanent interest in that faithful tribe."

During the winter of 1862–63 grim fears circulated among the Indians on the reservation. Memories of what had happened to the Wallawallas, Yakimas, and other tribes filled the villages, and both the treaty and nontreaty bands were astir with rumors that in the spring the troops would make war on any settlement that resisted eviction. In January 1863 the grand old patriot of the Nez Perce nation, Looking Glass of Asotin—the great Meiway Apash Wyakaikt, who had befriended Bonneville, humbled Pambrun, opposed Spalding, and resisted Stevens—died, and his son succeeded him, taking his

37. Fort Vancouver, W. T., November 25, 1862, Benjamin Alvord Collection, Oregon Historical Society, Portland, Ore.

name and hanging his father's small, round trade mirror around his neck. The junior Looking Glass, although a warrior and buffalo hunter who often went to the plains, was not as forceful as his father had been, and he stood in the shadow of Tipyahlanah Kaupu, the Eagle From the Light. The latter, together with Big Thunder, White Bird, and Joseph, were the principal spokesmen of the antitreaty faction, and they upbraided Lawyer during the winter months, charging that the pro-white policies that he and his followers had pursued had brought the tribe to its present crisis. Lawyer snapped back that the anti-treaty chiefs had no respect for the laws of God or the American government and that they were bad leaders, and the controversy only widened the breach in the tribe.

Nevertheless, Lawyer could not ignore the fears that filled his own people. From white friends he learned of Nesmith's speech in the Senate, and heard that not all the members of that law-making body had supported the proposal for a new treaty, but that some had voted against it. It gave him heart, seeming to indicate to him that the Americans might not be united and that Rector and Alvord, perhaps, had been acting for Nesmith alone, and had not spoken with the full authority of the United States government and its laws. If that proved to be the case, he and his followers could decline to accept a revision of the Stevens treaty, and the government would not move troops against the villages. At any rate, he and the other friendly headmen had no choice but at least to meet the negotiators; and when Anderson pressed them for a date for the council, they finally said they would see the superintendents at Lapwai on May 10, 1863.

In the meantime, the whites had been closing a tighter vise around the reservation. Pushing east from the Blue Mountains of Oregon, miners had made rich strikes in the Powder River Valley and had opened a new mining region south of the Wallowa Mountains. Late in the summer of 1862 prospectors had crossed the Snake River and, braving the hostility of the Shoshonis and Bannocks, who were desperately trying to keep whites out of their country, had found gold in the Boise Basin. In the fall a new rush had started to that area. To connect with the various discoveries that now hemmed the Nez Perces on the west and south, a port had come into being at the mouth of the Umatilla River, and a network of pack trails and roads was being blazed from the Columbia River to the Boise Valley, and from the Grande Ronde to the Snake. Although no miner is known to have entered the Wallowa Valley, prospectors were traveling freely through the Cayuse and Umatilla lands and exploring the mountains and canyons on the borders of Joseph's country. Farmers and stockmen, eager for trade closer to the new mines, and also with emigrants from the East who still used the Overland Trail, moved up the

Umatilla and across the Blue Mountains, and settled in the Grande Ronde Valley, just west of the mountain barrier that hid the Wallowa country.

At the same time, a new force with a subtle but powerful threat to the Indians came into being. Since the previous winter, the miners in the Nez Perce country had felt their remoteness from the Washington Territory's seat of government on Puget Sound, and had urged the creation of a new territory of their own. The proposal had been rejected several times, but with the discovery of the Boise mines and the large increase of population in the regions east of Walla Walla in 1862, the demand could no longer be opposed. On March 3, 1863, Congress established the Territory of Idaho, embracing all of the present states of Idaho and Montana and almost all of Wyoming, and a week later President Lincoln appointed William H. Wallace, Washington Territory's delegate to Congress, as the first governor of Idaho. White public opinion now had a powerful political weapon with which to bring increased pressure against the Nez Perces; the miners would have politicians of their own in the territory and the national capital to force federal policies and action in support of their interests against those of the Indians.

Superintendent Calvin Hale was already aware of this new pressure when he left Olympia on May 1, 1863, for the treaty council at Lapwai. He had heard of Wallace's appointment, and he stopped at Portland, understanding that Wallace was on his way there by steamer from San Francisco and assuming that the new governor would join him as one of the treaty commissioners. Although Wallace did not arrive, Hale went on to Idaho with a sense of responsibility to the political power represented by the new government of the miners and the authority of Lincoln's appointee. Since November, Rector had retired as Superintendent of Indian Affairs in Oregon, and Hale chose as his fellow commissioners for the council two Indian agents, Charles Hutchins, whom he had previously sent from the Nez Perces to the Flatheads, and S. D. Howe. To make "a good effect" on the Indians, and lend support to the commissioners, Alvord assembled six companies of troops at Fort Lapwai under the command of Colonel Justus Steinberger.[38] The troops included elements of the First Oregon Cavalry Regiment, as well as federalized units from Washington and California, and although their presence strengthened Hale's hand against the Nez Perces, Colonel Steinberger and his officers were meticulously careful to assume a posture of fairness and neutrality during the council proceedings. About a mile from the fort the soldiers established a huge tent city, laid out in streets, to accommodate the large numbers of Indians expected at the meeting.

38. General Alvord to Senator Nesmith, Fort Vancouver, W. T., July 25, 1863, Benjamin Alvord Collection, Oregon Historical Society.

Hale reached Lapwai on May 11, but because the lateness of spring had delayed the Indians' planting, he found few Nez Perces present. To his dismay, however, he learned that many of them had also stayed away deliberately because of reports, circulated by "evil disposed persons," that the commissioners would not come, that the soldiers at Lapwai were there to drive the Indians from their lands by force, and that the Civil War had broken up the American government in the East. Meeting immediately with Lawyer, he persuaded the head chief to spread the word through the tribe that the reports were false, that the commissioners had arrived and were waiting to begin the meeting.

During his visit to the reservation the previous year, Hale had been told by Timothy and some of the other headmen of the Lawyer faction that they would like to have Henry Spalding back on the reservation. Spalding had still been living on his claim on the Touchet River, maintaining contact with Timothy and other Christian Nez Perces and hoping for an appointment that would permit him to reside on the reservation and that would pay his expenses. No appointment had come, and in November 1861, after the discovery of gold, Spalding had written to his old friend A. T. Smith, suggesting that the two of them join William Geiger and go to the Nez Perce country to prospect.[39] That scheme had come to nothing, and when Timothy had finally told Hale in 1862 that Spalding's return would be a good influence on the Indians, he had probably been transmitting a suggestion by the former missionary. At any rate, Hale had agreed that Spalding's presence on the reservation might be desirable, and in the spring of 1863 the 60-year-old pioneer, accompanied by his second wife, had gone as government schoolteacher to the Lapwai agency, where many of his Indian friends had given him a warm and tearful welcome.

Now Hale enlisted him, together with Robert Newell, as official interpreters for the council. The selections bothered Lawyer. Marcus Whitman's nephew, Perrin Whitman, had been official interpreter on the reservation during Hutchins' term as agent, and Lawyer and the other headmen considered that his understanding of the Nez Perce language was better than that of either Spalding or Newell. Perrin and his wife and daughter had since moved to the lower Columbia; but on May 13 Lawyer, Utsinmalikin, Spotted Eagle, and Captain John called on the commissioners and asked them to send for Whitman to be the interpreter at the council. "They stated," Hale said, "that it was possible they might have some plain, some hard things to say, and the Commissioners on the other hand might have the same to reply. Whatever might thus be spoken by either party, they wished to be just as plainly or sharply interpreted." Spalding and Newell, the Indians felt, "might very

39. Drury, *Spalding*, p. 374.

naturally be led to soften some of the harsh expressions which might be used, from motives of the best character, in order to avoid disagreement of difficulty. Especially they desired that the labor should not devolve upon Mr. Spaulding, as he was their Teacher, and they did not wish to put harsh words into his lips." Also, they explained, the nontreaty bands might object "if the Interpreter should be taken solely from those living in their midst, being considered liable to the charge of favoring the views of one party more than the other." [40]

Lawyer and his followers had good grounds for their concern. Many of the Indians believed that the troubles that had followed the 1855 Walla Walla council had occurred because the interpreters had not accurately translated what either side had said. They wished no misunderstanding this time, especially since Lawyer had worked out a particularly delicate line of resistance that was based on questions that would require clear and unmistakable answers. Also, Lawyer knew that neither Newell nor Spaulding were friendly to the nontreaty leaders. Spaulding characterized them as "heathens," and was hostile to them—especially to Joseph, his erstwhile convert. If Lawyer was to assert his dominance over those chiefs at the treaty meeting, he recognized that he could give them no opportunity to claim to the different villages that he and the white men had been in collusion. Whitman, he knew, would be acceptable to all as a neutral.

Although Spaulding was distressed, and from that time on behaved in a jealous and unfriendly fashion to Whitman, Hale agreed to the request of Lawyer's group and sent Agent Anderson to the Willamette Valley to try to hire young Perrin. Meanwhile, the commissioners had arrived at an important conclusion. After talking to Anderson and others at the agency, they had decided "that it would be impossible to find, outside of their own reservation, a region of country suited to this people, upon which there could be any reliance for a permanent abode, besides, if there were, it would have been of no avail, for they would have refused to enter into any arrangement whatever, upon terms that would have required them to leave their own country." Having recognized that fact, and noting that "Agent Anderson elicited such information as led to the inference that the most suitable place for the future Reservation was to be found along the valley of the Clearwater, especially along the main Stream and South Fork, with the tributaries flowing into it

40. Unless otherwise noted, all quotations concerning the treaty are from two documents: "Synopsis of the Preliminary and Official Proceedings of a Council held in the valley of the Lapwai," and a covering letter from Superintendent C. H. Hale to William P. Dole, Commissioner of Indian Affairs, Washington, D.C., dated Olympia, June 30, 1863, and providing background to the account of the official proceedings. Both are in the National Archives, Record Group 75.

from the South," they tried to gather data about that region, but discovered that no white man could tell them much about it, and that even those "who had been longest in the country had but limited knowledge of [the] character or capacity" of the tribe's largest village, Kamiah. Therefore, accompanied by a Nez Perce guide, Hale made a tour for himself up the Clearwater.

"At all points," he wrote, "we found Indian villages or camps, with their patches of wheat, corn, peas and potatoes." Kamiah, where Lewis and Clark had stayed almost sixty years before and where the Asa Smiths had once lived, extended along the Clearwater "for a distance of about ten miles, and varying from half a mile to two and a half miles in width. It is nearly evenly divided by a beautiful stream, about half the size of the Lapwai, coming in from the South West, through what is known as Lawyers Canon. With this Stream, they are able to irrigate the entire plain, which is dotted with numerous Indian farms, exhibiting encouraging signs of thrift. Their wheat, corn, peas and potatoes were growing luxuriantly . . . Numerous and extensive bands of horses and quite a number of cattle were grazing along the borders of the plain, and on the sides of the lofty hills, which hem it on the South."

Hale returned to the agency, convinced that he could compress all of the Nez Perces into a reservation based on the Clearwater, its South Fork, and the Lapwai Valley, embracing a region of low farmland and high grazing country situated compactly between the Pierce and Oro Fino mines on the north and the Elk City and Salmon River mines on the south, but containing no country desired by the miners. He outlined the boundaries of the new reserve on a map, and by May 21 was ready to meet with the Indians. Still, there were delays. Some 1,000 Nez Perces had reached the treaty grounds, but an outbreak of influenza struck them, and the commissioners had to wait till a doctor came out from Lewiston to administer medicine and quell the epidemic. During the next few days more Indians arrived, although—with the exception of some members of Big Thunder's band—they were all followers of the Lawyer faction. Big Thunder himself was very sick, and Hale noted that the old shaman was "induced to consent" to let the physician visit him and prescribe medicines, which he took without protest.

Besides Nez Perces, the Indian camp contained friends and relatives from some of the tribes that had been smashed in the wars of the 1850s. A group of Palouses and Yakimas showed up one day, and after stalking about in an unfriendly manner and insulting the commissioners, they settled down among Big Thunder's people. Hale considered that they were up to no good, and he had some of Colonel Steinberger's men eject them from the area.

On May 25 Lawyer's people were willing to begin the council, although Perrin Whitman had not yet arrived. Neither had the anti-treaty bands of Eagle From the Light, Joseph, White Bird, or Koolkool Snehee, but Hale felt that he had sent them adequate notice and that he was no longer bound to wait for them. Soon after he had opened the first session, however, he announced, "This talk is for the whole Nez Perce nation, not for a part, but for every man who has an interest here." As the meeting got under way, he assured the Indians that the troops were there to protect them and not to drive them away from their homes. Then he came bluntly to the purpose of the council, informing the Nez Perces that the government desired them to relinquish part of their present reservation and "take a new Reservation, smaller than the one you now hold." He delineated the boundaries upon which he had decided, and explained that "the lands in the valleys shall also be surveyed into lots, so that each of you can have a farm in his own right, and have it secured to him by a paper, just as the whites do, then nobody can disturb you . . . The rest of your Reservation we propose to buy. Those of you who live on that portion of it, which is to be relinquished, will be paid for the improvements you have made, such as your fields that are enclosed and cultivated."

The headmen made no reply. Hale had designed the reservation so as to enfold within its borders almost all the villages of the friendly bands and as many as possible of the anti-treaty groups; and if they had just been thinking of protecting the riverbank sites of their settlements, few of the chiefs present would have had reason to complain. But the tightly drawn boundary lines looked to them like the confining walls of a corral. Joseph and some of the Snake and Salmon river nontreaty people were not there to see that their entire lands were to be taken by the whites. That would be their concern, and they would protest. But where were those "heathen" bands to be put? Inside the new reservation, on the lands of Lawyer, Utsinmalikin, Big Thunder, and others. Everyone would be squeezed together, Christian, "heathen," treaty, and nontreaty bands. There would be fights and turmoil. And what of the hills and mountains and valleys being relinquished? Where would men roam to hunt, where would women gather camas? Where would freedom be found?

The first session ended, and the Indians shuffled away, deeply troubled. The next day Hutchins described the proposals in more detail. The valley land would be divided into twenty-acre lots, with each Nez Perce family receiving one lot. The agent spent considerable time enumerating the payments that would be made, the buildings built, the services rendered, if the Nez Perces signed the new treaty. When Hutchins had finished, Hale asked the chiefs if there was anything they did not understand. It was suddenly time for the headmen to expose the flaw that would save them. Lawyer was silent, but he had primed Utsinmalikin to ask the delicate question. The old chief, who had once ordered Asa Smith to leave Kamiah, rose. "When," he asked Hale, "did the order for this proposition, you have made, come from your

Government? I feel responsible to the Government, and wish to know if this comes from it, when it came, whether in the fall, in the winter or this spring? State it distinctly for we wish to know."

Now was the moment for an expert interpreter. Was this council the doing of the President, or of Nesmith? Unaware of what the Indians were getting at, Hale felt insulted. Launching into a long history of the gold rush, the government's desire to protect the Indians from conflict with the whites, and the orders he had received from Washington, he ended angrily, "We are here by the authority, and under the instructions of our Government." It failed to satisfy the chiefs. Lawyer rose and in a shrewd speech that bristled with sarcasm told the commissioners that he and his people were governed by laws, that they were there that day "to adhere to the treaty that has been made, and which we on our side have kept. Not one of us is grasping at shadows, or the simple sayings of any outsider . . ." He was not one of the anti-treaty troublemakers, he reminded Hale, and "those who will cast off all law, if any do, I will not acknowledge as belonging to me, they would be considered by me as outlaws." So much for Joseph and the anti-treaties, but ". . . you have broken the treaty [of 1855], not we . . . That engagement was made with us for 20 years, with the boundary as made by your Government. We understand very well what 20 years mean . . . This winter we were told that Colonel Nesmith was in Congress at Washington; we learned what he said there; I understood that there was a division of opinion on Colonel Nesmith's proposition, part were in favor of it, and part were not. Here we are listening to what you say again, before the 20 years are ended . . . Perhaps by contemplating you will find something that is wrong in your proposition . . ."

It was a good try, but it could only be a try. The government was behind Nesmith, and behind Hale. "This proposition is from the Government," the Superintendent repeated. "We are expected to fix upon such boundaries as can be understood, and protected, and to make such a Treaty as can be carried out." He ignored comment on the failure of the government to adhere to the old treaty, but promised to have the Stevens document read out loud the next day. Somewhat nettled by the opposition of the head chief, whom he had been led to believe would help and not hinder him, he adjourned the session.

The next day he appeared with a copy of the 1855 treaty. It was obvious that hearing it read out loud would embarrass him, and he began the session with a stream of awkward explanations and apologies. "We do not claim that in all respects the Treaty has been carried out," he said. He listed the monies already appropriated, puncturing his accounting with such remarks as, "How much of that money was sent here and expended I do not know. I have endeavored to find out, but have not been able to . . . I cannot be expected to account for the monies received, before I became the Superintendent, about a year ago. I do not know about it . . . There are perhaps some deficiencies in the expenditure of the first years' appropriations, we do not know how much. But whatever it may be, if any, it will undoubtedly be made good." He did not say what made him think that he or anyone else could get the Congress to make good the deficiencies; and overlooking the fact that he was just another passing figure in Nez Perce history, who would have no more to say about what happened after his departure than had any Superintendent before him, he glibly assured the chiefs that, in time, they would receive everything that Stevens had promised them. Futhermore, he guaranteed that what they received for this new treaty would be in addition to everything that was already owed to them.

The 1855 treaty was then read aloud, after which Lawyer completely demolished Hale. Opening a small pocket notebook, the head chief read some of Stevens' statements that he had written down, word for word, at the Walla Walla council eight years before. "My friends," Lawyer quoted Stevens as saying to the Indians at that time, "we have assembled under the influence of Laws, and that which shall be permanent and straight . . . The Creator is looking down upon us, and I expect to say the truth." Hale heard Lawyer out in silence, and then adjourned the session.

The anti-treaty bands had not yet arrived, but the commissioners were already in trouble. The next morning, May 28, Lawyer and his followers showed up in great excitement, because they had just learned that some white men had moved onto reservation land near Lewiston and were erecting buildings. Hale saw a chance to prove his good intentions and ingratiate himself with the tribe. He appealed at once to Colonel Steinberger to send troops to remove the invaders. Steinberger moved swiftly; the whites were ejected and their structures demolished and thrown into the river. But the action did not help Hale. When the council met, Lawyer was ready to give the Superintendent the tribe's answer. After a lengthy summation, in which the head chief reviewed the history of Nez Perce relations with the whites, and the tribe's assistance to Americans in times of crisis and war, he listed the violations that had already occurred on the reservation, suggesting that the only matters to be discussed were payments for the townsites of Lewiston, Oro Fino, and Elk City, and for the many ferries that white men had established within the reservation's boundaries. These, he implied, the government could buy and pay for. As for Hale's proposal that the tribe sell most of its land and live on what was left, "I fear there would not be enough . . . there will be crowding," and he concluded, "I will now give you the great answer. Dig the gold, and look at the country, but we cannot give you the country you ask for."

Some historians have believed that Lawyer was merely being a good politi-

cian and was sparring with Hale for a better price. Hale himself thought that
the episode of the white trespassers that morning had had much to do with
Lawyer's refusal "so early and so decidedly." Neither was true; the headmen
had counciled the previous night and, recognizing that they could no longer
question Hale's authority but must give him an answer to take to the President, were now showing him their hearts with honesty. They had never, at
any time during the winter, considered selling their lands, and the idea was
still unthinkable to them. Utsinmalikin spoke when Lawyer had finished, and
made the point clearly: "That boundary then made [in 1855]," he said to
Hale, "we considered permanent, sacred, and according to law . . . We
thought it was to remain forever. With pleasure we have listened to the
words brought from the President from time to time. Hence the reason I
asked you the other day, whether propositions so unlike the other, came from
him. I say to you, you trifle with us. The boundary was fixed, and we have been
under it and thought it permanent. We understood that the whole of our
reservation was for us, to cultivate and to occupy as we pleased. We cannot
give up our country. You but trifle with us. We cannot give you the country, we cannot sell it to you." These were not the words of a bargainer. Nor
was the plea of the next speaker, a headman named Hohots Stortee, known to
the whites as Billy: After recounting Stevens' promises, he said, "Now you
come with other propositions. It does not look as if they came from the Government; it cannot be—it is so different from what Governor Stevens said to
us, as to our boundary . . . It does not look good, it looks crooked. My people say, it is *not* good . . . We have answered you, we cannot sell our
country."

The chiefs' opposition left Hale in a helpless position. He argued with a
long, purposeless speech, admitting that what the headmen had said about
Stevens' word was true, but insisting that the President at the time had let the
Nez Perces keep a large portion of their country which they did not use, simply because the white men did not need it at that time. The President
thought, however, that "if the time should come when that, which you could
not use, might be needed," the Indians would be willing to sell. Now times
had changed. The Government wished to protect the Nez Perces from the
miners. "By making the Reserve smaller, it is believed, that you can be the
better protected." As he went on, the absurdity of his arguments, suggesting
that bands like that of Joseph did not need the Wallowa, and that the main
reason for the reservation was to separate the Nez Perces from the whites,
became apparent to him, and he ended by pretending to resent the way the
Indians had questioned his authority. "If you have made up your minds," he
said testily, "that is the end. We are sorry that you have so hastily decided
this matter. All that we say to you, and that you say to us, will be reported to

the President . . . if you do not recognize our authority, it is useless for us to talk any further to you."

The council recessed, but no one went home, and six days later, on June 3, the Indians asked for another meeting. Meanwhile, Perrin Whitman had arrived, and a huge throng of anti-treaty Indians under Joseph, Eagle From the Light, White Bird, Big Thunder, and Koolkool Snehee had reached the Lapwai grounds. More than 3,000 Indians had gathered when the commissioners reconvened the council. In the interval since the adjournment of the last meeting, the white negotiators had collected their wits, and Agent Howe, thinking principally of the anti-treaty newcomers in the audience, opened the session with a clear and frank summation of the government's position. If gold had not been discovered on the reservation, he told the Indians, there would have been no reason to wish to change the boundaries established by the 1855 treaty. But what no one could have foreseen in 1855 had come to pass, and now there were problems for both the Indians and the government. "Many of your difficulties," he explained, "are caused by the extent of your Reservation, a few of you living at one place, and a few at another, so that you are scattered and divided. Whilst you continue in this way, it is impossible to protect you, as we wish, and as it is important for you, that you should be."

When he had finished, the leaders of both the treaty and anti-treaty factions of the tribe retired from the council and deliberated together in an amicable discussion. After a while they returned and announced that they were willing to sell the portions of the reservation on which gold had been discovered, as well as the land on which Lewiston was situated, with the country around it for about ten or twelve miles. That was exactly what the Lawyer group had already proposed, and inasmuch as the anti-treaties had agreed to go along with it, it represented a victory for Lawyer within the tribe. But it dismayed the commissioners, who told the Indians "that they could not entertain such a proposition." Hale adjourned the council again, and recognizing that he had reached an impasse, decided to try something new. He wrote to the Commissioner of Indian Affairs in his covering letter to the account of the council proceedings:

> I . . . concluded to try private conferences with the Chiefs, where, by direct questions and answers, there would be better opportunity of ascertaining their true feelings, meeting their objections, removing their doubts, and explaining to them such matters as they were liable to misunderstand. The difference was soon perceivable. They had thought our speeches to them might mean something different; they had been afraid that we would deceive them. Private conversations thus held, separately with the chiefs of each faction, resulted satisfactorily. On

the part of the friendly ones, an agreement to accept the terms proposed by the Commissioners, with some slight alterations as to boundary, and a few items in the way of further consideration, was at length had . . . On the part of the disaffected bands, their chiefs gave an unequivocal assent to the main features of the Treaty, so far as they were concerned, only that their pride would not permit them to come in with the Lawyer party, and sign the Treaty. Quil-quil-se-ne-na, Eagle of the Light and Hin-ma-tute-ka-kike or Big Thunder, each came of their own accord, in private conference, and asked that it might be reported to their Great Father at Washington, that they did not refuse to sign the Treaty, out of any disrespect or want of friendly feeling towards him, to the Commissioners, or the people of the United States, but that their refusal was solely, on account of difficulties amongst themselves. Besides, they alleged that it was not necessary for them to sign it, as they were not called upon, by the conditions of the Treaty, to surrender anything to the Government, as their lands were almost entirely included in the proposed new Reservation. They did not need provisions or presents, they were not poor, they were rich. They wished the Treaty to be made, and expressed their belief, that it would be for their best interests as a people. After thus opening their hearts, in which they seemed to be sincere, manifesting nothing of that haughtiness which marked their behavior on their first arrival at the Council Ground, they took leave of us in the kindest manner.[41]

Without knowledge of this summation by Hale, which is published here for the first time, much nonsense has been written in the past about how the treaty finally came to be signed, and who signed it and who did not. Using Hale's account as a frame of reference, the official minutes of the proceedings can now be followed to show what actually occurred.

After the adjournment of the June 3 session, the minutes record, Hale first conducted separate, private conversations with "the leading chiefs of the friendly Indians." Hale's summation says that in those meetings he was assisted by Henry Spalding and Perrin Whitman, who went beyond their duties as interpreters "to explain fully to the Indians the matters proposed for their consideration, and the advantages to accrue to them." The commissioners' line to each of the Indians was perhaps the same; only two of the chiefs, Timothy of Alpowa and Jason of Asotin, had to move; all the rest were already situated within the proposed new reservation. By isolating the headmen from each other in those private sessions and hammering at them, one by one, the commissioners and the interpreters must gradually have overcome

41. Hale to Commissioner Dole, Olympia, June 30, 1863, pp. 19–21.

the Indians' opposition. Then the offer of a "further consideration" must have been helpful in securing a capitulation. Lawyer had undoubtedly been the first man to meet with the commissioners, and it is likely that his principal request had been to make the new reservation a little larger so that the bands would not be so crowded together. The commissioners had apparently complied with his request by making "some slight alterations as to boundary." There is no record of any special personal "consideration" offered to the head chief; but the treaty itself shows that most of the payments, buildings, and improvements were to go to his village. It also reveals some of what was given to others: Timothy, for instance, who was almost considered a white man and was allowed to continue to live with his family on his farm at Alpowa, was promised $600 to build himself a new house, and two other headmen were promised houses and salaries of $500 each.

The friendly chiefs did not surrender on the first night, but the commissioners must have been satisfied with the progress they had made. The next day, when the council met, Hutchins spoke and addressed his remarks principally to the anti-treaty chiefs, with whom the commissioners had not yet met in private. Knowing that their people were more inclined to roam than were the more settled farmers of the Lawyer faction, Hutchins assured them that "they were to be as free as the Whites, to go where they pleased throughout the whole country, to hunt, to fish, to gather berries and dig cammas. They could take their horses and cattle, to graze them, on any lands outside, not in the occupancy of the whites." In answer, the minutes note, "Two or three of the disaffected chiefs said a few words but in such a haughty, and incoherent manner as to be unable to understand the half of what was said."

When the session ended, the commissioners resumed their private talks with Lawyer's headmen, but found to their distress that there had been some backsliding since the previous evening. The problem seemed to lie in the friendly Indians' fear of the anti-treaty chiefs, who had recognized that Lawyer's people had weakened during their conversations with the commissioners and had accused them of being cowards. Hale understood that threats had been made and, fearing that the anti-treaty bands would have their way, and perhaps even threaten Lawyer's people and the commissioners with violence, sent a dispatch to Colonel Steinberger, asking him to send a detachment of troops to the council grounds. He argued again with the friendly chiefs, won them back to support of the treaty, and promised to protect them against the other bands.

The soldiers, whom the Nez Perces had originally regarded as guardians against the whites, now became an instrument of coercion. About one o'clock that night, a detachment of twenty Oregon cavalrymen under Captain George Currey arrived on the council grounds. All was quiet, except at one lodge where fifty-three headmen, representing both the treaty and nontreaty bands, were debating the proposed treaty. Currey dismounted and, with the aid of an interpreter, listened in. "The debate," he wrote in his official report, "ran with dignified firmness and warmth until near morning, when the Big Thunder party made a formal announcement of their determination to take no further part in the treaty, and then with a warm, and in an emotional manner, declared the Nez Perce nation *dissolved;* whereupon the Big Thunder men shook hands with the Lawyer men, telling them with a kind but firm demeanor that they would be friends, but a distinct people. It did not appear from the tone of their short, sententious speeches, that either party was meditating a present outbreak. I withdrew my detachment, having accomplished nothing but witnessing the extinguishment of the last council fires of the most powerful Indian nation on the sunset side of the Rocky Mountains." [42]

Captain Currey did not overestimate the significance of the momentous event he had observed. In a formal manner, all of the headmen, including the members of the Lawyer party, had agreed that Lawyer no longer had the right to regard himself as spokesman or head chief of the anti-treaty bands. The political system fastened on the tribe by Elijah White in 1842 was dead. For many years, not all of the bands had accepted the authority of the head chief; but the tensions after the Whitman massacre and during the period of the wars of the 1850s had, at least, forced the bands to acknowledge the head chief as tribal spokesman in councils with the whites. Now even that was ended, and the fact should have been communicated immediately to the commissioners. That it was not must be blamed on Lawyer, whose willingness to allow the white negotiators to believe that they could use his signature to bind every Nez Perce band was fraught with serious consequences for the people of Joseph, White Bird, and others who did not sign the treaty, and who lived outside the boundaries of the new reservation.

Neither Joseph nor White Bird had had anything to say during the two sessions of the council they had attended. Both of them were deadset against the treaty, which would have taken their lands away from them, and they could sense that Lawyer and most of his followers, who would lose nothing, would give them little support. There was no reason for them to participate in a council aimed principally against themselves, and after the all-night session that Currey had witnessed, they started their bands back to their homes, secure in the belief that Lawyer could no longer speak for them or sign a treaty that would sell their lands. It was an innocence and trust that they would regret.

When the council convened on June 5, Agent Hutchins directed his remarks at the anti-treaty chiefs who had caused Lawyer's people to backslide

42. Report of the Adjutant-General of Oregon, 1865–66, p. 18.

the day before. Only three of the anti-treaty leaders remained. "We wish now," Hutchins said, "to talk to Quil-quil-se-ne-na, Eagle of the Light, and Big Thunder, and what we say is for them, and not for the other Nez Perces, but we want all to hear what we say to you." It was now the time for threats and coercion. "We heard your talk yesterday," Hutchins went on, "and have considered it. What you said convinces us, that you are not good men to the Law, and that you are bad counsellors to your young men . . . You shall not poison the hearts of the other Nez Perces. The Government will protect them against your bad designs, and . . . will punish you terribly . . . You talked a little yesterday, but you did not say much when you spoke . . . You answer us with crooked words . . . You have told the Nez Perces, that when they take the blankets and clothing given them by the President, that they are putting their lands on their backs and when they eat the Beef and the Flour [offered as annuities by the government] that they are eating up their country. When you say that, you lie . . . Lawyer and his Chiefs who wish the welfare of their people, begin to see that it will be wise and good to accept our propositions, and if you do not choose to make the arrangement with them, we will make it without you."

At that point it would have been well if Lawyer or another headman had interrupted to inform the commissioners of the development of the night before. But no Indian said anything, and Hutchins continued, establishing the ground for the recognition of Lawyer and his followers as the only signers the Americans would need for the Nez Perce treaty. "When the new arrangement is made," he threatened the anti-treaty chiefs, "the good Nez Perces will be wise, and rich and happy. You will be poor and miserable—and you will make your children poor and miserable. They will see that you have caused it, and when you are dead, they will curse you, because you did not secure these things, to make them happy, as the wise chiefs did for their children . . . if you persist in your disloyalty, we shall not regard you as Nez Perces, for the white men think that to be a Nez Perce, means that you are good men."

The anti-Lawyer headmen sat through this harangue without seeming to be upset. They were used to American promises, lies, and threats. But there was a difference now. "Is that the way we are?" asked Big Thunder. His mind may have filled with memories of the days when he had ridden with Hudson's Bay Company brigades, when he had frolicked with American mountain men at the Green River, when he had sung for a missionary's biscuit to give to Joe Meek, when he had made Spalding know who was chief at Lapwai . . . But it was all in the past, and that was the difference. His freedom was gone; he was old, sick, surrounded by the conqueror, and without the power to defy anyone. Speaking for the anti-treaty leaders, he again raised the question of the commissioners' authority, but intimated that his principal concern was whether he would have enough land on which to live. He was answered patiently by Robert Newell, the best friend of Big Thunder's son-in-law Bill Craig and the white man at the conference whom the old Lapwai chief most trusted. Newell's remarks, giving the stamp of authority to the commission, went a long way toward breaking down the hostility of the nontreaties. When the former mountain man had finished, Big Thunder, making almost his last documented appearance in history, said simply, "I am very sick, and spitting blood, excuse me." He left the council grounds, but that night came to see the commissioners privately. When they convinced him that his lands lay within the boundaries of the new reservation, and that he would not have to give up any of his country, he surrendered, though refusing to put his mark on the treaty because—as Hale wrote in his summation —he did not wish to lose face to Lawyer.

Hutchins' threats had the same effect on Koolkool Snehee and Eagle From the Light. Both of them maintained their opposition for the public record, then left the council and later came privately to see Hale. Assuring themselves that their lands lay within the new reservation, they gave their support to the treaty, but refused to sign it. After the departure of the last of the anti-treaty leaders, whatever residue of resistance to the agreement remained among Lawyer's people vanished quickly. One after another, the head chief's followers—Utsinmalikin, Spotted Eagle, Billy, Jason, Timothy, Captain John, and others—rose to announce their eagerness to accept the treaty.

On June 9 Lawyer and fifty-one members of his faction signed the document. There is an interesting point about the signers of this treaty. In the night meeting of the nation's chiefs, which Captain Currey had witnessed, fifty-three headmen were in attendance, representing most of the top leadership of both the treaty and nontreaty bands. Several of the leaders were not at the council, including Three Feathers and Red Heart, the latter being an anti-treaty man who was in the buffalo country at the time. Of the chiefs who had come to the council, however, not a single anti-treaty leader signed the 1863 document; yet, somehow, Hale and his fellow-commissioners, with Lawyer's assistance, rounded up fifty-one men to give the treaty the appearance of having the support of almost all the important men in the nation.[43]

43. McWhorter, *Yellow Wolf*, pp. 35–36 n., and *Hear Me*, p. 109 n., says that two Nez Perces who signed the treaty were not of the Lawyer element and were "trapped unawares." He names them as Waptastamana (Black Feather), a shaman, and Hohots Stortee, sometimes spelled Ha-haich-tuesta (Bear on Top). The latter, however, was definitely a Lawyer man and was known to the whites as Captain Billy. He lived at a crossing on the Salmon River, opposite Rocky Canyon. The minutes of the council, identifying him both as Ha-haich-tuesta and Billy, pp. 71–72, show him speaking unmistakably in support of Lawyer. Also, see the Report of the Commissioner of Indian

Another point worth noting is that Hale secured the signature or the agreement of every headman whose lands the treaty would not affect, but did not secure the signatures of Joseph, White Bird, or any leader, save Timothy and Jason, who lived outside the borders of the new reservation. And Timothy and Jason were both treated as white men who could continue to dwell as private residents in their old homes.

In announcing the signing of the treaty, Hale wrote proudly to the Commissioner of Indian Affairs that whereas the old Nez Perce reservation covered "ten thousand square miles, or six million four hundred thousand acres" the new one "is reduced to a little over twelve hundred square miles, or about eight hundred thousand acres." "The amount thus relinquished," he boasted, "is very nearly six millions of acres, and is obtained at a cost not exceeding eight cents per acre . . . In the tract of country relinquished is much that is exceedingly valuable, by reason of its gold and silver mines, whilst many of its valleys, and much of its uplands, will be found desirable and necessary for agricultural and grazing purposes." Actually, the Nez Perces gave up 6,932,-270 acres, and the new reservation of 784,996 acres was slightly more than 10 per cent the size of the old one. Its boundary generally followed the valley of the main Clearwater from just west of Lapwai Creek to a point south of the junction of the Middle and South forks, then west to Lake Waha, and north to the point of beginning. Taken from the Nez Perces were all of the Wallowa, Imnaha, and Grande Ronde country of Oregon, the valleys of the Snake and Salmon rivers, including such places as Asotin and Alpowa, the Camas Prairie, the upper waters of the Clearwater and its tributaries, and the trails to the Bitterroot Valley. By the treaty's terms, all of the bands were required to move on the reservation within one year after the document was ratified. The government promised to pay for improvements on any of the relinquished lands, but the Indians could sell such improvements in the way of farms or buildings to white men, if they preferred to do so. Tillable acreage on the new reservation was to be allotted, and the tribe would hold the rest of the land in common. The government would pay the tribe $265,000 for the ceded land, but more than half of that sum would be appropriated in four installments to finance removal and to pay for the plowing and fencing of the allotments—a diversion of payments, in part, from bands that were relinquishing land to those that were not! In addition, $50,000 was to be paid the first year after ratification in the form of agricultural equipment and livestock. Other funds were promised for a sawmill, schools, a hospital, a blacksmith's shop, headmen's salaries and houses, and the payment for horses that

Affairs (1866), p. 193, where Agent James O'Neill speaks of "Ha-harts-tuesta, or Captain Billy, the chief on Salmon river, being the largest owner of cattle, having some five hundred head . . ." O'Neill's annual report, Lapwai, July 20, 1866.

members of the Lawyer faction had sold to government troops on credit during the wars of the 1850s. Finally, the Nez Perce signatories gave white men the right of access to the new reservation to build public roads, ferries, and inns anywhere they chose on the Indians' land.[44]

The treaty was a fraudulant act on the part of both Lawyer and the commissioners. On the one hand, Lawyer and his followers had no right to sign away the lands of the other bands, and they knew it. In later years, when young Joseph began to protest the sale and it seemed that the government might be thinking of an investigation, Lawyer complained weakly that he had not meant to represent any of the bands that had not signed the document. But there is nothing in the record of the treaty proceedings or the documentation surrounding the treaty to indicate that the old head chief did not know exactly what he was doing in 1863. On the other hand, the commissioners followed a time-worn and deceitful procedure for extinguishing title to Indian land when the rightful owners refused to sell. The precedent had been set long before by Anthony Wayne and William Henry Harrison in the Ohio Valley, and the treaty of 1863 was of the same cloth. Nor can it be said that Hale and his fellow-commissioners sincerely believed that Lawyer was empowered to speak and act for the whole tribe: too much effort was made to coerce the anti-treaties; too much plotting went on with the Lawyer faction; and, in the end, a bold lie was broadcast in the assertion that the entire tribe had agreed to the treaty. That statement was conveyed to Washington without qualification. Actually, Joseph and the other nonsignatory bands outside of the new boundary line literally had their lands sold from under them by Lawyer who, in return for his betrayal, was promised a disproportionate share of the treaty's beneficence.[45]

44. One article in the treaty also granted a tract of land at Lewiston to Robert Newell. The former mountain man may have asked his Nez Perce friends to seek this special consideration for him, as Craig had done at the 1855 Walla Walla council. In addition, approximately $3,600 in Nez Perce payments under the 1855 treaty reached Hale during the council, and he distributed it to the friendly headmen at the conclusion of the Lapwai meeting.

45. It would seem proper today that federal officials recognize the great harm that still accrues to the Nez Perces as a result of the government's continuing to accept the Stevens-Hale versions of history. In *Joseph's Band of the Nez Perce Tribe v. The United States*, 95 C. Cls. 11 (1941–42), a suit filed before the Court of Claims by the Joseph Band, which maintained that it had been deprived of the Wallowa Valley without its consent and without compensation, the court held that under the 1855 treaty the Wallowa lands were reserved to the Nez Perce tribe as a whole, using as reasoning the facts that there must have been power in the tribe to act as a whole with reference to all lands of the tribe or of any of its bands, otherwise Joseph, a signatory to the 1855 treaty, would have been relinquishing lands which he and his band did not own (the Palouse River area), and that the same situation must have held true in 1863, so that the dissent-

The treaty drove the last wedge between the two elements of Nez Perces—those who were on the reservation and who accepted, with increasing help-lessness, the position of being an oppressed group among white men, and those who were off the reservation and tried to avoid contact with whites and continue as much as possible their old ways of life with the least interference. Lawyer held sway over the first group, though he was mildly challenged from time to time by the jealous and cantankerous Big Thunder. A month after the signing of the treaty, Lawyer and Captain John visited Judge Mat-thew Deady in Portland. "L. Said Big T. did not amount to much," Deady wrote to Senator Nesmith after the meeting. "He only had three chiefs, while he, L., had 46." [46] In January 1867 Big Thunder at last died, and then Law-yer had no opposition.

But developments on the reservation were not altogether to Lawyer's lik-ing. White civilization was planting itself firmly over the hills and valleys of central Idaho, and to "the Bostons" the Indians who hung around the white men were pestiferous creatures who should be moved far away to some re-mote reservation. In July 1863 Lewiston was proclaimed the temporary capi-tal of the new territory. Roads were run through the Indians' country, and inns and trading establishments were built upon it. The opening of the ceded lands, even before the treaty of 1863 was ratified, brought farmers and stock-men spreading over the landscape along the borders of the proposed new re-serve, and swarms of newly arrived families in buckboards looked with fear and contempt at the Indians along the roads. The livestock of the newcomers grazed across the hills onto Indian lands, and friction occurred over the use of grass and springs. Racial conflict increased steadily, stemming from a multi-tude of causes. The Indians came to regard the period as a "crimson" one, when the whites asserted their superiority over them, and their own rights

---

ing minority, including the members of Joseph's band, was bound by that treaty even if it did not sign it. This reasoning is a perversion of the historical facts. It is beyond belief that Joseph signed the treaty of 1855 with intent to give up anything. He signed it to retain the Wallowa. As evidence that he never considered that he gave up anything, there is the fact that he steadfastly refused to accept any sort of payment from the gov-ernment. What happened along the Palouse River was none of his business. And from that line of reasoning, it would follow that what happened in the Wallowa was none of Lawyer's business. Members of the Bureau of Indian Affairs in Washington to this day, however, provide questioners among the public with the Stevens-Hale version of what occurred at the two treaty councils.

46. "I, The Lawyer" by Clifford M. Drury, New York Westerners *Brand Book*, 7 (May 1960), 16. It is too bad that Dr. Drury rushed this brief and fragmented biog-raphy of Lawyer into print before he had done more research on his subject. Lawyer deserves a first rate biographical study. Much of what is in the present volume on Law-yer, for instance, is omitted in Drury's work.

disappeared. In the years after the signing of the treaty more than twenty-five Nez Perces are known to have been murdered; perhaps one or two white men were slain.[47] But the Indians were without political or legal protection, and their own ability to defend themselves had vanished.

The acculturation of the reservation Nez Perces proceeded swiftly. It might be tempting to say that in the post-1863 period they became like white men, but it would not be correct. They were still between two worlds, mixing the traits of the two cultures. Most of the treaty Indians farmed and raised wheat or livestock, but almost all of them, in addition, continued to fish and gather camas, kouse, and berries. Many hunted in the Bitterroots, and a few continued to go to the plains to fight and hunt buffalo with the nonreservation bands. Some built cabins, but a majority still dwelled in hide and mat lodges. Increasingly, they took to wearing white men's clothes, and Christianity and education both began at last to make significant headway among them. For a while, Spalding exercised a dominant influence in both departments. After the treaty of 1863 the old missionary and his second wife taught at the government school at Lapwai, using the New Testament as a textbook. Spalding, however, soon became ensnarled in personal quarrels with Perrin Whitman, the government agents, and others, and in 1865 he was dismissed from Lapwai and the school was closed. Two years later Catholics came to the reservation, but Lawyer and his followers made it clear that they would not be welcomed, and for a while the priests had to be content with settling in Lewiston and ministering to whites. Eventually, however, they won converts among the Indians, and in 1872 they finally established themselves on the reservation. In 1868 a school was reopened for the Indians, and in the fall of 1869 the children of reservation Nez Perces began to attend government-supported boarding schools, where it was believed the instructors could more effectively isolate the youngsters from the cultural influences of their Indian families.

The following year an upsurge in Christian influence struck the reservation. Four young Yakimas from a Methodist mission on the Yakima reservation visited the Nez Perces and began to preach the Christian gospel. Spalding was able to return to the reservation in 1871, both as a government Superintendent of Instruction and as a missionary of the Presbyterian Board of Foreign Missions; and aided by a young newcomer, Henry T. Cowley, he accelerated the work begun by the Yakimas and aroused the reservation Nez Perces to a great spiritual revival, baptizing more than two hundred Nez Perces, including the member of the tribe who had been his first friend and sorest trial, old Tackensuatis, or Rotten Belly, whom he now named Samuel.

47. For a detailed record of the violence against the Nez Perces during this period, see McWhorter, *Hear Me*, pp. 118–26.

Under a government policy of the early 1870's that placed reservations in the care of specific religious denominations, education and spiritual instruction went hand in hand at Lapwai and Kamiah, the two principal centers on the reservation, and Spalding was at last happy. The government built a church at Kamiah in 1873, and by the time that Spalding terminated his preaching there, he claimed to have baptized more than 600 Nez Perces in all. In 1873 old Spokan Garry asked him to visit his tribe, and Spalding accepted the invitation. After fanning the sparks of the Christian revival among those people, he returned to Kamiah, and then to Lapwai, where he died on August 3, 1874, at almost 71 years of age. His work in Christianizing the treaty or reservation Nez Perces had finally succeeded; churches, congregations, and native preachers and elders were now permanent features of the Lawyer faction of the tribe.

The leaders of the nonreservation element, meanwhile, clung to what remained of their independence. They had never accepted annuities or gifts from the government, and that gesture helped them maintain their feeling of self-respect. They and their people were still free, and proud to be so; and when the government again failed to live up to its promises, and annuities and funds guaranteed by the treaty of 1863 failed to arrive, their young men jeered at the treaty bands that had sold their country for nothing. Often they appealed to young, resentful members of the Lawyer faction, and defectors constantly joined them. ". . . many, very many . . . young men" were going to the nontreaty side, Agent O'Neill reported from Lapwai in 1865, complaining again the following year that the nontreaty element, numbering altogether about 1,000 people, "every day . . . is increasing in strength."[48]

The government's lack of control over the nontreaty Indians often alarmed the whites. There were frequent rumors that the band of White Bird would rise up and kill the Salmon River settlers, or that Eagle From the Light was about to join with the Blackfeet and Crows and exterminate the miners in western Montana, where another great gold rush had occurred during the mid-1860s. The fears were never realized, for the nontreaty groups were becoming merely islands in a sea of whites, and their leaders appreciated the military hopelessness of their position. Their bands rode to buffalo, fought the Sioux, and counted coup on the Montana plains as in former days; but their war chiefs would not have dared to counsel the people to war upon the overwhelming number of Americans who surrounded them. Moreover, despite their wish to isolate themselves as much as possible from contact with the Americans, their own economic well being rested on the near presence of the whites. Few of the nontreaties farmed; but they raised livestock and sold horses and cattle to the whites, some of the Indians even accumulating

48. Reports of the Commissioner of Indian Affairs (1865), p. 236; (1866), p. 194.

personal hoards of gold or cash from their sales. Many of them traded regularly at white men's stores and bought arms, food, hardware, presents for women, and sometimes liquor. In this position the liberty they valued was characterized by their ability to roam where they pleased over land that had always been theirs, as well as by their freedom from government control. Yet some of it was a delusion. Until the treaty of 1863 was ratified, no one could force them to come on the reservation. But in areas that had been ceded by the treaty, and that were attractive to whites—like the valleys of the Snake and Salmon rivers and the Camas Prairie—their hold on the land was already being contested. There were whites who would not wait for ratification, but came in to squat among the Indians whenever and wherever they wished to do so. In other regions like the Wallowa, that were still unknown to white men, the Indians had a longer period of grace. But in any case ratification inevitably put a time limit on Nez Perce freedom everywhere.

The tensions of the period—marked by the constant specter of white pressure, interracial friction, and the threat of oppression and extermination—had meanwhile contributed to the rise of a new faith of hope among various Indian bands in the Northwest. It was a gradual and natural evolution from the old religious beliefs of the tribes, but it had new ideas and ritual that showed Christian influences, and its chief practitioner was a Wanapum shaman named Smohalla, who lived at Priest Rapids on the Columbia River. A short, thickset hunchback who had been born about 1815 near the site where Donald McKenzie built Fort Nez Perces in 1818, Smohalla was an able and impressive speaker, who also possessed the power of self-hypnosis. Between the hostility of jealous Indian headmen and of whites who had regarded him as a troublemaker, he had led a wretched existence, and had finally moved with a small following of Indians to a fishing settlement in the bleak and barren country of Priest Rapids.

There, in the decades of the 1850s, when the Indians of the Columbia were living in fear of the American soldiers, Smohalla had gone on a sacred-vision quest. From it, and from lengthy periods when he had mysteriously disappeared, and when his followers had seen him in self-hypnosis and had considered him dead, he had gradually gained prominence as the teacher of a new doctrine of promise, supposedly communicated to him in the afterworld. It was both a belief and a way of life, which whites came to call the Dreamer faith, for its principal directives and promises came to its followers in dreams. In brief, it called on the Indians to abandon the customs and clothing of the white man and return to the Indian ways of their own ancestors. By doing so, and by following certain pure and sacred rules of behavior, they would be rewarded with a new and happy day, when the dead Indians of former times would return to life and the hated white man and his works would disappear from their lands. Smohalla preached his faith in a tule mat longhouse on the sandy, windswept banks of the Columbia, employing hand drums, flags, special songs and dances, a bell, and other sacred symbols to give mysterious ritual to his ceremonies. His important *Washat* dance was of particular significance; by participating in it, he said, believers would help hasten the day when the Indians would regain their land and freedom.

The Dreamer faith was not unlike the desperate religions of hope that had flared briefly among dying Indian cultures elsewhere on the continent. Indians of the times of Pontiac and Tecumseh had been rallied by native prophets with special faiths and dances that would bring back dead warriors and cause the disappearance of the white men. In the 1880s another prophet, Wovoka, a Nevada Paiute, would give the Plains Indians what the whites would call the Ghost Dance—still another last, flickering promise of restored freedom and dignity. But each so-called religion came out of its own special environment and circumstances, and Smohalla's faith, giving a dramatic new dimension to ancient Sahaptin beliefs and ways of life that already included sacred vision quests and contact with the supernatural through dreams, spread quickly among the more dejected of the Sahaptin peoples of the Columbia Basin.

White men were at a loss at first to know what the new movement signified, or how dangerous it might be to them. Major J. W. MacMurray of the United States Army, who visited Smohalla at a later date, quoted the native prophet's soul-stirring preachment to his followers:

> Those who cut up the lands or sign papers for lands will be defrauded of their rights and will be punished by God's anger. . .
>
> You ask me to plough the ground! Shall I take a knife and tear my mother's bosom? Then when I die, she will not take me to her bosom to rest.
>
> You ask me to dig for stone! Shall I dig under her skin for her bones? Then when I die I cannot enter her body to be born again.
>
> You ask me to cut grass and make hay and sell it and be rich like white men! But how dare I cut off my mother's hair? [49]

This hearkening to the old bond between the Indian and his land, reminding the Indians of their sacred attachment to the supreme chieftaincy of the earth, their mother, circulated among many of the bands—among the crushed and powerless peoples of eastern Washington as well as the strong Nez Perce groups that were still off the reservation in Idaho and the Wallowa Valley of Oregon. To some whites it sounded like defiance of the American and his civilization, even a plot—spread under the guise of religion—to weld

49. James Mooney, *The Ghost-Dance Religion*, Bureau of American Ethnology, 14th Annual Report (Washington, D.C., 1896), p. 721.

rebellious Indians into an insurrectionary force. Although some Nez Perces in both treaty and nontreaty bands were moved by Smohalla's preachings, however, few of them showed more than a temporary curiosity in the ritual and the strange new ideas, like the resurrection of the dead, that the prophet had added to their own traditional spiritual beliefs. Nevertheless, as Smohalla gained notoriety the Americans came to regard all non-Christian Nez Perces as followers of the Priest Rapids hunchback, calling them Dreamers and equating them with the anti-treaty, anti-Lawyer faction. All the members of Joseph's band in the Wallowa were characterized as Dreamers, and white men came to distinguish them by their hair, for they, like Smohalla's followers, refused to cut their hair, white-fashion, but wore it long and brushed it in a roll above their forehead.

Despite the gulf that separated them from Smohalla, the anti-treaty Nez Perces were inspired by the patriotic phases of the prophet's teachings. Although it was not a call to violence, the hunchback's faith told them to hold on and believe. There were also a purity and simplicity to his doctrine that made the actions of the Lawyer group seem dark and foolish. The Indians who had turned to Christianity had become agriculturists and had cut the bosom of their mother. Then they had sold their mother, the great chieftaincy of all. Now they were in trouble.

Lawyer and his followers at the time were indeed in great trouble. After all the promises and threats made by Hale and Hutchins at the Lapwai council in 1863, the Americans were proving no more faithful than they had been after the treaty of 1855. In 1864 Congress failed to ratify the new treaty, and no funds reached the Nez Perces, not even payments for the 1855 treaty. In that year a new territorial governor, Caleb Lyon, an eccentric and a rogue, arrived at Lewiston to succeed William Wallace, who had been elected to Congress as delegate from Idaho. On August 21, 1864, less than two weeks after he reached his post, Lyon attended Spalding's Sunday service and met Lawyer, who made a long speech to him, listing his grievances: The Nez Perces had agreed to the Stevens treaty, the head chief complained, "and now nine years have passed, and little part of the stipulations on the other side has been complied with . . . I did not know a crook in them, but they have become crooked . . . we have no church as promised; no school house as promised; no doctor as promised; no gunsmith as promised; no blacksmith as promised . . . I stand here, as it were, naked so far as these promises are fulfilled." Lyon appeared to be touched, and appealed to Lawyer for a little more patience. But only ten days later, showing the depth of his insincerity and rascality, he wrote his good friend and mentor, John P. Usher, the Secretary of Interior: "You will find an account of my talk with Sawyer [sic]. I want the permission of the Department to run the agency for the good of the Indians . . . Please have that instruction given me. Do not fail when the treaty with the Nez Perces goes before the Senate again. Make the amendment instead of 'the mouth of the Hatwa[i] creek' have it read 'to within one mile of the mouth of the Hatwae creek'. The reason is there are some 'good washings' that I wish to get hold of for our benefit that can not be done without this amendment is made for Arthur & myself. It is now a secret . . . I am buying through a 3d party the land from the Indian who owns it . . ." [50] That was just the beginning of the new governor's deceit. Holding also the office of Superintendent of Indian Affairs in Idaho, he schemed to get Lawyer's good will by ordering the construction of a church on the agency grounds. But he avoided paying the laborers, and they soon abandoned the project. Two years later, after a helter-skelter career in which he did nothing for Lawyer's people, Lyon fled the territory, taking with him $46,418.40 of funds appropriated by Congress for the Nez Perces.

The cheating of the treaty bands continued year after year. Indian agents came and went at Lapwai. Each one complained about the irregularities and defalcations of his predecessors, and each one departed with Nez Perce money. James O'Neill, the agent from 1864–68, absconded with $10,000. Lieutenant J. W. Wham, who served in 1869, was accused of scandalous frauds and so was Wham's successor, Captain D. M. Sells.[51] It was the pattern of the times, and although Lawyer and his subchiefs complained often and bitterly about the government's failure to pay salaries and annuities, to erect promised buildings, and to provide services, the persons to whom they complained always had others whom they could blame. The patience of Lawyer and the treaty headmen was remarkable; they were the principal victims, because they had been promised special considerations in the way of salaries, houses, and other favors for their signatures. But many of their people had also come to look forward to a schoolhouse, fenced and ploughed lands, and other benefits of the white man's way of life. Their pressure, together with the taunts of the nontreaty Indians, fell on Lawyer, and there was nothing he could do save plead with whoever would listen to him.

The 1863 treaty itself traveled a rocky road. After a four-year delay it was finally ratified by the Senate on April 17, 1867, and signed by President Andrew Johnson on April 20. By that time Lawyer and his followers were eager for a new council to air their many complaints, which now included

50. "Grievances of the Nez Perce," *Idaho Yesterdays*, 4 (Fall, 1960), 6–7. Elmo R. Richardson, "Caleb Lyon: A Personal Fragment," *Idaho Yesterdays*, 1, No. 4 (1957–58), 4. An interesting reflection seems cast on the honesty of Lincoln's Secretary of Interior.

51. The charge against Wham did not seem to hurt him. In 1871 he was sent as agent to the Brulé Sioux after being recommended by the Episcopal Church as a good man and a Christian. See Hyde, *Red Cloud's Folk*, pp. 187 ff.

such assorted items as distress over the white whiskey sellers who were corrupting the Indians, and anger with timber cutters who were chopping down trees on the reservation and taking lumber without paying for it. Lawyer no longer relied on getting satisfaction from the local Indian agents, and wanted to see the President himself, thinking that the head of the American government would surely recognize the many injustices the Nez Perces had suffered. In 1865 he had written an appeal to President Lincoln, which a white friend in Portland had taken east with him. The letter had reached the capital after Lincoln's assassination, and nothing had come of Lawyer's effort. But word of the head chief's restlessness got through to the Indian Bureau in the annual reports of the Lapwai agents, and the awareness of his discontent raised a complication in Washington soon after the ratification of the treaty in 1867. President Andrew Johnson had hardly signed that document when the government wished to amend it to acquire some of the reservation land near the agency for a permanent military post. Knowing of the Nez Perces' feelings, the Commissioner of Indian Affairs sent a special agent, George C. Hough, to meet with Lawyer and his people and try to iron out difficulties. Hough counciled with the head chief and some 1,500 of the treaty Indians at Lapwai from June 21 to 27, but accomplished nothing. To the agent's announcement that the treaty of 1863 had finally been ratified, Lawyer replied bluntly, "The treaty of 1855 has not been lived up to, and we have no faith that this will be lived up to." He still wanted to talk to the President directly.

On November 20 he addressed another personal appeal "To the President of the United States and others of the Government," stating "Myself the Lawyer am anxious to visit Washington with an Interpreter & one or more of my Chiefs. Have pity on me and give me permission to do so at the expense of the Government." [52] Agent O'Neill forwarded the letter to the capital, and on January 3, 1868, the Commissioner of Indian Affairs, still charged with securing agreement to the amending of the treaty for a military post, authorized O'Neill to bring Lawyer and three of his headmen, together with interpreters, to Washington. [53] O'Neill enlisted Robert Newell and Perrin Whitman as interpreters, and in March 1868 the three white men left for the East with Lawyer, Utsinmalikin, Timothy, and Jason.

It was the first time that Nez Perces had gone to Washington, and Newell's diary reveals their excitement and wonder at seeing the great populated centers of the American nation. But the former mountain man, now 61 years old, was also going east for the first time in many years, and he was making use of

52. Office of Indian Affairs, Letters Received, Idaho Territory, O-36 (1867), National Archives.
53. Office of Indian Affairs, Letters Sent, Vol. 85, pp. 214–15, National Archives.

the visit to lobby for an appointment for himself as the Nez Perce agent to succeed O'Neill.[54] The group traveled by way of Portland, San Francisco, and Panama, and reached New York on May 14. ". . . truly a wonder," wrote Newell. "I went to the Metropolitan Hotel to the Theatre the grandest Sight I ever saw." The next day the travelers went to Washington. "Saw wonders on my way houses Towns. O everything." They reached the capital on the day of the vote on Johnson's impeachment, ". . . a day long to be remembered," said Newell. On May 17 Newell recorded that both Lawyer and Utsinmalikin were unwell. The next day Newell saw General Grant and "had a fine interview." On May 18 he went to market with Timothy and Jason "who was surprised to see the throng of people & vegitables. The people stare at the Indians. Saw Secty of Int. and others." Two days later Newell was received by the President who "paid me quite a compliment as a Pioneer." On May 22 he recorded that "Utes—the Indian quite sick," and on May 25 he entered the solemn note that "Utes-sin-ma-le-kin died today of Tyfoid fever." A day later his diary reads: "Utes-sin-Malikin Buried at the Congressional Ground four Carriages attended by Friends." Somehow, word got home later that Utsinmalikin had been resisting the treaty amendments in Washington, and a story, attributed to Timothy and repeated by anti-treaty Nez Perces, still circulates among members of the tribe to the effect that Utsinmalikin had been shoved from a high window and killed—although Newell's diary seems to give the truthful version of the death of the old headman of Kamiah.[55]

54. Newell had been seeking the job for sometime, but a problem with alcohol had not helped him. On July 25, 1863, General Benjamin Alvord had written Senator Nesmith: "I am satisfied that Dr. Robert Newell was mainly influential in effecting the treaty with the Nez Perces Indians— After *full enquiry*, I told Gov. Wallace when he left for Lewiston, that I withdrew all opposition to Dr. Newell's appointment as *Agent* to the Nez Perces *Indians* . . . I believe that he will take care of his habits sufficiently to attend to the business, and he has won the place by his labor of love among that interesting tribe . . ." Fort Vancouver, W. T. Benjamin Alvord Collection, Oregon Historical Society.

55. The excerpts from Robert Newell's diary of 1868 are used with the kind permission of its owners, Mr. and Mrs. Chester Wiggin of Lewiston, Idaho. The document also contains the following interesting biographical material, entered under the heading "Family Record of Robert Newell" in Newell's handwriting:
Robert Newell born March 30, 1807.
Married Kitty M. (a Nez Perce) July 27, 1833.
Francis Ermatinger Newell born on Green River, South Pass, June 14, 1835.
William Moore Newell, born March 30, 1838, died March 29, 1855.
Marcus Whitman Newell, born April 17, 1840.
Robert Newell Jr., born February 27, 1842, died August 23, 1863.
Thomas Jefferson Newell, born November 25, 1843.

The other members of the delegation remained in Washington all of June and July, sightseeing, having their "Degarytype" taken, calling on senators, the President, and high officials of the administration, and straightening out the matters that had brought them to the capital. On several occasions Lawyer and his colleagues were able to discuss "the non Compliance of Treaty Stipulations"; at other times they worked on "altering the lines of the Reservation" and settling on amendments to the treaty. On June 18 "Lawyer got a little tight." On June 25 the head chief was homesick. That same day Newell saw General Grant again and remarked that he "is a quiet reserve man and look well for a man who is to run for President." On July 9 Lawyer, Timothy, and Jason petitioned President Johnson to have Newell appointed agent for the Nez Perces, and on July 22 the President nominated Newell for the post. On August 11 "Lawyer Timothy and Jason got tight late at night," but they continued work the next day at the Indian Department, and soon signed amendments to the treaty that gave the government land at Lapwai for a military reservation, but compensated the Indians with promises to replace Indian school funds that had previously been stolen, to protect the timber on the reservation, and to provide additional twenty-acre lots off the reservation if the reserve did not prove large enough to supply enough good agricultural land for all the Indians. On August 22 the group left Washington and returned home by way of New York, Chicago, Omaha, and Boise. Along the Platte River, where troops were protecting the building of the Union Pacific Railroad from forays of the Sioux, Newell, the old mountain man, was moved to note, "I never saw such humbug about Indian matters by Government," and near Fort Bridger, he recorded wistfully, "Saw Wind river mountains and much of the old country of former days which brought to mind many incidents of my former life." The country had changed. Even the capital of Idaho had already been moved from Lewiston to Boise, and that city, he found, was a bustling outfitting center for the southern mines. On September 22 the group reached Lewiston, and three days later Newell took over as agent at Lapwai.

The ratification of the treaty and its amendments heralded a more stable period of development for the reservation Nez Perces. Money began to come through, and schools were finally opened. Newell's tenure was brief; the government replaced him as agent in June 1869, and he died at Lapwai in November, following to the grave by barely two months his old trapper companion, Bill Craig, who died after a paralytic stroke. President Grant's policy

---

First wife died January 3, 1845.
On June 28, 1846, married Rebecca Newman who was born May 20, 1832.
On June 25, 1869, married Mrs. Jane M. Ward.

at first was to staff the Indian reservations with military men, and the two officers, Wham and Sells, held brief sway at Lapwai after Newell. In 1869 pressure of church leaders and reformers in the East, who were opposed to a government policy that seemed dedicated to the extermination of Indians by armed might, forced the adoption of a so-called "peace policy" in the Administration's dealing with the Indians, and the next year Grant ordered reservations placed under the supervision of different religious denominations, whose Christian standards and benign care, it was expected, would halt white oppression and injustices that caused Indian resentments and hostility, end the corruption in the Indian Service, break up tribal bonds and institutions, and hasten the conversion of Indians to Christianized farmers.

At first, the Nez Perce reservation was assigned to the Catholics, who had finally won permission to establish a church on the reserve. But the Presbyterians protested, arguing that they had been the first and most active workers among the Nez Perces, and the government finally authorized them to name the new agent and administer affairs on the reservation. The man they selected, John B. Monteith, a determined, strong-willed son of a Presbyterian minister, took over at Lapwai in February 1871. The year before, Lawyer had ended his reign as head chief of the treaty bands. He had been showing his advanced years, and his followers had urged him to give way to a younger and more vigorous man who enjoyed more contacts and respect among the youthful elements of the treaty bands. On April 18, 1870, a council had been held and Jacob had been selected to succeed Lawyer. But Jacob was only a half-hearted Christian for whom Monteith had little respect, and under the new agent Lawyer continued to exercise influence in reservation affairs.

Monteith and Lawyer together brought about the final disintegration of the cultural heritage and bonds of the treaty Nez Perces. The era of the mining rush was over, and the day of the American homesteader and the solid, God-fearing pioneer family had arrived in the region. Fortified by the strength and influence of their numbers, Monteith encouraged whatever would hasten the assimilation of the Nez Perces into the surrounding white culture. Unlike his predecessors, he was an honest man; but under his administration missionaries and teachers deliberately made the Indians ashamed of their own traditions, history, culture, and lore. Old ways and beliefs were frowned upon, ridiculed, and prohibited. The treaty Nez Perces were led, pushed, and pulled to become like whites—and yet they were not accepted as equals by the American settlers around them. Bereft of their own culture, their strength, self-respect, and dignity, they became a subjugated and lost people, a second-class minority in their own homeland.

During those years of dissolution in the early 1870s, Lawyer had many little problems for Monteith: white men constantly trespassed on Indian lands and sometimes appropriated their gardens, springs, and livestock; Indians could get no justice in the white men's courts, since Indians could not testify against whites; white traders and store owners got young Indians drunk, then cheated and robbed them and turned their heads to ideas of going on the warpath and killing whites. There was also one large problem: despite the ratification of the treaty, the Dreamer or "heathen" bands were still off the reservation and uncontrolled. They were a thorn to the good Nez Perces, said Lawyer; they turned young men of the treaty bands against the Law and the Christian Indians and the Americans. The treaty chiefs could do nothing about the "heathens"—particularly those of White Bird's band along the Salmon and Joseph's band snug in the Wallowa—as long as they were allowed their freedom. Lawyer continued to denounce them, and the years went by . . .

Then, on January 3, 1876, Lawyer died at Kamiah, at about 82 years of age. He was buried in the cemetery of the small church at that settlement and was mourned by many of the whites as well as by the leaders of the treaty bands. Rising from a buffalo hunter and a shrewd talker who had learned English and become useful as an interpreter and intermediary, he had worked his way into position as the Nez Perces' most important and forceful leader. Although he had not done well for all of his people, neither had the government done well for him. Despite the accommodating role he had played, the Americans had repaid him with only small and niggling favors, and in his later years he had lived close to want. On his death, hypocritical whites, knowing they had lost a valuable tool, called him a patriot. Many of the Christian Indians used the same term but with more justice. As a shepherd, who had genuinely believed that any course but accommodation of the powerful Americans would lead to the destruction of his people, Lawyer had skillfully guided his tribe through years of dangers, almost to the safe shore of assimilation. But he had presided over the destruction of the cultural pride, dignity, and heritage of large numbers of Nez Perces, and had robbed them of their self-respect as humans. The Dreamers did not mourn his passing. They were still proud of their Indianness, proud of their own ways, and jealous of their freedom. They did not want assimilation. To them Lawyer had been a traitor, "a tobacco cutter," who had opened one door after another to lying, thieving, murdering conquerors. The treaty Nez Perces were finished as an independent people. But the nontreaty part of the tribe was still vital and defiant. One year after Lawyer's death, the head chief's legacy exploded in the thunder of what he had striven for so long to avoid—war with the Americans. To the so-called Dreamers, the tragic conflict was proof that Lawyer had caused the Nez Perces more harm than good.

Part III. The War

II

The Wallowa

PRESENT-DAY Wallowa County, encompassing the northeastern corner of Oregon, coincides almost exactly with the territory once regarded as home by the Joseph, or Wellamotkin, band of Nez Perces. It covers 3,145 square miles, almost three times the size of Rhode Island, yet little of it is good for farming. A large part of it is mountainous, and another large part is knifed by a network of lava-rimmed canyons that are among the deepest and most rugged in the world. Even its most habitable portion, the relatively flat valley drained by the meandering Wallowa River and its feeder streams, has an altitude ranging from approximately 2,500 feet to above 4,000 feet, limiting the growth of crops to a short season. But the grasses in the canyons and along the great expanse of plateau that borders them are rich, and nowhere in the United States, perhaps, is there better natural grazing country.

Originally, many small Indian groups and families, each one independent, had occupied the region; but gradually they had drawn together, and by 1860 all of them, totaling about 60 men and possibly twice that number of women and children, looked upon Joseph as their headman. In the spring of each year the Indians came up from their scattered camps in the warm canyons, gathered kouse in the Chesnimnus area and other high meadowed regions in the northern part of the district, and then moved south to the Wallowa Valley, with its sparkling lake and river, where they laid in a store of salmon and spent the summer in the hills and on the prairie beneath the Wallowa Mountains. In the fall they returned to the Chesnimnus and northern wooded areas to hunt deer and bear and, as cold set in, descended again to the shelter of the deep canyons. Winter grass in the canyons, spring and fall grass on the plateau, and summer grass in the valley provided their large herds of horses and cattle with year-round feed, while the beauty of the region and the lushness of its bounty satisfied the Indians' spiritual and material needs. Occasionally, some of the Indians traveled to the Umatilla Valley in the west to visit friends and relatives among the Cayuses and Umatillas, or went in the opposite direction to hunt buffalo in Montana and to stop along the way at villages of treaty and nontreaty Nez Perces in Idaho. But no place seemed so good to Joseph's people as the Wallowa, and on occasions when the agents at Lapwai tried to argue them into moving onto the reservation, in accordance with the treaty of 1863, they retorted that they loved the land in which they lived and would never give it up.

Through the 1860s no white man seriously bothered them. Over the mountains to the west, white settlement began in the Grande Ronde Valley in November 1861, and seven months later a settler named Fred Nodine, searching for some strayed horses, found an Indian trail and followed it to a hill, overlooking the Wallowa. Seeing five or six Indians and "several thousand horses," he withdrew quickly, telling his friends that he "considered it best to give up the chase." In 1863, after Joseph returned from the treaty session at Lapwai, he worriedly erected a line of poles surrounded by rock piles three or four feet high as boundary markers along Wallowa Hill, above the Wallowa and Minam rivers on the Grande Ronde Valley side of his territory. It was from this direction that settlers would most likely press toward the Wallowa, and Joseph meant to make it clear to them that there was a line beyond which they would have no right to go. At about the same time, according to a story that agent Monteith later reported to Washington, the elderly chief destroyed the copy of the New Testament that Spalding had given him many years before, thus symbolically breaking his final bond with white men and with the Christian Indians who had done Lawyer's bidding and signed the treaty at Lapwai.[1]

By the end of 1864 there were some 500 settlers in the Grande Ronde Valley, and some of them had a vague idea that to the east was a hidden region of lush pastureland. Two French trappers, known as Charles LeVar and Louis Yabor, who had taken a pair of Nez Perce sisters as wives, had gone into the Wallowa country with the Indians and were living in dugout cabins; but the farmers and stockmen in the Grande Ronde still regarded the Wallowa as part of the Nez Perce reservation and, with plenty of land for their own needs in the Grande Ronde, had no reason to risk trouble by invading the Indians' country. In the summer and fall of 1866, however, a party of government surveyors under William H. Odell surveyed a Base Line through the

1. Report of John B. Monteith to F. H. Walker, Commissioner of Indian Affairs, August 27, 1872. Lapwai Agency Files.

Wallowa Valley. In his field notes under date of September 16, 1866, Odell wrote: "This line passes through the beautiful Wallowa Valley . . . about 6 miles wide and 40 long . . . Narrow streams of clear cold water put down from the high snow mountains just to the South. Timber is to the S. and W. and along the banks of the streams. A large part of the Valley is well adapted to agriculture, while the low grassy hills to the N. and E. furnish extensive range for stock. The finest of trout and salmon abound in the streams, and the surrounding mountains give evidence of plenty of game. Here I found many Indians camped upon the banks of the streams, taking great quantities of fish, while their large herds of horses quietly grazed upon luxuriant grass. This valley should be surveyed as soon as practicable, for the wigwam of the savage will soon give way to the (whites). Instead of the hunting and fishing grounds of the red man the valley will teem with a thriving and busy population." [2]

Although the treaty of 1863 had not yet been ratified, Odell seemingly expected no trouble from the Indians. He made no mention of having difficulties, but Joseph's people were obviously disturbed by his intrusion, and one of the members of the government party, Levi Rouse, later reported that the Indians kept pulling up the stakes and scattering the rock monuments that the surveyors erected. Odell's report aroused further curiosity about the Wallowa among the Grande Ronde settlers, but still they made no move to look it over. Then on May 28, 1867, a month after President Andrew Johnson signed the treaty of 1863, the United States General Land Office, accepting the assurance of the treaty commissioners that the Nez Perces had sold the Wallowa Valley, included it in the public domain and directed that it be surveyed preparatory to being opened for settlement.

Surveyors worked in the valley, without interference from the Indians, in the summer and fall of 1867 and laid out eleven townships. They were back the next year, and again in 1869. At the same time, the agents at Lapwai made several attempts to induce Joseph to leave the valley and bring his people onto the reservation in Idaho. The old man resisted them peaceably but firmly. Yet he knew that a crisis was building up for his band. By 1869 he was growing blind and had to ride double on horseback behind an Indian boy. As his strength and vision faded, he sought to inspire his two sons with his own determination to hold the Wallowa. The sons were Hin-mah-too-yah-lat-kekht (Thunder Traveling to Loftier Mountain Heights) and Ollokot (Frog), the former carrying the name of his mother's brother, and

2. "Field Notes of the Survey of the Base Line" by William H. Odell, U.S. Deputy Surveyor, under Contract No. 114, July 2, 1866, Wallowa County Clerk's Office, Enterprise, Oregon. Courtesy Miss Marjorie Martin, County Clerk.

the latter bearing a Cayuse name by which one of old Joseph's half-brothers had been known.[3]

Hin-mah-too-yah-lat-kekht, 29 years old in 1869 and the older of the two sons, was already assuming some of the responsibilities of leadership from his failing father. He was a large, heavily built man, six feet, two inches tall, with handsome, noble features. Born in a cave near the mouth of Joseph Creek in 1840, he had been taken as a babe to Spalding's mission, baptized, and apparently given the name Ephraim by the Spaldings. During his first seven years he had been at the Lapwai mission on many occasions, and had begun to receive some education and Christian training from the missionaries. That had come to an end with the Whitman massacre, and after 1847 he had been raised by the shamans and teachers of his own people in the Wallowa Valley. He had inherited his father's compassion, tolerance, and mild, gentle disposition, and had developed as a civil rather than a hunting or military leader. He carried himself with dignity, could speak in council with eloquence and logic, and, despite his youth, was already known among the nontreaty bands as a sagacious man. The younger, more impetuous Ollokot was his perfect complement, gay, fun-loving, and daring, an able hunter who was winning the respect and following of the band's hunters and braves. Both brothers, like most of the Nez Perces, wore a mixture of Indian and white men's clothes, but combed the hair above the forehead in the upswept curl of the Dreamers, letting the rest hang long or gathered in two braids.

As the decade of the 1870s began, the crisis in the Wallowa approached. The surveyors' glowing descriptions of the valley circulated through the Northwest, and along the Pacific coast several families afflicted with poor health pulled up stakes and headed for the Grande Ronde, intending to push on and establish new homes in the higher, drier, healthier country of the Wallowa. In the Grande Ronde, however, they met confusion and uncertainty. Officially, there seemed to be no doubt that the Wallowa was public domain and that the Indians had no right being there. The region had already been surveyed into sections, and some of the surveyors said that the valley was open for settlement. But the Indians were still there, and there were rumors that in a short time the government would enforce the treaty of 1863 and remove the Indians from the land they had supposedly ceded. Until then, it seemed best to wait. In the fall of 1870, however, pasturage in parts of the Grande Ronde showed signs of exhaustion. Oldtimers and newcomers alike felt the crowding in that valley, and during the winter of 1870–71 some of them thought increasingly of the lush grasslands they had heard about in the Wallowa. In the spring of 1871 a few stockmen finally made up their minds to beat the rush into the new rangeland, and by the end of May two men,

3. See below, p. 668, n. 49.

William McCormack and Neil Keith, had driven their herds across the mountains and into the Wallowa. Several more followed them in the summer and fall, some coming in merely to look over the region and locate claims before settling permanently the following spring, others driving their horses and cattle in to the new grasslands. None were disappointed. McCormack and Keith located homesteads far up the valley on Hurricane Creek and remained there during the winter. Families, including the Mastersons, Tulleys, McNalls, and Findleys, selected choice lands lower down in the valley, where the bunchgrass on the rolling hills north of the river was stirrup high.

Meanwhile, old Joseph—the benign Tuekakas of Samuel Parker and Henry Spalding—died, apparently in August 1871, in his camp in the fork of the Wallowa and Lostine rivers at the lower part of the valley. He was buried at once on a hilltop above the camp, but that same night was reinterred at the foot of the hill. The Indians built a fence of poles around his grave, and within the fence erected another pole, with an arm at its top, and painted it red. From the arm they hung a bell that rang in the wind, and was used by Dreamers to signify moments of great import. One of the headman's horses was killed and slung by a crosspole above the grave. Settlers saw the grave and freshly slain horses for several years. About 1874 a white man stole the bell, and in 1886, long after the Nez Perces had been ousted from the Wallowa, the persons who then owned the property on which old Joseph was buried opened the grave and took the chief's skull. Later, it was exhibited in a dentist's office in Baker, Oregon.[4]

4. The facts regarding Old Joseph's death and the subsequent robbing of his grave were compiled in interviews with early settlers by the late J. H. Horner, historian of the Wallowa and resident of Joseph, Oregon. According to Horner, in notes on file in the County Clerk's Office in Enterprise and in displays in the historical museum in Joseph, the bell was taken by George Morrison, son of a Grande Ronde minister in Cove, Oregon. Regarding the taking of Joseph's skull, Horner wrote: "In about July, 1886, L. Pfefferle, a traveling dentist, who had an office in Boise City, Idaho, and later moved to Baker City, Oregon, where he practiced, came into Wallowa Valley driving a buggy. His wife was a sister of [A. V.] McAlexander [who in 1876 had settled on the property containing Joseph's grave], and they stopped at their home and did some dental work for Mrs. McAlexander. One afternoon while they were there Pfefferle and his wife, Melinda, McAlexander, and his wife and father went up to the grave and dug into it and took the skull. Pfefferle and his wife took it down to the river where they made a fire and heated water and boiled the skull to get the dirt off . . ." Pfefferle retained the skull and displayed it, according to Horner, "in his dental office, at Baker City, which he had marked, Chief Joseph's skull."

In 1926 Horner and others, with the permission of the Nez Perce tribe, moved the remains of Old Joseph to a new grave at the foot of Wallowa Lake. When the original grave was opened, it was seen that the skull was indeed missing. Despite this outrage, McAlexander himself had once assured the young Chief Joseph that he had always

Old Joseph was completely blind when he died, and Hin-mah-too-yah-lat-kekht had already assumed full leadership of the Wallowa Nez Perces. He was now 31, was married to the daughter of a Lapwai headman, and had a 6-year-old daughter of his own. Before the old chief died, he had again exhorted his sons never to abandon their ancestral home. Hin-mah-too-yah-lat-kekht, who spoke the Chinook Jargon rather than English, recounted his father's dying plea in an interview he gave an eastern magazine in 1879, two years after the Nez Perce war. The interpreter and editor put the Indian's words into polished English, and the magazine ran it thus: "My son," said old Joseph, "my body is returning to my mother earth, and my spirit is going very soon to see the Great Spirit Chief. When I am gone, think of your country. You are the chief of these people. They look to you to guide them. Always remember that your father never sold his country. You must stop your ears whenever you are asked to sign a treaty selling your home. A few years more, and white men will be all around you. They have their eyes on this land. My son, never forget my dying words. This country holds your father's body. Never sell the bones of your father and your mother." To that, Hin-mah-too-yah-lat-kekht added, "I buried him in that beautiful valley of winding waters. I love that land more than all the rest of the world. A man who would not love his father's grave is worse than a wild animal." [5]

Time, unfortunately, had already run out for Joseph's people. Even as the old chief died, the first settlers and their cattle and horses were coming through the Wallowa canyon from the Grande Ronde and crossing the high hill to the new range. Those who returned to the Grande Ronde to spend the winter of 1871–72 came back with their families, and with additional settlers, in 1872. Their first view of the Indian paradise from the top of what they called Emigrant Hill delighted them. "Here was a sight more beautiful than anything that they had witnessed in crossing the Rockies, grander than the

---

cared reverently for the grave of the old leader. Young Joseph had been allowed to visit the valley in 1900, long after his military defeat, and had stopped at his father's grave. At that time, so the story went, tears had welled in his eyes when McAlexander had showed him how carefully he had protected the grave (James McLaughlin, *My Friend the Indian*, New York, 1910, p. 366). Some Americans have enjoyed a ghoulish pride in owning and exhibiting the skulls of dead Indian leaders; as already noted, similar savagery was practiced on the remains of Osceola, Black Hawk, and Kamiakin, among others.

5. Chief Joseph, "An Indian's View of Indian Affairs," *North American Review* (April 1879), p. 419. This interesting and powerful document, Joseph's version of the crimes against the Nez Perces, was widely reprinted under the title "Chief Joseph's Own Story." The precise words obviously are not those of Joseph, but the ideas, with allowance for some misunderstandings and errors made by the interpreter and editor, are those of the chief.

9. The Wallowa, 1870–77

WASHINGTON

OREGON

Toohoolhoolzote's Band

SALMON R.

SNAKE R.

HELLS Canyon

OREGON

IDAHO

LIGHTNING CR.

CANYONS

Imnaha

IMNAHA R.

TULLY CR.

CORRAL

FENCE CR.

SNAKE RIVER

IMNAHA RIVER

LITTLE SHEEP CR.

BIG SHEEP CR.

FOREST

CHESNIMNUS CR.

Young Joseph's Birthplace, 1840

JOSEPH CR.

GRANDE RONDE R.

Wilhautyah Murder

WHISKY CR.

V A L L E Y

Enterprise

PRAIRIE CR.

Joseph

Alder Slope

HURRICANE CR.

Wallowa Lake

Emigrant Hill

WALLOWA R.

Wallowa

First Grave of Old Joseph

Lostine

LOSTINE R.

WALLOWA RIVER

Old Joseph's Boundary Markers

MINAM R.

WALLOWA MTS.

BLUE MTS.

Cove

Union

GRANDE RONDE R.

Elgin

[La Grande]

PROPOSED RESERVATION FOR JOSEPH'S BAND, 1873

Sierra Nevadas or even the lofty Shasta in whose sight mother had lived a number of years," wrote H. R. Findley about his pioneer parents, Alexander B. and Sarah Jane Findley, who hauled their wagonbox full of household possessions to the summit of Emigrant Hill in May 1872.

> Diamond Prairie like a huge emerald diamond lay in the immediate foreground. Grand evergreen clad mountains crowned with snow capped peaks towered like mighty sentinels guarding the valley on the South and Southwest and on the South East the rugged Seven Devils were mirrored in a sky blue background while on the East were miles and miles of bunch grass covered hills and valleys which ran on and on in undulating waves to finally meet the horizon in a field of azure blue.
>
> They noticed the luxuriant growth of former years of bunch grass and commented on the thousands yes tens of thousands head of cattle it would feed.
>
> It seemed to them that they had reached the end of their rainbow trail, the trail that they had followed all the way from St. Joseph, Missouri, through desert and plain, over mountain and valley, across treacherous rivers and dangerous mountain passes, all the way to the Willamette valley and then back to Eastern Oregon again and here they were looking at their promised land, their land of opportunity, for here were hundreds of stock ranches waiting for some one to claim them and one of them was to be theirs.[6]

Old Joseph's sons must have seen the first intruders in 1871, during the weeks before and after their father's death. They made no remonstrance, however, and went down to the canyons to winter. When the Indians returned to the valley late in the spring of 1872, the whites were there in larger numbers. McCormack and Keith had wintered in cabins at Hurricane Creek on Alder Slope above the present town of Enterprise. Three stockmen had moved into the Prairie Creek region farther up the Wallowa River Basin. One man, Henry Schaeffer, was even settling at Wallowa Lake at the head of the river, while many others were moving onto claims along the lower part of the Wallowa, closer to old Joseph's grave, near the present towns of Lostine and Wallowa. Cabins were going up, and large herds of cattle and horses dotted parts of the flatland and some of the hills.

The Indians held council for a long time and apparently talked to some of the whites. The latter learned that old Joseph had died, and they called the new chief, Hin-mah-too-yah-lat-kekht, Young Joseph. In their confusion some of them sometimes mixed the two sons and called them both Young Jo-

6. H. R. Findley, "Memoirs of Alexander B. and Sarah Jane Findley," *Chief Joseph Herald* (Joseph, Oregon, November 21, 1957), p. 3.

seph. But in time the name Joseph settled on the tall, intent civil leader, who spoke most often for the band. This man, also, was something of a surprise to the whites. He was not at all the kind of menacing savage their fears had led them to expect of all Indians. There was something "civilized" about him. He spoke intelligently and with moderation; he argued, but he was patient and kind; he seemed to believe that the day of Indian war against the whites was over, and that the two races must somehow try to find ways to settle their problems peacefully. Even in the tension that the white invasion brought to the Wallowa, he often showed that he wanted to be friendly, visiting some of the settlers' homes, sitting in polite conversation in the Chinook Jargon with the women, and playing genially with the children. Although some of the settlers were thorough Indian-haters and wanted nothing to do with the Indians, others became fond of Joseph, and a few gradually came to regard him as a good and trustworthy friend.

The new chief, however, could not ignore what was happening to his people's country. He told the settlers that his father had never sold the Wallowa and that it still belonged to the Nez Perces. Although he wanted no trouble, he said, there would be quarrels and conflicts, and he might not always be able to control the passions of the younger men. The whites listened to him, but replied that his version of the 1863 treaty was not the one that they had heard. According to their information, the United States had bought the valley, and they had a right to be there. Even if they were to leave, other people would come and claim the good land they would abandon. The people in the Grande Ronde, they pointed out, needed this range; pasturage in the Grande Ronde was giving out, the fall of 1871 had been very dry, and the Grande Ronde stockmen faced the prospect of no winter feed in the future for their herds. Surely, they argued, there was room for both whites and Indians in the Wallowa.

Joseph made no headway in his entreaties, and during the summer the Wallowa settlers further entrenched themselves. In August some traders from the Grande Ronde entered the valley to sell whiskey to the young Indians. Fearing trouble, a few of the more responsible settlers dumped the liquor in a stream, which was thereafter called Whiskey Creek, and ordered the vendors out of the valley. In the middle of the month Joseph finally acted, calling on the settlers for a formal council. Some forty or fifty Indians and almost as many whites met on August 14. The settlers chose Joseph Johnson, who was fluent in the Chinook Jargon, to speak for them, and the whites discovered that among the Indians present were Eagle From the Light and a few members of the Idaho nontreaty bands, who had come to give support to the Wallowa Indians. Joseph did most of the talking for the Indians, beginning with a plea that the settlers take their hay and leave the valley at once. When Johnson replied that the whites had the government's permission to live in the Wallowa, an argument commenced over whether the Indians had actually sold the region. Finally, Johnson asked Joseph if the Indians planned to drive the settlers out. The young chief said no, the Nez Perces were friends of the white men and wished to remain so, but the whites must leave. Johnson replied that they would not leave and, as a solution, proposed that the Indians join in sending a delegation of whites and Nez Perces to Lapwai to consult with the agent about the official status of the valley. Joseph declined the invitation but, feeling certain apparently that the reservation officials would explain the truth, that his father had not signed the 1863 treaty, agreed to wait for the white men to return.

The settlers dispatched A. C. Smith and J. H. Stevens to Lapwai with news of their problem, and agent John Monteith hurried over to the valley to see what was happening. He met with Joseph on August 22 and wrote that the young chief told him "that his father had never traded off that country and on his dying bed, about a year ago, bequeathed the whole country to him for his band." [7] Monteith had mixed feelings. As a Presbyterian and a friend of Lawyer and the Christian Nez Perces, he had little patience with the Dreamers and wanted to bring them on the reservation, where he would be in a better position to control their movements and end their influence and troublemaking activities. But at the same time he knew little about what had happened at the treaty sessions of 1855 and 1863, and there was a strong doubt in his mind as to whether the government had actually extinguished Indian title to the Wallowa in 1863.

During Monteith's session with Joseph the chief suggested that the two men meet the next day in a council with the settlers, and the agent agreed to do so. The new meeting occurred on August 23, with some thirty settlers and eighty Indians present. Many of the Nez Perces, Monteith noted, came with their faces painted. Again Joseph explained that the Wallowa belonged to his people, and insisted that the whites must leave. When Monteith tried to argue that "as far as I know from laws and treaties, the country was sold to the government, that it had been surveyed and brought into the market, and the government would protect the settlers," Joseph replied that it was a lie to say that his father had sold the valley. Nevertheless his appeals to Monteith to order the settlers to leave got nowhere; and when the agent finally convinced him that he had no authority to oust the whites, but proposed, instead, that the whites and Indians both use the valley and observe each other's rights and live in peace, Joseph asked Johnson how much land the settlers wanted. Johnson said the government allowed each man 160 acres, or one half mile square,

7. Monteith to F. H. Walker, Commissioner of Indian Affairs, August 27, 1872, Lapwai Agency Files.

and illustrated by pointing out a plot of that size on some neighboring land. He said nothing about the additional grazing land the settlers would use, and when Joseph saw how small 160 acres were, he laughed and replied, "If that is all, you and your Klutchman [wife in the Chinook Jargon] and Papooses can stay and live in peace. It's all right." [8]

Relieved that the trouble was ended, for the time being at least, Monteith returned to Lapwai and wrote a report of the council to the Commissioner of Indian Affairs at Washington, stating, "It is a great pity that the valley was ever opened for settlement . . . If there is any way by which the Wallowa Valley could be kept for the Indians, I would recommend that it be done." His opinion was noted by T. B. Odeneal, Superintendent of Indian Affairs in Salem, Oregon, and by the Indian Bureau in Washington, where wheels began to grind slowly. Meanwhile, although more settlers entered the valley in the fall, the Indians withdrew to the canyons with the onset of cold weather, and there were no difficulties during the winter. By spring, however, action had commenced in Washington. A serious war, dramatized by the sensational murder of government peace commissioners which white men had regarded as typical Indian treachery, had broken out with the Modocs near the Oregon-California border, and the conflict had fanned a new wave of fear throughout the Northwest of all off-reservation Indians, including those of the Wallowa. Indian Bureau officials who had received Monteith's letter had examined the documents of the Nez Perce treaty of 1863 and had decided that the Wallowa might well prove to be another trouble spot. To avoid a new war, Odeneal and Monteith were ordered, by direction of the Secretary of Interior, to meet with the Joseph band. The Indians, the Department advised, should be urged to move onto the Nez Perce or Umatilla reservation, but if they refused, they should be asked what part of the Wallowa they wanted for themselves and what part they would give up—thus reflecting the government's uncertainty at that time over its right to the title of the Wallowa.

Odeneal and Monteith met with Joseph and his people at Lapwai on March 27, 1873. There were familiar exchanges concerning the question of whether the Nez Perces still owned the Wallowa, and Joseph's intense sincerity and force of logic soon convinced the government men that something had definitely gone awry in 1863. At one time in the Nez Perces' history, they learned, the tribe had "had no head chief, but were divided up into bands" and "each band had a chief or head man, and each claimed, occupied and held the land within certain natural boundaries." At some point, white men had apparently designated Lawyer as the tribe's head chief, and Lawyer had signed away the Wallowa. But had he had the right to do so? Joseph said no.

8. Portland *Oregonian*, August 29, 1872.

Granting that the Indians might have had the force of truth on their side, Odeneal and Monteith abandoned their attempt to persuade Joseph to move onto the Nez Perce or Umatilla reservation and turned the discussion to the possibility of allowing the band to remain in the Wallowa.

Joseph eventually left the council the victor, and Odeneal and Monteith reported to Washington that "The question for the Government to decide is as to whether the title of these Indians was extinguished by the so-called supplementary treaty of 1863, in which they took no part . . . If any respect is to be paid to the laws and customs of the Indians then the treaty of 1863 is not binding upon Joseph and his band. If so, then Wallowa Valley is still part of the Nez Perce reservation; this being the case, then the Government is equitably bound to pay the white settlers for their improvements and for the trouble, inconvenience and expense of removing from there." [9] Concerning the Wallowa country, the agents noted that the region was too high, anyway, for successful agriculture; early frosts hampered the growth of grains and gardens. Nevertheless, the area provided excellent range for stock raising, and they suggested that, as a solution, it could be divided between white stockmen and the Indians. The whites should be allowed to settle along the lower part of the Wallowa Valley, and the Indians should retain the upper valley and the lake. That section should be considered part of the Nez Perce reservation, set aside for hunting and summer use by all the tribe.

The recommendations were received in Washington, and were approved. On April 30, 1873, H. R. Clum, Acting Commissioner of Indian Affairs, wrote to Odeneal that the Secretary of Interior was preparing an executive order for the President's signature, "setting apart this vally for the exclusive use of said Indians and that white settlers be advised that they are prohibited from entering or settling in said vally." At the same time, he informed Odeneal that authorization would be forthcoming to appraise the value of improvements made by the settlers in the Wallowa so that Congress could pay them and extinguish their rights. The wheels now ground quickly. A little more than a week later, on May 10, 1873, Commissioner W. W. Curtis of the General Land Office ordered the United States Surveyor General at Eugene City, Oregon, to take steps to prevent further settlement of whites in the Wallowa Valley "until the Nez Perce Indian title may have been extinguished." On June 9 the Secretary of Interior forwarded the executive order to the White House for President Grant's signature, establishing a "reservation for the roaming Nez Perce Indians in the Wallowa Valley, in the State of Oregon." Something, however, had become mixed up in the Bureau of Indian Affairs, and the boundaries of the new reservation proved to be totally different from those proposed by Odeneal and Monteith. Instead of giving the Indians the lake and the upper part of the river, and the settlers the lower

9. Report of the Commissioner of Indian Affairs (1873).

prairies, the awards were just the opposite. The Indians received the northern part of the region, which happened to include the lower portion of the Wallowa Valley, where most of the whites had located, as well as the route of access to the valley from the Grande Ronde, while the settlers were given the southern section of the district, including the headwaters of the river, the lake, and the mountains. Little of that region would have been useful to the whites, even if they had been granted access to it.[10] Either the maps in Washington were imperfect, or no one in the capital knew the Wallowa situation well enough to understand what was being done, and the error was not detected. On June 16 Grant signed the order, making the new reservation official: "It is hereby ordered," the document read, "that the tract of country described be withheld from entry and settlement as public lands, and that the same be set apart as a reservation for the roaming Nez Perce, as recommended by the Secretary of Interior and the Commissioner of Indian Affairs."

Meanwhile, Joseph's people had come up from the canyons at the end of the winter of 1872–73, and some of his young men had become embroiled in quarrels with white stockmen over the right to use certain portions of the range, as well as over the ownership of individual strayed animals. The older Nez Perces calmed their young men and counseled them to let the white men have their way; but the conflicts, frequently heightened by warriors' threats to oust the settlers by force, aroused fears among the whites that the Indians were planning to massacre them. As the Indians withdrew to the northern part of the Wallowa, trying to stay away from the white men and avoid contacts that might lead to bloodshed, the settlers' fears multiplied, and early in May a flurry of rumors and gossip caused a groundless panic in the valley. On May 7 the settlers assembled in an emergency meeting and formed a volunteer militia unit, electing James A. Masterson as captain. About two miles above the present town of Wallowa they hurriedly constructed a stockade. At the same time they sent word of their fears to the Grande Ronde Valley, announcing that "we only propose protection to ourselves against depredations of unfriendly Indians. And then WAR TO THE KNIFE." [11] Although the Indians stayed out of sight, the settlers' alarm continued to feed on rumors, and one family after another gradually packed up and left the Wallowa for the safety of the Grande Ronde. ". . . seven or eight wagons," reported the

10. The official wording of the reservation boundaries reads: "Commencing at the right bank of the mouth of the Grande Ronde River; thence up Snake River to a point due east of the southeast corner of Township One south of the base line of the surveys in Oregon, in Range No. 46, East of the Willamette Meridian; thence from said point west to the fork of the Wallowa; then down said West Fork to its junction with the Wallowa River; thence down said river to its confluence with the Grande Ronde River; thence down the last named river to the place of beginning" (Fee, *Chief Joseph*, p. 70).

11. *Mountain Sentinel*, LaGrande, Oregon, May 17, 1873.

LaGrande, Oregon, *Mountain Sentinel* on May 31, "with men, families, stock, dogs and cats, were leaving hurriedly and singing:

> 'Run nigger, run nigger and try to get away,
> For it is high time, for it is almost day.
> Come along, get out of the Wallowa
> Before Old Joseph kicks up a row.' "

In the same issue of May 31 the *Mountain Sentinel,* published in the Grande Ronde, carried word of the creation of the new reservation. "Those who have not heard the news as published in other papers giving the Wallowa Valley to the Indians, will almost be struck dumb with the intelligence that such is the case," it announced. "And that the man Ordeneal, Supt. of Indian Affairs, stinks in the nostrils of every decent man east of the Cascades, for the dirty part he has acted in robbing the settlers of Wallowa of their homes, their everything. Were he today to put in an appearance among those whom he has so fouly wronged, [he] would pay the penalty with his worthless life."

The news from Washington caused consternation and fury among the settlers, who convinced themselves that they had entered the Wallowa in the first place only on the assurance that it was public land. Fear of the Indians gave way to a hatred of them, as well as of "the Indian-coddling government," and most of those who had left the valley doubled back to save their homes by maintaining physical possession of them. Indignation meetings were called, and resolutions were passed to stay put and defend homesteads and claims "against the savages or any other corrupt power." By the end of June, however, when three government land commissioners arrived in the Wallowa to appraise the settlers' improvements, the temper of many of the people had changed. Some insisted that they had nowhere else to go; but many others were willing to itemize their improvements and, announcing that they would only move after they received their money, hinted that they intended to make the government pay dearly. The land commissioners went to work and, according to the Portland *Oregonian* of July 3, 1873, "visited every section and heard every statement to be made to them, then placed an estimate on the amount due the claimants." In all, they noted eighty-seven farms entered or occupied in the Wallowa and listed improvements, including irrigation ditches, worth a total of $67,860.

Still, there were many who had no intention of moving. With friends in the Grande Ronde, they wrote letters and brought pressure on officeholders, and the latter, in turn, readily adopted their cause against the Indians, who were neither voters nor contributors to political parties. Urged on by newspapers, individuals, and citizens' associations like the Wallowa Road and

Bridge Company and the Prairie Creek Ditch Company, which had already begun to build roads and irrigation ditches in the valley, members of Oregon's Congressional delegation lodged protests with the Department of Interior. But the settlers got their most telling assistance from Oregon's governor, Lafayette F. Grover, who listened to their version of the situation in the Wallowa and on July 21 sent an outraged letter, full of misstatements and distorted history, to Secretary of Interior Columbus Delano.

Although Old Joseph had made it plain to I. I. Stevens, as well as to Indian agents and other white men during the 1860s, that he had signed the 1855 treaty because it had recognized the Wallowa as the homeland of his people, and although no other Nez Perce band had ever suggested that the region belonged to any but Joseph's Indians, Grover followed the line of reasoning of the 1863 treaty commissioners and told the Secretary that by the 1855 treaty the Nez Perce reservation had become "the common property of the whole tribe." Having thus repeated the argument which Stevens had invented and established as fact, the Governor blithely concocted a new piece of deceit. Although Joseph had never accepted annuities or other payments from the government, Grover stated baldly and flatly that he had. "Joseph and his band," he informed the Secretary, acknowledged that the reservation belonged to the whole tribe "by accepting the benefits of the treaty of 1855." With the legal background settled to his own satisfaction, he went on: "The treaty of 1863 is the organized action of the Nez Perce tribe, in relation to land in which the whole tribe had a common interest." Then, with total disregard for the current situation, he wrote in capital letters: "JOSEPH'S BAND DO NOT DESIRE WALLOWA VALLEY FOR A RESERVATION AND A HOME . . . The reason for this is obvious; they can have better land and a more congenial climate at a location which has been tendered them upon the Nez Perce reservation. This small band wish the possession of this large section of Oregon simply for room to gratify a wild, roaming disposition and not for a home." He ended his letter with an official demand, on behalf of the State of Oregon, that "preliminary steps" be taken to rescind the executive order that President Grant had signed.

The high-powered protests from Oregon's governor and Congressional delegation placed the Secretary of Interior in an awkward position. He knew little about the Joseph band of Nez Perces, but it was plain that a handful of Indians was not worth the hostility of Oregon's political leaders. With the President, the Party, and the elections of 1874 to think about, he ordered the Commissioner of Indian Affairs to reexamine the problem. Although the officials in the Indian Bureau were perplexed, they agreed that Odeneal and Monteith might have misled them, and they set about obediently to make a new study of the Wallowa situation.

Monteith, meanwhile, had informed Joseph of Grant's executive order. The division of the region between the settlers and the Indians disappointed the young chief, who was as confused as the settlers were by the boundaries of the new reservation. But he was willing to try sharing the country with the whites, and he promised to keep his people and their herds at a distance from the settlers. There was no chance, however, that he could succeed. The whites were not going to abandon any part of the Wallowa, at least until the government paid them for their homes, and all summer they and the Indians gravitated naturally to the river valley and the neighboring prairies—the Indians' traditional summer grounds and the whites' best summer range. Friction was constant; herds became intermixed; the whites charged the Indians with stealing their animals, and the Indians retorted with similar accusations. Indian cattle trampled the settlers' gardens, the settlers made threats, and the Indians replied that the whites had no right being there. As the settlers hung on, the conflict worsened. A few of the whites, anxious to avoid violence, did their best to settle the quarrels and keep the Indians peaceful. Some of them acknowledged the illegality of the whites' continuing presence in the valley and, touched by Joseph's genuine desire to prevent warfare, hoped to show him that they, too, wished to be friendly. But the temper of public opinion was swinging away from this moderate group, not only in the valley but throughout the Northwest. In the Wallowa, hatred for the Indians festered, as hotheads and agitators among the settlers continued to fan the frustrations of those families who felt that the government had sold them out to the savages. Many of those people taunted the Indians, called them "saucy and impudent," and held meetings at which they threatened to make war on Joseph's Indians and exterminate them.

In March 1873 the Commissioner of Indian Affairs had appointed a three-man group to conduct a general investigation of the condition of the various tribes in Idaho and adjacent territories, and on August 2 this board, headed by John P. C. Shanks and including Governor Thomas W. Bennett of Idaho, had met briefly at Lapwai with Joseph. There had been disturbances on the Lapwai reservation at the time over Catholic efforts to wean treaty Nez Perces away from the Presbyterians; and although the commissioners seem to have had little discussion with Joseph about the problem of the Wallowa, one portion of their conversation with him concerning the new reservation that Grant had established for Joseph's band had impressed them deeply.

"Do you want schools or school houses on the Wallowa Reservation?" they had asked him.

"No," he had answered. "We do not want schools or school houses on the Wallowa Reservation."

"Why do you not want schools?"

"They will teach us to have churches."

"Do you not want churches?"

"No, we do not want churches."

"Why do you not want churches?"

"They will teach us," Joseph had said, "to quarrel about God, as the Catholics and Protestants do on the Nez Perce reservation and at other places. We do not want to learn that. We may quarrel with men sometimes about things on this earth, but we never quarrel about God. We do not want to learn that." [12]

His frank replies had caused the commissioners to observe in their report that arguments among Christian sects in front of Indians were bad. But they had said nothing about the urgent problems confronting the Wallowa Indians. As the hostility of the settlers intensified, Joseph grew uneasy and later in the fall traveled again to Lapwai to complain to Monteith. By that time a change had occurred there too. In Idaho and eastern Oregon, popular sentiment was building up in favor of the "wronged" families in the Wallowa. Joseph and the nontreaties were now almost everywhere considered to be troublemakers; they were termed potentially dangerous, and their position was likened to that of the Modocs just before war had broken out with those Indians. Moreover, it was asserted that as long as the Nez Perces were allowed to live off a reservation, they would exert a bad influence on natives who were already on reservations, posing the threat of a general uprising throughout the interior country. Newspapers were already warning people to be ready for a large-scale Indian war, and in Idaho volunteer units were training and the governor had requisitioned federal rifles and ammunition for them.[13]

Monteith felt the sting of public displeasure that seemed to hold him accountable for a government decision that had favored hostile Indians and victimized white men. Blame appeared to be leveled at him from three directions: from the Indian Bureau whose reexamination of the executive order implied censure of his original recommendation; from the citizens of the Northwest; and from Lawyer's Indian followers on the reservation, who smarted over Joseph's victory that gave the Dreamers and the nontreaties a renewed influence over their own people. By the time that Joseph got to Lap-

12. Annual Report, Department of Interior (1873), pp. 526–27.

13. On April 13, 1874, Idaho's governor, T. H. Bennett, who had been so impressed the year before by Joseph's reason for not wanting churches on the Wallowa reservation, wrote Indian Commissioner E. P. Smith complaining that the settlers in southwestern Idaho were terrorized by the annual gatherings of Indians, including Nez Perces, in the Weiser, Payette, and Boise river basins, and asking that they all be placed, and kept, on reservations (*Nez Perce War Letters*, ed. Eugene B. Chaffee, Idaho Historical Society, Fifteenth Biennial Report, Boise, 1936, pp. 42–43).

wai with his complaints about the impossibility of the situation in the Wallowa, Monteith had shifted his position and was acknowledging that Joseph
belonged on the Nez Perce reservation in Idaho. Accommodating himself to
the questioning that had already reached him from Washington and to the
winds of public opinion in the Northwest, he had written the Commissioner
of Indian Affairs on September 9, 1873: "The Department cannot too soon
take the necessary steps toward those living outside the reservation . . . The
treaty of 1863, as also the treaty of 1868, provides for the location of the Indians and it should be done at as early a day as possible. Some measures ought
to be adopted whereby the Indians can be prevented from going to the
buffalo country." [14]

When Joseph reached Lapwai, Monteith bewildered him by making
him the scapegoat for his own uncomfortable position. The agent was
impatient with the chief, showed him no sympathy, and ignoring the fact
that he had told Joseph that the President had confirmed part of the Wallowa
to the Nez Perces, rebuked him for the troubles in the valley and said they
were proof that the Indians should be forced to come on the Idaho reservation. Joseph argued in vain against the agent's "forked tongue" and, as a last
recourse, asked to be allowed to go to Washington and tell the President the
truth of what was happening in the Wallowa. Monteith refused his request,
and Joseph returned angrily to the valley, where he gathered his people and
took them down in the canyons for the winter.[15]

With the Indians out of sight, fears again grew among the settlers that Joseph was planning to massacre them. But as no word arrived regarding government payments for their improvements, none of the whites made a move
to leave, and confusion increased when nine new settlers drove into the valley
and, showing their contempt for Grant's executive order, took up claims far
up the Wallowa River on reservation land. Despite the tensions and restlessness, the Indians made no appearance during the winter, and in the spring of
1874, when the weather warmed, the settlers gradually relaxed and sowed
more grain than ever before.[16] In May they were suddenly cheered by news

14. Report of Secretary of Interior (1872–73), House Executive Document, *1*, 43rd
Congress, 1st Session, p. 613.

15. Monteith to Commissioner Walker, November 22, 1873, Lapwai Agency Files.

16. The principle planting was of spring oats. The settlers' economy in the Valley
was still a primitive and precarious one. The families had gardens and berry patches,
and raised hogs and cattle. Venison and fish were plentiful, and the people and their
herds had no difficulty subsisting. But there was no income from cash crops, and no
money with which to buy supplies or other necessities outside the Valley. To solve
this problem, many of the settlers took part time or seasonal jobs for pay at sawmills
or other enterprises in the Grande Ronde Valley or at Walla Walla. Nevertheless, white
civilization in the Wallowa took forward steps. The first postoffice was established on

from Washington of a change in their status in the Wallowa. On May 18 Commissioner of Indian Affairs Edwin P. Smith wrote Senator James K. Kelly of Oregon, the same man who as the leader of Oregon volunteers at Walla Walla in 1855 had been responsible for the vicious murder of Peopeo Moxmox, assuring him that "nothing more would be done toward establishing a reservation there, and that the settlers in the Wallowa Valley would not be molested in any way by the Indian department . . . the whole valley is now open for settlement by the whole people." [17]

On both legal and moral grounds the United States government's reversal was the signal for the start of a new chapter in its indefensible record of dealings with the Nez Perces. Grant's executive order of 1873 was still the law, yet the Indian Bureau had now notified the whites that it would not enforce the decree. At the same time, it withheld that information from the Indians. Joseph was not informed of the new development and for more than a year was permitted to believe that the government still recognized the existence of a reservation for the exclusive right of the Indians within the Wallowa. It puzzled and angered him that Monteith would do nothing to oust the settlers, and when the chief and his people came out of the canyons and found more whites rolling into the valley and settling on Indian land late in the spring of 1874, he found it increasingly difficult to restrain his young men. Once more there were bitter altercations. The whites again insisted they were right, and the Indians charged them with lying. At one point a delegation of settlers rode to Lapwai to complain that the Indians had talked "saucily" to the settlers and were gathering to make trouble. A unit of troops hurried to the Wallowa, found no evidence of hostile intention on the part of Joseph, and left. But Joseph was in deep difficulty. Members of other nontreaty bands were visiting his people, telling them of murders and other injustices committed by white men, and questioning whether they should take up the gun together to defend their rights.

Ollokot, now the respected leader of Joseph's young braves, helped his brother point out the folly of war. But early in July, when the band traveled to the Weippe Prairie to dig roots and participate with other Nez Perces in the annual social gathering, some of Lawyer's people told Monteith that the

---

April 10, 1873, near the present town of Wallowa. A Sunday School was organized, and in the fall of 1874 a petition was granted to create a voting precinct, called Wallowa, within the Valley. At the same time, W. W. White was appointed the first justice of the peace. See Findley, *Chief Joseph Herald*, Joseph, Oregon, December 26, 1957, and January 2, 1958.

17. Senator James K. Kelly to Senator James H. Slater, May 18, 1874. *History of Union and Wallowa Counties of Oregon*, pp. 480–81. As this chapter will make clear, not all the settlers were happy with the news. Some had become anxious to receive cash payments for their improvements, and get out of the Valley.

nontreaties were going to have a "talk" there. Believing that the Dreamers might be plotting an uprising, Monteith requested an escort of a company of troops and, under their protection, showed up at Weippe. The council of nontreaty leaders took place; but in the presence of the agent and the soldiers, the headmen, including Joseph, merely voiced their grievances. The meeting ended peacefully, and Monteith and the troops returned to Lapwai, satisfied that they had forestalled trouble. A little later, however, the nontreaty bands met again, this time at Tepahlewam (Split Rocks), the meadows at the head of Rocky Canyon on the Camas Prairie near present-day Grangeville, Idaho, where Nez Perce bands often gathered and where the Sahaptin peoples had rendezvoused for their historic truce meeting with the Shoshonis in 1806 after Lewis and Clark had left the Nez Perces. Among the leaders present for the new meeting, about which Monteith was unaware, were Joseph, Ollokot, White Bird, Looking Glass, Red Owl, and a tall, powerful hunter and warrior named Toohoolhoolzote. A fiery orator, and a proud man, whose intense spiritual beliefs caused the whites to regard him as a hostile Dreamer medicine man, Toohoolhoolzote was the leader of a small band of nontreaty Nez Perces that lived in a mountainous district known as Pikunan along the Snake River south of the mouth of the Salmon River. Three of the tribe's most respected warriors—Rainbow, Five Wounds, and Grizzly Bear Ferocious— were asked to speak on the question of whether the nontreaty Nez Perces, joined by some of the Cayuses in the Umatilla Valley and Moses' people in eastern Washington, should go to war against the whites. The three young men counseled against a war, and when Looking Glass and Red Owl also said that they did not wish to fight the white men, no one else offered an opinion, and the council ended.[18]

Although the Wallowa band had most about which to complain, the result of the meeting undoubtedly pleased Joseph, who knew the hopelessness of an armed struggle. But on his return to the Wallowa the situation seemed worse than before. There were new quarrels between the Indians and the settlers, and on one occasion the two sides almost came to blows over the use of certain pasture lands. For a while the whites barred the Indians from the area in question, threatening to start a shooting war if the Indians approached. Cooler heads among the settlers finally prevailed upon their companions to withdraw, and the episode ended without bloodshed. Joseph did his best to

18. After the council, some of the nontreaty Indians, including possibly Ollokot and other members of Joseph's band, went to the Montana plains on the invitation of the Crows. There, in a big battle against the Sioux, Looking Glass gained distinction in combat. His leadership of the Nez Perce fighting men gave mighty aid to the Crows. There is no evidence that Joseph was in the battle, or even in the buffalo country, at that time.

calm the Indians and to remain personally friendly with some of the less truculent whites. He continued to drop in on farmers' homes, take meals with their families, fondle their children, and discuss problems in an amicable way that demonstrated his sincerity in searching for a solution that would be acceptable to both the Indians and whites.[19] But despite his efforts, tension continued high, and early in August the settlers appealed again for the protection of troops. Two companies of cavalry under Colonel John Green rode into the Wallowa, unconcerned with such legal niceties as whether they were invading unceded Indian land. Their presence brought about a sullen peace, and at the approach of winter, when the Indians withdrew to the canyons, the troops left the valley.

On September 1, 1874, meanwhile, a brave and nationally known general officer of the Civil War, Oliver Otis Howard, destined to become Joseph's chief antagonist, had assumed command of the Department of the Columbia at Fort Vancouver. A deeply religious and moralistic man, known as the "Christian general," Howard had lost his right arm at the battle of Fair Oaks. Returning to active service, he had participated in many of the great battles of the war, including Antietam, Fredericksburg, Chancellorsville, and Gettysburg, and had led two Army Corps on Sherman's march through Georgia. He had not been one of Grant's favorite officers; at both Chancellorsville and Gettysburg his XI Corps had crumbled disastrously, and despite his pluck it had been hard to tell whether he had been the victim of bad luck or of his own weaknesses. After the war he had served as Commissioner of the Bureau of Freedmen and Refugees in the capital, and had then campaigned against Cochise and the Apaches in the Southwest. Compared to the trials he had already faced, the problem of the Wallowa was of small moment to him in 1874, but in time it would test him sorely and overshadow everything else in his record.

In the spring of 1875, during a visit to the Umatilla reservation, Howard met Joseph for the first time. While he was with the agent, the General was informed by John McBean, now the interpreter on the reservation, that the Nez Perce leader and ten members of his band were at one of the Cayuse camps on the reserve and wished to have a talk with him. Howard had already heard of Joseph from his predecessor, General Jefferson C. Davis, at Fort Vancouver, who had told him that he expected that the situation in the Wallowa would one day lead to war. Howard said he would be glad to see the

19. In an article, "Chief Joseph: He Met White Men Half Way," in the Portland *Oregonian*, January 26, 1947, J. H. Horner and Grace Butterfield tell of an episode in June 1875 when Joseph saved the daughter and crippled wife of an itinerant Baptist minister named William Webber from drowning in the Wallowa River. The settlers, said the authors, appreciated Joseph's brave act.

Nez Perce, and a half hour later the eleven Indians approached, "noticeably tall and stout for Indians." They came "in single file," he said, "Young Joseph ahead. One after another took the agent's hand, and then mine, in the most solemn manner. Joseph put his large black eyes on my face, and maintained a fixed look for some time. It did not appear to me as an audacious stare; but I thought he was trying to open the windows of his heart to me, and at the same time endeavoring to read my disposition and character." Joseph may have heard a rumor that the President had changed his mind about the Wallowa, for he had only one question for Howard. "I heard that Washington had some message for me," he had the interpreter ask the General. Howard answered: "There is no word from Washington." Then he added, "We are glad to see you and shake you by the hand." Joseph had nothing else to say. If he had been trying to find out the truth of a rumor, he had first gauged Howard and had then got his answer. Later, it might have looked like a lie, but at this time Howard, in truth, would not have known what Joseph was trying to get at. As the two men looked at each other, in fact, Howard felt that somehow an impulse of mutual respect and understanding ran between them, and he said, "I think Joseph and I became then quite good friends." A moment afterward, the Indians took formal leave of the General, and the Nez Perce chief led his companions back to the Cayuse camp.[20]

Sometime later, Joseph finally learned the bad news about the Wallowa. On June 10, 1875, President Grant accepted the recommendation of the Department of Interior and issued a new proclamation, formally rescinding the executive order of 1873 and reopening the Wallowa Valley to white settlement.[21] When news of the decree reached Monteith, he sent for Joseph and

20. O. O. Howard, *Nez Perce Joseph* (Boston, 1881), pp. 28–29.

21. On a number of occasions in the recent past the Bureau of Indian Affairs has seemed unaware of the history, as recounted in this chapter, that led to the rescinding of Grant's executive order in 1875. On March 28, 1931, for instance, Commissioner of Indian Affairs C. J. Rhoads provided a United States senator with the following distorted version of what happened: "The lands in question were set apart for the use of the roaming Nez Perce Indians, by executive order of June 16th, 1873. These Indians never moved onto or occupied these lands, and for that reason by executive order of June 10th, 1875, these lands were restored to the public domain" (J. H. Horner's notes in the County Clerk's Office, Enterprise, Oregon, pp. 59–60). More recent communications by members of the Department of the Interior indicate continuing official ignorance on the subject. The problem can be traced to the annual report of the Department of Interior for 1877, p. 407, where the erroneous information first appears, and which apparently continues to be the source of the government's position. "Chief Joseph . . . showed a disposition neither to settle upon the Wallowa reserve nor to respect the rights of property of the whites whom he encountered in his unrestricted roving," it says. Hence, Grant's order of 1873 was revoked. It says nothing of the Grover letter or of other political pressure that led to the rescinding of the 1873 decision.

told him of the President's new decision. "At the first interview," the agent wrote, "he was inclined to be ugly and returned to his camp very much dissatisfied with the action of the Government. In the course of the week he came back and talked more reasonably."

The news made Joseph's position more difficult than before. If he was dissatisfied with the betrayal, many others in his band were furious. The chief and his followers rode back to the Wallowa and, ignoring Monteith's plea to come onto the Idaho reservation as quickly as possible, called a council of all the leaders of the nontreaty bands. The meeting was held at a favorite campsite which the settlers called Indian Town, close to the center of white settlement at the forks of the Wallowa and Lostine rivers. The visitors included Eagle From the Light, White Bird, Looking Glass, and Toohoolhoolzote. An Indian named Johnnie, who reported some of the proceedings to white friends, said that Toohoolhoolzote was the angriest of all the men present. Apparently, he, Eagle From the Light, and White Bird spoke for armed defense against the whites. But the other speakers, including Joseph, Ollokot, and Looking Glass, still argued that it was foolhardy to start a war, and when the shamans also counseled caution, the group as a whole agreed to continue to try to live in peace with the settlers.[22]

In the meantime, Monteith had become fearful that a clash might occur in the Wallowa and, as much to protect the Indians as the whites, had urged that troops be sent back to police the valley. Howard responded by dispatching two companies of cavalry. One of the officers who rode into the area, Captain Stephen C. Whipple, met Joseph on several occasions and after conducting his own inquiry into the history and current status of the Wallowa problem, wrote a report for Howard that was sympathetic to the Indians and to their claim to the valley. The district, he pointed out, was "only fit for stock raising, as a business, and not desirable for that in consequence of the long winters." Furthermore, "one of the most enterprising, reliable and best citizens" had told him that the settlers had been willing to sell out and move, and that many were disappointed that the government had decided against the reservation, and would therefore not be paying them to move. Regarding the Indians, while it was true, he said, that they were Nez Perces, meaning that they were part of the tribe that had signed the treaty of 1863, "my opinion is they have for many years formed a somewhat separate and independent community, claiming this valley as their peculiar possession and permanent home . . . Old Joseph . . . to his last hour . . . asserted to his children and friends that he had never surrendered claim to this valley, but that he left it to them as their inheritance, with the injunction never to barter it away . . . This band of Indians are by no means a vagabond set. They are

22. Findley, *Chief Joseph Herald* (January 2, 1958), p. 4.

proud-spirited, self-supporting and intelligent; and if it is possible that Indians can rise in the social scale; I know of none who give better promise of rewarding an effort in that direction . . . At the time Joseph visited me," he added, ". . . he asked earnestly if I had nothing more to say, to which I replied in the negative. He looked disappointed, and after a short silence he said he hoped I could tell something of a possible doubt of their being obliged to relinquish this valley to the settlers. I told him the case was decided against the Indians by higher authority than that of any army officer. This declaration did not make the countenances of the Indians more cheerful." [23]

Whipple's comments impressed Howard, and he forwarded them to the War Department, adding sympathetically in his own report for 1875: "I think it a great mistake to take from Joseph and his band of Nez Perces Indians that valley. The white people really do not want it. They wished to be bought out . . . possibly Congress can be induced to let these really peaceable Indians have this poor valley for their own."

With Governor Grover and the state politicians committed to getting the Indians onto the Idaho reservation, the current session of Congress could have been induced to do no such thing. Grant's Secretary of Interior, also, had endured too much embarrassment already, and his new verdict seemed to be final. Local officials in the Grande Ronde accepted it as such. For some time, pending a clear decision from Washington, they had delayed granting a permit to construct a toll road into the Wallowa; now they issued the permit, and A. C. Smith and M. B. Reese started a construction crew at work, building a wagon road directly past the stone monuments that old Joseph had once erected as boundary markers of his land. Young Joseph protested to Smith. Despite the fact that Smith was generally fair and sympathetic to the Indians, and was one of the few white men whom Joseph respected, the chief got nowhere with him. Smith was within his rights, and if Joseph had a complaint, Smith told him to take it to the government.

Joseph did nothing about it, and with the troops in the valley, the summer and fall passed peacefully. Only five new settlers entered the Wallowa that year, and one of them established a claim on Alder Slope above the present town of Enterprise. At the approach of winter the Indians returned to the canyons and the cavalry left the valley. Just before Christmas, Joseph and most of the members of his band journeyed to the Lapwai area to visit relatives. While they were there, the settlers in both the Wallowa and the

23. Whipple's report was dated August 28, 1875. His statement concerning the settlers' willingness to move and their disappointment that the government had decided against the reservation is corroborated in detail in the memoirs of Alexander B. and Sarah Jane Findley, as recounted by H. R. Findley, in the *Chief Joseph Herald* (April 3, 1958), p. 4.

Grande Ronde valleys experienced a scare, this one based on a misunderstanding and a hoax. In the last week of December farmers in the Grande Ronde sent out an appeal for troops; Joseph and his Indians, they said, were driving off the settlers' livestock in the Wallowa and were threatening a general uprising. Hurrying out of the fort at Walla Walla on New Year's Day, two troops of the First Calvalry under Lieutenant William R. Parnell made an uncomfortable, forced march across the Blue Mountains to the Grande Ronde, through below-zero temperature and snow up to four feet deep. At the same time, Monteith, puzzled by the appeal, journeyed to the Wallowa from Lapwai and insisted that Joseph and his people were in Idaho, not more than twenty miles from the agency. After an investigation, it was discovered that the scare in the Wallowa had been occasioned by a few elderly Indians who were wintering in the Imnaha canyon. Some stray cattle owned by settlers had mingled with the Indians' horses, and the Nez Perces had cut them out and tried to drive them back to the whites, lest the latter accuse the Indians of rustling. Some settlers had seen them and, thinking the worst, had raised an alarm. In the Grande Ronde, the scare had been deliberately amplified, Parnell learned, to lure the troops to that valley so that the farmers could sell them feed and provisions at profiteering prices. Feeling no kindness toward the settlers who had ruined their New Year's Day celebration, the cavalrymen returned across the mountains to Walla Walla.[24]

Joseph finally came back to the canyons, and in March 1876 took his band to the Umatilla reservation for a visit to the Cayuses. Although the agent and whites in the vicinity watched the Nez Perces suspiciously, Joseph's purpose seemed to be nothing more sinister than to participate in horse races. A short time later, he and his people returned to their home canyons, and in June they came up to the plateau as usual and established camps in the root-gathering meadows of the Chesnimnus area in the north, which the Indians called Chesnimax (Thorn Brush Mountain). Several hunting parties were sent out to bring back meat, and at least one of them made an appearance in the valley, camping for a while in the forks of the Wallowa and Lostine rivers. But the settlers' feeling was high against them, and after a quarrel over the Indians' ponies, which apparently knocked down some of the farmers' fences and got into grain fields, the Indians withdrew and disappeared toward the north.

Violence, avoided for so long, was now in the offing. On June 22 one of the farmers, A. B. Findley, missed five of his horses that had been grazing on the open range. After a long search, he came on tracks that looked like those of his animals and followed them to the upper part of Whiskey Creek. Nearby,

24. Monteith to Commissioner Smith, February 2, 1874. Also, account by Major W. R. Parnell in Cyrus Townsend Brady, *Northwestern Fights and Fighters* (New York, 1907), p. 91.

he saw an Indian camp and assumed that the Indians had taken his animals. He rode back to the settlements for help and returned with three men, including two brothers, Wells and Oren McNall, both of them bitter Indian-haters who had had several altercations with Nez Perces. They found no one at the camp but, discovering some deer carcasses hung up in the trees, believed that a hunting party was in the vicinity and would eventually come back for the meat. As it was late, the white men decided to return home and come out again after daylight with more settlers.

The next morning, June 23, Findley and Wells McNall started out ahead of the others, intending to watch the Indian camp until the reinforcements came up. The details of what happened after the two men reached the camp have been the subject of controversy ever since, and the truth will never be known. Several different Nez Perce versions exist. One states that a hunting party of eight Indians had returned to the camp to get the deer. When they saw the two white men approach, all but a young Indian named Wilhautyah (Wind Blowing) got on their horses and started to leave. Wells McNall leaped from his horse and tried to hold Wilhautyah. There was a scuffle, McNall called to Findley to shoot the Indian, and the latter did so, killing the Indian. Another Indian version says that the two white men dismounted a short distance from the camp, saw Wilhautyah in a tree trying to untie one of the carcasses, and shot him down. No contemporary account by the two white men exists, but years after the event, two versions of Findley's side of the story appeared in print. Although there are discrepancies in those two tellings, they are in the main similar to each other; and since official documentation by contemporary investigating agencies seems to bear out some of their principal points, none of them complimentary to the white men involved, they are perhaps close to the truth of what occurred.

According to the more detailed of the two accounts, Findley and McNall waited near the camp until they saw three Indians approaching. Then they rode down to meet them. The whites were sure that the Nez Perces knew where the missing horses were, and their attitude alarmed the Indians. Although the Nez Perces had always been friendly with Findley, they intensely disliked McNall. Small, wiry, and only twenty-one years old, he was known to them as a quarrelsome troublemaker. At one time, it was said, he had tried to sell whiskey to the Indians. Later, he had barred Indians from using one of their accustomed fishing sites, which was near his home at the mouth of Whiskey Creek. Ollokot and a white interpreter had visited him at the time to warn him to halt his bullying, but it had served no purpose. Now, McNall's presence with Findley must have betokened trouble, and it came quickly.

Findley told the Indians that he suspected them of having taken his horses, and asked that two of them go back to the settlements with him and hold a council over it with the white men. While they argued about it, another Indian approached on horseback. The three Nez Perces, according to the white men's story, had rested their guns against a tree, and during the argument Findley and McNall—they said—got between the Indians and their weapons. Suddenly, according to their version, Wilhautyah made a move to pick up a coil of rope, but lunged instead at McNall's gun. The truth may be that, on the contrary, McNall lunged at Wilhautyah's gun. At any rate, the two men engaged in a desperate wrestle while Findley covered the other Indians. As McNall fought for his life, he kept crying to Findley to shoot Wilhautyah, but the white man held his fire. Finally, McNall, out of breath and screaming curses at Findley for not shooting his opponent, began to weaken. Findley said that McNall's weapon went off, and when he saw McNall fall, he thought he had been shot. At the same instant, he said he saw the Indian reach for McNall's gun. Despite the fact that it would now have had no bullet in it, he feared he too was about to be shot and, drawing a bead on Wilhautyah, killed him. McNall was unhurt. He got to his feet just as the mounted Indian came up. The two white men backed away, got on their horses, and rode off.[25]

Near the settlements they met the reinforcements who were just starting

25. Findley, *Chief Joseph Herald*, January 30, February 6, 13, 1958. The second—and somewhat different—version of Findley's side of the story, written by a son, here identified as H. K. Findley, appears in McWhorter, *Hear Me*, pp. 610–14. Nez Perce versions can also be found in *Hear Me*, pp. 123, 124, 129–30, and 619–20. Various dates are given for the killing, but the *Chief Joseph Herald* account and official inquiries into the matter make it June 23. An article in the *Mountain Sentinel* (LaGrande, Oregon, July 1, 1876), also refers to the killing as having occurred "last week." This account, a brief one though perhaps more authentic than any other, because of its immediacy, says that "McNall and one of the Indians engaged in a scuffle over one of the guns belonging to the Indian and in the struggle, it was thought McNall, shot the Indian in the leg. This enraged the Indian beyond all reason, and McNall . . . could not handle him." So Findley shot him. This version gets some confirmation from Monteith's report of the episode, written on July 31, 1876, to the Commissioner of Indian Affairs. "Some four weeks ago," he wrote, "while a party of four of said band were hunting in the Wallowa Valley they met two white men and got into a dispute about something. The white men proceeded to take the firearms from the Indians . . ." (*Hear Me*, pp. 135–36). See also Duncan McDonald's version in the *New Northwest*, Deer Lodge, Montana, April 26, 1878. In this account, which Nez Perces gave McDonald, the two white men came on two Indians at the hunting camp, disarmed them, and picked a fight with them. Wilhautyah arrived during the scuffle, tried to help the other two, and was killed. There is ample reason to believe that the Indians would not have set their weapons against a tree, as Findley's account says.

out to join them. Findley's recital of what had happened must have cast doubt on the wisdom and justice of his act, for some of the settlers blamed him at once for a rash deed. All the whites were alarmed. The dead man, Wilhautyah, was well known to the settlers as a close friend of Joseph. Some of the whites even thought mistakenly that the dead Indian was Joseph's personal medicine man, and fear that the Indians would seek revenge spread rapidly. That night the whites near the mouth of Whiskey Creek barricaded themselves in the home of Ephraim McNall, who had built his cabin like a blockhouse, with chinks through which the men could fire. No Indians appeared, however, and in the morning the worried settlers induced Wells McNall to ride to the county seat of Union in the Grande Ronde, and tell officials what had happened. Findley and the rest of the settlers in the area meanwhile scouted cautiously through the countryside. They saw no sign of Indians that day or the next, but on the third day after the killing Findley was bewildered to discover his five missing horses grazing quietly near his home. His embarrassed plea that the Indians must have sent the animals back did not please the other settlers, whose fear of what the Indians intended doing was now heightened by an angry feeling that Findley and McNall were to blame for the crisis.

The Indian witnesses to the murder, in the meantime, had returned to the Chesnimnus area, possibly carrying Wilhautyah's body with them. There was consternation and anger in Joseph's camp, and the young men and grieving woman cried out for the extermination of the settlers in the Wallowa. Within a week, however, a Nez Perce arrived from Lapwai with word that Monteith had heard of the murder, that he was also grieving about it and was angry with the settlers, and that he wished to see Joseph. The chief considered the message for several days, then journeyed to Lapwai. Monteith now seemed to be on his side. Joseph told him that the Indian witnesses to the shooting had informed him that the fight had started because the two white men had seized the Nez Perces' guns during a dispute about something. "I . . . advised him to let civil authorities deal with the murder in accordance with our laws and told him I thought justice would prevail," Monteith wrote to the Commissioner of Indian Affairs in Washington. "I told him to keep his people quiet and that all would end well . . . Joseph seemed to care but little for the man killed and seemed satisfied with the state of affairs . . ." he added.[26]

The last statement was unjustified and had no basis in fact. Joseph was not that unfeeling about the murder of one of his people, and of a close friend at that. What he conveyed to Monteith was his willingness to try to calm the

26. Monteith to Commissioner J. Q. Smith, July 31, 1876. See McWhorter, *Hear Me*, p. 136.

passions of his people. After Joseph had left Lapwai to return to the Wallowa, the agent on July 3 informed General Howard of the new crisis, terming the killing of Wilhautyah "willful, deliberate murder," and asking him to send troops to the valley "to protect the Indians while fishing." [27] The news disturbed the General. He wired Captain David Perry, commanding the troops at Lapwai, to visit the Wallowa, "see the chief Joseph, and do what was necessary to preserve the peace." [28] At the same time, he directed his own assistant adjutant general, Major Henry Clay Wood, to go to Lapwai, investigate the matter, and report his findings to him.

Wood was already familiar with the historic and legal background of the Wallowa conflict. Six months earlier, at the request of Howard, he had made a lawyer's study of the causes of the unrest in the valley, and on January 8, 1876, had submitted a brief to the General that he had titled "Joseph and His Land Claims, or Status of Young Joseph and His Band of Nez Perce Indians." His conclusion, after studying the thorny treaties of 1855 and 1863, had been noteworthy: "In my opinion," he had said, "the non-treaty Nez Perces cannot in law be regarded as bound by the treaty of 1863; and in so far as it attempts to deprive them of a right to occupancy of any land its provisions are null and void. The extinguishment of their title of occupancy contemplated by this treaty is imperfect and incomplete . . . It remains for the commissioner of Indian Affairs to solve the problem of a politic and just disposition of the non-treaty Nez Perces. Except that I suggest a departure from the temporizing policy, and a conciliatory and just, yet speedy solution of the problem, I have no matured sentiments to present." [29]

Shortly after Wood had given his brief to Howard, the General had received a letter from a prominent Presbyterian minister in Portland, the Reverend A. L. Lindsley, who had maintained frequent communication with Monteith and Presbyterians on the Idaho reservation and knew something about the Wallowa problem. Lindsley had reached a conclusion similar to that of Wood. The Joseph band's "title has never been rightfully extinguished," the clergyman had written Howard. "In fact, the fair construction of treaty stipulations confirms the Indian title . . . The treaty of 1863 was not adopted by the Nez Perce Tribe, but by a part only . . . The Government is bound by its own engagement to fulfill the original Treaty, until it can procure an honorable discharge from its obligations." Lindsley had gone on also to propose the appointment by the government of a commission of qualified men to ". . . settle the whole matter before war is even thought of" by negotiating

27. Howard and McGrath, *War Chief Joseph*, p. 97.
28. McWhorter, *Hear Me*, p. 141.
29. H. Clay Wood, *Status of Young Joseph and His Band of Nez Perce Indians* (Assistant Adjutant General's Office, Portland, Oregon, 1876), p. 45.

with the Indians "for the relinquishment of all their land-claims by fair purchase . . ." [30]

Wood's brief and Lindsley's letter, coming on top of Captain Whipple's
first-hand report, which had also been sympathetic to Joseph's people, had
had a strong effect on Howard. Wood had examined the validity of Joseph's
claim with a wholly objective disinterest, and as a lawyer, the officer had been
moved to conclude that the band's title to any part of the Nez Perce reservation of 1855, including the Wallowa, had not been extinguished in 1863.
Lindsley, a voice of conscience in the Northwest and a moral force to which
the religiously inclined Howard would have been particularly attentive, had
further interested the General with his proposal of a commission, a suggestion
that had seemed an admirable way to solve the Wallowa problem. Soon afterward, Howard's thinking had become settled on the matter. Taking the position that Grant's second executive order would have to stand as final and that
the whites could no longer be ousted, he had decided that the government
should end the conflict in the valley as promptly as possible by extinguishing
the Indians' rights to all off-reservation lands through a fair and just purchase
of those claims from every band that had not signed the 1863 treaty. Such a
settlement, he had determined, should be brought about by a commission like
the one proposed by Dr. Lindsley.

This line of thinking, which became Howard's unrelenting policy, had
within it the seeds of infamy. Wood, Lindsley, and Howard all believed that
their motives regarding Joseph's band were just and fair and that, compared
to those who wished to drive Joseph from the Wallowa without further
negotiations, they showed a decent concern for the Indians' legal and moral
rights. But there were serious deficiencies in their thinking. Aware that Joseph's people still had a claim to the Wallowa, they proposed simply that the
government pay for that claim—and then put the Nez Perces on the reservation. What if Joseph refused to sell? Then, wrote the Reverend Lindsley to
the General, "harsher measures" would be justified. Wood's brief, suggesting
an end to the government's "temporizing policy," implied the same thing, and
Howard, in his future actions, showed that he had totally abandoned his position of 1875, at which time he had said that it had been a mistake to take the
Wallowa from the Indians. Now he would take it, by negotiation and payment if possible, but by force if necessary. Moreover, by having the government accept and promptly execute his policy, he would make inevitable an
injustice that might have been avoided. Up to then, the government's indecisiveness—opening the valley to settlement but not forcing the Indians onto the

30. Howard's 1876 Report to the War Department. See also Merrill D. Beal, *I Will
Fight No More Forever* (Seattle, 1963), p. 35, and McWhorter, *Hear Me*, pp. 140–41.
Lindsley's letter was dated January 9, 1876, the day after Wood had submitted his
brief to Howard.

reservation—reflected continuing confusion in Washington over the validity of Joseph's claim. How long that situation might have existed if Howard had not brought it to a head by endorsing Lindsley's proposal for a commission and an enforced cession of the area is problematical. Sooner or later, it would seem, the crisis in the Wallowa would have grown even worse than it was. But the possibility would have remained for a fair settlement, not based on the use of force, and a final decision might still have been made under a different administration, returning the valley to the Indians or dividing it again— but in a more reasonable fashion—between the Nez Perces and the whites, whose number in that huge area even close to a century later totaled fewer than 8,000. With Howard, the hope of a peaceful solution disappeared. He had the same goal as I. I. Stevens and the commissioners of 1863: the government must get the land from the Indians. There was an interesting difference, however, between the thinking of the earlier negotiators and that of Howard and Lindsley. Both of the latter had consciences, sympathized with the pitiable situation of Joseph's people, and secretly sided with them. But in the face of public opinion, which demanded the Wallowa for the settlers, they deluded themselves into believing that they had found an honorable answer. Neither one of them could have believed it seriously. Howard, the "Christian general," from that moment on cast in the role of Devil's advocate in behalf of the settlers for whose cause he had scant tolerance, became increasingly tormented and, in trying to justify himself by becoming the principal instrument of injustice to Joseph, only wracked his soul the more. His behavior then, and his writings in later years, make that plain.[31]

By July 1876 the General's policy had taken form, and he had already made his proposal to Washington for the appointment of a commission, when the news of Wilhautyah's murder in the Wallowa reached him. Shortly afterward, Major Wood left Fort Vancouver for Lapwai, sending instructions ahead to have Joseph and his brother, Ollokot, meet him there. At Captain Perry's request, Joseph was sent for again, and on July 22 he and Ollokot, accompanied by some forty of their people, met Wood at the Lapwai agency. At this meeting, attended also by Lieutenant Parnell from Walla Walla, Perry and assistant surgeon Jenkins A. Fitzgerald of Fort Lapwai, Monteith, and Joseph's brother-in-law, Reuben, who was now also the head

31. See, e.g., Howard's tortured attempts to explain the causes of the war against Joseph in his books, *Nez Perce Joseph* (Boston, 1881), pp. 30–33, and *My Life and Experiences among Our Hostile Indians* (Hartford, Conn., 1907), pp. 240–44. In many factual matters the two books disagree with each other, and neither is entirely reliable. As evidence of Howard's personal distress they are more interesting; they reveal points of view whose hollowness Howard himself could not have failed to recognize. Note also his "Comment on Joseph's Narrative," written in 1879 in reply to Joseph's "An Indian's View of Indian Affairs," and published in Brady, *Northwestern Fights and Fighters.*

chief of the treaty Nez Perces, Joseph made a strong and favorable impression on Wood.

It was true, Joseph told him, that "one of his brothers had been killed by whites in Wallowa Valley; that the Indian who was killed was much respected by the tribe, and was always considered a quiet, peaceable well-disposed man; that the whites who killed him were bad, quarrelsome men, and the agressive party; that the whites in the valley were instigated by those in authority, and others in Grande Ronde valley, to assault and injure the Indians while fishing and hunting in that section of country; that he wished the white who killed the Indian to be brought to the agency, to be there confronted with his accusers. Joseph said," Wood went on in his summary of the council, "that among the Indians the chiefs controlled the members of their bands, and had power to prevent bad Indians from doing wicked things and in case of their doing so to punish them; and if the chiefs did not restrain or punish bad Indians, they themselves were responsible for their bad acts; and he reasoned that those in authority over the whites had or should have, the same control over their men; and hence the white authorities in the vicinity of Wallowa Valley and elsewhere were directly responsible for the killing of his brother; that his brother's life was of great value; that it was worth more than the Wallowa valley; that it was worth more than all this country; that it was worth more than all the world; that the value of his life could not be estimated; nevertheless, that now, since the murder had been done; since his brother's life had been taken in Wallowa valley, his body buried there, and the earth there had drunk up his blood, the valley was more sacred to him than ever before, and he would and did claim it now as recompense for the life taken; that he should hold it for himself and his people from this time forward forever, and that all the whites must be removed from the valley." [32]

Wood was deeply touched. These were the reasoned words of a patriot, and there was a strain of humanitarianism in the military man that responded to Joseph's plea. Parnell, already impatient with the settlers over the trick they had played on him in January, undoubtedly shared Wood's sympathy for the Indians. Both men found it easy, moreover, to talk to Joseph. He made no threats, and bore little resemblance to the sullen, resentful Indians with whom military leaders had clashed on the plains and in the Southwest. The tall, handsome Nez Perce knew his rights, yet spoke with restraint and dignity. When he had finished, he was followed by Ollokot, who "spoke almost to the same purpose as his brother, except that he did not want the whites, Findley and McNall tried and punished for their crime, but wished them to leave that section of country that he might never see them more . . ."

32. Major H. Clay Wood, *Supplementary to the Report on the Treaty Status of Young Joseph* (Assistant Adjutant General's Office, Portland, Oregon, 1878), pp. 2–4.

The talks of the two Nez Perce leaders, Wood could see, had caused discomfort to Monteith, who had announced earlier that Joseph did not care about Wilhautyah's death and seemed "satisfied with the state of affairs." The presence of the treaty Nez Perce, Reuben, also caused tension, and the next day the military men met again with the two brothers, but this time at Fort Lapwai and without asking Monteith or Reuben to attend. The discussion was even fuller and more frank than that of the day before, as Joseph and Ollokot recounted their version of the tribe's history that had led to the conflict with the whites in the Wallowa.[33] Wood then revealed to the Nez Perces that General Howard was recommending to Washington that the President appoint a commission of five men to hold a council with Joseph and settle all difficulties. Until the General received an answer, Wood said, the Wallowa Indians would do best for their cause if they tried not to have further trouble with the settlers, but let the courts of the white men bring Findley and McNall to justice.

Joseph and Ollokot agreed. When the meeting ended, the two brothers and the members of their band who had accompanied them to Lapwai put on an equestrian show, with military-like maneuvers, and then started back to the Wallowa. Wood and Parnell departed also, leaving behind a miffed agent, who wrote a bitter letter to the Indian Bureau complaining of interference by the military men in a field that he felt was rightfully his own. He had successfully pacified Joseph, he protested, but "up comes the General's Adj't" all the way from Portland, holding councils with the Nez Perce chief, informing him that five commissioners may be sent, and stirring him up with a feeling that "it must be a matter of great importance . . ." Now Joseph would think that the whites were afraid of him, and he would push his claim more strongly. Monteith, who learned what Wood had told the Indians about Howard's proposed commission, felt that that recommendation was also an interference. If such a commission were necessary, he wanted it understood that he should have had the right to propose it. And now that it was proposed, he objected to the men whose names had been suggested for it by Howard, as he had heard; and he urged, instead, that it be composed of Joel Palmer, the Reverend E. R. Geary, who had secured his own appointment as agent at Lapwai, and himself.[34]

33. At this time, apparently, Ollokot produced a "quite accurate" map he had made, showing the band's claim in the Wallowa. This, and another one he showed Wood, were covered with drawings of animals, people, and guns, and depicted the slaying of Wilhautyah. See McWhorter, *Hear Me*, pp. 156–58.

34. McWhorter, *Hear Me*, pp. 136–39, quoting Monteith's letter to Commissioner J. Q. Smith, July 31, 1876. One of Monteith's complaints, also, was that the military's attention to Joseph created dissatisfaction among the treaty Nez Perces "who see so

Meanwhile, although Wells McNall had gone to Union to inform county authorities of the killing in the Wallowa the day after it had occurred, Howard had learned that neither McNall nor Findley had yet been arrested. Since that was the first thing to be done to reassure Joseph, Howard wrote to District Judge Brainard at Union, requesting that he have the two settlers held and tried in District Court for the murder of the Indian.[35] Then, when Wood arrived back at Fort Vancouver and submitted his summary of the Lapwai council, Howard filed his own annual report to the War Department in Washington, attaching copies of both of Wood's briefs, adding his endorsements to them, and renewing his recommendation for the appointment of a five-man board of commissioners to extinguish the land claims of the non-treaty Nez Perces.

His report was mailed on September 1. By then two months had passed since Monteith had promised Joseph at Lapwai that white men's courts would bring justice to the killers of Wilhautyah, and a month had gone by since Howard had written to Judge Brainard. Still, the two settlers in the Wallowa had not been arrested. In July members of Joseph's band had appeared in the valley and caused great excitement by pitching their camp at Indian Town and practicing what the settlers thought were war maneuvers—wild riding and target shooting—in full view of the whites. At night the Indians had increased the settlers' fears by constant drumming and dancing. In August, Joseph himself had arrived at Indian Town and had somewhat eased the tension by visiting the Findleys and asking, in a surprisingly friendly manner, to hear their version of the murder of Wilhautyah. From the conversation, Findley got the idea that the Indians had decided not to blame him but were angry only with McNall, who, they claimed, had started the fight and caused the murder on Whiskey Creek by grabbing Wilhautyah's gun and then forcing Findley to shoot the Indian.

---

much consideration shown to the 'non-treaties' . . ." Monteith's petulance, of course, got him nowhere. Despite his initial sympathy for Joseph's band after the murder of Wilhautyah, he was in the position of a man marking time. He wanted Joseph on the reservation, but his superiors—still uncertain about the legal status of the Indians' claim—had not yet given him orders to force them out of the Wallowa. The commission proposed by Monteith may eventually have solved the problem in the Valley more justly than the one appointed by Washington, perhaps recommending the restoration of the Wallowa to Joseph, or a reasonable division of the region between whites and Indians. The consequences of either decision are too "iffy" to contemplate. All that is relevant is what actually happened—a shameful "mailed fist" ejection of Joseph and his people. Monteith, for jealous reasons only, objected to the proposal for a commission that began the train of events leading to that ejection, but eventually he got his own marching orders and fell in line with Howard.

35. La Grande *Mountain Sentinel*, July 29, 1876.

But on September 1 Joseph and various Indian messengers suddenly showed up at most of the homes in the valley and, in a stern and threatening mood that indicated that the members of the band had lost patience with the white man's justice, ordered the settlers to meet the Indians in a council the next day at the forks of the river and to bring both Findley and McNall with them. The seriousness of the new situation stunned the settlers. A number of them gathered the next morning at Ephraim McNall's cabin and, after advising Wells McNall and Findley for their own safety not to go with them, rode to Joseph's camp at the forks. The Indians were angry not to see McNall and Findley, but they agreed to a council with the whites. With James Davis, one of the settlers, serving as interpreter, the two sides engaged in an excited discussion the rest of the day. Joseph and the other Indians were insistent now that the settlers could no longer remain in the valley but would have to leave by the following Sunday. They must also turn over McNall and Findley for trial by the Indians. As it was their country, they maintained that they had jurisdiction over it, and stated that if an Indian killed a white man, the whites tried him; therefore when whites killed an Indian, the Indians had a right to try them—particularly when the whites made no move to do so themselves.[36] The settlers refused to accept the demands, and the meeting broke up angrily—though peaceably—with an agreement for Joseph and his followers to meet again with some of the settlers, this time including Wells McNall and Findley, the next day at Ephraim McNall's home.

Excitement rose the following morning when one of the settlers reported seeing sixty or seventy Indians, armed, painted, and stripped for war, riding on the hills. Certain that Joseph was planning a surprise attack, a number of families, including the A. B. Findleys, again took refuge in Ephraim McNall's blockhouse-like cabin. Soon afterward the Indians, with Joseph and Ollokot at their head, swooped down from the hills and surrounded the house. There were seven men inside, with some thirty rifles previously supplied to the settlers by Union County officials. Most of the guns were propped against the walls with their muzzles sticking through firing chinks, and the frightened settlers ran from one to another of them, jiggling them to make the Indians think that their numbers were greater than they were. Ephraim McNall had remained outside, and he parleyed boldly with Joseph,

36. See the letter of Henry Rhinehart, a Grande Ronde settler who came to help the Wallowa whites, in the *Chief Joseph Herald* (March 12, 1958), p. 4. Rhinehart's letter, dated September 12, 1876, recounted what he had heard of this council at the forks. "You will see the force of their argument," he wrote, referring to the Indians. ". . . They were very indignant to say the least when they found that Findley and McNall were not to attend their Council, and that the whites still refused to give them up after so polite and urgent request."

telling him that Wells McNall was not in the cabin. The Indians made no hostile move, but continued to encircle the house. For a time nothing happened. Then some Indian women arrived. One of them was Wilhautyah's daughter. She went suddenly to the cabin door and opened it, but two of the white women inside hastily ejected her.

Early in the afternoon six more settlers rode up, and another heated discussion began outside the house. Joseph repeated his demands of the day before, and again the settlers refused to agree to them. Finally, the Indians prepared to leave, telling the whites that unless they gave up McNall and Findley and left the Wallowa by the following Sunday, the Indians would burn their houses and drive them out. Just before the Nez Perces departed, Wilhautyah's daughter went again to the cabin door and, pushing it open, asked to see the man who had killed her father. When Findley came to the door, she stared at him for a moment and then turned and walked away. Joseph then rode over and asked Findley to come with the Indians and let them try him. The settler had been visibly affected by the confrontation with Wilhautyah's daughter. He started to go with Joseph, but the other whites interceded quickly and would not let him leave.

The Indians at last rode away, reminding the settlers of their warning; and that night, under cover of darkness, the Wallowa Justice of the Peace, W. W. White, and a youth named Gerard Cochran were sent racing to the upper parts of the valley to warn the whites in that area to band together for safety. At the same time, Ephraim McNall was dispatched to Fort Walla Walla to summon military help. At the post, McNall was turned down. Lieutenant Albert G. Forse, in command at the fort, telegraphed Fort Vancouver for instructions. Either Forse, remembering previous false alarms, was not impressed by McNall's panicky state and communicated that judgment to Portland, or Howard's headquarters itself decided against the dispatch of troops. McNall was told that Joseph was a peaceable man and would not harm the whites, and that no soldiers could be sent. Failing to move the federal officers, McNall headed frantically for the Grande Ronde, stopping wherever he knew people to ask them to round up volunteers and hurry to the Wallowa. By Wednesday, September 6, groups of armed men were on their way from several communities. When news of what McNall had done reached Fort Walla Walla, Forse changed his mind. Thinking that he had better go to the Wallowa now, if only to protect the Indians, he notified Fort Vancouver of the new situation, and set off with a troop of forty-eight cavalrymen.

In the valley, meanwhile, Joseph had moved his people to a camp at the foot of Wallowa Lake near the present town of Joseph. Units of Grande Ronde volunteers had been arriving at Ephraim McNall's, and on the afternoon of Saturday, September 9, some forty of the Wallowa settlers and

Grande Ronde reinforcements organized themselves into a militia unit and elected William Boothe captain and Henry Rhinehart sergeant. Then they sent Rhinehart and thirteen men to the upper valley to help the settlers there. In that region, tension was coming to a head. A couple of days previously, Joseph had heard of a threat made against him by one of the two messengers dispatched from Ephraim McNall's to warn the upper valley settlers. The pair had run into a Umatilla Indian, and when the Indian had told them that Joseph was angry, Gerard Cochran, known apparently as a young braggart, had boasted that if Joseph did not behave himself, he would bring men over from the Grande Ronde and kill all the Indians. Furthermore, he had said that he personally would kill Joseph, scalp him, and wear his scalp on his bridle. The Umatilla had taken Cochran's words seriously and had got a report of the conversation to Joseph, who had learned soon afterward of the arrival of the Grande Ronde volunteers at McNall's. To the Indian, Cochran's threat did not seem idle.

In the evening of the same day that Rhinehart and his volunteers started up the valley, Joseph and a large part of his band, with all the young warriors again stripped and painted for war, surrounded the home of Reese Wright at Alder in the upper valley, near the present town of Enterprise. A number of the settlers in the region had gathered there for safety, and Gerard Cochran and the Justice of the Peace, W. W. White, were with them. The Indians were accompanied by two white men, James Davis, the interpreter, and Thomas H. Veasey, who lived at Alder and was known as a friend of Joseph's people. At the Indians' approach the Justice of the Peace went under a bed in Wright's cabin, and Cochran hid in a log barn. The other settlers were frightened at first, but when they heard what Cochran had said that he would do to Joseph and realized the cause of the chief's anger, they hauled Cochran and White from their hiding places and promised the Indians to get the two men out of the valley. Joseph seemed satisfied, but he reminded them of the next day's deadline for all the settlers, and told them that everyone must leave. He asked where the men from the Grande Ronde were, and one of the settlers said later that he heard the chief state that if the Grande Ronders wanted to fight, he would meet them halfway the next day.[37]

37. The Cochran story, recounted in considerably fuller detail from the reminiscences of participants in the affair, can be found in J. H. Horner's notes in the County Clerk's Office, Enterprise, Oregon. It is not certain, however, whether the Indians who visited the Wright cabin were led by Joseph or Ollokot. Since a large number of the band, including women, were present, and since one of the sources for the story was Veasey, who knew the difference between Joseph and Ollokot, I am inclined to believe that Joseph was there. However, many of the settlers often called both of the brothers Joseph, and the Indians themselves say that Ollokot led the group. McWhorter, *Hear Me*, p. 618, also throws doubt on whether Joseph actually said that he would be willing to fight the Grande Ronders. Although I have noted the

The Indians soon left, and Wright and the other settlers lost no time in piling into wagons and starting for the lower valley. On the way, they were met by Rhinehart and his men, who escorted them back to the ranch of the Tulley brothers, where many of the settlers of the lower and middle parts of the Wallowa had agreed to concentrate. Forse and his cavalrymen had already arrived there, after their hurried ride from Fort Walla Walla, and at 8:45 the next morning, Sunday, the lieutenant moved his troops, accompanied by most of Boothe's militia company, up the valley to Veasey's home at Alder. The interpreter, Davis, was staying with Veasey, and Forse enlisted them both to guide him to Joseph's camp, about seven miles away.

Forse left the troops and volunteers at Veasey's and traveled alone with the two men to the foot of the lake, where they came on Joseph and members of his band "mounted and posted" on a bluff. It took some time to arrange an interview, but Forse and the chief finally met on top of the hill. Joseph told the lieutenant that the cause of the trouble was the murder of Wilhautyah, but said that he would be satisfied if a white man's court gave Findley and McNall a fair trial. Forse asked him why he had made threats at Reese Wright's cabin, and Joseph replied that it was because the whites had boasted that they intended to kill and scalp him and his people. When the officer asked him why he did not go on the Lapwai reservation, Joseph informed him that "in the interview with Major Wood at Lapwai in July the subject was mentioned and that it had been referred to Washington, and that a commission of five men were to come from there and decide the matter." Realizing that he "might be interfering in some agreement between Joseph and the Government," Forse said, "I let the subject drop."

At the same time, the lieutenant told the chief that he should keep his horses and Indians up near the lake and away from the settlers, and designated Hurricane Creek as a line beyond which the Indians should not go except to travel to the Grande Ronde for supplies, and then only "two bucks" should go at a time. To all of this, Forse said, Joseph acceded, "and to show his good faith he would throw away the bullets they had put in their guns for the purpose of killing the Whites, who had come to kill him. He did this by forming his Indians in single rank, and discharging their pieces." [38]

---

remark, as reported in a letter from Lieutenant Albert G. Forse to the Assistant Adjutant General, Department of the Columbia, Portland, Oregon, from "Upper Wallowa Valley," September 11, 1876 (copy in J. H. Horner's notes), I, too, question whether any white man present, save the interpreter, James Davis, who was with the Indians, could have understood Joseph well enough to have reported accurately what he said.

38. Forse's letter to the Assistant Adjutant General, September 11, 1876, in Horner's notes. Also, narrative of E. S. McComas, editor of the *Mountain Sentinel*, in *History*

When the meeting ended, Forse, Veasey, and Davis returned to the troops and volunteers. The cavalrymen established a camp in the valley, and on Forse's assurance that his men could keep the peace, the militia unit disbanded and the settlers started back to their homes. On the day after his meeting with Joseph, Forse sent word to Wells McNall and Findley, advising them to go to Union and give themselves up. He had promised Joseph that he would ask them to do so, he said, and the security of all the whites in the valley depended on their compliance. The two men acquiesced and on September 14 appeared before Judge Brainard in Union. Findley was charged with manslaughter and released in $250 bail. No charge was filed against McNall, who was held to have been defending himself against the Indian. On the same day, Forse had another meeting with Joseph in the Wallowa, informing him that the two settlers had given themselves up to a court, according to his promise, and urging the chief to send the two Indian witnesses of the killing to Union to present their version of what had happened. Joseph was afraid that the whites would harm the Indians, but he agreed finally when Forse offered to place them in the care of one of his noncommissioned officers. The next day the two Indians left for the Grande Ronde with a corporal named Funk.

Nothing came of the hearing. For some reason the Indians did not testify, and Judge Brainard freed Findley, ruling that he had acted in self-defense.[39] The verdict disturbed Findley, who knew that the Indians would not be satisfied. At his own request he was heard in October by a grand jury at Union, but was again exonerated. By the end of October he was back with his family in the Wallowa, and the case was ended.

------

of Union and Wallowa Counties of Oregon, pp. 157–59. Again, it may have been Ollokot, rather than Joseph, with whom Forse met at the lake. McWhorter, *Hear Me*, p. 618, quotes the version of an Indian informant who definitely says that Forse met Ollokot there, and not Joseph. This version also differs greatly from that of Forse concerning what was said at the meeting, although both accounts agree that the Indians were afraid that the whites planned to attack them, and had assumed a posture of defense rather than offense. Once again, however, it must be remembered that both Davis and Veasey, who were there, knew Ollokot from Joseph and were favorable to the Indians' side. The reminiscences in Horner's notes have Veasey in particular fairly well substantiating Forse's account of what happened.

39. The annual report of the Commissioner of Indian Affairs (1876), p. 45, quotes Monteith: "The Indian witnesses refuse to appear in court against the murderer." Monteith's letter is dated August 31, 1876, which, strangely, was prior to the September excitement in the Valley and to Forse's successful plea to Findley and McNall to surrender themselves. But Findley (*Chief Joseph Herald*, February 27, 1958, p. 4) also says that the Indians refused to testify against Findley, intimating that the Nez Perces held McNall, rather than himself, guilty and, unable to secure justice against McNall, did not want to punish Findley.

Peace, meanwhile, had settled over the valley. A new company of troops under Captain Stephen Whipple entered the Wallowa to relieve Forse and his men for the winter. Whipple established a camp on Bear Creek, near the present town of Wallowa, and soon afterward had a meeting with Joseph. At its conclusion the officer told the settlers that Joseph had stated that he would never spill any white man's blood in the valley. Although the Indians still claimed the Wallowa and Forse had had no legal right to pen them in any special part of it, Joseph looked forward hopefully to a final decision by Howard's five-man commission from Washington that would restore the valley to his band. Meanwhile, he would be patient and keep his horses and people obediently on their side of the Hurricane Creek line. The chief's statesmanlike restraint under the provocations of the settlers once again impressed Whipple. He had more respect for Joseph than he had ever had, he told the whites in the valley, and he added that the Indian was a very pleasant and reasonable man, but firm.

Those qualities of Joseph, acknowledged even by many of the settlers, were on the eve of their greatest testing. During the month of September, General Howard had gone to Washington, the object of his visit, according to a dispatch in the LaGrande *Mountain Sentinel* of September 30, "being the adjustment of the troubles between Whites and Indians in Wallowa Valley." Using the recent crisis in the Wallowa as leverage, Howard pressed, through the War and Interior Departments, for his five-member commission. On October 3, 1876, Secretary of Interior Zachary Chandler acceded, naming three easterners, David H. Jerome of Michigan, A. C. Barstow of Rhode Island, and William Stickney of Washington, D.C., as well as Howard and his assistant adjutant general, Major Wood, as members of the board. The three easterners knew nothing about the Wallowa Valley or the Nez Perces. According to a contemporary observer, who met them after they reached Idaho, they had "not a speck of Indian sense, experience, or knowledge." [40] It made no difference. Jerome was titular chairman of the group, but Howard was to give it its purpose and direction. And he and Wood both knew what they wanted. Innocent and unknowing, trusting in the commission and in Wood's plea to put faith in the justice he would receive from the board, Joseph was about to learn that in the United States there was nothing sacred about a man's home if the man was an Indian. The commission proceeded to the Northwest under orders—in line with Howard's recommendation—to meet with the nontreaty Indians "with a view to secure their permanent settlement on the reservation . . ."

40. Mrs. John B. Monteith, Lewiston *Morning Tribune*, Lewiston, Idaho, January 22, 1933.

12

"The Earth Is My Mother"

On the plains of Montana, Custer had been defeated in June, and in the fall chagrined troops were floundering in pursuit of the Dakota leaders, Crazy Horse and Sitting Bull. Sensitive to the political embarrassment that hostile Indians had caused the Administration, the members of the commission to the Nez Perces traveled by way of Chicago, San Francisco, and Portland, and arrived at Lapwai on the night of November 7, 1876. Monteith had carried out orders to "lose no time in sending for the non-treaty Nez Perce Indians, and especially for Joseph and his band, to be there at that time."[1] Not a single nontreaty band had appeared, however, although Joseph and his people were known to be on their way.

While the commissioners waited, they listened to complaints of the treaty Nez Perces, examined the reservation area around Lapwai, and discussed the background of the Wallowa problem with Monteith. Either at that time or during the ensuing council the agent appears to have given the commission a full and startling briefing on the role the Dreamer faith seemed to be playing in the difficulties he was having with the nontreaty bands. Howard would have been able to add to whatever Monteith told the commissioners. The General had heard much about the Dreamers from Major N. A. Cornoyer, the agent on the Umatilla reservation, and from the Reverend James H. Wilbur of the Yakima reserve. Like Monteith, they had been having troubles with Indians who would not come to—or stay on—their reservations, and they were even more outspoken than Monteith in blaming their problems on the influence of Dreamer "magicians," who, under the hunchbacked

1. Annual Report, Department of Interior (1877), p. 607 (Report of the Commission to the Nez Perce Indians).

Smohalla, the Indian they regarded as the chief of all the demons in the region, appeared to them to be uniting Indians of many different tribes in a religious movement dedicated to the extermination of the whites.

Cornoyer had already poured out his problems to Howard concerning what he called "renegades," including Chief Homli, the leader of a remnant band of Wallawallas that would not stay on the Umatilla reservation; and Wilbur, a Methodist minister who insisted that all Indians on the Yakima reservation become Methodists, had blamed Smohalla and his heathenish teachings for every example of Indian defiance—including Joseph's stubbornness in not going onto the Nez Perce reservation. Wilbur, tyrannical in his efforts to stamp out native religious beliefs, had maintained that Joseph was part of an intertribal conspiracy directed by the Dreamer shamans, and that the government had a responsibility to suppress Dreamer influences and put Joseph's people on the Idaho reservation, by force if necessary, where Monteith could Christianize them.

None of the agents knew what they were talking about. In their attempts to convert Indians, all had met resistance from Indians who agreed, partly at least, with Smohalla's teachings. But the Indians were not acting in concert, and the spiritual ideas of some of the bands, including those of Joseph's Nez Perces, derived from their own ancestral beliefs, and differed sharply from Smohalla's preachings on major points—notably on the promise of the resurrection of dead Indians. Smohalla had no control, direct or indirect, over Joseph. Yet at Lapwai the information that stemmed from the three reservation agents caused all the commissioners except Wood to believe that Joseph was a pernicious disciple of a native cult that was threatening the peace and security of the Northwest. "He [Joseph] and his band," they reported to Washington, "have fallen under the influence of the 'dreamers' (Smohollah,) a modern spiritualistic mysticism, known of late among the Indians of this region, and represented in his band by his 'medicine-man' or magician, who is understood to have great power over him and the whole band." Smohalla, they underscored darkly, was a "new-fangled religious delusion . . . a kind of wizard." [2]

On November 11 the commissioners heard that Joseph and his band were seven or eight miles away, and Monteith, accompanied by Jerome and James Reuben, an English-speaking treaty Nez Perce who had been enlisted to serve as interpreter during the council, went out to hurry the Wallowa Indians along. James Reuben was the son of old Reuben, who had operated a ferry and grown wealthy during the gold rush, and of Joseph's sister, Elawinonmi, who lived on the Idaho reservation with the Reuben family. Translating for

2. Ibid., p. 609. Quotations from the council report that follow in my text are taken from this same source.

Jerome, young Reuben asked Joseph why he moved so slowly. "My business, even now, does not demand haste," Joseph replied. It did not sit well with Jerome, who had made a long trip to get there and was already eyeing the Oregon Indian as a second Sitting Bull.

Two days later Joseph reached Lapwai, arriving with Ollokot and the band's shamans at the head of a mounted column of Indians, who wheeled up almost with military precision. The council began at once in the mission church on the agency grounds. Joseph and his people, some sixty men, including a few members of other nontreaty bands who had come with him, took seats in the left aisle; the center and right were crowded with treaty Nez Perces from the reservation. Joseph was self-confident, certain that he had no reason to fear or look with distrust upon the row of white commissioners facing him. He respected Howard and Wood. The other men, also, were not like the Wallowa settlers or Grande Ronde officials. They had no personal interest in the valley but came direct from the President in Washington. They would listen with open hearts, he was sure, and would decide fairly.

Within the first few moments he realized differently. In their opening speeches the commissioners asked him to give up the Wallowa, citing a number of specious reasons for doing so: the Nez Perces had sold the area to the United States government in 1863; it now belonged to the State of Oregon, which would not cede it back to the federal government for a reservation; the President could not protect the Indians in their quarrels with the settlers; it was too cold an area for the Indians; a part of the valley had already been opened for settlement, and even if the present white men left, others would come. Despite all, however, the commissioners added that the government would "in a spirit of generosity . . . treat for an adjustment of present difficulties."

Joseph and his people must have been stunned. There were ready answers for each of the commissioners' arguments: the 1863 "sale" was open to question; if that were so, the government had had no right to give the area to Oregon, and the state had no legal basis for its claim; if the land were returned to Joseph, the area could be divided sensibly between Indians and whites, or the latter could be evacuated after being paid for their improvements; if the Wallowa was too cold for the Indians—a ridiculous argument to people who had inhabited it for generations—what made it warm enough for the settlers? To any white man with integrity, the hypocrisy of the commissioners would have been embarrassing. But Joseph rose with dignity and spoke of a fundamental matter the commissioners had overlooked: a man's unwillingness to be driven from his home.

". . . the Creative Power, when he made the earth, made no marks, no lines of division or separation on it," the commission's report quoted him as saying. "The earth was his mother. He was made of the earth and grew up on its bosom. The earth, as his mother and nurse, was sacred to his affections, too sacred to be valued by or sold for silver and gold. He could not consent to sever his affections from the land that bore him. He asked nothing of the President. He was able to take care of himself."

The commissioners could not help being moved by Joseph. "The serious feeling and manner in which he uttered these sentiments was impressive," they reported, noting that he was "usually calm and sedate, when animated marked and magnetic." But his eloquence, at the same time, nettled them, and they began to resent their inability to dominate him. The President, they told him, "was not disposed to deprive him of any just right or govern him by his individual will, but merely subject him to the same just and equal laws by which he himself [the President] as well as all his people were ruled." Such a statement was foolish too: Indians on reservations were wards, not citizens, of the nation and were subject to the orders of agents, who rarely accorded them any of the rights enjoyed by white Americans, including the freedoms of religion and movement. Joseph was aware of this; the oppression of the treaty Nez Perces was a daily reminder to the Wallowa band of what happened to Indians when they accepted a reservation status. But when he replied again that he would not risk such a fate for his own people by accepting a reservation, he gave Howard a legalism on which to claim a righteousness for his policy of force.

"Indian Joseph and his malcontents denied the jurisdiction of the United States over them," he wrote. "They were offered everything they wanted, if they would simply submit to the authority and government of the United States agents." [3]

Joseph's appeal, that his people wished to continue in the Wallowa as free people, without molestation, could not be accepted. Council sessions continued during the next two days, and the commissioners became increasingly frustrated. At one time they thought they had weakened the resistance of both Joseph and Ollokot, but they were wrong. Joseph later said that his reasoning about his right to the Wallowa should have been clear to the commissioners, and he illustrated it by showing what he had tried to convey to them.

"Suppose a white man should come to me and say, 'Joseph, I like your horses, and I want to buy them,'" he said. "I say to him, 'No, my horses suit me, I will not sell them.' Then he goes to my neighbor, and says to him: 'Joseph has some good horses. I want to buy them, but he refuses to sell.' My neighbor answers, 'Pay me the money, and I will sell you Joseph's horses.' The white man returns to me and says, 'Joseph, I have bought your horses,

3. Howard, *Nez Perce Joseph*, p. 30.

and you must let me have them.' If we sold our lands to the Government, this is the way they were bought." [4]

His argument was irrelevant to the commissioners. Howard had proposed that the government pay Joseph to move, but Joseph was not going to move. The flaw in Howard's policy was now revealed. Further talk only convinced the commissioners that they could get nowhere with this stubborn Indian, and they lost patience with him. "What shall we say to the President when we get back?" Jerome asked him. "All I have to say is that I love my country," Joseph replied. "Suppose several thousand men should come from Oregon with arms, what would you do?" Howard said. "We will not sell the land. We will not give up the land. We love the land: it is our home," Joseph repeated. "We came all the way out here from the East to ask you, by the Great Father's orders, if you would go on the reservation at Lapwai," Jerome concluded bitterly. ". . . That is our final statement . . . If you come to a better point of view notify the agent at Lapwai."

The council ended, and Joseph and his band left Lapwai for the Wallowa. The chief had given no ground; the commissioners had made no decision and issued no orders; the situation, Joseph thought, was no worse than it had been. At least, the band still had its freedom in Wallowa.

But the commissioners were not finished with their work at Lapwai. Joseph, it had been proved to their satisfaction, was under the influence of the Dreamers. They had seen him talk to his older shamans, "sorcerers," who obviously guided him according to the plans of Smohalla. While the Wallowa Indians made their way home, the commissioners wrote their report for Washington, holding that Joseph and his band were under the spell of Dreamer "fanaticism" and summarizing the following recommendations for the Department of Interior:

(1) Dreamer teachers should be confined to their own agencies and suppressed, or exiled to the Indian Territory in present-day Oklahoma.

(2) The military should occupy the Wallowa Valley at once, while the agent continued his efforts to settle Joseph's band in severalty on lands still vacant on the Idaho reservation. (Although few allotments had yet been surveyed on the reservation, even though the treaty of 1863 had called for that to be done, the commission, in effect, was urging that Joseph's approximately sixty males trade the Wallowa for some sixty plots of twenty acres each.)

(3) Unless they moved "within a reasonable time," Joseph's people "should then be placed by force upon the Nez Perce reservation."

(4) If the Wallowa Indians "overrun land belonging to the whites and commit depredations upon their property, disturb the peace by threats or otherwise, or commit any other overt act of hostility," force should be used

4. "Chief Joseph's Own Story," p. 16.

to bring them into subjection and place them on the Nez Perce reservation.

(5) The same provisions should apply to all other nontreaty bands of the general region, including Nez Perces, Palouses, Yakimas, and Umatillas.

Monteith, it was urged, should be fully instructed to carry out these recommendations and to rely at all times on the department commander (General Howard).

Four of the commissioners signed this report and sent it to Washington. Although Howard's hand was clearly discernible in it, his subordinate, Major Wood, did not fully subscribe to its harsh intolerance and filed his own minority report. It recommended that, although Joseph's people would ultimately have to be removed from the Wallowa, force should not be used to put them on the reservation until the Indians committed an overt act of hostility.

Before leaving Lapwai, the commissioners also took official note of the government's continued failure to live up to its obligations to the treaty Nez Perces, an embarrassment which they thought ought to be rectified, especially in view of their recommendations concerning Joseph's band. Four white men, for instance, were occupying large tracts of reservation land in violation of the treaty of 1863; measurements had not yet been taken for Indian farms as provided for by the same treaty; and, wonder of wonders, the Nez Perces who had helped the Oregon volunteers during the Indian war of 1856 had not yet been paid for their services or for their horses.

Monteith was pleased with the commission's recommendations. If approved, they would give him authority, backed by military power, to enforce Joseph's removal to the reservation. Once he had the Indians there, he could control the Dreamers, smash the influence of the "heathen" element, and make faster progress in turning the entire tribe into settled, Christianized farmers.

Unaware of the commission's action, Joseph, meanwhile, took his people into the Imnaha canyon for the winter. Despite the presence in the valley of Captain Whipple and his troops, conditions remained uncertain, and only fifteen new settlers moved in, while a number of oldtimers closed up their homes and went to live temporarily with relatives and friends in the Grande Ronde.

On January 6, 1877, Commissioner of Indian Affairs J. Q. Smith sent Monteith word that the recommendations of the commission had been approved, and were to be carried out. The agent was directed to send reservation Nez Perces to Joseph's people to urge them to come in "at once and in a peaceable manner," giving them "a reasonable time to consider and determine this question." Monteith was also to request the military occupation of the Wallowa Valley "in the interests of peace," and to ask General Howard for any aid he needed. The Interior Department, Commissioner Smith informed the agent, was simultaneously notifying the War Department of its decision, but he warned Monteith that "should violent measures become necessary . . . report thereof must be submitted to this office for the consideration of the Department when more definite understanding will be issued."[5]

Monteith moved quickly. His idea of "a reasonable time" was April 1, and he sent four treaty Nez Perces, Joseph's brother-in-law and nephew, old Reuben and James Reuben, his father-in-law, Whisk-tasket, and old Captain John, the reliable pro-white of the wars of the 1850s, to warn Joseph to come onto the reservation by that date. The four treaty Indians found Joseph's camp in the canyon and startled the chief with the agent's demand. They tried to persuade him that he would find a better life on the reservation and that his people would suffer great harm if they remained in the Wallowa, but Joseph was deaf to their pleas. "I have been talking to the whites many years about the land in question, and it is strange they cannot understand me," he said. "The country they claim belonged to my father, and when he died it was given to me and my people, and I will not leave it until I am compelled to."

The treaty Indians returned to Lapwai with Joseph's reply. In the meantime Monteith had written to Washington, notifying the Commissioner of Indian Affairs of his April 1 deadline to Joseph and recommending "that the officer in command of the troops who are to occupy Wallowa Valley, in the interest of peace, be instructed to call on Joseph and inform him that unless he goes on the Nez Perce reserve on or before April 1, 1877, he will be forced to do so by the soldiers, and also inform him that he must remain on the reserve, not leaving it without a pass from the agent at Lapwai. This would have a tendency to hurry him up and show him that the department is in earnest. If he is allowed to have his own way this time, it will only make him more stubborn in the future." Now, with Joseph's answer to the four treaty Indians, Monteith wrote a postcript, telling the officials in Washington that "I think, from Joseph's actions, he will not come on the reserve until compelled to. He has said so much to the Indians who have moved on the reserve, calling them cowards, etc., that he would be lowering himself in his own estimation, as well as in that of his immediate followers, did he not make some show of resistance. By making such resistance, he could say to the other Indians, 'I was overpowered, and did not come of my own choice,' in case he is forced on the reserve."[6]

Gone now were all thoughts that Joseph had any rights, that the government ought to purchase his claim, or even that, once on a reservation, an In-

5. Text in J. H. Horner's notes, County Court House, Enterprise, Oregon.
6. Report of the Secretary of War (1877), *1*, 115–16.

dian could enjoy "the same just and equal laws" as the whites. Joseph's adamancy had dispelled the shams of peaceful negotiations; there was nothing left to Monteith and Howard but the use of force, based on the false fear that Joseph was committed to armed resistance.

Still the War Department in Washington was hesitant. A government order to bring the Sioux onto reservations by force had started the plains war of 1876 that had resulted in Crook's rugged battle at the Rosebud and Custer's defeat at the Little Bighorn, and the military wanted no more public criticism of cruel and impulsive action against Indians, or of bungled operations undertaken on the recommendation of a civilian Indian Bureau whose agents were often incompetent and untrustworthy. On January 13, 1877, the War Department, obliging the Interior Department directed Howard to occupy the Wallowa Valley, but the Secretary of War cautiously reminded Interior Department officials that the role of "the military authorities was merely protecting and aiding them in the execution of their instructions."[7] A short time later General Irwin McDowell, commander of the Division of the Pacific at San Francisco, also warned Howard: "As this question of the removal of Joseph's band is a very delicate and important one, the division commander directs it to be done under your personal direction if practicable . . . It is, therefore, of paramount importance that none of the responsibility of any step which may lead to hostilities shall be initiated by the military authorities."[8]

The advice that the Army meant to proceed with caution slowed Howard. But when, in response to his orders, he sent directions to Fort Walla Walla for the continued stationing of troops in the Wallowa, the Walla Walla newspapers and others in the area learned of his dispatch and printed stories of a war about to be launched against the Indians. The resulting uproar alarmed the General, and he had Major Wood wire Fort Walla Walla from Fort Vancouver on March 1: "Please correct impression in Walla Walla newspapers that campaign against Joseph has been ordered. Indians so informed may begin to strike against scattered families. Troops go as they have gone before."[9] Howard also knew nothing yet of Monteith's April 1 deadline, and when the agent questioned him impatiently about his plans to force Joseph out of the Wallowa, the General answered him meticulously on March 12, saying, "I do not understand how we can take the offensive at all until further instructions from Washington," and adding that he was glad the agent had not set any final date for Joseph and his band to be on the reservation.[10]

7. Beal, *I Will Fight No More Forever*, p. 306 n.
8. Report of the Secretary of War (1877), *1*, 587.
9. Fee, *Chief Joseph*, p. 96.
10. Report of the Secretary of War (1877), *1*, 587.

Nevertheless, both men were already adjusted to the prospect that they would have to use force against the Wallowa Indians. The agent had given Joseph his ultimatum, explaining to Washington that April 1 was as good a date as any, since the Indians "can come one time just as well as another, having nothing to hinder them in moving"—a glib statement that overlooked the problems the Indians would have in trying to move their families and live-stock across the Snake and Salmon rivers during the torrential spring run-offs. And on March 13, when General McDowell wired Howard, "Are you expecting hostilities at Wallowa?" Howard replied, "Hostilities threatened; believe measures taken will prevent . . ." [11] The following day he took action to set the "measures" in motion, ordering two companies of the First Cavalry at Fort Walla Walla, with two Gatling guns, ammunition, and a thirty-day supply of rations, to prepare to occupy a strategic position at the juncture of the Wallowa and Grande Ronde rivers, ready to hit Joseph at the first sign of hostility.

It was Howard, not Joseph, who was threatening conflict. The four treaty Nez Perces whom Monteith had sent to Joseph had greatly alarmed the people of the Wallowa band. Surely, Joseph told them, the interpreting of his words at the November council had not been true; the commissioners could not have understood him correctly. On March 17 he sent Ollokot to see Monteith at Lapwai. The Wallowa Indians, Ollokot assured the agent, did not want to fight; there had been a misunderstanding at the Lapwai meeting. "I have eyes and a heart, and can see and understand for myself that if we fight we would have to leave all and go into the mountains. I love my wife and children and could not leave them," the tall, young warrior asserted. He urged the agent to arrange another council for the Indians with General Howard at Lapwai.[12]

At the same time, Joseph asked his friend, Young Chief, the Cayuse, to make a similar request in his behalf to Major Cornoyer, the agent on the Umatilla reservation. In March, Cornoyer met Howard at Walla Walla and told him of the Nez Perce's distress, adding that the Cayuse headman had told him that Joseph wished to come to the agency for a talk. Howard encouraged him to see Joseph, and later that month, when Cornoyer was in Portland and again saw Howard, he told the General that he was to see Joseph as soon as he got back to the reservation. Howard was interested to know Joseph's thinking, and he directed his aide-de-camp, Lieutenant William H. Boyle, to go to the meeting and report back to him.

The interview at the Umatilla agency occurred on April 1, Monteith's original deadline, which had now proved to have no meaning. Instead of Joseph, Ollokot arrived, accompanied by a few other members of the band, in-

11. Fee, *Chief Joseph*, p. 97.
12. Monteith to Commissioner J. Q. Smith, March 19, 1877.

cluding an elderly shaman. Nothing of significance resulted. Cornoyer and another white man who was present both said later that Ollokot had come with the impression that Howard would let the Wallowa Nez Perces settle on the Umatilla reservation, where the Dreamers and non-Christian Indians, many of them related to Joseph's people, were more numerous than at Lapwai. Ollokot was in a friendly, pleasant mood, but Boyle, according to Cornoyer, snapped at him sternly, setting him right by telling him that Howard wanted him to prepare to move onto the Nez Perce reservation, and Ollokot became angry and termed Boyle and Howard liars.[13] Whatever actually took place, the lieutenant went to Fort Walla Walla and telegraphed Howard that Joseph understood—perhaps from Ollokot's meeting with Monteith on March 17 at Lapwai—that he could have another council with the General, and that the Indian leader would be at Walla Walla with his people on April 20.[14]

Howard agreed to the meeting, and on April 16 left Portland for Walla Walla. At Wallula he made appointments to see the troublesome Smohalla and Homli at later dates, when he would try to talk them into going onto reservations and prevent them from "joining the non-treaty Nez Perces of Joseph." Then he went up the Walla Walla Valley, past the site of Whitman's old mission at Waiilatpu, to the place of council at the fort. Again Ollokot showed up, explaining that his brother, Joseph, was ill and could not appear, and again the interview was inconclusive. The General made it clear to Ollokot and the other Indians, however, that the government had indeed decided that the Wallowa Nez Perces would have to go on a reservation, and that there was nothing he could do about it—although the agent, as a concession, would be willing to give passes to obedient Indians to visit the Imnaha Valley part of each year to fish and hunt. Ollokot must have felt the net closing around his people, and for a while he and the Indians with him thrashed desperately, trying to make counter proposals which they hoped Howard

13. See the account of Captain W. C. Painter in McWhorter, *Hear Me*, pp. 152–55. Painter, sympathetic to the Joseph band, claimed he was at the meeting and that Ollokot started out willing to move on the Umatilla reservation, but ended by accusing Howard of talking with a forked tongue. Where Ollokot would have got the idea that the Nez Perces could move on the Umatilla reserve is not known; Howard and the other commissioners at Lapwai in November 1876 had even recommended abandoning that reservation, moving the Indians on it to the Lapwai reserve, and opening the Umatilla lands to white settlers.

14. Howard, *Nez Perce Joseph*, p. 37. In a report filed to the War Department Howard stated it somewhat differently, asserting that Boyle had wired him that Ollokot wished to see him, and desired him to appoint the time and place. Howard had misunderstood the wire, he said, and had thought Boyle had meant Joseph, rather than Ollokot (Report of the Secretary of War 1877, *1, 590*).

would accept. The Nez Perces "seemed at first to wish to join the Umatillas," the General said, "then it appears there was a project (probably originating with white men) to combine the reservation Indians of Umatilla with the non-treaty Nez Perces, and ask for them thus joined the Wallowa and Imnaha country giving up the Umatilla reserve." Howard guessed that settlers who wanted the rich Umatilla country were behind that proposal, and he turned it down. "I replied that the instructions are definite," he reported, "that I should send troops very soon to occupy the Wallowa, and proceed to Lapwai as soon as possible in execution of my instructions." [15]

Ollokot, who "manifested a good disposition," still sparred politely but anxiously, and at length asked if the Wallowa Indians and all the nontreaty Nez Perce bands could meet Howard once more when he was at Lapwai. The suggestion sat well with the General, who felt that Monteith should now "take the initiative in dealing with the Nez Perces" and use the proposed meeting to work out with the Indians the details of their entrance onto the reservation and the finding of places for them to establish new homes. The conference at Lapwai was agreed upon for twelve days later, and the council at the fort ended. "Really matters did not look much like war . . ." Howard wrote.[16]

Ollokot and his people returned to the Wallowa and told Joseph that Howard was of the same mind as Monteith, and that the General meant business. There was a discussion between the brothers over what to do. The two men were close to each other, and Joseph regarded Ollokot as his most trusted confidant and counselor. Ollokot, moreover, was the leader of the warriors; when he agreed to a decision with Joseph, he helped to see that the more headstrong younger men accepted it. According to an Indian named Yellow Wolf, who was Joseph's nephew, Ollokot could hold out little hope for

15. Ibid., p. 590. The meeting at Fort Walla Walla was also attended by Young Chief, the Cayuse, who was apparently the one who made the proposal that the Indians of the Umatilla reservation move into the Wallowa with Joseph's people (Howard, *Nez Perce Joseph*, p. 43). Also present at this council were Cornoyer and his agency interpreter, John McBean, the husband of Timothy's daughter, Jane, and the former post interpreter at Fort Walla Walla.

16. Howard, *Nez Perce Joseph*, p. 43. The Nez Perce version of this meeting, as related by Duncan McDonald in 1878, differs in a few particulars from Howard's account. In the discussion between Howard and Ollokot, according to the Indian telling, the Nez Perce leader pretty well held his own against the General, and said at the end of the meeting: "This is where we were born and raised. It is our native country. It is impossible for us to leave. We have never sold our country. Here we have all we possess, and here we wish to remain." To that Howard replied that he wanted to have all the Indians at Lapwai in ten days for a big talk. Thus the Lapwai council, in this account, resulted from Howard's demand rather than from Ollokot's request. *New Northwest*, Deer Lodge, Montana, October 18, 1878.

changing Howard's mind at Lapwai. "Government wants all Indians put in one place," he told Joseph. "If you say, 'Yes,' I will bring in the stock and we will go there. If the white officers ask what you will do, you answer, 'Nothing to talk about. Ollokot has settled everything.' " [17] Joseph listened to him; but since the bands of White Bird, Looking Glass, and the other nontreaties would be at Lapwai, he decided that he would go anyway, and perhaps together all the chiefs could make Howard see that the government still did not understand the truth.

Meanwhile, the General and Agent Cornoyer went from Walla Walla to Wallula on the Columbia River, where they held a council with Smohalla and a large group of the prophet's followers, including the "renegade" Homli. Some of those weak and impoverished Indians asked about the Wallowa situation, but Howard warned them to move onto reservations as quickly as possible and not to get themselves involved in Joseph's problem, which he was about to settle with troops if necessary. Then the General went up the Snake River by boat to Lewiston, reaching that town, whose population since the heyday of the gold rush had shrunk to a few hundred people, on April 26. He held a conference with Monteith and Captain David Perry, commander of the post at Lapwai, making plans for the forthcoming council and the removal of the nontreaty bands to the reservation. The hour had struck, he told Monteith, "to concert measures of cooperation." The council would take place on May 3; on that day the agent should have his letter prepared requesting the assistance of the military commander of the district to enforce his orders to the bands.

Howard mde a brief trip back to Wallula to use the telegraph to Fort Vancouver, but by May 2 he had returned to Fort Lapwai, a few miles from Monteith's agency buildings. Troops, meanwhile, had been given their marching orders, and the day before, Captain Stephen Whipple, with two companies of cavalry, had left Fort Walla Walla for the juncture of the Wallowa and Grande Ronde rivers to establish a camp and prepare to strike wherever necessary. Monteith also had his letter ready for the General. Under date of May 3, 1877, it read: "I would respectfully request that you assist me in the removal of Joseph's and other roving bands of Nez Perce Indians to and locate them upon proper lands within the boundaries of the Nez Perce reservation by the use of such troops as you may deem necessary." Howard was satisfied. On the eve of the council with the nontreaties, all seemed in good order. "Positive *instructions* had come," he wrote, "and *obedience* was required." [18]

On the morning of May 3 Joseph and Ollokot, accompanied by their

17. McWhorter, *Yellow Wolf*, p. 37.
18. Report of Secretary of War (1877), *1*, 117. Howard, *Nez Perce Joseph*, p. 56.

friend, Young Chief of the Cayuses, and some fifty members of the Wallowa Nez Perce band, arrived at Lapwai. They approached the fort in a column, the men in the lead, the women and children behind them, all painted and dressed in their beaded and decorated Indian finery, and singing proudly. The bold show, a demonstration of the Indians' faith in themselves, must have stirred glowing memories among the crowds of treaty Nez Perces who gathered to watch them. Once, Nez Perces by the hundreds had appeared in the same self-confident manner at councils with white men. Now, the small Wallowa band of Chief Joseph was parading all that was left of the independence and self-respect of the nation. Their singing, "sad, like a wail, and yet defiant in its close," said Howard, moved some of the white women who had come to watch the council proceedings to ask in fear, "Do you think Joseph means to fight?" Howard thought not, noting that the Indians carried no arms save a few tomahawk pipes, probably relics of the days of the Hudson's Bay Company trade.[19]

The Indians circled the buildings of the post, and then Joseph, Ollokot, Young Chief, and the principal men of the Wallowa band, with dignified and serious features, joined Howard in a large hospital tent that had been prepared, with its flaps raised, to accommodate the council. Only a few members of the garrison were in evidence; most of the troops had been ordered to stand by in their barracks under arms. With Howard were his aides, Lieutenants Boyle and Wilkinson, Monteith, and the interpreters, James Reuben and Perrin Whitman, the latter the nephew of Marcus and the interpreter at the treaty of 1863. None of the other nontreaty bands had yet arrived. There were still snow and slippery trails in the mountains, and the Indians were coming in slowly. Joseph had no wish to let the council begin without them, for he would need their support. But suddenly the meeting was under way. Howard would rush it, band by band, and as soon as the Wallowa Indians were in the tent, he had the proceedings commence. While the treaty Nez Perces, most of them in white men's clothes, crowded around to watch, Father Cataldo from the nearby Catholic mission on the reservation gave a brief prayer in Nez Perce. At its close Joseph protested to Howard: "Another band of Indians, White Bird's from the Salmon country, are coming . . . They will be here tomorrow. You must not be in a hurry to go till all can get in to have a talk."

The General replied that there was no reason to wait. "Mr. Monteith's instructions and mine are directly to YOUR people," he said. ". . . We will not wait for White Bird; instructions to him are the same; he can take his turn." Two of the older Nez Perces rose and, giving voice to the gravity with which the Wallowa Indians regarded this climactic moment in their fortunes,

19. Howard, *Nez Perce Joseph*, p. 52.

cautioned Perrin Whitman. "On account of coming generations, the children and the children's children, of both whites and Indians, you must interpret correctly," one of them warned. The other also wished to be sure that this time the whites did not misunderstand the Nez Perces' minds. "We want to talk a long time, many days, about the earth, about our land," he said.[20]

Howard nodded and said he would listen with patience, "but you may as well know at the outset," he added, "that in any event the Indians must obey the orders of the government of the United States."

The Indians' features must have sharpened. The broad-shouldered and full-bearded officer, whom they called Atim Keunim (Cut Off Arm), looked friendly and kind, but no matter what the Nez Perces said, he was going to give them orders. They remained silent, and Monteith, tall and 35 years old, rose and read his instructions to them, then addressed them in a manner emboldened by the presence of the General. "I sent out Reuben and some others to your camp, and invited you to come in. Now you must come, and there is no getting out of it . . . General Howard will stay till matters are settled."

The Nez Perces were confused. Alone and anxious for the support of the other bands, they sparred for time. Ollokot, who had been half-reclining beside his brother, pushed himself to his feet and spoke quietly, but with emotion. "We have respect for the whites; but they treat me as a dog, and I sometimes think my friends are different from what I had supposed. There should be *one law* for all."

His hurt feelings ruffled Howard. "Agent Monteith and myself are under the same government," he replied. What it commands us to do, that we must do . . . If the Indians hesitate to come to the reservation, the government directs that soldiers be used to bring them hither." He could see that he was getting nowhere. The Nez Perces did not want to decide until the other bands arrived. When the older men persisted in arguing with him, he warned them to give good advice to their people and not to speak to him in an insult-

20. Despite the Indians' fears of furthur misinterpretation, it is certain that we do not know exactly what their spokesmen said at the council. The record is filled with discrepancies concerning even the language that Howard used. For instance, the Report of the Secretary of War (1877), *1*, 593, containing Howard's official version of what was said, quotes him as telling Joseph that he would not wait for the arrival of White Bird, as I have noted. Yet four years later, in his book *Nez Perce Joseph*, pp. 53–54, the General quoted himself as telling Joseph that he would wait for White Bird if Joseph desired it. The Indian versions of the council do not help much, for they are almost completely at variance with the facts as Howard reported them. In my account of the council proceedings, I have tried to draw judiciously from the two Howard sources—although I am sure that neither one of them conveys adequately the ideas and words of the Indians—and to note, in addition, the significant differences in the Nez Perces' versions of what occurred.

ing way, or he would arrest them and send them to the Indian Territory. Then, when they "took alarm, and changed their tone," he agreed to adjourn the council till the next day, content that he could cope with all the bands at once. So far, he had successfully handled "malignity and noisy opposition. Against these," he said, "fearless sternness always produced the most whole-some and immediate consequences." [21]

The next morning White Bird and many of his followers reached the fort. The old hunter and warrior, whose real name, Peopeo Kiskiok Hihih, actu-ally meant White Goose, was past seventy, yet he walked with an alert bear-ing that some whites termed stately. A shaman as well as the civil leader of nontreaty Nez Perces in a part of the Salmon River gold regions, he carried the symbol of the medicine man, the wing of an eagle, which he customarily held against his nose. Although he was distrustful of whites and faced them with a stern look, he was mild-mannered and quiet, and did not favor a war.

Other new arrivals included the powerful old man Toohoolhoolzote and members of his band, from the hills along the Snake south of the mouth of the Salmon River, and Looking Glass, from the Middle Fork of the Clear-water, who was accompanied by some of his nontreaty relatives from his fa-ther's village at Asotin on the west side of the Snake. Toohoolhoolzote—active, restless, and unafraid of any white man—came like a grizzly at bay, contemptuous of the Christian Nez Perces, resentful of a soldier who, he had heard, planned to tell him to go on a reservation, and ready to outargue any-one who attempted to deprive him of his freedom. An able Dreamer orator, with a deep, gutteral voice, he had been chosen, apparently, to be the principal spokesman for the nontreaty bands. Even Joseph, it seemed, had agreed to abide by whatever answers the older man gave to Howard.[22] Less rancorous than Toohoolhoolzote was Looking Glass, known to his own people as Allalimya Takanin, now about 45 years old and standing almost six feet tall. Proud, muscular, and opinionated, he was one of the tribe's most respected hunting and war leaders, and basked in the prestige he had won by his prowess in a battle against the Sioux on Pryor's Fork of the Yellowstone River in 1874. Nevertheless, he was a realist about the whites; he knew their num-bers and strength, and he, too, wanted no war with them.[23]

After a treaty Indian known as Alpowa Jim had opened the second session

21. The foregoing has been based primarily on Howard, *Nez Perce Joseph*, pp. 54–56.
22. See below, p. 675.
23. McDonald says that Looking Glass and his neighbor Red Owl (Koolkool Snehee) were "in the mountains hunting" during the time of the council, "and neither they nor their people had any intimation of what Howard proposed to do with them." Howard's many specific references to the presence of Looking Glass during and immediately after the conference, however, show that McDonald was in error.

with a prayer, Monteith read the newcomers his instructions from Washington. Joseph introduced White Bird to Howard and then announced that Toohoolhoolzote would speak for all of the nontreaty bands. Monteith had told the General about the fiery old man, calling him one of the most dangerous of the Dreamer teachers, and Howard watched him suspiciously. Toohoolhoolzote lived up to the agent's warning about him. He spoke with a "plentiful flourish of words and illustrations," the General said, "but with no attempt at conciliation even in manner." From Toohoolhoolzote's point of view there was nothing to conciliate; he was fighting for liberty, which Americans themselves had long accepted as having no alternative but death.

"I have heard about a bargain, a trade between some of these Indians and the white men concerning their land," the Indian said. "But I belong to the land out of which I came. The Earth is my mother."

"The Nez Perces did make such an agreement," replied Howard, "and as the commission from Washington explained last fall, the nontreaty Indians being in the minority in their opposition, were bound by that agreement, and must abide by it."

The old Indian grew "more surly," said Howard. "You have no right to compare us, grown men, to children," he complained. "Children do not think for themselves. Grown men do think for themselves. The government at Washington, cannot think for us." [24]

It was an echo of Spokan Garry's rebuke to I. I. Stevens at the Spokan

24. Howard, *Nez Perce Joseph*, p. 59. McDonald quotes Toohoolhoolzote as follows: "You are always talking about *Washington*. I would like to know who Washington is? Is he a Chief or a common man, or a house, or a place? Every time you have a council you speak of Washington. Leave Mr. Washington, that is if he is a man, alone. He has no sense. He does not know anything about our country. He never was here. And you are always talking about your soldiers. What do we care about your fighting qualities? You are chief, Howard, and I am elected by the Nez Perces to speak for them and do the best I can for my people. Let us settle the matter between you and me" (*New Northwest*, October 25, 1878). Toohoolhoolzote may not have used just those words, but it is probable that the quotation reflects what he said more accurately than does Howard's version. The old man, a mountaineer who had had little contact with the white men's civilization, was talking from the heart about things he knew; yet Howard treated him with contempt and hostility, and kept threatening him with the use of force. The whites lived in fear that the Indians were the aggressors and would rise up in violence, but it was precisely at this point that Howard best demonstrated that it was he who was threatening war and would precipitate violence. By the end of the council, every Indian present had the idea that Howard wanted to make war on them, and waited only for an excuse. They tried not to give him that excuse, but when it came, their knowledge that the General would now fight them and that they, at last, had no choice but to defend themselves against him made the war inevitable, as will be seen.

council in 1855. Howard's feeling of racial superiority was being unmasked. The nontreaty Indians recognized the General's discomfort and felt good that the truthful and fearless Tohoolhoolzote was speaking for them. As he went on, they nodded with "Ah's" of agreement, watched the white men for signs of weakness, and glanced at each other with satisfaction. Howard could see what was happening and became uneasy. In the background, pressed around the tent, the treaty Indians of Lapwai were growing alarmed; the old Dreamer agitator was stirring up the nontreaties, making them excited. The general was furious with Toohoolhoolzote, but it seemed too dangerous to begin suddenly to argue with him. "The Great Spirit Chief made the world as it is and as he wanted it, and he made a part of it for us to live upon. I do not see where you get authority to say that we shall not live where he placed us," the old man continued.

When Toohoolhoolzote's anger had finally died and he had finished talking, Joseph asked Howard for a postponement to another session, and the General was glad to comply, even proposing that since the following two days were a Saturday and Sunday, the next meeting should be held on Monday. From the manner of the Indians, he had decided privately, "it would be wise to have the troops that were already on the march in position."

The nontreaty leaders agreed to his suggestion, and the session ended.

That night Howard sent a rider to Fort Walla Walla with a message for Whipple's troops in the Wallowa to march to the mouth of the Grand Ronde River, where they would be closer to Lapwai; for a company of cavalry under Captain Joel G. Trimble to hurry from Walla Walla to Lewiston; and for another company to come from Fort Vancouver to Fort Walla Walla. Under Toohoolhoolzote's "saucy" provocations, the menace seemed to be rising, and it did not lessen during the week end. The nontreaties moved off to their camps, but the area around the post was filled with rumors and alarms. Treaty Indians, employed as servants at the fort, reported that the Dreamers were meeting in council and making all sorts of hostile threats. On Sunday the Christian Indians at Lapwai went to church, and later they told the whites that Joseph and his people were spending the day chanting war songs.

By Monday, May 7, Howard's fears had grown. Many newcomers had arrived during the recess to swell the ranks of the nontreaties. The most important of them were members of two bands of Palouses who still lived at their ancestral homesites on the lower Snake River, ignoring demands that they go onto the Yakima reservation. One of the bands, residing at Wawawai on the Snake, was led by a 37-year-old Dreamer prophet named Husishusis Kute (Little Baldhead), also known as the Preacher, who claimed he had lost some of his hair when he had been slightly wounded by a cannonball while helping the Americans during Colonel Wright's campaign against the Spokans. Husis-husis Kute was a noted speaker, and although he had no opportunity to talk during the ensuing council session, it is believed that the nontreaties had intended him to be a second orator after Toohoolhoolzote. The other Palouse group was led by a 34-year-old warrior named Hahtalekin, who was also known as Taktsoukt Ilppilp (Red Echo). He was headman of the largest Palouse band that still lived in freedom, and dwelled at the junction of the Snake and Palouse rivers, in the location that had seen so much of the white man's history since David Thompson had stopped there and John Clarke had hanged an Indian on the spot in 1813.

Before the session opened that morning, many of the nontreaties joined in a colorful equestrian display at the fort. Bolstered by the new arrivals, they seemed to the whites and treaty Nez Perces who watched them more self-confident and threatening than before. Nor did it ease Howard's tension when he learned that a messenger had arrived for Joseph with word that troops were marching through the Wallowa, where the chief had left many of his women and children without a guard of warriors. Joseph was disturbed, but he and Ollokit both came to the council again. When the meeting began, Monteith, who had worried during the week end over the support the Indians had given Toohoolhoolzote's "Dreamer talk," tried to assure the nontreaties that the government would not interfere with their religious rites, except when a *tewat* (shaman) proved to be a bad teacher and counseled disobedience. If he had meant to neutralize Toohoolhoolzote's effectiveness in the ensuing session, he failed. As soon as the agent finished, the old Indian was on his feet again to plague Howard. The General had lost patience with him, and was already describing him as a "cross-grained growler" and a "large, thick-necked, ugly, obstinate savage of the worst type." [25] He was, "if possible," said Howard, "crosser and more impudent in his abruptness of manner than before. He had the usual long preliminary discussion about the earth being his mother, that she should not be disturbed by hoe or plough, that man should subsist on what grows of itself, &c., &c. He railed against the violence that would separate Indians from lands that were theirs by inheritance. He repeated his ideas concerning 'chieftainship,' chieftainship of the earth. Chieftainship cannot be sold, cannot be given away . . ."

Howard had no idea what the Indian was talking about, but he had had enough of it. Toohoolhoolzote's words, arguments, and imagery, his thoughts and spiritual beliefs, claiming that the earth itself was a chief, were Indian, and they were stirring the rows of nontreaty Indians into restlessness again. The time had come to halt the old man.

"We do not wish to interfere with your religion," the General snapped at

25. Report of the Secretary of War (1877), *1*, 593.

him, "but you must talk about practicable things. Twenty times over you repeat that the earth is your mother, and about chieftainship from the earth. Let us hear no more, but come to business at once." [26]

It was not easy. Howard's hasty words precipitated an angry quarrel between himself and the Indian. At first, Toohoolhoolzote tried to go on in his earlier vein: "You white people get together, measure the earth, and then divide it . . . Part of the Indians gave up their land. I never did. The earth is part of my body, and I never gave up the earth."

"You know very well that the government has set apart a reservation, and that the Indians must go upon it . . ." Howard replied.

The Indian glared at the General and said something in a low voice. Howard asked the interpreter what he had said. "He demands," said the interpreter, " 'What person pretends to divide the land, and put me on it?' "

The murder of peace commissioners by the Modoc Indians several years before flashed through Howard's mind. Despite the fact that the newspapers of the Northwest had been putting pressure on him, urging him to be stern and uncompromising with the Nez Perces, and to avoid a repetition of the Modoc affair, he had met with the Indians, listened to them, and tried to be considerate. Now, there had been enough "insolence" from them. He was bitter and angry.

In the most decided voice, he said, "I am the man. I stand here for the President, and there is no spirit good or bad that will hinder me. My orders are plain, and will be executed."

The rest of the Indians stirred. "Signs of anger and bad blood began to appear." Looking Glass became evasive, and White Bird indicated support for Toohoolhoolzote. Howard sensed their pleasure at the old man's defiance. "I perceived that I must, somehow, put in a wedge of separation, and curb their unruly tendency," he said. So he faced Toohoolhoolzote squarely and demanded, "Then you do not propose to comply with the orders of the government?"

"So long as the earth keeps me, I want to be left alone," the old man replied. "You are trifling with the law of the earth."

"Our old friend does not seem to understand that the question is: Will the Indians come peaceably on the reservation, or do they want me, in compliance with my orders, to put them there by force?" said Howard.

"I never gave the Indians authority to give away my lands," Toohoolhoolzote answered.

"Do you speak for yourself alone?" the General asked.

26. Howard, *Nez Perce Joseph*, p. 64. The quotations at the council for the rest of the day are from this source, though it is improbable that they correctly reflect Toohoolhoolzote's words and thoughts.

The Dreamer turned to him fiercely. "The Indians may do what they like, but I am not going on the reservation."

Howard at last lost his temper. "This bad advice is what you give the Indians," he exclaimed. "On account of it, you will have to be taken to the Indian territory [Oklahoma] . . . I will send you there if it takes years and years . . ." He turned to the other Indians. "Will Joseph and White Bird and Looking Glass go with me to look after the land [meaning, choose new homes for themselves on the reservation]? The old man shall not go; he must stay with Captain Perry."

"Do you want to scare me with reference to my body?" Toohoolhoolzote demanded.

"I will leave your body with Captain Perry," Howard retorted.

The General called for a messenger. None came at once, so he took the old Indian by the arm and, aided by Captain Perry, propelled him angrily across the post grounds to the guardhouse. Toohoolhoolzote offered no resistance, and the two officers handed him to the guard who took him into the building. The rest of the Indians watched in silence, as Howard and Perry returned and faced them. "Will you go with me to look for reservation land?" the General asked again.

For a moment, none of the chiefs replied. Then, one by one, they nodded. Howard, said Yellow Wolf later, had showed them the rifle.[27] It was go on the reservation now, or fight. Still, none of the headmen wanted war.

"With this satisfactory conclusion," Howard reported in words ironically reminiscent of those of I. I. Stevens at Walla Walla in 1855, "the council again adjourned."

There is a question concerning the dialogue between Howard and Toohoolhoolzote that led to the old man's arrest, an act that lay heavily on the hearts of every nontreaty Indian present and that was a contributing cause soon afterward to the start of the war. It was bad enough that Howard failed to understand the depth of Toohoolhoolzote's spiritual beliefs, and that he lost first his patience and then his temper. But in the exchanges between the two men there must also have been considerable misunderstanding, possibly caused by the interpreters. There are a number of discrepancies in the reports of the language used, even between the official War Department summary of the meeting and the account in the book, *Nez Perce Joseph*, both of them written by Howard, presumably, from the same verbatim transcript of the council proceedings. But the Indians' versions of what they understood was said are totally different from Howard's. They report such things as the General cutting the old man short and telling him to "Shut up," and, later, shoving him angrily over some Indians who were sitting on the ground. True or not,

27. McWhorter, *Yellow Wolf*, p. 41.

they are significant, for if they reflect the Indians' point of view, they make more understandable the brooding resentment and hatred of Howard that the nontreaties carried with them from the council. They had come to the meeting as free men, to talk as equals with Howard, to try to persuade the military man of the injustice of what he was demanding of them. They left in humiliation, with their last illusion of fair treatment by Americans totally shattered.[28]

Their homelands, they now knew, were gone. There was no way, short of war to the death, to save them. On May 8, the day after the council, Howard and an entourage that included Lieutenant Wilkinson, two cavalrymen, a treaty Nez Perce named Jonah Hayes, and an interpreter, stopped at the camps of the nontreaties and picked up Joseph, Looking Glass, and White Bird to look over the reservation and select new sites for their bands.[29] They rode up Lapwai Valley, where Howard hoped to resettle Joseph's people, and above the mouth of Sweetwater Creek came on the thrifty farms, totaling 700 acres, of two white families, the Finneys and Caldwells, who were squatting on the reservation. After stopping for lunch at the Caldwells, Joseph showed an interest in the area. Although he said he told the General at that time that he had no right to the white men's farms and did not want to take their property, a search during the rest of the day failed to find other

28. See above, n. 24. Besides McDonald's account, other Indian versions of the council are found in McWhorter, *Yellow Wolf*, pp. 37–41, and "Chief Joseph's Own Story," pp. 17–19.

29. McDonald, still saying that Looking Glass was not present, related that the three chiefs who rode with Howard were Joseph, White Bird, and Husishusis Kute. The accounts in the reports of the War and Interior Departments, and in *Nez Perce Joseph*, however, refer so frequently and specifically to Looking Glass that, again, McDonald must have been in error—although Howard gave no explanation of why Looking Glass had to make the tour with him, since he already lived on the reservation. At the same time, other points made by McDonald are worth noting. After the general put Toohoolhoolzote in the guardhouse, McDonald said, Howard told the other chiefs that they had ten days in which to get themselves on the reservation. "Then and there," he went on, "Joseph, Sr. [as distinguished from Ollokot], spoke to Howard. 'You give us ten days to move our livestock and property. You must be joking. I notice when you want to move it takes a long time to do it, especially when there are rivers to cross. I notice whenever you go after Indians in time of war it takes you months to cross a river. I want you to understand that we have more horses than the soldiers ever had in the Indian wars; we want time. Ten days is no time for us. When the generals have a handful of soldiers and a few animals to cross a river, it takes them weeks and months to cross. We have plenty of children, women, horses and cattle, and the rivers are high.' This is the only speech," said McDonald, that "Joseph, Sr., ever made during the year 1877." Howard had his way. "I don't want any humbugging," McDonald quoted him as replying to Joseph. "Do as I tell you to do—move immediately to the reserve." *New Northwest*, November 15, 1878. As related, the time limit in the end was thirty days.

land in the valley not occupied by treaty Indians, and Howard realized that he would have to evict the whites.

The group started back to the fort that afternoon, the chiefs apparently resigned to their fate, and even—according to Howard—laughing and talking "in the most friendly way." [30] White Bird wanted to test his roan against Wilkinson's horse, and "we had quite a horse race," the General reported, although he did not say who won. If there was cheerfulness, however, it was on the surface. Looking Glass gave no more than an indication of the weight on the chiefs' hearts when he suddenly rode over to Howard and begged him to release Toohoolhoolzote. He and White Bird, he promised the General, would be responsible for their friend's good behavior, and Howard could shoot them both if Toohoolhoolzote violated the officer's trust. Howard listened to Looking Glass but rejected his plea, saying that he intended keeping the old man in the guardhouse until the Indians settled the question of their new homes.

That evening he was satisfied that his stern policy was proving successful. Jonah and the interpreter told him that there was no question any more regarding the nontreaties' willingness to settle on the reservation, that Joseph and his people would take the land from the mouth of the Sweetwater to the head of Lapwai Creek, including the farms of the two white squatters, that White Bird wished to live near Looking Glass on the upper Clearwater, and that Husishusis Kute would bring his Palouses to the lower Clearwater, just above the Lapwai agency. Pleased that "matters appeared to be taking a good turn," Howard, now joined by Captain Perry and six cavalrymen, picked up White Bird, Looking Glass, Joseph, and Ollokot early the next morning and rode across the hills to Kamiah with them. The Indians, he said, were in even better humor than the day before. Looking Glass, who was laughing, told the General that he did so "from real joy," and added, "I shall never forget our ride along these paths."

Although that chief had not signed the 1863 treaty and had sided ever since with the nontreaties, his lands on Clear Creek of the Clearwater's Middle Fork, above present-day Kooskia, were just within the eastern border of the reservation, and there was no need for his people to resettle. White Bird wished to be close to Looking Glass, however, and after staying overnight at Kamiah, the group searched the next day some eighteen miles up the Clearwater past the Kooskia region, finally finding an unoccupied site suitable for

30. During this ride, according to McDonald, "Howard said to White Bird, 'What made you a chief? I am a chief because I lost my arm while fighting in big battles and fought bravely.' Joseph and White Bird were surprised at these remarks, and said amongst themselves 'Howard is anxious for war'" (*New Northwest,* November 15, 1878).

the followers of both White Bird and Toohoolhoolzote. Then they started back for Lapwai, Howard leaving them temporarily to ride to the Caldwells and Finneys to discuss the eviction of the two families from their Lapwai Valley farms, and rejoining the Indians that night at a camp along the trail. The next evening, May 12, they were back at Lapwai, where Howard was greeted by Captain Joel Trimble, who had arrived at the post with his company of cavalry from Walla Walla to reinforce Perry. At the same time, the General learned that Captain Whipple and the two cavalry companies in the Wallowa were camped near the mouth of the Grande Ronde River, pursuant to Howard's orders of May 4.

Both items of information, learned soon afterward by the nontreaties in their camps nearby, created excitement among the Indians. Rumors spread that Howard was going to use the troops to drive the nontreaties onto the reservation. Joseph was particularly alarmed by the report of Whipple's new position on the lower Grande Ronde, which was close to his own winter camp in the canyon, and he hurried to the post to ask for protection for his people who were waiting for him in the canyon. Lieutenant Wilkinson assured him that the troops would not harm the Indians, and Joseph, in turn, reiterated his promise to move peaceably to the reservation.

On May 14 Howard called all the nontreaties together at the post for a final discussion of the terms of removal. Although Toohoolhoolzote was still sullen with rage, the General at last satisfied the headmen by releasing the old man. The Indians greeted their former spokesman happily, joshing him for a soldier's white shirt that he had received in the guardhouse, and calling him a bride because of a Nez Perce custom in which a newly married woman received a new dress from her husband's family.[31] Their joy, however, was short-lived. As soon as the Indians had gathered around the post adjutant's office, Howard announced that they would have thirty days, and no more, in which to come onto the reservation. The nontreaties were crestfallen. Several of them protested, especially Joseph, who argued that he would need more time to gather his stock from the canyons and ridges of the Wallowa and cross the Snake and Salmon rivers, both of which would be approaching flood-tide. But Howard was adamant, and "in a haughty spirit," according to Joseph, replied, "If you let the time run over one day, the soldiers will be there to drive you on the reservation, and all your cattle and horses outside of the reservation at that time will fall into the hands of the white men." [32]

The Indians could not get Howard to change his mind. Every day's delay, the General told them, risked the possibility of an armed conflict with impatient settlers. That very morning, he informed them, he had received a letter

31. McWhorter, *Hear Me*, p. 173 n., quoting the Nez Perce War Singer.
32. "Chief Joseph's Own Story," p. 19.

from whites on the Salmon River, complaining of the continued presence in that area of Nez Perces of "unruly character," who were members of White Bird's band. He had the message read in full to the Indians, citing it as proof of the need for speed. Letting them hear the settlers' charges, he thought, "strengthened their decision to come on the reservation," but it actually heightened their resentment. They smoldered over it, and members of White Bird's band told each other that the writers of the petition were the people who were making them give up their country. In time, these Indians would prove by their actions against the settlers on the Salmon River how wrong Howard had been in having the letter read to them.

Before the meeting ended, Joseph told Howard that he had decided that he would rather settle on the upper Clearwater near Looking Glass and White Bird. Howard was willing to comply; it relieved him from having to evict the Finneys and Caldwells from Lapwai Creek, and he believed that it might be better, after all, to place the nontreaties as far as possible from Lewiston, where there was white "hostility even against the friendly reservation Indians." He distributed "protection papers" to the chiefs, which called on white men to treat the Indians justly during their removal, but sensing that Husishusis Kute was the only man with whom he would have trouble, he gave Monteith that man's protection paper to hold until the Palouse Dreamer demonstrated his good intentions. Because that Indian and his band had the farthest distance to travel, however, he permitted them thirty-five days to come on the reserve.

On May 15 the Indians set off sadly for their homes, and Howard prepared to leave for Portland. "Having now secured the object named, by persuasion, constraint and such a gradual encircling of the Indians by troops as would render resistance evidently futile, I thought my own instructions fulfilled," he reported. "The execution of further details I leave in perfect security to the Indian agent at Lapwai and Captain Perry whom I put into my place for this work." [33] He reached his own home, snug with his family, in Portland on May 19, and two days later wired the division commander, General McDowell, in San Francisco: "Non-treaty Nez Perces constrained compliance with orders of government. Thirty days allowed to gather scattered people and stock." [34]

Joseph and Ollokot, meanwhile, trailed back with their followers to the mouth of Joseph Creek, where the rest of the members of the band were waiting for them. Whipple's troops were camped nearby on the Grande Ronde, and Joseph found his people highly excited. Their alarm roused a war fever among some of the young warriors, who met and talked secretly, telling each other in anger, "General Howard has shown us the rifle. We answer,

33. Fee, *Chief Joseph*, p. 110.
34. McWhorter, *Hear Me*, p. 173.

'Yes.' We will stir up a fight for him. We will start his war!" [35] At the same time, Toohoolhoolzote and his people came down from the hills to join Joseph's band, and the old chief, still outraged by Howard's conduct, gave support to Joseph's young men, urging them to fight rather than let themselves "be driven like dogs from the land where they were born." But Joseph, Ollokot, and the elders of the Wallowa band knew the impossibility of gaining anything by a war. They called a council and spoke against bloodshed, and proposed moving at once. Toohoolhoolzote and some of the younger men continued to cry out their anger, recounting the wrongs of the white men and pleading for resistance. "It required a strong heart to stand up against such talk," Joseph said, "but I urged my people to be quiet, and not to begin a war." In the end the chief's reasoning, supported by that of his brother, won reluctant acceptance, and the word was carried among the lodges by the crier: "Everyone get ready to move to our new home. Round up horses and cattle, as many as can be found."

The people were resentful and bitter, but they hurried to obey the council's order. It was a difficult task. The band's thousands of horses and cattle were spread across a vast, rugged expanse of canyons, ridgeslopes, prairies, forests, and meadows. Those that were found were driven down to the lower end of the Imnaha Valley, but many were missed. What the Indians were trying to do in thirty days could have taken them half a year. It was a sad farewell, also, to their homeland, to the valley and lake where their fathers and fathers' fathers had summered, to the meadows where they had gathered roots and hunted, to the canyons that had sheltered their winter camps and stone corrals, and to the snowy mountains and the Wallowa River, where Old Joseph and many others of their people lay buried. It was farewell to their sacred sites, farewell to their dead, and farewell to the land they loved, the most beautiful valley in the world.

They trailed down the steep draws to the Imnaha, down Fence Creek, down Corral and Tully Creek, driving cattle and horses before them. They carried what possessions they could, food, cooking pots and household ware used in their lodges, clothing, blankets, leather articles, ceremonial and war regalia that had seen the times of the fur trade and the proud hunts and battles on the plains, tools, parfleches, tipi covers, horn bows and arrows, powder and guns. The huge stores of roots and whatever else they could not take with them they cached in the canyons, thinking hopefully that the exile might not be forever, that somehow they could come back, if only for a visit for a short time each year.

In the valley, the settlers were overjoyed. The Indians were going; the

35. Quotations in this paragraph are from McWhorter, *Yellow Wolf,* p. 41, and "Chief Joseph's Own Story," p. 20.

Wallowa, at last, was to be the domain of the white man. Some of the stock-men rode cautiously after the Indians, stopping on high land to spy on their withdrawal. Occasionally, they came on Indian stock, overlooked by the Nez Perces. No one knows how many head of horses and cattle were appropriated silently by the settlers, driven back to the rangeland in the valley, or rounded up in the canyons, after the Indians had departed.[36] There were alarms, also, as before. Still taking every precaution, Howard sent word to the valley that, until the Indians were safely under control on the Idaho reservation, the set-tlers ought to evacuate the Wallowa and take refuge in the Grande Ronde Valley; the Indians, he warned, might well get their families and livestock across the Snake River and then return to seek vengeance on the whites in the Wallowa. The message caused a panic, and many of the families fled to stockades at Summerville and Elgin in the Grande Ronde, where they were joined by Captain Whipple and one company of cavalry, withdrawn from the mouth of the Grande Ronde River to guard against a return of the In-dians.[37]

In the lower valley of the Imnaha, Joseph's people, meanwhile, turned from the lava-walled canyon near the river's mouth and drove their stock over a steep, grassy divide and down to the Snake above the Imnaha's mouth. The river was a raging torrent, carrying the melted snowpacks from its head-waters. The idea that Howard had forced them to cross the rivers at that time of the year, when they were at their highest and most dangerous level, en-dured as an angry memory among the Indians. Joseph had pleaded with the General to let the band stay in the valley until the fall when the rivers would be lower and more tranquil; but Monteith, remembering perhaps that he had originally asked the Indians to come in before April 1, at a time of year when the rivers would also have been low, and when most of the Indians' livestock would still have been in the canyons where the Nez Perces could have rounded them up more easily, had wanted no further delay. Any postpone-ment, he had warned Howard, would look like a victory for Joseph and would have made him more difficult to handle.

36. In 1881 Helen Hunt Jackson, in *A Century of Dishonor*, p. 131, stated that white men attacked some of the retreating Indians in the Valley and took their cattle. Although she provided no source for this story, many writers since then have repeated the charge, and some of the Nez Perces have agreed that it happened. I have found nothing to confirm it, however, and an account by Captain John W. Cullen, which is among J. H. Horner's papers in the County Court House at Enterprise, Oregon, paints a picture of too much fear among the settlers at that time to suggest that they would have risked getting close enough to the Indians to fight them. Moreover, it seems plausible that a fight of this nature would have found its way into the lore of Wallowa County and the war. In fact, it probably would have been embroidered into quite a yarn!

37. *Chief Joseph Herald* (April 24, 1958), p. 4.

Several of the younger Indians, prodding their horses into the swirling current of the Snake, tested it and managed to get across. Gradually, more of the band followed them, making rafts and bullboats out of buffalo robes, and piling children and old people on top of the baggage. Three or four ponies, guided by riders and swimmers, towed each of the tossing craft across the torrent, while the passengers held on fearfully. Around them, the women and younger men clung to the backs of struggling mounts, urging them on toward the opposite shore. When the herds of livestock were driven into the turbulent water, eddies and high waves caught many of the riderless animals and swept them off downstream. For two days the struggle continued. The tumultuous river scattered people, possessions, and animals for thousands of yards along the Idaho bank. The noise of the river, roaring across rapids in the canyon, combined with the cries of the children, the shouts of horsemen, and the bawling of cattle. Eventually, all of the people were across safely, but many of their possessions had gone whirling off in the current, and a large part of their herd of horses and cattle had perished.

The band members rested for a while on the Idaho bank, collecting their goods and letting their animals graze. Then they trailed up the steep draw of Divide Creek and headed for the Salmon. When they reached that river, they decided not to try crossing their cattle at once. Leaving the animals under the guard of a few herders, the people successfully ferried themselves and most of their horses to the opposite shore, and moved up Rocky Canyon to Tepahlewam, Split Rocks, the ancient rendezvous site at the camas meadows beside Tolo Lake, about six miles west of Grangeville, Idaho. There, on June 2, the people of Joseph and Toohoolhoolzote found the other nontreaty bands, and with twelve days remaining before they had to be within the borders of the reservation, now only a few miles from where they were, they went into camp for a last gathering in freedom.

It was a fatal pause. Many of the Indians had come with White Bird, riding sad-heartedly and heavily laden with all their possessions from their ancestral homes farther south along the Salmon River. A few members of the bands of Looking Glass and Koolkool Snehee (Red Owl), who would not have to move, had traveled westward across the Camas Prairie from their settlements in the Kooskia region of the upper Clearwater to participate in the final rendezvous of the nontreaties. There were Palouses also, a small detachment from the lower Snake. Altogether, with the people of Joseph and Toohoolhoolzote, some 600 Indians were present, more than two-thirds of them women, children, and old men.

While the women dug camas roots, the men played the bone game, raced horses, and sat around talking of the evil times that had fallen upon them. Their angry pride rose as they discussed the injustices of the white men, the unpunished murders of their people, the imprisonment of their spokesman, Toohoolhoolzote, and the haughty orders of General Howard. The most bitter Indians were the followers of White Bird; Indian-hating settlers and miners had overrun their lands along the Salmon River, had cheated, robbed, and killed their friends and relatives, and—as they remembered from their last meeting with Howard—had written the government to drive the Nez Perces from the Salmon River country. Night after night the Indians recounted the long list of wrongs, and among the younger men passions began to burn for a release of their feelings of hurt and humiliation. But the chiefs and older men remained firm against starting any trouble. They restrained those who cried for revenge, urging them to wait for the return of Eagle From the Light and the warriors who were off in Montana hunting buffalo. "Then will be decided what to do if war breaks," they counseled.[38]

But as the days passed, a warlike spirit crept across the camp and tension increased. The young men rode around feverishly, racing past the tipis and hanging over the sides of their horses as if they were on war parties on the plains, firing their guns, and showing that they were eager and daring, and not afraid. At night, drumming filled the air, and the people chanted and danced. Looking Glass and Koolkool Snehee were alarmed. They wanted no war, and they urged the other headmen to keep their young men in check. On June 10 those two chiefs returned to their own people at their villages near Kooskia, but Looking Glass continued to worry, and three times apparently he sent an emissary to Tepahlewam to tell the other leaders to quiet the hot-heads.[39] But the memories of a generation of insults and persecution were welling up strongly among the freemen, and now, on the eve of what was beginning to seem like imprisonment, their self-restraint was about to snap.

On June 12, 1877, with only two days of liberty left, a large number of the Indians staged a war parade through the camp. Two young members of White Bird's band, Wahlitits (Shore Crossing) and his cousin, Sarpsis Ilppilp (Red Moccasin Tops), were riding double on a horse at the rear of the column. Both youths were the heirs of trouble with white men. Sarpsis Ilppilp was a grandson of Tomahas, one of the Cayuse murderers of the Marcus Whitmans. Wahlitits was the son of a Salmon River headman named Tipyahlanah Siskan (Eagle Robe), who had been murdered in March 1875 by a white man named Larry Ott. Eagle Robe had originally befriended Ott, giving him part of his land on which to settle. Soon afterward, Ott had begun erecting a fence around Eagle Robe's garden, claiming it as his own. When the Indian had protested, Ott had wounded him mortally with his six-shooter.

38. McWhorter, *Yellow Wolf*, p. 42.
39. *New Northwest*, November 15, 1878.

Before he had died, Eagle Robe had urged Wahlitits not to seek revenge but to let the cruel white man live.

Ott had never been brought to justice, but there had been nothing unusual about that. Although murders and other wrongs against the Indians had been commonplace in the Salmon River district, the law had never worked in behalf of the Nez Perces. Like many other Indians in the district, Wahlitits had learned to bury his hurt deep within himself. But his resentment had not died, and his heart still burned with anger against the white man who had killed his father.

As he and Sarpsis Ilppilp followed the parade through the camp, their horse stepped on some kouse roots spread out to dry on a canvas in front of the tipi of a man named Heyoom Moxmox (Yellow Grizzly Bear). The Indian shouted bitterly at Wahlitits: "See what you do! Playing brave you ride over my woman's hard-worked food! If you are so brave, why don't you go kill the white man who killed your father?"

The words stung the young man. He stopped and looked back at Yellow Grizzly Bear. "You will be sorry for your words," he said.[40]

That evening, according to Nez Perce friends of Wahlitits,the youth wept, explaining to those around him that he had not killed Larry Ott because he had not wanted to give the white men an excuse to harm other Indians in retaliation. But Yellow Grizzly Bear's taunt had reopened his wound. His honor as a man had been impugned. During the night the spirit of revenge permeating the camp fed his emotions, and by dawn he had made up his mind to show his courage.

Early in the morning he and Sarpsis Ilppilp enlisted Wahlitits' 17-year-old nephew, Wetyetmas Wyakaikt (Swan Necklace), also of White Bird's band, not telling him their plans but asking him to come along on a ride as "horse holder" for them, and rode out of camp on two horses. Heading down White Bird hill and up the Salmon River, they stopped at the Slate Creek home of two settlers named Cone who were friendly to Indians, and bought some food. When they tried to purchase ammunition, however, they were turned

---

40. In 1878 Duncan McDonald published an entirely different version of this taunting of Wahlitits, claiming that the young man was "a gay Lothario," who played fast and loose with various Indian maidens. Finally, said McDonald, the relatives and friends of one of the girls took exception to his conduct and called him a coward, lacking the manliness to kill the white man who had slain his father (*New Northwest*, June 21, 1878). Nez Perces who were present at Tepahlewam called this story untrue and said that white men had made it up—and so it seems from a reading of McDonald's implausible-sounding account. White men who knew nothing about what was occurring at the Indian rendezvous also appear to have started a story that Wahlitits and his companions the next day were drunk. The Nez Perces vigorously denied this, saying that there was no liquor in the camp at that time.

down. Continuing on, they made for Larry Ott's home on the Salmon River. Ott was not there, and although they searched all day, they could not find him. Toward evening, they picked up Wahlitits' wife, who had not yet left her dwelling place on the Salmon River, and revealing to her and Swan Necklace that they were on a mission to slay white men who had mistreated Indians, rode some eight miles above the mouth of Slate Creek to the home of an elderly white man named Richard Devine. The latter had been guilty of brutal conduct to Indians. He customarily set his dogs on any Indians who passed near his home, and had once slain a crippled Nez Perce named Dakoopin. The four Nez Perces, filled with hatred for this man, hid behind some rocks near his house during the night. Early in the morning Wahlitits and Sarpsis Ilppilp gave their horses to Swan Necklace to hold and, pushing in the door of Devine's house, found him there and shot him dead.

The first slaying stoked their passions. With war feathers and strips of red flannel in their hair, and paint daubed across their faces, they rode on toward John Day Creek of the Salmon and killed a rancher named Henry Elfers, who had also been known for his hostility to Indians. They took one of Elfers' horses, a roan stallion that he had used as a racehorse, and, hurrying to his house, helped themselves to his guns and ammunition. Some women were in the building, but the Indians did nothing to them and rode away. Within a short time they had slain two other Indian-hating white men, Robert Bland and Henry Beckroge, and wounded and chased into the brush a whiskey-selling store owner named Samuel Benedict, who had once killed a drunken Nez Perce and wounded two others, and who was notorious for shortchanging and cheating Indian customers.

Recrossing the White Bird divide, the exhilarated Indians then headed back toward the Tepahlewam camp, proud of the way they had avenged their people. Several miles short of the rendezvous area, they stopped at a stream known as Round Willow, deciding that it would be unwise to return to the bands and involve them in the blame for what they had done. If the white men were to seek revenge, they did not want the rest of the people to suffer. But they sent Swan Necklace riding to the camp to tell their friends what had happened and to inform them that they intended to kill more of the bad whites along the Salmon the next day. Astride Elfers' roan stallion, Swan Necklace entered the sprawling village that evening, June 14, and rode past the lodges, calling out to various Indians what had occurred, and showing off the stallion as proof of what he was telling them.

Excitement spread through the camp. Joseph and Ollokot were not there, although Joseph's wife, lodged in a tipi in a place separate from the others, had just given birth to a baby girl. With a party of four men—including one known as Welweyas, "a half-man-and-half-woman, who dressed like a woman," and two women, Joseph's older daughter, Hophoponmi (Sound of Running Feet), and Ollokot's wife, Wetatonmi—the two Wallowa leaders had recrossed the Salmon River to the cattle herd several days before to butcher some animals and bring back meat.[41] The other chiefs and some of the older men were in one of the lodges, holding another council and talking again of whether to go on the reservation the next day or take up arms. The speakers were counseling against a war, pointing out how weak the Indians were against the whites, and suggesting once more that they wait until summer, when the best warriors would be back from the buffalo country and all the bands could hold a council at Weippe and decide what to do.

In the midst of their talk, someone called to them from the next tipi: "You poor people are talking for nothing! Three boys have already started war! They killed a white man on Salmon and brought his horse to this camp. It is already war." [42]

The council ended abruptly. Swan Necklace was questioned closely, and in a short time several men were on their horses, riding through the camp and calling on others to prepare themselves to join the attacks the next day against white men on the Salmon who had been enemies of the Indians. The war spirit rose, although the response was not a united one. Many of the people were confused and frightened, sure that General Howard and the soldiers would be on them at any moment. Some began to gather their goods, intending to strike their tipis and flee to a hiding place, but the chiefs held them in the camp, urging them to wait through the night.

The next morning, still unaware of what had happened, Joseph and his party came up Rocky Canyon from the Salmon with twelve horses loaded with meat. An Indian fighting man named Two Moons came riding out to meet them, calling, "War has broke out. Three white men killed yesterday!" Joseph was horrified. For a moment he sat stunned, then, with Ollokot and the other men, hurried to the camp, finding most of the tipis down and the people packing their horses to leave. The two Wallowa leaders rode frantically among the Indians, urging them to stop and wait till the army came. They would explain to Howard, they said, that the bands were not to blame for the killings, and the white officer would then not hold all of them guilty. But the younger followers of White Bird and the other headmen objected to such talk; they had lost patience with the cowardly peace words of the Wallowa chiefs and now regarded Joseph and Ollokot with distrust, looking on

41. McWhorter, *Hear Me*, pp. 195–96, quoting narrative of Wetatonmi. McWhorter also quotes another Indian version of this cattle-butchering excursion to the effect that the Wallowa chiefs had gone with nine other men to kill the cattle, which had been bequeathed to them by a headman who had died the year before (p. 197).
42. McWhorter, *Yellow Wolf*, p. 45.

them as they had once looked on Lawyer—wondering if the two brothers, also, would be traitors to the people. They turned away angrily from the Wallowa headmen and harangued the women, children, and old men to hurry to safety, while the braves sought revenge on the whites. One by one, the families ignored Joseph and Ollokot and moved off, leaving behind the members of the Wallowa band and some thirty-five other Indians, most of them instructed by their headmen to watch the brothers and see if they abandoned the nontreaties and went to Lapwai or Kamiah with the Christian Indians on the reservation.

In the meantime, sixteen young men and Chuslum Moxmox (Yellow Buffalo Bull), the father of Sarpsis Ilppilp and a noted veteran of fights on the plains, rode out to Round Willow and joined the original raiders. Roused to a lust for vengence, they returned to the Salmon, wreaking bloody retribution on some fourteen or fifteen whites in the country between White Bird and Slate creeks. With the exception of one member of Joseph's Wallowa band, Lahpeealoot (Geese Three Times Lighting on Water), all were Salmon River Indians, followers of White Bird, with a score of atrocities and wrongs to avenge. Calling again at the store of Samuel Benedict, whom Wahlitits had previously wounded, they killed Benedict and a companion named August Bacon, and frightened away the owner of a neighboring store and some friends who were there. Then they looted and wrecked both buildings, scattering gold dust from the cash boxes and helping themselves to kegs of whiskey. In a short time, many of them were reeling and boasting in a drunken frenzy. Looking for more victims, they slew a man named Harry Mason, who a few months before had used a blacksnake whip on two unarmed Indians; cut down settlers named James Baker, William Osborne, and François Chodoze; and attacked and burned the home of a family named Manuel. Mr. Manuel and his little daughter, mistaken for a boy by the Indians, were wounded and got away; but Mrs. Manuel disappeared, her body presumably consumed in the flames of her burning home.[43]

The killings continued for two days, and the Indians, sodden with alcohol, at last rejoined the rest of the people of White Bird's band, who by that time had trailed down from the Camas Prairie to White Bird Canyon. The district had been almost emptied of whites. Word of the murders had raced up the creeks and across the hills, from one farm and cabin to another, and white families had streamed north as fast as they could go, abandoning their homes, gardens, and possessions and heading for the settlements on Camas Prairie on

43. Various legends and accounts grew up regarding the fate of Mrs. Manuel. Some of the Nez Perces even said that they held her captive for a month and killed her in Montana. For various Indian and white versions of this second Nez Perce raid on the Salmon River, see McWhorter, *Hear Me,* pp. 207–18.

the road to Lewiston. In the Slate Creek area some sixty-five people, including twenty-five Florence miners who had been warned of the Indian actions by a Nez Perce woman named Tolo, manned a stockade at the home of the Cone brothers. Not all the settlers and miners had been hostile to the Indians; the Nez Perces later told of one stockman named Wood who had invited Yellow Bull and the other raiders to come into his house. He had agreed with them that the government and the whites had cheated them and that justice was on their side, and he had advised them to stay in the rough Snake River country and "meet the soldiers and fight them." [44] The whites who fled north found no safety there either; by then Camas Prairie was also engulfed in violence. The bands that had left Tepahlewam had originally headed northeastward across the prairie to a large cavern known as Sapachesap on Cottonwood Creek, about a mile above its junction with the South Fork of the Clearwater River not far from the villages of Looking Glass and Red Owl.[45] At the same time, the headmen had left scouts behind them to watch all the trails and roads that came from Lewiston to the white men's settlements on Camas Prairie and in the Salmon country farther south.

Joseph, Ollokot, and the members of the Wallowa band had remained at Tepahlewam overnight, worrying what to do. The brothers were still opposed to war, but their hopes for peace were fading quickly. About ten in the evening some white horsemen were heard in the darkness, and a bullet ripped into Joseph's tipi. Some of the Indians ran outside with their rifles, but the attackers whirled about and rode away. The Indians stayed on guard the rest of the night, and at dawn they heard another shot far in the distance. By then the brothers had made up their minds. They had vigorously opposed a war with the whites and had done everything possible to avoid it, enduring injus-

44. Ibid., p. 228. Still another version of the Salmon River raids, that of one of the Cone brothers, was published by Bailey, *River of No Return*, pp. 252–60. It gives an interesting account of the Slate Creek stockade and of Tolo's all-night ride to Florence for help. The Indian name of Tolo, or Too-lah, according to this account, was Alablernot. She thought the Nez Perces' action in starting the war was madness. Cone's figuring for the number of people in the stockade makes it about 90, but on June 30, after the 25 Florence miners had arrived on the scene, the Slate Creek group sent a call to Governor Brayman of Idaho for weapons. The appeal was signed by 30 men, apparently all who were capable of bearing arms, and said that there were 30 women and children in the stockade. Among the signers, incidentally, was Larry Ott, the man perhaps most responsible for the start of the Indian war. Chaffee, *Nez Perce War Letters*, pp. 55–56.

45. The Cottonwood Creek cave, Sapachesap, received its name, meaning Drive-In, about 1806, when a large broup of Bannock invaders of the Nez Perce country were trapped within it. The Nez Perces lit a fire at the mouth of the cavern and smothered many of those inside; the rest of the Bannocks were forced into the open and killed. See McWhorter, *Hear Me*, p. 15.

tices, persecution, and provocations with an almost superhuman patience. Now the war was coming, and it was not their fault. Announcing that they would not desert the other nontreaties in their moment of peril, Joseph moved among the Wallowa people and with a heavy heart told them to pack up and prepare to go to Sapachesap to join their friends. The chief had come through hours of travail like those experienced at another time by the Virginian Robert E. Lee. The die was cast to follow his heart.

At Sapachesap the Wallowa band was welcomed by the others. The newcomers learned of raids and gunfights that had already occurred on Camas Prairie, and heard that one Indian had just been killed. Joining an avenging party, Yellow Wolf and a group of other young men of Joseph's band rode out to get the dead Indian's body and to kill the white man who had slain him. They shot one settler before they returned to the camp. The skirmishing made the headmen recognize, however, that the area was not going to be safe for the people, and the chiefs decided to move. Some of the Indians, possibly including Joseph and White Bird, went the rest of the way down Cottonwood Creek to the South Fork of the Clearwater, hoping to find safety in the country of Looking Glass and Red Owl. According to one story, Looking Glass met them near present-day Stites and turned them back, telling them angrily that he had warned them to restrain their young men, and that now he wanted no part of the war and did not wish them to involve him in their troubles.[46] At any rate the chiefs, uneasy about remaining on the Cottonwood, decided to go to White Bird's country, and on June 16 headed their people south to White Bird Canyon, known to them as Lahmotta. There, behind two buttes at the bottom of a long draw of treeless, rolling land, the nontreaties set up a new camp along White Bird Creek, hopeful that somehow before General Howard sent his soldiers against them, the military officer would establish contact with them and let them explain to him just what had happened.

It was an unrealistic hope. The countryside was in terror; white settlers were crying for arms, ammunition, and troops; and Howard was notifying the nation that another Indian war had broken out in the West. The murders at Salmon River and on the Camas Prairie had come as a shock to the General. All information from the Wallowa had told him that Joseph had been moving peaceably to the reservation and would be within its borders by the deadline time. In his mind Joseph had been the principal menace among the Nez Perces. He was the strongest and most stubborn of the nontreaties, and Howard had automatically thought of him as the leading force among the Indians. In that regard he had been following and had been helping to form public opinion. The Wallowa band was the proudest, the most cohesive and

46. Duncan McDonald, *New Northwest*, November 22, 1878.

ablest led, and the most demanding of all the off-reservation groups. And Joseph was its chief and spokesman. Therefore, the Wallowa leader who had been so much in the public eye during the 1870s—resisting removal to the reservation, holding his own against settlers and government agents, and making trouble that had reached to Washington—must inevitably be the key to the behavior of all the nontreaties.

The General had just arrived back at Lapwai from Portland when the outburst on the Salmon River had occurred. He had left his home on May 30 and, in an attempt to prevent the Dreamer bands of Columbia River Indians from uniting with Joseph and giving the Nez Perces support if the Wallowa Indians did try to resist going on the reservation, he had stopped at the Yakima reservation and had met again with Smohalla, Moses, and the leaders of other bands that were still living outside reserves. Warning them that if they had any plan to aid Joseph in a general uprising, they had better forget it, since the Wallowa Nez Perces were now definitely on their way to the Idaho reserve, he had wrung from them promises to go onto reservations themselves. Then he had continued on to Lewiston and Fort Lapwai, reaching the military post on June 14. Captain Perry, with two troops of the First U.S. Cavalry, F and H companies, numbering about 120 men, was still in command, and he and Agent Monteith had both reassured Howard that all was still quiet—Joseph seemed to be acting in good faith, and the Indians were coming onto the reservation without trouble.

Toward evening of the same day, however, a rider had appeared with a disquieting communication from Mount Idaho, the principal settlement on Camas Prairie, located on the higher ground of its southern border, a few miles south of Grangeville. The message, signed by Lloyd P. Brown, a man who had squatted there in 1862 when it had still been a part of the Nez Perce reservation, had told of the alarm of several settlers who lived near Rocky Canyon. The nontreaties had been gathered at that place (Tepahlewam), and had become so "insolent" and threatening that the settlers had moved over to Mount Idaho to be closer to other whites. Some of the Indians, the message had said, had boasted that they intended to fight the soldiers. About one hundred Indians had staged a grand parade and had gone through "the manoeuvres of a fight." Other Indians had come into Mount Idaho that very day and had tried to buy powder and ammunition. Brown's letter had been dated June 14, and Wahlitits and Sarpsis Ilppilp had already been embarked on their angry mission of revenge, but the whites at Mount Idaho had not yet heard of the slayings on the Salmon River. In conclusion, Brown had merely asked that soldiers be sent by Perry to remove the Indians "from the neighborhood, and quiet the feelings of the people." [47]

47. Howard, *Nez Perce Joseph*, pp. 90–91.

Encouraged by Howard, Perry had dispatched several cavalrymen and an interpreter to Mount Idaho to see what the trouble was and, if possible, to hurry the Indians along, for they should have entered the reservation that day. The group had departed from Fort Lapwai at dawn on June 15 but had soon returned, escorting two excited Indians whom they had met on the road. Both, it seemed, had belonged to reservation bands, but had been visiting the nontreaties at Tepahlewam and had heard of the killings on Salmon River. In considerable alarm, Howard and Perry had taken the Indians to the agency, and after a hasty conference with Monteith and several leaders of the treaty Nez Perces, who had still insisted that Joseph would not fight, they had sent Reuben and Joseph's father-in-law, Whisk-tasket, to talk to the Wallowa chief and see what was happening. The Indians had ridden off at full speed but had reappeared at the fort at about half past four in the afternoon with two messengers from Mount Idaho, whom they had met on their way. One was a halfblood named West, who had handed Howard a letter written by Lloyd Brown at seven that morning.

The communication had been desperate. The evening before, the people of Mount Idaho had started a courier to Lapwai; near Cottonwood House on the Camas Prairie, Indians had intercepted him, wounding him and forcing him to turn back. Soon afterward, Brown had said, some settlers in the Cottonwood area had tried to flee to Mount Idaho, but Indians had attacked them also, killing or wounding them all. At the same time, reports had arrived at Mount Idaho that whites had been murdered on Salmon River. "One thing is certain," Brown had written. "We are in the midst of an Indian war . . . We want arms and ammunition and help at once. Don't delay a moment . . . Send to Lewiston, and hasten up. You cannot imagine a people in a worse condition than they are here."

A second message, written an hour later, had been carried by the other courier, an Indian who had said that he was a brother of Looking Glass. That dispatch, also signed by Brown, had repeated the call for help and had added the information that men had just returned to Mount Idaho with the Cottonwood settlers who had been wounded the previous night. Teams also had been attacked on the prairie and had been abandoned. "Stop the stage and all 'through travelers,'" Brown had pleaded. "Give us relief . . . Hurry up; hurry!" [48]

Howard had responded at once. He had known nothing of what had been happening on the Indians' side, but the settlers' appeals had told him, as clearly as he had wished to know, that Joseph had started the war which he had apparently been so long in planning. In an ultimate act of slyness and treachery, the chief had tried to fool Howard. Instead of fighting in the Wal-

48. Ibid., pp. 94–96.

Iowa, where Whipple's soldiers had been close at hand, he had pretended to go on the reservation, but, just short of it, had struck with savagery where there were no troops.

At eight o'clock that evening Howard had started the two companies of cavalry at Lapwai, ninety-nine troopers under Captains Perry and Joel Trimble, for Mount Idaho. The rest of the garrison, a handful of soldiers, he had kept with him to defend Lapwai if that became necessary. Both the agency and the post had become the scenes of excitement and confusion, as whites and reservation Indians had crowded in from the surrounding region, wondering what was happening and fearing that Joseph and his warriors were about to attack them. Their alarm and the dangerously exposed situation in which the countryside had suddenly been plunged had moved Howard to take further measures for his security. As the troops had departed, he had sent his aide, Captain Wilkinson, hurrying by a commandeered stage to Walla Walla with news of the outbreak and with orders for reinforcements. The orders had included commands to Whipple to hasten his cavalry from the Wallowa to Lapwai; to Fort Walla Walla to rush infantry by steamer from that post to Lapwai; and to Portland to send more troops and three months' supplies to Lewiston "at once." In addition, Howard had given Wilkinson a message to telegraph from Walla Walla to General McDowell in San Francisco, detailing what had happened and ending "Think we will make short work of it." [49]

Perry, in the meantime, hurried his column of cavalry through a rainstorm to the Camas Prairie. With him were a mule train, traveling in his rear, a half-blood interpreter named Joe Rabusco, and a group of ten unarmed Nez Perces, including Whisk-tasket, who hoped to act as intermediaries between Joseph and the troops and convince the nontreaties to stop fighting. The column sloshed through mud and rain all night, and by nine in the morning of June 16, after passing a looted prairie schooner and other signs of violence, reached the abandoned Cottonwood area, where the troops rested for several hours. It was fifteen miles farther to the village of Grangeville, close to Mount Idaho, and they arrived there near evening, being greeted just outside the town by the excited settlers who had been waiting for them.

As they rested again and ate dinner, they heard the details of what had occurred on the prairie. Two days before, on the evening of June 14, a reservation Indian youth who had been visiting Joseph's people at Rocky Canyon had arrived in fear at the home of Arthur Chapman, a white man who was married to a Umatilla Indian and was well known to the Nez Perces, and had informed him that White Bird's people had begun killing the Salmon River

49. Ibid., p. 98.

settlers.[50] Chapman had ridden to Mount Idaho with the news, and a man named Lew Day had volunteered to carry the information to Lapwai. He had been too late. The nontreaties had started to break up their camp at Tepahlewam, and Indians had already begun to move across the prairie to Sapachesap. After passing Cottonwood safely, Day had been intercepted by a small group of Indians, who had fired at him and slightly wounded him. He had turned about and raced back to the Cottonwood ranch of B. B. Norton, which was used as a stage stop and tavern and was known as Cottonwood House. On his return flight he had overtaken and panicked a group of teamsters who were packing flour from Lewiston to Mount Idaho. Indians had already stopped them and had let them go without harm, but the packers had now dumped their loads and had made full haste to Mount Idaho.

At Cottonwood House Day had spread the alarm, and a frightened group of whites had piled into a wagon and started through the night, accompanying the wounded Day to Mount Idaho. Elsewhere on the road, another pair of freighters, Luther P. Wilmot and P. H. Ready, who had been hauling whiskey from Lewiston to a Mount Idaho saloon, had been chased by Indians. The two had managed to unhitch their teams and get away on fast horses, abandoning their freight to the Indians. The Nez Perces had been overjoyed with their find and had proceeded to get drunk. Soon afterward some of them, riding across the prairie, had sighted the wagon of the refugee party from Cottonwood and had given chase. They had shot the horses, bringing the wagon to a halt, and had wounded some of the terror-stricken whites. Several people had managed to get out of the wagon and had tried to escape in the darkness. Two children had got away, but the Indians had discovered the others and, inflamed by alcohol, had assaulted them brutally and killed some of them. The rest of the party had huddled behind the dead horses, keeping up a desultory fire against the Indians during the rest of the night. Several more whites had been killed and wounded before the Indians, who could have overwhelmed the members of the group if they had decided to rush them, had finally broken off the fight and ridden away. Early in the morning the children who had escaped had reached Grangeville, four miles distant, and had told the settlers of the attack. Rescuers had ridden out, and had just been able to place the survivors on horses when Indians had reap-

50. Chapman, generally called "Ad" Chapman by the settlers, knew the Whitebird area well. For some years he had lived on Whitebird Creek, at the mouth of Chapman Creek, which was named for him, and in 1871 he had applied for a permit to build a toll road across the mountains from Mount Idaho to Whitebird. His acquaintance with the Indians and his knowledge of their language made him useful as an interpreter for the whites, but as an officious, self-styled "expert" about Indian matters he left much to be desired; and the nontreaties—who were forced to accept his services after the war—held him in contempt.

peared. After an exchange of shots, the whites had got away and had finally reached Mount Idaho safely.

During that day the settlement had filled with refugees from all parts of the prairie. A volunteer unit of twenty men had been formed under the captaincy of George Shearer, a former major in the Confederate army, and its members had scouted the nearby countryside for Indians. One group of Nez Perces had been discovered raiding an abandoned house, and an Indian had been riddled with bullets and killed. He had been the Nez Perce whose body Yellow Wolf's party had retrieved.

The situation, the settlers told Perry, had been quiet this second day, June 16. The troops had entered the prairie in the morning; and at about 11 A.M., as if the Indians knew the soldiers were coming, they had been seen leaving the prairie, trailing south in the direction of the White Bird crossing of the Salmon River. But there was much to avenge. The tales of the night of terror on the prairie, the shock of the deaths of friends and neighbors, including Lew Day, who had finally been mortally wounded during the attack on the wagon, and the vivid recitals of atrocities committed on the Cottonwood party by the group of drunken Indians, had roused the settlers to fury against the Nez Perces. The people held Joseph personally to blame for the uprising and called his Wallowa Indians "Red Devils." Less than forty-five years before, Captain Bonneville, the first white man known to have entered the homeland of Joseph's people, had praised those Indians for the "loving-kindness" with which they had treated him. There were aging Nez Perces with young Joseph who could remember Bonneville in that golden age of their happiness. Now, to the settlers, they were "fiends" and "savages."

Perry rested only a few hours at Grangeville. With restraint and judicious conduct, he could still have avoided a war. His orders had been merely to protect the settlers, which was what he was doing where he was. He might have sent his treaty Nez Perces to Joseph and White Bird, found out what had actually happened, and effected a peace parley in which he could have convinced the chiefs to surrender the men who had committed the murders and take the rest of the people peaceably onto the reservation. But the settlers of Grangeville and nearby Mount Idaho crowded around him impatiently and urged him to follow the Indians at once and punish them the next morning before they could cross the Salmon River and reach the sanctuary of the mountains. Arthur Chapman, more voluble than the others, told the Captain that he knew the Indians well; they were cowardly scoundrels, he said, and the settlers could easily whip them if they had enough arms.

Perry required little urging.[51] A group of eleven citizen volunteers under

51. "The Battle of White Bird Cañon" by Brigadier General David Perry in Brady, *Northwestern Flights and Fighters*, pp. 113–14. Perry said: "it was decided that to make

George Shearer was formed, principally to show the officer the route to White Bird Creek, and at 9 P.M. the troops were on the march again. About midnight they reached the summit of Whitebird Hill and stopped once more, intending to launch their attack at dawn. As they started to dismount in the darkness, "there came from the timber, just off to one side, the shivering howl of a coyote," said one of Perry's sergeants. "That cry was an Indian signal, enough to make one's hair stand straight up." [52]

The howl came from a nontreaty sentinel, one of several who had been directed to watch the summit and warn the Indian camp of the approach of soldiers or armed settlers. A few moments later a sentinel named Seeskoomkee came racing down the canyon to the Nez Perce village, crying, "Soldiers coming this way! Soldiers coming this way!" [53] On top of the hill the troopers, the civilian volunteers, and the treaty Nez Perces waited in quiet, wondering about the coyote howl.

The route of attack did not favor Perry. The troops would have to ride down a long, grassy draw of treeless, rolling land, opening to broad perspectives, and flanked here and there by ridges and hills. At the bottom of the slope, behind two buttes, lay the Nez Perce camp. When the warning came, the headmen were uncertain what to do. All of them still wanted to make peace. There was worried talk through the early morning hours, and six men were finally detailed to take a white flag of truce forward and try to arrange a peaceful meeting when the soldiers appeared. At the same time, the old men, women, and children were directed to drive in the stock belonging to the different bands, while the warriors were told to prepare to defend the people. As dawn approached, the young men stripped for battle and, mounting their ponies, sought hiding places to the right and left of the draw to wait and see what would happen. The total manpower of the Indian bands was about 150, but many of the men were lying helplessly drunk from the whiskey they had seized on the Camas Prairie and at Benedict's store on the Salmon River, and

---

the attempt to overtake the Indians before they could effect a crossing of the Salmon River was not only the best, but the *only* thing to do. It was also suggested that the Indians would most likely begin crossing at once and I would thus strike them while divided." He therefore is seen to have had no idea of trying to contact them peacefully.

52. Narrative of Sergeant John P. Schorr of Company F, in McWhorter, *Hear Me*, p. 235.

53. McWhorter, *Yellow Wolf*, pp. 50, 52–53. Seeskoomkee (No Feet), an Indian of unknown tribal origin, had lost his feet and one hand when he had been a slave of Kamiakin's. The Yakima chief had purchased him from some tribe farther west, and one freezing night had left him outdoors, pinned by traps, to punish him for stealing. Later, Kamiakin had given him his freedom and sent him to the Nez Perces. Seeskoomkee was an expert rider, despite his handicapped condition. He went through the whole Nez Perce war and escaped to Sitting Bull's camp in Canada.

would be unable to fight. Others had no weapons or were too aged, sick, or frightened to use them. Altogether, not more than sixty or seventy Indians— armed with bows and arrows; shotguns; old, muzzle-loading, fur trade muskets; and a few modern rifles—rode out to prepare for battle.

The nature of the terrain, offering numerous hiding places for flanking attacks, should have put Perry on his guard. But Arthur Chapman and other volunteers who knew the country assured him that the slope eventually opened up into a comparatively smooth valley, and as dawn broke Perry started his men confidently forward on a horse trail that led down the draw. First Lieutenant Edward R. Theller and eight men rode ahead as a scouting guard; the unarmed treaty Nez Perces came cautiously in the rear.

As the descent continued, the advance quickened.[54] Theller, moving across the open ground, topped a ridge and sent word back to Perry that he could see the Indians. Perry immediately formed his men into line at a trot. Suddenly, as the troops rounded a small hill, the Indian truce team led by a Nez Perce named Wettiwetti Howlis (Vicious Weasel) appeared directly in front of them. Behind the men with the white flag were other Nez Perces, sitting on their horses waiting to see what would happen. There was an instant of surprise. Perry himself may never have noticed the group; he made no mention of it in his report, but said only that he saw Indians "coming out of the brush." Arthur Chapman, wearing a broad, white hat like a sombrero, and riding boldly ahead of the volunteers, did see the truce team. It was another brief moment when war might have been averted. Then the opportunity was past. Raising his rifle, Chapman fired twice at the Indian group. The Nez Perces backed away, unharmed; an elderly Indian named Otstotpoo (Fire Body) behind them fired in return, killing one of Perry's two trumpeters; and the fight was on.

As Indians began shooting from all directions, Perry hastily deployed his men in a line across the draw, placing the volunteers on a high, rocky knoll to his left. The company in the center dismounted, letting men in the rear lead their horses into a valley, and the company on the right under Trimble remained mounted.

The battle, fought without plan by the Indians, lasted only a few moments. On the left a group of sixteen Nez Perces, led by Two Moons, swept from behind a hill and galloped straight at the volunteers, sending them flying in

54. On the way down, the troopers were startled by a white woman and two small children, whom they found hiding in the brush, starving and in rags. They were Mrs. Benedict and her children, who had escaped when the Indians had killed her husband at Salmon River. She apparently pleaded with the officers not to lead the men into the canyon, as they would all be massacred. After the battle the stunned troopers picked her up at the summit and gave her a horse. McWhorter, *Hear Me*, p. 235.

panic back up the draw and exposing Perry's whole line. At the same time, Ollokot and a large group of warriors, including Wahlitits, Sarpsis Ilppilp, and a young friend named Tipyahlanah Kapskaps, all flaunting their bravery by wearing identical long red blanket coats that made them good targets for the whites, emerged from cover on the right and, firing as they came, charged into Trimble's mounted troop, frightening the horses and disorganizing the cavalrymen. The men in the center, seeing Indians and confusion all around them, gave way and made a sudden rush for their horses. Perry galloped from one side of the line to the other, trying to halt individual squads, but as soon as he faced one about, Indians charged in from its uncovered flanks and forced it to abandon its position. In a few minutes the entire command was cut into small groups, its members fighting desperately for their lives. Eighteen men under Lieutenant Theller tried to make a stand but were driven against a rocky wall and wiped out. The rest of the troop disintegrated into a rabble that fled up the canyon, pursued by Indians. On the way up, some of the nontreaties overtook the reservation Nez Perces and captured three of them. Then they joined in a chase after the whites, who were finally able to reach the summit and regroup for a stand, four miles from Mount Idaho, in a field owned by a rancher named Johnson. The Indians gradually gave up the fight and returned down the canyon to their camp, and Perry withdrew his battered troops and volunteers to Grangeville, where he sent a messenger racing to Lapwai with news of what had happened. On the battlefield lay Lieutenant Theller and thirty-three enlisted men dead, a third of the command. The Indians had had only three men wounded, one merely cut by a rock during a fall, and none killed. Equally important for the future, they retrieved sixty-three rifles and a large number of pistols from the battlefield.[55]

One year after Custer's defeat there had been another shattering Indian "massacre" of regulars. The war had started with an explosion that shocked Washington and drew people's attention in every part of the nation to Joseph and his Nez Perces.

55. A memorial marker on the Whitebird Battlefield today reads: "Before you to the westward lies the historic White Bird battle ground of the Nez Perce Indian War in which 34 men gave their lives in service for their country June 17, 1877. Beneath this shaft lies one of these men who rests where he fell." The wording, it would appear, should be changed to clarify that while the whites died bravely in the service of their country, the Indians also fought bravely *for* their country.

13

The Patriots

ON THE MORNING after the fight the embattled bands, still in their camp at the foot of White Bird Canyon, were cheered by the arrival of a small group of buffalo-hunting Nez Perces, just returned from Montana. They were some of the experienced war leaders for whom the nontreaties had been waiting, and they were led by two of the tribe's ablest and most respected plains warriors, Wahchumyus (Rainbow) and Pahkatos Owyeen (Five Wounds). With the new arrivals, the chiefs and elders of the different bands went into council. The three treaty Nez Perces who had been captured were brought before them and angrily scolded, warned that if they helped the soldiers again and were caught, they would be whipped. Then they were released and told to go home. The discussion turned to what to do next. It was obvious that Howard's soldiers would be coming after them again, and the principal problem was how to stay out of their way. Rainbow and Five Wounds suggested that the bands cross the Salmon and stay in the mountains on the other side of the river. If the troops crossed after them, they could then double back at another place on the river, cross the Camas Prairie in the soldiers' rear, and go to the Clearwater River. They could lead Howard's men a good chase, and could fight them again wherever it seemed well to do so.[1]

1. McWhorter, *Yellow Wolf*, p. 69. Ever since the close of the Nez Perce war (which some writers have termed not a war, since the Nez Perces were merely fighting defensively), numerous histories, personal reminiscences, fragmented studies, and other works have been written and published about it. No part of the tribe's history has been so thoroughly documented and argued about, and it is fair to say that it has been done almost to the point of exhaustion, so that there is little new—save interpretation, based on the knowledge of Indian culture—that can be added today. My

The plan was adopted, and the bands moved several miles up the Salmon River to a good crossing place at Horseshoe Bend near the mouth of Slate Creek. The settlers of that region were still in a stockade at the Cone ranch, and Indians, carrying flags of truce, came over on two occasions to visit the frightened whites. The Nez Perces were friendly. They told about the fight at White Bird, and some of them gave money to the settlers, saying that the soldiers were after them and they might never come back, and asking the whites to pay the debts they had run up at the Slate Creek store.[2] Then, on June 19, most of the nontreaties crossed the Salmon and ascended the high hills to a sheltered site on Deer Creek, where they established a new camp. Some thirty warriors were left behind, directed to return to Tepahlewam and keep a watch on Camas Prairie for the soldiers.

At Lapwai and Lewiston, meanwhile, all was in turmoil. The countryside had been alive with rumors of disaster even before Perry's messenger had come racing into Fort Lapwai from Grangeville, and the news he carried caused a panic. Word sped from settlement to settlement, and in all directions families abandoned their homes and, keeping a sharp lookout for hostile Indians, hurried to Lewiston. At Kamiah the missionary and other whites evacuated the region and hastened across the hills toward Lapwai with a protective guard of Christian Nez Perces led by Lawyer's son, James. Miners came down from the mountains and the upper Clearwater, and stockmen rode in from the hills, all of them filled with alarm and full of stories of armed Indians lurking along the trails and in the woods. The reservation Nez Perces, most of them as frightened as the whites, were caught between two enemies. Most of the panicked settlers regarded every Indian suspiciously, and in a series of false alarms shot at some of them and manhandled others.

Howard was stunned by the magnitude of what had happened. His first thought was of the danger of a general Indian uprising. Joseph's success

account, a synthesis of the chronology drawn from many different sources, may, within the context of the entire work I have done, provide a clearer appreciation of this climactic episode in the affairs of the Nez Perces, and of the people who participated in it. All the works on which I have based my narrative of the struggle appear in the bibliography, and some are specially cited in these notes. Of all that has been published, however, the following, in my opinion, are the most valuable for an understanding of the full conflict: McWhorter's *Hear Me, My Chiefs* and *Yellow Wolf*, especially for the Indian side; the Report of the Secretary of War (1877) and Howard's *Nez Perce Joseph* for the soldiers' side; and Beal's *I Will Fight No More Forever* for an objective summation (though with some errors and little understanding of Indian culture). Chester Anders Fee's *Chief Joseph* is an excellent detailed account of the white men's military moves, but Fee's version of the Indians' side, playing up Chief Joseph as a military genius, is entirely fictional. Many accounts of individual actions, most of them used by McWhorter and Beal, are either cited in these notes or appear in the bibliography.

2. Bailey, *River of No Return*, p. 257.

would embolden others, and although the General trusted the leaders of the Christian Nez Perces, he envisioned reservation Indians by the hundreds, as well as Dreamers from tribes throughout the interior country, marching to join the hostiles. There would be armed Indian bands everywhere, burning, looting, and killing, appearing suddenly from hiding places, and as quickly disappearing. With only twenty regulars at Fort Lapwai and Perry's battered survivors at Grangeville, he faced an emergency that might rapidly scandalize the nation.

His appraisal of the situation and desperate messages to Walla Walla, Fort Vancouver, and San Francisco for the dispatch of reinforcements set troops in motion toward Lewiston from all parts of the West. Whipple was already hurrying from the Wallowa with his cavalry, and 107 infantrymen were coming up the Snake River from Fort Walla Walla aboard the steamer *New Tenino*. By June 21 both groups had reached Howard, affording him some relief. But he needed more soldiers, and General McDowell and the War Department responded to the crisis. Units were ordered to Idaho from barracks in Washington, Oregon, and California; an outfit of artillerymen, returning to the States from Alaska, was diverted up the Columbia River; and as far away as Georgia companies of the Second U.S. infantry were entrained for the new Indian war. At the same time, the Northwestern governors called for volunteers to help the regulars. Militia companies were enrolled in Oregon and Washington and were sped toward Lewiston. In Idaho alarms spread through the entire territory, and Governor Mason Brayman was bombarded with notices of the formation of volunteer units and with appeals for arms and ammunition. The Governor's excited encouragement of home defense added to the feeling of emergency. "Hostile" Indians were seen everywhere. Settlers in the Weiser and Payette valleys south of the scene of violence were sure that Howard would push Joseph and his Nez Perces toward them; and if that did not happen, there were enough suspicious-looking Indians already in those areas to menace the whites.[3] Stockades rose in numerous places, and demands went out to round up every Indian not on a reservation. In the Boise Valley, the Owhyee River country, and all the way east across southern Idaho, militia companies prepared for war against Paiutes, Bannocks, Shoshonis, and Nez Perces—any Indian that seemed threatening—and regulars marched from Arizona and California to defend Boise.

Nor was that all. As the nontreaty bands, concerned now only with avoid-

3. See Chaffee, *Nez Perce War Letters*. Typical of the temper of the times was a letter to Governor Brayman from the settlement of Indian Valley in the Weiser Basin, June 20: "There are 50 women & children here about one half corralled at Abernathy's in Middle Weiser & the rest here . . . Every kind of business is Suspended in all these valleys. We want help in time shall we have it? . . . Those Indians are blood thirsty . . ." (pp. 92–93).

ing troops and protecting their people, congregated in the hills above the
west bank of the Salmon River, tales of the excitement in Idaho spread with
exaggeration and embroidery through eastern Washington and caused a reign
of terror in that region. Farm families in exposed areas fled to Colfax, Walla
Walla, and other towns or took refuge on islands in rivers; stockades went
up; and from the Palouse prairie to Spokane and the Colville Valley, whites
imagined themselves suddenly on the verge of a war to the death against
Dreamer bands led by Joseph. Gradually, as the Spokans and other Indians
demonstrated their peaceful intent, the panic subsided; but no part of the interior country felt fully safe until Joseph's whereabouts were known with
certainty.

Howard himself soon realized that there were no signs of a general uprising, and that the strategic placing of regulars and a posture of watchful defense by the settlers and their volunteer units would effectively deter the
danger of such a calamity. The sole enemy, with one possible exception, now
seemed to be the cluster of nontreaty bands that had whipped Perry, and that
the General—like everyone else—assumed were led by Joseph. The possible
exception was Looking Glass, whose people were still quietly going about
their business at their villages and gardens near Kooskia. But Looking Glass
had been a nontreaty, and many of the Christian Nez Perces from Kamiah,
not far from Looking Glass's village, had come into Lapwai with frightened
stories about threats that Looking Glass's people had made to them. At the
right time, the Christian Nez Perces warned, Looking Glass would attack
both the soldiers and the peaceful Nez Perces. For the moment, however,
Looking Glass could be overlooked. The job was to strike Joseph, who, un-
opposed, had freedom of movement to carry his war anywhere he wished—
back to the Wallowa and the Oregon settlements, up the Snake or Salmon
into southern Idaho, or eastward across the mountains.

As his reinforcements arrived, Howard got his plans under way for a punitive expedition against the hostiles. Colonel Alfred Sully of the 21st Infantry
was called to Lapwai to assist in the defense of the Lewiston area, and at noon
on June 22 Howard personally led 227 regulars, 20 civilian volunteers, and a
large group of packers and guides out of Fort Lapwai to search for Joseph
and beat him. The regulars included Whipple's two companies of cavalry,
five companies of the 21st Infantry, and a company of the 4th Artillery,
while the volunteers were a mounted unit from Walla Walla under the command of Captain Tom Page. For armament, Howard had two Gatling guns
and a mountain howitzer.

The expedition reached the deserted Norton ranch at Cottonwood on June
23 and lay over there the next day, which was Sunday, while Howard tried
to ascertain where Joseph was. During the day Perry arrived from Grange-

ville with information that the nontreaties were still in camp near White Bird Creek. The next morning Howard sent his infantry to Johnson's ranch near the head of White Bird Canyon, where Perry had first been able to make a stand after his defeat, and with Perry and the cavalry the General rode to Grangeville and Mount Idaho. There he enlisted some citizen volunteers to guide Trimble and a troop of cavalrymen via Florence and a circuitous route through the mountains to join the Slate Creek settlers, who were still with the Florence miners in their stockade, and thus get behind Joseph's people in the south. After reassuring the families at Mount Idaho that he would soon take care of the Nez Perces, Howard and the rest of the cavalrymen joined the infantry at Johnson's ranch, and the next morning went to the head of White Bird Canyon.

Nez Perce scouts had already sighted Howard's men, and taking a shortcut across the mountains, Yellow Wolf and another Indian had reached and crossed the Salmon about two miles below White Bird Creek. Climbing a butte that overlooked the nontreaties' camp, they waved a red blanket, the signal that the soldiers were coming.[4] Howard, meanwhile, sent his infantry and a company of cavalry, preceded by skirmishers and covered by flankers, cautiously down the canyon. The artillerymen and the second company of cavalry stayed with Whipple and Howard at the summit, while the Walla Walla volunteers, guided by Arthur Chapman, scouted the hills to the right of the canyon. The Indian camp at the foot of the hill was seen to have been abandoned, and as no Indians were sighted, most of the day was spent in finding and burying the bodies of the men who had fallen in the battle on June 17. Despite stories that circulated to the contrary, none of the bodies, according to the most reliable sources among the troops, were discovered to have been mutilated.[5]

In the afternoon Chapman and Page, riding out on a promontory along the Salmon, sighted the Indians across the river. The report of the nontreaties' new position placed Howard in a quandary. It started to rain heavily, and he moved his command back to Johnson's ranch for the night, marveling at Joseph's tactics. Clever movements, such as this one, by the Indians, which Howard ascribed to the Wallowa chief's brilliance and which he publicized in his reports and in briefings to war correspondents who began to reach the theater of war, soon created the image of an Indian Napoleon. "The leadership of Chief Joseph was indeed remarkable," he wrote of this first surprise information given him by Chapman and Page. "No general could have chosen a safer position, or one that would be more likely to puzzle and obstruct a pursuing foe. If we present a weak force he can turn upon it. If we

4. McWhorter, *Yellow Wolf*, pp. 63–64.
5. See McWhorter, *Hear Me*, pp. 256–59.

make direct pursuit he can go southward toward Boise, for at least thirty miles, and then turn our left. He can go straight to his rear, and cross the Snake at Pittsburg Landing. He can go on down the Salmon, and cross at several places, and then turn either to the left, for his old haunts in the Wallowa Valley, or to the right, and pass our flank, threatening our line of supply, while he has, at the same time, a wonderful natural barrier between him and us in the Salmon . . ." [6]

Despite his knowledge that the Indians could recross the Salmon in his rear and cut his supply lines, Howard chose to risk that gamble and plunge after the game. After sending Perry and a group of men back to Lapwai for more ammunition and supplies, he took his command—now reinforced by 175 more infantry and artillerymen rushed from Fort Lapwai—down the canyon the next day, June 27, and prepared to cross the Salmon. From their position along the river, the troops could see Nez Perce scouts on the hills across the stream, and could hear them shouting back and forth to each other. At one point, as Howard's men were trying to carry a cable across the river in a boat, a group of mounted Indians rode out from canyons and from behind buttes and came charging down the slope. They pulled up opposite the soldiers, and when James Reuben, the Christian Nez Perce who was serving as a scout for Howard, called across to them that they were cowards, they shook their rifles and yelled back to him that they were fighting for their homes, their women, and children. "Come over," they taunted him. "We will scalp you . . . You are growing fat, eating Government food!" Some of the soldiers began shooting, and the Indians fired back. None of the bullets found a mark, and a few moments later, when the Nez Perces saw Howard's artillerymen coming down the bluff with the howitzer, they broke off the fight. "We will give them this road. Do not bother them," their leaders counseled. "Let them come across . . . If they come to our side, we can fight them if we want." The Indians scurried up the slope again and returned to the bands. That night the nontreaties moved their position. While the warriors remained behind to watch for soldiers, the headmen and the people climbed higher into the mountains and made a new camp.

Four days passed before Howard was ready to cross the river. In the meantime, Captain Tom Page's Walla Walla volunteers went home, relieved by a new unit that arrived from Dayton, Washington, under Lieutenant Colonel George Hunter. On June 29 Howard received disquieting information about his rear. "Positive information is obtained that Looking Glass, who, with his people, has stood aloof from the hostiles, has been furnishing reinforcements to them of at least twenty warriors, and that he proposed to join them in person, with all his people, on the first favorable opportunity," he wrote. This

6. Howard, *Nez Perce Joseph*, pp. 145–46.

Route of the Indians

WASHINGTON / IDAHO

SNAKE R.

POTLATCH R.

CLEARWATER R.

NORTH FORK

OROFINO CR.

•Pierce

Lewiston

Lapwai Agency

Fort Lapwai

LAPWAI CR.

NEZ PERCE RESERVATION

Weippe Prairie

LOLO TRAIL

Road from Lapwai to Mt. Idaho

Kamiah

LAWYER'S CR.

Mt. Misery

[Kooskia]

Attack on Looking Glass's Village, JULY 1

SNAKE RIVER

GRANDE RONDE R.

WASHINGTON

OREGON

JOSEPH CR.

Cottonwood Fight JULY 4·5

[Stites]

Sapachesap

MIDDLE FK.

Rains' Defeat

Cottonwood House (Norton's Ranch)

Craig Billy Crossing

SALMON R.

BILLY CR.

COTTONWOOD CR.

Nez Perce Camp JULY 11

CLEAR CR.

Battle of Clearwater, JULY 11-12

GRAVE CR.

ROCKY CANYON

Tolo Lake

Grangeville

DIVIDE CR.

Tepahlewam Rendezvous

Johnson's Ranch

Mt. Idaho

Joseph's Crossing of Snake

SNAKE RIVER

Battle of Whitebird, JUNE 17

Whitebird Hill

WHITE BIRD CR.

SOUTH FORK

TULLY CR.

CORRAL CR.

FENCE CR.

LIGHTNING CR.

DEER CR.

Horseshoe Bend

IMNAHA R.

Pittsburg Landing

SLATE CR.

SALMON R.

WALLOWA VALLEY

OREGON / IDAHO

•Florence

10. THE OUTBREAK OF WAR, 1877

information, which he later rephrased to read, "Forty bucks have just left him [Looking Glass] to join Joseph. He is only waiting his favorable chance," was given him by "our friendly Indians" and was either a deliberate falsehood or the figment of some frightened Indian's imagination. But Howard, about to cross the river, believed the worst and, taking no chances, ordered Whipple's two cavalry companies to take the Gatling guns and arrest Looking Glass "and all other Indians who may be encamped with or near him, between the forks of the Clearwater, and turn all prisoners over, for safe-keeping, to the volunteer organization at Mount Idaho." [7]

Whipple and his men rode off late in the night of June 29 for Looking Glass's village. The next day some of Howard's men tested the Salmon. Colonel Hunter and two companions swam across, carefully reconnoitered the hills, and returned to report that the Indians had moved farther into the mountains and the army could probably cross without interference. A group of regulars then made the crossing in a skiff, carrying a line to the other shore, and a short time later advance units ferried across in two boats, fastened by ropes and rings to the cable, while other men commenced forcing horses and mules into the current. During the day another volunteer group, a Lewiston, Idaho, company under Colonel Edward McConville, arrived and was sent to Slate Creek to join Trimble's men and help guard Howard's southern flank from a surprise attack during the main crossing of the river the next day.[8]

Once again the Indians knew what Howard was doing. While the troops were testing the river, the Nez Perce chiefs gave orders to the people to pack up and prepare to break camp. The pine-covered country they would travel through was extremely rough, and to hurry out of the soldiers' way they would have to leave much behind. Caches were made, and large stores of provisions and equipment, including flour, roots, sugar, axes, bags, and kettles, were hidden along Deer Creek.[9] The next morning, when all was ready, scouts were detailed to stay behind and watch the soldiers, while the main body of Nez Perces started across the high, mountainous plateau. Herding between 2,500 and 3,500 horses, and shepherding women, children, old peo-

7. Report of the Secretary of War (1877), *1*, 120. Howard, *Nez Perce Joseph,* pp. 148–49.

8. McConville's Report to Governor Brayman, August 1877, in Chaffee, *Nez Perce War Letters,* pp. 62–63.

9. About a month later, long after the Indians had gone from the area, Mount Idaho volunteers under Luther P. Wilmot scoured the Deer Creek campsite and discovered many of the caches. In frank reports to Governor Brayman, written on August 3, Wilmot told how his men destroyed what the Indians had left, and complained that "a great many persons," finding horses that the Indians had lost in their flight, were "getting up and branding" the animals to keep them for themselves (Chaffee, *Nez Perce War Letters,* pp. 73–74).

ple, and the sick, the bands paralleled the Salmon River northward and in a remarkable journey of some thirty-six hours hurried almost twenty-five miles over steep, rugged country, finally descending to the Salmon at a place known as the Craig Billy Crossing.[10] In their rear, far up the river, the scouts had seen Howard's men finally get across the Salmon soon after the bands had left Deer Creek. Chasing after the families, they brought word that the soldiers were now on the same side of the river. The chiefs were satisfied; at Craig Billy Crossing they would recross the Salmon and leave the troops in the mountains.

The day of the Nez Perces' departure from their Deer Creek camp, and of Howard's crossing of the Salmon, was July 1, a Sunday, and violence of the most vicious and stupid kind was flaring elsewhere. After leaving Howard on the night of June 29, Whipple had hurried his cavalrymen to Mount Idaho, where he had picked up about twenty citizen volunteers under D. B. Randall to guide him to Looking Glass's village near the junction of Clear Creek and the Middle Fork of the Clearwater River, just above the present town of Kooskia. Whipple had wanted to arrive at the Indian village by dawn of July 1, but the sun was already up when he reached the wooded crest of the hills above the unsuspecting settlement. He dismounted his cavalrymen, left his Gatling guns on top of the hill, and started the troops and volunteers down the slope in a skirmish line toward the village, which lay on the opposite side of the creek.

It was a prosperous settlement of tipis, horse and cattle herds, and culti-vated gardens, plowed and planted with potatoes, corn, squash, melons, and other crops. Here and there was rail fencing. Some members of the band, which was made up of about forty men and perhaps three times that number of women and children, possessed milk cows. Most of the people were Dreamers and had no use for the Christian Nez Perces; but Looking Glass had convinced them that they had nothing to gain by a war, and he had kept them aloof from the difficulties of the other nontreaties.

As the whites started down the hill, the Indians saw them. Immediately the Sunday morning calm of the village was shattered. Looking Glass was in his tipi, having breakfast with some of his men. He sent one of them, Peopeo Tholekt (Bird Alighting), to tell the troops that his people were living peace-fully and wanted no trouble. The Indian crossed the creek and met the whites part way up the hill. Whipple was surrounded by the Mount Idaho volun-

10. This crossing, at the mouth of Billy Creek, had once been the home of the Nez Perce Indian known as Salmon River Billy. His son, Luke Billy, now lived there in a cabin. But a ferry had also existed at the site during the gold rush, and a good trail still led from the crossing toward Craig Mountain and the main road between Lewiston and Camas Prairie. Hence the name of the place, which was also called Craig's Ferry.

teers, who were itching for revenge for all that had happened to them on Camas Prairie. They gave Peopeo Tholekt little chance to talk. One of them shoved his gun against the Indian's ribs and demanded, "You Looking Glass?" When the Indian convinced them that the chief was in his tipi, one of the volunteers named Washington Holmes, who spoke Nez Perce, ordered him angrily to go back and get him. Peopeo Tholekt rode back quickly, but the Indians in the village had seen how the whites had threatened him, and Looking Glass said he did not trust the soldiers. He asked Peopeo Tholekt and another man to return to the troops and urge them once more to go away. It did no good. The two Indians planted a white cloth on a pole between Looking Glass's tipi and the creek and rode out bravely to the waiting soldiers. Again, the volunteer insisted that Peopeo Tholekt was Looking Glass, and made a motion to shoot him. The interpreter interceded, however, and Whipple and several of the other men told the Indians to lead them into the camp. They rode to the white flag, when Whipple halted and ordered Peopeo Tholekt to get the chief. Peopeo Tholekt entered Looking Glass's tipi and was talking to him again when a shot rang out. A volunteer, apparently recognizing an Indian against whom he had a grudge, had fired at him, wounding him in the left ankle.

The shot galvanized the trigger-happy volunteers. Whipple and the men waiting to see Looking Glass raced back to the other side of the stream, and firing broke out all along the hillside. Whipple did nothing to stop it, and as the bullets peppered the village, Indian men, women, and children emerged from the tipis in terror and scattered in all directions. Some grabbed horses and galloped away, and others ran up the hills and hid. Several of the people were wounded, but managed to drag themselves into the brush. One Indian woman flung herself into the Clearwater with her child, and both were drowned in the swift current. After a few moments the soldiers and volunteers advanced down the hillside, still firing sharply, and, charging across the stream, entered the deserted village. Chagrined by the escape of Looking Glass and his people, Whipple ordered the settlement and its gardens destroyed. Men tried to fire the leather tipis, but were only able to burn two of them. They trampled the gardens, smashed, battered, and ripped the Indians' possessions, and rounded up some cattle and more than 700 head of horses, which they drove back with them to Mount Idaho.

It was a senseless and inexcusable attack. Whipple later reported to Howard that "an opportunity was given Looking-Glass to surrender, which he, at first, promised to accept, but afterwards defiantly refused . . ." But Whipple never talked to Looking Glass, or gave any of the Indians an opportunity to convince him of their genuine desire to stay out of the war. As a result of the precipitous action, Peopeo Tholekt said, "Of course that settled it. We had to have a war." After the soldiers and volunteers had left, congratulating themselves on the day's work, the Indians came back from the hills and other hiding places to the ruined village. Led by Looking Glass, who now burned with hatred against Howard's soldiers, they gathered what possessions they could salvage and, accompanied by Koolkool Snehee, who had also tried to remain at peace but was now willing to fight, prepared to join the other nontreaties in war against the whites. The result of the day's action was clear to Howard, when he heard about it. "Of course," he wrote, "we thus stirred up a new hornet's nest." [11]

Having a belligerent Looking Glass in his rear, ready to pounce on the Camas Prairie and cut Howard's supply line to Lewiston, might have concerned Whipple that evening, but there were more problems ahead. Near Mount Idaho, at midnight, he received a message from Howard, who had crossed the Salmon River that day, ordering him to proceed at once to Norton's abandoned ranch at Cottonwood, join Perry, who would be coming from Lapwai with supplies, and watch for Indians in case, under pressure from Howard's force, they recrossed the Salmon and came up again on the Camas Prairie. The next morning Whipple marched his regulars to Cottonwood and had his men prepare rifle pits and defensive positions.

It was now July 2, and during the same day the nontreaties, well out ahead of Howard, who was just starting his pursuit of them through the mountains, crossed the Salmon at the Craig Billy Crossing.[12] Leaving the river, they moved up to a sagebrush flat known as Aipadass, west of Cottonwood, and camped for the night. Early the next morning two youthful citizens, William Foster and Charles Blewett, dispatched by Whipple as scouts to look for signs of Indians, came on a warrior named Seeyakoon Ilppilp (Red Spy), who was standing guard at some distance from the Nez Perce camp. In an exchange of shots the Indian killed Blewett, and Foster raced back in alarm to Cottonwood to warn Whipple. The captain immediately ordered a squad of ten cavalrymen under Second Lieutenant Sevier M. Rains to return to the area with Foster and another citizen guide, scout the strength and position of the Indians, and rescue Blewett if he were still alive. Almost simultaneously, Red Spy, who had apparently pursued Foster far enough to glimpse Whipple's position at Cottonwood, had returned to the Indian camp with news that soldiers were close by. A party under the experienced war leaders, Rainbow and Five Wounds, set off at once to see what the situation was. Topping a ridge that overlooked the prairie, the Indians sighted Whipple's tents at

11. The account of Whipple's attack on Looking Glass is drawn principally from McWhorter, *Hear Me*, pp. 262–74, which gives versions by both Indian and white participants. See also Howard, *Nez Perce Joseph*, p. 149.

12. See below, p. 676.

Cottonwood. They dismounted quickly and prepared for battle, unwrapping their medicine packs, "wherein lay our strength," said Two Moons, and singing "in low tone our war songs, derived from the Spirit Powers." [13]

As they started forward over hilly ground, furrowed here and there by gulches, the Indians saw Rains's column approaching in their direction. The Nez Perces broke into a charge and were almost on the column when the cavalrymen saw their danger and turned and fled. The troopers were too late. Six of them were shot dead from their horses. The rest galloped up a hill and flung themselves among some rocks to try to make a stand. The Indians halted and, dropping out of sight in a ravine, circled around the soldiers. One of the warriors, Tipyahlanah Kapskaps (Strong Eagle, one of the trio of "red coats" at the White Bird battle), ran to another position and, popping into the open by a dead tree, acted as a decoy and drew the soldiers' fire. A moment later, the main body of Indians crawled up behind the whites and killed them all. The warriors, according to the Nez Perces, were then ready to go on and attack Whipple's camp, but Rainbow and Five Wounds told them that they had achieved enough for that day, and directed them to return to the bands.

In the meantime Whipple had started his whole command on the trail of his scouting detachment, intending to attack the Nez Perces when Rains found them. He was shocked when he came on the scene of the fight and discovered every member of the unit slain. His report to Howard said that Indians in large force were still in sight but disappeared when he had his men dismount and deploy for battle. At any rate he recovered the bodies of the thirteen dead men, and, shaken by recognition of his perilous situation—separated from Howard and exposed to the main body of nontreaties in his front and Looking Glass in his rear—withdrew to Cottonwood. Ordering his men to stay on the alert in their rifle pits, he dispatched two men to Howard with news of what had happened. That night other couriers arrived at his position from Fort Lapwai with word that Perry and a squad of about twenty men were on their way with a train of ammunition and supplies. Fearing that the Indians would overwhelm the small group, Whipple hurried his entire command at dawn the next morning, July 4, toward Lapwai to meet and protect Perry. The two units met eight miles out on the road and started together for Cottonwood, being joined after a few miles by Arthur Chapman, George Shearer, and four other citizens, who had heard of the fate of the Rains detachment from Whipple's messengers to Howard and had ridden anxiously from Grangeville to discover how serious the situation was. The

13. Two Moons's account of the fight, in McWhorter, *Hear Me*, pp. 282–83. My version is based on McWhorter's *Hear Me*; his "Yellow Wolf," pp. 71–74; and Howard's *Nez Perce Joseph*, p. 151.

citizens started back to Cottonwood with the troops, and shortly afterward the men began to see Indians on the surrounding hills. By the time the members of the column reached Cottonwood, warriors were all about them. As senior officer, Perry took command, and during the rest of the day the troops held off the Nez Perces with a desultory fire from their rifle pits. Late in the afternoon, according to Shearer, some of the Indians almost overran the pits, but a few bursts from Whipple's Gatling gun finally induced them to break off the engagement and return to their camp, and the skirmish ended without casualties.[14]

The next day the story was different. The headmen decided to move their camp across the Camas Prairie toward the South Fork of the Clearwater River, stopping for the night at a spring called Piswah Ilppilp Pah (Place of Red Rock). It would be a dangerous journey; the families, driving their large herds of stock, would have to pass between Grangeville and Cottonwood, moving directly across the front of the soldiers' entrenchments at Norton's ranch. Orders were given to a group of about fourteen young Indians to precede the main body and act as a protective screen between the troops and the families. The rest of the warriors, including the older and more experienced fighting men, would shepherd the bands across the prairie, ready to fight if the troops broke past the younger men. At almost the same time that the Nez Perce families started boldly down the mountain, driving their stock toward the prairie, a group of seventeen citizen volunteers led by D. B. Randall—whose men had triggered the attack on Looking Glass's village five days before—left Mount Idaho to help the soldiers at Cottonwood. Whipple's two messengers to Howard, now returning to Cottonwood from the General, were on the prairie road ahead of them and, when within three miles of Cottonwood, sighted the Indian screening party. Although chased by the Nez Perces, they reached Perry's rifle pits safely. The seventeen mounted men behind them were less fortunate. As they came down the road, they suddenly saw the Indian screening group drawn up in a line across their route. Randall halted his volunteers a moment, then ordered them to charge through the Nez Perces and race to Perry's camp, which they could see three miles away.

The decision cost Randall his life. The men charged down the road, and the Nez Perces gave way, letting them through. Then the warriors galloped after them, pulling up on them and forcing the volunteers to veer off the road and run for a place to make a stand. The whites were able to establish a defensive position, and from eleven in the morning until mid-afternoon kept up a fire that held off the Indians. Randall and another volunteer were killed, and two others were wounded. None of the Indians was killed, but two were

14. "The Skirmish at Cottonwood," an eyewitness account by George Shearer, ed. Francis Haines, *Idaho Yesterdays, 2* (Spring, 1958), pp. 6–7.

wounded, and one of them, an older man named Weesculatat (sometimes called Mimpow Owyeen, or Wounded Mouth), died that evening, the first Nez Perce to lose his life in battle. Watching from Cottonwood, Perry and his troops could see the plight of the volunteers, but despite the fact that two of Randall's men got through to the rifle pits and pleaded for help, Perry refused to move out and risk another White Bird debacle. Finally, after George Shearer dashed safely by himself from the rifle pits to Randall's beleaguered citizens, Perry ordered Whipple and some of the troops to go to the volunteers' relief. By the time they reached Randall's men, Weesculatat's bad wound had convinced the Indians to break off the fight, and they were withdrawing. Far in the distance, the main body of Nez Perces and their livestock, having first moved south toward Rocky Canyon to get away from the fighting, were now hurrying east across the prairie past Grangeville, leaving scouts to protect their rear. The screening party had done its job, and the Nez Perces had the Camas Prairie to themselves. As Whipple's men returned to Cottonwood with Randall's volunteers and the dead and wounded, the young Nez Perce fighters left the scene of the skirmish and, carrying Weesculutat, who had paid with his life for his people's safety, rode hurriedly after the bands.

Perry's tardiness in coming to the aid of the volunteers caused hard feelings against him among the civilians, and Perry later faced a court-martial for not having sent help earlier to Randall. Although personal reminiscences of the episode by citizen participants described the captain as having been rattled and frightened during the siege of the volunteers, the court-martial exonerated him with the judgment that, in refusing to endanger his supplies for Howard at Cottonwood, he had acted correctly.[15] For the moment, however, despite bitterness toward the officer on the part of Randall's men, the situation on the prairie was too tense for recriminations. That evening at six o'clock a mounted troop of Lewiston volunteers under Edward McConville and Dayton, Washington, volunteers under George Hunter, fifty men in all, rode up as reinforcements. They had been with Howard across the Salmon River, but the General had sent them to help guard the prairie as soon as he had received Whipple's message about the wiping out of Rains's detachment. Perry now had to inform the newcomers that the Nez Perces had slipped past him and were well on their way to the Clearwater, probably to link up with Looking Glass. Nothing had gone right anywhere. The Indians had outmaneuvered everybody.

Howard himself that evening could not have been in a more awkward situation. He had crossed the Salmon on July 1 and, ordering Trimble and Mc-

15. See Shearer, p. 7, and Luther Wilmot's account in McWhorter, *Yellow Wolf,* pp. 80–83.

Conville's volunteers to join him from Slate Creek, had found the Nez Perce trail through the mountains and had started in pursuit of the Indians. It had been a tortuous, floundering, and vain march after an enemy who, on July 2, the very day that Howard got moving, had already recrossed the Salmon almost twenty-five miles away. Where the Indians had been able to move quickly, even with their women and children and huge herd of livestock, the troops had found it rugged going, clambering painfully to the plateau and then marching laboriously across the precipitous, pine-covered mountains, part of the way through driving rain and mud. On the evening of July 4 Whipple's messengers had reached the General with the dispiriting news that the quarry was across the Salmon and threatening the Camas Prairie, and Howard had ordered McConville and Hunter and their volunteers to descend to the Salmon, cross at Rocky Canyon, and hasten to Whipple's assistance. The volunteers had made the crossing the next morning, but on starting up Rocky Canyon had run into rearguard scouts of the main body of Nez Perces, who were then edging away from Cottonwood and preparing to strike eastward across the Camas Prairie. McConville had avoided an ambush by taking his volunteers up another route, farther south, to Johnson's ranch, and later in the day, after the fighting at Cottonwood had ended and the Nez Perces had crossed the prairie, he had headed north and had finally reached Perry.

On the same day Howard and the main body of the army had arrived at the Craig Billy Crossing, where the Nez Perces had ferried the Salmon three days earlier. Howard was desperate. The Indians were now at large, free to move anywhere they chose, able to threaten the settlements and his own line to Lapwai, and opposed—if they were opposed—only by small, uncoordinated detachments of regulars and volunteers, any one of which might be trapped in a repetition of the White Bird disaster. What was worse, he could not get his own troops across the Salmon at the Craig Billy Crossing. The river was boiling and churning, and he had no boats. He had his artillerymen tear down Luke Billy's hut on the shore and make a large raft from its timbers, but the swift current snapped a restraining cable and swept the raft away. There was nothing to do but turn around and go back over the entire dreadful mountain trail to the White Bird Crossing, where he had left his boats. The wearying and frustrating retrograde march took him three days. By the evening of July 8, the advance units of his column, having ferried back across the Salmon and trooped up White Bird hill, appeared again at Grangeville. The rest of the soldiers, some of them riding in farm wagons rushed by settlers to the White Bird Crossing, trailed in soon afterward.

Howard was back where he had started, having had to retrace every step of his route since he had left the Camas Prairie on June 27. The failure of his punitive expedition, coming on the heels of the White Bird battle, exposed him to a burst of angry criticism. Newspapers and civilians, stung by the Nez Perces' victories on the Camas Prairie, heaped accusations of incompetence on the General and his officers. At the same time, the public, first in areas remote from danger but eventually even in the theater of war itself, began to accord grudging praise to the Nez Perces, and especially to Joseph, who was supposedly directing the Indians' movements. Howard was already of the opinion that he had a shrewd and able strategist opposed to him, but the public also could now see how the Indians had fooled the army, and, following the same line of thinking as Howard, ascribed the Nez Perces' "masterful" success to the intelligence of the Wallowa chieftain who had been so well publicized before the outbreak of the war. In addition, reports from fair-minded people at Slate Creek and other scenes of conflict related that the Nez Perces had been conducting themselves in an unusual manner for Indians "on the warpath," refraining from scalping or mutilating bodies, treating white women and noncombatants with humanity and even friendliness, and otherwise adhering to what was considered the white man's code of war. The giving of money to the settlers by Nez Perce warriors to pay their debts at Slate Creek, for instance, was considered unprecedented, and this and other examples of surprisingly ethical behavior were credited to Joseph, whose dignity and decency at prewar councils were recalled by those who had attended them.[16]

The truth was that the Nez Perces' military successes were resulting from a combination of overconfidence and serious mistakes on the part of army and volunteer leaders, the vast and rugged terrain that gave the Indians great freedom of movement and made pursuit difficult, the democratic and group aspects of Indian culture that nurtured individual initiative and self-reliance—though always in behalf of the group—and, to a very great extent, the Nez Perces' intense courage and patriotic determination to fight for their rights and protect their people. Indian strategy and tactics had played a strong role, but at each step of the way these were discussed and agreed upon in councils of all the chiefs and experienced war leaders and were carried out on the field by the fighters. Joseph sat in the councils, but since he had never been a war chief, his advice carried less weight than that of men like Five Wounds, Rainbow, and Toohoolhoolzote. On the march and in battle Joseph, like the much older White Bird, took charge of the old men, women, and children, an assignment of vital importance and sacred trust, while Ollokot and the experi-

16. A typical expression of public sentiment, recorded even as early as June 26 before Howard's ill-starred Salmon River expedition, was that of a settler named E. B. Whitman, who wrote the Lewiston *Teller:* "Chief Joseph's magnanimity may save us, and that is all" (Beal, *I Will Fight No More Forever*, p. 71).

enced warriors led the young men on guard duty or in combat. The whites had no way of knowing this, and, as events continued to unfold, the legend that Nez Perce strategy was planned and executed by one man, Joseph, was spread far and wide by the hapless forces opposing him and was accepted without question by newspaper writers and the American public.

The humaneness of the Nez Perces, at the same time, did not surprise the few persons in the Northwest who best knew the tribe and its history. For almost fifty years the Nez Perces had been allies and companions of the Americans. They had lived with trappers, studied under missionaries, aided American military forces, and frequented the settlements and homes of miners and farmers. The white men's way had been working to "civilize" the Nez Perces since the days of the Indians' grandfathers. But a more fundamental humanity of their own was in their marrow. Lewis and Clark had noted it; Warren Ferris and the mountain men had written about it; and Bonneville and Samuel Parker, among others, had lauded it. The Nez Perces had needed no white men to give them a code of decency. Their conduct stemmed from their own group notions of right and wrong, and the idea that Joseph was responsible for the behavior of the warring bands was simply another part of the gathering myth.

At Grangeville, Howard had no time to respond to his critics. On July 6, the day after the skirmish at Cottonwood, McConville's volunteers had escorted Randall's survivors and their dead and wounded to Mount Idaho, and two days later, after organizing the Grangeville, Mount Idaho, Lewiston, and Dayton, Washington, volunteers into a single "regiment," McConville, its new commander, had led its members, some eighty strong, after the Indians. McConville had sent a message to Howard that his small group would pick up the trail of the Nez Perces and keep them under surveillance until the regulars could catch up and help surround them. But the restless volunteers had become disgusted with the troops and had undoubtedly hoped to find and defeat the Indians on their own.[17] By the time Howard reached Grangeville, the impatience of McConville's men had led them into another debacle.

Since the fight with Randall's party, the Nez Perces had crossed to the South Fork of the Clearwater, setting up a camp on the flats along the west

17. McConville's dispatch to Howard apparently expected the General's approval of his movement, but at the same time it must have indicated the volunteers' impatience with the army's bumbling efforts. See Howard's comment: "The enterprising volunteers, who had become a little disgusted with the slowness of regulars, and angry at their own fearful discomfiture near Cottonwood, had suddenly left us and started on an independent movement" (*Nez Perce Joseph*, p. 155). On July 8 McConville recorded that he received a message from Howard, "confirming my movements, and directing me to keep him informed of the where abouts of the Indians" (Chaffee, *Nez Perce War Letters*, p. 65).

side of the river at the mouth of Cottonwood Creek, just above the present town of Stites. Soon after their arrival, Looking Glass and his entire band had joined them, giving them another forty fighting men but also raising to more than 500 the number of women and children who would have to be protected from the soldiers. A large number of Indians had then trailed off to Kamiah, where they had forced James, Lawyer and some of the treaty Indians to ferry them across the Clearwater to a Dreamer religious meeting with some Nez Perces who had just returned from Montana. When the meeting had ended, the Indians had heard that a group of white soldiers had been seen on Doty Ridge, atop a round hill called Possossono (Water Passing, named for a nearby spring), near the juncture of the South and Middle forks of the Clearwater.

The soldiers were McConville's volunteers, who had arrived from Mount Idaho the previous evening, July 8. They had already discovered the Indians' camp five miles farther south, but had realized that they were not strong enough to attack it. Sending a dispatch to Howard to come quickly, McConville had had his men dig rifle pits and prepare to defend the hill. Now the Indians had learned of the volunteers' presence.

Nez Perces under Rainbow, Five Wounds, and Ollokot rode up and all through the afternoon of July 9 ringed McConville's position, exchanging long distance shots with his men. At dusk the Indians withdrew, but several hours after dark, they came back, crawling closer to the rifle pits, maintaining an harassing fire on the besieged whites, and finally making a sortie on their horse herd and running off some of the animals. At daylight the Indians were gone again, but at seven the weary volunteers sighted them returning once more, this time forming a line as if preparing to charge. The Nez Perces changed their minds, however, and eventually rode away, and late that afternoon a small group of civilians under George Shearer, sent by Howard to assist McConville, broke past a number of Indians who tried to intercept them and reinforced the volunteers.

The battle by then was over. Although there had been no casualties, Mc-Conville's men were frightened and tired and had already dubbed their hill Mount Misery. McConville kept them in their positions through another night, waiting to hear from Howard, who had told Shearer that he would soon arrive with the full army to fall on the Nez Perces. By the morning of July 11, however, the volunteers were running out of provisions, and at noon, when McConville had still had no word from the General, he gave them the order to return to Mount Idaho. The Nez Perces had taken forty-three horses from the command, many of them animals seized by the volunteers during the attack on Looking Glass's village. Of those the Indians had not taken, most were inferior horses. The men placed all their saddles on the lank animals, and the unit marched disconsolately back to Mount Idaho.

The failure of their expedition depressed the volunteers, but, unknown to them, their efforts were to have a beneficial result. For several days the Indians had focused their attention on these men, possibly thinking that Howard and his army would soon come marching eastward across Camas Prairie to join them. Scouts had watched in that direction, but no regulars had appeared. Finally, the Indians had relaxed their vigilance, keeping an eye on the volunteers but making no effort to drive them away.

This lack of belligerence was a reflection of the state of mind of the Indians. There were five bands now in the camp by the South Fork of the Clearwater, those of Joseph, White Bird, Looking Glass, Toohoolhoolzote, and Husishusis Kute. There was no such thing as a unified command. Each band looked to its own headman for advice and counsel. At a time of action, any warrior might follow any individual war chief he respected, and at the same time any man might refrain from fighting. Under these conditions there had been considerable unity of purpose during the periods of stress and chase through which the bands had passed. But ever since the murders on the Salmon River, the bands had essentially been engaged in maneuvers to evade and escape the soldiers. Individuals had participated in small belligerent actions; but each large engagement, directed by the war leaders, had been fought to defend the people. This aim still persisted. The bands were running, and the chiefs had no thought but to stay out of the way of the troops. The camp on the South Fork of the Clearwater was in a bad strategic position if a battle had to be fought over it. But the bands had already cached many of their supplies and possessions and, with their scouts watching toward the west for Howard, planned to be ready to continue their retreat if the soldiers were sighted. Meanwhile, they saw no sense in risking the lives of their warriors against McConville's men on Doty Ridge. As long as the volunteers were pinned there, without adequate horses, they were harmless. The presence of the volunteers, in a way, therefore lulled the Indians and left them open to a danger they did not foresee.

The peril to them, in turn, developed accidentally. McConville's message that he had found the Nez Perce camp galvanized Howard, and without delaying at Grangeville he took up the pursuit of the Indians. His command, including the cavalry of Perry and Whipple, who joined him from Cottonwood, now numbered four hundred regulars and more than 150 civilian scouts, volunteers, and packers. The army was guided by Arthur Chapman, who knew the Camas Prairie well but who for some reason—despite McConville's call for help—led the troops along a more southerly line, so that they reached the South Fork of the Clearwater well above the Nez Perce camp and McConville's force on Doty Ridge. The route of march may well have been by design, but neither Howard nor anyone else ever explained why the army did not go straight to McConville's position. A hint that Howard may have known what he was doing exists in a single manuscript account by Luther Wilmot, one of McConville's men, who with a companion left the volunteers on Doty Ridge and found Howard's camp far south on the river. There, Wilmot said, he worked out a battle plan with the General, by which Howard would circle the Indians and attack them from the east side of the Clearwater while McConville would strike them simultaneously from the west. Wilmot and his companion, however, got into an argument with Perry over the officer's past actions and, riding off in a huff, failed to get the message to McConville. The latter, as we have seen, withdrew therefore to Mount Idaho, uninformed of what was happening.[18]

Whatever the facts were, Howard, at any rate, crossed the South Fork, climbed his men to high ground, and moved north in a line paralleling the river. In order to skirt the heads of deep ravines that plunged to the Clearwater from the 2,000-foot high plateau, he had to march his column well inland, so that the men could not see over the edge of the bluffs. Trimble and a company of cavalry scouted ahead, leading the way across rough ground and through thick stands of woods. At a little after noon on July 11, just when McConville's men were leaving Doty Ridge for Mount Idaho, Howard's troops broke into more open country and marched past a ravine-gashed, grassy tableland, covered with boulders and dotted with clusters of pine trees. Trimble's advance scouts caught a glimpse of two Indian herders driving some horses through the trees at the edge of the bluffs, but though the word was passed back, the column continued to move ahead. At almost the same time, one of Howard's officers left the middle of the two-mile-long column and rode to the rim of the bluff, about a quarter of a mile to the left of the troops. Down below, on the opposite side of the river, he saw the Nez Perce camp.

The Indians seemed relaxed and unconcerned. Some of them were racing their horses; others were bathing in the river, and the rest were cooking and lolling about their leather lodges. The officer hurried the word back to Howard, who for a moment thought that it might be a village of reservation Nez Perces. By the time he got to the edge of the bluff to view the camp for himself, he knew the truth. Some of the Indians had already learned that the soldiers were above them and were running through the camp, hurrying for their guns, cartridge belts, and horses. Behind Howard, the army column was

18. Beal, *I Will Fight No More Forever*, pp. 70–71, from the manuscript account by Luther P. Wilmot in the Yellowstone National Park Library.

strung out, still marching unknowingly toward the north. The General dispatched a messenger ahead with orders for the howitzer and Gatling guns to wheel toward the rim and open fire on the village. In a short time a shell from the 4-inch howitzer whizzed harmlessly over the camp, and the battle, on a field of nobody's choosing, was on.

In the first moments the Indians at the village separated into several groups, a large number of Nez Perces driving the horses up the Clearwater away from the troops. Two parties of warriors, stripping hastily for fighting and throwing cartridge belts around their waists and over their shoulders, gathered at either end of the camp to defend the people. Another group, swelling eventually to twenty-four fighters and led by old Toohoolhoolzote, raced impetuously up the river, away from the position of the howitzer, crossed the stream on their horses, and hastened up the wooded slope of a ravine, arriving at its head to see soldiers farther north advancing toward the edge of the bluffs. Having finally stopped his column, Howard had turned his men to the left and was starting some of them toward the rim for a charge down the slope. Toohoolhoolzote's warriors sized up the danger at a glance. Galloping after the fiery, old man, they crossed another ravine, tied their horses to some trees, and scrambled up to the flatland. Crawling hastily behind rocks, they got between the soldiers and the edge of the bluffs and began shooting. Their fierce and accurate fire stopped the troopers abruptly. The soldiers, many of them poor shots, insufficiently trained, and facing fire for the first time, faltered as some of their companions fell, then retreated and sought cover. With his attack temporarily halted, Howard continued to bring back the various units of his column that had marched farther north, forming them into a line against the Indians. Dismounted cavalrymen joined the infantry and in a series of short, sharp assaults pushed toward the Nez Perces, none of whom could be seen save when they popped suddenly from behind rocks to dash to different positions.

Finally, as they were about to be flanked, Toohoolhoolzote's men abandoned their stand and ran back to the ravine for their horses. But their determined resistance had lasted long enough to save the camp. Realizing that the soldiers were being fought off on top of the hill, the two groups of warriors guarding the families finally headed for the battle. Numbering altogether fewer than eighty men and led by the bands' ablest war chiefs, including Rainbow, Five Wounds, and Ollokot, they forded the river and swarmed up the ravines south of where Toohoolhoolzote's men had been fighting. As the original twenty-four warriors withdrew—mounting their horses and crossing the ravine to the more southerly tableland where some of the Indian reinforcements were beginning to appear—Howard saw the new threat and extended his line toward it. At the same time, another group of the newcomers charged out of the woods farther north. In the column's lead, Trimble had finally turned and begun a reverse march, coming on Howard's main pack train, which had halted to await orders. Trimble had started it south, toward the middle section of the column, when the newly arrived Indians hit it. The warriors killed two of the packers and, for a moment, threatened to capture the entire train. Then cavalrymen under Perry and Whipple arrived and drove them off.[19]

The confused movements of the different elements of his column and the intense firing on both sides convinced Howard that a large force was opposing him. Gradually, the Indian sharpshooters, concealed in positions that formed a great semicircle whose wings were along two ravines with the center hidden in woods along the edge of the bluff, forced Howard to erect a long, sprawling elliptical defense of his own, with most of his men facing toward the bluffs and the ravines, and some guarding the rear. In a small depression in the center, barricaded by piled-up saddles, blankets, and ration and ammunition boxes, he established his headquarters, ordering the supply train, protected by Trimble and a company of artillerymen, to seek shelter on high ground in the rear.

The battle raged through the rest of the day. Under a broiling July sun the troops dug rifle pits with their trowel bayonets and piled rocks and earth into protective parapets. Shooting from prone positions, they kept up a steady but largely ineffective fire against the Indians. The latter, also, were well concealed behind trees and rocks, though occasionally individuals ran across the open, or charged suddenly on horseback from the woods or a ravine to flaunt their bravery in a wild gallop past the front of the soldiers. The lines generally were widely separated, and the firing, at distances of up to 600 yards, resulted in few casualties on either side. During the afternoon Howard launched several assaults, and with the help of his howitzer managed for a time to drive the Indians from small sections of the ravines and from some of their positions in his front. But groups of warriors, some on foot and some mounted, continued to come back, often getting close to the troops. Their sudden appearances led to spirited shooting and abrupt movements by Howard's men, who were shifted to face their threat and drive them away. On several occasions the howitzer and Gatling guns were used to scatter them, but once, it was later charged, the confusion was so great that the artillerymen mistook some of their own units for Indians and fired toward them, wounding at least one man.

In the heat the troops suffered from lack of water. There was a single spring on the plateau, but Indian sharpshooters kept it under fire, and the sol-

19. Major J. G. Trimble, "The Battle of the Clearwater," in Brady, *Northwestern Fights and Fighters*, p. 142.

diers were unable to reach it. The Nez Perces, meanwhile, were supplied by women, who from time to time carried water up the hill to them from the river. In one corner of the plateau, toward their rear, the Indians had a concealed "smoking lodge," a shelter protected by an overhanging cliff and a stone wall, in which the chiefs, older men, and other "no fighters" smoked and counciled during the battle. Occasionally, warriors abandoned the fighting and came to join them, arguing whether to continue the fight, and usually being shamed into returning to the battle. A stir occurred in the middle of the afternoon when one of the treaty Nez Perces who were with Howard suddenly deserted the troops and dashed across to the Indians' lines. There had perhaps been some communication between the warriors and the treaty Nez Perces with Howard, for the deserter, Elaskolatat, known to the whites as Joe Albert, was the son of Weesculatat, the Nez Perce who had been killed in the fight with Randall's volunteers at Cottonwood and, learning of his father's death, had decided to join the warring bands. Shedding the white men's clothes he wore, he immediately charged back to the fighting with a mounted group of warriors and received a bullet wound in his thigh. At the same time, it is believed, two or more men deserted the Indian side during the conflict and, deciding that they had had enough of the war, fled the battlefield and sought safety with treaty Nez Perces.

As darkness fell, Howard's army of approximately 560 men was still under siege by the less than 100 Indians. During the night the firing quieted save for occasional flurries of shots, when men on either side thought they saw figures moving in the gloom. Many of the Indians went back to the village to guard the families and the horse herd, and arguments began over whether to move away and escape or continue to fight the next day. The war chiefs had their way; the Nez Perces, they convinced the others, had Howard and his men trapped, and they could permanently end his chasing them if they stayed there and beat him the next day. On top of the hill, Howard, in the meantime, kept his men busy, shortening their lines, digging new rifle pits, and strengthening their rock barricades. In the darkness, several soldiers got through safely to the spring and returned with buckets of water for the thirsty troops.

By daylight, Howard had decided that he would have to seize the spring. The howitzer was brought into play, shelling the area around the water, after which an assault was launched against the positions of the Indians who covered it. After a short fight the warriors were driven back, and the spring was finally secured for the troops. For a while, as Indians returned from the village to the battlefield, the firing on both sides was as sharp as the day before. But the time of decision was approaching. The soldiers were becoming weary, attrition was taking its toll of dead and wounded, and provisions could not last forever. There was no other army to rescue the troops, and thoughts of Custer's last stand were crossing the minds of some of the men. By mid-morning Howard planned an assault to try to break out of his uncomfortable position. His plan was to pierce the Indians' right wing, then wheel the attacking line to hit the Indians from the rear while other troops struck them from the front. The attack was delayed, and in the meantime a development on the Indians' side began to favor him.

The protracted fight from fixed positions had been an unusual action for Indians. Rarely, in the history of any tribe since the days of Pontiac, had Indians surrounded troops and held them patiently under siege for so long a time, especially when they had suffered casualties of their own. Howard's men had already remarked on the unprecedented nature of the siege, and were again ascribing it to the unusual generalship of Joseph. But now the Indians' impatience was asserting itself, and disastrous bickering was breaking out among the Nez Perces. Increasingly during the morning, warriors questioned the chiefs, saying that their principal aim should be to protect the people and get them away without losses, and that there was no sense in continuing the battle and endangering more lives. Gradually, men gave up the fight and rode back to the village, not caring if the others called them cowards. The soldiers at length noticed the Indians' fire decreasing but thought little of it, believing that the enemy was merely waiting for something to happen. But the Nez Perce lines continued to thin, as warriors defied the taunts of the braver ones and abandoned their positions.

By 2:30 in the afternoon Howard was ready to launch his attack but suddenly held it up when he saw a supply train, escorted by a company of cavalry, approaching the river toward the south. He sent a unit of his own men to escort it safely up the bluff and past the Indians to his own lines. On the way back, however, the escorting unit turned suddenly to its left and charged the right flank of the Indians' positions. This area had been held by some of the best warriors, including Five Wounds and the "Three red coats" of the White Bird battle, Wahlitits, Sarpsis Ilppilp, and Tipyahlanah Kapskaps, the first two being the youths who had started the war by their foray on the Salmon River. The Indians offered firm resistance, and for a moment almost flanked the attacking troops. But Howard was now alert to his opportunity. A member of General McDowell's staff from San Francisco had arrived with the new pack train to observe Howard's conduct of the war, and under his eye the General suddenly ordered a vigorous attack all along the line. Troops moved out, some of them to the support of the unit already engaged on the army's left and the rest against the center and left of the Indians' lines. To the soldiers' surprise, the weakened Indian lines offered little resistance. Most of the Nez Perces who were left, seeing that they would be overrun, broke and fled, racing down the slope to the village. On the right, two Indians, Yellow Wolf and Wottolen, held out longer than the others but soon had to run for their lives.

Moments earlier the chiefs had sensed that the defections in their lines would spell defeat, and they had sent Joseph down the hill to the village to help the people get away. Joseph had scarcely reached the camp when the warriors began coming down the slopes and ravines after him, riding through the trees and tumbling headlong over rocks and bushes, trying to escape the soldiers' bullets. They crossed the river and found the families hastening away in confusion. Shots from the howitzer were bursting among the tipis, and women, children, and old people were gathering possessions, mounting horses, and driving loose stock from the camp. Yellow Wolf came on Joseph's wife, Toma Alwawonmi (Springtime), trying to manage her horse. Joseph was nowhere about, and his baby daughter, born at Tepahlewam, was lying on the ground wrapped in its *tekash* (cradleboard). Yellow Wolf handed the child to its mother and helped them get away.[20]

On the hill the soldiers kept up a hail of fire after the retreating Indians, then moved down the ravines to the river opposite the Indian camp. The cavalry under Perry found the steep descent difficult going, and by the time the troopers reached the river the Indians were in full flight into the hills on the opposite shore. Leaving the infantry on the east bank, the cavalry forded the river, but instead of pursuing the Indians they entered the abandoned camp and waited for orders. As Howard started to make his descent, he thought he saw Indians returning to fight, and he sent a message to Perry to return for the infantry and ferry them across the stream on their mounts. Perry did so, but the Indian threat did not materialize and the entire army eventually pulled up and made camp around the deserted tipis.

The troops swarmed through the village, noting the vast amount of equipment and supplies left by the Indians. Blankets, robes, cooking utensils, flour, and jerked beef had been abandoned. Fires still burned, and meals were still cooking. Some of the men discovered the Indians' caches and broke them open. "There was gold dust, jewelry, and fine silver tableware, some of which I judged dated from an early Hudson's Bay period," said one of the officers. The volunteers ("it was marvelous how many citizens seemed to arrive," the same officer added) helped themselves to souvenirs, priceless heirlooms and treasures of the vanished bands, and burned what they did not want.[21]

McDowell's staff officer immediately composed a wire to be sent to his superior in San Francisco, praising Howard for the "vigor" of the movements

20. McWhorter, *Yellow Wolf*, p. 97.
21. McWhorter, *Hear Me*, p. 322, quoting a letter from Colonel H. L. Bailey.

and actions during the closing moments of the battle, and Howard himself framed a wire to McDowell, announcing that he had won an important victory in which the "Indians fought as well as any troops I ever saw . . ." McDowell soon afterward replied to Howard that the dispatches "gave us all great pleasure," and added, "I immediately repeated them to Washington, to be laid before the Secretary of War and the President. These dispatches came most opportunely, for your enemies had raised a great clamor against you . . ." He referred to the unrest that Howard's previous lack of success against the Nez Perces was occasioning, for in Washington, according to the Associated Press, Howard's removal was under consideration by the Cabinet. The Clearwater battle would now be trumpeted as a victory, and Howard would be saved.[22]

But it was a hollow victory. Howard had had thirteen men killed and twenty-seven wounded, two of them fatally, while the Nez Perces counted four dead and six wounded. The Indians had got away with most of their horses and many of their possessions, but, most importantly, they had got away intact. On the heels of the conflict, while he was congratulating himself on his success, Howard committed one of the most grievous blunders of the campaign. Instead of hounding the Indians, dispersing the shattered bands, and breaking up the last of their resistance, he let them go, satisfying himself that he could not overtake them before dark and postponing pursuit until the next day. By that time he was too late, and the opportunity to end the war had slipped past him.

In the hours after the battle, the Indians moved down the Clearwater and drew together again at evening in a camp near Kamiah, within sight of the subagency buildings on the Nez Perce reservation. Few of the Indians thought they had been whipped, or were in a defeatist mood, but division persisted among them over whether to stand and fight or continue to run away. Those who counseled the latter course were the strongest voiced, but even they knew that sooner or later they would have to get away from Howard for good and find safety and peace again for the families. The next morning, aware that the army would soon be appearing, the bands made bullboats and crossed to the east bank of the river, swimming across their large herd of horses which still totaled between 2,000 and 3,000 animals. The last of the people were still crossing late in the afternoon, when Indian pickets left in the hills behind them, signaled with their blankets that the soldiers were coming

22. The material in this paragraph is in McWhorter, *Hear Me*, pp. 324–25, and is contained in *Claims of the Nez Perce Indians*, Senate Executive Document No. 257, 56th Congress, 1st Session, pp. 37, 39–40. Howard's July 12th dispatch to McDowell from "Camp Williams, left bank South Fork Clear Water, near mouth of Cottonwood, I.T., July 12," is in the *New Northwest*, December 13, 1878.

into sight. The vanguard of Howard's pursuing troops, cavalrymen under Perry and Whipple, had crossed the high ground between Cottonwood Creek and Kamiah and were coming down to the river in two columns. Near the Indians' crossing place, the columns merged to pass beneath the flank of a high bluff at the river's edge. By then, the Indians had all crossed the river and had hurried up the hills and out of sight. Those who wanted to fight now saw another opportunity. As the troopers rode along the stream, warriors suddenly opened fire on them from their hiding places across the river. The unexpected attack caused panic among the cavalrymen, who jumped from their horses and ran for cover, or galloped in disorder back in the direction from which they had come.

By the time that Howard and his main command appeared on the crest of the hills and started a descent to the river, the cavalrymen had regained their nerve and were returning the fire. The howitzer and Gatling guns were brought into play, and the warriors gradually gave up the fight and chased after the families, who had established a camp out of artillery range on top of the hill. The long distance firing of the skirmish had been mostly noise; the only casualty was a soldier who had been slightly wounded. That night Howard established his own camp along the river, opposite the place where the Indians had disappeared, and he stayed there all the next day, July 14, sending out reconnoitering parties and planning his next move. Treaty Nez Perces, including old Captain John and James Reuben, were still with him, serving as scouts, and they informed him that the warring bands would undoubtedly move next to the camas grounds of the Weippe Prairie, from where they might try to escape over the Lolo Trail to Montana. The treaty Nez Perces knew of another crossing of the Clearwater, lower down on the river at present-day Greer, and a short-cut trail up the hills on the opposite shore that would bring the troops to the Weippe Prairie ahead of the warriors. The information delighted Howard, and, when at 3:30 in the afternoon Colonel McConville and his regiment of mounted volunteers arrived from Mount Idaho, he ordered the newcomers to be ready to march downriver the next morning with three companies of cavalry, cross the river, and get behind the Nez Perces' at Weippe Prairie. The rest of the troops would cross at Kamiah and push the enemy toward the trap.

Early on July 15 the cavalry and volunteers moved out, accompanied by Howard himself. The troops climbed the hills, heading in a westward direction to fool the Indians and make them think they were returning to Lapwai. Then, when they thought they were out of sight of Indian spies, they veered downriver, intending to cross by Dunwell's Ferry near present-day Greer. They had gone only six miles when a messenger overtook them to report that the Nez Perces had broken their own camp and started for the Lolo Trail.

Furthermore, an Indian sent by Joseph had come down to the river and had
called across to ask on what terms the Nez Perces could surrender. The news
threw Howard into confusion. Guessing that the Nez Perces had managed,
after all, to see his movement toward Dunwell's Ferry and would now beat
his men to Weippe Prairie, he ordered the cavalry and volunteers to continue
to the ferry and guard it against its use by hostiles who might come back and
try to flank the army. Then he returned to his camp to see what Joseph's
emissary wanted.

The intent of that Indian, a warrior named Zya Temoni (No Heart), was
apparently not serious. Howard said he talked to the messenger, and Monteith reported later that the General laid down terms of unconditional surrender, to be followed by trials and the punishment of Joseph's people. The
Nez Perces themselves said that Zya Temoni never even crossed the river to
talk to Howard and that if he had called out anything about surrendering, he
had done so in derision. Some critics thought that Howard misplayed his
hand by offering terms so harsh that the Nez Perces were forced to continue
retreating, and the war had to go on. But it is doubtful that Zya Temoni
spoke for anybody but himself or that his appearance was anything more
than a boastful gesture. The conference, at any rate, ended suddenly when a
shot rang out—it was never established whether from the rifle of a soldier or
of a concealed Indian—and Zya Temoni slapped his thigh in a sign of contempt for the troops and galloped away.[23]

Howard thought soon afterward that the Indian's appearance had been a
ruse to divert the army and hold it in camp, for at noon the bands, as reported
earlier to him, had started for the Weippe Prairie, fifteen miles away. They
decided to move not because they saw the General's downriver sortie but, according to Yellow Wolf, because the warriors who had wanted to fight had
finally lost patience with the soldiers. "No use staying here," they had said.
"They do not want to cross and fight us." [24] The Indians reached the camas
grounds late in the afternoon and met a band of about twenty Nez Perce
men, women, and children under a nontreaty headman named Red Heart.
Those people had been on their way back from the Montana plains to their
homes near where the battle of the Clearwater had just been fought at
present-day Stites, and had learned of the war for the first time only three
days before. Although friendly to the people of the warring bands, they were
like the members of Looking Glass's band before Whipple had attacked, and
they had planned to stay at Weippe and avoid becoming entangled in the

23. Howard, *Nez Perce Joseph*, p. 169. Beal, *I Will Fight*, p. 312 n., quoting letter
from Monteith to Indian Commissioner Smith, July 31, 1877. McWhorter, *Hear Me*,
p. 329.
   24. McWhorter, *Yellow Wolf*, p. 104.

fighting. Now the war was suddenly upon them. After a brief meeting with the newcomers, they decided to leave Weippe, go down to Kamiah, and seek safety with the treaty Indians on the reservation. A few of Looking Glass's people under a chief named Three Feathers also decided that they had had enough of the fighting and, joining Red Heart's band, said farewell to the war group and started back to Kamiah. At the Clearwater the next day they were identified as Dreamers and nontreaties by the Christian reservation Nez Perces and were seized as prisoners of war by Howard's soldiers. Despite their protestations of peaceful intentions, they were herded to Kamiah, where their horses and equipment were taken from them; and they were then marched with unnecessary cruelty for sixty miles on foot to Fort Lapwai. All of them, women, children, and old men, numbering thirty-three persons and including the aged Chief Jacob, a follower of Lawyer's, who had signed the Stevens treaty of 1855, were sent by steamer to Fort Vancouver, where they were held in confinement until April 1878. They were the only prisoners Howard took during the war, and although his official report pretended that they were hostile, the Nez Perce tribe to this day counts the treatment of Red Heart's people as one of the most unjust of the General's actions.

At Weippe that evening of July 15 the chiefs, war leaders, and principal spokesmen of the different bands finally faced the question of what next? At a council of great significance, Looking Glass, supported by warriors who were familiar with the buffalo lands, urged that the people cross the Lolo Trail and go to the plains country of the Crows. Looking Glass knew that tribe well. He had fought with them against the Sioux, and they had once taunted him for the docile way in which the Nez Perces had let the white men over-run and steal their lands in Idaho. The Crows, he thought, were talking of making war against the Americans themselves; and even if they did not do so, there was much to be said for going to them. This war had been an Idaho affair, fought against the Idaho people, who were enemies of the Nez Perces. The Montana whites would be different. They were not enemies of the Nez Perces and would not fight them. Looking Glass knew many of the white men in the Bitterroot Valley and other places in Montana. They were friendly to him, and he would show the other chiefs that if the Indians be-haved themselves in Montana and acted peacefully, as they always did when they went for buffalo, the whites would leave them alone, and there would be no fighting there. Then they could go on to the Crows and find a tempo-rary place of safety in their plains country in the Yellowstone Basin, where white settlers and their forts and soldiers were few and widely scattered. Moreover, Looking Glass is also thought to have argued, if they found no safety with the Crows, the bands could then go on to Canada, the Old Woman's Country (the domain of Queen Victoria), and join Sitting Bull.

That Sioux chief and his followers, some of the Nez Perce buffalo hunters had learned, had found safety in Canada the previous winter after the American soldiers had defeated the Sioux in eastern Montana. The Nez Perces could join them, if they had to. Then when the hard feelings in Idaho blew over and the troubles were forgotten, the bands could come home again.[25]

White Bird, Toohoolhoolzote, and Hatalekin, the latter having arrived with sixteen Palouse warriors to join the Nez Perces after the battle of the Clearwater, were moved by Looking Glass's reasoning and agreed to his proposal. Joseph and the men of the Wallowa band were not so sure. Going to Montana would take their people even farther from the Wallowa. They were homesick for the valley. All through the previous weeks, memories of the land they had abandoned had made their hearts ache. As they had trailed back and forth along the Salmon and across the Camas Prairie, their minds had been on the other side of the Snake River, and they had dreamed of the Wallowa and reassured each other that some day the bad times would end and they would find a way to go home again. There was something ominous now about going even farther away to the remote Montana country. It was as if they were again saying farewell to the Wallowa, but this time for a distant exile, and for all time. Soon after the council, stories circulated among the treaty Nez Perces that Joseph made an impassioned speech to the other chiefs against leaving Idaho. "What are we fighting for if not for our own country?" he is supposed to have asked. But nothing about what he actually said is known for sure. On the other hand, Looking Glass, it is certain, pressed his proposal with vigor and officiousness. He spoke with optimism and self-confidence; and since no one else had either of those feelings at the moment, the members of the council finally went along with him by unanimous consent and told him to become the war leader of all the bands and guide the people until they got to the Crows. There is some evidence that when the meeting broke up, Joseph and the Wallowa leaders were displeased with Looking Glass's overbearing manner and conceit, but decided to remain silent and accept his leadership. White Bird and Toohoolhoolzote were too old to become the war leaders, and both men may have been persuasive in convincing Joseph and Ollokot that by seniority and experience Looking Glass was next in line. At the same time, the brothers apparently recognized that they could not leave the protection of the other bands, for if they abandoned the war and Howard captured them, the General would undoubtedly

25. Ibid., pp. 112–13, quoting Yellow Wolf as saying that at this Weippe council one of the chiefs told the people that they might join Sitting Bull in Canada. However, Duncan McDonald, basing his information on an interview with White Bird in Canada after the war, said that even after the Nez Perces crossed the Lolo Trial, they thought that Sitting Bull still retained possession of the Yellowstone country and that they might join him there (*New Northwest*, December 27, 1878).

hang them. In the days that followed, however, the Wallowa Indians found many reasons to be irritated by Looking Glass, and made many sarcastic jokes about his egotism, his desire to have his own way, and the fact that he never seemed to like an idea unless he had thought of it first himself.

That night, after the council, the chiefs rode through the camps, telling the people of their decision and warning them not to shoot any white man in Montana, or steal their cattle, for the Nez Perces were going to leave the war behind them in Idaho. Those were strong directions, they announced, and if the people obeyed them there would be no fighting in Montana. The next morning, July 16, the bands packed and broke camp. Five young volunteers were directed to stay at the prairie for three days and warn the families if Howard's men started after them. Then, with Looking Glass in supreme command, the Nez Perces, numbering about 200 men and almost 550 women and children, driving a herd of more than 2,000 horses as well as pack animals that bore all the worldly possessions left to the patriots, started up the wooded foothills of the Bitterroots toward the high Lolo Trail that led to Montana. It was a moment to add to many others, the beginning of a trek into exile by another American Indian people. To the Nez Perces it could also have been a time of ironic memories. At that very spot, Weippe Prairie, only seventy-two years before, their fathers had welcomed and succored the starving members of the Lewis and Clark Expedition, the first Americans to come to their homeland. They had made a treaty of alliance and friendship with those men and had remained loyal to their word. Now Weippe Prairie was the last of their part of the earth to see them leave. Behind them were the South Fork of the Clearwater and Kamiah, where only forty-four years before—and there were men among the refugees who could remember that time—Nez Perces had brought the ailing Samuel Parker, and had told him they hoped he would find a suitable place among their villages to build a mission. Now the river and the Camas Prairie, and all the countryside around, was lived on by whites who said it was their land. How had the Indians lost it, and the whites taken it? How had it happened so quickly? One people out, and another one—newly arrived—in, as though they had always been there. It was too much for the mind to comprehend, this robbery of a people's home.

On the same morning, July 16, aware that he could no longer cut off the Indians at the Weippe Prairie, Howard ordered the cavalry and volunteers back from Dunwell's Ferry. With the help of some treaty Nez Perces the horses of the returned units were swum across the river that evening to a point opposite Howard's camp, and a force was assembled under Major Edward C. Mason to follow the Indians' trail the next morning for a two days' march, to engage the Nez Perces in battle, if possible, and, if not, at least to

discover whether they were heading for Montana. The group was a formidable one, composed of the cavalry troops of Perry, Trimble, Jackson, and
Winters, the volunteer regiment under McConville, and a dozen or more
treaty Nez Perces headed by old Captain John, who was still anxious to help
American soldiers against Indians, even though they were his own people.
With Arthur Chapman, the Nez Perce scouts, and McConville's volunteers
riding at its head, the column left the river at 4 A.M.

Following the Indians' trail, the troops crossed Lolo Creek, reached the
Weippe Prairie, and by mid-afternoon were on the thickly wooded western
end of the Lolo Trail near Musselshell Creek and about three miles from Oro
Fino Creek, where the gold rush had begun in 1860. Indian signs were numerous and fresh, and McConville ordered the treaty Nez Perces to move out
ahead and scout the trail. Those men ran into a disastrous ambush. Sometime
earlier, Wahlitits, riding in the rear of the bands' long column, had spied the
pursuing soldiers. At word of his warning, the Indians had held a council, and
Rainbow and sixteen warriors had ridden back along the trail to set a trap,
while the bands had continued to hurry ahead. The warriors had concealed
themselves in the woods flanking the trail and had soon heard the treaty Nez
Perces coming along, examining tracks on the ground. The presence of the
Christian Indians, still helping the army, had infuriated the warriors. If they
had held their fire, they might have caught the principal elements of Mason's
troops and inflicted perhaps a greater defeat on the army than the one at
White Bird. But Rainbow was too angry to remain silent. He took aim and
fired at one of the treaty Nez Perces. The other warriors then opened fire.
One of the treaty scouts was killed, two were wounded—one of them dying
later from his injuries—and the rest of them fled back to the volunteers. The
man killed in the woods was John Levi, the son of the Nez Perce who had
formerly lived with Timothy at Alpowa, and one of the Nez Perces who had
aided Colonel Steptoe in 1858.

The sounds of the shots brought McConville's men to a halt. When the
frightened Nez Perce scouts reached the volunteers, McConville sent Chapman back to Mason and the regulars who were far in his rear. Mason brought
his own men to a halt and sent Winters and his company up to McConville
with orders for the two units to reconnoiter the woods for the enemy. They
did so, coming on the bullet-riddled body of John Levi but seeing no signs of
the warriors, who had already left to hurry after their people. The entire
military column, from McConville and Winters at the head to Mason's cavalry units in the rear, was immobilized. Mason made no move to send his main
body forward to aid McConville, many of whose men imagined that they
were in great danger. After standing the troops idly in the thick timber for
some time, Mason regrouped the units and took them all back to Howard's

camp at the Clearwater, reaching there the next morning and reporting that he had carried out his instructions, ascertaining to his satisfaction that the Nez Perces were on their way to the buffalo country in Montana. "This," Howard reported, "really ended the campaign within the limits of my department."

It was a note of finality that was not final. Oregon and Idaho had been cleared of the warring Nez Perces, but Howard could not suddenly wash his hands of the affair. More than 700 Indians, "on the warpath," were still at large. The War Department was responsible for them, and Howard and the large number of troops that had been placed at his disposal were the most effective force anywhere near the hostiles. On receipt of the news that the Nez Perces were leaving Howard's Department of the Columbia, General William Tecumseh Sherman, Commanding General of the Army, who was then on an inspection tour of military posts along the Yellowstone River in Montana, wired McDowell in San Francisco to have Howard continue the pursuit of the Indians regardless of military district boundary lines.

The one-armed general, weary from the unsuccessful chase, would have appreciated a rest. But continued criticism in the press, which he knew was making its mark on his superiors and on the Administration in Washington, scored him angrily for letting the Nez Perces get away, and demanded that he hurry after them. Despite both the criticism and the order from Sherman, however, Howard delayed, trying to form a plan of action. He knew little about the Lolo Trail, but dread reports of its ruggedness convinced him that it was an even worse trail than the one he had followed south of the Salmon River, and that it would be almost impossible to move his artillery and equipment over it quickly enough to overtake the Indians. In addition, there were other problems. All about him, in the recent theater of conflict, there was the possibility of further uprisings by other Dreamers; the country, from the Nez Perce reservation to the settlements along the Columbia River, was insecure. He did not think he had enough troops yet to do everything that was required of him—and, besides, the men who would be pursuing the Nez Perces would first need supplies.

In his camp on the Clearwater he gradually worked out a plan of operations. He would leave a small garrison at Kamiah to guard against a return of the warring bands, and would march his main command to Fort Lapwai, pick up supplies, and then hurry to Missoula by way of the Mullan Road, which followed the easy, water level route of the Clark Fork River. At Missoula he would strike south to intercept and defeat the Nez Perces somewhere on the eastern side of the Lolo Trail. At the same time, he would leave the Camas Prairie and the Snake-Salmon-Columbia River regions, still exposed to potentially hostile Indians, to Major John Green, who was marching north through

Idaho with troops from Fort Boise, and to Colonel Frank Wheaton, who was hurrying to the Northwest by transcontinental railroad and steamship from San Francisco with the 2nd Infantry from Georgia.

He had scarcely decided on that plan when he had to abandon it. Hurrying to Lapwai ahead of his troops, he received a message that a few hostile Nez Perces, apparently from the bands crossing the Lolo Trail, had reappeared briefly on the Camas Prairie, set some farmhouses on fire, and made off with a number of horses. The reports were confused; there were charges that white men or treaty Nez Perces had originally stolen the animals from their owners, and that the raiding Indians—who might or might not have been members of the warring bands—had only been reclaiming what had rightfully belonged to them. But the episode raised a new alarm among the reservation Nez Perces and the Camas Prairie settlers that Joseph's Indians were not crossing the Lolo Trail, after all, but would reappear in the hills to strike them at any moment, and their fears caused Howard to order his troops to stay at Kamiah and continue to guard the crossings of the Clearwater.

The state of unrest now made it impossible, in the General's mind, to abandon the region before reinforcements arrived to take over guard duty from his own men. At Fort Lapwai, he supervised the dispatch of supplies to his troops for their march to Montana, took a brief rest, and then returned to Kamiah. Leaving only a small unit at the river crossing, he withdrew the rest of his men to the vicinity of Mount Idaho and established a camp to wait for the arrival of Major Green's troops from Boise. As the situation remained quiet, he became convinced that the Indians were definitely crossing the Lolo Trail, and at length he worked out a new plan to put into effect as soon as Green appeared. He would take his own men directly over the Lolo Trail in pursuit of the Indians. Major Wheaton, who was momentarily expected at Fort Walla Walla with the 2nd Infantry, would take the Mullan Road, see to it that Smohalla and "the Columbia River renegades" stayed at peace, despite rumors that some of them had already joined the warring Nez Perces (an exaggeration of the report that Hahtalekin and his sixteen Palouses were now with the hostiles), and proceed to Missoula by way of the Clark Fork River route. Eventually, east of the Bitterroots, the two columns would link forces or, if they were fortunate, trap the Nez Perces between them. Major Green and his men, meanwhile, would hold themselves in reserve, patrolling and guarding the Clearwater-Salmon-Snake country, watching out for a return of the hostiles, protecting the settlements against Indians who might turn hostile once Howard left the region, and maintaining intercommunication between the two columns that were marching to Montana.

On July 25, Howard wired McDowell of his plan, and at the same time sent a dispatch for relay to the Army's Department of Dakota, which included Montana, stating that he would start across the Lolo Trail on July 30 and asking that troops in Montana be sent to block the eastern exit of the trail and keep the Nez Perces on it. "If you simply bother them and keep them back until I can close in," he said, "their destruction or surrender will be sure." The message was a belated one, for the Nez Perces at the time were already at the eastern end of the trail, and settlers and soldiers in the Missoula region and other valleys of western Montana—as we will see—were well aware of the Indians' arrival. But Howard's wire accelerated the entry of a new unit of Army regulars into the war. On July 21 General Philip Sheridan's headquarters of the Division of Missouri in Chicago had telegraphed Colonel John Gibbon, in command of the 7th Infantry at Fort Shaw on the Sun River in Montana, to undertake the protection of the settlements of western Montana against the Nez Perces. Gibbon, a vigorous and efficient leader of volunteers in the "Iron Brigade" in the Civil War and a veteran of the recently concluded campaign against the Sioux, now gathered additional men from Forts Benton and Baker and on July 28 set off hurriedly for Missoula via Cadotte's Pass over the northern Montana Rockies.

On July 26, meanwhile, Howard started his men back to Kamiah from the Camas Prairie, and the next day the first units crossed the Clearwater. On July 28 the head of Major Green's column from Boise finally arrived. The newcomers included three companies of cavalry and twenty Bannock Indian scouts, recruited in southern Idaho and led by a Bannock named Buffalo Horn, who had served as a scout for Generals Crook and Miles in their campaigns in Montana against the Sioux and Cheyennes. Major Green himself, with two companies of infantry, was still back in the mountains at Florence, but Howard felt no need to wait for him. The new arrivals were strong enough to commence the job of policing the country he was about to leave. All action now after his long delay, he sent another wire to McDowell's headquarters, asking, "Cannot troops at Missoula or vicinity detain Joseph till I can strike his rear? . . . My troops will push through rapidly."

Still, there was delay. The next day, July 29, was a Sunday, and Howard and some of his men attended religious services at Kamiah conducted in Nez Perce and English by Archie Lawyer, a Christian Nez Perce and the son of old Lawyer. The Bannocks, long the hated enemies of the Nez Perces, with whom they had clashed in battle along the Idaho-Montana border as recently as 1872, were also invited to the services. Buffalo Horn was a belligerent young warrior, and the following year he would shock his white friends by leading the Bannocks in a fierce war against the Americans in southern Idaho. He still had no use for Nez Perces, Christian or non-Christian, and would readily have scalped one of them if he had found him alone. But he and his companions came warily to the church and sat grimly through Archie Lawyer's sermon.

At 5 A.M. on the following morning, Howard's 700 men, forming a column more than two miles long, finally began climbing the hill toward the start of the Lolo Trail. Arthur Chapman and a group of treaty Nez Perces, still serving as guides and scouts, again rode in the lead. It was going to be a desperate march. During the gold rush era, a party of axemen had labored to widen and clear part of the trail. Since then, few people save members of buffalo-hunting Indian parties had used the route, and the trees and underbrush had again taken over. It was still the same winding, precipitous, high ridgetop trail that Lewis and Clark and John Work had followed. Parts of it led through thick forests where the trees were so close together that packhorses could scarcely squeeze through. Much of it was up and down steep, rocky grades, clogged with boulders, undergrowth, and fallen trees. In places the path clung to precipices, and the way was perilous. To make it worse for Howard, it was pouring rain when he started, and his men and horses slid and rolled on muddy inclines. Getting the artillery and strings of pack mules up the hills and through the deep woods tested his men's patience. But the column forced its way along, and by evening, with the skies clearing at last, the troops reached Weippe. Howard reported that he had another problem that day: the Bannock scouts had become tired and had decided not to go with him. Buffalo Horn, however, had finally induced all but three of them to go along—the inducements perhaps being promises of Nez Perce booty and scalps—and the Bannocks had fallen into line. Also with the troops, the General reported, was a newspaper correspondent named Sutherland.

The first day's trials were only a taste of what lay ahead. Next day the troops began the ascent of the main Lolo Trail, and the difficulties commenced in earnest. Trees and undergrowth, choking the route, held up the artillery and mule strings, and Howard's men wondered how the Indians, with all their horses and baggage, had ever got through. Howard had sent his engineer officer, Captain William F. Spurgin of the 21st Infantry, to Lewiston to recruit fifty axemen. Although the General had heard that they were on their way, he had not waited for them. Now he wished that he had. Spurgin's group of fifty-two men, designated skilled laborers and soon to be called "skillets" by the soldiers because of their ability to hack roads through the wilderness, finally overtook the column on August 2. After that, they made good time, plodding laboriously but at an average rate of only sixteen miles a day, across the dangerous saddles and ridges of the mountain wilderness which Howard later said, "None of us will ever forget." Lewis and Clark, searching anxiously for the Nez Perces, had once said the same thing about the tortuous trail, but Howard now left no evidence that he was aware of history's ironic turn. On August 8, nine days after he had left the Clearwater, he started the troops on the descent into Montana and approached the trail's eastern exit.

By then, he was far in the rear of the Nez Perces, who had also taken nine days to travel the same distance and had reached the wooded eastern slope of the range on July 25, five days before Howard had even started his pursuit. Much, then, had occurred in Montana.

Ever since the war had begun in Idaho, the whites in the mining towns and farm settlements on the eastern side of the Bitterroots had closely followed the news of the conflict, fearful that it would move their way. The Nez Perces, and some of the war leaders themselves, were no strangers to many of the Montana towns. Buffalo-hunting bands from Idaho had regularly traveled back and forth from the Clearwater to the plains, passing peacefully through the settled valleys and stopping to trade at stores. The Nez Perces had always been friendly to the Montana whites, and some of them had become acquaintances of various farmers and merchants. On occasion, white men had invited Nez Perces into their homes to share meals with their families. They had willingly cared for and stored Indian horses and camping equipment, which the Nez Perces wished to keep east of the Bitterroots. And at least once, Looking Glass had had a doctor in the small frontier town of Missoula treat his eyes. But Indians at war would be a different and dangerous people, and because the Montana citizens recognized that their part of the country, familiar to many of the warriors, would be an obvious escape route for the Nez Perces if Howard forced them from Idaho, they hoped that the troops could end the war west of the Bitterroots.

At the same time, the Montana settlers feared that if hostile Nez Perces came into their midst, they would arouse a war fever among their own Indians, the Flatheads, who had always been docile but who had also been friends of the Nez Perces and had recently been given cause of their own to be resentful of the whites. Since the I. I. Stevens treaty of 1855, the Flatheads had fared little better than the Nez Perces. To get his treaty signed, the impatient Stevens had allowed Chief Victor to remain temporarily in the Bitterroot Valley above the juncture of the Lolo Fork, but the treaty document had empowered the President to decide at any time in the future whether to grant the Flatheads permanent possession of the valley or force them to go to the Salish reservation farther north in Montana.

In the early 1870s settlers who had moved into the valley had raised an unwarranted alarm about the Flatheads, and a commission headed by the future President, James A. Garfield, had gone to the Bitterroot in 1872 for a treaty council with the Indians. In a meeting reminiscent of the one with the

CANADA

MILK R.

Bear Paws,
SEPT. 30-OCT. 5

BEAR
PAW
MTS.

Col. Miles'
route from
Ft. Keogh

Cow
Island,
SEPT. 23

LITTLE
ROCKY
MTS.

MARIAS R.

DIVIDE

TETON R.

Fort
Benton

MISSOURI R.

SUN R.

Fort Shaw

MISSOURI R.

JUDITH R.

Lewistown

zle,
-28

Helena

Judith
Gap

MUSSELSHELL R.

Deer
Lodge

Canyon
Creek,
SEPT. 13

Butte

Three
Forks

BIG HOLE R.

Crows and
Bannocks

Billings

YELLOWSTONE R.

Hole,
UG. 9

Fort
Ellis

 loward's
Route

Bannack

BEAVERHEAD R.

Virginia
City

MADISON R.

GALLATIN R.

A B S A R O K A S

CLARK FK.

BIG HORN R.

Bannack
Pass

Targhee
Pass

YELLOWSTONE
PARK

LAMAR R.

Heart
Mtn.

SHOSHONE R.

Monida
Pass

CAMAS CR.

Camas
Meadows,
AUG. 20

BIRCH CR.

11. THE ROUTE OF THE FIGHTING PATRIOT BANDS, 1877

Nez Perces at Lapwai in 1863 the second and third ranking chiefs of the Flat-heads, Arlee and Adolphe, had signed an agreement to evacuate the valley and move to the reservation, but Victor's son, Charlot, the principal chief, had refused to sign or move. Although Garfield and the other commissioners had fraudulently reported that Charlot had signed the document, explaining lamely that they had done so because they had believed that Arlee would eventually persuade the top chief to go to the reservation, the government had not forced Charlot from the valley, and he had remained there with his people, surrounded by white men and nursing hurt feelings.[26] He had made no trouble, however, and, recognizing the increasing power of the settlers in the Bitteroot, had maintained peaceful relations with them, but the outbreak of the war in Idaho had inevitably made many of his white neighbors worry whether he would join the Nez Perces. Eventually, Peter Ronan, the Indian agent on the Flathead reservation at Jocko, after winning pledges from the reservation Indians to remain at peace, had journeyed to the Bitterroot and secured a similar promise from Charlot. The chief, in fact, had assured Ronan that if the Nez Perces appeared in Montana, he would help protect his white friends against hostile actions by the Idaho warriors. Still, doubt persisted—about him as well as about the restless young Flathead men on the reservation.

There was great alarm in Montana when it was learned that the Indians had escaped from the troops at Clearwater. Now, for a certainty, it was felt, the beaten Nez Perces, angered by their drubbing and looking for revenge against whites, would stream across the Lolo Trail. Rumors swept through the valleys, increasing the fears, and the territory's governor, Benjamin F. Potts, realizing that only a handful of regulars were stationed in Montana west of the Rockies, telegraphed President Hayes for authority to raise a force of 500 volunteers. The War Department turned him down with an assurance that federal troops could take care of the situation, but neither the Governor nor the settlers felt at ease.

A new federal post was being constructed at Missoula, and Captain Charles C. Rawn had arrived there a month before with a small detachment of the 7th

26. Peter Ronan, *Historical Sketch of the Flathead Indian Nation* (Helena, Montana, 1890), pp. 64–66; and Michael Harrison, "Chief Charlot's Battle with Bureaucracy," *Montana, the Magazine of Western History* (Autumn, 1960), pp. 27–33. Note a curious twist: Lawyer, who signed for the Nez Perces in 1863, had a Flathead father; Arlee, who signed for the Flatheads in 1872, was partly of Nez Perce descent. Charlot was able to remain in the Bitterroot Valley until 1890, but that year the government finally forced his weak and helpless band, now bereft of allies and friends, to leave its ancient homeland and move to the Salish reservation, forty miles north of Missoula. Thus the Americans rewarded the Bitterroot Valley Flatheads for their eighty-five years of intense and loyal friendship to white men.

Infantry from Gibbon's headquarters at Fort Shaw, which was east of the Rockies. On July 18, bothered by the reports that the Nez Perces were headed his way, Rawn sent Lieutenant Francis Woodridge and four enlisted men to scout the Lolo Trail for signs of the Indians. When they failed to return, he dispatched another lieutenant, C. A. Coolidge, with one soldier and several citizen volunteers, to look for them on July 21. The two scouting parties met the next day on the eastern end of the Lolo, and Woodridge's unit reported that it had reconnoitered the trail as far as the Clearwater, meaning probably its Lochsa branch west of the Lolo Pass, and had seen no sign of the Nez Perces. But shortly afterward four Indians came in sight, and the soldiers and volunteers surrounded them and took them prisoner. They proved to be three Nez Perces and a mixed-blood named John Hill, who was the son of a Nez Perce woman and the halfblood, Delaware Jim. All of them were members of a small Nez Perce band that resided in the Bitterroot Valley with the Flatheads. They had been in the mountains, they told their captors, and had fallen in with the Nez Perce warriors who were crossing the trail from Idaho and would soon be appearing. The war bands had apparently advised them not to go down the mountain alone, but they had not wanted to become involved in the war and had done so anyway.

Woodridge and Coolidge sent a messenger hurrying to Rawn with the news and, taking the four noncombatant Indians as captives, also returned to Missoula. Rawn telegraphed the news to Fort Shaw, and was directed to intercept the Nez Perces and hold them on the Lolo Trail. At the same time, the report of the danger spurred Governor Potts, even without authority from Washington, to issue a call for volunteers. Defense groups had already been formed at Missoula and at Stevensville, Corvallis, Hamilton, and Skalkaho in the Bitterroot Valley, but as the *Weekly Missoulan* cried out Potts's call with the headline, HELP! HELP! COME RUNNING!" settlers and miners hurriedly organized units in Deer Lodge, Helena, Butte, and Virginia City and started for Missoula.

On July 24, meanwhile, Rawn with five officers and thirty enlisted men hastened to the mouth of Lolo Creek, where he met some 35 Bitterroot Valley settlers who had left their wives and children in Fort Owen at Stevensville. There was an impatient parley in which the settlers tried to convince Rawn that the whites were too few to defeat the Indians, and that if they attempted to do so and failed, the Bitterroot would be laid waste and all the people there killed by the irate Nez Perces. Rawn had his orders, however, and could not accept the settlers' plea to let the Nez Perces pass by without interference. As he started his regulars up the Lolo, determined to halt the Indians, the settlers went with him, realizing reluctantly that they had no choice but to help the troops and trust to luck.

True to Charlot's promise, the Flathead chief and twenty of his followers had also showed up and said that while they did not wish to fight the Nez Perces, they would help to try to make them surrender or go back to Idaho. The whites welcomed the Flathead contingent, which included old Delaware Jim, and gave them pieces of white cloth to tie around their heads to distinguish them from the Nez Perces.

The latter by then had crossed the summit of the trail and had started their descent from the mountains. Scouts, riding in advance, sighted Rawn's men, and after a harmless exchange of shots, galloped back to alert the Indians. Rawn selected a narrow spot in the canyon about six miles above the mouth of Lolo Creek, and on the morning of July 25 commenced felling logs for a barricade. More volunteers, eventually swelling the total to about 200, arrived from Missoula and the Bitterroot Valley and joined the preparations for defense.

The Nez Perces, meanwhile, camped at Woodman's Prairie, about two miles above Rawn's position. During the 25th, Looking Glass, White Bird, and Joseph, confident that the Montana people would talk peaceably with them, went down to the barricade with a white flag. The troops and volunteers held their fire and watched in awe as the chiefs, unafraid, rode up, dismounted, and shook hands with Rawn. For a moment, the Nez Perces inspected the half-built fortification, only two or three logs high in places, and laughingly called it a corral. Then, with Delaware Jim interpreting for them, they parleyed with the officer and delegates of the volunteer companies. To the whites, who regarded the Indians as hostiles, the Nez Perces' conduct seemed unreal. Stating that the Indians had left the war behind them and did not wish to fight their friends in Montana, Looking Glass promised that if Rawn allowed them to pass the barricade, unmolested, they would march peaceably through the Bitterroot Valley to the buffalo country. When Rawn replied that he could not let them go by unless they surrendered their arms, White Bird objected, recalling the war of 1858—which Rawn undoubtedly knew nothing about—when Colonel Wright had persuaded Palouses, Yakimas, Spokans, and Coeur d'Alenes to surrender their arms and had then hanged many of the Indians. The discussion reached an impasse. Stalling for time to allow Howard and Gibbon to reach the scene, Rawn suggested that he and Looking Glass meet again the next day at a point between the two camps and out of rifle range of both of them. The Indians agreed, and rode back up the trail.

The next day, July 26, Governor Potts appeared from Missoula and accompanied Rawn and an escort of some fifty men to meet the Indians. The Nez Perces were waiting at the lower end of Woodman's Prairie. The whites halted, and Rawn, Governor Potts, and Delaware Jim rode forward. As the

Nez Perce warriors formed a watchful line opposite the whites, Looking Glass, Joseph, and one or two others rode out to Rawn. The meeting lasted about half an hour; during its course the volunteers, soldiers, and warriors sat tensely on their mounts, fingering their rifles and eyeing each other's ranks nervously.

The parley was fruitless. Rawn later said that he repeated his demand that the Indians surrender their arms, and that Looking Glass told him that he would have to talk to his people. The chief, according to the officer, asked for still another council on the following day, and Rawn, still stalling for time, was agreeable to the request. The second council, held on July 27, was similarly without result.

The actual conversations between Looking Glass and Rawn at both meetings are shrouded in confusion and conflicting testimony by both Indians and whites.[27] Some Indians said later that when Looking Glass and his escort re-

27. Despite the existence of numerous personal reminiscences by Indians and whites of what happened at the eastern end of the Lolo Trail—or perhaps *because* of the existence of so many of them—no episode of the Nez Perce war is more unclear today. The reminiscences are often in total disagreement concerning dates, chronology, participants in meetings, what was said and not said, etc. To begin with, some accounts state that the units of Woodbridge and Coolidge captured John Hill and the Bitterroot Valley Nez Perces on July 22, while others say that Rawn and his regulars captured them on July 25. Many Indians and whites claimed that the Nez Perce chiefs came down for a council the same day that Rawn arrived on Lolo Creek, that it was the only council held, and that the Indians moved around the barricade the next day. McWhorter, in *Hear Me, My Chiefs,* was so sure, after gathering evidence in the twentieth century from surviving Indian and white participants, that there was only one council that he deprecated a Montana state historical marker at the site of "Fort Fizzle" which stated that the troops had occupied it for three days, and said flatly, "The Nez Perces, of course, made only one night camp" (p. 356 n.). However, Rawn, whose official report makes no mention of the presence of Governor Potts and, in addition, seems to have got every date wrong, spoke of two distinct councils; Captain J. B. Catlin of the Skalkaho volunteers said, "there was a parley for a couple of days"; W. B. Harlan, a volunteer from Como in the Bitterroot Valley, spoke of formal councils on two successive days; and Duncan McDonald, who got his information from White Bird, related the details of three meetings, the first one being with a captain of the volunteers. It is puzzling even to know with whom Rawn had his councils. All accounts mention Looking Glass, while some include White Bird and Joseph, and some do not. Certain of the accounts, including those of Indians, tell of the Nez Perce disposition to fight their way past the barricade if necessary; but Joseph, Yellow Wolf, and other Indians thought that Looking Glass had effected a truce or peace agreement with Rawn. See below, n. 28.

Among the known facts the following seem definite: Rawn began construction of his barricade on July 25, and the Indians marched around him on July 28. Beyond that, my narrative rests on a comparison of the various accounts written about the event by participants, and on a careful working out of their corroborative details. I have noted turned to the Nez Perce camp after one of the parleys, the chiefs and warriors formed a circle around him to hear his report. When Looking Glass told them of Rawn's repeated insistence that they give up their arms, arguments are supposed to have broken out. Rainbow and Sarpsis Ilppilp, according to Two Moons, called out that they would not lay down their guns or stop fighting. Joseph—White Bird later told Duncan McDonald—proposed that they simply try to march past the white men in peace, but that if they had to fight, they should fight. There were probably undercurrents of jealousy and distrust of Looking Glass present in the camp, for he could not seriously have tried to persuade the warriors to give up their guns. Objecting to advice from Joseph, Looking Glass was said by White Bird to have asserted to the Walowa chief that the bands had made him their leader and that he would get them past the barricade without fighting.

Looking Glass's confidence, as reported in White Bird's account, tends, in turn, to explain versions of still other Indians, including Joseph himself, who got the idea that Looking Glass had made some sort of agreement with Rawn. The military officer, they thought, had assured the Nez Perce spokesman that if the Indians maintained the peace, no one would attack them in Montana.[28] Although it is improbable that Rawn actually did make such an agreement, some of the Montana citizen volunteers—most of whom were becoming increasingly frightened and irritated with the officer's stubbornness—eventually came to a similar conclusion and believed that he had finally given the Nez Perces permission to pass the barricade but had withheld that information from the volunteers.

Whatever he told Looking Glass, however, Rawn returned from the second council to find about 100 of the Bitterroot Valley volunteers deserting the barricade and starting for their homes. They had learned of Looking Glass's promise not to attack the settlers, and after discussing it had finally decided, according to Rawn, that "no act of hostility on their part should provoke the Indians to a contrary measure." Rawn tried to hold them, but

---

many of those accounts in the bibliography, but the following, I think, are the most important: Rawn's report in the Report of the Secretary of War (1877), *1*, 548; the reminiscences of Sergeant Charles Loynes, Captain John L. Humble, Two Moons, and Wottolen in McWhorter, *Hear Me*, pp. 347–54; W. B. Harlan's reminiscence in Alva J. Noyes, *In the Land of Chinook* (Helena, Montana, 1917), pp. 63–69; Amos Buck, "The Battle of the Big Hole," *Contributions of the Historical Society of Montana* (Helena, 1910), 7, 119–20; McWhorter, *Yellow Wolf*, p. 107; and Duncan McDonald in *New Northwest*, December 27, 1878, and January 10, 1879.

28. See Chief Joseph, "An Indian's Views of Indian Affairs," *North American Review*, *128* (April, 1879), 426: "We then made a treaty with these soldiers. We agreed not to molest any one and they agreed that we might pass through the Bitter Root country in peace."

they had no stomach for a fight against the Indians, and they continued to leave "in squads of from one to a dozen." Sometime that day, also, Governor Potts decided that he could be of no further assistance on the scene and returned to Missoula.

Early the next morning, July 28, Looking Glass gave the signal to the bands to start down the canyon. The Indians' tactic, again ascribed erroneously to Joseph's military genius, was in reality a logical course for the freedom-bent Nez Perces to have agreed on. If they were to get by the barricade without fighting, they would have had to do exactly what they did do. Ordering the warriors to move into a screening line among the trees and rocks on the northern slope of the canyon overlooking the white men, the chiefs led the families up a gulch, also on the northern side of Lolo Creek, about half a mile upstream from the soldiers' position. Climbing to the top of the mountain, they turned east again and hurried the people along with the livestock, high above the barricade and the screening line of warriors.

The flanking movement met with no difficulty. Six whites, detailed early in the morning to climb the mountain and spy on the Nez Perces' camp, saw the Indians start off up the gulch and were almost cut off by the Indian column before they could get back to Rawn with a report of what was happening. One of them, a Bitterroot Valley settler named W. B. Harlan, claimed later that Rawn had been drinking that morning and refused to believe the report, remarking that "The trouble in this camp is that there are too many God Almightys in it." Nevertheless, the Indians were soon seen high on the mountain, hastening past the barricades toward Sleeman Creek and the Bitterroot Valley. Some of the whites began shooting at the Nez Perces, and the warriors in the screening line returned the fire from their hiding places on the lower part of the slope. Rawn finally took action, ordering the volunteers to charge the Nez Perces. Between thirty and forty men responded, but the Indians had disappeared before the whites had got halfway up the wooded hill.

Rawn then reorganized his men into a skirmish line across the canyon and led them downstream toward the creek's mouth, where he had stationed a small rearguard. On the way down, Charlot and the Flathead Indians left for their homes, and more of the volunteers deserted the regulars. Several miles down the canyon, the whites caught a glimpse of the Indians, who by then had descended the mountain and were again following the creek to the Bitterroot Valley. Instead of risking a fight, Rawn halted his men until the last of the Indians disappeared. By the time the whites reached the canyon mouth, the Nez Perces had had brief firefights with Rawn's small rearguard and with an isolated and frightened group of volunteers; had captured three citizens and let them go with an admonishment to return to their homes and tell everyone that the Nez Perces would not harm the settlers; and had started without further opposition up the broad, open Bitterroot Valley. Outmaneuvered and outnumbered, Rawn, now left with only his small force of regulars and some twenty Missoula volunteers, marched unhappily back to Missoula to wait for Gibbon and Howard. As word of what had happened spread through the settlements, the citizens' fears were momentarily eased by admiration for the Nez Perces and laughter at Rawn. The humor of the frontier people pictured the regular officer as a nitwit, and they dubbed his bypassed barricade "Fort Fizzle." [29] Rawn, in turn, had to have a scapegoat of his own, and he blamed the Bitterroot volunteers for deserting him just when he needed them. The conduct of the people of the Bitterroot during the ensuing days played into his hands and aroused the scorn of settlers in other parts of western Montana. But the situation was too dangerous for the bickering to last, and fast-moving events quickly put the Lolo Trail episode into the background.

29. Not everyone laughed at Rawn. "Wipe out the disgrace that has been put upon us, and never let any regular officer again command Montana Militia," Chauncy Barbour, editor of the *Weekly Missoulan,* wrote to Governor Potts on July 31 (Beal, *I Will Fight,* p. 102). Three days later, however, as Beal points out, Barbour changed his mind and wrote again to the Governor, telling him that it had been wise that no hasty action had been taken, for it would have resulted in the ravaging of the region: "our people . . . congratulate themselves that our welfare was in the hands of discreet men," he said. Regarding "Fort Fizzle," the last remains of its logs were consumed in a brush fire in 1934.

14

"This Most Wonderful of Indian Wars"

ON THE FIRST EVENING in the Bitterroot Valley, the bands camped eight miles above the mouth of Lolo Creek near the ranch of J. P. McClain on the route to Stevensville and Skalkaho. A group of about fifty citizen volunteers, on their way to their homes from the Lolo debacle, blundered into the Indian camp but were reassured by Looking Glass that the Nez Perces bore them no ill will. "I give you my word of honor," the chief told them, "that I will harm nobody." The white men continued on, much relieved, and helped spread the word through the Valley that the Idaho Indians were no longer on the war-path and would travel peacefully past the settlements.

That same evening three Indians arrived at the camp from the north and called at the tipi of a Nez Perce named Left Hand, a relative of Eagle From the Light. They were two treaty Nez Perces, Grizzly Bear Boy and his brother, Horn Hide Dresser, and a Yakima with the olden name Owhi; and the three had been serving as scouts for Colonel Nelson Miles in the Sioux country of the Yellowstone. They had heard about the Nez Perce war and, deserting Miles, had made their way to the Flathead reservation, where they had met Eagle From the Light, who even before the outbreak of the war had become disgusted with conditions in Idaho and had settled down with Flat-head friends. At the suggestion of Eagle From the Light, they had come south to meet the warring bands and propose to them that they head north, pass through the Flathead reservation, and cross into Canada, only a short distance away, where they could find safety.

Left Hand sent for the chiefs and war leaders of the different bands, and a council took place to consider Grizzly Bear Boy's message. White Bird, Toohoolhoolzote, Red Owl, and several others thought it a good idea to change the plan of march and take the short route to Canada. But Looking Glass would have nothing to do with it. After seeing Charlot with Rawn's men, he no longer trusted the Flatheads and thought that the Nez Perces might find themselves having to fight their way past their former friends on the Flathead reservation. In the Bitterroot Valley, he assured the others again, there would be no war, and from the Bitterroot all the way to the Crow country they would pass no settlements or forts and could travel in safety. In the part of Canada north of the Flathead reservation, moreover, times would be hard, for the Indians would find no buffalo west of the Rockies. On the Montana plains the families would have plenty to eat. The people could hunt in safety, dry their meat, and eventually return to their homes. Supported by Five Wounds and Rainbow, who also felt more secure in their knowledge of the Crows and the route to their country, Looking Glass had his way, and the council agreed to abide by the original plan.

Grizzly Bear Boy and his companions elected to stay with the warriors, even though their proposal was turned down, and the next day the bands headed up the valley toward Stevensville. During their last days on the Lolo Trail, their five-man rearguard had overtaken them and reported that Howard was not pursuing them. It seemed now that they had surely left the soldiers in Idaho and that the war was over, and they traveled leisurely, satisfied at last that no one was chasing them. Near Stevensville, Looking Glass and some of the warriors visited Charlot to show that they wished to be friendly and to ask him where the bands could camp. Charlot pointed out a place to them, but he upbraided Looking Glass for having the blood of white men on his hands, and the Nez Perce chief decided to ignore him.

The bands remained in the vicinity of Stevensville for two days, July 29 and 30. Many of the white families, not trusting the reports of the Indians' friendliness, continued to huddle in the old fort that John Owen had built, but a number of merchants kept their stores open in the town and did a thriving business with the Indians. The Nez Perces bought flour, sugar, coffee, and tobacco and paid scrupulously for their purchases with gold dust or currency which they had accumulated in their trade with white men before the war. There was minor trouble when one of the merchants violated an agreement among the store owners and sold some whiskey to an Indian. When the latter became drunk, Looking Glass had him seized and sent to camp under guard, and thereafter, it was said, the chief himself patrolled the streets to see that the Nez Perces behaved themselves. The whites of the Bitterroot Valley, already under criticism for the action of their volunteers at "Fort Fizzle," received renewed blame for their trade with the warring bands, but they replied sharply that the Indians, who needed provisions and supplies, would have raided and ravaged the area and taken what they wanted, anyway, if the stores had been shut to them.

About this time, some ten or twelve Nez Perces, including several women and children, who lived in the Bitterroot Valley joined the bands, believing apparently that the fighting was over and intending merely to travel to the buffalo country with the big group. The new contingent included Tom Hill, another of Delaware Jim's sons, and a footloose, half French, half Nez Perce hunter who had several names, including Lean Elk, Little Tobacco, and Hototo, but who was best known to white men in many frontier towns in Montana as Poker Joe, because of his love for that game. A short, voluble man with a loud voice, Poker Joe, according to one story, had been on his way across the Lolo Trail on a visit to Idaho when he had heard of the outbreak of the war. He had turned back to Montana and had accidentally gashed his leg with a knife in the mountains. When white men had seen him limping after his return, they had accused him of having been in one of the battles in Idaho. Their refusal to believe his story had irked him, and when the warring bands had come along, he had decided to join them.[1] As a brave and impulsive fighter, he was a welcome addition to the warriors, but his knowledge of the country east of the Bitterroots and his ability as a leader would soon make him even more valuable to the Indians.

On July 31 the Nez Perces took up their slow march again, traveling at a rate of about twelve miles a day. At Corvallis and Skalkaho they found that the whites had constructed sod and log stockades to protect the women and children. The Indians rode up and examined the forts, and their friendliness and amusement reassured the settlers, some of whom were even said to have visited the Indian camp and sold bullets to the warriors. Again, the Nez Perces traded at the stores and called at the homes of several settlers. At Corvallis, a youth named Amos Chaffin admired a beaded jacket worn by one of the Indians, whom he thought was either Looking Glass or White Bird, and told his nine-year-old nephew, Moses, "If we ever get into a fight with these fellers I'm goin' to get me that fancy jacket." [2] Farther up the valley, on August 5, some of the young men of Toohoolhoolzote's band went off on their own and rifled the deserted cabin of a man named Myron Lockwood, taking some flour, coffee, a few shirts, and several other articles. When the Indians returned to the camp, boasting of their plunder, Looking Glass

1. Statement of Camille Williams in McWhorter, *Hear Me*, p. 360.

2. Soon afterward, Amos Chaffin, as a citizen volunteer, participated in the battle of the Big Hole. After the fight Moses asked him, "Uncle Amos, where's the Chief's jacket?" Amos replied: "By grabs, I had all I could do to keep my own jacket." Letter from Glenn Chaffin, Corvallis, Montana, to the author, September 24, 1962.

irately made them leave three of their horses in Lockwood's field, first branding the animals with Lockwood's iron.

With that exception, the Nez Perces displayed perfect conduct toward the whites throughout their march up the valley. The settlers could scarcely believe their luck, and outsiders who heard what was happening wondered incredulously again at the apparent humanitarianism of Chief Joseph. Even stories of thefts by the Indians proved groundless; charges that horses and camping equipment were taken from some homes evaporated when it was revealed that the property had belonged, in the first place, to buffalo-hunting Indians who had left their animals and possessions in the care of white friends earlier in the year.

At the upper end of the valley, where the hills began to close in on the route, the Nez Perces passed the sacred Medicine Tree, a tall and stately yellow pine which the Salish and Sahaptin peoples had respected for generations and which Indians had pointed out to white explorers, trappers, and traders earlier in the century. A huge horn of a mountain sheep, its tip partly imbedded in the trunk of the tree eight feet above the ground, gave the tree its reputation for possessing a strong spiritual power, and Salish and Sahaptin travelers felt its spell and often sought its aid in ensuring success in hunts, fights, or other ventures on which they were embarked. To some of the Nez Perces the region seemed charged with the supernatural, and in this part of the valley several of the warriors, beginning to show signs of restlessness from the slow pace with which Looking Glass was leading them, gave voice to ominous feelings. Wahlitits, who had started the war, rode around one morning, calling loudly that he had had a dream in which he had seen himself killed. "I will be killed soon!" he cried. "I do not care. I am willing to die . . . I shall not turn back from the death. We are all going to die!" Another fighter named Peopeo Ipsewahk (Lone Bird) twice announced his own dreams, warning the chiefs of disaster if they continued the slow pace. "My shaking heart tells me trouble and death will overtake us if we make no hurry through this land! I can not smother, I can not hide that which I see. I must speak what is revealed to me . . . Why the idea these chiefs travel slowly? Maybe our enemies are now overtaking us, and we get whipped! We should keep going! . . . Move fast! Death may now be following on our trail!" Even Yellow Wolf said: "there was something—a feeling some of us could not understand." [3]

Looking Glass scoffed at their fears. Howard had been left behind in Idaho, and the Indians had seen that the Montana people wanted no war with

3. McWhorter, *Yellow Wolf*, pp. 108–09, and *Hear Me*, pp. 363–64. The handsome Medicine Tree still stands by the side of Highway 93, eleven and a half miles south of Darby, Montana, but the ram's horn has disappeared, chopped off at some time in the past by a drunken lumberjack who wanted to hang it in a saloon in Hamilton, Montana.

them. The families were safe, and they would be safe all the way to the Crows, he said. Brushing aside the warnings, he continued the slow march, leading the bands through Ross Hole, which had been named for Alexander Ross, and up and over the Continental Divide near present-day Gibbons Pass to the head of Trail Creek, which ran down into the Big Hole Valley. On the night of August 6 the Indians camped on Trail Creek, and the next day began the descent to an old campsite known by its Salish name, Izhkumzizlakik Pah (place of the "picket pin," an animal smaller than a ground squirrel), and used for decades by Salish and Nez Perce hunting parties on their way to and from the plains. The bands reached the site, a level prairie on the Big Hole River at the junction of Trail and Ruby creeks just below the slope of the mountains, on the evening of August 7, and Looking Glass announced that they would stay there the next day. Ever since the battle of the Clearwater, when the people had had to abandon their tipis, they had been sleeping in the open, and the halt was to give them time to rest and cut and dry new lodge and travois poles before starting across the flatter and more open country.

Once again, historic memories might have stirred among the older Nez Perces. In the Big Hole they had hunted with Shoshonis and Flatheads, and had fought the Piegans and Bloods. Across the valley, Nez Perces less than fifty years before had trailed with Hudson's Bay Company brigades and American mountain men. They had been there with Finan McDonald, Alexander Ross, Peter Skene Ogden, Jim Bridger, Tom Fitzpatrick, Jedediah Smith, and many other white friends. Now, the companionship and frolic of those days—unknown to the settler whites and the soldiers of Howard and Rawn—were gone.

The large Indian pony herd, still numbering almost 2,000 animals, was pastured part way up the hill, and the next morning the families commenced working and having a good time. It was their first moment of peace since the start of the war, and most of the Indians were relaxed. Not so much as one picket was out, even to stand watch over the horse herd. But among some of the warriors the uneasiness had not disappeared. Ominous dreams were still being reported, and even a few men who had not had supernatural signs of warning felt that it was wrong to take no precautions. Several of the warriors met in council that morning and decided to send scouts back along the trail to be certain that soldiers had not followed the families. But when they tried to borrow fast horses for the riders, they were turned down brusquely. Five Wounds got into an argument over it with Looking Glass, but the chief was adamant in his opposition to the scouting party, fearing perhaps that the warriors would shoot someone or indulge in an unwise action that would give the Montana whites an excuse to make war on the bands. He remembered the way the fighting had started in Idaho, and he finally had his way. "All right,

Looking Glass," Five Wounds said, giving in to the chief's decision. "You are one of the chiefs! I have no wife, no children to be placed fronting the danger that I feel coming to us. Whatever the gains, whatever the loss, it is yours." [4]

During the day the people cut and peeled lodge poles and raised new tipis. A few of the men went hunting, but most of them lolled about the camp, playing the stick and bone game, while the women dug camas roots and set them to baking in pits in the ground, and the children raced happily along the bed of the stream. Several times individuals in the camp thought they saw white men looking down at them from the top of the hill. But they shrugged it off, confident that they were only curious settlers or, perhaps, even some of Rawn's men who had followed their trail from Lolo Creek. Even if they were soldiers, there could not be many of them, and if they had meant to attack them, they would have done so already. At night the fires were lighted, and the families sought warmth around the flames. Some of the men began to chant, and many of the people danced and rode around on horses, happy at last to be in the open country, away from the hostility of settlers. Their hearts were light; there was nothing to fear any longer. Near the creek, some boys who were playing a game in the chill night air suddenly noticed two men wrapped to their eyes in gray blankets, standing close by and silently watching the camp. They realized that they were white men, and in fright they stole away from the creek and ran to their tipis. They were too afraid to tell anyone, and soon they could see that the white men were gone. Still, they said nothing about it to the grownups, but wrapped themselves in their own blankets and went to sleep. Gradually, the dancing stopped, the flames of the fires died, and quiet settled over the starlit camp. It was the night of August 8.

Five days before, Gibbon had reached Fort Missoula from Fort Shaw. Gathering up Rawn's command, Gibbon had halted only for the night. On the morning of August 4 he sent a messenger up the Lolo Trail to Howard, informing him that he was pursuing the Nez Perces at once. Then with 17 officers and 146 enlisted men of the 7th Infantry, he started for the Bitterroot Valley. He went as fast as he could go, carrying his infantry—whenever the roads permitted it—in mule drawn supply wagons, driven by local settlers. On the first day his column covered twenty-five miles and reached Stevensville, where he picked up a mountain howitzer at Fort Owen and added it to his train. The next day he rolled into Corvallis, enlisted a guide named Joe Blodgett, who was familiar with the Ross Hole and Big Hole country, and met with some volunteers who wanted to go with him. There had been an

4. McWhorter, *Hear Me*, p. 369.

argument among those men. Their captain, J. L. Humble, had opposed their going after the Indians. The Nez Perces could have wiped out the whites in the valley when they had passed through it a few days before, he had reminded them. Instead, the Indians had shown themselves to be friendly, and now it would be wrong to participate in an attack against them. He had finally agreed, however, to present the volunteers' offer to Gibbon, and to lead them as far as Ross Hole. Gibbon rebuffed the volunteers at first, telling them curtly that he did not want to encumber his troops with citizens, but later he changed his mind and agreed to let them come along. When the news reached nearby Skalkaho, volunteers in that locality had the same argument with their captain, John B. Catlin, but finally persuaded him to lead them to Gibbon's column. The group overtook the army the next day, and although Gibbon frowned on their coming, the Skalkaho citizens fell in line also, swelling the number of volunteers with the army to about seventy-five men. In later weeks, when Catlin was asked why he had turned on the Indians who had treated the Bitterroot Valley settlers so kindly, he replied that he had wanted to punish the Nez Perces for what they had done to the whites in Idaho. More likely, however, most of the citizens who now volunteered so eagerly were simply swept up by the excitement of an adventure and by the hope of acquiring Indian horses and gold dust after they had defeated the Nez Perces.

On August 6 Gibbon reached Ross Hole, where Captain Humble, true to his word, left the Corvallis volunteers and turned back. Other citizens had meanwhile dribbled away from the army, and more of them now lost heart and departed with Humble. The command of the remaining settlers, numbering thirty-four men, was assumed by Catlin. That afternoon Gibbon found a use for the citizens. Recognizing that some of them knew the country well, he sent Catlin and ten companions scouting ahead to see if the Nez Perces had crossed the divide to the Big Hole or were still on the western side of the mountains. Catlin took his men far enough to determine that the Indians had crossed the summit toward the Big Hole and then made camp on top of the mountain to wait for the troops. The army labored up the slope with its wagons and howitzer the next day, and late in the afternoon joined Catlin. That evening Lieutenant James H. Bradley, another veteran of the plains campaign against the Sioux, set off on a night march with Blodgett, about thirty regulars, and Catlin and his entire group of volunteers, to cross the Divide, try to locate the Indian camp, and, if possible, stampede the Nez Perces' horses. The men found the trail obstructed by fallen trees, and daylight overtook them before they had sighted the Big Hole Basin. Bradley hid the men in an area off the trail and, after eating breakfast, started forward again with two of the regulars. After a while, the three men heard the sound of axes; climbing a tall tree, Bradley sighted the open country and the Nez Perce camp, nestled in a meadow at the foot of the mountains about a mile to the northeast. Indian women, at work in the woods near the base of the hill, were unconcernedly cutting down pine trees for lodge and travois poles.

Bradley and his companions hurried back to the other men and sent a messenger to Gibbon with news of the Indians' location. The word spurred the army forward, and at evening Gibbon and his column reached Bradley's hiding place, six miles from the Nez Perce camp. Gibbon put out pickets and ordered the men to rest until eleven P.M. At that hour he started the troops and volunteers forward in the darkness. The howitzer would make noise, crunching over the brush along the trail, and he left it, together with his supply train and all the horses except his own and that of his adjutant, Lieutenant C. A. Woodruff, directing that the cannon and a mule loaded with rifle ammunition be sent forward to him the next morning. The command marched for five miles in silence, reaching the rim of the mountain, and then moved northeastwardly on a descending trail along the hillside for another mile, until the men were directly above and west of the Indian camp. They were suddenly in the midst of the large Nez Perce pony herd that had been pastured on the slope without a guard, but as the troops halted and remained quiet, the animals gave no sign of alarm and gradually moved up the hillside above them. Stringing out the soldiers and volunteers along a twelve-hundred-yard front on the trail, Gibbon settled them down to wait for dawn, when they would charge the village. It was now the early hours of August 9.[5]

There was a stir in the night, when Indian women came out of the tipis,

5. I am indebted to Jack R. Williams, former superintendent of the Big Hole Battlefield National Monument, Wisdom, Montana, and to his colleagues for supplying me with copies of original narratives and other documents pertaining to the battle of the Big Hole, and for accompanying me helpfully over the terrain of the conflict. These members of the National Park Service have done a superb job in marking the battlefield so that visitors may easily grasp the course of the action. In addition, "The Siege Area Trail Guide," which they compiled, is a model of accuracy, interest, and clarity. Acknowledgment is due also to the earlier work of Lucullus McWhorter, who visited the battlefield with several Nez Perce veterans of the fight and painstakingly erected stakes and drew identifying charts so that future generations might know just where everything happened. McWhorter returned on three other occasions and finished the job in 1938. Many Nez Perce veterans of the war refused ever to revisit the battlefield. One of the last Indian survivors of the conflict, Josiah Red Wolf, was viewing the Whitebird battlefield in Idaho with the author and others in May 1963 when he was more than ninety years old, and said that he would never go back to the Big Hole, where so many of his relatives had been killed. The bridge in time was almost unbelievable. As the aged Indian was talking about the bitterness of the 1877 conflict, which was still vivid in his mind though it had occurred eighty-six years before, several people near us were listening on a portable radio to the report of the descent of an astronaut from outer space.

built up the fires, and chatted a moment. Then they returned to their lodges. About 3:30 in the morning, light began to appear in the eastern sky, and the soldiers could more easily make out the village. Eighty-nine tipis, most of them leather but a few of canvas, were strung out along the east bank of the river in a V, with its apex to the north. The stream, which the men would have to ford to reach the camp, ran toward the north, twisting roughly parallel to the mountain, about a quarter of a mile from its base. Between the foot of the mountain and the river was a rough area of spongy marsh, grasses, and willow-grown ravines, or sloughs, where the creek had once run. A short distance to the southwest a higher benchland, densely grown with pines, jutted out like a point from the mountain base toward the stream. From that elevated table, pines and willows grew down to the bottomland along the creek.

Gibbon's attack was aimed at the entire line of tipis. His left wing under Lieutenant Bradley and including Catlin's volunteers, would strike the northern, or lower part of the village; two companies of infantry would hit the center; and Captain William Logan and other infantrymen would assault the upstream, or southern, part of the camp. Two companies, including Rawn's, would come in as reserve. While the men waited, Gibbon had an idea of detaching some of his men to drive away the Indians' horse herd. But Blodgett dissuaded him from dividing his forces, telling him that he was fighting Nez Perces not Sioux, and would need every man in the attack. Just before the assault, however, Gibbon again changed his mind and sent a few men to try to run off the horses as soon as the battle started. Some of the volunteers, it was said, also wanted to know if they should take prisoners. The reply, they understood, was that Gibbon wanted no Indian prisoners. He had not come to parley, to try to persuade the Indians to surrender, or to take captives. He had come to kill.

As the eastern sky lightened, he gave the order for the advance to start, and the men began working their way in silence down through the woods and out across the willow-covered bottomland. Their skirmish line was moving cautiously about two hundred yards from the creek when an aged Indian named Natalekin appeared on horseback from the tipis and started toward them in the gray dawn. The old man was on his way toward the horse herd. It was said later by the Indians that at about the same time Hahtalekin, the Palouse, had also started for the horses but, catching sight of the soldiers, had retreated to the tipis to wake his companions. Old Natalekin, however, had poor eyesight. He saw some figures ahead of him in the gloom, leaned forward on his horse to make them out, and the next instant was shot from his horse by a burst of fire from four volunteers.

The rifle cracks commenced the assault. Firing volleys into the sleeping village, the long line of whites charged suddenly toward the stream, cheering and shouting. The Indians came awake with a start, hearing the crash of fire and the rain of bullets tearing through the lodge covers. Some of the warriors lay dazed, trying to gain their senses; others grabbed their weapons, or ran into the open without arms. Screaming with fright, Indian women seized their babies and children and stumbled out of the lodges, to be met by the troopers' fire. The soldiers waded the river, up to their waists, and came at the tipis, firing and clubbing at everything that moved. On the right, the first lines of soldiers entered the village, colliding with warriors who tried to hold them off. Men fought at close quarters, the Indians firing guns and bows and arrows from clumps of bushes, and the soldiers making good targets. In the pandemonium, bullets splattered everywhere. Many of the troopers shot accidentally at women and children; some did so deliberately. The soldiers' line was not long enough to encompass the southern end of the camp, and warriors and their families gradually got around the troops' flank. One by one, and in small groups, the Indians escaped on foot and on horseback, running for the creek and the woods, where they stopped to get their breath and see about fighting back.

In the center, the troops also swept into the village. The fighting swirled around the tipis, then the warriors, bleeding from wounds, came through the soldiers' lines, following the panic-stricken women and children into the willows and underbrush along the stream. Many of the people were severely injured, but there was no time to care for wounds. The village and the banks of the river were littered with dead, and more persons were being hit each moment. On the left, Gibbon's attack was less successful. Again the line did not reach the end of the village. Worse still, Lieutenant Bradley was killed in the first moments of the attack. Without a leader, the volunteers and soldiers faltered as Indians stood their ground and fought back desperately from the tipis. The whites were gradually forced toward their right, allowing the Indians to move around their flank toward the creek and hills. Once more, families made their escape through the brush while sharpshooters gained positions from which to pick off individual soldiers. The intense fire from this flank slowly pushed the troops toward the center, where other soldiers had stopped fighting and were trying unsuccessfully to set the tipis on fire. The lodge coverings were tough, and wet with frost. The soldiers slashed at the walls, and finally some of them—still sheltering frightened and injured women and children—caught fire and sent up flames and smoke. Into this melee came the troops from the left.

By that time the chiefs and war leaders were rallying the fighters who had escaped from the south and center of the village. Some Indians said they heard old White Bird shouting, "Why are we retreating? Since the world was made brave men fight for their women and children. Fight!" [6] The Nez Perces' re-

6. Duncan McDonald, *New Northwest*, January 24, 1879.

newed fire from the southern flank and the woods on the hill caught the troops in an exposed position. Some of the soldiers left the village and came back to the stream, and fighting flared again in the willows, where warriors were trying to protect their families. At the height of the fury, Gibbon crossed the river. As he entered the village, his horse was shot, and he himself received a flesh wound in his left thigh. At the same time, his adjutant, Lieutenant Woodruff, was wounded. Soldiers milled about, subjected to a crossfire from both ends of the village. Several of the company officers were down, dead or wounded. There was no semblance of order, or of a skirmish line. Gibbon sensed the danger of an Indian counteroffensive and of a panic among his troops. He had seen the elevated benchland at the base of the mountain, slightly to the southwest, and now he ordered a retreat toward it.

It was eight A.M. One of the volunteers said he heard a shout, "Charge that point and rake the brush with your rifles!" The word passed from group to group, and the troops hastened south to the wooded hill. The soldiers and volunteers downriver had the worst of it, being exposed, during their withdrawal, to an Indian sharpshooter who picked them off with deadly accuracy from a tree on the slope above them. But the retreat was orderly, and the men were able to get their wounded safely up to the flat benchland. Those in advance had a brief firefight with Indians already in the woods, but finally they cleared the area. When Gibbon arrived, he ordered the men to form a square defense and dig entrenchments behind logs and boulders with their Rice trowel bayonets. Captain Catlin, one of the last to reach the position, saw the thick stand of trees around them, excellent hiding places for Indian snipers, and exclaimed, "Who in hell called a halt here?" When he was told that Gibbon had ordered it, he snapped, "I don't give a damn. It's a hell of a place to camp." [7]

While the men were digging in, the Indians began to swarm up around them. The battle had suddenly reversed itself. In a few moments, shots were coming in at the soldiers from all sides. The surrounding terrain, as Catlin had seen, favored the Indians, who could choose hiding places and shoot at any soldier who showed himself. A Nez Perce firing line gradually built up around Gibbon's men, and a siege began.

The village, meanwhile, became the scene of tears and mourning. With the soldiers gone, the women, children, old people, and some of the warriors came back to the tipis. Some thirty Indians had been killed in the camp, twenty more along the creek, and still others on the opposite side of the river. Every family had had a loss. Hahtalekin, the Palouse leader, was dead. Wahlitits, the youth who had started the war by avenging his father, had been killed, resisting the soldiers' first charge at the south end of the village.

7. John B. Catlin, *The Battle of the Big Hole,* Montana State Historian's Annual Report (Missoula, Montana, 1927), p. 12.

He and his wife had run out of their tipi and had dropped flat on the ground in a slight depression behind a log. From there, the young warrior had shot at soldiers emerging from a stand of willows. Finally he had raised himself slightly, and a trooper had killed him, the blow of the bullet spinning him on his back. His wife, although wounded at the same time, had seized Wahlitits' rifle, killed one of the soldiers, and then been killed herself. One of the most grievous losses was Rainbow, the beloved war leader. His *wyakin* had told him that he would never be slain in a battle fought after sunrise. When it was known that his body had been found in the willows at the lower part of the camp, a hush came over many of the warriors, and their hearts began to feel pain. Two Moons, Five Wounds, and many other fighters risked the soldiers' bullets to make their way to where the fallen hero lay, and when they saw him, they assured themselves that he had died early, before the sun had risen. Five Wounds, the close companion of Rainbow in many brave fights against the Assiniboines and other tribes on the plains, seemed to empty of life. He began to cry, mourning, "My brother has passed away. I too will now go, as did his father and my father die in war. They lay side by side where the battle was strongest. And now I shall lay down beside my brother warmate. He is no more, and I shall see that I follow him." The other warriors knew what it meant; soon Pahkatos Owyeen, the great Five Wounds, would also be no more.

There were many wounded to care for. The wives of both Ollokot and Joseph had been badly hurt. Just before the troops had abandoned the village, Two Moons, hiding at the creek, had met Joseph. The Wallowa chief had had no gun, but had been shielding his baby who had been born at Tepahlewam. For a second time during a battle, the child was being saved. "Skip for your life," Two Moons had cried to his chief. "Without the gun you can do nothing. Save the child!" [8] Earlier, Joseph had been seen with No Heart on the hillside across the stream, driving the horse herd farther up the hill and to the north, away from the soldiers. A youth named Black Eagle had sighted the chief, barefooted and without leggings, wearing only a shirt and a blanket, trying to save the horses. No Heart, the man who had mocked Howard and his troops at the Clearwater crossing at Kamiah, had been killed by a Nez Perce sharpshooter, who had thought in the confusion that he was a Flathead Indian trying to make off with the Nez Perces' herd. Soldiers, ordered by

---

8. McWhorter, *Hear Me*, p. 385. The Indian side of my narrative is based almost entirely on reminiscences of the warriors and Indian women, as recorded by McWhorter and published in *Hear Me, My Chiefs* and *Yellow Wolf*. The few surviving Nez Perce veterans of the war period, including Sam Tilden, Albert Moore, and Josiah Red Wolf, to whom I was privileged to talk in the 1950s and early 1960s, were able to add little to what McWhorter had already published.

Gibbon to round up the animals, had also come up the hill, but warriors had driven them away, and Joseph had finally herded the horses out of the troopers' reach. Later, after Gibbon's men had retreated to the timbered flat, Joseph and others had headed the horses back to the camp, and now, with the troops out of the village, the Wallowa chief was carrying out his responsibility as guardian of the families.

The people, it was realized, would have to run again. The lodges, out of sight of the troops' besieged position on the hill, were safe for the moment from the soldiers' bullets, but there was much to be done quickly. Amid the cries of the wounded, and the wailing of those who mourned for the dead, Joseph hastily supervised the preparations to move. It was a somber time, full of grief and passion. Nothing was said of Looking Glass. All that had happened was regarded in silence as his fault. He was in disgrace, and would no longer be allowed to lead. The women, aided by some of the men, tearfully gathered the slain members of their families and tried to bury them in the sides of old stream runs, clawing down piles of earth from the overhanging banks to cover them. Then they made their packs and quickly pulled down a few of the tipis. Some of the horses were fitted with travois poles, and the badly wounded, who were unable to ride, were strapped to the crosspieces. At noon, the column of families and the pony herd, accompanied by Joseph and old White Bird, started off to the south, keeping along the western rim of the Big Hole Basin, under the mountains, and leaving the warriors behind to hold the soldiers until the people were safely away.

On the wooded hill, the battle lost none of its fierceness. The first group of warriors around the troops was reinforced by others, and during the morning the Indians kept up a steady fire on the positions of the soldiers and volunteers. Whenever they showed themselves, men on both sides were hit. Toward noon a group of mounted Indians near the trail above the fighting spied Gibbon's howitzer train and ammunition mule coming along the hillside. As the warriors rode to intercept the newcomers, the howitzer was fired twice. Before the soldiers could load it again, the Indians were on top of them, killing one of the members of the detail and wounding two others. The rest of the soldiers picked up the wounded men and escaped back up the trail, leaving the cannon train and the ammunition mule, packed with two thousand rifle cartridges, to the Indians. Looking Glass's warrior, Peopeo Tholekt, who had now ridden up, wanted to wheel the cannon down the trail and use it against the troops' entrenchments. But when its wheels got hung up on a rock, Peopeo Tholekt dismantled it and buried its barrel. Later, Poker Joe rolled it over a bluff into some brush. The captured rifle ammunition was taken down to the other warriors, who found that they could use it in the Springfield rifles they had picked up from dead soldiers on the battlefield.

The siege continued throughout the day, gradually decreasing in intensity but continuing to claim lives. Early in the afternoon, Sarpsis Ilppilp, Wahlitits' companion in the first raids on the Salmon River, was shot through the throat and mortally wounded. He had been fighting with Tipyahlanah Kapskaps (Strong Eagle), the third of the "three red coats" of the White Bird battle, and when Sarpsis Ilppilp dropped, Strong Eagle made an unsuccessful attempt to pull him out of range of the soldiers' bullets. Word was passed back to others, and old Yellow Bull, the father of Sarpsis Ilppilp, anxious lest the troops capture his son's body and mutilate it in revenge for his actions on the Salmon River, offered the youth's white wolfskin neckpiece, considered to have strong spiritual power, to anyone who rescued his son. After several men had been wounded trying to save the warrior—who in the meantime had expired—a strong fighter named Tahwis Tokaitat (Bighorn Bow) finally dragged the body to safety, but later he saw Yellow Bull give the wolfskin neckpiece, instead, to Sarpsis Ilppilp's mother, who was considered to be a "magician," or shaman.

Shortly afterward, Five Wounds was killed. Pensive and silent ever since the death of Rainbow, he had joined an attack on one sector of the troops' trenches. As the Indians wormed their way carefully up the hill, Five Wounds suddenly stood up and, having finally made up his mind to die, rushed blindly up the bluff toward the soldiers. Some of his companions tried to head him off, but failed. At the top of the hill, Five Wounds drew a volley of fire and was instantly killed, his spirit, according to the watching Indians, soaring after that of Rainbow. The attack was called off, and the Indians withdrew sadly to the base of the hill.

Cut off and without prospect of early relief, the soldiers' position worsened rapidly. Men ran out of water, and could do nothing to ease the thirst of the wounded, whose cries and moans filled the air. Toward evening, some of the Indians set fire to the grass at one part of the entrenchments, intending to blind the troops with smoke and then rush in on them. The soldiers saw what they were doing and shouted to each other in fright that the Indians were about to burn them out. But the green grass refused to burn quickly, and the fire went out before it reached the troops.

As night settled over the siege area, many of the Indians withdrew and started after the families. About a dozen of the younger men remained in the darkness with Ollokot, determined to hold the soldiers where they were so that the families could have a night of peace. They kept up an occasional fire on the troops, but Gibbon noticed the relative tranquillity and was able to get two messengers successfully past the Indians, on their way to Deer Lodge and the Salmon River. The rest of the men stayed in their holes, and the suffering continued. The waiting Indians heard the wounded throughout the night moaning and crying, but Gibbon, injured himself, had neither doctors nor medical supplies with him. The soldiers were wracked also by hunger, thirst, and cold. Earlier in the day Lieutenant Woodruff's horse had been killed within the lines. It had been quickly butchered, but the raw meat had not gone far among the command. Now there were no fires, no coffee, and few blankets. The men huddled in misery under the cold, starlit sky. Gradually, said Yellow Wolf, "the night grew old, and the firing faded away." Near dawn, a horseman came cautiously down the mountain trail, hallooing softly in the darkness for Gibbon. He was a messenger named Oliver Sutherland, sent by General Howard, who was hurrying through the Bitterroot Valley. At noon that day Sutherland had reached Gibbon's men who had been standing, six miles back on the trail, waiting with the supply train. The panicked survivors of the Indian attack on the howitzer had just got back to those men with news of the battle. Nevertheless, after sending a messenger to Howard, Sutherland had pushed ahead to find Gibbon. The silence now made him think that the battle was over. Luck was with him, for the Indians did nothing to intercept him and he finally found the circle of Gibbon's troops. At daybreak, having held the soldiers through the night, Ollokot mercifully gave up the siege. Firing two rapid volleys at the troops, he and the last of the warriors rode off after the bands.[9]

Gibbon's men, cut up and dazed, were in no condition to follow. Twenty-nine soldiers and volunteers were dead and forty were wounded, two of them mortally. Seven of the seventeen officers were casualties. Howard and some of his men, coming up hurriedly the next morning, found the troops still in a state of shock, standing watch over the newly dug graves of the dead and trying to ease the pain of the groaning wounded.

The Indians' losses at the Big Hole had also been high. Between sixty and ninety Nez Perces had lost their lives, including twelve of the best warriors. Most of the casualties had been women and children slain during the initial attack on the tipis. It had been a shattering blow to each of the families and bands. They could not forgive Looking Glass, who had lulled them into a false sense of security, but their hearts were also filled with bitterness toward the whites. The Bitterroot Valley settlers had betrayed their trust by partici-

9. Some writers have maintained that the Indians broke off the siege because they were afraid that army reinforcements were on their way and would overwhelm them. This is not accurate. The warriors did not turn tail. At this time, it must be remembered, the bands were again flight-minded. The families had left during the day, and the warriors were anxious to be with them, in case they needed protection. They had penned up the soldiers long enough to let the bands escape, but danger could now come at the refugees from any direction, and they might need help. It was time to go and guard them. To many of the whites the lives of the Indian women and children were cheap; but not so to the Indians, who loved them as any men love the members of their family.

pating in the attack. The Montana people, they now knew, were against them, the same as those in Idaho. The Nez Perces were not safe, and their enemies, it was shown, would kill not only their bravest warriors but their women and children also. Among some of the Indians there were torn consciences. Joseph, whom fate had propelled along almost against his will, later said: "The Nez Perce never make war on women and children; we could have killed a great many . . . while the war lasted, but we would feel ashamed to do so." [10] Joseph was ashamed to kill anyone; he had opposed it on moral grounds, and the prospect of a future in which the people would have to kill to stay alive haunted him. He would continue to move on grimly with the others, seemingly numb at times, almost as if he did not know where he was going or what he was doing. But the savagery of the whites' attack at the Big Hole and the wanton slaughter of the women and children had confirmed his worst fears about the war, and he could no longer object to the wild, young warriors. There were groups of them now who banded together, their respected leaders dead. They were "heap mad, bad Injuns," as some of the other Indians told white men whom they met in the days to come. They were lamenting and angry, looking for revenge and knowing that the Nez Perces could trust no white man. Although Joseph and a few of the other chiefs may have disapproved of their actions, they would no longer have the heart or ability to control them. [11]

At the battlesite, Howard once again took command of the chase. The General had been camped at the hot springs near the eastern end of the Lolo Trail when Gibbon's messenger from Fort Missoula had reached him on August 6 to tell him that Gibbon had started after the Nez Perces but would need one hundred more men and hoped the General could hurry them to him. Howard had immediately dispatched Sutherland to overtake Gibbon and inform him that "General Howard is coming on, as fast as possible by forced marches, with two hundred cavalrymen, to give the needed reinforcement." [12] Then the General, with the cavalry and Bannock scouts, had struck out ahead of his main column and had reached the Bitterroot Valley on August 8. After arranging for wagon transportation for his infantry, he

10. Chief Joseph, "An Indian's View," p. 427.

11. It is not hard to understand the Nez Perces' point of view. They had fought a series of defensive actions in Idaho, trying to stay away from the troops. In Montana their relationship with the whites had led them to believe that no one would attack them anymore. Suddenly they discovered that everyone—even those to whom they had been friendly—was after them, attacking them at every opportunity, killing their women and children, not even wishing to council with them first, but hitting them, and hitting them again. Why? For what? The Nez Perces had not been making war on the whites. But the whites had declared war on the Indians, and would not let them be.

12. Howard, *Nez Perce Joseph*, p. 185.

and the cavalry had hastened up the valley, camping just short of Ross Hole on the night of August 9. Early the next morning, becoming anxious about Gibbon (for whom the fight was just ending), Howard had left in advance of most of his cavalry and, accompanied by forty men, including the Bannock scouts, had traveled fifty-three miles, up the mountainside and across the Divide. Messengers sent to him from the battlefield had missed him, taking another trail back to the valley, but when he had made camp that evening on Trail Creek, seven of the Bitterroot volunteers, who had fled from the siege lines the day before and were on their way home, had straggled in and informed him of Gibbon's plight. Howard's horses had been too exhausted to travel any farther that night; but the next morning at 4 o'clock the General had sent the Bannock scouts off in advance to look for ambushes. Howard had left soon afterward, the volunteers refusing to return with him, although one of them had a desperately wounded brother whom he had abandoned in the siege lines. At 10, Howard had finally reached Gibbon, and elements of his army had streamed in after him.

The General's command stayed with Gibbon until the morning of August 13, its doctors helping to care for the wounded and prepare the survivors for a return to their bases via the Deer Lodge Valley. Catlin and the Bitterroot Valley volunteers went home, glad to leave the battlefield alive and not envying a small group of newly arrived settlers from the Bitterroot who attached themselves to Howard's units and announced boldly that they would go on with the troops. Buffalo Horn and his Bannocks were responsible for a fierce spectacle that disgusted many of the whites. With shrieks of triumph, the Bannocks pulled out the half-buried bodies of the Nez Perces, scalped and mutilated them, and then put on a series of scalp dances at night. Howard and the other officers were dismayed but apparently did nothing to halt the indignities. In time, one of the men, Howard reported, suggested that they do something about the dishonored Indian corpses. "Oh, general," he said, "let us bury them; the settlers on the Big Hole below will desert their ranches if we leave 'em here." Howard's comment in reply was that warfare was horrid, "but Indian massacres, outrages, and brutality, and Indian rule, which is war, are a thousand times worse." [13] The Nez Perces, with justice, could have viewed such a remark as more of Howard's hypocrisy.

When the General finally got moving, he was once more far in the rear of his quarry. On August 9, after leaving the fighting, the bedraggled column of Nez Perce families, bearing their seriously wounded on travois, crawled all afternoon in a southwesterly direction through the Big Hole Valley, staying close to the mountains on the valley's western border and camping that evening twelve miles from the battlefield at a place called Takseen (Willows) on

13. Ibid., p. 211.

Lake Creek. The plight of many of the injured was desperate. At the camp, separated by her husband, who was still fighting, Ollokot's wounded wife, Aihits Palojami (Fair Land), died, leaving a baby boy whom the chief and she had named Tewatakis, or Tuekakas, after his noted grandfather, Old Joseph.[14] Others had died during the march, and more were to die in the following days. Some were buried along the trail. A few who were close to death or were too sick or old to continue the flight begged, according to the ancient custom of the people, to be left behind in the camps, so that they would not hold up the bands and imperil the lives of the rest of the people. Here and there, Howard's pursuers came on the abandoned Nez Perces, and as the soldiers stood by, the Bannock scouts inevitably murdered and scalped them with glee.

Riding rapidly, the warriors from the battlefield reached Lake Creek and overtook the families before all of them had left camp on the morning of August 10. The bands were in a quandary. They would no longer accept the guidance of Looking Glass; and Rainbow, Five Wounds, and some of the others to whom they would have looked for leadership were dead. The man best able to lead them from where they were was Poker Joe, who had joined them in the Bitterroot Valley. The Nez Perces would still go to the Crows, although many of them talked persuasively now of continuing the flight into Canada and joining Sitting Bull's camp. At any rate, Poker Joe knew every trail in Montana, as well as the route to Sitting Bull, and he could give orders for the march without arousing the jealousy of any of the individual bands. The people would still move under the leadership of their own headmen, and the warriors would ride in any group they wished, with or without particular war chiefs giving them directions, but Poker Joe would be the overall leader of the column.

Because of the condition of the wounded, the bands moved slowly on August 10 and 11. On August 12 they finally left the Big Hole Valley, crossed a divide, and trailed south along Bloody Dick Creek to Horse Prairie. Gibbon's messengers had already spread word of the direction in which the Nez Perces had headed when they had withdrawn from the battlefield, and settlers in Montana's Horse Prairie and Idaho's Salmon and Lemhi river valleys, across the Continental Divide from Horse Prairie, were in a state of alarm. Stockades were erected at Bannack City near Horse Prairie and at Junction near the present town of Leadore, Idaho; and riders and small expeditions galloped through the countryside, warning outlying settlers that the Nez Perces were approaching.

The alarms failed to stir some of the ranchers who thought they could take

14. The boy lived through the war and died at the age of 16 on the Colville Indian reservation in Washington.

care of themselves. They had horses, however, and groups of Nez Perce warriors went after their animals. The Indians could use all the remounts they found, and, besides, they had no intention of leaving horses in their rear for the use of pursuing soldiers. On Horse Prairie young warriors killed five white men, probably in fights over their stock, and drove off 250 head of horses. They entered a few ranch homes, ransacked the buildings, but seemed interested only in taking materials that would serve as bandages. That afternoon, leaving terror and tall stories of "massacres" behind them, they trailed westward across Bannock Pass. Reentering Idaho, they moved down Cruikshank Canyon, and at 10 o'clock on the morning of August 13 the vanguard of their column appeared before the settlers' stockade at Junction on the Lemhi River. Many of the white families along the Lemhi had hastened downriver to Salmon City, site of the old wintering grounds of the Nez Perces, Flatheads, and American mountain men. There, a leading citizen of the little town, Colonel George L. Shoup, who had participated under J. M. Chivington in the sad massacre of Cheyenne Indians at Sand Creek, Colorado, in 1864, had directed the building of fortifications against the possibility of the appearance of the Nez Perces. The Lemhi Shoshonis were on a reservation in that area, and Colonel Shoup and other settlers had taken pains to visit their chief, Tendoy, and win his pledge that these descendants of the band of Cameahwait, who had met Lewis and Clark and their own member, Sacajawea, in this region in 1805, would cooperate with the whites. The Shoshonis followed the example of the Flatheads and became still another Indian people to take the part of the white man against their former Nez Perce friends and allies.

Nor were they the only Indians to seek white favors from the Nez Perces' troubles. On the same day—as news of the Nez Perces' arrival in the Lemhi sped through eastern Idaho—the Indian agent at the Fort Hall reservation, near the site of Nathaniel Wyeth's old post, telegraphed Washington that he could enlist 200 Bannocks and Shoshonis on that reserve to fight the Nez Perces. "They would do good service," he wired. "It would be good for the Agency to have them thus employed." Later in the month, Chief Washakie, leader of the Shoshonis on Wyoming's Wind River reservation, who had aided General Crook against Crazy Horse's Sioux at the Rosebud the year before, also offered to turn out his warriors to fight the Nez Perces, and in time, as the Nez Perces would discover, the Crows and Cheyennes would be among their enemies too.[15]

With a friendly Lemhi Shoshoni acting as an intermediary, the stockaded settlers at Junction arranged a council with Looking Glass and White Bird, who assured the whites that the Indians would not harm them. The Nez

15. Beal, *I Will Fight No More Forever*, p. 151.

Perces made a noon camp in the vicinity and called on Tendoy, who wanted nothing to do with them and urged them to hurry out of the area. There were reports, however, that at this time somebody—either a Lemhi Indian or a white man—sold some cartridges to several of the warriors for profiteering prices. After the noon rest the Nez Perce fighting men, having some sport, lined up and charged at the stockade, breaking to the right and left around the frightened defenders, and circling back laughingly to their camp. Not a shot was fired, and soon afterward, when the Indian column trailed off again, up the Lemhi toward the southeast, the barricaded settlers breathed a sigh of relief and sent a messenger to Bannack City to announce their safety and report the direction the Indians had taken.

It was still August 13, and Howard's troops, accompanied by three officers and fifty men of Gibbon's command, had just started from the Big Hole battlefield that morning in pursuit of the Nez Perces. Soon after the General had left the scene of the fight, units of volunteers from Deer Lodge, Helena, and Butte had arrived with doctors and ambulances. Sixty-two of the volunteers took out after Howard later in the day, and caught up with him on August 15. Howard, meanwhile, heard of the Nez Perce shootings on Horse Prairie and learned that the Indians were turning westward toward Idaho, as if they planned to return home. But the General still had two treaty Nez Perce horse herders with him, Captain John, the loyal pro-white, and Meopkowit (Baby, or Know Nothing), called Old George, both of whom had daughters with the patriot bands, and they assured Howard that the Nez Perces were not on their way home, but would definitely circle eastward farther south, along a familiar route which they had often traveled, and head for the buffalo country. Convinced that this was the actual Nez Perce plan, Howard refrained from pursuing the Indians, but worked out a plan to intercept them when they turned eastward. Staying east of them, he would hurry south, cross Monida Pass, and plant himself across the east–west route that the Indians would take from the Lemhi area to the vicinity of Yellowstone Park.

Putting his plan in motion, he hurried southward on August 14, passing Bannack City, where the anxious townspeople watched his column march by, and the next night camped in Horse Prairie Valley. There, for a moment, he had a difficult time. The volunteers from Helena, Butte, and Deer Lodge overtook him, and crowding about his tent, severely criticized him for the slowness of his movements and for his decision not to turn westward and catch up with the Indians. Things got worse for him when Horse Prairie citizens and volunteer messengers from the Lemhi Valley rode breathlessly into camp, announcing that the Nez Perces had appeared at Junction and were threatening the citizens there and at Salmon City. If Howard hurried westward, they pleaded, his troops could trap the Indians in front of the fort at Junction. The

General finally gave in and began preparations to turn westward, but soon after midnight, the messenger dispatched from the Junction stockade arrived with his report that the Indians had left that area without doing damage and were hurrying southeastward as fast as they could go. The clamor ceased immediately, and the next morning the volunteers, now seeing the wisdom of Howard's plan, set off hurriedly with the regulars, heading for Monida Pass and hoping to trap the Indians on the east–west road.

The Nez Perces, meanwhile, were also moving quickly. Ascending the Lemhi Valley from Junction, they crossed present-day Gilmore Divide and started down Birch Creek toward the eastern end of the Snake River plains. In the Birch Creek Valley they had another shooting spree, which raised an additional alarm against them. A train of several freight wagons, hauling liquor and supplies to Salmon City, appeared in their path. The freighters were friendly and stopped for a noon meal with some of the Indians. The chiefs hoped that no trouble would occur, but some of the warriors were definitely hostile and taunting and a fight suddenly started, possibly over an Indian's attempt to seize the freighters' supplies or their horses and mules. There were two Chinese passengers with the wagons, and one story said that after the Indians made the Chinese get down on all fours and bob about like horses, they tried to force the white men to do the same thing. The latter objected, and the Indians began shooting at them. However the quarrel started, the warriors, still inflamed by what had occurred at the battle of the Big Hole, killed five white men, then discovered and opened the whiskey barrels. In an ensuing melee among the Indians, one Nez Perce was mortally wounded by a drunken companion, the freighters' horses and mules were herded off by the warriors, and the wagons were turned into a bonfire. One white man, who managed to escape, and the two Chinese, whom the Indians turned loose, made their way to safety, spreading new panic through the countryside with their story of the "massacre."

The killings angered the chiefs, but the attack was blamed on the warriors' feeling about the Big Hole, and the headmen could do nothing to control the young men. The bands hurried on, circled around the southern flank of the mountains, and headed eastward on a route paralleling the state road toward Targhee Pass and Yellowstone Park. On August 17, beating Howard to the point where he had hoped to intercept them, they reached the junction of the north–south stage road from Bannack City and, scaring the stagekeeper and some assistants into hiding in a nearby lava cave, camped on Beaver Creek, north of present-day Dubois, Idaho. Howard and his troops were still in Montana, just north of Monida Pass. The Helena, Butte, and Deer Lodge volunteers, deciding that the General was traveling so slowly that he would never overtake the Indians, had left him to return home and help swell the criticism that was again mounting against Howard, but that evening a new group, fifty-five volunteers from Virginia City, joined him. The troops were now only a day's march behind the Nez Perces, but Howard must have realized that the Indians might slip past him, if they were not doing so already. Figuring that the Nez Perces would try to cross the Continental Divide at Targhee Pass and then head through the Yellowstone National Park toward the buffalo country, he debated hurrying directly eastward across Montana from where he was, getting to the Targhee Pass ahead of the Indians, whose road would be a slightly longer one. Settlers and stagemen, however, flocked to his camp that evening and, appealing for protection along the road through Idaho, persuaded him to keep to his original plan and move southward across Monida Pass before turning east. Muffing an actual opportunity to get ahead of the Nez Perces, he sent only a token force of forty regulars and some scouts under Lieutenant George Bacon via the shorter Montana route to Targhee Pass, giving them orders to hold the Indians until he could strike them from the rear. The next day, joined by still another new unit— fifty cavalrymen under Captain Randolph Norwood from Fort Ellis, near Bozeman—he moved his cavalry in advance of the slower-moving infantry south across Monida Pass, and in the evening reached the Beaver Creek campsite which the Indians had left that morning. Norwood's men, members of a special detachment of the Second Cavalry, had been sent personally by General Sherman, who had stopped at Fort Ellis on his inspection trip and had studied the flight of the Nez Perces. Howard's reports had indicated that his pursuing troops would soon be able to intercept the Indians and, sensing no crisis, Sherman had dispatched the fresh unit of cavalry to assist in the pursuit. The next week, unaware that there was any danger to the Yellowstone, the Army's commanding general, accompanied by a small guard, went off on a pleasure tour of the national park.

Norwood's men reached Howard just in time for a battle—but not one of the General's choosing. On August 18 Buffalo Horn and his Bannock scouts brought word that they had sighted the Nez Perce camp, now only fifteen to eighteen miles ahead of the army, in the Camas Meadows west of present-day Island Park Reservoir in the northeast corner of Idaho. The meadows were a large, grassy region, crossed by two brush-bordered streams and rising on the north to foothills that extended out in ridges and on the east to a wild area of lava knolls. On August 19, as the Nez Perces left this area, Howard moved in, establishing his headquarters that evening on one of the knolls east of the two streams. Behind him, the Virginia City volunteers established their camp between the two creeks, while Norwood's company and forty infantrymen bivouacked west of them. Other companies of cavalry were flung out around Howard's position.

Rearguard scouts of the bands, meanwhile, had brought word to the Nez Perces during the day that the soldiers were again close upon them. The night before, at Camas Prairie, a wounded man named Black Hair had had a strong vision in which he had seen the warriors going back over the trail to the army camp and coming away successfully with the soldiers' horses. When the people, now camped again only fifteen miles ahead of Howard, learned that the troops were spending the night at Camas Prairie, a council of the warriors was called. Black Hair's vision was considered, and it was decided to try to capture the army's stock. Before midnight, a group of twenty-eight fighting men started back over the trail. Before dawn, they stopped near Howard's camp and the war leaders, including Ollokot, Looking Glass, and Toohoolhoolzote, planned the attack. There was a discussion over whether to go the rest of the way on horses or on foot. Then Ollokot, pointing out that daybreak was approaching, led them ahead on horses until they got almost upon the sleeping soldiers. Some of the young men finally dismounted and crept quietly among a herd of animals, cutting them loose and removing bells from those that wore them. Other Indians stood watch over nearby tents, and the rest waited to stampede the herd away. Suddenly, a sentry heard a sound and called out a challenge. It apparently frightened an impulsive Indian named Otskai (Going Out), who fired his rifle. The shot brought the troops awake and spurred the Indians to action. Yelling, shooting, and waving buffalo robes, the warriors circled the animals, heading them away from the soldiers, and in a thundering rush drove them out of the camp and toward the north.

It took several moments for Howard and his men to know what was happening. The pickets, the General understood, had heard the sounds of horsemen before one of the soldiers had called out his challenge, but they had thought that the noise was from Lieutenant Bacon's men, who might have been returning from Targhee Pass. The Virginia City volunteers, tasting their first alarm, found that half of their horses had vanished, and they scrambled in panic across one of the streams, seeking the protection of the regulars. Cavalrymen struggled to get dressed in the dark, and then could not find their arms. The horses and mules that were still tethered kicked and reared in fright, adding to the din and confusion. By the time that Howard had mounted three companies and ordered them in pursuit, the Indians were far down the trail.

As daylight broke, the warriors discovered to their disgust that instead of unseating Howard's cavalrymen, the principal purpose of their raid, they had taken some 200 of the General's mules. But it would hobble the army's pack train of supplies and ammunition, and the Indians consoled themselves when they saw that some of the volunteers' horses had traveled along with the mules. About eight miles from Howard's camp, the Indian rearguards sighted the troops coming after them. Several of the Indians hurried the drive, pushing the animals more quickly toward the Nez Perce camp but losing in their haste about twenty of the mules, which cavalrymen later overtook and rounded up. The rest of the warriors deployed behind a lava ridge to hold back the soldiers. Some of them waited in a long line on the open sagebrush flats, five hundred yards beyond the ridge, while others hid along the flanks of the hill.

In their pursuit, the three companies of cavalry had hurried forward in parallel columns but had become so widely separated that they had lost contact with each other. Norwood's fifty men of Company L of the Second Cavalry, the center group, eventually got far out ahead of the others and were alone when they reached the ridge. Advance riders of the unit topped the hill, saw the Indian barrier, and withdrew quickly. The troopers then dismounted, gave their horses to a few of the men who took them to the rear, and cautiously made their way to the summit of the ridge, where for half an hour they kept up an ineffective, long-range exchange of shots with the Indians. On the flanks, meanwhile, the other companies ran into sharp fire from Nez Perces on the hill, thought they were ambushed, and fell back. Their withdrawal was a signal to the warriors to press forward and intensify their attack, and the regulars of the two outside companies broke in confusion and fled. Indian marksmen now subjected Norwood's company to crossfire, and those men in sudden panic raced down the ridge and across five hundred yards of open ground to a thicket of cottonwoods and jagged rocks, where their horses were waiting for them. There they made a stand, subjected to the fire of hidden sharpshooters but fighting for four hours from rock-protected rifle pits and effectively holding off the warriors. Elsewhere, the troopers deserted the scene and headed back to Howard's camp. After several miles they came on the General, who was hurrying along with reinforcements. Howard turned the men about, and they went back to look for Norwood. By the time the General and his men, advancing in a skirmish line across the sagebrush and lava knolls, found the embattled company, the warriors had broken off the fight and were riding away to the Indian camp, which had not moved during the day.

No Indians had been killed in the battle, and only a few had suffered slight wounds. Howard had lost one dead, and had had eight men wounded, two of them mortally. But once again the General had let the Nez Perces get away. Despite the disgust of Buffalo Horn and the Bannock scouts, who wanted to continue the pursuit of the Nez Perces, Howard returned to his camp at Camas Meadows, stayed there another night, and the next morning sent the wounded, under guard of most of the volunteers, to Virginia City. Then his men loaded their baggage on every animal still available to them and started off toward Targhee Pass. His mind was on Lieutenant Bacon, supposedly standing guard at the pass, but even that part of his plan went awry. Bacon had reached the pass the day before, while Howard's cavalrymen had been fighting their battle, but after scouting around for Indians had decided that the Nez Perces had taken a more southerly route and were probably crossing Teton Pass to the Jackson Hole country. Abandoning his blockading position, Bacon had started back toward Howard, but he stayed off the main route and managed to miss Howard as well as the Indians.[16] On August 22 the Nez Perces moved by him, unseen, crossed Targhee Pass, and arrived on the upper Madison River at present-day West Yellowstone. The following day the Indians ascended the Madison River into the national park.

Howard himself reached Henrys Lake on the west side of Targhee Pass on August 22, still only a day behind the Nez Perces. The evening before, Captain S. G. Fisher and a new group of Bannock scouts, recruited at the Fort Hall Reservation, had caught up with the army, and early on the morning of August 23 Howard sent them ahead to the pass, hoping they would find Bacon still holding the Nez Perces on the western side. Fisher and the scouts discovered no sign of the Indians or of Bacon, and rode across the pass. Soon afterward, Howard arrived at the gap and realized with some bitterness that Bacon, too, had failed and that, once again, the Nez Perces had evaded him. He wanted to continue the chase, but now, at last, his army came to a halt. His 300 infantry men were exhausted from their long, hurried march from the Clearwater. Their supplies were low, their summer uniforms were ragged and torn, and although it was growing colder, they carried only thin blankets and had no overcoats. Some of the men were barefoot, others wore moccasins of burlap, and the rest were trudging in shoes that were wearing through. Even the cavalrymen were weary from the pursuit. Howard's medical officer, supported by other staff officers, urged a three-day rest for the men, and Howard acceded to their request. As it was, he knew the command had a pressing need for supplies, fresh mounts, and new pack animals. Ordering Fisher and his scouts to stay on the trail of the Nez Perces in the park, keeping him informed of the refugees' progress toward the east, he established a rest camp for his men at Henrys Lake, and sent several of the Montana volunteers to Virginia City, sixty miles away, to purchase horses for his column. At the same time, all the rest of the Montana volunteers and packers departed for their homes, and the cavalry companies of Captains Norwood and Cushing, driving the command's worn-out horses and mules, left for Fort Ellis with Howard's order to resupply themselves and proceed to Crow Agency on the Montana plains, northeast of Yellowstone Park, ready to rejoin the campaign and help trap the Nez Perces when they emerged on the plains from the park. Then Howard hurried with his son, Guy, and an escort to

16. Ibid., p. 163.

Virginia City to send dispatches to his superiors and to oversee the reequip-
ping of his army.

   The General's pursuit of the Nez Perces had now become a national
drama. To some it was a joke, tinged with bitterness and blame for Howard
or with admiration for the Nez Perces, depending on the point of view.
Satirists and funsters, delighting in the David-Goliath aspects of the struggle,
mocked the tribulations and bunglings of the pursuers. Time and again the
Indians, burdened with baggage, women, children, and a large horse herd,
had outrun and outwitted the best that the army could put against them, and
the easy way in which a small number of Indian warriors had doubled back
and stolen Howard's mules from under his nose had seemed to the wags to be
comic opera at its best. Others saw no humor in the situation. "Of one thing
we feel confident," said the *Idaho Semi-Weekly World*, echoing sentiment in
many of the towns in both territories that had felt the war, ". . . General
Howard ought to be relieved and someone else placed in command of the
forces." [17] A number of newspapers, catching the spirit of impatience and
disgust of the volunteers who had come home after serving with Howard,
berated the General for incompetence, blunders, and a failure to move fast
enough, but also gave space to salute a remarkable enemy. ". . . we cannot
forbear testimony to their prowess as warriors and the splendid military intellect that is leading their little handful of men, women, children and possessions from one remote land to another, through an enemy's country and with
five times their number of soldiers to intercept and pursue them," said the
Deer Lodge, Montana, *New Northwest* about the Nez Perces. ". . . their
peaceable, leisurely and audacious march through the Bitterroot Valley; their
quick recovery from surprise on the Big Hole, and tremendous fighting
thereafter; their inexplicable conduct in killing without scalping or mutilating . . . their surprise of the vastly superior force of Howard's cavalry and
capture of a large portion of his train at Camas Meadows, are incidents that
go to make up the inexplicable features of this most wonderful of Indian
wars . . . Their warfare since they entered Montana has been almost uni-
versally marked so far by the highest characteristics recognized by civilized
nations . . ." [18]

   Similar comments heightened an interest in the war in the cities of the East.
Harper's Weekly and other well read periodicals had their engravers make
portraits of Joseph, the supposed leader of the Nez Perces, depicting him fancifully as a noble red man in the Fenimore Cooper–Felix Darley tradition,
and their writers composed biographies of the Wallowa chieftain, together

   17. Issue of August 17, 1877. Ibid., p. 141.
   18. Quoted in the Lewiston, Idaho, *Morning Tribune*, July 28, 1957, in one of an il-
luminating series of articles on the Nez Perce war by Jack Wilkins.

with explanations of the causes of the war and accounts of the Indians' almost unbelievable exploits in their great, fighting retreat, which made Joseph something of a combined national hero and military genius, and swayed the public's imagination in behalf of the valiant refugees.[19]

None of this sat well with the Administration or the Army. Defenders of Howard pointed out that he was humane and was trying to avoid an unnecessary loss of lives on both sides. But as the long trail of bitter injustices that had driven the Nez Perces to hostility were publicized and became better known, the government received no laurels, and as one military detachment after another, officered by seasoned veterans of the Civil War, floundered in the chase, the impatience of Howard's superiors increased. The General was not his own best advocate. In San Francisco, General McDowell fretted restlessly over Howard's excuses for his failures to trap the Indians. Yet Howard kept writing to him with complaints and appeals for assistance from other commands. "Is it worthwhile for me to pursue them further from my department unless General Terry or Crook will head them off and check their advance?" he asked McDowell, as the Nez Perces moved across Montana toward the plains.[20] While he was in Virginia City, Howard got a sharp reply from McDowell, advising him to make his own plans and stop relying on help from others who were still far away.

At the same time, General Sherman had reached Fort Shaw on the Sun River in Montana after a pleasant tour of Yellowstone Park—leaving it only a few days before the Nez Perces entered it—and Howard wired him from Virginia City: "What I wish is from some eastern force, the hostiles be headed off . . . My command is so much worn by overfatigue and jaded animals that I cannot push it much further. If Miles, or Sturgis, is near by . . . I think I may stop near where I am, and in a few days work my way back to Fort Boise slowly . . ."

19. In its issue of August 18, 1877, *Harper's Weekly*, for instance, had said the following about the Nez Perce war: "Joseph, who leads the hostile Indians of his tribe, is not properly a chief, but merely a scalawag Indian who has gathered a band of disaffected warriors about him for the purpose of making a war of rapine and plunder on the whites. He is none the less dangerous, however, for want of legitimate rank and authority. He possesses great influence over the disaffected members of his tribe." But only two weeks later, in its issue of September 1, the same periodical carried a large, though unrealistic, portrait of Joseph, engraved "from a sketch by an army officer," and an article entitled "Chief Joseph" that included the following: "Our portrait of the redoubtable Indian warrior . . . shows him to be a man of intelligence and strength of character. He is certainly a shrewd and active fighter, and his influence over the Indians is very great . . ." After reviewing the history of the tribe and the causes that led the Nez Perces to hostility, the article adds, "And it must be allowed that they have a great deal of right on their side."

20. Beal, *I Will Fight No More Forever*, p. 142.

Sherman, feeling the heat of public opinion to which Howard himself seemed indifferent, replied on the same day, August 24: "I don't want to give orders . . . but that force of yours should pursue the Nez Perces to the death, lead where they may. Miles is too far off, and I fear Sturgis is too slow. If you are tired, give the command to some young, energetic officer . . ."

The rebuke from his old commanding officer of the Civil War stung Howard. On August 27 he answered Sherman: "You misunderstood me. I never flag . . . You need not fear for the campaign. Neither you nor General McDowell can doubt my pluck and energy . . . We move in the morning and will continue till the end . . ."

Sherman relented, his reply making Howard feel better. "Glad to find you so plucky," the Commanding General wired him on August 28. "Have every possible faith in your intense energy, but thought it probable you were worn out, and I sometimes think men of less age and rank are best for Indian warfare. They have more to make . . ." [21]

Nevertheless, the situation on the plains made Sherman anxious. The Sioux and Cheyennes had just been whipped in a costly campaign and, though forced onto reservations, the defeated tribes were restless and showing signs of breaking out again. Sitting Bull was an unconquered menace who might at any moment come riding back from his sanctuary in Canada. Crazy Horse, the Oglala hero, seemed preparing to storm loose from the Red Cloud Agency and lead his Dakotas back to their hunting grounds in the Powder River country. The emergence of the hostile Nez Perces on the plains, flaunting their successes over the soldiers, might be the signal for new uprisings by all the tribes. Tension was high in the Department of Dakota, and McDowell's messages to Sherman evidenced little faith in Howard's ability to cope with a crisis. The next day, August 29, Sherman did some second thinking and wrote Howard a letter authorizing him to transfer his command to the 7th Infantry's Lieutenant Colonel C. C. Gilbert, then at Fort Ellis. Gilbert left Fort Ellis with a detachment of troops on August 31 but missed Howard in Yellowstone Park. Although he hunted him through the mountains, he never did find him, and finally he returned to Fort Ellis, leaving Howard still in charge of the chase.

At the same time, further advice from Sherman assured Howard that, despite his worries, adequate steps were being taken by troops of the Department of Dakota to hem Yellowstone Park and trap the Nez Perces wherever they tried to emerge from it. On the north, two companies of the Second and Seventh Cavalry, led by Lieutenant Gustavus C. Doane and accompanied by Crow Indian scouts, had been ordered into the campaign by Colonel Miles and would be sent to block the park's exit at Mammoth Hot Springs. On the

21. Report of Secretary of War (1877), *1*, 13.

east, Colonel Samuel D. Sturgis, with six companies of Custer's old command, the Seventh Cavalry, 360 troopers strong, was also being sent by Miles to guard the Clark Fork River route, while Major Hart, with five companies of General George Crook's Fifth Cavalry and 100 scouts, would watch the Shoshone River exit near present-day Cody, Wyoming. Another of Crook's officers, Colonel Wesley Merritt, with ten companies of the Fifth Cavalry, was on the Wind River, and Miles, though still far-removed from the scene, at Fort Keogh near present-day Miles City at the mouth of the Tongue River, would be ready to move quickly with a large force wherever necessary. A veritable ring of troops, hastened into position with the aid of the telegraph —a white man's facility of intelligence information not available to the Nez Perces—was being formed to stop the Indians; and with Howard driving them from the west, the refugees, it was believed, would now certainly be caught, the threat of renewed trouble with the plains tribes would be nipped, and the criticism of the Army would cease.

On the morning of August 27 Howard began his pursuit again, leading his refreshed troops over Targhee Pass and into Yellowstone Park. The Nez Perces, meanwhile, had moved up the Madison River, aware that Howard's Bannock scouts were trailing them. Poker Joe had counseled the choosing of a shorter route across the park than the one with which he was familiar, and from the Firehole River he was not entirely sure of the way across the deeply wooded mountains to the Yellowstone River. The park had been established by Congress in 1872. Although it was still little changed from its original wild state (no funds had been appropriated for roads or other facilities), it was already popular with tourists and campers and there was something incongruous about an Indian war being waged within its confines. Several parties of tourists and many individuals, dimly aware that Howard was chasing Chief Joseph's Nez Perces somewhere west of the park, were wandering blithely among the Yellowstone's scenic wonders when the Indians burst upon them. The encounters were lively and dramatic and produced some of the most lurid stories of the war.

While they were hunting for the route east, the Nez Perces came on the first of the whites, an elderly prospector named John Shively. He told them that he knew the way to the Crow lands east of the park, and they swooped him up and pressed him into service as a guide. That night, August 23, near their camp at the junction of the Firehole River and the stream now known as Nez Perce Creek, Yellow Wolf and several scouting companions saw the light of a campfire, and the next morning surprised a party of nine tourists from Radersburg, Montana, and a prospector who was with them. The party, including a Mr. and Mrs. George F. Cowan and Mrs. Cowan's brother and sister, Frank and Ida Carpenter, were just concluding a happy vacation. The Nez Perces were unwilling to leave any white person behind them who might report their movements to the pursuing scouts and soldiers, and they took the entire group, fearful and trembling, up Nez Perce Creek with them. Shively guided the column for half a day toward Mary Mountain. There the Indians got their bearings, and although Shively stayed with the Nez Perces for a week, they no longer needed his services.

The Indians did nothing to the old man, but they gave the members of the Radersburg party an experience that haunted them for years. Their original captors had warned the tourists that some of the Indians were "heap mad" about the deaths of their people at the battle of the Big Hole, and regarded all whites, citizens and soldiers alike, as enemies of the Nez Perces. Traveling up the forested mountain, the Indian column became strung out, and the frightened whites soon found themselves surrounded by some of the angrier young warriors. When two of the whites successfully ducked away through the trees and escaped from the Indians, raising the threat that they might inform Howard of the Nez Perces' position, some of the Indians lost their temper and shot at Cowan and another of the tourists. Poker Joe arrived to halt the fray, but Cowan, who seemed to be dead, and his injured companion, who got away, were abandoned in the woods. Three other members of the party also escaped, but those who were still with the Indians traveled along with the different bands and found the rest of their stay with the Nez Perces a nightmarish experience. That afternoon, having passed Mary Lake and Mary Mountain, the Nez Perces descended the hills to Hayden Valley, upriver from the falls of the Yellowstone, and made their camp near the Mud Volcano. Mrs. Cowan and Carpenter spent the night by the campfire of Chief Joseph himself, and although Mrs. Cowan was distraught over what had happened to her husband, she seemed somewhat reassured to be under the protection of the humane chieftain about whom all Montana was talking. Her brother tried unsuccessfully to engage Joseph in conversation, she said. The chief was "sombre and silent," but she added: " 'The noble red man' we read of was more nearly impersonated in this Indian than in any I have ever met. Grave and dignified, he looked a chief." [22]

The next morning the Indians forded the Yellowstone and the chiefs decided to release Mrs. Cowan and her companions. With two horses, the bedraggled tourists made their way down the river, over Mount Washburn, and to the north of Tower Falls, where with great relief they met a detachment of soldiers. In time, all the other members of the party were found.

22. Heister D. Guie and Lucullus V. McWhorter, *Adventures in Geyser Land* (Caldwell, Idaho, 1935), p. 295. This book contains an annotated reprint of *The Wonders of Geyser Land* by Frank D. Carpenter, published in Black Earth, Wisconsin, in 1878, as well as narratives by other members of the tourist party, an account by Yellow Wolf, and various papers relating to the experiences of the Radersburg group.

Even Cowan, shot in the forehead by the angry warriors, survived and, despite a series of desperate adventures in the wilderness, finally returned home to his wife, who had given him up for dead.

Just before releasing their prisoners, the Indians had captured another white man, a soldier named Irwin who had recently been discharged from the army at Fort Ellis. The Nez Perces kept him with them, and that afternoon he traveled along reluctantly with the Indians' main column as it crossed from the eastern side of the Yellowstone River to Pelican Creek, north of Yellowstone Lake. From there, the bands, still led by Poker Joe, ascended Pelican Creek into the mountains in a northeasterly direction, made their way via the headwaters of Lamar River to Cache Creek, and headed through the high passes of the wild Absaroka Range toward the upper waters of the Clark Fork River that eventually ran down to the Yellowstone River on the plains.

Three small parties of Nez Perce warriors, meanwhile, had remained behind in the park. When he had been captured, Irwin had told the Indians of another group of tourists who had been camped in Hayden Valley north of the Nez Perce position, and the warriors, intent on dispersing spies and acquiring their horses, had gone looking for them. As the column of families headed eastward toward the mountains, the three groups of Indians roamed northward, down the Yellowstone River, and soon came on the tourists. They were a party of ten men from Helena, and they had previously sighted the Nez Perces fording the Yellowstone River. In fear they had retreated toward the north and had made a camp in the timber at Otter Creek near the Upper Falls of the river. There, two of the warrior groups fell on them, killing one tourist and sending the others—two of them wounded—flying through the woods for their lives. Most of the survivors eventually rendezvoused at a cabin at Mammoth Hot Springs, near the northern exit of the park, but two of the white men wandered westward to the Madison River, where a supply train for Howard's army found them. When those two men failed to reach Mammoth Hot Springs, their worried companions sent a party looking for them. The raiders by then had come down to the vicinity of Mammoth Hot Springs and had ransacked and burned a ranch and made off with a number of horses. Now, once again, they came on the Helena men and attacked both of their groups, the searchers as well as those who had stayed at the cabin. The members of the search party lost their horses but escaped with their lives. At the cabin the Indians killed one of the tourists and chased his companions away. After dark that same evening the warriors returned to the cabin and looted it.

Meanwhile, Lieutenant Doane's column of cavalry and Crow scouts had entered the park north of Mammoth Hot Springs and had reached the ranch which the Nez Perces had fired earlier in the day. Doane had received orders to mark time at that point and wait for Colonel Gilbert, who was on his way to try to find Howard and take command of the pursuit, but the lieutenant sent a detachment of ten troopers and a guide under Lieutenant Hugh L. Scott to search for the Indians. According to Yellow Wolf, one of the raiders, the soldiers arrived at Mammoth Hot Springs while the Nez Perces were ransacking the cabin. There was a short skirmish in the darkness, the Indian said, after which the Nez Perces rode away with their captured horses. The next day Scott's men found more of the raiders' handiwork. Proceeding toward Baronett's Bridge at the crossing of the Yellowstone, east of Mammoth Hot Springs, the soldiers came on two prospectors, who had crossed the mountains from Colonel Sturgis' Seventh Cavalry, which was lying in wait for the Nez Perces near the Clark Fork River. The two men, with an Indian guide, had entered the wilderness from the east to try to discover the whereabouts of the Nez Perces and then report back to Sturgis. Instead, the raiding warrior groups had found them, killed their Indian guide, and shot one of the prospectors in the neck. The shaken spies now had a rough idea where the Nez Perces were, but they were unable to return to Sturgis, and that officer and his troops never did get the information they needed.

It was now the first week of September, and Howard and his command were approaching the same part of the park. The General's lumbering column had followed Fisher and his Bannock scouts directly over the route the Nez Perces had taken from the Madison to the Yellowstone River, going up Nez Perce Creek and crossing Mary Mountain. In the rear of the main body of troops, the Idaho axemen under Spurgin had earned their title, "Skillets," by hewing a road through the wilds for Howard's wagon train. On September 1, Fisher's scouts had come on the discharged soldier, Irwin, whom the Indians had just released, and the next day Irwin had talked to Howard. He had given the General valuable information on the Nez Perces' route and had suggested that the troops could gain on the Indians by going down the Yellowstone to the crossing at Baronett's Bridge and then heading east via the Lamar River and Soda Butte Creek, an easier and faster route to the Clark Fork River than the wild, timber-clogged one that the Nez Perces were taking. With Spurgin and his axemen traveling more slowly in the rear, cutting a road for the wagons through the difficult wilderness and negotiating canyons by lowering the vehicles with ropes and hauling them up the opposite sides, Howard took Irwin's advice and hurried his fighting men down the Yellowstone to the crossing at the bridge. He reached there on September 5, just behind the Nez Perce raiders who had burned part of the bridge before galloping eastward to overtake the bands, now high in the mountains.

Howard was confident that he knew the Nez Perces' position and route and that his short cut would soon bring him into the mountains close on the

Indians' rear. Fisher had been having trouble with his Bannock scouts, many of whom had finally come back to one of Howard's camps, where they had stolen some of Spurgin's horses. The General had placed the Bannocks under arrest, but they had told him fearful stories of Fisher's difficulties trying to follow the Nez Perce column. Becoming anxious lest Fisher lose the Indians' trail, Howard had sent one of his own scouts, J. W. Redington, to find him. Redington had done so, and had returned to the General with news that Fisher had taken him to a ridge from where he had been able to see the Nez Perces, still heading toward the upper waters of the Clark Fork. The report had relieved Howard, who was now convinced that, with Sturgis waiting east of the mountains, he at last had the Nez Perces in a trap.

Repairing the burned bridge, Howard directed Spurgin to take the wagon train to Fort Ellis via Mammoth Hot Springs, then turned his troops eastward up the Lamar River. The nation's press had reported every detail of the events in Yellowstone Park, and the succession of sensational occurrences had raised the public's interest in Joseph's retreat higher than ever. Now, military spokesmen, as confident as Howard, let it be known that the chase was nearing its climactic moment. A net of troops, commanded by the most experienced Indian fighters in the West, finally had the Nez Perces surrounded. To the War Department and to citizens who studied maps of the wild, mountainous mass on the northeast corner of Yellowstone Park, it was certain this time that there could be no escape for the Indians.

Yet it happened. To the consternation of the Army and the glee of thousands of the American public who were now secretly rooting for the little group of refugee Nez Perces, the Indians again accomplished the unbelievable. How it occurred—whether by a deliberately planned and well executed maneuver by the Indians, by a grievous blunder on the part of Sturgis, by an accident, or by a combination of all three—was argued for years. Although it was never made clear whether Indian scouts learned that Sturgis was ahead of them, this much may be concluded: trying, at least, to throw Howard off their trail, the Nez Perce leaders—Poker Joe and the council of headmen and chiefs—devised a shrewd but simple tactic that fooled Sturgis and let the bands slip past him.

Howard, hastening up the Lamar River and Soda Butte Creek, knew nothing of what was going on ahead of him. His route, which followed part of the present-day highway from the park to Cooke City, Montana, was a relatively good one for much of the way. Crow and Shoshoni Indians had traveled the trail for generations. John Colter may have taken it in 1808 on his way back to Manuel Lisa's post from the vicinity of the Tetons. Many other trappers had used the route during the heyday of the mountain fur trade, and miners, based at Cooke City and working at diggings in the Absarokas, had moved along it with familiarity for a number of years before Howard's troops went over it. The General made good time along it and was soon in the high country of the divide, moving from the headwaters of Soda Butte Creek to those of the Clark Fork.

The heights of the Absarokas were a wild, tangled region of many rocky ridges, overlooking meadowed passes and deep gorges. The Clark Fork and the Shoshone River (at that time called the Stinking Water, for the evil-smelling thermal area of "Colter's Hell" in the river valley near present-day Cody) both headed on the eastern slopes, the Clark Fork commencing well north of the Shoshone but eventually approaching it near Heart Mountain, then turning away from it again, and proceeding northeastwardly through a deep, narrow canyon toward the plains in Montana. Sturgis and his six companies of the Seventh Cavalry, together with a unit of Crow scouts, sat near the mouth of the Clark Fork Canyon. Sturgis, advanced in years, had lost a son at the Little Bighorn and hated Indians. His troops, the inheritors of Custer's guidons, were anxious also to vindicate the Seventh's honor that had been sullied at the Little Bighorn. The Indians for whom they were waiting were not Sioux and had had no hand in Custer's defeat, but that did not matter—they were Indians; and although they had women and children with them, they would pay for what Sitting Bull and Crazy Horse had done.

As Sturgis waited, receiving no information from west of the mountains, he grew worried. Perhaps the Nez Perces were not coming toward him but had turned north and were going down the Lamar River within the park. Perhaps they were on the Shoshone, and were heading east, south of his position. His scouts told him that the Clark Fork Canyon looked impassable. There was no trail through it, and the walls came so close together in places that a caravan like that of the Nez Perces would scarcely try to move through it. Possibly, after all, the Indians were not coming down the Clark Fork. No messengers got through to Sturgis from Howard with information that would help him, and his own messengers and scouts had a succession of disasters. Somewhere, up in the heights, Nez Perce warriors were intercepting the go-betweens. "Every white man in those mountains could be counted our enemy," said Yellow Wolf.

On September 8 Sturgis sent out two scouting parties to reconnoiter the upper waters of the Shoshone River. One group returned with news that on the Shoshone its members had come on two miners whom Sturgis had sent into the mountains as scouts the day before. One had been killed by Nez Perces, and the other was dying. The second party came back soon afterward with definite word that it had sighted the Nez Perces moving on a trail in the direction of the Shoshone River. The two pieces of information decided

Sturgis. The Indians must be coming down the Shoshone, rather than the Clark Fork. Moving south quickly, he reached the Shoshone and, putting his troopers on the alert for a sudden confrontation with the Nez Perces, started them up the river along a trail that led into the mountains. On September 10, high in the rocky wilds, he came suddenly on the plainly marked path of the Indians and knew the worst. The Nez Perces had started along a trail to the Shoshone, pretending that they would take that river, and then, milling their ponies about in every direction and trying to cover their movements, they had turned abruptly north and headed toward the Clark Fork. What was even more demoralizing for Sturgis were signs, farther on, which showed that Howard's army was now also ahead of him, in full pursuit of the Indians. Howard's scouts under Fisher, he learned later, had followed the Nez Perces to the place of their milling, then, after some confusion, had managed to find the new trail to the north. When Howard came up, Fisher was able to point the General's column in the right direction, and Howard, thinking that Sturgis was still waiting at the mouth of the Clark Fork River, had hastened after the Indians, certain that he was compressing a trap.

There was nothing for Sturgis to do but hurry after Howard and the Indians. The trail led through a narrow, rocky canyon, almost as dark as a railroad tunnel, according to Howard's aide, Lieutenant C. E. S. Wood. The troopers of both commands could scarcely understand how the Indians had found the canyon, or got through it with their baggage and horse herds. At places, Howard noted, "rocks on each side came so near together that two horses abreast could hardly pass." Whether Poker Joe had been familiar with the route or had come on the canyon by accident is not known; but it had provided the Indians with a well-hidden passage through which to double back past Sturgis without being detected by his scouts, who had been moving on a parallel route but in the opposite direction, almost within the sound of a rifle shot from the Nez Perces.

On the evning of September 11, to Howard's amazement and Sturgis' embarrassment, Sturgis caught up with Howard in the lower valley of the Clark Fork River. The mountains were behind them, the trap had failed, and the Nez Perces were free again, fifty miles ahead of their two commands and starting across the plains. Once more the pursuit would have to begin. Although their chagrin was great, the two officers sent couriers, one overland and the other down the Clark Fork and Yellowstone rivers, to Colonel Miles, who had once been Howard's aide-de-camp, telling him what had happened and appealing to the younger man to hasten with his force from his cantonment at the mouth of the Tongue River and cut northwestwardly across Montana to intercept the Nez Perces. The refugee Indians, Howard believed, would now try to join some hostile band of Sioux, but if Miles could get in front of them and detain them, he and Sturgis, he promised, would come up and finish the job.

After dispatching the couriers, Howard transferred two mountain howitzers on pack mules and about fifty of his cavalrymen to Sturgis' command, and let that officer start off again in the lead of the chase. The horses of the Seventh Cavalry were in better condition than his own, and he recognized that the troopers under Sturgis were chafing over their embarrassment and were anxious to restore the good name of their outfit. At daybreak on September 12, Sturgis started forward again, his scouts well ahead of him, and that day traveled sixty miles through rain, down the leveling valley of the Clark Fork toward the Yellowstone.

The lower reaches of the Clark Fork, as well as the neighboring area along the Yellowstone, were sparsely populated, and Sturgis' men came on a trail of Nez Perce depredations. The warriors still regarded all whites as their enemies and, ranging in advance and along the flanks of the fleeing column of families, had had several brushes with miners, trappers, and ranchers who lived in lonely cabins and dugouts. On the Clark Fork three miners had been slain and another wounded. A few miles down the Yellowstone from its junction with the Clark Fork, two men had been killed and some horses taken; and farther down the river, at Coulson near present-day Billings, more white men had been murdered and a saloon burned.

The most dramatic episode was a playful one. Crossing the Yellowstone late in the afternoon of September 12, the bands moved a short distance down that river and camped. The next morning, about two miles below the place of crossing, some of the warriors came on a stagecoach that had just arrived at a station on the Bill Brockway ranch. The three passengers, including Fanny Clark, a popular vaudeville performer of the frontier towns, were warned by the station operators who had seen the Indians approaching in the distance, and everyone managed to escape into the brush before the Nez Perces arrived. From their hiding place, the whites watched the Indians scatter the mail, loot and burn the station, and then make off gaily with the stagecoach and horses. The vehicle was driven to the main Indian column, just getting under way, where it took up its position in the rear, young warriors enjoying great sport in riding atop it and guiding the horses back and forth in all directions across the plains.

Sturgis' troops, now more than 400 strong, had meanwhile crossed the Yellowstone that morning. Shortly afterward, scouts, following the Nez Perces' trail, caught sight of the Indian column as it turned north from the river, about four miles from the crossing point, and headed up Canyon Creek. Howard's scout, J. W. Redington, could scarcely conceal his amusement at the spectacle of the stagecoach, following blithely along about half a mile in the column's rear. "On its box," he said, "was a Nez Perce driver with nearly half a dozen other Indians squatting on the roof, with their war horses hitched on behind." [23] The scouts had little time for entertainment, however. Their word of how close Sturgis was to the Indians soon brought the command down the river in a galloping chase, and the Nez Perces, suddenly aware of their danger, abandoned the stage and moved quickly to protect their people.

The lower part of Canyon Creek was a dry stream-bed that ran through a broad, sagebrush plain until it reached the Yellowstone. Six miles north of the Yellowstone the creek's bed emerged from a canyon—really a wide, rocky valley between rough palisades of rimrock. The Indians had been heading for this so-called canyon, intending to ascend through it to higher and hillier country along the Musselshell River, an area long familiar to Nez Perce buffalo-hunting bands. Now, as waving, red blankets gave the alarm of "Soldiers coming," the families quickened their flight, beating the large pony herd toward the protective mouth of the canyon, three or four miles ahead of them. In their rear warriors deployed behind rocks and in washes and depressions to cover their retreat.

As the Indians began to fire, the troopers slackened their pace and gradually came to a halt, returning the long-distance shooting. One of the howitzers came up and fired one shot, which fell short of the withdrawing Nez Perce column. Then Sturgis, dismayed by the crackling shots of the interposing warriors, ordered his forward companies to dismount, form a skirmish line, and advance on foot. It was a tactical error which, according to one soldier, made some of the men weep with frustration and which, in the end, cost Sturgis whatever chance he may have had to accomplish anything. As the troops moved forward across the sagebrush, they could see the main column of Nez Perces approach the canyon's mouth in the distance. One group of cavalrymen, still mounted, made a long, flanking charge on the left, trying to reach the base of the bluffs, ascend them, and cut off the Nez Perces in the canyon. Led by Captain Frederick W. Benteen, a veteran of Custer's command at the Little Bighorn, the mounted troopers, suffering the severest casualties of the engagement, were twice thrown back by warriors who were already on the bluffs, firing from behind rocks and trees.

On the sagebrush flats, at the same time, Sturgis, using field glasses, could see the Nez Perce column moving into the canyon. Slowly, the warriors in his immediate front began to give way, riding back toward their people. The soldiers moved out after the Indians, but their horses were not brought up to

23. McWhorter, *Hear Me*, p. 457, quoting J. W. Redington, *The Stolen Stage*, pp. 70–76.

them, and the troopers became so exhausted hurrying across the rough ground on foot that they failed to keep up with the Indians or offer Benteen any assistance. One by one, the Nez Perce warriors entered the canyon and took up new positions along the rimrock walls and atop the bluffs, continuing to cover the escape of the families. By the time the troops reached the canyon mouth, the Indian column was far within its depths. The soldiers came to a halt again, held in check by the dangerous crossfire of the warriors. Gradually, individual Indians broke off the fight and rode away, still covering the retreat; and at length, apparently, only a single Nez Perce, a man named Teeto Hoonnad, remained behind, his deadly shooting still holding up Sturgis' entire command. By the time the cavalrymen's horses had been brought up, even Teeto Hoonnad had left. The weary troopers followed the Indians for a while, exchanging long-range shots with a few warriors; but as dusk approached, Sturgis ordered the chase abandoned and withdrew his men to the mouth of the canyon, where they camped for the night.

There were recriminations among the soldiers over the Seventh Cavalry's newest failure, and many of the troopers blamed Sturgis for a lack of aggressiveness. Sturgis, in turn, blamed the officer in command of his forward companies for not moving fast enough across the sagebrush to assist Benteen and catch the retreating Indians in a crossfire. But the dismounting of the cavalrymen had been the fatal error. Sturgis had lost three men killed and eleven wounded in the skirmishing, and the Indians claimed later that their total casualties had been three men wounded. During the hasty withdrawal, also, the Nez Perces had had to abandon some thirty or forty horses that had become lame, and it is possible that they had lost others that were picked up by Sturgis' Crow scouts.

On the morning of September 14 Howard, who had heard about the fight, arrived at the mouth of the canyon with fifty of his cavalrymen. There was nothing he could do, and while he waited for supplies and for the rest of his command to catch up, he sent Sturgis forward again in pursuit. With Bannock and Crow scouts in the advance, Sturgis moved up the canyon, finding that the retreating Nez Perces had blocked the trail in many of its narrower places with trees, rocks, and brush.

The Nez Perces, meanwhile, had emerged from the canyon the previous night and had made camp on the hilly ground north of it. In the morning the families had started off early, heading for the Musselshell, while a number of the warriors had trailed back to watch for Sturgis' troops. Instead of soldiers, they ran into Bannocks and Crows, the scouts of the commands of Howard and Sturgis, now combined in a unit of somewhere between fifty and two hundred warriors. On the Yellowstone, while the bands had been traveling toward Canyon Creek, it is believed that they had been overtaken by a group of Sturgis' Crow scouts. After being reminded of the help the Nez Perces had given them against the Sioux Indians, the Crows had given the Nez Perces some ammunition as an assurance of their friendliness and had promised to fire their guns in the air over the Nez Perces' heads if they were ever forced into battle with them.[24] Now the Nez Perces' faith in those former allies ended in another stern disillusionment. Actually, the entire Crow nation could not be blamed for what happened, for the majority of the Crow people had nothing to do with the white man's war against the Nez Perces. But Looking Glass had convinced the bands ever since they had left Idaho that the Crows would be their friends, and when Sturgis' scouts rode at the Nez Perce warriors the day after the Canyon Creek affair, the angry reaction of Yellow Wolf was typical of that of all the Nez Perce refugees: "My heart was just like fire," he said.[25]

For two days Ollokot and the Nez Perce warriors were forced to engage in desperate, running fights with Crow and Bannock raiders, who clung to the rear and flanks of the moving column, darting in and out in harassing attacks on the people, looking for loot and trying to capture the horse herd. Several brief, sharp skirmishes occurred, and once the Crows tried to raid the Nez Perce camp while the women were packing in the morning. From time to time the Crows made off with Nez Perce horses, and they killed one warrior and shot down two old men who had strayed from the column. But they failed to arrest the flight of the bands; and after taking some drubbings in the fierce skirmishes, far out ahead of Sturgis' main command, they gradually gave up their harassment and drifted away, the Crows making off for their homes and the Bannocks falling back to the soldiers' column. They had been of little value to the white pursuers, but their treacherous, snapping attacks made the Nez Perces feel more bitterly toward them than toward the soldiers.

On September 17 the Nez Perces crossed the Musselshell and continued north through the Judith Gap toward the Missouri River. Gone, now, was all idea of finding a haven on the buffalo plains. If there had been a lingering hope that they could settle down on their old hunting grounds along the Yellowstone and Musselshell, the hostility of the Crows had dashed it. Their goal at last was Canada, where Sitting Bull, according to Poker Joe, would welcome them to his camp in exile. The bands traveled quickly, but the pace of their flight and all the shocks and sad experiences of the past three months of running from danger were beginning to tell on them. The people were tired and losing heart. The promises of safety were always receding, and the place of final stopping was taking them ever farther from their homeland. A trail of

24. Edward S. Curtis, *The North American Indian,* 7 (Norwood, Massachusetts, 1911), quoting Yellow Bull, p. 167.
25. McWhorter, *Yellow Wolf,* p. 187.

graves of loved ones lay behind them, and sick and elderly Indians in increasing numbers were giving up, staying behind in camps in the morning or dropping out of the column during the day and wandering off to nearby hills to die alone and unseen. The Crows and Bannocks found some of them, and the soldiers came on others. If the dropouts had not already died, the Indian pursuers killed them. At the same time, the bands' horses were becoming lame and jaded, and the refugees were leaving many of them behind. Other animals were straying away, and the people could no longer take the time to look for them.

When the chiefs went into council during the stops, there was divided opinion. Some of the leaders, like Looking Glass, were pointing out that the Nez Perces were tired and needed a rest. They had outdistanced the soldiers who were far behind them. The bands could go more slowly, and camp for longer hours. Other men, like Poker Joe, remembering Looking Glass's counsel that had led to the deaths at the Big Hole, argued that they could not slacken their pace until they had crossed the border. Only then could they rest in safety. Little is known about Joseph at this time, but there is evidence among the reminiscences of some of the Indians that he had begun to assume a larger stature in the minds of the people of all the bands. For three months he had been the sturdy and reliable guardian of the camp, caring tenderly and efficiently for the women, children, and old people. Their affection and respect for him had grown, and there is more than a suspicion that, although he had not been one of the war chiefs, his wisdom and energy in directing their movements during their many moments of crisis had been responsible in great measure for the fact that they had come this far and were still alive and free.

At the Musselshell on September 17 those who said the column could slow down seemed right. The Nez Perce pace had been too fast for Sturgis and Howard, who were far in the rear and desperately in need of supplies and fresh horses. But on that same day, more than 150 miles to the east, one of the couriers whom Howard had sent from the Clark Fork on September 12 reached Miles at Fort Keogh at the mouth of the Tongue River. Miles, who was married to a niece of General Sherman, was regarded by his fellow officers as ambitious and "something of a glory chaser" like Custer, but also as a vigorous and competent soldier.[26] On receipt of Howard's appeal for assistance, he moved with dispatch, assembling another pursuit force and ferrying it at once across the Yellowstone, ready for a dash northwestward across Montana to cut off the fleeing Nez Perces. His command, 383 men strong, included three companies of the Second Cavalry, three of the Seventh Cavalry, five of the 5th Infantry four of which were mounted, a company of scouts, and thirty Cheyenne Indians. For armament he had a breech-loading Hotchkiss

26. Beal, *I Will Fight No More Forever,* pp. 200–01.

gun and a twelve-pound Napoleon cannon.[27] His plan was to hurry to the junction of the Musselshell and Missouri rivers, then head west along the Missouri and intercept the refugees before they could cross that river. Sending couriers to Forts Peck and Buford on the Missouri to direct that a steamboat and supplies meet him at the mouth of the Musselshell, and to Howard to tell him what he was doing and to caution the utmost secrecy about his movements, he took off at a rapid pace on the morning of September 18. The Nez Perces, meanwhile, continued to travel quickly, passing through Judith Basin between the Judith and Snowy mountains and seizing some fresh horses and jerked buffalo meat from a band of Crows whom they encountered along the way. Heading due north toward Canada, some two hundred miles distant, they rode through country familiar to many of their buffalo hunters and on the night of September 21 camped near the Reed and Bowles Stockade, close to the site of present-day Lewistown, Montana. Some of the hunters had traded with Reed in the past, and they rode over to see him, spending the evening in a friendly way and telling him of some of their exploits and adventures. The next day they continued on, following the Snowy Mountain foothills and heading down Dog Creek. They covered seventy-five miles in thirty-six hours, and about noon on September 23 reached the Missouri opposite Cow Island Landing. Shallows about the island had made it a well-known Indian fording place, but it was also the head of navigation for steamboats unable to ascend farther up the river to Fort Benton. On the northern shore vessels had previously deposited some thirty tons of government freight and twenty tons of private supplies, intended to be picked up by bull trains from Fort Benton for western Montana and Canadian settlements and posts. The depot was guarded by four civilians and about a dozen soldiers of Company B, 7th Infantry, under Sergeant William Moelchert. The whites, living in tents and already warned that the Indians were coming their way, had dug a rifle pit behind an earthen breastwork from which to defend the dump.

The Indians moved slightly upriver to a point above the mouth of Cow Creek. Then as a precaution against an attack by the whites, about twenty warriors crossed the Missouri ahead of the families and stood guard against the soldiers while the main column came across. Moelchert and his men remained quietly behind their defenses, and the Indians and their pony herd passed along quickly, heading two miles up Cow Creek, where they made a camp. When the column had disappeared, two members of the group of warriors who were still standing guard rode over to the rifle pit and made a sign that they wished to parley. With one of the civilians acting as interpreter, they asked Moelchert for supplies from the stockpile, offering to pay him for

27. Virginia W. Johnson, *The Unregimented General* (Boston, 1962), p. 193.

whatever he gave them. Moelchert at first refused, telling them that he would be violating his orders. But when the Nez Perces persisted, pleading that their people were hungry and promising that, in return, the Indians would not molest the small guard detail, Moelchert gave them a side of bacon and half a sack of hardtack from the provisions of his own men.

The meagerness of the gift irritated the Indians, and near sundown some of them began shooting toward the rifle pit from a nearby bluff. The shots struck two of the civilians, and the rest of the whites slid hurriedly behind their defenses. In a few moments, as dusk descended, men on both sides were firing at each other. The Indians could have overrun the soldiers with ease, but they were more interested in raiding the depot and securing much-needed food and supplies for their people. Under cover of the darkness and the desultory shooting, Nez Perce men and women helped themselves during the night, carrying off sacks of flour, sugar, rice, and beans, and pots and pans, and using a coulee on the north side of the freight pile to scurry back and forth in safety from the dump to their camp. The chiefs, it was said, did not approve of the looting, but the people convinced themselves that they were at war with all whites and that what they were doing was fair, and no one halted their attempt to replenish their provisions and supplies. When the Indians had taken all they wanted, a few of the young men—"bad boys," said Yellow Wolf—set fire to the rest of the dump. The shooting continued on and off during the rest of the night, but at dawn, the chiefs ordered the warriors to stop the firing and return to camp. As the Nez Perces rode away, Moelchert and his men convinced themselves that they had forced the Indians to retreat. Later, Moelchert even claimed that the skirmish had held up the Nez Perces' flight and had contributed to the capture of the Indians. Besides the two civilians, one warrior had been wounded during the shooting.

The bands started off again at an early hour, heading for a pass between the Little Rockies and the Bear Paw Mountains. Late in the morning an advance group of warriors sighted a long, oxen-drawn freight train loaded with supplies. They rode at the train, killed three of the teamsters, chased the rest away, and began to ransack the supplies. Meanwhile, unknown to them, a column of thirty-six mounted volunteers and one regular under Major Guido Ilges, the 7th Infantry's commander at Fort Benton, had been reconnoitering the countryside, looking for the Nez Perces. The military unit had arrived at the Cow Island Landing soon after the Indians' departure that morning, and had ridden boldly after the Nez Perces, following their trail north. Just as the Indians were hacking at the freight wagons, Ilges and his men appeared on the hills and began shooting at the families' rearguard. The warriors hastily burned the wagons and rode to cover the column's rear. After a brief skirmish in which one of the volunteers was killed, Ilges decided to retreat to

Cow Island, announcing later that the Nez Perces were excellent long-range sharpshooters. The Indian column had continued to hasten forward during the fighting, and the warriors caught up to it.

Sometime during the day, perhaps at the noon camp, the chiefs went into council again. According to the warrior Many Wounds, "Looking Glass upbraided Poker Joe for his hurrying; for causing the old people weariness; told him that he was no chief, that he himself was chief and that he would be the leader. Poker Joe replied, 'All right, Looking Glass, you can lead. I am trying to save the people, doing my best to cross into Canada before the soldiers find us. You can take command, but I think we will be caught and killed.' "[28] None of the other chiefs seemed to object. The people and horses were undoubtedly tired, the weather was growing colder, and the long, hurried marches were sapping the strength and morale of the Indians. Howard, moreover, was now believed to be at least two days behind them. The column could move more slowly and make camps earlier in the day, giving the warriors a chance to hunt and the people an opportunity to regain their strength and enjoy themselves in recreation. So, once more, Looking Glass had his way and assumed the leadership of the march.

This time his command proved fatal. Under his direction, the bands made an early camp that afternoon, and again each day for the next four days. On September 28, after passing the main range of the Bear Paws, they met a hunting party of Assiniboines, whom the Nez Perces called "Walk-Around Sioux," and, camping near them, exchanged a friendly visit with the plains tribesmen that afternoon and evening. The column continued north the next morning, and at noon reached Snake Creek, a narrow, twisting stream that ran north across the barren, almost treeless plains to the Milk River. Hunters in advance of the families had killed some buffalo, and Looking Glass told the people that they could camp there, eating and resting, until the next morning. The warrior Wottolen objected to the early halt, saying that he had had a dream the night before that soldiers would attack them the next dawn. But Looking Glass laughed at him and brushed aside his objection.

The campsite, near a northern flank of the Bear Paws, was bleak and desolate. The cold arctic wind of approaching winter, carrying with it a hint of snow, whipped across the plains, and the people moved down between low bluffs and rocky ridges to the shelter of a crescent-shaped hollow along the creek. Within the depression was a network of slightly deeper coulees and ravines, some of them wide trenches from five to ten feet deep. Protected from the wind, the bands made their camps on a line of flats running from south to north along the creek. Joseph's was the most southerly camp, set up

28. Many Wounds to Lucullus McWhorter, August 1935, quoted by McWhorter in *Hear Me*, pp. 473–74.

between two coulees and under the slopes of ridges on the south and east. Just north of him, across a coulee, were the camps of Looking Glass and White Bird, and across another shallow draw were Toohoolhoolzote's people. Poker Joe camped with Joseph and Ollokot; Husishusis Kute and the surviving Palouses stayed with Looking Glass; and Koolkool Snehee was with White Bird. There were no trees in the area and but little brush along the stream for fuel, but buffalo chips were plentiful, and the Indians soon built fires to cook the buffalo meat. The people settled down gratefully, eight miles from the crossing of the Milk River near present-day Chinook, Montana, and less than forty miles from the Canadian border.

Miles, meanwhile, had reached the confluence of the Missouri and Musselshell rivers on September 24, six days after leaving Fort Keogh. With the assistance of a steamboat, he ferried some of his troops across the Missouri, intending to march two columns upriver, one on each side of the stream, looking for the Nez Perces. The next day, soon after he had released the steamboat and let it start downriver, three men arrived in a small mackinaw boat with news that the Nez Perces had crossed the Missouri at Cow Creek, sixty miles west of Miles, on September 23. Recognizing that his only chance to intercept the Indians now lay in his ability to march quickly northwestwardly toward the Canadian border, he fired a signal shot from his cannon that brought the steamer back to him, and hurriedly ferried the rest of his command across the Missouri. Then, sending word of his movement to Howard, who was following the Nez Perces' trail northward from the Musselshell to the Missouri, he left his wagons and Napoleon gun to follow as quickly as possible and started the troops on a four-day race to head off the Indians.

His column moved rapidly and in silence across the cold, northern plains, skirting the eastern side of the Little Rockies. North of that range, he turned more westwardly around the northern flank of the Bear Paws, sending scouting parties ahead of him. On September 29 a messenger reached him from Major Ilges, telling the direction the Nez Perces had taken from Cow Creek. Miles thought he might now be ahead of the Indians, but the next morning, September 30, at six o'clock, a group of Cheyenne scouts under Louis Shambow picked up the day-old trail of the Nez Perce families headed north. Shambow sent word back to Miles and proceeded to follow the trail with the rest of his ten-man Cheyenne detail. A few miles farther on, two of the Cheyennes, Bobtail Horse and Buffalo Hump, sighted a group of Nez Perces running buffalo. Shambow's men watched them for a while. The Nez Perces, they thought, soon discovered that they were being watched but nevertheless went on with their hunting. Eventually, the Nez Perces butchered their kill and trailed off to the north with the meat. Shambow and the Cheyennes followed at a distance until the Nez Perces disappeared in a hollow along Snake

Creek about five miles distant. Confident that he had located the Nez Perces' camp, though he could not see it, Shambow directed the Cheyennes to wait there with him for Miles.[29]

The latter, meanwhile, had received word of the discovery of the trail and had ordered his men to prepare for battle. Before eight o'clock the command reached Shambow and with the scouts moved forward eagerly to a mile or two of the hollow. At that distance Miles made out the Nez Perces' position and could see a confused movement in the Indians' horse herd, pastured on the northeast side of the creek. The Nez Perces were hidden somewhere among the coulees and ravines along the stream bed, but they had probably discovered the soldiers' presence and were getting the horses ready to move. The troops had no time to lose. As the Cheyennes stripped for battle, Miles gave quick commands. Companies A, D, and K of the Seventh Cavalry, composed partly of veterans of the Little Bighorn, would lead the charge with the Cheyennes, striking the southern end of the Nez Perce village. Mounted companies B, F, G, I, and K and a detachment of D of the 5th Infantry would support the 7th. Companies F, G, and H of the Second Cavalry would accompany the charge but swing to the left, circle the camp, and drive off the Nez Perces' pony herd.

The trumpets blew "double quick" and the attack began, the men starting off at a trot but picking up speed. Half a mile from the camp the troopers were at full charge, thundering down on the Nez Perces.

The Indians knew they were coming. While the people had been eating their breakfast earlier, Tom Hill, the mixed-blood, and several Nez Perces had hurried into camp, announcing that they had seen stampeding buffalo, a sure sign of soldiers. Hill and his companions had spent the preceding night in the Assiniboine camp farther south and had probably been the hunters whom Shambow and the Cheyennes had sighted. The Nez Perce group, however, had not seen the Cheyennes, and when some of the people began to panic, Looking Glass rode around, reassuring them that no troops could be near them and telling them, "Do not hurry! Go slow! Plenty, plenty time. Let the children eat all wanted!" [30] A number of the families were still not satisfied but caught up their horses and began to pack. The rest of the people accepted Looking Glass's word. The women gradually got their possessions together, and the children went back to playing, some of them making mudballs along the stream. Less than an hour later, a scout was seen riding quickly toward the camp from the south. He stopped on a high bluff and waved his blanket

29. Shambow's account in Noyes, *In the Land of Chinook*, pp. 74–75. Also, author's interview with John Stands in Timber, Northern Cheyenne tribal historian, August 1964.

30. McWhorter, *Yellow Wolf*, p. 205.

wildly, signaling, "Enemies coming!" Immediately the village was plunged in confusion. Those who were already packed and had their horses with them streamed hastily out of the hollow and started toward the north, driving a large number of animals ahead of them. Joseph and many others who were not yet ready to leave ran toward the herd, intending to mount the rest of the families and get them moving north as fast as possible. Some of the warriors also hastened toward the horses, looking for their war ponies. The rest of the men, seizing rifles and cartridge belts, climbed the slopes on the south and east sides of the camp and scrambled into hiding places in depressions and behind rocks, from where they could hold off the enemy until the families got away.

They were just in time to see a mass of soldiers and horses coming at them across the plains, the hooves of the animals, said Yellow Wolf, pounding the earth like the rumble of a stampede. As the wall of enemies reached two hundred yards from them, the Nez Perces opened fire, their explosion of shots shattering the ranks of the cavalrymen. Troopers and horses went down in confusion. The dramatic charge crumpled. Men drew rein, milled, and turned to get out of the deadly fire. Yellow flashes of shots pocked the smoke on the slightly rising ground ahead of them, and the troopers of the Seventh beat backward quickly, leaving their dead and wounded behind them.

To their left the men of the Second Cavalry, accompanied by some of the Cheyennes, had swept past them, raced around the western side of the camp, and crashed at full gallop into the Nez Perce horse herd. Joseph and other people, women, warriors, youths, and old men, were already there. The noise of the shooting had frightened the animals just before the collision, and they were rearing, turning in circles, and moving away from the din. Some of the Indians were trying desperately to head groups of ponies back to the camps; others were searching for their mounts; many had found them and were half on and half off the frightened animals. As the troopers and Cheyennes stormed into the herd, the shock scattered Indians and horses. Some Nez Perces managed to ride away, fighting. Others struggled with their mounts, Cheyennes, and cavalrymen at the same time. The troopers scarcely paused. Their order was to drive the animals away. After a momentary struggle, many of them pushed on, driving between 300 and 400 of the Indians' horses across the plains in front of them. The Cheyennes and a number of soldiers stayed behind, caught in a wild, swirling melee with the Nez Perces. On the plains, the troopers with the horses broke into details. Two of them rounded up more of the Indians' animals and herded them with the original group into a hollow, safely distant from the fighting. A few of the cavalrymen, chasing down a valley, sighted Nez Perces trying to escape toward the north. They hurried after them, shooting at some but losing most of them.

The Indians, including Joseph, who had been fighting for the horses were soon compelled to run for their lives. Racing from the enemy fire, they scattered among the coulees and ravines. Many of the Indians were unarmed. Joseph, without a weapon, had got on a horse, but the animal was wounded and Joseph was scratched and singed by bullets. He finally made it back to his tipi, where his oldest wife handed him his rifle, saying, "Here's your gun. Fight!" With other men, he ran through the coulees to take up a firing position. On the higher ground, Ollokot, Poker Joe, and other Nez Perces squirmed behind rocks, facing outward to guard the northern and eastern flanks of the village. A few Indians, seeing heavy fighting at the south end of the camp, made it all the way back through the hollow to help the warriors who were holding the soldiers on that front.

The initial assault against the high ground on the south had cost the Seventh Cavalry dearly. Fifty-three of 115 men who had made the charge had been killed or wounded by the Nez Perce riflemen. Troop K, with 60 per cent of its men casualties, was leaderless, its captain killed instantly and its second in command mortally wounded. Two other officers, including Captain Edward S. Godfrey, veteran of the Little Bighorn, were also down. Sixteen cavalrymen in all lay dead in front of the Nez Perce positions as the Seventh withdrew. Miles came up, shocked by what had happened. An officer approached him, shouting hysterically, "I'm the only damned man of the Seventh Cavalry wearing shoulder straps who's alive!" The Nez Perce fire was still intense, and Miles had to think quickly. Wheeling the unscarred 5th into line, he ordered its men to sweep the ridge and storm the village. The mounted infantrymen started forward and charged almost to the edge of the hollow. There the Indians halted them. The soldiers dismounted and, holding the reins of their horses, fought from kneeling positions. It was no use. They suffered more casualties, and finally remounted and retreated. The hidden Nez Perces were impregnable, their shooting too accurate for the troops. Even Miles's Hotchkiss gun, rushed along to a ridge northwest of the village, had been put out of action by Indian marksmanship that cut down two of the mules and killed one of the riders. The gun was temporarily abandoned as the rest of the detail scurried to escape the Nez Perces' bullets.

Miles had no choice but to order his men to take cover and reply, shot for shot. A thin line was extended around the village to ensure the Indians' entrapment, and the cavalrymen dug shallow pits for themselves with their trowel bayonets. The Nez Perces' fire was still effective. "From their concealment, they sent shots with unerring aim at every head exposed," said Lieutenant Henry Romeyn of G Company of the 5th. James Snell, one of Miles's scouts, was more emphatic. "I never went up against anything like the

Nez Perces in all my life and I have been in lots of scraps," he said; and Louie Shambow, who had led the Cheyenne scouts, echoed him: "Those Indians were the best shots I ever saw." [31]

To Miles time was pressing. North of him, perhaps fifty miles above the border, was the camp of his old adversary Sitting Bull, with some 2,000 Sioux. Joseph had probably got a rider off to him, appealing for help; and if he had not, the Nez Perces who had escaped would inevitably ask the Sioux to ride south and save their people. With fewer than 400 men, many of them already battered and out of action, Miles was in a dangerous position. He would have to overrun the Nez Perces before Sitting Bull could arrive.

The impasse preyed on him, and shortly after noon he ordered another charge. Companies A and D of the Seventh and G of the 5th, all under Lieutenant Romeyn, were directed to strike at the Indian village from the southwest, sweep the Nez Perces eastward from the stream bed, and drive them from their water supply. The troopers started forward in a sudden burst, cheering, but again a Nez Perce fusillade struck them, and they faltered. Romeyn and many of the men were hit. Company I, which was ordered to assist them, shared the same fate. One group reached the Indians' firing positions and was driven back with casualties, but about a dozen soldiers went careening down into the hollow, charged into Joseph's camp, and fought at close range with the Wallowa chief and his people. Three Nez Perces and three troopers were killed at the lodges. The rest of the soldiers were finally driven out of the hollow again, leaving their dead companions in the Indian camp.

Miles's casualties, mounting at an alarming rate, finally forced him to abandon hope of an immediate victory. Reluctantly, he ordered his men to dig in for a siege. From time to time, some of the Indians tried to creep close to where the soldiers were digging, but the troopers drove them back. As darkness approached, the firing slackened. The wind blew harder, the cold increased, and flakes of snow were in the air. In the soldiers' rear, out of range of the Nez Perces' fire, Miles set up tents and established a field headquarters. The Hotchkiss gun was retrieved, brought to a new position, and fortified by a sod breastwork. Soon it was firing toward the Indian village. It was annoying, but it did no damage.

With the coming of night some of the Indians stayed on the slopes, digging rifle pits with trowel bayonets they had captured at the Big Hole. In the darkness they maintained a watch against another soldier attack, and from time to time shattered the stillness with shots at shadows opposite them. Other Indi-

---

31. Johnson, *The Unregimented General*, p. 200, quoting from Henry Romeyn, "The Capture of Chief Joseph and the Nez Perce Indians," *Contributions to Montana Historical Society*, 2 (Helena, 1896), and accounts of James H. Snell and Louie Shambow in Noyes, *In the Land of Chinook*, pp. 115, 76.

ans who had been trapped on the plains or in the coulees during the day straggled back to their families, bringing word of their losses. A toll was taken, and it was found that 22 Nez Perces, including men, women, and children, had been killed. The brave, good-natured Ollokot was dead, hit by a bullet during the fierce fighting in the morning while he had been firing from behind a rock on the ridge above White Bird's camp. Old Toohoolhoolzote had been slain, and so had Poker Joe, the latter shot mistakenly by an Indian sniper who had thought he was a soldier. More good warriors had fallen by error. In one case the Palouse Dreamer, Husishusis Kute, had deliberately picked off three Nez Perces in a draw far southeast of him. He had believed they were Cheyennes, and with each shot he had exclaimed proudly, "I got him!"

In the camps, the wounded Indians were laid out under buffalo robes. Tragedy and gloom filled the hollow. The horse herd was gone. If the people were to escape, they would have to rush on foot through the soldiers' line. The idea was debated and rejected. Too many women and children would be killed. Some of the warriors, going alone, might make it, but no brave man would abandon the families. The one hope lay with Sitting Bull, and in the darkness six men who knew the plains people were detailed to get past the soldiers, find the Sioux, and appeal for help. The six said good-by to the others, moved up the hollow toward the north, and disappeared. The rest of the people buried the dead at the camps and prepared for more fighting while they waited. With knives and camas hooks the women scooped shelter pits in the walls of the coulees and ravines, digging deeply into the earth to fashion snug caverns, connected in some places by tunnels. As the people worked, snow began to fall in earnest. There were no fires or lights, and the Indian children cried in the cold. The bitter night dragged on, and the snow became heavier. On the slopes, the warriors deepened their rifle pits. By morning, five inches of snow carpeted the plains, covering the stiffened bodies of the dead. The wind howled, and the storm continued. The sharp cracks of occasional shots across the lines could scarcely be heard.

In the eerie bleakness the battle resumed. Guns flashed, and the smell and smoke of powder hovered close to the ground. Shots from the Hotchkiss gun burst harmlessly in the hollow. Manning the rifle pits, each warrior was an island of resistance but also a lonely, symbolic figure of the once great Nez Perce nation, now brought to its gallant fighting finish. "I felt the end coming," said Yellow Wolf. "All for which we had suffered lost! Thoughts came of the Wallowa where I grew up. Of my own country when only Indians were there. Of tipis along the bending river. Of the blue, clear lake, wide meadows with horse and cattle herds. From the mountain forests, voices seemed calling. I felt as dreaming. Not my living self. The war deepened.

Grew louder with gun reports. I raised up and looked around. Everything was against us. No hope! Only bondage or death! Something screamed in my ear. A blaze flashed before me. I felt as burning! Then with rifle I stood forth, saying to my heart, 'Here I will die, fighting for my people and our homes!' " [32]

Toward noon the snow and gale slackened. Miles and one or two troopers reported later that the Indians displayed a white flag, but the Nez Perces denied that this happened. Miles, however, was becoming increasingly worried about Sitting Bull. Also, he wanted the glory of capturing the Nez Perces for himself, and Sturgis and Howard were both coming up. If Sturgis got there first, he would share the credit with Miles; if Howard arrived, it would be worse, for the General, as the senior officer on the field, would take command of all the forces and assume the honors. In an attempt to force the issue quickly, before other Indians or troops could reach the scene, Miles decided to try to get Joseph to surrender. He put up a white flag of his own. Yellow Wolf said that the Indians made no response at first, and the flag went down. Soon it went up again, he said, and a voice called over to the Nez Perces in the Chinook Jargon, "Colonel Miles would like to see Chief Joseph."

White Bird, Looking Glass, and some of the war chiefs held a hurried council with Joseph, who told them that he wished to talk to Miles. The other Indians were hesitant, concerned that Joseph's pacifism would lead him to agree to stop the war and deliver them all to the soldiers. To White Bird and Looking Glass surrender was unthinkable. They remembered again what Colonel Wright had done to the Spokans, Coeur d'Alenes, Palouses, and Yakimas after they had stopped fighting. Now, they were sure that Howard and the Americans would hang the Nez Perce leaders. But Joseph insisted that he would only find out what Miles wanted and would then come back and tell the other chiefs. Tom Hill, the mixed-blood who spoke English, was sent across the lines to tell Miles that Joseph was willing to speak to him. After a short time, Hill came halfway back, accompanied by Miles and several soldiers, and called that it was all right for Joseph to come out. The Wallowa chief, followed by two or three warriors, rode up from the hollow and joined Miles. Several Indians aimed their rifles at the American commander from their hiding places, ready to shoot Miles if he did anything to Joseph.

Using Hill as interpreter, Joseph and Miles had a brief parley. Miles apparently asked Joseph to surrender. The chief replied that he would not surrender, but wished to be allowed to return peaceably to the Wallowa. Miles may have given some indication that the Indians would be sent back to Idaho, but only after their unconditional surrender. Exactly what was said cannot be known, for no two accounts give the same story. Tom Hill reported that the

32. McWhorter, *Yellow Wolf*, p. 212.

discussion led to no agreement. Lieutenant Lovell H. Jerome, who was with Howard, thought that Joseph said that he was willing to give up, but that he would first have to return to his camp and talk to the other chiefs. Perhaps the interpreting was faulty and the two sides got different ideas of what was being said. Even so, the various accounts go on to give different versions, also, of what occurred following the parley. Lieutenant Jerome said he followed Joseph back to the Indian camp, where the chief explained the proposed surrender to the Indians. They raised some questions, Jerome said, and he suggested that Joseph take "20 or 30 guns he had collected" and, with some of the chiefs, come over to Miles's camp. The Indians did so, according to his account. They all had a long talk with Miles and finally agreed to bring their people up out of the hollow and surrender their guns. As the Indians started back, Miles turned to Joseph and said, "You stay here, and we will have some coffee." Joseph waited, and soon discovered that Miles was holding him a prisoner. Jerome, meanwhile, went to the Indian camp to see that none of the Nez Perces cached their guns before surrendering. When the Indians realized that Miles was detaining Joseph, they seized Jerome and held him in retaliation.

Miles's report, which says only that the Colonel "detained" Joseph, casts no light on the episode. But there are other versions that disagree completely with Jerome's account. None of the Indians' narratives, including those of Joseph and of Tom Hill, mention Joseph's return to the Nez Perce camp with word of Miles's surrender terms, the chiefs' pilgrimage to Miles's lines, or their agreement to a surrender. Those accounts, which corroborate each other substantially enough to provide a more reliable picture of what occurred, indicate that after the preliminary parley, Joseph—either at once, or slightly later, following another appeal from Miles—crossed into the soldiers' lines for a longer talk with the American commander. With Tom Hill again interpreting, Miles apparently pointed out the Indians' impossible situation and once more urged Joseph to surrender, promising that if the Indians gave up their horses and guns, he would escort them to Tongue River. There, they could spend the winter in peace, like the plains bands that had previously surrendered to him, and in the spring they could return to Idaho. Joseph answered that his people would only give up half their guns; they would need the rest of them in order to hunt. There was an argument over this, and Joseph again said he could not surrender. When the chief got up to go, Miles, feeling suddenly frustrated, ordered several troopers to detain him. Hill was allowed to go back to the Nez Perces. Joseph himself implied that Miles kept him in a tent all night. But some of the Indians who repeated what Joseph told them when Miles finally did release him said that he was taken to the army's mule herd, where his hands were tied behind his back. His feet were also bound and drawn up behind his back, and he was rolled in a blanket on the ground.

Whatever actually happened, the negotiations, initiated by Miles, ended with Joseph a prisoner in the American camp. His seizure was an inexcusable violation of the flag of truce by which Miles had lured the chief to his lines. According to Jerome, however, "That was Miles's way . . . He also did this with Geronimo in the Apache affair." [33]

At about the same time Jerome was captured by the Nez Perces. Jerome's story, as already stated, was that Miles had expected that the Indians were about to surrender and that the Colonel had directed him to watch and see that none of the Indians buried their arms before coming out of the hollow. There is no other explanation for Jerome's wandering within the Indian lines. When the Nez Perces realized that Miles was holding Joseph a prisoner, the situation became tense, and some of the Indians wanted to kill the Lieutenant. Yellow Bull and Wottolen restrained them, however, and the officer, allowed to retain his sidearms, was given food, water, and a sheltered dugout in which to make himself comfortable. The news of his seizure angered Miles, whose advantage in holding Joseph was now nullified. For the time being, however, the Colonel did nothing about exchanging the two men.

That afternoon, as the storm wore away, Miles sent a small detachment northward to scour the plains for Nez Perces who had escaped. The unit eventually overtook and captured a number of refugees, whom they brought back to Miles. More importantly, the cavalrymen's activity was interpreted by Assiniboines who were still in the region as permission for them to kill any Nez Perces they found. Soon afterward those "Walk-Around Sioux," only recently hosts to the Nez Perces, met some cold and starving escapees. Instead of giving them help, they slew two of them and drove the rest away.

The same afternoon, Miles's wagon train and Napoleon cannon arrived. The artillerymen had difficulty firing the piece into the hollow, but they stood the cannon almost on end, elevating the muzzle and sinking the tailpiece

33. McWhorter, *Hear Me*, p. 489 n. This episode, one of the most dramatic of the entire war, is also one of the most difficult to follow. Miles's skimpy report is of no help. Jerome gave his account in New York City in 1930, when he was 80 years old. It was published by Fee in *Chief Joseph*, pp. 337–39, but Fee's narrative, in the same volume, ignores it completely. Tom Hill's version, differing from that of Jerome's, can be read in the *Memorial of the Nez Perce Indians, Residing in the State of Idaho to the Congress of the United States*, Senate Document No. 97, 1st Session, 62nd Congress, pp. 31–32. Yellow Wolf's account, supporting that of Hill, is in McWhorter, *Yellow Wolf*, pp. 214 ff. See also "Chief Joseph's Own Story," pp. 25–26, and McWhorter, *Hear Me*, pp. 487–90. Despite the Indian assertions that there was only one parley, Howard's aide, Lieutenant C. E. S. Wood, definitely understood from Miles that he had had two different conferences with Joseph. See Fee, *Chief Joseph*, p. 328.

in a pit and, converting it into a mortar, shortened its trajectory. Soon shells were exploding in the Indians' camp, sending fragments flying against the slopes and causing more terror among the coulees and shelter pits. Although some of the Indians were struck, no one was killed by the bursting shell fragments.

The night brought more snow. On both sides of the lines entrenchments were extended and deepened. In the Nez Perce camp the suffering increased. "Children cried with hunger and cold," recalled one of the Indian women. "Old people suffering in silence. Misery everywhere." Ollokot's mourning second wife, Wetatonmi, added: "We slept only by naps; sitting in our pits; leaning forward or back against the dirt wall." [34] On the soldiers' side, behind the men in the seige pits and trenches, there were fires, hot food, tents, and blankets.

On the morning of the third day, October 2, the rifle fire slackened. Both sides now husbanded their ammunition while they watched anxiously toward the north, wondering if Sitting Bull and his Sioux were on the way. At one time Miles got a scare and the Indians a sudden thrill. Black dots appeared on the distant hills, looking like an army of riders. As the Indians and troops strained to make them out more clearly, the dots were seen to be buffalo, not Sioux.

Early in the afternoon Joseph and Jerome were exchanged. Miles had offered to return the chief if the Indians would first release Jerome. The Nez Perces had said no; Miles must first bring Joseph to a halfway point between the lines. Then they would take Jerome to the same place. A white flag went up on the soldiers' side, and several men walked out with Joseph. They stopped on a buffalo robe, spread halfway between the lines. The chiefs and a few of the older warriors escorted Jerome to meet them. The Lieutenant and Joseph shook hands. Then each party walked back to its own lines. For a while Joseph seems to have been held suspect by White Bird, Looking Glass, and a few of the war chiefs. They wondered what he had told Miles, and he had to insist several times that he had not offered to stop the war.

There was steady but not heavy firing the rest of the day, and also the day after. No one on the Indians' side talked surrender, but as the siege dragged on and the cold and hunger and misery continued, the people's spirits flagged and their hope of rescue all but died. The children scarcely moved, but lay in the shelters, crying and sobbing with hunger. The older people's minds became numb; they slept and dreamed of far-away homes, scenes of warmth, and loved ones. When they awoke, they knew with a start that they had been dreaming of the dead. Joseph, once the guardian of the large camp, was silent amid the suffering. Again, his mind must have told him that the right thing to

34. McWhorter, *Hear Me*, pp. 485–86.

do was what he could not do. His great heart hurt for the travail of the people.

The fifth day, October 4, was cold and blustery. That morning, a cannon shell made a direct hit on a shelter pit, burying four women, a little boy, and a girl of about twelve. The Indians dug frantically to get them out. The girl and her grandmother were found dead. The other people were rescued. Those two casualties were the first Nez Perces killed since the initial day of the siege, a reflection of the effectiveness of the shelter pits.

Late in the afternoon of the same day, Miles was chagrined by the arrival of Howard. The general, with two aides, his son Guy and Lieutenant C. E. S. Wood; his Idaho scout and interpreter, Arthur Chapman; the two treaty Nez Perces, Captain John and Old George; and a detachment of seventeen men had pushed on ahead of Sturgis and the rest of the troops to try to help Miles effect Joseph's surrender. Howard was confident that his appearance would do the trick. The Nez Perces would now know that his own troops were about to arrive to seal their doom, and Captain John and Old George, who had daughters with Joseph's people, could act as intermediaries and convince the hostiles to give up.

There was some confusion and bitterness among Howard's men concerning Miles's attitude toward the General. Miles, they thought, had failed to send messengers to Howard, informing him of what was happening, but they understood, at the same time, that couriers had gone from the battlefield to Sturgis. It seemed apparent to them that Miles had needed Sturgis' help but had not wanted Howard to arrive and take command of the siege. Actually, the Colonel's dispatch bearers had missed the General and reported to the slower-moving officers in his rear, but Miles's own welcome to Howard betrayed his feeling of disappointment. He was curt and unfriendly at first, but the one-armed General, who had come so far and experienced so many hardships to reach this moment, told him, "You shall receive the surrender. Not until after that will I assume command." Then, according to Lieutenant C. E. S. Wood, who thought that Howard's generosity was an injustice both to the General and to the long-suffering members of his command, Miles brightened suddenly and became cordial to the older man, whose aide-de-camp he had once been.

The following morning, Friday, October 5, Howard and Miles met to plan the procedure for securing the Nez Perces' surrender. Although Miles had previously given terms to Joseph, he undoubtedly reviewed them with Howard. It is not known what was said between Howard and Miles concerning the ultimate disposition of the bands, but it is certain from the later testimony and actions of every principal on the battlefield, including Howard, Miles, Wood, and Joseph, that the military leaders conveyed to the Nez Perces the promise that they would first take them to Tongue River for the winter, and that when the weather permitted it, they would then return them to the Northwest. In his earlier conferences with Joseph, Miles (said Wood) "had promised in clear terms that if Joseph surrendered, he and his people would be returned to their own country." With the understanding that this meant the Idaho reservation, and not the Wallowa, Howard not only could—but felt that he had been ordered to—support that commitment. In one of the telegrams that McDowell had sent him before Howard's troops had started the leg of the pursuit through Yellowstone Park, McDowell had said explicitly, "When captured, care for them as prisoners of war in your own Department." That, to Howard, meant that he should return the Indians to the Idaho reservation. In the negotiations with Joseph, the Indian leader may have received the erroneous impression that he could go back to the Wallowa. Obviously, the military leaders could not have committed themselves to that. But there was no question that Joseph could count, at least, on a return to the Northwest. "Everybody," said Wood, "took this as an accepted fact, including the old Indians, Captain John and Old George, and the interpreter, Chapman. It was one of those accepted facts . . ." [35]

After the conference, Chapman was called and told to direct Captain John and Old George to cross with a white flag to the Nez Perce camp and inform Joseph and the chiefs that Howard had arrived, that his troops were only a day's march away, and that if the Indians surrendered, they would be treated honorably as prisoners of war. There would be no trials or executions, and the people would be given food and blankets. In the blustery weather the two treaty Nez Perces, both of them in white men's clothes but with feathers stuck jauntily in the bands of their hats, mounted their horses and, holding a white flag aloft, rode cautiously toward the hollow. As they neared the Nez Perces' lines, old Captain John, still known to the Dreamers as Jokais (Lazy, or Worthless), called out anxiously, "All my brothers, I am glad to see you

---

35. "The Pursuit and Capture of Chief Joseph" by Charles Erskine Scott Wood in Fee, *Chief Joseph*, pp. 328–29. For the Indians' understanding of what was said to them on this point, see McWhorter, *Hear Me*, p. 494. Whether Joseph understood that he would go back to the Wallowa, or to Lapwai, is open to question. In "Chief Joseph's Own Story," p. 26, he is quoted as saying, "General Miles said to me in plain words, 'If you will come out and give up your arms, I will spare your lives and send you back to the reservation.'" Shortly afterward, however, he said, "General Miles had promised that we might return to our country with what stock we had left" and "I was told we could go with General Miles to Tongue River and stay there until spring, when we would be sent back to our country" (p. 27). By "our country," he may have meant the reservation, but one will never know. Joseph's exact words for this article went through the mill of a translation by Arthur Chapman and a polishing by a professional editor.

alive this sun!" One of the warriors wanted to shoot the two men, but others interfered, and the messengers were allowed to come slowly down the slope to the camp. There, Joseph and his people surrounded them. Captain John smiled weakly at the crowd of hostile faces and tried to look friendly. "We have traveled a long ways trying to catch you folks," he said. "We are glad to hear you want no more war, do not want to fight. We are all glad. I am glad because all my sons are glad to be alive. Not to go in battle any more."

The two reservation Indians rattled on, finally delivering the message Chapman had given them. "Listen well what I say," said Old George. "I heard General Howard telling, 'When I catch Chief Joseph, I will bring him back to his own home.' "

Chief Joseph, Yellow Wolf says contemptuously, "sent those two Indians back where they belonged."

But as soon as they were gone, a council was called. There was divided opinion. The arrival of Howard, heralding the appearance of reinforcements for Miles and the possibility of an attack that would overwhelm the Indians, had taken the final heart out of many of the suffering people. Looking Glass, White Bird, and many of the warriors, however, still opposed surrender, fearing that Howard would not live up to his word but would hang the leaders. In the middle of their debate Yellow Wolf said they heard General Howard calling to ask why the Indians were not giving up. Shortly afterward, the two treaty Nez Perces reappeared with their white flag and said that Miles wanted to speak to Joseph. Joseph replied that they were having a council to decide what to do, and the two messengers joined the meeting. One of them again made a short speech, telling them that Miles wished to remind them of the many efforts he had made to convince them that he wished to end the war.

This seemed to relieve Joseph, who had apparently been accused by the others of having offered, four days before, to surrender the Nez Perces to Miles. "You see, it is true," he said to the council members. "I did not say, 'Let's quit!' General Miles said, 'Let's quit.' And now General Howard says, 'Let's quit.' You see, it is true enough! I did not say, 'Let's quit!' "

"When the warriors heard those words from Chief Joseph," said Yellow Wolf, "they answered, 'Yes, we believe you now.' "

It was a significant point to the Indians, for to their understanding Joseph was saying that they would not be surrendering, but would merely be agreeing with Miles and Howard to end the fighting. It would be a draw, and they could go back to their homes with honor.

Still, many of the surviving leaders repeated that they wanted nothing to do with Howard, and they continued to argue that Joseph was merely deluding himself. White Bird's people later informed Duncan McDonald that Looking Glass lectured Joseph sternly. "I am older than you," he told the

Wallowa chief. "I have my experiences with a man of two faces and two tongues. If you surrender you will be sorry; and in your sorrow you will feel rather to be dead, than suffer that deception . . ." Joseph, however, turned away from him. Every band could now make up its own mind what to do. Every individual, in fact, was free to make his own choice. Joseph looked about the camp, gazing at the people in the shelter dugouts. "The white captain has made good talk all right," he said. "Many of our people are out on the hills, naked and freezing. The women are suffering with cold, the children crying with the chilly dampness of the shelter pits. For myself I do not care. It is for them I am going to surrender."

"I will never surrender to a deceitful white chief," Looking Glass said. White Bird agreed with him, and the two headmen planned to steal off with their people, at the first opportunity, and try to reach Sitting Bull's camp.[36]

The ill-starred Looking Glass never made it. A few minutes after the council broke up, someone called to him that a mounted Indian was approaching across the plains from the north. It was one of Miles's Cheyennes, but Looking Glass sprang up to see for himself, and thought it was a messenger from Sitting Bull. As he turned excitedly to call out the news, he was struck in the forehead by a bullet and killed instantly, the last casualty of the battle. While the Indians gathered about the slain chief's body, Joseph and a few warriors followed the treaty Nez Perces across the lines for a preliminary talk with Howard and Miles. Joseph apparently let them know that the Indians still feared Howard's intentions, and Miles reputedly reassured the chief that "Howard will forget all this," and that he, Miles, would guarantee to protect the Indians and after the winter send them all back home.

With that promise, Joseph returned to his people to tell them that he was about to stop the fighting, and that the soldiers would give them good treatment. Then, about 2 o'clock in the afternoon, he took his rifle and solemnly mounted his horse. Followed by five of his warriors on foot, he rode slowly up the hill at the south end of the village toward a spot between the creek and the site of the Seventh Cavalry's first charge. Howard and Miles were waiting there for him. A little behind them were Wood, Guy Howard, and another officer, and near them were Arthur Chapman and an orderly. In the rear, some distance away, was a courier with his horse, ready to carry Miles's report of surrender to Fort Keogh.

As Joseph appeared over the brow of the hill, the officers noted that his head was bowed as if he were listening to his companions, who "leaned on his knees at each side of his horse talking earnestly." Joseph's rifle was across his knees, and his hands were crossed on the pommel of his saddle. The Indians were "a picturesque and pathetic little group," said Wood. A bullet scratch

36. McWhorter, *Hear Me*, p. 495.

had left a scar on Joseph's forehead, and there were bullet scratches also on his wrist and across the small of his back, as well as bullet holes in his sleeves, the body of his shirt, and one of his leggings.

When the group reached the summit, Wood reported:

> those on foot stopped and went back a little, as if all was over. Then, nothing but silence. Joseph threw himself off his horse, draped his blanket about him, and carrying his rifle in the hollow of one arm, changed from the stooped attitude in which he had been listening, held himself very erect, and with a quiet pride, not exactly defiance, advanced toward General Howard and held out his rifle in token of submission. General Howard smiled at him, but waved him over to Colonel Miles, who was standing beside him. Joseph quickly made a slight turn and offered the rifle to Miles, who took it. Then Joseph stepped back a little, and Arthur Chapman stepped forward so as to be between the group of two— Howard and Miles. I was standing very close to Howard with a pencil and a paper pad which I always carried at such times, ready for any dictation that might be given. Joseph again addressed himself to General Howard . . .

With Chapman doing the interpreting, and Wood taking down the translation, Joseph began to speak:

> Tell General Howard I know his heart. What he told me before, I have it in my heart. I am tired of fighting. Our chiefs are killed. Looking Glass is dead. Toohoolhoolzote is dead. The old men are all dead. It is the young men who say, "Yes" or "No." He who led the young men is dead. It is cold, and we have no blankets. The little children are freezing to death. My people, some of them, have run away to the hills, and have no blankets, no food. No one knows where they are—perhaps freezing to death. I want to have time to look for my children, and see how many of them I can find. Maybe I shall find them among the dead. Hear me, my chiefs! I am tired. My heart is sick and sad. From where the sun now stands I will fight no more forever.

Joseph's sad and beautiful words affected the officers. His phrase "He who led the young men" referred to his own brother, Ollokot, whom Howard had known and respected. There was a moment of silence. Then Joseph drew his blanket over his head. The war was over.[37]

37. My account of the surrender scene is based on the eyewitness description of Lieutenant C. E. S. Wood, published in Fee, *Chief Joseph*, pp. 329–30. However, the text which I use of Joseph's speech, one of the most famous ever made by an American Indian, is not the one given by Wood in Fee's book, and an explanation is required. While Wood stated that he wrote it down as Chapman translated it, he noted that he later gave the original to the Adjutant General of the Army for his personal collection

During the rest of the afternoon other Nez Perces streamed up from the hollow. Some buried their guns in the ravines, but most of them carried them to the soldiers and surrendered them, raising an arm toward where the sun shone wanly, to indicate no more war. The troops fraternized with the Indians, trying to show their friendship and respect for a brave and manly foe. Roaring fires were built, hot food and blankets were distributed, and the shivering and starving people were revived by the warmth and cheer in the soldiers' camp.

There were still holdouts. White Bird and his followers lingered in the hollow, continuing to believe that Joseph would be hanged. Men, women, and children of other bands stayed among the shelter dugouts with them, determined not to give up. After darkness, many of them made their way silently out of the ravines in groups and started north toward Sitting Bull's people, moving on foot as fast as they could go. Old White Bird himself led the largest party. Later, other Indians, including Yellow Wolf, stole away on mounts and came after them.

Those who departed were sad to leave the others behind. "It was lonesome, the leaving," said Ollokot's surviving widow. "Husband dead, friends buried or held prisoners. I felt that I was leaving all that I had but I did not cry. You know how you feel when you lose kindred and friends through sickness-death. You do not care if you die. With us it was worse. Strong men, well women, and little children killed and buried. They had not done wrong to be so killed. We had only asked to be left in our own homes, the homes of our ancestors. Our going was with heavy hearts, broken spirits. But we would be free . . . All lost, we walked silently on into the wintry night." [38]

Altogether, counting the large group that had escaped on the first day of the battle, a few who had slipped away during the course of the fighting, and

---

of great Indian speeches. "I have done my best now to reconstruct it from memory," Wood said, referring to the version in Fee's volume. In its issue of November 17, 1877, however, only a little more than a month after the surrender, *Harper's Weekly* carried a text of the speech in an article that accompanied engravings of the surrender scene. "Our artist," said the article, "was the only person present who committed the proceedings to writing, and took the reply as it fell from the lips of the speaker." By that date, November 17, Wood had been in Chicago, where he had written an account of the surrender for a newspaper. He also had the original text of the speech still with him. It seems certain, therefore, that Wood was the source of the article, of the text of the surrender speech, and of the drawings in *Harper's Weekly* of November 17, and since this is the earliest version of the speech that I have found, taken apparently from Wood's original transcription, I have used it.

There has been some debate in the past, also, concerning the identity of the artist who drew the *Harper's Weekly* sketches, or at least provided rough drawings for the finished sketches. The periodical identified him as "an officer of General Howard's staff." I cannot see how it could have been anyone but Wood.

38. McWhorter, *Hear Me*, p. 511.

these last parties that escaped after Joseph's surrender, it was estimated that a total of 233 Nez Perces, including 140 men and boys and 93 women and girls, got away from the Bear Paw battlefield. The refugees suffered from cold, hunger, and fatigue. Many wounded people were among them, struggling along in pain. At the Milk River the various groups met sympathetic Crees and halfbloods, who gave them food and moccasins and treated them kindly. Some of the stragglers died on the plains from exposure or from their wounds, and others, including the warrior Tipyahlanah Kapskaps, ran into Assiniboines and Gros Ventres, who murdered them. Still others, overtaken eventually by some of Miles's cavalrymen, were rounded up and herded to Tongue River, where they were added to Joseph's group. But most of the refugees, including White Bird and Yellow Wolf, made it safely to Sitting Bull's Sioux, who welcomed them as fellow-victims of the Americans. A large Sioux war party, it was discovered, had actually started south to aid the beleaguered Nez Perces. Indians who had escaped from the Bear Paws on the first day of the battle had arrived and pleaded for help. But the Sioux had misunderstood their sign language, thinking that they had meant that the battle was on the Missouri River, which Sitting Bull thought was too far away. Another group of refugees had struggled in later, however, and when they had been able to pinpoint the actual location of the fight, the Sioux leader had organized a rescue group. But it had started south too late. On the way its members had run into White Bird's people, and they had learned that Joseph had surrendered.

At the battlefield the prisoners totaled 418: 87 men, 184 women, and 147 children. Viewing the Indians, still unbowed and proud in the belief that the soldiers had not defeated them, Miles gained a respect for the Nez Perces that he would never lose. "The fight was the most fierce of any Indian engagement I have ever been in," he wrote his wife. ". . . The whole Nez Perce movement is unequalled in the history of Indian warfare." [39]

Although he rushed a courier to Fort Keogh with an announcement of the surrender that claimed all the credit for himself, he could sympathize with what Howard had experienced. The Nez Perces, leaving Idaho with approximately 750 persons, including women, children, and sick and old people, with all their baggage and a huge horse herd, had conducted an unprecedented 1,700-mile retreat, fighting almost all the way. Altogether, the Indians had battled some 2,000 American regulars and volunteers of different military units, together with their Indian auxiliaries of many tribes, in a total of eighteen engagements, including four major battles and at least four fiercely contested skirmishes.[40] They had had at least 120 of their people killed, including

39. Johnson, *The Unregimented General*, pp. 207–08.

40. There may be a difference of opinion over skirmishes that I have included or omitted, but my list is: Whitebird; the attack on Rains; the Cottonwood skirmishing;

approximately 65 men and 55 women and children, and they had slain approximately 180 whites and wounded 150. Man for man, they had proven themselves better fighting men and marksmen than the soldiers or volunteers, many of whom were poorly trained marksmen and had no stomach for combat.

The Nez Perce war, in fact, emphasized the truth of what few writers even to this day will acknowledge, that the romanticized "Indian-fighting army of the West," glamorized by such persons as Frederic Remington, was a poor and uninspired army. The great numbers of warriors have been used to explain away the greatest of all Indian victories over that army, the defeat of Custer at the Little Bighorn. But the Nez Perces and other tribes won many victories when the odds were even or were against them; and what triumphs the army scored were gained more often than not because the soldiers' attacks were made on unsuspecting villages of men, women, and children, or because the whites' firepower was overwhelming. With the examples of what the Nez Perces did in combat when troops did not surprise them, it seems certain that they would have escaped from the soldiers—or badly thrashed them —had they been ready for them at the Clearwater, the Big Hole, and the Bear Paws. Even so, an appreciation of what they did accomplish exposes as myth much of what has been written about the post-Civil War armies that fought the Indians on the plains.

In the end, the war that Howard had brought on by his policy of force cost the United States $1,873,410.43, not including the losses of private individuals.[41] The Nez Perce survivors of the struggle, once a rich and self-sufficient people, were made destitute, and thereafter they became burdens to the American taxpayer. The Indians had lost their horses, cattle, guns, personal possessions, savings of gold dust and cash, homes, freedom—everything but their honor. With their defeat the history of the Nez Perces as an independent people came to an end. On October 8 Miles started the prisoners to Fort Keogh. The Colonel and the American nation did not know it, but among the dispirited captives were three Nez Perces with a distinguished white forebear. They were Halahtookit (Daytime Smoke), an aged son of Captain William Clark, and his daughter and granddaughter. The "Bostons" who had followed their illustrious ancestor into the valleys of the Snake, the Clearwater, the Imnaha, and the Wallowa finally owned the country.

---

the fight with the Mount Idaho volunteers; Mount Misery; the Clearwater; the skirmish at the Clearwater crossing; the ambush of Mason's column; the Fort Fizzle skirmishing; the Big Hole; the Horse Prairie skirmishing; Camas Meadows; Yellowstone Park skirmishing; Canyon Creek; fights with the Crows; Cow Creek; the skirmish with Ilges; Bear Paws.

41. Senate Executive Document, No. 14, 45th Congress, 2nd Session, Washington, D.C. (1879), p. 40.

Chief Joseph—An Epilogue

IT WAS AFTER THE WAR that Chief Joseph became the monumental symbol of the Nez Perces. They were terrible days for the defeated, full of dejection and suffering, and through the despair and hardship Joseph rose to greatness, never ceasing his efforts to win fair and just treatment for his people. Fairness seemed so simple: merely adherence to the promise Howard and Miles had made to the Indians at the Bear Paws. You will go home in the spring, the officers had said to them. But the defeated Nez Perces did not go home.

Miles took the column of the surrendered Indians to Fort Keogh. On the way he came to know Joseph better, hearing from the chief's lips the background of the war, and all that the Nez Perces had done to try to avoid hostilities. His respect for his prisoners was already high, but their integrity and manliness, as expressed principally through Joseph, still noble, dignified, and persuasive, now made a mark upon him. The Nez Perces "were the boldest and best marksmen of any Indians I have ever encountered. And Chief Joseph was a man of more sagacity and intelligence than any Indian I have ever met," he wrote.[1] By the time the troops and Indians reached Tongue River, Miles was anxious to become their champion. As it turned out, the Nez Perces would badly need one.

In the policy of General Sherman there was no leniency or charity for Indians. The commander of the armies viewed war as hell, and to his mind the only way to treat an enemy was to crush him totally and destroy his ability and desire ever to make war again. During the Civil War that uncompromising policy had made Sherman an effective and winning general. He had visited the same policy on the Indians. "The more we can kill this year," he had said in 1867, "the less will have to be killed the next war, for the more I see of these Indians, the more convinced I am that they all have to be killed or be

1. Nelson A. Miles, *Serving the Republic* (New York, 1911), p. 181.

maintained as a species of paupers." [2] The saying "The only good Indian is a dead Indian" was attributed to him, and whether or not he believed in genocide, he encouraged his subordinate, Sheridan, and many of the regular officers on the plains to treat Indians ruthlessly in combat and without mercy after their defeat.

The Nez Perces were now to feel Sherman's heel. As a military man he could admire their campaign; and his report of the war, prepared for the War Department at the request of the Senate, helped to confirm the public's feeling that Joseph and the Nez Perces had indeed contributed an epic to the history of the American Indians. The campaign, said Sherman, had been "one of the most extraordinary Indian wars of which there is any record. The Indians throughout displayed a courage and skill that elicited universal praise. They abstained from scalping; let captive women go free; did not commit indiscriminate murder of peaceful families, which is usual, and fought with almost scientific skill, using advance and rear guards, skirmish lines, and field fortifications." Nevertheless, they had to be punished and their ability and inclination to oppose whites ever again had to be smashed. The Nez Perce leaders, he said, "should be executed," and the rest of the captives "must never be allowed to return to Oregon, but should be engrafted on the Modoc in Indian country [Indian Territory]." [3]

In Chicago, General Sheridan concurred with Sherman's recommendations and suggested that the Nez Perces should be confined as prisoners of war at Fort Leavenworth until the Indian Bureau could find a place for them in the Indian country or somewhere else "not in Oregon." The generals' proposals were approved in Washington by the War and Interior departments, which feared the political difficulties of sending the war bands back to their homes. Indictments for murder had been issued in Idaho against many of the hostiles and their leaders, and feeling was still high against Joseph and the nontreaties throughout the late theater of war. Miles, however, learning what was in the wind, objected. "The Nez Perce trouble was caused by the rascality of their Agent, and the encroachment of the whites," he wired E. A. Hayt, Commissioner of Indian Affairs, "and [I] have regarded their treatment unusually severe. Joseph can tell you his own story . . ." [4] The Colonel's protest had no effect. Although he emphasized the promise that he and Howard had both given the Nez Perces, he was ignored by Sherman. Howard himself turned against the Nez Perces. In Chicago he took offense at Miles's report of Joseph's capture, which gave no credit to himself. He authorized his aide, Lieutenant C. E. S. Wood, to write a full and more exact story

2. *The American Heritage Book of Indians* (New York, 1961), p. 366.
3. Beal, *I Will Fight No More Forever*, pp. 243, 336 n., 265.
4. Ibid., p. 265.

of the surrender, but its publication in a Chicago newspaper got him in trouble with Sheridan. In the process of extricating himself, Howard endorsed the recommendations of Sherman and Sheridan regarding the prisoners, easing his conscience with the rationalization that White Bird's escape to Canada had rendered null and void the promise to Joseph to return the surrendered Indians to their homes.

By November 1 Miles had his orders. He was to send the Nez Perces down the Yellowstone and Missouri rivers at once to Fort Lincoln near Bismarck. The Colonel, torn by a feeling of sympathy for the Indians, had to obey. The prisoners now numbered 431 (cavalrymen had captured and brought in a group of escapees who had been trying to reach Canada), and a flotilla of fourteen flatboats took the wounded and ill down the river to Fort Buford at the mouth of the Yellowstone. Joseph and the rest of the captives rode overland with Miles and a military escort. It was a dreary and painful trip for both groups. The Indians' spirits drooped as they realized that another betrayal was afoot. At Fort Buford their fears mounted when they learned that they were to go down the Missouri to an American city. Now the warnings of Looking Glass and White Bird were remembered: the white chiefs' tongues were forked; the Indians would be thrown into prison and hanged.

The groups continued downriver by flatboat and wagon train and reached Fort Lincoln on November 16. The Indians' state was pitiful. One of the flatboatmen said they were so frightened that they became helpless. "They sat up a moaning chant no dout their death chant," he said.[5] But instead of receiving punishment, they were treated in Bismarck as heroes. The citizens of the city, reflecting the nation's admiration for their gallantry, flocked to cheer them. The Indians' ragged and forlorn condition touched the whites, who gave them food in the town square. A special banquet was held for Joseph, the invitation, published in the *Bismarck Tri-Weekly Tribune* on November 21, 1877, reading:

> To Joseph, Head Chief of the Nez Perces.
> Sir:
>   Desiring to show you our kind feelings and the admiration we have for your bravery and humanity, as exhibited in your recent conflict with the forces of the United States, we most cordially invite you to dine with us at the Sheridan House in this city. The dinner to be given at 1½ p.m. today.

The growth of the Wallowa chief as a legend, even in his own day, was under way. A photograph taken of him in Bismarck by F. J. Haynes—later one of the most famous photographers of Yellowstone Park and the American West—quickly became a best seller all over the country.

5. Fred G. Bond, *Flatboating on the Yellowstone, 1877* (New York, 1925), p. 19.

While Joseph banqueted at the Sheridan House, citizens took others of the Indians to dine elsewhere in town. Some of the Nez Perces were too depressed to eat. "The appearance of all," said the flatboatman who was with them, "was heart rending sad." An Irish waitress expressed the general sympathy for them. "The Devils to put those people under soldiers guard," she said.[6]

In Bismarck, Miles made another effort to help the Nez Perces, wiring an appeal to Sheridan to be allowed to take a delegation of their leaders to Washington. Sheridan, with the concurrence of Sherman, the Commissioner of Indian Affairs, and the Secretaries of War and Interior, turned him down. Telling Joseph that he had tried to abide by his promise but could no longer help him, Miles said farewell to the prisoners and left for St. Paul. On November 23 the Nez Perces, now reassured at least that they were not going to be executed, were put aboard a train for Fort Leavenworth. The cars were crowded, and the train had to make frequent stops at water tanks for the Indians to slake their thirst. Ironically, at one stop the train pulled away without Joseph, and it was some time before it was discovered that he was missing. The train stopped and backed up, and in time Joseph was seen hurrying down the tracks after it. There had been no thought in his mind of escape.[7]

The Nez Perces reached Fort Leavenworth on November 27 and were placed in a miserable and unhealthy location between the Missouri River and a swampy bottomland. General John Pope had urged that they be held at Fort Riley, where comfortable and healthier quarters were available, but again Sherman and Sheridan—almost as if they had deliberately selected the spot "for the express purpose of putting an end to Chief Joseph and his band," said one observer—had overruled that suggestion and settled on Leavenworth. "It was simply horrible," the same writer reported. "The 400 miserable, helpless, emaciated specimens of humanity, subjected for months to the malarial atmosphere of the river bottom, presented a picture which brought to my mind the horrors of Andersonville. One-half were sick, principally women and children. All were filled with the poisonous malaria of the camp." [8] By the following July at least 21 Nez Perces had died of sickness in the pesthole.

Shortly after the Indians reached Leavenworth, Joseph began his long and tireless effort for justice. On December 10 he and seven other Nez Perces addressed a petition to the government, pleading to be returned to Idaho or, at least, to be given the right to select land in the Indian Territory. Sherman wrote "Disapproved" on the petition and reprimanded the officer at Leavenworth who had forwarded it. At the same time Sherman pressed the Indian

6. Ibid., p. 22.
7. *Chief Joseph Herald*, July 24, 1952, courtesy Grace Bartlett, Joseph, Oregon.
8. McWhorter, *Hear Me*, pp. 529–30.

Bureau to decide where to put the prisoners permanently and to take them off the budget of the War Department.

In the warm weather of spring the suffering and misery of the Nez Perces at Leavenworth increased. Word of their plight managed to reach Washington from time to time, and on May 27, 1878, Congress appropriated $20,000 for the Indian Bureau to move them to the Quapaw Indian reserve in Kansas Territory. Late in July they were finally transferred to Indian Bureau jurisdiction and were taken by train, and then wagons, to an impoverished 7,000-acre tract of sand and sagebrush on lands purchased from the Miami and Peoria Indians. Commissioner Hayt had blithely assured Congress that the Indian Territory would be no hardship for the Nez Perces, "as the difference in temperature between that latitude and their old home is inconsiderable." [9] But he had had no idea what he was talking about. The Nez Perces' new home was almost as bad as Leavenworth had been. Used to the cool mountain air of the Northwest, the Indians withered in the barren southern plains country, which they called Eeikish Pah (the hot place). Sanitation was bad, no medicines were available, and the people continued to sicken. By October 47 more Nez Perces were dead.

Meanwhile, in Canada, individuals and small groups of Nez Perces, filled with longings for home, began to leave Sitting Bull and head for Idaho. Their wanderings were long and difficult. They had to travel in secrecy, forage for food and horses, and sometimes fight for their lives. Soldiers and vigilantes hunted them and forced them to hide in the woods and mountains. Often, men, women, and children traveled together, finding little help from white men or other Indians. Some were killed; others moved for years like animals, seeking temporary concealment on one Indian reservation after another. From time to time they straggled into the Lapwai reservation, where, without a place to live, they finally surrendered to the agent or allowed the officious Nez Perce Indian police to take them in. The Christian Nez Perces generally frowned on the returned nontreaties, calling them fools and troublemakers who deserved what had happened to them. The reservation was solidly under the influence of the missionaries, who worked closely with the agents, and the church-going Nez Perces encouraged the authorities to send the Dreamers and "wild ones," as the missionaries called the war veterans, to Joseph's group in the Indian Territory. Although some of the officers at Fort Lapwai felt sorry for the returned Indians, those in charge could not help them, and Yellow Wolf and many other Nez Perces who had made their way painfully home from Canada were sent off under guard to "the hot place." White Bird and some of his close followers never did come home. The old Salmon River chief stayed in Canada, and about 1882, when his shamanistic skill failed to

9. Annual Report, Department of Interior (1877), p. 409.

save the lives of two sick Nez Perce children, he is believed to have been shot dead by their father—which, according to Yellow Wolf, was the "law among all the tribes." [10]

Joseph, meanwhile, continued to exercise his role as the guardian and spokesman of the exiled people. His appeals for attention to their miserable condition gradually pricked the conscience of officials in Washington. Commissioner Hayt and a party, making an inspection of Joseph's camp in October 1878, readily observed the distress of the Nez Perces. Although Joseph pleaded for the government to live up to Miles's promise and return the Indians to Idaho, saying that all of them would die if they were left in the unhealthy, hot country, Hayt replied that it would be impossible to send them home. Instead, he took Joseph and Husishusis Kute on a 250-mile trip, looking for a better location on the southern plains. They finally found a more agreeable tract of 90,710 acres of fertile and timbered bottomland on the Ponca Indian reserve near present-day Tonkawa, Oklahoma; and although Joseph complained that the site was little better than where they were, and that his people would die there also, he agreed to move if Hayt got Congress to appropriate money for the transfer. Shortly afterward, a Congressional investigating committee arrived. Its chairman, of all people, was Lafayette Grover, the former Oregon governor who was now a United States Senator. With brazen indifference to the role he had played in reducing the Wallowa Indians to their present state, he unctuously assured Joseph that he was his friend and would try to help him if he would give up his hope of returning to Oregon.

As a dedicated pleader for his people, the conquered and powerless Joseph was a more impressive figure than he had ever been. He towered morally over the whites who came to see him; and when they returned to Washington, they took with them the unforgettable memory of a humanitarian who spoke with the passion and courage of a fighter for freedom, and the wisdom and dignity of a stateman. One visitor, Indian Inspector General John O'Neill, was persuaded that Joseph should have a personal hearing from President Hayes, and through O'Neill's efforts the chief was given permission to come to Washington in January 1879. He was accompanied by Yellow Bull and Arthur Chapman, who had taken a government job as interpreter for the exiles. The capital was interested in seeing the great Indian "Napoleon," and on January 14 Joseph spoke to a large assemblage of cabinet members, congressmen, and diplomats. His account of the causes of the war, his people's trials, and their present difficulties was eloquent and moving. The impact of his appeal, repeated soon afterward in an interview published in the *North American Review*, stirred everyone who heard or read it:

10. McWhorter, *Hear Me*, p. 524.

"I have shaken hands with a great many friends," he said, "but there are some things I want to know which no one seems able to explain. I cannot understand how the Government sends a man out to fight us, as it did General Miles, and then breaks his word. Such a Government has something wrong about it . . . I do not understand why nothing is done for my people. I have heard talk and talk, but nothing is done. Good words do not last long until they amount to something. Words do not pay for my dead people. They do not pay for my country, now overrun by white men. They do not protect my father's grave . . . Good words will not give me back my children . . . Good words will not give my people good health and stop them from dying. Good words will not get my people a home where they can live in peace and take care of themselves. I am tired of talk that comes to nothing. It makes my heart sick when I remember all the good words and all the broken promises. There has been too much talking by men who had no right to talk. Too many misrepresentations have been made, too many misunderstandings have come up between the white men about the Indians. If the white man wants to live in peace with the Indian he can live in peace. There need be no trouble. Treat all men alike. Give them all the same law. Give them all an even chance to live and grow. All men were made by the same Great Spirit Chief. They are all brothers. The earth is the mother of all people, and all people should have equal rights upon it.

"You might as well expect the rivers to run backward as that any man who was born free should be contented penned up and denied liberty to go where he pleases . . ."

The fact that Joseph had not alone been responsible for the outstanding strategy and masterful successes of the war was irrelevant. The surrender speech had confirmed him in the public's mind as the symbol of the Nez Perces' heroism. But his appeal, now being delivered before the bar of world opinion, was lifting Joseph far above the level of a mere Indian war chief.

"I know that my race must change," he went on. "We cannot hold our own with the white men as we are. We only ask an even chance to live as other men live. We ask to be recognized as men. We ask that the same law shall work alike on all men . . .

"Let me be a free man—free to travel, free to stop, free to work, free to trade, where I choose, free to choose my own teachers, free to follow the religion of my fathers, free to think and talk and act for myself—and I will obey every law, or submit to the penalty."

Joseph met the President, the Secretary of Interior, and other officials, and pleaded with all of them to honor Miles's pledge at the Bear Paws. His powerful appeals stirred emotions and consciences, roused people outside of the government to take up his cause and sign petitions in his behalf, but—for the time being—failed to achieve their purpose. The indictments were still out in Idaho, and the War and Interior departments were certain that trouble would break out in the Northwest if Joseph and his people were sent home.

The trio returned to the Quapaw reserve, and in June 1879 the Indian Bureau moved the Nez Perces to the new Oklahoma site that Hayt had found for them. It was scarcely an improvement. They had inadequate shelter and little medicine, and the fall rains and winter cold caused more illness and death. Practically every child born in the new place of exile died. At one time, a visitor counted the graves of one hundred children. One of them was the resting place of Joseph's little daughter, who had been born at Rocky Canyon on the eve of the outbreak of the war.

In 1879, also, three Christian Nez Perces, Archie Lawyer, James Reuben, and Mark Williams, arrived from Lapwai under government auspices to teach and preach to the exiles. They had a mite of success in bringing Christian comfort to some of the women and old men, but most of the war veterans had little interest in their instruction. Lawyer and Williams soon sickened in the climate and returned home, leaving Reuben to continue as a teacher.

As time dragged on, Joseph's efforts began to bear fruit in the East. Miles, now a general, had never abandoned his concern over what had happened, and in 1881 he appealed to President Hayes to return Joseph's Indians to Idaho. Other individuals and groups—Howard's former aide, C. E. S. Wood, the Indian Rights Association in Philadelphia, and the Presbyterian Church —also began campaigns to persuade the government to send the Nez Perces back to their homes. Newspapermen and other visitors to the exiles interviewed Joseph, inspected the Indians' condition, and kept their cause before the public. By 1883 Joseph's future had become a national issue. Letters, telegrams, and appeals flowed into Washington, and in May of that year the government finally allowed James Reuben to take twenty-nine persons, two of them old men and the rest women and orphans, back to the Lapwai reservation.

The following year Congress approved the return of all the people at the discretion of the Secretary of Interior. The Commissioner of Indian Affairs, convinced that the people of Idaho still held Joseph and his band accountable for the murders on the Salmon River and Camas Prairie, incongruously directed that that group of exiles should be sent to the Colville reservation in northeastern Washington, while the Looking Glass and White Bird Indians could go to Lapwai. Fears among Indian Bureau personnel in Washington and the Northwest delayed the return for several months, but on May 22, 1885, 268 Nez Perces, the remainder of all who had surrendered almost seven years before, or who had been captured after the war, entrained at Arkansas City. Ill, ragged, and worn, but still nobly proud in the satisfaction that they had been the patriots of their people, 118 of them finally reached Lapwai, where they received a mixed welcome. Some of the reservation Indians cried with joy. Others were not sure that they wanted the newcomers. Yellow Wolf understood that the division among the exiles was based on whether an Indian was willing to be a Christian, and he claimed that only those who agreed to embrace Christianity were sent to Lapwai. He was not correct, for the Lapwai contingent included Dreamers as well as those willing to be instructed by the missionaries. At any rate, the returned exiles found a deep division on the reservation. Although the missionaries were still influential, there had been considerable backsliding among the Indians. The situation was much as it had been during the days of Spalding, with constant hauling and tugging between Christians and so-called "heathens." Native religious beliefs and practices, though trampled on and "thrown away" again and again, had not died. The returned Dreamers found many sympathetic friends, and their own presence for a while helped to strengthen the antimissionary group.

At Colville, 150 Nez Perces, including Joseph, eventually found a new home along Nespelem Creek. It was not managed easily. The Colville reservation had been created in 1872, and a variety of Salish and Sahaptin peoples of northeastern Washington had been dumped on it from time to time. The reservation agent was dismayed by the arrival of the Nez Perces, and he backed the Salishan Sanpoils in their objections to the newcomers. Troops finally had to be called from Fort Spokane to get Joseph's people peaceably settled.

Until 1900 Joseph viewed this abode as a temporary one, and he made repeated efforts to be allowed to return to the Wallowa. His appeals were regularly denied, but he refused to abandon hope. In 1889 the allotment of land began on the Lapwai reservation. Joseph and his people could have come to Lapwai then and received allotments, but they refused. The Indians on the reservation at last settled down on their own plots, and although they protested that they would be left with no grazing country, the surplus reservation land was sold to white men. Gradually, the present form of intermixed Indian and white holdings and white land leases of Indian property took shape. In 1891 the reverent and good Timothy died. The division among the tribe over Christianity continued after his death, and in mild form it has persisted to this day.

In 1897 white squatters began to encroach on Colville reservation lands near Joseph's people, and the chief went to Washington to complain. He met President McKinley and General Miles. During the same trip he was invited to New York to participate in the dedication ceremonies of Grant's Tomb. His visit received great publicity, New Yorkers lionized him, and he rode in a place of honor in the dedication parade with Miles, Howard, and Buffalo Bill. More importantly, he reopened his plea for permission to return to the Wallowa. Miles and others took up his cause, and the Indian Bureau promised to investigate the possibility of such a move.

In August 1899 Joseph himself, accompanied by some of his followers, made his first visit to the Wallowa since the war. Four little towns existed along the river, and the valley was dotted with ranches and farms. Joseph was taken in hand by his old acquaintance, A. C. Smith. The chief received a polite reception wherever he went, but after telling a public meeting of his desire to buy a tract of land in the valley for his people, he was informed that no one would sell a foot of property for an Indian reserve. Still, the chief did not give up. In 1900 the Indian Bureau sent Inspector General James McLaughlin to see him at Nespelem. The two men journeyed to Wallowa to look over the situation. Again, Joseph received a courteous welcome. He visited his father's grave, where his eyes misted, then drove up to Wallowa Lake with McLaughlin. A. C. Smith and several of the valley's citizens met them there, and at that point Joseph's hopes finally ended for all time. The people of Wallowa, McLaughlin was bluntly told, did not want the Indians back— ever.

Joseph returned to Nespelem to die in exile. His death came on September 21, 1904, while he was sitting in front of his tipi fire. The Colville agency physician reported simply that he had died of a broken heart.

Today, the Nez Perces are still disunited. Some of the descendents of Joseph's followers have moved to the Lapwai reservation from Nespelem, but many of them still live in permanent exile on the Colville reservation, where Joseph is buried. At Lapwai the history since 1900 has been one of numerous factions and controversies, most of them stemming from the white man's pressures and interferences. They have revolved generally around problems of land ownership, claims, divisions of government payments, religious freedom, and proposals for the development of the tribe's human and economic resources. The tribe now carries some 2,100 members on its rolls, but about 700 of them have moved off the reservation and live among white men. The others—like numerous Indians elsewhere—are a bypassed and largely ignored people for whom the affluence of the rest of the American nation has little meaning. They operate or lease their small, and often uneconomic, individual land holdings, find occasional employment in the lumber and other industries around Lewiston, or spend their time helplessly and without aim at a level barely above subsistence. To give them motivation and opportunity, their leaders—officers and members of a periodically elected tribal executive committee—are anxiously seeking the means to adopt and carry out an overall reservation development program that will provide them with adequate education, health facilities, vocational training, managerial know-how, credit, and sources of employment to raise their standard of living and bring them into the mainstream of American life. Up to now the Bureau of Indian Affairs, still carrying out minimum treaty obligations to them, has had no money for such a modern Point Four type program for them.

For many years, under the domination of latter-day missionaries and agents who ended the institution of chiefs and tried to exercise more authority than the chiefs ever did, the Christian majority on the reservation deliberately turned its back on tribal culture and history. Lawyer and his achievements were respectfully remembered, but little pride was manifested—openly, at least—in the non-Christian eras or personages of the tribe's past. Hohots Ilppilp, Apash Wyakaikt, Metat Waptass, Tipyahlanah Kaupu, Koolkool Snehee, and many other of the war and buffalo-hunting chiefs were forgotten, or nearly so. Joseph, White Bird, and Toohoolhoolzote were referred to in front of whites as if they had been disgraces to the tribe. On Decoration Days in the past, Nez Perce children at Lapwai even placed flowers on the graves of soldiers who had fought the warring bands.

All that has now changed. With the passage of time, Joseph and the patriots have emerged as the true heroes of all the Nez Perce tribe, and many Lapwai reservation people are proud to trace their lineages to Joseph, White Bird, and others who led the fighters for freedom on the great retreat.

The whites, on the other hand, have lost almost all knowledge of the Indians who helped to make the dramatic history of the land in which they live. Few of the people of the town of Asotin, Washington, ever heard of Apash Wyakaikt, the elder Looking Glass, who once welcomed Bonneville to that area. Among most white men in Lewiston, Clarkston, Orofino, Grangeville, Kamiah, Kooskia, and Stites, the names Tackensuatis, Kowsoter, Tuekakas, Hin-mah-tute-ke-kaikt, Pahkatos Qohqoh, Utsinmalikin, or Kaupu mean nothing. There are no memorials to Rainbow, Five Wounds, Ollokot, or Poker Joe, whose bones lie in unknown graves far from their homelands. In the Wallowa, still sparsely populated by fewer than 8,000 people, the name Chief Joseph Days has been given to an annual rodeo and celebration. Umatillas, Nez Perces, and other Indians enter the valley to participate in the three-day affair. But the non-Indians in the rodeo grandstands, not knowing that several generations ago their fathers took away from the Indians their war horses and unfenced grazing country, can be heard saying, "Indians just can't ride as well as whites." Lewis and Clark, Jim Bridger, and Howard's troopers, of course, could have told them a thing or two, and Kentuck and Ollokot could have showed them. But they are dead.

DISCUSSION NOTES

CHAPTER 1. Their Hearts Were Good

4 (text, p. 9). The meaning of "Chopunnish," and why Lewis and Clark called the tribe Pierced Noses, are both worthy of note. In August 1805, before the explorers had crossed the Bitterroots and reached the Nez Perce country, they had conversed about the country and native peoples ahead with a band of Shoshonis on the Lemhi River of eastern Idaho. The Shoshoni headman, Cameahwait, Lewis' journal reads, "further informed me that he had understood from the persed nosed Indians who inhabit this ¡river [the Salmon] below [west of] the rocky mountains that it ran a great way toward the seting sun and finally lost itself in a great lake of water which was illy taisted, and where the white men lived [the Pacific Ocean]." Thwaites, 2, 380, August 20, 1805.

This is the first known record of the use of the tribe's designation as pierced noses, but unfortunately the notation in Lewis' journal is clothed in confusion. In the explorers' original manuscript the reference is found under the date of August 14, 1805, in Lewis' handwriting. However, just before it occurs, there is an interlineal memorandum, possibly added later by Clark, which reads: "This part to come in the 20th, related to Captain C. thro' the interpreter," which apparently meant the expedition's interpreter Touissant Charbonneau, who understood Hidatsa and would have translated his wife's (Sacajawea's) version of what the Shoshonis said, she speaking both Shoshoni and Hidatsa. (Codex F, pp. 104–09, of the original manuscript journals at the American Philosophical Society, Philadelphia.)

If the conversation had taken place on August 20, as Thwaites assumed it had, Clark would have heard the Shoshonis refer orally to the Nez Perces as Pierced Noses. If the interlineal memorandum is wrong and Lewis actually had the conversation on August 14, Clark, Charbonneau, and Sacajawea had not yet reached the Shoshonis to interpret Cameahwait's words, and Lewis would have been conversing by sign language which his interpreter George Drouillard read for him. The sign for the Nez Perces was made by closing the fist of the right hand and, with forefinger extended to the left, passing it horizontally beneath the nose, as if indicating a pierced nose. It is uncertain today whether the sign referred to a pierced nose or had another meaning, although Flatheads and other Salish peoples said that it meant "pierced noses." James A. Teit, *The Salishan Tribes of the Western Plateaus*, ed. Franz Boas, 45th Annual Report, Bureau of American Ethnology (Washington, D.C., 1930), p. 147. At any rate, it is likely that that is the way Drouillard would have read it for Lewis.

There is no doubt, as my narrative will make clear, that some of the Nez Perces did pierce their noses and wear bits of decorative shell in their nostrils. Meriwether Lewis twice said it, and it seems that that is why the explorers gave the name to the first people they saw who practiced nose piercing. The fact that French Canadians, independently of Lewis and Clark, a short time later also called the tribe by the same name (though in French) suggests that Lewis and Clark had not erroneously applied the name to a people that did not pierce their noses, as some persons have maintained.

When the explorers first met the Nez Perces at Weippe Prairie, sign language was again used. It is not known whether the Nez Perces gave the pierced nose sign for themselves at that meeting. But the word "Chopunnish" must have been pronounced, as it could not have been conveyed by signs. Its meaning has never been clarified. My belief is that it may have been an attempt at pronouncing "Sahaptin," a Salish word used by the Flatheads and other Salish peoples to designate the Nez Perces as people who lived south of themselves. The British trader David Thompson and other fur men often noted that Nez Perces and Salish people used this term for the tribe, on occasion pronouncing it "Shaw-patin." For further comment, see nn. 8, 9 in the chapte

10 (text, p. 15). Walter W. Taylor, "Archaeology and Language in Western North America," *American Antiquity*, 27 (1961). Save where otherwise noted, the material on the prehistoric Nez Perces and their neighbors of the Columbia-Snake-Clearwater areas is based primarily on the following: B. Robert Butler's studies, *The Old Cordilleran Culture in the Pacific Northwest* (Idaho State College Museum, Pocatello, Idaho, 1961), and *Contributions to the Prehistory of the Columbia Plateau*, (Idaho State College Museum, 1962); L. S. Cressman and others, "Cultural Sequences at the Dalles, Oregon: A Contribution to Pacific Northwest Prehistory," *Transactions of the American Philosophical Society*, 50, Part 10 (1960); Richard D. Daugherty, "The Intermontane Western Tradition," *American Antiquity*, 28 (1962); and "Archaeology of the Lind Coulee Site, Washington," *Proceedings of the American Philosophical Society*, 100 (1956); Daugherty and Roald Fryxell, "Interim Report: Archaeological Salvage in the Lower Monumental Reservoir Area, 1962," *Report of Investigations, No. 21* (Laboratory of Archaeology and Geochronology, Washington State University, Pullman, 1962); and Earl H. Swanson, Jr., *The Emergence of Plateau Culture* (Idaho State College Museum, 1962), and "Early Cultures in Northwestern America," *American Antiquity*, 28 (1962).

Also, H. J. Spinden, "The Nez Perce Indians," American Anthropological Association, *Memoirs*, 2 (1908), 165–274; Joel V. Berreman, "Tribal Distribution in Oregon," ibid., 47 (1937); Verne F. Ray, "Tribal Distribution in Eastern Oregon and Adjacent Regions," *American Anthropologist*, 40 (1938); and Sven Liljeblad, *The Indians of Idaho*, Idaho Historical Series, 3 (Boise, 1960).

At the present time, extensive archaeological, anthropological, and linguistic research is under way that will add new information on the subject. I wish to thank the following persons who kindly provided information from their own research and studies: L. S. Cressman, head of the Department of Anthropology, University of Oregon, Eugene; Earl H. Swanson, Jr., associate professor of anthropology and director of the University Museum, Idaho State University, Pocatello; Sven S. Liljeblad, professor of anthropology, Idaho State University; Haruo Aoki, University of California, Berkeley, and Tokyo; and, for their guidance and aid, H. J. Swinney and Merle Wells, Idaho Historical Society, Boise.

17 (text, p. 23). Teit, *The Salishan Tribes*, pp. 167–68, 381–82. Early in 1810, when Nicholas Biddle was editing the journals of the Lewis and Clark Expedition for publication, he consulted William Clark and compiled a list of clarifying notes from the explorer. One of them read: "The Oalashoots [the present-day Flathead tribe] are not *The* Flat Heads, the Chopunnish are Pierced nose. The real Flatheads are those in the plains of Columbia below Chopunish to the Falls [of the Columbia River] . . ." Else-

where, in the same notes he wrote: "Some of the Chopuniesh are flatheads women chiefly the men lower down" and "Almost all the people whom we saw west of the Ry. Mounts. flatten their heads more or less. The Chopunniesh nation & Shoshonees confine the practice to the women, but it extends to many of the men even as we approach the falls & below that universal" (Jackson, *Letters of Lewis and Clark*, pp. 527, 500, 545). The journals kept during the Lewis and Clark Expedition frequently refer to the Nez Perces as Flatheads (Patrick Gass used no other name for them, save once when he called them "the Cho-no-nish"), and on occasion contain significant comments on the subject. On March 19, 1806, discussing head-flattening, Lewis wrote: "this is a custom among all the nations we have met with West of the Rocky Mountains . . . it is from this peculiar form of the head that the nations East of the Rocky mountains, call all the nations on this side, except the Aliohtans or snake Indians, by the generic name of Flat-heads."

How this name eventually came to be applied to one particular tribe, and to one that did not practice head-flattening, is not known, but I suspect that the Nez Perces may unwittingly have been the cause of it. Long before white men got across the Rockies, plains tribes told French and British traders that the country west of the mountains was inhabited by people who flattened their heads. A map published in London in 1768 in an anonymous work entitled *The Great Probability of a North-West Passage deduced from observations of the Letter of Admiral de Fonte*, and based on a 1762 map by the French geographer J. N. Delisle, shows "Tete Plats" living in the interior on the west side of the "High Lands" (the Rockies). It is only one of many maps with a similar legend; another, presented in 1785 to the American Congress by Peter Pond, a Con- necticut fur trader who had explored the Canadian Athabaskan country, shows a "Naberkistagon R.," approximately in the position of the still-undiscovered Columbia River, and below it the legend "flat-head Indians country." A copy of Pond's map is in the British Museum, Add. MSS 15332D.

When Lewis and Clark headed west, and when a short time later British traders began to cross the Canadian Rockies into the Columbia Basin, the plains tribes were still referring generally to the transmountain people, other than the Snakes, as head- flatteners. The bands they would have referred to were those they had seen and known: groups of Salish speakers who also included buffalo-hunting Nez Perces. The plains Indians, often regarding both peoples as the same, may have observed head- flattening Nez Perces in the Salish parties and applied the term to all members of the groups. By 1808 the British and French Canadians on the Columbia's tributaries knew that the Flatheads did not flatten their heads, but they called them that anyway, because every tribe they had previously met had used that term for those particular people.

There is abundant evidence, in addition, that many of the plains Indians continued to use the single name Flathead for both the Nez Perces and the present Flatheads for years after the whites entered the Northwest, and that white men did so too. As late as 1833, maps of the region showed the Chopunnish and Salish as two tribes of a parent Flathead nation that stretched from the Columbia River to the vicinity of the Con- tinental Divide. By that time, most white men in the Northwest, taking their cue from the British and French veterans who had already been there for many years, were also calling the two tribes by their present-day names, and the term Flathead, possibly attributable in the beginning to the Flatheads' Nez Perce allies, had settled permanently on the wrong people.

As a postscript, it is interesting to note that as late as 1837 head-flattening was being practiced by Cayuse Indians, with whom many Nez Perces intermarried. On March 30 of that year Narcissa Whitman, missionary to the Cayuses on the Walla Walla River of southeastern Washington, wrote: "they never raise a child here except they are lash tight to a board & the girls heads undergo the flatening process" *First White Women over the Rockies,* ed. Clifford M. Drury (Glendale. Calif.. 1963), *1,* 127.

22 (text, p. 29). An assertion that the Nez Perces developed the Appaloosa "breed" for war is widespread in the United States, and publicists and Appaloosa owners are spreading it ever wider. The story appeared all at once, full-blown but without satisfactory documentation, only in recent years, and its circulation—abetted by several uncritical publications—has had much to do with the increase in popularity of this "breed." Save for Meriwether Lewis' comment, the literature of the nineteenth century regarding the Nez Perces is barren of a single reference that could give support to the tale. One mention of a "Nez Perce horse" by the British fur trader John Work has been found, but he gave no explanation of what the horse looked like. No eyewitness artist, such as John Mix Stanley or Gustavus Sohon, who drew views of Nez Perce horsemen in the mid-1850s, or western photographers like W. H. Jackson, who pictured Nez Perces prior to 1877, showed them on spotted horses, although the Nez Perces undoubtedly did have some—as did other tribes in the Northwest. Owhi, the Yakima chief, for instance, was killed on one. John Owen, the Bitterroot Valley trader of the 1850s, mentioned a spotted horse that was ridden by "Salmon River Indians," who were probably Shoshonis. And so forth.

On the other hand, many references exist to non-spotted horses ridden by Nez Perce war leaders. The great warrior Rainbow, of the war of 1877, rode a bay war horse. *Harper's Weekly* field sketches of that war do not picture the Nez Perces on spotted horses. Typical of descriptions of the horses the Nez Perces *did* have at various times during the nineteenth century is the following, written by Henry Miller, editor of the *Oregonian,* who visited the Nez Perce country during the gold rush in 1861 and from Slaterville on the Clearwater River on June 4 reported: "The generality of the Nez Perce horses are much finer than any Indian horses I have yet seen . . . A great many are large, fine-bred American stock, with fine limbs, rising withers, sloping well back, and are uncommonly sinewy and sure-footed. Their best gaits are usually a gallop and walk. I have seen thousands of these horses grazing on the mountain, apparently the property of a few lodges. In one place—to be more exact—these lodging of common Indians—calling themselves poor—have six or seven hundred of them, running from common Cayuses to elegant chargers, fit to mount a prince . . ." "Letters from the Upper Columbia," *Idaho Yesterdays, 4* (1960–61), 21. Like other writers who commented on Nez Perce herds, Miller made no mention of spotted horses, which it seems plausible to assume he would have done had there been many of them in evidence.

Nez Perces with whom I have discussed the question say that their people undoubtedly did have some spotted horses and bred any particular one that caught their fancy, as they did with all other horses. They never heard, however, that spotted horses were specially bred for war, and I have been unable to find knowledge of such traditions among descendants of non-Indian pioneers in the Nez Perce country or among present-day members of plains tribes who were in frequent contact with Nez Perces—though Blackfeet say that some of their own people occasionally rode spotted horses (as portrayed in some of Charles M. Russell's paintings of plains Indians).

The horse ("A Palousy"), which many knowledgeable horsemen hesitate to call a distinct breed, is an outstanding and strikingly handsome one, well-suited for so color-ful a legend. It was named by white men in comparatively recent times after the Palouse district north of Lewiston, where many Indian horses formerly grazed.

30 (text, p. 37). In 1802, three years before Lewis and Clark reached them, there is a controversial account of some Nez Perces looking for the first time upon white men. The story is told in *A Topographical Description of the State of Ohio, Indiana Territory, and Louisiana,* written by a member of the United States Army, Colonel Jervis Cutler, son of the prominent land speculator Manasseh Cutler, and published in Boston, 1812. In the book are extracts from a journal which Cutler said he had re-ceived from a French-Canadian trader named Charles LeRaye, whom he had met in the West. LeRaye, Cutler explained. had been captured by Sioux on the Osage River in 1801 and, after many adventures, had accompanied some Hidatsa on a hunt to the Yellowstone River. The journal extracts tell how LeRaye and a French trader named Pardo had then gone with some Crows to the mouth of the Bighorn River. There, on October 11, 1802, they came on a village of 160 Crow warriors who "had lately been on a war expedition against a nation of Indians, who reside on the west side of the Rocky mountains, called Pal-lo-to-path, or Flatheads, and had returned with sixteen prisoners, and a number of scalps."

LeRaye related that the prisoners had "a singular practice of flattening their heads, which is different from any other nation of Indianes in this country." His description of the prisoners' head-flattening methods, which he said he saw in use on some of the "Pal-lo-to-path" children, fairly accurately reflected the custom of the Nez Perces and various Columbia River tribes at the time, but he went on to say, "These people are of a middle stature, well formed, and of a pleasant countenance. Their skin of an olive colour, hair lank and coarse, and the features regular and handsome. The men had a bone passed through the gristle of the nose, which separates the nostril, that ex-tended the width of the face. All the hair on their heads was pulled out, except a lock on the crown, which was left to grow its full length. This tuft of hair was divided into two parts, tied up in a short cue, and fell over each ear."

If the LeRaye account was not a hoax, it is probable that these were Nez Perces, captured on the western plains by the Crows—though the style of the hair and the use of a bone in the nose extending "the width of the face" do not conform with what is known of any Northwestern tribe. Certainly, Nez Perces were being taken prisoner by tribes that had contacts at the time with white men, either in Canada or on the Missouri, for in 1810 William Clark told his editor, Nicholas Biddle, that prior to the Expedition's arrival in the Nez Perce country "a few [Nez Perces] had seen white people but that was when taken prisoners" (Jackson, *Letters of Lewis and Clark,* p. 501).

Of particular interest in the LeRaye account is the use of the name "Pal-lo-to-path" for the "Flathead" prisoners who "reside on the west side of the Rocky mountains." Though that name has long since fallen from use, it was once applied both to the Nez Perces and to their Sahaptin-speaking relatives, the Palouse Indians, whose tribe evolved from unions of Nez Perces, Yakima, and Spokan Indians, and who occupied a number of villages mostly in the Palouse River region near the Nez Perces. Four years after LeRaye's alleged adventures, Lewis and Clark met the Nez Perces and in their journals and letters, as well as on some of their maps, often used the term "Pelloat pallahs," or slightly different spellings of it, when referring to the Nez Perces or to a certain one of their bands. On June 8, 1806, Lewis noted in his journal that "the band [of Nez

Perces] with which we have been most conversant call themselves pel-late-pal-ler," and on July 4, 1806, he said that he was joined by "a man of the Pallotepellows (*Pelloat pallahs*)" at the Clark Fork River near the site of Missoula, Montana. This man he identified unmistakably as a Nez Perce. Immediately after their return to St. Louis in September 1806, both Lewis and Clark wrote letters to the East Coast, announcing the accomplishments of their Expedition and using only the name "Pallotepallors" or "Pallotepalless" for the Nez Perces (Jackson, *Letters of Lewis and Clark*, pp. 328, 333, 339).

The name also appears in other Lewis and Clark material, sometimes referring to the entire Nez Perce nation, and somtimes to only a single, specific band of "1,600 souls," residing on the headwaters and above the forks of Idaho's Clearwater River, from where they "sometimes pass over to the Missouri." About December 1809 Charles Willson Peale, proprietor of Peale's Museum in Philadelphia, listed the articles from the Lewis and Clark Expedition which Jefferson had presented from time to time to the Museum. Peale apparently knew the Nez Perces only as "Pallatepallers" and used that name, or a different spelling of it, whenever he referred to them. One item, a Spanish dollar, he noted, had been "obtained by Captn. M. Lewis, from the Pallotepallers —a nation inhabiting Lewis's River [the Snake River] within the Plains of Columbia, who had never previously seen white-men" (*Letters of Lewis and Clark*, pp. 476–79).

Other uses of the name occur in the notes made by Nicholas Biddle during his editorial meetings with William Clark about April 1810. They indicate that on October 10, 1805, soon after the members of the Expedition had first met the Nez Perces, Lewis and Clark recorded the term "Palapallasin." On that day the explorers were at the junction of the Snake and Clearwater rivers and were summarizing the information they had already gathered about the Nez Perces. They did not enter the name "Palapallasin" in their journals, but they had apparently already heard it (*Letters*, p. 498). In a later note Biddle states that the "Pallotpallah" who lived above the forks of the Clearwater River were members of one of five bands of the Nez Perce nation (ibid., p. 526). Finally, on the map that appeared with the first published version of the Expedition's journals in 1814, the "Selloat pallah" Indians are shown living near the junction of the Snake and Columbia rivers, not far from the actual area occupied by the Palouse Indians.

Actually, the word *pello-ut* in the Nez Perce tongue referred to something greenish or murky on the surface of the water of the rivers, particularly near the junction of the Snake and Columbia, in contrast to *koos keich keich*, or the clearness of the Lochsa and Clearwater rivers. *Palloh*, or more accurately *pelu*, the last part of the term, referred to a person from a particular area, so that a Pellout palloh was a person whose village was on a part of the river where the water was greenish and not as clear as elsewhere. Generally, the name was used for people who lived down toward the Columbia, where the water of the lower Snake was greener in color. (I am indebted for this information to various Nez Perces, including Richard Halfmoon, Samuel Watters, Josiah Red Wolf, James J. Miles, and Albert Moore.)

The term in time is believed to have settled on the Palouse Indians, whose principal villages were on the lower Snake River. With justification they were called Pello-ut pelus by the Nez Perces, and "pelus" eventually became "Palouse."

After Lewis and Clark had returned to the States, their use of the word gained circulation even before their journals appeared in print. In 1807 *Stranger in America*, a volume of observations about the United States, was published in London by Charles

W. Janson and spoke of the "Pollotepallors." In western Canada in the same year the British fur trader David Thompson recorded the receipt of an account of the Lewis and Clark Expedition from some unidentified Americans who used the same term when referring to the Nez Perces. Thompson, in turn, titled the Salmon River the Pallahto-pallah on his own monumental map of the Northwest. It is not impossible that LeRaye or Cutler had also heard the name from returned members of the Lewis and Clark Expedition.

LeRaye, in addition, claimed that he met some Snake Indians and stated that "We were the first white people which either they [the Snakes] or the Flat-heads had ever seen," adding that the Flatheads crossed the mountains to hunt the buffalo with spear and bow and arrow. "The buffaloe is not found on the west side of the Rocky mountains, and there these people subsist on fish and roots." Later LeRaye returned to the Missouri, where in 1804 he said, "a report was spread among the Indians that a party, an army, as they called it, of soldiers were coming up the Missouri" (the Lewis and Clark Expedition). A year later, in April 1805, he was able to escape from the Indians with the help of another French trader, a Mr. Paintelle, who, he said had long resided among the Teton Sioux.

It is not possible to prove or disprove the authenticity of LeRaye's account. As George E. Hyde stated in *Red Cloud's Folk* (Norman, Okla., 1937, p. 27): "Of the score or more of traders mentioned by LeRaye not one is known in the records of the Upper Missouri fur-trade, and this man's [LeRaye's] account of the Tetons [Sioux] is a grotesque distortion of truth." However, Cutler or his printer might well have transcribed the traders' names erroneously, or they might have been men whom history has simply missed. Not all the trappers and traders on the upper Missouri River at that time are known to this day. The weight of evidence seems to be against the genuineness of the document, but there is so much in it that is accurate and convincing that, at worst, it is an interesting fictional account of much that had not yet been in print.

CHAPTER 2.   Fur Trade Embroilments

1 (text, p. 40). Blackfoot hostility to American trappers was long thought to have stemmed from this single act of Lewis' killing of the two Piegans, which occurred about four miles below the junction of Two Medicine and Badger creeks on the morning of July 27, 1806. However, the matter was more involved. The evening before, Lewis had told the Piegans that he had been "to the great waters where the sun sets [the Pacific] and had seen a great many nations all of whom I had invited to come and trade with me on the rivers on this side of the mountains, that I had found most of them at war with their neighbours and had succeeded in restoring peace among them." What he was thus announcing to the Piegans was that he had united their enemies and had invited them all to come over and trade with white men for guns and goods in territory which the Saskatchewan tribes considered their own. The arming of their western enemies was the last thing the Blackfoot tribes would have welcomed, but Lewis went on, explaining to the Piegans that he wanted them to "be at peace with their neighbours particularly those on the West side of the mountains and to engage them to come and trade with me when the establishment is made at the entrance of this river."

Decades after the event, an aged Piegan named Wolf Calf revealed to George Bird

Grinnell that he had been a youthful member of a party that might have been the one that clashed with Lewis. He explained that the white men with whom he fought had been the first ones to enter the lower country of the Blackfeet, and that the Indians' leader had directed the young men to try to steal some of the strangers' possessions. The Indians had done so, hoping, according to the code of the plains, to win praise for their daring. They had failed and lost two of their warriors and, feeling that they had been punished, had run away in chagrin. (Wheeler, *The Trail of Lewis and Clark, 2,* 311–12, quoting Grinnell.) But, again, more relevant and understandable was what this tale did not add: the consternation of the Indians over Lewis' declaration to them that the Americans intended to supply white men's goods, obviously including arms, to their western enemies, whom up to then they had had at a disadvantage. That would have been enough to turn the Blackfeet against the Americans and, from that moment on, keep them alert to try to stop Americans from having further contact with the western tribes.

Beginning the next year, with the arrival of the mysterious Zachary Perch group in western Montana and the movements of Charles Courtin and Manuel Lisa's men westward through the mountains, the Blackfeet were given adequate and continuing cause to believe that Lewis' threat was being carried out. The Blackfoot tribes did all they could to stop the Canadian traders from getting to the Kutenais and other western Indians, and it was logical that they would also try to block the Americans. Lewis had forewarned them, and their hostility of subsequent years was an effort to intercept or drive away whites who planned to trade with the Flatheads, Nez Perces, and Shoshonis. But there is another point: It is hard to believe that Lewis' brush with some members of a single Piegan band would—without other cause—have inflamed all the Blackfoot tribes, as well as their allies, the Atsinas and Sarcis, in a war to the death against all Americans. The proof seems furnished by the events of 1807. Blackfeet attacked the "Perch" group which had already established contact with the Flatheads and Nez Perces. But Lisa, who stopped that fall at the mouth of the Bighorn River far east of the mountains and showed no sign at first of pressing on and opening trade with the Blackfoot tribes' western enemies, had no trouble immediately with the Canadian war bands.

Evidence of this is contained in a previously unpublished entry by British trader James Bird under date of January 22, 1808, in the journal of the Hudson's Bay Company's Edmonton House on the North Saskatchewan River. After noting the arrival of "Twelve men, Fall [Atsina] & Blood Indians" at the House the previous day, Bird wrote: "These Indians inform us that a party of their young men who went on a War Expedition last Autumn discovered an American Settlement on the Banks of the Missisoury. The Americans they say received them in a very friendly manner, made them presents, and invited them to a general Meeting next spring with all the Tribes they have hitherto warred with, in order to settle a peace with them, and for the Purposes of Trade. They tell us that, the Americans promise to sell them a Gun for five Beavers & other Articles in proportion, that they value Buffalo robes &c., but add that, the Americans have no Spirits, the Article first in their Esteem, and that they delight too much in War to deprive themselves of Enemies by making the Peace proposed." (Hudson's Bay Company Archives B. 60/a/7, quoted by permission of the Governor and Committee of the Hudson's Bay Company.) That these Indians, only a year after Lewis had slain the two Piegans, met peaceably with Lisa's men is significant; for while the Bloods and Atsinas were allies of the Piegans, they apparently felt no compulsion to seek revenge for the dead Piegans.

It was only after John Colter and others who were employed by Lisa had gone farther west and established contact with the Flatheads and Nez Perces, even joining those tribes in battle against the Blackfeet, that the angered Canadian tribes turned against the trappers. Such a conclusion appeared as early as October 29, 1819, in the well-known report of Major Thomas Biddle to Colonel Henry Atkinson on the state of affairs in the fur regions of the upper Missouri. In his letter Biddle remarked: "It is an act of justice due to the memory of the late Captain Lewis, to state that the Black Feet Indians . . . were so convinced of the propriety of his conduct in the rencounter between him and a party of their people, in which two of them were killed, that they did not consider it a cause of war or hostility on their part; this is proved, in as much as the first party of Lisa's men that were met by the Black Feet were treated civilly." Instead, Biddle blamed the 1808 encounters between Colter and the Blackfeet for the Canadian tribes' hostility. (*American State Papers, Indian Affairs*, 2, 201.)

By 1824 Jedediah Smith and other Americans in northwestern Montana were witnessing Blackfoot hostility to the British as well as the Americans and were at last concluding rightly that the Canadian tribes' anger was directed against any trader who threatened traffic with the western Indians.

2 (text, p. 41). Many years of flirting with the idea of crossing the Rockies to the Kutenais had provided British traders with the first information white men had acquired of the Nez Perce Indians. On December 30, 1792, when Peter Fidler of the Hudson's Bay Company was near "Bull pond river or Stommix e pis con" on the east side of the mountains in southwestern Alberta, some "Muddy River Indians" (Piegans) arrived with news that there were some "Cottonahaw" Indians (Kutenais) at "Naw pew ooch e tay cots" River (Oldman River). Fidler and a companion, John Ward, accompanied the Piegans "on purpose to see these Indians, who had never seen an European before." (Hudson's Bay Company Archives E.3/2, fol. 16–16d. This and the quotation cited below are used by the kind permission of the Governor and Committee of the Hudson's Bay Company.) On January 30, 1793, after he had met the Kutenais, Fidler referred to one of them who spoke fluently five different Indian languages of tribes with whom he had resided—Snake Indian, Flathead, Mountain Crow, Blue Mud, and "Pauk way gooya." (Hudson's Bay Company Archives E.3/2, fol. 27d.) The Blue Muds, as will be clarified below, were the Nez Perces.

Some of the information Fidler gathered from the Kutenais in 1793 was incorporated by the English cartographer Aaron Arrowsmith on a map of "the Interior Parts of North America," which he produced in January 1795. Although that first map does not include mention of the "Blue Mud" Indians, it shows a "Great Lake River," flowing west of the Rocky Mountains toward the Pacific and terminating in the country of the "Long Hair Indians," who were probably an interior Salish band. Later, in 1801, Fidler himself noted "Blue Mud" or "Cum mun na tappee" people of sixty "tents" among tribes west of the Rocky Mountains on a map whose details were given him by a Blackfoot Indian. See *The American Heritage Book of Indians* (New York, 1961), pp. 324–25, where the map is reproduced with the permission of the Governor and Committee of the Hudson's Bay Company. The following year, 1802, Arrowsmith issued a revised version of his map of North America, and now showed the Great Lake River passing the countries of both the Blue Mud Nation and the Long Hair Nation, and connecting with the Columbia River by a dotted line.

This map and its portrayal of Fidler's information were utilized a couple of years later by Lewis and Clark. In 1805, while the members of that American expedition were still with the Mandans in present-day North Dakota, Lewis sent the War Department in Washington a map of his own which showed the lower Missouri along which he had already traveled, as well as certain features of the western regions which he had not yet reached. A copy of his map, made in the capital the same year by Nicholas King for the United States Government, reflects Lewis' reliance at that time on Arrowsmith's 1802 map, and thus on Fidler's original information. The Blue Mud Nation is depicted as inhabiting the country along the Great Lake River, which is now shown flowing into the upper Columbia River, and is probably meant to be the present-day Clark Fork River of northwestern Montana. The identity of the Indians as Nez Perces came in 1811; in that year North West Company trader Alexander Henry said that the Nez Perces were called by some "the Green Wood or Blue Earth Indians." *New Light on the Early History of the Greater Northwest*, ed. Elliott Coues (New York, 1897), 2, 712. The term "Blue Mud" undoubtedly referred to the bluish clay found along the Clark Fork and in the area around Lake Pend Oreille (Great Lake?). On September 9, 1809, for example, David Thompson made note of the blue clay he was using in the construction of his trading post at Lake Pend Oreille.

For further material on the subject see Carl I. Wheat, *Mapping the Transmississippi West* (San Francisco, 1957–58), *1*, 175–78; *2*, 32–37; Arnold Hague, "An Early Map of the Far West," *Science* (November 4, 1887), pp. 217–18; and Jackson, *Letters of the Lewis and Clark Expedition*, pp. 233–34, 237–38. Also note a reference to "Blue Mud Indians" by Lewis and Clark in 1805 (Thwaites, *Original Journals*, 6, 106).

Thompson's own moves to cross the Rockies to reach the Kutenais and other Columbia Basin tribes had dated from 1800. That autumn he had established contact in the mountains with a band of those Indians and had sent two Canadians, known to us only as La Gasse and Le Blanc, across the Divide to winter with them. These were the first two white men known to have crossed the Rockies south of Alexander Mackenzie's route, and although neither they nor Thompson left a record of the knowledge they acquired during that first winter in the upper Columbia Basin, Peter Fidler at the nearby Hudson's Bay Company's Acton House recorded scraps of information that he had learned about their trip.

The men, Fidler noted, were seventeen nights traveling by way of "the Source of the Saskatchewan in an oblique direction" before reaching the Indian tents. When west of the mountains and "opposite to the Head of the Saskatchewan," they traveled "along an old Track formerly cut by the Cottonahouse [Kutenais]—being the Northern most track they have." For want of use, the track proved difficult. Great numbers of wild horses were seen, but very few signs of beaver. During the greater part of the winter the two white men "tented opposite to the King or Nin nare tock que in the fine open country." While some of the Indians "passed over the Mountain to kill Buffalo" during the winter, others kept watch "in case of a surprisal by the Muddy river Inds. who were at this time declared & inveterate enemies." In their own country the Kutenais depended on jumping deer for food. The two Canadians further reported that the Kutenais, who treated them kindly, used guns, and that "the bow" was "much upon the Decline," an indication that some of them, at least, had acquired firearms from slain Blackfeet or had managed to slip past the Piegans and contact white men. The whole tribe, the Canadians thought, amounted to about seventeen tents; they understood that only about forty-five to fifty men could be mustered for war, and they reported that hardly any men had more than one wife, there being but few women. These Kutenais also possessed hatchets, kettles, knives, and other white men's goods traded formerly from the Blackfeet for horses. The two Canadians, Fidler concluded, had returned to the east side of the Rockies on May 23, 1801, having taken twenty-eight nights to reach "this side the Mountain betwixt the Sources of the Red Deers river & Saskatchewan." (Hudson's Bay Company Archives E.3/2, fols. 19d, 20, 20d. Used by permission of the Governor and Committee of the Hudson's Bay Company.)

In "The North West Company's Columbia Enterprise and David Thompson," *Canadian Historical Review*, *17* (1936), 266–88, the late Arthur S. Morton contended that David Thompson and Duncan M'Gillivray made a brief trip across the Rockies to the Columbia River in the spring of 1801. The matter has been debated without settlement ever since. Now, new evidence can at least clarify the record as it relates to Thompson. On April 7, 1844, as the United States–British controversy over Oregon was approaching a climax, Sir George Simpson, the Hudson's Bay Company's top official in Canada and at that time Governor-in-Chief of Rupert's Land, wrote to Richard Pakenham, the British Minister in Washington: ". . . in a conversation two years ago he [David Thompson] informed me he did not cross the mountains until the year *1806*" (Hudson's Bay Company Archives D.4/64, p. 107, used by permission of the Governor and Committee of the Hudson's Bay Company). Thompson's memory in 1842 may have been slightly faulty, or he may have been referring to the sending of his advance party across the mountains in 1806, because what is generally accepted as his own first crossing occurred in 1807. But the statement seems to be a clear indication that he did not cross in 1801, and it would appear to imply that no one else did either. The absence of references to a M'Gillivray crossing in the journals and records of any of the fur companies or of the various traders, including Thompson, together with Simpson's silence concerning such a trip, outweigh, I think, Morton's contention.

At the same time, it is likely that between 1801 and 1806 there were numerous unrecorded crossings of the mountains by partly civilized trappers and hunters, mixed bloods and eastern Indians, who worked part time as employees of the fur companies but more often struck off on their own, wandering alone or in small groups through the wilderness and marrying into bands of western Indians. They were illiterate and left no records, but the journals of Thompson and other traders indicate their increasing reliance on the knowledge which these independent trappers were acquiring of territory that was still officially unexplored.

Relying undoubtedly on their knowledge of Howse Pass (as he did later on their pioneering of the more northerly Athabaska Pass), Thompson finally sent an advance group under Jacques Raphael (Jaco) Finlay, the son of a Canadian trader and a Chippewa woman, to the Columbia in 1806, and followed him over the same Howse Pass route the following year. By that time, thanks to Peter Fidler, the Kutenais, La Gasse and Le Blanc, and presumably many unknown trappers and hunters, Thompson possessed a large store of information concerning the identities and approximate locations of various western tribes, including the Flatheads and "Blue Muds," or Nez Perces.

3 (text, p. 41). "Narrative of the Expedition to the Kootanae & Flat Bow Indian Countries, on the Sources of the Columbia River, Pacific Ocean, by D. Thompson on Behalf of the N. w. Company 1807," in T. C. Elliott, "The Discovery of the Source of the Columbia River," *Oregon Historical Quarterly*, *26* (1925), 43.

The primary source of material on Thompson is Tyrrell, *David Thompson's Narrative of His Explorations in Western America, 1784–1812*, cited above, p. 000. Portions of Thompson's journals, some with excellent biographical material and notes by their editors, have also been published. Two of the most valuable are Elliott Coues' *New Light on the Early History of the Greater Northwest,* already cited, and *David Thompson's Journals Relating to Montana and Adjacent Regions, 1808–1812,* ed. M. Catherine White (Missoula, Montana, 1950).

Other parts of Thompson's journals and writings have been published as follows: "Account of an Attempt to Cross the Rocky Mountains, by Mr. James Hughes, Nine Men & Myself" ed. F. W. Howay, *Queen's Quarterly, 40* (1933), 333–56; Elliott, "The Discovery of the Source of the Columbia River," cited above; "David Thompson's Journeys in Idaho," ed. T. C. Elliott, *Washington Historical Quarterly, 11* (1920), 97–103, 163–73; "David Thompson's Journeys in the Pend Oreille Country," ed. Elliott, ibid., *23* (1932), 18–24, 88–93, 173–76; "David Thompson's Journeys in the Spokane Country" ed. Elliott, ibid., *8* (1917), pp. 183–87, 261–64; *9* (1918), 11–16, 103–06, 169–73, 284–87; *10* (1919), 17–20; "Journal of David Thompson," ed. Elliott, *Oregon Historical Quarterly, 15* (1914), 39–63, 104–25.

In addition, see V. G. Hopwood, "New Light on David Thompson," *The Beaver* (Winnipeg, Summer, 1957), pp. 26–31; and "More Light on David Thompson," ibid. (Autumn, 1957), p. 58.

4 (text, p. 41). Thompson made no reference to this letter in his journal, but on November 10, 1807, the British trader at the Hudson's Bay Company's Edmonton House east of the Rockies in present-day Alberta made the following note in the fort's log: "Received a letter from Mr. John Peter Pruden in which he informs me that four men, whom he had sent to Acton House [the Hudson's Bay Company's post near the North West Company's Rocky Mountain House on the upper Saskatchewan River] . . . found there three men who had come from Mr. Thompson (N W Co) who it appears has built . . . in the Cootanaha country . . . The Cootanaha's delivered Mr. Thompson a Paper given them (when on a visit to a more southerly Tribe), by the Americans, of which following is a copy." (Hudson's Bay Company Archives B. 60/a/7, published by permission of the Governor and Committee of the Hudson's Bay Company.)

The Americans' letter to Thompson, as copied in the Edmonton House journal, began: "We the undersigned by the Power delegated to us by General Braithwaite Commander of all the new ceded Territories northward of the Illinois do hereby make known and declare the instructions we have received relating to Foreigners who may at present be carrying on a Traffic with the Indians within our Territories for Peltries, &c., or who may in future carry on a Traffic with the said Indians." Following that were listed in detail and in authentically phrased language eight regulations for trade on American territory between Indians and citizens of countries other than the United States. A ninth point read: "By information received at the Monden Village on the Mississourie we were given to understand that, some of the Subjects of Great Britain are about to carry on a Trade and traffic with the western Indians, we have therefore given a Copy of the above Instructions., Rules and Regulations to be observed in the Indian Traffic to the principal Chief of each of the indian Tribes the most likely to see these foreign Traders that, the said Traders may not pretend Ignorance that they are within the Jurisdiction of Congress." And a final, tenth point warned that the writers recognized no special British rights to "any of the Lands on the Pacific Ocean or to the Commerce of any of the Rivers that flow into the said Ocean, all of which we shall comprehend as within our said Territories until some further Explanation takes place on this head between the united States of America and the Court of St. James." See J. B. Tyrrell, "Letter of Roseman and Perch, July 10, 1807," *Oregon Historical Quarterly, 38* (1937), 391–97, and T. C. Elliott, "The Strange Case of David Thompson and Jeremy Pinch," ibid., *40* (1939), pp. 194–95.

The dates of the letter and of its receipt by Thompson appear to preclude the possibility that it could have been written by the members of any American group previously known to have been heading west that year. Charles Courtin, of whom more will be related shortly, was still too far east on the middle Missouri in July, and Manuel Lisa's large trapping party that included four veterans of the Lewis and Clark Expedition (Colter, Drouillard, Potts, and Wiser) was even lower down the Missouri, in the area of present-day Nebraska and South Dakota, at the time.

Yet there is no doubt that an American wrote the letter, that the Kutenais carried it to Thompson, that, without having answered it, he gave it or a copy of it to some of his men who, according to his journal, started back for the eastern side of the mountains on September 23, 1807, and that they delivered it to the Rocky Mountain House, where the Hudson's Bay Company men also saw it. The signatures on the letter were aliases and were undoubtedly designed to mask the real identities of the Americans, a fact that throws suspicion on the motives of the expedition. Historical records reveal no trace of the existence of a Lieutenant "James Roseman," a Captain "Zachary Perch," or a "General Braithwaite." The similarity of the names Zachary Perch and Zebulon Pike is obvious, but Pike was occupied with his expedition to the Southwest far from the Missouri and Columbia rivers at the time, and it is certain that he could not have been the writer of the letter.

Pike, however, did have a curious relationship to the document. A year and a half earlier, while exploring the upper Mississippi River, he had come on Hugh McGillis, a North West Company trader, flying a British flag over a fur post on Minnesota's Leech Lake. The American lieutenant, annoyed, had composed a set of regulations for McGillis to observe while trading on American territory. On his return to St. Louis in April 1806, Pike had given a copy of these regulations to his commanding officer, General James Wilkinson, who was also governor of Upper Louisiana. In content, they were remarkably similar to the demands in the letter which David Thompson had received at the Kootanae House in 1807. (Elliott, "The Strange Case of Thompson and Pinch.")

The "Perch" letter takes on additional drama when it is realized that the position it ascribed to "General Braithwaite" was actually held at the time by Wilkinson, a significance discussed in detail below, n 7.

7 (text, p. 42). Perpetually involved in devious schemes for personal gain, Wilkinson until recently was thought to have directed almost all his attention toward the Southwest. A summary of documentary evidence will reveal, however, that he had not overlooked the upper Missouri as a theater for his own aggrandizement, and that he might, indeed, have been the silent sponsor of the "Perch" expedition.

Some of Wilkinson's projects, including those that involved him with Aaron Burr, were so secret or so obscured by his intricate double dealing that his biographers have been able to learn little about them. On July 1, 1805, Wilkinson assumed office in St. Louis as governor of the upper portion of Louisiana Territory. On the very day that he arrived in the city, he formed a personal attachment with the Chouteau family, the most powerful fur partisans in St. Louis. Less than a month later he ordered one of his lieutenants, George Peter, and a military escort to accompany a fur-trading expedition up the Missouri to the Osage Indians. Although Peter was bent on a legitimate mission, his trip was also a reconnaissance venture to provide Wilkinson with information about the western country and the conditions and prospects of the Indian trade.

By the end of July, Wilkinson had become so well informed that he was writing the first of a series of alarmed letters to Secretary of War Henry Dearborn and Secretary of State James Madison on the inroads that British traders from Canada were making on the fur trade in the upper Louisiana Territory. At a time when Lewis and Clark, still outward bound on their expedition, had just passed the Great Falls of the Missouri, Wilkinson wrote Dearborn that a "Garrison should be established at the Mandan Towns or perhaps at the Falls of the Missouri, with an officer of the customs to seize whatever may be introduced by that Channel." *Territorial Papers of the United States,* ed. Clarence E. Carter, *13* (Washington, D.C., 1948), 172–74.

The British menace in the new United States territory continued to loom large in Wilkinson's thinking, and he wrote to Dearborn again on August 10, reminding him of the need to stop the traffic from Canada. As governor, he was showing a proper concern, but he also informed Dearborn that he had plans to send out expeditions from St. Louis to protect the Indian trade from the British, and added: "I shall take measures by a private Agent, & without expense to Government, to obtain a concession from the Panis in the course of the ensuing Winter" (Carter, pp. 182–83). Two weeks later he circularized the territorial officers in St. Louis for their opinions on whether to halt British trade on the Missouri, and after being sustained by their verdict that he should oppose the British, he informed Dearborn on September 7 that the situation was growing worse, and added, "I think we should lose no time in getting possession of the upper waters of the Mississippi & Missouri." (Wilkinson Papers, Chicago Historical Society, Vol. 2, p. 83.)

The next day, September 8, 1805, he wrote Dearborn: "I have equipt a Perogue out of my Small private means, not with any view to Self interest, to ascend the missouri and enter the River Piere jaune, or yellow Stone, called by the natives, Unicorn River, the same by which Capt. Lewis I since find expects to return and which my informants tell me is filled with wonders, this Party will not get back before the Summer 1807 . . ." (Carter, p. 199). The "Unicorn" was a confused reference to the Bighorn River, which French traders called the Grosse Corne.

In the same message, Wilkinson told Dearborn: "It is essential to the Public Weal in this quarter, that some extraordinary provisions should be made, to detect or repel the impositions daily practiced by . . . Zealous British Partizans . . ." Regarding the membership of the expedition he was sending up the Yellowstone, he wrote: "They are natives of this Town, and are just able to give us course and distance, with the names and population of the Indian nations and to bring back with them Specimens of the natural products." Then he added, "I have also engaged a bold adventurer, who served under me during the late Indian War, and is now a Pensioner of the U.S. (McClelan) to look at St. Afee in person pending the Winter—He will take his departure from the Panis Towns on the River Plate."

Here, some two months after he had taken office in St. Louis, were two Wilkinson ventures up the Missouri River, about which history is otherwise silent. Nothing is known about the group bound for the Yellowstone, although a month later, October 10 (too soon for word of it to have traveled so far, unless it had left at an earlier date), François Larocque, a North West Company trader near the Mandan villages, recorded that the Hidatsa Indians had informed him that fourteen American boats were on their way up the Missouri. There is no other reference in history to that flotilla. ("Journal of F. A. Larocque, June 2–October 18, 1805," ed. L. J. Burpee, trans. Ruth Hazlitt, *Frontier and Midland, 14, 15* [1934].)

The "bold adventurer" going to Santa Fe seems definitely to have been delayed for a year. He was Artillery Captain John McClallen of New York State, who was still on the official rolls of the Army when Wilkinson wrote that he was a "Pensioner," but who finally had his resignation recorded as of January 31, 1806 (Francis B. Heitman, *Historical Register and Dictionary of the U.S. Army, 1798–1903*, Washington, 1903, p. 655). McClallen had come to St. Louis with Wilkinson, but his status was a curious one. He had forwarded from the East under his own name a large amount of goods for the western Indian trade, but it was later revealed that the goods really belonged to Wilkinson, and that McClallen had only acted as the General's agent. Sometime in August 1806, a year after Wilkinson had written Dearborn about him, McClallen left St. Louis for the West. On September 17, just above the Grand River in the western part of present-day Missouri, Lewis and Clark, homeward bound from the Pacific, met him ascending the Missouri River in a large boat. He was "Somewhat astonished to see us return and appeared rejoiced to meet us," the explorers noted. McClallen told them that he was on "reather a speculative expedition to the confines of New Spain," and planned to go up the Platte, trade with Pawnees, Otos, and Comanches, convince them to guide him to Santa Fe, where he would trade for "silver and gold," and then return to St. Louis. He carried, Lewis and Clark noted, "a kind of introductory Speach from Govr. Wilkinson" for the Indians, and was conveying private trade goods belonging to Wilkinson. Whether this story was a cover for a different destination is not known. After the meeting with Lewis and Clark, McClallen disappeared, and history as yet knows nothing further about him.

McClallen might not have turned west on the Platte, but could have gone farther up the Missouri and wintered with the Mandans, recruiting more men and learning about Thompson's plans to cross the Canadian Rockies to the Columbia country. In the spring of 1807 the former artillery captain could then have ascended the Yellowstone or taken the Missouri to the region of the falls, where he could have followed in reverse the route that Lewis had used across the Continental Divide on his return trip in 1806. Somewhere, he could also have met friendly Flatheads and Nez Perces and given his first letter to a Nez Perce leader for delivery to Thompson.

The timetable would have been right, for whoever "Perch" was, it is probable that he would have had to leave St. Louis by the summer of 1806, the time when McClallen departed from that city. Moreover, the reference to "Braithwaite" in the "Perch" letter, the strict military writing, and the link to Pike's regulations all suggest a connection with Wilkinson, who, at the very least, must have known of the leaders of the expedition, since he granted licenses to all the traders who left St. Louis for the Missouri. The Lewis and Clark veterans allegedly with "Perch" may have been recruited at the Mandans and been men who had gone as far as those villages with the two captains in 1804. Or, less conceivably, they may have turned quickly around at St. Louis after Lewis and Clark had reached there and gone back upriver, overtaking McClallen in the spring of 1807 before he had left the Mandans. The post-Expedition activities of John Thompson, Joseph Field, and Pierre Cruzatte, all Lewis and Clark veterans, are not accounted for. Yet about 1825 William Clark listed each of them as having been killed since 1806. Had they been members of the "Perch" group and, with "Perch," been slain in Montana by Blackfeet?

There is no record of the return to St. Louis at any time of McClallen or of a party that could have been "Perch's." David Thompson himself supplied two hints of the possible end of the "Perch" group. On December 21, 1810, he wrote a letter to Alexander Fraser in Montreal in which he referred cryptically to an American "officer and 8 soldiers" killed by Piegans in the Columbia country (*Les Bourgeois de la Compagnie du Nord-Ouest*, ed. L. R. Masson, rep. New York, 1960, 2, 41). And years later, when referring in his "Narrative" to the death of the American trader Charles Courtin on the Flathead fork of the Clark Fork River in February 1810 (below, n. 11), he wrote: "During my time the Traders and Hunters from the United States were most unfortunate, there seemed to be an infatuation over them, that the Natives of the Plains were all skulkers in the woods, and never dared show themselves on open ground, and they suffered accordingly being frequently attacked on open ground and killed by the Peeagans until none remained." This statement, referring to "open ground" like that of the region of the present-day Moise National Bison Range and the Mission Valley, which stretch north of the Flathead River in the area of Dixon, Montana—a neighborhood of sporadic clashes between Blackfoot raiders and western Indians—perhaps also points to the location of the ultimate fate of the "Perch" expedition.

Finally, there is no record that, once McClallen left St. Louis in 1806, Wilkinson ever again gave him a thought, though the former artillery officer had with him trade goods belonging to Wilkinson. The total absence of all evidence, in short, suggests not only that McClallen never came back but that Wilkinson in time was able to destroy any papers he owned that referred to this secret venture.

10 (text, p. 45). On Wiser and Casé Fortin, see Letters, Reuben Lewis to Meriwether Lewis, April 21, 1810, Meriwether Lewis Collection; and Pierre Menard to Adrien Langlois, October 7, 1809, Kaskaskia Papers—both in Missouri Historical Society, St. Louis. Wiser in 1808 or 1809 may have got as far west as the present-day Weiser River, bequeathing his name to that stream in southwestern Idaho, as indicated by David Thompson's huge map of 1824–25, which calls it Wiser's River.

In Canada, James Bird at the Hudson's Bay Company's Edmonton House recorded Blackfoot versions of the attacks against Lisa's men in the Three Forks country. On October 2, 1808, when Fortin was heading for the safety of the Flathead country, Bird wrote: "Several Blood Indians arriv'd with Provisions, &c. Theese People it appears from a variety of Accounts, & some Spoils now in their Possession, discovered in their Summer War excursions, on a southern branch of the Mississoury two small Settlements which they plundered of goods to a considerable amount, besides about 300 Beaver skins. One of the men belonging to these Settlements was killed, & the rest (ten in number) after being stripped were permitted to escape—From some papers brought us by the Indians, the immediate Traders seem to have been Canadians; but from the situation of the Houses, & from the American Colors which were taken from them, it is concluded that they must have been subject to the United States." Ten days later, on October 12, Bird wrote: "Several Sussus [Sarcis, allies of the Blackfeet] arriv'd, most of the few Beavers they have brought, have been taken from the Settlements above mentioned, several of them are mark'd with the Initials of their former Owners (who we suppose to have been Freemen . . .)" On the following day he added: "A few Fall & several Muddy [Atsina and Piegan] Indians arrived. The Fall Indians have likewise plundered a small American Settlement on the Mississoury, & as they confess themselves, killed two of the men that belonged to it. Amongst other plunder, they have brought us a rifle Gun which, on account of its weight, they consider as of little Value." (Hudson's Bay Company Archives B. 60/a/8, published by permission of the Governor and Committee of the Hudson's Bay Company.)

11 (text, p. 45). Knowledge of Courtin, pieced together here for the first time, is of recent vintage. He is still a difficult man to identify. Only one known document carries his signature with its correct spelling, and many other references that allude to a man who must have been he, spell the name in a variety of ways.

Prior to 1806 Courtin, a French Canadian, had been active in the fur trade of the Great Lakes region, crossing occasionally from Michilimackinac to the upper Mississippi and the Missouri. On August 11, 1806, while homeward bound on the Missouri River, William Clark referred to a "Mr. Coartong" or "Ceautoin." It was during the explorers' meeting on the river with the west-bound American trappers from the Illinois country, Dickson and Handcock, and Clark noted that the two men had spent the previous winter with the Teton Sioux in company with a "Mr. Coartong (Ceautoin) who brought up goods to trade. The tetons robed him of the greater part of the goods and wounded this Dixon in the leg with a hard wad. The Tetons gave Mr. Coartong some fiew robes for the articles they took from him." Later, on September 14, Lewis and Clark passed a party of three young men, "Mr. Lacroy, Mr. Aiten & Mr. Coutau all from St. Louis," ascending the Missouri. Coutau was undoubtedly Coartong. At any rate, the following spring William Clark complained to a delegation of Sioux in St. Louis of their bad treatment of a man named Couteau or Courtean, who was also probably "Coartong." (Jackson, *Letters of Lewis and Clark*, p. 437.)

In 1807 a man who was very likely the same person was part way up the Missouri. On April 5 of that year the Missouri River trader Robert McClellan wrote from the Omahas' country to William Clark in St. Louis, mentioning the presence on that portion of the river of "a Certain Mr. Corter a Kenedian who obtained Licinus to Traide with the Suoix & Poncas for the year 1806. Proceeds On a voige this spring up the Missouri Expecting to Reach the falls be fore he stops." (Clark Papers, Missouri Historical Society; copy kindly furnished me by Donald Jackson.) The trader in question apparently had more trouble and did not get very far on his journey that spring. On June 22, 1807, a man signing himself "Charles Courtin" wrote a letter in French from the Arikaras' "village" on the Missouri in present-day South Dakota, complaining to "the Government of the United States of the evilness and bad disposition" of the Arikara Indians, who had plundered his goods. (To trade on the Missouri Courtin had had to swear allegiance to the United States and was now considered an American.) Courtin, who had been ascending the Missouri River with Joseph Gravelines, an interpreter whom Lewis and Clark, as well as James Wilkinson, had used on government missions, had reached the Arikaras on June 3 and had had trouble with those Indians. About June 14, Courtin also explained, "a certain hunter named Joseph Dickson who was descending the River" landed and also had difficulties with the Arikaras, one of whom shot at Dickson and missed. On June 22, the day he wrote his letter, Courtin related that Forrest Handcock had just arrived from the Mandans. Dickson and Handcock were, of course, the trappers Lewis and Clark had met ascending the Missouri in 1806. Colter had joined them but had come back alone. Apparently, also, Dickson and Handcock had separated, and were now rejoined at the Arikara villages, where Manuel Lisa would soon arrive and hire them.

At any rate, Courtin's letter reached Frederick Bates, acting governor of Louisiana Territory in St. Louis, and on August 2 Bates sent a translation of it to Secretary of War Dearborn with the note: "I do myself the honor of enclosing the translation of a letter which I have lately received from a French Trader at the Ricaras' Village . . . Of Courtin I know nothing; it is said that he is respectable" (National Archives, RG 107, B-280/3).

Sometime after writing the letter to the American government, Courtin seems to have continued upriver from the Arikaras' village. A letter of October 16, 1807, to William Clark from Nathaniel Pryor, who had just returned from the Missouri where he, too, had had trouble with the Arikaras in September, noted that an Arikara chief had given Pryor "a letter from Courtney, who had previously to the arrival of Lisa [who had also reached the Arikaras after Courtin had written his letter of June 22] been cruelly treated by these barbarians, and informed us that he alone had been friendly to that unfortunate Trader, who owed his safety and ultimate release to his friendly offices." (Jackson, *Letters*, p. 433.)

Courtin, it would appear, soon afterward reached the Mandan villages. He may have gone directly on—ahead of Manuel Lisa's 1807 expedition—and eventually have reached western Montana that year, or he may have wintered with the Mandans and headed west in 1808. A further clue to his movements is provided in a letter of December 14, 1809, by the St. Louis fur trader, Pierre Chouteau, to Secretary of War William Eustis after Chouteau's return from the Mandan villages. "Two days after my arrival at the mandan Village [on September 24, 1809]," Chouteau wrote, "Information was Given me, that three persons belonging to the British north west company were at the Village. I immediately sent forward an Express desiring them to await my arrival But they feared being detained and departed: they however Informed a white man who resides at the mandan Village, that the north west Company had erected a fort at the three forks of the Missoury. This information is believed to be true from the Circumstance of about thirty american hunters, who had used to visit the mandan Village, not being seen nor heard of since about Eighteen months" (Pierre Chouteau Letterbook, pp. 146–47, Missouri Historical Society). No North West Company fort was ever known to have been established at the Three Forks of the Missouri, but the other part of Chouteau's information is significant. Although Courtin was not in the employ of the North West Company, he may have left the Mandans alone, or with a large group of Americans, and proceeded up the Missouri toward the Three Forks, where by 1808 many of Lisa's trappers were beginning to congregate.

While at the Three Forks, Courtin had apparently built a structure of his own, for in 1824 Finan McDonald, leading a Hudson's Bay Company brigade through the area, referred to an old fort that had been erected in earlier years near the Three Forks by a man named "Corta" (Dale L. Morgan, *Jedediah Smith*, Indianapolis, 1953, p. 123). After a sojourn at the Three Forks, Courtin had crossed the Rockies to the vicinity of present-day Missoula, and was there long enough for his name to become temporarily attached to geographic features in the region. In the spring of 1812 David Thompson called the Hellgate canyon "the Defile of Courter," noting that it led eastward to the "road to the Buffalo by Courter's River," thus suggesting that Courtin had come to the Missoula region by that route. On maps by Thompson and Alexander Ross, another Nor'Wester, the portion of the Clark Fork between the Missoula area and the junction with the Flathead River is similarly labeled "Courtine Fork."

On February 24, 1810, Thompson learned from Pend d'Oreille Indians that Courtin, whom he called Courter, had been killed in a battle with Piegans in the open country near present-day Dixon, Montana. Thompson hurried to the deceased man's camp and paid off hunters and trappers who had been associated with him. One of Courtin's *engagés*, Pierre Gignon, had apparently been in Courtin's employ for about three years, for he was owed that much in wages. Another man, suddenly revealed to be in the area, was François Rivet, who had ascended the Missouri to the Mandan villages with Lewis and Clark in 1804. Possibly he had come west with Courtin, or even with the "Perch" party, which Thompson had said had included two men who had been with Lewis and Clark.

Thompson later explained that Courter was "a trader and Hunter from the U States" and added that the Indians "seemed to think that the imprudence of Mr. Courter, in going on the War Grounds, with a small party to hunt the Bison and set traps for the Beaver, which were numerous, was the cause of his death and the accidents to the Indians."

13 (text, p. 46). The route of the eleven men from the Snake plains to the Nez Perce country has been the subject of much speculation. Actually, they had started as three groups, had come together, and at some point below the confluence of the Snake and Weiser rivers in southwestern Idaho had decided that they would have a better chance of survival if they split into smaller parties again and took different routes. Seeking the "Flatheads," by which they meant the Nez Perce and Flathead peoples whom they knew vaguely lived north of where they were, and whom Lewis and Clark and Lisa's men had reported were friendly and well provisioned, one group under Robert McClellan left the Snake and climbed northeastwardly over the mountains. Two other groups under Donald McKenzie and John Reed continued into the great canyon of the Snake but after a while also climbed the mountains and managed to rejoin McClellan's party somewhere along the divide between the Snake and the Weiser. Together again, they had gone on across rugged country, passing west of Payette Lake, and eventually coming on the Little Salmon River, which the Indians called the Mulpah. Up to then, they had traveled twenty-one days in the wilds. Now on the little Salmon the going was easier, and it took them without further difficulty to the canyon of the main Salmon and the southernmost settlements of the Nez Perces. Hunt's diary merely records that "Mr. Mackenzie and Mr. Reed with their party had gone on" (down the Snake), while "Mr. McClellan, on leaving the small river [Weiser?] had crossed the mountains with the hope of falling in with the Flatheads." But an account in the *Missouri Gazette* of May 15, 1813, supplied by returned Astorians, states: "Messrs. Mackenzie, McLelan and Reed had united their parties on the Snake River Mountains, through which they traveled twenty-one days to the Mulpot River."

It is also possible that one or all of the groups had descended from the mountains to the upper valley of the Weiser River somewhat south of the Little Salmon and for part of the way had followed the relatively easy route used today by Idaho's Highway 95. It was an ancient Indian route, and after they had reached the Columbia, McKenzie and his men must have felt so surely that they had found a passable way between the Clearwater and the Shoshoni country of southern Idaho that they soon sent Reed back over it, and McKenzie himself used it in later days.

28 (text, p. 63). Ibid., pp. 55–56. Simpson's ideas when he wrote these comments, on the eve of the departure from the Flathead Post of the 1824–25 Snake country expedition, require further explanation. By that time, Simpson had visited the Columbia district personally and had changed his mind again and decided now to abandon all the interior posts, Spokane and Flathead as well as Nez Perces, as jumping-off points for future Snake trapping brigades. The 1824–25 group would be the last to leave from the Flathead Post. After trapping the Snake Basin, it was expected to cross Oregon and come out at Fort George. Thereafter, each brigade would leave from and return to the lower Columbia. Simpson offered several reasons for this revised plan. First, it would be much more economical to provision the expeditions at Fort George (later Fort Vancouver), which was supplied by sea, than to continue to send provisions for the brigades all the way up the Columbia to the interior. Second, the timing of the expeditions would permit furs brought directly to Fort George to be shipped to London

a full year earlier than when they were delivered to the inland posts. Third, Simpson concluded that the expeditions still wasted much time and used up provisions getting from the interior posts to the southern trapping country. Fourth, the use of Fort George would keep the men out of the country of the Sahaptins and avoid conflicts with those people. Fifth, the men's time would be better controlled; there would be a minimum of idleness between expeditions. And, finally, Simpson, laboring under mistaken ideas of geography, believed that the expeditions could take an easy route across Oregon, following the Umpqua River, which he thought might head in the Snake country. The unexploited regions of Oregon, he reasoned, would provide good trapping all the way from the Willamette to the Snake. Instead, the Hudson's Bay Company men soon discovered that the Umpqua headed west of the Cascades, that there was no easy route across Oregon, and that that territory was not as rich in beaver as Simpson had imagined. The brigades moved through Oregon, but circumstances forced them also to continue to use the interior posts. For a fuller discussion of Simpson's ideas see Davies, *Ogden's Snake Country Journal, 1826–27*, pp. xx–xliv.

34 (text, p. 67). "Journal of John Work," ed. T. C. Elliott, *Washington Historical Quarterly, 6* (1915).

Also with Work on this trip was David Douglas, the young Scottish botanist and discoverer of the Douglas fir, who had come to the Northwest in 1825 as a collector for the Royal Horticultural Society. Douglas had accompanied Work's party from Fort Nez Perces to the Clearwater River, and he described the Snake River canyon in the July heat as "superior to the deserts of Arabia" only in the "abundance of good water . . . That excepted, there is but little difference." At the Clearwater he reported the presence of "a camp of three different nations, upwards of five hundred men able to bear arms. One called Pelusbpa, one the Pierced nose (Chawhaptan) and Chamuiemuch." At first, he said, "a conference was held and ended favorably and with great splendour by dancing, singing, haranguing, and smoking. All were dressed in their best garments, and on the whole presented a fine spectacle . . ." During the period of horse buying, Douglas and another member of the party took a trip through part of the Nez Perce country, going to "the Blue Mountains." It is difficult to know exactly where they went. Douglas said they "set out in a south-easterly direction, the country undulating and very barren." The next day, he reported, they "reached the mountains" and "among some very large trees . . . the spot pointed out to me by the Indians where Lewis and Clarke built their canoes, on their way to the ocean, twenty-one years ago." If that were true, they had gone eastward across the high ground paralleling the Clearwater, and had descended to the grove where the American Captains had constructed their canoes. Soon afterward they returned to Work's camp, arriving in time to witness the excitement between Toupin and Charlie, which Douglas described as a tense affair in which the whites and Nez Perces faced each other with "guns cocked and every bow strung." After peace had returned, Douglas accompanied Work and his two men to the Spokane House. There, the botanist found old Jaco Finlay, who had built the post with Finan McDonald in the winter of 1810–11, living alone. Douglas went on to Fort Colvile with the Work party and later descended the Columbia River. See Wilks, *Journal Kept by David Douglas, 1823–27*, pp. 199–203, 255.

39 (text, p. 73). *The Journal of John Work*, ed. W. S. Lewis and Paul C. Phillips (Cleveland, 1923), p. 139. From time to time, a few white men continued to record other unflattering statements about Nez Perces. The authors were usually British, and although what they wrote were undoubtedly fair and objective observations ac-

cording to their own experiences and points of view, they were generally narrow and did not square with the feelings of the majority of Americans in the field, or with history itself. In August 1845, for instance, Joseph Burke, a British collector of botanical specimens, traveled among the headwaters of the Missouri for a short time with about fifty lodges of Nez Perces and spoke disparagingly of their war prowess. After telling a tale he had heard of how Crows had beaten Nez Perces with clubs the year before, and implying that the Nez Perces had been afraid of the Crows, he related that the Nez Perces now talked boldly about fighting some Bannocks but, instead, retreated during the night when they accidentally came on them. The Nez Perces "talked a great deal of their bravery—A thing they are by no means noted for," he said, adding that they were "the greatest talkers & the least doers, of any tribe in this country."

Some may have held that opinion of them, but few recorded it. The Nez Perces, who like other Indians boasted regularly of what they would do to enemies, had a notable self-confidence that may have seemed like a hollow cockiness and irritated men like Burke. That the Nez Perces took a drubbing from Crows on one occasion fades into insignificance in the full context of the battle history of the two tribes: Nez Perces were fighting Crows fiercely until the 1870s, sometimes winning, sometimes losing. Their unwillingness to fight the Bannocks was also of momentary importance. Possibly their shamans had warned them that the time was not right, but Burke would not have known of that. Mountain men, who on numerous occasions had seen Nez Perces fight impulsively and bravely against Bannocks and other enemies, certainly did not agree that they were not noted for their courage. The written record they left said just the opposite.

I am indebted to Dale L. Morgan for calling Burke's comments to my attention and for generously supplying me with a copy of his quotations, which are not included in the account of his travels published by Susan Delano McKelvey in her monumental and fascinating work, *Botanical Exploration of the Trans-Mississippi West, 1790–1850*, Arnold Arboretum of Harvard University (Jamaica Plain, Mass., 1955), pp. 792–817.

42 (text, p. 75). Lewis and Phillips, *Journal of John Work*, p. 87, spell the stream "Saloas River." However, the editors worked from a copy of the original manuscript made about 1908 by R. E. Gosnell of the British Columbia Provincial Library in Victoria for Professor E. S. Meany of the University of Washington; and the transcription, in this and several other significant instances, was inaccurate. The study of a photostat of Work's manuscript diary, kindly provided me by Willard E. Ireland, Provincial Librarian and Archivist at Victoria, clearly shows it to read either "Loloo's river" or "Leloo's river." Only the first vowel, either an *o* or an *e*, can be in doubt. Another transcript of the original, made by the British Columbia Provincial Library for Hubert H. Bancroft, is also in error, making it read "Le Louis." The matter has more than passing interest in its bearing on when and how this most famous trail in the Northwest, now again of national interest as part of the Nez Perce National Historic Park and the Lewis and Clark National Historic Trail, received its name. Work's manuscript shows that an approximation of Lolo was affixed to the stream that paralleled part of the trail as early as 1831, much earlier than has previously been thought. As to its derivation, there was a trapper referred to as "Lolo" with David Thompson in this area in 1809. In addition, General Ashley made note of a "Mr. Lolo," a trapper who bought some supplies from him at the 1825 rendezvous on the Green River (Morgan, *The West of William H. Ashley*, pp. 121, 124). He is there listed among a group of men who had previously deserted Ogden's brigade, and may have been Charles Loyer,

one of the freemen who had left Ogden to join the Americans. This same Loyer had also been a free hunter associated with David Thompson in the Flathead country in 1809. It is possible, although by no means definite, that Thompson's "Lolo" and Charles Loyer and Ashley's "Mr. Lolo" were all the same man and that he had spent enough time on or about the stream during the second two decades of the nineteenth century to bequeath his name to it and to the trail that for part of its way ran beside it. At the same time it might be noted that the Hudson's Bay Company listed among its employees in North America from June 1, 1821, to June 1, 1824, a Jean Baptiste Loyey and a Louis Loyey (Payette, *The Oregon Country*, p. 623), and in the early 1830s it employed an interpreter known as "Leolo" (perhaps Charles Loyer, now returned to the firm's employ) in the Columbia country. Finally, as late as 1854–55, Major John Owen employed an Indian named Lolo in the Bitterroot Valley (*Men and Trade on the Northwest Frontier*, ed. George F. Weisel, Missoula, 1955, pp. 96, 106).

Mention should also be made that Ralph S. Space, former Supervisor of the Clearwater National Forest and perhaps the most knowledgable student of the history of the Lolo Trail, believes that the route was named for Lawrence Rence, a trapper who was killed in the area by a grizzly bear. That story, which relates that the Indians could not pronounce the letter "R" and corrupted Lawrence Rence to Lolo, seems, however, to have originated only after American settlers had appeared in Montana in the 1860s. Although I have searched diligently, I have been unable to find a trace of a trapper named Lawrence Rence in the area as early as 1831. The rolls of the North West Company, the Astorians, and the Hudson's Bay Company do not include him, and he does not appear in any of the literature of the American fur trade.

CHAPTER 3.   Creatures So Far Below

1 (text, p. 82). There is a large literature on the religious influence of the Iroquois and French Canadians from eastern Canada on the Salish and Sahaptins, the basic sources being principally the writings of Father Pierre-Jean De Smet and other Catholic missionaries who arrived among the Salish and other peoples in the Northwest in the late 1830s and early 1840s. Unfortunately, because those writings reflect almost no awareness of influences emanating about 1829–30 from an Anglican mission school at Red River in central Canada, which I describe later in this chapter, it is difficult to reconstruct what the situation actually was prior to 1829. The western Indians undoubtedly must have become interested, to some extent, in knowing about the supernatural world of the Iroquois and the white men, although only insofar as they regarded such knowledge as a means to greater power and material advantages. But Salish memories in the '40s of what had happened in the '20s must have been blurred by the impact of the Red River school's influence of the '30s, which, documentary evidence shows, did affect them.

In 1839, for instance, after deputations of Iroquois and western Indians had made a series of journeys to St. Louis, Bishop Joseph Rosati of that city wrote that a band of twenty-four Iroquois under a man named Old Ignace La Mousse, who had left the Catholic mission of Caughnawaga on the St. Lawrence River in eastern Canada sometime between 1812 and 1820 and had crossed to the Oregon country and settled among the Flatheads, had been primarily responsible for arousing that tribe's first interest in Christianity. (See Lawrence B. Palladino, S. J., *Indian and White in the Northwest*, Lancaster, Pa., 1922, p. 8; and William N. Bischoff, S. J., *Jesuits in Old Oregon*, Caldwell,

Idaho, 1945, p. 9.) But eight years earlier on December 31, 1831, soon after the first of the series of western Indian deputations had reached St. Louis, Bishop Rosati had written that a Canadian familiar with the western natives had informed him that "the nation of Flat Heads . . . had received some notions of the Catholic religion from two Indians who had been to Canada, and who had related what they had seen" (Palladino, p. 11). This was obviously a reference to two Salish boys who had gone to the Anglican mission school at Red River—see below, p. 000.

Moreover, during the winter of 1824-25 Jedediah Smith, a deeply religious man, would have been sure to note devout signs among the Indians, particularly anything approaching the fervor and zeal of prayer and observance of the Sabbath that Wyeth, Bonneville, Ferris, and numerous others reported a decade later. Smith spent considerable time at the Flathead Post in the heart of the Salish country, and then journeyed south with Salish and Sahaptins, yet failed to remark on a Christian bent among them. At least, we must so infer from such evidence as William Ashley's letter about those peoples that was published in the *Missouri Republican* of St. Louis on June 7, 1827. As previously noted (above, p. 000), there is comment in the letter about the friendship of the Flatheads, but nothing about their religion. It was only after 1829, when the first natives returned from the Red River school, that a mass of reports began to appear of bands of Salish and Sahaptin Indians praying, observing the Sabbath, and showing startling signs of religious piety. In other words, there was something—other than the influence of the Iroquois, who had already been present for many years—that caused a profound change in the Indians' interest in Christianity after 1829.

Finally, Fathers François Blanchet and Modeste Demers, who crossed the Canadian Rockies and entered Oregon in 1838, the first two Catholic priests to reach the Salish and Sahaptin peoples, made no claim that the French Canadian voyageurs and Iroquois had done more than tell the Indians about the "French chiefs," or blackrobes. (See *Notices & Voyages of the Famed Quebec Mission to the Pacific Northwest*, ed. Carl Landerholm, Portland, Oregon, 1956, pp. 17, 18, 21, 22, 194.) If a Catholic influence, beyond that, had been instilled among any of the Northwest tribes, the letters of Blanchet and Demers would have reflected it. In that light, the writings of De Smet and others who wrote after 1840 probably refer to the religious devotion of the Catholic Iroquois who lived among the Salish prior to 1840, rather than to that of the Salish themselves. This and later chapters will attempt to make the point clearer.

For further Catholic writings on the subject, see: *Life, Letters and Travels of Father Pierre-Jean De Smet, S.J., 1801-1873*, ed. Hiram M. Chittenden and Alfred T. Richardson, New York, 1905; Nicholas Point, S.J., "Recollections of the Rocky Mountains," a manuscript text written by a scribe from Father Point's notes in the archives of St. Mary's College, Montreal, some of which was published in *Woodstock Letters*, *11* (1882), 298-321, and *12* (1883), 3-22; "The Rocky Mountains: Memoirs of Father Gregory Mengarini," *Woodstock Letters*, *17* (1888), 298-309, and *18* (1889), 25-43, 142-52; Gilbert J. Garraghan, S.J., *The Jesuits of the Middle United States* (New York, 1938); Peter Ronan, *Historical Sketch of the Flathead Indian Nation* (Helena, Montana, 1890); and, already cited, Palladino, *Indian and White in the Northwest* and Bischoff, *Jesuits in Old Oregon*.

26 (text, p. 95). Smith's information, contained in a letter he wrote from Kamiah in June 1839 only eight years after the Nez Perces went to St. Louis, is especially interesting: "I have recently been making inquiries of the natives concerning the origin of their notions concerning the christian religion & of the object of those who went

to the States as it was said in search of Christian teachers," he wrote. "Untill about ten years ago as near as I can learn from them, they knew nothing of the christian religion or of the Sabbath. My teacher [the Lawyer] tells me that they had indeed before this seen a flag flying at the Forts of the H.B.C. on certain days & that the men were shaved & dressed different from usual & were engaged in horse racing & gambling, but they knew not then that it was the Sabbath. They had also I think before this seen some white men in the mountains (catholics) who had told them some things, & before or after this some had learned to make the cross, (probably afterwards) & they had witnessed the celebration of christmas by firing of guns, carousing & intoxication. These were among some of the first ideas they had of religion.

"About ten years ago a young Spokan who goes by the name of Spokan Garry, who had been at the Red River School, returned. My teacher, the Lawyer, saw him & learned from him respecting the Sabbath & some other things which he had heard at the school. This was the first that he heard about the Sabbath & it was called by them *Halahpawit*. He returned & communicated what he had heard to his people. Soon after wh. six individuals set out for the States, in search as he says of Christian teachers. Two of this number turned back in the mountains & the other four went on & arrived at St. Louis when two died, one died soon after having left that place & one alone returned to tell the Story & he is now dead. With what motives these individuals went it is difficult to determine. To suppose that it was any thing but selfish motives, is to suppose that good can come out of the natural heart. Were I to judge of their motives by what I see now among the people I should say it was nothing but selfishness. Doubtless there was curiosity to find out something about the christian religion. There has been much said about the desire of this people for instruction but it is quite evident what it is for. It is not usually the common people that express much desire only the chiefs & principal men. These manifest a great fondness for hearing something new & telling of it & by so doing they gather many about them & increase their influence & sustain their dignity among the people. This has evidently been the case . . ." *The Diaries and Letters of Henry H. Spalding and Asa Bowen Smith Relating to the Nez Perce Mission, 1838–1842*, ed. Clifford M. Drury (Glendale, Calif., 1958), pp. 106–07.

49 (text, p. 110). Tuekakas (sometimes pronounced Ta-wait-akas), destined to become well known in Oregon history as Old Joseph, was born sometime between 1785 and 1790 near Wawawai on the Snake River, the son of a Nez Perce woman and a Cayuse leader named Wallamatkin from Oregon's Umatilla Valley. The couple dwelled for a while among the Cayuses near present-day Pendleton, Oregon; but before the birth of Tuekakas, the mother left the father and returned to her own country. Later she became the mate of a Nez Perce man named Takinploon (Meadow) of the Kallapoon family and, with her son, lived in the Wallowa Valley and in Joseph Canyon until she died, when Tuekakas was seventeen years old. His father, the Cayuse, sent for him, and the youth went to the Umatilla, where he lived for about a year with three half-brothers and a half-sister. All of them were younger than he: one, a man who later married a Wallawalla woman, was called Ollokot (Frog); and in time young Chief Joseph's brother, a hero of the war of 1877, was named for him. The other two, who became prominent Cayuse headmen named Tauitau and Pahkatos Qoh Qoh (Five Crows), were known to white men in a period of turbulence and violence as the Young Chief and Hezekiah, respectively. Eventually, Tuekakas returned to his mother's people in the Wallowa and became a part of his step-father's Kallapoon family. When he came of age, he took as his mate the daughter of the Kallapoon chief, a girl

named Khapkhaponimi (The Scrapings of Bark, or Loose Bark on Trees), who had three brothers. The oldest was named Hin-mah-too-yah-lat-kekht (Thunder Traveling to Loftier Mountain Heights), after whom his nephew, the famous Chief Joseph, was later named. Another, Metot Weptish or Metat Waptass (Three Feathers), became a brave and famous war leader; the third, about whom little is known, was named Isthis. Through these prominent connections, as well as because of his own ability and qualities as an orator and wise counselor, Tuekakas became spokesman for his father-in-law and eventually leader of the Kallapoon family and of all the Wallowa people, sometimes called the Kamooenim or the Wellamotkin band.

During his lifetime, Tuekakas had a number of mates, including a Wallawalla and a Cayuse, and children by at least four of them. By 1839, the year before Young Joseph was born, the missionary Henry Spalding had baptized four of Tuekakas' children, "Mary Noyes, Abigail, Hannah More & Manassa" (see Drury, *Diaries and Letters of Spalding and Smith,* p. 281), but modern Nez Perces seem to know of only five of Tuekakas' children altogether: The oldest, a daughter, who after the arrival of the whites was called Celia and then Sarah, married into the Blackeagle family of Lapwai. The second child, another daughter named Elawinonmi, became Mrs. Reuben. The third, Young Joseph, born in 1840, took the name of his mother's brother, Hin-mah-too-yah-lat-kekht. The fourth child, another boy, was called Smuguiskugin, Suk-kui Suk-kui, or Shugun, all terms for the color brown. In 1868 or 1869 he was shot by a jealous Nez Perce rival near Weston, Oregon, and died soon afterward in the vicinity of the Wallowa Valley. The fifth child known to modern Nez Perces was also a boy, who received the Cayuse name Ollokot, after the half-brother of Tuekakas.

I am grateful to many persons for help in the compilation of this biographical material—particularly to Gilbert Edward Connor, a descendant of Ollokot; Richard Half-moon and the late Otis Halfmoon; the late Joseph Blackeagle; Josiah Red Wolf; and Max Wilson and Mrs. Grace Bartlett, historians and residents of Joseph, Oregon.

I have also based the spelling of young Joseph's Indian name on an important document made available to me by the additional kindness of Mrs. Bartlett. It is an account by Mrs. Frances G. Hamblen of a visit to her home by Chief Joseph, a friend of her father's, in 1893. Mrs. Hamblen was then a young girl, and she immediately recorded a description of the visit, including the following bit of conversation: "I asked him [Chief Joseph] to tell me his Indian name—he merely grunted and shook his head. Having just read in Parkman's 'Oregon Trail' that it is exceedingly bad policy to give in to an Indian I persisted in my request. He must have concluded that I was in earnest, for suddenly he leaned toward me in his chair and told his name, waiting for me to repeat each syllable after him. 'Hin-mah-too-yah-lat-kekht.' The last syllable in true Indian style between a cough and a spit. When we had done this together several times—he told us what it meant. 'Hi-n mountains' he said, 'Hi-u' T-under (thunder) 'hi-u tunder in mts.' and with his arm he described the course of thunder which reached from the base, to the very summit of the mts. His voice, too, was deep and full." Like the names of most Indians, its pronunciation sounded differently to various white men, and there is no accepted "correct" spelling of it.

CHAPTER 4. Children of Grace

11 (text, p. 125). Two versions of this period of the history of the Nez Perces and Flatheads continue to be published to this day, each one based on the original source

writings of religious partisans and both of them overlooking or ignoring portions of the total historical material that is now available, as well as present-day knowledge of the culture of the Indians themselves at that time. In 1834 Ignace may have preferred priests for the Flatheads, but it does not appear that he could have been too concerned about which church Lee belonged to. Until missionaries actually settled in the North-west, ties to any one faith were too loose among the Iroquois and the white men in the mountains to engender extreme partisanship among the Indians; and Ignace's acceptance of Lee—for the time being at least—would have been understandable within the context of the period.

Ignace would not have been alone in possessing this unconcerned attitude. François Payette, a devout Catholic trader, had given his halfblood son, Baptiste, to Nathaniel Wyeth—a Protestant and, perhaps, even an agnostic—to take to the East and educate, and there were other examples of men in the isolated Northwestern fur trade who were not too particular about adhering strictly to the church in which they had been raised. Moreover, it is certain that until priests appeared on the scene, the Flatheads and Nez Perces themselves could not possibly have differentiated among Anglicans, Catholics, and American Protestants, no matter what some of the Iroquois and whites might have told them. Any teacher who could instruct them in the white man's re-lationship with the supernatural would have been acceptable. Dogmatic assumptions of whom the Indians wanted or did not want cannot be made without evidence; and the cultural evidence available shows that they could not, at that time, even appreciate that their relationship to a missionary would be different from that which they main-tained with traders. They would catch beaver for a missionary—as some of them promised to do for Lee—because he would be like every other American—a man who wanted beaver. That reference in Jason Lee's diary seems to indicate tellingly that Ignace's tutelage had not yet commenced to form clear images about teachers—real, pretended, or otherwise—in the Indians' minds.

In addition, it is necessary to question whether Bishop Rosati in 1839 was not dis-cussing a situation that might have existed by that year, but had not existed as early as 1835. From time to time in the early 1830s various Iroquois trappers and their half-blood families had been making their way to the States and settling, for a while at least, in a village of former French trappers and voyageurs that had been established in 1826 at the site of present-day Kansas City, Missouri (See Louise Barry, "Kansas before 1854: A Revised Annals," *Kansas Historical Quarterly, 28*, 1962, 179–80.) There, some of them, recorded as "Iroquois-Flatheads," had been baptized as early as February 23, 1834 (Garraghan, *The Jesuits of the Middle United States, 2*, 239). By 1836 the Indian population of the French village had increased, and on July 18 of that year a priest reported that he baptized 14 mixed-blood children, of part Iroquois, Flathead, and Kutenai parentage, who apparently were members of twelve families that had "lately come down from the Rocky Mountains." On a second visit to these people the priest said that he "found them all sick and, in despair of being able to live here, they were talking of going back to their mountains" (Barry, "Kansas before 1854," *Kansas Historical Quarterly, 29*, 1963, 54). These Indians, perhaps including Big Ignace and members of his family, may have traveled across the plains alone, since there is no known record of their having accompanied a fur caravan to the East.

What emerges is the possibility that until the arrival of priests in Montana after 1840, the Protestant missionaries found no opposition from the Flatheads and Nez Perces in that quarter because the Iroquois had not been as influential among them as Bishop

Rosati thought they had. Instead, for a number of years at least, the Iroquois and their families may well have been traveling east for personal reasons. They may have told the priests about the Flatheads with whom they lived and, before returning west, may have agreed to do their best to turn their Salish friends away from the Protestant missionaries and toward the Catholic faith. Their concern and zeal to carry out the request made of them, and to protect the Flatheads from the spreading Protestant influence, may then have motivated their trips of 1837 and later years, at which times perhaps they pled earnestly for help in the form of Catholic missionaries; but their original inspiration would thus have come from Catholic sources in Missouri, and not from their own partisanship, or from that of the Indians of the Northwest.

17 (text, p. 128). Reverend A. S. Atwood, *The Conquerors* (Cincinnati, 1907), p. 236. Even before Lee's death, controversy had arisen over why Lee had failed to return to the Nez Perces and Flatheads. The question was never satisfactorily answered. Lee was undoubtedly oppressed by the arid country of the interior and by the prospect of a lonely and difficult life among the nonagricultural Flatheads and Nez Perces whom he saw at the rendezvous. When he reached Vancouver, he was advised by McLoughlin to consider the Willamette. If there was to be an American missionary in the country, the Hudson's Bay Company Chief Factor wanted him under his eye, and south of the Columbia River, in country that might one day go to the United States. McLoughlin told him that the interior tribes were warlike and unpredictable. If Lee got into trouble, McLoughlin would have to rescue him. If he were killed, his death would have to be punished. It would be expensive and difficult. So McLoughlin urged Lee to examine the country to the south, where there were also souls to save; and when Lee saw the Willamette's fertile and hospitable countryside, with whites and pacified Indians already living there, he undoubtedly found it easy to accept McLoughlin's proddings.

Daniel Lee, who accompanied his uncle to the Willamette and later founded a mission at The Dalles on the Columbia, believed that McLoughlin was almost entirely responsible for Jason's decision. The British trader, he said, had pointed out to the missionaries that there would be difficulties in obtaining food and transporting building materials and implements to the Flatheads, who were six hundred miles inland from Fort Vancouver. Also, he had argued that the Flatheads were only a small tribe, who were becoming fewer in number each year because of their wars with the Blackfeet; and if the missionaries went to live with the Flatheads, the Blackfeet would regard them as allies of their enemies, and their lives would not be safe. It would be better, McLoughlin was said to have urged them, to use the Willamette as a base for missionary activities over a large country and among many tribes, rather than to risk everything by settling among one small and remotely situated people.

All of this may have been put to Lee in good faith. There was considerable truth in some of the arguments. But if McLoughlin repeated his advice to the various missionaries who followed Lee to Oregon in succeeding years, they failed to mention it or to accept it. Many of them headed back to the isolation, discomfort, and perils of the lands of the native peoples whom they had come to instruct, and they had a right to wonder about Lee, as some of them did. Dr. Elijah White, a Methodist who arrived in Oregon in 1837 to work with Lee, offered a simple explanation. After Lee passed by the Flatheads and saw the Willamette, Dr. White wrote, the missionary "found the mild, equable climate, and society, though small, of whites, more congenial to his habits than any thing he could expect in the section to which he had been sent" (Miss A. J. Allen, *Ten Years in Oregon*, Ithaca, N.Y., 1850, p. 125).

This comment provided a clue to Lee's character that was missed by many of those who puzzled about him. Before he left the East, he thought of his charges as souls to be saved. They were not really people to him, because he could not accurately visualize the western Indians whom he had never seen. When he met them, he was shocked. They were wild, alien, and frightening. As he looked at them at the rendezvous on Ham's Fork, he without a doubt entertained the same thought that other missionaries after him shared: You cannot Christianize a wild Indian. First, you must make him into a white man. You must hold him still and tie him up while you destroy his traditions, culture, and way of life. He must be unhorsed and taught to plow, raise livestock, and settle down in a farmhouse with windows and a door. He must wear white men's clothing, cut his hair like white men, learn to read and write the white man's language, and think like white men. It might be immoral and evil to destroy a people's culture, but the missionaries would not see it that way, for the Indians would have to be refashioned into white men before their hearts could possibly be opened to salvation. To assume that larger task, missionaries had to accept their charges as people, rather than souls. In the case of wild Indians, Lee could not bring himself to do that. His remarks and actions led many people to conclude that with regard to Indians, this preacher of God's word had the superior attitude of one who considered himself a member of a master race. It would have made him view the Nez Perces and the Flatheads whom he met at the rendezvous, and the Chinookan peoples who were around him in the Willamette, as members of an inferior, colored race, different and apart from the white man, and repellent to him. Later, he supplied a hint of this attitude in a letter about the Nez Perces. "The truth is," he wrote after a visit to those people a few years after a mission was finally established for them, "they are *Indians.*" And he underlined the noun meaningfully. On another occasion, he advised his colleagues at the mission in the Willamette: "Let not the Indians trifle with you, let them know that you must be respected, and whenever they intentionally transgress bounds, make them feel the weight of your displeasure." This was one of the results of the Nez Perce mission of 1831 that had sought white teachers. See Drury, *Henry Harmon Spalding,* p. 180.

CHAPTER 6.   Chiefs, Laws, and Massacre

5 (text, p. 204). That Fathers Demers and Blanchet were aggressively on the offensive against all the American Protestant missionaries in Oregon, from the Willamette Valley to the upper Columbia, is made frankly clear by their correspondence, edited by Carl Landerholm, and published under the title *Notices & Voyages of the Famed Quebec Mission to the Pacific Northwest* (Portland, 1956). The two priests, instructed to "take possession of those various places in the name of the Catholic religion," moved vigorously into one area after another where the Protestants had been trying desperately to instruct the Indians in Christianity, treated the Protestants as quacks and fakes, and turned many of the Indians against them, often splitting bands and villages into factions and creating added difficulties and dangers for the American ministers. The conflict must be viewed today with recognition of the bitterness and intolerance that existed between many Catholic and Protestant missionaries in the 1830s and 1840s, and it must be pointed out, in addition, that most of the Protestant missionaries in Oregon were also riddled with bigotry, and fought back against the priests in kind. But by visiting tribes among whom the Protestants were already at work, and informing the Indians that the Americans were false teachers, the Canadian priests initiated the conflict in Oregon, and behaved

injudiciously as well, since their attacks on the Protestants ran the risk of inflaming the Indians against the missionary families. For examples of the attitudes and actions of Fathers Demers and Blanchet against the Protestant missionaries, whom they called "self-styled ministers," "Bible colporteurs," and "selfish professors of false doctrines," see *Notices and Voyages*, pp. 33, 35, 54–56, 79–83, 91–92, 108–10, etc.

32 (text, p. 223). Whitman's arrival in St. Louis produced great interest in that city, and he gave a number of talks and aroused considerable enthusiasm among potential emigrants before he left for Washington, which was on his route to Boston. In the national capital he called on John C. Spencer, an old acquaintance from upper New York State, who had become Secretary of the Treasury, and Spencer introduced him to President John Tyler, Secretary of State Daniel Webster, and Secretary of War James M. Porter. The content of his conversations with those men is not known, but it is probable that Whitman gave them first hand information on conditions in Oregon, and urged support for the American position there. The ownership of Oregon was becoming a burning political issue, and the next year Polk was to be elected with the campaign slogan "Fifty-four, forty, or fight," the cry of those who wished the United States to acquire all of the Oregon country up to its northern boundary at the parallel of fifty-four degrees, forty minutes, which included present-day British Columbia. Whitman's proddings, therefore, were probably listened to with attention, although there is no evidence that he played a significant role in deciding government policy or actions.

From Washington, Whitman went to New York, and still wearing his western clothes, including a great buffalo coat with a hood, buckskin breeches, fur leggings, and boot moccasins, he called on Horace Greeley, editor of the New York *Tribune*, and discussed the subject of Oregon with him. Greeley was interested in meeting him and wrote a sympathetic editorial, stating: "We did not learn what success the worthy man had in leading the Indians to embrace the Christian faith, but he very modestly remarked that many of them had begun to cultivate the earth and to raise cattle." In New York, also, Whitman's incongruous garb made him the target of an unscrupulous cab driver, who fleeced him out of some money by taking him on a long, roundabout ride to his lodgings.

In Boston, where Whitman arrived on March 29, his clothing did not amuse some of the stern-faced members of the Prudential Committee of the American Board. One of them was so offended by his travel-worn, western garments that he handed Whitman some money and told him critically, "Go get some decent clothes." Drury, *Whitman*, p. 316.

47 (text, p. 234). The diaries of Mrs. Elkanah Walker and Mrs. Eells at Tshimakain, published by Drury in *First White Women over the Rockies*, Volume 2, make abundantly clear how ineffective those two missionary families were with the Spokans, despite the fact that the Spokans were the people who had sent Garry to Red River, and had thus been among the first Indians to show a great interest in Christianity. The Walkers and Eells, for instance, never successfully learned the Indians' language. In addition, they failed to establish any sort of a close relationship with the Indians, showing little understanding of or sympathy for the natives' ways, busying themselves much of the time with their own domestic problems. "How little time we bestow on Indians compared with what we do on ourselves," wrote Mrs. Walker on February 4, 1845. But on February 21 her husband wrote to the *Christian Mirror* of Portland, Maine, "If they [the Indians] should remain constantly about us the whole year, it would to all human view soon kill us. It is their leaving us for a part of the year that affords us time & opportunity to renew our strength & prepare for our labors anew." The Indians were

not foolish enough to be unaware of the lack of warmth on the part of the missionaries; and although they did not become hostile to the Walkers and Eellses, they gradually lost interest in them. Their faith in their own beliefs and their shamans continued strong; on several occasions when the missionaries tried to treat sick or injured Indians with white men's methods, the Indians refused their help and told them frankly that "their own medicine was best." Once, when Mrs. Eells was dangerously ill, the Indians even proposed solicitously that the missionaries apply to their own medicine man for help.

Under these conditions, the position of Garry himself became pitiable. The missionaries tried to use him as an interpreter during worship, and Garry attempted to oblige them. But the Spokans laughed at him, and he soon told Eells that he could not assist the missionaries any longer, since he could not withstand his people's ridicule. On May 22, 1844, six years after the Walkers and Eells had come to the Northwest, Archibald McDonald, the chief trader at nearby Fort Colvile, wrote tellingly to Edward Ermatinger: The missionaries "sent out by the A.B.C.F.M. still hold on, but, literally, do nothing" (*Family Letters of Two Oregon Fur Traders, 1828–1856*, ed. Paul C. Phillips, in *Frontier Omnibus*, p. 38).

69 (text, p. 248). Since 1841 Father De Smet and his Jesuit colleagues, far more understanding and tolerant of Indian culture and ways than the Protestants, had been winning many friends and converts, and establishing a string of missions among the tribes of western Montana and northern Idaho. In 1841, the year after De Smet had first met Lawyer and other Nez Perces, his assistant, Father Nicholas Point, had also begun to meet Nez Perces in the Bitterroot Valley. In January 1842, while on a hunt with Flatheads and Nez Perces, Point noted that he baptized an old Nez Perce chief called Charlemagne (because of his stature, courage, and authority); and a few days later, when a large party of Nez Perces joined the group, he organized a special catechism class for them. They met in the evenings in a shelter formed by two Nez Perce lodges, he wrote. But on January 19 Blackfeet wounded his interpreter, and Point "lost the help of his tongue at the very moment when frequent instruction would have been useful" (from Point's *Recollections of the Rocky Mountains*). De Smet and the Jesuits also extended their work westward to the lands of the Kalispels and Coeur d'Alenes, bordering the Spokan country, and filled the Walkers and Eells with fears. On February 9, 1842, Mrs. Walker wrote that "The Cour de Lain Chief came to invite Mr. E [Eells] to go to & teach his people. Garry came with him. They say half of this people are in favor of the priests & the other Mr. W [Walker] & E." The next day Eells went to the Coeur d'Alene country, but he returned five days later and never went back. The Jesuits were more aggressive, and their missions had great success among the different Salish peoples. By May 22, 1844, Archibald McDonald at Fort Colvile was writing Edward Ermatinger that the Jesuits had become "as thick as blackberries in this district" (*Frontier Omnibus*, p. 38). One of their missions, Sacred Heart, which Father Point established for the Coeur d'Alenes in 1842, was often visited by Nez Perces. At the end of November 1845, during the height of the Nez Perce and Cayuse unrest over Elijah Hedding's murder and the influx of American settlers, Point recorded that ten Nez Perce men of importance arrived at the Sacred Heart mission "to be instructed." He said that they were "half-civilized by Protestantism" and "appeared disgusted with everything having to do with Protestantism . . ." They stayed for ten days, listening to instruction and translating Catholic prayers into the Nez Perce language. They spent the evenings reciting to each other, trying to memorize their lessons far into the night. They wanted to be admitted to the fold, Point maintained, but "we judged it prudent to postpone for some

months the fulfillment of their desires, assuming of course, that their conduct would remain in accord with their promises." They went home, and Point learned later that "in each of their camps there came into use two kinds of prayers, one according to the Protestant manner . . . and another according to the Catholic manner . . . Since the latter are the most influential and most esteemed in every respect, there is reason to hope that soon all will walk in the right way" (from Point's *Recollections*).

CHAPTER 12.   The Earth Is My Mother

22 (text, p. 499). McWhorter, *Hear Me*, pp. 162–63, quotes an account by the Nez Perce Red Elk concerning a council held on the Salmon River, about ten miles above the mouth of White Bird Creek, in the fall of 1876, at which the nontreaty leaders appointed Toohoolhoolzote as their head speaker at future meetings with white negotiators. It is probable that this was the same meeting referred to by a Salmon River settler named Cone, who—by invitation of the Indians—attended it with three other white settlers. In this account of the meeting Cone related that the council took place during the holidays of 1876–77 at Horseshoe Bend of the Salmon River, and that the principal chiefs present were White Bird, Joseph, Looking Glass, and Roaring Bull, who may have been Toohoolhoolzote. The Indians had learned that they would have to move, and the council was called apparently to plan common action in resisting the government's order. The white men invited to the meeting were all known to be friends of the Indians. Three of them understood the Nez Perce language, and the Indians probably hoped that somehow they would be able to help them. See Bailey, *River of No Return*, pp. 253–54.

Regarding Toohoolhoolzote, Duncan McDonald, the halfblood Nez Perce trader who in 1878 first published the Indians' version of the Lapwai council with Howard, said that all the nontreaty chiefs and their people, with the exception of Looking Glass and Red Owl, were present for the first meeting of the council at Lapwai, and that before it commenced, they held a meeting of their own and selected Toohoolhoolzote, "who was supposed to be a smart, intelligent Indian," as their speaker. Ollokot, McDonald said, "was barred out, the Council deciding that he was not smart nor bold enough to represent them in a council with Howard," and, as a result, he "felt aggrieved at the action of his people in electing another instead of himself as Speaker . . ." (*New Northwest*, Deer Lodge, Montana, October 25, 1878).

McDonald was reporting sometime after the event, and from hearsay, which by that time may well have been twisted by months of emotional turmoil, and his facts were often far from accurate. But his account of the war and of the various councils and events that preceded it was the first one—and for seventy years almost the only one—to give a significant emphasis to the roles of Ollokot and the war chiefs of the other bands in what happened, and consequently was the first to downgrade the supposed military leadership of Joseph. A closer reading of what McDonald wrote also strangely downgrades Joseph even further, indicating that Ollokot was much more important—even before the outbreak of hostilities—than any historian, including Lucullus McWhorter, has said. It is important, however, in striving to make a correct assessment of Joseph's role and stature, that every source of information about him be analyzed, and in this connection it is worth noting that McDonald got his information about Ollokot and Joseph from White Bird and his people in exile in Canada after the war. Secondly, Joseph and Ollokot, it must be remembered, were younger and less tried and experienced than White Bird. They had been viewed before the war with distrust by the more warlike Indians of other bands, who saw the brothers constantly make compromises and preach peace with the white men, and who suspected that they would eventually abandon the other nontreaty bands. In the third place, White Bird did not agree with Joseph's wish to surrender at the end of the war and fled to Canada, still maintaining a defiant posture, while Joseph gave up. And, fourth, White Bird must have been chagrined that the Americans did not hang Joseph after the surrender, but treated him as the hero and genius of the Indian side. White Bird, who by that time may have thought more of the dead fighting leader, Ollokot, than of Joseph, perhaps deliberately understressed Joseph's role when talking to McDonald. At any rate, care must be taken in evaluating the versions of individual Indians on the subject. Members of Joseph's own band, like Yellow Wolf, who remained loyal to their headman, are more reliable on the matter than veterans—or descendants of veterans—of other bands.

CHAPTER 13. The Patriots

12 (text, p. 537). Sometime about this period a small group of citizen volunteers under John W. Cullen of the Grande Ronde Valley, fearful that Joseph might bring his warriors back to the Wallowa, rode cautiously across the Wallowa Valley and down the Imnaha to scout the Snake River crossing. Cullen's account, which may be found in J. H. Horner's papers in the Wallowa County Court House at Enterprise, Oregon, states that in the hills on the opposite side of the Snake the men saw many Indians and horses, seemingly ready to recross that river and return to the Wallowa. By popping into view from different parts of the bluffs and pretending to be more numerous than they were, the six members of the volunteer group, according to Cullen, deterred the Indians from crossing the Snake and returning to the Wallowa.

That Cullen's expedition occurred cannot be doubted, but his dates and some of his observations are garbled, and it is difficult to reconcile his account with what was actually occurring on the other side of the Snake. In the first place, Cullen stated that, on leaving the Grande Ronde, he and his men met Whipple and his cavalrymen still in camp in that valley. That would have dated Cullen's departure as having been prior to Howard's call to Whipple to come to Lapwai. The volunteers then went into the Wallowa canyon, camped there "two or three days," and finally proceeded to the Imnaha Valley via the Wallowa. There, some of the men became faint-hearted about going farther, and only five of the volunteers went on with Cullen to the hills above the Snake. From their vantage point these men sighted the Indians across the river, and Cullen stated that they could also see shooting over near Salmon River. He said it was now July 5, and the shooting was the battle between Randall's Mount Idaho volunteers and the Nez Perce screening party near Cottonwood. If that was so, the nontreaties would have been across the Salmon three days already, and would have been on their way to the Clearwater. Who the Indians were that Cullen and his men saw, and what they were doing, is puzzling, unless they were an isolated group that had left the main body and remained behind in the mountains between the Salmon and the Snake. Howard himself had been in those mountains for several days, and on July 5 was at the Craig Billy Crossing, in a position between the main body of Nez Perces and the Indians Cullen saw. Those few Nez Perces may have intended to try to return to the Wallowa, but it is not likely. Certainly Joseph and the main body of nontreaties had no intention of doing so, or they would already have done it. It is possible, of course, that Cullen was seeing some of the treaty Nez Perces who were with Howard's army.

BIBLIOGRAPHY

MANUSCRIPT MATERIALS

AMERICAN PHILOSOPHICAL SOCIETY, PHILADELPHIA: Lewis and Clark journals.

BANCROFT LIBRARY, UNIVERSITY OF CALIFORNIA, BERKELEY: Miscellaneous Idaho, Washington, Oregon, and California materials. Important collections include: H. H. Bancroft interviews with Oregon settlers; Lafayette Grover materials; John McLoughlin private papers; Oregon Territory archives; W. V. Rinehart account of First Oregon Cavalry; Sir James Douglas private papers and journals; Archibald McKinlay narrative.

CHICAGO HISTORICAL SOCIETY: James Wilkinson papers.

COE COLLECTION OF WESTERN AMERICAN HISTORY, YALE UNIVERSITY LIBRARY, NEW HAVEN, CONN.: Elwood Evans correspondence, papers, journals, and miscellaneous writings; George Gibbs letters; Lewis and Clark Expedition manuscript maps; Missouri Fur Company letterbook kept by Thomas Hempstead, 1821–23; Isaac I. Stevens correspondence and papers.

GLENBOW FOUNDATION, CALGARY, ALBERTA: Miscellaneous materials on central and western Canadian Indian and fur trade history.

HAWAIIAN MISSION CHILDREN'S SOCIETY, HONOLULU: Oregon missionary letters.

HUDSON'S BAY COMPANY ARCHIVES, LONDON: Peter Fidler maps and extracts from journals of 1792–93; extracts from James Bird's Edmonton Journals, 1807–08, 1808–09; various materials relating to David Thompson, Sir George Simpson, and fur trade personnel and subjects.

KANSAS STATE HISTORICAL SOCIETY, TOPEKA: William Clark material.

LEWIS-CLARK NORMAL SCHOOL, LEWISTON, IDAHO: Gold rush and Idaho material.

MANUSCRIPT DIVISION, LIBRARY OF CONGRESS, WASHINGTON: George B. McClellan papers; James Wilkinson correspondence; miscellaneous Indian materials.

MISSOURI HISTORICAL SOCIETY, ST. LOUIS: Frederick Bates papers; Chouteau collection; Pierre Chouteau letterbook; William Clark collection; Colonel Thomas Hunt's orderly book, Cantonment Bellfontaine, 1808–10; Pierre Menard material, Kaskaskia papers; Reuben Lewis material, Meriwether Lewis collection; miscellaneous materials, fur trade papers, and Indian papers collections.

MONTANA HISTORICAL SOCIETY, HELENA: William Moelchert correspondence.

NATIONAL ARCHIVES, WASHINGTON: Frederick Bates, James Wilkinson, Charles Courtin, Robert McClellan, Thomas Fitzpatrick, Nez Perce 1863 treaty, and other materials on explorations, fur trade, missions, Northwest settlement, surveys, military affairs, and Indian relations and wars in Records of the Bureau of Indian Affairs, Office of the Secretary of War, Office of the Chief of Engineers, Office of Indian Trade, Departments of State, War, and Interior, etc. Various manuscript cartographic and sketch materials in Office of Cartographic Records.

New York Public Library, New York: James Wilkinson papers.

New-York Historical Society, New York: Jacob Kingsbury orderly books.

Ontario Provincial Archives, Toronto: David Thompson materials.

Oregon Historical Society, Portland: Benjamin Alvord collection; miscellaneous Northwest materials.

Provincial Archives of British Columbia, Victoria: Extract from John Work journal, 1831–32.

St. Mary's College, Montreal: Father Nicolas Point's notebooks and drawings.

Smithsonian Institution, Washington: Gustavus Sohon drawings; miscellaneous Indian materials.

Spokane, Washington, Public Library: Copies of John B. Monteith letters; miscellaneous Nez Perce and Northwest Indian and historical materials.

Thomas Gilcrease Institute of American History and Art, Tulsa, Okla.: Alfred Jacob Miller notes; miscellaneous Indian materials.

Wallowa County Courthouse, Enterprise, Ore.: J. B. Horner writings; Wallowa County survey records and miscellaneous materials.

Washington State Historical Society, Tacoma: Gustavus Sohon drawings; miscellaneous materials on fur trade, Fort Vancouver, Oregon missions, I. I. Stevens, and Northwest Indian Wars.

Washington State University Library, Pullman: Lucullus V. McWhorter collection; William P. Winans correspondence.

Mr. and Mrs. Chester Wiggin, Lewiston, Idaho: Robert Newell diary, 1868.

NEWSPAPERS AND NEWS MAGAZINES

Bismarck (N.D.) Tri-Weekly Tribune
Bozeman (Mont.) Times
Chief Joseph Herald (Joseph, Ore.)
Chicago Tribune
Harper's Weekly
Helena (Mont.) Weekly Independent
Idaho Semi-Weekly World (Idaho City)
Kentucky Gazette and General Advertiser
Leslie's Weekly Illustrated
Lewiston (Idaho) Morning Tribune
Lewiston (Idaho) Teller
Medical Repository (New York): First Hexade, Vol. 6, 1803; second Hexade, Vol. 1, 1804.
Missouri Advocate and St. Louis Enquirer
Missouri Gazette (St. Louis)
Missouri Republican (St. Louis)
Mountain Sentinel (LaGrande, Ore.)
Niles Weekly Register (Baltimore and Washington)
The New Northwest (Deer Lodge, Mont.)
Philadelphia Evening Fireside, Vol. 2, No. 48, Nov. 29, 1806.
Portland Oregonian
Wallowa County Chieftain (Enterprise, Ore.)

BOOKS AND PERIODICALS

Abel, Annie Heloise, ed., *Chardon's Journal at Fort Clark, 1834–1839*, Pierre, South Dakota, 1932.

—— ed., *Tabeau's Narrative of Loisel's Expedition to the Upper Missouri*, Norman, Okla., 1939.

Abernathy, Thomas P., *The Burr Conspiracy*, New York, 1954.

Allen, Miss A. J., *Ten Years in Oregon*, Ithaca, N.Y., 1850.

Alter, J. Cecil, *Jim Bridger*, Norman, Okla., 1962.

American State Papers: Documents, Legislative and Executive, 38 vols. Washington, 1832–61.

Annual Reports, Commissioner of Indian Affairs, Washington.

Annual Reports, Secretary of Interior, Washington.

Annual Reports, Secretary of War, Washington.

Atwood, A. S., *The Conquerors*, Cincinnati, 1907.

Ault, Nelson A., ed., "The Papers of Lucullus Virgil McWhorter," *Friends of the Library*, Washington State College, Pullman, 1959.

Avery, Mary W., *History and Government of the State of Washington*, Seattle, 1961.

Bagley, Clarence B., ed., *Early Catholic Missions in Old Oregon*, 2 vols. Seattle, 1932.

Bailey, Robert G., *River of No Return*, Lewiston, Idaho, 1947.

Baker, Paul E., *The Forgotten Kutenai*, Boise, Idaho, 1955.

Bancroft, Hubert H., *History of the Northwest Coast*, Vol. 1, San Francisco, 1884.

—— *History of Oregon*, 2 vols. San Francisco, 1886–88.

—— *The History of Washington, Idaho, and Montana, 1845–1889*, San Francisco, 1890.

Barber, Floyd R., and Martin, Dan W., *Idaho in the Pacific Northwest*, Caldwell, Idaho, 1956.

Barry, J. Neilson, "Archibald Pelton, the First Follower of Lewis and Clark," *Washington Historical Quarterly, 19* (1928), 199–201.

—— "Lieutenant Jeremy Pinch," *Oregon Historical Quarterly, 38* (1937), 223–27.

—— "Madame Dorion of the Astorians," *Oregon Historical Quarterly, 30* (1929).

—— "The Trail of the Astorians," *Oregon Historical Quarterly, 13* (1912), 227–39.

Barry, Louise, "Kansas before 1854: A Revised Annals," *Kansas Historical Quarterly, 28* (1962), 167–204; *29* (1963).

Beal, Merrill D., *I Will Fight No More Forever*, Seattle, 1963.

Beal, Samuel M., *The Snake River Fork Country*, Rexburg, Idaho, 1935.

Beidleman, Richard G., "Nathaniel Wyeth's Fort Hall," *Oregon Historical Quarterly, 58* (1957), 197–250.

Berreman, Joel V., "Tribal Distribution in Oregon," *American Anthropological Association Memoirs, 47* (1937).

Biddle, Nicholas, ed., *History of the Expedition under Command of Captains Lewis and Clark*, Philadelphia, 1814.

Bingham, Hiram, "Introduction of the Gospel to N. West America," *Hawaiian Spectator* (October 1838).

Bischoff, William N., *The Jesuits in Old Oregon*, Caldwell, Idaho, 1945.

Blumenthal, Walter Hart, *American Indians Dispossessed*, Philadelphia, 1955.

Bolton, Herbert E., "Papers of Zebulon M. Pike, 1806–07," *American Historical Review,* *13* (1908), 798–827.

Bond, Fred G., *Flatboating on the Yellowstone, 1877,* New York, 1925.

Brady, Cyrus Townsend, *Northwestern Fights and Fighters,* New York, 1907.

Brosnan, Cornelius J., *History of the State of Idaho,* New York, 1935.

—— *Jason Lee: Prophet of the New Oregon,* New York, 1932.

Brown, William C., *Early Okanogan History,* Okanogan, Wash., 1911.

—— *The Indian Side of the Story,* Spokane, 1961.

Buck, Amos, "The Battle of the Big Hole," *Contributions to the Historical Society of Montana,* 7 (1910).

Burcham, Ralph, "Orofino Gold," *Idaho Yesterdays, 4* (Fall, 1960), 2–5, 8–9.

Burns, R. Ignatius, "The Jesuits, the Northern Indians, and the Nez Perce War of 1877," *Pacific Northwest Quarterly, 42* (1951), 40–76.

Burpee, L. J., ed., "Journal of F. A. Larocque, June 2–October 18, 1805," *Frontier and Midland 14, 15* (1934).

—— ed., *The Journal of François Antoine Larocque,* Ottawa, 1911.

Butler, B. Robert, *The Old Cordilleran Culture in the Pacific Northwest,* Idaho State College Museum, Pocatello, 1961.

—— *Contributions to the Prehistory of the Columbia Plateau,* Idaho State College Museum, Pocatello, 1962.

Butterfield, Grace, and Horner, J. H., "Wallowa Valley Towns and Their Beginnings," *Oregon Historical Quarterly, 41* (1940), 383–85.

Camp, Charles L., ed., *James Clyman, Frontiersman,* Portland, Ore., 1960.

Campbell, Marjorie W., *The North West Company,* New York, 1957.

Cannon, Miles, "Snake River in History," *Oregon Historical Quarterly, 20* (1919), 1–23.

Carter, Clarence E., ed., *The Territorial Papers of the United States, 13,* Washington, D.C., 1948; *14,* 1949.

Catlin, George, *Letters and Notes on the Manners, Customs, and Condition of the North American Indians,* 2 vols. New York, 1842.

Catlin, James B., "The Battle of the Big Hole," *Montana State Historian's Annual Report,* Missoula, 1927.

Cave, Will, *Nez Perce Indian War of 1877 and Battle of the Big Hole,* Missoula, 1926.

Chaffee, Eugene B., ed., *Nez Perce War Letters,* Idaho Historical Society, 15th Biennial Report, Boise, 1936.

Chalmers, Harvey, II, *The Last Stand of the Nez Perce,* New York, 1962.

Chase, Don M., *He Opened the West,* Sacramento, 1958.

Cheetham, Robert N., *David Thompson Sesquicentennial,* Sandpoint, Idaho, 1960.

Chief Joseph, "An Indian's View of Indian Affairs," *North American Review, 128* (April, 1879), 412–33.

Chittenden, Hiram M., *A History of the American Fur Trade of the Far West,* 2 vols. Stanford, Calif., 1954.

—— and Richardson, Alfred T., *Life, Letters and Travels of Father Pierre-Jean De Smet, S.J., 1801–1873,* New York, 1905.

"Claims of the Nez Perce Indians," *Senate Executive Document No. 257,* 56th Congress, 1st Session, Washington, 1900.

Clark, Dan E., "Pioneer Pastimes," *Oregon Historical Quarterly, 57* (1956), 313–49.

Clark, Ella E., "The Mythology of the Indians in the Pacific Northwest," *Oregon Historical Quarterly, 54* (1953), 163–89.

—— "George Gibbs' Account of Indian Mythology in Oregon and Washington Territories," *Oregon Historical Quarterly, 56* (1955), 293–325.

Clark, J. Stanley, "The Nez Perces in Exile," *Pacific Northwest Quarterly, 36* (1945), 213–32.

Clark, Malcolm H., Jr., "'Oregon' Revisited," *Oregon Historical Quarterly, 61* (1960), 211–19.

Clark, Robert C., *History of the Willamette Valley,* 3 vols. Chicago, 1927.

Clarke, S. A., *Pioneer Days of Oregon History,* 2 vols. Portland, 1905.

"Clearwater Gold Rush," *Idaho Yesterdays, 4* (Spring, 1960), 12–15, 18–26.

Coale, George L., "Notes on the Guardian Spirit Concept among the Nez Perce," *National Archives of Ethnography, 48* (1958).

Coan, C. F., "The First Stage of Federal Indian Relations in the Pacific Northwest, 1849–1852," *Oregon Historical Quarterly, 22* (1921), 46–89.

Coues, Elliott, ed., *The Expeditions of Zebulon M. Pike,* 3 vols. New York, 1895.

—— ed., *New Light on the Early History of the Greater Northwest,* 3 vols. New York, 1897.

Cox, Isaac I., "Opening of the Santa Fe Trail," *Missouri Historical Review, 25* (1930), 30–66.

Cox, Ross, *Adventures on the Columbia River,* 2 vols., London, 1831. Republished as *The Columbia River,* ed. Edgar I. and Jane R. Stewart, Norman, Okla., 1957.

Cressman, L. S., and others, "Cultural Sequences at the Dalles, Oregon: A Contribution to Pacific Northwest Prehistory," *Transactions of the American Philosophical Society,* Vol. 50, Part 10 (1960).

Cross, Osborne, *The March of the Mounted Riflemen,* ed. Raymond W. Settle, Glendale, Calif., 1940.

Curtis, Edward S., *The North American Indian,* Vol. 7, Norwood, Mass., 1911.

Cutler, Jervis, *A Topographical Description of the State of Ohio, Indiana Territory, and Louisiana,* Boston, 1812.

Damon, Samuel C., *A Journey to Lower Oregon & Upper California, 1848–49,* San Francisco, 1927.

Daugherty, Richard D., "The Archaeology of the Lind Coulee Site, Washington," *Proceedings of the American Philosophical Society, 100* (1956), 233–78.

—— "The Intermontane Western Tradition," *American Antiquity, 28* (1962).

—— and Fryxell, Roald, "Interim Report: Archaeological Salvage in the Lower Monumental Reservoir Area, 1962," Laboratory of Archaeology and Geochronology, Washington State University, *Report of Investigations, 21,* Pullman, 1962.

Davidson, Gordon C., *The North West Company,* Berkeley, Calif., 1918.

Davis, K. G., ed., *Ogden's Snake Country Journal, 1826–27,* London, 1961.

Davison, Stanley, "Worker in God's Wilderness," *Montana, Magazine of Western History,* 7 (January, 1957), 8–17.

Denhardt, Robert M., *The Horse of the Americas,* Norman, Okla., 1947.

DeVoto, Bernard, *Across the Wide Missouri,* Boston, 1947.

—— *The Course of Empire,* Boston, 1952.

—— ed., *The Journals of Lewis and Clark,* Boston, 1953.

"Diary of Asahel Munger and Wife," *Oregon Historical Quarterly, 8* (1907), 387–405.

"Diary of Reverend George Gary," *Oregon Historical Quarterly, 24* (1923).

"Diary of Reverend Jason Lee," *Oregon Historical Quarterly, 17* (1916).

Douglas, David, *Journal Kept by David Douglas, 1823–1827,* New York, 1959.

Douglas, J. S., "Jeremy Pinch and the War Department," *Oregon Historical Quarterly*, *39* (1938), 425–31.

Douglas, Walter B., *Manuel Lisa*, ed. A. P. Nasatir, New York, 1964.

Dozier, Jack, "The Coeur d'Alene Indians in the War of 1858," *Idaho Yesterdays*, *5* (Fall, 1961).

Drumm, Stella M., ed., *Journal of a Fur Trading Expedition by John C. Luttig*, St. Louis, 1920.

—— "More about the Astorians," *Oregon Historical Quarterly*, *24* (1923), 335–60.

Drury, Clifford M., *A Tepee in His Front Yard*, Portland, Ore., 1949.

—— *Elkanah and Mary Walker*, Caldwell, Idaho, 1940.

—— *First White Women over the Rockies*, 2 vols. Glendale, Calif., 1963.

—— "Gray's Journal of 1838," *Pacific Northwest Quarterly*, *29* (1938), 277–82.

—— *Henry Harmon Spalding*, Caldwell, Idaho, 1936.

—— "I, The Lawyer," The Westerners *Brand Book*, Vol. 7, No. 1, New York, 1960.

—— *Marcus Whitman, M.D.*, Caldwell, Idaho, 1937.

—— "Oregon Indians in the Red River School," *Pacific Historical Review*, 7 (1938), 50–60.

—— ed., *The Diaries and Letters of Henry H. Spalding and Asa Bowen Smith Relating to the Nez Perce Mission, 1838–1842*, Glendale, Calif., 1958.

Dunbar, Seymour, and Phillips, Paul C., eds., *The Journals and Letters of Major John Owen*, 2 vols. New York, 1927.

Eberstadt, Charles, ed., *The Rocky Mountain Letters of Robert Campbell*, printed privately for Frederick W. Beinecke, 1955.

Eells, Myron, *Father Eells*, Boston, 1894.

Elliott, T. C., ed., "David Thompson's Journeys in Idaho," *Washington Historical Quarterly*, *11* (1920), 97–103, 163–73.

—— ed., "David Thompson's Journeys in the Pend Oreille Country," *Washington Historical Quarterly*, *23* (1932), 18–24, 88–93, 173–76.

—— ed., "David Thompson's Journeys in the Spokane Country," *Washington Historical Quarterly*, *8* (1917), 183–87, 261–64; *9* (1918), 11–16, 103–06, 169–73, 284–87; *10* (1919), 17–20.

—— ed., "David Thompson: Narrative of the Expedition to the Kootanae and Flat Bow Indian Countries on the Sources of the Columbia River," *Oregon Historical Quarterly*, *26* (1925), 23–56.

—— "Last Will and Testament of John Day," *Oregon Historical Quarterly*, *17* (1916), 375–77.

—— ed., "Journal of Alexander Ross," *Oregon Historical Quarterly*, *14* (1913).

—— ed., "Journal of David Thompson, 1811," *Oregon Historical Quarterly*, *15* (1914), 39–63, 104–25.

—— ed., "Journal of John Work, April 30th to May 31st, 1830," *Oregon Historical Quarterly*, *10* (1909), 296–313.

—— ed., "Journal of John Work, November and December, 1824," *Washington Historical Quarterly*, *3* (1912), 198–228; *5* (1914), 83–115, 163–91, 258–87; *6* (1915), 26–49; *11* (1920), 104–14.

—— ed., "Journal of John Work's Snake Country Expedition of 1830–31," *Oregon Historical Quarterly*, *13* (1912), 363–71; *14* (1913), 280–314.

—— ed., "The Peter Skene Ogden Journals," *Oregon Historical Quarterly*, *10* (1909), 331–65; *11* (1910), 201–22.

—— "The Gun Powder Story, Letter of Archibald McKinlay," *Oregon Historical Quarterly, 12* (1911), 369–74.

—— "The Murder of Peu-Peu-Mox-Mox," *Oregon Historical Quarterly, 35* (1934), 123–30.

—— "The Strange Case of David Thompson and Jeremy Pinch," *Oregon Historical Quarterly, 40* (1939), 194–95.

Ellison, William H., ed., *The Life and Adventures of George Nidever, 1802–1883,* Berkeley, Calif., 1937.

Elsensohn, M. Alfreda, *Pioneer Days in Idaho County,* 2 vols. Caldwell, Idaho, 1951.

Estergreen, M. Morgan, *Kit Carson,* Norman, Okla., 1962.

Ewers, John C., ed., *Adventures of Zenas Leonard, Fur Trader,* Norman, Okla., 1959.

—— *Gustavus Sohon's Portraits of Flathead and Pend d'Oreille Indians, 1854,* Washington, Smithsonian Institution, 1948.

—— *The Horse in Blackfoot Culture,* Bureau of American Ethnology, Bulletin 159, Washington, 1955.

—— *The Story of the Blackfeet,* Bureau of Indian Affairs, Washington, 1952.

Explorations and Surveys for a Railroad Route from the Mississippi River to the Pacific Ocean, Vol. 12, Part 1, Washington, 1859.

"Fabulous Florence!" *Idaho Yesterdays, 6* (Summer, 1962), 22–31.

Farnham, Thomas Jefferson, *Travels in the Great Western Prairies, the Anahuac and Rocky Mountains, and in the Oregon Territory,* Poughkeepsie, N.Y., 1841.

Fee, Chester Anders, *Chief Joseph,* New York, 1936.

Ferris, Warren A., *Life in the Rocky Mountains, 1830–1835,* ed. J. Cecil Alter, Salt Lake City, 1940.

Findley, H. R., "Memoirs of Alexander B. and Sarah Jane Findley," *Chief Joseph Herald,* 1957–58.

Fisher, S. G., "Journals of S. G. Fisher, Chief of Scouts to General O. O. Howard during the Nez Perce Campaign," *Contributions to the Historical Society of Montana, 2* (1896).

Forse, Albert G., "Chief Joseph as a Commander," *Winners of the West, 12* (1936), 1–6.

Franchère, Gabriel, *Narrative of a Voyage to the Northwest Coast of America in the Years 1811, 1812, 1813, and 1814,* New York, 1854.

Frémont, John Charles, *Report of the Exploring Expedition to the Rocky Mountains in the Year 1842, and to Oregon and North California in the Years 1843–44,* Washington, 1845.

Frost, Donald McKay, *Notes on General Ashley,* Barre, Mass., 1960.

Fryxell, Roald, "A Radiocarbon Limiting Date for Scabland Flooding," *Northwest Science, 36* (1962).

—— and Daugherty, Richard D., "Late Glacial and Post Glacial Geological and Archaeological Chronology of the Columbia Plateau," Washington Laboratory of Anthropology, Washington State University, *Report of Investigations, 23,* Pullman, 1963.

Fuller, George W., *A History of the Pacific Northwest,* New York, 1947.

Garraghan, Gilbert J., *The Jesuits of the Middle United States,* 2 vols. New York, 1938.

Garrard, Lewis H., *Wah-To-Yah and the Taos Trail,* Cincinnati and New York, 1850.

Gass, Patrick, *A Journal of the Voyages and Travels of a Corps of Discovery under the Command of Capt. Lewis and Capt. Clarke,* reprinted. Minneapolis, 1958.

Ghent, W. J., " 'Jeremy Pinch' Again," *Oregon Historical Quarterly, 40* (1939), 307–14.

—— *The Early Far West,* New York, 1931.

Gibbon, John, "The Battle of the Big Hole," *Harper's Weekly, 39* (December 28, 1895), 2036.

Gilbert, Frank T., *Historic Sketches of Walla Walla, Whitman, Columbia and Garfield Counties, Washington Territory*, Portland, Ore., 1882.

Glassley, Ray H., *Pacific Northwest Indian Wars*, Portland, Ore., 1953.

"Gold in 1860," *Idaho Yesterdays, 3* (Fall, 1959), 14–15, 18–21.

Goulder, W. A., *Reminiscences: Incidents in the Life of a Pioneer in Oregon and Idaho*, Boise, 1909.

Gray, William H., *History of Oregon*, Portland, Ore., 1870.

"Grievances of the Nez Perce," *Idaho Yesterdays, 4* (Fall, 1960), 6–7.

Guie, Heister D., and McWhorter, Lucullus V., *Adventures in Geyser Land*, Caldwell, Idaho, 1935.

Hafen, LeRoy R., and Ghent, W. J., *Broken Hand: The Life Story of Thomas Fitzpatrick, Chief of the Mountain Men*, Denver, 1931.

—— ed., *To the Rockies and Oregon, 1839–1842*, Glendale, Calif., 1955.

Hague, Arnold, "An Early Map of the Far West," *Science* (November 4, 1887), pp. 217–18.

Haines, Aubrey L., ed., *Osborne Russell's Journal of a Trapper*, Portland, Ore., 1955.

Haines, Francis, "Where Did the Plains Indians Get Their Horses?" *American Anthropologist, 40* (1938).

—— "The Northwest Spread of Horses among the Plains Indians," *American Anthropologist, 40* (1938).

—— "The Skirmish at Cottonwood, by George Shearer," *Idaho Yesterdays, 2* (Spring, 1958), 2–7.

—— *The Nez Perces*, Norman, Okla., 1955.

—— "Tom Hill—Delaware Scout," *California Historical Quarterly, 25* (1946), 139–48.

—— Hatley, George B., and Peckinpah, Robert, *The Appaloosa Horse*, Lewiston, Idaho, 1950.

Hakola, John W., ed., *Frontier Omnibus*, Missoula, Montana, 1962.

Harris, Burton, *John Colter*, New York, 1952.

Harrison, Michael, "Chief Charlot's Battle with Bureaucracy," *Montana, the Magazine of Western History, 10* (Autumn, 1960), 27–33.

Heitman, Francis B., *Historical Register and Dictionary of the U.S. Army, 1789–1903*, Washington, 1903.

"Henry Miller: Letters from the Upper Columbia," *Idaho Yesterdays, 4* (Winter, 1960–61), 14–22.

Hines, Gustavus, *History of the Oregon Missions*, Buffalo, 1850.

—— *Oregon: Its History, Condition and Prospects*, Buffalo, 1851.

Hodge, Frederick Webb, ed., *Handbook of American Indians North of Mexico*, Bureau of American Ethnology, Bulletin 30, 2 vols. Washington, 1907–10.

Hopwood, V. G., "New Light on David Thompson," *The Beaver* (Summer, 1957), 26–31.

—— "More Light on David Thompson," *The Beaver* (Autumn, 1957), 58.

Horner, J. H., and Butterfield, Grace, "Chief Joseph: He Met White Men Half Way," *Portland Oregonian*, January 26, 1947.

—— "The Nez Perce-Findley Affair," *Oregon Historical Quarterly, 40* (1939), 40–51.

Horner, J. H., and Pfister, Grace, *Wallowa, the Land of Winding Waters*, Joseph, Ore., 1950.

House Executive Document No. 1, 33rd Congress, 1st Session, Part I, Washington, 1854.

House Executive Document No. 93, 34th Congress, 1st Session, Washington, 1856.

House Executive Document No. 38, 35th Congress, 1st Session, Washington, 1858.

House Executive Document No. 2, 35th Congress, 2nd Session, Washington, 1859.

House Executive Document No. 1, 37th Congress, 3rd Session, Washington, 1863.

House Executive Document No. 198, Part III, 42nd Congress, 2nd Session, Washington, 1872.

House Executive Document No. 307, 42nd Congress, 2nd Session, Washington, 1872.

House Executive Documents relating to Nez Perces, 43rd Congress, 1st Session, Washington, 1874.

Howard, Helen Addison, and McGrath, Dan L., *War Chief Joseph*, Caldwell, Idaho, 1952.

Howard, Joseph Kinsey, *Strange Empire*, New York, 1952.

Howard, O. O., *Famous Indian Chiefs I Have Known*, New York, 1907–08.

—— *My Life and Experiences among Our Hostile Indians*, Hartford, Conn., 1907.

—— *Nez Perce Joseph*, Boston, 1881.

Howay, Frederic W., ed., " 'Account of an Attempt to Cross the Rocky Mountains by Mr. James Hughes, Nine Men & Myself' by David Thompson," *Queen's Quarterly*, *40* (1933), 333–56.

—— ed., *Voyages of the "Columbia" to the Northwest Coast, 1787–1790 and 1790–1793*, Boston, 1941.

—— Lewis, W. S., and Mayers, J. A., ed., "Angus McDonald: A Few Items of the West," *Washington Historical Quarterly*, 8 (1917), 188–229.

Hunt, Garret, "Sergeant Sutherland's Ride: An Incident of the Nez Perce War," *Mississippi Valley Historical Review*, *14* (1927).

Hussey, John A., *The History of Fort Vancouver*, Tacoma, Wash., 1957.

Hyde, George E., *Indians of the High Plains*, Norman, Okla., 1959.

—— *Red Cloud's Folk*, Norman, Okla., 1937.

Innis, H. A., *The Fur Trade in Canada*, Toronto, 1956.

Irving, Washington, *Astoria*, Philadelphia, 1836.

—— *The Adventures of Captain Bonneville*, Edition of New York, 1904; ed. Edgeley W. Todd and reprinted Norman, Okla., 1961.

Jackson, Donald, ed., *Letters of the Lewis and Clark Expedition with Related Documents, 1783–1854*, Urbana, Ill., 1962.

Jackson, Helen Hunt, *A Century of Dishonor*, New York, 1881.

Jackson, W. Turrentine, "Indian Affairs and Politics in Idaho Territory, 1863–1870," *Pacific Historical Review*, *14* (1945), 311–25.

Jacobs, James R., *Tarnished Warrior*, New York, 1938.

James, Thomas, *Three Years among the Indians and Mexicans*, St. Louis, 1916.

Janson, Charles W., *Stranger in America*, London, 1807.

Jessett, Thomas E., *Chief Spokan Garry*, Minneapolis, 1960.

Johansen, Dorothy O., ed., *Robert Newell's Memoranda*, Portland, Ore., 1959.

—— and Gates, Charles M., *Empire of the Columbia*, New York, 1957.

Johnson, Virginia W., *The Unregimented General*, Boston, 1962.

Jones, Nard, *The Great Command*, Boston, 1959.

Josephy, Alvin M., Jr., ed., *The American Heritage Book of Indians*, New York, 1961.

—— "A Man to Match the Mountains," *American Heritage*, *11* (1960), 60–63, 81–85.

—— "The Last Stand of Chief Joseph," *American Heritage*, *9* (1958), 36–43, 78–81.

—— "The Lolo Trail," New York Westerners *Brand Book, 4* (1958), 82–85.

—— "The Naming of the Nez Perces," *Montana, The Magazine of Western History, 5* (Autumn, 1955), 1–18.

—— *The Patriot Chiefs*, New York, 1961.

Journal of Sergeant John Ordway, Wisconsin State Historical Society Collections, Madison, 1916.

Kaiser, Leo M., and Knuth, Priscilla, ed., "From Ithaca to Clatsop Plains: Miss Ketchum's Journal of Travel," Part 2, *Oregon Historical Quarterly, 62* (1961), 337–402.

Kappler, Charles J., ed., *Indian Affairs, Laws, and Treaties*, 2 vols. Washington, 1904.

Kip, Lawrence, *Army Life on the Pacific: A Journal of the Expedition against the Northern Indians, the Tribes of the Coeur d'Alenes, Spokans, and Pelouzes, in the Summer of 1858*, New York, 1859.

—— "The Indian Council at Walla Walla," *Sources of the History of Oregon*, Vol. 1, Part 2, Eugene, 1897.

Kirkwood, Charlotte M., *The Nez Perce Indian War under Chiefs Joseph and Whitebird*, Grangeville, Idaho, 1928.

Koch, Elers, "Lewis and Clark Route Retraced across the Bitterroots," *Oregon Historical Quarterly, 41* (1940), 160–74.

Lamb, Sydney M., "Linguistic Prehistory in the Great Basin," *International Journal of American Linguistics, 24* (1958).

Landerholm, Carl, ed., *Notices & Voyages of the Famed Quebec Mission to the Pacific Northwest*, Portland, Ore., 1956.

Larpenteur, Charles, *Forty Years a Fur Trader on the Upper Missouri*, ed. M. M. Quaife, Chicago, 1933.

Lee, Daniel, and Frost, Joseph H., *Ten Years in Oregon*, New York, 1844.

Leforge, Thomas H., *Memoirs of a White Crow Indian, as Told by Thomas B. Marquis*, New York, 1928.

Lewis, W. S., and Phillips, Paul C., *The Journal of John Work*, Cleveland, 1923.

Liljeblad, Sven S., *The Indians of Idaho*, Idaho Historical Series, 3, Boise, 1960.

McBeth, Kate C., *The Nez Perces since Lewis and Clark*, New York, 1908.

McKelvey, Susan Delano, *Botanical Exploration of the Trans-Mississippi West, 1790–1850*, Jamaica Plain, Mass., 1955.

McLaughlin, James, *My Friend the Indian*, New York, 1910.

McWhorter, Lucullus V., *Hear Me, My Chiefs!* Caldwell, Idaho, 1952.

—— *Yellow Wolf*, Caldwell, Idaho, 1948.

Mackenzie, Alexander, *Voyages from Montreal, on the River St. Lawrence, through the Continent of North America*, London, 1801.

Mackenzie, Cecil W., *Donald Mackenzie, King of the Northwest*, Los Angeles, 1937.

Madsen, Brigham D., *The Bannock of Idaho*, Caldwell, Idaho, 1958.

Manring, B. F., *Conquest of the Coeur d'Alenes, Spokanes and Palouses*, Spokane, 1912.

Masson, L. R., *Les Bourgeois de la Compagnie du Nord-Ouest*, Quebec, 2 vols. 1889–90; reprinted New York, 1960.

Mattes, Merrill J., *Colter's Hell and Jackson's Hole*, Yellowstone Library and Museum Association, 1962.

Meeker, Ezra, *Pioneer Reminiscences of Puget Sound*, Seattle, 1905.

Memorial of the Nez Perce Indians Residing in the State of Idaho, to the Congress of the United States, Senate Executive Document 97, 62nd Congress, 1st Session, Washington, 1911.

Merk, Frederick, *Fur Trade and Empire*, Cambridge, Mass., 1931.

Miles, Nelson A., *Personal Recollections and Observations*, Chicago and New York, 1896.

Mitchell, Elaine Allan, ed., "A Red River Gossip," *The Beaver* (Spring, 1961), 4–11.

Mooney, James, *The Ghost-Dance Religion*, Bureau of American Ethnology, 14th Annual Report, Washington, 1896.

Morgan, Dale L., *Jedediah Smith and the Opening of the West*, Indianapolis, 1953.

—— ed., "The Diary of William H. Ashley," *Bulletin of the Missouri Historical Society, 11* (1954–55), 9–40, 158–86, 279–302.

—— ed., *The West of William H. Ashley, 1822–1838*, Denver, 1964.

Morton, Arthur S., ed., *The Journal of Duncan M'Gillivray, 1794–95*, Toronto, 1929.

—— "The North West Company's Columbia Enterprise and David Thompson," *Canadian Historical Review, 17* (1936), 266–88; *18* (1937), 156–62.

Mullan, Capt. John, *Report on the Construction of a Military Road from Fort Walla-Walla to Fort Benton*, Washington, 1863.

Nasatir, A. P., *Before Lewis and Clark*, 2 vols. St. Louis, 1952.

"News From the Nez Perce Mines," *Idaho Yesterdays, 3* (Winter, 1959–60), 19–29.

Noyes, Alva J., *In the Land of Chinook*, Helena, Mont., 1917.

Oglesby, Richard E., *Manuel Lisa and the Opening of the Missouri Fur Trade*, Norman, Okla., 1963.

Oliphant, J. Orin, "Encroachments of Cattlemen on Indian Reservations in the Pacific Northwest, 1870–1890," *Agricultural History, 24* (1950), 42–58.

—— "George Simpson and Oregon Missions," *Pacific Historical Review, 6* (1937), 213–48.

—— ed., "Journals of the Indian War of 1855–56," *Washington Historical Quarterly, 15* (1924), 11–31.

Osborne, Douglas, "Archaeological Occurrences of Pronghorn Antelope, Bison, and Horse in the Columbia Plateau," *Scientific Monthly, 77* (1953), 260–69.

Palladino, Lawrence B., *Indian and White in the Northwest*, Lancaster, Pa., 1922.

Parker, Samuel, *Journal of an Exploring Tour beyond the Rocky Mountains*, Ithaca, N.Y., 1838.

Payette, B. C., ed., *The Oregon Country under the Union Jack*, Montreal, 1962.

Pettus, Terry, "Frolic at Fort Nisqually," *The Beaver* (Summer, 1961), 8–15.

Phillips, Paul C., ed., "Battle of the Big Hole," *Frontier, 10* (1926).

—— *The Fur Trade*, 2 vols. Norman, Okla., 1961.

Phinney, Archie, ed., *Nez Perce Texts*, New York, 1934.

Point, Nicholas, "Recollections of the Rocky Mountains," *Woodstock Letters, 11* (1882), 298–321; *12* (1883), 3–22.

Porter, Kenneth W., *John Jacob Astor, Business Man*, 2 vols. Cambridge, Mass., 1931.

Ray, Verne F., "Tribal Distribution in Eastern Oregon and Adjacent Regions," *American Anthropologist, 40* (1938).

—— *Cultural Relations in the Plateau of Northwestern America*, Southwest Museum, Los Angeles, 1939.

Reed, John C., *Gold-Bearing Gravel of the Nezperce National Forest, Idaho County*, Idaho Bureau of Mines and Geology, Pamphlet No. 40, Moscow, Idaho, June 1934.

Rees, John E., *Idaho Chronology, Nomenclature, Bibliography*, Chicago, 1918.

Relander, Click, *Drummers and Dreamers*, Caldwell, Idaho, 1956.

—— *Strangers on the Land*, Yakima, Wash., 1962.

Redington, J. W., "Scouting in Montana in the 1870's," *The Frontier, 13* (1932).

Report of the Adjutant-General of Oregon, 1865–66, Salem, Ore., 1866.

Rich, E. E., ed., *McLoughlin's Fort Vancouver Letters, 1st Series, 1825–1838,* Toronto, 1941; *2nd Series, 1839–44,* Toronto, 1943; *3rd Series, 1844–46,* Toronto, 1944.

—— ed., *Peter Skene Ogden's Snake Country Journals, 1824–25 and 1825–26,* London, 1950.

—— *The History of the Hudson's Bay Company, 1670–1870,* 2 vols. London, 1958–59.

Richardson, Elmo R., "Caleb Lyon: A Personal Fragment," *Idaho Yesterdays, 1* (Winter, 1957–58), 2–6.

Robertson, Frank C., *Fort Hall,* New York, 1963.

Roe, Frank G., *The Indian and the Horse,* Norman, Okla., 1955.

Rollins, Philip A., *The Discovery of the Oregon Trail,* New York, 1935.

Romeyn, Henry, "The Capture of Chief Joseph and the Nez Perce Indians," *Contributions to Montana Historical Society, 2* (1896).

Ronan, Peter, *Historical Sketch of the Flathead Indian Nation,* Helena, 1890.

Ross, Alexander, *Adventures of the First Settlers on the Oregon and Columbia River,* ed. Reuben G. Thwaites, Cleveland, 1904.

—— *Fur Hunters of the Far West,* 2 vols. London, 1855; republished Norman, Okla., 1956.

Santee, J. F., "Lawyer of the Nez Perces," *Washington Historical Quarterly, 25* (1934), 37–48.

Scott, Hugh Lennox, *Some Memories of a Soldier,* New York, 1928.

Senate Executive Document No. 39, 21st Congress, 2nd Session, Washington, 1831.

Senate Executive Document No. 90, 22nd Congress, 1st Session, Washington, 1832.

Senate Executive Document No. 40, 35th Congress, 1st Session, Washington, 1858.

Senate Executive Document No. 14, 45th Congress, 2nd Session, Washington, 1879.

Sheridan, Philip H., *Personal Memoirs,* 2 vols. New York, 1888.

Shields, G. O., *The Battle of the Big Hole,* Chicago, 1889.

"Spalding and Whitman Letters, 1837," *Oregon Historical Quarterly, 37* (1936), 111–26.

Spier, Leslie, *The Prophet Dance in the Northwest and Its Derivatives: The Source of the Ghost Dance,* General Series in Anthropology, 1, Menasha, Wis., 1935.

Spinden, H. J., "The Nez Perce Indians," *American Anthropological Association Memoirs, 2* (1908), 165–274.

Splawn, A. J., *Ka-mi-akin,* Portland, Ore., 1944.

Stevens, Hazard, *The Life of Isaac Ingalls Stevens,* 2 vols. Boston, 1900.

Stewart, W. M., "David Thompson's Surveys in the North-West," *Canadian Historical Review, 17* (1936), 289–303.

Stranahan, C. T., *Pioneer Stories,* Lewiston, Idaho, 1947.

Stuart, Granville, *Forty Years on the Frontier,* ed. Paul C. Phillips, 2 vols. Cleveland, 1925.

Sullivan, Maurice S., *The Travels of Jedediah Smith,* Santa Ana, Calif., 1934.

Sunder, John E., *Bill Sublette, Mountain Man,* Norman, Okla., 1959.

Sutherland, Thomas A., *Howard's Campaign against the Nez Perce Indians, 1877,* Portland, Ore., 1878.

Swan, James G., *The Northwest Coast,* New York, 1857.

Swanson, Earl H., Jr., "Association of Bison with Artifacts in Eastern Washington," *American Antiquity, 24* (1959), 429–31.

—— *The Emergence of Plateau Culture,* Idaho State University Museum, Pocatello, Idaho, 1962.

—— "Early Cultures in Northwestern America," *American Antiquity*, 28 (1962), 151–58.

Swanton, John R., *The Indian Tribes of North America*, Bureau of American Ethnology, Bulletin 145, Washington, 1952.

Taylor, Herbert C., Jr., and Hoaglin, Lester L., Jr., "The 'Intermittent Fever' Epidemic of the 1830's on the Lower Columbia River," *Ethnohistory*, 9 (1962), 160–78.

Taylor, Walter W., "Archaeology and Language in Western North America," *American Antiquity*, 27 (1961).

Teit, James A., *The Salishan Tribes of the Western Plateau*, ed. Franz Boas, Bureau of American Ethnology, 45th Annual Report, Washington, 1930.

"The Appeal of the Northwest Company to the British Government to Forestall John Jacob Astor's Columbia Enterprise," *Canadian Historical Review*, 17 (1936), 304–11.

"The Rocky Mountains: Memoirs of Father Gregory Mengarini," *Woodstock Letters*, 17 (1888), 298–309; 18 (1889), 25–43, 142–52.

"The Salmon River Mines," *Idaho Yesterdays*, 6 (Spring, 1962), 40–48.

Thwaites, Reuben Gold, ed., *Narrative of a Journey across the Rocky Mountains by John K. Townsend*, Early Western Travels, 1748–1846, 21, Cleveland, 1905.

—— ed., *Oregon: A Short History of a Long Journey by John B. Wyeth*, Early Western Travels, 1748–1846, 21, Cleveland, 1905.

—— ed., *Original Journals of the Lewis and Clark Expedition*, 8 vols., New York, 1904–05; reprinted New York, 1959.

Titus, Nelson C., "The Last Stand of the Nez Perces," *Washington Historical Quarterly*, 6 (1915), 145–53.

Tobie, Harvie E., *No Man Like Joe*, Portland, Ore., 1949.

Twenty-third Biennial Report, Idaho Historical Department, Boise, 1951–52.

Tyrrell, J. B., "David Thompson and the Columbia River," *Canadian Historical Review*, 18 (1937), 12–27.

—— ed., *David Thompson's Narrative of His Explorations in Western America, 1784–1812*, Toronto, 1916.

—— "Letter of Roseman and Perch, July 10, 1807," *Oregon Historical Quarterly*, 38 (1937), 391–97.

Victor, Frances Fuller, *Early Indian Wars of Oregon*, Salem, Ore., 1894.

—— *The River of the West*, Hartford, Conn., 1871.

Wagner, Henry R., and Camp, Charles L., *The Plains and the Rockies*, Columbus, Ohio, 1953.

Waite, Frederick C., "Medical Education of Dr. Whitman," *Oregon Historical Quarterly*, 37 (1936), 192–216.

Wallace, William S., ed., *Documents Relating to the North West Company*, Toronto, 1934.

—— ed., *John McLean's Notes of a Twenty-Five Year's Service in the Hudson's Bay Territory*, Toronto, 1932.

Warren, Eliza Spalding, *Memoirs of the West*, Portland, Ore., 1916.

Weisel, George F., ed., *Men and Trade on the Northwest Frontier*, Missoula, 1955.

Wells, Donald N., "Farmers Forgotten," *Idaho Yesterdays*, 2 (Summer, 1958), 28–32.

Wells, Merle W., *Rush to Idaho*, Bulletin 19, Idaho Bureau of Mines and Geology, Moscow, Idaho, 1963.

West, John, *The Substance of a Journal during a Residence at the Red River Colony, British North America*, London, 1824.

Wheat, Carl I., *Mapping the Transmississippi West*, San Francisco: Vol. 1, 1957, Vol. 2, 1958.

Wheeler, Olin D., *The Trail of Lewis and Clark*, 2 vols., New York, 1904.

White, M. Catherine, ed., *David Thompson's Journals Relating to Montana and Adjacent Regions, 1808–1812*, Missoula, 1950.

Winther, Oscar O., *The Great Northwest*, New York, 1952.

——— *The Old Oregon Country*, Stanford, Calif., 1950.

Winthrop, Theodore, *Canoe and Saddle*, Nisqually Edition, Portland, Ore., n.d.

Wood, Erskine, *Days with Chief Joseph*, Portland, Ore., n.d.

Wood, H. Clay, *Status of Young Joseph and His Band of Nez Perce Indians*, Portland, Ore., 1876.

——— *Supplementary to the Report on the Treaty Status of Young Joseph*, Portland, Ore., 1878.

Woodruff, C. A., "The Battle of the Big Hole," *Contributions to the Historical Society of Montana*, 7 (1910).

Young, F. G., ed., *Journal of Medorem Crawford*, Sources of the History of Oregon, 1, Portland, Ore., 1897.

——— ed., *The Correspondence and Journals of Captain Nathaniel J. Wyeth, 1831–1836*, Sources of the History of Oregon, 1, Parts 3–6, Eugene, Ore., 1899.

INDEX

Indians have been indexed under the most frequently used form of their names and cross-referenced from other forms.

ILLUSTRATIONS

1. Tuekakas (Old Joseph), headman of the Wallowa Nez Perces and father of Chief Joseph and Ollokot. Pictured when he was about 65 years of age in a drawing by Gustavus Sohon, a private in the U.S. Army on detached duty with Governor I. I. Stevens, at Walla Walla Council, May 29, 1855.

The above Name is written by Garry himself

Spokan Garry

Head Chief of the
Spokan Tribe

2. Spokan Garry: Educated and converted to Christianity by the British at Red River; returned to the Northwest and aroused an interest in the white man's religion among Nez Perces and other Indians. He was about 45 in this drawing by Sohon, made at the Walla Walla Council, May 27, 1855.

3. Hallalhotsoot (Lawyer), friend of the missionaries, head chief of the Nez Perces, and leader of the treaty faction of the tribe. He was about 60 when Sohon made this portrait of him at the Walla Walla Council, May 25, 1855.

4. Tamootsin (Timothy) of Alpowa, one of Henry H. Spalding's first converts. A loyal follower of Lawyer and a friend of the Americans. He is shown at about 55 in this drawing by Sohon made at the Walla Walla Council, June 7, 1855.

5. Tepyahlahnah Temoni (Eagle Heart, but called Spotted Eagle by the whites). A war and hunting leader of the Lawyer faction of the tribe and an ally of Americans during the wars that followed the Walla Walla Council. Drawn by Sohon at the Blackfoot Council near the mouth of the Judith River, October 18, 1855.

6. Hin-mah-tute-ke-kaikt (known as Thunder Strikes, Thunder Eyes, or Big Thunder), Nez Perce shaman and village head at Lapwai. He fought with Spalding, who built his mission on his grounds and called him James. He was also a buffalo-hunting Indian and the father-in-law of mountain man William Craig. Drawn by Sohon at the Walla Walla Council, May 29, 1855.

7. Hemene Ilppilp (Red Wolf), village headman at Alpowa on the Snake River. He was a host to Bonneville and to other early American visitors. Drawn by Sohon at the Walla Walla Council, May 30, 1855.

Looking-glass
Apash-wa-hay-ikt
Chief of the Nez-percé Indians

8. Apash Wyakaikt (Flint Necklace), known as Looking Glass, Sr., and Meiway (great chief). Headman of the Nez Perces at Asotin, he was one of the tribe's most respected war and buffalo-hunting leaders. He welcomed Bonneville, thrashed Pambrun at Fort Walla Walla, and opposed the missionaries and I. I. Stevens. Drawn after his dramatic arrival at the Walla Walla Council by Sohon, June 9, 1855.

Peopeo max-max.
Head Chief of the Walla-Walla Indians

9. Peopeo Moxmox (Yellow Bird, but called Yellow Serpent by the whites), headman of the Wallawallas and ally of Nez Perces. A friend of the fur traders and the father of the Christianized Elijah Hedding who was slain in California, he served with Frémont and was himself murdered while a prisoner of Oregon volunteers six months after Sohon made this portrait of him at the Walla Walla Council, June 7, 1855.

Five Crows (pahat kohokoho)
or She-ca-yah
Chief of the Cayuses

Head eye of others

10. Pahkatos Qoh Qoh (Five Crows), one of the headmen of a Umatilla band of Cayuse Indians. Spalding claimed him as a convert and named him Hezekiah. A half-brother of Tuekakas, he took a survivor of the Whitman massacre as a wife and was wounded during the punitive war against his people. Drawn by Sohon at the Walla Walla Council, June 11, 1855.

Weeah-To-nă-tee-ma-ny
called "the young chief
Head chief of the cayuses

Head eye of others

11. Tauitau, known as the Young Chief. Ally of Nez Perces, brother of Five Crows, and with him the leader of a Umatilla band of Cayuses. Drawn by Sohon at the Walla Walla Council, June 8, 1855.

12. Kamiakin, leader of Yakima patriots. A friend of Apash Wyakaikt and Peopeo Moxmox, he was feared and opposed by I. I. Stevens. Drawn by Sohon, probably at the Walla Walla Council.

Kamayakhen
head-chief of the Yakimas

13. Owhi, Yakima leader and rival of Kamiakin. Killed while a prisoner of American troops, 1858. Drawn by Sohon at the Walla Walla Council, June 3, 1855.

Ou-hi
Chief of the Yakima Indians

14. William Craig, mountain man. Settled down at Lapwai near his father-in-law, James, and became an agent for the Nez Perces. Drawn by Sohon, June 4, 1855, at the Walla Walla Council where Craig served as an interpreter.

15. Isaac I. Stevens, first Governor of Washington Territory. Enlisted Nez Perces in the Americans' wars against neighboring tribes. Photograph by Mathew B. Brady.

16. Henry H. Spalding, pioneer missionary to the Nez Perces. A figure of controversy and storm who divided the tribe.

17. General O. O. Howard. Led U.S. forces in the long pursuit of the nontreaty bands, 1877. Photograph from a broken glass negative by Brady.

18. Hin-mah-too-yah-lat-kekht (Thunder Traveling to Loftier Mountain Heights), known to the whites as Chief Joseph, led the Wallowa Nez Perces through the war of 1877. One of the most famous of all American Indian leaders, he delivered the surrender speech for his people at the Bear Paws. Less than two months later, aged 37 and bound for exile, he posed in Bismarck, North Dakota, November 1877, for this photograph by F. J. Haynes.

19. Ollokot (Frog, or Little Frog), at center, is believed to have posed for this photograph with another Nez Perce and a Cayuse at the Umatilla Agency in 1876 as the Wallowa conflict was building to a climax. The brother of Chief Joseph, Ollokot was leader of the Wallowa warriors.

20. Chief Joseph at his home in exile after his return to the Northwest. The Colville Reservation, Nespelem, Washington, 1903. Photograph by T. W. Tolman.

21. Independence Day gathering of Nez Perce patriots in exile: July 4, 1903, on the Colville Reservation. Photograph by T. W. Tolman.

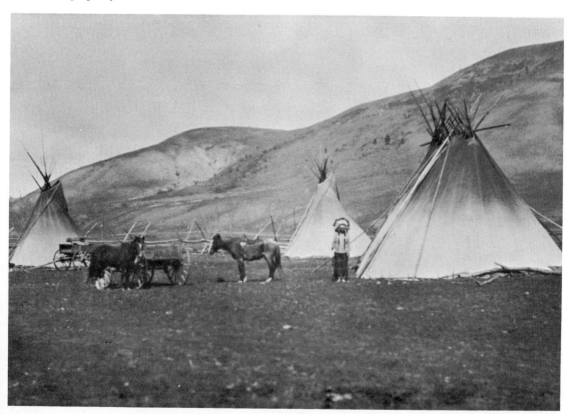

22. Chief Joseph, 63 years old, the year before his death in exile: July 4, 1903, Nespelem, Washington. Photograph by T. W. Tolman.

23. Joseph, Nez Perce Patriot and Statesman.

24. Jesse Red Heart, a modern-day Nez Perce, on an Appaloosa stallion decorated for a Lewiston, Idaho, parade. Photograph by Al Munson.